R320.956

POLITICAL DICTIONARY OF TH

ARAB WORLD

Minoa Library

Minoa, New York

SHIMONI, YAACOV   03/30/92
POLITICAL DICTIONAR\RAB WORLD
(5) 1987 R320.956
0116   95 550138 01 4   (IC=1)

POLITICAL DICTIONARY
OF THE
ARAB WORLD

POLITICAL DICTIONARY OF THE ARAB WORLD

Yaacov Shimoni

MACMILLAN PUBLISHING COMPANY
NEW YORK

Collier Macmillan Publishers
LONDON

Copyright © 1987 by G.G. The Jerusalem Publishing
House Ltd., 39 Tchernechovski Street, Jerusalem, Israel.

All rights reserved. No part of this book may be reproduced
or transmitted in any form or by any means, electronic or
mechanical, including photocopying, recording, or by any
information storage and retrieval system, without
permission in writing from the Publisher.

Macmillan Publishing Company
A Division of Macmillan, Inc.
866 Third Avenue, New York, N.Y. 10022

Collier Macmillan Canada Inc.

Library of Congress Catalog Card Number:
87 – 12392

Set, printed and bound by
Keter Publishing House, Jerusalem

Printed in Israel

printing number
1 2 3 4 5 6 7 8 9 10

Library of Congress Cataloging-in-Publication Data

Shimoni, Yaacov, 1915–
   Political dictionary of the Arab world.

   "In cooperation with the Dayan Center for Middle
Eastern & African Studies, Tel Aviv University" — T.p.
verso.
   Rev. ed. of: Political dictionary of the Middle East
in the 20th century. 1974.
   1. Arab countries — Politics and government —
Dictionaries. I. Shimoni, Yaacov, 1915– . Political
dictionary of the Middle East in the 20th century.
II. Merkaz Dayan le-limude ha-Mizra.h ha-tikhon
.ve-Afri.kah. III. Title.

DS37.S53   1987   909'.C974927   87-12392
ISBN 0-02-916422-2
ISBN 0-02-916423-0 (combined set)

FOREWORD

This book was written in the belief that there is a need for a concise political compendium on the Arab World in the present and recent past, a single volume in which the reader can find condensed information, alphabetically arranged, on countries and peoples, on national and political movements, parties and leaders, on ideas and ideologies, on disputes and wars, alliances and treaties.

To some extent, this Dictionary is a revised and updated edition of the *Political Dictionary of the Middle East in the 20th Century*, 1972, which I edited with the late Evyatar Levine (who dealt with the entries concerning Israeli and Jewish matters), and its second edition, 1974, with a supplement edited by Itamar Rabinovich and Haim Shaked. However, this new book deals with the Arab World, not the Middle East; it does not include Israel, which has been treated separately in the *Political Dictionary of the State of Israel* edited by Susan Hattis Rolef (Macmillan, 1987); nor does it include Turkey, Iran and Cyprus (except for matters linked or relevant to Arab affairs), while entries on Northwest Africa, the *Maghrib*, have been added. In some measure I have drawn upon the entries in the 1972 and 1974 books, written by area specialists (who are listed at the end of this Foreword) and a few new entries were also written by specialists; they are listed below.

This Dictionary appears under the auspices of the Dayan Center/Shiloah Institute of the University of Tel Aviv. An advisory editorial committee, composed of Prof. Itamar Rabinovich (chairman), Dr. Ami Ayalon, Prof. Uriel Dann, Daniel Dishon and Prof. Haim Shaked, has given me its counsel; and the research specialists of the Institute, and others, have reviewed the entries and suggested corrections and improvements. I am most grateful to all of them and to Edna Liftman, Assistant to the Head of the Dayan Center, who organized that cooperation. The responsibility for all the entries rests, of course, with me.

Although called a Dictionary, this book could not possibly be a simple compilation of indisputable data. An account of the recent history of Lebanon or Egypt; a description of the Arab-Israel conflict; political biographies of Nasser, King 'Abdullah, 'Arafat or Qadhdhafi; an analysis of Pan-Arabism, the status of Islamic law in the Arab countries, or the *Ba'th* movement — these are not items of lexicography but essays in political-historical writing. I have striven to present as accurate and objective a picture as possible, fully aware that complete objectivity is unattainable. Some errors may be unavoidable in a book like this. Corrections, amendments and suggestions will be warmly welcomed.

The Dictionary covers the 20th century up to the mid-1980s. But it does so from the point of view of people living today: more attention and more space is devoted to events closer to us in time than to the happenings of the first quarter of the century. The years before World War I, in particular, are treated as an introductory period. Geographically, the centers of the Arab world — the "Fertile Crescent" and Egypt, and to some degree Arabia — are treated more extensively than Northwest Africa. Selecting the entries involved, of course, a measure of subjective judgment. The general criterion was what the intelligent reader could be expected to look for in a volume of this kind. Therefore certain important matters are not listed separately because they are not associated with some key word which the reader is likely to seek, although it is hoped that he will find them covered in entries on countries, movements, ideas.

The Dictionary is not in any sense a *Who's Who*. A limited number of entries are devoted to leading personalities — kings, presidents and prime ministers, to the extent that they exerted significant historical or political influence, and others who helped to shape the character and fate of the countries of the Arab world. These, however, are not official, formal biographies, but rather attempts to record and assess political character and influence. At the last minute a large number of items, mainly biographical sketches, had to be deleted because of limitations of space.

A certain amount of duplication is unavoidable and often necessary in a dictionary, because many matters or events are relevant to more than one entry. I have endeavored to limit duplication by extensive cross-references; but there has been no attempt to eliminate it entirely, the assumption being that the reader will want to find in any one entry all that he wishes to know on a particular subject, without having to jump constantly from one part of the Dictionary to another. An asterisk (*) has been used to indicate that a name or term has a separate entry.

Arabic terms and names present problems of spelling and transliteration. I have employed the transliteration normally used in the international press, with some amendment towards a more correct transcription. For example, the guttural aspirate (Arabic: *'ayn*) is always indicated by an inverted apostrophe ('), except where a name is commonly transliterated without it (e.g. Iraq). The non-guttural aspirate (Arabic: *alif*) is reproduced as an apostrophe (') only where it is needed to separate two vowels *(Ra'uf, Feda'i)*. To simplify matters, diacritical marks have not been used: ض is d, ز and ظ are z or dh. A certain freedom has been exercised — within the spirit of the Arabic language — where vowels are concerned, and the generally accepted usage has been followed: Nasser (not Nasir); Hussein, Feisal, but Bahrain, Kuwait. The same goes for the doubling of consonants: Hussein, Hassan, Nasser (though the s is not doubled in Arabic), but Feisal, Asad. A liberal attitude has also been adopted towards "wrong" but accepted transliterations: Ottoman, not 'Uthmani; 'Oman, not 'Uman. Names well known in "wrong" transliteration are also in general left in their usual and accepted form, such as Chamoun (not Sham'un) or, in particular, North African names (Bourguiba — not Abu Raqiba, Boumédienne — not Abu Midyan). There is, therefore, no full consistency — which is, indeed, unattainable.

With Arab names, the last has been taken as the family name and the entry appears accordingly: Nuri Sa'id under Sa'id, Nuri (except in the case of kings and princes, generally known by their first name: Hussein bin Talal under H; Feisal Ibn 'Abd-ul-'Aziz under F). The Arabic definite article *al-* is disregarded in the alphabetical listing; thus Jamal al-Husseini will be found under H. In the text the article is used or dropped at will: Badr or al-Badr, Husseini or al-Husseini. Names composed of 'Abd-ul- ("Servant of") and one of the epithets of God ('Abd-ul-Fattah, 'Abd-ul-Rahman) are regarded as one name and therefore appear under A (e.g. Gamal 'Abd-ul-Nasser under 'Abd-ul-Nasser, Gamal).

Abbreviations used throughout the book are the following: the name of each entry is indicated in the text by its initials. A. stands for Arab, AC for Arab countries, ASt for Arab States, ME for Middle East.

Thanks are due to those who took part in the technical preparation of the volume — secretaries, typists, proofreaders, many of them faced with material of a dauntingly unfamiliar kind. The English style editing was done with great patience by Roberta J. Buland and Dave Levinson.

The maps were prepared by Carta and Chaim Eytan.

I would also like to express my gratitude to the Bronfman Program at the Dayan Center for the generous support which made much of the work invested in this volume possible.

Jerusalem, August 1987   Y.S.

List of Contributors to the *Political Dictionary of the Middle East in the 20th Century*, 1972, and the Supplement of 1974, whose entries I have used to some extent:

Prof. Shlomo Aronson; Prof. Gabriel Baer; Eliezer Beeri; Dr. Joseph Ben-Aharon; Dr. Hayyim J. Cohen; Dr. Shaul Colbi; Prof. Uriel Dann; Prof. Joseph Eliash; Vita Epstein; Prof. Hagai Erlich; Baruch Gilead; Asher Goren; Oded Gross; Dr. Haim Herzog, President of the State of Israel; Prof. Yehuda Karmon; Prof. Aaron Kleinman; Dr. David Kushnir; Dr. Joseph Lador-Lederer; Prof. Aharon Layish; Prof. Hava Lazarus-Yafeh; Dr. Avigdor Levi; Dr. Netanel Lorch; Sara Lulko-Israeli; Prof. Emanuel Marx; Yuval Arnon Ohanna; Prof. Yehoshua Porat; Prof. Itamar Rabinovich; Zvi Rafiah; Prof. Yaacov Ro'i; Dr. Susan Hattis Rolef; Joseph Rothschild; Prof. Amnon Sella; Zeev Shif, Journalist; Yaacov Shimoni; Prof. Sasson Somekh; Albert Soud'i; Esther Soueri; Ori Stendel, Jurist; Oded Tavor; David Tourgeman; Prof. Jehuda Wallach; Prof. Michael Winter; Ehud Yaari, Journalist; Samuel Yaari; Tamar Yegnes; Hannah Zamir.

The following specialists have contributed to the present volume:
Dr. Shai Feldman, Senior Researcher, Jaffee Center for Strategic Studies, Tel Aviv University (*Israel's Lebanon War, 1982*, in the entry *Arab Israel Wars*).
Dr. Dori Gold, Senior Researcher, Jaffee Center for Strategic Studies, Tel Aviv University (*United States Interests and Policies*).
Dr. Yohanan Manor, Information Department, World Zionist Organization (updating *French Interests and Policies*).
Dr. Sergio I. Minerbi, Israel Ministry for Foreign Affairs (*European Economic Community*).
Dr. Yaacov Ro'i, Associate Professor, Department of History, Tel Aviv University (updating *Russian Interests and Policies*).
Yehudit Ronen, Dayan Center for Middle Eastern and African Studies, Tel Aviv University (updating *Libya* and *Sudan*).
Prof. Benjamin Shwadran, Department of Middle Eastern and African History, Tel Aviv University (*Oil in the Arab Countries*).
Dr. Rachel Simon, Dayan Center for Middle Eastern and African Studies, Tel Aviv University (co-author, *Algeria, Tunisia* and *Morocco*).

A

'Abbas, Ferhat (1899–1985) Algerian nationalist leader. A pharmacist by profession, trained at the University of Algiers, 'A. became active in public affairs in the 1930s and was several times elected to those Algerian administrative and financial assemblies to which an Algerian Muslim was eligible. At first, he opposed Arab Algerian nationalism and advocated full equality for Algerian Muslims and Algeria's integration in France, perhaps with a measure of local autonomy. Disappointed by the failure of the reforms instituted by the French "Popular Front" government after 1936, 'A. gradually shifted to a more autonomist position and in 1938 founded a *Union Populaire Algérienne*; but his influence was limited. After serving with the French army in 1939–40, he was also personally disappointed by the lack of equal opportunity and reward granted to him by Vichy-France. After the landing of Allied forces in North Africa, 1942, he presented in Dec. 1942 a message to the French and Allied leaders, proposing a new régime of equality, full freedoms, a vaguely formulated measure of autonomy and Algerian participation in government; these demands were reformulated in Feb. 1943 in a "Manifest", co-signed by a group of Algerian leaders. 'A. was invited in May 1943 to present detailed proposals, but nothing came of these talks. In 1944 he founded an organization, *Amis du Manifeste de Libération*, which was re-formed in Apr. 1946 as the *Union Démocratique du Manifeste Algérien*, UDMA, calling for an autonomous Algeria in federation with France, and seen as a rival and an alternative to *Messali Hajj's more extremist organization. 'A. was now considered anti-French and was several times imprisoned. During those years he despaired of the prospects of federation with France and turned into an advocate of full independence. In 1956, when the armed revolt was in full swing, he escaped to Cairo, where part of the *FLN leadership maintained its headquarters, and joined the FLN. He played no major part in the military operations, but when the FLN set up a Provisional Government of the Algerian Revolution, in Cairo, in Sept. 1958, he was named Prime Minister. 'A. was, however, unable to accommodate himself fully to the policies and the leadership style of the FLN command, and in Aug. 1961 he was dismissed. He took no active part in the final negotiations for independence. In Sept. 1962 he became President of independent Algeria's first National Assembly. But his opposition to the course the Algerian leadership was taking deepened and in Aug. 1963 he resigned, bitterly denouncing the totalitarian, "Castroist" trends that had become dominant, the "confiscation of power" by *Ben Bella and his FLN associates (though he could not make that denunciation fully public). He remained in alienated opposition and without a part in power when Ben Bella was overthrown in 1965 by *Boumédienne. In 1976 he was placed under house arrest. This, however, was later relaxed and he was able to publish, in France, several books (*Autopsie d'une guerre*, 1980; *Le Jeune Algérien* — a collection of older essays — 1981; *L'Indépendance confisquée* — his denunciation of Ben Bella's and Boumédienne's régimes — 1984). In 1984 'A. was fully rehabilitated, but now over 80 years old he did not resume any political activity. He died in 1985.

'Abbas Hilmi (1874–1945) Ruler of Egypt (Khedive), 1892–1914, as 'Abbas II, succeeding his father, Tawfiq. 'A.H. was considered to be anti-British and in covert contact with Egyptian nationalists, Islamic revivalists and pro-Turkish elements. His relations with the British administration eased after Lord Cromer was replaced as British "Agent and Consul-General" (*de facto* Governor) by Lord Gorst in 1907. But friction continued. With the outbreak of World War I and the proclamation of a British protectorate, in 1914, 'A.H. was deposed and went into exile in Turkey. In 1922, his properties were confiscated and he and his family were forever barred from returning to Egypt. He continued cultivating clandestine contacts and political intrigues, but did not return to play an active role in Egyptian politics. (Excerpts from his memoirs were serialized in the Egyptian daily *al-Misri* in 1950.)

'Abbud, Ibrahim (1900–1983) Sudanese officer and statesman, President of the Sudan 1958–64. His ancestry is described as tribal (in differing versions). Educated at Gordon College and Military College and commissioned in 1918, 'A. served with the Sudan Defense Force established by the British in 1925. During World War II, he served with the Sudanese contingent in the British Army in the Libyan, Ethiopian and Eritrean campaigns. When the Army command was "Sudanized", he became, in 1954, Deputy Commander-in-Chief, and with the attainment of independence — Commander-in-Chief, 1956–64. In Nov. 1958, 'A. staged a *coup d'état* — reportedly with the encouragement of the outgoing Prime Minister — and became President, Prime Minister and Minister of Defense, while remaining Commander-in-Chief of the Armed Forces. His régime was conservative and oppressive and had no clear ideological orientation beyond its aspiration to stability and gradual economic improvements. In his foreign policy 'A. was moderately pro-West with a growing neutralist tinge. After having suppressed several attempts to oust him, 'A. was toppled in October 1964 in a *coup d'état* led by civilian politicians and supported by some army officers. He first continued as a figurehead President, but resigned after three weeks and retired from public life.

'Abd-ul-'Aziz bin (Ibn) 'Abd-ul-Rahman of the House of Sa'ud — see Ibn Sa'ud.

'Abd-ul-Hadi Large, prominent Palestinian-Arab clan, centered in Nablus and its rural surroundings. For several generations its sons have provided a long line of administrators for the Ottoman-Turkish Empire, British-mandated Palestine, the Kingdom of Jordan, and local-municipal government, as well as notables active in public and political affairs. In the struggle dividing Palestinian-Arab politics, in the 1920s and 1930s, into two rival camps, the *Husseinis or *Majlisiyyin* (supporters of the Supreme *Muslim Council) vs. the *Nashashibis or *Mu'āridin* (the Opposition), the 'AuH clan — which is not very closely knit — endeavored to maintain an independent, neutral position. Among its many prominent members: 'Awni *'AuH; Fakhri 'AuH — a "black sheep" and outlaw who became one of the top commanders of the guerrilla bands in 1936 and a deputy to Fawzi *Qawuqji. In 1938, when the guerrilla had turned into internal terrorism, he was one of the commanders of the opposition's counter-terror groups, the "Peace Gangs". He was assassinated in 1943. Ruhi 'AuH (1885–1954) served in the Ottoman diplomatic and consular corps, rose to senior positions in the Palestinian administration under the British Mandate, and became a Minister in the Government of Jordan (Foreign Minister 1949; Justice 1949 and 1952–53).

'Abd-ul-Hadi, 'Awni (1889–1970) Palestinian-Arab, later Jordanian, lawyer and politician. Active since his student days in the pre-World War I *Arab national movement in the Ottoman Empire, 'A. was a member of the *al-*Fatat* nationalist secret society and among the organizers of the Arab nationalist congress of Paris, 1913. He was one of Amir *Feisal's secretaries during his short-lived administration in Damascus, 1919–20, and accompanied him to the Paris Peace Conference. He then served Amir *'Abdullah in Transjordan. 'A. returned to Palestine in 1924, worked as a lawyer and became one of the chief spokesmen of the Palestinian-Arab nationalist movement — for some years as a member of the *Arab Executive. He had some — politically unproductive — contacts with Zionist leaders. In 1932 he founded a Palestinian branch of the pan-Arab *Istiqlal* (Independence) party (which never attained much influence); as its head he joined the *Arab Higher Committee that directed the Arab rebellion of 1936–39, and served as its secretary, but was arrested and went into exile, 1937–41. In the command of the later stages of the rebellion, from Damascus and Beirut, he played no major role. In Nov. 1945, 'A. joined a new Arab Higher Committee, but in the internal disputes of 1946–47 he opposed the *Husseini leadership, withdrew from the Committee and for some time joined the opposition's rival "Higher Arab Front" (1946). In September 1948 he was appointed Minister for Social Affairs in the abortive "Government of all Palestine" established in Egyptian-occupied Gaza, but resigned soon, and settled in Jordan. He served as Jordan's Minister (later Ambassador) to Egypt, 1951–55, and was a Senator, 1955–58. For a short time in 1956 he was Minister of Foreign Affairs and Justice, and in 1958 — one of Jordan's representatives on the Federal Council of the abortive Jordan-Iraq *Arab Federation. After 1958 he lived in Cairo and served for some time as chairman of the *Arab League's Judicial Affairs Committee. Parts of 'A.'s private papers were published in 1974 in Beirut.

'Abd-ul-Hamid II (1842–1919) Sultan of the Ottoman Empire 1876–1909. His biography, reign and deposition by the Young Turks are outside the scope of this Dictionary. His reign had a considerable impact on developments in the Arab world. Sultan 'A. fostered *Pan-Islamic ideas and policies, emphasizing his position as *Caliph of all Muslims and the loyalty owed to him and the Empire by the Arabs, as Muslims. 'A. initiated the construction of the *Hijaz Railway to serve the pilgrims to Mecca and strengthen all-Islamic ties.

'Abd-ul-Ilah bin (Ibn) 'Ali (1912–58) Regent, 1939–53, and Crown Prince, 1953–58, of Iraq. Born in Hijaz to Sharif *'Ali, the eldest son of Sharif *Hussein, both later Kings of Hijaz, 'A. moved to Baghdad with his father in 1925, when Hijaz was conquered by *Ibn Sa'ud. When King *Ghazi of Iraq, his cousin and brother-in-law, died in 1939, he became Regent of Iraq on behalf of the infant King *Feisal II; and when Feisal attained his majority, in 1953, 'A. assumed the title of Crown Prince, retaining considerable influence. He was strongly pro-British throughout his political life. In 1941, during the rule of Rashid *'Ali and the officers of the "Golden Square", he was deposed and fled Iraq, returning with the victorious British Army. He was considered, with Nuri *Sa'id, by anti-British opinion on the Right and Left as a symbol of reaction and subservience to foreign imperialist domination. 'A. fostered abortive plans for a *Greater Syria or a *Fertile Crescent Federation and was believed, in the 1950s, to aspire to the throne of Syria. 'A. was killed during the revolution of July 1958, and his body was torn to pieces by the mob.

'Abdullah bin (Ibn) 'Abd-ul-'Aziz (b. 1921? 1923?) Sa'udi prince, one of the sons of *Ibn Sa'ud; (his mother came from the *Rashid clan of the Shammar tribes — whose state the Sa'udis overpowered in 1921); Crown-Prince and First Deputy Prime Minister since 1982. 'A. belongs to the inner circles of ruling Sa'udi princes and is considered to head a conservative faction (as against the "moderate" and "pro-American" advocates of fast development). He served for some time as Governor of Mecca and, from 1962–63, as Deputy Minister of Defense. Since 1962–63 he is commander of the National Guard. When Prince Khaled became King and Prime Minister, in 1975, 'A. was appointed Second Deputy Premier, and with Khaled's death and the accession of King *Fahd, June 1982 — Crown Prince and First Deputy Premier. He is therefore supposed to accede to the throne when Fahd dies — but some foresee a potential struggle with Prince Sultan b. 'Abd-ul-'Aziz. 'A. is reported to be married to a Syrian woman (said to belong to the *'Alawite sect and to be a relative of President *Asad). In recent years he has advocated — against the "pro-Western" faction within the dynasty — closer Sa'udi cooperation with the Arab states, including the radical ones (e.g. Syria); he has also become rather more active in Arab politics and has several times tried, without much success, to mediate in the Lebanese crisis, the Syrian-Iraqi dispute, and between Syria and the United States.

'Abdullah Ibn (bin) Hussein (1882–1951) Amir 1921–46, King 1946–48 of Transjordan, King of Jordan 1948–51. Born in Mecca as second son of Sharif *Hussein ibn 'Ali, scion of the Prophet Muhammad's Hashemite clan of the Quraishi tribe. 'A. received his education in Istanbul, where he lived from 1891 to 1908 with his father under Ottoman surveillance. He was active in Arab cultural circles and reportedly in contact with semi-clandestine Arab nationalist groups in Istanbul. When his father was allowed to return to Mecca, as Amir, after the Revolution of the Young Turks, 'A. went with him. He stayed in Istanbul again, as Deputy for Mecca in the Ottoman Parliament, 1912–14. On his way back to Mecca he met British officials in Cairo to explore the prospects of a British-aided rebellion against Ottoman rule. When his father launched the *Arab Revolt in June 1916, 'A. took a leading part in it. From 1917 he also served his father, who had assumed the title of King of Hijaz, as political adviser and Foreign Minister. (It was, however, his younger brother *Feisal who was considered the leading figure and who represented Hussein in the peace negotiations.)

In Mar. 1920, at an Arab nationalist congress in Damascus that proclaimed Feisal King of Syria, a group of Iraqi nationalists offered 'A. the crown of Iraq. This corresponded to vague Hashemite concepts of three Arab Kingdoms — Greater Syria; Iraq; and Arabia — ruled by Hussein's sons and federated under King Hussein, but the British, whose zone of influence or domination was to include Iraq, did not seem to favor 'A. as ruler of Iraq. When the French foiled the plans for an

Arab Kingdom in Syria and compelled Feisal to flee Damascus in July 1920, 'A. assembled troops in Northern Hijaz, planning to march through Transjordan to Damascus to restore Arab-Hashemite rule to Syria. He reached Ma'an in November 1920 and entered 'Amman in March 1921. As the British wished to avoid an armed clash between their Hashemite allies and the French, yet felt obliged towards the Hashemites, the then Colonial Secretary Winston Churchill proposed to 'A. that he settle in Transjordan as Amir of that territory and renounce his plans regarding Syria and the French as well as his claims to the Iraqi crown.

'A. accepted the British proposal and in April 1921 became Amir of Transjordan. In 1922, the League of Nations endorsed that settlement, within the Palestine *Mandate — with the clause referring to the Jewish National Home made, upon Britain's proposal, inapplicable to Transjordan. On these terms Britain recognized Transjordan in May 1923 as an autonomous Amirate. 'A. gradually established an administration — conservative, with some preference given to Beduin tribal chiefs, with the Amir as a powerful, benevolent patriarch — a fully fledged government, an army (the *"Arab Legion", British-officered), a constitution (1928), first representative institutions (later developing into a bicameral Parliament). He remained closely linked to the British, dependent on their aid, with a loyalty which he proved during World War II, when he sent his Army to assist in the suppression of Rashid *'Ali's rebellion in Iraq (1941). Indeed, many Arab nationalists regarded 'A. as a British puppet, and many foreign countries doubted his independence even after it was formally granted by Britain in May 1946. On that occasion, 'A. assumed the title of King and changed the name of his realm from Transjordan to Hashemite Kingdom of Jordan; in 1947 he granted a new Parliamentary constitution.

Throughout his reign, 'A. continued to cherish the vision of a *"Greater Syria", i.e. a union of Syria, Lebanon, Palestine and Transjordan — under his crown — and a *Fertile Crescent Federation of that Greater Syria with Iraq, and to cultivate Syrian and Palestinian-Arab politicians that might support his scheme. 'A. publicized these plans mainly after World War II; some elements in Syria, Iraq and Palestine supported them, but most Arab political opinion was hostile. Egypt, Syria and Sa'udi Arabia strongly opposed any "revisionist" plans to change the inter-Arab *status quo*, and even 'A.'s Hashemite cousins and allies in Iraq did not fully back him. The French, who also violently rejected the "Greater Syria" scheme, saw it as a British plot — and so did most Arab opinion. Yet, while some British service branches seem to have supported 'A.'s aspirations to some extent, official British policy never fully backed them.

'A. maintained good relations with the leaders of Jewish Palestine and the Zionist movement over many years. In the early 1930s he favored and invited Jewish settlement in Transjordan — but the British Palestine administration foiled these plans. From 1946 towards the final Palestine crisis, 'A.'s contacts with the Zionist leaders intensified and finally led to a secret agreement — unwritten and vaguely general: 'A. — though preferring an autonomous Jewish entity within a Palestinian-Jordanian Kingdom under his crown — would not resist or impede the partition of Palestine and the creation of a Jewish State (in accordance with a UN decision then expected), while the Jews, and nascent Israel, would not hinder 'A. from taking over the Arab part of Palestine — in fact, while they would not actually assist him, they encouraged such a take-over; and cooperation, a sort of alliance, would be maintained. Reports or rumors of that agreement inevitably reached the Arab countries, and the resolve to foil it and prevent 'A. from taking over part of Palestine, in league with the Jews, played a major role in the all-Arab decision of May 1948 to invade Palestine (as against a previous decision not to involve the regular armies). In 1947–48, 'A. proved unable to keep his pledge to the full: he told his Zionist contacts (Golda Meir met him in Nov. 1947, and in a last meeting, later widely reported, in May 1948) that he could not resist the pressure to join the all-Arab camp. The British, too, while generally in sympathy with his ideas, seem to have advised him to take over the Arab part of Palestine in concert with all-Arab moves rather than in a separate agreement with the Jews. He therefore sent his army into Palestine, along with the other Arab forces. Moreover, in a symbolic gesture he was appointed Commander-in-Chief of all the invading forces; the title, however, was purely nominal. 'A.'s

"Arab Legion" took over large parts of Arab Palestine meeting virtually no resistance. 'A. avoided, however, attacking Israel in the areas allotted to her by the UN plan — a decision coordinated with the British commanders of his forces and conveyed by them to Israel. Fighting did take place in Jerusalem, its vicinity and on the road leading to it — areas not allotted to Israel by the UN plan and not covered by 'A.'s accord with the Zionist leaders. When hostilities ceased, 'A. resumed contacts. In Apr. 1949, while official armistice talks were being held in Rhodes, the most difficult points were settled in secret negotiations directly with the King. These talks continued and led to a draft non-aggression pact, readied for signature early in 1950. 'A., however, again reneged when mounting pressure by the Arab states culminated in a threat to expel Jordan from the Arab League.

In return for this renunciation of a pact with Israel, the Arab states acquiesced in the annexation of Arab Palestine by Jordan which they had violently opposed. Late in 1948 'A. had begun to turn the military take-over of the Arab part of Palestine (except for the *Gaza Strip, occupied by Egypt) into a full annexation. He had in fact been invited to do so by congresses of Palestinian-Arab notables and local leaders orchestrated by his long-standing supporters, the *Nashashibi-led opposition, and unopposed by an extremist leadership that had largely gone abroad and was totally discredited by the defeat of 1948. In 1948 he reaffirmed, with stronger emphasis, the new name of "The Hashemite Kingdom of Jordan" (with former Transjordan as the "East Bank" and Arab Palestine as the "West Bank") and appointed a large number of Palestinians to senior posts in his administration. This process culminated in a formal act of annexation proclaimed in Apr. 1950. The incorporation of the Palestinian Arabs wrought a basic change in the sociopolitical character and climate of the Kingdom: it introduced modern, urban, nationalist politics and a highly active, fermenting, traumatized population — many of whom regarded 'A. as a collaborator with the British and the Jews, a traitor to the Arab cause. 'A. was assassinated by a Palestinian in July 1951, while entering al-Aqsa Mosque in Jerusalem for prayer.

'A. published his Memoirs in 1945 (abridged English translation: 1950), and a supplementary volume shortly before his death (English: 1954).

'Abd-ul-Nasser, Gamal (1918–1970) Egyptian officer and statesman, President of Egypt 1956–70. Born in Bani Mor, Asyut district, son of a postal clerk, he graduated from secondary school, in Cairo, in 1936, and from the military academy in 1938. He served in Sudan, and from 1941 as instructor at the military academy. After advanced training at the staff college, he commanded a battalion in Egypt's expeditionary forces in the 1948 Palestine war. He was besieged with his battalion in the "Faluja Pocket" — a siege lifted only with the armistice agreement of 1949. In 1951 he was promoted to the rank of colonel and appointed lecturer at the military college.

Nasser was a leading member of a clandestine group of "Free Officers" conspiring to remove Egypt's old leadership whom they held responsible for the humiliating defeat of 1948 along with the other ills of Egypt. On 22 July 1952 they mounted a successful *coup* and took power, forming a Revolutionary Council. General Muhammad *Nagib was appointed to head the Council; according to some, he was a figurehead only, admitted to the plotters' junta at the last stage, while its real leader was Nasser (others dispute that version). In Sept. Nagib took the Premiership. Rivalry soon developed between Nagib and Nasser — a struggle both for power and the shape and character of the régime to be established. Nagib wished to revert to a parliamentary system and permit the political parties to resume activities, while N. envisaged an army-led populist one-party régime. N. had his way: in Jan. 1953 all political parties were banned and a single organization — the "National Liberation Organization" — established, with N. as its Secretary-General. In May 1953, N. was also appointed Deputy Secretary-General of the Revolutionary Council, and in June — Deputy Premier and Minister of the Interior (while Nagib became President and retained the Premiership).

In Feb. 1954 the struggle between N. and Nagib came to a head. N. became Prime Minister and tried to remove Nagib; but Nagib staged a come-back and deposed N.; demonstrations and counter-demonstrations took place and rival army units moved into position. In Apr. the struggle was resolved: N. became Prime Minister, while Nagib remained President but was stripped of all real power; in Nov. 1954 he was dismissed from that post, too, and put under house arrest. N. now took action against the remnants of the old political parties, seen as nuclei of potential opposition, by conducting a series of purges and trials. Harsh measures were taken particularly against the *Muslim Brotherhood. An attempt on N.'s life, in Oct. 1954, was ascribed to them and they were severely suppressed; their leaders were put on show trials and some of them were executed.

For N.'s reforms, from 1952, and his measures of nationalization, see *Egypt. From 1955–56, his policies were presented as a new doctrine of "Arab Socialism". N. also set about to reshape the political régime. In Jan. 1956 a new constitution was proclaimed, and in a June referendum N. was elected President for a six-year term. With the merger of Egypt and Syria, in Feb. 1958, he was elected President of the *United Arab Republic (UAR). After the dissolution of the UAR in Sept. 1961 he insisted on retaining for Egypt the official name of UAR and remained "President of the UAR". N. convened a congress of "popular forces" in 1962, founded a new ruling party — called the *"Arab Socialist Union" — and formulated a National Charter as the basic, Arab-Socialist, doctrine of the party and the nation. In May 1965 N. was elected President for a second six-year term.

In their first years of power, N. and his team had appeared moderate and pragmatic in their foreign and inter-Arab policy. In 1964 they reached a final agreement with Britain that had eluded all previous governments for some eight years, and obtained the abolition of the Treaty of 1936, the evacuation of British forces and the termination of any special privileges for Britain. They also conceded, in 1952–53, to the Sudan the right of self-determination — which all former rulers had denied. Even in Israel they were, at first, seen as moderates with whom a *modus vivendi* appeared possible — had they not denounced the old régime for its disastrous military intervention in Palestine in 1948, and were they not noticeably reticent on anti-Israel rhetoric?

In the mid-1950s, however, all this seemed to change and N. began adopting increasingly activist, extremist-revolutionary policies. His growing inclination towards the "Third World" and a neutralist position led him to oppose Western plans for a Middle East defense alliance linked to the West, the *Baghdad Pact (indeed, Egypt had opposed such pacts before his time, too). The ensuing confrontation with the West coincided with N.'s first appearance as a leading actor on the international scene — at the *Bandung Conference of Asian leaders, 1955, his meetings with Tito and Nehru, and his emergence as one of the architects of a neutralist bloc. It also induced him to conclude an arms deal with Czechoslovakia, 1955 — marking a budding alliance with the Soviet Bloc. In 1956 the USA retaliated by denying her aid to the *Aswan High Dam, N.'s pet project (and inducing the World Bank to do likewise). This step led N. to obtain the aid denied by the West from the USSR, and to nationalize the *Suez Canal. The confrontation with the West culminated in the Anglo-French invasion, the *Suez War; Israel's participation in that invasion was also a turning point in N.'s attitude to peace prospects with Israel (though N. himself repeatedly pin-pointed Israel's retaliatory raid on Gaza, in Febr. 1955, as that turning point). From that crisis of 1956 N. emerged triumphant, as the leader of a small, newly independent nation that had successfully withstood imperialist aggression, and his international standing was much enhanced. In Dec. 1957, a first Afro-Asian solidarity conference (non-governmental) was held in Cairo. In 1961, N. took part in the founding conference of the *Casablanca Bloc, and in a *neutralist summit meeting in Belgrade. In 1963, he participated in a summit conference founding the *Organization for African Unity — which held its second congress in 1964 in Cairo. Later in 1964, the second conference of *non-aligned nations was also held in Cairo, with N. among its leaders. In 1958, N. also paid his first visit to the Soviet Union.

From the mid-1950s, N. took an increasingly activist line also towards the Arab countries. Egypt had always seen herself as the center of the Arab world. In his booklet *The Philosophy of the Revolution* (1954) N. himself had described her position at the center of three circles: Arab, Islamic, and African. But gradually, N.'s policies tended to impose — by fostering *"Nasserist" pressure groups in the Arab countries; by Egyptian pressure; by subversion; and if needed, by force — an Egyptian hegemony, in terms of both her inter-state power position and her revolutionary Arab-Socialist doctrine. This process is described in detail in the entry *Egypt, as is N.'s direct military intervention in the Yemen civil war, 1962.

There were ups and downs, tactical shifts, in that activist-interventionist Arab policy. Moreover, statements and policies advocating all-Arab unity based on the inter-Arab *status quo*, cooperation between differing régimes and mutual non-interference (as provided for in the Arab League Charter) coincided with policies aimed at the overthrow of conservative régimes and assertions that such régimes had to go and that only progressive-revolutionary, Arab-Socialist states could cooperate. N. himself and his followers perhaps did not perceive the contradiction. Anyway, after the debacle of the Yemen expedition and the general failure to subvert Arab governments and create régimes in the Nasserist image (as even in countries with Arab-Socialist leanings, such as Algeria, Syria, Iraq and later Libya, national self-interest and particularist tendencies soon prevailed), N. from the early 1960s tuned down his interventionist statements and policies and cooperated with the conservative régimes in renewed efforts at all-Arab cooperation (e.g. regular "summit" meetings from 1964). Yet, harsh statements that no cooperation was possible with "reactionary" régimes also recurred.

In 1966–67, when preparing for war against Israel, N. revived and reinforced his alliance with Syria and in May 1967, after making war inevitable by proclaiming a blockade of the Straits of *Tiran and ordering the UN Emergency Force to withdraw from *Sinai, he imposed a close alliance on Jordan, too, and compelled King Hussein to toe his line. The frenzy of the *Six-Day War, June 1967, orchestrated by carefully built-up mass enthusiasm, brought N. to the pinnacle of his all-Arab leadership; all the Arab countries fervently backed him and many sent troops or equipment to aid Egypt. When the war turned into defeat, N., taking personal responsibility, resigned; but stormy mass demonstrations — seemingly spontaneous, but no doubt carefully staged — "forced" him to retract the resignation (some think that the resignation was calculated in the first place to provoke a public demand for his return). Thus he turned even that day of bitter defeat into a personal victory. N. had indeed become Egypt's sole leader and large masses could not envisage their country without him at the helm.

In the three years left to N. after 1967, his policies were less flamboyant, somewhat subdued — but there was no basic change and the contradiction between his pragmatic position at the center of the inter-Arab *status quo* and his radical revolutionary inclinations, with occasional interventionist sallies, was never resolved. N. supported, for instance, the *PLO's build-up of its state-within-a-state in both Jordan and Lebanon and prevented the governments of the two countries from taking effective measures against it, imposing a precarious co-existence embodied in agreements with the PLO that were formulated under his sponsorship (and never kept by the PLO). When that co-existence broke down in Jordan and King Hussein confronted the PLO in desperate battle, in 1970, N. "mediated", but in fact sided with the PLO and acted to discredit and ostracize King Hussein. N. also led Egypt into an ever-increasing dependence on the Soviet Union (with thousands of Soviet technicians and advisers, civil and military, in Egypt).

N.'s attitude to Israel and to the prospects of an Arab-Israel settlement also remained ambivalent and contradictory. He accepted Security Council Resolution 242 of 1967, calling for peaceful co-existence of Israel and the Arab states (interpreting it, as most Arabs did, as providing for Israel's *total* withdrawal from *all* territories occupied in 1967) and did not join the hawkish "Rejection Front" (Syria, Iraq, the PLO, Algeria) that refused in principle to co-exist with Israel in any form. Yet he always refused to negotiate with Israel and seldom spoke of the possibility of peace with her. It was N. who formulated the "Three Noes" of the Khartoum summit, 1967 (no peace, no negotiations, no recognition). In numerous speeches he stated that he would not be satisfied with the "removal of the results of the aggression of 1967" (i.e. Israel's withdrawal from the territories occupied), but would continue to struggle for the "removal of the results of the aggression of 1948", i.e. for the destruction of Israel's very existence. He repeatedly said: "What was taken by force, can be regained only by force". And he continued, in his last years, conducting a "war of attrition".

N. died, suddenly, in September 1970. His image has dimmed somewhat since his death. His successors, principally Anwar *Sadat, at first maintained that their policies though differing from his, were a loyal continuation — or at most a correction, an adaptation — of those bequeathed by him; but gradually they took their distance from N. and allowed previously hidden aspects of his rule to be revealed and harsh criticism to be publicly voiced concerning the failure of his economic policies, particularly the state enterprises; the all-pervading corruption; and mainly, the oppressive character of his régime, the police state he created — the suppression of the freedom of speech, organization and the press, the unlawful detention and torture of adversaries. And though "Nasserist" factions still exist in several Arab countries (e.g. Syria, Lebanon), and in Egypt herself, where many remember N.'s rule with nostalgia, "Nasserism" as a doctrine has lost most of its attraction and force.

Final judgment must be left to history. Yet there can be no doubt: N., Egypt's top leader for 18 years, endowed with unusual charisma and wielding an immense, though controversial, influence throughout the Arab world, one of the architects of international non-alignment, was a towering figure among the leaders of modern Egypt and the Arab world and has left a distinctive mark on the history of his country and the Middle East.

'Abduh, Muhammad (1849–1905) Egyptian Muslim thinker, one of the initiators and main leaders of the renaissance of Islamic thought and its reform and modernization. After the failure of the 'Urābi revolt, 1882, he went into exile and published the *Pan-Islamic journal al'Urwa al-Wuthqa* ("Faithful Support") in Paris — together with Jamal-ul-Din al-Afghani (1839–97), the founder of the *Pan-Islamic movement, by whom he was strongly influenced. 'A. called for a renewal of Islamic values and their adaptation to modern life; he advocated, for instance, the abolition of polygamy. He maintained that there is no contradiction between the tenets of Islam and those of modern Western civilization, and that the Islamic renaissance he advocated was the answer to Western criticism and an effective defense against the encroachment of Western values. In 1888, 'A. was permitted to return to Egypt, appointed a judge in the Muslim *Shari'a courts and a member of the board of al-*Azhar University and of the Legislative Council. In 1899 he was made Grand *Mufti of Egypt. His ideas and writings — intensely debated by supporters and opponents — had a considerable influence on the Islamic movement and Arab nationalism.

Abu --- (Arabic: Father of ---). Calling a man Father of his first-born son as an honorific added to his name is a widespread custom in Arab society. In most cases, the honorific is known only to close acquaintances; in some, it becomes public knowledge — particularly in underground organizations, where the honorific may serve as a *nom de guerre* (Abu 'Amār — Yasser *'Arafat; Abu Lutf — Faruq Qaddumi). In many instances, the *nom de guerre* is used rather than the real name (Abu Iyad — Salah Khalaf; Abu Jihad — Khalil al-Wazir; Abu Nidal — Sabri al-Banna; and many other *PLO activists). There also many family names with "Abu ---" — such as *Abu-(a)l-Huda, Abu-(a)l-Fatḥ, or in the North-African form (usually with the French transcription) *Bourguiba, Bouteflika, Boucetta; these stay in the family, in contrast to the honorifics and *noms de guerre* which are tied to the person bearing them.

Abu Dhabi The largest and most populous of the seven sheikhdoms or principalities of the *Trucial Coast (Trucial 'Oman) federated since 1971 as the *United Arab Emirates (UAE). AD's territory — some 29,000 sq.mi. (75,000 sq.km.) — is mostly unsettled desert, saline or covered by sand. Her borders are not finally defined and in several areas they were disputed by her neighbors. In one such dispute, with Sa'udi Arabia, AD in 1955 occupied al-*Buraimi oasis by British-led military action (together with 'Oman, which got half of the oasis); Sa'udi Arabia reluctantly relinquished her claim in 1974. Other disputes, with *Qatar and *Dubai, were settled amicably in the 1960s. In the 1974 agreement, AD ceded to Sa'udi Arabia, in return for Buraimi, a 50 km.-long strip in her extreme West, giving Sa'udia access to the Persian Gulf between AD and Qatar; it is, however, not clear whether the deal has been fully implemented.

AD's population was variously estimated, until the 1960s, at 20–40,000; a census of 1968 put it at 46,000. By the 1980s it had grown, in the wake of the rapid development of her oil economy, to an estimated 450,000 — most of it, according to some estimates, up to 80%, foreign workers and migrants (Arab, and mainly Pakistani). The majority of the population — some 250,000 according to latest estimates — live in the capital, AD, developed since the late 1960s as a modern city. This modernization — and the large proportion of foreign workers — have created serious social problems.

The Sheikh of AD, of the al-*Nuhayan family, was under British protection from the 19th century (see *Trucial Coast), with a British political officer stationed in AD. The present ruler, Sheikh *Zayed ibn Sultan, assumed power in 1966, toppling his brother, Sheikh Shakbut (alleged to be a tyrant and to stand in the way of progress and development), with British help. Since 1966, AD has maintained a small military force. In 1971, Britain withdrew, letting her protectorate lapse, and AD formed, with the other six Sheikhdoms, an independent federation, the United Arab Emirates (UAE). She became — in constant rivalry with Dubai — the dominant power within the Federation (to a degree that it is sometimes difficult to distinguish between actions taken by the ruler and his government on behalf of AD and those taken on behalf of the UAE). AD town is the temporary capital of the UAE (a new federal capital is to be built on the AD-Dubai border). AD's ruler, Sheikh Zayed, was elected by the Council of Rulers as President of the UAE, and re-elected in 1976, 1981, 1986, to 5-year terms; his son, the Crown Prince, became Deputy Premier, and from 1977 Deputy Commander-in-Chief, another member of the family taking over his cabinet post. Generally, AD's leaders want the Federation to become tighter and stronger vis-à-vis its component parts (while Dubai prefers it to remain loose). Apart from the Sheikh's traditional informal consultations, AD has not developed representative institutions of her own (an appointed Consultative Council representing the UAE as a whole). Strict Islamic law is in force.

Oil concessions were granted in 1939 and 1953, and oil was struck in 1962-63. For data on the rapid growth of oil and gas production and revenues see *oil. An oil refinery was inaugurated in 1982; so were two gas liquefaction plants (one, for offshore gas, on Das island), and gas collection and processing installations. Plans for a petrochemical industry had to be cut back in the oil recession of the 1980s.

Economic development remained mainly linked to the oil and petrochemical sector — though various other schemes were being planned. Communications were greatly expanded and a network of modern roads was built; a port was also constructed (though it could not become a major deep-water port). Social services and institutions — schools, hospitals etc. — were also energetically developed. In 1971 an "Arab Development Fund" was set up through which AD dispenses aid and credits — mainly to Arab, but also to some Asian and African, countries.

Abu Mussa A small island in the *Persian Gulf involved in international disputes. In 1906, an iron-oxide mining concession in AM granted by the Sheikh of *Sharja, one of the *Trucial Coast sheikhdoms, to a German company caused a flurry; Britain compelled the Sheikh to cancel the concession and a British landing party removed the Germans. In recent years, Sharja's ownership of AM has been disputed by both the Trucial Coast Sheikhdom of *Umm al-Qaiwain and Iran. Umm al-Qaiwain mainly claimed offshore oil rights (and had already granted a concession to a US company, while Sharja had given a rival concession to a competing US company). Iran claimed actual territorial possession of the island — no doubt with an eye to its strategic location near the Straits of *Hormuz. When British protection was removed from Sharja, in 1971, Iran forcibly occupied AM in Nov. 1971 (and the near-by Tanb islands belonging to *Ras al-Khaima) — as she had forewarned. Iran endorsed, however, the offshore oil concession previously granted by Sharja, and agreed with Sharja to share equally the revenue derived from it. Offshore production began in 1974.

'Aden Town and harbor at the western end of the south coast of the Arabian peninsula, since 1967 capital of *South Yemen. Acquired by Britain in 1839 and developed as a coaling and supply station for ships, 'A. was administered by the Government of Bombay province until 1932, and by the Government of India 1932-37; it became a separate Crown Colony in 1937. In 1963 'A. joined the short-lived Federation of *South Arabia as one of its member-states and its Governor's title was changed to High Commissioner for 'A. and the 'A. Protectorates. In 1967, when the Federation was transformed into the independent People's Republic of *South

Yemen, 'A. became part of the new state and its capital.

'A. colony had an area of 75 sq.mi. and occupied two peninsulas around a natural bay — 'A. proper on the eastern side, "Little 'A." on the western, and the separate town of Sheikh 'Uthman at the head of the bay; there, and farther inland on territory of the Sheikhdom of 'Aqrabi, a new town was built as the capital of the South Arabian Federation and later of South Yemen; it was called al-Ittihad (Union or Federation), and after 1967 Madinat al-Sha'b (People's Town). 'A. harbor — a free port since 1850 — became, after the opening of the *Suez Canal, one of the busiest ports of the world (with over 6,200 ships p.a. docking in the mid-1960s — but since the late 1960s it declined). An oil refinery was built in 1952–54 by the Anglo-Iranian Oil Company and later expanded; by the late 1970s its capacity reached 8 million tons p.a. 'A. also served as a principal British air and naval base until 1967.

'A. was a small fishing village when occupied by the British in 1839. The bunkering station and the British base, and later the oil refinery and the growing trading center, caused an increasing influx from the tribal hinterland (the 'A. Protectorates — see below), the Yemen and other countries, and 'A.'s population grew to 47,000 in the 1940s, and over 200,000 in the 1950s; it is now estimated at c. 340,000 — of whom 35–40% are Yemenis, nearly 10% Indians and Pakistanis and almost 10% Somalis. There was also a small Jewish community of c.1,000, mainly of Yemenite Jews, most of whom had left by 1967, after anti-Jewish disturbances and the British evacuation. The urban population of 'A. town provided the main growing and fermenting ground for the nationalist agitation of the late 1950s and the 1960s that led to the creation of independent South Yemen (see there).

In the hinterland of 'A., petty sultans, sheikhs and amirs were gradually brought under British protection during the 19th and early 20th centuries. For these "Western" and "Eastern" 'A. Protectorates — most of which joined the Federation of South Arabia and all of which were absorbed in 1967 in the People's Republic of South Yemen — see *South Yemen, *South Arabia, *Hadhramaut.

'A. colony and Protectorate also included the Red Sea islands of *Qamaran and *Perim, as well as *Socotra and the *Kuria Muria islands in the Arabian Sea. Qamaran now belongs to Yemen, Perim and Socotra — to South Yemen, Kuria Muria — to 'Oman.

'Aflaq, Michel (b. 1910) Syrian political thinker, founder and chief ideologist of the *Ba'th party. Born in Damascus, a Greek-Orthodox Christian, 'A. studied in Paris and was close to the Communist Party. In the late 1930s he developed his own brand of revolutionary-Socialist Arab nationalism, stressing the aim of immediate all-Arab unity. In the 1940s he organized, together with Salah-ul-din *Bitar, a group of like-minded students and young intellectuals as the "Arab Renaissance (al-Ba'th) Party". The party first appeared on the political scene in the Syrian elections of 1947: 'A. stood as a candidate, but failed. In 1949 he served briefly as Minister of Education (in Hashem *Atassi's government, following the Sami *Hinnawi coup), but was again defeated when he stood for Parliament. He remained Secretary-General of the Ba'th party when it merged, in 1953, with Akram *Hourani's "Arab Socialist Party" and in 1959 authoritatively summarized the party's doctrine in his book In the Ways of the Ba'th. In the factional struggles that split the party after it came to power through the coup of Mar. 1963, 'A. sided (with Bitar) with the "civilan" wing considered more moderate — i.e. with the faction that lost out in Syria — in the 1966 coup of the "military wing" — and won in Iraq. In 1966, 'A. left Syria. He continued leading the "National (i.e. all-Arab) Command" of the Ba'th seated in Beirut and Baghdad — to which the Syrian party no longer paid allegiance. In 1967, 'A. emigrated to Brazil, abandoning all political activity; but late in 1968 he went to Baghdad to resume his position of leadership. In 1970 he left Baghdad in protest against Iraq's failure to send troops against Jordan in support of the Palestinian guerrillas; but in 1974 a reconciliation was effected and he returned to Iraq. While highly respected as an ideologist and party intellectual, 'A. does not seem to have retained much effective influence on party and state policies (determined by political and military interests, as judged by a junta of officer-politicians, rather than by ideology or doctrine).

Africa Relations between the AC and Black A. have been strong since the Middle Ages — across the Red Sea, from Egypt to Sudan and farther south, and from the *Maghrib across the Sahara. The Arabs spread Islam; they were the chief traders (including the slave trade); and there was some migration.

In recent decades, the AC supported A.'s struggle for independence and Cairo was the center for several liberation movements. The African AC took part in pre-independence African conferences and organizations and later in the efforts to create an association of independent African countries (at a first conference, Accra 1958, five of the eight participant states were Arab). When initial splits into rival blocs — the radical *Casablanca Bloc, 1961, vs. the pro-Western Monrovia Group, 1961 — were overcome and the "Organization for African Unity", OAU, was founded in May 1963, all six African AC (Egypt, Sudan, Libya, Tunisia, Algeria and Morocco) — or eight, if we count semi-Arab Somalia and Mauritania (nine with Djibouti from 1977) — joined it and acquired a strong influence within it. The ASt were also active in various semi-governmental or non-governmental associations (women; youth; writers; journalists, etc.) — most of them including Asian countries and termed Afro-Asian. Most of these groups had, in addition to their geographical, Afro-Asian, definition, a strong neutralist flavor and some were considered Communist "fronts"; the main popular formation was the "Afro-Asian Peoples' Solidarity Organization", frequently meeting in Cairo. Since the late 1960s these Afro-Asian activities have slackened, mainly because of intra-Asian and -African disputes and the Sino-Soviet conflict.

The ASt vigorously campaigned for OAU support against Israel — and succeeded to a large extent. From 1967 the OAU constantly condemned Israel's occupation of Arab territories — despite good relations with Israel of most African countries; and after the failure of a mediation attempt by four African Presidents (Cameroon, Senegal, Nigeria and Zaire) in Nov. 1971, the AC persuaded all African states except Malawi, Lesotho and Swaziland to sever relations with Israel from 1972, and mainly in Oct.–Nov. 1973 (since 1982 relations with Israel were re-established — so far by five: Zaire, Liberia, Ivory Coast, Cameroon and Togo). The OAU also mediated in several inter-Arab or Arab-African disputes — Morocco-Algeria, with partial success; Western *Sahara and Libya-Chad with no success; it hardly intervened in Sudan's dispute and war with her southern Black-African tribes, the Ethiopia-Somalia dispute and the Ethiopia-Eritrea one and its repercussions on Ethiopia-Sudan relations. Arab-African relations remain close, though Africans tend to resent the inadequacy of Arab aid, Arab "Big Brother" attitudes and Libyan interference in neighboring African countries.

Afro-Asian conferences, organizations See *Africa.

agrarian reform See *Land Reform.

Ahmad bin Yahya (Hamid-ul-Din) (1895–1962) Ruler of Yemen and Imam of her Shi'i-*Zeidi community, 1948–62. The eldest son of Imam *Yahya, he was groomed for the succession and entrusted with various state missions (as a prince, he bore, like all the Imam's sons, the title *Seif-ul-Islam*, "Sword of Islam"). In his campaigns against rebellious tribes in the 1920s and 1930s, he acquired a reputation of cruelty. When his father was assassinated, in Feb. 1948, A. was chosen by the ruling Zeidi notables — the *Sada* (see *Sayyid) — to succeed him as Imam. He continued strengthening the central royal power — building a modern army, subduing recalcitrant tribes, reducing the influence and power of the *Sada*. In Aug. 1955 he had to suppress, with the help of his eldest son Muhammad al-*Badr, a *coup* attempt launched by rebellious officers and *Sada* as well as two of his brothers, Seif-ul-Islam 'Abdullah and Seif-ul-Islam 'Abbas (who were both executed). A. continued slowly to establish regular foreign relations, with both superpowers eager to respond. In his later years, A. was plagued by illness and delegated much of his power to his son al-Badr and his brother Seif-ul-Islam Hassan. His death, in Sept. 1962, triggered the revolution that toppled Yemen's monarchy.

Ahmadiyya A religious community derived from Islam, founded by Mirza Ghulam Ahmad of Qadian, India (d. 1908), who claimed to be a manifestation of Krishna, Jesus (who, according to him, died in India), Muhammad and all the prophets, and the *Mahdi of Islam. The publications in which he expounded his doctrine show traces of Hindu influence and, mainly, of Islamic mysticism. After the death of his successor (*Kha-*

lifa), Hakim Nur-ul-Din, in 1914, the A. split into two main groups. The main faction, also called Qadiani, has its center in Rabwah, Pakistan, and branches in many countries, especially in India, Pakistan and West Africa. It engages in vigorous missionary activity. This group considers Mirza Ghulam Ahmad as the "Seal of the Prophets", i.e. the last prophet — a title usually accorded to Muhammad. The smaller faction, the "Lahoris", centered in Lahore, Pakistan, and also active in missionary work, is closer to orthodox Islam and regards the Founder as an innovating Islamic thinker rather than a Prophet.

The A. claim to be the true community of Islam. They believe in the Qur'an — which one of the leaders of the smaller A. groups, Muhammad 'Ali (d. 1951) translated into English — and the basic tenets and commandments of Islam (interpreting *Jihad* — as do some orthodox Muslims, too — as "effort" for the sake of Islam rather than specifically Holy *War*). They expand through missionary efforts and publish much material expounding their doctrine. Muslim leaders generally denounce the A. and regard them as infidels, outside Islam. There have been instances of persecution and pogroms — e.g. in Pakistan in 1953 and again in 1974. Their activities have been banned and their institutions closed in Syria (1958) and Uganda (1975); in Pakistan they were outlawed altogether in 1974 (though their community continues to exist). Estimates of the number of A. vary between 1 million and 4 or 5 million; the A. themselves claim to number c.10 million (4–5 million in Pakistan alone).

al-Ahram Egyptian daily newspaper and publishing house. The paper was founded in 1876 by the brothers Salim and Bishara Taqla, immigrants from Lebanon, first in Alexandria and from 1898 in Cairo. Gradually, al-A. became Egypt's largest, most important and most prestigious newspaper, with its own network of correspondents in foreign countries, a rich variety of information and articles, a high level of responsible journalism, and well-developed printing techniques. Politically al-A. was neutral, with no party affiliation, but usually supported the government of the day. Among its editors were well-known writers, e.g. the poet Khalil Mutran, Daoud Barakat, Kamel Shinawi. After the Free Officers' *coup* of 1952 the paper declined, but when Muhammad Hassanein *Heykal was appointed chief editor, in 1957, it recovered its leading position. In 1960 al-A. was nationalized, together with all other Egyptian papers, and later was regarded as the semi-official mouthpiece of the Government, although Heykal maintained his own, independent line, usually to the right of the Nasser régime's main line. From the later 1960s the paper branched out, establishing a publishing house and several research institutes (e.g. one for Strategic Problems, and another for Palestine Studies). In 1974, Heykal was dismissed as chief editor and chairman of the board because of his "Nasserist" opposition to *Sadat and his régime. 'Ali Amin became editor for some time, and since 1975 the editorship has changed hands (Ahmad Baha'-ul-Din, 'Ali Hamdi Gamal, Ibrahim Nafe'). The chairmanship of the board, taken over in 1974 by Deputy Premier 'Abd-ul-Qader Hatem, has also changed hands (Ihsan 'Abd-ul-Quddus, Yusuf Siba'i & al.). Estimates vary as to al-A.'s circulation: it was thought to be 100,000 and above in the 1940s and 1950s, 250,000 or more in the 1960s, and since the late 1970s is claimed to be 700,000.

'Ajman The smallest of the seven sheikhdoms or principalities of the *Trucial Coast (Trucial 'Oman) now forming the *United Arab Emirates. Area — 97 sq.mi. (250 sq.km.). 'A.'s population — mostly nomadic, with some engaged in fishing — was less than 5,000 until the 1960s; it is estimated, in the 1980s, at about 35,000. The ruler belongs to the sheikhly family al-Nu'aimi. Since the 19th century 'A. was under British protection. When Britain renounced her Protectorate over Trucial 'Oman and the sheikhdoms formed the Federation of the United Arab Emirates in 1971, 'A. joined that Federation — remaining, in fact, a rather junior partner. An oil exploration concession granted in 1962 to a small American company expired in 1967. In 1970 a new concession was granted to the American Occidental Company; but no oil strikes have so far been reported.

al- (sometimes also el-, following its pronunciation in spoken Arabic, or ul-, in combined forms, following the rules of Arabic grammar) — the definite article — is frequently used in Arabic names. Al- is nearly always part of names deriving from places of origin (al-Misri or al-Masri, al-Hijazi, al-Baghdadi, al-Halabi) or from occupations (al-Najjar, al-Khayyat, al-Dabbagh); it is more or less optional in patronyms (which preceded family names): Ahmad al-Hussein or Ahmad Hussein. Its use fluctuates in modern family names: Anwar al-Sadat, Hafez al-Asad, Riad al-Sulh, but Rashid Karameh, Kamal Junblat, and in many names its use is optional; foreign-language press and publications tend to drop it and speak of Sadat or Asad, where in Arabic al-Sadat or al-Asad would be used. In this Dictionary al-, where used, is not taken account of in the alphabetical order — i.e. look for al-Husseini under Husseini, al-Suweidi under Suweidi; we have added a hyphen after al-, for the sake of convenience, though there is none in Arabic. We have disregarded, as does written Arabic, the rule by which the *l* in al assimilates, when pronounced, to certain letters — e.g. we write al-Numeiri, not an-Numeiri; al-Sallal, not as-Sallal; al-Dawalibi, not ad-Dawalibi; 'Abd-ul-Rahman, not 'Abd-ur-Rahman. In names constructed on the pattern of 'Abd-ul-Rahman, 'Abd-ul-Qader (i.e. The Servant of God — with "God" replaced by one of God's epithets) the 'Abd-ul-epithet combination is considered as one name (hyphens added for the sake of convenience); the same goes for combinations like Salah-ul-Din, Dia-ul-Din, Dia-ul-Haqq. Look, therefore, for all 'Abd-ul-epithet combinations under A. (Where a contrary usage has become dominant — like Nasser, instead of the correct 'Abd-ul-Nasser — cross references are given).

al-'Alami, Mussa (1897–1984) Palestinian-Arab politician. Son of a prominent Jerusalem family (his father, Feidi al-'A., 1815–1924, was Mayor of Jerusalem 1906–09 and represented the Jerusalem District in the Ottoman Parliament 1914–18), 'A. studied law at the American University of Beirut. He joined the Legal Department of the Palestine Government, attaining the senior position of Government Advocate. He took some part in the Arab nationalist movement, but was not very active. He was related to the *Husseini family and considered close to the Husseini political camp, but was never fully identified with any faction. In the mid-1930s — before and during the rebellion — he met Jewish leaders for talks on the possibility of an Arab-Jewish agreement, but the talks were abortive. In 1937 he was dismissed from government service because of his alleged involvement with the leadership of the Arab rebellion, and exiled himself to Syria and Iraq; he returned to Palestine in 1941. In the absence of a Palestinian-Arab representative body, he was appointed by the conveners of the *Arab League to represent the Arabs of Palestine at the Preparatory Conference of *Alexandria, Oct. 1944, and at the foundation of the Arab League, Mar. 1945. In 1945, he was also appointed to a new (or re-constituted) Arab Higher Committee, as a neutral notable not identified with any faction, but soon withdrew from the committee and the factional struggle around it, to devote himself to two special independent projects: he founded Palestinian-Arab Information or propaganda offices in London, Washington, Beirut and Jerusalem, selecting mostly younger intellectuals — without paying attention to their factional or clan affiliation; and he initiated a "Constructive Scheme" to develop the Palestinian-Arab village and its lands so as to prevent the sale of Arab lands to Jews (as against an Arab "National Fund" (*Sanduq al-Ummah*), established by a rival faction, that planned to attain the same goal by the purchase of such lands). Both his enterprises were approved and supported by the Arab League. Both collapsed in the Arab-Jewish war of 1948.

After the war, 'A. devoted himself to a training farm for Palestinian-Arab youth, particularly orphans, near Jericho, supported by funds from abroad — a remnant of his "Constructive Scheme". Reports of his involvement in political activities in Jordan — e.g. as a co-founder of a branch of the *al-*Ba'th* party or a faction sponsored by Iraq — were never substantiated. After 1967 he lived in London and 'Amman, paying visits to Jerusalem and Jericho. In 1971 he returned to Jerusalem, but took no part in public life. He died in 'Amman in 1984.

'A.'s book "The Lesson of Palestine" (*'Ibrat Filastin*), 1949, was one of the first to analyze the deeper social reasons for the Arab defeat in Palestine. A full-length biography of 'A., by Geoffrey Furlonge (virtually his autobiography, as told to the writer), appeared in London in 1969.

'Alawis, 'Alawites (or Nusseiris) Islamic sect, apparently derived from the *Isma'iliyya version of the *Shi'a. Little is known of their origin. Some see the 'A. as descendants of an ancient Canaanite people who, surviving in the isolated mountains of Syria, were only marginally influenced by Christianity and Islam and retained many pagan Syrian customs. They adopted the Arabic language and the Islamic faith, in its Isma'ili version, in the Middle Ages and then became a separate sect. Parts of their tenets are secret, known only to the initiated; they reportedly believe in a holy trinity of 'Ali, the Prophet Muhammad and Salman al-Fārisi (i.e. the Persian — one of the Companions of the Prophet). Some Muslims regard them as marginal to, on the fringes or even outside of, Islam; in Syria, however, they are generally regarded, for purposes of personal status jurisdiction, as Shi'i Muslims; their recognition as Muslims is at least implied in the fact that the Head of State — who must according to the Constitution be a Muslim — is since 1971 an 'A., Hafez al-*Asad (but some Muslim protests were voiced against his election).

Most of the 'A. — c. 75% — live in Syria, while the rest are mainly in the *Alexandretta (*Hatay) and Cilicia regions of southern Turkey, and some in northern Lebanon. In Syria, the 'A. are the largest minority group, 10–12% of the total population — at present about 1 million. Most of them live in mountain villages in the Lataqia district, on the north-western coast, also known as the 'A. region or the Mountain of the Nusseiris; they form about two-thirds of the district's population, though they are a minority in its capital, Lataqia.

Under Ottoman rule the 'A. enjoyed a measure of local autonomy; but in the mid-19th century the Ottoman government began tightening its control (e.g. 'A. were now tried in Muslim-Sunni courts). When France established her Mandate in Syria, 1920–22, the 'A. region was recognized as an autonomous territory under a French governor, and the French endeavored to advance the 'A. economically and culturally. In 1936, the 'A. state became part of Syria — with partial autonomy. This special autonomous status ended with the departure of the French, 1944–46.

A disproportionally large number of 'A. serve in the Army and its officers' corps, as the French encouraged the enlistment of members of the minorities in the Special Forces they established (i.a. as a means to curb the nationalist tendencies of the Arab-Sunni majority) and many 'A. saw a military career as a way to social and economic advancement. Since the 1950s many 'A. officers joined the *Ba'th party and its cells in the officers' corps, attracted by the party's emphasis on supra-communal nationalist-secular values. When the Ba'th officers seized power in 1963, more 'A. joined. As a result, 'A. are disproportionally numerous among Syria's political and military leaders — e.g. *Jadid, *Asad (President since 1971), 'Umran, Ibrahim Makhus, 'Ali Douba, 'Ali Haidar, 'Adnan Makhluf, Mahmud Khuli — to a degree that many speak of Syria's "'A. régime" or "'A. rulers". Yet, the 'A. remain economically and culturally Syria's most backward community.

In northern Lebanon, 'A. form the backbone of the faction supporting Syria to the hilt and frequently give battle to Muslim-Sunni fundamentalist groups in Tripoli. In Turkey, on the other hand, 'A. do not display strong communal cohesion or aspirations (in Turkish terminology, all Shi'i Muslims, non-'A., are often erroneously called 'A.).

Aleppo (Ḥalab) Syria's second city and the main center of North Syria. Population (1979 estimate) 919,000. At the cross-roads between Syria, Mesopotamia and Anatolia, linking the Euphrates valley with the Mediterranean, A. has been a strategically and economically important city since antiquity. In the Middle Ages it was a vital trading and communications center for Mediterranean Europe's commerce with the East. Since the last century its economic activity and its industry (mainly textiles, cement and food products) have surpassed those of Damascus. In the Ottoman empire, A. was the capital of a province (vilayet). From 1921 to 1924 it was the capital of a "State of A." formed by the French under their Mandate for Syria; in 1924–25 that state was merged with the "State of Damascus" to form Syria. Throughout recent history A. and Damascus have been rivals. Population figures were running neck to neck, until Damascus began overtaking A. in the 1960s and 1970s. During the years of active political and parliamentary life in the 1940s and 1950s, all factions had their A. branches; but A. was the center, mainly, of the "People's Party" that used to compete for power with the Damascus centered "National Bloc" (later the "National Party") and provided several Prime Ministers. Under the rule of the Ba'th party, since 1963, A.'s position has somewhat declined. Reviving its old opposition to the rulers of Damascus, A. has also become one of the main centers of Muslim-Sunni resistance to the rule of the *Ba'th* (brutally suppressed in the 1970s).

Alexandretta Province (named in Turkish *Hatay) and town and port (in Turkish: Iskenderun) in South Turkey, at the head of the Eastern Mediterranean Bay of A. The area was included, as a district with special status *Sanjaq*) in French-mandated Syria, 1921–39, and handed to Turkey in 1939, after a protracted crisis. The A. district, under Syria, had an area of 1,814 sq.mi. and a population (in the late 1930s) of c. 220,000, with c. 30,000 in A. town. Of this population, c. 40% were Turks — according to French estimates, while Turkey claimed a Turkish majority.

In the Franklin-Bouillon Agreement of 1921 that fixed the Syro-Turkish border, A. was allotted to the "State of *Aleppo" within French-mandated Syria, as a district with a special régime and official status for the Turkish language. When, in 1924, the "State of Aleppo" merged with the "State of Damascus" into Syria, that special régime was retained. In 1936, when a Franco-Syrian treaty was negotiated providing for Syrian independence and the end of the French Mandate, Turkey opposed the inclusion of A. in an independent Syria, claiming she had ceded it to the French Mandate only and demanding separate statehood for it, while France and Syria insisted on its retention by Syria. The dispute was raised at the League of Nations which decided in 1937 on a compromise: A. would form a separate entity independent in internal affairs and with its own constitution, linked to Syria concerning currency, customs and foreign affairs only; Arabic and Turkish would both be official languages, and Turkey would enjoy special rights in A. port; no military bases or fortifications were to be constructed. Attempts to implement this formula did not solve the problem, but led to unrest and violence between Turks and Arabs in the district. While France, preoccupied with the mounting European crisis and eager to retain Turkish friendship, was a weak defender of Syria's position, Turkey acted systematically and forcefully to gain control of A. Turkish armed forces entered the district in 1938. Under Turkish pressure an electoral law was passed that gave the Turkish inhabitants a majority in the House of Representatives. A Turk was elected President, and a Turk appointed to head an all-Turkish government. Turkey abrogated her acceptance of League of Nations supervision. The district was given an official Turkish name, Hatay, linked to the Turkish currency and postal services, and subjected to Turkish law. In June 1939 France ceded the district to Turkey.

Turkey's annexation of A. caused an outcry in Syria; demonstrations against Turkey and France demanded the return of the territory, but to no avail. Syria has never recognized Turkey's possession of, and sovereignty over, the district; her maps include A. within Syrian territory; and from time to time she demands its return. Usually, however, the dispute is dormant; it has not prevented Syria from establishing and maintaining normal, friendly diplomatic relations with Turkey (implying, at least, a *de facto* acceptance of Turkey's territory and borders). The other Arab states, too, while verbally and in principle supporting Syria's claim, are usually silent and keep the dispute quite dormant.

Alexandria Protocol After nearly two years of preparatory talks on "Arab Unity", i.e. on the ways to link the ASt's then existing in some kind of joint organization, the leaders of the seven ASt's then independent or nearly-independent — Egypt, Iraq, Sa'udi Arabia, Yemen, Transjordan, Syria and Lebanon, with a representative of the Palestine A's in attendance — met in Sept.–Oct. 1944 in A. for a full-dress Preparatory Conference. The Conference recommended the establishment of a "Commonwealth (or League) of Arab States" and resulted in a Protocol signed by five of the states on 7 Oct. 1944. The Sa'udi and Yemeni representatives were not empowered to sign without the endorsement of their kings. The A.P. laid down the principles to guide the association envisaged, and its main points were embodied in the Charter of the *Arab League in Mar. 1945. Chief of those was the conception of the League as an alliance of independent and sovereign states rather than a federation, and the rejection of any changes in the inter-A. territorial *status quo*. An appendix on Palestine stressed the Palestine A.'s right to independence (with no mention of autonomy or a special status for the Jewish community in a future independent Palestine) and pledged all-Arab help in their struggle. Another appendix confirmed Lebanon's right to full independence and the inviolability of her territory and borders. This appendix was demanded by the leaders of Lebanon, who feared annexationist designs on the part of Syria.

Algeria (Arabic: al-Jazā'ir — the islands). A republic on the southern coast of the western Mediterranean, bordering on Tunisia and Libya in the east, Niger, Mali and Mauritania in the south, and Morocco in the west. Area: 920,000 sq.mi. (2,381,741 sq.km.), over four-fifth in the western Sahara desert. Population: 18.24 m. at the last census, 1977 (including some 828,000 Algerians living in France), 1983–84 estimate — 20–21 m. Most of the population is Muslim (Sunni of the Maliki school), and the majority speak Arabic, which is the official language. The remainder, mainly in the Kabylia highlands east of Algiers, speak *Berber. (Those with Berber as mother-tongue are estimated at 4–6 m; the number of those still conscious of Berber descent — difficult to evaluate — is variously estimated at 25–50%, i.e. 5–10 m.). Capital: Algiers (2.2. m. — 1982–83 estimate).

HISTORY From the 16th century A. was under nominal Ottoman sovereignty. In fact, local governors ("Dey") ruled the coastal strip, while in the region inland tribes and local chiefs were hardly controlled by the Dey. The name Algiers (al-Jaza'ir) applied to the town rather than a country. As local pirate chiefs greatly disturbed Mediterranean shipping and trade, the European powers conducted several punitive campaigns in the early 19th century. In July 1830 35,000 French troops landed in Algiers, following an economic dispute and the humiliation of the French Consul by the Dey — but mainly because of the need of the French King Charles X and his right-wing government to gain some credit abroad in order to strengthen their power-base at home. In 1831, they deposed the Dey. In 1834 France established an administration for the "regions of North Africa in French possession". Local rebellions against the French occupation were widespread. The most important one was led by the Berber chieftain 'Abd-ul-Qader (1807–83), whom France had to recognize in 1834 as Amir of a West-A. district — but his rebellion continued and was finally suppressed only in 1847. 'Abd-ul-Qader was taken to France, and when released in 1852, he settled in Damascus. He is regarded as a national hero and the father of Algerian nationalism. In 1966 his remains were solemnly transferred to A. Outbreaks of militant opposition to the French continued throughout the 19th century. As a result of these rebellions the local Muslim population was reduced — according to some estimates by some 3 m. The settlement of French and European colonists was organized, and land was confiscated or bought for them, reaching an estimated 2 m. acres by the 1870s, nearly 6 m. acres between the world wars, or 25–30% of all cultivated land, including most of the best lands. French settlers also became dominant in trade, finance and industry. Frenchmen and Europeans numbered c. 800,000 on the eve of World War I — against a local Muslim population of 4.5–5 m.

A. was administered as part of France, but French citizenship was not granted to the local population — non-French in language, and ethnically, in its Muslim religion, in its customs, laws and social structure, and largely uneducated and illiterate. An exception was made for the Jewish community which received French citizenship in 1870 under a decree of French Justice Minister Adolphe Crémieux. A.'s Muslims were French subjects, but could obtain French citizenship on certain conditions only — including the attainment of defined educational levels, the renunciation of their status under Muslim personal law, and the acceptance of French laws and customs. Very few made use of that right. Representative bodies established in A. were limited to French citizens, and their powers were advisory only. In 1900 A. was granted administrative and financial autonomy; a "Financial Delegation" — two-thirds European, one-third Muslim — was to advise the Governor-General concerning the budget, the financial administration of A.'s three *départements* (Algiers, Oran, Constantine), and credits for economic development.

In the early 20th century, the socio-economic, cultural and legal gap between the French and the local population widened. A growing group of Muslims who studied abroad, both in France and in AC's, intellectuals who came in touch with European politics and Arab nationalism, started to give a political shape to their grievances. In 1924 Hajj Ahmad Messali (Messali Hadj) founded a nationalist society in Paris, "The North African Star", and a newspaper, which had left-wing and communist tendencies, and influenced mainly A.'n workers in France. Its links with the Communists were severed in 1927 and

Messali developed traditional-Muslim tendencies. The French closed the society in 1929, and Messali was imprisoned several times. In 1933 he was among the sponsors of a congress which called for the complete independence of A. In 1937 Messali Hadj founded the "Parti Populaire Algérien" (PPA). Islamic circles were also active in nationalist politics and in 1931 founded a Society of (Religious) Scholars (Jam'iyyat al-'Ulamā') which combined Muslim modernism with Arab-A.'n nationalism. These early attempts at nationalist activity had only a limited influence on the Muslim population, and the groups formed did not represent the local population either in the municipal and regional councils in A. or in the French parliament.

The victory of the Popular Front in France in 1936 gave rise to some hopes that integration with France on a basis of equality might be achieved. But the Blum-Violette Plan, which intended to grant full citizenship to a growing number of A.'ns was dropped due to the strong opposition of French right-wing circles, especially among the French settlers and the civil service in A.

World War II put a temporary halt to nationalist activities. The Vichy régime, strongly supported by the French settlers in A., was hostile to A.'n nationalist sentiments. Anti-Semitism, however, was common to both groups, and the anti-Jewish legislation of the Vichy administration, and the cancellation of the 1870 Crémieux Decree in Oct. 1940, were supported by the Muslims. The Crémieux Decree was re-enacted in Oct. 1943, after the Allied take-over.

Following the Allied Forces' landing in A. in Nov. 1942, nationalist activity resumed. On 22 Dec. 1942 a group headed by Ferhat *'Abbas presented to the French authorities and the Allied military command a memoradum calling for the establishment of an A.'n constituent assembly elected by all the population. In Feb. 1943 these demands were published in the form of the "Manifesto of the A.'n People", calling for immediate reforms, full equality and the participation of the Muslims in the administration. Further demands in May 1943 called for the postwar creation of an A.'n state with a constitution determined by a constituent assembly. The Free French administration in A. rejected all these demands but following De Gaulle's arrival in A. tried to calm Muslim discontent by reforms. A statute of Mar. 1944 granted c. 60,000 Muslims the right to acquire French citizenship and take part in French elections (as a separate "college" — against c. 450,000 in a European "college", each "college" to send the same number of deputies); only 32,000 Muslims accepted inscription. The Muslim share of seats in the mixed regional and municipal councils was set at 40%. Any further discussion of A.'s future was refused by the French authorities. Shortly afterwards, 'Abbas founded a political party, "Amis du Manifeste de la Libération" (AML), calling for the foundation of an autonomous A.'n republic, federally linked to France. The AML, supported mainly by middle-class Muslims, was dissolved in mid-1945 and 'Abbas was arrested, following the brutal suppression of riots at Setif in May 1945, which claimed the lives of many Muslims (estimates varying from 1,000 to 15,000 or more). In Mar. 1946 'Abbas was released under an amnesty, and established the "Union Démocratique du Manifeste Algérien" (UDMA), calling for the establishment of an autonomous, secular A.'n state within the French Union. The veteran PPA also returned to politics in 1944 and gained many followers among the masses. In 1946 Messali Hadj re-formed it as the "Mouvement pour le Triomphe des Libertés Démocratique" (MTLD). This party was more radical than the UDMA and called for the creation of a separate sovereign A., the election of a constituent assembly, and the evacuation of French troops.

On 20 Sept. 1947 a new constitution came into force. It provided French citizenship and the right to vote to all A.'ns, including women, without obliging them to renounce their personal status under Muslim Law, and recognized Arabic as an official language. It set up an A.'n Assembly divided into two "colleges" of 60 members each, one representing 1.5 m. French citizens, 550,000 voters (inclding 60–70,000 Muslims), the other representing the rest of the population (some 9 m. Muslims, 1.3–1.5 m. of them voters); each college was to send 15 representatives to the French National Assembly and 7 to the Senate. In the mixed municipal councils in A. the voters of the first college had 60% of the representation, and those of the second college, representing a much larger population — 40%, as before. A "Governing Council" was also established, composed of the President of the Assembly, one of his deputies (from the other college), two other Assembly representatives, one from each college, and two appointed by the Governor-General.

The new constitution did not satisfy the nationalists, who by now aspired to independence. They were also disappointed by the mode of its implementation. They gained a majority in the second college in the Oct. 1947 municipal elections, but failed in the Apr. 1948 elections for the A.'n Assembly: the MTLD was 9 seats, the UDMA 8, while the rest of the 60 deputies of the second college were "independents". The nationalists claimed that the French administration had interfered with, and rigged, the elections. This failure of the nationalists in elections to the French parliament, the A.'n Assembly and other institutions continued.

These developments caused much frustration among the nationalists and many despaired of achieving their aims through political-constitutional means. In 1947 several younger members of the MTLD formed an "Organisation Secrète" (OS), which started to collect arms and financial means and built up a network of cells throughout A. in preparation for an armed insurrection and the establishment of a revolutionary government and in 1949 launched an attack on Oran. In 1950 the OS was discovered and most of its leaders were arrested. A nucleus, however, survived in the Kabyle region, renown as a stronghold for dissident activities. Among its leaders were *Ben Bella, Hussein Ait Ahmad, Muhammad Khidr, and Belkacem Krim.

The establishment of the OS marked the growing split in the MTLD between leaders conducting traditional political activity, represented by Messali Hadj who was gradually losing ground, and more militant younger nationalists. An open breach occurred in Mar. 1953 when 9 former OS members established a "Conseil Révolutionnaire pour l'Unité et l'Action" (CRUA), which regarded the MTLD and Messali Hadj personally as traitors, and advocated militant operations towards an immediate revolt. Egypt had a profound influence on the CRUA and Cairo became the center of A.'n underground activities. From Mar. to Oct. 1954 the CRUA held a series of meetings in Switzerland where plans for an insurrection were worked out. Revolutionary A. was divided into six regions (*wilaya*), each headed by a military commander. The revolt was launched on 1 Nov. 1954 by the "Front de Libération Nationale" (*FLN) formed from the CRUA. The MTLD failed in its attempt to form a military organization of its own ("Mouvement National Algérien" — MNA), and most of the national groups gradually merged with the FLN. The FLN was headed by a 9-man command (among them Ben Bella, Rabah Bitat, Khidr, Muhammad Boudiaf, Ait Ahmad, Belkacem Krim). The revolt, which started in the Aurès region, spread in early 1955 to the Constantine area, Kabylia and the Oran region of West A. By the end of 1956 all the settled areas of A. were in revolt.

As the rebellion progressed, a rift developed between the FLN leaders in Cairo, some of whom were later captured and imprisoned, and the command in the field. This rift was also apparent later, after A. reached independence. In Aug. 1956 the FLN held a congress in the Soummam valley in Kabylia, to which most of the leaders outside A. were unable to come. The congress formed a coordinating committee, composed mainly of the commanders of the six military regions, and a "Conseil National de la Révolution Algérienne" (CNRA) as a representative body of all the nationalist groups with supervising, quasi-parliamentary functions. Two-thirds of the CNRA members were to be revolutionaries from inside A. The congress also drew up a socialist program for the future of A. and approved military plans for the continuation of the rebellion.

The French tried to quell the revolt by police action and military force. They also sought to persuade Egypt to stop supporting the revolt and offering Cairo as asylum and part-headquarters to the FLN leadership. Electrified barriers were set up along the Tunisian and Moroccan borders, to prevent FLN infiltration. France also tried to step up the political integration of A., coupled with socio-economic reforms. But this was not enough anymore for most of the rebels and the bloody revolt, fought mercilessly by both sides, continued. By 1956–57 the A.'n rebels numbered some 60,000. When leaders of Morocco and Tunisia, independent by now, started to plan for a North-African federation linked with France, FLN leaders participated in the negotiations. But in Oct. 1956 five of them, on their way from Morocco to Tunisia, were kidnapped to Algiers by their French pilot and arrested; they included Ben Bella, Khidr, Ait Ahmad and Boudiaf (Rabah Bitat had been caught earlier). One of the results of their removal from the leadership of the revolt was an increase in the influence of the commanders inside A., many of them Berbers, and especially that of Belkacem Krim.

The growing radicalism of the FLN, and the support it received from the non-aligned states and the Eastern bloc, caused a backlash from the Army and the French settlers. On 13 May 1958 Army officers and settlers rebelled, bringing about the collapse of the French Fourth Republic and the return to power of General de Gaulle. The settlers believed that de Gaulle would enforce the complete integration of A. into France, as they advocated. At first, de Gaulle indeed stepped up military operations against the FLN. But, realizing the stubborn strength of A.'n nationalism, he soon began moving towards accepting A.'n independence.

The FLN, while stepping up its warlike operations, in Sept. 1958 set up a Gouvernement Provisionnel de la République Algérienne (GPRA) in Tunis, headed by Ferhat 'Abbas (replaced in Aug. 1961 by Ben Youssef Ben Khedda) and including Ben Bella and the other interned leaders.

Since 1955 the A. problem was debated each year in the UN. No feasible solution acceptable to both sides was reached, but the continued debate put much pressure on France and encouraged the rebels. In late 1958 de Gaulle ordered the release of the interned FLN leaders into house arrest in France, and a number of other imprisoned rebels were also released. The French settlers, army and right-wing rejected this move, which they regarded as a step towards negotiations with a terrorist organization. In 1958, a new election law granted the A.'n Muslims a decisive majority among the deputies to be elected to the French National Assembly (48, against 21 Europeans). The FLN-guided nationalists did not put up candidates, and all Muslims elected were integrationists or non-political (but several soon dissociated themselves from the integrationist bloc). French proposals for cease-fire negotiations with no pre-conditions were rejected by the FLN leaders, who insisted on a full discussion of the future of A.

During 1959 de Gaulle hardened his view that the policy of integration was futile. On 16 Sept. 1959 he offered the A.'n people a cease-fire and self-determination in the form of a referendum to decide on one of three solutions: full integration with France, autonomy within the French community, or independence with no links to France. The French colonists rejected this proposal; the FLN government accepted it in principle, demanding further negotiations (with the FLN represented by the five imprisoned leaders). In Jan. 1960, after bitter right-wing propaganda against de Gaulle, the colonists in A. rebelled against him. Since they lacked the support of the army, the attempt was suppressed within nine days. A few officers suspected of supporting the rebellion were removed from A. In the summer of 1960 preliminary talks were held with the FLN near Paris, but they were abortive. Right-wing opposition grew, and during de Gaulle's visit to A. in Dec. 1960 disturbances broke out and violence against Muslims erupted. In reaction, the latter staged mass demonstrations, displaying FLN banners in public for the first time. In Jan. 1961 a referendum was held on de Gaulle's policy in A. The French electorate approved it by a 75% majority, but following an FLN call to boycott the referendum, only 58% of the electorate in A. participated, 69% of whom supported de Gaulle.

The proposal to hold an A.'n referendum on self-determination was now renewed. The French resumed secret talks with the FLN in Feb. 1961 — at first through the Tunisian President, Habib *Bourguiba, as intermediary, and from May-June 1961 in direct negotiations in Evian. As a token of goodwill, the French also freed 6,000 A.'n detainees and declared a ceasefire. In their first phase, the negotiations again failed, as the FLN insisted it would discuss future relations with France only after the referendum and stop fighting only after an agreement on FLN demands had been reached. It also demanded an immediate definition of the territory of A., insisting on the inclusion of the Sahara. Meanwhile, right-wing elements within the army and the colonists in A. had in early 1961 formed an "Organisation Armée Secrète" (OAS) to resist a negotiated settlement and the transfer of power to A.'ns. On 24 Apr. 1961 four generals — Challe, Zeller, Jouhaud and Salan — staged an army *coup* in Algiers, but it failed, as most officers remained loyal to de Gaulle. Following the failure of the Evian talks, both the FLN and the French army stepped up their operations, to which were now added those of the OAS against local Muslims. The OAS aimed, if it could not prevent A.'s independence, at least to partition A. and keep the rich agricultural, industrial and urban regions French.

While the fighting continued, negotiations with the FLN were resumed in Oct. 1961. They concluded in Evian on 18 Mar. 1962 with a ceasefire agreement and a declaration of future policy providing for the estalishment of an independent A. after a transitional period. Individual rights and liberties, including those of French citizens, were safeguarded, and France and A. were to cooperate. France was to retain a naval base in Mers el-Kebir for 15 years and nuclear testing grounds in the Sahara for 5 years. The ceasefire came into force the same day, and Ben Bella and his colleagues were released. A provisional government was established, headed by 'Abd-ul-Rahman Fares, who remained in Paris until July. The real authority in A. was in the hands of the remnants of the French army and administration, and of the FLN. The OAS made a last attempt to foil these developments by it ordering the evacuation of those regions it could not hold and inflicting upon them a policy of "scorched earth". Its commander, General Salan, was captured on 20 Apr. Following renewed FLN violence and reprisals, increasing numbers of Europeans and most of the Jewish community left A. for France. Secret negotiations between the FLN and the OAS revealed a split within the latter, and on 17 June the OAS decided to end its resistance. In the referendum, on 1 July 1952, 99.7% voted for independence, and de Gaulle proclaimed A. independent on 3 July. The new state was admitted to the *Arab League in Aug., and to the UN in Oct.

As full independence was realized, splits within the nationalist leadership became more and more evident — between the FLN's Provisional Government (GPRA) and the Fares Government established under the Evian Agreement, between various political factions, and between the politicians and the military commanders. The latter, in turn, were split between commanders of forces stationed in neighboring Tunisia and Morocco and now entering A. and the guerrilla leaders inside A. Tensions with the GPRA had already surfaced in Mar. 1962, when the release of the five threatened the position of Ben Khedda as Prime Minister. There were also ideological differences: a faction headed by Ben Bella and Khidr advocated Nasserist, leftist, anti-Western policies, while Boudiaf, Ait Ahmad and Belkacem Krim were more moderate. The military forces outside A., numbering some 30–35,000 fighters, were commanded by Houari *Boumedienne. The guerrilla formations inside A. were virtually independent of each other, and this fact weakened their political impact. Ben Bella and his followers were identified with the army outside A., Belkacem Krim, Boudiaf and Ait Ahmad with the guerrillas inside, and particularly with the Berber elements in the Kabyle mountains. Shortly before the declaration of independence the wider Revolutionary Council (CRNA) was convened by Ben Bella in Tripoli and proclaimed the "Tripoli Programme" for the new state in June 1962. This called for large-scale agrarian reform, including the establishment of cooperative state farms, a state monopoly on external trade, and a neutralist, anti-colonialist foreign policy; the FLN politbureau was to be superior to the government. Following the declaration of independence, authority was divided between three bodies: the official Provisional Government, headed by Fares; that of the FLN, headed by Ben Khedda; and the Politbureau of Ben Bella. In Aug. 1962, Ben Bella and the Politbureau took, in fact, governmental powers, with Ben Khedda's acquiescence, while the Fares Government was eclipsed. During the summer, Boumedienne and the "outside" forces, with Ben Bella's support, won against the "inside" guerrillas, and rebellious resistance by two of the six *wilayas* was overcome by a "compromise" which in fact established Ben Bella's primacy. Boudiaf, Belkacem Krim and Ait Ahmad had by now virtually become opposition leaders.

General elections were held on 20 Sept. 1962. The FLN presented a list of 180 candidates, all loyal to Ben Bella, and made sure no rival list would challenge it. Some 99% vote in favor of this list and for the proposal that the National Assembly elected would also function as a Constituent Assembly. On 25 Sept., the Assembly was opened, and Ferhat 'Abbas became its President; the GPRA ceased to exist and Ben Bella became Prime Minister, with Rabah Bitat as his deputy and Boumedienne as Minister of Defense. In Nov. 1962 the Government banned the PPA (which Messali Hajj had tried to revive when he was released by the French in May 1962), the Communist Party and the "Socialist Revolution Party" in which Boudiaf and Ait Ahmad attempted to rally the opposition. Ben Bella further consolidated his rule in Apr. 1962 by taking the position of FLN Secretary-General. In Aug. 1963, the National Constitutional Assembly adopted a constitution — Presidential, with a single party, the FLN, nominating the candidates for the five-year-term National Assembly — which was endorsed in a referendum in Sept. The same month, Ben Bella as the only candidate, was elected President; he also retained the Premiership. His main opponents inside the FLN had by now resigned their seats and positions, amongst them Muhammad Khidr, Ferhat 'Abbas, and Rabah Bitat. Ben Bella also tightened his control of the trade unions. More of his opponents were dismissed or imprisoned. Yet, opposition factions within and without the FLN kept growing, as well as resistance in the Kabyle mountains which in mid-1964 turned into armed rebellion. However, Ben Bella succeeded in dividing his rivals, wooing some to his side. Some rebel leaders were captured, with others Ben Bella reached compromise settlements. Boudiaf, Khidr, Ait Ahmad were formally expelled from the FLN, the two former joined Belkacem Krim in exile, Ait Ahmad was captured — but released in spring 1965, as Ben Bella tried to effect a reconciliation with the opposition.

On 19 June 1965 Ben Bella was deposed by Boumedienne in a bloodless *coup*. Boumedienne had come to oppose Ben Bella's economic policy, his tendency to become a Third World leader and his dictatorial inclinations, including his treatment of former colleagues and rivals from the pre-independence era (Ben Bella was kept in detention, later house arrest, until 1980, when he went into exile). Supreme authority now passed to a 26-member Revolutionary Council headed by Boumedienne. A government was formed on 20 July, with Boumedienne as Prime Minister and Minister of Defense, and *de facto* President; several ministers had also served under Ben Bella or been dismissed by him. Boumedienne thus tried to re-unite the FLN and end internal divisions. His régime remained socialist, but tried to stabilize the economy; its foreign policy was non-aligned and actively anti-colonialist. Gradually, the régime became more "technocratic" and less dogmatic. But numerous former FLN leaders seceded, and among the veterans only Bitat remained. Several opposition organizations were set up in exile in Europe. Their influence on A.'n politics was negligible — but a number of their leaders were assassinated (obviously by agents of the régime), including Khidr (1967) and Belkacem Krim (1970). The growing power of the technocrats at the expense of veteran warriors prompted several *coup* attempts in 1967–68. These failed because key positions in the army were held by young professionals loyal to Boumedienne. The rise of the technocrats gradually weakened the FLN as well, but only in 1974 did he decide to reorganize and reactivate it.

In the economic field, state intervention increased and a public sector was fostered and the nationalization of foreign enterprises, that had begun under Ben Bella (e.g. French-owned land), continued; in 1966–67, for instance, foreign-owned mines, several US oil companies, and properties of absentee owners were nationalized. More US oil companies were nationalized in 1970. This active socialist policy culminated in the "Agrarian Revolution" of 1971. The redistribution of private estates and the nationalization of food distribution met considerable resistance from those injured. Students were involved in these conflicts which in 1975 erupted in violent clashes at the Algiers University (with the speed and depth of "Arabization" of studies as another issue of conflict).

Until 1976, Boumedienne did not seek popular support through the ballot, and only local and provincial elections were held in 1967 and 1969 respectively. In June 1976 a new "National Charter", drafted by the FLN leadership and a "National Conference", was approved in a referendum, and in Nov. a new Constitution was similarly endorsed (with no basic change from the one of 1963). In Dec. 1976 Boumedienne was elected President (as single candidate), and in Feb. 1977 elections were held for a National Assembly of 261 FLN-selected members. Efforts were made to reactivate the FLN.

In his neutralist foreign policy, Boumedienne tried to cultivate relations with both France and the USSR. In 1966 agreements were signed with France providing technical and educational aid to A. for 20 years. Large numbers of A.'ns worked in France, and France continued to assist the A. army, which was also aided by the USSR. Relations with the USA were often disturbed; diplomatic relations were severed in 1967 and resumed only in 1974. Yet, trade, some US investments, and the service of US experts — e.g. in the development of oil and gas resources — continued. Boumedienne's anti-colonial line and support of national liberation movements were most evident in his African policy. Gradually, A. adopted harder policies towards France. French military and naval bases had to be handed over, despite the Evian Agreement, by 1967–68. A hard line towards France was most evident in the economic sphere, and especially in the oil-industry. When the two principal French companies — Compagnie Française de Pétroles (CFP) and Entreprise de Recherches et d'Activités Pétrolières (ERAP), who together accounted for some two thirds of A.'s fast-developing oil production — refused to increase the posted price on which their payments to A. were based, the Government in July 1970 unilaterally fixed a new price. Following futile discussions between the two governments, A. in Feb. 1971 took over a 51% holding in both French companies, and all of their gas and pipeline interests. Only after lengthy talks was compensation agreed upon in Dec. 1971, and the French companies became junior partners of the A. state oil concern, Sonatrach, in return for guaranteed oil supplies. This controversy also aroused much ill feeling against the A.'ns working in France — 700,000 at the time.

Concerning the Palestine question A.'s stand was hard-line and militant. She sent troops to fight Israel alongside Egypt in 1967 and 1973. She hosted Palestinian guerrilla leaders and was part of the *"Rejection Front" holding that no peace with Israel should be negotiated. She rejected Egyptian President Anwar *Sadat's peace initiative of 1977 and his peace agreement with Israel of 1979, and severed relations with Egypt.

A.'s relations with Morocco were troubled by a border dispute over the Colomb-Bechar and Tindouf areas — and general antagonism concerning the character of their régimes and inter-Arab and international policies. The border dispute led in the early 1960s to armed clashes and in 1963 to a brief war. The crisis was defused by mediation of the Organization of African Unity, but not finally solved; the disputed areas remained under Algerian sovereignty. A.'n-Moroccan relations were aggravated by the conflict over Western (formerly Spanish) *Sahara. A. has since 1975 supported the establishment of an independent state and actively aided the liberation movement there — the *Polisario; in 1976 she recognized the Sahara Arab Democratic Republic (SADR) — all this in bitter conflict with Morocco who annexed this territory in 1976 and 1979 (and who claims that the Polisario rebel forces are armed by and based in A.).

On 27 Dec. 1978 Boumedienne died. Since he had held all key positions without nominating a deputy, the President of the National Assembly, Rabah Bitat, automatically became temporary Head-of-State for 45 days. Within the FLN leadership, two men were seen as the chief candidates for the succession: Foreign Minister, 'Abd-ul-'Aziz Bouteflika, regarded as a moderate, and Muhammad Salah Yahyawi, the administrative head of the FLN, a more radical socialist. Yet the man chosen for the Presidency was Col. Chadli (al-Shadhili) *Benjedid, the commander of the Oran military district, considered more neutral within the FLN and acceptable to all factions. He was elected in Feb. 1979, as the single candidate. Benjedid at first anounced no changes in the accepted socialist and nationalist policies. His administration, however, was less centralized than Boumedienne's. Thus he nominated a Prime Minister, Col. Muhammad Ben Ahmad 'Abd-ul-Ghani — the first since independence (replaced in 1984 by 'Abd-ul-Hamid Ibrahimi). Constitutional changes adopted by the National Assembly by mid-1979 made the appointment of a Prime Minister obligatory and reduced the President's term from six to five years. The new régime was also more lenient on the opposition (weakened in any case) and many political prisoners were released, including Ben Bella, who went into exile in Oct. 1980. On the other hand, a campaign against corruption and inefficiency was launched in 1980–81 and numerous officials of all ranks were arrested and put on trial. In 1980 changes were made in the FLN machinery, strengthening the President's control over it. The Politbureau was reduced from 21 to 7 members, all selected by the President as FLN Secretary-General, and the party's committees were reduced from 12 to 5. Many former leaders were dropped from prominent positions in the FLN and replaced by the President's men. The party's grip over the trade unions was strengthened by a decision that all union officials must be card-carrying members of the FLN.

General elections were held in Mar. 1982; while the single list was still FLN-vetted, only 55 of the 281 assembly members were said to be FLN activists. President Benjedid was re-elected in Jan. 1984 and appointed a new Prime Minister, 'Abd-ul-Hamid Brahimi, who had previous experience in industrial and economic management. Issues in dispute in the early 1980 were a stepped up "Arabization" of all instruction and public life, and Berber demands, centered in the Kabyle region, to allow a cultivation of Berber language and culture. There was also some unrest of Islamic-fundamentalist groups, suppressed by the Government in a rather lenient manner. In 1985–86 there were signs of a less doctrinaire and more pragmatic policy. A new "National Charter" was adopted by an FLN congress in Dec. 1985 and endorsed by a referendum in Jan. 1986; it put emphasis on agriculture and small, light industry, recommended the dismantling of state-run giant conglomerates, and stressed A.'s historic roots and traditions, linking her socialism to Islam and turning away from "scientific", Marxist doctrines. But it did not envisage a multi-party liberal system, and did not mention Berber culture and traditions. A.'s international and inter-Arab policies also appeared to become rather more moderate. She was no longer an active member of the "Rejection Front", and though she did not resume official relations with Egypt, she seemed to foster growing *de facto* links with her.

'Ali bin Hussein (1880–1935) King of Hijaz, 1924–25. The eldest son of *Hussein b. 'Ali, the *Hashemite Sharif of Mecca and later King of Hijaz, 'A. led, together with his brothers *Feisal and *'Abdullah, the Hijazi *Arab Revolt (the "Revolt in the Desert") against the Turks, 1916, but played no major role in operations. The Hashemites' vague plans for an *Arab Federation to be established after the defeat of the Turks envisaged 'A. as ruler of Hijaz (with his brothers ruling Syria and Iraq, and their father as overall king or Caliph). Therefore 'A. remained with his father in Mecca while Feisal and 'Abdullah left for the countries of the *Fertile Crescent to claim them. 'A. seems to have had little influence on his father's policies. When the Hashemite Hijazis' conflict with *Ibn Sa'ud, the *Wahhabi ruler of *Najd, culminated in 1924 in armed clashes and the defeat of the Hijazis, King Hussein, to save the throne for his dynasty, abdicated in favor of 'A. and went into exile. 'A., however, could not save the Kingdom and Mecca was conquered by the Sa'udis late in 1924. 'A. renounced the throne late in 1925 and left Hijaz, thus ending Hashemite rule in Hijaz (which became part of Sa'udi Arabia). 'A. spent the rest of his days in Baghdad, at the court of his brother King Feisal I. His daughter 'Aliya (d. 1950) married Feisal's son King *Ghazi (King *Feisal II thus was his grandson), and his son *'Abd-ul-Ilah was Regent of Iraq from Ghazi's death in 1939 until Feisal II reached the age of 18 in 1953.

'Ali, Rashid See *Kilani, Rashid 'Ali.

'Ali, Salem Rubai' (1934/35–1978) South Yemeni politician, President of South Yemen 1969–78. A school-teacher and law student, 'A. was active in the 'Aden nationalist movement against British rule — first as a youth leader, and from 1963 within the main and extreme nationalist faction, the *FLN — on its leftist-Marxist wing linked with the *Arab Nationalist Movement (*Harakat al-Qawmiyyin*). When South Yemen became independent in 1967, under the NLF, 'A. was suspected of factional plotting and went into exile. In June 1969 he took part in a successful *coup* against President Qahtan al-*Sha'bi and his faction, and became chairman of a new Presidential Council (which he continued purging and re-shaping in 1970 and 1971). From 1970, he was also a member of the NLF Central Committee and Executive. 'A. was considered pro-Chinese (as against a pro-Soviet faction headed by 'Abd-ul-Fattah *Isma'il), and during his rule South Yemen remained leftist-extremist in her international and inter-Arab policies. But he was reported to have gradually mitigated his views and become more pragmatic and moderate, later described as "rightist"; and the rivalry between him and Isma'il grew more pronounced. In June 1978 'A. became involved in a strange drama that has never been clarified: a special envoy he sent to A.H. *Ghashmi, the President of (North) Yemen, assassinated al-Ghashmi with explosives he carried in his diplomatic brief-case (and was himself killed). According to one version, 'A. had apparently tried to enlist al-Ghashmi's help in a *coup* he was planning, but his plot had been discovered and his envoy caught and replaced. At the same time, a brief struggle took place in 'Aden: according to one version — an attempt on 'A.'s part to oust his rival 'Abd-ul-Fattah Isma'il and his faction, with the help of the army; in another version — a *coup* by Isma'il, aided by the NLF's People's Militia, to oust 'A. 'A. was defeated and executed.

Allon Plan A set of general ideas for the future of the areas occupied by Israel in 1967, formulated in 1967, immediately after the *Six Day War, by Yig'al A. (1918–80) — a former commander in the Israel Army (and the Hagana and Palmah, the defense organizations that preceded it), in 1967 Minister of Labor, later Foreign Minister and Deputy Premier. The AP was never officially adopted as government policy, nor was an official or authorized version published (A. summarized its general lines in an article in the American quarterly *Foreign Affairs*, Fall 1976; in 1984, an Israeli research institute published a fuller study of the Plan). But it had a considerable influence on the thinking of the Israel Labor Party and the governments formed by it. In general outline, the AP provided, within the context of a peace treaty, for the return to Egypt of *Sinai — except for Sharm al-Sheikh and a connecting land bridge from Eilat, the Rafah area, and a narrow strip along the *Negev-Sinai border, which Israel would retain, and the return to Jordan and/or a Palestinian entity linked with her of most of the *West Bank, with the *Gaza Strip added. The Plan envisaged the retention by Israel, as a strategic border and security belt, of most of the *Jordan River Valley — the "West Bank" to be connected to Jordan (the "East Bank") by a corridor in the Jericho area — as well as the eastern slopes of the Judean desert towards the *Dead Sea, the Etzion Bloc south of Bethlehem (owned and settled by Jews before 1948) and certain border areas. According to some estimates, the areas to be retained would amount to c.40% of the West Bank. Jewish settlement in the occupied areas was directed, under Labor-led governments, up to 1977, mainly to those areas which Israel would under the AP seek to retain. The AP's provisions for Sinai lost their relevance after Israel, under the terms of the peace treaty of 1979, returned to Egypt all the territory occupied, including the areas the AP wished to retain. As to the West Bank and Gaza, confidential contacts between Israeli leaders and King *Hussein have not elicited an inclination on his part to envisage an agreement along the lines of the AP. Yet, at least some Israeli leaders, mainly in the Labor Party, are still guided in their thinking by the general lines of the Plan.

al-Amal (Arabic: Hope). Political organization and militia of the *Shi'i community in Lebanon (South Lebanon, the *Biqā' and Beirut). Traditionally, the community was led and represented, in addition to its religious-spiritual leaders, by notables of competing clans, frequently in bitter rivalry, and had no "militia" of its own. In the mid-1970s, however, in the face of the increasing role played by "militias" organized by other communities (particularly the Christian-Maronite *Phalanges), the growing domination of South Lebanon by the Palestinian guerrilla establishment, and the civil war of 1975, younger Shi'i leaders felt the need to set up their own organization. Chief among them was Sheikh Mussa al-*Sadr, one of the top religious dignitaries (who disappeared, and was probably murdered, in Libya in 1978). The organization first appeared under different names (e.g. "The Disinherited" or "The Oppressed") and was mainly local, with little centralized leadership, but in the late 1970s al-A. emerged as *the* Shi'i organization. At that time it also acquired a military character it had not at first possessed and became a "militia" first and foremost. Al-A. was strongly influenced by the Shi'i religious leadership, and later also by the community's new, younger political leaders, chiefly Nabih *Berri (re-elected chairman in 1986). But it is doubtful whether Berri fully controls it since the actual command remains largely local.

During the main phase of the civil war, 1975–76, al-A. was not identified with either of the rival camps and took little part in the fighting, restricting itself to defending Shi'i villages and quarters. Gradually, however, it moved closer to the "Leftist", Syria-oriented camp, and from 1983–84 Berri was in alliance with that camp's leader, Walid *Junbalat, though it was an uneasy, unstable alliance sometimes shaken by bloody clashes. When the "leftist" coalition formed, in 1984, a "Government of National Unity", Berri joined it, pressing for and obtaining the establishment of a special Ministry for South Lebanon with himself at its head. But while being a Cabinet Minister, he has actually remained in opposition, foiling the Government's effort to impose control on the areas controlled by al-A. In Feb. 1984, and again in Apr. 1985, al-A. wrested control of West Beirut from opposing factions (mainly Muslim-Sunni) and government forces, and though it later accepted a degree of army control it has remained the dominating force there, supported by Syria. In 1986 al-A. forcibly resisted the re-establishment of *PLO control over the Palestinian camps in South Lebanon and Beirut, and bloody battles continued for many months, despite Syrian attempts to work out and impose a settlement.

Al-A. has come under the increasing influence of extremist trends guided by *Khomeini's Shi'i-revolutionary régime in Iran — a radicalization manifested also, from 1983–84, in growing Shi'i guerrilla attacks on Israeli forces occupying South Lebanon (who had at first been welcomed as liberating the South from the yoke of PLO domination). The radicals, who have established, with Syria's connivance, a stronghold in the Syrian-occupied al-Biqā' region, appear in different factions ("Islamic Amal"; "Hizb-ullah"; the "Islamic Jihad" seems to be a fictitious "front" of extremists). Their actual representation within and control of the A. leadership is disputed. A. half-concealed struggle seems to be taking place, and Berri and conservative-moderate Shi'i leaders are under strong radical pressure, the more so as some of the top religious leaders sympathize with the extremists. (Libya, in general a close ally of Iran and the extremists, remains the object of bitter hostility, and even terrorist attacks, on the part of al-A. because of her alleged role in the disappearance and assassination of Sheiki Mussa al-Sadr).

'Amer, 'Abd-ul-Hakim (1919–1967) Egyptian officer and politician. Graduated from the Military Academy in 1938 and served in the Palestine War of 1948. One of the founders of the "Free Officers" group that planned and mounted the *coup* of July 1952; member of the Revolutionary Council it established. Promoted General, and appointed Commander-in-Chief of the Armed Forces in June 1953; from 1954 also Minister of War. With the union of Egypt and Syria in 1958, 'A., promoted to the rank of field-marshal, became Vice President and War Minister of the *UAR. When opposition to the régime increased in Syria, he was sent there in 1960 as special commissioner to enforce the will of the central government. After the dissolution of the UAR in 1961, he continued serving as Minister of War in Egypt, becoming also a member of the Presidential Council in 1962. In 1964 he was appointed First Vice President and Deputy Commander-in-Chief of the Armed Forces. In June 1967 he was considered responsible for the Egyptian débacle in the *Six Day War and resigned, or was dismissed. In Aug. 1967 he was accused of plotting a military *coup* and was arrested; he committed suicide in prison in Sept. 1967.

'A., who came from a wealthy peasant family and himself acquired quite a fortune and extensive landed property (he was also involved in some questionable deals), was considered "Right-wing" within the officers' junta, conservative in his political leanings, and upper-class in his life-style. He had reservations regarding the populist-socialist régime *Nasser introduced, as well as Egypt's growing alliance with the USSR, and strove to enhance the leading role and special status of the armed forces and their top commanders. On this account he clashed several times with Nasser; yet his divergent tendencies never crystallized to become a rival doctrine and in the end, he always went along with Nasser's decisions. Until the final crisis of June 1967 he was linked to Nasser in close personal friendship and was considered nearest to Nasser of all the Free Officers' group.

American policies, interests See *United States.

al-'Amri, Hassan (b. 1916) Yemeni officer and politician. Received his military education in Iraq, graduating in 1939. 'A. took part in the *coup* of Sept. 1962, was a member of the Revolutionary Council and became one of the leaders of the Republican government, as Minister of Transport, 1962, and Communications, 1963. Later in 1963 he became Vice-President and in 1964 briefly Prime Minister. However, he opposed and rivalled the then top leader of Republican Yemen, 'Abdullah *Sallal. 'A.'s faction, while staunchly anti-Royalist, was considered somewhat more conservative, fostering strong ties to the great tribal federations, and rather more reserved towards the Egyptians, who then controlled Yemen through their military aid and expeditionary force. When the Egyptians wished to extricate themselves from the Yemen war, in 1965, they made 'A. Prime Minister, removing Sallal into semi-detention in Egypt. In 1966, when Sallal returned, 'A. lost the Premiership and was taken, in his turn, to Egypt, where he was kept in semi-detention. In Oct. 1967, following Sallal's fall, he returned and was appointed a member of the Presidency Council (to 1971), Prime Minister (to 1969) and Commander-in-Chief. He led the Republican forces that saved the capital San'a from being taken by the Royalists (Dec. 1967–Feb. 1968). In 1971 he again became Prime Minister, but was ousted after a week or two both as Premier and as member of the Presidential Council — officially because he was involved in an unsavory incident and accused of murder. The real reason for his overthrow was, reportedly, that he had fallen foul of his powerful tribal allies and was trying to abolish the consultative-representative institutions that served as a stronghold of the tribal leaders and a brake on the government. After three years of exile 'A. returned to Yemen in Jan. 1975; he has not regained a position of influence or power.

al-Ansar (Arabic: the Assistants, Supporters — originally of the Prophet Muhammad.) The militant supporters of the Mahdiyya Order in Sudan. See *Mahdi, Mahdiyya.

anti-Semitism Arab governments and spokesmen usually assert that there can be no A. among the Arabs, as they are themselves "Semites". This assertion, however, disregards, by semantic casuistry, the real problem. Arabic is, no doubt, a Semitic language; and the European inventors of the doctrine of races, claiming the existence of a Semitic "race", would have to include the Arabs in that imaginary Semitic "race". But A. means, most specifically, anti-*Jewish* instincts, feelings or doctrines. And, though in the Middle Ages the fate of the Jews in the Arab countries — as a "protected people" (*Ahl al-Dhimma*) without civic rights — was undoubtedly better than that of the Jews in the Christian world, such anti-Jewish feelings do exist in the Arab countries. They have been intensified by the dispute over Palestine between Arab nationalism and Jewish nationalism (*Zionism) and, since 1948, the *Arab-Israel conflict. Recent Arab history contains instances of pogroms, anti-Jewish violence, persecution (see *Jews in Arab Countries), some of which were triggered by the Arab-Israel dispute. The two stock-in-trade props of A. appear in Arab A., too: the blood libel (i.e. the horror-tale that Jews use the blood of non-Jewish children for baking their Passover bread) was raised in several 19th-century pogroms; and the belief in a world-wide Jewish, or Zionist, conspiracy to dominate the world is wide-spread. German Nazi propaganda in the 1930s and 1940s helped spread these notions, and was eagerly absorbed. Arab A. is noticeable after the end of World War II, too. Anti-Semitic Nazi literature continues being printed and distributed (German Nazi experts for some time served as advisers to Egyptian and Syrian information departments). Nazi-style caricatures of "The Jews" continue appearing in the press of Arab countries, including Egypt — even after her peace agreement with Israel. Hitler's *Mein Kampf* in Arabic translations has been reprinted. The *Protocols of the Elders of Zion* — a notorious forgery "documenting" the Jewish plot to take over the world — continues being printed and distributed in Arabic. An anti-Semitic bias can be discerned in school textbooks and in indoctrination material of the armed forces. Arab top leaders avoid showing such bias — and in recent years stress that they are fighting Zionism and Israel only, and not the Jews, and even invite the Jews who left the Arab countries to come back. However, anti-Jewish clichés keep reappearing in speeches by Arab political and religious leaders, and in the press.

'Aqaba Jordan's only port, at the head of the Gulf of 'A. A small village during the Ottoman period, with no record in history (biblical Eilat and 'Etzion-Gever seem to have been situated slightly farther to the north), 'A. became known in 1906 through the "'A. Incident" arising from a dispute between Britain (acting for Egypt) and Ottoman Turkey over the *Sinai Peninsula. The friction was caused by a Turkish attempt to move troops into the *Taba area near 'A. which Britain considered part of Egyptian Sinai. The Sultan had to submit to a British ultimatum and acquiesce in the inclusion of the whole of Sinai in Egypt. The 'A.-Rafah demarcation line then drawn later became the border between Egypt and British-mandated Palestine. The nearly identical line from Rafah to 'A.'s Israeli "sister"-town of Eilat was the Egypt-Israel armistice border, 1949–67, and is since the Peace Agreement of 1979 the Egypt-Israel border (possession of the little post of Taba, west of 'A.-Eilat, has remained in dispute).

In 1917 'A. was occupied, with British assistance, by troops of Sharif *Hussein's *Arab Revolt (advancing as the right wing of General *Allenby's British and allied forces). Until 1925 the town was administered by Hijaz, and though its status was ambiguous, Amir *'Abdullah of Transjordan acquiesced. In 1925, however, when Hijaz was taken by *Ibn Sa'ud from its *Hashemite King Hussein, 'Abdullah's father, 'Abdullah annexed 'A. (and Ma'an, a town farther inland, and the area between the two towns), claiming his father had transferred the area to him; Britain encouraged and supported that step. The Sa'udis did not formally agree to that incorporation of 'A. in Transjordan, but acquiesced. Formal Sa'udi agreement was accorded in 1965, when Jordan and Sa'udia demarcated their frontier — exchanging some strips of land (with Jordan also gaining a length of coastline south-east of 'A.).

After 1948, when Jordan could no longer use the ports of Palestine, now Israel, the port of 'A. was developed — largely with West-German and British aid. In the late 1970s it handled more than 3 million tons of cargo annually. In 1960 'A. was linked to 'Amman by a modern highway, in 1975 — by a railway; a modern airport was built in the 1970s. In 1985 a car ferry service was opened between 'A. and Nuweiba' in Sinai, to facilitate Egypt-Jordan overland transport. In the mid-1980s a large oil pipeline from Iraq to 'A. was being planned. During the years of border tension and Arab sabotage incursions into Israel, Jordan ensured that no such activities took place in the 'A.-Eilat area, in order not to endanger 'A. and its port.

The *Gulf* of 'A. played a critical role in the *Arab-Israel conflict since Egypt blockaded the Straits of *Tiran at its entrance, closing the Gulf to Israeli and foreign Eilat-bound shipping, from 1950–51 (claiming that the Straits were entirely within Egyptian territorial waters). This blockade was one of the contributory causes of the *Sinai Campaign of 1956. Freedom of navigation was ensured from 1957 under the supervision of a *United Nations Emergency Force. It was the expulsion of that force and the re-imposition of a blockage on the Gulf of 'A. by *Nasser in May 1967 that triggered the *Six Day War. Since 1967 navigation in the Gulf is free again — since Mar. 1979 with Egypt's consent, under the terms of the Israel-Egypt Peace Treaty.

Arab, Arabs The Arabic term *al-'Arab* originally referred to the nomads of the Arabian desert. Traces of this original usage survive to this day: all Beduin tribes are called "'Arab al-" ('Arab al-Tarabin, 'Arab al-Ta'amira meaning the Beduin tribe of T. Tribes of pure A. descent sometimes resent the fact that tribes of mixed descent, e.g. with Negro or Turcoman blood, are also called "'Arab al-"). However, with the A.-Muslim conquests of the 7th and 8th centuries and the spreading and gradual domination of the Arabic language throughout the area conquered, the term acquired a new meaning, generally accepted today: all members of the A. nation. There is no official, commonly accepted definition of that A. nation. As it has absorbed, over the centuries, most of the pre-Arab inhabitants, of different ethnic-national character, it cannot be defined in terms of ethnic (let alone "racial") descent. The usual, reasonable working rule is to define as A. all those who speak Arabic as their mother tongue, feel themselves (and are seen by others) to be A., and are formed by the heritage of A. history and civilization (and do not possess, though speaking Arabic, a different national identity — such as the *Jews in Arab countries).

A. in that definition form the majority in the Arabian peninsula and its northern rim, the *"Fertile Crescent" — with the exception of Israel and the Kurdish regions of Iraq (all these countries are called *al-Mashriq*, "The East"); and in the countries of North Africa, north and east of the Sahara (the countries west of Libya, sometimes defined to include Libya, are called *al-Maghrib*, "The West"). In the Maghrib strong pre-A. and non-A. *Berber elements survive, partly retaining their non-Arabic languages. Estimates vary as to their share in the population, the actual use of their language and the degree of their separate national consciousness. In any case, the Arabic language and A. consciousness dominate. To a much lesser extent residues of a pre-A. national consciousness survive in Egypt (see *Pharaonism), among certain groups and tribes in Sudan (even outside the wholly non-A. South), in Lebanon (see *Phoenicianism), and among some of the ancient oriental Christian communities in Syria and Iraq — some of which used, until recent times, Syriac-Aramaic not only in their liturgy but also as a spoken tongue. In Iraq, the names assumed by some of the ancient Christian communities evoke pre-A. national memories (*"Assyrians", *"Chaldeans") — but there seems to be no conscious cultivation of pre-A. national sentiments. Anyway, except for the Berbers, such non-A. national memories seem to be marginal and no counterweight to the complete domination of the A. nation in its realm. Wholly non-A. populations included in ASt's are, mainly, the *Kurds of Iraq and the African tribes of Southern Sudan.

Beyond that A. realm, A. populations exist in Israel, in the Turkish province of *Hatay (*Alexandretta) and other border regions in southern Turkey, and in *Khuzistan, the south-western part of Iran (sometimes also called Arabistan). Semi-A. populations — sometimes with Arabic as second language or *lingua franca*, though not as a mother-tongue — are found in several African countries bordering on the A. domain, such as Chad, Niger, Mauritania, Djibouti, Somalia and Eritrea.

All the ASt's have achieved full political independence, most of them after a protracted struggle with colonial or semi-colonial protecting powers. A. nationalists claim some of the areas with partly A. or semi-A. populations beyond their borders — such as the whole of Palestine (i.e. the elimination of Israel); Turkish Hatay; Iranian Khuzistan; the northern part of Chad. Mauritania, Somalia and Djibouti have joined the *Arab League and wish, presumably, to be counted among the A. countries.

The A. nation does not form one united A. state but is politically divided into 21 separate states with a combined population of c. 190 million (1984 estimate — including c. 8 million in the three non-A. member-states of the Arab League). Several powerful factors — a common classical language, literature and civilization (including the heritage of Arab Islam, though this is, in terms of religious belief, not shared by the non-Muslim parts of the nation), and a common national consciousness and history — unite the populations of these 21 states and make of them one nation. Other elements — different spoken dialects, separate statehood and interests, divergent histories — make for the growth of particular entities and may turn the A. in their various countries into separate nations (Egyptian, Syrian, Iraqi, Moroccan etc.). Opinions differ as to whether the unifying or the dividing factors are stronger and which trend will prevail. All A. political leaders, and many literary and cultural leaders, stress the unity of the A. nation, and great efforts have been made to enhance that unity, give it political expression, and increase inter-A. cooperation (see *Arab Nationalism, *Pan-Arabism, *Arab Federation).

Arab boycott (of Israel) Palestinian-Arab leaders began using an economic B. as one of their weapons in the early days of the Palestine dispute. They campaigned, in the 1920s and 1930s, for a complete B. of Palestinian-Jewish products and services, and sometimes tried to enforce that B. by violence. However, these efforts failed to stifle the development of the Jewish community — and in some fields even stimulated it. Moreover, many Arabs, Palestinian and non-Palestinian, continued using Palestinian-Jewish products and particularly Jewish services (doctors, hospitals, lawyers). In Dec. 1945, however, the newly established League of Arab States proclaimed a complete economic B. of the Jews of Palestine — and the Arab states had the means to enforce that decision: from the end of 1945 onwards the B. was embodied in the legislation of the various Arab countries. In 1948 it was automatically transferred from the Jews of Palestine to the State of Israel. Since the early 1950s it has been organized and supervised by special B. offices of the *Arab League.

The direct, primary B. of Israeli goods and services is fully applied. It prevents all communication, all trade — though some Israeli products may reach Arab markets camouflaged under foreign labels or smuggled in with labels removed. This rupture of all ties between Israel and her neighbors, her natural trading area, has undoubtedly hurt Israel's economy to some extent — an extent that cannot be estimated in figures, since it cannot be determined how much trade there would have been without the B.

The main efforts of the AB offices have been directed to a secondary B.: to persuade enterprises in non-Arab countries not to do business with Israel. The B. offices generally "permit" ordinary trading with Israel — though they request foreign companies to supply them with full information about their transactions with Israel, and frequently also about Jews among their shareholders, directors and employees. But in some cases they use pressure to prevent even ordinary trade — e.g. in Japan, where major enterprises, apprehensive of damage to their interests in Arab countries, submit to that pressure and refrain from exporting to Israel. The main object is to prevent foreign enterprises from investing in Israel, building plants, granting franchises, or engaging in any kind of cooperation beyond trade. Companies that violate the instructions of the B. offices are blacklisted and themselves threatened with B.

Several Western governments have taken steps against B. pressures, e.g. by banning certain B. practices and obliging their enterprises to report any request by B. offices for information (e.g. the Ribicoff Amendment of 1976 to the US Internal Revenue Act, and 1977 and 1979 amendments to the US Export Administration Act; more modest French Legislation of 1977, implemented only since 1984; similar decrees in the Netherlands). But none has completely outlawed the submission to B. demands. B. pressures are applied in a haphazard and inconsistent way. Some companies that insist on their rights and refuse to submit are not hurt, especially if they are large and powerful and the Arab states need their cooperation; others quietly find ways around the B. by forming subsidiaries for their operations in Israel, or by camouflaging such operations. Yet, some enterprises have, over the years, submitted to the AB — closing their plants in Israel or refraining in the first place from investing and operating in Israel. Again, as there is no way of determining what part the fear of the AB plays in a foreign company's decision not to operate in Israel, the actual damage done to Israel cannot be estimated.

The AB is also applied to international shipping and aviation: ships and airplanes calling at Israeli ports are barred from Arab ports (exceptions being made for some tourist cruise ships), and planes en route to or from Israel cannot overfly Arab territory. However, attempts to impose a complete B. on shipping companies and airlines that also serve Israel were not pursued when they met with firm resistance. Sometimes attempts are made to extend the B. to international conventions, congresses and organizations — again, in a rather haphazard way. At the UN, its agencies and other international conventions, where Arab representatives sit together with those of Israel, efforts are frequently made to oust Israel — but this is a matter of general Arab policies in the Arab-Israel dispute rather than a specific issue of the AB. The B. offices have also tried, again in a haphazard and arbitrary way, to boycott foreign artists, and bar their films, records etc., if they are deemed to have too close ties to Israel.

Since 1967, the B. apparatus has not found effective solutions for the problem posed by the Israel-occupied areas: how to prevent the infiltration of Israeli goods among the products of the Palestine "West Bank" and Gaza (that should not be boycotted), or how to ensure that the Arabs of the occupied territories are not hurt by the B. of Israel. In general, AB operations seem to have slackened somewhat in recent years — particularly as Egypt since 1979 no longer takes part in them.

Arab Federation Plans to unite all or several Arab states in a F. have been part of *Arab nationalism from its inception, though they were, at the beginning, vague and usually referred only to the formerly Ottoman countries of the *Fertile Crescent, and sometimes the Arabian peninsula, but did not include Egypt and the Arab areas of North Africa. The *Hashemite princes who led the *Arab Revolt of World War I and represented Arab nationalist claims at the peace negotiations intended, though they never formulated clear-cut, detailed plans, to establish a federative Kingdom consisting of Arabia (in the first place *Hijaz, Greater Syria and Iraq, each ruled by one of them — *'Ali, *Feisal and *'Abdullah, the sons of Sharif *Hussein, with their father as overall king [and Caliph?]). When despite these plans the area was divided into separate states — at first semi-independent and under European tutelage — the Hashemites and their followers continued nurturing the idea of a Hashemite-led F. Thus, the Iraqi statesman Nuri *Saʿid presented a F. plan in 1942, while Amir (later King) *ʿAbdullah of Jordan propagated a *Greater Syria scheme under his crown. Non-Hashemite plans for a similar F. or union were marginal and feeble — e.g., Antoun *Saʿādeh and his *Syrian Nationalist Party's idea of a Great Syria, inspired by a specifically Syrian nationalism and aspiring to a unitary, not a federal, state of an authoritarian, fascist-oriented pattern. The non-Hashemite ASt's of Saʿudia, Egypt (after she became active in inter-A. affairs in the mid-1930s) and Syria opposed the formation of an AF, rejecting any change in the inter-A. territorial and political *status quo*. Their position determined the character of the *Arab League, founded in 1945, as a close alliance of independent states rather than an instrument for union or F., and the revisionist-Federalist Hashemites acquiesced.

In the 1950s the initiative for closer inter-A. union, for far-reaching, even revolutionary, changes in the *status quo*, passed to the rival camp: to Egypt, by now *Nasserist, to Syria, increasingly under the influence of the *Baʿth faction, and, from 1969 and the 1970s, to Libya's *Qadhdhafi. But *their* pressure for closer union was no longer Federalist. True to their Leftist-revolutionary doctrines, abhorring F. as a liberal Rightist-reactionary device, they aspired to full union on a unitary pattern — on this, Nasserism and Baʿthism were of one mind, though differing on many other issues. Yet, when Egypt and Syria merged in the *"United Arab Republic" (UAR) of 1958, which had some federal features, but was basically unitary and centralist, they allowed Yemen to join them in a F. — the "F. (or Union) of Arab States" (*Ittihad al-Duwal al-ʿArabiyya* — the Arabic language, otherwise so immensely rich, has no separate terms for "Union" and "F." and uses *Ittihad* for both), to be open for other Arab countries to join. This F. never got off the ground.

Hashemite-ruled Iraq and Jordan regarded the formation of the Syro-Egyptian union as a threat and, as a counter-move, immediately formed a F. of their own, the "Arab Union" (*al-Ittihad al-ʿArabi*), proclaimed on 14 Feb. 1958. That Union, in contrast to the UAR, was to be a true F., with each component state to retain its identity and sovereignty. A Constitution, published in mid-Mar., laid down that the Head-of-State would be King *Feisal II of Iraq, with Jordan's King *Hussein as his deputy, each to remain King in his own country; the capital would rotate semi-annually between Baghdad and ʿAmman; a federal Parliament would be appointed from among the members of the two Parliaments, twenty from each; foreign affairs, defense, diplomatic representation would be a joint, federal matter, citizenship would remain separate. This Constitution was endorsed by both Parliaments in Mar. 1958, and the Jordanian and Iraqi Constitutions were accordingly amended. The Federal Parliament met in May (with a Jordanian President and an Iraqi Vice-President), and a Federal Government took office the same month, with the Iraqi Nuri al-*Saʿid as Prime Minister and the Jordanian Ibrahim *Hashem as Deputy-Premier, the Iraqi Tawfiq al-Suweidi as Foreign Minister (with a Jordanian Deputy) and the Jordanian-Palestinian Suleiman *Touqan as Minister of Defense (with an Iraqi Deputy). However, before the new "Arab Union" could make its mark, it was swept away by the Iraqi revolution of July 1958. When the revolutionary junta abolished the monarchy and killed the royal family and some of the Union's leaders, including Nuri Saʿid, Touqan and Ibrahim Hashem, Hussein hurriedly annulled the Union. Fears that the new Iraqi régime would insist on Iraq-Jordan unity and try to extend its revolution to Jordan proved unfounded, and Iraq acquiesced in the dissolution of the Union.

When the UAR broke up, in 1961, with Syria seceding, Egypt and Syria tried (after a period of Egyptian recriminations and severed relations), despite their dislike for the idea of F., to remake their union in a federal pattern — this time with Iraq as a third partner. The idea of a Syro-Iraqi F. had been much talked about in the 1940s and 1950s — but Iraq at that time was a Hashemite kingdom, Egypt and the Syrian mainstream and Left always strongly objected, and these schemes had never approached realization. In 1963, however, both Syria and Iraq were ruled by the *Baʿth*, and it was on *Baʿth*ist initiative that the plan for a triple F. was devised. The federal pattern served the *Baʿth*ists as a compromise, a bridge between their bitter, disappointing experience of full merger with *Nasser's Egypt and their persistent desire for closer union. In April 1963, therefore, Egypt, Syria and Iraq agreed to form a new

"United Arab Republic" — which was to be entirely federal in structure, leaving each member-state its identity and institutions. Yemen again adhered to the F., in June 1963. But by that time a bitter dispute had broken out between Nasser and the *Ba'th*ists in Syria, and in July the agreement was abrogated. In the fall of 1963 Syria and Iraq agreed on plans for an economic union and a joint command, towards a future F., without Egypt; but these plans, too, were cancelled in Apr. 1964 (Iraq had ceased, in Nov. 1963, to be *Ba'th*-ruled). Now it was Egypt's turn to try F. with Iraq — without Syria: in May 1964, Nasser and President *'Aref of Iraq agreed to establish a joint Presidential Council and political command and fully coordinate their economic and military policies towards full (federal) union within two years. Yemen again joined, in a separate agreement with Egypt. The joint Council was formally established and 'Aref began to adapt Iraq's policies and institutions to Egypt's, but after Iraq had again become *Ba'th*ist, it was abolished in July 1968.

A new attempt at F. with Egypt at its center was made from 1969–70 — this time with Libya (revolutionary and unionist since Colonel *Qadhdhafi's *coup* of 1969) as a main partner. In Dec. 1969 the leaders of Egypt, Libya and Sudan (also populist-revolutionary since *Numeiri's *coup* of 1969) proclaimed the "Tripoli Charter" under which the three countries would closely coordinate their policies. In Nov. 1970 they announced plans for a fully fledged F. and Syria announced her decision to join. In Apr. 1971 the "F. of Arab Republics" (*Ittihad al-Jumhuriyyāt al-'Arabiyya*) of Egypt, Libya and Syria — Sudan had opted out at the last moment — was proclaimed; it was endorsed by plebiscites in the three countries and went into effect on 1 Jan. 1972. The FAR had a full range of federal institutions: a Constitution, a Presidential Council (the three Heads of State), a Federal Assembly (its members delegated by the National Assemblies in Egypt and Syria; as Libya had no such assembly, the Revolutionary Council selected her delegates) and a Federal Council of Ministers. It was to have one common flag, a national anthem and a capital, a joint Defense Council and common diplomatic representation abroad; diplomatic representatives among its members were replaced by "liaison officers".

Yet, though duly installed and officially existing, the FAR never got off the ground, never became a living body. Apart from the intrinsic difficulties of F. between countries so different, so unequal, it was mainly Libyan-Egyptian relations that caused its failure. Col. Qadhdhafi was pressing for full Libyan-Egyptian union within the FAR, and in Aug. 1972 he persuaded President *Sadat (who had replaced Nasser in 1970, between the conception of the FAR and its birth) to agree to the proclamation of such a union, to be implemented by Sept. 1973. As Sadat wanted to go slow, and probably had second thoughts on the plan itself, Qadhdhafi went on a barnstorming tour of Egypt in June-July 1973, appealing directly to the Egyptian public behind the back of its government, and later in July organized a "spontaneous" march of Libyan masses into Egypt. His fiery speeches had little success in Egypt, where the whole operation was bitterly resented. In Aug. 1973, Sadat reaffirmed the merger agreement — but it was clear by now that he had no intention of going through with it, and it was never implemented. Relations deteriorated, bitter recriminations, accusations of Libyan plots etc., led to the severance of relations, military confrontation, border clashes, and, in 1977, actual warfare. After Sadat's visit to Israel, Nov. 1977, Libya was in the forefront of those Arab states denouncing Sadat and clamoring for Egypt's expulsion (as was Syria). In Dec. 1977 Syria and Libya expelled Egypt from the FAR, dismissed Sadat as its President and transferred its Headquarters from Cairo to Tripoli. As Qadhdhafi continued referring to the validity of the FAR, Egypt's National Assembly in Dec. 1984 passed a bill abolishing it. Libya and Syria may still consider themselves formally federated (with Libya pressing for full union), but in reality, the FAR has ceased to exist.

Other attempts at F. between various ASt's have been made from time to time — sometimes as a means to improve hostile relations rather than to cement existing close ones. Talk of a Syro-Iraqi F. in the 1940s and 1950s and plans of 1962–64, and their abortion, are described above. Plans for a Syro-Iraqi F. were revived late in 1978 — at a time when the two countries, under rival *Ba'th* régimes, were bitterly hostile and in dispute — though both were opposed to Sadat's peace initiative towards Israel. F. was apparently seen as a means of conciliation and of forging a united front against Egypt. But this attempt, too, failed and was soon called off. Efforts to effect a reconciliation between Syria and Jordan, embroiled in bitter conflict, also led, in 1976, to proposals for a Syro-Jordanian F., and, in Dec. 1976, even to an agreement in principle; but nothing came of that scheme.

The most active and persistent protagonist of union or F. plans was Col. Qadhdhafi of Libya. He worked, from 1969–70, for F. with Egypt and Syria (and at first with Sudan, too), as described above. He pressed for full union with Egypt, 1972–73, until a formal agreement was reached which was subsequently cancelled. He offered some kind of union to Malta (1971). He persuaded President *Bourguiba of Tunisia, in Jan. 1974, to agree to a Libyan-Tunisian union (an agreement that had to be undone with great caution by Bourguiba's associates). He pressed for full union with Syria, and in 1980 agreed with Syria's *Asad to form a united Syro-Libyan state — an agreement that remained a mere declaration. In 1981 Qadhdhafi offered union to Chad. He repeatedly put out feelers to Algeria regarding the prospects for a merger or F. And, in Aug. 1984, he agreed with the King of Morocco — with whom he had been in bitter dispute — to establish a Libyan-Moroccan F. This union, which did not look realistic in the first place, was abrogated by Morocco in Aug. 1986. In short, nothing came of Qadhdhafi's fervent unionist scheming.

In contrast to these highly publicized F. plans, Egypt and Sudan in the 1970s and early 1980s quietly strengthened their relations to a degree that amounted to near-confederal arrangements. Since the early 1920s Egypt had regarded the "Unity of the Nile Valley" as one of her main national aims and endeavored, in a bitter struggle with Britain, to extend the reign of the Egyptian crown to Sudan, without consulting the Sudanese or granting them the right of self-determination. In 1954–55 the revolutionary officers' régime, in agreement with the Sudanese political parties, conceded self-determination, and Sudan chose independence. It may be assumed that Nasser and his associates did not really renounce Egypt's aspirations to union with Sudan, but wisely decided that they would be better served by friendly cooperation with an independent Sudan. For some years Sudanese resentment and suspicions of Egyptian big-brother attitudes and the cultivation of pro-Egyptian factions marred relations; but gradually the moderate policy of 1954–55 paid off. *Numeiri's revolutionary régime of 1969 concluded an agreement of coordination, with federal intent, announced late in 1970. Sudan's need for Egyptian assistance, political and military, against suspected Libyan plots enhanced the trend towards closer cooperation, and though Sudan withdrew from the plan for F. with Egypt, Libya and Sudan, 1970–71 (see supra), bilateral cooperation with Egypt grew. In July 1976 a Defense Pact was concluded, finalizing a process of co-ordination agreed upon in 1974. In 1979 Sudan refused to toe the all-Arab line and break relations with Egypt. In Oct. 1982, a ten-year agreement for "Integration" was signed, under which a joint "Nile Valley Parliament" was set up, with 60 members of each of the two National Assemblies delegated to meet twice a year in joint session. While arrangements did not amount to a F. (and policy coordination was far from complete — Egypt had, for instance, serious misgivings concerning Numeiri's enforcement of Islamic Law, since 1983), the trend was towards confederation. It remains to be seen whether the overthrow of Numeiri in Apr. 1985 and the policies of Sudan's new régime — whose statements seemed cooler towards Egypt but were sometimes contradictory — will alter that trend.

Another case of a planned inter-state merger or F. is the long-standing scheme for a union of Yemen and South Yemen. Both countries have always regarded themselves, in principle, as parts of one, greater Yemen. While the British ruled what is now South Yemen (then — 'Aden and the 'Aden Protectorates), Yemen claimed those territories and the nationalists in 'Aden strove ultimately to join Yemen. But when South Yemen attained independence, in 1967, and union with Yemen became feasible, it was not implemented: the two countries were too different in character and régime, and Yemen — rather conservative even under her post-1962 republican government — suspected that a union might turn into a take-over by the Leftist revolutionaries of South Yemen. The decision to merge the two countries was reaffirmed in principle in 1970, 1972 and 1979, though tension sometimes led to armed clashes and twice, in 1972 and 1979, to actual war. Usually, South Yemen is pressing for union, while Yemen drags her feet (her reluctance being enhanced by Sa'udia, on whose support and aid Yemen depends). The merger plan stands, with both sides frequently reconfirming its principle and joint committees and presidential meetings preparing the ground, but there has been no actual advance towards its implementation.

Additional F.'s were in fact — like some of those described — cases of re-structuring one country or creating one state out of smaller pre-state entities. Such a local F. was set up in 1951 by *Tripolitania, *Cyrenaica and Fezzan, which formed the F. Libya; this federal constitution was amended in 1962 and power was somewhat centralized, and after the revolution of 1969 the F. was abolished altogether and Libya became a unitary state. In 1959 six small sheikhdoms of the *'Aden Protectorate formed, under British guidance, a "F. of Arab Emirates of the South", renamed in 1962 *"South Arabian F." and expanded to include 'Aden itself and most of the Protectorate principalities. This F. attained independence in 1967 as the Republic of South Yemen, and lost its federal character (which had been opposed by the 'Aden nationalists), becoming a unitary state. In 1971 the seven British-protected sheikhdoms of the *Trucial Coast (Trucial 'Oman) formed a F. and attained independence as the *United Arab Emirates — the only ASt. that retains a federal structure. This category of local F.'s would include a F. or confederation between Jordan and a future Palestinian-A. entity in the part of Palestine occupied since 1967 by Israel — a confederation discussed (and agreed in principle, but not finalized) by King Hussein of Jordan and *PLO leader Yasser *'Arafat in 1982–83 and reaffirmed in 1985. Should this agreement materialize — which is doubtful since large parts of the PLO oppose it — the two parties may take quite divergent positions as to its interpretation and the nature of the confederation.

Most of the F. plans described concerned actually two or several states, though some of them were proclaimed open for additional AC's to join, and were thus far removed from the original idea of an *all*-Arab F. or union. This idea seems to have become a vision of a far-away ideal future rather than an attainable political goal.

Arabia The Arabian Peninsula, with an area of 1.1 m. sq. mi. and an estimated population of c. 22 m., is bounded by the *Red Sea and the Gulf of *'Aqaba in the west, the Gulf of *'Aden and the Arabian Sea in the south, the Gulf of *'Oman and the *Persian Gulf (called by A.'s the Arabian Gulf) in the east, and the Syrian and Iraqi deserts in the north. A. is mostly desert, except for the south-west (*'Asir, *Yemen) and the south-east ('Oman). 75% of A. belongs to *Sa'udi Arabia; other political entities are located along the southern and eastern coast: Yemen, *South Yemen, 'Oman, the *United Arab Emirates (UAE), *Qatar and *Kuwait (and the offshore islands of *Bahrain, usually considered part of Arabia).

Arabic The language of the *Arabs, a Semitic tongue which originated in the Arabian Peninsula and spread through most of the Middle East and North Africa, mainly after the Muslim-Arab conquests, from the seventh century. Written, literary A., shaped by pre-Islamic poetry and principally by the Koran (*Qur'ān*) and medieval Islamic literature, retains the main structure, qualities and vocabulary of ancient, classical A. Yet it has adapted itself to modern use with astonishing flexibility and has created a rich vocabulary answering the needs of contemporary scientific and social-political terminology. There is a great difference between written, literary A. (*Fusha* — pure, or *Nahwi, Nahawi* — grammatical, correct) and spoken A., divided into many dialects and differing from the written language in grammar, syntax, vocabulary and pronunciation. The dialects themselves are so different that their speakers, if they cannot use *Nahawi*, might find it difficult to communicate with each other.

Written A. is used in literature, official documents, the press, broadcasts, films, as well as in contacts between educated Arabs from different countries, at conferences and in speeches. In everyday life, even educated Arabs use the spoken tongue in its local form. There are, however, ways of slightly mixing the two levels of the language. Newscasters often add certain spoken forms or idioms to their generally literary A., and many leaders mix into their speeches certain elements of spoken A., each creating his own style. The dualism of literary A. vs. spoken dialects has caused much discussion among Arab nationalists. Some writers advocate the use of the spoken tongue in fiction; plays have been written in dialect, and some novelists put dialogues in spoken A. in their novels that are otherwise written in classical A. Some favor transforming the various dialects into fully fledged written languages — a position that sometimes has undertones of separatist-particularist nationalism (thus, e.g., in Lebanese *Phoenicianism or Egyptian *Pharaonism); some also recommend latinizing the A. script. All these, however, have remained a small minority, while the majority insist on the use of *Fusha*, pure classical A., as the only language of writing and communication. The fact that written A. is a powerful factor uniting the Arab nation, while the cultivation of spoken dialects might lead to separatism, is an important element in that majority position, added to its fundamental respect for the heritage of Arab civilization and its continuity. Academies of A., in Cairo, Damascus and Baghdad cultivate the language and its development; their suggestions for new terms, and sometimes changes and corrections, are not, however, always found acceptable by the public.

Arab-Israel conflict The A-I.C., from 1948, the year Israel came into existence, is essentially a continuation of the A.-Jewish dispute over Palestine. When modern Zionist settlement began in the 1880s, good neighborly relations were maintained in most cases with adjacent A. villages and Beduin tribes, and A.'s from neighboring areas and from other parts of Palestine were attracted to settle near the new Jewish villages, seeking employment and trade. There were instances of Arab resistance, mostly non-political, by peasants, tenants or Beduin shepherds who feared the settlements might affect their ownership, tenancy or grazing rights. Bands of robbers and marauders also attacked the settlers, who were considered weak (sometimes derogatorily called, in Arabic, "Children of Death"), until they posted armed guards who formed the nucleus for later organized self-defense. Such clashes were sporadic and did not turn into organized violence or a national struggle until after World War I. However, politically-minded urban notables, professionals and students, and an incipient press (making its first, tentative steps at the beginning of the century), perceived the political contents of the settlement efforts: Zionism's goal of a Jewish homeland, a Jewish state in Palestine — though it seemed impractical and remote at that time — and opposed them. Such opposition — at meetings, in pamphlets and articles, and in protests and petitions to the Ottoman authorities to prevent Jewish immigration and settlement (to which the authorities at times acceded) — were motivated either by awakening A. nationalism or by Mulsim-Ottoman considerations; no clear distinction was made, and on this issue there was no contradiction between the two trends. When A. nationalist societies began forming, from c. 1908, in the A. parts of the Ottoman Empire, some of them inscribed opposition to Zionist aspirations on their program. The Zionist leadership and local leaders of the Jews of Palestine, on their part, established contacts with A. leaders, mainly those — in Egypt, Beirut, Istanbul — advocating a decentralization of the Ottoman Empire, in an effort to reach an understanding and find ways of cooperation, but no full agreement was reached.

1. FROM 1917 TO 1936. Both A. and Jewish national aspirations entered a new phase with the dismemberment of the Ottoman Empire at the end of World War I, and the *Balfour Declaration of 1917. Palestine was defined by the victorious powers as a political entity (such as had not existed for many centuries) — an entity linked, from the outset, with the internationally backed plan to establish a Jewish National Home. A Pan-A. national leadership — King *Hussein of Hijaz and his sons, first and foremost Amir *Feisal, who were accepted at the Peace Conference as representing the A. national movement and its claim to independence (though Feisal received a formal A.-nationalist mandate only in 1920, when a Syrian-A. national congress proclaimed him King of Syria, meaning a *Greater Syria that would incorporate Lebanon, Palestine and Jordan) — regarded the Jews of Palestine and the Zionist movement as potential allies. They saw no contradiction between the Jewish enterprise in Palestine and A. independence in the rest of the A. homeland — according to their plans, in a Federation (that might include the Jewish commonwealth in Palestine — their plans were not detailed and explicit). They also hoped to obtain the assistance of influential world Jewry. After Feisal met the Zionist leader Chaim Weizmann several times in Palestine and during the Paris Peace Conference, they concluded the *Feisal-Weizmann Agreement of Jan. 1919, in which

the A. and Jewish national movements recognized each other's justice and pledged mutual support and cooperation. On several points the agreement was vague and open to conflicting interpretations, but its essence was clear: the future A. State and a Jewish Palestine were to be two separate entities which would cooperate and be reciprocally represented, and the A. nationalist movement and the Zionist enterprise were to support each other.

The agreement's legal validity was in doubt. Feisal had added, in his own hand, in Arabic, that it would be valid only if all A. national demands were satisfied — and at the time they were not, though the Arabs have since attained the full independence they sought. Also, Feisal's mandate to speak for the A. nationalists of the *Fertile Crescent countries was dubious. Most A. nationalist leaders have always denied the agreement's validity — claiming, alternatively, that it was a Zionist forgery; that Feisal was deceived by *Lawrence and other advisers and did not understand what he was signing; and that he was not entitled to speak for Arab nationalism. Yet, it remains a moral and historical fact that when A. and Jewish nationalism first appeared as realistic, effective political movements, they did so as friends and allies, and that early A. nationalism did not oppose the creation of a Jewish Palestine or regard it as an enemy.

The Feisal-Weizmann Agreement was not implemented and left no real mark on future events: the Pan-A. kingdom or federation in whose name Feisal spoke was never established, and Palestinian-A. leaders, as well as most nationalists and governments in the AC's, turned against the Zionist enterprise in a decided and uncompromising way. Feisal himself and some of his advisers continued, quietly and not very energetically, mostly through British contacts, seeking ways to accomodate a Jewish Palestine within a greater A. Federation. Zionist leaders maintained contact, in the same general direction, with Pan-A. leaders — such as the Syrian-Palestine Office in Geneva and its counterpart in Cairo (Shakib *Arslan, Ihsan Jaberi, Habib Lutfallah, Riad al-*Sulh and others). But these men were, in the 1920s, politicians in exile, devoid of authority and power — and, anyhow, anti-Zionist views gradually began dominating even among them. Jewish efforts to foster moderate Arab leaders and organizations inside Palestine prepared to reach an accomodation had scant success. As the A-I.C. intensified, and an extremist leadership gained control among the Palestine Arabs, exerting heavy pressure and silencing most dissidents, moderate opinions and a preparedness to seek an accomodation with the Zionists soon became views not to be expressed in public, not even by those inclined towards them (with few notable exceptions).

The political organization of the Palestine Arabs is described in the entry *Palestine Arabs. Zionism, and the British Mandate based on the Balfour Declaration and the obligation to assist in creating a Jewish National Home were, from the outset, opposed by all parties and organizations. Their argument was clear and simple: the country belonged to the people living in it, of whom the majority was A., and it was entitled to immediate independence as an Arab state. No Jewish immigration or settlement were to take place without the consent of the country's owners (and that consent was refused). The British and the world powers had no right to promise a land that was not theirs, and their promise to the Jews was null and void. Zionist counter-arguments — that the Jewish people had a historical right to the land; that only in Palestine could it set up its homeland to right a historical injustice of two thousand years and to prevent further persecution; that the rights of the A. majority should be weighed not against those of the Jews already in the country but against those of the whole Jewish people; that the development of the country would benefit — indeed was already benefiting — both peoples; that the Jewish National Home was being created out of nothing, mostly in uninhabited swamps and deserts; that no A. had been, or would be, expelled, and that A. civil rights and freedoms would be scrupulously honored — all these claims failed to assuage A. opposition.

The organized political resistance, which induced the Palestinian-A. leaders to reject and boycott all representative institutions proposed by the British Palestine authorities, also led, from the outset, to increasing violence against the Jews. In Apr. 1920 and May 1921 demonstrations and incitement, partly Islamic-religious (e.g. at the annual popular celebrations of "Nabi Mussa" near Jerusalem, Apr. 1920), turned into anti-Jewish, pogrom-like, riots and attacks on several settlements. In Aug. 1929, riots and what was officially called "Disturbances", including attacks on Jewish settlements, and a massacre of the old-established Jewish population of Hebron, were prolonged and more intense. They were again motivated to a significant extent by Muslim religious fears and incitement and derived from a conflict over the Western ("Wailing") Wall and claims that the Jews sought control of the Temple Mount, al-Haram al-Sharif. The riots of 1929 led to a protracted investigation of the problem of the Western Wall by a British commission of inquiry, and to be White Paper of 1930 which marked a pronounced pro-A. turn in British policies, restricting Jewish immigration and settlement (parts of the White Paper were cancelled, or reinterpreted, as a result of Jewish pressure). Another inquiry, into land and agrarian problems, also questioned further Jewish settlement and was therefore seen as advantageous to the A. cause.

2. THE ARAB REBELLION, 1936–39. The sharp increase in Jewish immigration after Hitler's rise to power in Germany in 1933 aggravated tensions and led to further A. violence. Riots in Oct. 1933 were nipped in the bud. But in Apr. 1936, renewed "disturbances", coupled with a general strike and the proclamation of a total boycott of all Jewish goods and services, turned into a general Arab rebellion. An "Arab Higher Committee" was formed by all A. parties to lead the rebellion with the Mufti of Jerusalem, Hajj Amin al-*Husseini, who had emerged as the top leader of Palestinian-A. nationalism, as chairman. Guerrilla squads ("gangs", *'Issābāt*) proliferated, and attempts were made to impose a centralized military command (see *Palestine Arabs).

In Aug. 1936 an army of several hundred volunteers from AC's, mainly Syria and Iraq, under Fawzi al-*Qawuqji, penetrated Palestine and established itself in its northern and central regions, principally in the Nablus-Jenin-Tulkarm "Triangle". Many Jewish settlements, Jewish quarters of the mixed towns, and particularly inter-urban communications, were attacked. The Government reinforced its police (largely composed of A.'s, part of whom sympathized and collaborated with the rebels) by some British troops, but its reaction during that phase was restrained and rather feeble. The Jews stepped up their settlement and immigration efforts (including the beginnings of organized illegal immigration, i.e., without Government "certificates") and, in the face of the Arab boycott, expanded their economy to penetrate those branches then exclusively in Arab hands. Their underground and formally illegal self-defense organization, the *Hagana*, which had until the 1930s been based mainly on the local defense of each settlement, gradually became a fully fledged, though poorly equipped, military organization with a central command. It maintained, however, a policy of restraint and static defense and refrained from active, offensive reprisal action against the centers of the guerrilla bands in the A. villages — mainly for moral-ethical reasons, as reprisals would hurt innocent villagers, among them women and children. This issue engendered much controversy and led to a split in the *Hagana*, with the more extremist advocates of an activist strategy seceding and forming a "National Military Organization", *Irgun Tzeva'i Le'umi, IZL*.

The rebellion of 1936 failed to achieve its objectives, and hurt the A. community perhaps more than it hurt the Jews and the Government. As the A. leadership could not simply call it off, thus admitting defeat, it was arranged, with British assistance, for the rulers of the AC's to call on the Palestinian A.'s to end their strike and armed resistance while they, the A. rulers, would struggle for the Palestinian-A. cause. That appeal was issued in Oct. 1936 by the Kings of Iraq and Sa'udi Arabia and the Amir of Transjordan, with the Imam of Yemen associated but not fully participating (Egypt, it should be noted, as yet took no part in that all-Arab action). The appeal was heeded, and the rebellion halted (temporarily, as it soon emerged). Qawuqji's volunteer army withdrew.

Throughout the later 1920s and the early 1930s the ideological content of the conflict hardly changed. In the face of the increasing number, power and self-confidence of the Jews, no A. thinker came forward with new ideas for a solution, beyond the demand for an immediate take-over by the A. majority, with the Jewish minority frozen in its status (if not expelled or liquidated) with no more immigration or acquisition of lands — a formula that did not correspond to the facts of power and realities. The Zionist leadership maintained contacts with A. leaders, inside and outside Palestine, even during the rebellion; but there was no breakthrough. Unofficial Jewish personalities suggested, in various versions, a formula based on far-reaching concessions by the Jews, amounting to a renunciation of plans for a Jewish majority and a Jewish state: a Bi-national State based on perpetual parity in all future government institutions. This idea did not arouse much enthusiasm among the Zionists; but had there been an Arab leadership willing to accept it, many Jews might have supported it — provided that immigration and settlement could continue within its framework — and it could have served as a basis for fruitful negotiations. Other proposals, going even farther by suggesting a definite predetermined ceiling for the Jewish population, in absolute numbers or fixing a percentage, was not acceptable to Jewish public opinion — the more so as the A. notables contacted regarded a Jewish population of 35% or at the utmost 40% as the highest ceiling that could be discussed. Anyway, the Palestinian-A. leadership showed no interest in a bi-national or parity-based solution. The Zionist leadership continued therefore seeking a formula based on the old Feisal-Weizmann conception: a Jewish Palestine within a Pan-A. or ME framework that would satisfy A. national demands, create a sense of A. strength and security, and be able to accomodate a Jewish commonwealth. But this conception, too, proved unacceptable to most A. leaders (for a few notable exceptions see below).

In July 1937 a British Royal Commission under Lord *Peel published the recommendations it had submitted after careful investigation. As both the A. and the Jewish peoples were entitled to independence in Palestine and as agreement on joint independence in a single state was, the Commision thought, unattainable, it proposed to partition the country into a Jewish State, an A. State that would be united with Transjordan, and an extensive zone (including Jerusalem) that would remain under British administration. The Zionists, while rejecting the specific, detailed boundaries proposed for the Jewish state, were prepared (following a majority decision of the Zionist Congress, after a bitter debate) to discuss the Peel scheme — i.e. they accepted the principle of Partition. The A.'s, however, totally rejected it — including the *Nashashibi-led opposition faction that might have acquiesced in Partition, despite their public rhetoric, had it been firmly decided upon and vigorously implemented.

The struggle against the Partition proposal was one principal reason, though not the only one, for the resumption of the Arab rebellion in 1937.

While the Palestine-A. rebellion in its second stage, 1937–39, became increasingly ferocious (including mounting internal terrorism against dissidents, and counter-terror by the "Peace Gangs"), it achieved no military success, and in 1939 it died down. At the same time, however, the extremist A. leadership reaped a significant political victory because the British, in their weakness vis-à-vis the Fascist-Nazi Axis and the mounting European crisis, applied a policy of appeasement to the ME, too. In 1938 they repealed the Partition plan and initiated new consultations with the leaders of the Palestine A.'s (including those of the outlawed Higher Committee, who were exiles under warrant of arrest) and the ASt's. As the A. leaders refused to attend a round-table conference together with the Jews, such a conference was held, early in 1939, in London, in separate sessions, with the operative emphasis on the Anglo-A. consultation. The result was the British White Paper of 1939 which, though it was never officially endorsed by the A.'s, virtually accepted the main A. demands since it envisaged independence soon for a Palestine under full control of its A. majority, with the Jewish population frozen — Jewish immigration to be very limited for a short while and subsequently stopped altogether, and land purchase limited to those areas already with a Jewish majority.

In those years, the ASt's increasingly assumed the leadership of the Palestine struggle and the representation of the Palestine A.'s. While up to the mid-1930s they had contented themselves with giving moral-political and some financial support, they now began exerting active political, even military efforts. Qawuqji's army of volunteers of 1936 was recruited and dispatched with the connivance of the Arab governments at the very least. The intervention of the A. kings in Oct. 1936, as yet without Egypt, was an important milestone. Inter-A congresses and committees in support of the Palestine A.'s proliferated and acquired a semi-official character, with increasing participation of parliamentary and government representatives. This transfer of the leadership to the ASt's was hardly resisted by the Palestinian A.'s, exhausted by their struggle and internal terror and with their most prominent leaders in exile or detention. It culminated in the London Conference of 1939, now including Egypt. At all stages, from 1936, Britain encouraged, even initiated, this transfer of the decision-making from the Palestine A.'s to the ASt's.

3. FROM 1939 TO 1948. Palestinian-A. leaders, numbed into inactivity since 1939, resumed some activity from 1943–44. The Husseini faction opposed the creation of a new representative body and the resumption of fully fledged political activities in the absence of their top leaders — an obstacle that was removed only in 1945–46. Until then, efforts were directed mainly to prevent the sale of A.-owned land to Jews. Two rival bodies were set up for that purpose: a "National Fund" (*Sunduq al-Umma*), which offered to buy any land in danger of being sold to Jews; and Mussa *'Alami's "Constructive Scheme", which sought to prevent such sales by the general, agricultural and social development of the Arab village. The latter scheme was supported by the A. League, but neither of the two achieved much success. From 1945 on, much effort was also devoted to reinvigorated political propaganda, and information offices were set up, with the support of the A. League, in London, Washington, Jerusalem and Beirut.

The A.'s resumed full political activity in 1946 when the Palestine issue began moving at high speed: an Anglo-American Committee of Inquiry, 1946 (its report, Apr. 1946, recommending a future bi-national independence based on equal representation); an abortive Anglo-American scheme (the "Morrison-Grady Plan", July 1946, recommending semi-autonomous A. and Jewish cantons); another Anglo-A. conference (boycotted by the Palestinian-A. leaders in its first session, Sept. 1946, but attended in its second session, Jan. 1947); Britain's decision to hand over the Palestine problem to the UN (Feb. 1947); a special session of the UN, from 1947; the UN Committee of Inquiry (*UNSCOP, Apr. to Aug. 1947); the struggle against a UN decision favoring Jewish statehood; the UN resolution of 29 Nov. 1947 to partition Palestine and establish a Jewish state and an A. state, to

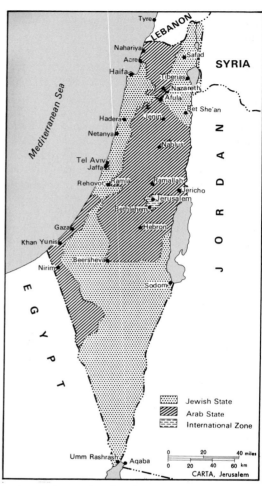

Palestine: the Jewish and Arab states according to the 1947 UN resolution

form an economic union, and an internationalized Jerusalem; and the preparations for the final fight to prevent the implementation of that decision. Since 1942 the Jews had unequivocally demanded full independence and statehood, with their mainstream majority accepting partition as the price, and there were no further contacts between their leaders and the mainstream-extremist Palestinian-A. leadership.

In the A. camp, four conflicting attitudes were discernible: a) A very few individual statesmen acquiesced in the establishment of a Jewish state or even supported the idea: men such as the Egyptian Isma'il *Sidqi, a former Prime Minister; the Syrian ex-Premier Husni Barazi (who secretly recommended that solution to the Anglo-

American Committee); some leaders of the Nashashibi-led Palestinian-Arab opposition (also in secret); the leaders of the Catholic-*Maronite church in Lebanon, one of them, Archbishop Ignatius Mubarak, even in public (in 1946, a secret written agreement with the Maronite Patriarch provided for cooperation between nascent Israel and the Lebanese Maronite community). But these individual dissenters had no influence on the course of events.

b) Some statesmen realized that the only realistic way to prevent total Jewish independence was to offer far-reaching autonomy, cantonal or confederal, in the framework of an A. federation. The leading Iraqi politician Nuri *Sa'id, many times Prime Minister (including several months in 1946–47), thought along these lines. He had presented a plan for a Fertile Crescent Federation, containing partial Jewish autonomy in Palestine, in a "Blue Book" in 1942 — but his ideas were rejected by the other ASt's, and he did not insist. King *'Abdullah of Jordan went much farther than that. Planning to take over the A. part of partitioned Palestine, he was prepared to do that in cooperation with the Jews, and while he preferred Jewish autonomy or semi-independence under his crown, he was ready to accept full Jewish independence. In 1946–47 he concluded an informal and unwritten agreement along these lines with the Zionist leaders. He kept that accord secret, but it soon became widely known or at least rumored — the more so as 'Abdullah kept telling the other A. rulers that he reserved to himself "freedom of action", which everyone understood to mean fredom to take over the A. part of Palestine — and efforts to foil his plans played a significant role in A. decision-making. 'Abdullah eventually kept his agreement with the Jews only in part. He ordered his army to join the other A. armies in invading Palestine in May 1948, so as to achieve his goal by nominally co-ordinating his moves with the A. sister-states rather than by open co-operation with the Jews. But he did not attack the area earmarked for the Jewish state (though his forces fought bloody battles over areas outside that region, mainly Jerusalem and the access road to it — areas not included in his agreement with the Jews), and his divergent policies were a most important factor in the war of 1948.

c) The mainstream, the ASt's and the A. League, in effect accepted the British White Paper of 1939, though they never officially said so. They claimed speedy independence for an A.-majority, A.-ruled Palestine — with full civic rights for the Jews, but no autonomy, no further immigration and no land-acquisition (a policy that was clear and rigid but paid no heed to political realities).

d) The Palestinian-A. leadership was more extreme: it wanted independence immediately, and it was not prepared to commit itself to accept all the existing Jewish population and to assure it civic and minority rights in the future A. state.

From 1946–47 it was clear to both A.'s and Jews that the final struggle would be decided by force of arms. The Jews had their volunteer force, the *Hagana*, still underground and illegal, reinforced since 1942–43 by a regular "Striking Force" (*Palmah*). There were also the "dissident", more extremist, formations of the IZL ("Irgun", see *supra*) and the "Fighters for the Freedom of Israel" (called by the British the "Stern Gang"). The Arabs of Palestine formed two rival para-military youth organizations in 1946: *al-Futuwwa* of the Husseini faction, and *al-Najjada* for the opposition; late in 1946 the A. Higher Committee decided to merge the two and in 1947 it brought an Egyptian officer as commander, but the merger was half-hearted and never got off the ground. It was obvious that these organizations were no match for the well-organized Jewish forces, even if unity could be imposed and that Arab victory was feasible only with the help of the armed might of the ASt's.

The ASt's had, indeed, declared, before and after the UN decision of Nov. 1947 on the partition of Palestine, that they would resist and foil that decision by all means, including military force. They were, however, not keen to involve their regular military forces and to invade Palestine. The decision-making rested mainly with Egypt, Iraq and Syria, with the two latter pressing for action, while 'Abdullah kept his own counsel and reserved his freedom of action, Lebanon had little military force, and Sa'udi Arabia and Yemen were on the sidelines. In addition to the regular meetings of the Arab League Council, special emergency conferences were held at Inshas (by the Heads-of-State) and Bludan, 1946, and Sofar and 'Aley, 1947. At all these meetings the ASt's — who were already imposing a total boycott on Palestinian-Jewish goods and services since 1946 – resolved to grant the Palestine Arabs every possible form of aid: finance and arms, volunteers and logistic assistance, but to avoid the direct involvement of their regular armed forces (though the Bludan Conference added several secret decisions that went somewhat farther). They began implementing these decisions late in 1947, appointing the Iraqi General Isma'il Safwat as commander-in-chief of all volunteer forces and a former Iraqi Premier, General Taha al-Hashemi, as Inspector-General, and nominating an inter-Arab committee to direct and supervise the armed struggle in Palestine. Yet the implementation of the measures decided upon fell far short of plans and was half-hearted and irresolute. Each state followed its own policies and tactics, and none fully trusted the others; funds were allotted grudgingly; arms provided (mainly rifles) never matched the quantities requested and promised; a united volunteer force was never recruited, and the armed volunteers who did go to Palestine in early 1948 were not coordinated with the all-Arab Committee, nor were their commanders appointed by that committee. On the whole, the "unofficial" all-Arab aid, until May 1948, thus was a failure. At the same time, the Palestinian A.s' own resistance, which had broken out after the UN decision of 29 Nov. 1947 but had, despite numerous attacks on Jewish quarters, settlements and inter-urban communications, achieved no major military success, collapsed in March-Apr. 1948.

The failure of A. guerrilla operations and the collapse of the Palestinian-A. body politic induced the ASt's to decide, despite previous decisions to the contrary, on the invasion of Palestine by their regular forces. This decision was taken in mid-April and was finalized only in the second week of May. The chiefs-of-staff of the armies advised delaying the invasion, since the armed forces were not ready and first needed considerable increases in equipment, but they were overruled by the political leaders. Egypt had the decisive vote in that decision – and she was undoubtedly motivated, at least in large part, by the resolve to foil 'Abdullah's separate and dissident plans, which he forcefully reiterated in April, indicating that his forces would invade on their own to take over the Arab part of Palestine. To keep him in line, he was appointed commander-in-chief of all invading forces – an appointment that was mainly nominal and was not effectively implemented. Egyptian army leaders later insisted, in their efforts to absolve the armed forces of responsibility for the debacle of 1948, that the decision to invade had been imposed on them, against their better judgment, by Premier *Nuqrashi and his government; Nuqrashi claimed that King *Farouq had forced his hand.

The military struggle within Palestine, and the failure of A. operations, created two new problems that were to bedevil A-I relations for years to come. a) In the course of operations, the Jewish forces did not stick to the precise UN-proposed boundaries of the future Jewish State, which were militarily indefensible (with their "crossing points" – see map; the UN had, indeed, not considered defense needs, assuming that partition would be implemented in peace and mutual cooperation); but rounded out and expanded the territory allotted to them, adding c. 2,600 sq. mi. to the c. 5,400 sq. mi. envisaged. b) A refugee problem was created. From about Feb. 1948, the fabric of Palestinian-A. society began collapsing, its leadership crumbling, and refugees started streaming from the Jewish-controlled areas into the A.-held parts and the neighboring AC's. Among the first to flee were most of the local leaders, including many military commanders, the wealthy and upper-class, professionals and the intelligentsia. By April-May, 200–250,000 refugees had left – nearly one third of the A. population of the Jewish-held area; 300–400,000 more left after the A. invasion of May 1948. Most A. spokesmen maintain that these refugees were forcibly expelled by the Jews; Israel has always vigorously denied this. During the operations there were doubtlessly instances of Jewish pressure, of forcible evacuation – particularly of villages which resisted their incorporation into the Jewish State and served as bases for A. military operations; but by and large the exodus was a spontaneous movement, caused by fear and the confusion and violence of bloody war and triggered by the visible departure of nearly all the leadership, the élite, that was clearly understood as a signal, if not as an outright instruction. In some instances explicit instructions were given, as in the well-documented case of Haifa, where local Jewish and A. leaders were preparing an agreement to spare the city a murderous civil war, but an envoy sent to Damascus to obtain the endorsement of the A. top leadership returned with a rejection of any such agreement and a definite instruction to evacuate the city. The evacuation was carried out with the assistance of the British authorities.

4. FROM 1948 TO 1956. The War of 1948 began on 15 May, when the Mandate ended and Israel declared her independence with the invasion of the nascent state by the regular forces of the seven independent AC's, Egypt, Iraq, Syria, Lebanon, Jordan, Sa'udia and Yemen — Sa'udia with a token contingent, Yemen only nominally. (For its military events, see *Arab-Israel Wars.) The war inflicted grievous losses on Israel's fledgling army, still poorly equipped and hardly organized, and on her civilian population. For two to three weeks the situation was critical, but the end result was a defeat for the ASt's: they were unable to prevent Israel's birth and consolidation, and Israel was able to hold on to all the territory allotted to her under the UN plan, expel A. forces from parts they had occupied (except for a small corner on the upper Jordan occupied by Syria), and add c.2,600 square miles (including the Western, Jewish-inhabited part of Jerusalem, where the UN had been unable to establish an internationally-administered separate unit, as the partition plan had provided).

The war ended with Armistice Agreements concluded in Feb.-July 1949, separately, with Egypt, Lebanon, Jordan and Syria. Iraq refused to conclude any formal agreement with Israel, but empowered Jordan to take charge of the Iraqi forces and their withdrawal. The Armistice Agreements, negotiated under the chairmanship of UN mediator Ralph Bunche (for details see *Arab-Israel Wars), were based on the existing lines as they had emerged from the war. The Agreements were defined as steps toward the restoration of peace, banned any "warlike or hostile act", affirmed "the right of each party to security and freedom from fear of attack" and laid down that "no aggressive action shall be undertaken, planned or threatened against the people or armed forces of the other" side; the Armistice line was not to be crossed. The Agreements emphasized, on the other hand, that they would not "prejudice the rights, claims and positions" of the parties as to "the ultimate peaceful settlement of

Map of Armistice Lines, 1949

the Palestine question" and that the Armistice lines were "not to be construed in any sense as a political or territorial boundary". Mixed Armistice Commissions were set up, chaired by UN-appointed officers and aided by UN observers, to supervise the correct implementation of the Agreements and deal with complaints.

For the State of Israel, with its existence established and its independence recognized by most nations, the A.-Jewish dispute over Palestine was ended: an entity named "Palestine" had ceased to exist — after a brief 30 years. Part of it was now Israel, while the rest was part of Jordan (the annexation, a fact since 1948–49 was formally proclaimed in Apr. 1950), or occupied by Egypt. Of the Palestine A.'s, who had rejected the offer to establish their own state in part of Palestine; 150,000 were citizens of Israel; more than 700,000 were citizens of Jordan (c.600,000 in Palestine, including c.200,000 refugees from Israel-held areas, and nearly 100,000 refugees in Transjordan — not counting pre-1948 Transjordanians of Palestinian origin); c.250–300,000 were in the Egyptian-occupied *Gaza Strip (with no Egyptian citizenship conferred upon them), including 150–200,000 refugees from Israel-held areas; and 100–150,000 refugees were in Lebanon and Syria. The dispute was now between Israel and the ASt's — and Israel thought it could, and should, be settled speedily. Israel had no claim on the ASt's other than requesting their acquiescence in her independence and the transformation of the Armistice into a lasting peace.

The ASt's and the A.'s of Palestine took a completely different position. Officially, they insisted on two main demands: a) Israel should withdraw to the borders blueprinted by the UN plan of Nov. 1947, and b) the refugees should be allowed to return. Israel rejected both demands. The new borders — that could be changed, under the Armistice Agreements, by consent only — had been established as a result of war, and because the UN blueprint took no account of defense needs and was militarily untenable, and there was no going back to that blueprint. Besides, who had a better claim to these areas than Israel, since the Palestinian A.'s had rejected a state of their own? As to the refugees, Israel was prepared to permit an agreed number of them to return (the figure of 100,000 was proposed from 1949 on); she was also prepared to pay compensation for land and unmovable property left behind (tentative estimates of the value of that property were made by a UN commission, and Israel made no appeal against its findings). But a return of all the refugees, or a free choice for all those who wished to return, was out of the question. The refugees had left of their own will, rejecting the option to stay and become citizens of Israel. Having fought Israel's emergence, they would be a hostile element that would not only fundamentally alter the character of the state but would work for its destruction. Moreover, Israel later claimed, after the large-scale movement of Jews from the Arab countries to Israel, a population exchange had in fact taken place; and throughout History problems created by similar population movements had never been solved by repatriation and the re-creation of large hostile and disruptive national minorities, but the solution had always been resettlement in the countries chosen by the refugees in the hour of decision (recent, cruel examples — Central and Eastern Europe after World War II, or India/Pakistan 1947). The bulk of the refugees should, in this case too, be resettled, with international help, in the AC's, the homeland of their own nation, with which they had thrown in their lot.

The ASt's rejected out of hand Israel's arguments and proposals, including the offer of partial refugee repatriation and compensation for those not repatriated. Moreover, they refused to meet with Israel in any direct negotiations; nor were their demands coupled with firm assurances that their acceptance would lead to peace and neighborly relations. In this deadlocked situation the UN continuously tried to help, but with little success. The General Assembly and its committees, as well as UN special agencies, held incessant debates. The iron-clad majority against Israel that developed after 1967, with annually repeated condemnations, had not yet coalesced in those years, 1949–67; but UN majority opinion was not favorable to Israel's policies. No clear stand was taken on the border question, but the UN tended to favor the refugee's right to choose between repatriation and compensation, and adopted many resolutions in that sense. A General Assembly resolution of Dec. 1948 granted that right to those refugees "wishing to live at peace with their neighbors", and one of 1950 recommended "the reintegration of the refugees into the economic life of the Near East either by repatriation or resettlement". Many similar resolutions were adopted year after year. While these resolutions were linked to a general desire to achieve peace in the Middle East, they did not stress or elaborate the basic issues of peace and co-existence or call for A.-Israel negotiations. At any rate they had little effect.

The UN also set up institutions to deal with the A-I dispute. In 1948 it appointed a mediator, the Swedish Count Folke *Bernadotte; but his proposals proved unacceptable to the parties, and to the UN General Assembly as well. In Sept. 1948, Bernadotte was assassinated in Jerusalem by a dissident extremist group of the Jewish underground. The American Ralph Bunche succeeded him as acting mediator and successfully chaired the Armistice negotiations; with their completion he ceased his activities. Since 1948–49 the UN sent officers from various nations as Truce (later Armistice) Observers and Supervisors ("UNTSO"). Late in 1948, the UN appointed a *"Palestine Conciliation Commission" (PCC), composed of representatives of the USA, France and Turkey. The PCC convened a conference in Lausanne in 1949, but the ASt's refused to meet Israel, and the "Lausanne Conference" was no more than separate talks. It achieved nothing. The parties agreed on a protocol which provided for the UN blueprint map of 1947 to be regarded as a starting point for discussion, but the A.'s interpreted that as an acceptance of the 1947 map, while Israel considered it only as an opening for negotiations. Further low-profile efforts of the PCC had no success either, and while it was never officially disbanded, it gradually faded away. In Dec. 1949, the UN established a *"UN Relief and Works Agency for Palestine Refugees" (UNWRA), to aid and rehabilitate the refugees. For over 35 years now, that agency has been providing housing (in camps), food rations, education and health services; but its efforts to advance to rehabilitation and resettlement yielded virtually no results, mainly because the ASt's resisted them. In 1949, when it was still believed that resettlement was politically feasible, perhaps within the framework of a major ME development scheme, the PCC commissioned a group of experts to survey the economic prospects and work out such a general scheme. Its report — the "Clapp Report", presented in Dec. 1949, envisaged the solution of the refugee problem, through resettlement linked with a major general development project, within one year. The ASt's, however, wanted no link between the refugee question and their economic development, and nothing came of the Clapp Report.

Behind the scenes, efforts were made to break the deadlock by secret Arab-Israel contacts. Those with King 'Abdullah of Jordan were re-established while the war was still on; the Armistice with Jordan was in fact concluded in secret talks with the King himself behind the screen of the official negotiations in Rhodes. Continuing contacts yielded a secret draft non-aggression pact, ready for signature in early 1950; but as rumors of the planned pact leaked, the ASt's threatened Jordan with expulsion from the A. League and total boycott — and the King reneged and made a deal: he renounced the pact with Israel in return for all-A. acquiescence in his annexation of the A. part of Palestine. Further contacts with 'Abdullah were cut short by his assassination, in July 1951. Among other secret contacts, those with Egypt's *Nasser looked promising. As the "Free Officers" seemed to follow a moderate policy, the new régime was cautiously welcomed in Israel and secret contacts were made through various middlemen. However, nothing came of these attempts. (One of the contributory reasons for that failure may have been an abortive attempt by Israel's secret service, in 1954, to foil a *rapprochement* between Egypt and the West, and the evacuation of British troops, by covert sabotage acts against Western and American institutions in Egypt — an operation that caused a deep and protracted political crisis in Israel.) In 1949, Husni *Za'im, Syria's new military leader, made contact with Israel indicating his wish to discuss a possible peace settlement; but these contacts were cut short by Za'im's fall and execution. Israel also maintained covert contacts with forces outside the Arab mainstream, such as the Christian Maronites in Lebanon and their para-military organization, the *Phalanges, and exiled leaders of *Kurd nationalists.

The hostility of the ASt's led them — beyond the political struggle and the propaganda and indoctrination linked with it — to take various practical anti-Israel steps, such as a complete boycott (see *Arab Boycott). Egypt also closed the *Suez Canal to Israeli shipping and to foreign ships en route to or from Israel. Against her obligation, under the Convention of *Constantinople of 1888, to keep the Canal open to ships of all nations, even in time of war, she cited article X of that Convention permitting her to take measures for her security. In Sept. 1951, the UN Security Council condemned the closure of the Canal as unjustified interference with the freedom of navigation and called on Egypt to terminate these restrictions, but Egypt did not heed that (binding) decision, and the Canal remained closed to Israel-bound shipping. Egypt imposed a similar blockade on the Straits of *Tiran, the entrance to the Gulf of *'Aqaba. After acquiring the islands of Tiran and Sanafir from Sa'udi Arabia, in 1950 (promising, at the time, not to interfere with the freedom of navigation in the Gulf), she claimed the right to close the Gulf entrance as it was entirely within her territorial waters. Several attempts by ships of different flags to defy the blockade and reach Eilat, Israel's port at the head of the Gulf, failed and Eilat remained blockaded (until 1956).

There were also, from 1949, frequent border clashes. Some of them were "ordinary" clashes of army patrols or exchanges of fire between army border positions. Most of them, however, were incidents caused by infiltration and terror and sabotage acts by small groups of A.'s. At first, these infiltrations were haphazard and there seemed to be little organization behind them, but gradually they grew into what Israel called organized terrorism and the Arabs — "guerrilla" (see *Palestine Arab guerrilla organizations, *Feda'iyyun). Israel maintained that these attacks were organized and aided, supported, or at least connived at, by the Arab states, their armies and secret services. These claims, usually denied by the Arab states, could not be proved in most cases when complaints were aired at the Mixed Armistice Commissions, where the UN Truce Observer usually cast the decisive vote, as each side maintained its version. In any case, these commissions and the UN observers could only record and censure breaches of the armistice, but had no power to prevent or remedy them. The commission's work was also frequently interrupted — thus Israel from 1952 to 1957 participated only in emergency sessions of the Israel-Syrian commission, and from 1957 boycotted it completely (as Syria insisted that the commission consider also the demilitarized zones — see *Arab-Israel Wars — which Israel held to be outside its authority). From 1956 to 1959 Israel boycotted the Israel-Jordan commission, and from 1956 she regarded the Israel-Egypt commission as abolished.

As complaints were unavailing and the ASt's took no action to prevent acts of infiltration and sabotage (but Israel maintained, even encouraged them), Israel increasingly took recourse to retaliatory raids across the armistice lines. The first major reprisal action of that kind was taken in Oct. 1953 against Qibya village on the Jordan-held *West Bank; many others followed. One of them, against Gaza in Feb. 1955, was later frequently cited by Nasser as a turning point inducing him to abandon hope for a settlement with Israel. The ASt's usually complained about such reprisals to the Security Council, and as the reprisals were undoubtedly breaches of the armistice by Israel's regular forces (while the sabotage intrusions that triggered them were on a much smaller scale and there was no proof that the ASt's and their armies were behind them), Israel was frequently condemned.

5. FROM 1956 TO 1967. The growing scale and frequency of sabotage intrusions, the continuing Egyptian blockade, and a threatening build-up of Arab military forces — since 1955–56 with Soviet help — orchestrated by increasingly bellicose Arab statements and policies and enhanced by a series of Egyptian-led inter-Arab military pacts, imbued Israel with a sense of encirclement and imminent mortal danger. To pre-empt that danger Israel in October 1956 took military action and launched the *Sinai Campaign — which, as was later revealed, was prepared in collusion with Britain and France and coordinated with their *Suez War. Israel forces swiftly occupied all Sinai (see *A.-I. Wars), but halted 10 miles East of the Suez Canal — conforming to a pre-agreed Anglo-French ultimatum. In early Nov., the UN General Assembly called several times for an immediate cease-fire and the withdrawal of all invading forces. Heavy pressure was exerted by both the United States and the USSR, with the latter adding dire threats of unilateral military intervention. But the UN also established a *"United Nations Emergency Force" (UNEF), to supervise the cease-fire and separate the forces; Israel assumed and demanded that UNEF would also ensure the freedom of navigation in the Gulf of 'Aqaba. Israel therefore accepted the withdrawal order. By Jan 1957 her forces had withdrawn from all Sinai, except for Sharm-al-Sheikh, the coastal post controlling the Straits of Tiran; Israel retained this position and a strip on the East coast of Sinai connecting it with Eilat, pending the receipt of assurances concerning the freedom of navigation in the Gulf. Israel also retained Gaza, demanding an assurance that UNEF would administer it for a suitable period ("until a peace settlement is concluded": Premier Ben Gurion) and would prevent its

re-transformation into a base for hostile intrusions. After more negotiations with the UN and the USA, Israel in Mar. 1957 withdrew her forces from those last positions, too. The effectiveness of the guarantees she had received was dubious: the Secretary-General of the UN could not give iron-clad guarantees — on the contrary, Egypt's agreement to the stationing of UNEF on her soil had been given on the explicit condition that it would be withdrawn as soon as Egypt demanded it. The United States promised to "support" the freedom of navigation, to exercise it and to join with others to ensure its general recognition. She expressed "confidence" that Egypt would abide by her obligations and would no longer bar Israeli shipping from the Gulf or the Suez Canal, and said that the assurances Israel was asking for should be given effect after her withdrawal. She also supported a UNEF presence in Gaza and participation in its administration — "with the approval of Egypt". All this did not amount to full, effective guarantees. Gaza was immediately evacuated by UNEF and handed back to the Egyptian military administraton; the freedom of shipping in the Gulf of 'Aqaba was maintained until 1967; the Suez Canal remained closed to Israel and Israel-bound shipping.

Thus, the freedom of navigation in the Gulf of 'Aqaba and the prestige of a swift military success, were Israel's only achievements in the Sinai Campaign. Otherwise, the A.-I. situation after 1956–57 remained much as it had been before. Politically, the A.'s remained adamant in their hostility. Moreover, those regarding Israel as a foreign body, a "spearhead of Western imperialism", and an aggressor, found their opinion confirmed by her collusion with France and Britain, and by her pre-emptive action. Border clashes, intrusions and sabotage acts continued. And so did military preparations and a build-up of forces by the ASt's, first and foremost Egypt.

Three new elements were added in the late 1950s and early 1960s. a) A. guerrilla operations were now conducted by newly coalescing Feda'iyyin organizations such as al-*Fatah. These organizations were inspired by a tendency to revive a Palestinian-A. entity — an ideology that fully developed after 1967 but had its beginnings in the early 1960s, symbolized by the foundation of the *Palestine Liberation Organization (PLO) in 1964 (see *Palestine Arabs).

b) As clashes between Israel and the Feda'iyyin sharpened again, A. regular forces, particularly Syrian and Jordanian, were increasingly drawn into them and sometimes incidents escalated into serious battles. From 1964 on, escalating Israeli reprisals sometimes involved the use of the air force.

c) The problem of the waters of the *Jordan River became an acute, critical issue. That problem had come close to an agreed solution in the mid-1950s when experts of both Israel and the ASt's involved had agreed to the *Johnston Plan, but the agreement had then been rejected by the A. leaders for political reasons. Israel now prepared to implement her part of the scheme — unilaterally, but conforming to the principles and water-quantities of the Johnston Plan — and began pumping from the Sea of Galilee. As the ASt's could not, short of war, prevent Israel from doing so, they devised a plan to divert the sources of the Jordan — the *Baniyas in Syria and the *Hasbani in Lebanon — so that their waters would no longer reach Israel. This plan was approved at the First A. Summit Conference in Jan. 1964, and work on the diversions began early in 1965. However, as Israel made it clear that she would consider any diversion as a hostile act and take firm action, underscoring that warning by several deliberate strikes at the diversion points in Syria when border incidents presented an occasion, the ASt's backtracked. Syria, and particularly Lebanon, made the continuation of the diversion work conditional on full all-A. military guarantees, which the ASt's, and especially Egypt, were not prepared to give, considering that they were not ready for full-scale war. Diversion works, while not officially cancelled, therefore slowed to a snail's pace and virtually ground to a halt. Yet, the issue was perceived in Israel as a permanent vital threat.

The increasing tension, and Israel's sense of encirclement and mortal threat, in 1966–67, were similar to those of 1956. New Egyptian-led military pacts, including joint commands and explicitly directed against Israel (Egypt-Syria, Nov. 1966, Egypt-Jordan, May 1967, with Iraq joining immediately); a growing concentration of forces on Israel's borders, accompanied by intensified threats; and an ever-increasing incitement of the masses to a Holy War, created a deepening impression that a strangling noose was closing in on Israel. Incidents kept escalating, particularly on the Syrian front, including an air battle in Apr. 1967. This time there was no collusion with outside powers: Israel felt she was quite alone. When Nasser, on 16 May 1967, deliberately took the final step of escalation by ordering the UN Force out and declaring a renewed blockade of the Straits of Tiran, and the great powers did not intervene, Israel pre-empted the imminent Egyptian-and-A. attack. On 5 June 1967 her forces attacked and destroyed the Egyptian air force and marched into Sinai. Syria joined Egypt in this *Six Day War; so did King *Hussein of Jordan — disregarding Israel's appeal to stay out and her guarantee that Jordan and her forces would not be attacked. Several other ASt's sent token contingents (see *Six Day War).

6. FROM 1967 TO 1973. The Six Day War (for its military events see *A.-I. Wars) left Israel in occupation of the whole of Sinai up to the Suez Canal (which was blocked by ships sunk, and kept closed by Egypt), of the Syrian *Golan Heights, and of the A. part of Palestine, i.e. Jordan's *West Bank and Eastern Jerusalem, and the Egypt-occupied *Gaza Strip. At first, Israel was prepared, and offered, to restore all the occupied territories — with the exception of East Jerusalem, which was immediately declared united and incorporated with Israeli West Jerusalem — in return for a complete and contractual peace. This offer, however, elicited no response from the ASt's. On the contrary, an A. League summit meeting at Khartoum, in Sept. 1967, while calling for a "political solution" (as against A. extremists who held that no settlement with Israel was possible and that the only solution was her destruction), reiterated the Nasser-formulated "Three No's": no peace with Israel, no negotiations and no recognition. Israel's position thereupon hardened: The Right-wing opposition openly strove to annex and incorporate in a "Greater Israel" — "The Whole Eretz Israel" in Hebrew — all the occupied parts of Palestine, as well as the Golan, and perhaps also Sinai or parts of it. The Government was still prepared to negotiate, within the framework of a peace agreement, the return of most occupied territories, but not necessarily all of them; the Armistice lines of 1949, explicitly defined as not constituting final political borders, were not sacrosanct, and at any rate they were invalidated by the war of 1967. New, agreed borders had to be negotiated. A general indication of what Israel might wish to retain (most of the Jordan Valley, the eastern slope of the Judean desert, the Etzion block of former settlements south of Jerusalem, Sharm al-Sheikh on the Straits of Tiran and a strip on the East coast of Sinai connecting it to Eilat) was outlined in the *"Allon Plan" which dominated the ruling Labour Party's thinking, though it was never formally adopted. Israel began establishing settlements in the occupied areas — at first semi-military villages based on the Labour-Zionist aversion to purely military occupation and the glorification of settlement of the land, and until 1977 mostly in those parts that Israel intended to retain under the Allon Plan. Israel also instituted a policy of "Open Bridges" unprecedented in modern history: she permitted, even encouraged, economic links between the occupied West Bank and Jordan, imports and particularly exports, financial ties, and a constant, though controlled, movement of mutual visits. West Bank and Gaza A.'s also began to find employment — mostly menial, in agriculture, construction and services — in Israel. Soon those working in Israel were 35–50% of the West Bank and Gaza labor force and contributed 20–25% of the occupied areas' GNP. For the ASt's, on the other hand, Israel's withdrawal from all the territories occupied in 1967 soon became a cardinal demand, a pre-condition for any political settlement.

In the wake of the 1967 war there was a surge of specifically Palestinian-A. nationalism, and the ASt's increasingly supported its demands. As the "West Bank" and the Gaza Strip, the remaining heartland of Arab Palestine, were now occupied by Israel — and additional refugees, estimated at 250–350,000 (including more than 100,000 refugees from 1948) had left the area, most of them to Jordan — the demand for the return of these areas came to mean not specifically their return to Jordan or Egypt but the establishment of an independent Palestinian-Arab State. The PLO standing for that demand, grew into a strong organization — and was taken over, in 1968–69, by the various "Feda'iyyin" guerilla groups, becoming a roof-organization of these groups. It was fully supported by the ASt's — though it was in bitter conflict with Jordan and Lebanon since 1969–70 (see *PLO, *Jordan,

*Lebanon) — and was recognized in 1974 by the A. League and all its member-states as the sole legitimate representative of the Palestine Arabs.

The UN and the great powers resumed their efforts to find a formula for an Arab-Israel settlement soon after a cease-fire ordered by the Security Council had ended the war. These efforts were now even more difficult, as the Soviet Bloc, except for Rumania, had severed relations with Israel, while six radical Arab states had broken relations with the USA, whom they accused of collusion with Israel. Attempts by the Soviet Bloc and anti-Israel Third World countries to get the UN to order an immediate Israeli withdrawal, with no settlement and no conditions, failed both in the Security Council and the General Assembly, while the UN was nearly unanimous in condemning the incorporation of East Jerusalem in Israel and demanding its annulment. In Nov. 1967, the Security Council, after protracted wrangles, unanimously adopted Resolution 242 — which became the principal document concerning the A.-I.C., agreed to by the UN, the great powers and most of the states of the region. It stressed the need for "a just and lasting peace in which every state in the area can live in security", and "the inadmissibility of the acquisition of territory by war", and called for a withdrawal of Israeli armed forces "from territories" occupied (in the French version: from *the* territories — "*des territoires*"), the "termination of all claims or states of belligerency and respect for and acknowledgment of the sovereignty, territorial integrity and political independence of every state in the area", guarantees for the freedom of navigation through "international waterways", and a "just settlement of the refugee problem". Israel accepted Resolution 242, stressing that it called for withdrawal "from territories" and not from "*the*", or "all", territories occupied — versions that had indeed been deliberately rejected — and that the withdrawal was to be part of a peace settlement to be negotiated and agreed. Most ASt's also accepted the Resolution — though some of the more radical ones remained ambiguous, and the PLO rejected it (principally because it spoke of refugees only without acknowledging Palestinian-Arab rights to independence and statehood). But all A. spokesmen interpreted it as ordering the withdrawal of Israel from *all the* territories occupied, and without the need for prior negotiations or peace agreements.

Resolution 242 also requested the UN Secretary-General to designate a "special representative" to promote agreement and assist peace efforts; he appointed the Swedish diplomat Gunnar Jarring. Such efforts were even more urgent as hostilities between Egypt and Israel were resumed soon after the war; it was mainly artillery shellings by Egypt, to which Israel replied by counter-shellings and air raids (in Oct. 1967, e.g., the Suez oil refinery was destroyed). Throughout 1968 these artillery duels and air raids continued, and in 1969 they intensified and came to be called "War of Attrition". In July 1969 Nasser openly proclaimed such a war and declared that the "phase of liberation" had begun. Early in 1970 Israel escalated the confrontation by air-bombing Egypt in depth. Egypt now set up batteries of a new weapon: Soviet-supplied (and mostly Soviet-manned) surface-to-air missiles (SAM), which caused the Israel air force grave losses. Soviet pilots also began operating Egyptian (Soviet-supplied) war-planes and got involved in confrontations with Israeli planes.

The crisis was also aggravated by a freak incident: in Aug. 1969 a Christian fanatic set fire to the al-Aqsa mosque in Jerusalem. A. and Islamic leaders refused to accept Israel's assurance that the arsonist was a demented Australian tourist, and suspected an Israeli plot against *al-Haram al-Sharif*, the Temple Mount sacred to Islam. An Islamic summit conference held in protest in Rabat, Morocco, was the beginning of a permanent organization for regular meetings of Islamic Foreign Minsters. Other marginal issues also exacerbated tension. A. apprehensions of Israel as an aggressive power with expansionist designs was enhanced by the strong ties Israel was developing with many countries of Black *Africa, much resented and opposed by the ASt's. They also bitterly resented the secret (but known) military aid Israel was extending to the anti-A. rebellions of the *Kurds in Iraq and the African tribes in South Sudan.

Israel had to confront not only Egypt: frequent clashes occurred on her borders with Jordan, Syria and Lebanon, too. Most of these clashes derived from actions by Palestinian-A. Feda'iyyin — called terrorists by Israel, resistance guerrillas by the A.'s — and from Israeli counter-operations and reprisals. Attempts to organize violent-permanent resistance within the occupied territories were curbed — in the West Bank by the end of 1967, and in Gaza by 1971–72, and while there were occasional incidents, the occupied areas were, on the whole, quiet until the 1980s. Sabotage and terrorist squads came from across the borders — from Jordan and Lebanon, where the PLO was building an ever-growing establishment of guerrilla bases and a huge organizational infra-structure, a veritable state-within-the-state (Syria kept the Palestinians on her soil under strict control and permitted them no independent action). Jordan clashed with the guerrilla establishment when it increasingly endangered the state and its régime, and expelled it after a bloody war in 1970–71. From that time on Lebanon became the main and virtually only base for PLO operations. As terrorist attacks increased in scope and intensity, so did Israel's counter-action — air raids, brief punitive incursions, commando operations, all mainly in Lebanon. Israel was frequently condemned for these incursions by the UN Security Council. Palestinian-A. terrorists also began hijacking civilian airliners — at first Israeli ones (the first case: July 1968), but increasingly foreign ones, outside the ME — and attacking planes and passengers in international airports. Operations of this kind culminated in a spectacular simultaneous hijack of several international airliners in Sept. 1970 (timed to coincide with the decisive battle against Jordan) and a suicide attack (by Japanese terrorists allied with the PLO) on passengers at Lod (Tel Aviv) airport in May 1972. Other terrorist operations also increasingly took place outside the immediate arena. There were attacks on Israel Embassies; the assassination of Israeli athletes at the Olympic Games at Munich, Sept. 1972; the seizure of the Saʻudi Embassy in Khartoum and the murder of the American Ambassador and other foreign diplomats in Mar. 1973. From c.1972, the mainstream PLO leadership dissociated itself from terrorism in foreign countries and air-hijacks and ordered them to stop; but the extremist factions within the PLO continued. Israel's secret services, in their struggle against terrorism, in those years turned to methods of counter-terror, such as seeking out and killing terrorist leaders (e.g. in a commando raid on Beirut in Apr. 1973).

The political deadlock was not broken in the years after 1967. In the A. position certain changes were perhaps discernible: a) Extremist slogans calling for the extermination of Israel ("throwing the Jews into the sea") — which had damaged the A. case in world public opinion and deluded the public at home — were gradually discarded; the struggle was to be aimed not at the residents of Israel and their annihilation or expulsion but against their state and what the A.'s considered its expansionist aggression — though the acceptance of Israel's rightful existence, even after total withdrawal from the territories occupied, was only vaguely circumscribed by the moderate ASt's and avoided or rejected by the extremist ones and the PLO.

b) As the stress was now put on withdrawal to the pre-1967 borders, the former insistence on the 1947 blueprint was muted (although it has not altogether disappeared). It was implied, and sometimes explicitly stated, that a settlement should be sought with an Israel withdrawing to the borders of 1949–67, i.e. the Armistice lines. There was also less emphasis on the demand to permit the return of the refugees — although this demand was not dropped.

c) There was now a growing emphasis on the demand for a Palestinian-A. state. Before 1967 the stress had been on the elimination of Israel, implying the erection of an A.-dominated Palestinian state on her ruins — but all references to the "West Bank", the A. part of Palestine annexed by Jordan and forming half of the Kingdom, had been blurred so as not to antagonize Jordan, and no group or movement in the West Bank itself had explicitly advocated secession and the creation of a separate Palestinian independence. This restraint was abandoned after 1967 and most of the ASt's began speaking of a Palestinian state based mainly on the occupied areas to be vacated, the West Bank and Gaza — and their demand for Israel's withdrawal with its implied acceptance of Israel in her pre-1967 borders logically could mean: only in the West Bank and Gaza. This position — seldom clearly spelled out — was not fully shared by either Jordan or the PLO. Jordan did not abandon her claim that the occupied West Bank was part of her kingdom and should be returned to her. However, King Hussein had to accept Palestinian claims to self-determination, at least in part. From 1972 he advocated a federal structure for his kingdom, with the Palestinian West Bank as a semi-independent constituent part, and in 1974 he had to bow, at least officially, to the all-A. recognition of the PLO as the sole legitimate representative of the Palestinian A.'s.

The PLO never formally accepted the restriction of future Palestinian independence to the West Bank and Gaza, in co-existence with Israel, but insisted on its claim to all Palestine. In 1968 it adopted a revised "National Charter" (or Covenant), which clearly spelled out that claim. It defined Palestine in her British-mandated boundaries of 1917–48 as the homeland of the Palestinian Arabs (alone) and denied Israel any right to exist. It negated even the existence of a Jewish nation and of "historical and spiritual ties between Jews and Palestine", and denied to the bulk of Israel's population the right to stay in the future Palestine state, accepting as "Palestinians" only those Jews living in Palestine before "the beginning of the Zionist invasion" — defined in other resolutions as 1917 — and their descendants. And it laid down that "armed struggle is the only way to liberate Palestine". This Charter has never been abrogated or revised, though changes in the thinking of the PLO leadership have been reported or implied. In 1974, the PLO National Congress decided to establish an "independent combatant national authority" in "every part of Palestine that is liberated". This was interpreted by some as implying the PLO's readiness to be content with a Palestinian-Arab state in the West Bank and Gaza that would co-exist with Israel — but such a readiness was not spelled out in the resolution of 1974, nor has it been clearly stated since.

Diplomatic efforts by the UN and the great powers, particularly the USA, from 1967 on, were of no avail. UN Special Representative Jarring met fundamentally opposed positions on the part of the two sides: Israel wanted to *negotiate* a peace agreement on the basis of Resolution 242 and "secure and recognized borders" as mentioned by the Resolution (usually adding the Word "agreed": secure, recognized and *agreed* borders). The ASt's saw the Resolution as self-implementing and insisted on total and immediate Israeli withdrawal, with no need for negotiations. In March 1969 Jarring suspended his efforts. Talks by the four great powers, from Apr. 1969, and by the two super-powers, in the course of the year, were also of no avail (particularly as the Soviet Union presented plans to be imposed, with no need for negotiations or acceptance by Israel, which was unacceptable to the US). In Oct. 1969, the US Secretary of State, W. Rogers, presented to the USSR a plan, also presented to the Middle East disputing parties, and published, in Dec. As the *Rogers Plan was based on Israel's near-total withdrawal on the Egyptian and Jordanian fronts (it did not deal with the Israel-Syrian border), with negotiations on certain details only, and on freedom of return for the refugees, it was rejected by Israel; it was also rejected by the ASt's and the USSR — as being excessively pro-Israel. As the "War of Attrition" escalated, with increasing Soviet involvement, the US presented, in June 1970, urgent proposals for an immediate cease-fire, a 50 km wide military stand-still zone on both sides of the Suez Canal and the resumption of the Jarring mission (the "Rogers Plan II"). These were accepted by Egypt and Israel — the latter persuaded by a secret message from President Nixon, with far-reaching US assurances (24 July). The cease-fire ran into another crisis when on 7 Aug., the day of its implementation, Egypt moved new missiles into the stand-still zone, whereupon Israel re-suspended her participation in the Jarring talks. This suspension was lifted, after further US assurances, late in Dec. 1970.

In Feb. 1971 Jarring submitted a plan to Egypt and Israel, requesting at a first stage a clear Egyptian commitment to end all belligerency (including the assurance of freedom of shipping through the Suez Canal and the Straits of Tiran) and an Israeli one to total withdrawal to the former Palestine-Egypt border. Egypt, now under President *Sadat, replied favorably, though she hedged her commitment to the freedom of navigation by making it subject, for the Suez Canal, to the *Constantinople Convention of 1888, and for the Straits of Tiran to "the principles of international law", both of which she had cited in the past to justify the denial of passage. Egypt also demanded a prior Israeli commitment to the repatriation of the refugees. Israel replied that she was committed to withdraw "to the secure, recognized and agreed boundaries to be established in the peace agreement", but would not withdraw to the pre-June 1967 lines. Concerning the refugees she was prepared to negotiate compensation and Israeli participation in the planning of their "rehabilitation in the region" (i.e. not repatriation). The Jarring mission was thus again deadlocked; Jarring maintained his contacts and continued his efforts, but in July 1973 his mission was abandoned. From the spring of 1971 on, US Secretary Rogers attempted to mediate an interim agreement on the reopening of the Suez Canal based on a partial withdrawal and an agreed military de-escalation — a proposal in which Sadat had evinced interest and which Israel was prepared to discuss; but nothing came of these efforts either.

7. FROM 1973 TO 1977-78. The lack of diplomatic progress, the complete deadlock of 1971–73, led Egypt and Israel to diametrically opposed conclusions and conceptions. Egypt was preparing a military assault — intended, if full victory could not be achieved and the occupied areas could not be reconquered by force, at least to break the deadlock and force an intolerable situation to be reopened to movement, new negotiations, and a renewed involvement of the great powers. Israel's leaders deluded themselves into thinking that an A. military assault was impossible, that Egypt and the ASt's would have to acquiesce in the occupation for a long time, and that Israel could sit it out. The concerted attack by Egyptian and Syrian forces on 6 Oct. 1973, prepared under the guise of maneuvers, therefore caught Israel by surprise (and later had critical repercussions for Israel's internal politics, causing a deep upheaval). The *October War (Yom Kippur War in Israeli, War of Ramadan in A. terminology) initially brought Israel to the brink of defeat, with the Bar-Lev Line destroyed and Egyptian forces in Sinai, and Syrian forces in the Golan. But Israel rallied, despite grievous losses, crossed the Suez Canal and established her forces on Egyptian territory west of the Canal, while paralyzing and besieging the Egyptian Third Army east of the Canal, and drove the Syrian forces out of the Golan, occupying an additional strip of Syrian territory (for the military events see *Arab-Israel Wars). A massive US air-lift had enabled Israel to overcome the critical setbacks of the first days, while Egypt and Syria had received similarly massive supplies from the USSR (though Egypt later denied this). When a cease-fire, proclaimed by the Security Council on 21 October, was finally imposed, on 25 October, after dire Soviet threats and heavy American pressure, Israel felt she had been deprived by the great powers of a decisive victory over Egypt and Syria. The other ASt's had all declared their solidarity with Egypt and Syria, and some had sent token forces. Jordan had been excused from direct, frontal participation in the war, but had sent an armored force to aid Syria; a substantial Iraqi contingent that had been dispatched to Syria arrived too late to play a significant role in the battle.

The October War was in military terms, ultimately, a defeat for the A.'s; but it was seen by Egypt and the ASt's as a victory. Indeed, they could mark three important achievements: a) They had proved that Israel was not invincible in battle and that their forces were capable of mounting a well-planned, ably led and bravely fought military operation — thus wiping out what many A's perceived as a stain on their shield of honor: the shame of previous defeats, and making negotiations, and perhaps a reconciliation, with Israel possible for Egypt. b) They had enhanced their weight and influence in the international arena by causing a world crisis and deeply involving the great powers — the more so as they cleverly linked the A.-I. dispute with the global oil crisis that erupted at the same time. After the sudden upsurge of oil prices (dictated by the producing countries, many of them A.), the A. oil countries declared an oil boycott on countries they defined as hostile, while promising reductions and concessions to "friendly" countries — threats and promises taken seriously by the industrial countries of the West, though the A. oil countries were quite incapable of implementing them. c) Egyptian forces had broken into the territory occupied since 1967 and established themselves at least in a small part; thus the deadlock was broken and things began to move — at least on the Israel-Egypt front.

The UN Secretary Council re-established, in October, a UN Emergency Force (UNEF) — like the one that had existed from 1957 to 1967. The Council also reaffirmed, in its Resolution 338, its Resolution 242 of 1967, adding a call for immediate A.-I. peace negotiations, under "appropriate auspices" (which Resolution 242 had not spelled out). Most of the diplomatic effort, however, was exerted by US Secretary of State Henry Kissinger who served as an untiring mediator, "shuttling" innumerable times between Cairo, Jerusalem and Damascus, and cajoled the disputing parties into agreeing to the partial settlements evolved under his guidance. Egyptian and Israeli senior officers were meeting under UN auspices since the end of October at Kilometer 101 on the Suez-Cairo road, on the cease-fire line. In Nov. a "Six Point Agreement" was reached that dealt with the reinforcement of the shaky cease-fire and, mainly, with food and non-military supplies to the besieged Third Egyptian Army, East of the Suez Canal, and the town of Suez. Further talks ran into difficulties and were suspended. Late in Dec. 1973 a Conference optimistically termed "Peace Conference" met in Geneva under the co-chairmanship of the Russian and American Foreign Ministers and the UN Secretary-General, with Egypt, Jordan and Israel attending (Syria refused to participate, and no Palestinian-Arab representatives were invited). Speeches and statements were exchanged, but no progress was achieved. An Egypt-Israel Military Committee also met in Geneva to discuss an agreed separation of forces or disengagement. Agreement on this, however, was reached not at Geneva but at "Kilometer 101", under Kissinger's auspices, in Jan. 1974 and implemented in Feb.-Mar. Under its terms Israel withdrew her forces from Egypt West of the Canal, accepted the presence of Egyptian forces in Sinai, East of the Canal, up to the line of the October cease-fire, and lifted the siege of the Egyptian Third Army; a 10-km buffer-zone under UNEF was established, to separate the two armies; in strips East and West of that zone Egyptian and Israeli forces were "thinned out" and limitations imposed on their equipment. Syria maintained a hard line and clashes continued, with Israeli air raids in reply, but a Disengagement Agreement was eventually reached late in May 1974. Israel withdrew from the territory captured in October 1973, and from the town of Quneitra and an adjacent area held since 1967. A buffer zone was established, manned by a "UN Disengagement Observer Force" (UNDOF), and limitations on the strength of forces and their equipment were accepted for a 10-km strip and a further 25-km zone on each side. Syria refused to undertake to prevent Palestinian-Arab guerrillas from operating from her territory, but was believed to have given an informal, verbal undertaking to Kissinger.

Continuing efforts by Kissinger to proceed from the Disengagement Agreement to further stages were unsuccessful for a year and a half. But in Sept. 1975 an Egyptian-Israeli Interim Agreement was signed providing for a further withdrawal in Sinai and the establishment of a new UN buffer zone, moved farther to the East. Egyptian forces moved East into what had been the buffer zone. Egypt and Israel set up one surveillance and early-warning station each in the new buffer zone, with a third such station set up by the US and manned by American civilian technicians. The oil fields and installations in the Abu Rudeis area on the Red Sea coast were restored to Egypt, demilitarized and with a civilian UNEF-supervised administration. In this Interim Agreement the parties also reaffirmed that they would not resort to the threat or use of force or military blockade and that the conflict should be solved by peaceful means. The Agreement provided for free passage through the Suez Canal of Israel-bound cargoes (on non-Israeli ships); towards the Agreement, the Suez Canal was reopened in June 1975. This Interim Agreement was made possible by new US assurances to Israel, set down in a formal "Memorandum of Understanding" (and balanced by parallel US assurances to Egypt).

There was no comparable progress in Israel-Syrian relations. Secret and informal contacts with King Hussein of Jordan, based mainly on the general lines of the "Allon Plan", continued in the years after 1973, but they yielded no agreement. During those years the political position and status of the PLO grew perceptibly stronger, as outlined above. In the 1970s the PLO put more stress on its conception of the future Palestine as a "secular and democratic" state — though it had not amended its Charter to accept the Jews of Israel as future citizens. Given the absence of secularism and the dubious character, or even the suppression, of democracy in the constitutional and political structure of most ASt's as well as the PLO's own record (e.g. the systematic elimination-by-assassination of dissenters and the use of cruel violence in inter-factional rivalries), Israel regarded that slogan as a public relations ploy and did not take it seriously. The "secular and democratic" formula did, however, impress liberal and leftist circles in Europe and the West, and the élite of the "Third World", and many supported the PLO in its quest for self-determination and independence for the Palestine Arabs (now usually referred to as "the Palestinians").

This shift of opinion clearly affected the UN, too. Its General Assembly and its special agencies grew increasingly anti-Israel, and year after year condemned Israel's occupation of Arab territories, her practices as occupying power, her anti-terrorist reprisals and raids. The Assembly specifically denounced Israeli settlements in the occupied areas as illegal (July 1979, endorsed by the Security Council in Mar. 1980, and since reiterated). In Nov. 1975 the Assembly even denounced Zionism, the Jewish nationalist movement that had founded Israel, as "racism". From 1969 on the General Assembly demanded the right of self-determination for the "Palestinians", i.e. the Palestinian A.'s. ("the inalienable rights of the Palestinian people" — Dec. 1968). In Nov. 1974, Yasser *'Arafat was invited to address the General Assembly and the same year the PLO was accorded observer status and the right to participate in debates.

Throughout these years, attacks by Lebanon-based terrorist squads inside Israel continued, generally on civilian "targets" like schools, buses and apartment blocs, with occasional attacks abroad — e.g. at embassies or airports, and hijackings of airliners. So did Israeli counter-operations, preventive, deterrent or punitive. In July 1976, a spectacular Israeli commando operation at Entebbe, Uganda, rescued a hijacked French airliner with its captive, mostly Israeli passengers. Raids on Palestinian guerrilla bases in South Lebanon culminated, in Mar. 1978, in a three-month occupation of a strip of Lebanese territory up to the *Litani river. The UN Security Council, besides ordering Israel's withdrawal, created a UN force, *UNIFIL, to supervise the withdrawal and help prevent further hostilities. When Israeli forces withdrew, they handed over control of that strip to a Lebanese, mostly Christian, militia under Major Sa'd *Haddad equipped, trained and supported by Israel. Since 1976, Israel's northern border was kept nearly open — at "the Good Fence" — for the inhabitants of South Lebanon's border zone (whose normal ties to the rest of Lebanon had been virtually cut by the Lebanese civil war and PLO domination) to sell their produce and seek supplies, medical help, employment, and there was much fraternization. Israel's secret ties to the Christian Phalanges also grew stronger and gradually came into the open.

Efforts to achieve further Egypt-Israel progress were stalled. Attempts to reconvene the Geneva Peace Conference failed. Another round of Soviet-American talks yielded a joint statement (1 Oct. 1977) that was rejected and resented by Israel, and was not followed up. In Israel, a Right-wing government under M. Begin had replaced the 30-year rule of Labour-led coalitions in May 1977, and the new government opposed Labour-led Israel's preparedness to withdraw from the bulk of the occupied territories and aspired to the incorporation of the occupied parts of Palestine in Israel.

8. FROM 1977 TO 1982. The deadlock was dramatically broken by Egypt's President Anwar Sadat. In Nov. 1977 he surprised Israel, the Arab countries and the world by visiting Israel — openly and publicly. The visit, that had been prepared in secret contacts (in which reportedly President Ceausescu of Rumania and King *Hassan of Morocco had some part), turned into a dramatic and highly emotional state visit. In addition to meeting Israel's leaders, government and opposition, Sadat addressed a solemn meeting of the Knesset, Israel's Parliament, offering peace and normal relations against a withdrawal from all territory occupied in 1967 and an agreed, negotiated solution to the problem of the Palestine A.'s. In substance, Sadat's proposals were thus not very different from the position of the other moderate ASt's. His great achievement was, first, as he also himself put it, a psychological breakthrough, cutting the vicious circle, by meeting the Israeli "enemy" and talking to him face to face; and second, spelling out what other A. leaders at best implied: a preparedness to accept Israel and co-exist with her in peace and normal relations once she agreed to the far-reaching concessions he demanded. He made it clear, though, that he would not conclude a *separate* peace but would consider an eventual agreement as being within the context of, and a first step towards, a general Israel-Arab settlement.

Sadat's historic visit of Nov. 1977 ended with an agreement to negotiate a peace accord. In Egypt, Sadat's move and the agreements ensuing later were opposed by the Nasserist intelligentsia, the extreme Left and the Islamic fundamentalists; but public opinion in general seems willingly to have accepted them — as shown, later, in 1979, in a National Assembly vote and a Referendum. The ASt's, however, immediately began moves to ostracize and isolate Egypt; these moves culminated in 1979 in the rupture of relations and the suspension of Egypt's membership in the Arab League and all other inter-Arab bodies (see *Egypt, *Arab League).

Israel-Egypt negotiations proved difficult, despite the euphoria and the good will of Nov. 1977. They were conducted under the good offices and mediation of the USA and required a great deal of American persuasion and cajoling, with the personal involvement of President *Carter. After several rounds of talks that yielded no agreement, Sadat, Begin and Carter closeted themselves in Sept. 1978 at the US President's "Camp David" — and there, after 12 days of hard negotiation, the *"Camp David Agreements" were signed on 17 Sept. One was a "Framework for Peace in the Middle East", committing the parties to an active search for "a just, comprehensive and durable settlement of the ME conflict through the conclusion of peace treaties based on Security Council Resolutions 242 and 338" and respect for the "sovereignty, ...integrity and ... independence of every state in the area and their right to live in peace within secure and recognized boundaries, free from threats or acts of force"; to achieve this, and implement Resolution 242, negotiations were needed (as Israel had always insisted, and the Arabs had denied). Egypt and Israel agreed that for a transitional period of up to five years a régime of autonomy should be established in the West Bank and Gaza (for "the inhabitants", as Israel insisted, meaning: not for the territory); Jordan would be invited to join the negotiations on the details and the self-governing authority, and the Egyptian and Jordanian delegations might include Palestinians acceptable to all. The five-year transitional period would begin with the inauguration of the self-governing authority, whereupon Israeli armed forces would withdraw to "specified security locations". During that transitional period Israel, Egypt, Jordan and the elected representatives of the inhabitants of the West Bank and Gaza would negotiate and agree on "the final status of the West Bank and Gaza and its relationship with its neighbors", while simultaneously Israel and Jordan, "joined by the elected representatives of the...West Bank and Gaza", would negotiate an Israel-Jordan peace treaty. The "solution" negotiated "must also recognize the legitimate rights of the Palestinian people and their just requirements".

A second agreement laid down a "Framework for... a Peace Treaty between Israel and Egypt". It provided for Egyptian sovereignty up to the international border between Egypt and Mandated Palestine and the withdrawal of Israeli armed forces from Sinai (Israel's negotiators had failed to obtain Sadat's assent to an Israeli presence at Sharm al-Sheikh and the Sinai east coast — not even in the form of a lease recognizing Egyptian sovereignty, or as a joint Egyptian-Israeli presence — or to Israel's retention of an area of Israeli settlements in the north-eastern corner of Sinai, with the new Israeli town of Yamit). Three major airfields built by Israel in Sinai were to be used by Egypt for civilian purposes only. Free passage of Israeli ships through the Suez Canal, the Gulf of Suez, the Straits of Tiran and the Gulf of 'Aqaba was assured. Certain limitations were to be imposed on the size and equipment of military forces in Sinai. UN forces were to be stationed in parts of Sinai (this was later changed to a "Multinational Force of Observers", US-directed and not under UN auspices). After the signature of the peace treaty, "complete, normal relations" would be established between Egypt and Israel, "including diplomatic, economic and cultural relations", and "economic boycotts and barriers to the free movement of goods and people" would be terminated. The Camp David Agreements were accompanied by several letters exchanged by the Egyptian, Israeli and US heads of government. In one of them, Sadat insisted that "A. Jerusalem is an integral part of the West Bank" and "should be under A. sovereignty", and, while the city should be undivided and under a joint municipal council, "all the measures taken by Israel are null and void and should be rescinded". In Dec. 1978 Sadat and Begin jointly received the Nobel Peace Prize.

Efforts to widen the scope of the Egypt-Israel agreement and use it as a basis for resumed negotiations for a general A.-I. peace, failed. Late in Nov. 1978, an invitation issued by Sadat to Jordan, Syria, Lebanon, as well as the USSR, to join a

Cairo Conference preliminary to the resumption of the dormant "Geneva Peace Conference" was rejected. This was inevitable, since all the AC's and the Soviet Bloc rejected the Camp David Agreements, and some of them were taking first steps to foil their consummation and to ostracize and boycott Egypt should she insist on carrying them out. The Cairo Conference of Dec. 1978 was therefore attended only by Egypt, Israel and the USA. Even so, it made no progress. An agreed draft of the peace treaty had been completed by Nov. 1978, but objections raised in both Jerusalem and Cairo prevented its final endorsement. Difficult negotiations continued for months, with active US mediation, until, finally, the Peace treaty was signed on 26 Mar. 1979. It conformed to the framework laid down in the Camp David Agreement. It was accompanied by several annexes, agreed minutes and letters. Thus, agreed minutes further interpreted Article V, dealing with the freedom of navigation, and Art. VI — which said, after much wrangling that "in the event of a conflict between... obligations under the present Treaty and ...other obligations, (the former) will be binding and implemented". A joint letter committed Sadat and Begin to start, within a month from ratification, negotiations on the "modalities for establishing the elected self-governing authority (administrative council)" for the West Bank and Gaza — with Jordan, if she accepted the invitation to join — with the intention of completing them within one year.

The peace treaty was ratified, and went into effect, on 25 Apr. 1979. The Israeli withdrawal from half of Sinai, set for Dec. 1979, was duly implemented (with the town of al-'Arish handed over far in advance, in May), and the total withdrawal was completed, in accordance with the treaty, in Apr. 1982 (with Yamit and the settlements dismantled and destroyed by Israel). Israel-flag ships began passing through the Suez Canal in Apr. 1979. The normalization of relations went into effect in Jan. 1980. Ambassadors were exchanged in Feb. The boycott laws were repealed by Egypt's National Assembly the same month, and some trade began to develop (although it was much less than Israel had hoped for). In Mar. 1980 regular airline flights were inaugurated. Egypt also began supplying Israel with considerable quantities of crude oil. A US-led Multinational Force of Observers (MFO), with early warning stations etc., to replace UNEF (which had ended operations in July 1979), was in place in Mar. 1982, but no major incidents called for its intervention.

Peace was thus reigning between Egypt and Israel — and Egypt, since Oct. 1981 under President Husni *Mubarak, loyally maintained it despite Arab pressures and her own strong desire and interest to rejoin the Arab family of nations and resume its leadership, and despite disappointing vicissitudes and crises in Egypt-Israel relations. For the establishment of normal, friendly relations — beyond an official state of peace — had hit obstacles which the two parties have thus far been unable to overcome. Talks on the autonomous régime for the West Bank and Gaza were stalled soon after they opened in 1979, both on the substance of the autonomy envisaged, with Egypt's and Israel's views divided by a very wide gap, and on procedure (e.g. Israel's insistence that some sessions should be held in Jerusalem, which Egypt refused), and have, despite several attempts to revive them, not been resumed. A dispute on the small area of *Taba, adjacent to Eilat, has not been resolved. Egypt resented, and was embarrassed by, Israel legislation finalizing the annexation of East Jerusalem (July 1980) and the extension of Israeli law to the Golan, i.e. its *de facto* annexation (Dec. 1981), as well as the Israeli air raid on an Iraqi nuclear reactor in June 1981. Her resentment was aggravated by Israel's invasion of Lebanon in June 1982. In Sept. 1982 Egypt recalled her Ambassador, leaving the Embassy headed by a lower-level diplomat, and virtually froze the process of normalization and the cultivation of trade, cultural relations, etc. She repeatedly indicated that the Ambassador would be reinstated and relations unfrozen only after Israel withdrew from Lebanon, the Taba dispute was settled, and progress was made on the Palestinian-Arab issue, i.e. West Bank and Gaza autonomy. Israel bitterly resented the withdrawal of Egypt's Ambassador and demanded his reinstatement. She also saw a violation of the spirit if not the letter of the peace agreement in the halting of the normalization process and complained that even before Sept. 1982 Egypt had permitted her press and public institutions and organizations to conduct vicious anti-Israel propaganda, and had hampered all efforts to cultivate trade and cultural relations. American efforts to mediate or informally assist in an improvement, an unfreezing, of relations, were only partially successful. An agreement to submit the Taba issue to arbitration was reached in Sept. 1986, and the same month Egypt's President and Israel's Premier met — for the first time in five years — and Egypt appointed a new Ambassador.

The Egypt-Israel peace agreement of 1979 caused no improvement on the other A.-I. fronts — on the contrary, the "Rejection Front" of extremist ASt's hardened its stance and managed to draw most ASt's into total opposition to that agreement and an anti-Egyptian position. Thus the A.-I. confrontation was aggravated. While the Israel-Jordan front was quiet and the "open-bridges" policy of close Jordan-West Bank relations was maintained, PLO terrorist attacks from South Lebanon (and abroad) continued. Israeli counter-operations, commando and air raids against the PLO establishment in Lebanon, which inevitably hurt also the Palestinian and Lebanese civilian populations, were intensified. They often led to clashes and air battles with Syrian forces stationed in the *Biqā', East Lebanon; thus, Syrian planes were shot down in air battles in June 1979 and Apr. 1981; in the latter clash, near Zahla, Israel let herself be drawn into battle to protect and assist operations by the Christian *Phalanges — with whom relations had grown into a secret alliance that was being revealed in these years. In July 1981, a cease-fire arranged for South Lebanon through US mediation informally included a halt to Palestinian attacks from Lebanon on Israel; but in 1982 Israeli air raids on PLO targets in Lebanon again intensified.

9. FROM 1982 TO 1985: LEBANON. On 6 June 1982 Israeli forces invaded South Lebanon, in a large-scale operation designed, so Israel announced, to liquidate the PLO's military-terrorist establishment entrenched there and to halt c. 40 km from the border, occupying an area wider than that seized in the previous operation of 1978, which had stopped 20–25 km from the border at the *Litani River. The local population, including its Shi'i-Muslim majority, largely welcomed the invading troops as liberators from the near-domination of South Lebanon by the PLO that had become oppressive. However, after the initial target was achieved, within a few days, Israeli troops continued their advance (for the military events see *A.-I. Wars), occupying most of the Shuf, the mountainous region southeast of Beirut with its mixed *Druse and Christian population, advancing in the Biqā' (eastern Lebanon), reaching the southern outskirts of Beirut, and cutting the Beirut-Damascus highway in several places. When a cease-fire took hold, on 25 June (a first cease-fire, on 11–12 June had not been effective), Israeli troops had linked up with Christian Phalange forces and reached the coast north-east of Beirut, encircling the capital. Without occupying Beirut itself, they were moving freely in Christian-dominated East Beirut and virtually besieging Muslim- and PLO-dominated West Beirut. Despite an initial resolve to avoid clashes with Syrian forces in Lebanon, they had clashed in the Biqā', around the Beirut-Damascus road, and in air battles.

Behind these expanded operations — which were clearly contrary to the originally announced and endorsed plans, and later caused deep rifts and a grave internal crisis in Israel — a grand political design was discernible: not content with the elimination of PLO terrorist bases, Israel apparently intended to help the Christian Phalanges achieve a dominating position and restore Christian predominance in Lebanon, to shape a permanent alliance between Israel and a Christian-dominated Lebanon and reach at least non-belligerent co-existence and security agreements if not a formal peace. This plan seemed to approach realization when, in Aug. 1982, the term of Lebanese President *Sarkis having expired, the militant young Phalange leader Bashir *Jumayyil was elected President.

In the meantime, the immediate aim — common to Israel and the Phalanges, and accepted by the Government of Lebanon — was to eliminate the PLO not only from the south but from all Lebanon and particularly from West Beirut, to where many PLO fighters had retreated from the south, and where the leadership maintained its headquarters and main institutions. Cut off and besieged, the PLO leaders were prepared to negotiate an orderly evacuation with the Lebanese Government. Agreement was reported early in July, but could not be finalized and negotiations dragged on. The USA — which had not opposed UN Security Council calls for a cease-fire and the withdrawal of Israeli troops, but condoned Israel's operation in its first, limited version and viewed with some sympathy even its expanded, grand-design version — had in June again sent a senior diplomat, Philip Habib, to mediate. In July the US announced that Marines would be sent to supervise, and assist in, the evacuation of PLO forces, and stepped up efforts to reach an agreement on that evacuation. At the same time Israel intensified her pressure, shelling and bombing West Beirut — thereby arousing much condemnation and strong US objections. Her forces also entered several suburbs of Beirut. In mid-Aug. agreement was reached on the evacuation of the PLO, and troop contingents were sent by the USA, France and Italy to assist and supervise it. The evacuation of c.11,000 PLO fighters was completed — by sea to Tunisia, Algeria, Yemen, South-Yemen, and overland to Syria — on 1 Sept. PLO headquarters and institutions were transferred to Tunis. About 3,000 Syrian troops were also evacuated from West Beirut. The evacuation did not apply to PLO men in Syrian-occupied Northern and Eastern Lebanon — an estimated 10–15,000.

Israel's grand design, however, soon ran into a serious crisis. On 14 Sept. 1982 newly-elected President Bashir Jumayyil was killed in a terrorist attack on the Phalanges' headquarters. Israeli forces entered West Beirut the same night. Two days later Phalange fighters, in revenge for the murder of their leader, entered the Palestinian camps of Sabra and Shatila in West Beirut and massacred nearly 500, including some women and children. Israel, whose forces had entered West Beirut "to ensure order and security", was seen by many as bearing at least a large share of the responsibility. A high-level Israeli inquiry later confirmed that Israeli army and political leaders should have been alert to the danger of Phalange revenge (a Lebanese inquiry yielded no serious insight); some charged certain Israeli leaders with connivance in, or even encouraging, the massacre, but that charge was not substantiated in the inquiry. The "multi-national" forces, that had withdrawn from Beirut in mid-Sept., now returned. Israeli troops evacuated Beirut late in Sept., maintaining a liaison office, nearly an Embassy, in a suburb.

On 21 Sept. Amin *Jumayyil replaced his murdered brother Bashir as President. The new leader was much less militant as a Phalangist fighter for Christian predominance and tended to seek a compromise and national reconciliation, and an accomodation with Syria; he was also much less identified with, or sympathetic to, Israel. When Israel-Lebanon talks on the withdrawal of Israeli forces began, in Dec. 1982, the new régime no longer shared the basic conception that Israel had hoped to work out with Bashir and his associates: that Israel's withdrawal would be accompanied by, even conditional on, a formal agreement on border security and the prevention of terrorism from Lebanese soil, as well as a non-belligerent co-existence or a *de facto* peace with close liaison and possibly open borders and normalized relations. Negotiations were protracted and difficult and required much American mediation. The Agreement, finally signed on 17 May 1983, fell short of Israel's expectations, but went a long way to satisfy her minimum requirements: the state of war was terminated and mutual respect for the two countries' independence and territorial integrity proclaimed, with the existing international boundary recognized. The "existence or organization of irregular forces, armed bands, organizations, bases, offices or infrastructure" aiming at "incursions into or any act of terrorism in" the other party's territory and threatening its security were to be prevented, as were "entry into, deployment in, or passage through" the parties' territory, air space and territorial waters of "military forces... or equipment hostile to the other party". Previous Lebanese agreements enabling such a presence and activity were declared null and void. Israeli forces were to withdraw from all Lebanese territory within three months from the ratification of the agreement (simultaneously with Syrian and PLO forces — a condition not explicitly spelled out but informally understood, and confirmed in an Israel-US exchange of letters). Lebanon would establish a special Security Zone, whose southern part, a 15-km wide strip from the Israel border nearly to the Litani (and *de facto* a further area up to the Zahrani river), would be policed by an "Army Territorial Brigade" that would incorporate "existing local units" (i.e., in fact, Major Haddad's South-Lebanese forces set up and maintained by Israel), while its northern part, a further 30 km wide, up the Awali river, was to be policed by a regular army brigade. The UN force (UNIFIL) would be transferred to that northern area. A Joint Liaison Committee, with US participation, would supervise these measures, assisted by joint supervisory teams and patrols. Israel would maintain a Liaison Office in Lebanon, and Lebanon was granted the right to do likewise in Jerusalem. An agreement would be negotiated on the "movement of goods, products and persons" (i.e. *de facto* normalization), while in the meantime existing patterns of such movement would continue.

The agreement of May 1983 was never ratified by Lebanon and therefore did not go into effect. It was vehemently opposed by Syria and her allies within Lebanon, President Jumayyil's opponents, headed by the leaders of the Druze and Shi'ites, and as Jumayyil felt compelled to seek a compromise with his adversaries and set up a government of national unity, the demand for its annulment was one of the main issues discussed at the lengthy negotiations on intra-Lebanese reconciliation (and Jumayyil had not been enthusiastic about it in the first place). Eventually, when a Lebanese conciliation agreement was concluded and a government of National Unity established (Feb. 1984, see *Lebanon), the May 1983 agreement was formally annulled by Lebanon on 5 Mar. 1984. The Israeli Liaison Office, transferred in 1983 to a northern suburb of Beirut in the Christian area controlled by the Phalanges, was ordered to close down in July. Israel's vision of coordination and friendly, near-normal relations with a Lebanese government in full control of its country had been shattered.

Since the summer of 1983, with the May 1983 agreement inoperative and eventually abortive, Israel had to envisage a unilateral withdrawal of her troops — if possible, in coordination with the Lebanese government and army. Her resolve to accelerate that withdrawal was enhanced by two acute considerations: a) her occupation entailed a degree of responsibility for regions torn by a violent inter-communal and inter-"militia" struggle - a responsibility that she was unable and unwilling to take on. This concerned, particularly, the Shuf, southeast of Beirut, where Christians and Druze were engaged in a deadly race for predominance and physical control — each side accusing Israel of favoring and arming the other. Israel had indeed allowed her Christian-Phalangist allies to send their militias to take control of the Shuf; but she had contacts with the Druze leadership, too, despite its outwardly extremist anti-Israel and pro-Syrian stance (Israel's own Druze population was displaying strong sentiments of solidarity with its Lebanese-Druze brothers, exerting pressure and even clandestinely sending volunteers, including deserting Druze soldiers of the Israeli Army).

b) From 1983, guerrilla or terrorist attacks on Israeli forces in Lebanon were increasing — perpetrated by Palestinian fighters from the Syrian-held parts of Lebanon who succeeded, or were permitted, to infiltrate the Shuf and areas further south, as well as by an incipient Lebanese resistance. The latter was mostly Shi'i. The Shi'is of the south, who had initially welcomed the Israeli forces, were increasingly resentful of the continuing occupation, the ensuing separation of the south from the rest of Lebanon, and the security measures imposed. The organized Shi'i movement, "al-*Amal", with its militias, was increasingly turning against Israel, parallel to its growing radicalization in internal Lebanese affairs. In addition, extremist *Khomeini-inspired groups were competing for the leadership of the Shi'i community and organizing a violent terrorist campaign against Israel as well as against US and French troops and institutions, and in the internal Lebanese struggle.

All efforts to coordinate Israel's withdrawal with the Lebanese government and army to ensure an orderly take-over failed. The Government was unwilling to agree with Israel on such lines, insisting on a total and unconditional withdrawal — for political reasons and because of pressure by its internal opposition and by Syria. It was also incapable of taking over and imposing its rule on the rival militias. Israel therefore, in Sept. 1983, withdrew from the Shuf and the Kharrub region (southwest of it, including the coastal area) to a new line on the Awali River, north of *Sidon (positions in the east, the Biqā', were maintained). Israel's unilateral withdrawal was then blamed for the anarchy, the bloody fighting, the mutual massacres that broke out in the Shuf between Christians and Druze (and ended with the full take-over of the region by the Druze and the elimination of much of its Christian population).

After the annulment of the Israel-Lebanon agreement in 1984, the situation stagnated — with resistance and terrorist attacks increasing (and Israel's resolve to withdraw as speedily as possible enhanced by her change of government, in Sept. 1984, and the establishment of a Labor-led coalition). American efforts to help arranging for new talks on a coordinated withdrawal met with persistent obstacles and failure. When Israel-Lebanon negotiations were finally resumed, in Nov. 1984, they were bound to fail, as the two parties held totally incompatible conceptions. For Israel, withdrawal remained linked, even if her desire for a political settlement and a degree of normal neighborly relations was unfulfilled, to security arrangements that would at least prevent the re-transformation of Lebanon into a base for hostile, terrorist activities. She doubted whether the Lebanese army — barely in control of all Beirut, since July 1984, and incapable of enforcing security even there, and as yet unable to move into the Shuf and the coastal plain south of Beirut (where it attempted gradually to take over in Jan. 1985 only) — would be capable of ensuring security and preventing hostilities. Israel re-proposed the arrangements envisaged in the May 1983 agreement: a southern zone, in which the Israel-trained and equipped "South Lebanon Army" (commanded, after Haddad's death, by General Antoine Lahad) would do that job, in coordination with Israel and under her supervision (if possible as a territorial brigade of the Lebanese army); and a northern zone where the UN Force would be stationed. Lebanon, stressing that the talks were purely military and had no political implications, accepted the need to enforce security and prevent any hostile activities, but insisted that this was the task of the Lebanese army alone. She adamantly rejected any role for Israel's "South Lebanon Army" and the transfer of UNIFIL from the border to an area further inside Lebanon and insisted on a total and unconditional withdrawal, with no coordinated security arrangements and thus no "gains derived from the invasion". (The Government thus adopted the position pressed upon it by the Lebanese opposition and by Syria).

As pressure mounted on the Israeli home front to speed up the withdrawal and extricate the country from an operation that had turned into a failure, and as there was no prospect of agreement with a Lebanese government, Israel announced in Jan. 1985 — while guerrilla and terrorist attacks, now nearly all Shi'i, increased daily — her decision to withdraw unilaterally, in three phases, with subsequent security arrangements to be imposed unilaterally. The first phase — withdrawal from the Sidon area — was completed in mid-Feb. 1985, the second — the Tyre region, to the Litani, the central area of South Lebanon around Jezzin and Nabatiyya, and the southern Biqā' — in Apr. 1985. The last stage, completed by June 1985, left Israel in control of a "Security Zone" 5–10 km. (3–6mi.) wide, with a population of c. 150,000 mostly Shi'i. This zone was policed by the 2,000–2,500-strong "South-Lebanese Army" trained and maintained by Israel, with Israeli forces sending patrols but keeping no (or nearly no) permanent positions. (The UN Force, UNIFIL, was stationed in parts of the same area.) Lebanon protested and demanded the complete evacuation of all Lebanese territory up to the international frontier, and the UN repeatedly backed that demand. Clashes with Shi'i militias — both al-Amal and more extremist *Hizbullah* groups — and re-constituted PLO squads continued to some extent, and so did Israeli punitive or preventive patrols in the area beyond the Security Zone. Israel has so far kept the Security Zone under her military control.

10. FROM 1982 TO 1985: OTHER FRONTS. On the other A.-I. fronts, and in the A.-I. confrontation in general, there was some movement in the 1980s, deriving mainly from three variables: the shifting fortunes and positions of the PLO; diplomatic initiatives by both A. and foreign statesmen (and the moderate stance of the Israeli government, Labour-led from 1984 to 1986); and the gradual reassertion by Egypt of a leading role in inter-A. and ME affairs, coupled with the emergence of a bloc of moderate ASt's led by Egypt and Jordan.

Little change occurred in three aspects of the situation. (a) An incessant stream of resolutions condeming Israel continued flowing from the UN General Assembly and the UN special agencies, mostly concerning retaliatory raids, the occupation and malpractices in its administration, and Palestinian-A. rights (in the Security Council similar resolutions were usually prevented by a US veto). (b) Terrorist attacks continued — up to June 1982 mostly from Lebanon (mainly shelling of Israeli border villages by katyushas), and later, on a smaller scale, by clandestine infiltrators. Cases of stoning or attacking traffic in the West Bank also increased. (c) There was no basic change in the West Bank and Gaza, but as the occupation continued with no solution in sight and Israeli settlements kept spreading, there was a growing sense of frustration and bitterness, and increasing small-scale violence (see *Israel Occupied Territories). Generally, developments in the West Bank and Gaza raised deep concern, among their A. inhabitants and in the AC's alike (and among Israeli moderates), lest Israel was creating facts that might prove irreversible and serve to make future negotiations meaningless.

Among those concerned and eager to assist breaking the deadlock was the USA. Her leaders saw the Palestinian-A. problem as the key to a general settlement, and a transitional régime of autonomy in the West Bank and Gaza, in accordance with the Camp David Agreements, as the best way to a solution. Vigorous American efforts to reactivate the stalled Egyptian-Israeli talks on that issue failed in 1982. Finally, President Reagan publicly presented his ideas on 1 Sept. 1982. The "Reagan Plan" proposed a five-year transitional régime of "full autonomy" for the West Bank and Gaza, under an elected self-governing Palestinian authority with Israeli settlement in the occupied areas frozen. During that transitional period final solutions should be worked out. It was for the parties concerned to negotiate them, but the US opposed both annexation by Israel and the establishment of an independent Palestinian state and thought "self-government... in association with Jordan" offered "the best chance for a ... just and lasting peace". The conflict should be resolved, on the basis of Resolution 242, "through negotiations involving an exchange of territory for peace"; the "extent to which Israel should be asked to give up territory (would) be heavily affected by the extent of true peace and normalization and the security arrangements offered in return". Jerusalem should "remain undivided, but its final status should be decided through negotiations".

The Reagan Plan was rejected by the radical ASt's, the PLO, and Israel. The moderate Arab states saw some positive points and a possibility to work out a compromise, or a combination, with their own plans; so did the Israeli Labor opposition (that came to lead the government for two years in 1984). The Americans hoped, mainly, that King *Hussein of Jordan would come round to join American-initiated negotiations based, if not on the Camp David Agreements (which Hussein would not accept) then at least on the Reagan Plan. But King Hussein could not bring himself so to decide. Though the idea of Palestinian-A. self-government in association with Jordan conformed to his own plans, he kept delaying and, after some vague intimations of general support, in Mar. 1984 gave the US a negative reply. He preferred to rejoin the all-A. mainline which rejected direct negotiations with Israel and insisted on an international conference (with the participation of the USSR and the other permanent members of the Security Council, as well as the PLO), a total withdrawal by Israel and a Palestinian-Arab state.

The ASt's remained divided on the Palestine issue. Egypt, at peace with Israel, was outside the camp, excommunicated and boycotted — though she informally wielded great influence. The "Moderates" — Jordan, Morocco, Tunisia — did not offer clearly wrought plans of their own and hesitated to diverge from the mainline. The "Rejectionists" — Syria, Libya, South Yemen, and parts of the PLO (Iraq had seceded from that group, and Algeria was gradually moderating her position) — saw no need for any negotiations or any diplomatic initiative, as the only solution was complete victory over Israel. A new diplomatic initiative came from Sa'udia, assuming the leadership of the central, mainline camp. In Aug. 1981, Crown Prince *Fahd, in an interview, made public a new 8-point plan: total Israeli withdrawal from all the occupied areas, with all settlements to be dismantled; Palestinian refugees to have the right to return; an independent Palestinian state, with Jerusalem as its capital — evidently: in the territories vacated by Israel, though that was not said — after a brief UN takeover not exceeding a few months; after that, the "right of all states of the region to live in peace" would be recognized; the UN "or UN member states" would guarantee the implementation of these principles. Commentators saw in that formula an implicit acceptance of Israel (as one of "all states of the region"), though the Fahd Plan did not mention Israel, negotiations with her or the conclusion of formal peace agreements.

Efforts to have an all-A. summit conference endorse the Fahd Plan failed, as the Rejectionists refused to go along, and the 12th Summit, at Fez, Nov. 1981, was suspended in disarray. Eventually, the Summit reconvened in Sept. 1982, only Libya absenting herself, and unanimously endorsed the Fahd Plan with certain amendments. These were mainly two: a) The Security Council was to guarantee "peace among all the states of the region, including the independent Palestinian state" (the "recognition of the right" of all states to live in peace being eliminated); b) The position of the PLO as the sole and legitimate representative of the Palestinian-A. people was re-endorsed and stressed. The Fahd Plan has since become the main policy guideline accepted by all the Arab states (except Libya, though even she has not explicitly rejected it).

The pivotal role of the Palestinian A.'s in any future settlement was accepted by the USA (and most other countries, and world public opinion), and stressed by the Arab states. The latter insisted that the PLO alone was to speak for the Palestinians, while Israel and the US refused to see the PLO as a partner for peace negotiations as long as it had not accepted Resolution 242, Israel's right to exist and the principle of peaceful co-existence with her, and renounced terrorism. The PLO itself was in disarray since 1982. 'Arafat and his PLO mainstream al-*Fath, while not bowing to Israeli and US demands for a total reorientation of Palestinian-A. policies, seemed to grope for a way to join negotiations for a general settlement on the lines of the Fahd Plan. In Feb. 1985 Hussein and 'Arafat concluded an agreement on a future Palestinain-Jordanian confederation and joint action towards a peace settlement, based on the Fez (Fahd) Plan and "all" UN resolutions, and to be negotiated by a joint Jordanian-PLO delegation (see *PLO, *Jordan). Since the Hussein-'Arafat Agreement did not contain a PLO commitment to peaceful co-existence with Israel and a renunciation of terrorism, and as it envisaged an international conference rather than direct negotiations, Israel could not regard the Agreement as a serious plan for peace. Neither could the US, though she welcomed the agreement as a positive step, since it implied the acceptance by the PLO of Resolution 242 and the principle of a peaceful solution (an implication sometimes denied by PLO spokesmen).

While the extremist Arab states and PLO factions rejected the Hussein-'Arafat Agreement, President Mubarak of Egypt welcomed it as an opening for peace negotiations and began to promote further steps. He called for direct negotiations between Israel and a joint Jordanian-Palestinian delegation, whose Palestinian members would be nominated by but not members of the PLO (an "amendment" that the PLO could not explicitly accept). He urged the US to take the lead and initiate such negotiations, and proposed, as a first stage, US talks with a Jordanian-Palestinian delegation. But 'Arafat was unable to get the Agreement endorsed by the PLO, and in Apr. 1987 the PLO abrogated it, reiterating its rejection of Resolution 242 and its demand for an international ME conference in which it would be independently represented.

Efforts for a peace conference continued — the US had come round to support it, and the Labor Party half of Israel's coalition government seemed ready to acquiesce in an international conference as an umbrella "accompanying" and endorsing direct negotiations though the right-wing half and the government as a whole firmly opposed it. But as the PLO was unwilling to declare its acceptance of UN Resolution 242 and of Israel's right to exist, and as no Jordanian-Palestinian delegation acceptable to the US could be agreed upon, there was no progress.

Arab-Israel Wars The violent, military or semi-military clashes that erupted from time to time between Palestine A.'s and Palestine Jews, 1920–48, before the establishment of Israel, and particularly the A. rebellion of 1936–39, are described in the entry *Arab-Israel Conflict.

1. THE WAR OF 1948

Phase I: Prelude The A.-I.W., of which one can properly speak only from 15 May 1948 onwards, was preceded, while Palestine was still under British administration, by bloody clashes that gradually turned into a full military confrontation. Arab violence broke out on 30 Nov.–1 Dec. 1947, the day after the adoption of the UN resolution on the partition of Palestine and the establishment of independent Jewish and A. states and an international enclave of Jerusalem. Jewish buses were attacked, in Jerusalem a Jewish commercial quarter was burned and looted, and clashes soon spread. The pattern of violence was largely similar to the rebellion of 1936–39: local guerrilla squads ("gangs", 'isabat), frequently reinforced by men of neighboring villages or townquarters recruited *ad hoc* ("*faz'a*"), attacked Jewish traffic, settlements and outlying quarters — usually by small-arms' sniping and bomb-throwing. While Jewish traffic was much affected, attempts to capture settlements (Kfar 'Etzion, Tirat Tzevi, Kfar Szold) failed. The Jewish defense forces, the *Hagana*, still underground, concentrated on defensive measures, limiting retaliation to those directly involved in assaults, and began only gradually to take offensive action against centers of A. military formations; but the dissident *Irgun* tended to retaliate indiscriminately (e.g., by planting a bomb in an Arab market). British security forces intervened only sporadically — primarily to protect their own installations and forces — as Britain, on her way out, was unwilling to assume responsibility for enforcing partition or safeguard security and order in the inevitable troubles. Individual British deserters perpetrated several terrorist attacks on Jewish targets, including the Jewish Agency buildings, the *Palestine Post* newspaper, and houses on a central Jerusalem street.

In Jan. 1948 an A. volunteer force under Fawzi al-*Qawuqji entered Palestine and took over A. areas in the north and center, while other volunteers, mainly from among the *Muslim brothers in Egypt, entered the Hebron-Bethlehem area in the south. Qawuqji's force — calling itself the "Army of Deliverance" (*Jaish al-Inqadh*) — was c. 2,000 strong in Jan. and reached an estimated strength of 5–8,000 by Apr. It sent officers and small detachments to A. quarters in mixed towns liable to be conquered by the Jews, such as Haifa and Jaffa, and attacked Jewish settlements in the north (Tirat Tzevi, Mishmar Ha'emek, Ramat Yohanan). While it failed in these operations, it had more success in its attacks on Jewish traffic along major routes, and so had other guerrilla formations. In early 1948 Jewish Jerusalem was virtually cut off from the coastal plain (and from supplies and reinforcements), the Western Galilee from Haifa, the *Negev from Tel Aviv. Qawuqji also attempted to impose on the various local guerrilla formations a military command structure and centralized planning and discipline. These efforts had only partial success, as several local commanders — such as Hassan Salama in the Ramle-Lydda area or 'Abd-ul-Qader al-*Husseini in the Jerusalem region — refused to accept his overall command. Qawuqji seemed to have no backing from the political leadership, dominated by the Husseini faction (by now mostly abroad), and the *Arab League and its all-Arab military committee, which had decided to send volunteers and supply them with arms and logistic support, did little to enhance his position.

Early in Apr. 1948 the *Hagana* High Command decided to seize the initiative in order to gain effective control of the territory allotted to the Jewish State and secure communications within it and with Jewish settlement outside it. "Operation Nahshon" reopened the road to besieged Jewish Jerusalem — but the *Hagana* had not decided to hold the hills and villages controlling the road, outside the area earmarked for the Jewish State, and in mid-Apr. Jerusalem was again under siege. The *Hagana* captured the whole of Tiberias, where the Jewish quarter in the Old City had been besieged (18 Apr.); Haifa (22 Apr.); the area connecting Tel Aviv with outlying quarters; the A.-inhabited Qatamon and Sheikh Jarrah quarters in Jerusalem (the last had to be re-evacuated following a British ultimatum); Western Galilee; and all of Safad, where, too, the Jewish Quarter had been besieged. A Jewish take-over of Jaffa had been prevented by British intervention (the town surrendered later, in May). A. attacks continued, and some of them caused heavy loss of life (such as that on a convoy to the University Hospital on Mount Scopus — seen as a reprisal for the Deir Yassin attack — see below), but they did not achieve any change in the balance. In Apr. the exodus of A. refugees, that had begun in Feb., triggered mainly by the visible departure of most of the leadership and the social élite, gathered momentum. It was further accelerated and enlarged by reports of a massacre perpetrated by the *Irgun* in an attack on the village of Deir Yassin near Jerusalem — an attack (the only one of its kind by Jewish forces) strongly denounced by the *Hagana* and the Jewish leadership.

By late Apr. 1948 it was clear that Palestinian-A. resistance was ineffective, with the fabric of leadership and society disintegrating, and the Army of Deliverance virtually beaten. It was these developments — together with indications that King *'Abdullah of Jordan was planning to invade Palestine and take over the A. part, in agreement with the Jews — that induced the ASt's in May to order their regular armies to intervene, thus changing previous decisions to aid the Palestine Arabs but stop short of an invasion by the regular armies. The decision, taken against the advice of the military chiefs, was predominantly Egypt's and was, as claimed later, imposed by King *Farouq.

Phase II: 15 May to 10 June 1948   On 15 May Tel Aviv was bombed by Egyptian planes, and the regular armies of five ASt's — Egypt, Jordan, Iraq, Syria and Lebanon — invaded Palestine. Jordan's *Arab Legion was in the country before, considered by the British as part of the legitimate security forces; it was removed to Transjordan on 15 May, but was back on 16 May as an invading force. The all-A. plan envisaged the Egyptian forces moving north, in the coastal plain, towards Tel Aviv, the Syrian, Lebanese and Iraqi forces converging, through Galilee, on Haifa, and Jordan's Arab Legion approaching the coastal plain from the east, after occupying A.-inhabited central Palestine and Jerusalem; but the Legion did not in fact cross the partition line.

The *Hagana*, now the Israel Defense Army, exhausted by the fighting of the preceding months and as yet without air force, artillery or armor, hastily mobilized forces to block the invasion, but the situation was critical. The Egyptian Army moved along the coastal plain, attacking Jewish settlements on its path and eventually capturing some (Yad Mordekhai, Nitzanim), while bypassing others (Nirim, Kfar Darom). Its advance was halted near Negba, 35 km from Tel Aviv (with the help of the first fighter planes which had arrived the same day from Czechoslovakia).

Jordan's Arab Legion — which had captured the settlements of the 'Etzion Bloc, south of Bethlehem as well as the power plant at the Jordan-Yarmuk confluence before 15 May (Beit Ha'arava and the Potash Works at the northern end of the Dead Sea, and two settlements north of Jerusalem were evacuated) — entered the eastern, A. part of Jerusalem and captured, after bitter fighting, the isolated Jewish Quarter of the Old City. It failed, however, in its attempts to penetrate the Jewish new city. The Legion also occupied the foothills between the coastal plain and the Jerusalem Hills and repulsed *Hagana* attempts to dislodge it from Latrun which commanded the road to besieged Jerusalem. The Jews built an alternative road — nicknamed the "Burma Road" — through which Jerusalem was saved from starvation or surrender for lack of arms and ammunition.

The Syrian army occupied some territory south of the Lake of Galilee, with the settlements of Massada and Sha'ar Hagolan, but was halted at the gates of Deganya. Farther north, the Syrians crossed the Jordan south of the Huleh Lake, at the Bridge of Jacob's Daughters, capturing some territory near Mishmar Hayarden. The Lebanese army occupied Malkiya (at the bend where the frontier turns sharply to the north), but thereafter took little part in operations. Iraqi formations failed in their attempts to take Jewish settlements on the middle course of the Jordan, but besieged and by-passed them and deployed in central Palestine in the Nablus-Tulkarm-Jenin "Triangle". Neither their attempts to advance into the coastal plain nor Jewish attacks on Jenin had much success.

By early June the A. offensive had lost momentum, and confident expectations of a speedy victory, backed by much expert world opinion, had evaporated. Jewish forces had suffered heavy casualties but had not collapsed. They held most of the territory allotted to Israel (except for the southern coastal areas taken by Egypt, and the Syrian bridgehead), and Jewish Jerusalem. When the Security Council ordered a truce of 28 days, both sides accepted, and the truce went into effect on 10 June.

Phase III: 8 to 18 July   When fighting resumed on 8 July, the situation had changed. The Israel Defense Forces had been consolidated and some heavy equipment, purchased before May but held up by the British blockade, had reached them. Israel now took the initiative to round out the territory she controlled — disregarding some of the details of the UN blueprint-map which she considered obsolete, as that patchwork-map had been based on a peaceful implementation and an economic union and was indefensible in armed conflict. "Operation Dekel" (Palm) led to the capture of Lower Galilee, including Nazareth. "Operation Brosh" (Cypress) failed to eliminate the Syrian bridgehead near Mishmar Hayarden. An attempt to capture the Old City of Jerusalem also failed. On the central front, "Operation Dani" took Ramla and Lod (Lydda) — including the vital airfield. The second cease-fire intervened before Latrun and the hills leading to Ramallah could be captured and the corridor to Jerusalem widened, as planned. In the south, the Egyptians again succeeded in closing the main road to the Negev; Israel devised a secret alternative route to be used at night, but failed to dislodge the Egyptians. Yet, the initiative had passed to Israel, and it was reportedly in response to an A. request that Britain proposed at the Security Council a new truce — this time of unlimited duration. This came into effect on 18 July.

Phase IV: 19 July 1948 to 7 Jan. 1949 The truce was uneasy, and efforts by the UN mediator, the Swedish Count *Bernadotte, to work out a political compromise plan were unsuccessful. Bernadotte's proposal to exclude the *Negev from the Jewish state aggravated Israel's concern for that area which she considered a vital part of her territory. When Egyptian forces tightened their blockade of the Negev, heavy fighting broke out and, in "Operation Yoav" (15 Oct.), Israel succeeded in opening the road, capturing Beer Sheva on 21 Oct. Egyptian forces in the Hebron mountains and south of Jerusalem were now isolated. Simultaneously, "Operation El Hahar" (To the Mountain) widened southward the precarious narrow corridor to Jerusalem.

As A. irregulars, who had never accepted the truce, and the remnants of Qawuqji's forces continued harassing Jewish settlements in Galilee, Israel mounted a counter-attack. "Operation Hiram", a pincer movement from Safad in the East and the coast in the West (29–31 Oct.), took western Upper Galilee (and also some adjacent Lebanese territory). In Oct.-Nov. Israeli forces also reduced the area held by the Egyptians in the southern coastal plain. "Operation Horev", in Dec., was designed to expel Egyptian forces from Palestine. Israeli forces outflanked the Egyptians, advancing southwards through the desert, crossing into Sinai at 'Auja, capturing Abu 'Ageila and reaching the sea southwest of the Gaza Strip. As Egyptian territory was now involved, Britain threatened to intervene against Israel, invoking the Anglo-Egyptian treaty (which Egypt had not invoked), and British-US pressure compelled Israel to withdraw from Sinai. She regrouped her troops East of the Gaza Strip, posing an obvious threat to the last main stronghold of Egyptian forces in Palestine. An Egyptian brigade remained cut off and besieged in a pocket around Faluja (one of its staff officers was a young major named Gamal *'Abd-ul-Nasser).

The UN Security Council had called, on 16 Nov., for a new truce and negotiations on an armistice. On 5 Jan. 1949 Egypt agreed, and, as fighting on the other fronts had long ceased, the other Arab states followed suit. On 7 Jan. a truce took effect, and on 13 Jan. armistice negotiations began in Rhodes under the chairmanship of the acting UN mediator, Dr. Ralph Bunche.

The War of 1948 — for Israel: the War of Independence — caused very heavy Israeli casualties: over 6,000 dead (4,500 soldiers and nearly 2,000 civilians), almost 1% of the population. A. casualties have been estimated at c. 2,000 for the invading regular armies and an unknown number of Palestinian irregulars (the figure of 13,000 has been mentioned but no reliable figures are available).

Armistice A "General Armistice Agreement" with Egypt was signed on 24 Feb. 1949. It served as a model for similar agreements signed with Lebanon (23 Mar., at the border point of Naqura), Jordan (3 Apr., in Rhodes) and Syria (20 July, at the border point of the Bridge of Jacob's Daughters). For the general principles of the Armistice Agreements — their definition as transitional stages towards permanent peace; their non-aggression clauses; their definition as purely military, with no prejudice to an ultimate settlement — and the arrangements for UN observers and Mixed Armistice Commissions see *Arab-Israel Conflict.

The Agreements contained specific provisions different from case to case. With Egypt, the armistice line was defined as identical with the southern international border of Palestine, apart from the Gaza Strip — which remained under Egyptian control. Al-'Auja and its vicinity were demilitarized and designated as the seat of the Mixed Armistice Commission. The Egyptian brigade besieged at Faluja was evacuated. With Lebanon, too, the armistice line was identical with the international border; Israel evacuated the small area her forces had occupied during the fighting inside Lebanon.

Matters were more complicated with Jordan. Here, with no previous border, the whole length of the dividing line had to be negotiated — an issue that was resolved, behind the screen of the official Rhodes negotiations, in secret talks with

King 'Abdullah. The King ceded to Israel certain strips of territory in the coastal plain and the Wadi 'Ara hills that were not actually held by Israel (they had been held by Iraqi forces, but Iraq had refused to negotiate an armistice and handed to Jordan the responsibility for the area occupied by her). Jordan also gave up claims she had raised concerning the border in the southern Negev and accepted the line as requested by Israel, along the middle of the 'Arava valley. Several issues concerned Jerusalem — e.g. free movement on "vital roads" (the one from the coast to Jerusalem, via Latrun — for Israel; the East Jerusalem-Bethlehem road — for Jordan); free access for Israel to Jewish Holy Places in East Jerusalem (particularly the Western Wall), to the cemetery on the Mount of Olives, and to the University and Hospital on Mount Scopus (forming an enclave in Jordan-held territory); the operation of the Latrun pumping stations supplying water to Jerusalem, and of the railroad to Jerusalem; the provision of electricity to the Old City of Jerusalem. On these problems agreement was reached "in principle" only. It was agreed that a special committee should work out detailed arrangements. But this committee was never established and the matters listed were not resolved. The Hospital and University on Mount Scopus, e.g., could not operate — though they were maintained by Israeli caretaker crews supplied and rotated by UN-supervised convoys. Jews had no access to their Holy Places in Jerusalem.

Negotiations with Syria were difficult, as she was the only A. country to hold territory allotted to the Jewish State under the UN resolution and refused to hand it over. The deadlock was resolved by a deliberately vague formula establishing demilitarized zones in these areas, which were to be evacuated by Syrian forces. Elsewhere the armistice line followed the international border. From 1949 to 1967, the Demilitarized Zones caused frequent clashes and a state of almost permanent crisis. Israel regarded them as part of her sovereign territory, with limitations only on military forces and installations, as specified, while Syria considered them as areas in which she had special rights and which did not finally and fully belong to Israel (she disputed, for instance, Israel's right to divert Jordan waters in the Demilitarized Zone). Syria also insisted that the Demilitarized Zones were under the jurisdiction of the Mixed Armistice Commission, which Israel denied (though conceding certain rights of supervision to the chairman of the commission — but not to the commission itself, with its Syrian members). Israel stopped in the 1950s attending the commission.

2. THE SINAI CAMPAIGN (OCT. 1956)

In 1955–56 Israel felt a growing apprehension of encirclement engendered by increasing sabotage raids, especially across the Egyptian armistice lines; the Egyptian blockade of *Eilat and the Gulf of *'Aqaba, imposed since 1954; the build-up of Egyptian forces, enhanced since 1955 by major arms deals with the Soviet Bloc and accompanied by threatening speeches; the growing tension generated by the *Baghdad Pact of 1955 and the *Suez crisis of 1956. When, in Oct. 1956, Jordan joined a Syro-Egyptian military pact and a Joint Command was set up, Israel felt that the encirclement was complete and posed an immediate mortal danger. Israel resorted to preemptive military action. This operation had been secretly co-ordinated with Britain and France and their plans for military action against Egypt in the context of the conflict over the Suez Canal.

On 29–30 Oct., Israeli parachutists seized the Mitla Pass. Subsequently, three columns set out across the Sinai desert, tactically supported by the air force. One, striking south from Eilat, took Sharm al-Sheikh, commanding the Straits of *Tiran. Another advanced across central Sinai towards Isma'iliyya. The northern column outflanked the *Gaza Strip, turned back to take it and mop up its Egyptian forces, and then turned southwest along the coastal road towards Qantara. As the Egyptian air force was unable to intervene in full strength because of the simultaneous Anglo-French assault, Egypt's massive forces in Sinai were completely routed within 100 hours. An Egyptian destroyer was also captured off Haifa. Other AC's, defense pacts notwithstanding, did not take part in the war.

Heeding a pre-arranged Anglo-French "ultimatum", Israel's forces halted 10 mi. east of the Suez Canal. As the Security Council was paralyzed because of the veto power of the two permanent members themselves involved, the UN General Assembly, with the USA and the USSR in a rare show of unanimity, called on 2 Nov., and again on 7 Nov., for the immediate withdrawal of Israeli forces to the armistice lines, along with that of the Anglo-French forces which had in the meantime invaded the Canal Zone. The USSR threatened to use force if the resolution were not heeded. On 4 Nov. the Assembly decided to create a *UN Emergency Force (UNEF) to replace the withdrawing troops. On 8 Nov. Israel agreed to withdraw upon the conclusion of arrangements with the UN concerning UNEF. By 22 Jan. 1957 she had evacuated all the territory occupied expect for the Gaza Strip (Egyptian-occupied since 1948, but not Egyptian territory) and the eastern coast of Sinai facing the Straits of Tiran. Concerning these areas Israel insisted on safeguards for free navigation and freedom from attacks and sabotage raids across the lines. In Mar. 1957 the UNEF was deployed along the borders, including the Gaza Strip, and in Sharm al-Sheikh, to provide such safeguards — though its terms of reference in that respect were rather vague. Israel also obtained certain diplomatic assurances; but those given by the Secretary-General of the UN were vague and non-committal — a face-saving formula rather than a binding guarantee — and separate US assurances also fell short of full guarantees. When Israel completed her withdrawal in Mar. 1957, the Gaza Strip was, contrary to Israel's expectations, immediately handed over to Egypt, and hostile incursions were soon resumed. Freedom of navigation through the Straits of Tiran was maintained until May 1967 (when its re-abolition by Egypt was among the main causes of the Six Day War).

3. THE SIX DAY WAR, JUNE 1967

A.-Israel tension, increasing steadily in the mid-1960s, because of intensified sabotage raids and shellings of Israeli border villages, and the dispute over the *Jordan waters, rose to a fever pitch in 1967, particularly on the Syrian front. On 7 Apr. Israeli planes struck at Syrian artillery positions and shot down six Syrian MIGs. Syria complained bitterly to Egypt that the latter had not rushed to help her ally, particularly in view of their new military pact of Nov. 1966. Egypt now announced that she would not tolerate any further Israeli action against Syria and massed large formations of troops and armor close to the Sinai-Israel border. Her Soviet ally encouraged her in these war preparations and warned her of alleged Israeli troop concentrations against Syria (denied not only by Israel but also by the UN observers). Both the A's and the Russians interpreted mid-May statements by Israeli leaders as threats against Syria.

In mid-May President Nasser deliberately brought the crisis to a head. On 16 May, he requested the immediate withdrawal of the UN Emergency Force (UNEF) from the borders and the Straits of Tiran, and, on 18 May, from the whole of Sinai. The UN Secretary-General complied with the request. On 21–22 May, Nasser reimposed a blockade on the Gulf of 'Aqaba, closing the Straits of Tiran to all shipping to and from Eilat — a step which Israel had repeatedly stated she would regard as *casus belli*. These Egyptian measures were accompanied by threatening, bellicose speeches, tauntingly challenging Israel to war and proclaiming that Egypt was now strong enough to win. Public opinion was deliberately inflamed and mass demonstrations excitedly called for war. Leaders of the other ASt's rallied around Egypt, making equally bellicose speeches. On 30 May, King Hussein of Jordan, under intense pressure, joined the Syro-Egyptian military pact and joint command, and on 4 June, Iraq followed suit. The USA and several other maritime nations proclaimed that they regarded the Straits of Tiran as an international waterway open to free passage of ships of all nations, and reserved their right to use it, but took no effective steps to make President Nasser change his decision, or to break the blockade. Nasser, on his part, declared that any attempt to break the blockade would be considered an act of war. The blockade — itself an act of war — seemed to be a fact, and the encirclement appeared complete.

On 5 June, Israeli airplanes mounted a rapid, massive attack against Egyptian air fields and air force concentrations, and Israeli armor moved into Sinai. Syrian airfields were attacked the same day. A message was sent to King Hussein warning him to stay out of the war and pledging that Israel would initiate no action against Jordan. The warning went unheeded and Jordan joined the war (moving, first, to occupy the UN Headquarters south of Jerusalem). During that first day, both the Egyptian and the Syrian air forces were largely destroyed, losing over 400 planes (against 19 Israeli planes), and Israel won complete aerial superiority.

Simultaneously, Israeli forces attacked Gaza, where bitter fighting took place, and advanced into Sinai — in three columns; towards al-'Arish in the north; Abu 'Ageila and its elaborate fortifications in north-central Sinai, where a major battle was fought; and al-Qusseima in the center farther south. Sharm al-Sheikh was taken from the sea, and parachutists landed without opposition. By the end of 6 June, the Egyptian retreat had become a rout, and when the third day of fighting ended Israeli forces had taken all of Sinai, up to the Suez Canal, and the Gaza Strip.

Jordan's entry into the war met swift Israeli counter-action. On 5 June, Israeli forces took the UN Headquarters and linked up with the isolated outpost on Mount Scopus. The following day they attacked Jordanian positions in East Jerusalem (restraining the inevitable artillery and armor operations out of respect for the Holy Places). On 7 June, East Jerusalem was taken, including the Old City, and so was most of the *West Bank, the Jordan-annexed part of Palestine.

On 7 June, the Security Council, after much wrangling, called for a cease-fire. Israel accepted, and so did Jordan; Egypt initially rejected the cease-fire, but acceded on 8 June. Syria, however, which had intensively shelled border villages and unsuccessfully attempted to capture one of them, refused to accept the cease-fire — relying on the tremendous tactical advantage of her heavily fortified positions on the crest and slopes of the *Golan Heights which dominated all of eastern Upper Galilee. Israeli forces thereupon attacked Syrian positions, and after 20 hours of intensive uphill fighting captured the Golan Heights up to and including Quneitra. Now Syria, too, accepted the cease-fire, effective from 10 June.

In less than six days, Israel had routed the armies of three ASt's supported by several other AC's (with token contingents in some cases; Iraq sent 4 brigades, but they played no major role). In addition to the 400-plus aircraft destroyed on the first day, well over 500 tanks were destroyed or captured; A. military equipment lost included c. 70% of the three armies' heavy armament. Egyptian casualties were over 11,000 killed, and 5,600 were taken prisoner; King Hussein claimed that Jordan had lost 6,000 men — though other estimates were considerably lower; and Syria lost nearly 1,000 men. Israel lost over 20 airplanes and over 60 tanks, and her casualties were over 700 killed.

The war left Israel occupying an area over three times her pre-1967 size, with an A. population of nearly one million (in addition to her own 400,000 A. citizens). For the political struggle ensuing — see *Arab-Israel Conflict.

4. THE WAR OF ATTRITION, 1969-70

Border friction resumed soon after the Six Day War and intensified in 1968-69, particularly on the Egyptian front. It was mainly Egyptian artillery shelling, to which Israel reacted by countershelling, after some months also air raids and sometimes commando raids. In 1969-70 these hostilities escalated and came to be called "War of Attrition". In July 1969 Nasser explicitly declared such a war, adding that the "phase of liberation" had begun. In Dec. 1969-Jan. 1970 Israeli air raids developed into strategic bombing in depth, far inside Egypt. The Egyptians installed new Soviet surface-to-air missiles, largely manned by Soviet crews, which managed to down several of the raiding planes; Soviet pilots reinforced the Egyptian air force and began taking part in operative missions. Though Israel had built a network of fortifications, "bunkers" etc., the "Bar-Lev Line" (completed in Feb. 1969), casualties were heavy. On Israel's side more than 1,000 were killed from June-July 1967 to 1970 (more than in the Six Day War), while Egyptian casualties were estimated at over 10,000 — also a figure nearly as high as that of the war.

As the danger of further escalation mounted, including a possible direct involvement of the Soviet Union, fervent efforts were made, particularly by the USA, to obtain a cease-fire (if not a more general settlement). Finally, proposals made by the US Secretary of State (sometimes called *"Rogers Plan Two") in June 1970 were accepted, providing for a cease-fire and a military stand-still zone on both sides of the lines. They went into effect on 7 August, but as Egypt moved missiles forward the same day, breaking the stand-still zone agreement, a new sharp crisis erupted. That violation was never corrected, but finally the cease-fire took hold; the confrontation continued, and occasional incidents occurred, but the "War of Attrition" in its acute phase was over.

5. THE WAR OF OCT. 1973 ("OCTOBER WAR"; "YOM KIPPUR WAR"; "RAMADAN WAR")

Indications, in Sept. 1973, of a major A. build-up on both the Egyptian and Syrian fronts were interpreted in Israel as parts of military exercises (such as were frequently staged, particularly on the Suez Canal front). This assessment conformed to Israeli intelligence estimates that the A. armies were not ready for a major war, that their leadership was not capable of launching one, and that, anyway, an assault across the Suez Canal was not feasible. It also tallied with general conceptions of Israel's leaders who failed to perceive the imperative urgency of the occupation issue for the ASt's, the fact that A., and particularly Egyptian, leaders could not possibly acquiesce in the occupation of important parts of their territories for a long time. The military intelligence assessment was aided by deliberate Egyptian and Syrian deception.

When intelligence confirmed, early on 6 Oct., that war was to break out the same day, only hours were left to complete the mobilization ordered on 5 Oct. (a task made easier by the fact that on that day, Yom Kippur, the Day of Atonement, Israel's entire manpower was available at home or in the synagogue). Thus, when Egyptian and Syrian forces launched an all-out attack, at 14:00, Israel's army was not fully prepared, and the situation was critical.

Syria mounted air attacks and heavy artillery shellings, and moved three divisions with some 1,400 tanks into the Golan, with two more divisions ready to follow. Facing them was an Israeli line of outposts, each with a small force of tanks — a total of, initially, 180 tanks. One of these posts on Mount Hermon was overrun by a helicopter-landed Syrian force and surrendered (later causing a bitter controversy in Israel), and three were evacuated. Syrian forces advanced deep into the Golan, in two main thrusts: one along the main northeast-to-southwest axis of the central Golan leading from Quneitra to the Bridge of Jacob's Daughters; this force reached the Nafakh area, some 10 km from the Bridge. The other advanced along the parallel axis farther south, the road leading from Rafid towards the Lake of Galilee; this force reached the area of El Al and also moved northwest, along the disused Tapline and the road parallel to it, to reinforce the first force in the Nafakh area. However, Israeli counter-attacks, from 8 Oct., leading to bitter fighting and heavy losses on both sides, succeeded in halting the Syrian advance on both axes and pushing the Syrians back. By 9–10 Oct., Syrian forces had retreated to the Khushniyya area, still inside the Golan, and by 10 Oct. they were pushed out of the Golan.

On 11 Oct., Israeli forces continued their counter-attack into Syrian territory, in two thrusts: one, in the north, crossing the lines in the area of Jubata, advanced up to Mazra'at al-Jinn; the other, farther south, in the central sector, advanced along the main Quneitra-Damascus road beyond Khan al-Arnaba and turned southeast, reaching al-Kanaker and Kafr Shams. In that area they were attacked by two Iraqi armored divisions which had reached the battle area. Despite heavy fighting in which the Iraqis lost some 80 tanks, they were unable to dislodge the Israeli forces; nor could a Jordanian armored brigade that joined the Iraqis on their left flank on 12 Oct. Israeli forces consolidated their positions when paratroopers captured the dominating hill of Tell Shams on 13 Oct. The position lost on Mount Hermon was recaptured on 21–22 Oct., and Israeli forces advanced, taking several Syrian outposts on the Mount. In naval operations the Israelis destroyed much of the Syrian navy and gained control.

When a cease-fire was accepted on 22 Oct., Israeli forces occupied some 600 sq.km. of Syrian territory beyond the Golan and had the entire area between the battlefield and Damascus within the range of their guns. Losses had been very heavy, on both sides. Syria had lost over 3,000 dead (with some estimates much higher), 600–800 tanks (some estimates: more than 1,000; President Asad himself mentioned 1,200 tanks lost), much of her artillery, c. 160 planes, and her elaborate missile system was largely destroyed; about 370 Syrian soldiers were taken prisoner. Israel had lost over 770 dead and some 250 tanks (of which some 150 could later be repaired); more than 2,400 soldiers were wounded; 65 were taken prisoner. For the military-political aftermath of the war — Syria's refusal to attend the Geneva "Peace Conference" of Dec. 1973, the negotiations on "Disengagement", US Secretary of State Kissinger's "shuttle" mediation, and the Disengagement Agreement reached on 30 May 1974 and implemented in June (including withdrawal of Israeli forces from Syrian teritory occupied beyond the Golan) — see *Arab-Israel Conflict.

Egypt's attack was precisely simultaneous with Syria's: at 14:00 on 6 Oct., five Egyptian divisions began crossing the Suez Canal, about 70,000 troops against less than 500 Israeli troops holding the Bar-Lev Line in widely dispersed outposts. When Israeli armored forces, hastily mobilized, rushed to counter-attack, they found the Egyptians established on the eastern side of the Canal and came under heavy attack, particularly by anti-tank missiles that caused heavy casualties. Egypt's dense anti-aircraft missile system frustrated operations by the Israeli air force and caused it heavy casualties. Efforts to relieve small units besieged in isolated outposts of the Bar-Lev Line also led to heavy casualties. By the third day most of the Bar-Lev Line had been captured or abandoned (the most northerly positions, in the area of Baluza, held out throughout the war; the most southerly one, at Port Tawfiq, held out for most of the week but surrendered after running out of ammunition and supplies). The Egyptians set up three major bridgeheads across the Canal: one in the north, based in Qantara (the Second Army), one in the center, based in Isma'iliyya (Second Army), and one in the south, in the area of the Great Bitter Lake and opposite the town of Suez (Third Army). While these forces continued consolidating their positions and pressing farther east, and while Israeli forces were still in disarray, no major offensive was mounted to capture the strategic points dominating the area: the Mitla Pass and the Gidi Pass (an omission that caused much controversy within the Egyptian military leadership: some top generals had strongly advocated such an operation, as had Syria). A tank offensive on 14 Oct. that might have led in that direction was halted by the Israelis with heavy losses among the attacking tanks. Egyptian efforts to advance southeastwards along the Gulf of Suez towards the Abu Rudeis oil fields were also foiled. Egypt was reported to have lost over 300 tanks in these two offensives.

Israeli counter-attacks, from 8 Oct., attempted to regain the eastern bank of the Suez Canal, but were held by the Egyptians in pitched battles with heavy losses. On the night of 15–16 Oct., however, Israeli paratroopers crossed the Canal north of the Bitter Lake and established a bridgehead on its western, Egyptian, side. On the morrow they were joined by elements of an armored brigade which began to widen the perimeter. Attempts to secure and widen a corridor on the eastern bank so that larger forces, including those moving down from the northern sector, could cross the Canal, met determined Egyptian resistance. But the routes to the bridging area, and a corridor leading to them, were cleared by the northern division on 16–17 Oct., bridges were built, and on 17–18 Oct. the northern force crossed the Canal. On 19 Oct. a division from the southern sector also crossed, bringing Israeli forces on the west bank to three divisions. (The operations leading to the crossing, and the decision-making and command process involved, led to bitter controversy in army command circles and public opinion.) Egyptian counter-attacks on the west bank, from Isma'iliyya southwards, on 17–18 Oct., failed. During those days the Israeli air force also regained, in large-scale air battles, the upper hand.

While Israeli forces on the East bank continued their efforts to clear widening areas of Egyptian troops and strongholds, with no more than partial success in the center and north, but surrounding and cutting off the Egyptian Third Army in the south, those on the western bank advanced, in heavy fighting, in three prongs: northwards from the bridgehead, reaching the outskirts of Isma'iliyya; southwards towards the Genifa Hills and Suez town; and southwards behind the Genifa Hills towards al-Adabiyya on the Gulf of Suez. The southern forces reached, and cut, the Suez-Cairo road on 22 Oct., and the same day closed the ring by taking Adabiyya. They also entered Suez town, believing that firing had ceased there, but came up against Egyptian strongpoints and suffered heavy casualties. Except for Suez town, Israeli forces now held a continuous area of some 1,600 sq.km. inside Egypt, from the outskirts of Isma'iliyya to Adabiyya on the Gulf of Suez. The Israel navy also had, in several encounters, gained the upper hand and controlled both the coastal waters of the Mediterranean and the Gulf of Suez.

The super-powers had supported their clients with urgent and massive military supplies: the Russians, who had resumed large-scale military aid to Egypt, after much controversy, in Feb. Mar. 1973, greatly stepped up their supplies in Oct., by sea and in a massive airlift (reportedly

15,000 ton by air, in over 900 flights, and 63,000 ton by sea); and the USA began rushing supplies to Israel — after some controversy as to the timing and extent — in an airlift, from 14 Oct. (a reported 22,000 ton). Both super-powers, and the other powers, were working in the UN Security Council for a cease-fire, with the USSR pressing for speedy decisions — reportedly in response to a Syrian request (but there was confusion on that point, as Egypt objected to a cease-fire in the early stages of the war, when matters seemed to go well, and Syria thereupon denied having requested one). After much wrangling, the Security Council decided on a cease-fire on 21 Oct. When the fighting did not stop, it reiterated its urgent call on 22 Oct., coupling it with another general-political resolution on peace in the Middle East — Resolution 338, which reconfirmed Resolution 242 of Nov. 1967, adding a call for immediate "negotiations between the parties concerned under appropriate auspices". Fighting still continued, with the Egyptian Third Army trying to break out of the Israeli ring and Israel consolidating her forces' positions around Suez-Adabiyya. On 24 Oct. the Soviet Union, angry with the delay, reportedly threatened massive intervention and US forces were put on world-wide alert against that threat. But on 24 Oct. the fighting ceased.

The cease-fire left Egypt in possession of two major bridgeheads on the east bank of the Suez Canal, to a depth of some 10 km, an area of more than 1,000 sq.km. — but her Third Army, in the southern sector, 20,000 troops with some 300 tanks, was surrounded and cut off, saved from complete defeat and surrender by the cease-fire. Israel was left in possession of the 1,600-km.-area on the east bank described above. Losses had been heavy. Egyptian casualties were thousands killed — according to some estimates up to 15,000 — and 8,000 taken prisoner; Egypt had lost more than 650 tanks, according to some: 1,000, more than 180 planes, 6 missile speedboats, much heavy artillery. Israel had lost, on the Egyptian front, nearly 2,000 killed and 5,000 wounded, some 700 tanks, and much artillery; some 240 Israeli soldiers were taken prisoner. On both the Egyptian and Syrian fronts Israel had lost 2,700 killed, and 305 taken prisoner, more than 800 tanks, some 120 aircraft, and much heavy artillery.

For the military-political aftermath of the war — the Six-Point Agreement of 11 Nov. at "Kilometer 101"; the Geneva "Peace Conference" of 21 Dec. 1973; the Disengagement (or Separation of Forces) Agreement of 18 Jan. 1974 and its implementation by 5 Mar. — see *Arab-Israel Conflict.

In purely military terms, the October War, that began with heavy, even critical setbacks for Israel (which led to soul-searching investigations, bitter controversy and political crises), ended with a clear Israeli victory — though Israel was denied its final fruits (the elimination of the Egyptian Third Army, the capture of Suez town) by the cease-fire imposed by the great powers and the Security Council. Yet, politically and in terms of morale, the war was perceived by the Arabs, and particularly by Egypt, as a major victory: its initial operations, and first and foremost the crossing of the Suez Canal, were seen as brilliant feats of military valor; they had proved the Arabs' ability to plan and execute complex military operations; they had done away with the legend of the invincibility of the Israeli armed forces; they had cleansed the Arabs' shield of honor of the stain of previous defeats and restored a sense of Arab self-confidence. The war also broke the deadlock of Israel's unmovable occupation of the territories captured in 1967 and established a significant Egyptian presence at least in part of these territories. It thus, politically and morally, broke through a psychological barrier — and enabled Sadat to envisage steps towards a peaceful settlement (to begin with a settlement of Egypt's own Sinai problem even before a comprehensive solution of all A.-Israel issues was attained).

6. THE LEBANON ("PEACE FOR GALILEE") WAR, 1982

For the events that led to Israel's invasion of Lebanon (— see *Arab-Israel Conflict, *Lebanon). The invasion began on 6 June, with Israeli forces advancing northward on three axes: one along the Mediterranean coast, one in the central mountain region, and one in the eastern sector, near the Lebanese-Syrian border. A fourth important axis would later develop in the Biqā' valley. The operational instructions to the forces were to destroy PLO assets while avoiding a confrontation with Syrian forces in the Biqā'.

At the end of the first day, Israeli tanks and mechanized forces reached the Qusseima bridge on the Litani River, some 17 mi. north of the border, while some infantry units advanced further north towards Sidon. On the central axis Israeli forces conducted a flanking movement towards the PLO-held town of Nabatiyya, some 6 mi. north of the border, and by nighttime an IDF infantry unit had taken the Beaufort Castle, a PLO artillery stronghold on a hill-top. On the eastern axis, the IDF moved towards Hasbayya, a town 7 mi. north of Metulla, Israel's northernmost town.

On 7 June, the IDF continued its advance along the coastal axis, reaching the outskirts of Damour, some 14 mi. south of Beirut. The Israeli navy meanwhile conducted a vertical flanking operation, landing tank and infantry forces at the mouth of the Awali River. On the central axis, Israel's forces took Nabatiyya and continued their advance to areas east of Lake Qar'un. In the eastern sector, IDF forces positioned themselves on the Hasbayya-Kaukaba line, 7 mi. northeast of Metulla. The Syrians moved their First Armored Division into the Biqā', to an area north of Hasbayya and southeast of Lake Qar'un. A number of limited encounters with Syrian forces had already taken place on the second day of the war, including some artillery exchanges in the eastern and central sectors, a short air battle over Beirut, and an exchange of tank fire west of Jezzin.

After two days of advance, the IDF was halted on 8 June, along the coast, at the outskirts of Damour. South of that area, other units fought a difficult battle with PLO guerrillas entrenched in Tyre, Sidon and a number of refugee camps. The IDF's advance was also slow in the eastern sector, from Hasbayya to 'Ein 'Eita. The IDF continued its advance in the central sector, moving north of Jezzin and west of Lake Qar'un, reaching Ramlaya and 'Ein Zahalta, 4 mi. south of the Beirut-Damascus highway.

On 9 June, the invasion of Lebanon turned into a full-scale confrontation with Syria, particularly in the air and in the suppression of air-defense. In a preemptive strike, the Israeli Air Force destroyed 17 of the 19 SAM batteries which Syria had installed in the Biqā'. An unprecedented air battle also took place, with the participation of 150 fighter aircraft; 29 Syrian MiG-21s and MiG-23s were shot down. Armored warfare took place in the Qar'un Lake area, both south of Jezzin and in areas southeast of Qar'un, and heavy fighting in the vicinity of 'Ein Zahalta, south of the Beirut-Damascus highway, with very slow Israeli progress. On the coastal axis, the IDF conquered Damour and reached Khalde, south of Beirut airport. The Syrians meanwhile moved some forces out of Beirut, to strengthen their defences along the highway.

On the following day, a full scale confrontation with Syria developed on the ground as well. In the early morning, the largest tank battle of the war began north and northeast of Lake Qar'un, between an Israeli armored corps and the Syrian First Armored Division. The IDF prevailed, its forces moving north towards Jubb Jenin. In another large-scale air-battle some 25 Syrian MiGs were shot down. The IDF continued its slow advance along the coastal axis, meeting Syrian and PLO resistance north of Khalde, 2 mi. south of Beirut airport. On the central front, Israel's tank forces were halted by heavy Syrian resistance in the mountain passes of the 'Ein Zahalta region.

Thus, when a cease-fire came into effect at noon on 11 June, Israeli forces were positioned about 2 mi. south of Beirut airport on the coastal front; a few miles south of the Beirut-Damascus highway in the 'Ein Zahalta area; in the vicinity of Jubb Jenin — well below the highway — in the Biqā', and in Kafr Ququ on the eastern axis near the Lebanese-Syrian border.

The "Crawling" Stage The cease-fire declared by Israel and Syria on 11 June did not bring a halt to Israel's operations against the PLO. There was now a "crawling" stage, initially meaning Israeli movement to cut off the PLO in West Beirut from its Syrian suppliers. At first, this involved artillery exchanges between the IDF and PLO forces south of Beirut. On 13 and 14 June Israeli tank and paratroop units completed the encirclement of Beirut by linking up with the Christian Phalangist forces in East Beirut. They also won control of Beirut's exit to the Beirut-Damascus highway and reached the proximity of the presidential palace at Ba'abda and the outskirts of Beirut airport. This was achieved in heavy battle, involving Syrian tank and anti-tank commando forces. On 15 June IDF forces began to "crawl" five miles east of Beirut, to the Jamhour region, in an effort to extend eastward their control over the Beirut-Damascus highway. Syria had meanwhile reinforced her positions along and south of the highway, especially in the 'Aley-Bahamdun-Shtaura region. On 17 June Israeli forces continued their movement east and southeast towards 'Aley, and on 19 June artillery duels took place between IDF and PLO forces in Beirut, while IDF and Syrian artillery exchanged fire in Kafr Quq, near the Lebanese-Syrian border. On 20 June the PLO and Syria withdrew their forces from Beirut airport, and Israeli forces gained control of the airport without a battle.

The second part of the "crawling" stage began on 21 June with a major battle initiated by the IDF against Syria's reinforced tank and commando units in an effort to gain control of the Beirut-Damascus highway in the 'Aley-Bahamdun area. Israel's advance was slowly gaining momentum; the battle raged for almost a week. When it ended, Israel had gained control of the highway to a point just east of Bahamdun.

The Siege of Beirut The siege of Beirut, aimed at forcing the PLO and the Syrian forces to evacuate the city, took place throughout July and most of August. This included artillery, naval and air bombardment of PLO positions in Beirut, as well as incremental advances into the western parts of the city. On 23 July Israeli forces intensified their air and naval bombardment. On 3 August, IDF infantry entered the Hayy al-Salum neighborhood in southwest Beirut, the following day it encircled Burj al-Barajina; after a 20-hour battle, Israeli forces, advancing a little more than a mile, gained control of the al-'Uzai quarter and the museum area. On 11 and 12 August, the Air Force conducted a massive bombardment of Beirut. The following day, the PLO agreed to withdraw under the protection of a multi-national force. This withdrawal commenced on 25 August. PLO chairman Yasser *'Arafat left Beirut on 30 August, as did the Syrian brigade positioned in the city. By 4 September the evacuation of all PLO and Syrian forces from Beirut was completed and the multi-national force was withdrawn.

The "Holding" Stage The expulsion of the PLO and the Syrians from Beirut was followed by a "holding" stage. On 14 September, Israel's ally, President-elect Bashir *Jumayyil, was assassinated. Israel's reaction was to order the IDF into West Beirut, officially: to keep order. On 17 September, Phalange forces entered the Sabra and Shatila refugee camps and massacred several hundred Palestinians. Under heavy US pressure, Israel began to withdraw her forces from Beirut on 19 September, and the multi-national force — including some 1,800 US Marines — returned to take their place.

For about a year after September 1982, the IDF's main task was to hold on to its positions pending the outcome of the negotiations. Militarily and politically it still had to cope with three types of threats — first, Syria's entrenched military forces in Lebanon, which now included some three divisions (two armored, one mechanized), and a number of independent brigades and commando units, totalling the equivalent of over four divisions. Against some 350 tanks in Lebanon before the war, Syria now had some 1,200 tanks positioned in the Biqā', both north and south of the Beirut-Damascus highway. Although this force still lacked air and air-defense cover, its inferiority in these realms was alleviated to some degree by the introduction of Soviet SA-5 systems into Syria in late 1982. Overall, the Syrians enjoyed an impressive defensive capability against the IDF in the Biqā'.

The second problem the IDF had to face was the intense conflict between the Maronite Christians and the Leftist Druze, led by Walid *Junbalat, in the Shouf mountains. Since the area was under Israeli control from late June 1982 for over a year, the IDF often found itself in cross fire between the warring factions.

Finally, the IDF also had to cope with an escalation of resistance or terrorist activity in Lebanon. Small armed terrorist units remained in Israeli-held territories of Lebanon, while others infiltrated through the areas held by the Syrians, the Christians, and the multi-national force. Moreover the resistance or terrorist squads were increasingly Shi'is. The result was that while the war relieved the towns of northern Israel (at least temporarily) from the danger of terrorist attack, the IDF was under attack by terrorist resistance in Lebanon. One account noted 256 terrorist incidents against the IDF in Lebanon between September 1982 and April 1983. Resistance continued after Israel's unilateral withdrawal to the Awali river in September 1983. On 4 November, a suicide-terrorist operation conducted by Syrian-backed Shi'is destroyed the IDF's headquarters in Sidon, killing 36 Israelis. Terrorist operations intensified as Israel implemented a staged withdrawal from South Lebanon in late 1984 and early 1985. They diminished only after April 1985, when the IDF completed its withdrawal from all of Lebanon except for a narrow security zone north of the Israeli-Lebanese border. The IDF officially withdrew to the international border in early June 1985 — but claimed freedom of patrolling and security operations in that security zone where it also continued to support a local, mostly Christian, "South Lebanese Army" (See *Arab-Israel Conflict, *Lebanon, Saʻd *Haddad).

Arabistan See *Khuzistan.

Arab League The "L. of A. States" (*Jāmiʻat al-Duwal al-ʻArabiyya*) was founded, after a Preparatory Conference at Alexandria (Oct. 1944), in Mar. 1945, in Cairo, by the seven ASt's then independent or on the threshold of independence: Egypt, Iraq, Saʻudi Arabia, Yemen, Transjordan (from 1948: "Jordan"), Syria and Lebanon. The following countries joined subsequently: Libya (1953), Sudan (1956), Tunisia and Morocco (1958), Kuwait (1961), Algeria (1962), South Yemen (1967), Bahrain, Qatar, the Union of Arab Emirates, ʻOman (1971), Mauritania (1973), Somalia (1974), and Djibouti (1977). (The last-named three countries are non-Arab, or at most semi-Arab.) The *Palestine A's were represented at the founding conference (by a notable appointed by an all-Arab committee) and enjoyed observer status; after the establishment of the *Palestine Liberation Organization (PLO), 1964, it assumed that status of a permanent observer, and since 1976 it enjoys full membership. Thus the A.L. has, since 1977, 22 members: 21 states (*all* the independent A. states, and three non-A. or semi-A. states), and the PLO.

The foundation of the A.L. was inspired by age-old visions of Arab Unity (see *Pan-Arabism, *Arab Federation). It is, however, not a federal body and has no power over its member-states. All federal or unionist ideas were rejected, even during the preparatory talks, 1942–44, by most of the seven founding states, particularly by Egypt, Saʻudi Arabia, Syria and Lebanon, who believed that the only feasible association was one of sovereign countries retaining their full sovereignty (the British, who had encouraged these talks, were not basically adverse to federal schemes, but went along with the majority). The L. has, therefore, no binding power over its members. According to its Charter, decisions of its Council are binding only on those member-states voting for them. Before agreeing to join the L., Lebanon requested, and obtained, a specific recognition of her independence and territorial integrity — against potential Syrian plans (suspected, but not spelled out) to annex her or her Muslim-majority North, South and East; this recognition formed an annex to the *Alexandria Protocol which prepared the L. Charter. Another annex pledged A.L. support for the Palestine A.'s in their struggle.

Egypt was — until 1979, when her membership was suspended because of her peace agreement with Israel — the most influential, the dominant power in the A.L. The L. headquarters were in Cairo — until 1979, when they were transferred to Tunis. The Secretary-General was always Egyptian: ʻAbd-ul-Rahman *ʻAzzam 1945–52, ʻAbd-ul-Khaleq Hassuna 1952–72, Mahmud *Riad 1972–79; in 1979 a Tunisian, Chedly Klibi (al-Shadhili al-Quleibi), was appointed. Deputy Secretaries-General and Secretariat staff are recruited from all member-states. The budget is raised by the member-states according to a percentage-scale that is adjusted from time to time.

The A.L. has drafted and initiated many projects for all-Arab co-operation and co-ordination in the economic, cultural, social, technical, military and political fields. While many of these schemes have not — or not fully — materialized, a limited degree of co-ordination in various spheres has been achieved. Thus, all-Arab projects have been planned — and implemented in varying degrees — for a Development Bank (from 1959), a Development Fund (1972–73), a mining company (1975), a Monetary Fund (1977), a joint shipping company and a maritime transport corporation (oil tankers, 1972–73), communications' satellites. An Organization of Arab Oil-exporting Countries (*OAPEC) was set up in 1967–68. An Economic Union was planned from 1964–65, designed gradually to develop, within 10 years, into a Common Market. Most of these projects wre not directly under the auspices of the A.L., but were arranged by some of its members in various combinations; the L., however, was instrumental and a clearing ground for many of them. The L. also arranged for aid to be given, in very large amounts, by the rich AC's (mainly Sa'udia and the oil principalities of the Persian Gulf) to the "confrontation countries", i.e. those bordering on Israel (Egypt, Jordan, Syria, Lebanon), and the PLO — after the wars of 1967 and 1973, and again in 1978–79 (this time excluding Egypt).

In military matters — mainly the armed struggle with Israel — the AC's involved mostly preferred to follow their own policies and conclude bilateral or multilateral pacts with other AC's rather than operate through the L. A "Collective Security Pact" was signed in 1950 — intended mainly to give more binding power to L. decisions — but it played no major role.

The L.'s main function has always been to present a common political front towards the outside world and to conduct information and propaganda work. It enjoys, since 1950, observer status at the UN and maintains information offices in several capitals. Its propaganda centered mainly on issues and areas where A. demands had not been fully satisfied — Syria and Lebanon in the 1940s; Morocco, Tunisia and Algeria in the 1950s; 'Aden and the Persian Gulf in the 1960s; and the Palestine problem and the A.-Israel dispute permanently. The A.L. directs and supervises the economic boycott of Israel and those trading with her (see *Arab Boycott) and finances Palestinian-A. organizations (though that function has passed mainly to the individual AC's). It initiated and directed the establishment of the Palestine Liberation Organization (PLO), in 1964. It also decided to set up a Joint Military Command of the forces pitted against Israel, from 1964; but the Command did not in fact direct joint operations.

Within the A.L. divergent or conflicting trends have always formed rival blocs. In the 1940s and 1950s, an Egyptian-Syrian-Sa'udi bloc was guarding the inter-A. *status quo* against a *Hashemite Iraqi-Jordanian bloc with federalist-revisionist plans. In 1956–57 Jordan was compelled — by Egyptian, and by internal-leftist, pressure — to join the Syro-Egyptian alliance; but in 1957 King *Hussein halted that trend. At the same time, sharp differences with Nasserist Egypt induced Sa'udia to move out of the Egyptian camp. As Hashemite federal schemes became obsolete after 1958, there was a Sa'udi-Jordanian rapprochement. A new, different confrontation shaped rivalries throughout the 1960s: an Egypt-led "progressive", socialist and neutralist bloc (Egypt, Syria, Iraq, Algeria, South Yemen) versus a conservative, "reactionary" group (Sa'udia, Jordan, Morocco) — and now it was Egypt and her allies that were revisionist, fostered unionist schemes and revolutionary changes in the countries of the rival bloc.

The late 1950s and early 1960s were years of crisis for the A.L. Egypt's *Nasser repeatedly asserted that there could be no true cooperation with the reactionary régimes and that A. unity could be created only after "progressive" forces had taken over all A. countries; there were incessant complaints of Egyptian subversion, plots, attempts at political assassination (including that of Heads of State — e.g. Sa'udia, Tunisia, Jordan); in 1962 an Egyptian expeditionary force intervened in a civil war that had erupted in Yemen, and soon it clashed with Sa'udia, up to nearly open warfare between the two countries. A degree of inter-A. reconciliation was achieved in the mid-1960s (with newly instituted "summit" meetings added to the L. Council as the main inter-A. forum, beginning with the First Summit, 1964), when the failure of Egypt's operations in Yemen and of her subversive scheme elsewhere had sobered Nasser's interventionist zeal, while the mounting A.-Israel crisis caused all A. countries to rally around Egypt. Egypt's gradual return to more conservative, mainline inter-A. policies, begun in Nasser's last years, fully unfolded, after Nasser's death (1970), under his successors. (For the abortive Egypt-Libya-Syria Federation of 1971 and the deterioration of Egypt-Libya relations, see *Federation of Arab Republics.)

After 1973 inter-A. differences centered mainly around the Palestine problem and the ways to settle it; the rift between conservatives, now including Egypt, and revolutionary Leftist régimes did not disappear — and largely corresponded to that on the Palestine issue. Against the mainstream, led by Egypt and Sa'udia, and the moderates (Jordan, Morocco) stood a bloc of extremist countries that saw no need for any negotiated settlement and envisaged a solution only through a total defeat of Israel. That group — Libya, Syria, Iraq, Algeria, South Yemen, parts of the PLO — called by its adversaries "Rejection Front" and by its adherents "Steadfastness and

Confrontation Front" — formally constituted itself when it held in 1977 and 1978 three separate summit meetings (but Iraq walked out of the first and took no further part). That was after Egypt's President *Sadat had stunned the A. states (and the world) by visiting Israel, Nov. 1977, and embarking on direct negotiations for peace with Israel — regarded by most A. countries as a separate peace and a betrayal of A. unity. While some A. countries were reluctant to break with Egypt and counseled moderation (thus, reportedly, Jordan and Sa'udia), they went along, eventually, with extreme decisions: as Egypt refused to heed strong warnings unanimously issued in 1978, went ahead and signed a peace treaty with Israel (Mar. 1979), the A.L. unanimously suspended her membership, transferred the L. headquarters to Tunis, and decided to sever all official relations and boycott Egypt; only three A.L. countries — Sudan, 'Oman and Somalia — maintained diplomatic relations with Egypt (but even they dared not vote, formally, against the decisions taken). The boycott was never fully implemented (see *Egypt), and even political relations were maintained, at least with some A. countries, by semi-official representatives or "interest sections" in foreign embassies (some of them headed by diplomats of Ambassadorial rank); and gradually, some of these relationships grew close, even intimate — thus with Jordan and Iraq (whom Egypt aided in her war with Iran). While official diplomatic relations had not yet been resumed, by 1986, with Iraq, Sa'udia or Morocco, as some had expected, Jordan resumed official relations in Sept. 1984, and so did Djibouti in 1986.

Yet, Egypt was isolated, excluded from the A. family of nations — and the A.L. was but a rump, without its strongest, leading member (who remained, even outside the L., the center of the A. world) and with its efficacy and prestige greatly reduced. Within the L., the old division continued: a mainstream, led by Sa'udia, a moderate wing — Jordan, Morocco, the three who had maintained relations with Egypt — and the "Rejectionist" camp. The latter was now perceptibly weaker: Iraq had dropped out (mainly under the pressure of her war with Iran, since 1980 — in which Syria and Libya supported Iran, while Iraq was badly in need of all-A. support and aid); Algeria was also drifting away; and the PLO was split, with its extremist factions remaining allied with the Rejectionists, while the 'Arafat faction was close to the Moderates and Egypt; only Syria, Libya and South Yemen remained — and they were isolated.

While the A.L. had to accomodate, throughout the years, such differences, such rival blocs, among its members, acute disputes sometimes impeded its coherence. Thus the L. sessions themselves were boycotted by Tunisia 1958–61, Iraq 1961–63, Egypt 1962–63, Libya several times; even summit meetings were sometimes boycotted — thus the 6th, Nov. 1973, by Libya and Iraq; the 11th, Nov. 1980, by all Rejectionist countries and Lebanon; the 12th, in its first session, Nov. 1981, by the Rejectionists and several others, and in its second session, Sept. 1982, by Libya; the Rejectionists also boycotted an "Extraordinary" Summit in Aug. 1985; Egypt was absent from the 9th summit, Nov. 1978, even before the suspension of her membership. The fact that diplomatic relations were frequently severed between various AC's also impeded their cooperation in the framework of the A.L. As to the various inter-A. disputes themselves, the L. was usually unable to prevent, arbitrate or even mitigate them, and its Charter's provisions for arbitration have hardly been used. Thus the L. had little say in the Yemen War (1962–67); it did not mediate when Algerian and Moroccan troops fought each other (1963) or in the dispute over Western *Sahara; all-Arab attempts to settle the clashes between the Palestinian guerrillas and Jordan and Lebanon (1968–71) were not conducted by the L. or within its framework. Complaints by A. states against Egyptian or UAR subversion or aggression (Sudan 1958; Tunisia 1958 and onwards; Lebanon 1958; Jordan 1958 and onwards; Iraq 1959; Syria 1962; Sa'udia 1963; Morocco 1963) were useless — and the complainants frequently chose to turn to other bodies, such as the UN Security Council. The only inter-A. clash in which the L. directly mediated or assisted the wronged party was the defense of Kuwait against Iraqi threats (1961).

Thus, the efficacy and the success of the A.L. have been limited both in inter-A. political and military co-ordination and in the sphere of cooperation projects. Various measures have been proposed from time to time to amend its constitution so as to make it more effective — e.g. to substitute majority decisions for the rule of unanimity and to make its decisions more binding; but so far nothing has come of such proposals. Suggestions have been made, from time to time, to supplement — or even to replace — the L. of A. *States* by a L. of A. *Peoples*; in the early 1960s Egypt began to institutionalize such a body — but she did not persist and allowed the new organization to fade away; after the suspension of Egypt's membership, Sadat also proclaimed, in 1980, the foundation of a "L. of A. and Islamic Peoples" — but his successor dropped the plan and dissolved that body in 1983. Anyway, the A.L. has been a useful instrument of A. policies, and even its detractors have not seriously proposed its abolition.

Arab Legion (*al-Jaish al-'Arabi*) Military formation established in Transjordan in 1920–21 by British administrators and officers — with a strength of c. 1,000 men. Commanded by Lt.-Col. F.G. Peake (Pasha) (1886–1970) until 1939, and by Sir John B. *Glubb (Pasha) from 1939 to 1956, the A.L. was enlarged from 1940 to c. 8,000 men. It was considered to be the most effective A. military force. In 1941, A.L. units assisted the British re-occupation of rebellious Iraq. When Transjordan became independent, in 1946, the A.L. became her regular army. But as British subsidies continued financing it and British officers retained its top command posts, many A.'s (and others) continued regarding the A.L. as an instrument of British imperial interests. Glubb's dismissal, in 1956, and the handing-over of the top command to Jordanian-A. officers was seen as the completion of Jordan's independence and the end to special British privileges. In 1969 the A.L. was renamed the "Jordanian Armed Forces".

Arab Nationalist Movement (*Harakat al-Qawmiyyin al- 'Arab*) See *Arab Nationalism.

Arab national movement, nationalism Feelings of national pride, endeavors to cultivate the nation's heritage and traditions, resistance to foreign rule, have been prevalent among A's as among all nations, for a long time. An ANM in the modern sense, however — i.e. a movement based on the conception that "nations", and the A. "nation" among them, were entitled to independence, and that states should be formed on the basis of "nations" (and not, for instance, religion or dynastic allegiance), and organizations with the defined aim of attaining independence and establishing an A. nation-state (or states) — emerged only at the beginning of the 20th century. (It had been preceded by Egyptian N., and by stirrings of an Algerian NM against French rule — but these were principally Muslim, and Egyptian and Algerian rather than A., in their conception and aims).

The ANM was rooted in, and preceded by, a movement of cultural and literary renaissance in the 19th century mainly centered in the Levant (and to some degree in Egypt), strongly influenced by the penetration of Western civilization and inspired by European romantic nationalism and national liberation movements. Among the leaders of that renaissance were Christian-Arab literati and educationalists, such as the Lebanese Butros Bustani (1818–1883) and Nassif Yāzeji (1800–1871). European and American Christian missionaries also significantly contributed to that renaissance, particularly by the development of educational institutions and technical instruments (printing presses, textbooks). The national renaissance was later strongly influenced by the modernist Islamic revival movement (Jamal-ul-Din al-Afghani, 1839(?)–1897; Muhammad *'Abduh, Rashid *Rida, 'Abd-ul-Rahman al-Kawākibi, 1849–1903) — perhaps without fully realizing the inherent conflict between supranational *Pan-Islamism and extra-religious AN, two conceptions that run parallel or overlap in some areas.

A politically motivated ANM began organizing in the first decade of the 20th century — in the Arabic-speaking parts of the Ottoman Empire, i.e. mainly in the *"Fertile Crescent" (the Levant and Iraq) and among students and young officers and officials from that area and the Arabian peninsula in the capital Istanbul (Egypt and Arabic-speaking North Africa were, at that time, outside the scope and target-area of incipient AN). The organizers were influenced by the revolt of the Young Turks (1908), which, at first, seemed to open the way to a liberalized, de-centralized régime.

When the new rulers imposed a centralist and Turkish-nationalist régime, some of the new A. societies grew increasingly antagonistic and began envisaging full A. independence and the dissolution of the Ottoman Empire; others strove for Arab autonomy within a decentralized

Empire. This difference coincided with the divergence described between Islamic influences and A. nationalist motivations; for radical AN necessarily demanded a struggle for full independence and the abolition of Turkish rule, while Islamists were bound to be loyal to the Muslim empire, to the Ottoman Sultan in his capacity as Khalifa (Caliph), the head of the whole Islamic community. This ideological dichotomy was never fully resolved, though in fact the loyalists seemed to have the upper hand in the A. parts of the Empire. Nor did the A. societies in these initial stages work out a clear definition of their aims: did they aspire to one national state for all the AC's? to several separate states? to a Federation of several ASt's? and what precisely was the area covered by their AN, what was the extent of their future independent state or states?

The ANM at its initial stage consisted of various clubs or societies — such as the "Ligue de la Patrie Arabe" (Paris 1904), headed by Najib 'Azuri; the "Literary Club" (al-Muntada al- Adabi) (Istanbul 1909); the "Decentralization Party" (Cairo 1912); the "Reform Committee" (Beirut 1912); al-Qahtaniyya (1909, founded by 'Aziz 'Ali al-*Masri); the "Arab Pact" (al-'Ahd, founded 1914 by the same, with its members mainly young army officers); the "Young Arab Society" (al-Fatāt, Paris 1911 — among its founders the Syrian Jamil *Mardam and the Palestinian 'Awni *'Abd-ul-Hadi); the last three were clandestine. Al-Fatāt, which called for full Arab independence, was perhaps the most important among these groups. In 1913 it organized an A. nationalist conference in Paris which is regarded as an important landmark. Members of these organizations later became prominent in the leadership of the ASt's. At the time, they were a small group, with an active membership hardly exceeding 100, a few hundred supporters, and little influence. They did not arouse any popular movement for A. independence, let alone an insurrection against the Ottoman rulers — even during World War I, when the international and military situation presented an opportunity. Arrests and trials of their members and other A. notables conducted by the Turkish authorities in 1916–17 and resulting in a number of death sentences and executions were preventive rather than punitive.

An A. insurrection arose, during World War I, from a different source: *Hussein bin 'Ali, the Sharif of Mecca, of the *Hashemi clan, rebelled in 1916, after preliminary contacts with the British and with their support (see *Arab Revolt). The Sharif, and particularly his sons *Feisal and *'Abdullah, had had contacts with the A. nationalist societies. In his exchange of letters with the British he stipulated the establishment of an independent A. state, or A. states, in the Arabian peninsula and the Fertile Crescent, after the dissolution of the Ottoman Empire. He obtained British support, though that support remained rather vague, envisaged a measure of British (and French) tutelage for the future A. state(s), and was not finalized in a hard and fast agreement. The A. nationalists in the Fertile Crescent probably sympathized with the Sharif's revolt, but did not support it by a simultaneous rebellion in their countries, and only a handful of A. officers in the Ottoman army joined the revolt — deserting, or recruited as prisoners. Among them were 'Aziz 'Ali al-Masri, who became the revolt's chief-of-staff for a short time, the Iraqis Nuri Sa'id who succeeded him, Ja'far al-'Askari, Jamil al-Midfa'i, 'Ali Jawdat al-Ayyubi, the Syrian Nassib al-Bakri. In 1918, Prince Feisal and his troops, advancing into Transjordan and Syria as the right wing of the British and allied forces under General *Allenby, were allowed to enter Damascus and establish their headquarters and an Arab administration there.

Hussein and his sons were regarded by the victorious powers as the legitimate spokesmen of AN. Amir (Prince) Feisal represented them at the Peace Conference, while many of the officers from Iraq and Syria who had joined the revolt — and others who had rallied to them in 1918–19 when they were advancing into Transjordan and Syria — became their advisers and members of the governmental bodies they set up. In 1919 a group of these officers and politicians — most of them members of the al- Fatāt club — created an "Arab Independence Party" (al-Istiqlal). In 1919 and 1920 Syrian-Arab national congresses were organized which supported Feisal's claims and proclaimed him King of Syria (including Lebanon and Palestine), while delegates from Iraq invited his brother 'Abdullah to become King of that country.

The character of AN in the post-World War I period was determined by the settlement imposed by the allied powers. The Hashemite princes' design for one ASt, or a Federation of ASt's in Arabia and the Fertile Crescent under their rule was not implemented. Separate semi-independent states under British and French tutelage were set up instead in Iraq, Syria, Lebanon and Transjordan (with Palestine under a British *Mandate, to become a Jewish National Home, and Hashemi rule in Arabia contested by the rising Sa'udi power). NM's arose in each of the states created in the formerly Turkish area, each struggling for full independence from Britain and France — sympathetic to, and supporting, each other, but separate. For the Palestine A's there was the additional struggle against Zionism and the Jews of Palestine — a struggle also supported by the emerging ASt's and their NM's. NM's and the independence struggle in Egypt and North Africa also gradually became part of, and involved in, that AN. This country-by-country fight for full independence achieved its main goal, in most cases by stages, by the 1940s and 1950s, except for the case of Palestine. By that time all Arab countries were fully independent (in South Arabia and the Persian Gulf the process was achieved in the 1960s and 1970s), and the last vestiges of foreign, imperial privileges, military bases, unequal treaties were eliminated.

The original plans of the ANM for a greater, united all-A. entity (see *Arab Federation, *Pan-Arabism) continued to be fostered by A. political writers and thinkers — such as the Egyptian 'Abdul-Rahman *'Azzam and the Syrians Sati' al-Husri and Constantine (Qusti) Zureiq. In terms of practical politics, they survived mainly in schemes of the Hashemite rulers of Iraq and Jordan for a Fertile Crescent Federation or a *"Greater Syria". In the 1920s, a "Syria-Palestine" Representation in Europe also spoke for pan-Arab nationalism; it was vaguely linked to these Hashemite plans but had little political effect and gradually faded out. These Hashemite schemes were revived in the 1940s, but they found little support in the "target" countries of Syria, Lebanon and the Palestine A.'s. British backing, always suspected by the French and many Arabs, was at best partial and half-hearted, and the Hashemite plans never got off the ground. They were, anyway, adamantly opposed by most AC's, and particularly by Egypt, Syria and Sa'udia. When, in 1945, the *Arab League was founded, it was based on close cooperation between independent AC's and the rejection of all "revisionist", federal schemes. Pan-AN in its Hashemite version lost its relevance with the assassination of Kings *'Abdullah (1951) and *Feisal II (1958) and the elimination of Hashemite rule in Iraq (1958).

From the 1950s, pan-AN appeared in new, invigorated, radical versions — postulating an all-AN (*Qawmiyya*) that transcends the patriotism of specific AC's (*Wataniyya*). The shock of the A. defeat in Palestine, 1948, was a main catalyst in that re-emergence of all-AN. The new trends were Leftist, Socialist in inclination, partly inspired by "New Left", Maoist-Castroist thought. One of them was the "Movement of Arab Nationalists" (*Harakat al-Qawmiyyin al-'Arab*), clandestinely organized from c. 1949–50, at first mainly among students, e.g. at the American University of Beirut; among its underground and never clearly identified leaders was the Palestinian George *Habash. The *Qawmiyyin*, gradually moving farther left, aimed at the elimination of the conservative Arab régimes and the creation of revolutionary Arab unity; they advocated violence and terrorism against foreign interests, Israel, Arab conservatives and dissenters. They were closely linked to Palestinian-A. guerrilla groups, with Habash's *"Popular Front for the Liberation of Palestine" (PFLP) as their sister-organization, and had some influence on the radical nationalists of South Yemen, the ruling NLF. Factional splits among the Qawmiyyin were frequent, and while their underground cells may still be active, little has been heard of them since the 1970s.

Another trend of pan-A. Leftist-revolutionary N., with a rather more elaborate ideology published in detail, was the "Arab Renaissance" (*al-*Ba'th*) group. This faction regarded the existing ASt's as temporary entities only, bound to be merged into a united all-A. state — by revolutionary violence or subversion if need be. The Ba'th group, at its inception mainly students and young intellectuals, cultivated ties to younger officers, particularly in the Syrian and Iraqi armies. It was these clandestine officers' cells that transformed the little club of intellectuals into a politically significant faction and enabled it first to push Syria into union with Egypt (1958), then to assist in

Syria's secession from that union (1961), and finally to seize power, through military *coups*, in Syria (1963) and Iraq (1963 and, after losing power later the same year, again in 1968). It maintains branches outside Syria and Iraq, too, but except for Lebanon, these are illegal underground cells. For further developments concerning the *Ba'th*, its rule and its splits — see *Ba'th. Since the 1960s the *Ba'th*, enmeshed in the power politics of the two countries it rules, has contributed very little to the development of all-AN, its original *raison d'être*.

Pan-A. revolutionary N. in the 1950s and 1960s found its strongest expression in Egyptian *Nasserism and in the teachings of Libya's *Qadhdhafi. The Egyptian officers' régime, in power since the *coup* of 1952, was at first moderate and restrained in its foreign policies. In the 1950s, under the leadership of Gamal *'Abd-ul-Nasser, it turned increasingly activist in inter-Arab affairs, attempting to impose on the other ASt's a régime in its image — "Arab Socialism", populist-totalitarian single-party state socialism, leftist-neutralist in international affairs. The ideology of "Arab Socialism" — called "Nasserism" by others, not by its own leaders — developed pragmatically, growing out of Egyptian political needs, and was never laid down as a formal, complete doctrine; and though Nasser and his aides encouraged "Nasserist" factions in other Arab countries, no all-Arab Nasserist party was ever created, and rival Nasserist factions often fought each other. Even in Egypt the régime was based on the state bureaucracy rather than on the single party (which never got off the ground). Nasserism had some affinities with *Ba'thism*, and the Syrian A. Socialists pressed for union with Egypt, achieved in 1958, in the hope that a joint doctrine could be worked out and that the pragmatic Nasserists would accept *Ba'thist* ideological guidance. But after the union, the Egyptian's determination to impose their centralist single-party system and state bureaucracy on the united state soon caused a clash with the Syrian *Ba'thists* and led to Syria's secession in 1961.

In the 1950s and the early 1960s Egyptian Nasserism operated chiefly through subversion, causing innumerable complaints and disputes. Nasser justified such methods by repeatedly proclaiming that true inter-A. cooperation and unity could be achieved only by "progressive" Arab-Socialist régimes and that conservative, "reactionary" régimes would have to be swept away. Yet at the same time he was pragmatic enough to enable the Arab League, and cooperation with the self-same "reactionary" régimes, to continue. After the dissolution of the Syro-Egyptian union, the failure of all Egyptian-Nasserist attempts to topple conservative régimes and impose all-A. unity according to Nasserist prescriptions, and the frustration of Egypt's military intervention in Yemen (1962–67), Nasser's all-A. unionist fervor cooled considerably, and Nasserism lost much of its momentum. After Nasser's death in 1970, Egypt's rulers abandoned revolutionary A.-Socialist unionism, and though Nasserist trends still have some influence in Egypt, and rival Nasserist factions exist in Syria and Lebanon under various A.-Socialist or Socialist-Unionist labels, Nasserism has faded away or at least lost its impact.

Libya's Mu'ammar *Qadhdhafi, in power since his military *coup* of 1969, developed his own version of AN — a mass-oriented populist-totalitarian semi-Socialism, fervently nationalist with strong Islamic emphasis, pressing for immediate moves towards all-A. unity (and based, though strictly anti-Communist, on a firm alliance with the Soviet Bloc). Qadhdhafi's doctrine and policies, laid down in a "Green Book" (1976 and 1978), led him into unrelenting efforts to unite Libya with various AC's, coupled with subversive, even terrorist, activities that brought him into constant conflict with the very countries he wanted to merge with Libya — Egypt, Sudan, Tunisia, and Morocco (see *Libya, *Qadhdhafi).

AN, the assertion of A. independence and power (since World War II with strong leanings to non-alignment) and the construction of modern, stable, economically and socially developed nation-states (in many cases with populist or socialist tendencies), has remained the dominant force in A. thinking, sentiment and policy. AN has, like other independence movements, its difficulties with the process of nation-building, the problems of régime and administration, of good government and social development. It has not completely overcome, for the sake of the nation's unity, divergent or particularist allegiances — regional, tribal, and mainly communal-religious. Minority communities tend to feel a dominant, first-priority allegiance to their community, while many simple, uneducated Muslim A.'s hardly distinguish between "Muslim" and "A.", instinctively regarding only a Muslim A. as fully and really A. The upsurge, in recent years, of strong, radical Islamic trends has added to this problem. Wide strata of the Muslim-A. population do not, perhaps, perceive the intrinsic dialectic tension, and even contradiction, between extra-religious AN and supra-national Islamism, but leaders, policy-makers, intellectuals do, and try to cope with the problem in various ways — e.g. by emphasizing the basic link between Islam and the A. nation, the fact that Islam became a world religion through the medium of the A.'s genius and their language, and the A.'s achieved greatness through Islam. But in terms of ideology and doctrine, AN has never clearly resolved this issue. However, these problems do not detract from the dominant position of AN in A. thinking and politics.

All-AN, *Qawmiyya*, A. unionism, remains an aspiration, a potent emotion, a dominant ideological trend. Actually and historically, *Wataniyya*, the N. of the various AC's, determines policies. The two trends go side-by-side in dialectical interplay, contradicting each other and yet influencing and complementing each other. Some elements unite all A.'s, from Casablanca to the Persian Gulf, forging them into one nation; other elements make for increasing divergence and the emergence of separate A. nations — Egyptian, Syrian, Iraqi, Algerian, Moroccan etc. The historically dominant trend seems to be towards growing all-A. cooperation; but this increasing unity is a close alliance rather than a move towards federal or unionist merger. Though ideologically and emotionally the stress may be on all-AN and many A.'s may balk at the assumption that the separate ASt's are borne by separate AN's, actual A. unity and the N. inspiring it are based, as the Arab League is, on the acceptance of, and respect for, the sovereignty and integrity of separate, individual A. nation-states.

Arab Revolt (also "The Revolt in the Desert") The uprising of *Hussein ibn 'Ali, the Sharif of Mecca, and his sons *'Ali, *'Abdullah and *Feisal, of the *Hashemite clan, against the Turkish-Ottoman Empire during World War I, June 1916. The AR was preceded by an exchange of letters between Hussein and Sir Henry McMahon, the British High Commissioner in Egypt, in which the latter promised British support for Arab independence after the war (for details see *McMahon-Hussein Correspondence). Britain financed the AR with £200,000 per month and supplied arms, provisions and direct artillery support; she also sent guerrilla experts, among them the legendary T.E. *Lawrence. The AR army started with an estimated 10,000 Hijazi Bedouin, reinforced by an additional 30–40,000 semi-attached and recruited occasionally; its final strength was estimated at c. 70,000. Several Arab (Syrian and Iraqi) officers of the Ottoman army — deserters or prisoners — joined the AR, but their number remained very small. For a short time, the Egyptian 'Aziz 'Ali al-*Masri served as Chief-of-Staff, and for some time — the Iraqi Nuri al-*Sa'id. The rebels took Mecca (with British artillery support) and 'Aqaba (with British naval support); al-Madina remained in Turkish hands, but was cut off. The AR's main operation was sabotaging the *Hijaz Railway, the principal Turkish supply route to Western Arabia. When the British and allied forces, under General Allenby, advanced into Palestine and Syria, 1917–18, the rebel army formed their right wing. It was allowed to enter Damascus first, raise the A. flag and establish an A. administration, semi-coordinated with the allied military administration of occupied territories. Though this A. Government was suppressed and evicted in 1919–20 by the French, the princes heading the AR became the principal and recognized spokesmen for the A. national cause at the peace conference. Their connection to the A. nationalists of the *Fertile Crescent was tenuous, and their claims and demands were not fully realized (see *Arab Nationalism; *Syria; *Hussein b. 'Ali, *Feisal, *'Abdullah); yet the AR is to this day seen as the Golden Age of A. Nationalism, the cradle of A. independence. Several of the officers of the AR became spokesmen and leaders of the ASt's in the 1920s and 1930s, and they continued glorifying the memory of the revolt (helped by the impressive, though not quite reliable, writings of Lawrence).

Arab Socialism See *Socialism, *Nasserism.
Arab Socialist Union From 1962 to 1976–77 the only legal political organization in Egypt. It was preceded, as the single party

intended to provide popular support for the post-1952 officers' régime, by the "National Liberation Organization", 1953–58, and the "National Union", 1957–62, which were considered to have failed in their task. The ASU was closely integrated in the new constitutional pattern devised by *Nasser (see *Egypt). Its leadership was chosen indirectly: village and township committees sent representatives to regional committees whose delegates formed district committees which in turn elected the national leadership. The ASU leadership nominated the single-party candidates for election to the National Assembly, as well as a single candidate as President of Egypt. The ASU Executive Committee consisted of President Nasser, his Vice-Presidents and the other top leaders of the Government. Its Secretary-General (sometimes styled chairman) was for some time Nasser himself, for most of the time 'Ali *Sabri, and after Nasser's death in 1970 several Secretaries followed each other in rapid changes. The ASU, like its predecessors, remained part of the official establishment rather than an independent popular organization and had little influence of its own, but in the late 1960s 'Ali Sabri gradually shaped it into a power instrument for himself and his Leftist faction (and was dismissed in 1969).

In the hidden struggle for the succession, after Nasser's death, the ASU was considered the center of "Nasserist" opposition to President *Sadat, and in 1971 its leadership was purged and new functionaries were appointed. In the course of Sadat's liberalization moves various trends and factions that had developed within the ASU began asserting themselves in 1975, and in 1976 three trends (or "platforms", *minbar*, pl. *manābir*) were permitted to constitute themselves formally within the ASU: a Right-wing-Liberal faction, a Leftist one (headed by Khaled *Muhyi-ul-Din), and a center or mainstream (considered to be the Government faction and headed by the Prime Minister). In the elections for the National Assembly, Oct. 1976, candidates were presented by these ASU "platforms": the center won an overwhelming majority, the Rightist-Liberals 12 (of whom several immediately joined the center), and the Left 2. Late in 1976, fully fledged parties were permitted, and a party law of June 1977 regulated their formation. The ASU thus lost its monopoly; its Right wing became the "Social Liberal Party", its Left — the "Progressive-Unionist Rally". In 1978, President Sadat established his own "National Democratic Party" — and the mainstream faction of the ASU, which by now called itself "Egypt Party" (*Misr*), decided to merge into it. It was formally dissolved in May 1980.

Arab summit conferences Since 1964, the Heads of the ASt's have been meeting, irregularly, at the top level (in addition to the regular sessions of the *Arab League Council, held at the level of Foreign Ministers or Permanent Representatives). The first SC, in Jan. 1964 in Cairo, was convened in an effort to overcome inter-A. dissension and disputes which the regular meetings has been unable to resolve. The following ones had the same purpose and were meant to ensure a minimal, basic all-A. consensus. A decision to hold a SC every year was not implemented. So far 12 SC's have been held — the last at Fez, Morocco, in Sept. 1982. Efforts to convene another fully fledged SC have since been foiled by inter-A. dissent. An "extraordinary" SC was held in Aug. 1985 in Casablanca, but few of the major Arab Countries were represented by their Heads-of-State, and five boycotted it altogether.

Arab unity See *Pan-Arabism; *Arab Federation; *Arab Nationalism.

'Arafat, Yasser (b. 1929) Palestinian-Arab politician and guerrilla leader. A distant relative of the prominent *Husseini family, 'A. was educated in Egypt and graduated from Cairo University as an engineer. In the 1950s he was chairman of the Palestinian Students' Union centered in Gaza and was active as a political organizer while working in Kuwait as an engineer, 1957–60 (reportedly after briefly serving in the Egyptian army in 1957). In the late 1950s 'A. was a co-founder of the *al-*Fatah* guerrilla group forming in the Palestinian-A. diaspora in AC's and among students in Europe; he emerged in the 1960s as its chief leader. When in mid-1968 the *Palestine Liberation Organization (PLO) became a roof-organization of various guerrilla groups, al-Fatah gained control of the organization and in Feb. 1969 'A. became chairman of its Executive Committee and the PLO's main leader and commander-in-chief. In this capacity he was recognized by the ASt's as the top leader of the Palestine Arabs, particularly since the 1974 all-A.

summit of Rabat recognized the PLO as sole legitimate representative of the Palestinians. He attends all-A. summit conferences, maintains permanent contact with A. heads-of-state and Government leaders and is treated as a head-of-state; Third World, non-aligned, Islamic states and organizations similary recognize him. Many other countries, while not formally recognizing his status, also treat him as the authorized spokesman and leader of the Palestine Arabs; in Nov. 1974 he was invited to address the UN General Assembly. He constantly travels between Arab capitals and frequently visits other world centers.

As head of *al-Fataḥ* and from 1969 of the PLO, 'A. led the planning and execution of continuous sabotage and terror operations in Israel (which began, according to *Fataḥ* chronology, in Jan. 1965), abroad, and against international aviation. From the mid-1970s 'A. and his mainstream faction disapproved of hijacking and terrorist operations against foreign aircraft; but as chairman of the PLO he remained responsible for such operations continued by the PLO's more extremist factions, as well as for the frequent assassinations of dissenters and factional rivals within the PLO. 'A. was the chief architect of a large PLO organization and transformed it, with the huge funds put at his disposal by the ASt's, mainly the rich oil countries, from a feeble association of small guerrilla bands into a wealthy, multi-branched establishment conducting military, economic-financial, social, medical and educational operations. He thus built a veritable state-within-a-state in Jordan and Lebanon — without their consent and against their interest — and brought about a critical confrontation with these countries (see *PLO, *Jordan, *Lebanon).

In the course of Israel's Lebanon war, from June 1982, the PLO establishment was expelled from South Lebanon and evacuated from West Beirut (late Aug. 1982 — see *PLO; *Lebanon; *Arab-Israel Conflict), and 'A., while stepping up his constant travels, established his headquarters in Tunis. He maintained a command base in Syrian-occupied East Lebanon (the *Biqā') and North Lebanon (Tripoli), but Syrian-instigated anti-'A. factions within the PLO and *al-Fataḥ* rebelled in 1983, led by Abu Mussa and Abu Saleh. The rebels, with Syrian army support, expelled 'A.'s forces from the Biqā'; 'A. personally was expelled from Syria in June 1983. As 'A. rallied his forces in Tripoli and the Palestinian camps around it, fighting soon spread to that area; 'A. was defeated by the Syrian-supported rebels, and in Dec. 1983 the remnants of his forces were evacuated from Tripoli (to Yemen, South Yemen, Algeria, Tunisia) and 'A. returned to Tunis. But while the Tunis Government allowed him to maintain his political and administrative headquarters there, it objected to the presence of military/terrorist commands and operative departments, and these were dispersed in various Arab countries.

'A. has always been considered, within the PLO, a man of the center, the mainstream. He was not a moderate; he saw "military" action, i.e. sabotage and terrorism, as the main method of struggle, and he was instrumental in the formulation of the PLO Charter of 1968 — a very extremist document totally denying Israel's right to exist, negating any link between the Jews and Palestine and refusing any kind of compromise or co-existence. But against various rival PLO factions, particularly the Leftist ones of *Habash and *Hawatma with their Marxist-Maoist doctrines, and those linked to extremist-rejectionist ASt's, 'A. insisted that the unity of the Palestinian movement must be maintained at all costs and that all internal social-ideological struggles concerning political orientations should be postponed. Such a position is considered by Leftists as right-wing; indeed, 'A.'s own inclination was patently conservative, with a measure of Islamist tendencies.

Since the 1970s, 'A. has been considered by many observers as moderate. He opposed terrorism against foreign countries and international aviation, as practised by the extremist factions. He initiated, in 1974, a resolution by the PLO National Council stating that the PLO would establish a "national authority" in any part of Palestine vacated by Israel; and though that resolution did not renounce the claim to *all* Palestine or pledge peaceful co-existence of the proposed Palestinian "national authority" with Israel — nor did 'A. himself commit himself to such a co-existence — some observers interpreted it as implying that 'A. and the PLO might content themselves with a Palestinian state in part of Palestine, in co-existence with Israel. 'A. in some of his many and often conflicting statements also began to emphasize political solutions, implying that he would prefer diplomatic struggle to military-terrorist operations. He spoke of joining international efforts to negotiate a settlement; he hinted that even Security Council Resolution 242, considered by most countries as the key to any settlement, might be acceptable if amended to recognize the national rights and aspirations of the Palestine Arabs, i.e. an independent state. 'A. did not object to all-Arab plans (e.g. the *"Fahd Plan" or the Fez Summit Resolution of 1982 advocating a settlement based on the recognition of the Palestinians' right to independent statehood and acquiescence in the peaceful existence of "all states in the region", i.e. by implication: of Israel, too. 'A. advocated and held meetings with Israelis — primarily those of the dovish Zionist Left or the anti-Zionist Communists; such contacts were based, explicitly, on the acceptance of the Jews of Israel as inhabitants of the country (contrary to the PLO Charter) and, implicitly, on the assumption that some settlement between Israel and the Palestine Arabs is feasible (again contrary to the PLO Charter). Yet 'A. has so far been unable to commit himself clearly to co-existence with Israel, to renounce terror, or to accept Resolution 242, and has frequently invalidated or counter-balanced moderate statements by renewed expressions of extremism.

Since 1982, 'A. negotiated with King *Hussein of Jordan, mainly on two issues: a confederation between the future Palestinian entity and Jordan; and joint Palestinian-Jordanian action towards a general peace settlement, possibly a joint negotiating delegation. They reached an agreement in Feb. 1985; but rejected by the traditional PLO factions, it was abrogated by the PLO in Apr. 1987 (see *PLO, *Jordan).

'A., who in 1978–79 had fully supported the all-A. steps against Egypt, also resumed, since 1982–83, close relations with President *Mubarak's Egypt — to a point that there was talk of a "moderate bloc" formed by Egypt, Jordan and 'A.'s wing of the PLO. Yet here, too, 'A. was unable unequivocally to accept Mubarak's proposals, and in Apr. 1987 he had to accept the radicals' demand to suspend relations with Egypt.

'A.'s status and position were questionable since 1982. He lost his main base of operation in South Lebanon and was reduced, except for some marginal, indecisive terrorist ventures, to a feeble travelling diplomacy. His "moderate" policies and his *rapprochement* with Jordan and Egypt deepened the rift with Syria — a rift that had originated with 'A.'s refusal to submit to Syrian guidance, Syria's refusal to accord the PLO full freedom of action — and the extremist, Syria-guided factions of the PLO. The *Fataḥ* rebellion of 1983 deprived 'A. of his last power base in the Biqā' and the Tripoli area and caused a deep, perhaps irreversible, split within the PLO. It was fully supported by some of the extremist factions, while the two Leftist ones of *Habash and *Hawatma half-sympathized with it and tried to mediate. The rebels and their supporters demanded 'A.'s dismissal, and boycotted all meetings and sessions of the 'A.-loyal PLO. In Nov. 1984 'A. succeeded in convening, in 'Amman, a session of the National Council that was attended only by 'A.-loyalists; it endorsed 'A.'s policies and his leadership. Since 1985–86 he has also re-established, despite near-constant clashes with the Shi'i *Amal militia, a strong presence of his PLO wing in the Palestinian-A. camps in South Lebanon and Beirut. In Apr. 1987, 'A. achieved a reconciliation with some of the radical factions within the PLO. To achieve this, he had to accept some of the policy changes they demanded (mainly concerning PLO relations with Jordan and Egypt). Syria and the factions guided by her were not reconciled with 'A.

'A.'s status remains in doubt: beyond his own inability to commit himself and take firm decisions, he represents, and is able to commit, only part of the PLO, and his policies are frequently disputed even within the camp of his loyalists and by some of his close associates. However, Palestinian A.'s in general, as well as A. and world public opinion, still seem to regard him as the chief and the most representative Palestinian-A. leader.

ARAMCO (Arabian-American Oil Company) A consortium of American oil companies — Standard Oil of California; Texas Oil; Standard Oil of New Jersey (later ESSO, EXXON); and Socony Vacuum — formed in the mid-1940s to produce oil in Sa'udi Arabia. See *Oil in the Arab Countries.

'Aref, 'Abd-ul-Salam (1920–66) Iraqi officer and politician. President of Iraq, 1963–66. Son of a Sunni middle class family of Baghdad, 'A. was trained as a professional officer. He served with the Iraqi expeditionary force in the Arab-Israel war of 1948. He was a leading member of the "Free Officers" group that overthrew the monarchy in July 1958 and commanded the task force that took over Baghdad. *Qassem, the leader of the junta, appointed him Deputy Commander-in-Chief, Deputy Prime Minister and Minister of the Interior — i.e., in fact, Number Two of the new régime. However, as 'A. was strongly *Nasserist, advocating union with Egypt (the UAR), and obviously aspired to the top leadership, he soon fell out with Qassem. In Sept. 1958 he was dismissed, and in Nov. he was arrested and put on trial; in Feb. 1959 he was sentenced to death by a "People's Court" for plotting against the régime and planning to assassinate Qassem, but the latter did not confirm the sentence, and in 1961 'A. was set free. He was one of the organizers of the *coup* of Feb. 1963 (together with officers of the *Ba'th group) that overthrew Qassem, and became President. As long as the Ba'th officers were in control, his powers were nominal only; but in Nov. 1963 he ousted the Ba'th group in a bloodless semi-*coup*, and henceforth he exercised real power.

As President, 'A. at first endeavored to model his régime on a Nasserist pattern and sought a close association with Nasser's Egypt. In May 1964 he agreed with Nasser to establish a political union with Egypt, with a Joint Presidential Council and close military and economic co-ordination. In July he decreed measures of far-reaching nationalization, on the Egyptian model, and established an "Arab Socialist Union" as a single party. However, the union with Egypt, scheduled to be fully consummated within two years, did not materialize, as 'A. insisted, in effect, on Iraq's complete independence. Iraq's transformation on the Egyptian pattern was also half-hearted and incomplete and 'A. soon ceased advancing it; few of the nationalization decrees were put into practice, and the ASU did not come into being. 'A. followed no clear ideological line; his policy was based on nationalism and a pragmatic, rather conservative state socialism. Though most of his colleagues and supporters were army officers, he entrusted the Premiership to a civilian ('Abd-ul-Rahman al-*Bazzaz, Sept. 1965). 'A. and Bazzaz were keen on solving two issues troubling Iraq — but failed on both: an agreement with the *Kurdish rebels was reached in June 1966, but was not implemented; and an agreement with the Iraq Petroleum Co. was signed in 1965, but was not ratified by Iraq because of leftist and nationalist pressure. 'A. was killed in Apr. 1966 in an air crash (and succeeded by his brother 'Abd-ul-Rahman 'Aref, who was overthrown in July 1968).

armed forces in the Arab countries Most states throughout history regarded the possession and development of AF as a chief attribute of statehood, as needed for defense, and as the main instrument of power, both externally and internally. The modern ASt's, looking back on deeply rooted traditions of martial feats and warrior pride, are no exception. Those Arab-inhabited countries which formed defined entitites or states already in the 19th century — Egypt, Tunisia, Morocco — possessed AF, and the modernization of these AF was an important part, and sometimes a chief instrument, of the general modernization and development of the country concerned. The modern Egyptian army, for instance, founded by Muhammad 'Ali in 1816, served that ruler and his descendants in their efforts to build a modern Egypt (semi-independent under Ottoman suzerainty). As the countries concerned came under Western, semi-colonial tutelage — Tunisia in 1881, Egypt in 1882, Morocco in 1912 — their AF were re-formed under the tutelage and command of the French or British protecting power. Egypt's AF had been reduced, under the pressure and supervision of the powers, in 1841 and in the 1870s. They had staged, in 1881–82, under Ahmad 'Urābi (usually spelled 'Arabi in foreign publications), the first officers' *coup d'état* in recent Arab history and had been defeated by the British. They had also been defeated — together with British forces — in 1882–83 by the *Mahdi in Sudan, and had been formally disbanded in 1883. After being re-formed under British patronage, they reconquered the Sudan, together with British forces and under British command, in 1896–98.

In World War I, no Arab AF as such participated, except for the mostly Hijazi tribal fighters recruited by the Sharif *Hussein in the *"Arab Revolt" who were gradually shaped, with British help, into an army; and small Libyan-*Sanussi units the British helped organize — mainly in Egypt. There were, of course, thousands of Arab soldiers in the Turkish-Ottoman AF on one side,

ARMED FORCES OF THE ARAB COUNTRIES

Country	Regular	Reserves	Total	Tanks	Other Armored Fighting Vehicles	Artillery Pieces	Surface-to-Surface Missile Launchers	Combat Aircraft	Transport Aircraft	Helicopters	Surface-to-Air Missile Batteries	Naval Surface Combat Vessels	Submarines
	Personnel (all branches) 1,000 men												
Egypt	453	400	853	2500	3600	2200	12	608	97	204	131	129	12
Iraq	520	480	1000	5000	3500	3500	36	615	65	435	70	56	—
Jordan	80	30	110	1095	1460	600	—	115	18	54	20	10	—
Libya	101	?	101	3000	2000	2000	100	565	67	200	100	48	6
Sa'udi Arabia	89	—	89	450	3000	580	—	195	97	107	15	62	—
Syria	500	340	840	4100	3500	2300	53	650	32	235	150	40	2
Sub-total: Major Armed Forces	1743	1250	2993	16,145	17,060	11,180	201	2748	376	1235	486	345	20
Algeria	120	—	120	700	1300	700	25	295	57	99	30	59	2
Bahrain	3	—	3	—	145	8	—	6	—	19	—	20	—
Kuwait	12.5	—	12.5	260	480	58	4	62	7	40	4	55	—
Lebanon	35.5	—	35.5	100	300	150	—	15	2	38	—	12	—
Morocco	129	—	129	395	1595	688	—	84	38	128	—	20	—
'Oman	24	—	24	45	66	108	—	38	37	31	—	26	—
Qatar	7	—	7	24	195	14	—	17	4	22	—	49	—
Sudan	75	—	75	590	444	223	—	45	28	57	5	20	—
Tunisia	30.5	—	30.5	180	245	70	—	8	12	47	—	26	—
United Arab Emirates (UAE)	49	—	49	178	665	94	—	44	29	57	7	53	—
Yemen (YAR)	37	—	37	850	500	320	—	99	15	35	14	15	—
South Yemen (PDRY)	27.5	—	27.5	700	450	300	24	135	12	49	9	25	—
TOTAL: All Arab Armed Forces	2,293	1,260	3,543	26,167	23,745	13,993	254	3,596	616	1,857	555	725	22

Abridged version of a table prepared by Dr. Zeev Eytan, Jaffee Center for Strategic Studies. Data mainly from *The Middle East Military Balance*, 1985 (Mark Heller ed., Aharon Levran, Zeev Eytan), published for the JCSS by the *Jerusalem Post* and Westview Press (Boulder, CO). Partly revised and updated to early 1986.

and of Arab North-Africans in the French forces. In the semi-independent AC's that emerged after the war, under British and French tutelage, AF were speedily established — but they were under British and French control at first, and their transfer to full national control formed part of the nationalist struggle for the attainment of full independence. The Egyptian AF were officially commanded until 1924 by the British Governor-General of Sudan, concurrently bearing the title *Sirdar* of the Egyptian AF. From 1924–25, their command was fully Egyptian, but the British continued to exercise *de facto* control, at least until the conclusion of the Anglo-Egyptian Treaty of 1936 and in some measure even after it. An Iraqi Army was established in 1921, under Iraqi command; but here, too, the British wielded a large measure of control, at least until the Anglo-Iraqi Treaty of 1930 recognized Iraq's full independence. The British also raised, outside the framework of the Iraqi AF, special "levies" for internal security. The *"Arab Legion" established in Transjordan in 1920 gradually became Jordan's national army; but it was British-commanded and financed until 1956. The "Sudan Defense Force", established in 1925 by the British, was also British-commanded. So were, later, paramilitary guards or levies set up by the British in areas they still controlled in a semi-colonial way (the Western 'Aden Protectorate, 1937; the "Hadrami Legion" in the Eastern 'Aden Protectorate, 1940; the "Trucial Scouts" in Trucial

'Oman, 1955). The AF of independent Muscat and 'Oman were also British-officered. In Palestine under the British Mandate no AF were established beyond the police and a small Palestinian-Transjordanian Frontier Force, TJFF (Palestinian volunteer units in World War II — mostly Jewish, from Sept. 1944 the "Jewish Brigade", and some 9,000 Arabs — were part of the British Army). The French in Syria and Lebanon kept even tighter direct control of the "*Troupes Spéciales*" they established in 1926. Of the countries of the Arabian peninsula not under formal foreign tutelage, Yemen had a small, primitive army. King Hussein's Hijazi AF seem to have reverted to mainly tribal levies — and were overrun in 1924–25 by the *Wahhabi-Sa'udi conquest of Hijaz. The Sa'udi forces conquering most of Arabia were tribal fighters and the *Wahhabi *Ikhwan* (Order of Brethren); Sa'udia began establishing modern, organized AF only after World War II.

The Arab AF under imperial tutelage, in the 1920s and 1930s, served mostly internal purposes — the suppression of tribal unrest (e.g. in Iraq) or rebellious minorities (e.g. the Kurds in Iraq), and the preservation of law and order. Their leading officers also began appearing as contenders for power and staging the first military *coups* — in Iraq, 1936 (see *Army Officers in Politics). Foreign operations, exclusively inter-Arab, were confined to the Arabian peninsula (Wahhabi-Hijazi clashes, 1919–20; Wahhabi raids on Iraqi, Transjordanian and Persian Gulf border areas; the Wahhabi-Sa'udi conquest of Hijaz, 1924–25; Sa'udia's war against Yemen, 1934); they were traditional tribal warfare and raids rather than military operations of modern AF. The Iraqi AF seem to have had a hand in the organization of *Qawuqji's volunteer force for the Palestinian-Arab rebellion of 1936. No Arab AF were involved in World War II — except for operations of the Iraqi AF against their British ally that were suppressed in May 1941 in a short war, and the dispatch of units of Jordan's Arab Legion to support the British forces in that war.

After World War II, as imperial tutelage was drawing to its end, the Arab AF became instruments of fully independent states. British guidance and interference virtually ceased with regard to Egypt's and Iraq's AF. Jordan, independent since 1946, asserted growing control of her "Arab Legion", though it remained British-officered and British-financed until 1956–57. After a bitter struggle, France in 1945–46 handed to Syria and Lebanon the command of her *troupes spéciales*, which became the two countries' national armies. Similar developments in the *Maghrib*, "French" North Africa, came later, from 1956–57. The main preoccupation of the Arab AF in the later 1940s was their growing involvement in the Palestine struggle — preparations and the provision of training, arms, volunteers, logistic support from 1946–47, and finally full armed intervention in May 1948 (see *Arab-Israel Conflict, *Arab-Israel Wars).

The principal A. armies were at that time comparatively small forces — Egypt: 30–35,000, increasing by 1949–50 to 60–80,000; Iraq: 25–30,000; Syria: 10–15,000; Jordan: 8–10,000. These forces possessed the usual arms and branches, though the air forces, armor and mechanized units were still in the initial stages of development (Jordan set up an air force only in the 1950s. The AF command, in its angry efforts to explain the Palestine defeat of 1948, particularly in Egypt, claimed, and tried to prove in trials that ended in convictions, that the procurement and supply of equipment had been sabotaged by corruption.

A tremendous upsurge in the strength of the Arab AF, and particularly in the modernization of their equipment, especially concerning the air force, armor, and sophisticated air defense systems, began in the mid-1950s and the early 1960s. (In 1950 the USA, Britain and France agreed to keep the inter-Arab and Arab-Israel military balance, and co-ordinated and limited their sales of weapons. However, these limitations were breached by incipient Arab arms purchases from the Soviet Bloc, from 1955; they were soon eroded in the West, too.) The permanent cause and target of Arab efforts to improve their AF and their equipment, was the increasingly bitter confrontation with Israel. The assertion of stiffening neutralist or non-aligned policies by Egypt and Syria (and Iraq, since 1958), and apprehensions that the Western powers might try to foil these independent policies, even by military intervention — apprehensions aggravated by the Anglo-French *Suez campaign of 1956 and by continuous efforts to impose on the Arab states Western-led anti-Soviet defense pacts (see *"Baghdad Pact") — reinforced the will to develop the strongest possible AF. The fact that the countries concerned were ruled by military juntas may have further strengthened that resolve.

From 1955–56, Egypt and Syria increasingly turned to the Soviet Union as a source of weapons, military equipment, training, expert advice, instructors and technicians. Iraq joined that new orientation after 1958 — as did Algeria and South Yemen after attaining independence (1962 and 1967) and Libya after the *coup* of 1969. During the 1960s, and particularly after the *Six Day War of 1967 and again during and after the *October War of 1973, unprecedented quantities of Soviet arms and equipment flowed to Egypt and Syria, and also to Iraq, Libya and Algeria. In Egypt, and even more so in Syria, whole sectors of the military establishment — e.g., sophisticated air defense and missile systems — were organized and supervised, and partly manned, by Soviet personnel. The number of Soviet military technicians and experts in Egypt were estimated before 1969–70 as about 5,000. During the "War of Attrition", 1969–70, the USSR sent, in response to President *Nasser's appeal, an air defense division, comprising Soviet-manned surface-to-air missiles (SAM) and 150 fighter aircraft. In the early 1970s the number of Soviet military experts was estimated at 15–20,000 in Egypt and 5–7,000 in Syria. The huge supplies of Soviet arms depended mostly on Soviet credits and created an ever-increasing indebtedness to the USSR.

In Syria, the flow of Soviet arms — and the resulting dependence on Soviet replacements, parts, instructors, credits — continued through the 1970s and 1980s. Egypt under *Sadat, on the other hand, changed course in the 1970s. Sadat, complaining bitterly about the inadequacy of Soviet aid and about increasing Soviet interference, in July 1972 terminated the services of over 15,000 Soviet technicians, i.e. expelled them. Yet he had to depend on Soviet aid again in 1973, before and during the October War, and received new massive supplies of Soviet arms, including fighter planes, advanced surface-to-air and surface-to-surface missiles and rockets, and modern tanks (as did Syria). But Sadat increasingly turned to the West (France from 1972, Britain, and in the later 1970s mainly the USA) and began re-equipping Egypt's AF with American weapons (with US grants and credits). Iraq's dependence on Soviet arms had also been modified when the USSR took a neutral position in the Iraq-Iran War, since 1980, and the supply of Soviet weapons, and particularly the highly sophisticated systems Iraq required, was greatly reduced. Iraq therefore increasingly turned to France, and gradually also to other Western powers (motivated also by political reasons — see *Iraq.

The Arab countries not allied with the Soviet Bloc, like Jordan, Sa'udia and Morocco after she attained her independence in 1956, also greatly increased the strength and modern equipment of their AF, but they did so later than Egypt, Syria and Iraq, and to a much smaller extent. Tunisia, Lebanon, Sudan, Yemen did not make similar efforts to build very large AF and equip them with hyper-modern weaponry — though both Sudan and Yemen received Soviet arms (and in both of them the AF played a decisive role in internal political events). Jordan, after a brief Leftist lurch in 1956–57, which included the dismissal of the British commander of her Army and the termination of its special links with Britain, remained allied with the West — now with the USA rather than Britain; she depends on American and Western (British and French) equipment and American aid, though she considers, and negotiates, the purchase of Soviet arms when American ones are denied to her. The strength of her AF grew to c. 80,000. Sa'udia transformed her tribal levies into a modern army in the 1950s, with US aid in training and instruction. She did not need financial aid, as did the other Arab countries, and even herself aided those others; as her oil income rose, in the 1960s and 1970s, she made large military purchases, equipping her AF with the most advanced and sophisticated defense systems from Western sources, mostly US but also British, French, Italian and German. So did Kuwait, on a much smaller scale, after attaining independence in 1961. Kuwait, however, took a neutralist stance, though most of her equipment was British, and some American and French, and in the 1980s purchased some Soviet arms, too. As the other Persian Gulf principalities — Bahrain, Qatar, the United Arab Emirates — attained independence in 1971, they also began building small AF, with

British, American and French equipment. In the mid-1980s efforts were made to establish joint defense units of the "Gulf Cooperation Council" consisting of the three last-named countries, Sa'udia, Kuwait and 'Oman. The Sultanate of 'Oman also has its own small AF, built with British aid and officered by Britons under contract. All these Gulf countries had ample means to finance advanced equipment for their AF from their oil revenues.

A special case is that of Lebanon's AF. Never of great strength (until the 1970s — 15–17,000 men, in the 1980s increased to a nominal 33–35,000), they were for internal reasons hardly able to make war against a foreign enemy. Their participation in the Arab-Israel war of 1948 was limited, almost as a token-force only, and they took no part in later wars. They offered hardly any resistance to the Israeli forces invading Lebanon in 1978 and 1982 (though various non-governmental militias did). Lebanon's AF could not even enforce internal security, as they were caught up in the country's communal problems. Their top command was mostly Christian-Maronite, and the Maronites' share in the force was higher than in the population; but a large part of officers and men belonged to other communities, Christian, Muslim (Sunni and Shi'i) and Druse. The Army was thus in danger of breaking apart whenever it was used in an intercommunal conflict. In the civil war of 1958, the President and the High Command, realizing that danger, decided not to involve it. Nor were the AF used, for similar reasons, to prevent the takeover of South Lebanon by Palestinian guerrillas, in the late 1960s and the 1970s, or to impose the Government's will and control upon them. In the civil war since 1975 the leadership took the same line, and the AF were not used to enforce law and order. But the internecine fighting was stronger than that decision, and the Army disintegrated, whole units joining their community or simply deserting. When the Army was rebuilt, in the late 1970s and early 1980s, it did not become, despite several agreements to that effect, a united supra-communal force. Its several brigades are essentially communal — Christian-Maronite, Muslim-Shi'i, Druze; they tend to obey orders from the leadership of their community and its militias and frequently take part in the intercommunal fighting on the side of "their" community's militia. Other brigades are Syrian-dominated. Efforts to re-create a united non-communal force heeding the Government's command have so far failed.

In recent decades the AF of the Arab states have also been used in several inter-Arab operations. Sa'udi troops clashed in 1955 with a British-led 'Omani force, over possession of the *Buraimi oasis. 'Omani troops fought South Yemeni units aiding rebels in *Dhofar in the 1960s. South Yemen was involved several times in border fighting with Yemen, which escalated in 1972 and again in 1979 into short real wars (ended by all-Arab mediation). An all-Arab force composed of Sa'udi, Egyptian (UAR), Sudanese, Jordanian and Tunisian troops was dispatched in 1961 to Kuwait, to defend her against Iraqi annexation threats. In 1962, Egypt sent an expeditionary force to Yemen, intervening in that country's civil war and supporting its revolutionary republican régime (leading also to clashes, and nearly to war, with Sa'udia). The force was finally withdrawn in 1967. Algerian and Moroccan troops clashed in a brief border war in 1963. A Syrian force crossed into Jordan in 1970, to intervene on the PLO's side in the Jordan-PLO fighting; it was repelled by the Jordanian AF and by American and Israeli threats of intervention. Since 1975 Moroccan troops have been operating against *"POLISARIO", the guerrilla of the *"Sahara Arab Republic" — formerly Spanish Sahara, which Morocco claims as her own — operations that also create Moroccan-Algerian tension and sometimes lead to clashes. Repeated clashes between Libya and Egypt briefly escalated into warlike operations in 1977.

Syrian troops openly and massively intervened in 1976 in Lebanon's civil war, after protracted semi-clandestine intervention without regular troops. This Syrian intervention force was transformed, the same year, into an "Arab Deterrent Force" with troops from several Arab countries (Sa'udia, Sudan, Libya, Yemen, South Yemen). Some of these Arab troops were soon withdrawn, and all of them were out by 1979; but even while the force — variously reported to number 25–40,000 men — was nominally all-Arab, its bulk was Syrian. From 1979, the force was virtually Syrian only, though the Arab League continued extending its term as an "all-Arab" force — extensions from which several Arab states dissociated themselves. The Government of Lebanon several times requested Syria to withdraw her troops, but as there was no formal Arab League decision to disband the "all-Arab" force, Syria did not comply. In the June 1982 Israeli invasion of Lebanon Syrian troops clashed with Israeli ones; those in Beirut, Southern and Western Lebanon were evacuated in Sept. 1982, but Syria maintained her troops in Northern and Eastern Lebanon (the Tripoli-'Akkar region and the Biqā'), and in effect occupied these areas.

All these military operations concerned inter-Arab problems and disputes. The exceptions — apart from the *Arab-Israel wars — were Libya and Iraq. Libya conducted military operations in neighboring Chad since the mid-1970s. In 1973 she occupied, and later annexed, a strip of territory — the "Aouzou Strip" — which she claimed as part of Libya. In the later 1970s her support of one of the warring factions in Chad led her into full military intervention. Her forces continue occupying large parts of northern Chad — despite several agreements (involving also France) to end that occupation. Iraq has, since Sept. 1980, been embroiled in a bloody all-out war with Iran, which began with an Iraqi invasion of southwestern Iran (the *Shatt al-'Arab and southern *Khuzistan). As Iran was in turmoil after its Islamic revolution, her AF in disarray because of cruel purges, and her equipment run down, Iraq had a distinct advantage in modern war-equipment and the personnel to operate it. Iran had greater reservoirs of man-power, and the fighting fanaticism instilled by the Islamic régime. In 1981–82, Iran succeeded in recapturing most of the territory lost to the invaders, and a stalemate ensued (during which Iraq's military capacities, particularly those of the air force which had so clear an advantage, did not show at their best). The war extended also to third parties, as Iraq, her own ports destroyed or crippled, and her oil exports by sea halted, made a determined effort to hurt Iran's oil exports by paralyzing her oil ports and loading facilities and shipping access to them, and from time to time bombed foreign oil tankers approaching Iranian ports. Iran retaliated by bombing oil shipping *en route* to and from ports on the Arab side of the Persian Gulf. No determined action was taken by the international community against either of the two warring rivals to prevent such practices. The war, though at a stalemate, led to cruel bombing and shelling of towns and civilian populations and caused heavy casualties. Figures are unrealiable, but Iranians killed are estimated at far over 100,000 and even up to 250–300,000, Iraq lost over 50,000 killed, some estimates reaching 70–125,000, while hundreds of thousands were wounded. Iranian complaints of chemical warfare and the use of poison gas by Iraq seem to be borne out by foreign and international investigations. Since 1983–84 Iraq seems to be ready for a cease-fire and a negotiated settlement based on the re-confirmation of the pre-war borders and the evacuation of all territory conquered. Iran, however, insists on far-reaching demands and refuses to negotiate with the present Iraqi régime. Mediation efforts have so far been unsuccessful.

All these foreign operations by Arab AF have been, except for the Arab-Israel wars and the Iraq-Iran war, relatively minor. The Arab states no doubt kept their AF ready for inter-Arab or international crises and disputes. Sa'udia and the ASt's of the Persian Gulf, for instance, felt responsible for the security of the Gulf and apprehensive of potential Iranian designs; Jordan feared possible Syrian moves against her; the West Sahara crisis led to near-constant tension between Morocco and Algeria; Libya's neighbors had to be alert for new Libyan schemes. Yet, it was principally against Israel that the AF of the main Arab powers were poised; it is in this context that one should understand the abnormal size, the disproportional share of budget and GDP, the constant modernization and development of the AF of Egypt (though at peace with Israel since 1979), Syria, Iraq (though since 1980 using, and needing, her AF in war against Iran), Jordan, Sa'udia, Libya and to a degree even Algeria. Iraq, Syria, Egypt, and even Libya dispose of numbers of tanks (2,500–5,000 each) and aircraft (550–650 each) equal to or surpassing most major European powers. For a breakdown of Arab AF and their equipment see the table.

Armenians Armenia and the A. themselves are outside the scope of this Dictionary. There are, however, sizable groups of A. in several Arab countries, particularly Syria and Lebanon, and some in Jerusalem. Most of these migrated from the Turkish parts of Armenia after large-scale massacres of A. in 1894–96 and in 1915–16, and after the A.-inhabited parts of Eastern Turkey were re-occupied by post-war, Kemalist Turkey in 1920; more A. came in 1939 from *Alexandretta when it was annexed by Turkey. Of the estimated total of c. 6m. A., over 4m. live in Soviet Armenia and 1.5–2m. in an A. diaspora, including more than 0.5m. in Arab countries: 2–300,000 in Syria, 150–200,000 in Lebanon, 40–50,000 in Egypt, and a few thousands in Iraq and Jordan (of the rest, some 200,000 reside in Iran, c. 60,000 in Turkey — mostly in Istanbul, nearly no A. having remained in the originally A.-inhabited eastern parts of Turkey, more than 500,000 in the USA, 200,000 in Latin America, 400,000 in Europe, mostly France; Jerusalem has c. 2,000 A.). After World War II, the Soviet government encouraged the A. of the diaspora to return to Soviet Armenia. Some 200,000 did so, among them, according to unverified and conflicting reports, more than 100,000 from Arab countries. The return movement ceased after a few years.

The A. in the Arab countries are well integrated in the economic life of the host countries. Many have become citizens and most of them speak Arabic; but they have not become part of the Arab nations, as they jealously preserve the coherence of closely knit A. communities. In Lebanon, the A. are recognized, within the communal structure of the state, as a community entitled to representation. In 66-member and 77-member Parliaments there were 3 A.-Orthodox deputies and 1 A.-Catholic, in the 99-member chamber — 4 A.-Orthodox and 1 A.-Catholic; some Lebanese Governments contained an A. Minister. However, the A. take little part in Lebanese political struggles, such as the civil war since 1975.

The A. are Christians. Most of them belong to the A. Orthodox Church, which is *Monophysite. The head of the church bears the title Catholicos and resides in Etchmiadzin in Soviet Armenia. In the 11th century the Catholicos moved to Sis, in Cilicia, and when his successor later returned to Etchmiadzin, the seat of Sis was maintained — with a measure of rivalry between two Catholici in their two seats. In the 1920s the seat of Sis was transferred to Antalias in Lebanon. The A.-Orthodox Church also has a Patriarch in Constantinople and one in Jerusalem. A minority of A. joined the Catholic Church, as a semi-autonomous community, from the 12th century; this *"Uniate" was reformalized in 1740. The number of A.-Catholics is estimated at c. 5% of all A., and most of them live in the European and American diaspora, and c. 50,000 in the Arab countries — most of them in Lebanon.

The A., particularly those in the Arab countries, maintain communal organizations of their own, including political parties. There are two main parties: *Hantchak*, and *Tashnak* — both with shifting ideologies and allegiances. In recent times, *Hantchak* is considered Leftist, sometimes with Communist leanings, while *Tashnak* is considered Right-wing and pro-Western and describes itself as Social-Democratic. A third party is *Ramkavar* (about whose political tendencies reports differ). An A. terrorist organization, the "Armenian Secret Army for the Liberation of Armenia (ASALA)", operates against Turkish institutions, diplomats, etc., mainly in Europe and America; it is said to cooperate with the *PLO and international terrorist organizations.

army officers in Arab politics The Armed Forces were systematically westernized and modernized in the ME from the 19th century, and their officers became a power group imbued with a modernist-nationalist mentality, a sense of mission, and leadership ambitions. As the AC became independent, they tended to follow the pattern of officers' *coups* set in Turkey (1908, 1920) and Iran (1921). A predecessor *coup* was staged in Egypt in 1881–82 by Col. Ahmad 'Urābi ('Arabi). The main *coups* are described in the entries on the various AC. A brief list would include: Iraq 1936 (Bakr *Sidqi), 1937; Syria 1949 (*Za'im; *Hinnawi; *Shishakli), 1951 (Shishakli), 1954, 1962, 1963 *(*Ba'th)*, 1966 *(Ba'th)*; Egypt 1952 (*Nagib, *Nasser); Iraq 1958 (*Qassem), 1963 (Ba'th, *'Aref), 1968 *(Ba'th)*; Sudan 1958 (*'Abbud), 1969 (*Numeiri), 1985; Yemen 1962; Libya 1969 (*Qadhdhafi); Algeria 1965 (*Boumedienne). All these *coups* involved purges and the detention and/or exile of deposed rulers; some of them were bloody (e.g., the Iraqi one of 1958).

Changes in the régimes set up after these *coups* could no longer be effected by political-constitutional means but were usually semi-*coups* — such as the accessions to power by Iraqi juntas of colonels in the later 1930s (the "Golden Square") and their installation of the Rashid 'Ali

*Kilani government, 1941, or *Asad's takeover in Syria in 1970. Such semi-*coups*, which cannot be precisely defined, have been frequent. A list of failed *coups* would also be extensive.

Many of the officers' *coups* had reformist tendencies, promising clean and efficient government and fundamental economic and social reforms, often in the direction of state socialism, and nearly all of them were nationalist-neutralist in their orientation. Many of them had their régime endorsed by plebiscite and established mass organizations, single parties and People's Assemblies. See in the entries on the various countries.

Arsalan (often spelled **Arslan**); also called Yazbaki. Clan of Lebanese *Druze notables, whose chiefs bear the hereditary title of Amir; until the late 19th century — the semi-feudal lords of the south-western regions of Mount Lebanon, centered in the al-Gharb area east of Beirut. Since the 17th and 18th centuries, the A. clan headed one of the rival factions competing for the overall leadership of Lebanon's Druze community — mainly against the *Junbalat clan. The Arsalan-Junbalat rivalry became pronounced in the late 19th century, after the elimination of the semi-Druze Shihab dynasty, with whom the A.'s had been allied. During the French Mandate, the A.'s were usually opponents of the Mandatory régime; some of them took an active part in the Pan-Arab nationalist movement and opposed Lebanon's separate status. Thus — 'Adel A. (1882–1954), a right-wing Syrian politician, briefly Deputy Premier and Foreign Minister in 1949. Since 1943, however, they have supported the unwritten "National Pact" and the Maronite-led establishment based mainly on a Maronite-Sunni coalition. Their leader was Majid A. (1904–83), from 1937 many times a Minister, usually Defense Minister. As the Junbalats increasing became the chief spokesmen of Druze demands and opposition, the A.'s influence declined, particularly during and since the civil war from 1975 onward (in which they tried not to become involved and, in contrast to the Junbalats, maintained no real organized "militia"). Since the death of their chief, Majid A., in 1983, and the succession of his son Feisal A., this decline has been aggravated by the lack of strong leadership and an organized military force.

Arsalan, Shakib (1869–1946) Syrian Pan-Arab writer and politician, of Lebanese-Druze origin. A district governor under the Ottoman Empire, A. remained loyal to the Sultan and joined the Arab nationalists only after World War I. In the 1920s A., mostly in exile, was active in the "Syro-Palestinian Congress", which strove to keep Pan-Arab endeavors alive, and was a leading member of its permanent delegation in Geneva. He edited the Pan-Arab weekly *La Nation Arabe* and cultivated contacts with world statesmen (including unsuccessful talks with Zionist leaders). A. later became close to Fascist tendencies and maintained strong ties with Italy and Nazi Germany. He also converted to Islam and drew nearer to Pan-Islamic views. Among his numerous writings many concern Islamic topics, including a detailed biography of the modern Islamic thinker Muhammad Rashid *Rida. A. returned to Syria in 1937, but took no active part in Syrian political affairs. During World War II he returned to Switzerland, where he resumed his contacts with the Axis powers and called on the Arabs to collaborate with the Axis.

al-Asad, Hafez (b. 1928[?]) Syrian officer and statesman, President of Syria since 1971. Born in Qardaha near Lataqia, of *'Alawi origin, A. became a professional officer in the air force. In the 1950s he joined the clandestine officers' cells linked to the *Ba'th party. He took a leading part in the *coup* of Mar. 1963 that brought the *Ba'th* officers to power, and became commander of the air force (promoted to the rank of *Fariq*, Lieutenant-General, in 1968). From 1965 A. was a member of the *Ba'th* High Command — both the "national", i.e. all-Arab, and the "regional"-Syrian one. In the incessant factional struggles that rocked the Syrian *Ba'th* and caused frequent changes in party, army and government leadership, A. sided with the "military" faction of the extreme, doctrinaire "Left" which opposed the *'Aflaq-*Bitar- Hafez faction then in control. He was one of the leaders of the *coup* of Feb. 1966 carried out by the military wing and became a leading figure in the régime established after the *coup*, serving as Acting Defense Minister. However, A. soon fell out with Salah *Jadid, the top leader of the new team, and his associates, and formed a "nationalist" faction. He opposed Jadid's doctrinaire Leftism, rejected rigid ideological definitions and preferred a pragmatic approach to political and economic issues. He opposed total identification with the Soviet Union, chafed at Syria's growing isolation within the Arab world and aimed at closer all-Arab co-operation and a stronger emphasis on the fight against Israel. In Feb. 1969, in a bloodless semi-*coup*, A. gained control of the government and party command, but accepted — reportedly on Egyptian and Russian advice — a compromise providing for a coalition and leaving some of his adversaries in positions of power (e.g. Nur-ul-Din al-*Atassi as President and Prime Minister). When, however, the power struggle resumed, A. seized full control in a semi-*coup* in Nov. 1970 — and this time he kept power, purging and dismissing his opponents and detaining their leaders (for over ten years, as it turned out). He assumed the Premiership, retaining the Defense Ministry, and became Secretary-General of the Ba'th. In Feb. 1971 he nominated a "People's Council", and that Council appointed him President, after the Ba'th command had nominated him. In Mar. 1971 a plebiscite endorsed that election, with A. as the only candidate and 99.2% of the votes in his favor. He was re-elected in Feb. 1978, and for a third seven- year term in Feb. 1985.

Since 1971 A. has given Syria a régime of remarkable stability, with the reins firmly in his own hands. He continued an economic policy of nationalization, a pragmatic state socialism, and kept Syria's economy on an even keel. He established firm constitutional patterns: a Constitution was adopted in 1973, and elections for a People's Council were held, from 1973, every four years — with a Ba'th-led "National Progressive Front" (including the Communist Party) as the only permitted party list, but with Ba'th-approved independent candidates admitted. In fact, the Ba'th apparatus was in firm control, with A. himself as its undisputed chief, and behind the façade of semi-democratic and populist institutions the régime was harshly authoritarian, underpinned by a powerful all-pervasive secret police.

Opposition, apart from exiled politicians, came mainly from orthodox and fundamentalist Muslim-Sunni groups, such as the outlawed *Muslim Brotherhood, and it was aggravated by the fact that A., the Head of State, and many of his close associates belonged to the heretic *'Alawite sect. A. ruthlessly suppressed the Brotherhood (see *Syria) and broke its resistance. Other political and factional struggles were conducted semi-clandestinely within the ruling army and party junta. These intrigues turned into a bitter fight for the succession, as A.'s health deteriorated, since 1983.

In his foreign and inter-Arab policies, A. at first effected a measure of *rapprochement* with the all-Arab main line, taking Syria out of her isolation. He reinforced relations with Egypt, joining in 1971 a *"Federation of Arab Republics" with her and Libya, and entering a close partnership with Egypt towards and during the October 1973 war against Israel. He also obtained all-Arab endorsement for his military intervention in Lebanon in 1976. But then he adopted increasingly hard-line, extremist policies, leading Syria back into the isolation from which he had sought to extricate her. Differences with Egypt had emerged even during the October War; they deepened when Syria joined the "Rejectionist" camp (see *Arab League, *Arab-Israel Conflict) and became its mainstay, and they turned into complete estrangement after *Sadat's moves towards peace with Israel, from 1977, when Syria headed the extremist camp clamoring for Egypt's boycott and expulsion. Tension and mutual hostility between Syria and Iraq mounted under A., to a point that Syria supported Iran against Iraq in the Gulf War, since 1980 — contrary to the all- Arab line. Syria's Arab-endorsed intervention in Lebanon turned into a permanent occupation of northern and eastern Lebanon, and though A. took care not to be dragged into the Lebanese quagmire he became the arbiter of Lebanese internal affairs, through client factions' "militias", and acquired near-total domination of Lebanon (without being able fully to control the situation, end the civil war and get his plans implemented).

Towards Israel A. took a very hard line — though he strictly adhered to disengagement agreements reached and also prevented terrorist attacks from Syrian soil (while encouraging such raids from Lebanese territory). He strove to attain "strategic equality" with Israel, opposed American peace plans, totally rejected Egypt's peace with Israel, and vehemently objected to the Jordanian King's efforts to work out a formula for peace negotiations. His relations with Jordan, aggravated by those efforts and by King

Hussein's alliance with the *PLO under *'Arafat, were anyhow far from friendly — though there were ups and downs, and periods of *rapprochement* in 1975–76 and again from late 1985. A.'s bitter dispute with 'Arafat, originating in the latter's refusal to accept his guidance and subject the PLO to Syrian dictates, was exacerbated by 'Arafat's moderate line and accomodation with Jordan. A. cultivated PLO factions subservient to Syria, instigated and supported an armed revolt within the PLO's main faction, *al-Fataḥ*, in 1983, and waged a war against the PLO forces loyal to 'Arafat, expelling them from Syria and Syrian-occupied eastern and northern Lebanon. Despite his opposition to his predecessors' close alliance with the USSR, A. further cemented that alliance and made Syria even more dependent on the Soviet Union.

In contrast to the erratic flamboyance of Libya's *Qadhdhafi, his close ally, A. conducted both his authoritarian rule of Syria and his extremist foreign policies with cool calculation and suave tactics. Whether A.'s policies of Leftist-authoritarian extremism were ultimately successful, only History will judge; in their execution, in any case, A. proved himself a master-politician.

al-Asad, Rif'at (b. 1936) Syrian officer and politician, a brother of President Hafez al-*Asad and one of the contenders for his succession, deeply involved in an internal power struggle. See *Syria.

'Asir A region on the Arabian coast of the Red Sea, between Yemen and Hijaz, consisting of a coastal plain ("al-Tihama"), with Jizan as its chief town and port, and a mountainous hinterland with the towns of Sabya and Najran. In 1910 the ruler of Sabya, al-Sayyid Muhammad al-Idrissi of the *Idrissi sect and dynasty, rebelled against the Ottoman Sultan. He was defeated with the help of Sharif *Hussein of Mecca, but was saved by Italian intervention. During World War I he rebelled again, in concert with British agents who promised him independence; agreements to that effect were signed in Apr. 1915 and Jan. 1917. When, after the war, the British army withdrew from the coast of Yemen, they allowed Sayyid Muhammad to occupy al-Hudeida, Yemen's chief port. In northern 'A. the *Wahhabi *Sa'udis used a local insurrection to occupy the Abha region in 1919, and again, permanently, in 1923. After Sayyid Muhammad's death in 1923, 'A. was weakened by a dispute over the succession. *Wahhabi-Sa'udi influence continued penetrating from the North, and Yemeni-*Zeidi tribesmen conquered Hudeida (1925). In 1926 the weakened, quarrelling Idrissi princes asked for Sa'udi patronage, and in 1933 'A. was formally annexed by Sa'udi Arabia. The Imam of Yemen disputed that annexation and claimed 'A. Yemeni raids, from late 1932, were encouraged by Italy. In 1934 they led to a war in which Ibn Sa'ud defeated the Imam. The peace treaty of Ta'if allotted 'A. to Sa'udia. During the Yemeni civil war, 1962–67, Egyptian planes occasionally bombed Najran, claiming that it was part of Yemen. While Yemen could not seriously challenge Sa'udi possession of 'A., she maintained vague claims until Mar. 1973, when a border agreement reconfirmed Sa'udia's possession.

Assyrians Alternative name for the Nestorian Christians — surviving, in the 19th century, mainly in the Zagros mountains of Kurdistan in eastern Anatolia, between Lake Van and Lake Urmia, and in northern Mesopotamia (an area divided after World War I among Turkey, Iran and Iraq).

The Nestorian Church seceded from the main body of Christianity after the Council of Ephesus, 431, when Nestorios, the Patriarch of Constantinople, and his followers rejected the doctrine of the divine nature of Christ confirmed at that Council. The description of the Nestorians as A. came into use much later; the implied link to the A. of antiquity has no proven historical basis (except that *all* inhabitants of northern Iraq may trace their origins in part to the A. and Babylonians of old). The Nestorians-A. spoke an Eastern Syriac-Aramaic tongue, but today its use is largely confined to their liturgy. In the course of the centuries the A., divided into several tribes, became a small minority struggling for survival in their remote mountain strongholds, against the dominant Muslim populations and other hostile communities. Their number — estimated at c. 100,000 in the 19th century — also dwindled because of defections to other Christian creeds — mainly to the Catholic Church, through the *Uniate (the *Chaldeans), and since the 19th century to Protestant churches.

Until World War I most A. lived within the

Ottoman Empire. During the war they were suspected of having connections with enemy countries — Britain, and mainly Russia — and were harassed and persecuted. After repeated attacks by Turks and Kurds, some 50–70,000 A. crossed into Iran, led by their Patriarch, the Catholicos, and joined the Russian forces occupying northern Iran. When the Russians occupied parts of eastern Anatolia, the A. collaborated with them, and when the Russians withdrew, they were exposed to Turkish retaliation. At the end of the war, more A. left for Russian-governed areas of the Caucasus. A main group of A. marched to join the British forces in Iraq, followed by their families, and some 50,000 of them were placed by the British in refugee camps in Iraq, where many perished. Many of the men were employed by the British as guards, later organized into special levies.

Vague plans, between the end of World War I and the victorious emergence of Kemalist Turkey, to form an independent state for a Syriac-language nation — the A., the Chaldeans and the Syrian-Orthodox *Jacobites — came to naught. A. who tried to return to their ancestral homes were soon re-expelled by the Turks. They settled in a few areas in northern Iraq vacated by Turks and Kurds, but these were too small to maintain all the A. In 1932, when the British Mandate in Iraq ended, many of them were practically still refugees.

In independent Iraq the A. met with considerable Iraqi animosity, as they were clamoring for autonomy and were, moreover, identified with the intensely unpopular armed levies employed by the British. Their Kurdish neighbors were also hostile. Soon, bloody clashes broke out, and in Aug. 1933 hundreds of A. were killed in a massacre. An exodus of thousands followed; some 4,000 migrated to America, about 6,000 to Syria, and some to Lebanon. The French, with the support of the League of Nations, tried to settle some of the A. in Syria, but independent Syria discontinued that project. Other settlement schemes proposed in the League of Nations did not materialize. 30–35,000 A. remained in Iraq; gradually, and particularly since Kurdish rebellions were resumed in northern Iraq in the 1950s, many of them moved to Baghdad. Of those settled in north-western Iran, too, many moved to the cities, principally to Tehran. The A. were not active in the Iraqi (or Iranian) nationalist movement or other political organizations. Some of them joined Communist groups. In recent decades no further crises have hit the A. in Iraq and they seem to have settled down. Moreover, in Apr. 1972 the Iraqi *Ba'th régime, in the course of efforts to come to terms with Iraq's restless minorities (and to create the impression that the partial autonomy given to the Kurds was part of a larger scheme), granted the Syriac-speaking communities — i.e., the A. and the Chaldeans — a measure of cultural autonomy. Little has been heard of the actual implementation of that decree.

The number of Nestorian A. is estimated at 100–150,000: 15–30,000 or more in the Soviet Union (where they have no republic or autonomous area of their own); c. 80,000 in the ME — 35–40,000 in Iraq, 20–30,000 in Iran, c. 15,000 in Syria; the rest reside in countries of Europe and America (c. 10,000 in the USA).

The Nestorian ecclesiastical hierarchy is headed by the Catholicos, who always bears the title "Mar Sham'oun" (as the successor of the Apostle Simon Petrus) and whose office passes from uncle to nephew. The Catholicos' seat, since the 8th century in Baghdad, was in recent centuries in Mosul; but in 1933 Mar Sham'oun XXI Eshai fled (or was exiled) to Cyprus, from where he later went to the USA, maintaining little contact with his flock in the ME. His permanent absence — and also the fact that he broke the rule of celibacy by marrying — caused a schism, and in 1968 part of the A. clergy in Iraq elected the Metropolitan Bishop of Baghdad as (rival) Catholicos. Mar Sham'oun Eshai was assassinated in California in 1975.

Aswan Dam The first dam on the *Nile River in Upper Egypt constructed by British engineers in 1898–1902 near A. It partially controlled the Nile floods and made possible the transfer of large tracts of land from basin-flooding to permanent irrigation. Its height was raised in 1907–12 and again in 1933–35, and its storage lake held c. 5,500 m. cubic meters (mcm). Several more recent development schemes were based on that original AD, such as an electric power station and a fertilizer plant, both opened in 1960.

Egypt's most important and most publicized development project since the mid-1950s was the construction of a new, much bigger AD (the

"High Dam"), five miles south of the original structure. Work was begun in 1960 and completed in 1970, and the High Dam and its power plant were formally opened in Jan. 1971. One of the world's largest man-made lakes, named Lake Nasser, formed behind it, 360 mi. long, covering c. 2,000 sq. mi. and holding 140–160,000 mcm. The regulated release of its waters added 1.5–2m. acres to Egypt's irrigated area and transformed additional areas, estimated at 700,000 to nearly 1m. acres, from partially irrigated one-crop land into permanently irrigated land with several crops each year. The High AD's power plant had a generating capacity of more than 2m.kw., producing up to 6,000m. kwh. per annum (first estimates of 10,000m. kwh. proved excessive). That power contributed significantly to Egypt's industrialization, with several plants constructed near the AD, and enabled the linking of all Egypt's villages to the national power grid. The cost of the construction of the AD was estimated at c. $1,500m.

Lake Nasser flooded agricultural land and villages with a population of more than 100,000, mostly *Nubian, about half of them in Sudan. Egypt paid compensation to Sudan, and both countries resettled the displaced villagers elsewhere; a large part of them later drifted back and re-established villages on both shores of Lake Nasser. The lake also inundated several sites of ancient Egyptian monuments; the best-known among them, the temple of Abu Simbel, was lifted to higher ground, at tremendous cost, by an international operation with contributions from many nations.

The regulation of the Nile's seasonal floods through the High Dam and its storage lake, and the resulting expansion of perennial irrigation, have also had negative side-effects. In the absence of the silt deposited by the Nile in its annual flood before the AD was erected, stronger erosion along the river and an increase in soil salinity have set in. It is also feared that Egypt's coastline might recede and sea-water might seep in. The incidence of Bilharzia has also increased. Sardine fishing off the Egyptian coast was also affected to a degree not yet clearly ascertained. The Government of Egypt is endeavoring to counteract these negative effects of the AD.

The AD project in its initial stages was the subject of an international crisis. Following Egypt's arms deal of 1955 with the Soviet Bloc, the USA and the International Bank in 1956 cancelled plans to aid the project financially. Egypt reacted by nationalizing the *Suez Canal, declaring that its revenues would be used to finance the construction of the AD — a step that led to the Anglo-French *Suez War of 1956. Egypt also turned to the USSR with a request for aid — and the USSR responded. Soviet credits — variously estimated at 220–1,300m. rubles, 300–500m. or more, about one quarter of the cost — were the project's main source of foreign finance, and Soviet engineers and technicians took a leading part in its design and construction, using mainly Soviet equipment and supplying most of the machinery needed. USSR President Podgorny attended the festive opening of the AD. In the later 1970s much of the machinery turned out to be deficient, most of the power turbines were not properly operating and in constant need of repair. After the change that had occurred in Egypt's political orientation, American experts began executing the repairs needed and replacing parts of the machinery with American equipment.

al-Atassi Syrian land-owning clan of notables which provided many leaders of modern Syria. It was centered in Homs and wielded considerable influence in all of northern Syria. When Syria had a parliamentary régime and political parties were operating, leaders of the A. clan were often in opposition to the mainstream of the nationalist movement and the Damascus government. In the 1940s they were among the founders and leaders of the "People's Party".

The following were prominent members of the family: Hashem al-A. and Nur-ul-Din al-A., both Presidents of Syria — see entries below. 'Adnan al-A. (b. 1905), the son of Hashem al-A. — in the 1950s among the leaders of the "People's Party" and Minister in several governments. Accused, in 1956–57, of playing a leading rôle in an "Iraqi-British-American plot", tried and sentenced to death in Feb. 1957 (commuted to prison for life), pardoned by Nasser in Sept. 1960 and released into forced residence in Cairo, he did not return to play an active part in Syrian politics. Feidi al-A., also a leader of the "People's Party" in the 1950s and a Minister in several governments. He was accused in 1956–57 of involvement in the Iraqi plot mentioned, tried (*in absentia*, as he had fled) and acquitted. He was not further active in Syrian politics. Feisal al-A., one of the leaders of the military *coup* which overthrew Adib *Shishakli in Feb. 1954, but not among the leaders of the régime that followed. Dr. Jamal al-A., active as a young psychiatrist and lecturer in the *Ba'ath group and for some time editor of its organ *al-Jumhuriyya* (which was closed in 1959 under Nasser). He later drifted away from the Ba'th and became a leader of the Nasserist "Arab Socialist Union"; in the numerous factional splits of that group he headed, in the 1960s and 1970s, a faction that refused to cooperate with the Ba'th and its government and was one of the founders of an anti-Ba'th "National Progressive Front" in exile. Col. Louay al-A. (b. 1926), close to the Ba'th officers' group, he was, after the Ba'th *coup* of 1963, briefly Chief of Staff and President of the Revolutionary Council, but was removed in July 1963 in the course of Ba'th-Nasserist and intra-Ba'th factional struggles.

al-Atassi, Hashem (1874?–1960) Syrian politician, three times President of Syria. Educated in Istanbul, A. served as district governor in the Ottoman administration. In 1920 he chaired the nationalist Syrian-Arab Congress and was for a short time Prime Minister of the government Amir *Feisal tried to set up in Damascus. Under the French Mandate he was one of the leaders of the "National Bloc" which fought for Syrian independence. He headed the delegation which signed the Franco-Syrian Treaty of 1936 providing for Syria's independence with certain privileges for France — a treaty that was not ratified by France and remained abortive. He was President of Syria, 1936–39. In the 1940s A. drifted away from the mainstream Damascus faction of the National Bloc. He took no active part in the final struggle for complete independence, 1945–46, and the Syrian governments that ensued. In 1949, after *Hinnawi's *coup*, he became Prime Minister, and in Dec. 1949, following *Shishakli's *coup*, President; but Shishakli was the real ruler, behind the scenes, and the President's powers were limited, almost nominal. When the politicians failed in their struggle with the dictator, A. resigned in 1951 and began working for the overthrow of Shishakli. Following Shishakli's fall, A. returned to the Presidency in 1954; but as real power was again in the hands of shifting officers' cliques, he was frustrated, resigned in Sept. 1955, and retired from politics.

al-Atassi, Nur-ul-Din (b. 1929?) Syrian politician. President of Syria 1966–70. A physician (Damascus University, 1955), A. was close to the *Ba'th group. After the Ba'th officers' *coup* of 1963 he became Minister of Interior, 1963–64, Deputy Prime Minister, 1964–65, and member of the Revolutionary Council and the Presidential Council, 1964. In the struggle between rival Ba'th factions he was close to the extremist-Leftist "military" group, and after that faction came to power in the *coup* of Feb. 1966, he was made President and Secretary-General of both the "national" (i.e., all-Arab) and "regional" (Syrian) command of the Ba'th party (the wing ruling Syria). From 1968 to 1970 A. also served as Prime Minister. In the struggle between the factions of Hafez al-*Asad and Salah *Jadid, he sided with the latter, but tried to mediate. After Asad's semi-*coup* of 1969, A. retained his posts, as part of a compromise settlement; but when Asad took full control in Nov. 1970, A. was dismissed from his three posts as President, Prime Minister and Secretary-General, and imprisoned. There were conflicting reports concerning his release. He was reportedly offered a release late in 1980, but was returned to jail or house arrest when he refused to cooperate. Apparently he was released later, but was not allowed to return to political activities.

al-Atrash Clan of traditional leaders of the *Druze in the Jabal al-Duruz (Druze Mountain) region of South-East Syria. According to one tradition the family is of Kurdish origin, lived in Lebanon and moved to the Syrian Druze Mountain in the 1860s. Its heads were semi-feudal *de facto* rulers and were sometimes appointed governor of their district (thus, Salim al-A. — head of the clan and the Mountain since 1914, was recognized as governor by both Amir *Feisal's short-lived régime and the French, 1920–21; he died in 1923). In recent decades the clan has lost much of its status and influence.

Prominent in the last generation or two: Sultan al-A. (1886?1891?–1982) emerged in the 1920s as main leader, though he never held official positions. He was close to Amir Feisal and later to his brother Amir *'Abdullah of Transjordan and supported the latter's *"Greater Syria" scheme. He triggered and led the Druze revolt of 1925 that turned into a general Syrian uprising, and subsequently spent ten years in exile in Transjordan. He returned to Syria in 1937. Though respected as a legendary leader and pulling strings behind the scenes, he was not openly active in Syrian politics. He was reportedly instrumental in the uprising that led, early in 1954, to the overthrow of *Shishakli.

Sultan's brother Zeid al-A. (b. 1905) was also active in the revolt of 1925, but did not become a major leader. He was in exile in Transjordan, for some time as Chamberlain to Amir 'Abdullah, returned to Syria in 1937 and served in the army and police. In the mid-1950s he was accused of being involved in an "Iraqi-British-American plot" and put on trial in 1957. Sultan's son Mansur al-A. (b. 1925) did not attain his father's position as leader of the clan. He was, from the 1950s, close to the *Ba'th group and served as a minister, 1962–64, and briefly, in 1964, as a member of the Presidential Council. After the take-over by the Ba'th's extremist military faction in the coup of 1966 he was detained. He was released in 1967 and has since not been active in Syrian politics.

Hassan al-A. (b. 1905), carrying the title "Amir", was a member of Parliament several times, a district governor (including the district of Jabal al-Duruz, 1937–42), and a minister in 1942–43 and in the 1950s. Since the rise to power of Leftist officers, in the 1950s, and the Ba'th group since 1963, he has not been active in politics, but he was suspected of plotting against the government and detained several times. In 1957 he was tried, in absentia, for involvement in an "Iraqi-British plot" and sentenced to death (commuted to prison for life). In 1968–69 he was tried again — this time for involvement in Salim Hatum's abortive coup of 1966. He escaped to Jordan but was kidnapped in 1968 by Syrian irregulars. He was sentenced in 1970 to two years of prison but released on account of his age.

Other well-known members of the clan were Farid al-A. (1916–74) — a popular singer and composer of hit songs, and his sister Amal al-A. (1917–44, known as Ismahan) — a singer and movie-star killed in Cairo in a mysterious accident; since she was involved in high society intrigues, murder was suspected.

al-Azhar Famous center for the teaching of Islam, in Cairo, founded in 970 by the Fatimid conquerors of Egypt as a mosque and center of Shi'i-*Isma'ili preaching and teaching. Under the Sunni Ayyubids al-A. was transformed, in the 12th century, into a Sunni orthodox center. Since the 16th century it has been regarded as the principal institution of Islamic religious teaching. From the 19th century onwards several attempts were made, both from inside and outside al-A., to reform its medieval methods of teaching. These efforts reached their peak with "Law No. 103" of 1961 which transformed al-A. into one of Egypt's five state universities. It now admits women and has several faculties of secular studies. Its main function, however, has remained that of religious teaching and preaching. Al-A. trains Islamic judges, preachers etc. (Qadis, Muftis, Khatibs) for many Muslim countries — to a great extent on its own or Egyptian government scholarships — and sends out teachers. It issues legal-religious opinions and decisions (Fatwa), in response to questions from all over the Islamic world. It arranges conferences and publishes Islamic writings and periodicals, the best known of which is the monthly Majallat al-A., and it encourages Islamic missionary work, especially in Africa and the Far East. The 'Ulama' of al-A. are also involved in politics, promoting the domination of Islamic teachings and the Islamic law (the *Shari'a) in Egyptian society and legislation. They usually cooperate with the government. In *Nasser's days, for instance, they propounded the doctrine of Islamic Socialism, while in recent years they strongly support the efforts of Presidents *Sadat and *Mubarak to strengthen the country's conservative-Islamic foundations while combating radical Islamic organizations (like the *Muslim Brothers — a group that al-A. has opposed since its inception — and more extremist groups). Al-A. also issued Fatwas serving Egypt's foreign policies — e.g., a decree denouncing Iraq's anti-Egyptian and pro-Communist leaders (1959), and several Fatwas against Israel, including calls for *Jihad (holy war) against her. Al-A.'s publications also contain anti-Semitic material. In 1979, however, an al-A. Fatwa justified and endorsed Sadat's peace treaty with Israel.

In recent years, al-A. has about 20,000 university-level students (several thousands — foreign), and c. 100,000 at primary and secondary schools affiliated to it.

al-Azhari, Isma'il (1900? 1902?–69) Sudanese politician. Educated at Gordon College,

Khartoum, and the American University of Beirut, A. served in the Sudan Department of Education, 1921–46. In 1938 he organized the "Graduates' General Congress", the association of graduates of Gordon College and intermediate schools, most of them civil servants, that formed the nucleus of Sudan's nationalist movement. A. himself was its secretary. In 1943 he organized Sudan's first political party, the *Ashiqqa'* (Brothers). He and his group favored union with Egypt, collaborating with the *Khatmiyya order. In 1952, various "Unionist" factions merged in the "National Unionist Party" and A. became its President. The NUP won the 1953 elections, during the transition period towards self-rule, and in Jan. 1954 A. became Sudan's first Prime Minister. Although in principle favoring union with Egypt, he and his government led Sudan to independence in Dec. 1955–Jan. 1956. He continued as independent Sudan's Prime Minister, heading a coalition, but in July 1956 lost his majority and became leader of the opposition until the fall of the parliamentary régime in 1958. In 1961–62 he was detained by General *'Abbud's military régime. A. played a part in the 1964 *coup* which restored civilian-political government. In 1965 he was elected a member, and later permanent chairman, of the Presidential Council, i.e. Head-of-State, a post he held until *Numeiri's *coup* of May 1969. The new régime kept him under house arrest until his death in Aug. 1969.

al-'Azma, Yussuf Syrian politician, scion of a family of Damascus notables. In 1920, 'A. was Minister of War in Amir *Feisal's short-lived administration. When the French Army advanced on Damascus from Lebanon, he organized and commanded an Arab force of soldiers and volunteers to resist the French. The force was defeated and largely annihilated at the Maisalun Pass, and 'A. was killed in the battle. After his death he became a national hero and a symbol of the resistance to French rule. "Maisalun Day", 26 July, is a day of national mourning in Syria.

Other members of the al-'A. clan were also active in the nationalist movement and held various government positions in Syria. Thus Nabih al-'A. was an activist in Pan-Arab nationalist organizations, but did not find a prominent place in independent Syria's establishment. 'Adel al-'A. (died 1952), also active in the nationalist struggle, became a governor and, in 1948–49, a Minister. Bashir al-'A. was briefly Prime Minister in 1962.

al-'Azm, Khaled (1960–65) Syrian politician. Scion of a wealthy family of Damascus notables which dominated the city in the 18th century and continued to provide administrators and notables. Al-'A. was an independent, not belonging to the mainstream "National Bloc" that led Syria to independence and governed her in the first years after independence; sometimes he formed short-lived parliamentary factions of his own. He was a Minister in many governments and several times Prime Minister — in 1941–42 under the French Vichy régime; 1948–49 (until removed by the *coup* of Husni *Za'im); 1949–50; and 1951 under *Shishakli. In 1955–57 he served as Minister of Defense, Finance and Deputy Prime Minister. Although himself a wealthy land-owner and industrialist, he vigorously fostered close ties between Syria and the Soviet Union and was therefore considered by some as a "Leftist". 'A. was not among the advocates of Syro-Egyptian union, and when the two countries merged into the United Arab Republic in 1958, he ceased political activity. After Syria's secession in 1961 and the re-establishment of her independence, he became once more Prime Minister, in 1962–63. He was overthrown by the *Ba'th officers' *coup* of Mar. 1963 and went into exile in Lebanon, where he died. A volume of al-'A.'s memoirs was published posthumously in 1973.

'Azzam, 'Abd-ul-Rahman (1893?–1976) Egyptian diplomat and politician. Studied medicine in London, but did not become a practising physician. From his youth an active Arab nationalist, 'A. for some time joined Libyan guerrillas resisting the Italian conquerors, after 1911–12. He was a member of Parliament, 1924–36. At first he was an adherent of the *Wafd*, but since the 1930s he joined the anti-*Wafd*ist camp and was, among its various factions, particularly close to 'Ali *Maher. From 1936 to 1945 'A. joined Egypt's diplomatic service — first as Minister to Iraq, Iran and Sa'udia, and from 1940 as Minister to Turkey; in 1939 he briefly was counselor to the Arab delegations to the London Conference on Palestine. His diplomatic service was interrupted for a year, when he joined 'Ali Maher's Government, 1939–40, as Minister of *Waqf* (religious endowments), and later of Social Affairs. Since the early 1930s 'A. actively advocated an "Arab orientation" of Egypt's policy, promoted her involvement in pan-Arab affairs, and himself took part in several all-Arab congresses and in continuous efforts at all-Arab organization. He combined a fervent Pan-Arabism with pronounced Islamic tendencies. When, in 1945, the League of Arab States was established, 'A. became its Secretary-General and chief architect. He served as Secretary-General until 1952. As he was *persona non grata* with the Nasserist régime, he was not politically active since 1952 and even absented himself from Egypt. He returned in 1972, but did not resume political activities. His memoirs were serialized, in Arabic, in Egyptian and Lebanese weeklies in 1950 and 1972.

B

Ba'ath See *Ba'th.
Bab al-Mandeb (Arabic: Gate of Lament) Straits connecting the *Red Sea and the Gulf of 'Aden (the Indian Ocean) — of great strategic importance, particularly since after the opening of the *Suez Canal they became the main thoroughfare from the Mediterranean to India and the Far East. The Straits are divided by *Perim Island into a shallow 2.2 mi. wide eastern channel and a western one, deeper and 17.4 mi. wide. They are bordered on the Arabian side by South Yemen and Yemen, and on the African side by Ethiopia and Djibouti. They were controlled by Britain from 1851 through her possession of Perim. Since gaining control of Perim and part of the eastern coast in 1967, newly independent South Yemen has several times threatened to impede the freedom of shipping through the Straits for political reasons, e.g. to prevent the passage of Israeli or Israel-bound shipping; South Yemen reportedly permitted Palestinian-Arab guerrillas to establish themselves, for that purpose, on Perim (Yemen did the same for the *Qamaran Islands farther North). An Israel-bound oil tanker was shelled, probably by guerrillas, in June 1971. Reports, in 1972–73, of an Israeli military presence on islands near the African coast, were denied. During the *October War of 1973 the Egyptian navy tried to close the Straits to Israel. In Nov. 1973 it was reportedly agreed to remove that blockade — though the matter is not mentioned in the published text of the "Six Point Agreement". The B. al-M. Straits are not mentioned in the Egypt-Israel Peace Treaty of 1979, but they were reportedly discussed in the negotiations leading to it and it was agreed that freedom of shipping through them should be safeguarded.

Babism See *Baha'is.
al-Badr, Muhammad (b. 1926) Yemeni prince, Imam of Yemen (i.e. head of the *Zeidi community and ruler of the state), 1962–70. Eldest son of Imam *Ahmad b. Yahya, Prince al-B. served his father in various capacities, both consultative and executive. His status and influence increased after he succeeded, in 1955, in rallying the northern Bakil and Hashed tribal federations to save his father from defeat by a serious rebellion. In 1956 and 1958 he visited Russia and China as his father's representative (and got the reputation of being somewhat "Leftist" and of pushing Yemen towards growing links with the Soviet Bloc). In Imam Ahmad's absence, e.g. in 1959, al-B. acted as Imam, and in 1961 his father formally appointed him Crown Prince. On the death of Imam Ahmad, in Sept. 1962, al-B. became Imam. A week later he was overthrown by an officers' *coup* and reported killed. But early in Oct. he reappeared in the northern mountains and soon rallied various tribes to lead them into war against the Republic proclaimed in San'a. In the civil war that ensued, he retained or recovered control of parts of Yemen — changing with the shifting fortunes of war. He was generally supported by the northern Zeidi tribes, and by Sa'udi Arabia (while Egypt sent an expeditionary force to support the Republic). But his control of his own Royalist camp was precarious, and other princes, mainly his uncle Prince Hassan b. Yahya, frequently had to support (or, virtually, to dispute) his flagging leadership. A sick man, Imam al-B. had to go for a cure in Sa'udia and was out of Yemen during the critical period of Nov. 1966 to Sept. 1968. Late in 1966 his power was formally reduced, in his absence, by the formation of an "Imamate Council" under Prince Muhammad b.

Hussein. Early in 1969, however, al-B. resumed power. The Royalist-Republican reconciliation that ended the civil war in 1970 by-passed him, as it was based on the general acceptance of a republican régime, the abolition of the Imam-King and the permanent exclusion of the royal Hamid-ul-Din family. Al-B. has not formally abdicated, nor has he renounced his claims and titles; but he acquiesced in the abolition of the royal régime and the Imamate and went into exile in London. No serious efforts to restore the royal Imamate have been reported.

Badran, Mudar (b. 1934)   Jordanian administrator and politician. After rising to a senior position with the Royal Court and, mainly, in the security services, B. became a Minister in 1973 and Prime Minister 1976–79 and 1980–84.

Baghdad Pact   Unofficial name for a defense treaty ("Pact of Mutual Co-operation") concluded between Iraq and Turkey on 24 Feb. 1955. That treaty had been preceded by a Turkish-Pakistani agreement of Apr. 1954 and bilateral military aid agreements between the USA and Turkey, Iraq and Pakistan in Apr.-May 1954. Britain, Iran and Pakistan joined the BP in 1955, while the USA, its prime mover and main source of support and finance, considered herself an associate member. The BP was the cornerstone of Western, particularly American, plans for a ME defense system. Overtures for regional defense arrangements had been rebuffed by Egypt and other ASt's in 1951. Negotiations were resumed in 1953–54 — and now emphasized the defense of the "Northern Tier" (Turkey-Iran-Pakistan), with Iraq as the connecting link to the AC's. They culminated in the BP. But Iraq was the only Arab member-state. Attempts to get other ASt's to join were rather half-hearted, as the stress was now on the "Northern Tier" conception, and failed.

The BP was vigorously denounced by Egypt as introducing great-power rivalries and the cold war into the Middle East, dividing the Arab world and threatening Egypt with encirclement. Egypt began the creation of a counter-alliance, and the division of the Arab states into rival camps hardened. Egypt's alienation from the West culminated in 1955–56 in her alliance with the Soviet Bloc. Efforts to attract AC's to join the BP, half-hearted as they were, caused a major crisis in Jordan late in 1955, and contributed to the fear of Western, Iraqi and Turkish "plots" that drove Syria in 1957–58 into union with Egypt. Thus, the BP failed in its main purpose: to erect a barrier against Soviet penetration of the Middle East. It was, in fact, counter-productive.

Iraq's revolutionary, anti-Western government, after General *Qassem's *coup* of July 1958, formally withdrew from the BP in Mar. 1959. In 1959 the resultant rump alliance was renamed "Central Treaty Organization" (*CENTO) and shifted its emphasis to schemes of economic and social co-operation. In 1964 it established a "Regional Co-operation for Development" group (RCD). However, having lost most of its political and military significance, CENTO-RCD had but little impact. In Feb. 1979 Iran too, now revolutionary, withdrew. As the group now had little meaning, Turkey and Pakistan also withdrew and CENTO ceased to exist.

Baghdad Railway   A project to extend the Anatolian Railway to B. and the Persian Gulf. In 1899, Sultan *Abd-ul-Hamid II granted a concession to the Deutsche Bank and the German-Anatolian Railway Company — in line with the Ottoman government's plans to improve communications within the Empire. The BR project was, however, an object of intense rivalry between German, French and British companies. In 1903 a definite concession was granted to the newly formed BR Company, in which German interests predominated. Britain, France and Russia, apprehensive of expanding German power and fearing for their own interests, remained hostile to the project, but ultimately reached agreements with Germany. Britain, the principal objector, stipulated in agreements concluded with the Ottoman Empire and Germany in 1911–14 that, contrary to the original plans, the railway should not extend beyond Basra to the Persian Gulf. The diplomatic activity generated by the BR project continued for 15 years, from 1899 to the outbreak of World War I, creating several minor crises. The construction of the line was hampered by technical and financial difficulties. By 1917 it had been completed from the Anatolian side up to Nuseibin (on what later became the Turkish-Syrian frontier) and working from the south, from Baghdad to Samarra. The Nuseibin-Mosul-Samarra gap, c. 300 mi., was closed only in 1939–40, under the auspices of France and Britain (as the Mandate powers in Iraq and Syria), and the first Istanbul-B. train rolled in July 1940. (By that time, railways in general, and the BR in particular, had lost much of their strategic-imperial import.)

Baha'is Adherents of an eclectic religion founded in Persia in 1862–63 by Mirza Hussein 'Ali, "Baha'-ullah" (1817–92). Baha'ism grew out of Babism, a sectarian deviation of Shi'i Islam that was proclaimed in 1843 by 'Ali Muhammad of Shiraz (1819–50) "Bab-ul-Din" or "The Bab" ("The Gate of the Faith", the forerunner of salvation and the end of days). The Bab was considered to be a heretic and was executed, and his followers were persecuted and deported. The B., whose creed stresses the unity of all religions, world peace and universal education, are also considered by many Muslims as heretic deviators from Islam. They were sometimes banned and persecuted in Persia and other Islamic countries. Baha'-ullah himself was deported and taken by the Ottoman authorities to Acre, in Palestine (1868). At present Baha'ism is outlawed in Morocco, Egypt and Syria (since 1960), and Iraq (since 1970); in Iran the B. are considered to be non-believers and are harassed or persecuted by the Islamic régime.

The B. spiritual leadership is the "Universal House of Justice", composed of nine "Hands". The main leader or Guardian, after Baha'-ullah's death, was his son 'Abbas Effendi, 'Abd-ul-Baha' (1844–1921), who was succeeded by his grandson Shogi Effendi (1896–1957). The latter was followed by his uncle Amin Effendi (1881–1974), whose leadership was disputed. The B. revere the tomb of the Bab, in Haifa, and that of Baha'-ullah, in Acre, as holy places. The B. developed vigorous missionary activities and attracted many followers in the West. Their number is variously estimated at 5 m. or more (they claim over 10 m.), of whom 50–100,000 live in Iran (they claim 700,000 to 1 m.) and a few thousands in Arab countries.

Bahrain Group of 33 islands in the Persian Gulf, between the Qatar peninsula and the Sa'udi Arabian coast (the largest island is about 12 mi. from the coast). Area: 230 sq.mi. The population is concentrated mainly on two islands: B. itself and Muharraq, which are connected by a causeway, and numbers 351,000 according to a census of 1981; later estimates put it at up to 400,000. According to the census, it included 115,000 foreigners, mainly A.'s from other countries, Persians, Pakistanis and Indians; later estimates counted up to 200,000 foreigners — 40–50% of the population and the work force. The indigenous inhabitants are mostly A., though a considerable part claim Persian origin and an estimated 10–20% speak Persian as their mother-tongue, and Muslim — with about 170,000 Shi'is constituting c. 60% of the indigenous population. More than half of the population lives in the two main cities: Manama, the capital, and Muharraq.

B. Island has been settled since ancient times because of its springs and oases. Before the A.'s named it al-B. (The Two Seas), it was known as Dilmun. Since the Middle Ages it was famous for its pearl fishing. After some decades of Portuguese rule in the 16th century, B. was ruled intermittently by Persia (1602–1782). While Persia continued claiming sovereignty, the ruler since 1783 has been an A. sheikh (since 1971: "Amir") from the house of al-Khalifa; the present Amir is Sheikh 'Issa ibn Salman al-Khalifa (b. 1933; ruler since 1961). A Government was formally constituted in 1971, with the ruler's brother, Sheikh Khalifa ibn Salman, as Prime Minister and several other members of the ruling family among the Ministers.

In the 19th century Great Britain became the dominating power in the Gulf and established, by several treaties and particularly one of 1880, a Protectorate over B. too. She also installed a military and naval base (expanded in 1966, towards the liquidation of the British base in *'Aden). When Britain announced, in 1968, her decision to renounce her Protectorate and withdraw her forces from the Persian Gulf in 1971, Iran revived her old claim to sovereignty over B. She agreed, however, to a public opinion poll to be supervised by the Secretary-General of the UN. Such a poll took place in Apr. 1970, and a decisive majority favored independence. Iran acquiesced. But under her new, Islamic-revolutionary régime, since 1979, she resumed claims and subversive activities, now in the name of Islamic fundamentalism. B. planned to join a federation of Arab Gulf principalities (see *Trucial 'Oman, *United Arab Emirates), but then withdrew, preferring separate independence — which she proclaimed in Aug. 1971. Since 1981 she is a member of the "Gulf Co-operation Council" established in that year by Sa'udia and the five Gulf principalities. The British base was officially abolished in 1971, but B. kept her facilities at Britain's disposal in a more limited way. Moreover, in 1971 she granted similar facilities to the USA, amounting virtually to a naval base. This agreement was terminated in 1973, for 1976–77, and in mid-1977 the US base was handed over. Certain "minor" facilities, however, remained at the disposal of the US.

Demands for a measure of popular government and free political organization have been voiced in B. since the 1930s, but attempts to establish elected councils were not entirely successful. In the 1950s and 1960s, such demands were renewed, and the ruler set up partly elected advisory councils for health, education etc. In the late 1960s and early 1970s, political agitation revived — supported or triggered by foreign workers with *Nasserist, *Ba'th, *PLO leanings and by underground groups considered "Leftist", mainly Shi'i, partly based abroad and supported by foreign interests (South Yemen, Iraq). This led to unrest and riots that were suppressed. However, late in 1972 the ruler granted a measure of self-government: a Constituent Assembly was elected (with government ministers and appointees of the Amir joining the 22 elected members), and in 1973 a Constitution was duly proclaimed. Under that constitution, elections for a National Assembly were held in Dec. 1973. In 1974–75, however, agitation was resumed by a "Popular Front" that was considered subversive, Leftist and linked with foreign revolutionary plots, but had supporters within the National Assembly. In 1975 the Assembly was dissolved and has not been re-constituted since. In Dec. 1981 an attempt to topple the régime and set up an Islamic republic on the *Khomeini pattern — reportedly instigated and organized by Iran — was foiled. There has been no major unrest since.

B.'s economy, in the past principally fisheries and pearl fishing, has been based mainly on oil since the 1930s, and since the 1960s on banking services and a measure of industrialization. An American company discovered oil in 1932 and started production in 1933 — for data on production and revenues (never very large and fully nationalized since 1979) see *oil. Oil revenue has been declining in the 1980s. Yet it has provided the bulk of B.'s national income and government revenue and made possible the gradual development of other branches of economy.

The port of Manama was developed as a free port and serves the entire region; an international airport was built. A 15 mi., $1,200 m. causeway connecting B. to Sa'udi Arabia and financed by the latter, was opened in Nov. 1986. A large drydock was built, after much controversy and against a vigorous counter-bid by Dubai, by the Organization of Arab Petroleum-Exporting Countries (*OAPEC), and opened in 1977. An aluminium plant, based on imported raw materials, was built with the participation of American and German companies, and opened in 1971. Since the mid-1970s B. has become a major financial center, with some 70 international banks operating, many of them as "offshore" banks. Foreign banks are now the second-biggest employer.

al-Bakr, Ahmad Hassan (1912? 1914?–1982) Iraqi officer and politician, President of Iraq 1968–79. B. belonged to the group of "Free Officers" who plotted and carried out the revolution of July 1958; but, favoring a more active Pan-Arab policy and an Iraqi-Egyptian union, he soon fell out with *Qassem, the new ruler, and was removed from the army. He took a leading part in the *Ba'th-led *coup* that toppled Qassem in Feb. 1963 and became Prime Minister. When his *Ba'th* Government was dismissed by President 'Abd-ul-Salam *'Aref, in Nov. 1963, B. continued serving the new régime for a few weeks as Deputy Premier, but resigned in Jan. 1964. While probably not belonging to the inner core of the original *Ba'th* officers' group, he was in close contact with them. In July 1968 he led a group of *Ba'th* men and other officers in a *coup* that toppled 'Abd-ul-Rahman 'Aref, and became President. Less than two weeks later he ousted his non-*Ba'th* partners, Col. 'Abd-ul-Razzaq Na'if (Nayef), then Prime Minister, and his group. In the *Ba'th* régime that ensued he assumed, in addition to the Presidency, the premiership and the supreme command of the armed forces, and also became chairman of the Revolutionary Command Council. B. and his associates consolidated the *Ba'th*'s rule by cruel purges, first of non-*Ba'th* opposition nuclei, then of intra-*Ba'th* factional rivals, and an all-pervasive secret service. He kept the Iraqi *Ba'th* firmly in the hands of the "Right", anti-Damascus wing and took an extremist line in inter-A. affairs, making Iraq a mainstay of the "Rejectionist" camp, while seeking, inside Iraq, an accommodation with the *Kurd rebels (an agreement he reached with them in Mar. 1970 later broke down) and the Communists (with one of whose factions he concluded, in 1973, a "National Front" pact — but whom he suppressed again in 1978–79). In the Iraqi Ba'th's internal factional struggles B. was considered close to the "rightist" group, but he tried to position himself above the factions, mediating between them and keeping them together, leaving the purge and the in-fighting to his chief lieutenants. Among those, Saddam *Hussein (al-Tikriti) emerged dominant, since the early 1970s, eliminating his rivals one-by-one. In fact, due to deteriorating health, B. was losing control since the mid-1970s and turning into a figurehead, while Saddam Hussein became the real ruler. In July 1979, what had been a fact was openly formalized: B. resigned all his posts — officially for reasons of health, in reality probably ousted by Saddam Hussein, who took over all power. B. spent his last three years in retirement, shunted aside and nearly forgotten.

Balfour Declaration A statement of 2 Nov. 1917 in which British Foreign Secretary Arthur Balfour informed the Zionist Organization, through Lord Rothschild, that "His Majesty's Government view with favor the establishment in Palestine of a national home for the Jewish people, and will use their best endeavor to facilitate the achievement of this object, it being clearly understood that nothing shall be done which may prejudice the civil and religious rights of existing non-Jewish communities in Palestine, or the rights and political status enjoyed by the Jews in any other country".

If the BD's intent was to bring Palestine, after the defeat of the Ottoman Empire, under British administration, it contradicted the *Sykes-Picot Agreement of 1916 which envisaged an international administration for Palestine. But the allied powers eventually associated themselves with its main purpose, and it was incorporated in the *Mandate for Palestine, 1922. The Zionist leadership later charged that Britain failed to fulfil her obligations under the BD and the Mandate, and the Mandate Commission of the *League of Nations was also frequently critical of the British administration in that respect.

A. spokesmen have always totally rejected the BD, maintaining that Britain had no right to dispose of a country that was not hers and that the BD was therefore illegal. A. leaders also claimed that Palestine had been included in the area earmarked for an A. independent kingdom in the *McMahon Correspondence with Sharif *Hussein; but this claim is disputed by British spokesmen and has remained controversial.

Bandung Conference In April 1955 the first conference of the independent states of Asia and Africa convened in B., Indonesia. Its leading initiators were the Prime Ministers of India (Jawaharlal Nehru), Pakistan, Indonesia, Burma and Ceylon. High-ranking delegations from 29 countries attended — 23 from Asia and 6 from Africa; of these 9 were ASt — 6 from Asia and 3 from Africa. Among them were the major leaders of Asia and Africa — Nehru, Chou En-Lai, Sukarno, U Nu, Nkrumah, Sihanouk, Pham Van Dong, *Nasser. The participants included all the then independent Asian and African nations — except Israel and Korea, who were deliberately excluded; "Nationalist China" (Taiwan), which would not attend a congress recognizing the People's Republic of China as representing China; the Asian republics of the USSR; and Mongolia. Both South and North Vietnam attended. As to Israel, the sponsors of the BC, led by Nehru and U Nu of Burma, wished to invite her; but when the ASt threatened to boycott it if Israel were invited, they gave in.

The BC was meant to mark a new era, the appearance on the stage of history of hitherto oppressed nations, and the end of colonialism. It deliberately avoided any discussion of controversial political issues and stressed mainly the newly-won independence of the nations of Asia and Africa, their cooperation, and the struggle against colonialism where it still ruled. It solemnly endorsed the "Five Principles" *(Panch Sila)* formulated by Nehru (in his joint statement with Chou En-Lai of China, June 1954): mutual respect for the territorial integrity and sovereignty of all states; non-aggression; non-interference in the internal affairs of other states; "equality and mutual benefit"; and peaceful coexistence. It called for economic and cultural cooperation and proclaimed its support for the principles of human rights and self-determination, the abolition of colonialism, and world peace. Among specific "anti-colonial" struggles mentioned and supported was Yemen's position on *'Aden and the "the southern parts of Yemen known as the Protectorate". The final declaration expressed support for "the rights of the A. people of Palestine" and called for the implementation of the UN resolutions on Palestine and a peaceful settlement.

It also denounced the "persistent denial to the peoples of North Africa of their right to self-determination," supporting the right of Algeria, Morocco and Tunisia to independence, and called for the admission to the UN of Asian and African states not yet admitted (including, in the A. world, Jordan and Libya).

The countries participating in the BC had differing political and ideological orientations, and the Conference did not discuss these issues, let alone adopt decisions concerning them, but the general trend was unmistakably towards *neutralist attitudes, *non-alignment. In fact, the border-line between Asian-African, i.e. geographical and non-ideological, criteria and the emergence of the BC as the nucleus of a neutralist movement was blurred. This double function of the BC became even more evident in the years that followed it. Attempts to organize the nations of Asia and Africa in a permanent body failed, as did efforts to convene another gathering of all Asian-African governments, a "second BC" (while non-governmental Afro-Asian organizations were established — see *Africa). A group of non-aligned nations, on the other hand, held several conferences and established a near-permanent bloc (see *non-alignment) — and regarded these activities in large measure as a continuation of the BC.

The BC was the stage for the first appearance of several leaders in the international arena. Thus the People's Republic of China appeared for the first time at a major international gathering, and her Prime Minister, Chou En-Lai, made important contacts and emerged as a major leader on the world scene. The same goes for several AC; particularly for Egypt's Gamal *Abd-ul-Nasser the BC marked his first appearance on the international scene, his emergence as a major leader and co-founder of the neutralist bloc, and the beginning of a more activist Egyptian foreign policy.

Baniyas One of the three main sources of the *Jordan River; its spring, yielding c. 120m. cubic meters (mcm) p.a., is situated about 1.25 mi. east of the border between Mandated Palestine and Syria, on the slopes of the *Golan Heights occupied since 1967 by Israel. The B. carries c.150 mcm p.a. contributing about one-third of the water carried by the upper Jordan. Some 10 mcm were used for local irrigation on the Syrian side, and the tentative Jordan waters agreement of 1954 (the *"Johnston Plan") envisaged expanding that irrigation and reserved 20 mcm p.a. for that purpose. In 1964–67, the ASt planned, and began, to divert the waters of the Jordan sources from Israel. The B. would have been diverted southwards along the slopes of the Golan to the *Yarmuk River where its waters would join the reservoir planned on that river, to be used in both Jordanian and Syrian projects. Diversion work was disturbed several times by Israeli military action, brought to a standstill, and finally stopped in 1967. B. village, at the source, was the Hellenistic Paneas, renamed in Roman times Caesarea Philippi.

al-Banna, Hassan (1906–49) The founder of the *Muslim Brotherhood in Egypt, 1929, and its "Supreme Guide" *(al-Murshid al-'Aam)*.

Barazani (or **Barzani**) Kurdish tribe and clan in Iraq, leaders of Kurdish rebellions. Originally a branch of the Muslim-Sunni Naqshabandi order (see *Dervish Orders), the B.'s assumed the characteristics of a tribe in the 19th century. Their center is the village of Barzan, c. 50 mi. north of Erbil. The B. sheikhs, always involved in feuds with rival Kurdish clans and in constant competition for predominance among the tribes, were traditional, semi-feudal, tribal-type leaders of their community, maintaining a sort of *de facto* semi-autonomy in their mountain valleys, closely linked to related tribes across the border in Iran. Whenever a government — Ottoman, British (for Iraq), or Iraqi — tried to impose tighter control, they resisted. They were thus frequently, even usually, in a state of semi-rebellion that often erupted into fully-fledged revolt. This near-constant rebellion gradually established links to Kurdish nationalist groups in the towns or in exile and grew into a revolutionary nationalist upheaval. The B. tribal sheikhs thus turned into national, though never uncontested, revolutionary leaders.

Since 1915 the head of the tribe was Sheikh Ahmad B. (died 1969) — a religious eccentric often considered mentally disturbed. In the 1920s, he was not the top leader of the Kurds (that place was taken by Sheikh Mahmud, a non-B.). During the 1930s and early 1940s he was identified with the leaders of the Kurdish rebellions, but later he again faded out of the political and military struggle.

The leader of the Kurds in their national struggle since the late 1930s was Sheikh Ahmad's younger brother, Mulla Mustafa Barzani (1901/2/4?–79). Involved in the rebellion, he was jailed with his brother Sheikh Ahmad in the early 1930s and spent the years following in and out of prison, and in exile (mainly in Iran). He returned in 1943 and assumed the leadership of a new rebellion. In 1945–46 he again crossed into Iran, and in 1946 he commanded the army of the short-lived Kurdish Republic of *Mahabad. After its collapse he escaped with a band of followers to the USSR (though he was no Communist; the Soviet Union had supported the Mahabad Republic). He stayed in Russia until permitted to return to Iraq after *Qassem's *coup* of 1958. He and his men supported Qassem against both Nasserist and Communist attempts to take over, but he himself was not permitted to leave Baghdad. When Kurdish hopes were disappointed by the Qassem régime and a new rebellion began fermenting, B. escaped to the Kurdish mountains in 1960 and assumed the leadership of the rebellion that re-erupted in 1961. The military fortunes of that rebellion were changing, but Iraq's armed forces were unable to liquidate it. B. had obtained significant aid from the Shah of Iran and was able to use Iranian territory as a supply base and staging area. He also reportedly got aid, training etc. from Israel.

While B.'s leadership remained essentially traditional and tribal, he maintained a firm alliance with political nationalist groups and formally headed the modernist-socialist "Kurdish Democratic Party" that led the national struggle since the 1950s. Yet his leadership was beset by both tribal and political-factional rivalries and defections, and his rivals (such as Jalal Talabani who headed a faction considered Leftist) frequently collaborated with the Iraqi authorities. Throughout the rebellion B. conducted, on and off, negotiations with Iraq, offering to end the rebellion in return for far-reaching autonomy for the Kurds. An agreement conceding a large part of B.'s demands was reached in June 1966; but as it was not implemented, the rebellion re-erupted in 1968. A new agreement, even more far-reaching, was signed with the *Ba'th régime in Mar. 1970 (see *Kurds). Again, the Kurds held that it was not honestly implemented, and in Mar. 1974 B.'s fighters, the *Pesh Merga*, resumed battle. But in Mar. 1975, Iraq reached an agreement with Iran which provided, *inter alia*, that the Shah stop his aid to the Kurdish rebels. As the Shah did so and closed his territory to the rebels and their supplies, the rebellion collapsed and on 20 Mar. 1975 B. announced its end in defeat. B. himself was among more than 100,000 refugees who escaped to Iran. He later went to the USA, where he died in 1979, a refugee and a broken man.

One of B.'s sons, 'Ubaid-ullah, was reported to be collaborating with the Baghdad Government. Two others, Idris and mainly Mas'ud, tried since the late 1970s to rebuild the Kurdish Democratic Party and resume armed resistance. Mas'ud B. is reported to collaborate, against the Iraqi régime, with Khomeini's Iran (while a rival Iranian wing of the Party, rebelling against Khomeini, collaborates with Iraq). Idris died in Jan. 1987.

bases, foreign (military/naval/air) The right to maintain military forces and permanent MB in the countries of the ME was for many years an important policy aim of the great powers. It was to be attained either forcibly, through colonial or semi-colonial occupation, as usual until World War I, or by agreement with the host country, as preferred since World War I.

In the pre-World War I period Great Britain maintained forces and MB in Egypt (since 1882), in 'Aden and several islands nearby (since 1839), and in the Persian Gulf (since the 1820s), as well as in Cyprus (since 1878) and Somaliland (since the 1880s); France — in Algeria (1830), Tunisia (1881) and Morocco (1912 — *de facto* since the beginning of the century); Italy — in Libya (1912), as well as in Somalia and on the Eritrean coast of the Red Sea (since the 1880s). Spain had B. in Morocco — under a protectorate imposed in 1912, and in several towns on Morocco's Mediterranean coast that she considered to be Spanish territory. The main development of FMB occurred between the two world wars. Italy maintained her MB in Libya and Eritrea (also conquering Ethiopia in 1935–36). Britain kept and expanded her MB in Egypt (mainly in *Alexandria port and the *Suez Canal Zone), 'Aden and the Persian Gulf, and obtained new ones in Iraq, Palestine and Transjordan. France maintained her MB in the Maghrib and acquired new ones in Syria and Lebanon. Britain's military presence was sanctioned in Iraq, Palestine and Transjordan by League of Nations *Mandates; it was approved by the host country in Iraq (treaty of 1930), Transjordan (treaties of 1928, 1946 and 1948), and Egypt (treaty of 1936) — but these treaties, signed by Iraq and Egypt after protracted negotiations, remained controversial, and a struggle for the restriction or abolition of Britain's military presence continued. France's MB were sanctioned in Tunisia and Morocco by the protectorate treaties, and in Syria/Lebanon by a League of Nations Mandate; a treaty of 1936 containing Syrian and Lebanese approval of France's military presence was never ratified by France and remained abortive. Spain's Moroccan B. were sanctioned by the protectorate.

During World War II Britain's military presence was strengthened (an Iraqi attempt to expel British troops and occupy their B. by military force was defeated in 1941). France's presence was weakened by her defeat in 1940: her forces in the Maghrib and Syria/Lebanon collaborated, under the Vichy régime, with the Axis powers or were virtually neutralized; late in 1942 American and allied forces occupied Morocco and Algeria, and Tunisia was taken over by the German army — to be conquered in 1943 by British and allied forces; Syria/Lebanon was occupied in 1941 by British and Free French forces, and a Free-French military presence was established. Italy was expelled from Libya, Somalia and Eritrea (as well as Ethiopia); in Libya Britain and Free France established a military presence and B. The USA, apart from her operations in Morocco and Algeria established a MB in Libya and modest, auxiliary military presence in the Persian Gulf. (The presence of US, British and Russian troops in Iran, 1941–46 is outside our scope here.)

After World War II the nationalist struggle for the abolition of foreign-imperial MB intensified, and eventually all FMB in AC were liquidated. France was compelled to withdraw her forces from Syria and Lebanon in 1945–46 (the USA and particularly Britain supporting the two countries' insistent demand). French B. and forces were evacuated from Morocco and Tunisia in 1961 and 1963 — after the failure of an attempt to maintain a privileged relationship and MB even after the two countries had attained full independence in 1956. The withdrawal of French B. and forces from Algeria, agreed when that country became independent in 1962, was completed in 1968. The handful of troops France kept in the Fezzan area of southern Libya were withdrawn in 1956, at Libya's request. The withdrawal of Spanish B. and troops from Morocco was agreed, as a by-product of France's withdrawal and Morocco's independence, in 1956. It was completed in what had been the northern Spanish Protectorate in 1958, and in the southern Protectorate (Tarfaia region), 1961 and in the Ifni enclave, 1969; it did not apply to the "Presidios" on the Mediterranean coast, around Ceuta and Melilla, considered by Spain, though not by Morocco, as being part of her territory.

Britain's MB were also liquidated one by one. Her presence in Palestine ended in 1948. In Egypt, her MB outside the Suez Canal Zone were handed over in 1947. As to those in the Canal Zone, and the presence of her troops there, it was agreed in 1954, after a long struggle, to evacuate them — while civilian British technicians would maintain the B. The military evacuation was completed in 1956, but the agreement to leave British technicians at the Suez Canal B. was invalidated by Egypt in 1956–57 following the Suez crisis and the Anglo-French invasion. The two British MB in Iraq, Habbaniyya and Shu'eiba, were relinquished in 1955 following an Anglo-Iraqi agreement, to be turned into joint B. under the *Baghdad Pact. That agreement lapsed when Iraq withdrew from the Baghdad Pact in 1959. In 1956–57 Jordan terminated her special military links with Britain, including the financing of Jordan's army, the *"Arab Legion", by Britain and the employment of British officers under contract as commanders of that army. The British base in 'Aden was abandoned in 1967, when independence was granted to South Yemen. Libya had agreed in 1953 to lease to Britain MB (mainly at al-'Adem and Tobruk); in 1964 it was agreed, at Libya's request, to terminate Britain's military presence, and her troops evacuated Tripolitania in 1966 and Cyrenaica in

1968, but kept the two main bases. Late in 1969, Libya's new revolutionary régime demanded their liquidation, too, and they were handed over in Mar. 1970. In the Persian Gulf, Britain relinquished her protecting presence in Kuwait in 1961; in 1971 she renounced it in the whole Gulf area and liquidated her MB at *Bahrain and *Sharja (with certain facilities reportedly remaining at her disposal in Bahrain). Britain maintained a special military relationship with 'Oman (formerly "Muscat and 'Oman"), with British officers, on contract, commanding the country's armed forces, and some MB (including one on Masira island in the Arabian Sea). It was, however, agreed in 1976 to close these B. in 1977 — though certain "facilities" were to remain at Britain's disposal.

The USA had, prior to World War II, no MB in AC. During the war, however, several B. were set up in Morocco from 1942–43 to serve war operations; the US kept these B. after the war, but handed them over, in agreement with Morocco, in 1963 — though certain facilities remained at her disposal. Under a 1954 agreement the US obtained an air base in Lybia ("Wheelus Field"); at Libya's request it was evacuated in 1970. The US also built a B. at *Dhahran in Sa'udi Arabia, completed in 1946; the lease, formalized in 1951, was terminated in 1961, and the B. was returned to Sa'udia in 1962, with certain aviation privileges remaining at US disposal. In 1971 the US obtained certain naval facilities, never called a B., in Bahrain; that country announced their termination in 1973, and in 1977 the B. was handed over — again with certain facilities retained. In 1980, when the US was planning to set up a "Rapid Deployment Force" for the defense of the Persian Gulf and the ME, 'Oman and Somalia (as well as Kenya) reportedly agreed to put certain air and naval "facilities" — never officially called B. — at her disposal. These US plans did not fully materialize, but some military installations were constructed on 'Oman's shores, in her *Ras Musandam exclave, and on Masira island. Egypt also agreed in principle to allow the US to construct "facilities" on the Red Sea coast, mainly at Ras Banas. Major construction was delayed by disagreements over details, but some work seems to have been done. The US was reported to enjoy additional facilities, *inter alia* for electronic surveillance in Egypt and Sa'udia.

The USSR never admitted to the possession of MB in the AC. She kept, however, a considerable number of military personnel as instructors, advisors and technicians in several AC — Egypt and Syria since the late 1950s, later also Iraq, Algeria, Somalia, Libya and South Yemen — to aid the defense and the armed forces of these countries. In the course of these aid operations it was frequently reported that Soviet military personnel served the USSR's own strategic and military aims and that military installations of the countries aided — such as the ports of Alexandria and Mersa Matruh in Egypt, Lataqia in Syria, airfields in both countries, air and naval facilities in South Yemen ('Aden and *Socotra island) and Libya — were at Russia's disposal, though not amounting to fully fledged MB. Egypt terminated the Soviet military presence in 1972, and Somalia did likewise in 1977. Iraq seemed to have moved away, in the 1980s, from her close links with the USSR. A Soviet military presence, officially advisory and defined as technical aid, continues in Syria, Libya and South Yemen.

al-Ba'th (Arabic: Renaissance) Pan-Arab socialist party. It originated in Syria, which has remained the area of its main activities and influence. It has ruled Syria since 1963, and Iraq, by a rival faction, since 1968. The B.'s doctrine is radically Pan-Arab; it regards the various ASt as temporary entities to be replaced by a united all-A. state — by revolutionary violence or subversion if need be. Accordingly, its own parties in the AC are but "regional", local branches, subject to a "national", all-A. command. In fact, as the B. has been deeply split since 1966, with two rival all-A. commands, one Syrian and one Iraqi, the "regional" leaderships in Syria and Iraq determine its policies. The B. slogan is "Unity, Freedom, Socialism — One A. Nation, the Bearer of an Eternal Mission". While the party's Pan-A. vision is unequivocal and simple, its socialist doctrine is rather vague and avoids clear-cut social, economic and ideological definitions. It is based on far-reaching nationalizations, a mixed economy of state and private enterprise (with the state as the stronger, determining partner), and a populist semi-totalitarian régime. It claims a single-party monopoly not for itself but for a "national-progressive" front headed by the B. and comprising other groups acceptable to the B. as "Socialist-Unionist" (usually including the

Communists), and bans all other political organizations. The B. was originally secularist. In its political practice it has come to terms with the Islamic character of the A. state, but it opposes and suppresses extremist-fundamentalist Islamic groups — Sunni in Syria, Shi'i in Iraq. In Syria this issue is aggravated by the fact that the B. leadership, from the President down, contains a disproportionally large number of *'Alawis — a sect on the margins of Shi'i Islam, considered by most Muslims as heretic and by many as outside Islam.

The B. was founded in the mid-1930s, as a small group of students and young intellectuals, by two teachers from Syria studying in Paris: Michel *'Aflaq, who became its chief ideologist, and Salah-ul-Din *Bitar, later Prime Minister of Syria. The first congress of the "A. Renaissance Party" (Hizb al-B. al-'Arabi), still a small group of young men, was held in 1947. In 1947 and 1949 party members stood unsuccessfully in Syrian elections; its Secretary-General 'Aflaq briefly served in 1949 as Minister of Education. In 1953 the party merged with Akram *Hourani's "A. Socialist Party", to become the "A. Socialist Renaissance Party" (Hizb al-B. al-'Arabi al-Ishtiraki). It played a part in the overthrow of Adib *Shishakli's dictatorship in Feb. 1954. In the Syrian elections the same year it won 15 seats, and in the following four years its influence steadily increased in Syria and spread also to Jordan, Lebanon and Iraq. The party's attraction for young intellectuals and officers probably was its bold, crisply formulated ideology, its Pan-A. doctrine, its anti-imperialist, anti-capitalist slogans, its anti-Israel extremism; but its real political influence, its transformation from a small group of debating students and young intellectuals into a powerful faction with clout, were due to the following it was able to recruit among army officers. Whenever the B. seized power, it was through *coups* made by army officers and wherever it was able to hold that power, it was the B. army officers who wielded it (assisted by the all-pervasive secret police they established). This link with officers' juntas was forged in Syria and Iraq; where it did not exist — in Jordan, Sudan, Yemen or Tunisia — the B. remained an ineffective group of plotting, subversive intellectuals. Once in power, however, the B. officers were guided by state and army interests and the exigencies of power politics rather than by B. ideology.

In 1957, the Syrian B. officers were one of the pressure groups pushing Syria towards union with Egypt in the *United Arab Republic (UAR), Feb. 1958. The B. expected to become the ruling party and the ideological mentor of the new state; but President *Nasser insisted on the dissolution of all parties other than his single-party "National Union", and of the B. in particular. Nasser's doctrine of Arab Nationalism, and since the late 1950s Arab socialism, was perhaps influenced by B. ideology; but he never acknowledged that debt and remained suspicious of and hostile to the B. as a political organization. During the period of the UAR, the B. maintained some underground cells, but its leaders were gradually eliminated from positions of power and influence. Their growing opposition was one of the chief reasons for Syria's secession from the Union in the army *coup* of Sept. 1961.

The B. officers were bitterly disappointed with the new secessionist régime which turned Rightist, did not afford them positions of power and relapsed into constant factional friction and intrigues. In Mar. 1963, they were the principal partners of a new army *coup* in Syria. At the same time, in Feb. 1963, B. officers in Iraq joined hands with (non-B.) 'Abd-ul-Salam *'Aref, toppled 'Abd-ul-Karim *Qassem's military régime and took up key positions in the new government. The B. was now in power in both Syria and Iraq, though it had to share that power with other factions.

Despite the trauma of the abortive merger with Egypt, the B. had not written off either its general unionist doctrine or its aim to unite, specifically, with Egypt; indeed, it was troubled by the secessionist role it had played in 1961. It now advocated a rather looser, federal union — contrary to the basically centralist, anti-federal tendency of its brand of nationalism. In Apr. 1963 the Syrian and Iraqi B. régimes together worked out a new agreement with Egypt for a tripartite federal union, to be called, again, "United Arab Republic", and prepared a detailed draft constitution. This federation plan remained abortive, mainly because within the coalition ruling Syria since the *coup* of Mar. 1963 a bitter, violent power struggle had erupted between the B. and the Nasserists: the latter were purged, and mutual hostility reached a pitch that made a reconciliation impossible. In Nov. 1963, the Iraqi B., weakened by bitter factional struggles, was ousted from the Government by President 'Aref.

In Syria, the B. has retained power since 1963. But it was split into rival factions that struggled for power and even carried out military *coups* against each other. One faction, headed (politically and militarily) by Gen. Amin *Hafez and (ideologically) by Michel 'Aflaq, was considered "Rightist" and less rigidly doctrinaire. It ruled Syria until Feb. 1966 and controlled the "national", all-A. leadership and the Iraqi B. A rival, "military" faction, more leftist-extremist and doctrinaire, was headed by Generals Salah *Jadid and Hafez al-*Asad. They gradually gained control of the Syrian "regional" command, and in Feb. 1966 ousted the Hafez-'Aflaq group in another military *coup*. The new rulers removed not only Syria's political and military leaders but also the all-A. leadership, including the party's founders 'Aflaq and Bitar, and set up their own, rival all-A. national command. In Iraq the B. again came to power, in a *coup*, in July 1968 (in partnership with non-B. officers; these were ousted after two weeks and the B. alone assumed total power). The Iraqi B. remained linked to the national leadership ousted in Syria, and on its part purged its pro-Syrian faction. Bitter Syrian-Iraqi hostility ensued.

The "military" faction in power in Syria since Feb. 1966 soon split, with Gen. Asad heading a new faction that judged Jadid and his associates (Zu'ayyin, Makhus, Nur-ul-Din al-*Atassi) to be too leftist-extremist, denounced Syria's isolation in the inter-A. arena, and wanted a stronger Pan-A. policy. The rift was obviously motivated by ideological dissension only in part and revolved principally around power. In 1969 Asad gained control in a semi-*coup*, but agreed to a compromise leaving his rivals in leading positions. In Nov. 1970 he took full control, in another semi-*coup* and ousted and detained the leaders of the defeated faction. In 1971 Asad became President of Syria and Secretary-General of the B. (both the Syrian-"regional" and his wing of the "national" all-A. command). He has ruled Syria since 1970–71.

The Damascus and Baghdad B. parties and governments have remained bitterly hostile (a hostility based only partly on intra-B. doctrinaire dissension and rooted in a geopolitically motivated struggle for predominance in the *Fertile Crescent). Both wings use the name of the B. party and doctrine, but their organizations are completely separate (B. branches outside Syria and Iraq, e.g. in Lebanon, also split accordingly). Both rule their respective countries with an iron fist — nominally at the head of a "National Progressive Front", but in fact as totalitarian single parties. Both have instituted elected National Assemblies or "People's Councils" — in Syria since 1973 (replacing appointed councils that preceded the elected body), in Iraq since 1980. In both Syria and Iraq the B. party has become a tool serving a ruling group of officers, headed by Asad in Syria and by Saddam *Hussein in Iraq.

The Iraqi B. régime has shown some pragmatic flexibility. It has, for instance, endeavored to solve Iraq's Kurdish problem with a degree of moderation and a readiness to compromise unusual in Iraqi politics (see *Kurds). Iraq has also in the 1980s mitigated her foreign and inter-A. policies, despite her B. ideology. Needing A. and Western aid in her war against Iran, since 1980, she has seceded from the *"Rejection Front", loosened her ties with the USSR and sought a *rapprochement* with both the West and pro-Western ASt's, including ostracized Egypt. Syria, on the other hand, has remained hard-line and extremist in both international and inter-A. affairs and particularly vis-à-vis Israel. In fact, she has drifted back into the same isolation in inter-A. relations from which Asad himself sought to extricate her in 1970 — to a degree that she supports Iran in her war against Iraq, contrary to the position of most AC. Syria under Asad and the B. has also suppressed Muslim-Sunni fundamentalist resistance with unprecedented brutality — a policy aggravated by the fact that her régime is dominated by heretic 'Alawis. Factional, ideologically motivated (or ideologically coated) struggles within the Syrian B. seem to have ceased under Asad. Rivalries and clashes within the ruling group — e.g. over Asad's succession — are hardly connected with B. party ideology.

Outside Syria and Iraq, B. branches exist in Lebanon — split into (weaker) pro-Iraqi and (stronger) pro-Syrian wings. As Syria operates in Lebanon directly, and dominates her, and therefore hardly needs the type of agent a local B. branch could provide, the Lebanese B. dos not seem to wield much influence. In Jordan, a B. party was briefly legal in the 1950s and sometimes represented in Parliament (party membership of the elected deputies remaining blurred and in doubt).

Most of the time, the party has been illegal and underground, and does not seem to possess any strength or influence. Among the A.'s of Palestine (West Bank and Gaza), party affiliations and leanings are so blurred and obscure that B. influence cannot be determined reliably. Illegal, underground B. cells may exist in some other AC — Tunisia, Sudan, Yemen, South Yemen; but they do not seem to wield influence. As an all-A. political movement or ideological tendency, the B., apart from being in power in Syria and Iraq, seems to have faded over the last decade.

al-Bazzaz, 'Abd-ul-Rahman (1913–73) Iraqi politician and jurist. A Sunni Muslim, born in Baghdad, B. studied law. A fervent nationalist, he was detained in 1941, after the defeat of the Rashid *'Ali régime, for his anti-British and pro-German attitude. From 1955 he was Dean of the Baghdad Law College. In 1957, he was again arrested for "Nasserist" anti-régime activities. After the July 1958 revolution of General *Qassem, B. was among those pushing the new régime towards Nasserist policies and in 1959 was arrested for his suspected involvement in a Nasserist plot. After Qassem's fall in 1963, he became Ambassador to Cairo (briefly) and London, and in 1964–65 served as Secretary-General of *OPEC (the Organization of Petroleum Exporting Countries). In Sept. 1965 B. was appointed Deputy Premier and Foreign Minister, and two weeks later became Prime Minister, retaining the Foreign Ministry. He tried to restore civilian-political rule and thus soon fell out with the army officers really in control. B. was the chief architect of an agreement of June 1966 with the Kurdish rebels that made far-reaching concessions to the *Kurds and granted them partial autonomy. The agreement was never implemented as it proved unacceptable to most of the nationalist military establishment, and the controversy around it contributed to B.'s fall, in Aug. 1966. After the *Ba'th *coup* of July 1968, B. was arrested for plotting with the Western powers. He was released in 1970 and went into exile, to England, where he died in July 1973.

Bedouin, Beduin Arab nomads, organized in tribes. The term B. (Arabic: Badawi, pl. Badu), denoting an inhabitant of the desert (Arabic: Badiya), is used chiefly by the settled population. The B. refer to themselves as "Arabs" — and indeed, that term originally meant only, or mainly, the nomadic tribes of the Arabian peninsula. To this day, B. tribes are called "'Arab al-(name of tribe)", and most tribes claim descent from the early tribes of the peninsula. There are some tribes that are not A., such as the Qashqai in Iran, the Tuareg in the Sahara, or Turcoman tribes in northern Syria and Iraq, and quite a few tribes of mixed descent, e.g. with some Negro blood, particularly in Sudan and North Africa; pure-blooded Arab tribes look down on those and resent their being called "'Arab al--".

The classical, fully nomadic B. tribe lives in tents and raises camels. It has no fixed, permanent camping place; its wandering and grazing area is more or less firmly established by tradition — but rival tribes have clashed throughout history over disputed wandering areas and grazing and water rights. B. tribes also used to raid trade caravans, often collecting payment for protection. Throughout history B. tribes raided the settled lands in the areas bordering the desert. Whenever the countries concerned were weak, politically and militarily, B. incursions gained control and established their domination — often settling in the process. Many villages in Iraq, Syria, Jordan and Palestine are fully or partly of B. descent. In recent history, with the states of the area growing stronger and more effectively administered, such B. raids and incursions have become rare and virtually impossible. Moreover, in the course of modern development, pasturing on arable land — always a bone of contention between B. and the settled farmers — is being prevented, the settled and cultivated area extended, farming villages are established, and the B. are in retreat.

The B. themselves are in a constant process of transition to sedentary life, a process much accelerated in the last century. The transition usually begins with the raising of sheep and goats in addition to camels; then — grazing cattle; gradually, plots of land are sown, shifting and irregularly at first, then permanently; dwellings are built — shacks at first, for storage and for occupation during part of the year, when the tribe or family reaches that place in its migrations, and finally, houses for permanent occupation. Most governments of the region encourage and support that process of settlement (though it often raises complex problems of land ownership). There are few fully nomadic, camel-raising tribes left by now. Most have become semi-nomadic, at various stages of the transition process, and some are fully settled, though in many cases animal husbandry remains their main source of livelihood. All semi-nomadic tribes, and most settled ones, retain their tribal identity and organization long after they have ceased to be fully nomadic B.

The basic unit of B. social organization is the tribe (*'ashira*) — though the migrating unit often is the extended family rather than the whole tribe. Frequently several tribes form a large tribal federation (*qabila*). The tribe, usually claiming descent from a legendary common ancestor, is headed by the *sheikh*, who wields wide authority over his tribesmen, including their personal and family affairs. In tribes settling on the land, the sheikh sometimes secures the formal ownership of the land, changing from a *primus inter pares* into a semi-feudal landlord and large-scale employer and contractor. The sheikh is nominally elected by the heads and elders of all the families of his tribe; in fact, his position in most cases is hereditary. Modern governments often reserve for themselves the right to appoint, or at least to confirm, the sheikh.

B. tribes have developed their own customs and lore, often described in literature and travelogues, such as their renowned hospitality (a social convention strictly necessary in the conditions of the desert). They also have their own tribal law, based on collective tribal and family responsibility, and the treatment of all conflicts as civil disputes to be settled between man and his fellow, or between the families concerned, rather than criminal matters to be prosecuted by the state or society. Thus, murder or sexual offences are matters to be settled by the family of the transgressor and that of the victim — either by revenge or by a truce (*sulḥa*) based on the payment of compensation. While there are countless cases of blood feuds, deriving from revenge and counter-revenge, inter-tribal or intra-tribal, the general trend is to prefer the compensation-and-truce process, usually with the help of mediating tribal judges and elders. Large parts of this tribal law, particularly customs concerning revenge killings or truce-and-compensation, and killings for sexual offences affecting family honor (such as the murder of women for extra- or pre-marital relations), have been adopted also by a wide sector of the settled rural population. Tribal law poses a delicate problem to all governments of the region: can they condone murder if committed under rules of tribal custom, thus creating in effect different systems of law for different sectors of the population — or should they treat tribal revenge and honor killings as ordinary murder, thus alienating the B. (and large parts of the rural population)? No government has fully solved this dilemma; most have sought some *de facto* compromise. While constitutions and laws do not provide for special, different treatment for B., the courts often show special consideration for their customs, regarding them at least as extenuating circumstances. So did Western powers in semi-colonial administrations, with the British particularly fond of B. customs and nostalgically eager to preserve them.

The nomadic and semi-nomadic B. have remained a disturbing, anomalous element in the administration of many AC's — though their share in the economy and their role in the social fabric have continuously decreased. Modern communications, particularly air transport, have made irrelevant the B.'s control of desert routes and abolished their function as chief suppliers of meat and beasts of burden. Modern administration and enhanced security have made raids and the collection of protection payments well-nigh impossible. Semi-desert grazing lands are continuously narrowed down by development, river irrigation schemes, and the expansion of cultivated areas. The gradual settlement of the B. breaks up their tribal coherence — the more so as in recent decades the growing Arabian oil industry has turned many B. into industrial workers and dispersed them. Yet, those B. remaining nomadic and semi-nomadic are not easily integrated into ordinary administration, tax collection, compulsory army service, health and education services; that integration has in most AC remained partial.

It is difficult to establish the number of B. A normal census does not reliably cover them and, moreover, it cannot be determined with certainty which semi-nomadic B. should still be counted as B., or at which point of the sedentarization process settled or half-settled tribes cease to be B. Some estimates put the number of B. tribesmen in the AC and Israel at c. 7–8m. In the Arabian peninsula there are c. 4m., less than 20% of the population. In Iraq, estimates range from 2–2.5m. to about one quarter of the population (which would be c. 3.5m. in the mid-1980s). In Libya, B. form about one third, i.e. 0.7–1m. Syria's B. are variously estimated at 200–300,000; Jordan's — at 200–250,000 or 7–10% of the population; Egypt's number c. 200–250,000 (including c. 60,000 in the *Sinai peninsula); Israel's — c. 60,000 (40,000 in the southern desert, the Negev, the rest mainly in Galilee; the former are in the process of settlement in townships being built for them, the latter are virtually settled).

In some AC provision is made for B. representation in Parliament (sometimes through nomination by councils of tribal chiefs rather than through general elections); thus in Syria's election law of the 1950s. In Jordan two — and lately three — special constituencies ensure tribal B. representation in Parliament. Specific political influence of B. tribal leaders seems to survive in few AC: in Sa'udia and the Persian Gulf principalities; in Jordan, where B. form a large part of the army — originally created as the "Arab Legion", a specifically tribal force — and dominate its officers' corps, and where they have always been the backbone of the King's conservative régime and his loyal allies in his struggles with Leftist agitation, political ferment and Palestinian guerrillas; in Yemen, where the *Zeidi tribal federations were the last support of the royalist régime and continue to wield a restraining conservative influence in the Republic; and perhaps in Libya.

Beirut Capital, largest city and main port of Lebanon. Its population is estimated at about 1m.; Greater B., with suburbs c. 1.5m. The city, which in the Ottoman empire was the capital of the province (*vilayet*) of B. — and not included in the autonomous district of Lebanon, 1861–1914 — became part of Lebanon in 1920, when the French created "Greater Lebanon". Until the 1960s, the population was about one-half Christian, one-half Muslim; Sunni Muslims were the largest single community, c. 35%, followed by Armenians (24%), Greek-Orthodox (11%), Maronites (8%), Shi'i Muslims (7.5%). Since the 1970s the communal structure of the city's population seems to have greatly changed by a large increase in its Muslim-Shi'i component — *inter alia* through a constant influx of Shi'is from South Lebanon, partly as refugees; in recent years, the Shi'is claim to be the largest single community and to form together with the Sunnis a Muslim majority. During the civil war since 1975 B. was virtually divided into two separate cities, the Christian-majority East, and the Muslim West, with a heavily barricaded "Green Line" dividing the two parts. Transit was restricted to a few crossing points that were often closed by nearly constant mutual shelling and sniping on the part of rival "militias". This division and civil war was further aggravated from 1982–83.

In 1984 and 1985 Shi'i militias (al-*Amal) seized control of West B. and despite agreements to hand it over to the army, kept control until Syrian troops took over in Feb. 1987. B. also contained, on its outskirts, several large Palestinian quarters — originally refugee camps but gradually transformed into armed *PLO guerrilla strongholds. One of these, Tel al-Za'tar, was taken and destroyed in Aug. 1976, after a two-month siege, by Christian militias with Syrian army support. In two others, Sabra and Shatila, Christian *Phalange militias carried out a bloody massacre in Sept. 1982; the same two camps and Burj al-Barajna were again attacked, and partly destroyed, in May-June 1985 by Shi'i *Amal* forces, but in 1985–87 the *Amal*-PLO battle over the camps continued. During the civil war, and particularly since 1985, B. became the scene of numerous abductions and murders, also of foreigners, by terrorists. Its academic institutions, including several well-known foreign ones (such as the American University of B. and the French Jesuit University of St. Joseph), were paralyzed by these developments. The civil war also affected, and largely paralyzed, B.'s port and airport, Lebanon's main gates to the outer world. Since 1985, the airport has been in the hands of militias and guerrillas, and most international airlines have stopped using it. B.'s position as a major financial and banking center has also been destroyed by the civil war.

Ben Barka, Mehdi (1920–65) Moroccan nationalist leader and politician. One of the younger leaders of the *Istiqlal* party, BB served as chairman of the Consultative Assembly, 1956–59, that preceded the establishment of elected representative and legislative bodies. Within the *Istiqlal* he headed a leftist faction opposed to the traditional leadership, and in 1959 he seceded with his faction and founded the *Union Nationale des Forces Populaires*. Accused of involvement in subversion and plots, he soon went into exile in France. In 1963–64 he was tried *in absentia* and sentenced to death, though the King later pardoned him. In Oct. 1965 BB disappeared in France and it was generally assumed that he was abducted and murdered by the Moroccan Secret Services (though his body was never found). The "BB Affair" caused a grave crisis in French-Moroccan relations for several years. In Jan. 1966 the French issued an arrest warrant against Muhammad Oufkir, the Moroccan Minister of the Interior and Head of the Secret Services. A trial was held in France from Sept. 1966; of the accused, Oufkir was absent, but one of the heads of the Secret Service, Ahmad Dlimi, gave himself up. Sentence was pronounced in June 1967: Oufkir was condemned to imprisonment for life, and Dlimi was acquitted. The French-Moroccan crisis over the "BB Affair" was patched up in 1969.

Ben Bella, Ahmad (or sometimes **Muhammad** (b. 1916? 1918?)   Algerian politician and leader of the nationalist revolt. President of Algeria 1963–65. BB emerged as a nationalist leader after World War II. After serving in the French Army during the war, he joined the MTLD party led by *Messali Hajj, which advocated full independence for Algeria. He soon began advocating armed struggle and set up, with a group of like-minded associates (Belkacem Krim, Muhammad Khidr, Hussein Ait-Ahmad), an underground "Organisation Spéciale" for that purpose, thus breaking with Messali and the MTLD. In 1950 he was arrested and sentenced to seven years imprisonment. He escaped in Mar. 1952 to Cairo and established there the headquarters of the groups preparing an armed revolt. In 1953 his *"Organisation Spéciale"* turned into a *Conseil Révolutionnaire pour l'Unité et l'Action*, out of which grew the *Front de Libération Nationale*, *FLN, in 1954. When the FLN opened the armed revolt in Nov. 1954, BB was its most prominent leader. In Oct. 1956, when BB was flying from Morocco to Tunis, the French secret services arranged for the pilot to land at Algiers and arrested BB and four other rebel leaders, including Khidr and Ait-Ahmad. While BB was in prison in France and could no longer directly lead the rebellion, his colleagues kept his place in their leadership bodies and apparently managed to consult him; he was named, for instance, Deputy Premier in the FLN's Provisional Governments of 1958 and 1961.

BB was released in Mar. 1962, with the French-Algerian agreement and cease-fire. He immediately assumed a vigorous leadership — and took bold positions in the factional splits that developed. He advocated leftist-neutralist, anti-Western policies on *Nasserist lines and a one-party state socialism, with the party dominant; in the rift between the guerrillas inside Algeria and the rebel army under *Boumédienne entering Algeria from Tunisia he backed the latter. In June 1962 he convened the FLN leadership in Tripoli, Libya, and imposed his line. He ignored the two rival governments struggling for control — the one set up provisionally by the French-Algerian agreement, and Yussuf Ben-Khedda's FLN government, and imposed his own politbureau's control (with the FLN government acquiescing). In Sept. 1962 the provisional arrangements were ended and BB formed the government of independent Algeria. He continued imposing his strict, hard-line rule and began suppressing all oppositional trends within and without the FLN. In Apr. 1963 he became Secretary-General of the FLN in addition to the Premiership. In Sept. 1963 BB was elected President in a referendum, as the only candidate, nominated by the FLN; he kept the Premiership, too, but from 1964 ceased using the title Prime Minister and treated his government as a Presidential one. He made Algeria an ally of the Soviet Bloc (he received the Lenin Peace Prize in 1964) and a mainstay of the Leftist-neutralist camp, aspiring to a position of leadership in that camp.

BB's harsh policies and his suppression of opposition leaders with a proud fighting FLN record caused much unrest and dissatisfaction. In June 1965 he was overthrown by his associate and protégé Boumédienne, and imprisoned. His confinement was eased from 1979, after Boumédienne's death, and in Oct. 1980 he was released. He refused, however, to associate himself with the régime in power and soon went into voluntary exile in France. Since 1980 he has been linked with various opposition groups in exile —

according to some reports with an increasingly Islamic and pro-Libyan line; but these groups, factionally split, do not seem to have much impact on political realities in Algeria. In 1982 he co-founded an "International Islamic Commission for Human Rights".

Ben-Jedid, Chadli (al-Shadhili) (b. 1929) Algerian officer and politician, President of Algeria since 1979. Born in eastern Algeria into a peasant family, BJ received no higher education. According to French reports never confirmed by Algerian sources, he served in the French Army in the early 1950s. He joined the *FLN forces of the armed revolt in 1955 and rapidly rose in rank, soon named Colonel. In 1961 he was appointed to *Boumédienne's General Staff of the rebel army in Tunis, and from 1962 was a member of the Revolutionary Council. In the factional struggles of 1962–63 he supported Boumédienne (and therefore *Ben-Bella), and was named commander of the Constantine region. From 1963–64 he commanded the Oran region for fifteen years and, while supporting Boumédienne, ruled it with a strong hand and as his personal fief. He took no part in ideological debates or factional struggles.

When after the death of Boumédienne in Dec. 1978 the struggle for the succession seemed to be deadlocked — mainly between Salah Yahyawi, considered leftist-radical and the candidate of the FLN party cadres, and 'Abd-ul-'Aziz Bouteflika, considered more moderate and a "technocrat" — BJ emerged as the Army's candidate and a generally acceptable compromise. In Jan. 1979 he was nominated by the FLN as the single candidate for the Presidency and in Feb. he was elected in a referendum. As President, he kept the Defense Ministry to himself. He appointed a Prime Minister — the first separation of the Premiership from the Presidency since 1962–63. He was also elected Secretary-General of the FLN. He was re-elected President, as the only candidate, in 1984. BJ seemed to rule with a firm hand. He purged the FLN, the government and the army of elements he considered extremist or undesirable. While he made no major changes in Algeria's policies of state socialism and radicalism, he fostered the influence of "technocrats", seemed to de-emphasize ideological-doctrinal elements and to relax Algeria's régime in some measure. He also toned down Algeria's radical foreign policies, e.g. gradually dissociated her from the inter-Arab *"Rejection Front".

Berbers The ancient, pre-A. inhabitants of Northwest Africa (the *Maghrib*). Their language belongs to the Hamitic group and is related to ancient Egyptian. After the A.-Muslim conquest in the 7th and 8th century the B. accepted Islam, many of them in the version of the *Ibadiyya sect or school (though they retained many pre-Islamic customs), and became the spearhead of its further expansion into Spain and West Africa. They also gradually adopted the Arabic language, but their own B. language continued to be widely spoken, particularly in remote areas, where the B. also maintained their own tribal structure.

The number of B. today cannot be reliably established. The majority of the Maghrib population is of full or part B. descent; but estimates vary as to the number of those still retaining a degree of B. distinctiveness, consciousness and the B. language. Some estimates put their number at more than 50% of Morocco's population, and c. 50% of Algeria's, others estimate it at 30–40% in both countries. In Tunisia there are very few B., and in Tripolitania (Libya) — where an estimate of 1917 still thought them to be a majority — they are today considered to be 5–10%. The distinctive character of the B., and their particularist, conservative tendencies, were preserved in the remote mountain areas rather than in the cities and villages of the lowlands. The French in Morocco, during the period of their domination, tended to foster B. particularism, and some conservative local B. leaders collaborated with them against the nationalists (see *Morocco). No organization or political party explicitly represents B. interests or cultivates B. nationality. The trend of contemporary history seems to enhance A. hegemony, the integration of the B. in the Arabized society of the modern Maghrib, and the decline of their conscious B. distinctiveness. Yet, B. particularism, and resentment of Arabization and A. domination, are still flickering. Some conservative political groupings in Morocco have a B. flavor. Some factional struggles in Algeria, particularly in the Kabyle region, in the 1950s and 1960s, also had distinct B. undertones. In Algeria, demonstrations still occur of B. resistance to the Arabization of higher education, and defiant efforts are being made to foster B. traditions and the B. language (whose use in the media is banned).

Bernadotte, Count Folke (1895–1948) Swedish nobleman, related to the royal dynasty; prominent as President of the Swedish Red Cross in efforts towards the end of World War II to obtain the release of Scandinavians and others, including Jews, fom German concentration camps. Appointed by the UN, in May 1948, as Mediator in the Palestine conflict, B. recommended the merger of the A. part of partitioned Palestine with Jordan, the annexation of the *Negev, the southern part of Palestine (earmarked in the UN partition plan for Israel), to the A.-Jordanian state, in exchange for Western Galilee (to remain in Israel's possession though originally earmarked for the A. state), and the repatriation of the A. refugees who had fled from Palestine during the war of 1948. The first version of the "B. Plan" provided for Jerusalem to be annexed to the Arab state; a second version recommended its internationalization (as had been laid down in the UN partition plan). B. also suggested that Haifa be made an international port, and Lod (Lydda, al-Ludd) an international airport.

The B. Plan raised opposition from both Israel and the ASt. It was discussed by the UN, and published, in September 1948. Its territorial suggestions, though supported by Britain, were rejected by the General Assembly's Political Committee in Dec. 1948.

B. was assassinated in Sept. 1948 in Jerusalem by members of a Jewish dissident terrorist group. The murderers were never tried. An advisory opinion of the International Court of Justice determined Israel's formal responsibility, and Israel paid compensation to the UN.

Berri, Nabih (b. 1937? 1940?) Lebanese lawyer and politician, political leader of the Muslim-Shi'i community. Born in Freetown (Sierra Leone), where his father had migrated, B. was returned to the town of his family's origin, Tibnin in South Lebanon, and brought up there. He later studied law at the Lebanese University of Beirut. He was, in his student days, active in the Ba'th Party and frequently visited Damascus. For some time he was President of the students' union. Later he studied for some time at the Sorbonne in Paris, lived with his father in Sierra Leone, and then went to the USA. There he married a Lebanese-American, but later divorced her; his divorced wife and some of their seven children remained in the USA (he remarried in 1982).

B. returned to Lebanon in 1975 and joined the Shi'i leader Sheikh Mussa *Sadr and his recently formed para-military organization, al-*Amal. During the civil war that erupted in 1975, the Shi'is of Lebanon — until then a backward community that had not been given a fair share in the distribution of political power — began asserting their strength and organizing to claim the power due to them. B. gradually became one of their main younger leaders. He soon became a member of al-Amal's Political Committee, then its Secretary-General (1978) and its chairman (1980); and though his direct control of the organization and its militia remained in doubt, he has emerged as the chief Shi'i leader.

In the civil war itself, from 1975, the Shi'is did not actively join either of the rival camps and restricted their militias, al-Amal and local guards, to the protection of their villages and quarters. There were tension and frequent clashes between them and the Palestinian *PLO guerrillas dominating South Lebanon. In the early 1980s, however, and particularly after the Israeli occupation of South Lebanon in 1982 and with the increasing Shi'i resistance to that occupation, B. allied himself to the "Leftist", anti-Government camp led by the Druze chief Walid *Junbalat. He did not formally join the several "National Front" coalitions set up by Junbalat in 1983 and 1984, but he joined their efforts to force on the Christian-led Government a pro-Syrian and anti-Israel policy and far-reaching changes in Lebanon's political structure, which officially aimed at the abolition of the communal structure, but in fact at the enhancement of the Shi'i and Druze share in that structure and the creation of Shi'i-ruled and Druze-ruled districts (parallel to the Christian-ruled "canton" of Mount Lebanon). When these efforts succeeded, under Syrian pressure, and a "Government of National Unity" was set up in Apr. 1984, B. joined it as Minister of Justice. He refused, however, to take his seat until he was given the additional post of a Minister of State for South Lebanon, aiming at total control of that region. Even after that he did not fully participate in the work of the Government, boycotting most of its sessions — together with Junbalat — and sabotaging its efforts to impose unified control. He resided for much of the time in Damascus.

In 1984–85, his Shi'i "militias" in violent, military operations against both the Army and Government (of which he was a member) and local Sunni "militias" (*al-Murabitun*) took control of West Beirut and its southern suburbs and, after the withdrawal of Israeli troops, of the southern coastal plain and most of South Lebanon. These operations were conducted in cooperation with Junbalat's Druze forces, and in July 1985 he cemented that alliance in a "National United Front" — but his Shi'is sometimes clashed with those forces, too, in the struggle for full control. From May–June 1985 B.'s forces attacked the Palestinian guerrilla camps of Beirut and South Lebanon.

B. became internationally known through his part in the June 1985 hijack of an American airliner by Shi'i extremists and the detention of its passengers and crew as hostages. He acted partly as mediator, partly as negotiator for the hijackers, adopting their demands, sent his *Amal* men to take over partially from the extremist hijackers, and together with Syria, eventually took credit for the release of the hostages. In Dec. 1985 he and Junbalat agreed with a leader of the Christian "Lebanese Forces" on a plan for a new political structure for Lebanon, in line with Syria's conceptions and demands; but the agreement was rejected by the Christian leadership and remained abortive (see *Lebanon).

B. is considered by many as essentially a moderate with limited aims: the enhancement of the Shi'i share in power, and full Shi'i control of South Lebanon and the *Biqā'. Towards Israel, too, he may content himself with the achievement of a full Israeli withdrawal from Lebanon and oppose attacks on Israel herself, though he refuses to establish fully fledged contacts with Israel and reach an agreement with her. He opposes any return of an armed PLO presence in South Lebanon and Beirut. But he is under constant pressure from more extremist Shi'i groups (*Hizb-ullah, al-Amal al-Islami, al-Jihad al-Islami*) inspired and directed by Iran's *Khomeini and his partisans — groups which clamor for control of the Shi'i community and its *al-Amal* militias, for much more extreme political aims (the transformation of Lebanon into an Islamic state, and total war against Israel). Therefore B. may himself adopt more extremist positions so as to maintain his leadership.

Bevin, Ernest (1881–1951) As British Foreign Secretary 1945–51, B. was deeply involved in many ME and A. issues, and particularly the Palestine problem (see *Arab-Israel Conflict). Three agreements informally bear his name: the B.-Bidault agreement of Dec. 1945 providing for the evacuation of French and British troops from Syria and Lebanon; the abortive Anglo-Egyptian B.-Sidqi agreement of Oct. 1946 (see *Egypt), and the abortive Anglo-Italian B.-Sforza agreement of 1949 on Libya (see *Libya).

al-Biqā' (Arabic: the Valley). The valley, or plain, in eastern Lebanon, between Mount Lebanon and the Anti-Lebanon mountains in Syria; the *Orontes (al-'Āssi) river flows through it, to the north, and the *Litani to the south; in European languages the B. is also called Coele-Syria. The B., one of the six provinces of Lebanon, has a Muslim majority, with *Shi'i Muslims forming the largest single community, c. 35%. In two districts — Baalbek (the provincial capital) and Harmal — Shi'is are the majority (60–70%). In the southern district of Rashaya, the *Druze are the largest community. Among the Christians, the Greek-Catholics are the strongest community, mainly in Zahla and the Harmal district.

The B. was not part of the autonomous district of Lebanon under Ottoman rule, 1861–1914; it was joined to "Greater Lebanon" in 1920 by the French, together with the Muslim-Sunni North Lebanon, Muslim-Shi'i South Lebanon, and the city of Beirut — an "annexation" that created serious problems as it was not readily accepted by either the Muslim population concerned or Syria. The territorial integrity of "Greater" Lebanon was, eventually, formally accepted and guaranteed by all ASt., including Syria, in the *Alexandria Protocol of 1944, upon Lebanon's insistence and as a pre-condition for her joining the *Arab League.

Syria continued regarding the B. as a region of crucial strategic importance for her security. During the Lebanese civil war from 1975 onward, as the effective authority of the Lebanese Government was waning, Syria in fact imposed on the B. and its local government a kind of protectorate. This was intensified after Syria's full military intervention in 1976, until it became *de facto* full Syrian control and nearly direct Syrian administration. The southern part of the B., occupied by Israel in 1982, reverted to that Syrian administration after Israel's withdrawal in 1985. Under that Syrian umbrella, the B. was in the 1970s a major center of Palestinian-Arab guerrilla camps and bases. The Syrians and pro-Syrian Palestinian formations expelled those loyal to *'Arafat, in military operations in 1983, and the B. became the main base of the extremist, Syria-guided organizations exclusively. Since the early 1980s Iranian "volunteers" and "Revolutionary Guards" sent by *Khomeini have also established themselves, with Syrian permission, in the B. and turned it into the main base for extremist Shi'i factions (*al-Jihad al-Islami, Hizb-ullah, al-Amal al-Islami*). The B. is also Lebanon's main center of marijuana (hashish) cultivation — officially illegal.

Bitar, Salah-ul-Din (1912–80) Syrian politician. Born in Damascus to a prominent family, B. studied physics at the universities of Damascus and Paris and worked as a teacher. In 1940, together with Michel *'Aflaq, he founded among Syrian and A. students and intellectuals in Paris, a leftist-nationalist Pan-A. group, *al-*Ba'th al-'Arabi* (A. Renaissance), and became editor of its organ, *al-Ba'th*. When the *Ba'th* group became a political party of growing importance, in the late 1940s and the 1950s, B. was one of its chief leaders. In 1954, after the overthrow of *Shishakli, B. was elected to Parliament. In 1956–57 he was Foreign Minister and worked, with his *Ba'th* associates, for the union of Syria and Egypt. When that union was established, in 1958, B. became Minister of State for A. Affairs, and later Minister of National Guidance, in the Government of the *UAR. He resigned in 1959, when *Nasser began curbing the influence of the *Ba'th* leaders and drove them into opposition. In 1961, after Syria's secession from the UAR, B. lost in the elections. After the *Ba'th* officers' *coup* of 1963, B. became Prime Minister, serving as his own Foreign Minister, too. As the *Ba'th* government increasingly turned into an officers' régime, with the civilian politicians and ideologues gradually losing whatever influence they had, B. had to step down late in 1964 for General Amin *Hafez; he also lost his position in the *Ba'th* party high command. With the decline of Hafez, B. briefly became Prime Minister again in Jan. 1966, but was overthrown in the Feb. 1966 *coup* in which the *Ba'th*'s Leftist "military" faction seized power. He was arrested, but escaped to Lebanon. He was expelled, together with 'Aflaq, from the *Ba'th* party — i.e., from the faction now ruling Syria.

In his Lebanese exile, B. was not active in the rival wing of the *Ba'th* controlled by 'Aflaq and linked with the Iraqi *Ba'th* régime, and later he moved to Paris and dissociated himself from both wings of the *Ba'th*. In 1969 B. was sentenced to death, *in absentia*, by a Syrian court, but in 1971 he was pardoned. In the late 1970s he briefly returned to Syria, but finding co-operation with the *Asad régime impossible, he soon left again for Paris, where he became the rallying point for various dissident groups in exile. B. was assassinated, in Paris, in July 1980 — according to anti-Syrian *Ba'th* spokesmen: by the Syrian secret service.

Black September Palestinian-Arab terrorist group. See *Palestine-Arab Guerrilla Organizations.

Boumédienne, Houari (Hawari; original name: Muhammad Boukharouba) (1925? 1927? 1932?–78). Algerian officer and politician. Born in the 'Annaba (Bone) region of eastern Algeria as the son of a farm laborer, B. was later said to have studied Arabic literature at Tunis University and Cairo's al*Azhar. He stayed on in Cairo, working as a teacher. It was there that he met *Ben Bella and other leaders of the incipient Algerian revolt; in 1954 he joined their *FLN and soon became one of the revolt's commanders. In 1955 he landed in Western Algeria with a group of rebels and soon headed the rebel formations in the Oran region. He later returned to FLN headquarters, now in Tunis, became a member of the Revolutionary Council set up in 1956, and in Mar. 1960 was appointed Chief-of-Staff of the rebel army. After the French-Algerian Agreement of 1962 he led that army into Algeria; half-hidden tensions between the guerrillas inside Algeria and the rebel army outside now erupted. B. firmly insisted on the primacy of the regular rebel army entering Algeria from Tunisia and soon armed clashes broke out; he also became involved in factional struggles, vigorously backing Ben Bella. In July 1962 he was dismissed by the FLN Prime Minister Ben Khedda, but, firmly backed by Ben Bella, he ignored this order, marched into Algiers and imposed the rule of his army and Ben Bella's faction. When Ben Bella set up the first government of independent Algeria in September 1962, B. became his Defense Minister and from Sept. 1963 also Deputy Prime Minister and Number Two of the régime (and some thought that he held the real power). But tension developed between him and Ben Bella; Ben Bella did not trust B. and saw him as a rival, and B. loathed Ben Bella's factionalism and his treatment of former comrades-in-arms, his allures of grandeur and his aspirations to all-A. and African leadership.

In June 1965 B. overthrew Ben Bella in a *coup* and imprisoned him. He set up a new Revolutionary Council with himself as chairman. He was now Head-of-State and Prime Minister — without formally assuming these titles — and remained Minister of Defense. For nearly eleven years he ruled Algeria without seeking a formal institutionalization or popular endorsement of his titles and positions. Only in 1976 he convened a FLN leadership conference and had it draw up a new "National Charter", which was endorsed by a plebiscite; a "National Conference" under that Charter enacted a new constitution, and under that constitution B. was elected President, as the only candidate, in a referendum of Dec. 1976.

In his over thirteen years as Head-of-State, B. made no major changes in Algeria's policies. He put less emphasis on ideology and doctrine and stressed the internal régime and economic rather than foreign and international policy, but his régime remained strict, allowing no deviation from the line he laid down and keeping power within the group of his associates. He purged not only the establishment within Algeria, but during his rule — i.e. probably under his orders — prominent opposition leaders in exile were eliminated by assassination, including Muhammad Khidr and the revolution's most prominent leader after (or with) Ben Bella, Belkacem Krim. His state socialism remained leftist-radical and his alliance with the Soviet Bloc, international leftist neutralism and the inter-A. "Rejection Front" was firm. While B. had not much charisma, his leadership was unquestioned until his death in Dec. 1978.

Bourguiba, al-Habib (b. 1903) The most prominent leader of Tunisian nationalism, who led Tunisia to independence. President of Tunisia since 1957. Born in Monastir, B. studied law in France and began practising as a lawyer. He was active in the nationalist movement represented by the *Dustur* (Arabic: Constitution) Party. In 1934 he was among a group of younger activists who seceded from the party, dissatisfied with its traditional leadership and lack of vigor, and founded the *Neo-Dustur* Party which soon became the chief spokesman of Tunisian nationalism. B. was imprisoned in 1934–36 and again from 1938. He was released in 1942 by the German occupiers of France (and from Nov. 1942 also of Tunisia). His official biographers are silent concerning his relations with the Germans after his release; he seems to have collaborated with them to some degree, but this has not been fully clarified. In 1945 he escaped renewed French surveillance and harassment and went to Cairo, where the nationalists of the three Maghrib countries established their headquarters. In 1950 he went to France to negotiate, but when these talks failed he was again arrested. For the final negotiations on Tunisia's independence, 1954–55, he was released but kept under surveillance. During those years B. had to face more extremist elements within his movement — both the guerrillas fighting an armed struggle, and a faction of the *Neo-Dustur* led by his rival Saleh Ben Yussuf — but he won out.

After Tunisia attained partial independence in 1955 and full independence in Mar. 1956, B. was elected President of the Constituent Assembly in Apr., and the same month he formed the first government of independent Tunisia, keeping the Defense and Foreign Minister posts himself. With the abolition of the monarchy in July 1957 he was proclaimed President of Tunisia (though the Constitution was completed and adopted only in 1959). He was re-elected President as the only candidate in 1959, 1964, 1969 and 1974, and in Mar. 1975 was proclaimed President for life. As President he also kept the Premiership until Nov. 1969.

For the three decades since his assumption of the Presidency, B. has been the supreme leader of Tunisia, determining the character and policies of the state, its organization and its administration. He decided to give T. a modernist and moderate, liberal, pro-Western shape. He abolished polygamy, restricted the rule of Islamic law and its institutions and made the secular institutions of the state supreme. He intervened personally several times to prevent pogroms or mob excesses against T.'s Jews. Despite several sharp conflicts with France, he kept T. close to France and the USA, with the French language and French cultural influence nearly dominant. While supporting all-A. cooperation, he had little sympathy for Pan-A. rhetoric or for the radical leftist-"progressive" régimes and doctrines prevalent in several AC, such as Egypt or Algeria. He frequently clashed with Egypt's *Nasser. In the spring of 1958, on the eve of T.'s admission to the *Arab League, he accused Egypt, and Nasser personally, of assisting in plots to subvert T. and assassinate him (the reference was to Saleh Ben Yussuf, his leading rival, who had found asylum in Egypt since 1956); in Oct.–Nov. 1958 he repeated these accusations in public speeches, severed relations with Egypt and ordered T.'s representative to walk out of the first A. League meeting attended by T., denouncing the League as Egypt's tool. In 1961 he resumed relations with Egypt and returned to the League, but relations remained cool.

B. did not conform to all-A. positions on Israel. Although he had no sympathy for Israel, he held that the ASt did not have the military power to solve the conflict by war and that they should negotiate with Israel and peacefully co-exist with her if she accepted their conditions. As to these conditions and demands, B. hardly differed from other A. leaders; but the prospect of peaceful co-existence he held out in public was in the 1950s and 1960s unusual and unacceptable to the ASt. His dissent reached a peak in the spring of 1965 during a tour of the ME when he expounded his ideas to journalists, students and political circles in Egypt, Jordan and Lebanon and formulated them into a plan. There was a storm of protest, the ASt denounced him and recalled their ambassadors, he was called a traitor and informed that T.'s participation in A. League sessions was undesirable. B. dissented also on other issues. In 1965 he refused to sever T.'s relations with West Germany, as most ASt did, and throughout the early 1960s T. was the only AC to accept Mauritania's independence. In 1966 B. again severed relations with Egypt; he also absented himself from the all-A. summit of Casablanca, 1965. In the crisis of 1967 and the *Six Day War B. returned to the fold and declared his solidarity with Nasser. But after the war relations reverted to the old pattern: B. was sharply critical of Nasser's Egypt, boycotted A. League meetings and severed relations with Syria in 1968. After Nasser's death in 1970 relations with Egypt improved. B. also mended relations with Algeria. Those with Libya, on the other hand, sharply deteriorated; the strange episode of the proclamation of a Tunisian-Libyan merger, in Jan. 1974, which B., ailing and very old (and his facilities declining?), was apparently persuaded by *Qadhdhafi to accept, aggravated Tunisian-Libyan tension when the merger was cancelled soon after.

The liberal image B. was trying to impart to Tunisia, and to himself, was not borne out by his internal régime. He installed and maintained a *de facto* one-party system, and though in recent years rival parties have been permitted, B.'s *Neo-Dustur* (since 1964: "Socialist *Dustur*") has remained in full control and the only party represented in Parliament. And within the party, and the government, B. rules with an iron fist, ousting and purging anyone not wholly conforming to his wishes (see *Tunisia). The impression is also that B. resents anyone of his aides and associates growing too strong or independent; thus he dismissed Prime Ministers Ladgham (1970), Nouira (1980, after nearly ten years of Premiership), Mazali (1986, after over six years). Even within his own household his rule is harsh (and he seems to fear plots and intrigues); in 1986 he divorced his wife (whom he had married in 1962 after divorcing his first, French-born, wife) amidst rumors of a wide-spread intrigue, and he broke with his son, al-Habib B. Jr., who had served him in senior posts for many years. Yet, B. is very old and has been ailing for years. His succession is T.'s major problem; it is wide open and in doubt, as B. has not allowed anyone to grow strong in his shadow.

Boycott See *Arab boycott

Britain, British interests and policies in the Arab countries Great B. first became involved in the ME in the 16th century, when the English mercantile system, European power struggles and B. imperial dictates prompted the expansion of interests and control to the eastern periphery of the Mediterranean. The resulting commitments, reinforced by strategic considerations, created a string of garrisons and naval bases from

Gibraltar, under B. control since 1704, to the Indian subcontinent and beyond. As the ME was ruled by either the Ottoman Empire or the Persian Empire, B. traders and statesmen sought to establish amicable relations with both. In 1553, Sultan Suleiman gave English merchants permission to trade within his realm on the same terms as were then enjoyed by the French and Venetians, and in 1578 the first B. ambassador presented his credentials to the Sublime Porte. Similarly, in 1566–68, Shah Tahmasp gave English merchants the right to live and trade in Persia. Subsequent penetration of the ME thus came from the two directions of the Mediterranean and the Persian Gulf. The India Office was concerned with Persia and the maritime corridors to India, while the Foreign Office involved itself in Turkish affairs.

By the 19th century the Ottoman Empire had declined so much that it became known as "the Sick Man on the Bosphorus" and posed before European diplomacy a sensitive "Eastern Question": what arrangements should replace the Ottoman Empire in the event of its demise? Great B. was reluctant to see the Turkish domains, and especially Constantinople and the Dardanelles, come under the control of either France or Russia. As a result, the survival, sovereignty and territorial integrity of the Turkish Empire were cardinal principles of B. foreign policy. B.'s commitment to Turkey often involved her in the external and domestic affairs of the Empire. Through the Treaty of Paris, 1856, the Convention of London 1871, and the Congress of Berlin, 1878, B. endeavored to ensure Turkish security, and British interests, by peaceful means. Yet on several occasions B. used force: against France, 1798; in ending the Egyptian Muhammad 'Ali's defiance of the Sultan, 1839; and against Russian expansion during the Crimean War, 1854–56.

French and Russian designs on Turkish territory heightened London's appreciation of the ME and actually led to an extension of B. control. Napoleon's invasion of Egypt in 1798 alerted B. to the vulnerability of her lines of communication to India as well as to Egypt's strategic importance. The Sultan of *'Oman and the sheikhs of *Bahrain and *Kuwait subjected their foreign relations to exclusive B. control in 1891, 1892 and 1899 respectively; B. acquired Malta in 1815 and *'Aden in 1839. The *Trucial Coast, which had been brought under "Trucial agreements" against piracy in 1820 and 1835, was pacified under a "Perpetual Maritime Truce" in 1853 and became a B. protectorate. Once the dream of a *Suez Canal became a reality in 1869 (inspired by a Frenchman, Ferdinand de Lesseps), B. politicians realized its importance as the primary route between Europe and the Orient. At Disraeli's initiative, B. acquired a major share in the Canal and obtained a voice in its management. This was reinforced by the B. occupation of Egypt in 1882, transformed into a protectorate in December 1914. In 1878 B. exploited renewed Russo-Turkish friction by annexing Cyprus.

As European Powers began to compete for oil concessions, one of the first and most important concessions was granted to W. K. D'Arcy in 1901 by Persia; it was acquired in 1909 by the Anglo-Persian Oil Company, in which the B. Government possessed a controlling interest from 1914. B. interests also competed for railway concessions, although few materialized, and endeavored to frustrate rival powers' concessions, such as the German-controlled Baghdad Railway project. River navigation was also an important B. interest, especially on the Nile and Tigris-Euphrates systems. In Iran, B. exercised considerable influence, in constant competition with Imperial Russia. An Anglo-Russian Treaty of 1907 divided Iran into B. and Russian zones of influence.

Turkey's decision to side with Germany in World War I, 1914, induced B. to consent to the eventual partition of the Ottoman Empire. Russia was to take possession of Constantinople and the Straits (Secret Agreement of April 1915). According to the *Sykes-Picot Agreement with France and Russia, 1916, B. was to obtain possession of southern Mesopotamia with Baghdad, and Haifa and Acre in Palestine; central Iraq, the region that later became known as Transjordan, and southern Palestine (the *Negev) were to become a British zone of influence; B. was also to participate in an international administration of the main parts of Palestine. B. also sought contact with A. Leaders, to activate them against Turkey in the war and to protect B. interests in the A. world. London considered Sharif *Hussein of Mecca to be the most appropriate partner (though B. was since 1915 in local treaty relations also with *Ibn Sa'ud of *Najd, through the government of B. India). In the *McMahon-Hussein correspondence, 1915–6, B. gave her qualified support for A. independence, in return for which Hussein sponsored an A. revolt against the Ottomans. (For later differences as to the extent of A. independence see *McMahon-Hussein Correspondence.) In November 1917 B. issued the *Balfour Declaration which extended B. support to world Jewry for establishing a national home in Palestine.

The post-war settlement conferred upon B. *Mandates to administer Iraq and Palestine (including Transjordan). By 1920 B. enjoyed an unprecedented primacy in the ME. No other great power offered a challenge. In the wake of the Bolshevik Revolution, Russia's new leaders had renounced traditional territorial claims; the Turkish nationalists under Mustafa Kemal did not wish to restore the Turkish Empire; Germany was defeated; the USA did not want to play any part in the ME power game; France was weakened by the war effort and had to use force to assert her claim to Syria and Lebanon. Local A. nationalists, however, were unwilling to accept B. tutelage, and there were rebellions and unrest in Iraq (1920), Egypt (1919, 1921), and Palestine (1920, 1921). The several conflicting wartime undertakings — to Hussein, to France and to the Zionist movement — aggravated the problem. B. remained silent while France forcefully asserted her control over Syria and Lebanon in 1920.

Gradually national élites in Egypt and Iraq accepted the semi-independence granted them under B. guidance. B. authority was exercised in Egypt through a protectorate (*de jure* until 1922, *de facto* until 1936); in Palestine and Iraq through *Mandates confirmed by the League of Nations; and in Arabia and along the littoral of the Persian Gulf by direct treaty relationships with local sheikhs.

In an attempt to formulate a coherent policy, Winston Churchill, then Colonial Secretary, summoned B. authorities to a conference in Cairo in 1921; its decisions governed Ango-A. relations during the interwar period. B. interests and influence were to be ensured with minimal expenditure; the use of B. troops could be avoided, it was hoped, by the efficient employment of air power, local A. forces and monetary subsidies to various tribal leaders and rulers. Support was extended to Sharif Hussein in Hijaz and to his sons *Feisal enthroned by B. in Iraq, and *'Abdullah made Amir of Transjordan (created in 1921 as a semi-independent principality within the League of Nations Mandate for Palestine). As for Palestine, London initially felt confident that the Jewish and A. communities could eventually be brought to cooperate under B. rule; the Zionists considered the B. authorities in London to be well-intentioned, but most of the B. administrators in Palestine antagonistic; with the passing of time, B. tended to favor the A.'s, largely for political and strategic reasons. In the AC, B. interests were to be fostered by the creation of semi-independent states under indirect B. supervision or guidance rather than direct control; such High Commissioners as Gen. Allenby in Egypt and Sir Percy Cox in Iraq reflected this spirit. The plan was to guide the ASt gradually and peacefully to full independence while safeguarding B. imperial interests. The transition to independence, and the satisfaction of B. interests after its achievement, were to be laid down in treaties between B. and the countries concerned.

In the period after 1921 B. pre-eminence reached its peak. B. oil interests increased their involvement in the Persian Gulf area, and relations with Iran, Iraq, Kuwait and Sa'udi Arabia grew in importance. Friction developed between B. and the USA, as their oil companies vied with each other for access to the oil-rich countries and concessions, and American companies felt themselves excluded by B. imperial rule. By the mid-1920s, B. had to admit American companies to areas of her concessions and interests, such as Iraq and later Kuwait and in the 1950s Iran. In Bahrain and Sa'udi Arabia, American oil interests won the concessions on their own.

In the AC under B. tutelage the nationalists continued their struggle for more independence, to be codified in new treaties — separate and divergent in each country. For this process in Egypt — from B.'s 1922 unilateral proclamation of Egypt's independence with reservations, B. retaining authority for defense, the protection of foreign interests and the governance of Sudan, to the 20-year Treaty of 1936 — see *Egypt, *Colonialism. For the similar gradual emancipation of Iraq — from the Treaty of 1922 to the 25-year Treaty of 1930, Iraq's admission to the League of Nations in 1932 and the termination of B.'s mandatory responsibility — see *Iraq, *Colonialism.

B. continued to exert considerable *de facto* influence and her still-privileged position soon caused renewed resentment and agitation in both countries. In Iraq, anti-B. resentment played a rôle in a military *coup* led by Gen. Bakr *Sidqi in 1936, and in the late 1930s, the officers who *de facto* ruled Iraq were extreme nationalists and bitterly anti-British. Transjordan provided the least troublesome relationship. The Amir 'Abdullah cooperated with B. upon whom he was dependent financially and militarily. By the treaty of 1946, London recognized Transjordan as an independent kingdom, but continued to aid her financially and subsidize her army.

There were persistent rumors of B. support for a planned *Hashemite *"Greater Syria" or *Fertile Crescent Federation. The French, and anti-Hashemite Syrian and Lebanese politicians, certainly suspected such plans — as part of a secret B. scheme to oust France from the ME. In fact there was little B. involvement in Syria and Lebanon during the interwar period.

In Arabia, B. acknowledged Ibn Sa'ud's primacy after 1925, aquiescing in his conquest of Hijaz and the ouster of B.'s Hashemite protégés, Hussein and his son 'Ali; a treaty with Ibn Sa'ud was signed in 1927. B. influence endured in the Persian Gulf sheikhdoms. Efforts to gain influence in Yemen were not very successful.

The greatest test of British preponderance in the ME occurred in Palestine. For A. hostility towards the Mandate, the B. and the Jews; the A. rebellion of 1936; the 1937 partition plan — rejected by the A.'s and soon dropped by B.; the resumed A. rebellion, 1937–39; the Round Table Conference of 1939, including, at Britain's invitation, the Arab States; the White Paper of 1939 — see *Palestine Arabs, *Arab-Israel Conflict.

That B. had not gained the friendship of the A.'s was reflected in the sympathy which Italy and particularly Germany evoked in the region in the late 1930s. During World War II a group of Egyptian military officers and politicians were in contact with Italian and German officials; and Egypt's government only grudgingly granted B. the cooperation and facilities agreed to in the Treaty of 1936. The former Mufti of Jerusalem and some of his supporters took refuge in Berlin; and so did pro-Nazi politicians from various AC. In Iraq the pro-Axis government of Rashid *'Ali made war on B. in 1941, when B. insisted on using the facilities and privileges provided for in the Treaty; pro-B. leaders were reinstated after the suppression of the Rashid 'Ali régime. In June 1941, B. and Free French forces took Syria and Lebanon; Anglo-French antagonism soon reappeared — with B. openly supporting Syrian and Lebanese nationalists against the French. To secure Iran and deny her territory to the enemy, B. and Russian troops occupied the country in August 1941, and divided it into two zones — with B.'s Zone much larger than in 1907. 'Abdullah of Transjordan was loyal, and the Jews of Palestine, while fighting against B.'s White Paper policy, fully supported her war against Hitler, though B. was reluctant to form the 26,000 Palestinian-Jewish volunteers into a specifically Jewish Army, as they demanded (part of them were permitted to form a Jewish Brigade in 1944).

The end of the war found B. weakened and confronted by new challenges from the USSR. Several means were used to maintain influence if not actual power in the region. B. fostered the *Arab League, founded 1945; joined the USA in insisting on a complete and speedy withdrawal of USSR troops from Iran, 1945–46; put pressure on France to withdraw from Syria and Lebanon by supporting the local nationalists, 1943–46; tried to retain a degree of influence on the Palestine conflict; later promoted regional security organizations, such as the abortive *ME Defense Organization, 1951, and the ill-fated *Baghdad Pact, 1955; and even resorted to military force against Egypt during the Suez crisis of 1956.

Despite these efforts, B. was unable to arrest the rapid decline of her position in the ME. From the 1940s onwards, B. encouraged American involvement in the ME; she was overshadowed by the USA after 1950. In 1947 B. granted India independence, thus removing one of the major justifications for a strong B. presence in the ME. After final attempts to work out a Palestine solution acceptable to A.'s and Jews, B. admitted failure in 1947, relinquished her Mandate to the UN and withdrew from Palestine in May 1948. In 1950 she co-sponsored with the US and France attempts to control arms supplies and vaguely to endorse existing A.-Israel frontiers (the Tripartite Declaration); but these attempts were ineffective and, in any case, B. was no longer a chief factor. A grave Anglo-Persian crisis, 1951–53, over the oil concession, ended with a compromise — but B. lost her position of special influence.

In 1954 — B. signed a new treaty with Egypt (now under a revolutionary government), in which she agreed to evacuate the Canal Zone bases and renounced any special privileges. Egypt's nationalization of the Suez Canal in 1956 and the abortive Anglo-French Suez War — the last attempt to impose imperial wishes by "gunboat diplomacy" — highlighted the impotence of the two former imperial powers. Egypt now tore up even the inoffensive Treaty of 1954 and any special treaty relationship with B. ended. Sudan was granted self-determination in 1955 and assumed full independence without any special concessions for or treaty with B. In 1956–57, B.'s special position in Jordan was ended by the dismissal of Brig. *Glubb, the B. commander of Jordan's Army, and the replacement of B.'s subsidy for the army by Syrian-Sa'udi-Egyptian financial aid (which, however, was not implemented). B. re-assumed a temporary role in July 1958, when her troops were asked by Jordan to ensure the latter's independence; but her privileged position in Jordan was not restored.

In Iraq, attempts to replace the Treaty of 1930 with a new one, were abortive. That Treaty was terminated, when both B. and Iraq joined the Baghdad Pact, 1955. The revolution of 1958 ended B.'s privileges in Iraq. Kuwait won her independence in 1961 — by peaceful means and in agreement with B.; Kuwait immediately asked for B. protection against Iraq. In 1967 B. rule ended in the Crown Colony of 'Aden and the adjoining Protectorate. In 1970 B. completed the evacuation of her bases in Libya. Those in the Persian Gulf were liquidated and B. protection for the petty rulers of the Trucial Coast ended in 1971.

B. oil companies are no longer as powerful as they used to be. B.'s share among the foreign companies decreased from over 50% of production at the end of World War II to less than 30% in the 1960s. In any case, all foreign oil companies lost most of their special power when, after a long process of change in the conditions and concessions in favor of the producing countries, the latter began in 1973 unilaterally to determine prices and production terms; moreover, most oil production has since the 1970s been nationalized and the foreign companies continue working only as agents or operators on behalf of the producing countries and their national companies. B.'s primary interest in unimpaired access to the sources of oil in the region still endures, as does a desire to retain influence in the region through normal diplomatic channels. B. also remains a major supplier of arms, and attempts, sometimes, to use that position as a diplomatic lever.

B. takes part, in some measure, in Western efforts to sponsor a ME peace settlement; thus she participated in abortive Four-Power talks on the A.-Israel dispute in 1969–70, and tried to assist American efforts in the 1970s and 1980s. She also participates in Western attempts to insure free shipping in the Persian Gulf and still aids the armed forces of 'Oman. But she does so as a medium power, a junior partner rather than as a great imperial power. B.'s own diplomatic relations with the ASt were disrupted several times. Egypt, Sudan and Algeria severed relations in 1965 to protest her Rhodesia policy; Syria, Iraq and Sudan did the same in 1967 in connection with the *Six Day War (Egypt had no relations with B. at that time). Relations were later resumed. In recent years B. has severed relations with ASt she considered to be actively involved in terrorism — Libya (1984) and Syria (1986).

al-Buraimi Oasis in the Arabian peninsula, on the border between Abu Dhabi and 'Oman. Area: 13,490 sq.mi., pop.: c. 25,000 in eight villages of which six belong to Abu Dhabi, two to 'Oman. In the late 1940s, when it was reported that oil might be found in B., Sa'udi Arabia claimed the oasis, asserting that it had been ruled in the 18th and 19th centuries by the Sa'udi Sultans of Najd. This claim was disputed by Britain, as the power protecting Abu Dhabi and 'Oman, pointing out that in the Anglo-Sa'udi Treaty of Jedda (1927), in which the boundaries of the Sa'udi kingdom were fixed, al-B. had not been defined as Sa'udi. Behind the dispute, opposing interests of the oil giants were discernible: if B. belonged to Abu Dhabi and/or 'Oman, its oil would be covered by concessions held by subsidiaries of the largely-British Iraq Petroleum Co.; if it was Sa'udi territory, its oil would belong to the American "Aramco". In 1952, after a period of claims and counter-claims, Sa'udia sent a military force to occupy al-B. In 1954, arbitration was agreed upon, but it was not carried to a successful conclusion. In 1955 B. was taken by military forces of Abu Dhabi and 'Oman, under British command. Sa'udia protested and after severing relations with Britain in 1956 following the *Suez War declared that relations would not be resumed until the B. issue was settled. However, Anglo-Sa'udi relations were renewed in Jan. 1963 with the B. dispute still unresolved. Further diplomatic efforts, including mediation on behalf of the UN Secretary-General, were of no avail, and when Britain announced that she would withdraw her protectorate from the Persian Gulf sheikhdoms, Sa'udia in 1970 reasserted her claim to B. But when the British indeed withdrew, in 1971, creating a power vacuum, Sa'udia resolved to accord priority to a decisive improvement in her relations with the Gulf principalities and to ignore petty disputes standing in its way. In 1971 she promised the visiting Sultan of 'Oman that she would renounce her claim to B. That renunciation was formalized in a Sa'udi-Abu Dhabi border agreement of July 1974 (against certain concessions by Abu Dhabi in other border sectors).

Oil has in the meantime been found in B. The oasis has also been linked to Abu Dhabi by a modern highway and is being developed as a tourist resort.

Butrus-Ghali Prominent Egyptian Coptic family. The best-known of its sons was Butrus B.-Gh, Foreign Minister at the end of the 19th century, and in that capacity co-signatory, with Lord *Cromer, of the 1899 Anglo-Egyptian Convention which established the *condominium over Sudan. Later he was Justice Minister; in that capacity he was responsible for the trial, in 1906, of the Egyptians involved in the Dinshawi Incident, which aroused much resentment and nationalist agitation — and bitter hatred of B.-Gh personally and anti-Copt incitement. In 1908 B.-Gh became Prime Minister — Egypt's first and only Coptic-Christian Premier. As Prime Minister he advocated a 40-year extension of the *Suez Canal concession — which again caused violent nationalist agitation and was rejected by the National Assembly. B.-Gh was assassinated in 1910.

Wassef B.-Gh (1877–1958), the former's son, was Foreign Minister in several Governments of the *Wafd Party — in 1924–25, 1928, 1930 and 1936–37.

Mirrit B.-Gh, a grandson of the first-listed, a Wafdist and later, in the 1950s, an independent member of Parliament, published a book, *The Politics of Tomorrow* (1938, re-issued in 1951), a socio-political analysis of Egypt's basic problems, which aroused considerable attention and praise.

Butrus B.-Gh (born 1922), also a grandson of the first-listed, a jurist and a political scientist, educated in Cairo and Paris, since 1949 teaching at Cairo University, and the author of several studies of international problems. In 1977 he was appointed by President *Sadat as Minister of State for Foreign Affairs. He played an important part in the Egypt-Israel peace negotiations, and while he drove a hard bargain and adamantly stuck to positions laid down by Egypt's leaders (and some of his statements were resented in Israel), he strongly advocated, and acted for, peace. His influence in that direction was considerable and he was in fact the chief operative of Egypt's foreign policy, though formally he did not attain the position of Foreign Minister (the impression was: because he was a Copt).

C

Cairo (al-Qāhira) Capital and largest city of Egypt. Its population, estimated in the mid-1980s at over 12m., grew rapidly over the last half-century (from less than a million early in the century to 1.3m. in 1937, 5m. in 1966, 10m. in 1980). The annual influx, mostly from the countryside, adding an estimated 350,000 each year, and the infrastructure of the city — housing, water, sanitation, power, communications and traffic conditions — have not kept pace; large slums have been created and the city is overcrowded and badly congested. C. is the main center of A. literature and journalism, film and record production, and A. cultural activity in general. Its universities (the C. University — formerly Fu'ad I University, founded in 1908 and modernized in 1925; 'Ain Shams — founded 1950; a small American college, raised to university status in 1953; the famous Islamic University of al-*Azhar, founded 969) attract a large number of students from AC's.

C. was for many years the center and headquarters of British political institutions or agencies dealing with the ME, such as the "Arab Bureau" during and after World War I; the conference of British ME policy makers that designed the governance of Iraq, Transjordan etc., in 1921, took place in C. During World War II, a British Resident Minister for the ME had his seat in C. The city also hosted, even before Egypt's independence, several congresses and conferences, such as the Islamic Congress of 1926 (see *Pan-Islam). The *Arab League was founded in C. (Mar. 1945); its headquarters were located there until 1979 and most of its meetings were held, until 1977–78, in C. Other international organizations, particularly Afro-Asian ones, often held congresses and meetings in C., including the second summit conferences of both the Organization for African Unity (*OAU) and the *Non-Aligned States, both in 1964. The Afro-Asian Peoples' Solidarity Organization (AAPSO) was founded in C., in 1957, and had its headquarters there. C. also provided refuge and headquarters for several African liberation and/or revolutionary underground organizations, beginning, in the 1950s, with those of the French-ruled *Maghrib.

Among the political documents bearing C.'s name are: the "C. Declaration" of 1 Dec. 1943, in which Roosevelt, Churchill and Chiang Kai-shek defined their war aims, mainly in relation to the Far East; the C. Agreement of Nov. 1969, mediated (and imposed) by Egypt's rulers, which sought to define the relations between the Government of Lebanon and the Palestinian-A. guerrilla groups and provide rules for the latters' operations and conduct; and a similar C. Agreement with the *PLO imposed in Sept. 1970 through Egyptian and all-A. pressure on King *Hussein of Jordan (abortive).

Caliph (Arabic: *Khalifa*, Successor or Replacement), **Caliphate** (*Khilāfa*) The C. was the head of the Muslim community, succeeding the Prophet Muhammad in his political and social functions (as distinct from his prophetic mission, in which there can be no successor). After the Prophet's death in 632 the C. was first held by his companions the "Righteous" C.'s Abu Bakr, 'Uthman (Othman), 'Umar (Omar) and 'Ali, then by the Umayyad (661–750) and 'Abassid (750–1258) dynasties. The succession was frequently disputed and civil wars erupted around it from the early days of Islam. The most famous one was that around the C. 'Ali and his sons Hassan and Hussein which caused a permanent split and the emergence of *Shi'i Islam (and in which both 'Ali and Hussein were killed). Rival claims, splits, the emergence of semi-independent Muslim kingdoms in various parts of the empire, and the rise of military rulers at the C.'s center, especially from the 10th century, caused a decline in the office of the C.; various Muslim rulers arbitrarily assumed the title of C., and the last 'Abassid C.'s were mere figureheads. In 1517 the conquering Ottoman Sultan assumed the C., and his successors bore the title of C. concurrently with, and somewhat subordinated to, the Ottoman Sultanate. From the late 18th century the Ottoman Sultans reasserted, as C.'s, a general, at least spiritual, authority over all Muslims, including those outside the empire. Thus the Treaty of Küçük Kaynarca with Russia, 1774, stipulated that the Sultan retain such spiritual authority over the Muslim Tatars of the Crimea, which was granted independence. A similar provision was applied to Libya when, in 1912, Turkey ceded her to Italy. The Sultan's position as C. was further reasserted when, in the late 19th century, Sultan *'Abd-ul-Hamid II developed *Pan-Islamic policies, and it was incorporated in the Ottoman constitution of 1876.

During World War I, the Ottoman Sultan used his office as C. to arouse sympathy for Turkey among Muslims in the countries allied against her, e.g. in India, and stir up resistance to their governments' war effort. While such sympathy was created to a certain extent, it did not lead to rebellions or resistance. Moreover, loyalty to the Sultan-C., which prevailed, in general, in the Arab-populated countries of the *Fertile Crescent, did not deter the Muslim-A. Sharif of Mecca from rebelling against the Ottomans (see *Arab Revolt). Yet, after the war, rumors of allied plans to dismember the Ottoman Empire and abolish the C. led to the formation of a *Khilafat* movement in India from 1919 to protect the C. (Indian nationalists identified themselves with that movement). The abolition of the C., however, came not from the victorious allied powers but from Turkey's nationalists. They, led by Mustafa Kemal (Atatürk), fought against the Sultan and his government in 1919–23 (mainly because the Sultan had submitted to the Peace Treaty of *Sèvres, dictated by the allied powers, that would have dismembered Anatolia, the Turkish heartland). When the nationalists finally abolished the Sultanate, in Nov. 1922, they let the C. continue, appointing a relative of the deposed Sultan as C., but in Mar. 1924 they abolished the C. too (exiling forever all members of the Ottoman dynasty).

The abolition of the C., along with Kemal's policy of cutting nationalist Turkey's ties with her Ottoman-Islamic heritage, aroused puzzled hostility among the world's Muslims. Various Muslim rulers now began scheming to have themselves recognized as C.; King *Hussein of Hijaz openly staked his claim and proclaimed himself C. (1924), while similar plans regarding *Ibn Sa'ud, or Kings *Fu'ad and later *Farouq of Egypt, were rumored but never officially confirmed. Anyway, none of them gained much support. In 1926 an Islamic Congress was convened in Cairo to plan the renewal of the C., but it was not representative of all Muslims, failed to agree on a candidate, and dispersed with a call for future action. No Muslim consensus was achieved henceforth either, and as nationalism became the dominant trend, calls for the re-establishment of the C. diminished and were largely disregarded. Even the revival, since the 1960s, of Islamic tendencies and all-Islamic political organization (see *Pan-Islam) has not given rise to a significant movement for the renewal of the C.

Camp David Agreements Accords concluded in Sept. 1978 between Egypt and Israel, called CDA because the negotiating delegations, led by President *Sadat of Egypt and Israel's Premier Begin, closeted themselves for the last phase of their talks at the CD retreat of US President *Carter (wtho played an active and decisive rôle in the negotiations). The CDA, accompanied by a series of letters and annexes, consisted mainly of two documents — one setting out principles of a general ME, A.-Israel settlement and particularly the question of Palestine and the Palestine A.'s, and oné laying down guidelines for an Egyptian-Israeli peace treaty. For their contents see *Arab-Israel Conflict and *Egypt.

capitulations Agreements exempting foreigners, their personal status, their commerce, navigation and religious, educational and charitable institutions, from local jurisdiction. (The term derives from the chapters or paragraphs — Latin: *capitula* — of the agreements, not from "capitulation" in the usual sense.) The great medieval merchant powers — Genoa, Venice, Pisa — were first granted the right to exercise jurisdiction over their nationals in the Middle East in the 11th and 12th centuries by the Crusader princes, and later also by Byzantium. The Ottoman Empire, consolidating and expanding in the 15th and 16th centuries, and interested in the development of trade with Europe, took over and renegotiated such C. and concluded agreements with Genoa 1453, Venice 1454, France 1535, and England 1583. New Western states (e.g. USA, Belgium, Greece) were accorded similar C. rights as late as the 19th century. C. agreements were also concluded by the West with other Eastern countries, e.g. Morocco, Persia, East African rulers, and the Far East. Most C. agreements provided for consular jurisdiction or mixed tribunals.

For centuries, the C. were considered necessary to protect foreigners against arbitrariness, corruption or xenophobia of local rulers. Some autonomy for foreigners also tied in with the Muslim *Millet* system traditional in the Ottoman Empire which granted the non-Muslim communities jurisdiction in matters of personal status and wide autonomy in religious matters and the maintenance of educational and charitable institutions. The C. also encouraged foreign investment, in which the Ottoman Empire and other eastern countries were interested.

The C. were abolished, first, in the parts of the Ottoman Empire lost to countries gaining their independence or to the Western powers — e.g. Rumania 1877, Bosnia-Herzegovina 1880, Serbia 1882, Tripolitania (taken by Italy) 1913, Morocco (under a French protectorate) 1912. In independent Greece they were at first maintained, but gradually abolished from 1914. The settlement after World War I included the suspension of the C. in the Mandated territories of Syria and Lebanon, and of Palestine and Transjordan; the Peace Treaty of 1919 imposed the renunciation of C. rights on the defeated Central Powers, too. Soviet Russia voluntarily renounced any C. rights in 1921.

Where C. still remained, they were now resented, seen as illicit strongholds of Imperialism, and eventually abolished as a result of a nationalist struggle. In Turkey, the Western powers sought to maintain C. rights in the Peace Treaty of *Sèvres they imposed on the Sultan; but when the nationalists tore up that document, the West did not insist on C., and renounced them in the new Peace Treaty of *Lausanne, 1923. In Iran (1928) and Iraq (1931) the C. were replaced, under juridical reforms, by certain contractual arrangements. In Egypt they were abolished by international agreement: the Convention of *Montreux, 1937, provided for a transitional arrangement of mixed courts for a period of 12 years. That arrangement was duly terminated in 1949 and the last remnant of C. disappeared. When Syria and Lebanon, Jordan and Israel became fully independent, in the 1940s, no attempt was made to revive C. rights.

Carter, J.E. ("Jimmy") (b.1924) As US President from Jan. 1977 (elected Nov. 1976) to Jan. 1981, C. actively sought a comprehensive ME and A.-Israel settlement. He tended to recognize the Palestine A.'s' right to self-determination and saw the creation of a Palestinian autonomous entity as the center of a solution. He strove for a general ME peace conference, the resumption of the *Geneva Conference of Dec. 1973, and was prepared to readmit the USSR as a partner in these efforts. A joint US-USSR declaration of 1 Oct. 1977 was much resented in Israel and had, anyhow, little effect. C. was not a partner to the secret Egypt-Israel contacts of the fall of 1977, and President *Sadat's visit to Jerusalem in Nov. 1977 took him by surprise. Soon, however, he vigorously — and with a personal involvement unprecedented on the part of a world power's Head of State — joined the Egypt-Israel negotiations as an active mediator, with his Secretary of State Cyrus Vance, and played a crucial role in the talks that led to the *Camp David Agreements of Sept. 1978 and the Egypt-Israel peace treaty of Mar. 1979. C. also endeavored to strengthen ME defense capabilities, based on an informal alliance with the USA. In the "C. Doctrine" of Jan. 1980 he pledged US action (and aid) against "any attempt by any outside force to gain control of the Persian Gulf region". He also planned a US "Rapid Deployment Force" in the area, based mainly on the US navy, and obtained certain facilities for such a force in 'Oman, Somalia and Kenya, and to some extent in Egypt; the plan did not fully materialize.

Casablanca (Arabic: Dar al-Baida). Largest city and chief seaport of Morocco. Founded by the Portuguese in the 16th century, C. developed rapidly in the 20th century, when a modern port was constructed from 1913, and the city became the center of European, chiefly French, enterprise and of Morocco's Westernized sector. After World War II its population was estimated at c. 600,000; attracting large numbers of migrants from the rural areas and smaller towns, it is in the mid-1980s estimated at over 3m.

C. has been the venue of international conferences — e.g. the Third all-A. Summit of Sept. 1965 and the Extraordinary A. Summit of Aug. 1985 — and its name has been linked to several political events. In Jan. 1943 it hosted Churchill and Roosevelt for consultations on the grand strategy of World War II. In Jan. 1961 King *Hassan convened in C. a conference of African Heads-of-State, all of the radical, anti-Western camp, mainly on the Congo (Zaïre) problem (for the reasons for this short-lived departure from the King's usual conservative, pro-Western line — see *Africa, *Morocco). But only four Presidents attended: those of Egypt, Ghana, Guinea and Mali, with observers representing Algeria, Libya, the Palestinian A.'s (*PLO), and the Lumumba faction of Zaïre. This C. meeting proclaimed a "C. Pact" on the freedom and cooperation of African countries and tried to form a "C. Bloc". But the Bloc did not get off the ground; as it represented only the five countries of the C. meeting and Algeria, it acquired no major influence. Moroccan-Algerian border clashes in 1963 disrupted it (with Morocco charging Egypt, too, of aiding Algeria). The conservative Moroccan monarch's enthusiasm for a radical bloc cooled, and when the problem of Zaïre was solved, or decreased in significance, the C. Bloc withered away. By 1963–64 it had virtually ceased to exist.

Catholics in the Arab Countries There are c. 1.8m. C. in the ME. In the *Mashriq*, the eastern part of the A. world, over 85% of the C. belong to *Uniate Churches, i.e. parts of Eastern Christian communities that joined the C. church *en bloc*, maintaining a measure of autonomy concerning liturgy (including its language) and church organization and administration. Less than 15%

belong to the Roman-C. (Latin) church proper; some are descendants of converts of the Crusader period, most are more recent converts from the Eastern church communities — but proselytizing among the Eastern communities by the Latin church was banned by the papal Encyclica *Orientalium Ecclesiarum Dignitas* of 1894, and all such proselytizing was entrusted to the Uniate churches alone. (Terminology: what in European languages is called the Roman C. church is in Arabic "Latin"; Roman-C. in Arabic — *Rum-Katholik* — denotes the Uniate Greek-C. church.) The 85/15 proportion between Uniate-C. and Latin communities does not apply to the A. countries of North Africa: as Sudan and the Maghrib were not within the realm of the Eastern (Greek Orthodox, Byzantine) church and its schismatic offshoots, no uniate churches developed there either, and the C. there are all Latin. In Sudan, nearly all C. are among the negro tribes of the South, recent converts (19th and 20th centuries) of Latin-C. missionaries.

The Latin-C. church first appeared in the ME with the Crusaders and soon embarked on intensive missionary efforts — converting both individuals (to the Latin church) and, later, whole groups of Eastern Christians, through the Uniate described. Nearly all converts were Eastern Christians — not Muslims or Jews. The number of Latin C. in the ME is about 550,000 — c. 230,000 in the Maghrib (110,000 in Morocco, 60,000 in Algeria, 20–30,000 in Tunisia, 25–30,000 in Libya); c. 170,000 in Sudan; and c. 150,000 in the "Mashriq": Egypt 30,000, among the A.'s of Israel 10,000, the "West Bank" and Jordan 25,000, Lebanon 20,000, Syria 15,000, Arabia and the Persian Gulf 35–40,000, Iraq 5,000 (and also some 12–15,000 in Iran; some of these figures include foreign C.). Administratively, the Latin Patriarch of Jerusalem is responsible for the C. in Israel, the West Bank and Jordan (and also Cyprus). In other countries of the ME there are apostolic vicarates headed by apostolic administrators. The Latin-C. church maintains several educational, charitable and monastic institutions, particularly in Jerusalem and Bethlehem and in Lebanon (including two universities — the University of St. Joseph in Beirut, founded in 1875 out of a Jesuit college established in 1839, and the University of Bethlehem, raised to university status in 1973).

The Oriental C. (Uniate) churches comprise the *Maronites (500–600,000 — nearly all in Lebanon, or Lebanese migrants in the West); the *Greek C., also called Melkites (250–300,000 — nearly 200,000 in Lebanon, most of the rest in Syria, Israel and the West Bank); the *Chaldeans (c. 200,000 — almost all in Iraq; more Chaldeans are in India, estimated by some at 200,000 — but the distinction between various Eastern churches and their sectarian offshoots has become somewhat blurred in India); the *Coptic C. in Egypt (c. 80,000), The *Syrian C. (c. 60,000) and the *Armenian C. (c. 50,000) — Uniate offshoots from the Coptic, Syrian and Armenian "orthodox" *Monophysitic churches. Each of these six Uniate churches is headed by a patriarch.

Cemal Pasha (1872–1922) Turkish officer and politician, one of the leaders of the "Young Turks" (from 1908), from 1913 one of a "Triumvirate" ruling the Ottoman Empire (with Enver and Talat). The biography of C. (Jamal, if transcribed from the Arabic version) is outside our scope, but he played an important rôle, during World War I, in Syria and Palestine, serving concurrently, 1914–17, as commander of the Fourth Army and Military Governor of Syria with near-dictatorial powers. In that capacity he suppressed suspected subversion by A. nationalists and conducted several trials that led to the execution of some suspected rebels — precautionary rather than punitive, as there was no A. rebellion in Syria and Palestine. Several Palestinian Jews suspected of disloyalty were also tried or expelled. (At the end of the war, C. fled to Europe. He was assassinated by an Armenian in Tiflis.)

CENTO (Central Treaty Organization) New, official name given in Aug. 1959 to the defense alliance between Turkey, Iran, Pakistan and Britain (with the USA as associate and chief supporter) established in 1955 by the *Baghdad Pact. That former name had become inappropriate with the withdrawal of Iraq (revolutionary since July 1958) in Mar. 1959. With Iraq's withdrawal, C. is outside our scope. See *Baghdad Pact.

Ceuta (al-Sabta) Spanish town in northern Morocco, on the Mediterranean coast. C. and Melilla are the chief towns among the five "Presidios" and considered by Spain part of her territory. Morocco claims them, but has so far not pressed that claim. See *Morocco.

Chaldeans The branch of the Nestorian-*Assyrian church that joined the Catholic church through the *Uniate, retaining a measure of liturgical and administrative autonomy. The movement for union with Rome began after the Crusades, and the Uniate was effected in several steps, various dates being given as to its completion: 1552, 1778. The C. live mostly in Iraq, some in Iran, and small groups in Turkey, Lebanon and Syria; a C. church exists also in India. The C. community grew considerably after World War I through conversions of Assyrian refugees in Iraq. The number of C. is estimated at over 200,000 in Iraq — with another c. 200,000 in India (but as border-lines between various Christian sects in India have become blurred, that figure does not seem to be reliable). The C. church is headed by a Patriarch (the "Patriarch of Babylon") who used to reside in *Mosul, but transferred his seat to Baghdad.

Chamoun, Camille (Sham'un, Kamil) (1900–1987) Lebanese politician. President of Lebanon 1952–58. One of the top leaders of the *Maronite-Christian community. Born in Deir al-Qamar in southern Mount Lebanon (the Shuf) — a region that remained his home and power base until 1983, when in the civil war it was taken over by the Druze militias. C. graduated from the French Law College of Beirut (1925). He has been a member of most Parliaments since 1934. He became a Minister in 1938 (Finance) and again in 1943 (Interior). In that year he played an important rôle in the events leading to the "National Covenant" (see *Lebanon, *Maronites). In 1944 he was appointed Minister to Great Britain and in 1946 headed Lebanon's delegation to the UN, as Ambassador. Chamoun belonged to Bishara al-*Khouri's "Constitutional Bloc" that stressed Lebanon's Arab character and advocated her integration in all-Arab alignments and the termination of special ties to France. He was considered anti-French (and pro-British). In 1947–48 he served again as a Cabinet Minister. However, when President Khouri and the Government arranged, in May 1948, to have the Constitution amended so that Khouri could be elected to a second term, constitutionally barred (as he duly was, in 1949), C. resigned and joined the opposition. As resistance to Khouri during his second term increased and he was accused of corruption and malpractices, C. staged a semi-*coup* in the summer of 1952 that forced Khouri to resign. In Sept. 1952 C. was elected President, with 74 of Parliament's 77 votes.

As President, C. followed a policy of close relations with the West and cautious neutrality towards the other A. countries. His pro-Western attitudes brought him into growing conflict with the swelling tide of Leftist-*Nasserist tendencies inside and outside Lebanon. These forces also resented his authoritarian inclinations and accused him of rigging the elections of 1957. When Syria and Egypt merged in 1958, he stoutly opposed Leftist and Muslim trends pushing Lebanon to join the Syro-Egyptian camp. Clashes developed in May 1958 into a civil war, which was also fanned by rumors that C. intended, like his predecessor, to seek a constitutional amendment to secure his re-election for a second term. Lebanon complained to the UN Security Council against Syro-Egyptian intervention and C. requested the help of the US armed forces. In mid-July US Marines landed in Beirut. A compromise agreement that ended the civil war in Sept. 1958 included C.'s renunciation of any plan to run for a second Presidential term, and with the end of his term, the same month, he stepped down. He now founded a political party of his own, the "National Liberal Party", and remained an elder statesman and a powerful influence; but he returned to a governmental position only for a year as Minister during the civil war of 1975–76 and as Finance Minister in the "National Unity" Government since 1984 — both governments that did not really function.

In the years since 1958 C. has become a spokesman for the Christian camp resisting Lebanon's active integration in Pan-A. alignments and wishing to preserve her pluralistic character under Christian-Maronite leadership and her communal structure protecting that pluralism. This Christian camp was never politically united. In the 1960s C. and his National-Liberal Party established a "Triple Alliance" with the camp's other factions — Pierre *Jumayyil's *"Phalanges", and Raymond *Edde's "National Bloc", but their co-operation was never complete and the three factions frequently followed divergent policies. During the civil war from 1975 onward C. headed a rather loose "Lebanese Front" of various Christian-Maronite-dominated conservative factions that resisted a Muslim-Leftist takeover; but his chairmanship was little more than nominal and the real decisions were taken by the leaders of the factions and their "militias". C. and his party set up armed "militias" of their own — the "Tigers", active mainly in the area of his power base south-east of Beirut. In 1980, however, the Phalanges' hardening claim to complete domination and exclusive leadership of all Christian forces led to escalating clashes between them and C.'s "Tigers" and finally the "Tigers" were completely eliminated as a fighting force (their remnants were incorporated in the Phalanges-led "Lebanese Forces"). It is hardly surprising, therefore, that C. did not play an active rôle in the post-1982 régime headed by the Jumayyil brothers. When the Phalanges' and Bashir *Jumayyil's cooperation with Israel was at its height, in 1982, C. seems to have been somewhat more reserved (in the past, he had never openly advocated cooperation with Israel — though he had, in recent years, delegated his son Danny, groomed as his political heir, to maintain contact). Yet, when President Amin *Jumayyil reneged on his brother's policies and annulled the May 1983 agreement with Israel, C. opposed that step and recommended continuing Lebanon-Israel cooperation. However, he agreed to join, in Apr. 1984, the "Government of National Unity" Jumayyil was compelled to form — a government headed and dominated by C.'s leading adversaries; but he seemed to regard this as a token contribution to national reconciliation was not very active in the affairs of the Government or his Ministry.

C. published his memoirs in 1949 and, in a revised edition, 1963, as well as a book on the Lebanese crisis, in 1978.

Chehab, Chehabists See Shihab, Fu'ad.
China Until the 1950s, C. was not particularly interested in the AC and the ME; Israel was the only country of the region to recognize Communist C. (in Jan. 1950) — though no diplomatic relations were established. Most AC maintained official relations with Nationalist C. (Taiwan). In the 1950s C. extended her world-wide campaign for recognition to the AC — after promising contacts had been established at the *Bandung Conference. AC began recognizing the People's Republic, led by *Nasser's Egypt (1956), and severing their relations with Taiwan, and by the end of the 1950s and the early 1960s most of them had established official relations, with only Sa'udi Arabia, Lebanon, Jordan and the Persian Gulf principalities holding out. Gradually these conservative countries also recognized C. and established relations (Lebanon and Kuwait 1971, Jordan 1977, 'Oman 1979, UAE 1984); only Sa'udia, Bahrain and Qatar have no official relations with C.

C. was eager to foster and develop her newly won relations with the AC, in the first place with the leftist-populist-revolutionary ones like Egypt, Syria, Algeria, South Yemen. Since she had aided the Algerian rebels in their struggle for independence, relations with Algeria were cordial. In South Yemen, C. wielded for some years a particularly strong influence, in constant competition with the Soviet Union. C. also cultivated relations with the conservative ASt — Yemen (even before 1962, when she was still royalist and ultra-conservative), Morocco, Tunisia (with whom relations were marred by disagreements and an exchange of insulting statements in 1967), Jordan. C.'s eagerness grew as she endeavored to enlist Third-World support in her dispute with the Soviet Union, from about 1960. The ASt willingly responded to C.'s wish for close relations, while generally maintaining a cautious neutrality in the Sino-Soviet conflict. C. included several AC in the network of her foreign aid grants and credits, and sent several teams of expert technicians — though this aid never reached large proportions. C. has supported and aided Palestinian-A. guerrilla/terrorist organizations, both the *PLO and its various more extremist factions, and their leaders are frequent visitors to Peking.

It was evidently to gain A. support that C. shunned any relations with Israel. The grateful acceptance of Israel's recognition in 1950 was forgotten and Israel's proposals to establish full diplomatic relations, from 1955, were rebuffed. Trade and economic links were also rejected, Israelis were not admitted to C. and from the late 1950s a complete boycott was imposed on any contacts. Chinese anti-Israel statements sometimes went as far as to deny Israel's very right to exist. In recent years, while C. still professes full solidarity with the A.-Palestinian struggle against Israel, statements have been mitigated somewhat, *viz.*, should Israel withdraw from the occupied territories and accept an A.-Palestinian state C. would no longer refuse relations with her. Since the mid-1980s, Israeli visitors are admitted to C. Recent years have also seen repeated reports of C.-Israel economic deals — many of them concerning military equipment and know-how, and most of them clandestine; such reports have usually been denied.

The permanent problem besetting C.'s relations with countries of South-East Asia (at least up to very recently) — the contradiction between friendly relations with governments and simultaneous aid to Communist parties rebelling against these governments — has been less apparent in C.'s ME policy. It is assumed, for instance, that Chinese aid for subversive organizations in the Persian Gulf, frequently reported in the past, often in conjunction with South Yemen, was discontinued once official relations were established with 'Oman and Kuwait. Anyhow, C.'s links with Communist parties in the A. region have never been close. The Iran-Iraq war, however, has posed problems for C.; she is frequently mentioned as a major supplier of arms and aircraft to Iran, but she usually denies such reports. In any case, the AC and the ME in general, are not a high-priority area in C.'s policies: her political and economic links and interests there are limited as are her influence and power.

Christians in the Arab countries As Christianity spread, from its original home in Israel to the neighboring countries, that region — the "Fertile Crescent", or what is now the eastern part of the AC, the *Mashriq* — soon became the cradle and heartland of the eastern Christian world, overshadowed only by Byzantium. Its main cities — Alexandria and Antioch — were, besides Constantinople, eastern Christianity's spiritual and administrative capitals. The main body of eastern Christianity — later to be called the *Greek Orthodox church — was rent, from the 3rd century to the 5th, by schisms. The schismatic churches established — the Nestorians-*Assyrians, *Monophysites, Monothelites-*Maronites — all had their cradle and centre in this region (and "national" motivations, opposition to Byzantium-Constantinople's centralistic rule of the church, may well have been linked to the theological issues causing the schisms). At the time of the Muslim-A. conquest, in the 7th century, the majority of the population was Christian. Over the centuries following, a majority embraced Islam and became linguistically and culturally Arabicized, and those who remained C. — most of them also Arabicized — became a minority. Some, particularly in remote mountainous areas, retained their Syriac-Aramaic language, at least for liturgical purposes. The number of C. probably increased somewhat during the Crusades. From that time on, the *Catholic version of Christianity also penetrated the region — through direct conversion (mostly: of eastern C., not of Muslims or Jews) to the Catholic-Latin rite, or through the adhesion *en bloc* of whole communities, parts of the eastern churches (the *Uniate). Protestant communities were created, through the activities of missionaries (from English-speaking, German, Scandinavian countries), from the 19th century.

Today, the number of C. in the AC is estimated at 7–8m., 5–6% of the total population, with numerically significant communities only in Lebanon, Syria and Egypt, and among the Negro tribes of South Sudan. In Lebanon they constituted, according to the last census taken in 1932, c. 53% of the country's population with the Maronites as the largest single community (30% of the total, nearly 57% of the C.). They therefore had a predominant influence on the country's governance, in accord with its Constitution (which provides for a communal structure of parliamentary and governmental institutions) and an unwritten "National Pact" of 1943 (laying down, for instance, that the President should always be a Maronite C., as should the commander of the army). In recent decades, however, the proportion of C., and particularly of Maronites, has declined. While for political reasons no official census has been taken since 1932, C. are now estimated to form only 40–45% of Lebanon's population, Maronites — c. 25% (and some estimates are even lower). Egypt's C., most of them Monophysite *Copts, constitute about 7% of the population, over 3m. (but the Copts tend to claim a larger percentage). Syria's C. — about one-third Greek-Orthodox, one-third Armenians, one-third other denominations — form 8–10% of the population (some estimates put them at 13–14%). In Jordan, C. constitute 5–8%. C. are about 5% of Sudan's total population, but among the non-A., non-Muslim Negro tribes of the south C., mostly Catholics, are estimated at 15–20%. In all other AC, C. are small groups, less than 5%, and in the countries of the Arabian peninsula and the Persian Gulf there are virtually none, except for foreigners. In Israel, there are 90–95,000 Arab C. (2–3% of the total, c. 12% of the non-Jewish population).

In the Ottoman Empire, the *Millet system gave the C. communities a large measure of autonomy in their religious life, the administration of community affairs and educational and charitable institutions; matters of personal status, like marriage, divorce, guardianship etc., were under the jurisdiction of communal-ecclesiastical courts. In some countries — Jordan, Lebanon, Israel — this system still prevails, somewhat adjusted to conditions of modern life. In other countries it has been wholly or partially abolished. Thus Egypt has abolished C. religious courts, and Syria has restricted their authority. C. educational autonomy has also been curtailed and educational institutions, in large part owned and maintained by foreign missionaries, have been subjected to nationalization and expropriation measures and those that were not closed altogether have been placed under strict state supervision. Such restrictive measures derive in part from the growing emphasis on the Islamic character of the AC, and mainly from their nationalist-centralist and in part authoritarian régimes. Their suspicion of Western missionary institutions, seen as a continuation of European colonialism and as serving imperial interests, plays no small part.

A. C., mainly from Lebanon, Syria and Palestine, played an important role in the A. national movement, particularly in its early stages when it was a movement of enlightenment and literary revival rather than of political aspiration. As Muslims took over the leadership and the dividing line between A. nationalism and Islamic revival became blurred (see *Arab Nationalism, *Pan-Islam), and as A. nationalism became a political movement striving for statehood, and later in the independent ASt, C. have become less prominent in leading positions.

As a minority community in a region where communal-religious allegiances still are of vital, primary importance, the C. A.'s' attitude to A. nationalism has tended to be ambivalent. Some C., concerned lest totalitarian nationalism, sometimes coupled with Islamic fanaticism, impair the remnants of C. communal semi-autonomy or even endanger the survival of the A.-C. communities, tend to defend that semi-autonomy and to dissociate themselves from Pan-A. nationalism, at least in its more extreme manifestations. In Lebanon, the center of C. political awareness and activity, C. leaders, defending the C.-led pluralism of their country, have mooted the idea of Lebanon as a "C. National Home" and a center and refuge for all C. A.'s. A.C. also tend to see themselves as socially and educationally more advanced than their Muslim neighbors; they also remain closer to the West and its civilization. Other C. leaders, however, have displayed a radical A. nationalism — some of them perhaps out of an age-old minority instinct to over-compensate, to overstress conformity to the majority's ideals — assuming that the minority's survival is more safely ensured by integrating in the mainstream of the majority's policies than by resisting them. A debate on these issues has been openly conducted, for decades, only in Lebanon; C. leaders elsewhere do not like to discuss them frankly. But even if sometimes not fully and consciously realized, the problem of minority ambivalence undoubtedly exists in all AC.

Circassians One of the peoples of the Caucasus. Their region was ceded to Russia by the Ottoman Empire in 1829. After rebellions lasting until 1859 and the expansion of Russian control over additional regions in the Caucasus, many C., mostly Muslims, emigrated to the Ottoman Empire which willingly accepted and settled them. Some of them reached Thrace, in European Turkey, while most settled in the Asian, A.-populated parts of the Empire — Syria, Iraq, Transjordan, Palestine. These were partially assimilated by the A.'s. They maintained their language for two-three generations, but in recent decades it has given way to Arabic. Yet it is still spoken in some measure, and efforts are being made to revive and cultivate it and introduce its teaching in the schools. While the way of life of the C. in their villages and the region's towns is like that of the A.'s in whose midst they live, they have maintained their distinctive character and most of them live in C. villages.

The number of C. is estimated at 20–25,000 in Syria, the same number in Jordan, 10,000 in Iraq, 3,000 in Israel. Some C. villages in the *Golan

Heights were abandoned, and their inhabitants went to Syria, when Israel occupied the area in 1967. In Israel, there are two C. villages in Galilee (Kafr Kama and Rihaniyya), and the name "C." survives in several A. villages' names. The C. in Israel usually maintained good relations with their Jewish neighbors and took no part in the Palestine A.'s' struggle against the Jews. Like Jews and *Druze they are conscripted for compulsory military service (unlike Israeli A.'s, who may volunteer but are not conscripted). In Jordan, many C. serve in the army, and the officers' corps contains many more C. than their proportion in the population would indicate. They are also numerous in the civil service, and several C. have attained high political and governmental office (the more so as they are considered to be deeply loyal to the royal family and a mainstay of the régime). King Hussein's eldest daughter married a C.

The migrating C. were joined, in the 19th century, by a number of Chechens. In the course of time, the differences between these two related peoples disappeared and the Chechens were assimilated by the C.

colonialism Foreign countries were conquered throughout history and settlers sent out to the territories occupied. The ancient Greeks established "colonies" all over the Mediterranean islands and coasts, as did the Phoenicians and Carthage; the Muslim-A. conquests and the invasions of Mongol and Turkish peoples entailed, or were followed by, settlement. But usually the term C. is applied to overseas conquests and settlement since the 16th century — by Portugal, Spain, the Netherlands, Britain and France; Germany, Italy, Belgium followed in the 19th century. The USA never acquired "colonies" — except for some Pacific islands and the Philippines, never officially a "colony" (for the perception of US economic penetration and influence as indirect C. or Neo-C. — see below). Russian expansion into Siberia, Central Asia and the Caucasus, in the 19th century, can properly be defined as C., and Russia's pressure on and penetration of Iran and Ottoman Turkey as indirect C. Yet, as that expansion took place overland, into contiguous, adjacent territories, it is frequently excluded from accounts of great-power C. Russia has never exercised direct control over any A. territory; her post-World War II acquisition of far-reaching influence in some AC, may well be termed indirect C.

Direct C. in the narrow sense of the term — i.e. the definition of a territory as a "colony" owned and directly administered by the foreign power in posssession — applied to the A. region and the ME in three instances only: 'Aden colony, occupied by the British in 1839, ruled by the Governor of Bombay Province, later (1932–37) by the Government of British India, and from 1937 as a Crown Colony; Algeria, conquered by France in 1830, never termed a "colony", but annexed and considered an integral part of France; and Tripolitania-Libya, also not termed a "colony", but annexed in 1911–12 by Italy and administered, despite some abortive attempts to bestow partial autonomy, as part of Italy (though by a Ministry of Colonial Affairs). One might add Sudan, ruled since 1899 by a *"Condominium" of Great Britain and Egypt (herself *de facto* a British protectorate). Among the non-A. countries that joined the *Arab League should be added: Mauritania, a French Protectorate from 1903, defined as a colony in 1920 (renamed "Overseas Territory" in 1946, and a member of the "French Community" 1958–60); French Somali (Djibouti), a "French territory" or colony from the 1880s; and Somalia, acquired by Italy in the late 1880s and administered from 1905 until World War II as a colony. Colonists, settlers, were implanted mainly in Algeria and Libya (and also Tunisia); most of them left after independence.

All these instances of direct colonial rule have been eliminated: 'Aden is part of independent South Yemen (1967); Algeria is independent since 1962; Libya (captured from the Italians in World War II) — since 1951; Sudan since 1956; Mauritania since 1960; Djibouti since 1977; and Somalia (also taken from Italy during World War II) — since 1960.

C. in its broader sense, however, may also mean the imposition of a European power's domination by indirect rule, protectorates, or excessive control of economic assets and unequitable concessions (oil, other raw materials, railways, shipping, canals etc.). It was in that sense that C. prevailed for long periods throughout the A. region and the ME. As the Ottoman Empire grew weaker in the 19th century, the European powers increasingly intervened in its crises, Balkanic and Near-Eastern, imposing a measure of control or supervision and obtaining various concessions (a similar process affected Persia, which was divided in 1907 into British and Russian spheres of influence). In 1840 they imposed on the Ottoman Sultan and Muhammad 'Ali, the Pasha of Egypt who had rebelled against his suzerain and occupied Syria, a settlement making Egypt semi-independent. In the 1840s they began intervening in Lebanon, compelling the Sultan in 1860–61 to grant autonomy to the Mount Lebanon Christian-majority region. In the 1870s they imposed on Egypt an Anglo-French administration of her foreign debts, i.e. of her finances and economy, and in 1882 Britain occupied Egypt and took over her administration — in what she termed a temporary occupation, leaving the ruler, the "Khedive", in office and recognizing the Ottoman Sultan's suzerainty, but what amounted in fact to a semi-colonial protectorate; in 1914 such a protectorate was officially proclaimed. (These power interventions were sometimes made in concert, but often in rivalry and dispute — mostly between Britain and France.) In 1881, after increasing intervention and several crises between the powers, France imposed a protectorate on Tunisia, and in 1912, on Morocco (neutralizing Italy's objections by allowing her to annex Libya, and agreeing to a Spanish protectorate over parts of Morocco). During the 19th century Britain also imposed her protection, by a series of treaties, on the principalities and sheikhdoms of the Persian Gulf — Muscat-and-'Oman, Qatar, Bahrain, the Trucial Coast and finally, in 1899, Kuwait — and those of Southern Arabia (Hadhramaut and the 'Aden Protectorates), and parts of Somali ("British Somaliland"). Some of these protectorates involved nearly-direct colonial administration. Growing British links with *Ibn Sa'ud of *Najd, formalized in an agreement of 1915, and later, during World War I, with Sharif *Hussein of Mecca, led to alliances rather than formal protectorates, but in reality they were not partnerships between equals and had the flavor of great-power protectorates.

During World War I, the allied "Entente" powers planned to divide the non-Turkish areas of the Ottoman Empire, after victory in the war and the dismemberment of the Empire, into "spheres of influence", or even territorial possessions to be allotted to the various powers (see *Sykes-Picot Agreement). But as the principle of self-determination for all peoples had been proclaimed as one of the war aims, particularly by US President Wilson, and specific promises had been made (e.g. to the A. Sharif of Mecca) this could no longer be done in the old, straightforward imperial-colonial way. The compromise between the independence promised and imperial plans and interests was the system of the *Mandates, by which a Western power was charged by the *League of Nations to "guide" to independence "peoples not yet able to stand by themselves". Such Mandates were entrusted to Britain for Palestine (including Transjordan) and Iraq, and to France for Syria and Lebanon. In practice, the régime established by the Mandatory powers was a semi-colonial administration. Under British and French tutelage, semi-independent governments were gradually set up in the mandated territories, except for Palestine. Such governments already existed, and continued, in Egypt and in the French Protectorates of Tunisia and Morocco, but not in Libya, Sudan and the various parts of Somalia, where the administration was direct and colonial; the principalities of the Persian Gulf, under their British-"protected" sheikhs, had not yet evolved modern structures of administration and government.

The nationalists in the countries under such foreign tutelage regarded that governance, whatever its description, as a form of C. or imperialism and struggled to abolish it and attain full independence — and though the political élites, including most nationalists, cooperated in the establishment of semi-independent governments under that tutelage, it was the national struggle for its abolition that determined the political climate. The Western tutor countries strove to replace the mandate, or protectorate, with a treaty according a formally complete independence, while bestowing on the protecting power special privileges that would continue ensuring its imperial political, economic and strategic interests. The local semi-independent governments and political leaderships went along in the search for such treaty formulae (until the 1940s and 1950s) — including most nationalists, though they often opposed the actual terms of the treaty drafted.

For Anglo-Egyptian treaty negotiations, their failure and Britain's unilateral declaration of Egypt's independence; the Treaty of 1936; its abrogation by Egypt in 1951; the agreement of 1954 and its abrogation on 1 Jan. 1957 — see *Egypt. By 1957 Britain's special position and privileges and the last vestiges of semi-colonialist military British presence had ended. For the similar gradual liquidation of British semi-colonial tutelage in Iraq — the Treaty of 1922; that of 1930 and Iraq's independence; the war of 1941; the replacement of the Treaty by Iraq's accession to the *Baghdad Pact, 1955; and her secession in 1959 —see *Iraq. By 1959, Britain's semi-colonial privileges and imperial military presence had ended in Iraq, too. A similar process in Jordan took a smoother course, but the end result was not much different. For the Treaty of 1928, still giving expression to Britain's near-complete control; those of 1946 and 1948 recognizing Jordan's independence; and the abrogation of the Treaty in 1957 — see *Jordan. Despite a *de facto* alliance with Britain, and now increasingly with the USA, British bases, a military presence and special privileges were not restored.

France was always less enthusiastic than Britain concerning the replacement of semi-colonial control by treaties with independent states. For her unratified Treaties of 1936 with Syria and Lebanon, her renewed proclamation of their independence in 1941, and the final struggle of 1943-46 — see *Syria, *Lebanon. By 1945-46 all French bases and privileges and the last imperial-colonial military presence were liquidated with no preferential treaty (even before the parallel process concerning Britain was completed in Egypt and Iraq). For the end of France's Protectorates over Tunisia and Morocco in 1956 and the liquidation of the last French military bases in Morocco in 1961 and in Tunisia in 1963 — see *Tunisia, *Morocco. Algeria won her independence in 1962, after a 7-year rebellion, and the last vestiges of French privileges — military-naval bases and the use of Algerian desert territory for nuclear tests — were liquidated in 1968. Mauritania and French Somali (Djibouti) won their independence in the process of the decolonization of Africa — the former in 1960, the latter in 1977.

Italy's colonial possessions were conquered by allied forces in the course of World War II. A proposal to put Tripolitania (Libya) under an Italian trusteeship failed in 1949 to obtain the necessary two-thirds majority at the UN, and Libya became independent in 1951, after a provisional administration by Britain, and in the South by France, since the end of the war. Certain military bases that remained at the disposal of Britain, the USA and France were evacuated, the French one in 1956, and the British and American ones in 1970. Former Italian Somalia was put under a 10-year Italian trusteeship by the UN, in 1950, and became independent in 1960, merging with British Somaliland.

The few colonial possessions or semi-colonial protectorates remaining — all British — were liquidated in the 1960s and 1970s. The 'Aden Protectorates became a semi-independent federation in 1969, and 'Aden Colony joined that Federation in 1963. In 1967 Britain withdrew and the country became fully independent as "The People's Democratic Republic Yemen" (*South Yemen). The British Protectorate of Somaliland became independent in 1960 (and united with former Italian Somalia). Kuwait emerged from the British protectorate in 1961 and became independent. In 1971 Britain withdrew her protection and military forces and bases from the rest of the Persian Gulf sheikhdoms and those became fully independent — Qatar, Bahrain, 'Oman, and the 7 sheikhdoms of the Trucial Coast (who federated as the United Arab Emirates). Britain remained directly involved only in 'Oman, where British officers on contract continued to train and command the armed forces, at 'Oman's request.

The monopolies and preferential concessions, the economic domination obtained by Western companies since the late 19th century and particularly between the two world wars have also been regarded as an aspect of C. and imperialism. This economic C., too, has been on the decline since the 1950s and has largely been eliminated. This pertains particularly to the oil industry. Giant multinational Western oil companies ("The Seven Sisters") dominated most oil extraction in the ME, controlled the world market, and were able to determine, through agreements with the producing countries, the terms of their concessions, the oil price and the royalties they paid, making huge profits. In the 1950s most producing countries obtained agreements on an equal, 50:50, sharing of all profits — a process triggered by the bitter struggle of a radical government in Iran, 1951-52, and the nationalization of the

Anglo-Iranian Oil Co. A process of nationalization — by decree, or through the acquisition of a majority of shares in the companies operating in each country by the state (or by national oil companies set up by the state) — continued, escalating in the 1970s. In the 1980s most oil companies in the AC were wholly or largely owned by the state, and most foreign companies were operating as agents of the local government or under modest, greatly reduced concessions no longer conferring a dominating, semi-colonial influence. Since 1973 the local governments were also unilaterally (or in concert, through *OPEC — but without the agreement of the purchasing countries or companies), setting the official oil price (escalating it in 1973 and 1979–80).

Yet, with old-type C. thus eliminated in the ME, a climate of anti-C., an insistence that further struggle against C. is needed, prevails with most nationalists and many governments. It is argued that "Neo-C." still wields an undue, dominating influence, restricting the real independence of most countries of the "Third World" — through the domination and manipulation of world markets, particularly those for raw materials produced in Third World countries, through manipulative use of the aid and credits proffered and the military equipment sold by the developed countries, and through their domination of world banking and finance. Such charges are usually levelled against the West (and not, for instance, against the Soviet Bloc — though the acquisition of Soviet influence and power bases in some AC may well be termed indirect C.). They are aimed particularly at the USA rather than the former old-type colonial powers. To what extent such claims are just, and whether C. or Neo-C. still exists in the ME, is a matter of definition and terminology, and of political opinion.

Communism, Communist parties, in the Arab countries CP's were founded in the AC in the early 1920s. Some of them coalesced out of small groups, mostly of intellectuals, some dissolved and re-formed, and some were unorthodox C. or radical groups whose adherence to Russian-line C. and the Third International was doubtful or wavering. Different dates as to the actual establishment of fully fledged CP's are therefore given by different sources. The first were CP's in Tunisia and Morocco, in 1920 — but these were virtually branches of the French CP and were hardly considered as "Arab" CP's. An Egyptian CP was admitted by the Third International in 1921, though its actual foundation is usually put at 1922. The Palestine CP, though containing some A.'s, was mainly Jewish (see below). Syro-Lebanese and Iraqi CP's were established later in the 1920s.

These CP's were small groups with hardly any influence, and they were soon outlawed and went underground. They drew their members mainly from the intelligentsia, and largely from minority groups (A. Christians, Jews, Greeks, Armenians, Kurds) — a fact that further reduced their influence — and indulged in a great deal of internal, ideological disputes which frequently led to schisms. It was only in the 1940s, after the Soviet Union entered World War II as an ally of Great Britain and Free France (the powers *de facto* in control in the AC), that CP's were allowed to emerge from underground and became semi-legal. As they were considered by public opinion as representing, or at least close to, the Soviet Union — a power in which many nationalists set great hopes as a potential ally and supporter against the Western imperial powers — the CP's began attracting some support. This process was set back in 1946–47 when the USSR retreated from power positions and activist policies on the fringes of the ME (Iran, Turkey, Greece), and in 1948 when she supported the partition of Palestine and the emergence of a Jewish state and instructed the CP's to do likewise. It gathered new strength when the Soviet Union emerged in the 1950s as the close ally of the radical AC (Egypt, Syria, Iraq); but it flagged again when it became evident that the Soviet Union was dealing with the non-C. rulers of these countries and treating *them* as her allies, while largely ignoring or abandoning the CP's. The attitude to be taken towards those radical but non-C. régimes was much debated inside the CP's, causing splits and secessions. Since the mid 1960s the CP's, at least in their official mainstream factions, no doubt guided by Soviet advice, accepted the rulers of the radical AC as "progressive" and cooperated with them — for some time in Egypt, and mainly in *Ba'th*-ruled Syria and Iraq. The Syrian and Iraqi régimes reciprocated by setting up a "National Progressive Front" with the CP and other groups in 1972–73 and appointing CP men as Government Ministers. In Iraq this *Ba'th*-Communist cooperation ceased in the late 1970s, and the CP turned against the régime, went underground again and was suppressed. In Syria, cooperation continued and the country had C. Ministers in her governments until 1985.

Details concerning the CP's in the various AC are not always full and reliable. In Egypt, the CP was split in the 1940s and 1950s into rival factions — since 1952 mainly concerning the attitude to be adopted towards *Nasser's new revolutionary and progressive régime. The main faction, the "Democratic Movement of National Liberation" (MDLN or HDTW) at first granted the officers' régime its qualified support, while other factions opposed it. The régime, however, did not reciprocate, especially as it suspected the CP to be behind violent strikes in Aug. 1952, and from 1953 on suppressed its cells and arrested its leaders. Further waves of arrests occurred in 1956 and 1958 (the same year the CP reportedly reunited its various factions). Egypt's increasingly close relations with the USSR led to a softening in her attitude to the C.'s. In 1963–64 all C.'s in jail were released, and many joined Nasser's administrative and information establishment. In 1965 the CP formally disbanded itself and its members joined the régime's "Arab Socialist Union" as individuals. In 1972, under President *Sadat, two reported C.'s joined the Government; but most C.'s were assumed to have joined the growing opposition. When political parties were permitted in 1977, many of the C.'s probably joined the Leftist "Progressive Unionist Rally", and as they were suspected to be behind anti-Government agitation, the régime increasingly turned against them. In 1975 the Egyptian CP announced (in Beirut) that it had re-established itself, probably underground. Throughout these years no major Egyptian C. leader emerged.

In Syria and Lebanon a joint CP was founded in the 1920s, in years variously given as 1922, 1924, 1928, 1929–30. Though the party's legal position under the French Mandate was not quite clear, its spokesmen appeared quite openly, particularly in the freer and more cosmopolitan climate of Beirut. But they had very little influence and took no part in overt political-parliamentary activities, and the party itself remained underground. In 1943, when Syria and Lebanon became independent, the joint CP separated into a Syrian CP and a Lebanese one. In Syria the party was illegal, but after the fall of *Shishakli in 1954 it began to wield some influence behind the scenes. Its main leader, Khaled Bakdash, was elected to Parliament as an independent. The Chief-of-Staff from 1957, 'Afif Bizri, was at least a sympathizer, if not a card-carrying member. CP cells existed among army officers. Indeed, the fear of growing C. influence was one of the motives that impelled the officers who were the *de facto* rulers in 1957–58 to negotiate Syria's union with Egypt. During the three years of the Syro-Egyptian *United Arab Republic the CP, along with all other political parties, was suppressed. After Syria seceded from the UAR, 1961, the CP remained illegal; but after the *Ba'th coup* of 1963, and particularly the second one, of the Leftist "military" faction, in 1966, it became, without being officially legalized, a partner of the Ba'th régime in a "National Progressive Front" (1972). On the list of that Front it gained representation in the People's Assembly. From 1972 to 1985 there were also C. Ministers in the Syrian Government, usually two. A faction headed by Riad Turk and Danial Ni'ma opposed that collaboration with the A.-nationalist Ba'th from about 1969 and seceded in 1971 (finalized in late 1973). Ni'ma and some of his associates later returned to the party, but part of the seceding faction, under Turk, stayed out.

The CP in Lebanon gained some influence in the Trade Unions (Mustafa al-'Aris) and in intellectual circles; it was officially legalized in 1970. Its leaders were mostly Christian (Antoun Thabet, Farajallah Hilou, Ra'if Khouri, Georges Hawi), but some Muslims were also prominent ('Omar Fakhouri). In recent years it reportedly gained a strong foothold among Lebanon's Shi'is. The CP in 1972 put up candidates for Parliament, but none was elected. At first it had no "militia" of its own and was therefore not very active in the civil war of 1975 and onward, though ideologically it supported the radical, "Leftist" camp. Later, the existence of a C. armed militia was reported. In 1970 an extremist faction seceded and set up a "C. Action Organization", with armed squads of its own.

The strongest CP in the AC, after World War II, was probably that of Iraq. It was brutally suppressed in the 1940s and 1950s and some of its leaders were executed, but new leaders emerged and the party — though split into rival factions — was seen to extend its underground activities. After General *Qassem's revolution of July 1958, the CP collaborated with the new republican régime and gained some important positions in the army and administration. In 1959 the Party — and particularly its mostly Kurdish sections in the north — helped Qassem to suppress a *Nasserist plot and attempted *coup*. But when the C.'s demanded full and open partnership in the régime and continued penetrating key positions, Qassem half-suppressed them and tried to balance his régime between the C.'s and the Nasserists. After Qassem's fall in 1963, the CP was again suppressed — by both the *Ba'th* and President *'Aref's régime. Gradually, however, the *Ba'th* leaders, in power from 1968, sought to gain the co-operation of the CP — at least one or the other of its rival factions. The CP itself was split concerning such co-operation with the *Ba'th* rulers. In 1969–70 it was reported that of the party's three main factions — the "Central Command" of 'Aziz al-Hajj; the "Central Committee" of Zaki al-Kheiri and Baha'-ul-Din Nuri; and Salim Fakhri's group — the first co-operated with the authorities, while the second opposed such tactics. From 1969 to 1976 a C. leader, 'Aziz Sharif, was a Government Minister (but it was doubtful whether he was a card-carrying party member). From 1972 another C., later two, became Ministers. The growing *Ba'th*-C. coalition was formalized in 1973 in a "Progressive and Patriotic National Front". However, conflicting interests, mutual suspicion and old enmity were too strong for that *Ba'th*-CP cooperation to last. By 1978–79 the National Front was breaking down, and in 1979 the CP went underground again and turned anti-*Ba'th*, while the régime reverted to a policy of brutal repression. In the 1980s, the clandestine CP was co-operating with anti-Iraqi Syria, aiding the Kurdish rebels (with guerrillas of its own), joining anti-Government united fronts (in exile or underground), and supporting Iran in the Iraq-Iran war.

In Palestine in the 1920s the CP was a mainly Jewish underground group, strongly anti-Zionist. In its ideological support for Palestinian-A. nationalism it sought to cultivate an A. section and to hand the leading positions to A. C.'s. During the A. rebellion, 1936–39, the CP reportedly co-operated with the rebels — mainly its A. section, with Radwan al-Hilou ("Mussa", died 1975) emerging as its main leader. The Jewish section was thrown into confusion and the two sections were virtually separate — and both declined. When the CP became semi-legal during World War II, stress was laid on trade union activities through the "Arab Workers' Congress", and front organizations, mainly the "League for National Liberation". In 1947–48, the CP, guided by the Soviet Union, was the only Palestinian-A. group that did not oppose the partition plan and the creation of the State of Israel, but quite a few of its A. leaders did not go along with that line; most of the dissenters, including al-Hilou, were in the A. part of Palestine or went there as refugees from the areas that became Israel. The CP was the only A. group in Israel with unbroken continuity, with its accepted leaders (Tawfiq Toubi, Emile Habibi, Emile Touma) and its organ, the weekly *al-Ittihad*. In 1948 a united "Israel CP" was established. Israel was, at that time, the only country in the ME where the CP was legal and took part in elections. In the five elections from 1949 to 1961 it obtained 2.5–4.5% of the total vote, and 3–6 seats in the 120-member *Knesset*. Its main strength was with the A. voters, and among them it obtained 11–22%. In 1965 the CP split, largely on issues of loyalty to the state and the position on the A.-Israel conflict. The "Israel CP", largely Jewish in membership, soon dissolved, merging with other Leftist groups. The "New C. List", appearing for elections since 1977 as the "Democratic Front for Peace and Equality", became the main CP. Its members and voters were mainly A., though it retained several Jews among its leaders and members of Parliament. This New CP's share of the total vote remained 3–4.5%, and its *Knesset* seats 3–5; but it considerably increased its share of the A. vote: from 23% in 1965 to 38% in 1973 and nearly 50% in 1977, then back to 38% in 1981, 34% in 1984. It also controlled Israel's largest A. municipality, Nazareth, and several local and village councils. The NCP is fully aligned with Soviet policies, and largely espouses A. nationalist positions. Its considerable influence with Israel's A. population seems to derive from its A.-nationalist opposition to government policies and its championship of full equality and A. rights in Israel rather than from ideological support for its C. doctrines.

In Jordan, the CP is illegal and lacks influence, though in the *"West Bank", annexed in 1948–50 and held until 1967, there were Leftist-C. currents of opinion. In the elections of 1954 and 1956, C.'s participated in lists submitted by a "National Front" and two or three of those elected from these lists were considered C. The main leader of Jordan's CP, Fu'ad Nassar (who had spent many years in prison, exile or hiding), died in 1976 and no prominent new leader has emerged. After 1967, the CP of the "West Bank" was reportedly separated from the Jordanian one and reconstituted as the Palestine CP, but it is not quite clear whether it is fully separate and independent. The CP on the Israel occupied West Bank, with Bashir Barghuthi as its leader (and 'Arabi 'Awad, its Secretary-General, residing abroad), remains underground and illegal, but it operates among trade unions, professional and front organizations, and its influence seems to have increased in the 1970s and 1980s.

Among the Palestinian-A. organizations outside Palestine, Leftist-C. leanings exist in several groups, though they frequently tend to vague Maoist-Trotskyite ideas rather than orthodox, Moscow-oriented C. Such tendencies prevail, for instance, in *Habash's *"Popular Front for the Liberation of Palestine" and *Hawatma's *"Popular Democratic Front". The orthodox CP also appears, sometimes, among the organizations federated in the *PLO and taking part in its Palestine National Congresses. In the PLO's factional rivalries it sides with the Leftist, pro-Syrian groups, but, guided by Moscow, it is seeking an accommodation with *'Arafat. The CP keeps a low profile within the PLO. A CP representative, identified as such, was admitted to the PLO Executive Committee for the first time in Apr. 1987. As to guerrilla units, the CP's of Syria, Iraq, Lebanon and Jordan were several times reported to be setting up a joint formation of their own, *al-Ansar*, but little has been heard of actual operations of such a group, and they reportedly ceased in 1972.

In the Arabian peninsula, there may be underground C. cells in Kuwait, or perhaps even in Sa'udi Arabia — among the Palestinian A.'s and other foreign workers. But a significant C. presence exists in South Yemen only. There, the ruling party and the state apparatus are radical-leftist and C.-inspired — though, like the Palestinian organizations mentioned, of a Maoist-Castroist rather than an orthodox CP type. A small regular CP seems to have existed, but it merged with the ruling *NLF in 1975, and with the "Yemen Socialist Party", established to unite all factions, in 1978.

Sudanese C. had its beginnings in cells of Sudanese students in Cairo in the early 1940s. A Sudan CP was founded in 1944 — at first as a "National Liberation Front" (others set the foundation at 1948). It grew, based on both intellectual circles and the powerful Railway Workers Union in Khartoum and Atbara. Its chief leader was 'Abdul-Khaleq Mahjub. The party took part in the overthrow of General *'Abbud's military dictatorship in 1964 (which it had at first supported but which had begun suppressing it) and in the post-*coup* Government. In the elections of Apr. 1965 it won 11 seats in Parliament (all among the seats reserved for college graduates). However, its share in the government caused a bitter dispute which split the régime. Government and Parliament banned the CP late in 1965; the Supreme Court invalidated that act, but the régime refused to accept that verdict and to annul the ban. That controversy caused much unrest. Meanwhile the C.'s succeeded in establishing strong front organizations of professionals, students, women etc. In May 1969 they took part in *Numeiri's military *coup* and remained partners in the new régime, though it was not quite clear whether the four or five C. government ministers were card-carrying CP members or belonged to dissident factions or C.-leaning front organizations. When Numeiri began turning Sudan into a one-party state, that collaboration soured; some C.'s tended to go along with the régime, but Mahjub and the main CP opposed further collaboration and the self-dissolution of the party. In 1970, C. front organizations were outlawed, the C. ministers ousted from the government, Mahjub exiled to Egypt — and detained when he returned. In July 1971, Numeiri accused the CP of complicity in an abortive *coup*, arrested its leaders and executed the most prominent among them, including Mahjub and Shafe'i Ahmad al-Sheikh, and brutally suppressed all C. organizations. In 1978 some C. detainees were released, but the party remained illegal and underground. After the Apr. 1985 *coup* that toppled Numeiri, C.'s were reported to be part of the alliance of professional unions and former parties and to strive for a position of guiding influence within it, but there were no indications of C. gains. In the elections of Apr. 1986, the C. won 3 seats.

In Tunisia, the CP became independent of the French CP in 1934. It took part in the struggle for independence, but was not particularly prominent or influential. In independent Tunisia, from 1956, it at first operated openly, taking part in the elections of 1956 and 1959 without gaining a single seat. In 1963 it was banned — along with other parties, as the country adopted a single-party system. The ban was lifted in 1981, and CP candidates competed in the elections of the same year but again won no seat; the CP boycotted the elections of 1986. None of the party's leaders achieved great prominence.

The Algerian CP, too, was separated from the French one in 1934 (some sources say 1936). It ideologically supported the struggle for independence, but did not take a very active part in the guerrilla war of 1954–62. It tried to join with the *FLN, the main nationalist fighting organization, in a united front and to obtain representation and influence on the bodies directing the rebellion, but was kept at arm's length by the FLN. In the factional struggle inside the FLN, with the advent of independence, the C. supported *Ben Bella. But as the new state adopted a strict one-party régime, the CP was outlawed late in 1962. There have been few reports of underground activities; nor have reports been substantiated of CP support for, or participation in, some of the anti-régime organizations set up in exile, mostly in France. None of the Algerian C. leaders has achieved great prominence.

In Morocco, as in the two other Maghrib countries, the CP separated from the French CP in 1934. Its links with the nationalists and its participation in the struggle for the abolition of the French Protectorate were weak and partial. After Morocco became fully independent (1956), the CP was banned in 1959–60, and its appeal to the courts was rejected. As it continued some activities and several of its functionaries stood for elections, as independents, the ban was reiterated in 1964. In 1968, 'Ali Yata, who had emerged as the CP's chief leader, tried to get around the ban by founding a "Party of Liberation and Socialism" as a front for the CP; this party, however, was also banned in 1970. But a new, similar attempt succeeded in 1974: Yata's new front, the "Party of Progress and Socialism", was allowed to operate legally, hold congresses and participate in elections. It won no seat in 1976, but in 1977 Yata won a by-election, and in the 1984 elections the party obtained two seats. Yata's tactics of disguising the CP in front organizations resulted in several splits and secessions. One of the seceding splinter groups, the "Organization of Democratic Popular Action", was reported to have won one seat in the 1984 elections.

condominium Term used for the joint Anglo-Egyptian rule of Sudan, from 1899 to 1955 (though the expression does not appear in the Anglo-Egyptian Agreement of 1899 establishing that rule, after the country was reconquered from the *Mahdi).

Constantinople, Convention of A Convention signed in 1888 by the European powers, chiefly Britain and France, and the Ottoman Empire, ensuring free navigation through the *Suez Canal. As France objected to a British reservation which in effect suspended certain clauses for the duration of Britain's occupation of Egypt, the CC became effective only in 1904, after an Anglo-French understanding. Independent Egypt continued to recognize the CC's validity, and frequently cited its clauses concerning the security of the Canal to justify restrictions she imposed on the freedom of passage through the Canal (e.g., with regard to Israel) — see *Suez Canal.

The name "C. Agreement" is also usually given to an exchange of diplomatic memoranda, in Mar.–Apr. 1915, between Russia, Britain and France, in which Russia put on record her claim to annex, after victory in the war and the dismemberment of the Ottoman Empire, C., the Bosphorus and the Dardanelles, certain islands and coastal areas on both the European and the Asian shores. The Western powers agreed in principle, subject to reservations and counter-demands elsewhere. While claims to C. (and concerning Iran) are outside the scope of this book, British demands included a stipulation that "the Musulman Holy Places and Arabia shall. . . remain under independent Musulman dominion" (implying: under British tutelage). France put on record that she "would like to annex Syria together with the region of the Gulf of Alexandretta and Cilicia up to the Taurus range" (with Russia stipulating that "Syria" would not include Palestine — contrary to French notions). This C. Agreement became inoperative after the Bolshevik revolution.

Copts The ancient Christians of Egypt ("C." is a corruption of the word Egypt). The Coptic Church traces its foundation to St. Mark the Evangelist. With the schism at the Council of Chalcedon (451), the C. Church became *Monophysite. The C. probably were a majority in Egypt from the fourth to the seventh century. After the Arab-Muslim conquest, many converted to Islam and Egypt became a Muslim-majority country. Under Arab, Mamluk and Ottoman rule the C. were often discriminated against or persecuted. In the 19th century, with the growing modernization and Westernization of Egypt and the increasing influence of the Western powers, the C. gradually acquired a standard of wealth and education superior to that of the average Egyptian. Some C. were active in the Egyptian nationalist movement, but none attained top leadership rank. Modern Egyptian nationalism had, at least in some of its streams and factions, strong Islamic currents that erupted from time to time in anti-C. unrest or pogroms and Muslim-C. clashes. Independent Egypt professes a strict policy of non-discrimination — but C. frequently complain and are apprehensive of strong Islamic tendencies to base the Constitution and legal practice more extensively on the *Shari'a, Islamic law, which would relegate the C. to second-class status; and Muslim-C. clashes and anti-C. outbreaks occur even in contemporary Egypt. Egyptian Governments usually contain one to three C. Ministers — but only one C. has ever been Prime Minister (*Butros-Ghali, assassinated in 1910 amid scenes of anti-C. agitation). Other sons of the same Butros-Ghali family attained prominent positions. The most prominent C. in the nationalist leadership was Makram 'Obeid (1889–1961) who served in high government office, mainly as Finance Minister; he was prominent in the *Wafd Party, but seceded from it in 1942, forming his own "Independent Wafdist Bloc" (until 1953).

The C. in Egypt are officially said to number c. 7% of the population, at present more than 3m.; but some C. spokesmen claim a higher percentage, denouncing the official census figures, and many foreign observers estimate the C. of Egypt at c. 6m. Small C. communities, largely of Egyptian origin, exist in several A. and ME countries, and in Europe and the USA. The C. church is headed by a Patriarch — also called Pope (*al-Baba*) — whose seat, originally in Alexandria, was later transferred to Cairo; he must be approved by the Government. (In Sept. 1981, President *Sadat withdrew Government recognition from Patriarch Shenouda III, causing a grave crisis with the C. community which continued regarding the deposed Patriarch as its spiritual leader; he was reinstated in Jan. 1985 by President *Mubarak.) A small part of the C. community joined the Catholic church through a *Uniate in 1741. Protestant missionaries have also won C. converts.

The Ethiopian (or Abyssinian) church, which was originally a branch of the Coptic one, became autonomous by decree of Ethiopia's Italian conquerors in 1936. Liberated Ethiopia, after World War II, foiled efforts by the C. hierarchy to regain control and tutelage of the Ethiopian church, and affirmed its independence.

Cyrenaica The eastern part of Libya. The main center of the *Sanussi order, C. was semi-independent under Amir Idris al-*Sanussi, 1949–51. From 1951, it was one of Libya's three semi-autonomous units until 1962–63 when the federal system was abolished. See *Libya.

Czechoslovakia C's involvement in ME A. affairs has been, mainly, in three instances: (a) in 1948, C. supplied arms to emerging Israel, then engaged in war with the ASt's, and allowed the transit of arms and aircraft from other sources. (b) The Slansky trials of 1951–52, in which "World Zionism" was accused of espionage, subversion etc., inaugurated the Communist countries' new anti-Israel, anti-Zionist and to a large extent anti-Jewish policy (after a brief period of support for the creation of Israel). (c) Egypt's first arms deal with the Soviet Bloc, in 1955, was concluded with C., though the USSR herself had no-doubt backed and underwritten it and soon became the chief partner. Beyond these specific involvements, C. continuously supplies training and education for A. Communist cadres, and a place for rest, refuge, advanced training and re-indoctrination for their leaders.

D

Deir Yassin Palestinian-A. village near Jerusalem destroyed in Apr. 1948, in the A.-Israel war, by Jewish dissident fighters of the *Irgun* (IZL). The attack or massacre, which killed c. 250 villagers, including women and children, was strongly denounced by the Jewish leadership and its defense organization, the *Hagana*. Reports of the event spread among the A. population and added further impetus to a flight of refugees that had begun earlier. See *Arab-Israel Conflict, *Arab-Israel Wars.

Dervish (Darwish) orders Muslim mystics, *Sufis*, have since early Islamic days created brotherhoods or orders (*tariqa*, pl. *turuq* — literally "ways", "paths"), which have since the 12th and 13th centuries attracted and organized large groups, mostly city artisans. Local groups of adepts (*dervish* in Persian, *faqir* in Arabic) are led by a *khalifa* (substitute, deputy), who is in practice quite autonomous, while the head of the order, the *sheikh*, usually claiming descent from the founder of the order, is the supreme leader. "Specialists" among the brethren, often wanderers and beggars, reputed to perform miracles, sometimes live in monasteries (*zawiya, takiyya, khankah*). Ordinary members, laymen, usually from the lower classes, visit the tomb of their order's saint or patron (*wali*) and celebrate his anniversary (*mawlid*) with processions, dancing etc. The central practice of a Sufi ritual is the *dhikr*, the ever-repeated uttering of God's name or some religious formula, until ecstasy is attained. Some orders, such as the *Rifa'iyya* also take narcotics and add practices like walking on fire, devouring glass, playing with serpents etc.

The official Islamic establishment and the state authorities have always frowned upon such practices, as well as upon certain beliefs seen by them as superstitions, such as the veneration of saints, living or past, and the cult of their tombs. Moreover, orthodox Islam with its intellectual theology and its stress on Muslim Law (the *Shari'a*) as the central tenet of Islam, has retained reservations regarding Sufism's emphasis on religious feeling and gnostic experience — though Sufism has been a legitimate version of Islam since the great medieval theologian al-Ghazzali (d. 1111) reconciled Sufism and orthodox Islam. On the other hand, Sufism and Sufi orders have been particularly popular with some non-Arab Muslims, such as Turks and *Berbers (having been originally instrumental in their conversion to Islam).

Some Sufi DO's were particularly strong in Turkey — such as the *Bektashiyya*, the *Mevleviyya* (called the Whirling D.'s in Europe because of their ecstatic dances) and the *Nakshabandiyya* (popular among the *Kurds). All DO's were prohibited in 1925 by the Kemalist republic and their monasteries and mausoleums (*türbe*) were closed down. Yet the orders, underground and illegal, survived to some extent, and when the enforcement of secularization was relaxed, since the 1940s and 1950s, the three orders mentioned came to be accepted, though processions and ecstatic ceremonies remained forbidden. Orders considered to be extreme, such as the North-African *Tijaniyya* and the *Nur* or *Nurju*, were outlawed.

In Egypt, the DO were, until the 20th century, an important social force. The main indigenous orders are the *Ahmadiyya* (no connection with the *Ahmadiyya sect on the fringes of Islam) or *Badawiyya*, named after Sidi Ahmad al-Badawi, whose *mawlid* in Tanta is still a popular feast, and the *Burhaniyya* or *Brahimiyya*, named after Sidi Ibrahim of Dasuq. Also influential are the *Qadiriyya* (of Iraqi origin, and considered to be the earliest order still in existence, and close to orthodoxy), the *Rifa'iyya* (also of Iraqi origin), and the *Shadhiliyya* (an order of North-African origin). Early in the 19th century Viceroy Muhammad 'Ali established state control over the DO by creating a high council of the orders and nominating its head. Since then, a government permit must be obtained for the celebration of each *mawlid*. But both the government and the Islamic establishment centered around the al-*Azhar university failed in their efforts to curb those Sufi practices they considered offensive. Despite the changes in social values, the expansion of education, modernist development and westernization, the *mawlids* are still popular and some of the customs considered objectionable are still maintained. According to the head of the

Sufi Council, there are now 60 orders in Egypt, most of them off-shoots of the main ones mentioned. He presents them as a respectable establishment, loyal to the Government and opposed to religious innovation. Since 1958 the Council publishes a journal, to which even university professors have contributed. With the exception of one new order, the *Hamidiyya-Shadhiliyya*, which is centralized and cohesive, the orders are but loosely organized, and multiple membership blurs the distinction between them. Generally, however, membership — mostly from the lower classes — seems to be declining.

In the *Fertile Crescent, Sufi orders have never enjoyed influence or prestige comparable to their position in Egypt, Sudan or Turkey. There is little information about their present state, but apparently they are rapidly declining. The exception seems to be Iraq, where Sufism may be somewhat more alive. The tomb of 'Abd-ul-Qader al-Gilani (d. 1166) in Baghdad attracts *Qadiri* pilgrims. The *Rifa'iyya*, the *Nakshabandiyya* and the *Bektashiyya* have followers among both A.'s and Kurds in Iraq.

The *Sanussiyya* in Libya and the *Mahdiyya* in Sudan (and similarly the *Idrissiyya* in North Africa and later in *'Asir), founded in the 19th century, were movements similar to, and perhaps originating in, Sufi DO's, and they adopted some of the DO's methods, such as the training of propagandists in monasteries, a central hierarchial organization, the practice of *dhikr* and prayers peculiar to the order, as well as a general dislike of the orthodox theologians (*'ulama'*) and their emphasis on learning. The *Mahdiyya* at first called themselves D., and Europeans continued calling them so. But these orders were not Sufi DO's, but militant fundamentalist and revivalist movements — see *Mahdiyya, *Sanussiyya. Some true Sufi DO's are also active in Sudan — chiefly the *Tijaniyya*, the *Sa'diyya* and the *Ahmadiyya*, all of which came to Sudan from Egypt in the 19th century.

In the *Maghrib*, Northwest Africa, especially Morocco, DO's still have considerable influence, although it seems to be declining. The most important orders are the *Shadhiliyya* and its sub-orders, the *Tijaniyya*, and the *Darqawa*.

Dhahran Town in eastern Sa'udi Arabia, 10 km. from the Persian Gulf shore, on the Dammam-Riyadh railroad. A modern, planned city, built from the late 1930s on, mainly as headquarters for the Arabian-American Oil Co. ("Aramco") with a central air-conditioning system. It is inhabited chiefly by technicians and officials, and has a population of 15–20,000. D. is connected to the oil fields by a network of pipelines. It has a large international airfield built towards the end of World War II as an American base (completed only in Mar. 1946, after the end of the war), to which Sa'udia granted her *ad hoc* short-term approval, without formal treaty. A formal agreement concerning the US base was concluded in 1951 and extended for a further five years in 1957; on its expiry in 1962, the base was formally handed over, but the US retains certain facilities.

Dhofar Region on the south coast of the Arabian peninsula, on the Arabian Sea, between 'Oman in the East and the Hadhramaut region of South Yemen in the West. The chief town and port is Salala. D. is largely desert, with a mostly nomadic population estimated at 40–50,000, though some areas are cultivated. D. was for centuries under local tribal chiefs; the language spoken is an ancient South-Semitic dialect. Since the 1870s the Sultanate of 'Oman (then called Muscat and 'Oman) controls D. and considers it part of the Sultanate. But D., while heavily taxed, remained a neglected backwater and resisted 'Oman's rule. Local resistance coalesced in the 1960s into a "D. Liberation Front" (1965), renamed in 1968 (after South Yemen became independent and under her influence) "Popular Front for the Liberation of the Occupied Arab Gulf" (PFLOAG). The insurgents, now of leftist-revolutionary tendencies, enjoyed South Yemeni (and reportedly Chinese) support and were organized and equipped mainly in South Yemen. In 1974 they again renamed their organization, becoming the "Popular Front for the Liberation of 'Oman" (PFLO). The rebellion died down in the later 1970s, when 'Oman was able to step up her military operations — decisively aided by a strong Iranian expeditionary force of c. 3,000 men — and when Sa'udia prevailed upon South Yemen to stop her support. In Oct. 1982, 'Oman and South Yemen concluded an agreement to cultivate friendly relations and pacify their border in D. However, the PFLO, though no military rebel operations were reported in recent years, claims a continuing existence, holds conferences etc. At Salala, Britain and since 1980 also the USA, enjoy certain air and naval facilities (not amounting to a fully fledged military base).

Djibouti Country and port town in Northeast Africa (the "Horn of Africa"), on the Gulf of 'Aden. Since the 1880s a French territory or colony (for some time called "French Territory of the Afars and Issas" — after the two main tribal groups inhabiting it), the country became independent in 1977. It has an area of c. 9,000 sq.mi. (22–23,000 sq.km.) and a population that grew from c. 50,000 at the end of World War II to c. 350,000 in the mid-1980s — nearly all Muslims, divided about equally into 'Issas (of Somali origin) and 'Afars (part of the Danakil group of tribes). The population is not A. — though it includes an A. minority of a few thousands and Arabic is spoken to some extent as a second language. D. is therefore in itself outside the scope of this book; but as it has joined the *Arab League, in Sept. 1977, it belongs to some degree to the A. group of nations. It is not very active in the Arab League, endeavors not to become involved in inter-A. differences and blocs, and usually takes moderate positions. In July 1986, for instance, D. resumed official relations with Egypt (severed in 1979 by all but three ASt).

Druze(s), Druse(s) Sect, religious-national community, Arabic-speaking, in Syria, Lebanon and Israel, numbering an estimated 5–600,000. The D. sect, an offshoot of the *Isma'iliyya, developed in the 11th century around the figure of the Fatimid Caliph al-Hakim bi-Amr-Illah, regarded by his followers as an incarnation of the divine spirit. They were considered heretics and persecuted, and retreated to remote mountainous areas — Wadi al-Tim on the slopes of Mount Hermon, and later the southern parts of Mount Lebanon. There D. leaders, amirs, maintained a *de-facto* autonomous semi-feudal rule. Fakhr-ul-Din II (1585–1653), of the Ma'n dynasty, ruled, formally under the sovereignty of the Ottoman Sultan, most of Lebanon and parts of Syria and Palestine. His execution by the Turks, as a rebel, marked the end of the Ma'n dynasty's power. In the 18th century the house of Shihab gained ascendancy over rival feudal lords — though their D. descent and their loyalty to the faith were in doubt and some of the Shihabis converted to Christianity. Under the Shihabi Bashir II (1786–1840) the power of the D. amirs waned. Tension between the D. and their Christian-*Maronite neighbors mounted, especially in mixed areas where D. feudal clans lorded it over Maronite peasants. The Maronites — with French support — tried to end that feudal rule and gain control, while the D. — with British encouragement — strove to maintain or restore their predominance. This inter-communal strife led to violent clashes several times, notably in 1840, when power intervention — intended mainly to impose a settlement of the conflict between the Ottoman Sultan and his Viceroy in Egypt, and end the Egyptian occupation of the Levant — achieved a temporary respite only. Violence continued and in 1860 turned into a large-scale D. massacre of Christians; anti-Christian outbreaks spread also to Damascus. These events led to an intensified intervention by the powers, the dispatch of a French expeditionary force, and the creation of a semi-autonomous district (*Sanjaq*) of Mount Lebanon (see *Lebanon), where Maronites predominated, though D. formed a strong minority (c. 12%). In the 19th century two D. clans emerged as the chief contenders for leadership: *Junbalat (also Jumblat), and *Arslan (or Yazbaki).

D. had been drifting to the Hawran (Houran) mountains of southern Syria since the 18th century. In the 19th century this migration increased, impelled by the unrest described, until the Houran region became a major D. center and was called *Jabal al-Duruz*, the D. Mountain. Among the D. leaders there the al-*Atrash clan rose to prominence, and some of its sons were appointed by the Ottoman authorities as governors of the district. The French, ruling Syria under a League of Nations Mandate since 1920 (officially 1922), granted the D. Mountain in 1921 a degree of autonomy under the Mandate and appointed Salim al-Atrash as governor, a post he had also filled under the Ottomans since 1914. Incipient friction intensified on the death of Salim al-Atrash in 1923, and when the D. notables were unable to agree on a candidate, a French officer, Cpt. Carbillet, was appointed governor. Friction with him, objections to his administration and his attempts at reform, sparked off an uprising in the D. Mountain in 1925, which spread to the D. in the Mt. Hermon area. This "D. Rebellion" soon turned into a national Syrian revolt and heavy fighting took place before the French were able to put it down in 1927. The chief rebel leader, Sultan al-*Atrash, escaped to Jordan, returning to the *Jabal D.* only ten years later. Under the Syro-French agreement of 1936, *Jabal D.* became part of the Syrian republic, enjoying a measure of local autonomy. It lost that special status in 1944, with the departure of the French, and became an ordinary Syrian province.

The D. in Syria are c. 3% of the total population — 250–300,000 in the 1980s — most of them in the *Jabal D.*, where they form 80% of the population. They participated in Syria's national movement, but apart from triggering the revolt of 1925 and from Sultan al-Atrash's leadership of that revolt, their part was not prominent, nor was their share in the governance of independent Syria. Local autonomism and a traditional hostility to any centralistic government (now that of Damascus) remained strong, and the D. leaders' close ties with the Hashemite dynasty, and the British, made them suspect. They were indeed reported to have had a hand in several Syrian *coups*, e.g., that of Col. *Hinnawi in 1949, the overthrow of *Shishakli in 1954, rumored pro-Western and pro-Iraqi plots (1956–57), and a *coup* attempt by Col. Hatum (1966). Several D. officers reached senior rank in the armed forces (Muhammad 'Ubeid, 'Abd-ul-Karim Zaher-ul-Din, Salim Hatum, Fahd Sha'er, Talal Abu-'Asali) — but none of them became a first-rank Syrian leader. Under the régime of the *Ba'th military faction (from 1966) and of Hafez *Asad (from 1970–71) most senior D. officers were purged.

In Lebanon — the "Greater Lebanon", as created in 1920 — the D. form 6–7% of the population, 180–250,000 in the 1980s, most of them in the southern part of Mount Lebanon and South of the *Biqā' region, on the slopes of Mt. Hermon, around Hasbayya, a town which is also a D. religious center. Under Lebanon's communal constitution, they are represented in parliament, government and the civil service according to their share in the population; under a tradition created by the unwritten "National Pact" of 1943 the Defense Minister is usually a D.

Throughout the political history of modern Lebanon, the Arslan and Junbalat clans have competed for the community's secular-political top leadership (as distinct from the religious one) — with shifting factional alliances. Under the French Mandate, the Arslans were usually considered more militant, allied with the nationalist faction, while the Junbalats were more pliable and "pro-French". In independent Lebanon, from 1943, the Arslans confirmed their alliance with Bishara al-*Khouri's "Constitutional Bloc" and the factions succeeding it, striving to integrate the D. in the communal constitutional structure and safeguard their interests and position in that framework. The Junbalats gradually became more assertive; under Kamal *Junbalat, and after his assassination in 1977 under his son Walid *Junbalat, they turned into a near-permanent opposition, calling for the replacement of Lebanon's communal-structure constitution by a simple one-man-one-vote democracy. In fact, they were striving mainly for the enhancement of the D. position in the power structure and for fuller D. control of their power base, the Shuf district of southern Mount Lebanon. In 1949 Kamal Junbalat founded a "Progressive Socialist Party" (PSP), and from the 1950s he became increasingly left-leaning and *Nasserist. In the civil war of 1958, and again in that of 1975 and onward, his armed squads were part of the Nasserist-Leftist-Muslim camp, and Junbalat himself became a chief leader of that camp. There was near-complete identity between his D. "militias" and those of the PSP: the D. armed squads appeared as "Progressive-Socialist" ones, while Junbalat appeared as a Socialist leader, though he derived his strength from his position as a D. chieftain. In any case, in recent decades the Arslans' influence has much declined and J. has become the nearly undisputed leader of the Lebanese D.

In 1983, after the withdrawal of Israeli forces from the Shuf, the D. of the region, in a bitter war with the Christian *Phalanges, gained near-complete control and despite their call for the abolition of the communal structure, they created a virtually autonomous D. "canton". From 1983 to 1985 the D. (PSP) militias, in alliance with the *Shi'i *Amal (though sometimes in rivalry and clashes with them — as, indeed, the interests of the D. "canton" and those of the Shi'is clash on several issues), expanded the area of their predominance and took control of the coastal strip adjoining the Shuf, of the Iqlim al-Kharrub region further South, of additional areas of South Lebanon, and of the hills approaching Beirut from the South-East; they also helped the Shi'i forces to take control of West Beirut and its southern suburbs. The D. leaders were able thus to enlarge their power because they operated in close alliance with Syria, or as Syria's clients — though Syria could not rely on their full adherence to her advice or guidance. Since Apr. 1984, Junbalat has been a Minister in the Government of National Unity — but in fact he and his D. (or PSP) militia forces continued to oppose and sabotage the government of which he was a member (and most of whose meetings he persistently boycotted, though he did not resign). A few thousand D., on the slopes of Mount Hermon, reside within the "Security Zone" kept by Israel after her 1985 withdrawal from Lebanon.

In Israel, c. 70,000 D. (mid-1980s) constitute 1.5–2% of the population, c. 8% of the non-Jewish, Arabic-speaking population. Most of them live in 15 villages in Western Galilee and two on Mount Carmel; some of these villages are purely D., some have a mixed population of D., Muslims and Christians. Since 1967, four D. villages on the *Golan Heights, with a population of c. 15,000, have been under Israeli administration (but most of their D. inhabitants have refused Israeli citizenship). A long-standing friendship links Jews and D. in Israel. In Israel's War of Independence (1948) many D. helped the Jews against the invading A. armies. Since 1957, at the community's own request, D. are subject to compulsory military service (while Arab citizens may volunteer, but are not conscripted); many D. had volunteered before, and some D. attained senior rank in the army and police. In 1957 the D. were given the status of a distinct community with its own recognized communal-judicial institutions (under the British Mandate they had been subject to Muslim communal jurisdiction). First D. Qadis were appointed in the 1960s. Since 1970 D. matters are no longer handled by departments concerned with affairs of the A. minority. One or two D. are regularly elected to Parliament (the *Knesset*) — either on lists of the general parties or on lists appealing specifically to the A. and D. voter. Some teaching of D. religious traditions was introduced in D. schools in the 1970s, and in 1985 the creation of a chair for the D. heritage was announced by the University of Haifa.

Measures taken in Israel, at the request of the D. leaders, to treat the D. as a separate community rather than as A.'s, need not mean that the D. regard themselves as non-A. They are Arabic-speaking, and their cultural background and traditions are A., and their brethren in Syria and Lebanon consider themselves A. (though strong communal-autonomist sentiments persist). The Israel D. may register their ethnicity (in the population registry and identity cards) as either D. or A; but they tend to avoid a clear definition or even a frank discussion, as to whether they see themselves as a separate national entity — and it may be assumed that on balance most of them regard themselves as A. Their solidarity with the D. in Syria and particularly in Lebanon is strong. It was vigorously expressed during the Lebanese civil war and Israel's invasion of Lebanon, 1982–85, and even led to Israeli D. volunteering for service with Lebanese D. military formations and to a measure of tension between the D. and the Government on that account. Anyhow, the idyll of D.-Jewish friendship and of the integration of the D. in Israel has been troubled in recent years by growing D. complaints of discrimination and insufficient attention to their needs for economic and social development. While a "D. Zionist Association" continues fostering the full solidarity of the Israel D. with the Jewish State, a "D. Initiative Committee" represents D. claims and complaints in an increasingly assertive manner, and there is growing resistance to the conscription of the D. for military service.

The D. religion, though originally an offshoot of the Shi'i Isma'iliyya, is considered by most as having seceded from Islam. It is a secret cult; its tenets are fully known only to the Initiated, the Sages (*'Uqqāl*), who are the religious heads of the community (notables and political leaders may well be uninitiated, commoners — *Juhhāl*). The D. stress moral and social principles rather than ritual. Their house of prayer, the *khalwa*, is a small, modest structure. Their main holy days are the Feast of Sacrifice (*'Id al-Adha*), like that of the Muslims, and the Day of Pilgrimage (*Ziyara*) to the tomb of their legendary patriarch, the prophet Shu'aib (identified with biblical Jethro) at Hittin near Tiberias. The tombs of other saints, in Lebanon, Israel and the Golan, are also venerated. In the wake of the persecutions they suffered, and in line with their isolationist tendency, the D. are permitted by their faith to conceal their religious identity (*taqiyya* — camouflage, as also permitted to Shi'i Muslims). In both Lebanon and Israel religious guidance and leadership are vested in a Supreme Council of religious leaders.

Dubai (also **Dibai**) One of the seven sheikhdoms on the Trucial Coast of the Persian Gulf (*Trucial 'Oman) which in 1971 formed the federation of the *United Arab Emirates. Area: 3,900 sq.km. (1,175 sq.mi.) D.'s population grew rapidly with the development of its port and the discovery of oil — from a few thousands in the 1950s to 65,000 in the 1960s, 207,000 according to a census of 1975, and an estimated 280,000 in the mid-1980s, of which c. 80,000 live in the capital, D. (D. used to be the most populous of the seven sheikhdoms but was overtaken in the late 1970s by *Abu Dhabi). The majority of the population is foreign — estimates ranging from c. 75% up to 90%. Even the original, "indigenous" population consists largely of fairly recent immigrants, mainly fron Iran, creating a Shi'i majority. The rapid increase since the 1960s and 1970s resulted from the influx of foreign laborers — from Iran, AC such as Yemen, and mainly Pakistan and India. This large number of foreign workers without citizenship rights creates grave social, and potential political problems — though so far there have been no reports of serious actual unrest.

The Sheikh of D., of the *Maktum clan, was, in accordance with several 19th century treaties (see *Trucial 'Oman), under British protection, and D. was the seat of the British political officer responsible for the area. This British protection was removed in 1971 and D., along with the neighboring sheikhdoms, formed the independent UAE. The ruler since 1958 is Sheikh Rāshed ibn Sa'id al-Maktum, who has been concurrently Vice-President of the UAE since 1971, and since 1979 also her Prime Minister; his son, Sheikh Maktum, was Prime Minister of the UAE 1971–79 and became Deputy Prime Minister in 1979. Since the creation of the UAE there has been constant rivalry between the rulers of D. and Abu Dhabi for the primacy in the Federation — a rivalry also manifested in constitutional-ideological differences: Abu Dhabi strives for strong federal power, while D. is "autonomist", preferring stronger units and a weaker federation. In 1978–79 this conflict led to a serious crisis (and the addition of the Premiership to the positions held by the ruler of D. was part of the compromise solution achieved — see *UAE).

Oil concessions for onshore and offshore exploration and production were granted in the 1950s and 1960 to American, British and French companies, after previous concessions had expired or been returned with no results. However, D.'s rapid development began even before oil production started, with the construction of a large and modern deep-water port, "Port Rāshed", using the deep 15 km.-wide natural bay of D. and expanding the busy previously existing harbor. Construction began in 1968–69 and by 1972 the first phase was completed. By the mid-1980s the port had 35 berths and excellent facilities and had become the most modern port on the Persian Gulf. The construction of a second large modern port at Jabal 'Ali, combined with an industrial estate, was decided upon in 1976. With the first phase completed, the port was operating in 1980; ultimately over 70 berths were planned. D. also decided to construct a large drydock, intended mainly for oil tankers; and though the Organization of Arab oil-exporting countries (*OAPEC) decided to build its common drydock in *Bahrain rather than in D., the latter refused to renounce her project and proceeded on her own, from 1973. The D. drydock, one of the world's largest, was completed in 1979. A compromise had been reached late in 1977 that it would be operated jointly with OAPEC's in Bahrain, but it began operating only in 1983 — on its own, with a foreign company as operator. A modern international airport was also built. Oil was struck, offshore, in 1966, and production began in 1969; for production and revenue, and the process of nationalization — see *oil. Nearly all revenue derives from oil; but D. is creating several industrial projects including some oil-connected ones, such as a refinery (still in the planning stage) and a gas liquefaction plant at Jabal 'Ali (operating since 1980); an aluminium plant was opened in 1979.

E

Edde, Emile (1886–1949) Lebanese politician, President of Lebanon 1936–41. A *Maronite Christian, French-educated lawyer, E. was one of the advocates of the creation of "Greater Lebanon" in 1920. Later he realized that that addition of a large Muslim population, gravely affecting the Christians' primacy in Lebanon, was a historic mistake, and even contemplated a reduction in Lebanon's territory to restore that primacy (though such a view was hardly aired in public in his life-time).

E. served in the administration of the French *Mandate and was Prime Minister in 1929–30. In the 1930s he emerged as the leader of the camp that took a pro-French attitude, wanted Lebanon to remain a pluralistic, multi-community state, protected by France, with the Christian Maronites as the leading community wielding predominant influence, and opposed the notion that she was part of the A. world and should cultivate close ties with it and be integrated in pan-A. formations. E. was also willing to reach an agreement with the Jews in Palestine and with Zionism; he had several meetings with Weizmann and other Zionist leaders and agreed, in general terms, that Maronite-led Lebanon and Jewish Palestine should co-operate — though he concluded no formal agreement. In 1934, E. organized his camp in the "National Bloc" party, and in 1936 he was elected President, defeating Bishara al-*Khouri. He continued as Head-of-State even when the French suspended the Constitution, in Sept. 1939, and resigned only in 1941. With the restoration of a parliamentary régime in 1943, his supporters sought to have him re-elected as President, but eventually his candidature was not put to the vote (8 pro-E. members of Parliament absented themselves from the session that elected his rival Khouri). In the crisis of Nov. 1943, E. agreed to be appointed Head-of-State by the French. However, when British and American pressure compelled France to retreat and to reinstate the President, government and Parliament, E. was deposed, thoroughly discredited; in Mar. 1944 he was expelled from Parliament and his political career ended.

E.'s sons Raymond and Pierre continued to lead his "National Bloc" — but their views were not as clear-cut as their father's, their factional-tactical positions vacillated, and the party declined. Raymond Edde (b. 1913) has been a member of Parliament since 1953 (except for a defeat in the elections of 1964 — repaired in a 1965 by-election) and led the small parliamentary group of his party (usually 3–6 seats) in a loose "Triple Alliance" with *Chamoun's "National Liberals" and *Jumayyil's *Phalanges, but factional rivalries between him and both Chamoun and Jumayyil prevented the formation of a strong, stable bloc of Christian parties. In 1958–59 R.E. was one of the four Ministers of the compromise government set up after the civil war of 1958. He served again as a Minister in 1968–69, but usually he was in opposition. He was mentioned as a candidate for the Presidency in 1976 and again in 1982, but no formal candidature was put to the vote. For some years E. strongly opposed the use of Lebanese territory as an operational base by the Palestinian guerrillas and the "Cairo Agreement" of 1969 that was intended to regulate that use, and suggested an international peace force. He also opposed Syrian ambitions and policies in Lebanon, but he was prepared to compromise on the preservation of Lebanon's communal régime and Christian predominance. In the civil war since 1975 he did not actively support the Christian-conservative camp, and his National Bloc did not establish a militia. In recent years he mostly lives in France and is no longer politically active.

Pierre Edde (b. 1921) was a member of Parliament several times from 1951, and briefly served as Finance Minister four times, but usually was active mainly in the economic and financial arena.

Egypt A. country at the north-eastern corner of Africa, on the southern shore of the Mediterranean. (The official name, 1958–71, was "The *United Arab Republic" (UAR), 1958–61 in union with Syria; since Sept. 1971 it is "The Arab Republic of E."). Capital: *Cairo.

E.'s area is c. 1m. sq.km. (386,000 sq.mi.) — of which c. 59,000 sq.km. (23,000 sq.mi.), the *Sinai peninsula, are in Asia. The inhabited area is only 3.5% of the total, c. 35,500 sq.km. (13,500 sq.mi.) — in the *Nile valley and its delta, and a few oases. The rest of the country, east and west of the Nile valley, is desert. The northern border is the Mediterranean; in the east E. borders — in Sinai — on Israel and the Red Sea's Gulf of *'Aqaba-Eilat, and, in her main African part, on the *Red Sea and its Gulf of *Suez; in the south, the 22nd parallel constitutes the desert border with Sudan; and in the western desert E. borders on Libya. The southern border was determined in the Anglo-Egyptian *Condominium Agreement of 1899; the Sinai border was imposed in 1906 by Britain on a protesting Ottoman Sultan, who never renounced his claim to Sinai; and the western border was agreed upon with Italy, then in possession of Libya, in 1925.

E.'s population rapidly increased during this century — from c.10m. in 1900 to 15m. in the mid-1930s, 30m. in the mid-1960s, 38.2m. in the last census taken (1976); it passed the 50m. mark in 1986. The population continues increasing at c. 2.5% p.a., with a birth-rate of 3.6%. Nearly all Egyptians are Arabic-speaking. More than 90% are Sunni Muslims. Christian Egyptians, the *Copts, are c. 7% — more than 3m. in the 1980s — or more, as many Copts claim. Other minorities — Greeks, Italians, Jews — some of which had played an important role in E.'s economy, have almost disappeared since the 1960s, mainly because of the far-reaching nationalization of the economy; the exodus of the Jews was accelerated by the A.-Israel conflict; of more than 65,000 only a few hundred have remained.

E.'s population used to be mainly rural-agricultural, but the urban population, estimated at c. 20% early in the century and at 25% in the 1930s, is constantly increasing; it is estimated, in the 1980s, at c. 45% and migration to the towns continues (for Cairo alone, already the residence of c. 20% of all Egyptians, a rate of 300–350,000 p.a. is estimated). The percentage of those engaged in agriculture, estimated at c. 70% in the 1930s and still at more than 50% in the 1970s, continues decreasing and is estimated at c. 38% in the mid-1980s. Those working in industry are estimated at c. 15% (some place this figure as high as 30%, depending on the statistical definition of "industry"). More than 40% of the labor force is engaged in services. An estimated 3–3.5m. Egyptians are working and residing abroad, mainly in AC; the number seems to be declining in the mid-1980s owing to the recession in the oil countries. The share of agriculture in the national income, c. 40% in the early 1950s, is down to less than 25%, while that of industrial production is up to 15–20% (and according to some data, more than 35%, again depending on the statistical definition of industry). E.'s GDP is estimated in the mid-1980s at c. $30b., the national income p.c., about $600.

CONSTITUTIONAL STATUS   E. is now a Presidential Republic. She was under Turkish-Ottoman sovereignty from 1517, with local *de facto* rule exercised until 1803–05 by Mamluk governors (interrupted by Napoleon Bonaparte's French occupation, 1798–1801), and from 1803–05 by a dynasty of Governors (*Wali, Pasha*) that adopted in 1867 the title of *Khedive* (Viceroy). From 1882 E. was under a "temporary" British occupation — which *pro forma* recognized Ottoman sovereignty — and since 1914 under a British Protectorate, with the Khedive restyled Sultan. In 1922 Britain unilaterally proclaimed E.'s independence, and the Sultan assumed the title of King. A Constitution of a conservative parliamentary monarchy was adopted in 1923. In 1936, an Anglo-Egyptian Treaty affirmed E.'s independence. E. became a member of the *League of Nations in 1937, and a founding member of the *UN in 1945. After a July 1952 *coup* by a group of "Free Officers", the monarchy was abolished in 1953 (formalized, with a new Constitution, in 1956). Though the Constitution has since been changed several times (including three years of union with Syria, 1958–61), no basic change has occurred in E.'s character as a Presidential Republic.

POLITICAL HISTORY   At the turn of the 20th century, E. was ruled by a *Khedive* (Viceroy) of the dynasty of Muhammad 'Ali, nominally under Turkish-Ottoman sovereignty, and occupied by Britain; in fact, the British "Agent and Consul General", Cromer, ruled like a Governor, in a semi-colonial, indirect, conservative-paternalistic way. The British had occupied E. in 1882. E. under the Khedive Isma'il had become insolvent and Anglo-French supervision of her debts, in fact her economy, set up in 1876, led to increasing Anglo-French intervention and control. The Khedive was deposed in 1879 and replaced by his son Tawfiq. Unrest led by military officers culminated in 1882 in a semi-*coup* and the appointment of the officers' leader, Col. Ahmad 'Arabi (correct: 'Urābi), as Minister of War. As a result of that crisis Britain occupied the country, defeating military resistance by 'Arabi and the army.

Incipient Egyptian nationalism, which saw its beginnings in the 'Arabi revolt, was thus directed against the British and their occupation rather than against the Turkish sovereign, and some of the political parties that began organizing from c. 1900 had a pro-Turkish flavor, enhanced by a strong Islamic tendency. Egyptian nationalism was indeed to a large part linked with, and rooted in, a simultaneous movement of Islamic revival. It had, on the other hand, little connection with A. nationalism, and regarded itself as Egyptian rather than A. A. nationalists of the time also did not include E. in the AC whose autonomy or independence they demanded. The main parties of those years were the "Nationalist Party" (*al-Hizb al-Watani*), formed in 1907 and led by Mustafa Kamel (1874–1908) and after his death by Muhammad Farid (1868–1919), with nationalism, pronouncedly anti-British, as its main plank, and the "Nation Party" (*Hizb al-Umma*), also founded in 1907 and led by (Ahmad) Lutfi al-Sayyid (1872–1963), with Ahmad Sa'd

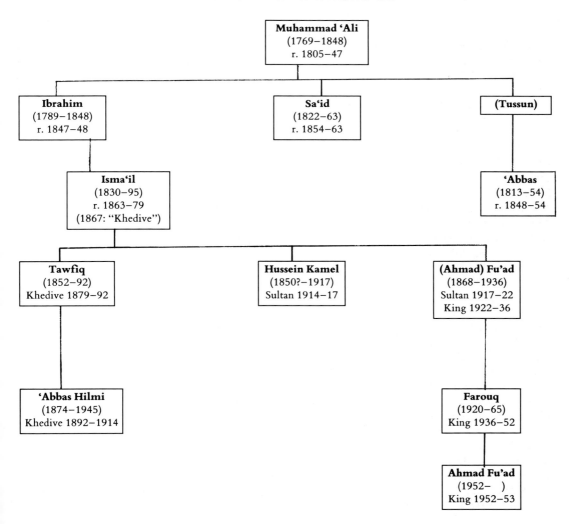

THE RULING DYNASTY OF EGYPT, 1805–1953

*Zaghlul, later E.'s national leader, among its junior leaders. The *Umma* Party professed a more liberal westernized nationalism, and aspired to a parliamentary-constitutional régime; it was not unwilling to let E. be guided for some time by Britain — and was regarded by its adversaries as Lord Cromer's pet or creation. In any case, Egyptian nationalism was intensifying and led to several incidents and clashes with a British administration that had little understanding and no sympathy for these national aspirations (for instance, the "Dinshawi Incident" in 1906).

When Turkey joined Germany and Austria in World War I, Britain in Dec. 1914 severed the formal link between E. and the Ottoman Empire and declared E. a British Protectorate, under a High Commissioner, promising to guide her towards self-rule. At the same time, the British deposed the Khedive, *'Abbas Hilmi, considered anti-British and involved in political intrigues, and replaced him with his uncle, Hussein Kamel, as "Sultan"; the new Sultan in 1917 was succeeded by his brother Ahmad *Fu'ad. During the war years Egyptian resentment against British rule intensified. The war effort imposed on the population economic hardships, soaring prices, martial law, and censorship; E. was Britain's main base in the war against Turkey, and Britain felt compelled to keep a tight rein and postpone any advance towards independence, while younger Egyptian leaders were pressing for that independence.

Towards the end of the war, a new nationalist group formed, led by Sa'd Zaghlul. This group, mainly men of the landed gentry, the commercial middle class and the intelligentsia and free professions, with influence in the villages, too, claimed that it — rather than the Sultan and his government — should represent E. in negotiations with Britain scheduled to be held in London. In Nov. 1918, a delegation laid that claim before the High Commissioner, Sir Reginald Wingate, and that delegation (Arabic: al-Wafd) became the nucleus of the *Wafd Party. When the British refused to recognize Zaghlul's group as the national leadership representing E., demonstrations and strikes broke out. In Mar. 1919, Zaghlul and some of his leading associates were exiled. But when violent riots followed, the British backed down. Wingate was replaced by General *Allenby, who adopted a policy of conciliation. Early in Apr. Zaghlul and his colleagues were released and allowed to go to Paris to place the Egyptian demands before the Peace Conference. However, when they arrived, the Conference had already recognized the British Protectorate (May 1919).

In May 1919, the British government appointed the Secretary for the Colonies, Lord Milner, to investigate the situation and suggest a new régime that would grant E. self-government under British guidance while safeguarding British and foreign interests. Milner, arriving in E. at the end of 1919, was boycotted by the nationalists and most public figures not connected with the palace or the government, but later contacted Zaghlul in Europe and in June 1920 held talks with him in London, offering E. independence on condition that a treaty guaranteeing British interests be signed. But no agreement was reached on the details of such a treaty. Milner presented his report late in 1920; it was published in Feb. 1921. Negotiations with a government delegation, 1921, reached no agreement on an Anglo-Egyptian treaty, and attempts to recruit leaders who would accept independence on British terms failed. In Dec. 1921, Zaghlul was again exiled; intensified nationalist ferment and renewed violence followed.

As no agreed solution seemed feasible, Britain on 28 Feb. 1922 unilaterally proclaimed E. independent. Four matters were reserved to the British government until agreement could be reached upon them: a. the security of British communications in E.; b. the defense of E. against foreign aggression; c. the protection of foreign interests and minorities; d. the administration of Sudan. The Egyptians refused to agree to that restricted independence, but in effect accepted it and began to establish their state institutions.

In Mar. 1922, Sultan Fu'ad proclaimed himself King (after a bitter struggle the British prevented him from taking the title of King of E. *and Sudan*). A Constitution was worked out by an appointed committee and promulgated in Apr. 1923, and a Parliament was elected (Sept. 1923 to Jan. 1924) — with the *Wafd* winning a decisive majority. The Constitution of 1923, after a bitter struggle between the nationalist radicals and liberals and the King and his conservative advisers, was a conservative one. The King was to appoint and dismiss the Prime Minister, to dissolve Par-

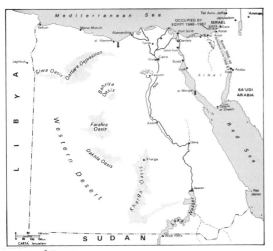

Map of Egypt

liament and postpone its sessions, to appoint the President of the Senate and one-fifth of its members, and had the right to veto all laws. Despite this, the *Wafd* became the defender of the Constitution, while the King and his conservative supporters viewed it as restricting their rule.

The 30 years of E.'s parliamentary monarchy saw a continuous struggle between the *Wafd*, as the main nationalist and radical-liberal party, and conservative anti-*Wafd*ist parties — usually supporting the King, and supported by him. The most important of those was the "Liberal-Constitutional Party", founded in 1922 by 'Adli Yakan, 'Abd-ul-Khaleq Sarwat, 'Abd-ul-'Aziz Fahmy, Muhammad Mahmud, Hussein Heykal; many of its leaders were seceding *Wafd*ists. A new split in the *Wafd* created, in 1937, the second major anti-*Wafd*ist party, the Saadist Party (commemorating Sa'd Zaghlul's name), led by Dr. Ahmad *Maher and Mahmud Fahmy *Nuqrashi. Usually, whenever a *Wafd*ist or neutral government was in power, the *Wafd* won the elections (1924, 1926, 1929, 1936, 1942, 1950); under governments of the anti-*Wafd*ist parties, it was they who won (1931, 1938 and 1945). But all pre-1936 *Wafd*ist governments (1924, 1928, 1930) were short-lived, as the King used his prerogative to dismiss them and dissolve Parliament. Several times election laws were changed, e.g. direct elections were replaced by indirect, and property, tax or educational restrictions were imposed — in the hope that such measures would reduce the *Wafd*'s influence; most of these changes were later abolished by *Wafd*ist or liberal governments. In 1930, however, ultra-conservative Prime Minister Isma'il *Sidqi abrogated the Constitution and enacted a new, much more conservative one. The *Wafd* and the Liberals boycotted the new régime and its elections; their resistance escalated into serious unrest and riots, and in 1935 the King gave in and reintroduced the Constitution of 1923. The elections of 1936 were overwhelmingly won by the *Wafd* — led by Mustafa *Nahhas since Zaghlul's death in 1927.

While the parliamentary-constitutional régime did not operate satisfactorily, nearly all Egyptian parties, and the King, were united in their desire to replace the semi-independence imposed in 1922 by full independence and to abolish Britain's four "reserved matters" by concluding a treaty regulating the issues in question, as Britain also wanted. Though there were tactical differences between the parties, and between them and the King, E.'s basic "National Demands" were presented by whichever government negotiated for her. Talks on an Anglo-Egyptian treaty failed in 1924, 1927 and 1929–30 mainly over the two principal demands: those concerning defense and the Sudan. E. demanded the evacuation of British forces and the handing-over of her defense to the Egyptian army alone, as well as the abolition of restrictions on the strength of that army and the transfer of its command (held *ex officio* by the British Governor-General of Sudan) to Egyptian hands. As to Sudan, E. demanded the replacement of the *Condominium by the "Unity of the Nile Valley", i.e. Egyptian rule over Sudan (as before the *Mahdi's revolt of 1881). Moreover, E. complained that she was deprived of her proper share in the joint administration of Sudan as provided under the Condominium Agreement of 1899. Her demands included the freedom for Egyptians to migrate to and settle in Sudan. These complaints were aggravated by a serious crisis in 1924. When the Governor-General, Sir Lee Stack, was assassinated, the British imposed reprisals: the withdrawal of Egyptian troops from Sudan; the conversion of Sudanese units of the Egyptian army into a Sudan Defense Force; the enactment of Sudan's budget without submission to E. for approval; the enlargement of irrigated areas in Sudan (implying the threat to strangle E. by cutting off the vital Nile flood-waters). E. now demanded, as a first step, the abrogation of these reprisals. Tension was eased in 1929 when Britain and E. reached agreement on the distribution of the Nile waters between E. and Sudan; but the basic dispute remained unresolved.

A breakthrough came in 1936. Britain was keenly interested in mending her fences in the ME in view of Italy's conquest of Ethiopia and general expansionism, and the growing aggressive strength of Nazi Germany. E. had observed Iraq attaining fuller independence through the Anglo-Iraqi treaty of 1930, proving that an accommodation with Britain — independence against certain, reduced privileges for Britain — was possible. The restoration of the parliamentary-constitutional régime in E. had been encouraged by Britain, and the latter now considered the *Wafd*, though strongly nationalist (or perhaps *because* of that), as the preferable partner for a settlement. King Fu'ad died in Apr. 1936, and as his son *Farouq was a minor, a Regency Council was set up. Elections in May 1936 brought the *Wafd* to power; for the resuming negotiations with Britain an all-party delegation had been formed even before the elections (excluding the old "Nationalist Party" — a group with little influence — which rejected any agreement with Britain). In Aug. 1936, a Treaty of Preferential Alliance was signed.

A 20-year Defense Pact allowed Britain to station a defined number of troops (10,000 land forces, 400 pilots, and ancillary personnel) on the Suez Canal — and for a limited time also in Cairo and Alexandria — until the Egyptian army be deemed by both parties to be able to ensure its defense and the security of navigation. In the event of war or imminent threat of war, E. was to aid Britain by furnishing her with "all the facilities and assistance in (her) power, including the use of (her) ports, aerodromes and communications". Sudan would continue to be administered under the Condominium Agreement — without pejudice to the question of sovereignty, and with Egyptian immigration unrestricted. The protection of foreigners and minorities was recognized as E.'s exclusive responsibility. Britain was to support the abrogation of the *Capitulations (extra-territorial privileges for foreigners; their abolition was agreed in the *Montreux Convention of 1937). The Treaty of 1936 thus completed E.'s formal independence. In May 1937, E. was admitted to the *League of Nations, on Britain's recommendation.

The honeymoon of general satisfaction was, however, brief — both internally and in Anglo-Egyptian relations. Young King Farouq, who came of age and took the reins in July 1937, tended even more than his father to play a dominant political rôle. Late in 1937 he dismissed the *Wafd* government, and under its successor the *Wafd* — which had been unable to fulfil popular hopes, and which had split in 1937 (seceding leaders founding the Saadist Party) — lost the elections of 1938, and non-*Wafd*ist governments followed each other. And Britain — though her former High Commissioner was now an Ambassador — continued interfering in Egyptian politics. She also did not fully adhere to the military clauses of the Treaty: the number of her troops still exceeded that stipulated, and those outside the Canal Zone were not withdrawn.

World War II further aggravated Anglo-Egyptian discord. As E. became Britain's vital ME base, military installations were further strengthened and the number of troops was increased. E. did not declare war on the "Axis" powers, though they violated her territory, reaching Mersa Matruh in 1950 and al-'Alamein in 1942, in a new offensive. Many Egyptian politicians, including the King and Prime Minister 'Ali *Maher, displayed sympathy for the German-Italian Axis, and some groups displayed openly Fascist tendencies — such as the "Young Egypt" Party (*Misr al-Fatat*), founded in the mid-1930s by Ahmad Hussein (1911–82). And the "facilities and assistance" stipulated in the Treaty were supplied but grudgingly. In 1940 Britain forced the dismissal of Premier Maher and the Chief-of-Staff, 'Aziz 'Ali al-*Masri, who was (rightly) suspected of contacts with the enemy; al-Masri was thereupon caught trying to escape to the Axis forces and was detained and put on trial (along with some other officers). Britain's intervention reached its peak in Feb. 1942, when she forced the King, by an ultimatum accompanied by a show of military force, to replace the government by a *Wafd*ist one.

In the later war years, E. became increasingly involved in regional A. affairs. Before then, she had — despite much sympathy and a measure of emotional-ideological solidarity — taken little part in A. nationalist struggles outside her borders. She first became officially involved when she responded to a British invitation to attend the London Conference of 1939 on the future of Palestine. In 1942–43, the British were actively interested to establish an all-A. alliance, hoping such an alliance would lead to A. moderation and support for Britain; and they realized that without E. such an alliance could not be built. Premier Nahhas consented to head the consultations that were to bring about the foundation of the *Arab League, 1944–45, and E. became (until 1978–79) the major and decisive force in the League, with Cairo as its headquarters and an Egyptian as its Secretary-General. E.'s growing involvement in A. affairs dragged her into the Palestine War of 1948, despite explicit decisions of 1946–47 not to intervene with regular forces and against the specific advice of the army commanders (see *Arab-Israel Conflict). Within the A. League, E. headed a group of states (with Syria and Sa'udi Arabia) which opposed all plans for federation or a revision of the map of the ASt and especially an expansion of the *Hashemite dynasty ruling Iraq and Jordan, and shaped the A. League as an association of sovereign states protecting the inter-A. status quo (a policy changed only in the late 1950s).

With the danger of an Axis victory receding, British intervention in E.'s political affairs lessened, and in Oct. 1944 King Farouq dismissed the British-imposed *Wafd* government. On 24 Feb. 1945 E. declared war against Germany and Japan, and thus became qualified to become a founding member of the UN; her forces did not engage in action (Premier Ahmad Maher, who had decided to declare war, was assassinated the same day).

In Dec. 1945, E. demanded the abrogation or radical amendment of the Treaty of 1936, to obtain the evacuation of British forces and the "Unity of the Nile Valley", i.e. Egyptian sovereignty over Sudan. Britain was prepared to discuss the replacement of the Treaty, even before its expiry in 1956, by a defense agreement that would satisfy her strategic requirements in the Canal Zone; for Sudan, she advocated eventual self-determination, with an advance towards self-government in the meantime. In 1946, Premier Isma'il *Sidqi reached an agreement with Foreign Secretary *Bevin under which Britain was to withdraw her forces within three years and a joint Anglo-Egyptian defense committee was to be established; Britain and E. were to prepare Sudan for self-rule and self-determination "within the framework of the unity between E. and the Sudan under the joint Egyptian crown". But this formula was interpreted by the two parties in contradictory terms: to the British, Sudan had been granted self-determination, while Egyptian-Sudanese unity was no more than a token formula; the Egyptians claimed that the Unity of the Nile Valley and Egyptian sovereignty had been conceded and self-determination was to be a symbolic act. When these contradictory interpretations were voiced in public, the agreement fell through and Sidqi resigned. The question of Sudan was raised in 1947 in the UN Security Council by Prime Minister *Nuqrashi, but the Council could reach no decision, and E.'s argument against self-determination for Sudan failed to sway world opinion.

The impasse in relations with Britain, and the growing radicalization of Egyptian politics, led the *Wafd* government, in Oct. 1951, unilaterally to declare the abrogation of the Treaty of 1936 and the Condominium of 1899, to proclaim King Farouq "King of E. and Sudan" (i.e. to declare E.'s sovereignty over Sudan), and to issue a draft constitution for Sudan envisaging self-government in internal matters while reserving defense and foreign affairs to E. At the same time, E. rejected Anglo-American proposals, with which France and Turkey were also associated, to join a *ME Defense Pact or "Supreme Allied Command for the ME" (SACME) and to solve the dispute over British troops and bases by placing the bases at the disposal of that ME Command. She also rejected new British proposals for a settlement of the Sudan issue. Late in 1951 the Government encouraged attempts to force the British out by popular resistance; clashes continued into 1952. In late Jan. 1952 Egyptian and British forces fought in Isma'iliyya, and on 26 Jan. serious riots in Cairo turned against foreigners and minorities ("Black Saturday"), martial law was declared, and the King dimissed the *Wafd* government held responsible.

The radicalization of Egyptian politics and the increasing violence were part of a more general malaise, a deep frustration with the social-political régime. The constitutional-parliamentary régime had not operated very well. In its 29 years, until it was overthrown in 1952, it had seen 10 elections and 38 changes of government, and only two parliaments had completed their term (1931–36, 1945–50). The rigging of elections, purchases of votes etc. had been frequently denounced, and big land-owners and strongmen had imposed their influence and delivered bloc-votes of whole villages. Economic and social problems were even more fundamental. The large increase of the population (from less than 10m. in 1900 to over 22m. in 1952) was not balanced by a parallel expansion of arable land so that the ratio of cultivated land and food production per inhabitant was in constant decline. Industry did not develop fast enough to catch up with population growth. Standards of life and nourishment were declining and poverty was spreading, while the gap between rich and poor widened. A constant stream of migrants from the villages to the cities created huge slums and a large sub-stratum of society not absorbed in gainful employment. Of the peasants, over 50% were landless tenants or agricultural laborers, and of those owning land the majority owned less than 1 *feddan* (acre) i.e. insufficient to feed a family, while some 12,000 big landlord families owned 37% of the land (and the captains of industry, banking and trade mostly came from the same families). The politicians and their parties all spoke of reforms and economic development, and the *Wafd* had a radical wing which probably meant it seriously and advocated a ceiling of 500 *feddan* on land ownership (radical Leftists wanted a ceiling of 50 *feddan*). But the political leaders came mostly from the big land-owning and capitalist families, and very little was done in the way of reforms or welfare-oriented development.

Egyptian politics were thus largely remote from the basic social and economic concerns of the people. The frustration created led to the growth of extremist extra-parliamentary organizations. The Communist Left was weak, and split into factions, and its appeal to the masses was diminished by the fact that many of its leaders were members of the minorities (Copts, Jews, Greeks). The Fascist "Young Egypt" is mentioned above. A more influential stream of extremism was the Islamic one. Among several associations, the *Muslim Brotherhood (al-Ikhwan al-Muslimun)*, founded in 1929 by Hassan al-*Banna, came to be the important one. In its efforts to teach and spread fundamentalist Islam and impose it on E.'s social fabric and state institutions, it also used violence, political assassination and terrorism, such as bombs in movie-houses etc. (for details see *Muslim Brothers; the Brotherhood also sent early in 1948, several squads of volunteers to fight with the Palestine Arabs against the Jews). In Dec. 1948, the Brotherhood was banned by Premier Nuqrashi and steps were taken to suppress it. Three weeks later, Nuqrashi was assassinated (the Botherhood's "Supreme Guide" Hassan al-Banna was murdered in revenge in Feb. 1949).

The ground was thus prepared for the overthrow of the régime by a group of army officers. The officers chafed under the failure of the Palestine War of 1948 and were convinced that the débacle had been caused by faulty political leadership and, principally, by wide-spread corruption, a generally rotten civil and military administration, sabotaged arms supplies and treacherous intrigues; they found their suspicions confirmed by an investigation, from June 1950, purges of senior officers (Oct. 1950) and trials (from Mar. 1951). The reinstatement of the most senior dismissed commanders, in May 1951, angered them and caused further ferment — as did the deepening instability of the régime, and what they saw as its general corruption, and the King's high life of debauchery. From c. 1950 a secret group of "Free Officers" formed. On 23 July 1952, that group staged a *coup*, led by General Muhammad *Nagib and Col. Gamal *'Abd-ul-Nasser (the latter apparently was the real leader, while Nagib, an older and more senior officer, had been asked to join as a figurehead). There was no resistance, and the officers' 12-member Revolutionary Council took over. The new rulers set up a civilian government headed by the veteran politician 'Ali *Maher. They forced King Farouq to abdicate and go into exile, transferred the crown to his infant son Ahmad Fu'ad, appointing a Regency Council, and suspended the Constitution. The new régime immediately declared its resolve to introduce far-reaching reforms, with land reform heading its lists. As Maher was reluctant to go along, a new government was formed in Sept. with Nagib at its head. A Land Reform

Bill was immediately enacted, restricting land ownership to 200 *feddan* (acres), with 100 *feddan* more for other members of the family. Another decree made the existence of political parties conditional on the approval of their programs and leaders by the government. The parties were ordered to reform and purge themselves and some, complying, began replacing their leaders. A considerable number of old-régime politicians were arrested, and trials for corruption, maladministration or treason were promised.

Later in 1952 the new régime faced a measure of political resistance and some of the parties, led by the *Wafd*, demanded the reactivation of the constitution and parliament. The ruling officers thereupon hardened their stance. In Dec. 1952 they abrogated the Constitution of 1923. They set up a special court to try ministers, parliamentarians and civil servants who had "betrayed the trust of the people". Some of the accused, including one ex-Premier, Ibrahim 'Abd-ul-Hadi, and several ex-Ministers and leading politicians, were sentenced in 1953 and 1954 to long prison terms and the loss of their political rights. In Jan. 1953, all political parties were dissolved and their property was confiscated, and the régime set up a political mass-organization of its own, the "Liberation Organization", with Nagib as President and Nasser as Secretary-General. In June 1953, E. became a republic, under a provisional constitution. Nagib was named President and Prime Minister and Nasser — Deputy Premier. There were also further arrests and purges — *inter alia* of officers and politicians charged with plotting against the new régime. Moreover, first rifts appeared within the new ruling team: among the plotters arrested was Col. Rashad Muhanna who had been close to the Revolutionary Council and a member of the Regency Council, from which he had been dismissed already in Oct. 1952; he was later sentenced to prison for life. More important: a major rift erupted between Nagib and Nasser. It was partly a struggle for power, but it also concerned policy. Nagib advocated an early restoration of a constitutional régime and the return of the army to its barracks, while Nasser strove to perpetuate a revolutionary-reformist régime led by army officers. Nagib was also more sympathetic to the Muslim Brotherhood, whom Nasser regarded as a chief adversary to be suppressed. In Feb. 1954, Nagib resigned, in protest, as President, Prime Minister and Chairman of the Revolutionary Council, and Nasser assumed the Premiership, leaving the Presidency vacant. But a semi-*coup* by groups of officers, supported by some members of the Revolutionary Council, chiefly the Leftist Khaled *Mohieddin (Muhyi-ul-Din), restored Nagib to the Presidency and after a few days to the Premiership as well. In Mar. 1954, the Revolutionary Council announced that in July elections would be held for a constituent assembly. The military régime would be lifted before these elections, and after them political parties would be re-permitted and the Revolutionary Council dissolved.

Nagib's victory was short-lived. Nasser and his supporters stirred up opposition within the armed forces, decrying the threat to the revolution and calling for the abrogation of the measures announced. Strikes, e.g. by transport workers, supported these demands. Late in Mar. 1954, the Revolutionary Council bowed to that pressure and postponed to 1956 the restoration of a constitutional-political régime. In Apr., Nagib was compelled to appoint Nasser Prime Minister, while his own authority as President was greatly reduced; and in Nov. 1954 he was dismissed and placed under house arrest (he was released in 1971 only, after Nasser's death). The Presidency remained vacant until 1956. With Nasser now as the main leader, further purges were carried out, in 1954, in the armed forces, regional and municipal councils, the press, and among politicians. More "free officers", members of the Revolutionary Council, assumed ministerial positions, a process that had begun in June 1953.

At the same time there was a contest between the régime and the "Muslim Brotherhood". The latter had welcomed the revolution of 1952 and had been treated with sympathy by the Revolutionary Council. The decree on dissolution of parties was not applied to the Brotherhood, as it was not considered a "party"; in Sept. 1952 it was even invited to join the government, but did not do so when the officers rejected two of its three nominees. Differences, however, soon became apparent. The Brotherhood demanded that the new régime adopt its principles and base itself on Islam; it also wanted a real share in power and policy-making and full freedom of action and organization. The officers rejected these demands; tension intensified after the establishment of the "Liberation Organization", as the officers would not allow another popular organization beside their own, while the Brethren — though weakened by internal struggles for the leadership — were not prepared to stop all activities. In Jan. 1954, Brotherhood-inspired student demonstrations led to clashes, the Brotherhood was outlawed and its leaders were imprisoned, Nagib released them and relaxed the ban, but when Nasser won, in Apr. 1954, efforts to eliminate the Brethren's influence resumed and the rift grew. Late in Oct. 1954, an attempt to assassinate Nasser was reported. The Brotherhood was now vigorously suppressed. Its leaders were tried in Dec. and sentenced to death, and though the "Supreme Guide", Hassan Isma'il al-Hudeibi, was reprieved, six of his associates were hanged. (The Brotherhood continued to exist underground, and in the 1950s and 1960s there were further purges, arrests and trials.) Nasser continued purges in the army, the civil service, the press and among politicians, consolidated his position as the uncontested leader, and began dropping members of the Revolutionary Council. In June 1956, a new Constitution was endorsed by a Referendum — a Presidential one, with no Prime Minister; it proclaimed Islam as the state religion and granted women the vote. Nasser was elected President, as the only candidate; a new popular mass organization, the "National Union", was entrusted with the nomination of all candidates for election.

In foreign affairs, the new régime displayed, in its first three years, a remarkably moderate attitude. It extracted the Sudan problem from its deadlock by agreeing to Sudanese self-determination and immediate steps towards self-government — in an accord between Nagib and Sudanese party leaders (Oct. 1952), endorsed by a formal agreement in Jan. 1953. That agreement, and Egyptian proposals for a three-year transition to self-government, were communicated to Britain in Nov. 1952, and in Feb. 1953 an Anglo-Egyptian agreement was signed (Sudan became independent on 1 Jan. 1956). With the Sudan dispute solved, the issue of British bases and troops was tackled. Talks on E.'s demand for their evacuation began in Apr. 1953, and led in Oct. 1954 to a formal agreement: Britain was to hand over the bases and evacuate her troops within 20 months, but was permitted to return troops and use the bases in case of an attack on a member-state of the Arab League or Turkey; British civilian technicians were to maintain the bases. With regard to the Palestine dispute, a certain pragmatism could be discerned — or at least Israeli leaders thought so. The new leaders were not identified with the régime that had involved E. in the war of 1948 and had denounced at least certain aspects of that involvement. Anti-Israel indoctrination, statements and propaganda seemed to diminish considerably — and in Israel there was hope that the new, pragmatic E. would accept Israel's existence and make peace. However, several attempts to arrange for E.-Israel meetings and talks yielded no results.

E.'s policy began changing in about 1955, and the main catalyst was an increasingly activist *Neutralism. E., like most newly independent countries of the "Third World", had always inclined to a measure of non-alignment, but this had not been a major tenet of ideology. When Nasser in 1953–54, in his booklet *The Philosophy of the Revolution*, formulated the principles of the new régime's policy, he saw E. in the center of three overlapping circles: the A., the African, and the Muslim ones; a "circle" of neutralist nations was not mentioned. In Apr. 1955, however, Nasser attended the *Bandung Conference of Asian and African countries; there he came into contact with leaders of the Afro-Asian world — Nehru, Chou En-lai, U Nu, Sukarno, Sihanouk, Nkrumah, Pham Van Dong and other prominent figures — and was accepted as one of them. In the wake of Bandung, when efforts were made to establish a neutralist bloc of nations, E. took a leading part and later hosted many conferences of that group — official, popular (e.g. the "Afro-Asian Peoples' Solidarity Organization"), and specialized (youth, women, writers). Nasser, indeed, was seen, with Nehru and Tito, as one of the "Big Three" of Neutralism.

E.'s new neutralist activism caused a growing estrangement between her and the Western powers. While neutralism later became quite respectable, the West, and particularly the USA, at that time still vigorously condemned it. Moreover, from 1953–54, the US and her allies resumed efforts to set up a *ME Defense Pact linked to the West, which resulted in 1955 in the establishment of the *Baghdad Pact. E. refused to join the proposed alliance and vigorously opposed the concept of a defense pact linked to the Western powers. She regarded the Baghdad Pact as a threat to her security and régime, suspected Western-inspired Turkish-Iraqi schemes to force the Pact on additional AC (Syria, Jordan), and began building a counter-alliance of her own, particularly with Syria. In 1955, she concluded an arms deal with the Soviet Bloc (Czechoslovakia, and the USSR behind her). This lit a red warning light in the West. Talks about large-scale Western aid for E.'s development, and particularly her pet project, the *Aswan High Dam, ran into difficulties, while the Soviet Union was reportedly offering her aid. In July 1956, the US and Britain withdrew their offer of aid and got the World Bank to do likewise. E. reacted by nationalizing the Suez Canal, a step that created a major international crisis. As negotiations for a settlement of the Suez crisis dragged on and showed little progress, Britain and France late in Oct. 1956 took military action, bombing and invading E.'s Canal Zone (see *Suez War). Israel — which perceived a much hardened Egyptian stance, suffered from frequent border raids which she saw as backed and organized by E. and an E.-imposed blockade of the Suez Canal, and since 1954−55 also of the Gulf of *'Aqaba, and felt a growing sense of encirclement — simultaneously invaded E.'s *Sinai, halting just short of the Suez Canal, as secretly pre-arranged with Britain and France (who used the Israeli invasion as a pretext for their intervention). The invasion failed, as international pressure, particularly US and Soviet, compelled the three countries to call it off and withdraw; a UN Emergency Force, *UNEF, was set up to supervise the withdrawal and stay on in Sinai.

From the crisis of 1956 E. emerged victorious and, having defeated an armed assault by imperial great powers, with her prestige much enhanced in the "Third World". Her stance of "Positive" (i.e. activist) Neutralism hardened and her relations with the Soviet Bloc became closer, while those with the West were at a low point. E. had severed relations with Britain and France on 1 Nov. 1956 and sequestrated the property of their citizens. She had also abrogated, on 1 Jan. 1957, the Anglo-Egyptian Agreement of 1954 concerning the maintenance and reactivation of the British bases. Relations with Britain were resumed in 1959, and restored to ambassadorial level in 1961 (they were severed again in Dec. 1965 because of the Rhodesia crisis and resumed late in 1967). Relations with France were resumed in 1963, after France had granted independence to Algeria and embarked on a pro-A. policy. Neither Britain nor France was able to recover former positions of political and economic influence in E. Diplomatic relations with West Germany were severed in 1965, along with 9 other ASt, in protest against German recognition of, and aid to, Israel; they were resumed in June 1972. Relations remained cold and hostile even with the USA, though she had supported E. in the crisis of 1956, turning against her principal European allies. E. suspected American intervention in the ME and intrigues to form a pro-Western bloc, resented the *Eisenhower Doctrine of 1957, and was irritated by US support for Israel. Soviet aid, on the other hand, both economic and military grew until E. became politically, economically and militarily dependent on the USSR in large measure.

Since the mid-1950s E. adopted an activist line in her A. policies, too, with the aim of forging inter-A. alliances under her guidance and leadership. In 1955 she concluded a military pact with Syria and Sa'udi Arabia, joined by Jordan and Yemen in 1956. With countries not inclined to shape their policies according to E.'s guidance, pressure was used (e.g. Jordan 1956−57). Moreover, in her desire to see "progressive" régimes in the image of her own established in all AC, E. began intervening in other AC, encouraging "Nasserist" groups and supporting their subversive schemes and *coup* attempts, up to and including attempts to assassinate "reactionary" leaders. Jordan in 1957, Lebanon in 1958, Iraq in 1959 complained of such interference, the two former even appealing to the UN Security Council and asking Britain and the USA to send troops. Sa'udia, Tunisia, Jordan complained of Egyptian-engineered attempts to assassinate their leaders. In fact, there was hardly an ASt that did not complain of Egyptian subversion and interference, expel Egyptian diplomats and military attachés, sometimes even sever relations with E.

While aiming at close co-ordination of like-minded "progessive" Nasserist régimes in all ASt, E. did not strive for territorial unions. Her merger with Syria and the formation of the

*United Arab Republic (UAR), 1958, was a deviation from her usual policy; indeed, E. did not initiate that union but was swept along by events in Syria. However, once the union was proclaimed, on 1 Feb. 1958, and endorsed by a plebiscite, once Nasser was President and a united government installed (with two "regional" governments administering local affairs in the "Egyptian Region" and the "Syrian Region" of the UAR), E. imposed her régime, her policies, her concepts on Syria, including the dissolution of all parties and their replacement with the single, state-run "National Union", with no consideration for Syria's susceptibilities and volatile politics. Syria's secession from the UAR, in Sept. 1961, after a *coup* by Syrian officers and politicians, was a deep shock for E. She denounced the secession as illegal, refused to accept Syria's renewed separate independence, walked out of the Arab League Council when that body recognized Syria's resumed separate membership and agreed to discuss a Syrian complaint against E. (Aug. 1962). E. also continued to call herself, officially, "UAR" and retained the UAR flag until 1971, after Nasser's death. A partial reconciliation took place in 1963, after the *Ba'th party came to power in Syria; E. and Syria negotiated, with Iraq also joining, an agreement to set up a new UAR — replacing the unitary régime that had failed in 1958–61 with a federal one, despite both sides' objections to the principle of federalism, generally considered "rightist" and reactionary. But unbridgeable differences between the Ba'thists and the Nasserists in Syria, with E. backing the latter, led to the failure of that new attempt at union. E. established full official relations with a separately independent Syria in 1966 only, when a close alliance and a defense pact were renewed.

Despite the trauma of Syria's secession from the UAR, E. continued her activist-interventionist A. policy. That reached its climax when E. intervened militarily, in Sept. 1962, in the civil war that had broken out in Yemen, by sending an expeditionary force to support the republican camp. That operation led to warlike clashes, nearly open war, with Sa'udia, who supported the rival, royalist camp in Yemen. This intervention tied down considerable Egyptian forces. It also deeply involved E. in internal political problems of Yemen, with E. arbitrating factional struggles, taking a hand in the nomination and dismissal of Prime Ministers and detaining in E. Yemeni politicians in disfavor. But her success was doubtful: E. was bogged down, but not really in control.

The near-failure of the Yemeni intervention, coming on the heels of the Syrian debacle, led in the mid-1960s to a tuning-down, a mitigation of E.'s inter-Arab interventionism. Anyhow, that interventionism did not succeed in the long run: not a single ASt replaced its "reactionary" régime by a "progressive", Nasserist one or fully accepted Egyptian guidance or predominance. Inter-A. reconciliation was also urgently needed in the face of escalating tension on the A.-Israel front. E. and Sa'udia, since the late 1950s her main adversary in inter-A. alignments, made serious efforts at reconciliation (including a settlement of the Yemen problem). The Arab League Council, the principal all-A. forum of deliberation, was complemented, and nearly eclipsed, by a new, highest-level forum: the "Summit" meetings of Heads-of-State (the first met in Cairo in Jan. 1964). In 1964, E. encouraged the creation of the *PLO. In Oct. 1964, E. agreed with Iraq, under the pro-Egyptian régime of President *'Aref, to establish a near-federal "Unified Political Command"; the plan was not fully implemented and withered, though it was officially abolished only in 1968. In Nov. 1966, E. concluded a new military pact with Syria, with a joint military command (but this time with no federal or union plans); in May-June 1967, Iraq and Jordan joined that pact (Jordan — under heavy Egyptian pressure). At that time, indeed, inter-A. differences seemed forgotten, as the whole A. world rallied behind E. towards the war with Israel that was clearly about to break out. Yet, even during those years of Egyptian inter-A. moderation, E.'s A. policy remained contradictory in concept and ideology. Even while working for reconciliation and cooperating with all ASt, Nasser did not abandon the distinction between "progressive" régime and "reactionary" ones and frequently proclaimed that E. was willing to cooperate only with progressive A. régimes, only with them was there a "unity of aims" and only with them true cooperation was possible, while the "reactionary" régimes were bound to be swept away by revolution.

The radicalization that characterized E.'s foreign and A. policy from the mid-1950s applied also to her internal and economic régime. The constitution of 1956 defined the régime as "democratic-cooperative-socialist", and the main plank of economic policy was the resolve to carry out a far-reaching nationalization of economic assets and build an ever-expanding public sector state economy. The nationalizations of 1956 applied only to British and French properties, and in some measure to Jewish assets; but that opened the gate. In 1960, banks were nationalized, and so were all newspapers. In July 1961, the land reform of 1952 was further tightened and the ceiling of ownership halved to 100 *feddan*; and a sweeping nationalization was applied to all remaining foreign assets, most industrial and mining enterprises, and all export-import trade. A huge state sector was created which became by far the largest employer and provided in the early 1960s c. 85% of industrial production and 35% of the GDP. The political régime also took a turn to the left. In Feb. 1962, a "National Congress" was convened, to formulate the country's basic policies; a "Charter for National Action" was laid before it in May and proclaimed late in June. That Charter elaborated the concept of "Arab Socialism", which now became the official doctrine, and initiated the "transitional stage of Socialism". The sole political organization, replacing the "National Union", was henceforth the "Arab Socialist Union" (ASU), to be built on wide-spread popular democracy, based on c. 7,000 "basic units"; it was to nominate the candidates for a National or People's Assembly. Such an Assembly was elected in Mar. 1964. A reorganization of the government in Sept. 1962, termed "Provisional Constitution", was expanded into a fuller Provisional Constitution, proclaimed in Mar. 1964; committees were to work out a permanent Constitution. Behind these elaborate constitutional arrangements, the régime was dominated — after the elimination, since 1952, of the old, pre-revolutionary political and economic élite — by a new élite: the "Free Officers". Though the original "Revolutionary Council" was no longer officially active, the nucleus of the officers' group — shedding some members and gradually admitting new ones — still was the leading group around Nasser, providing, in shifting compositions, the Presidential Council or the Vice-Presidents and the reservoir for top government positions. That group was gradually joined by a growing élite of "technocrats", the top managers of the expanding state sector of the economy. Their rule was underpinned — as became publicly evident in the 1970s, when criticism of the Nasserist régime was first permitted — by a dominant police and security apparatus.

The escalation of Arab-Israel tension in the mid-1960s led in June 1967 to the *Six Day War. For the Egyptian steps making that war inevitable — Nasser's May 1967 order to the UN Force to withdraw from Sinai; his re-imposition of a blockade on the *'Aqaba Gulf's Straits of *Tiran; Israel's encirclement by Egypt's military pacts with Syria and Jordan; and the stream of taunting bellicose speeches, accompanied by frenzied mass demonstrations, all threatening an imminent attack on Israel — see *Arab-Israel Conflict, and for the events of the war see *Arab-Israel Wars. When the fire ceased, with Israeli troops on the Suez Canal and in possession of all Sinai, and Egypt and her Syrian and Jodanian associates defeated, Nasser, accepting responsibility, resigned on 9 June. Following mass demonstrations imploring him to stay at the helm, he withdrew his resignation the same day. But E. was badly shaken, and Nasser's leadership impaired. He immediately carried out an extensive purge of the officers' corps, reportedly dismissing over 1,000 officers; among those resigning, or dismissed, were Marshall 'Abd-ul-Hakim *'Amer, Vice President and Commander-in-Chief, who had been considered "Number Two" of the régime and Nasser's closest aide, as well as the Chief-of-Staff and the commanders of the air force and navy; several senior officers, particularly of the air force, were put on trial for dereliction of duty and/or treason and found guilty in 1968. (When a later, post-Nasser, committee in 1977 investigated the reasons for the defeat of 1967, only a minority went along with that attempt to blame 'Amer and the military high command, while the majority ascribed the debacle to Nasser's policy and particularly the steps he took in May.) Nasser's new government had no Vice President until Dec. 1969, when Anwar *Sadat became sole Vice President. In Aug. 1967 a plot against the régime was discovered and the plotters, headed by Marshall 'Amer, former War Minister Shams-ul-Din Badran, Intelligence

Chief Salah Nasr, were arrested. 'Amer committed suicide, in prison; the others were sentenced in 1968 to long prison terms.

Egyptian policy for the following years was determined by the resolve to recover the territories occupied by Israel. First Israeli offers, in the summer of 1967, to withdraw in the context of a peace settlement, were rejected — as E. demanded an unconditional withdrawal prior to, and as a pre-condition for, any negotiations on a settlement. Nasser was instrumental in the adoption by the Arab League states, at their Khartoum summit meeting on 1 Sept. 1967, of a decision not to recognize Israel, not to make peace and not to negotiate with her until she had withdrawn from the areas occupied. E. accepted the UN Security Council resolution 242, in Nov. 1967, calling for Israel's withdrawal "from occupied areas" in the context of a "just and lasting peace" — but in her own interpretation: *total* withdrawal, with no need for negotiations. Nasser also formulated his hardening view that "what has been taken by force can be recovered only by force". E. continued therefore to conduct on the cease-fire lines a near-constant campaign of harassment, shelling etc.; this led to a grave crisis and a "war of attrition" in 1969–70, that was ended by a US-mediated new cease-fire and stand-still agreement only in late 1970. For all these developments see *Arab-Israel Conflict.

E. severed diplomatic relations with the USA in June 1967, on the outbreak of the war, and accused her of having covertly aided Israel in actual military operations; the US indignantly denied that claim, and E. never substantiated and gradually abandoned it, though her resentment of US general support for Israel persisted (relations were resumed in 1973-74 only). Relations with the USSR, on the other hand, became ever closer; President Podgorny and the Soviet Chief-of-Staff, in a symbolic gesture, visited E. in June 1967 and undertook to rebuild E.'s military might, and especially the air force and air defense. In the war of attrition, 1969–70, Russian SAM missiles, operated largely by Russian personnel, played a major rôle and Russian pilots flew Soviet-supplied planes, reportedly even on some operational missions. The number of Russian technicians and instructors, most of them military, reached a reported 15–20,000. Mutual visits were frequent (including Podgorny attending, in Jan. 1971, the festive opening of the Soviet-financed second stage of the Aswan High Dam), and an increasing number of Egyptian students and officers were trained in Russia and Soviet Bloc countries. Yet, relations were not always smooth. The extent and conditions of Soviet aid, and the measure of Soviet influence on E.'s policy, and the presence of so many Russians, and their behavior, caused friction. As to relations with Western Europe, there was, after France granted independence to Algeria and virtually ended her alliance with Israel, a remarkable *rapprochement* between E. and France. Relations with West Germany, broken in 1965, were further aggravated by E.'s recognition of East Germany in July 1969.

Gamal 'Abd-ul-Nasser, the man commonly recognized as the one great leader of both E. and the A. world, died suddenly on 28 Sept. 1970. The succession was contested — not in an open, public struggle, but as variously reported — by rival factions: a right wing tending to a liberalization of the economy and the régime, headed by Zakariyya *Mohieddin (Muhyi-ul-Din) and 'Abd-ul-Latif Baghdadi and supported by M. Hassanein *Heykal, the régime's foremost publicist, editor of al-*Ahram and since spring 1970 Minister of Information; and a left wing headed by 'Ali *Sabri and supported by Nasser's closest aides, the heads of his apparatus, such as Sha'rawi Gum'a and Sami Sharaf. To avoid a split and a bitter struggle, the inner group of leaders chose as a compromise candidate Vice-President Anwar *Sadat — whose views were close to the right wing, but who was considered a man of the center and the core of Nasser's team and capable of mediating between the factions. In Oct. 1970 Sadat was elected President for a six-year term, as well as leader of the ASU; he appointed 'Ali Sabri and Hussein Shafe'i as his Vice-Presidents and the diplomat-technician Mahmud Fawzi as Prime Minister.

The struggle avoided in 1970 soon broke out, as Sadat emerged not as a *primus inter pares*, a pale, faceless figurehead, as expected, but as a leader with his own strong concepts and intent on taking full power. In May 1971 he dismissed Vice-President 'Ali Sabri; thereupon six Ministers and several ASU top functionaries resigned in an attempt to force Sadat's hand that amounted, so Sadat announced, to a take-over plot by the leftist faction. Those resigning included the leading leftist Nasserists Gum'a and Sharaf, and also Gen. Muhammad Fawzi, former Chief-of-Staff and since 1968 Minister of War; the latter, however, did not carry with him the bulk of the officers' corps. The leaders of the Nasserist plotters — Sabri, Fawzi, Gum'a, Sharaf and c. 100 others — were now arrested, and their suspected followers were purged from the army, the government services and the ASU; the executive and the central committee of the ASU, seen as the center of the plot, were dissolved. In July, a new ASU congress was elected, and nominated a new central committee. The National Assembly expelled 18 members involved in the plot; but Sadat, not content with this purge, dissolved the Assembly in Sept. In Oct. 1971 a new National Assembly ("People's Council", *Majlis al-Sha'b*), was elected. Sadat also had a new Constitution drafted. It was endorsed, with certain amendments by the ASU central committee, and adopted in Sept. 1971 by a referendum. The new Constitution was little different from the provisional one of 1964; it retained a near-presidential system (limiting the President to two 6-year terms and permitting him to appoint a Prime Minister – which had become usual since 1961), a 350-member "People's Council", and the ASU as the single party; it reconfirmed Islam as the state religion and enhanced E.'s Islamic character by laying down that Islamic law (the *Shari'a) should be a main source of legislation; it restored E.'s name, now "The Arab Republic of E.", and her flag (abolishing the name and flag of the UAR). In Aug., the plotters were put on trial; sentences were announced in Dec. 1971: four to death, commuted to prison for life — including Sabri, Gum'a, Sharaf; Gen. Fawzi — life imprisonment commuted to 15 years; over 50 others — various prison terms (those still in jail were released from 1977, the last ones, including Sabri and Sharaf, in May 1981). No further major upheavals occurred in Sadat's team until 1973 — except for the dismissal, in Oct. 1972, of War Minister Muhammad Ahmad Sadeq (who had replaced Fawzi in May 1971, leaving his post as Chief-of-Staff, and was a strong contender for the "Number Two" position in the régime), apparently because he could not get along with the Russians and with Sadat's Russian policy.

His power and position assured, Sadat began changing E.'s régime and economic policy. He did so cautiously and at first without admitting that he was abandoning at least some of the principles of the Free Officers' régime and Nasserism. His measures were officially called a "correction" of the Revolution of 1952, a restoration of its true principles. They fully unfolded after 1973, but beginning steps were taken from 1971. First measures were intended to alleviate the harsh police-state features of the Nasserist régime — detainees were released in large numbers, the practice of detention without trial was nearly abolished, and the powers of the secret police and the security apparatus were restricted. More freedom of expression and the press was granted, and gradually the voicing of criticism (e.g. of the excesses of Nasser's security apparatus) was allowed. A certain liberalization applied to the economic régime, too: private capital, both Egyptian and foreign, was invited to invest and promised wider freedom of initiative, less state interference, and security against nationalization. Limitations on income, on the use of properties and profits, and of foreign currency earned, were lifted to a certain extent; the stress on, and preference for, the public, state-owned sector of the economy, and centralized planning was mitigated, a process of de-nationalization, e.g. the restoration of sequestrated properties to their former owners, was begun.

This "Opening" (*Infitāḥ*) of E.'s economic régime inevitably entailed a *rapprochement* — economic at first, but gradually political, too — with the West, and particularly with the USA, to whom E. began looking again for investments, equipment, technology and aid even while official relations with the US were still severed. Full relations were restored, and became increasingly closer, ony after 1973; but these new links with the US grew, and were fostered, from 1970–71 — the more so as the US was playing an active mediatory role in the Egyptian-Israeli confrontation.

The USSR remained E.'s chief ally, but relations were complex and sometimes troubled. The Russians would probably have preferred 'Ali Sabri as E.'s leader, and there seemed to be little sympathy between them and Sadat; the latter did not accept their guidance and suspected them of not sincerely supporting his policies. Yet, relations seemed close. President Podgorny came to

Egypt twice in 1971 — for the opening of the Aswan High Dam in Jan., and in May to sign a Soviet-Egyptian Treaty of Friendship, the USSR's first with an AC; but this treaty was seen by observers as an effort to shore up crumbling relationships rather than a sign of firm mutual confidence. Indeed, after Sadat had been to Moscow twice in Oct. 1971 and Feb. 1972, he unilaterally terminated the services of an estimated 15–10,000 Soviet experts, including all military ones, in July 1972, and the USSR immediately withdrew them. The main reason for this step, as Sadat later explained, was the Russians' unwillingness to give him a free hand and full support in his preparations for war against Israel. Yet, later in 1972 and in the spring of 1973 relations were re-normalized. Russian arms supplies, without which E. could not wage war, were resumed and stepped up, and during and after the *October War of 1973 the USSR gave Sadat full military and political support.

Sadat's A. policy was moderate, abandoning all attempts to impose Egyptian guidance and domination on other ASt (attempts that Nasser had already mitigated and virtually dropped in his last years). In inter-A. alignments E. now tended to a moderate-conservative bloc and cultivated closer relations with Saʻudi Arabia. Sadat continued a scheme for an Egyptian Federation with Libya and Sudan and/or Syria that had been initiated by Libya's *Qadhdhafi late in 1969 and accepted by Nasser. In Nov. 1970, E., Libya and Sudan announced their decision to establish a Federation, and Syria joined, and in Apr. 1971, with Sudan dropping out, E., Libya and Syria set up the *"Federation of Arab Republics". But the main initiative was Qadhdhafi's and Sadat seemed to go along half-heartedly — except for a joint Egyptian-Syrian military command that was re-established in Oct. 1971, as Sadat considered it desirable for the coming confrontation with Israel. The Federation did not get off the ground, though its institutions were formally established by 1972. Anyway, Qadhdhafi was no longer content with a loose federal association but kept pressing for full merger with E. — and Sadat, though clearly unwilling, went along, apparently not taking Qadhdhafi's erratic moves quite seriously. In Aug. 1972, the two Heads-of-State announced the merger of E. and Libya, to be endorsed by a referendum and implemented on 1 Sept. 1973. When preparations for that implementation made no progress, Qadhdhafi resorted to "direct action": in June 1973 he appealed, in a barnstorming tour of E., directly to the Egyptian public — with an obscurantist fanaticism that irritated his listeners; and in July he had Libya's "People's Committees" mount a mass march into E. (30–40,000 marchers with 2,000 trucks and cars were forcibly halted and returned to Libya). The merger was shelved by Sadat. Relations now soured and soon turned into open hostility. Though there was a brief reconciliation in 1974, E. from that year on accused Libya several times of plots, sabotage and terrorism; clashes occurred and in 1977 turned briefly into actual warfare.

Sadat's main preoccupation was with the continuing Israeli occupation of Sinai (and other Arab territories). In Feb. 1971, he told UN envoy Jarring, in a detailed memorandum, that E. was prepared to enter peace negotiations with Israel and commit herself to a list of requests submitted by Jarring (termination of belligerency; respect for Israel's sovereignty and territorial integrity; freedom of navigation in the Suez Canal and the Straits of Tiran; etc.) — provided Israel committed herself to a total withdrawal to the 1949–67 lines and to a "just settlement" of the refugee problem. As Israel would commit herself to a withdrawal only to "secure, recognized and agreed boundaries" to be negotiated, and not to the pre-June 1967 lines, the negotiations Sadat offered did not materialize. But while Israel could live with the situation, expecting to continue her occupation until a negotiated solution be found, E. could not. The ending of Israel's occupation and the restoration of E.'s territory — a vital policy matter of highest priority, a precondition for any future settlement, and a matter of national honor — could now, Sadat resolved, be achieved by military force only. From 1971–72 E. was preparing for war.

The *October War of 1973 is described in detail in the entries *Arab-Israel Wars an *Arab-Israel Conflict. From a military point of view, the war did not end with an Egyptian victory. But in a wider perspective, and certainly in Egyptian and Arab perception, it was a great achievement: Egyptian (and Syrian) forces had won battles against Israel, displayed impressive capabilities of military planning and leadership, and thus wiped off the stain of previous defeats and restored the pride and honor of E.'s armed forces. Even more important, the deadlock was broken, Israel's occupation dented, E. had recovered at least part of her territory — including the vital eastern shore of the Suez Canal — and Israel had accepted, in the Disengagement (or Separation of Forces) Agreement of Jan. 1974, the presence of Egyptian troops in Sinai, with a UN force manning a buffer zone between the two sides. The Suez Canal was reopened in Jun. 1975 (with Israel-bound cargoes allowed to pass it on non-Israeli ships). This was formalized in a further Interim Agreement of 1 Sept. 1975, reached after intensive mediation efforts by US Secretary of State Henry Kissinger, which also provided for a further Israeli withdrawal and an expansion of Egyptian- and UN-held zones of Sinai, as well as mutual limitations and a thinning-out of the forces close to the dividing line. It also restored to Egyptian administration part of the oil installations on the western shore of Sinai on the Gulf of Suez. However, efforts for a further advance towards a more permanent settlement had no success until Nov. 1977.

The deadlock was broken in Nov. 1977 by President Sadat's dramatic surprise visit to Israel (which had in fact been prepared by secret diplomatic contacts, with Sadat obtaining assurances that his main demands would be met). In his meetings with Israeli leaders, and his public address to a solemn meeting of the *Knesset*, Sadat offered complete peace and normal relations against a total withdrawal from all occupied territories and an agreed, negotiated solution to the problem of the Palestine A.'s. Sadat's proposals were thus, in substance, not different from previous positions held by E. herself and other moderate ASt. His great achievement was, first, a psychological breakthrough, cutting the vicious circle by meeting the "enemy" face to face and talking to him, and, secondly, spelling out what before had at best been implied: a preparedness to accept Israel and co-exist with her in peace, even co-operation, once she agreed to the concessions he demanded. Sadat made it clear, though, that he would not conclude a *separate* peace but would consider an eventual agreement as a first step towards a general A.-Israel settlement.

The E.-Israel agreements achieved after protracted and difficult negotiations — the *"Camp David Agreements" of 17 Sept. 1978 (a "Framework for Peace in the ME", and a "Framework for a Peace Treaty between Israel and Egypt"), and the Peace Treaty of 26 Mar. 1979 — are described in more detail in the entry *Arab-Israel Conflict. The total Israeli withdrawal from Sinai, to the former international E.-Palestine border, was to be followed by "complete normal relations... including diplomatic, economic and cultural relations". The "Framework for ME Peace" envisaged a Palestinian-A. autonomy, a self-governing authority in the West Bank and Gaza for a transitional period of five years, during which E., Jordan and elected representatives of the inhabitants would negotiate an agreement with Israel on the area's final status.

The Peace Treaty was ratified by E.'s National Assembly in Apr. 1979 and endorsed by a referendum the same month, and it went into effect on 25 Apr. 1979. Its implementation was completed by Israel's total withdrawal in Apr. 1982 (for details see *Arab-Israel Conflict). Peace now reigned between E. and Israel (in 1978, Sadat and Premier Begin of Israel had jointly received the Nobel Peace Prize) — and peace continued under Sadat's successor, *Mubarak, after Sadat was assassinated in 1981. But it was a "cold peace", disappointing to both E. and Israel. It was dampened by the total hostility of the A. world (see below); parts of Egyptian public opinion — the Left, Nasserists, Islamic fundamentalists, opposition groups, intellectuals — opposed it; and the general Egyptian public, which had at first accepted it, greeting the end of war with joy, and welcomed large streams of Israeli visitors with friendly curiosity, soon cooled off, disappointed that peace with Israel did not entail an immediate far-reaching improvement in E.'s general situation. The implementation of the ME Peace "Framework" ran into serious obstacles, and several disputes poisoned relations (details see *A.-Israel Conflict). Relations improved to some extent in Sept. 1986 when it was agreed to submit one of the disputes, over *Taba, to arbitration.

The ASt were stunned by Sadat's Nov. 1977 visit to Israel and his decision to embark on negotiations towards what they saw as a separate peace with Israel and a betrayal of all-A. solidarity. The radical ASt of the *"Rejection Front" immediately severed relations with E., and under their pressure all ASt except three (Sudan, 'Oman and

Somalia) did the same in Mar.-Apr. 1979 and suspended E.'s membership in the A. League and all inter-A. institutions; in June 1979 they transferred the headquarters or the League to Tunis and replaced its Egyptian Secretary-General, Mahmud Riad, by a Tunisian (for details on these developments see *Arab League).

Since 1979 E. was thus isolated from the A. family of nations which she had led before and of which she still was the largest and strongest member. The isolation was not complete. Trade, economic relations diminished somewhat, but continued; there was little new investment of A. capital from the oil-rich Persian Gulf countries, but of the funds invested, very little was withdrawn. Egyptian technicians, experts and workers continued working in AC — estimates of their number varying from 1.5m. to 3m. — and remitting their earnings to E. Communications, particularly air links, were somewhat reduced but, continued. A. tourism declined, but still was c. 40% of all foreign tourism, and hundreds of thousands of A. tourists continued visiting E. and frequenting Cairo's night-life. E. remained the center of A. book and film production, though her position as the main center of the A. press was no longer undisputed. Her exclusion from official all-A. associations, specialized and professional meetings of Ministers, officials etc., was complete, and even the "Islamic Conference Organization", the regular meetings of Foreign Ministers of Islamic states, suspended E.'s membership (but in Jan. 1984 it invited E. to resume her participation). Both E. and the ASt were unhappy with this situation and desired E. to resume her rightful place in the A. group of nations; but the ASt made this conditional on the abrogation of the Camp David Agreements and the Peace Treaty with Israel — a condition that E. rejected and regarded as an insult to her national honor. E.'s leaders also resolved that, though keenly interested in mending their A. fences, they would not petition for it but it was up to the A. League to cancel the suspension of her membership and re-invite her in. E. strengthened *de facto* relations with several conservative ASt such as Sa'udi Arabia, Jordan and Morocco (a measure of official relations were maintained in any case through "interest sections" in foreign embassies, some of them headed by Egyptian diplomats of ambassadorial rank). She fostered close relations with Iraq, aiding her financially, with military supplies, and even with volunteers in her war with Iran. She cultivated a certain patronage of the *'Arafat wing of the *PLO (after 'Arafat broke inter-A. discipline by paying a visit to E. in Dec. 1983). But the decisive step of re-establishing full, official relations with E., in defiance of all-A. policies, had been taken, by the time of writing, only by Jordan in Sept. 1984 and Djibouti in Sept. 1986. Subsequently, E.-Jordan relations became close.

In E.'s global orientation, Sadat wrought a major change by turning from an alliance with the Soviet Union to a growingly closer association with the USA. This process intensified particularly after 1973, culminating in President *Carter's partnership in the Camp David Accords of 1978 that led to the Peace Treaty of 1979. The resumption of official diplomatic relations, severed since 1967, was agreed in Nov. 1973, announced in Feb. 1974, and implemented in Apr. 1974. Mutual visits were exchanged at the highest level (Nixon, June 1974; Carter, Jan. 1978; Sadat, Oct. 1975, and several times later; Foreign Ministers frequently). US economic aid was resumed in 1973 and soon reached large proportions, until E. became, in the 1980s, the largest recipient of US aid after Israel; from 1976–77 the US granted E. also considerable military aid. US economic enterprise and investment in E., eagerly solicited, did not come up to E.'s hopes — largely because of the difficulties posed by E.'s bureaucracy and its tangled regulations — but assumed a certain role in E.'s economy. E. also became a partner in wider US policy and strategy plans, concerning both the A.-Israel peace process and US plans for the defense of the ME. When the US in 1979–80 conceived plans for a "Rapid Deployment Force" for emergencies, it was proposed that E. — with 'Oman, Somalia and Kenya — provide "facilities" for such a force (the use of the term "Bases" was carefully avoided). In Aug. 1980 it was agreed that such facilities be constructed, at US expense, at Ras Banas on the Red Sea. The scheme did not fully materialize, but it is reported that the US enjoys certain facilities such as the stationing of surveillance installations.

Relations with the USSR deteriorated after 1973. The Treaty of Friendship of May 1971 became a dead letter, and in Mar. 1976 E. annulled it. Later in 1977, E. recalled her Ambassador and left her Moscow embassy in the charge of a lower-level diplomat; in 1979 and 1981 she expelled members of the Soviet embassy, charging them with espionage etc., and in Sept. 1981 requested the withdrawal of the Ambassador himself and closed the Soviet Military Attaché's office, simultaneously terminating the contracts of most of the remaining Soviet technicians (some 5–700 reportedly departed). Relations on the ambassadorial level were restored in Aug.-Sept. 1984, but have remained cool.

After 1973 Sadat stepped up the pace of liberalization, the opening of E. to private and foreign enterprise, and "de-Nasserization". This brought about a certain upswing in economic activity, but could not, of course, solve E.'s basic economic problems — the limited area of agricultural land (which, it was assumed, had reached its upper limit, with 6–7m. acres cultivated and, with multiple cropping, up to 11m. acres cropped — projects for large-scale reclamation of the Western desert making little progress), as against the constant large increase of the population, with the resulting continuous decline in food production p.c.; the slowness of industrial growth, insufficient to absorb the surplus of the rural population no longer sustained by agriculture; the growth of an ever-expanding semi-urban population in and around Cairo, with no productive employment, no proper housing, and socially uprooted; an inflated, unproductive bureaucracy. Sadat's policies created a new class of entrepreneurs, displaying their wealth, and an increasing measure of corruption, while the standard of life did not markedly improve for the masses — despite high expectations, and the gap between rich and poor widened. The resulting social unrest frequently focussed on the problem of government subsidies for the price of basic food and fuel — subsidies that had to be cut or altogether abolished according to the new policies and all foreign and international advisers but that were vitally needed by the poorer masses. Attempts to reduce these subsidies and raise the price of basic commodities led to serious disturbances in Jan. 1975 and Jan. 1977, and the government had to retreat. The disturbances were blamed on Communists and other leftist groups, and steps were taken to suppress them.

The political liberalization that went with the general "opening" of the régime did not apply to the Communists (who in 1975 re-established an Egyptian Communist Party, half underground) and the radical Left. The measures taken against them were endorsed by a referendum in Feb. 1977. Another referendum, in May 1978, specifically restricted all political and media activity of Communists, and also of old-régime, pre-1952 politicians, and of those linked with the repressive security apparatus of Nasser's time, those who had abused democracy and corrupted political life, as well as atheists and "enemies of religion" — as specified in a law passed by the National Assembly after the referendum.

The liberalization did apply to Islamic groups. Sadat tended to favor a growing emphasis on E.'s Islamic character. Constitutional amendments endorsed by a referendum in Apr. 1979 included one establishing Islam and the *Shari'a* as *the* (no longer *a*) main source of legislation. Fundamentalists agitated for the imposition of Islamic law on E.'s social and legal fabric, and no-one dared openly oppose that proposal in the National Assembly, though many in fact opposed it; it was accepted "in principle" with its implementation deferred for committees and experts to work out the details. Various Islamic-fundamentalist groups mushroomed, and gained increasing influence, particularly among the urban lower classes. The Muslim Brotherhood was not formally re-legalized, but it began rebuilding its organization semi-legally. The Brotherhood, however, had become a rather conservative, almost moderate group; other groups, underground, were more extremist, aiming to enforce Islamic rule by force. Such groups repeatedly clashed with the security forces, and with adversaries, and also agitated against E.'s Christians, the Copts, and several times attacked them. One group — the "Islamic Liberation Party", *Hizb al-Tahrir al-Islami* — in Apr. 1974 attacked a military installation in what was seen as a Libya-linked plot to take over the government; it was suppressed, its leaders tried in 1975, and its main leader, Saleh Suraya, was executed in Nov. 1976. Another group — *al-Takfir wa'l-Hijra* — in July 1977 staged bomb attacks and kidnapped and murdered a former Minister; it, too, was suppressed, trials were swiftly held, and five leaders, including the group's chief, Shukri Ahmad Mustafa, were executed in Mar. 1978. Islamic extremists also infiltrated the armed forces. A cell of such extremists, not clearly identified with a certain organization, assassinated President Sadat in Oct. 1981. In subsequent riots they gained control of the town of Asyut until dislodged in heavy fighting. After a trial five of their leaders were executed. Sporadic unrest by Islamic extremists has continued.

This trend of Islamic organization, with its extremist outgrowths, was a by-product of Sadat's liberalization, which in its mainstream allowed a diversification of political organization. In Sadat's first years, the ASU, though purged of its Nasserist leadership, still was the only political organization permitted; but within it, different trends that had always existed were allowed in 1975 to organize themselves as "platforms" (*minbar*, pl. *manābir*) within the ASU. In Mar. 1976, three such platforms were formally constituted: a right-wing, "Socialist-Liberal" one; a left-wing "Progessive Unionist Rally", led by Khaled Mohieddin (*Muhyi-ul-Din), one of the Free Officers' Revolutionary Council of 1952; and a mainstream, centrist platform led by the Prime Minister and considered the government's faction. These platforms presented themselves to the National Assembly elections of Oct. 1976; the right-wing one got 12–13 seats, the left-wing 2, the center 270–80, and Independents-within-the-ASU c. 50. In Nov. 1976, Sadat decreed that the platforms might now organize as fully-fledged parties, and in June 1977 a party law was passed. The new multi-party system was endorsed, as an amendment of the Constitution, in a referendum in May 1980, and in 1977–78, the parties constituted themselves. The mainstream center of the ASU at first called itself *Misr* (i.e. "E.") Socialist Party; but in July-Aug. 1978 Sadat founded a new party, the "National Democratic Party", and the *Misr*-ASU immediately merged with the new party (the ASU was formally dissolved in May 1980). To the two other platforms now turned into parties was added a "Socialist Labor Party", led by Ibrahim Shukri, whose ideology and policy hardly differed from the ruling NDP. The *Wafd* also reconstituted itself in Feb. 1978, sometimes called Neo-*Wafd*; but as the authorities refused their assent to the party's elected leader, Fu'ad Siraj-ul-Din, and some of his associates, disqualified as pre-1952 politicians, the *Wafd* re-dissolved itself in June 1978. It re-emerged in Feb. 1984, when the government accepted Siraj-ul-Din (after the courts had so ruled).

Multi-party elections to the National Assembly (People's Council) were held in 1979 and 1984. They confirmed the NDP in its overwhelming majority. In 1979, the Socialist Labor Party won 29 seats, and the Socialist Liberals 3; the leftist NPUR won no seat. In 1984, none of these three groups won any seat and the *Wafd*, now back on the scene, was the only opposition represented; it won 58 seats — including 8 from the Muslim Brotherhood which, while not officially recognized, had made an unofficial election alliance with the *Wafd*. New elections in Apr. 1987 confirmed the NDP majority; the Socialist-Liberals, Socialist Labor and Muslim Brotherhood formed a coalition and won 60 seats, the *Wafd* won 36. In Sept. 1980 an Upper House was recreated — first since 1952: a Consultative Council (*Majlis al-Shura*) of 210 members, two-thirds elected, one-third appointed by the President.

In the executive, no major upheavals occurred between 1973 and 1981. During the war of Oct. 1973, Sadat dismissed the Chief-of-Staff, Sa'd-ul-Din Shadhili (Shazly) — a step kept secret until Dec. Shadhili went into exile and set up an organization of expatriates opposing and denouncing the government of E. He was replaced by 'Abd-ul-Ghani Gamassi, who later became Minister of Defense and Deputy Premier, 1975–78. In 1972 Sadat appointed Prime Minister Mahmud Fawzi as second Vice President (retired in 1974); Vice President Shafe'i was dismissed in 1975 and Husni *Mubarak, the commander of the air force, became Vice President. In 1973–74, Sadat served as his own Prime Minister, and from 1974 various loyal second-rank associates followed each other in that post. Sadat himself was re-elected as President in Sept. 1976.

Sadat's charisma, his paternalistic leadership and his popularity declined in his later years. High-pitched, rising popular expectations were frustrated and social and economic problems aggravated. He was denounced by the extreme Islamists, the Left, the Nasserists, and many intellectuals. He released his rivals of 1971 (making sure they would not return to positions of power or political influence), as well as most of those convicted after the 1967 war, but began taking harsher measures against his new adversaries. In Sept. 1981, he carried out large-scale purges and arrests — of Islamist extemists, and for the sake of "even-handedness" of Coptic leaders, too (including the dismissal and banishment of the Patriarch), of Nasserists and Leftists, and banned several journals. He had these measures endorsed by another referendum — but they were not popular.

Sadat was assassinated on 6 Oct. 1981 — on the reviewing stand of a parade celebrating the anniversary of the Oct. 1973 war — by Islamist extremists led by an army officer. There were few signs of genuine mourning. Vice-President Husni Mubarak took over and was, after a few days, duly elected President. Mubarak — a personality less flamboyant-charismatic than either Nasser or Sadat, a staid, pragmatic administrator rather than a popular leader — in general continued Sadat's policies, but endeavored to redress some of their outgrowths seen as harmful. He released many of those detained in Sadat's last purge. He tried to restrain excesses of the private sector, to curb corruption, and to re-impose stricter state controls. It is too soon to assess whether and how far he has succeeded. For Mubarak's foreign, A. and international policies see supra.

EDUCATION, CULTURE, PRESS E. is the most important cultural and educational center of the A. world. There are over 150 institutions of higher, post-secondary education, including 17 universities with a student population of over half a million — among them the al-*Azhar Islamic study center (founded 970); the University of Cairo (est. 1908, modernized 1925 and called, until 1952, "Fu'ad I University"); that of Alexandria (1942); 'Ain Shams (1950) and several more in Cairo, and several in provincial towns. There is also a small American University, founded in 1919 as a secondary school. Several thousand foreign students are also trained at some of these institutions, and thousands of Egyptian teachers work in AC. Since 1933, schooling is compulsory for all children aged 6–12, and a huge network of primary and secondary schools serves a student population of over 7m. Illiteracy, over 70% until the early 1970s, is still estimated at 50–60%.

E. is the center of literature, art, the production of books and records, theater and the film industry for the entire A. world. Her broadcasting stations are the largest and most powerful in the ME and transmit in many languages in addition to Arabic. Until the nationalization of the press in 1960, E. was the center of A. journalism, the home of a large, rich and until 1952 comparatively free press — dailies, literary monthlies (al-Kāteb, al-Hilal, al-Thaqāfa), and political weeklies (Akhbar al-Yawm, Akher Sa'a, al-Ithnein, al-Mussawwar, Rose al-Yusuf) — which were read in all the AC. There were also dailies and periodicals in English, French, Greek, Armenian. Most of these papers were politically independent, i.e. of shifting orientation and allegiance; political parties also founded organs, but those were never very successful. Since the nationalization of 1960, which concentrated all publications in several centralized publishing houses, with the NU / ASU as owner and manager, all the press has been controlled. Under the officers' régime since 1952, and culminating with the 1960 nationalization, many papers folded, or were closed down by the government — including all party organs and such old-established and respected dailies as al-Muqattam (since 1886–89) and al-Misri (1936). In 1975, in the course of Sadat's reforms, it was decided partly to de-nationalize the press, too, and hand 49% of the shares to the editorial staff and the workers of each paper. Political-editorial control was also somewhat relaxed, but the appointment and dismissal of editors remained de facto in the hands of the government. The most important dailies in recent years were al-*Ahram (founded 1875, edited from 1957 until his dismissal in 1974 by Muhammad Hassanein *Heykal) and al-Akhbar (founded 1952); these two papers had a circulation of over 700,000 each. Al-Gumhuriyya (1953) used to be the daily organ of the régime's party. The government, not always satisfied with the popular weeklies, also established two weeklies considered semi-official mouthpieces: Oktober (1976, edited until 1985 by Anis Mansur) and Mayo (1981), the organ of the NDP. Opposition groups also began publishing weekly organs of their own — al-Da'wa of the Muslim Brotherhood, and other Islamic periodicals, frequently banned; the leftist NPUR's al-Ahali; the Socialist Labor Party's al-Sha'b; a leftist-intellectual monthly, al-Tali'a (Vanguard), issued since 1965 with the encouragement of Nasser and the government by al-Ahram's publishing house, with

Lutfi al-Khouli as editor, was closed down in 1978 but re-permitted in 1984 (it does not appear regularly). These opposition organs are on a technically low level and do not seem to have much influence.

Eisenhower Doctrine US policy statement on the ME made by President E. on 5 Jan. 1957, requesting Congress authorization for US military and economic assistance to ME countries asking for such aid, and the use of the US armed forces to protect the independence and territorial integrity of any nation in the region "against overt aggression from any nation controlled by international Communism". Congressional authorization was given on 9 Mar. 1957.

The ED was put to the test by Jordan in Apr. 1957, when King *Hussein accused communist-controlled forces of attempting to overthrow him; the USA dispatched the Sixth Fleet to the eastern Mediterranean and began giving economic aid to Jordan. Following Gen. *Qassem's *coup* of July 1958 in Iraq, both Jordan and Lebanon invoked the ED and requested military aid, including troops. Britain sent paratroops to Jordan, and the US sent 14,000 marines to Lebanon. The ED was also linked to close US co-operation with *CENTO (formerly the *Baghdad Pact), agreed in Mar. 1959 in bi-lateral accords with Turkey, Iran and Pakistan. After 1959, it was not explicitly invoked again.

The ED was strongly denounced by radical-neutralist AC as imperialist interference, and it contributed to the suspicions and charges of US "plots" voiced in 1957–58. On the other hand, its effectivity was limited, as it applied only to "overt aggression" from outside each country, and not to the danger of internal leftist plots and takeovers.

Eritrea Region in north-eastern *Ethiopia, on the *Red Sea. E.'s area is 45,000 sq.mi. (117,000 sq.km.). Its population, estimated at c. 2m., is about equally divided between Christians and Muslims, with the eastern part predominantly Christian, the western part Muslim. E. was an Italian colony from 1889, under British occupation from 1941 until 1952, and federally united with Ethiopia since 1952, following a resolution of the UN General Assembly. The semi-autonomous federal régime was abrogated by Ethiopia in 1962, and an E. Liberation Front, split into rival factions, has since been conducting a guerrilla war for its independence. The guerrillas were at first mainly, but not entirely, Muslim. Some Eritrean Muslims consider themselves A. or semi-A., and Arabic is spoken to some extent as a second language, particularly in the coastal towns.

E.'s independence movement is politically supported by most ASt and its guerrillas are aided and provided with supplies, training and operational bases by some Islamic-conservative AC like Sa'udi Arabia and the Gulf principalities; Palestinian-A. guerrilla / terrorist organizations reportedly also aid the E. rebels. The leftist-revolutionary ASt, such as Syria and Libya, at first also aided them, reportedly with particular vigor; but Libya and South Yemen changed their stance when Ethiopia turned revolutionary and leftist, after 1974–75, and in 1981 concluded a pact with her, stopping all aid for the rebels. A. aid for the E. rebels has put a strain on A.-Ethiopian relations. The E. problem has particularly troubled Sudan and her relations with Ethiopia, since most arms and supplies for the rebels come from or through Sudan and, Ethiopia charges, some of their main bases are in that country. Since the early 1980s, Sudan has, for the sake of her relations with Ethiopia, officially closed down the political and organizational offices which the Eritrean rebels were maintaining in Khartoum and liquidated their military bases, forcing thousands of rebels to withdraw from Sudan. But Ethiopia claims that these official measures were not fully and sincerely enforced and that in fact the Eritrean rebels continue receiving at least some support from Sudan.

Ethiopia Herself outside the scope of this book, E. is in many ways involved in ME and A. affairs. She is the home and center of the Ethiopian Church which was for many centuries linked with, and hierarchically and administratively dependent on, the *Coptic Patriarchate in Egypt. Her relations with neighboring Sudan have been troubled for many years. Old border disputes have not yet been fully settled, and a mixed population on both sides of the border and wandering tribes aggravate the problem. Moreover, Sudan accuses E. of aiding the rebellion of African tribes in Southern Sudan and providing it with its main bases, while E. on her part charges Sudan with supporting and aiding the secessionist rebels of *Eritrea. The waters of the *Nile

River also are a potential source of serious friction: the Blue Nile, one of the two major sources of the Nile, and in terms of water quantities *the* main source, rises in Lake Tana in E. Should E. extensively tap its waters for her own development projects — and despite some Egyptian-Sudanese talks with her (and Kenya and Uganda) no binding agreement bars her from doing so — both Sudan and Egypt would be seriously affected. E. is also in near-permanent conflict with neighboring Somalia (which, though not A., is a member-state of the *Arab League) — a territorial dispute that leads to frequent clashes and sometimes to warlike operations (thus — in July 1977, and again in July 1982).

E. plays a leading part in the Organization for African Unity, OAU, in which the 6 African ASt (9, if Somalia, Djibouti and Mauritania are regarded as A.) are also active members, and the OAU headquarters are in her capital Addis Ababa, with the frequent and intense contact that involves. As long as E. was a kingdom, or an empire, under the "Negus" Haile Selassie, the Emperor followed conservative, "right-wing" African and international policies which sometimes created differences with the radical Arab-African states (Algeria, Egypt 1952–70, Libya from 1969, and sometimes Sudan). All ASt resented the close co-operation which the Emperor cultivated with Israel and which led to the presence of Israeli experts and technicians in E. (and, suspected, to a measure of military and secret service collaboration; A. reports, always denied, even spoke of an Israeli military presence on some Ethiopian coastal islands in the Red Sea). These ties with Israel were reinforced by ancient Ethiopian traditions of a common origin of E. and Israel (the Kings of E., bearing the title "The Lion of Judah", regarded themselves as descendants of King Solomon). Following most of the other African states, E. broke relations with Israel late in Oct. 1973.

After the Emperor was deposed (Sept. 1974) and the monarchy abolished (Mar. 1975), and particularly after Mengistu Haile Mariam emerged as the main leader of the junta ("Dergue") in power and officially became Head-of-State (Feb. 1977), E. joined the camp of radical, leftist countries and closely allied herself with the Soviet Union. This *volte face* removed some obstacles from the path to better relations at least with the radical ASt. Indeed, E. in Aug. 1981 concluded an agreement of friendship and cooperation with South Yemen and Libya, the most radical among the A.'s. This agreement was sometimes termed a military and defense pact, and Libya broke A. solidarity by supporting E. against Somalia and even sent her some military supplies. Yet, the pact with Libya and South Yemen does not seem to have become a major element in E.'s stance, and relations with the ASt in general have remained troubled, mainly on account of A. support for Somalia and the Eritrean rebels. Another irritant was the mass-transfer of 10–15,000 E.'n Jews ("Falashas") to Israel, organized from about 1981, and particularly in 1984, by American-Jewish bodies and Israel with the assistance of the US authorities. Jews who were helped to reach Sudan were airlifted from there, with the acquiescence of the Sudanese government (which ordered the operation halted when it became public). Mutual accusations were exchanged, with the E.'n authorities claiming they had not known of the operation and objecting to the exodus of E.'s Jews, and charging Sudan with collaboration in an anti-E.'n scheme.

Euphrates River Rising in Anatolia and passing through northeastern Syria, the E. then forms, with the *Tigris, the river system of Mesopotamia, now Iraq. Near Qurna it joins the Tigris, to form the *Shatt al-'Arab. Caravans followed its course from the Mediterranean to Baghdad and Basra, and a railroad along it is planned, but because of its shallowness and sluggish changes of course the E. played no role in navigation. Projects for flood control, irrigation and the generation of power were first carried out in Iraq: the Hindiyya Barrage, 1913, and the Ramadi Barrage (diverting flood waters into the Abu Dibbis depression and creating the Habbaniyya Lake), 1956; further major E. schemes in Iraq, long planned, have not been finalized. Turkey is developing a series of large-scale dams, and Syria has constructed, with Soviet aid, a large dam near Tabqa and created a 50 mi. long lake, "Lake Asad", storing 40,000m. cubic meters and slated to irrigate up to 1.75m. acres and generate over 600,000 kw.; construction began in 1968 and was completed in 1978. Both Turkey and Syria pursue their projects without any agreement on the distribution of the E.

waters either among themselves or with Iraq downstream; tentative talks did not lead to full-fledged negotiations, let alone agreement, and the issue is a potential source of conflict.

European Economic Community, EEC, European Common Market The EEC — established in 1957 by the Treaty of Rome with six members, and since 1 Jan. 1986 including 12 European states — is important to most AC as a source of supply and a market for their products. In 1980, trade with the AC represented 21.5% of the EEC imports (90% of them crude oil) and 15.5% of their exports. In 1983 the EEC (then with ten members) supplied 37% of the total imports of Egypt, 32% of Syria, 39% of Iraq, 35% of Sa'udi Arabia, while the share of exports sent to the EEC was 53% for Egypt, 31% for Syria, 29% for Iraq, 21% for Sa'udi Arabia. Trade with the EEC is particularly important for the *Maghreb countries. In 1983 the part of the EEC in their imports was 38% for Morocco, 55% for Algeria and 63% for Tunisia. The share of exports sent to the EEC was 52% for Morocco, 60% for Algeria and 61% for Tunisia. This trend was mainly due to traditional links with France.

In 1959, first contacts were made between the governing bodies of the EEC and ME countries with a view to establishing Preferential Trade Agreements or Association Trade Agreements. Turkey, Iran and Israel were the first to seek such agreements, while Lebanon was the first AC to sign a non-preferential commercial agreement with the EEC; in 1965 Egypt also signed a commercial agreement. In Mar. 1969 association agreements were signed with Tunisia and Morocco; Algeria declined, since she regarded the EEC as an "imperialist" group.

By Oct. 1970, agreements had been signed with Iran, Turkey and Israel. In the frame of the EEC's Mediterranean policy Israel signed an agreement on a free trade area for industrial products in 1975, becoming the only country of the region to give reverse preferences to the EEC. According to the same Mediterranean policy, Morocco, Algeria and Tunisia signed preferential cooperation agreements in 1976. Egypt, Syria, Jordan and Lebanon signed similar agreements a few months later. (Egypt had originally claimed that the EEC was a "neo-colonialist scheme" aimed at gaining control of the raw materials of the AC and stifling their industrial development.) According to these agreements the AC may export their industrial products to the EEC duty-free, with the exception of refined petroleum products and textiles, while their agricultural products benefit from some tariff reductions. The seven countries also receive financial aid; after modest beginnings, a five-year protocol of 1981 provided for 975m. ECU (European Currency Units — then equivalent to about $1,090m.) — 560m. as credits by the European Investment Bank at normal rates of interest, 155m. as special, favorable loans, and 260m. as grants. Sudan and the three non-A. or semi-A. countries of the A. League — Somalia, Mauritania and Djibouti — receive even better treatment, since they are included in the EEC's Rome Treaty with 63 African, Caribbean and Pacific countries; they receive financial assistance from the European Development Fund, all their products have free access to the European market, and a Stabilization Fund guarantees a stable income for some basic commodities produced by them.

During the October War of 1973, A. oil producing countries declared an oil embargo against Denmark and Holland. Although crude oil continued to flow regularly to all EEC countries, EEC governments panicked, fearing a total disruption of oil supply, and their Prime Ministers issued a joint statement on the ME (6 Nov. 1973), designed to assuage the ASt's position towards the EEC countries — e.g. by calling for an end to the Israeli occupation and the recognition of Palestinian-A. rights — the first of a series of similar statements. A European summit in Dec. 1973 decided to open a Euro-Arab dialogue with institutionalized meetings every six months. The immediate purpose of that dialogue was to assure oil supplies, limit oil prices to a reasonable level, recycle petrodollars back to EEC countries, and strengthen economic cooperation with the AC. The EEC countries also hoped to improve their political relations with the AC and, perhaps, to contribute to a ME settlement. The ASt were interested in the dialogue as a means to increase economic and political cooperation with the EEC, benefit from its economic strength and, perhaps, win its countries as allies. The dialogue got under way only in 1975 and made little concrete progress. Since 1979 its formal meetings have been blocked by the suspension of Egypt's membership in the A. League. (Actual relations between the EEC countries and the ASt, including a political dialogue, are conducted of course, bilaterally.) Some leaders of the EEC countries have also been meeting with *PLO leader *'Arafat and his associates.

In June 1980, the EEC issued another statement on the ME and the ways to achieve an A.-Israel settlement. That "Venice Declaration", which still is the basis of EEC policy on the ME, was considered by Israel to be strongly pro-A. — stipulating Israel's total withdrawal from occupied A. territories (with Jewish settlements in the occupied territories considered to be illegal), the recognition of the Palestinian people's rights to self-determination, and the association of the PLO in any negotiations.

While the EEC countries continue to strive for closer relations with the ASt, their dependence on A. oil has diminished in recent years. The increase of oil prices after the crises of 1973 and 1978–79 induced many European countries to take energy conservation measures and develop oil substitutes, thus reducing their demand for crude oil. Total EEC imports of crude oil and refined products diminished from a peak of 598m. tons in 1973 to only 299m. tons in 1984. The EEC countries' relations with the AC have also been adversely affected by A. terrorist operations in Europe, leading in some instances to the severance of official relations (Britain-Libya 1984, Britain-Syria 1986). On the other hand, most EEC countries, and the EEC as a community, were not prepared to take extreme measures against AC suspected of abetting terrorism (Libya, Syria) or to join such measures initiated by the USA.

F

Fahd Ibn 'Abd-ul-'Aziz (b. 1921/22) King of Sa'udi Arabia since June 1982. A son of Ibn Sa'ud (his mother— from the notable Sudairi tribal clan of Najd). Prince F. served as Minister of Education, 1953–60, during the reign of his half-brother *Sa'ud. In Oct. 1962, when his half-brother *Feisal ascended the throne, F. became Minister of the Interior, and from 1968 also Second Deputy Prime Minister. When Feisal was assassinated, in Mar. 1975, and another half-brother, Khaled, became King, F. was promoted to be Crown Prince and First Deputy Prime Minister; he retained the Home Ministry for half a year only. Upon Khaled's death, in June 1982, F. became King and Prime Minister.

F. is considered relatively liberal, an advocate of development and modernization, and moderate in his foreign policies. His name is linked to a plan for a ME peace settlement based on the total withdrawal of Israel from all the territories occupied in 1967, including the removal of settlements set up, and the establishment of a Palestinian-A. state, following which "all states of the region" would "be able to live in peace" (or their "right to live in peace would be recognized": versions differ) —implying A. acceptance of, or acquiescence in, the existence of Israel. This "F. Plan" was launched in Aug. 1981 by a press interview granted by F., then Crown Prince. It was one of the causes for the break-up of the 12th all-A. Summit at Fez, Nov. 1981, but was eventually adopted — with several significant changes (see *A.-Israel Conflict) — at the Summit's resumed, second session, Sept. 1982. Now usually called "Fez Plan", it has since been regarded as the A. master-plan for a ME settlement.

F.A.R. See *Federation of Arab Republics.

Farouq (1920–65) King of Egypt, 1936–52. The son of *Fu'ad, Sultan and later King of Egypt, F. was educated in England and Egypt. On the death of his father in May 1936, he succeeded to the throne; as he was a minor, a Regency Council ruled for him until July 1937. F. continued, even intensified, the struggle between the royal court and the *Wafd party and encouraged the rise of anti-*Wafd* parties, such as the existing Liberal-Constitutional Party and the newly created *Saadist Pary, and reportedly also extra-parliamentary right-wing groups. He was considered anti-British; during World War II he was reported to share the pro-Italian and pro-German sentiments that permeated the administration, the officers' corps and public opinion and led to several cases of desertion and treason. The British had to put pressure on him before he would honor Egypt's obligations under the treaty of 1936 and render the wartime assistance stipulated; it was also under pressure only that he dismissed subversive government and army officers. In Feb. 1942, the British forced F. to dismiss the government and appoint the *Wafd* leader Mustafa *Nahhas Prime Minister (F. removed him in Oct. 1944 — as soon as the British, the danger of an Axis victory having passed, ceased actively intervening in Egyptian internal affairs). The decision of May 1948 to have the Egyptian armed forces march into Palestine — in disregard of previous decisions not to involve the regular forces, and against army advice — was imposed on the government and the army, so their leaders later claimed, by F. personally. The defeat of 1948, and ensuing revelations of corruption in the palace, the bureaucracy and the army, undermined F.'s position, as did his luxurious life and his reputation as a playboy. In the crisis of 1951, when a *Wafd* government abrogated the Anglo-Egyptian Treaty, F. was proclaimed "King of Egypt *and Sudan*". In July 1952, F. was deposed in the officers' *coup* led by Gen. *Nagib and Col. *Nasser. He was allowed to go to Italy with his family. F. had three daughters, and a son from a second marriage, Ahmad Fu'ad (b. 1952). The latter was proclaimed King in 1952 (with a Regency Council ruling for him) — until the abolition of the monarchy in 1953. F., known throughout his life as a voluptuary, a gambler and man of the "jet set" and the night-club circuit, continued his "high life" in his Rome exile. He died in Rome in July 1965.

Fascism Few groups in the AC explicitly and openly advocated F. even in the heyday of European F. in the 1930s and early 1940s, and none have done so since the end of World War II. However, the social doctrine of F., its concept of the corporate state, its stress on nationalism, its rejection of the order imposed by the great powers after World War I, its hostility towards the liberal-democratic West and social democracy, and its hatred of the Jews (particularly in its German Nazi version), all these aroused in the 1930s and 1940s much sympathy among the A.'s, who were then in conflict with the British, the French and the Jews of Palestine. Fascist propaganda was broadcast mainly from Italy (Radio Bari) and then in increasing volume from Germany, and exerted considerable influence. Some A. politicians also were in secret contact with German and Italian agents. Groups considered strongly pro-Fascist or outright Fascist were "Young Egypt" (*Misr al-Fatat*), led by Ahmad Hussein (1911–82), and its "Green Shirts"; the *"Syrian Nationalist Party (*al-Hizb al-Suri al-Qawmi*) of Antoun *Sa'ādeh in Lebanon; and the "Nationalist Action Group" (*'Usbat al-'Amal al-Qawmi*) in Syria. Sympathy for F. and attitudes molded by it were widespread among younger army officers, especially in Iraq, where in the later 1930s a Fascist-inclined group of officers, the "Golden Square", ruled behind the scenes.

Sympathy for, and collaboration with, the Fascist powers increased, and was in part revealed, during World War II. The Egyptian Chief-of-Staff, 'Aziz 'Ali al-*Masri, was caught trying to cross the lines in 1940, and other officers and politicians were detained for similar plots or sympathies. In 1941 the Rashid 'Ali al-*Kilani government of Iraq made war against Britain and requested German help. Not a few A. politicians escaped to Italy and/or Germany — particularly after the fall of the Kilani government in Iraq and the Anglo-Free-French conquest of Syria, 1941, when these two countries no longer provided a haven for leaders sympathizing with the "Axis" powers — and joined Germany's and Italy's propaganda machine, and their efforts to recruit A. and Muslim volunteer units. These collaborators included the Palestinian-A. leader Hajj Amin al-*Husseini and several of his associates; the Iraqis Rashid 'Ali Kilani, Naji Shawkat, Yunis Bahri; the Syro-Lebanese Fawzi al-*Qawuqji; the Egyptians Prince Mansur Dawud, Dr. Tayyib Nasser, Dr. Mustafa Wakil. Some of them resumed political activities in the ME after the war, though most were not permitted to return to their own country as long as the Western powers or strongly pro-Western governments were in charge. None of them attained top leadership positions even after the AC ceased to be Western-dominated or pro-Western, in the 1950s — but the reason was not their war-time collaboration, for that association with Fascist Italy and Germany was not considered a black mark on an A. politician's record.

Fataḥ, Fatḥ See *Palestinian-Arab Guerrilla Organizations.

Fatwa Islamic law ruling, issued by a *Mufti* — usually in response to questions, but also on his own initiative. Such rulings frequently intend to lay down the proper Islamic response to social problems posed by new and changing circumstances — and thus must refer sometimes also to political or semi-political questions. Usually, though not always, the *Mufti* — who in most AC is government-appointed — conforms, in his F.'s on political issues, to the political positions prevailing in public opinion and taken by the government. Several F.'s, for instance, recommend *Jihad, Holy War, against Israel and recognize the Palestinian guerrillas as *Mujahidin*, fighters of a Holy War; other F.'s declare a *Jihad* against Communism to be a religious duty. A F. of an Egyptian *Mufti* rejects King *Hussein's plan of 1972 for a Jordan-Palestine federation as a violation of Islamic law; another justifies the assassination of the Jordanian Prime Minister Wasfi *Tall as an act of *Jihad*. Iraqi *Muftis* have proclaimed the war against Iran a Holy War and excommunicated *Khomeini. A Palestinian *Mufti* has excommunicated any A. selling land to Jews; the same has also excommunicated President *Asad of Syria. On the other hand, a F. by the head of Egypt's al-*Azhar Islamic college in 1979 ruled that the peace treaty with Israel was not incompatible with the Qur'an and Islamic law.

Feda'iyyun, Feda'iyyin (Arabic for suicide squads, commandos). A term based on medieval Islamic concepts, particularly of the *Shi'i-*Isma'ili branch of Islam and its *Hashashiyyin* (the "Assassins"). In modern times the term F. has come to designate sabotage groups, guerrillas, terrorists. The "Young Turk" revolutionaries had their F., and the term is widely used in Iran ("Fedayan Islam"), alternating with *Mujahidin* (Fighters of *Jihad, Holy War) — a term that has lately been preferred in Iran. In recent years the term F. has been applied mainly to *Palestine-Arab guerrilla organizations.

federalism, federations See *Arab Federation.

Federation of Arab Republics (*Ittihad al-Jumhuriyyat al-'Arabiyya*) A Federation — or rather Confederation — of Egypt, Libya and Syria proclaimed in Apr. 1971, endorsed by plebiscite on 1 Sept., and in effect on 1 Jan. 1972. The initiative for the formation of the FAR came from Col. *Qadhdhafi, Libya's leader since the revolution of Sept. 1969. Plans for close co-ordination were announced in Dec. 1969, at an Egypt-Libya-Sudan "summit" meeting (the "Tripoli Charter"), and at first included those three countries. In Nov. 1970, after *Sadat assumed the Presidency, it was decided to set up a fully fledged federation, and Syria, where *Asad had taken full powers, decided to join it. Sudan opted out on the eve of the formal proclamation of the FAR in Apr. 1971. In Egypt, the hard-core Nasserists objected to some aspects of the Federation, and the resulting crisis was one of the reasons for their ouster in May 1971.

The FAR had a full range of confederal institutions: a Constitution, a Presidential Council (the three Heads-of-State), a 60-member Federal Assembly (20 members delegated by each of the National Assemblies of Egypt and Syria and by the Revolutionary Council of Libya — which had no National Assembly), a Federal Council of Ministers resident in Cairo and headed by a Syrian Premier. It was to have a common flag, national anthem and capital, a joint Defense Council, and common diplomatic representation abroad. The three countries' diplomatic envoys to each other were to be replaced by "liaison officers".

However, though duly installed and officially existing, the FAR never got off the ground. Apart from the intrinsic difficulties of a federation between countries so different, so unequal, it was mainly the deterioration of Libyan-Egyptian relations that made it fail. Qadhdhafi was pressing for full Libyan-Egyptian union and in Aug. 1972 persuaded President Sadat to agree to implement such a union by Sept. 1973. As Sadat was dragging his feet and obviously had second thoughts, Qadhdhafi in June–July 1973 appealed directly to the Egyptian people, by a barn-storming tour of Egypt followed by a "spontaneous" mass march of Libyans into Egypt — operations that were resented in Egypt. Sadat in Aug. 1973 reaffirmed the merger agreement in principle, but it was never implemented. Relations deteriorated; bitter recriminations, and accusations of Libyan plots, led to a severance of relations, military confrontation, border clashes, and in 1977 to actual warfare. In Oct. 1973 Qadhdhafi denounced Egypt for limiting her objectives in the war against Israel instead of waging total war for Israel's destruction; after Sadat's visit to Jerusalem in Nov. 1977, he was in the forefront of those ASt denouncing him and demanding Egypt's expulsion and boycott (as was Syria). In Dec. 1977 Syria and Libya expelled

Egypt from the FAR, dismissed Sadat as its President and transferred its headquarters from Cairo to Tripoli. As Qadhdhafi continued referring to the validity and existence of the FAR, Egypt's National Assembly in Oct. 1984 passed a bill abolishing it. Libya and Syria have not formally abolished the FAR; but as they proclaimed, in Sept. 1980, a full union between them (which has not been implemented), the FAR may be considered superseded; it is in any case, not operative.

Feisal Ibn (bin) 'Abd-ul-'Aziz (of the House of Sa'ud) (1904/05–75) King of Sa'udi Arabia 1964–75. The second son of 'Abd-ul-'Aziz *Ibn Sa'ud (after the death of two elder half-brothers). In 1927 his father appointed him governor, later with the title Viceroy, of the *Hijaz, which had recently been conquered from the *Hashemite King *Hussein and his son *'Ali, and entrusted him with its integration into the Sa'udi kingdom. In 1928 F. was also made chairman of the Council of *'Ulama'* (Islamic savants), acting as an advisory State council. Prince. F. frequently represented Sa'udia in foreign affairs and negotiations and, with Ibn Sa'ud maintaining no formal Council of Ministers in the Western pattern, was considered a kind of foreign minister. In 1953, after the death of Ibn Sa'ud and the succession of *Sa'ud, F.'s elder half-brother, F. was designated Crown Prince, Deputy Prime Minister (the King himself taking the Premiership) and Foreign Minister. A half-concealed fight for power between Sa'ud and F. flared up in 1958, when Sa'udia experienced a severe economic crisis and a deterioration of relations with Egypt (with *Nasser and Sa'ud accusing each other of assassination plots). Sa'ud was forced to grant F. full powers in fiscal, internal and foreign affairs and to make him Prime Minister in 1962. F. instituted financial and administrative reforms, took saving measures and attempted to eliminate waste and corruption. He managed to retrieve the economic situation and pay all state debts by 1962. The struggle with King Sa'ud continued intermittently, with F. the virtual ruler. In 1964, Sa'ud demanded the restoration of his power, but F. refused and a new crisis ensued. On 2 Nov. 1964, the Council of *'Ulama'* deposed Sa'ud (who went into exile) and proclaimed F. King.

During his reign, F. promoted and accelerated the development and modernization of Sa'udi Arabia, made possible by the continuous growth of oil production, but made few changes in the ultra-conservative system of government. He followed a more active, nationalist inter-A. policy and became a much-respected all-A. leader. He endeavored to mend relations with Egypt (which had again deteriorated as the two countries were involved, since 1962, on opposing sides in the Yemen civil war), but frequently refused to go along with Nasser's policies and emerged as the leader of a bloc of conservative ASt moderately pro-Western. He also cultivated relations with the Islamic states and was instrumental in the formation of a permanent consultative group of these states from 1969–70. King F. was assassinated in Mar. 1975 by a nephew, Feisal Ibn Musa'id, who was executed for the murder.

Of F.'s 8 sons, several fill senior positions. Prince Sa'ud Ibn F. (b. 1941) has served since 1975 as Foreign Minister, Turki (b. 1945) is Director of Foreign Intelligence.

Feisal I, Ibn Hussein (1885–1933) King of Iraq, 1921–33. Born in Ta'if, Hijaz, as the third son of Sharif (later King) *Hussein of the *Hashemite dynasty, F. grew up in Istanbul, where his father lived in exile. He returned to Hijaz with his father in 1908, when Hussein was appointed Amir of Mecca. On the eve of World War I he established contact with A. nationalists in Damascus. When his father launched the *"Arab Revolt" in Hijaz, 1916, F. took command of the "Northern Army" which harassed Turkish forces in guerrilla operations and from 1917 advanced northwards into Transjordan as part of General Allenby's British and allied forces. F. and his contingent were allowed to enter Damascus on 1 Oct. 1918 and assume control of inner Syria in the name of A. nationalism and under the supervision of the Allies' provisional military administration. F. set up an A. government and administration, composed of and supported by A. nationalist leaders (some — with administrative experience in Ottoman-Turkish service). But France regarded Syria, under the war-time secret *Sykes-Picot Agreement, as her zone of control, and made it clear that she would not accept Syrian-A. independence free of that control. In the meantime, F. presented his dynasty's claim to an independent A. kingdom (or federation of kingdoms), and A. nationalist claims in general, at the Paris Peace Conference (where he also signed an agreement on future co-operation with the *Zionist leader Weizmann — see *Feisal-Weizmann Agreement).

In Mar. 1920 an A.-Syrian national congress proclaimed F. King of Syria (meaning a *"Greater Syria", including Lebanon, Palestine and Transjordan, though no borders were specified). At the same time, the *San Remo Conference of the allied powers confirmed French control of Syria by conferring upon her a *"Mandate" to administer that country. It would be idle to speculate whether an accommodation could have been found between French control and a semi-independent A. kingdom under F. (such as the British arranged in Iraq and Transjordan): French forces soon clashed with hastily assembled troops and volunteers of F.'s régime, and after a battle at Meisalun, in July 1920 F. gave up the fight and left Syria. As the British felt committed to the Hashemite dynasty, Colonial Secretary Churchill, on the advice of *Lawrence and the British "A. Office" in Cairo, secured for F. the Kingdom of Iraq. A "plebiscite" of notables was arranged in July 1921, and in Aug. 1921 F. was proclaimed King of Iraq.

During his reign, F. proved himself an astute politician. He had to tread carefully, to avoid alienating the nationalists, most of whom were anti-British and regarded the King and his dynasty as a foreign implantation; yet he remained on good terms with the British and was their loyal ally. He also continued, not very vigorously, to advocate a settlement with the Jews of Palestine within the framework of a general ME confederation or alliance. He promulgated an Iraqi Constitution in 1925, laid the foundations for an independent administration, at first under British tutelage, and led Iraq, through the Anglo-Iraqi Treaty of 1930, to formally complete independence and admission to the League of Nations in 1932 — the first Arab country to attain that status. In 1933 he tried to restrain mounting violence against the *Assyrian minority — an attempt that cost him much of his popularity and persuaded observers that he was losing his grip. F. died in Sept. 1933 and was succeeded by his only son, *Ghazi.

Feisal II, Ibn Ghazi (1935–58) King of Iraq 1939–58. The only son of King *Ghazi and grandson of *Feisal I (and, through his mother, of ex-King 'Ali of Hijaz, the brother of Feisal I), F. became King on his father's death in 1939, when he was not yet four years old. His uncle *'Abd-ul-Ilah (his father's cousin and his mother's brother) became Regent. During the crisis under the Rashid *'Ali régime in 1941 — when the Regent and other leaders of the conservative, pro-British régime fled — F. and his mother were in the power of the rebellious nationalist government, but remained unharmed. After the war, F. was educated along English lines, partly in England (Harrow). On coming of age, in 1953, F. assumed his royal-constitutional duties. In Feb. 1958 he became head of the short-lived *"Arab Federation" of Jordan and Iraq. F. was not a forceful personality and had no appreciable influence on his country's policies. He was murdered during the revolution of July 1958; his murder was probably planned, with the intention of depriving adherents of the old order of a possible rallying center.

Feisal-Weizmann Agreement In June 1918, the Zionist leader Prof. Chaim Weizmann, then in Palestine at the head of a Zionist commission to make a survey and preparations for the implementation of the *Balfour Declaration, followed a British suggestion and met Amir *Feisal Ibn Hussein, the leader of the *Arab Revolt, at the latter's camp between Ma'an and 'Aqaba in Transjordan, to discuss future cooperation between the Jewish and the A. national movements. Following the meeting, a statement by Feisal was published in *The Times* of 12 Dec. 1918, describing A. and Zionist national aspirations as compatible. Further talks took place during the Paris Peace Conference, and on 3 Jan. 1919, F. and W. signed a formal agreement. This provided for "the closest collaboration in the development of the Arab State and Palestine" (Preamble) and "the most cordial good will and understanding" between the two states (Art. I), whose boundaries would be determined by agreement (Art. II). The Balfour Declaration was endorsed (Art. III), and it was agreed (Art. IV) that "all necessary measures shall be taken to encourage and stimulate immigration of Jews into Palestine on a large scale, and as quickly as possible to settle Jewish immigrants upon the land", while the A. peasants and tenant farmers would be duly "protected in their right, and (...) assisted in forwarding their economic development". F. added a hand-written note making the implementation of the agreement conditional on the fulfilment of his demands concerning A. independence.

F. was later somewhat ambiguous concerning the Agreement he had signed, particularly his recognition of a Zionist-led Palestine as a separate, non-A. state, as expressed in the articles speaking of the boundaries between that state and "the A. state" and their cooperation. In an interview with *Le Matin* of 1 Mar. 1919 he said that persecuted Jews were welcome to Palestine under a Muslim or Christian government responsible to the League of Nations, but any desire to establish a Jewish state and claim sovereignty would lead to serious conflict. As the Zionists were disturbed by that statement, contradicting the F.-W.A., and sought clarifications, the matter was cleared up in a meeting between F. and an American judge, Prof. Felix Frankfurter, in the presence of F.'s British adviser, T. E. Lawrence, and a subsequent letter of 3 Mar. 1919, in which F. reassured the Zionists that "we are working together for a reformed and revived Near East, and our two movements complete one another... There is room in Syria for us both". (In 1929, asked about this letter, F. could not remember having written it).

A. nationalist spokesmen have never accepted the validity of the F.-W.A. Some claimed that it was a forgery. Others, admitting the fact that F. indeed signed the agreement and that the text of the document was unquestionably authentic, claimed that F. had been influenced or misled by Lawrence and had signed unaware of the agreement's implications, and that in any case he had no authority to sign on behalf of the A. national movement an agreement affecting the Palestine A.'s. In any case, the F.-W.A. was never implemented — a document of poignant historical interest but little or no impact on the march of events.

Fertile Crescent Informal, general term for the countries on the northern edge of the Arabian peninsula: Iraq, Syria, Lebanon, Palestine (Israel and Jordan). Before the dismemberment of the *Ottoman Empire in 1918, the FC, as part of that empire, was administratively divided into the provinces *(Vilayet)* of Basra, Baghdad, Mosul, Aleppo, Damascus and Beirut, the autonomous district *(Sanjaq)* of Lebanon, and the special district of Jerusalem; there were no units by the name of Iraq, Syria or Palestine. As protagonists of A. independence and leaders of the *A. Revolt during World War I, the *Hashemite Sharif *Hussein of Mecca and his sons *'Ali, *Feisal and *'Abdullah planned to include the FC in an Arab kingdom. They never spelled out their plans in detail, but apparently envisaged a federative structure consisting of two FC kingdoms, Iraq, and (Greater) Syria (including Lebanon and Palestine-with-Transjordan), to be united with a third one, in Hijaz, under a super-king. However, great-power arrangements during and after the Paris Peace Conference, 1918–20, divided the FC into semi-independent entities under separate *"Mandates", with Britain administering Iraq and Palestine (including Transjordan) and France administering Syria and Lebanon; these separate entities became firmly established and eventually independent states (Palestine was partitioned twice: in 1922, when Transjordan was separated, and in 1948, when Israel was founded).

However, the concept of the FC as a single political entity persisted. Plans for a FC Federation — in an Iraqi version presented by Nuri *Sa'id in 1942-3, or in King *'Abdullah's version, both envisaging the creation of a *"Greater Syria" as the first step — were bitterly opposed by France, which saw them as British-inspired plots, and by many A. nationalists. After Syria and Lebanon attained full independence, they, too, rejected these Hashemite schemes — and were joined by Egypt, Sa'udi Arabia and the *Arab League. The FC idea was partly realized in the Iraqi-Jordanian "Arab Federation" of 1958 (with the main element: Syria — missing), but that Federation was abolished later the same year, after Iraq's July 1958 revolution. (For details of these federative plans see *Arab Federation, *Greater Syria.)

Non-Hashemite or anti-Hashemite schemes for a "Greater Syria" and a FC union were propagated by Antoun *Sa'adeh's *"Syrian National (later "Social-National") Party" — a marginal Lebanese group with little influence. Radical-leftist Syria under the *Ba'th party advocated all-A. union rather than specifically FC federations; yet, in their search for new patterns of union after the dissolution of the Syro-Egyptian *United Arab Republic the Ba'th leaders agreed in 1963 to the creation of a Federation of Syria, Iraq and Egypt, and when that agreement remained abortive they played with the idea of a Syro-Iraqi union. Talks and tentative agreements on that line also remained inconclusive, the more so since Syria and Iraq, ruled by rival factions of the *Ba'th*, have been in dispute and mutually hostile since the late 1960s.

While a FC union or federation thus seems to have ceased to be a practical-political scheme (though remaining, perhaps, an idea, a vision), the FC has retained its importance as a sphere of influence, an arena of struggle for strategic control. Both Iraq and Syria aspire to a position of controlling influence and of predominance in the FC — and as Iraq has been since 1980 absorbed in her war with Iran, it is mainly Syria that seems to seek such control. Ba'thist Syria does not seem to scheme for a "Greater Syria" in terms of actual union or federation; but she seeks — and since 1984 holds — near-total control of Lebanon and aspires to far-reaching influence (at least negative and deterrent, to prevent policies unacceptable to her) on the inter-A. and international policies of Jordan and the Palestine A.'s, and strives to exclude a dominating influence of rival Iraq. Egypt and Sa'udi Arabia would, it may be assumed, be interested in preventing any one A. power — either Syria or Iraq — from dominating the FC.

Fez Plan, Fez Decisions A plan adopted in Sept. 1982 by the second session of the 12th A. Summit at F. and laying down guidelines for a ME, A.-Israel, settlement. The FP was an amended version of the "Fahd Plan" which had caused the break-up of the first session of the Summit in Nov. 1981. It has since been regarded as the master-plan for a settlement accepted by all ASt. For its contents see *Fahd and *Arab-Israel Conflict.

FLN, Front de Libération Nationale Algerian nationalist organization, founded underground c. 1954 by a group of younger, activists dissatisfied with the leadership of *Messali Hajj and other established nationalist leaders and their parties (the MTLD and PPA — see *Algeria). The younger group held armed struggle to be unavoidable and resolved to prepare for it. They formed an *Organisation Secrète* (or *Spéciale*) for that purpose in the early 1950s and later seceded from the MTLD and formed the *Comité Révolutionnaire pour l'Unité et l'Action* (CRUA), which transformed itself in 1954 into the FLN, led by Ahmad *Ben Bella, Belkacem Krim, Hussein Ait-Ahmad, Muhammad Khidr and others, and headquartered in Cairo and later Tunis. In Nov. 1954 the FLN opened armed struggle against France. It established a strong guerrilla force which developed into a full-fledged army, and also claimed the political leadership. It led an unrelenting armed struggle for over seven years and finally achieved Algeria's independence in 1962.

The FLN conducted and won an internal-factional struggle over the formation of independent Algeria's governing institutions and established itself as the country's single party dominating the government and providing all leading functionaries. In the process it eliminated all rival groups and also "purged" and ousted all factions within the FLN that opposed Ben Bella's dominant group (see *Algeria, *Ben Bella). The FLN has remained in that ruling position throughout the quarter of a century of independent Algeria. Its leadership and its congress determine the candidate for the Presidency and all candidates for the National Assembly, to be endorsed in elections which are in reality plebiscites to endorse prepared lists, and for most other leading positions.

FLOSY (Front for the Liberation of Occupied South Yemen). Underground nationalist organization in *Aden and *South Arabia, founded in 1966 through a merger of several underground groups, reportedly supported, or even sponsored, by Egypt. F. was a mainly urban movement, based in 'Aden town, and had strong links with the trade unions. Its aim was to liberate South Arabia (later South Yemen) from British rule and unite it with Yemen. F. was at first considered the most radical, and the main, nationalist faction; but it failed to develop a base in the tribal hinterland of 'Aden and evolve effective guerrilla formations.

In 1967, on the eve of independence, a more extremist group, the leftist *"National Liberation Front" (NLF), got the upper hand and eliminated F. in bloody fighting; F.'s leaders were detained or went into exile, mostly to Yemen or Egypt (thus, e.g., 'Abd-ul-Qawwi Makkawi). For some years Yemen continued sustaining F., but the organization, in exile or underground, had no more significant influence on events in South Yemen.

France, French interests and policies in the Arab countries F. interests in the ME are manifold and of long standing. F. was deeply involved in the ME in the era of the Crusades (1096–1291), assuming a leading part in eight of them. In 1535, François I signed a treaty of friendship with the Ottoman Sultan Suleiman I, which conferred upon France certain privileges or *capitulations, including French jurisdiction over French merchants, and virtually recognized F. as the protector of Latin Christianity in the Empire. The capitulations were further extended in 1740, and by Napoleon in 1802.

In 1798 Napoleon invaded Egypt, to cut off Britain from her Indian possessions. He conquered Egypt, then ruled by a Mameluk viceroy under Ottoman sovereignty, and advanced into Palestine and Syria. However, he failed to reduce Acre and was unable to proceed beyond Sidon on the Lebanese coast. In 1799 he returned to France, and by 1801 the French Army was forced to surrender to Britain. Though the expedition was spectacular, its main effects were in the cultural rather than the military domain. F. played an active role in the diplomatic and military maneuvers of the Great Powers concerning the conflict between Muhammad 'Ali of Egypt and the Ottoman Sultan in the 1830s, and in protecting the Ottoman Empire against Russia (the Crimean War, 1854–56).

F. granted her special protection to the *Maronites in Lebanon and intervened on their behalf in 1842–45 and again in 1860, when she exerted pressure upon the Sultan to establish Lebanon as an autonomous region, predominantly Christian; the Sultan had to concede this to F. and the other Western Powers supporting her. This led to a considerable extension of French political and cultural influence. F. interests were also active in the Ottoman Empire (railways, banking), Persia, and particularly Egypt. The *Suez Canal was devised and built by French engineers and largely with French capital. F., together with Britain, administered Egypt's foreign debts and was deeply involved in her economy. Even after the British occupation of Egypt (1882), which F. bitterly resented, French interests and influence in Egypt remained strong.

During the 19th century F. built her empire in A. North-west Africa, the *Maghrib, conquering Algeria in 1830 and incorporating her in F. as fully F. territory, and imposing a Protectorate, in reality a colonial administration, on Tunisia in 1881–83 and on Morocco in 1912. For these developments see *Algeria, *Tunisia, *Morocco. F. also had aspirations in East Africa, on the margins of the A. world. She acquired F. Somali or *Djibouti in the 1880s, and her attempts to expand her African possessions in the direction of southern Sudan led to a grave crisis with Britain (the Fashoda crisis, 1898). This crisis was resolved by F.'s retreat and the renunciation of any claims to Sudan, and the Anglo-F. *entente cordiale* of 1904.

F. claims to the Levant were put forward during *World War I. Under the *Sykes-Picot Agreement of 1916 F. was to obtain possession of the coastal strip of Syria-Lebanon and most of Cilicia in SE Anatolia, as well as a sphere of influence to include the Syrian hinterland and the *Mosul province of Mesopotamia, and a share in an internationalized administration of Palestine. But in Nov. 1918 the French and British prime ministers, Clemenceau and Lloyd George, signed an agreement by which F. waived her claim to the Mosul area in favor of Britain, in return for a share in the oil resources of the area (and further compensation in Europe). F. also had to acquiesce in a British *Mandate administration for Palestine. Plans for F. rule in Cilicia were re-affirmed in the Peace Treaty of *Sèvres with Turkey, 1920, but that treaty was torn up by the Turkish nationalists and the partition of Anatolia was abandoned.

In return for her concessions, F. was granted a Mandate over the whole of Syria and Lebanon, the distinction between direct administration in the coastlands and guidance-and-influence in the A. hinterland being dropped. In Nov. 1919 F. troops under General Gouraud replaced British troops along the Syrian coast. F. recognized Amir *Feisal's authority in the Syrian hinterland. However, when in the spring of 1920 Feisal accepted the Syrian crown, symbolizing complete independence, this was regarded by F. as a threat to her "rights" in Syria. General Gouraud's forces entered Damascus on 24 July 1920 and deposed Feisal, asserting F. supremacy in Syria. For the F. Mandatory administration in Syria and Lebanon, and its struggle with the nationalists, see *Syria *Lebanon. At first General Gouraud split the F. Mandate territory into four units: Greater Lebanon; the State of Damascus (including the Jabal *Druze district); the State of *Aleppo (including the *Alexandretta district); and the *'Alawi Territory of Lataqia. Jabal Druze was granted special status in 1922, and the *Sanjaq* of Alexandretta gained semi-autonomy in 1924; on 1 Jan. 1925 the states of Aleppo and Damascus were unified as the State of Syria. In 1925–26 F. had to suppress an armed rebellion in Syria.

F.'s endeavors to set up Western-type parliamentary institutions were more successful in Lebanon than in Syria. In treaties of 1936 the Léon Blum government granted Syria and Lebanon independence within three years, in return for a military pact stipulating the presence of French forces and bases and a privileged status for F. However, as a result of developments in F., such as the eclipse of the Socialist-led Popular Front and the preoccupation with the German and Italian danger, F. did not ratify the two agreements, reverting on the eve of World War II to unqualified colonial-type rule under the Mandate. The danger of the approaching war also induced F. to surrender the district *(Sanjaq)* of Alexandretta-*Hatay, with its 40% Turkish minority, to Turkey in June 1939 (see *Alexandretta). At the same time, F. and Turkey signed a pact of non-aggression and mutual assistance.

In World War II, after the capitulation of F. in June 1940, French administrators and officers in Syria and Lebanon under General Dentz threw in their lot with the Vichy authorities. An Italian Armistice Supervision Commission was stationed in the Levant, the presence of German and Italian troops was rumored, and Syria and Lebanon were expected to serve as the bridgehead of a fully fledged invasion of the ME. In June 1941, British and Free French forces occupied Syria and Lebanon in a brief campaign. On the day of the invasion General Catroux declared on behalf of Free F. the end of the Mandate and the independence of Syria and Lebanon, future relations with F. to be determined by treaty. A British statement endorsed his proclamation, and General Catroux was appointed "Delegate General and Plenipotentiary of Free F. in the Levant" (rather than the traditional "High Commissioner") and instructed to negotiate treaties with Syria and Lebanon. On 28 Sept. and 26 Nov. 1941, Catroux again proclaimed the independence of Syria and Lebanon.

However, the Syrian and Lebanese leaders, backed by the USA and particularly Britain, were no longer prepared to conclude a treaty conferring upon F. special privileges, while F. was not willing to grant full independence without such a treaty. A bitter struggle ensued. A grave crisis erupted in Nov. 1943, when the Lebanese government and Parliament formally abolished all articles of the Constitution limiting independence and granting F. special privileges. The F. arrested the Lebanese leaders, including President Bishara al-*Khouri and Premier Riyad al-*Sulh, but were compelled, mainly by a British ultimatum, to back down (the British Army being in war-time overall command of the region). Serious clashes again broke out in Syria early in 1945, as the F. refused to withdraw their troops from the Levant and to hand over to Syria the locally recruited "Special Forces". F. again had to retreat following a British ultimatum. Early in 1946, the evacuation of F. (and British) forces was discussed by the UN Security Council, and though no formal decision was adopted owing to a Soviet veto, F. and Britain consented to withdraw their forces from Syria by Apr. 1946, from Lebanon by Dec. 1946. This spelled the end of F. predominance in the Levant.

The evacuation of F. forces and the end of F. rule over Syria and Lebanon left F. deeply embittered towards Britain, whom she saw as the chief cause of her dislodgement from the ME. F. always suspected Britain of scheming for a *"Greater Syria" *Hashemite-led Federation designed to oust F. Some F. economic and cultural influence remained, especially in Lebanon, because of that country's strongly Christian character.

After World War II F. took part in the provisional Allied military administration of Libya. She administered Libya's South, Fezzan, adjacent to her possessions in Algeria, Niger and Chad, and maintained a military base there after Libya's independence in 1951. By agreement with Libya she evacuated that base in 1956, but retained some communication facilities until 1963.

F. voted in favor of the partition of Palestine on 29 Nov. 1947, but her recognition of Israel was delayed in order to allay A. sensitivities. F. officers served as UN truce observers in Palestine, 1948–49, and under the A.-Israel Armistice

Agreements from 1949. F. was elected in December 1948 to the UN *Palestine Conciliation Commission (PCC), with the USA and Turkey. Though F. had given generous assistance to survivors of the European holocaust, and had allowed the establishment of transit camps for Jews on their way to Israel and various Zionist activities during the struggle towards independence, her ties with Israel continued to be marked by restraint. F. persisted in regarding herself as a Muslim power, mainly in view of her North African possessions.

In the early and mid-1950s F. was engaged in a struggle over Tunisia's and Morocco's claim to independence — a contest resolved in 1955–56 by the termination of the F. Protectorate and both countries' complete independence. F.'s links with Tunisia and Morocco, and her influence remained strong; but initial F. attempts to preserve a position of institutionalized privilege failed. The struggle over Algeria was more violent and protracted and culminated in a rebellion and full warfare from Nov. 1954 until Mar. 1962, when Algeria, too, became independent. Egypt and most AC actively supported the Maghribi nationalists against F., and that support, particularly that for the Algerian rebels, affected F.-A. relations and induced F. to change her attitude and follow less pro-A. policies. The *Suez crisis of 1955–56 and Egypt's nationalization of the Suez Canal Company in July 1956, led F. to invade Egypt, in the *Suez War, together with Britain and in secret coordination with Israel's *Sinai War. Britain and F. failed to achieve their objective and were compelled to withdraw. Egypt and most AC broke off diplomatic relations with F. (while F.'s relations with Israel now became an intimate, semi-secret alliance). Egypt also nationalized all F. properties and interests.

The granting of independence to Algeria in 1962 paved the way for the resumption of normal relations between F. and the ASt; the last AC to restore relations was Egypt in spring 1963. De Gaulle, rejecting A. pressure, proclaimed a doctrine of "parallelism" to guide F.'s dealings with both Israel and the ASt. Gradually, however, the normalization of F.'s relations with the ASt and F. interests in the ME and North Africa and particularly in Algeria, e.g. the oil resources of the Sahara, caused F. to revert to a more pro-A. policy. This was revealed in a drastic change of attitude on the eve of the *Six Day War in May-June 1967. De Gaulle opposed any physical intervention in the Straits of *Tiran to protect the freedom of navigation, tried in vain to solve the crisis by great power consultations, and confidentially warned Israel not to start a pre-emptive war. On 3 June, F. placed a total embargo on the supply of arms and military equipment to the ME. Since Israel was the chief buyer of such equipment from F., the embargo was aimed almost exclusively at her.

When Israel did open a pre-emptive war, de Gaulle never forgave her for having "fired the first shot"; Israel's protestations that the closing of the Straits of Tiran constituted a *casus belli* and was planned as the beginning of her destruction, left the F. President unimpressed. At the UN, F. took a distinctly pro-A. position, demanding a total and unconditional Israeli withdrawal; and at a press conference in Nov. 1967 de Gaulle was severely critical of Israel (using the phrase "a chosen people with a domineering disposition", with its anti-Semitic undertone). In 1969 F. took the initiative for the abortive talks on the ME by the UN Ambassadors of the Four Powers. The reversal in F.'s attitude was praised by the AC, whereas relations with Israel steadily deteriorated. The embargo mainly affected 50 Mirage-V planes for which Israel had already paid. But following a retaliatory Israeli raid on Beirut airport on 28 Dec. 1968, de Gaulle placed a total embargo on arms supplies to Israel. The accession of Georges Pompidou to the presidency in 1969 did not lead to a substantial change in F. ME policy. Feelers put out at the end of 1969 with a view to reverting to a selective embargo were withdrawn when five gunboats, built for Israel but kept back by F. in accordance with the embargo, were taken out of Cherbourg harbor by an Israeli commando in Dec. 1969.

While maintaining her ME arms embargo against Israel (and refunding the amounts Israel had paid), F. broke it where AC were concerned. In Dec. 1969 she agreed to supply 110 Mirage jets to Libya (under her new, *coup*-born, *Qadhdhafi régime), claiming that Libya was not a "front-line" country facing Israel and was therefore not covered by the embargo. From the 1970s F. became a major supplier of arms to several ASt. She also continued taking pro-A. positions on various aspects of the A.-Israel conflict and in particular supported Palestinian-A. rights to participation in any negotiations, to self-determination, to "a homeland" (her Foreign Minister, Oct. 1975) or a state (Foreign Minister, 1981), and pushed the other countries of Europe, in the *EEC, in the same direction; F. influence was discerned, for instance, behind both the pro-A. EEC statement of Nov. 1973, the 1980 Declaration of Venice and the initiative for a European-A. dialogue. F. also supported the admission of the *PLO to various UN bodies (e.g. the conference on the Law of the Sea, 1974 — other EEC countries abstained). Among Europe's leading statesmen the F. were the first to meet with *'Arafat and other PLO leaders, and F. was among the first European countries to allow the PLO to open an office (1975). F. was unimpressed by, or indifferent to, Egyptian President *Sadat's peace moves of 1977 and voiced sceptical reservations about the *Camp David Agreements, since they provided no general settlement with all ASt. After the accession of President Mitterrand, 1981, F. followed a more balanced policy. She also took a modest part in the Multinational Force set up in Sinai in 1982 under an Egypt-Israel agreement.

The years of F.'s pronounced pro-A. policy on the A.-Israel issue affected several particular fields. Concerning the A. *Boycott of Israel, for instance, the F. National Assembly enacted a law against economic discrimination (1977); but an executive decree in effect neutralized the law with regard to "oil producing states of the Near East". Even in the fight against terrorism, which affected F. no less than other Western countries, F. was not a full partner. Indeed, it was rumored, though never confirmed, that she concluded, in about 1974, a secret "sanctuary agreement" with the PLO granting PLO men free passage through and residence in F. in return for a pledge that in F. herself no terrorist acts would be committed (a pledge that was not kept). In 1976, after the hijacking of a F. airliner en route from Israel to Paris and the Israeli rescue operation of Entebbe, F. refused to join the USA and Britain in a Security Council resolution condemning all air piracy. In 1977 many were aghast when F. deported, i.e. let go, a senior PLO terrorist leader, Abu Dawud, accused of planning the 1972 Munich Olympic Games massacre, whose extradition had been requested by both West Germany and Israel. Yet, in the 1980s F. herself became the arena of many acts of terrorism, Palestinian, Lebanese, Iranian and international, and had to take measures against it; but even now, many regarded her steps against terrorism as rather half-hearted.

F. still felt a special link to Lebanon — though the tradition of her special status and influence in that country had faded out. After the Israeli invasion of 1978, she joined *UNIFIL, the "UN Interim Force in Lebanon", and in Aug.-Sept. 1982 she allotted some 2,000 troops to a Multinational Force designed to assist and supervise the evacuation of Syrian and PLO forces from Beirut. F. also actively assisted the actual transportation of the evacuated PLO forces — both those from Beirut in Aug.-Sept. 1982, and those from Tripoli in Dec. 1983. When the Multinational Force was withdrawn in Feb.-Mar. 1984, F. sent c. 80 observers to monitor the intra-Lebanese cease-fire — a frustrating task, since that cease-fire was never fully operative. These observers were withdrawn early in 1986. Later, in Nov. 1986, F. also reduced her UNIFIL contingent from nearly 1,400 to about 500 and restricted its task to logistics and maintenance only. This gradual but far-reaching reduction in F.'s involvement in Lebanon was in large part the result of the increasing victimization of F. personnel by the Lebanese civil war and terrorism and its extension to F. Many F. officers and men were killed or wounded serving with UNIFIL, the Multinational Force or as observers; other Frenchmen were kidnapped and some of them murdered; a F. Ambassador was assassinated in Sept. 1981; 85 F. soldiers were killed by a terrorist car bomb at their headquarters in Oct. 1983. And it was in any case becoming increasingly evident that the presence of F. personnel could make no significant contribution to a solution of Lebanon's problems.

F. interests were also badly hurt by Iran's Islamic revolution (though she had given asylum to Khomeini in the years of his exile) and the Iran-Iraq war. Iran bitterly resented the fact that F. was a main supplier of arms to Iraq and granted asylum to leaders and organizations of the régime's foes, and refused to reach agreement on several disputes (outside our scope here) until F. changed that policy. In June 1986 F. did expel

Mas'ud Rajavi, the leader of the Iranian anti-régime *Mujahidin-i-Khalq*, but this step did not satisfy Iran's demands.

Since the early 1980s F. has been involved in a conflict with Libya over Chad. She has not accepted full responsibility for the defense of Chad, and has acquiesced in Libya's *de facto* domination of northern Chad, but she has sent a small contingent of troops and applied political pressure to halt any further expansion by Libya. An agreement of Sept. 1984 on the withdrawal of both F. and Libyan troops was broken by Libya, and F. reinstated her partial military presence and reconfirmed a "Red Line" at the 16th parallel which Libya would not be permitted to pass. (See *Libya.)

F.'s main interests in the AC have remained centered on the three Maghrib countries — Algeria, Tunisia and Morocco. Since the 1960s (the end of the Algerian rebellion and Algeria's independence, 1962; the F.-Tunisian Bizerta crisis of 1962; the agreement with Tunisia on former F. properties, 1965; the evacuation of F. bases in Algeria, 1967–68), there were no major crises in F.'s relations with the three countries — though those with Algeria were sometimes strained, for instance by the problem of Algerian migrants in F. and the fate of former Algerian collaborators. Problems of oil and natural gas development and production also troubled F.-Algerian relations. In 1965 an agreement was reached according to F. companies (which had been the pioneers of Algeria's oil development) a major share in the further, major expansion of Algeria's oil and gas economy. But, after several disputes over production and price policies, Algeria nationalized 51% of the F. companies' holdings, and all gas production, in Feb. 1971, and F. had to acquiesce. The F. companies now became junior partners of Algeria's national oil combine, but Algeria remained a major source of oil and particularly liquefied gas for F. Protracted wrangles over the price of gas were resolved by an agreement of Feb. 1982.

Besides variegated economic enterprises and the supply of arms, oil was indeed a major F. interest in the AC. F. companies had a 23.75% share in the Iraq Petroleum Company since its inception, and a 6% share in Iran's oil consortium since 1954; both these major holdings have since been fully nationalized and F. has become a mere buyer of Iraqi and Iranian oil. F. companies also operated or had a share in Abu Dhabi, Dubai, 'Oman, Qatar, Tunisia and Libya; some of these concessions have been formally nationalized, the foreign companies turning from concessionaires into operators, on behalf of the respective country's national oil company.

While the AC have remained a major source of oil and gas for F., F. (along with the rest of Western Europe) has become somewhat less dependent on A. oil in the 1980s — *inter alia* due to the vigorous development of nuclear power and the saving of energy. While she imported 125m. tons in 1979, of which more than 60% came from the ME, plus 4% from Algeria (not counting liquefied gas) and 3% from Libya, her oil imports in 1985 were down to 73m. tons — less than 20% coming from the ME, 5% from Algeria and 4% from Libya. (This reduction of F.'s dependence on A. oil may well be one of the reasons for the gradual mitigation of her pro-A. policies.)

Franjiyeh, Suleiman (b. 1910) Lebanese politician. President of Lebanon 1970–76. The powerful Christian-*Maronite F. clan, centered in Zagharta, northern Mount Lebanon, are the chief leaders of the Maronites in the north and largely in control of their region. They are in near-constant rivalry with the Maronite chiefs of central Mount Lebanon (*Khouri, *Edde, *Chamoun, *Jumayyil) over a leading role in general Lebanese-Christian politics. The main political exponent of the F.'s was SF's elder brother Hamid F. (1907?1909?–81), from the late 1930s a member of Parliament and many times Minister, frequently Foreign Minister, and in 1952 a candidate for the Presidency (he withdrew in favor of Camille Chamoun) — while SF acted as the organizer and strong-arm man of the clan and its armed guards. After Hamid F. suffered a stroke in 1957, SF became the main leader of the clan and entered politics. In the civil war of 1958 he aligned himself and his "militia" on the Nasserist side and against President Chamoun; but his political position was complex and shifting, and after 1958 he was considered pro-American or at least neutral. From 1960 he was a member of Parliament and served several times as a Minister (1960–61, 1968–70). In Aug. 1970 he was elected President, against Elias *Sarkis, the candidate of the strongest Parliamentary group, the

*"Shihabists"; the vote was 50:49 — the smallest majority ever.

SF did not become a strong President. He had publicly denounced the armed presence of the Palestinian guerrilla formations, and their operations from Lebanese territory, as a danger to Lebanon — both externally, for exposing the country to Israeli counter-operations, and internally, for endangering the cohesion of Lebanon's communal structure. But as President he took no action to avoid that danger; and when the dreaded crisis erupted, in Apr. 1975, and turned into a civil war, he was weak and indecisive. He did not order the army into action to defend the régime and public order, fearing (rightly, as it turned out later) that the army would split and break up if it became involved in the civil war; and he did not throw his support to the conservative, Christian-led camp, to whose leaders (Chamoun, Jumayyil) he remained deeply antagonistic, despite their crucial vote for his election. He stayed neutral and even evinced some sympathy for the leftist-revolutionary, mainly Muslim camp. From late 1975, F. became very close to Syria, recognizing her as the only power capable of mediating and imposing both an end to the civil war, and basic reforms as a more permanent solution. In Jan.–Feb. 1976 he evolved, together with Syrian President *Asad and his associates, a plan for reforms in Lebanon's political-communal structure. The plan was based on the abolition of the Christian majority in Parliament, which no longer corresponded to demographic realities, and its replacement by a 50:50 division of Parliamentary representation between Christians and non-Christians (Sunni, Shi'i and Druze), but retained the constitutional principle of pre-determined communal representation and the communal division of the main power positions as informally agreed in the "National Pact" of 1943. It has remained Syria's, and F.'s, basic formula for Lebanese reforms. When, in early 1976, the Asad-F. plan was rejected by the leftist-Muslim-Palestinian camp, F. encouraged, or even invited, Syrian armed intervention.

F.'s presidential term was slated to end in Sept. 1976. For some time, he resisted demands, reinforced by formal Parliamentary votes, to reaffirm that he would step down — maintaining that in the conditions of crisis and civil war no elections could be properly held and implying that his term should be extended (as Parliament had extended its own term). But eventually he bowed to pressure, his Syrian allies failing to support his bid for extension. In May 1976, a new Syrian-backed President, Elias *Sarkis, was elected, and in Sept. F. stepped down.

Out of office, F. maintained his position as the chief of the Maronites of the Zagharta region and North Lebanon, and built up his "militia", the *Marada*. The tension between him and the main Maronite leadership flared up in the late 1970s when the *Phalanges, the main military formation of that leadership, and the "Lebanese Forces" they had established, claimed exclusive control of all Christian militias, and F. refused to integrate his force. During the clashes that ensued, F.'s son Antoine (Tony) — a budding politician, member of Parliament since 1970, a Minister 1973–75, and his father's political heir — was killed, with his wife and small daughter, by the Phalangists; F. held the Phalange leaders of the Jumayyil clan personally responsible, and the old antagonism was aggravated by a bitter blood feud. When Bashir *Jumayyil was murdered in Sept. 1982, F. openly expressed joy. He had, anyway, bitterly opposed Jumayyil's policy of co-operation with Israel — before, during and after the Israeli invasion of June 1982 — and his election to the Presidency.

In July 1983, F. joined the Druze chief *Junbalat and the Muslim-Sunni leader *Karameh in a "National Salvation Front" founded to oppose President Amin *Jumayyil and his government and to step up resistance to the Israeli occupation. At the conference of national reconciliation of Oct.–Nov. 1983 (Geneva), and Mar. 1984 (Lausanne) F. was aligned with the Sunni, Shi'i and Druze leaders against President Jumayyil and the conservatives. However, his allies went beyond the "Asad-F. Plan" and demanded the gradual abolition of the communal representation system altogether, and a far-reaching limitation of the powers of the Maronite President for an immediate transition period and F., apparently re-discovering his Maronite allegiance, could not go along with that and parted company with his allies or at least dissociated himself to a large extent. F. remained close to Syria, but did not take part in the 1985 efforts of the Druze and Shi'i leaders to work out a reform plan. He rebuilt contacts with Maronite leaders — including even Chamoun (but not President Jumayyil whose resignation or dismissal he continued demanding), and also the new leader of the "Lebanese Forces", Elie Hobeika, who was no longer loyal to and dominated by the Jumayyil faction. In Sept. 1985 he re-submitted his own plan for reforms, which was in fact the old "Asad-F. Plan" of 1976; it was vaguely implied that it was no longer the plan of SF alone, an isolated former leader, but was backed by other Christian leaders. In the clashes between rival Christian militias that broke out in Jan. 1986, after Hobeika reached an agreement with the Druze and Shi'i militias that was repudiated by Jumayyil and the Phalanges, F.'s militia joined Hobeika and the Druze and Shi'i forces in their unsuccessful assault on Jumayyil and the Phalanges. Throughout recent years, F. seemed to indicate that he aspired to a new term as President, though he staked no formal claim.

Fu'ad (full name: Ahmad Fu'ad) (1868–1936) Sultan of Egypt 1917–22, King of Egypt 1922–36. The youngest son of the Khedive Isma'il (ruled 1863–79). In 1917 the British arranged for F. to succeed his brother Hussein Kamel as Sultan of Egypt — a title they had introduced in 1914, when they made Egypt a protectorate and deposed Khedive *'Abbas Hilmi. In 1922, following Britain's unilateral declaration of Egypt's independence, F. was proclaimed King (he relinquished his claim to the title "King of Egypt *and Sudan*" only under intense British pressure). During his rule, Egypt's government and nationalists continued to struggle for complete independence and a treaty with Britain recognizing and assuring it — a struggle in which the King did not play an overt part. While officially Egypt rejected the unilateral British declaration of her independence and the reservations limiting it, the foundations of independent Egypt's constitution (promulgated in Apr. 1923) and governance were in fact based on that declaration. The King and his Court desired a strictly conservative system of government with limited power for Parliament and its political parties, and throughout his reign F. struggled with the nationalist, radical *Wafd* party over this issue and strove to exclude the *Wafd* from power, preferring prime ministers from conservative circles close to him. During the last year of his life, in December 1935, F. reinstated the liberal-parliamentary constitution that had been suspended in 1930, thus opening the way for the *Wafd*'s return to power, and nominated an all-party delegation for negotiations with Britain that led to the Anglo-Egyptian Treaty of 1936; he did not live to see its completion. He died in Apr. 1936 and was succeeded by his only son, *Farouq. When the University of Cairo was modernized and turned into a Western-type institution, 1925, it was named "King F. University"; his name was removed in 1952–53, after the "Free Officers" revolution and the abolition of the monarchy.

al-Fujaira One of the seven sheikhdoms of *Trucial 'Oman which, until 1971 a British protectorate, in that year formed the Federation of the *United Arab Emirates (UAE). F. is one of the smallest of the seven — with an area of 450 sq. mi. (c. 1,050 sq. km.). In the 1960s its population was c. 10,000, in a census of 1975 — 26,000, and according to estimates of the mid-1980s c. 35,000. Situated on the east coast of the Trucial 'Oman peninsula, F. was in the past part of *Sharja (al-Shāriqa). In 1952 it was recognized by the British protecting power as a separate sheikhdom, but it still is closely linked to Sharja, under a cooperation agreement of 1960. F. is ruled by a Sheikh of the al-Shāriqi clan.

In 1966 a concession for oil prospecting was granted to a German company, and later the international Shell company took a 60% interest, but as no oil was found, the licence was cancelled in 1971. Other companies are prospecting for offshore oil. So far, no oil discovery has been reported. Thus, while F. benefits from some of the UAE's overall wealth and development, it has not enjoyed the spectacular growth of the richer, oil-producing members of the Federation, such as *Abu-Dhabi or *Dubai. An oil pipeline from the Abu Dhabi-Dubai area to F. and the development of a major oil port in F. is planned, to eliminate the need to ship the oil through the Straits of *Hormuz.

G

Gaddafi See *Qadhdhafi.

Gaza Strip The southern Palestine town of G. — an ancient settlement, named in the Bible as one of the five cities of the Philistines and the site of Samson's death — was a district capital under the British Mandate and the largest exclusively A. town of Palestine. It was mostly Muslim, with a small Christian community (a medieval Jewish community had declined in the 18th century, was revived in 1882, but had left after the disturbances of 1929). In 1948, at the end of the Mandate, its population was c. 40,000; during and after the war of 1948 it grew to over 100,000, due to the influx of refugees from the areas that then became Israel. In the mid-1980s, the town's population is estimated at 130–140,000 — and considerably more if adjacent refugee camps are included.

The region around the town, the "GS", was not, before 1948, an entity or a term in use. It is the area occupied by the invading Egyptian army in the war of 1948 (see *Arab-Israel Wars) — 25 mi. (40 km.) long and 4–9 mi. (6.5–14.5 km.) wide, an area of c. 135 sq.mi (350 sq.km.). The population in 1948 — including G. town — was 70-100,000; during and after the war grew to over 250,000, due to the influx of refugees. In 1967, when the region was occupied by Israel, it was estimated at c. 360,000, and in the mid-1980s at over 500,000, of whom c. 60% or more were refugees from the 1948 war and their descendants (precise figures are in dispute; *UNRWA, the UN Relief and Works Agency for Refugees, has over 400,000 on its registers). The economy of the GS itself could not support and employ so large a population, and from 1948 to 1967 a large proportion was unemployed and entirely dependent on the rations distributed by UNRWA. Since 1967, a growing number have found employment in Israel (about 50% of the labor force) and material conditions as measured in housing conditions and the possession of cars, refrigerators, washing machines and other electrical appliances etc., have much improved.

The Israel-Egypt Armistice Agreement of 1949, based on the positions held by the respective forces at the end of the fighting, confirmed Egypt's occupation of the GS. In contrast to Jordan, which annexed the part of Palestine she occupied, Egypt never annexed the GS; and though she claimed special responsibility for the area — even after 1967, when she was no longer in occupation — she never claimed it as part of her territory. In Sept. 1948, Egypt permitted an attempt to form in G. a "Government of All Palestine", claiming control of all Palestine, including Israel and the Jordan-occupied parts; but the attempt failed, and the "government" soon faded out, though a formal declaration that it had ceased to operate was issued, by the Arab League, only in 1952 (see *Palestine Arabs). Even while that government existed in G., Egypt did not grant it any self-governing control of the GS itself. That was administered by a Military Governor appointed by the Egyptian Minister of War. In 1958 the Governor appointed an Executive Council, including local notables, and a Legislative Council, partly nominated by indirect elections. Little was heard of the activities of these bodies.

Prior to the Suez-Sinai War of 1956, the GS served as a base for raids into Israel by guerrilla-saboteurs (*Feda'iyyin) aided or even dispatched, so Israel thought, by the Egyptian military establishment, and Israel mounted counter-raids; one of them, in Feb. 1955, was later cited by President *Nasser as a major reason for his conviction that no peaceful settlement with Israel was possible. These incursions from the GS were one of the main factors leading to the *Sinai Campaign of 1956, in the course of which the GS was occupied by Israel. When Israel was compelled to withdraw, early in 1957, the GS was returned to Egyptian military administration — contrary to Israel's expectations and to assurances she thought she had received; but a *UN Emergency Force, UNEF, was stationed there. The resumption of attacks from the GS and the concentration of large Egyptian forces, capped by Nasser's request to withdraw the UNEF, were among the chief reasons for Israel's pre-emptive attack of 5 June 1967 and the *Six Day War, in the course of which Israel again occupied the GS.

Since 1967, Israel administers the GS through

a Military Governor, later a Civil Administrator. During the first years of the Israeli occupation, the GS was a center of sabotage and terrorist activity — no doubt because of the large concentration of refugees and the social and economic frustration accumulated in the GS (much more than in the *"West Bank" taken from Jordan); this unrest was suppressed by 1972. Israel also attempted, from 1971–72, to tackle one of the reasons of unrest, by "thinning out" the overcrowded refugee camps and re-housing some of the inhabitants; this was denounced and resisted by some, but accepted by some. During the years of occupation, Israel has established settlements in the GS — some 14, with a population of c. 1,200.

Municipal elections, as held on the West Bank, were not held in G. The Mayor was dismissed in Jan. 1971, and the man appointed to replace him, Rashad al-Shawa, of the GS's chief clan of notables and considered a leading Palestinian-Arab moderate, was himself dismissed in Oct. 1972; he was reappointed in 1975, and dismissed again in 1982, but seems to be accepted by Israel as the chief spokesman for the GS. Political organization is not permitted by the Israel authorities; but it is assumed that part of the population inclines towards Jordan (with al-Shawa as their exponent), part sympathizes with the PLO mainstream (with Fa'iz Abu Rahma leading), and part with the "Rejectionist"-extremist factions of the PLO (led by Dr. Haidar 'Abd-ul-Shafi).

Material improvement, mainly through employment in Israel, has led to a measure of economic development; the economic situation was complicated by the involved political status of the GS. While West Bank produce was freely exported to Jordan, and through Jordan to A. and Persian Gulf countries, similar arrangements for the produce of the GS, particularly its citrus fruit, frequently met difficulties in Jordan.

The future of the GS is highly problematic. Though no Israeli government has officially committed itself, various spokesmen have indicated that even when withdrawing from the rest of the occupied A.-inhabited regions of Palestine (the "West Bank"), totally or partly, Israel would insist on keeping the GS. All A. spokesmen, on the other hand, maintain that the GS must be part of whatever Palestinian-A. entity emerges from a settlement, independent or confederated with Jordan. Some add a demand for an extra-territorial corridor between the GS and the West Bank. Egypt has sometimes informally suggested that the GS be the first region to apply the régime of autonomy agreed between Egypt and Israel; so far, nothing has come of that suggestion. In any case, Egypt does not claim the GS for herself and agrees that it should form part of the Palestinian or Palestinian-Jordanian entity to be created.

GCC See *Gulf Cooperation Council.
Gemayel See *Jumayyil.
Geneva Peace Conference An Arab-Israel "Peace Conference" called after the *October War of 1973, following UN Security Council Resolution 338 of 22 Oct. and mediation by Henry Kissinger, the US Secretary of State. That mediation was needed since both parties to the conflict originally objected to such a conference: the ASt rejected negotiations with Israel as long as Israel had not totally and unconditionally withdrawn from the territories occupied since 1967; and Israel wanted negotiations with each of the ASt separately, and without the direct participation of the UN or outside powers, particularly that of the USSR (the Security Council Resolution had called for peace negotiations "under appropriate auspices"). Eventually, Egypt and Jordan agreed to take part in a peace conference with Israel on condition that talks would not be direct and that other powers would be present. Syria refused to participate, while Israel had anyway refused to sit with Syria until the latter published a list of Israeli prisoners taken in the October War and allowed Red Cross representatives to visit them. The *Palestine A.'s were not invited to attend. The ASt had wanted Britain and France to be invited, but neither the USA and the USSR nor Israel agreed, and outside participation remained restricted to the UN, the USA and the USSR.

The GPC was opened on 21 Dec. 1973, with the Secretary-General of the UN, Kurt Waldheim, in the chair and the Foreign Ministers of the two superpowers, Kissinger and Gromyko, as co-chairmen. As the ASt refused to sit at one table with Israel, separate tables were arranged — with one left empty for a Syrian delegation. Opening speeches were made in public, the press attending and television cameras blazing. The speeches stated the known positions of the parties to the conflict (see *Arab-Israel Conflict) and gave no indication of new openings or progress towards a peaceful settlement. After the ceremonial opening the Conference was adjourned.

An Egypt-Israel Military Committee under the auspices of the GPC began meeting in G. on 26 Dec., with the commander of *UNEF, Gen. Siilasvuo of Finland, as chairman, to discuss an agreement on the separation of forces. But such an agreement was eventually reached, in Jan. 1974, elsewhere, through Secretary Kissinger's "shuttle diplomacy".

The GC has not met again. In recent years, efforts to reactivate ME peace negotiations and call an international conference for that purpose are sometimes termed attempts to reconvene the GC. The ASt, the USSR and some European powers favor its reconvention, but Israel prefers bilateral negotiations (though she does not reject, as clarified in 1985–86, an international conference as an umbrella to accompany direct negotiations), and the USA, not interested at all in re-inviting the USSR to take part in a ME settlement, does not press for another GC. In Sept. 1975 the US also gave Israel assurances that, should a GC be reconvened, she would co-ordinate her positions and the timing of the C. with Israel and ensure that the C.'s terms of reference would not be changed, that substantive negotiations would be bilateral, and that the C.'s purpose would remain "a negotiated peace".

Germany, German interests and policies in the Arab countries G. joined the Great-Power competition relatively late. Prussia had no interests outside Europe, and Bismarck's united G., from 1870–71, avoided acquiring colonies or spheres of influence in the ME or North Africa. Bismarck cultivated G.'s alliance with both Austria-Hungary and Russia, in spite of their rivalry over the Balkans, and avoided any involvement in the "Eastern Question". His removal by Kaiser Wilhelm II brought about the collapse of this system of treaties and launched G. on a course of imperialist competition. The Reich, preferring its Austrian alliance to agreement with Russia, intensified its interests in the Balkans and Turkey. In the 1890s German companies were building railroads in Anatolia, dreaming of a "Berlin-Baghdad axis" to the Persian Gulf, where oil prospecting had just started. Rivalry with Britain was now added to G.'s friction with France and with Russia.

From the turn of the century G., bolstered by a mighty navy, frequently engaged in activist demonstrations of her interests outside Europe. The Kaiser visited the ME in 1899 and stressed G.'s friendship with the Muslim nations. He showed interest in Zionist efforts to obtain a Palestine charter from the Ottoman Sublime Porte and received a Zionist deputation led by Dr. Herzl; however, in view of the Sultan's objections, he abandoned the idea of taking the planned Jewish land company under his protection. Increasingly concerned with G.'s growing strength and her activities in Turkey, Morocco and other sensitive areas, Britain, France and Russia reached agreement on the division of spheres of influence in Africa and Asia (1904–07) and formed an alliance. The race which developed between their *entente* and the Triple Alliance formed by Germany, Austria-Hungary and Italy later led to World War I. G. suffered two heavy diplomatic defeats over Morocco, first in 1905–06, when the preponderance of France's position in that country was recognized by most of the Powers at the Algeciras Conference, and again when the French Protectorate over Morocco was confirmed (1911). The Balkan Wars of 1912–13 increased tension between G. and Russia and deepened G.'s influence on the defeated Ottoman army. The Young Turks now in control of the Sultan's empire turned increasingly to G. for aid.

At the outbreak of *World War I in 1914, G. gave first priority to the European theater, but did her best to strengthen Turkey with arms and experts. G. generals — von der Goltz, Liman von Sanders and Kress von Kressenstein — directed Turkish military operations from Mesopotamia to Gallipoli and helped to mount an abortive Turkish offensive on the Suez Canal (1915). The contest for American public opinion that led England to issue the *Balfour Declaration, 1917, induced G. to consider a similar proclamation on behalf of Zionism, but her hands were tied by her support of the Turkish Empire. In Palestine, itself, during the war years under Cemal (Jamal) Pasha's ruthless rule, G. military advisers exercised a restraining influence.

After the war, G., defeated and rocked by upheavals during the Weimar period (1918–33), was no longer a power able to compete in any extra-European arena, and the upsurge of Hitler's "Third Reich" (1933–45) made no difference to this at first. Nazi Germany's gradual involvement in the ME and North Africa began in the wake of its pact with Italy (1936) and its support of Mussolini's expansionist policies in Ethiopia and East Africa. Palestine was of special interest to the Nazis in view of their intention to expel — and later to exterminate — the Jews; for some years they permitted the transfer of Jewish capital to Palestine under certain conditions. But they hoped that Jewish immigration to Palestine would add to Britain's difficulties in the ME. Nazi G. supported the Palestine A.'s against the Jews and Britain, established secret contacts with their nationalist leaders and enlisted their services as agents and spies. She also began aiding and supporting the A. nationalists everywhere, mounting a large-scale propaganda campaign — mainly anti-British and anti-Jewish — and acquired many supporters and agents throughout the AC, particularly among intellectuals and young officers (see *Fascism).

In *World War II G. became more directly involved in the ME, especially after Italy joined hostilities in 1940 — first in North Africa, where she had to step in militarily to help her Italian ally, and later by support to A. nationalists in Iraq and Syria. In Iraq, the government of Rashid 'Ali al-*Kilani, fighting Britain in 1941, appealed for G. military aid, but this failed to arrive in time. The G.-Italian Control Commission which had installed itself in Syria and Lebanon after the fall of France and established some air bases, tried to come to Rashid 'Ali's assistance, but the quick suppression of the Iraqi revolt and the 1941 conquest of the Levant countries by the British and Free French put an end to the immediate Italo-G. threat.

During the war, pro-G. sentiment and subversion in the AC crystallized into active collaboration. In Egypt, willing collaborators flocked to the G. side from the very start of the war — including a high proportion of army officers, from the Chief-of-Staff, 'Aziz 'Ali al-*Masri (dismissed for his connections with the Axis powers, and arrested while attempting to reach their lines) down to such junior officers as Anwar *Sadat. Quite a number of A. activists escaped to G., particularly after the defeat of the Rashid 'Ali régime in Iraq — Rashid 'Ali himself and the Mufti of Jerusalem, Hajj Amin al-*Husseini (for additional names see *Fascism). Pro-G. sentiment among A. nationalists in North Africa and the ME, already strong under the influence of G.'s initial victories over the British and French, reached its peak with Rommel's 1942 advance to the gates of Egypt. Hitler's anti-Jewish doctrine was a major attraction for many A.'s. Nazi G. made some attempts to deport the Jews of North Africa to death camps, but most of them escaped G.'s "Final Solution" because G. left Italy and Vichy France in political control.

After G.'s defeat in 1945, two separate, rival Gs. arose from the wreck of the Third Reich. East G. became part of the Soviet Bloc, West G. — of the US-led Western alliance, NATO, and the *EEC. In the early 1950s, West G. began to cultivate large-scale economic interests in the AC, particularly Egypt, and to grant considerable aid and credit guarantees. From the late 1940s, dozens, and sometimes hundreds, of G. experts, including known Nazis, worked for A. military industries, especially in Egypt, where they engaged in aircraft and rocket production, as well as intelligence and propaganda in Egypt and Syria. West G. was unable to prevent their departure, or escape, and their activities.

West G. tried to square her ME interests with the special character accorded to her relations with the Jewish people and Israel and the need to atone for Nazi crimes and the horrors of the Holocaust. Israel had put in a claim for compensation or restitution, forwarded to the two G. governments by the Allied Powers. While East G. did not respond to such claims, West G. did, from 1950. In 1952 a Restitution Agreement was signed, giving Israel c. $850 million in goods, mostly G.-made. Another agreement signed simultaneously settled personal claims of Jews for at least some of their despoiled properties and other damages suffered. By 1970, the sum involved about $8,000m., of which $1,500m. went to residents of Israel; 1986 estimates put the total of personal restitution paid at DM 77,000m. (32,000m. to Israelis), and total West G. aid to Israel at about $27,000m. With the signature of the agreements, West G. Chancellor Konrad Adenauer proposed the establishment of diplomatic relations with Israel. But Israel's Premier David Ben-Gurion felt the time for such normalization had not yet come. When Israel was ready for that move, at the start of the 1960s, the Bonn government balked, fearing G. interests in the AC might be harmed and the ASt might retaliate by extending recognition to East G.; to compensate for withholding diplomatic recognition from Israel, Bonn was ready to continue with economic, and later military, aid, while continuing to cultivate her political and trade relations with the ASt. Full diplomatic relations were finally established in 1965 and economic aid was set at $140m. p.a.

In the 1960s, the Soviet Union and East G. launched a concerted effort to obtain A. recognition for East G. and the latter granted large-scale ecoomic aid to Egypt, Syria, Iraq and Algeria and assisted several AC in various fields (particularly security and secret services). However, West G. was bound, under her "Hallstein Doctrine" to break with countries recognizing East G. (except the USSR); the ASt refrained therefore from formally recognizing East G. and establishing diplomatic relations — though they installed consular representations and fostered close *de facto* relations. In 1965, after West G. established diplomatic relations with Israel, all ASt except Morocco, Tunisia and Libya, severed relations with her. By 1974 all had resumed them. In the meantime West G., under Chancellor Willy Brandt, abandoned the "Hallstein Doctrine" in 1969, and foreign countries could now establish diplomatic relations with both West and East G. Nearly all ASt did so. No official relations between East G. and Israel have ever been established.

West G. continues to seek a reasonable balance between her commitment to, and special relations with, Israel and her considerable economic interests in, and desire for close relations with, the ASt. She imposes on herself, for instance, certain restrictions concerning the export of military equipment to the ASt. In her desire to play, perhaps, a positive role in the search for a ME settlement, together with her fellow-members of the *EEC, she takes positions regarded by Israel as rather too pro-A., based on the EEC's "Declaration of Venice" of 1980, such as a strong emphasis on the Palestine A.s' right to self-determination, i.e. a separate Palestine-A. state, and support for the participation of the *PLO in any negotiations. On the other hand, G.'s relations with several ASt are adversely affected by the suspected involvement of these ASt in terror acts perpetrated or planned on G. soil (including an attack during the Munich Olympic Games in Sept. 1972). Yet, G. steers a very cautious course; she denied the USA overt permission to use G. bases and airfields for the US airlift of arms to Israel during the October War of 1973 (though she refrained from public protests when the US did use G. airfields); she refused to join concerted action against Libya as proposed by the USA in 1986; and she gave only half-hearted support to Britain's strong diplomatic reprisals against Libyan and Syrian involvement in terrorism, in 1984 and 1986 respectively, and did not herself fully join them.

Gezira (*al-Jazira*, Arabic: island or peninsula.) The part of Sudan situated between the Blue *Nile and White Nile as they converge. Principal cotton-growing and development area of Sudan. Two British plantation syndicates received concessions, first granted before World War I, elaborated and formalized 1919, to develop and cultivate large areas in the G., through tenants guided and obliged to use modern methods of intensive irrigation and cotton production. Work started in 1925, after the completion of the Sennar Dam on the Blue Nile made perrennial irrigation possible. The area worked by the G. concession reached 400,000 acres in the 1930s. In 1950 the concessions expired and the enterprise was taken over by the government (the pre-independence Anglo-Egyptian administration). A new dam on the Blue Nile at Ruseiris, its first stage completed in 1966, made it possible to enlarge the area cultivated in the G. to over 2m. acres. The number of tenant families settled in the G. passed 100,000 in the 1970s; seasonal employment reaches c. 500,000. (For the Syrian region of the same name see *Jazira).

al-Ghashmi, Ahmad Hussein (1938/39–78) Yemeni officer and politician, President of Yemen 1978. Gh., himself of a leading clan of the *Zeidi Hashed tribal federation, was one of the officers serving as liaison between the post-1962 republican régime and the powerful tribes, but he was frequently in conflict with Sheikh 'Abdullah al-Ahmar, the Hashed federation's chief leader. After Ibrahim *Hamdi's *coup* of June 1974, Lt.-Col. Gh. was appointed Chief-of-Staff, Deputy Commander-in-Chief and member of the Military Command Council. When Hamdi was assassinated, in Oct. 1977 (according to some reports in Gh.'s house, or at least with his collaboration), he became Commander-in Chief and chairman of a three-man Military Command Council. He had to manoeuver between the powerful Zeidi tribal leaders on one side and urban leftist pressures, largely *Shafe'i, on the other. But he was seen as a conservative, close to the tribes and to Sa'udi Arabia. In Feb. 1978 he re-established an appointed "People's Constituent Assembly" that had been abolished by Hamdi, thereby responding to tribal demands; but he did not appoint the chief tribal leaders. Tribal fighting, in Mar. 1978, was seen by some as a rebellion, and in Apr. an officers' *coup* led by his associate on the Command Council, paratroop commander 'Abdullah 'Abd-ul-'Alem, had to be put down. In Apr. 1978, the Assembly decided to replace the Military Council by a Presidential Council and elected Gh. President. Gh. was assassinated in June 1978 by an envoy from South Yemen carrying a booby-trapped briefcase that killed Gh., and its bearer — a bizarre episode apparently connected with the South Yemeni factional in-fighting but never fully clarified.

Ghazi Ibn Feisal (1912–39). King of Iraq 1933–39. Born in Hijaz, the only son of Amir (later King) *Feisal, the third son of Sharif (later King) *Hussein, Gh. became heir apparent to the Iraqi throne when his father was installed as King of Iraq in 1921. He was educated in Iraq, with a brief, unhappy spell in England (Harrow). He succeeded to the throne in 1933, upon his father's death. He married his cousin 'Aliya, daughter of *'Ali ibn Hussein. Gh. was popular in Iraq for his A. nationalism and his reputed hate of the British, but carried little political weight; he had no influence on the officer cliques which succeeded one another as the real rulers of Iraq after 1936. Gh. was killed in Apr. 1939 in a car crash.

Glubb (Pasha), Sir John Bagot (1897–1986) British officer and writer, commander of the Jordanian Army 1939–56. G. served in Iraq 1920–30. In 1930 he went to Transjordan, where he raised Bedouin units within the *Arab Legion, the Transjordanian Army. He became the Legion's second-in-command and from 1939 its commander (from 1948 — Chief of the General Staff), attaining the Jordanian rank of *Fariq* — Lieutenant-General. Although he served Jordan under contract (not seconded from the British Army), the nationalists in Jordan and other AC regarded him as a symbol of British imperialist domination. They blamed him for the limitation of Jordan's military role in the Palestine war of 1948, her non-adherence to A. overall strategic-military plans, and specifically the A. Legion's failure to capture West Jerusalem, the loss of Ramle and Lydda, and Jordan's withdrawal from Umm Rashrash (to become Eilat) near *'Aqaba. As the tide of nationalism rose in Jordan and King *Hussein felt compelled to ally himself with Egypt and Syria, the King abruptly dismissed G. in Mar. 1956. G. retired to Britain. He wrote many books and continued expressing strongly pro-A. views, especially on the A.-Israel conflict.

Golan, Golan Heights Parts of the provinces of Quneitra and Fiq in south-western Syria, occupied since 1967 by Israel. In the Anglo-French negotiations on the Palestine-Syria border, 1920–23, the British claimed parts of the G. for Palestine, and it was agreed in Dec. 1920 that a triangle with its base on the Jordan from Lake Hula to the Lake of Galilee and the Lake itself, and its apex near Quneitra, should be part of Palestine; but in 1922 the British renounced that claim. In Syria, the G. area, never a defined administrative entity, was an economically and socially backward region. Its population by 1967 was variously estimated at 50–100,000 (Syrian spokesmen later claimed higher figures) and included several *Druze, *Circassian and *'Alawi villages.

After the Arab-Israel War of 1948, Syria fortified the GH. Commanding the Lake of Galilee, the Hula area and the upper Jordan Valley, artillery positions often shelled Israeli villages, traffic, the Hula drainage and Jordan diversion projects. In the *Six Day War, 1967, the GH were taken by Israeli forces after intense fighting — an area of c. 720 sq.mi. (nearly 2,000 sq.km.). Most of the inhabitants moved to Syria. Those remaining — 7–10,000 — were almost exclusively Druze; their number was estimated in the mid-1980s at c.15,000. Israel established about 30 settlements with a Jewish population of 8–10,000.

In the *October War of 1973 Syrian forces overran large parts of the G. but were repelled after several days of intense fighting, with Israel forces advancing into Syria beyond the G. and taking an area of c. 600 sq.km. After a "Disengagement" Agreement achieved in May 1974 with US mediation, Israel withdrew her troops from that area and from the town of Quneitra and an adjacent strip held since 1967. A buffer zone was established, manned by a "UN Disengagement Observer Force" (UNDOF), as well as a strip of territory on both sides in which forces and equipment would be limited (see *Arab-Israel Wars and *Arab-Israel Conflict).

Since 1967, Syria and all the ASt have demanded Israel's total withdrawal from the G. and the return of the area to Syria. In Israel, large sections of public opinion and official spokesmen claim the retention of the G. In Dec. 1981 a law was promulgated applying Israeli law to the G. — a measure seen as nearly-formal annexation. Most of the A.-Druze inhabitants have not responded to the invitation to take on Israeli citizenship, and some have actively resisted the order to take out Israeli identification papers, and a measure of tension has developed. On the other hand, as Syria bars infiltration, sabotage or terrorist operations directly from her territory, there have been very few such incidents in the G.

Greater Syria The A.-Syrian Kingdom which Amir *Feisal ibn Hussein tried to establish in 1918–20, and of which he was proclaimed king in Mar. 1920, was meant to include Lebanon and Palestine with Transjordan (Palestine, perhaps, as an autonomous or separate Jewish entity — see *Feisal-Weizmann Agreement), probably to be federated with Iraq in a *Hashemite Federation of the *Fertile Crescent. "S." proper, as she emerged under French tutelage, after Feisal was defeated and expelled, and as she later became fully independent, was confined to a smaller area.

The idea of a "GS", however, persisted. It was fostered by groups of A.-Syrian nationalists and mainly by the Hashemite dynasty, first and foremost by Amir, later King, *'Abdullah of Jordan. As long as the French ruled S., such schemes had little hope of realization. The French always suspected that the GS notion was a British plot to oust them from the area, and many A's also viewed it as a British scheme; but official British support for a GS plan was never more than partial and half-hearted.

During World War II, when it was becoming clear that French rule would not be restored, 'Abdullah revived the GS idea. Public overtures he made to Syrian leaders met negative reactions from many of them. In Nov. 1946, at a public session of Parliament, he declared his intention to work towards the union of "the natural GS", incorporating S., Jordan, Lebanon and Palestine, under his crown; he implied that he would offer the Jews of Palestine an autonomous status within his GS (but did not reveal that he was negotiating with them a secret agreement that went much farther). In 1947 he also published a voluminous "White Paper" on GS.

'Abdullah's scheme had very few open supporters. Among them were a faction of Aleppo politicians from the Syrian "People's Party" and a small group of Damascene politicians (Hassan al-Hakim, Munir al-'Ajlani et al.); some others suported the plan secretly. Publicly, the GS plan was attacked from all sides. Lebanon categorically refused to become part of a Muslim state. The ruling "National Bloc" in independent S. refused to renounce S.'s separate independence and turn her into a province of a Hashemite-ruled kingdom. The Sa'udis opposed any plan that might strengthen the Hashemites, their past enemies who might still dream of reconquering Hijaz. Egypt also opposed a Hashemite-led GS as an undesirable expansion of Hashemite power. Even Hashemite Iraq, nursing federative plans under her own leadership, gave 'Abdullah little support. The *Arab League, dominated by the Egyptian-Sa'udi-Syrian bloc, opposed GS or any other revision in the existing map of the independent ASt. Britain, 'Abdullah's ally and main support, did not really back this scheme of his — fearing both French and A. hostility. 'Abdullah's supporters and agents among the Syrian political factions were few, and their schemes and intrigues had little impact. And the Palestine Jewish leadership told him that despite their general sympathy for him as the only A. statesman planning peaceful co-existence with a Jewish State he could not expect any help from them for the GS scheme. The murder of 'Abdullah in 1951 put an end to the Hashemite GS plan (and the assassination of *Feisal II in Baghdad, in 1958, terminated all similar or alternative Hashemite schemes).

A different, non-Hashemite GS, based on the mystique of a pan-Syrian nationalism, was advocated by a marginal, mainly Lebanese, Fascist-leaning faction — Antoun *Sa'ādeh's *"Syrian Nationalist Party". In its erratic shifts, this group, though anti-Hashemite in its ideology, established some clandestine links with 'Abdullah's agents in the 1940s and 1950s. It was, in any case, without power or influence.

While the GS scheme as such has not been revived, the notion that Lebanon, Jordan and Palestine (or, in view of the existence of Israel, at least its A. part) should be united with, or dominated by, S. seems to be held also by radical S. led by the *Ba'th Party under President *Asad. They apparently do not strive for a straightforward merger of S. with the countries mentioned; but they seem to envisage a Syrian predominance and a far-reaching adaptation or conformity of their policies to Syrian guidance and prescriptions.

Greece, Greeks G.'s involvement in the ME — both politically, and concerning Greek populations — has been principally with Turkey and Cyprus (and is outside the scope of this book). Among the ASt it was only Egypt that had a sizable Greek population, created mainly in the 19th century. In the 1940s, the G. in Egypt numbered c. 120,000, mainly in Alexandria and Cairo. Most of them were employed in trade, banking, the crafts and clerical jobs, and some of them were prominent in business. They retained their Greek nationality and language. Under the radical officers' régime, since 1953, many G. began leaving because of the economic policies of the new régime, the take-over of foreign enterprises from 1956–57, and the nationalization and expropriation measures of 1961. By the 1970s, only a few thousand remained.

G.'s ME policy was largely determined by the need to protect the interests of the Greek minority in Egypt and Greek shipping and trading interests throughout the ASt, as well as to ensure a favorable A. attitude on the Cyprus issue. Thus G. denied Israel *de jure* recognition in 1948–49. She has persisted in a distinctly pro-A. policy and kept her relations with Israel at the level of a "Diplomatic Representative" — even after the disappearance of the Greek community in Egypt. The fact that she has been frequently embarrassed by Palestinian-A. terrorist operations on her soil, sometimes directed against Greek targets and interests, had made no change in her pro-A. policies.

Greek Catholics The branch of the *Greek-Orthodox community that joined the Catholic church *en bloc*, through the *Uniate, retaining a certain autonomy regarding both liturgy and its language, and church and community administration. (In Arabic, GC are *Rum-Katholik*, i.e. Roman-C., while those named Roman-C. in European languages are called *Latin*; the GC in the ME are also called Melchites or Melkites — from Syriac-Aramaic *Melk*, King or Emperor, i.e. State church — a description originally pertaining to the Orthodox church that stuck mainly to the GC).

The Uniate of parts of the Orthodox with the C. church took place in the 18th century — preceded and influenced by Uniates of other eastern communities, such as the *Maronites, and the protection afforded them by France. There are different versions as to precise dates: 1725, 1730, 1775. The new community was persecuted by the Orthodox church, backed by the Ottoman authorities; it was not recognized by the latter, and the first Patriarch appointed by the Holy See had to go into exile. It was only in 1837 that Patriarch Maximos III Masloum was recognized as the head of an independent GC community (*Millet*) and took residence in Damascus. In 1882, a GC Seminary was opened by the White Fathers at St. Anne's Church in Jerusalem and thereafter produced most of the educated GC priests; after Israel took East Jerusalem in 1967, it was transferred to Harissa in Lebanon.

The GC follow, mainly, the Byzantine rite. Those in the ME use Arabic as their liturgical language with a few Greek parts. The Church is headed by the "Patriarch of Antioch and all the East, Alexandria and Jerusalem", whose seat is in Damascus; the Patriarch, usually an A., mostly Lebanese or Syrian, is appointed by the Holy See. The incumbent, since 1967, is Maximos V, Georgios Hakim. There are GC communities in Greece, Cyprus, Eastern Europe and the Balkans, and among migrants in America. Those in AC and Israel, number c. 400,000: Lebanon — 250,000; Syria 90,000; Egypt 30,000; Jordan 5–10,000; and among Israel's A.'s 35–40,000.

Greek Orthodox The eastern branch of the official, main body of the Church of early Hellenistic and Byzantine Christianity, separated since 1054 from the Western, Catholic Church centered in Rome. Also called Melchite or

Melkite — from Syriac-Aramaic *Melk*, King Emperor, i.e. State church — mainly as against the *Nestorian and *Monophysite churches that split from it in the 5th century (but the term Melkite is mainly used for the *Greek Catholics). The main GO communities are in Russia, Greece, the Balkans and Cyprus, and in the European and American diaspora. As to the AC, there are no GO in the North-African West, the *Maghrib*, and very few in Egypt (after the exodus of the large *Greek community), and in Iraq; in Syria, Jordan and Palestine they are the largest Christian community, and in Lebanon — the second largest, after the *Maronites. The number of GO in the AC is estimated at c. 1m.: more than 450,000 in Syria, 3–400,000 in Lebanon, nearly 100,000 in Jordan and the Palestine *"West Bank", and c. 40,000 among the A.'s of Israel.

The GO Church has no overall Head, but comprises "autocephalous", i.e. autonomous, Patriarchates. In the ME there are four: Constantinople, Antioch, Alexandria, and Jerusalem. The Patriarch of Constantinople used to be considered *primus inter pares*.

Until the end of the 19th century, the four Patriarchs and their senior clergy were priests of Greek origin, though the majority of the faithful in the patriarchates of Antioch and Jerusalem were A.'s. Since 1899, however, the hierarchy of the Patriarchate of Antioch, with its center in Damascus, has been entirely Syrian and Lebanese A. (in 1964 and in 1969–70 serious splits between the bishops of the Syrian and Lebanese parts of the Patriarchate were patched up with difficulty). The language of liturgy, originally G., has become mainly Arabic. In the Patriarchate of Jerusalem the Greek character of the senior hierarchy has been maintained, and the A. GO community, supported by the lower clergy, has been struggling for many years to abolish, or at least reduce, that Greek character of their church.

In general, the GO have been considered the Christian community most firmly integrated and active in the A. national movement (as compared with autonomist, even separatist tendencies in the Maronite community for instance).

Gulf Cooperation Council (GCC) An alliance formed in Feb. 1981 by the six ASt on the *Persian Gulf — Sa'udi Arabia, United Arab Emirates, Kuwait, Qatar, Bahrain and 'Oman (but not Iraq) — to foster close economic, political, military, social and cultural cooperation. The GCC, with headquarters at Riyadh, has a permanent secretariat and holds regular meetings, in alternating capitals, of a "Supreme Council" (of the heads-of-state) and a "Ministerial Council" (of the Foreign Ministers). The GCC has been much preoccupied with the Iraq-Iran war and has endeavored to mediate. It tries to avoid openly taking sides in that conflict and to maintain normal relations with both Iraq and Iran, but it tends to accord a greater measure of sympathy and support to Iraq. See *Persian Gulf.

H

Habash, George (b. 1924–25–26?) Palestinian A. guerrilla leader and politician. Born in Lod (Lydda) to a Christian Greek-Orthodox family, H. graduated in Medicine at the American University of Beirut. After the A.-Israel war of 1948 he settled for some years in 'Amman. In the 1950s, he was one of the founders, and the ideological mentor, of the *"Arab Nationalist Movement" *(Harakat al-Qawmiyyin al-'Arab)* — an extreme nationalist, pan-Arab group, largely underground and never endowed with publicly identified leading bodies, that opposed the established A. governments and increasingly adopted Marxist-Maoist doctrines. In 1969 H. was a co-founder of the *"Popular Front for the Liberation of Palestine", an extremist guerrilla/terrorist formation strongly influenced by and connected with the ANM. The PFLP, of which H. has remained the leader, advocates all-out guerrilla war against Israel and opposes a political solution involving compromises.

H. is in bitter rivalry to the mainstream of Palestinian-A. politics and guerrilla/terrorism, led by *'Arafat, and cooperates only partly in their joint roof organization, the *PLO. In an Apr. 1987 reconciliation he rejoined the PLO National Council and Executive. See *PFLP, *Palestine Arab Guerrilla Organizations.

Haddad, Sa'd (1937–84) Lebanese officer. Born in Marj 'Ayoun, South Lebanon, a Christian of the Greek-Catholic community, H. joined the army as a professional officer. In 1976 he was appointed commander of the forces in South Lebanon, with the rank of Major. He strongly opposed the guerrilla/terrorist operations of the Palestinian A. *PLO from Lebanese soil, and its *de facto* control of South Lebanon, semi-secretly cooperated, from about 1976–77, with the Israeli army, and in 1978 assisted it in its occupation of South Lebanon, lasting three months and intended to eliminate the PLO bases. When the Israeli forces withdrew, he established, with their co-operation and aid, a "South Lebanese Army", SLA, to continue preventing the use and domination of the area by the PLO. The force H. commanded was equipped and trained largely by Israel. It numbered 1,500–2,000, mostly Christians (his efforts to recruit also Shi'is, who constitute the majority of South Lebanon's population, had but little success), and controlled a 15–30 km. wide strip of territory along the border. As his operations, and his collaboration with Israel, did not have the approval of the Lebanese high command (virtually non-operative because of the Lebanese civil war) and government (wielding little actual control, with the various regions ruled by rival "militias"), H. was dismissed from the army. He appealed, since he regarded himself as a loyal Lebanese patriot; the matter was never fully clarified, but he and those among his men who were Lebanese army soldiers seem to have continued drawing army pay. In 1979 H. proclaimed a "Free Lebanon" entity in the area under his control; but he apparently regarded that as a symbolic declaration only, for he did not actually establish such an entity, and maintained partial links with the Beirut government or its Christian components. In June 1982, H. and his force collaborated with the invading Israeli forces and took part in the military administration Israel set up in the occupied area. H. died in Jan. 1984 and the command of the SLA was taken over by General Antoine Lahad, a retired Maronite-Christian officer of the Lebanese Army.

Hadhramaut Region in the southern part of the Arabian peninsula, named after its main water-course, Wadi H., which flows south-eastward, for 248 mi. (nearly 400 km.), into the Indian Ocean and serves as the region's agricultural center and trade route. H. — a geographical term, not a political or administrative entity — contained until 1967 four principalities: Wahidi in the west, Qu'aiti and Kathiri in the center and Mahrah in the east, all part of the British "Eastern Protectorate" of 'Aden. H.'s main town and port is Mukalla.

In the 1930s *Ibn Sa'ud laid claim to H. or parts of it. There upon the British, to strengthen their hold, concluded over 1,300 truce and protection treaties with H. tribal chiefs between 1936 and 1939 and put an end to inter-tribal warfare (Harold Ingrams, who directed these operations, wrote several books on the region). The Sa'udi claim was not further pressed. When the British formed the Federation of *South Arabia, from 1959 onwards, Wahidi was the only Eastern Protectorate principality to join it (1962). In Sept.–Oct. 1967, all the H. Emirates were taken over by the *NLF and integrated into the People's Republic of *South Yemen. The Amirs were deposed and H. was divided into districts not identical with the former principalities in order to erase their separate identities and allegiances. H. had a small number of Jews, of whom very little is known. The H. Jewish community seems to have been liquidated in the course of the migration to Israel of the Jews of Yemen and South Yemen, but isolated groups possibly still exist.

al-Hafez, Amin (b. 1920/21) Syrian officer and politician. President of Syria 1963–66. Aleppo-born H. was a NCO in the French-Syrian "Special Forces" and in 1947 graduated from the Syrian Army's military academy. A veteran member of the *Ba'th party group of officers; H. was, after the *Ba'th* took power in the *coup* of Mar. 1963, recalled from his post as military attaché in Argentina to become Deputy Prime Minister and Minister of the Interior in the *Bitar cabinet. He soon emerged as the most prominent leader of the new régime. In July 1963 he became chairman of the Revolutionary Council, i.e. in fact Head-of-State, a post he retained when in May 1964 that body was reshaped as a Presidential Council. Concurrently he was, for some months in 1963, Defense Minister, Commander-in-Chief and Chief-of-Staff, and twice — Nov. 1963 to May 1964 and Oct. 1964 to Sept. 1965 — Prime Minister. In the factional struggles within the ruling *Ba'th* group H., though trying to stay above the factions and keep the régime united, gradually became identified with the "civilian" faction of *'Aflaq and Bitar considered more moderate and "rightist". In Aug. 1965, he ousted Salah *Jadid, the head of the extremist "military faction", from his post as Chief-of-Staff.

In Feb. 1966 H. was overthrown by a *coup* of Jadid's military faction, wounded and imprisoned. He was released in June 1967 and went into exile in Lebanon. There he took part in efforts to organize the ousted wing of the *Ba'th*. In 1968 his faction joined a "National Progressive Front" of several groups opposed to the Syrian régime. As his *Ba'th* wing retained control of Iraq, he moved, with 'Aflaq and others, to that country. In 1968 he was accused, in Syria, of involvement in 1966 and 1967 *coup* attempts and plots by Salim Hatum and tried *in absentia*; however, the verdict in that trial, in Jan. 1969, indicated that H. and some others would be tried separately. In Aug. 1971, he was sentenced to death, with four other leaders of the pro-Iraqi *Ba'th*, all *in absentia* (commuted in Nov. to life prison). H. has remained in Iraq, as a member of the leadership of the pro-Iraqi *Ba'th* wing and its "national", all-A. command. His formal post is not quite clear — in 1970, e.g., it was reported that he had been relieved of his official position (to ease the way for a reconciliation between the rival *Ba'th* wings?). But he remains involved in anti-Syrian activities on behalf of the Iraqi régime and the "National Alliance for the Liberation of Syria", a loose coalition of anti-*Asad factions.

Hamdi, Ibrahim (1939? 1943?–77) Yemeni officer and politician, President of Yemen 1974–77. H., son of a Qadi (Islamic judge) and trained as a Qadi, joined the army after the revolution of Sept. 1962, though the new Republican régime had at first detained him as a suspected Royalist. He held several command posts and served as confidential secretary to Gen. Hassan al-*'Amri, who was in the later 1960s several times Chief-of-Staff and Prime Minister. In Sept. 1971, Prime Minister 'Aini made him Deputy Premier and Minister of the Interior, and late in 1972 he became Deputy Chief-of-Staff with the rank of Lt.-Colonel. In June 1974, H. staged a bloodless *coup*, dissolved the Presidential Council (and the Consultative Council), and formed a new Military Command Council with himself as chairman, i.e. President. He was at that time considered a "Rightist" and closely linked with Sa'udi Arabia. However, in the complexities of Yemeni politics this label did not prove to be wholly fitting. H. did endeavor to foster relations with Sa'udia and managed to obtain increased aid from her, but he also took a "leftist" line in efforts to mend relations with South Yemen; and he clashed with Sa'udia's main allies in Yemen, the tribal federations of the North, and particularly the Hashed tribes who rose in rebellion — and was supported in that policy by the 1976-founded leftist and half-underground "National Democratic Front". In effect, H. was trying to establish himself as a strong leader able to keep both the tribes and the leftists in check. H. was assassinated in Oct. 1977 — together with his brother, Lt.-Col. 'Abdullah Hamdi, the commander of an élite brigade. The identity of the murderers was never established; but many assumed that they came either from the right wing and the tribes or, more probably, from a group of officers plotting for power.

Hasbani (Hebrew name: *Senir*). The northwestern source of the *Jordan River, originating in south-eastern Lebanon, near Hasbayya, about 12 mi. (20 km) north of the Israel-Lebanon border. The springs produce c. 120m. cubic meters (mcm) p.a., with the rains adding flash floods. The H.'s total 130–160 mcm provide about one third of the water carried by the upper Jordan. A small part of its water is used for local irrigation in southern Lebanon, and the abortive Jordan waters agreement of 1954 (the *"Johnston Plan") envisaged expanding that irrigation and reserved 35 mcm p.a. for that purpose. A. plans of 1964–67 for the denial of the Jordan waters to Israel by the diversion of its sources in Lebanon and Syria called for the diversion of the H. waters, partly through a tunnel to the *Litani River in Lebanon and partly in an open canal eastward to the *Baniyas in Syria (and thence, together with the waters of the Baniyas, to the *Yarmuk). These plans were foiled by Israel. See *Jordan River, *Arab-Israel Conflict.

Hashem, Ibrahim (1884? 1888?–1958) Jordanian politician, born in Nablus, Palestine. Prime Minister of Jordan 1931-38, 1945-47, 1955-56, Apr. 1957 (in times of crisis, as a loyal supporter of the King). As Deputy Prime Minister of the 1958 Jordan-Iraq *"Arab Federation" he was assassinated in July 1958 in Baghdad during the Iraqi *coup*.

Hashemite Kingdom of Jordan See *Jordan.
Hashemites, Hashemis, House of Hashem *Banu Hashem* are the family, or clan, of the Qureish tribe to which the Prophet Muhammad belonged. In the 20th century, the name H. has come to refer specifically to the family of the Sharifs of Mecca, from which came the Kings of Hijaz, Iraq, briefly Syria, and Jordan. They are descendants of the Prophet Muhammad through his daughter Fatima and his son-in-law 'Ali, and their son al-Hassan. They thus carry, like all descendants of that line, the title Sharif, and one of them usually bore the honorific Sharif of Mecca.

The Sharif *Hussein Ibn 'Ali (1852–1932) was appointed Amir of Mecca in 1908. In 1916, after obtaining promises of British support through an exchange of letters with Sir Henry *McMahon, the British High Commissioner in Egypt, he staged an *"Arab Revolt" against the Ottoman Empire and proclaimed himself King of Hijaz. In 1924 he took steps to declare himself *Caliph, but this was not accepted by the Islamic world. The same year he was defeated by *Ibn Sa'ud and abdicated in order to save his throne for his dynasty (he died in exile). His son *'Ali (1879–1935) succeeded to the throne of Hijaz, but after less than a year he was driven out by Ibn Sa'ud (he died in exile, in Baghdad). 'Ali's son *'Abd-ul-Ilah (1912–58) was Regent of Iraq, 1939–53; 'Ali's daughter 'Aliya (d. 1950) married King *Ghazi of Iraq.

Two other sons of Hussein founded dynasties. *Feisal (1885–1933) reigned for a short time in Damascus, 1919–20, and was driven out by the French. In 1921, by an agreement with the British endorsed by a sort of referendum, he became King of Iraq and reigned there until his death. His only son, *Ghazi (1912–39), who succeeded him, was killed in an accident. As Ghazi's son, *Feisal II (1935–58), was a small child, his uncle 'Abd-ul-Ilah acted as regent; when Feisal came of age and was crowned in 1953, 'Abd-ul-Ilah became Crown Prince. They were both killed in the July 1958 *coup d'état* in Baghdad, and the Iraqi branch of the H. came to an end.

Hussein ibn 'Ali's second son, *'Abdullah (1882–1951), was made by the British in 1921 Amir of Transjordan — a state they established for him in the framework of their *Mandate for Palestine. In 1946 he obtained full independence, took the title of King, and changed the name of Transjordan to "The H. Kingdom of Jordan". He re-emphasized the new name in 1948, when he occupied the A. part of Palestine, the *"West Bank" (formally annexed in 1950). 'Abdullah was assassinated in 1951 at the al-Aqsa Mosque in Jerusalem. His son *Talal (1909–72) succeeded him, but was deposed in 1952 when found to be mentally ill; he was hospitalized in Istanbul and died there. Talal's son *Hussein (b. 1935) has ruled Jordan since 1953 and has grown into one of the major statesmen of the ME. The crown prince is his younger brother Hassan (b. 1947) rather than his brother Muhammad (b. 1945). The eventual succession of Hussein's own sons might pose a problem, since only one of them — 'Ali (b. 1975) — was born from an A.-Jordanian-Muslim mother, while the mothers of two older and two younger sons were, though converted to Islam, of foreign origin (see table). In 1978 'Ali was named (second) Crown Prince, after the King's brother Hassan.

The leadership of the H. dynasty stood at the cradle of A. independence in the *Fertile Crescent after World War I with British assistance. When H. plans to found a single kingdom, or a federation of kingdoms, failed and the region was divided into separate states under British and French tutelage, the H. found themselves reigning (apart from Hijaz, until 1924) in two countries: Iraq and Jordan. The idea of reviving the original scheme and establishing a H.-headed kingdom or federation, and mainly to bring Syria, as well as Lebanon and Palestine (or at least its Arab part), under their domination, continued to animate some of them. 'Abdullah was the chief protagonist of this plan (see *Arab Federation, *Greater Syria, *Fertile Crescent). The Iraqi branch had similar plans in a different version, and its support for 'Abdullah's scheme was always in some doubt. Most ASt always opposed both versions, particularly Egypt, Syria, Lebanon and Sa'udi Arabia, and their opposition prevailed. British support for these H. plans was doubtful and at best partial; yet the French, and many A.'s, always suspected British plots behind them. These revisionist-expansionist schemes of the H. faded away after the assassination of 'Abdullah in 1951 and that of Feisal II and 'Abd-ul-Ilah in 1958. Another aim of the H. was perhaps to return to Hijaz and rule it; though this idea was sometimes broached, it never had serious prospects, and it was finally shelved in the late 1940s and the 1950s, when a H.-Sa'udi *rapprochement* took place.

The H. kings and princes were loyal allies of the British (perhaps with the exception of King Ghazi of Iraq, but he died too young to have much impact on the policies of his country). This

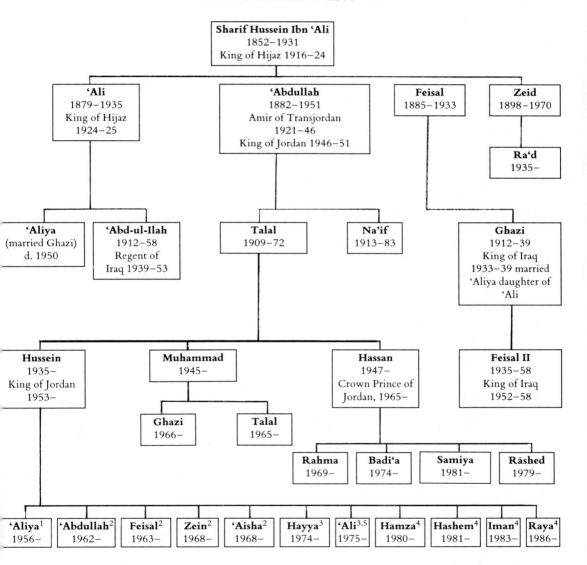

THE HASHEMITE DYNASTY

[1] Mother: Dina 'Abd-ul-Hamid al-'Awn, from another H. branch, whom Hussein married in 1955 and divorced in 1957.
[2] Mother: Tony Gardiner (after converted to Islam: Muna), whom Hussein married in 1961 and divorced in 1972.
[3] Mother: 'Aliya Touqan, whom Hussein married in 1972; died in 1977.
[4] Mother: Lisa Halabi (after converted to Islam: Nur-al-Hussein), whom Hussein married in 1978.
[5] Named in 1978 (second) Crown Prince after Hassan.

loyalty, and the fact that the very rule of the H. was arranged by the British, made them suspect for many A. nationalists who regarded them as collaborators or stooges of Britain (and, after the eclipse of the British Empire, of the USA). Some of the H. were also prepared to envisage an agreement and co-operation with a Jewish-Zionist Palestine and later with Israel, and actively to work for it — from the *Feisal-Weizmann Agreement of 1919, through 'Abdullah's long-standing friendly contacts with the Zionist leaders, his secret agreement with them in 1946–47 and his negotiations and (abortive) draft agreement with Israel in 1949–50, to Hussein's readiness, in principle, to accept peace and co-existence with Israel and his secret contacts with her several times. This attitude has made the H. further unpopular with radical A. nationalists.

The H. clan has several branches apart from the line of Sharif/King Hussein and his sons, and many of their members held state positions in Iraq. Thus Sharif Sharaf (1879/80–1955) was appointed Regent when the Rashid *'Ali régime deposed 'Abd-ul-Ilah in 1941; when that régime fell, he was interned and after the war went to Jordan, where he was named a Senator. Many held, or still hold, positions in Jordan — in the army, the Court, civil service and political posts. Among them, Sharif Hussein bin (ibn) Nasser, (1906–82), married to a daughter of King 'Abdullah, Ambassador, Chief of the Royal Court, and twice Prime Minister, 1963–64 and 1967. Sharif Nasser bin (ibn) Jamil (1927–79), born and educated in Iraq, an officer in the Iraqi army, later rose to senior position in the Jordanian army; Minister of the Royal Court 1961–63, Commander-in-Chief 1969–70, dismissed upon the demand of the Palestinian guerrillas (his sister married King Talal and became the mother of King Hussein). Sharif 'Abd-ul-Hamid Sharaf (1939–80), the son of the Iraqi ex-Regent Sharaf, Minister of Information, Ambassador to the USA and the UN, Prime Minister 1979–80; his brother Fawāz (b. 1938), Ambassador to the USA in the 1970s, Minister of Culture and Youth 1976–79. Sharif Zeid bin (ibn) Shaker (b. 1934), Commander-in-Chief of the Jordanian armed forces since 1976. Ra'd bin (ibn) Zeid, King Hussein's AdC, belongs to Sharif Hussein's direct line, being the son of the Sharif's youngest son Zeid (1898–1970), who never played a prominent role. King Hussein also took his first wife, Dina, in 1955, from the distant 'Awn branch of the H. clan (he divorced her in 1957).

Hassan II (b. 1929) King of Morocco since 1961. The eldest son of *Muhammad V, Ibn Yussuf, the Sultan (from 1959: King) of Morocco, Prince H. (also bearing, according to Moroccan custom, the honorific "Moulay"), received a French and Arabic-Muslim education at a college founded in 1941 for his and his brother's schooling, and later studied law at Bordeaux University. He became a close collaborator of his father the Sultan, but was reputed to sympathize with the nationalists. In 1953 he accompanied his father into exile in Madagascar and returned with him to Morocco in Nov. 1955, towards independence. In July 1957 his father appointed him Crown Prince; he also formally headed the armed forces as Chief-of-Staff. In May 1960 the King, assuming the Premiership himself, named Prince H. Deputy Prime Minister. In Feb. 1961 H. succeeded to the throne upon King Muhammad's death. He retained the Premiership until 1963 and resumed it from 1965 to 1967; after the attempted *coup* of Aug. 1972 he assumed the command of the armed forces and made himself Defense Minister (until 1973). King H.'s rule was conservative, but he introduced, after several attempts and experiments, a modern constitution of representative government and endeavored to keep leftist-nationalist factions within the establishment, sometimes as partners in coalition governments. He overcame two serious military *coup* attempts in July 1971 and Aug. 1972 and had to face a great deal of social tension and ferment, and sometimes subversion. Several times he resorted to harsh measures to suppress leftist factions and what he considered their subversive plots. His vigorous nationalist policy over the *Sahara issue, since the mid-1970s, seems to have made him much more popular even with leftist groups.

King H.'s foreign policy was also conservative — except for a brief demonstration of radical tendencies in the early 1960s (the *"Casablanca Bloc"). He fostered close relations with France and the USA. In inter-A. affairs, he kept Morocco within the moderate-conservative camp, and his relations with *Nasser's Egypt and the rest of the radical camp were sometimes tense; this applied particularly to Algeria where relations were troubled, in addition to Algeria's radical orientation, by border disputes and basic conflicts of interest (e.g. over Sahara), and Libya (despite the brief abortive confederate union with that country, 1984–86). King H. demonstrated his independence of thought by secretly aiding the preparations for Egyptian President *Sadat's peace moves in 1977 (though he felt compelled to join the other ASt in 1979 in severing relations with Egypt). He also showed his non-conformist moderation on the A.-Israel issue by permitting a measure of relations between the Jews of Morocco and Israel, by allowing visits of Israelis to Morocco, including public figures, and inviting Premier Peres of Israel to Morocco for talks in 1986.

Hatay See *Alexandretta.

Hawatma, Na'if (b.1934) Palestinian-Jordanian guerrilla/terrorist leader. A Christian born in Jordan, H. is a Marxist-Maoist. He was active in the extremist *"Arab Nationalist Movement" (al-Qawmiyyun al-'Arab) in the 1950s and 1960s and the *"Popular Front for the Liberation of Palestine" (PFLP) that grew out of it after 1967, and headed their Left wing. In 1969 H. set up his own organization, the *"Popular Democratic Front for the Liberation of Palestine" (PDFLP).

Heykal, Muhammad Hassanein (b. 1923) Egyptian journalist, writer and politician. After studying in Egypt (journalism, economics, law), H. worked as a reporter for several Egyptian papers (*Egyptian Gazette; Rose al-Yussuf*), reporting *inter alia* the desert campaign in World War II and the Greek civil war. He became prominent reporting the Palestine War of 1948 for *Akhbar al-Yawm*. In the early 1950s he was editor of *Akher Sa'a* weekly and later co-editor of the daily *al-Akhbar*, of which he became chief editor in 1956–57. After the revolution of 1952, he came close to *Nasser and his associates, and in 1957 was appointed chief editor of al-*Ahram, Egypt's most prestigious daily, considered the semi-official mouthpiece of the government. Gradually, H. became Egypt's most influential journalist and a close adviser and confidant of President Nasser. In 1970 he served for a few months as Minister of Information and National Guidance. H. was a loyal "Nasserist", identified with the régime, but kept, and was permitted to keep, a large measure of independent political thinking. According to his own account, he advised Nasser not to rely on an alliance with the Soviet Union exclusively but to cultivate better relations with the USA and the West, too, and also advocated a more liberal régime, a larger measure of democracy, press freedom etc. In the factional struggles within Nasser's team he was thus considered a right-winger.

After Nasser's death, in 1970, he soon fell out with President *Sadat — despite their personal friendship. Remaining a Nasserist, he denounced Sadat's deviation from, or betrayal of, Nasser's heritage. He opposed Sadat's all-out alliance with the USA; and he disapproved of Sadat's peace-making with Israel and the ensuing rift between Egypt and the ASt. In 1974 he was dismissed as editor and chairman of *al-Ahram* and barred from publishing his articles in the Egyptian press. In 1977–78 he was subjected to interrogations by the police and the state attorney, and for some months was denied the right to go abroad. In Sadat's Sept. 1981 purges he was detained, but was released later in the year by Sadat's successor, President *Mubarak. As he could not publish in Egypt, he began in 1975–76 publishing articles and regular columns in foreign newspapers, and from 1971 also published, in the West, several books on Egyptian and ME politics — and became well-known in the West.

While H. has not regained, under Mubarak's régime since late 1981, either his major influence on policy planning and decisions or his leading position in the Egyptian media, he seems to be on his way to resuming at least part of his activity in both fields. He is sometimes mentioned as a possible mediator between Egypt and her adversaries among the ASt (e.g. Libya).

Hijaz The western region of Arabia, since 1925 part of the Sa'udi Kingdom. H. extends from the Gulf of *'Aqaba and the border of Jordan to *'Asir, to a length of over 800 mi. (almost 1,300 km.) and a width of up to 200 mi. (320 km.). Area: 120-150,000 sq.mi. (320-390,000 sq.km.). Of the estimated population of 2-3m., more than half were nomads in the past, but in recent times many, perhaps most, have left the nomadic ways. Chief towns: Mecca, Medina, Jidda (Sa'udi Arabia's chief port on the Red Sea), Ta'if (a summer resort in the mountains), Yanbu' (an ancient small port recently developed and combined with an industrial estate, and the outlet of an oil pipeline from the Persian Gulf). H. consists of a narrow coastal plain, and a mountainous plateau inland, both largely barren, cultivation being possible only where water is available, near springs and wadis.

Since ancient times, a trade and caravan route, the "Frankincense Road" follows an inland line of depressions, with several oases, from South Arabia to the "Fertile Crescent" and Damascus. This road also was the main pilgrimage route to Mecca and Medina, and along it the Ottoman Turks built the *Hijaz Railway (in disuse since 1917). In recent years, a network of modern highways connects the main cities.

H. was part of the *Ottoman Empire from 1517, but effective Turkish rule was maintained chiefly in the holy cities Mecca and Medina and efforts were made to secure and control the pilgrims' route there and the coast. In the interior, authority was in effect in the hands of the tribal chiefs. The local *amir*, the Sharif of Mecca (of the *Hashemite clan), enjoyed a degree of autonomy, but his authority was limited. For Sharif Hussein Ibn 'Ali's revolt of 1916; his Kingdom of H., 1916–25; his defeat by *Ibn Sa'ud and the incorporation of H. in the Sa'udi Kingdom see *Arab Revolt, *Hussein Ibn 'Ali, *Hashemites. After the conquest of H., Ibn Sa'ud assumed the title "King of H. and Sultan of Najd" in 1926, changing it in 1927 to "King of H. and Najd" (until 1932, when the Kingdom was renamed "The Sa'udi Arabian Kingdom"). H. was at first administered as one unit and its governor, the King's son *Feisal, was given the title Viceroy. But later H. was divided into several provinces and disappeared as an administrative unit.

Hijaz Railway A 807 mi. (1,290 km.) long railway connecting Damascus in Syria with Medina in Hijaz, built in 1900-08 by Ottoman Turkey, with the help of German engineers. Its official purpose was to transport Muslim pilgrims to Mecca, and about a third of its £ 3m. cost was covered by contributions from the Muslim world. It may be assumed that the HR's chief initiator, Sultan *'Abd-ul-Hamid, also considered strategic-political aims and intended the HR to help consolidate his rule and prevent rebellion in the Arabian peninsula. He kept it out of the range of naval guns by building it not along the coast but in the interior, following the ancient caravan route, the "Frankincense Road". After the revolution of the "Young Turks" (1908), the HR was not completed, as planned, as far as Mecca and Jidda. A branch line was constructed to the Mediterranean, linking Der'a' in southern Syria to Haifa. During World War I, the guerrillas of the *"Arab Revolt" sabotaged the HR and destroyed many parts. It has never been fully repaired and only parts of it, in Syria and Jordan, are in use. Since the early 1950s, Sa'udi Arabia, Jordan and Syria have drafted joint programs to repair the whole HR and resume operation. International tenders were issued and contracts signed, and preliminary work was begun; but due to political and financial difficulties (cost estimates rising to $ 2,500m. or more), repair work has not progressed.

Hinnawi, Sami (1898? 1904–1950) Syrian officer and politician. In Aug. 1949, a colonel, he staged a *coup* against President Husni *Za'im, executed both Za'im and his Prime Minister Muhsin al-Barazi, and appointed himself Chairman of the Revolutionary Council and Chief-of-Staff. He allowed political activity to resume and in Nov. 1949 held elections. He was close to the "People's Party" *(Hizb al-Sha'b)* and encouraged its participation in the government. He initiated closer relations with the *Hashemite kingdoms, Jordan and especially Iraq, and was suspected of planning a union of Syria and Iraq. H. was deposed, in another *coup*, by Adib al-*Shishakli in Dec. 1949, and arrested; but he was soon released and allowed to leave for Beirut. There he was murdered in 1950 — reportedly in revenge for the killing of al-Barazi.

Holy Places Most places sacred to Islam are in the AC and Palestine. The city most holy to Muslims is Mecca, in the Hijaz, the birthplace of the Prophet Muhammad and the site of the Mosque of the Ka'ba (with the sacred black rock venerated since pre-Islamic days). One of the five main precepts of Islam is to make a pilgrimage *(Hajj)* to Mecca at least once. The second-holiest city is Medina (al-Madina), also in Hijaz, where the Prophet took refuge and where he is buried. Third is *Jerusalem *(al-Quds)*; there, on the Temple Mount *(al-Haram al-Sharif* — the Noble Sanctuary), stand *al-Masjid al-Aqsa* ("The Farthest Mosque") and the Dome of the Rock (also incorrectly called the Mosque of 'Omar). According to Muslim tradition, the Prophet was miraculously transported to this place, thence to ascend to heaven in the "Night of Ascension" (*Lailat al-Mi'raj*), while his winged horse, *al-Buraq*, remained tied to the Western Wall; this tradition, considered by some as post-Qur'anic in its main elements, emphasized the ties of Islam with Judaism and Christianity and created a custom of making a pilgrimage to Jerusalem, too. The Tomb of the Patriarchs in Hebron (*al-Khalil*) is also venerated by Muslims, particularly that of Abraham (*Khalil Allah*, "God's Friend"); a mosque, *Haram al-Khalil*, built in the 7th century on earlier, ancient foundations, enshrines the burial cave.

The Shi'i branch of Islam venerates as a HP also the tomb of Hussein, grandson of the Prophet, in Karbala in Iraq, near where he fell in battle, and its mosque. Another Shi'i HP is al-Najaf in Iraq — according to Shi'i tradition the site of the tomb of 'Ali, Muhammad's son-in-law and the fourth Caliph. Two additional towns in Iraq, al-Kazimain and Samarra, contain the tombs of later heads (**Imam*) of the Shi'a and are places of pilgrimage and centers of Shi'i-Islamic learning (so are al-Mashhad and Qum in Iran).

Muslim masses in most of the AC and Palestine also venerate many tombs of sages, prophets, saints, holy men — many of them legendary; many of them have their memorial days (*mawsim*, pl. *mawāsim*), when processions and memorial ceremonies are held; in Palestine, many of these sites and tombs are connected with biblical names and traditions. The Islamic establishment has never formally sanctioned this veneration of tombs, but neither has it ever denounced or banned it.

The *Druze venerate the tomb of Nabi (the Prophet) Shu'aib, their legendary ancestor identified with biblical Jethro the Midianite, Moses' father-in-law, at Hittin in Israel. Additional Druze HP are the tombs of Sheikhs 'Abdullah al-Tanukhi at 'Abayya in Lebanon, 'Ali al-Ya'furi on the Golan, Nabi Sablan near Hurfeish and al-Khidr near Kafr Yassif, both in Israel. The *Baha'is venerate the tombs of their creed's founders at Haifa and Acre in Israel.

For Christians, all of Palestine/Israel is the Holy Land. About 100 sites associated with events related in the Christian scriptures are considered specifically HP's, and churches were built on most of them. The most important HP's are in Jerusalem: the Church of the Holy Sepulchre at the traditional site of the Crucifixion and the Tomb of Jesus; the Via Dolorosa, with its stations; the Cenacle (the Room of the Last Supper), on Mount Zion; the Mount of Olives, with the Tomb of Mary, the Garden of Gethsemane and the Church of Ascension. In Bethlehem, there are the Church of the Nativity and the nearby Shepherds' Field, in Nazareth — the Catholic Basilica of the Annunciation, and the Church of St. Gabriel held by the Greek-Orthodox to be the site of the Annunciation. Other HP's in Galilee include the Church of Cana, the place of Christ's first miracle, and Mount Tabor, the site of the Transfiguration. The Lake of Galilee is associated with several miracles performed by Jesus and churches and chapels near its shore mark scriptural episodes such as the Sermon on the Mount and the multiplication of loaves and fishes. The River Jordan, the site of the baptism of Jesus, is considered sacred.

Several of these HP's are jointly owned by different Christian denominations and are the object of conflicting claims — thus the Church of the Holy Sepulchre, the Church of the Nativity, the Tomb of Mary and the site of the Ascension. The ownership of and worship at such sites, which created much inter-denominational conflict, are regulated by the *status quo* of 1757, as defined in 1852 by a Firman of the Ottoman Sultan. The British Mandatory Government, Jordan from 1948 to 1967, and Israel since 1967, adhere to the *status quo* (except for the Deir al-Sultan monastery adjacent to the Holy Sepulchre, in dispute between the Copts and the Ethiopians — which was handed by a Jordanian court to the Ethiopians, in 1950, returned to the Copts by King Hussein, overruling the court, then seized by the Ethiopian monks in 1970, with the acquiescence of the Israel Government; the case has been before the Israel Supreme Court and also appears in Egypt-Israel negotiations, with Egypt backing the Copts' claims for the restoration of their status).

For Jews, too, all the Land of Israel is The Holy Land. Especially sacred is the Temple Mount in Jerusalem, barred to Jewish worship; the adjacent Western (or Wailing) Wall is the only part of the site at which Jews pray. Jews also venerate the Tomb of the Patriarchs in Hebron and of Rachel near Bethlehem, the alleged Tomb of King

David on Mount Zion (sacred also to Muslims and Christians), as well as several tombs of ancient and medieval sages (such as Rabbi Shim'on Bar-Yohai in Meron, Maimonides and R. Me'ir Ba'al Haness in Tiberias etc.).

The Western Wall (and, to a lesser degree, the Tomb of the Patriarchs in Hebron) caused Jewish-Muslim, and Israel-A., conflict. Since June 1967, all HP are, under Israeli rule, accessible to all. However, the conflict over the HP's of the Temple Mount is by no means settled. A. Muslims — and most non-A. Muslims as well — cannot acquiesce in the occupation by Israel of Islam's third HP (though Israel allows the Temple Mount to be administered by a Muslim institution); and as most A. Muslims are citizens of countries in a state of war with Israel, they make no use of the right to visit that Israel would grant them (as she grants it to A.'s who cross the "open bridges" from Jordan). Moreover, Jewish fanatics and extremist groups clamor and scheme for taking actual possession of the Temple Mount, and A. Muslims are concerned lest an Israeli government acquiesce in such schemes or even adopt and support them.

Hormuz, Straits of The straits connecting the *Persian Gulf with the Gulf of 'Oman and the Arabian Sea — named after the town and island of H., close to the Persian shore, which served from 1594 to 1622 as a main center of Portuguese trade and naval control. The S. are bordered in the north by Iran, and in the south by *Ras Musandam, an exclave belonging to 'Oman. Their width at the narrowest point is 35 mi. (56 km.), or, if measured from the Persian shore islands, 24 mi. (37 km.). The S. are within the territorial waters of either Iran or 'Oman, as both claim territorial waters of 12 mi. The main shipping channel is closer to the 'Omani shore.

The SoH are the main thoroughfare for most of the Persian Gulf oil and before the Iran-Iraq war an oil tanker used to pass through them every 10–15 minutes, with nearly 20m. barrels per day, almost half of the oil consumed by the non-Communist world. The security and defense of the freedom of shipping through the S. were therefore vital. For threats to this security in the 1960s and 1970s and in the Iraq-Iran War since 1980, and the involvement of Iran and the great powers, see *Persian Gulf. A US-'Oman agreement of 1980 on defense cooperation and facilities for the US does not specifically refer to the SoH, though it includes US aid for the development of defense and naval installations in 'Oman's Ra's Musandam province and may be assumed to aim at the strengthening of the defense of the S.

Plans to circumvent the SoH by the construction of oil piplines to loading points beyond them have been thus far only partly realized. Sa'udi Arabia built a pipeline from her oil fields on the Gulf to Yanbu' on the Red Sea (opened in 1982); but with a capacity of 1.85m. barrels p.d., this pipeline takes care only of part of the Sa'udi production (the more so as part of its capacity has been put at Iraq's disposal). Plans for a pipeline across the *UAE's peninsula (formerly *Trucial 'Oman) that would enable oil to be loaded on the east coast of that peninsula, beyond the SoH, have not yet materialized.

Hourani, Akram (b. 1914) Syrian politician, lawyer and journalist. Vice-President of the UAR, 1958–59. Born in Homs, H. was active in various nationalist organizations. During World War II, he went to Iraq and reportedly participated in groups preparing and assisting Rashid *'Ali's seizure of power in 1941. In 1943 and 1947 he was elected to Parliament, profiling himself as a campaigner for agrarian reform and a defender of the oppressed tenants against the big landlords. For some time he edited a newspaper, *al-Yakza*. In 1948 he volunteered for service with *Qawuqji's "Army of Deliverance" against emerging Israel and saw action in Galilee. In 1949 H. supported all three military *coups* — first Husni *Za'im's, then *Hinnawi's against Za'im, and finally *Shishakli's. Under Hinnawi, late in 1949, he was re-elected to Parliament and served as a Minister in Hashem al-*Atassi's government. Under Shishakli, he was Minister of Defense in Khaled al-*'Azm's government. In 1949–50, he belonged to a loose "Republican Bloc" in Parliament, but in 1950 he founded his own party, the "Arab Socialist Party". That party merged in 1953 with the "Arab Renaissance Party" (*al-*Ba'th) and H. became, with *'Aflaq and *Bitar, one of the top leaders of the united "Arab Socialist *Ba'th* Party". He fell out with Shishakli and went into exile to Lebanon. In 1954, after Shishakli's fall, H. was re-elected, and in 1957 became President of Parliament. He was one of the architects of Syria's union with Egypt, 1958, and was named Vice-President of the *United Arab Republic (UAR) and Minister of Justice, Syria's top representative in the new union's government. But, together with his *Ba'th* colleagues, he soon became bitterly critical of the new Egyptian-dominated régime and its chief leader, *Nasser, and late in 1959 he resigned. After Syria's secession and the disbandment of the UAR, 1961, H. opposed the *Ba'th* party's efforts for renewed, federal union with Egypt. He left the party and, elected in Dec. 1961 on his own, local Homs list of candidates, tried to re-establish his Arab Socialist Party. During the *Ba'th* officers' *coup* of Mar. 1963 he was arrested, and when released went into exile to Lebanon. He has not returned to Syria since, but has been cultivating his faction in exile, as a potential alternative to Syria's military *Ba'th* régime, joining, since 1968, with various like-minded factions in an exiled "National Progressive Front".

Hussein Ibn 'Ali, Sharif (1852? 1853/54?–1931) Sharif of Mecca; King of *Hijaz 1916–24. A *Hashemite descendant of the Prophet Muhammad and hereditary bearer of the title Sharif of Mecca, H. was kept for years under surveillance in Istanbul by Sultan *'Abd-ul-Hamid. After the revolution of the Young Turks, 1908, he was allowed to return to Mecca and appointed Amir of Mecca. There was rivalry between him, *Ibn Sa'ud in *Najd, and the House of *Rashid, the chiefs of the Shammar tribes in Ha'il.

In 1914, H. contacted the British High Commissioner in Cairo to enquire about British help for a revolt against his Turkish-Ottoman sovereign. These contacts were renewed in 1915, when the British, engaged in war with Turkey, had become more interested in such a revolt. Apart from military and financial help for the rebellion itself, H. demanded a promise of independence for "Arabia". The British agreed in principle, but had reservations concerning H.'s territorial demands (see *McMahon-Hussein Correspondence); they also envisaged the future independent A. state or states tied to some British tutelage or protectorate. Without reaching a clear, written agreement, H. and his sons *'Ali, *'Abdullah and *Feisal in June 1916 launched the *"Arab Revolt", guerrilla operations against the Turks in Hijaz. He received British military and financial help, and his forces later advanced into Transjordan and Syria as the right wing of the British and allied forces under General Allenby.

At the end of World War I, H. sent his son Feisal to represent him at the Paris Peace Conference, where he was informally recognized as the chief spokesman for A. nationalist claims. Since his demands were not completely satisfied, and in protest against inter-allied imperial schemes, as embodied in the *Sykes-Picot Agreement, and the imposition of *"Mandates" instead of complete independence, H. refused to endorse the peace treaties. He also rejected, in 1920/21, British proposals for an Anglo-Hijazi treaty, including British aid and guarantees against outside attack, since he refused to endorse the arrangements made in Syria, Iraq and Palestine. As to the latter and Zionism, H. at first endorsed Feisal's readiness to reach an agreement and cooperate with the Zionists — see *Feisal-Weizmann Agreement — but later changed his mind. H. also refused to send delegates to a British-initiated conference in Kuwait, 1923, called to settle border problems in the Arabian peninsula. He thus threw away, step-by-step, Britain's vital support and protection and remained politically isolated.

In 1919/20, armed clashes erupted between Hijazi and Najdi-Sa'udi tribesmen, and H.'s Hijazis suffered defeat; H. was saved from a total débacle by British intervention with Ibn Sa'ud. After Turkey abolished the *Caliphate in 1924, H. proclaimed himself Caliph. He had not obtained the agreement or support of any major Islamic leader, and the proclamation was unrealistic; it caused consternation and anger among many Muslims, and especially among his Sa'udi-*Wahhabi neighbors. In Sept. 1924, the Sa'udis attacked, and H. was defeated. After the capture of Ta'if he abdicated in favor of his oldest son 'Ali, hoping thus to save the kingdom of Hijaz for his family. But in Oct. the Sa'udis took Mecca, and H. escaped to 'Aqaba ('Ali could not hold his kingdom and fled late in 1925). H. was taken by a British naval vessel to Cyprus and lived in exile there or with his son 'Abdullah in Transjordan. He died in 'Amman in 1931 and was buried in Jerusalem, in the precinct of the *Haram al-Sharif* (the Temple Mount).

Hussein bin (Ibn) Talal (b. 1935) King of Jordan. Born in 'Amman and educated at Victoria

College (Alexandria); and at Harrow, and Sandhurst Military Academy, in Britain, H. succeeded his father *Talal in 1952, when the latter was dethroned because of a mental illness. As he was a minor, a Regency Council ruled for him until May 1953, when he came of age and was crowned.

H. ascended to the throne at a time of crisis and had, in the first four years of his rule, to make important concessions to nationalist-"Nasserist" groups, concerning both internal and, mainly, foreign affairs. Thus he agreed in 1954 to an amendment of the constitution enabling parliament to dismiss the government by a simple majority. In Dec. 1955 he had to withdraw a decision to adhere to the *Baghdad Pact, bowing to politicians of the opposition and popular demonstrations. In 1956 he dismissed General *Glubb, the British commander of his army, who was viewed by A. nationalists as a symbol of Jordan's subservience to British imperialism. When a leftist-nationalist "National Socialist Party" won the elections of Oct. 1956, the King had to appoint its leader, Suleiman al-Nabulsi, as Prime Minister. Under this new régime he approved Jordan's adherence to an Egyptian-Syrian Defense Pact and Joint Command, and early in 1957 the abrogation of the Anglo-Jordanian Treaty and the replacement of British aid, particularly for his army, by Egyptian, Syrian and Sa'udi subsidies.

In 1957, however, H. halted the integration of Jordan into a Leftist-Nasserist bloc. He dismissed the leftist government — a step triggered by the government's decision to establish diplomatic relations with the USSR (which was then considered a "leftist" departure from traditional policies, though it later became normal, accepted policy). He averted, by a courageous personal confrontation, a subversive, apparently Egyptian-supported, officers' plot, reinstated conservative governments and army leaders and re-established a *de-facto* alliance with the West. In Feb. 1958, faced by the merger of Egypt and Syria, H. took a determined stand against what he conceived as a move to expand the power of the leftist-Nasserist ASt and acquire domination of the A. world. He created the Jordan-Iraq *"Arab Federation" and became its Deputy-Head. When that Federation collapsed in July 1958, as a result of the *coup* in Iraq, and Jordan felt isolated and threatened by *UAR intervention aided by subversion, H. asked Britain to send troops to protect Jordan; they stayed until Oct. He also complained to the UN Security Council against the UAR.

H. succeeded in preserving his throne in spite of numerous plots sponsored by Egypt or Syria. His relations with Nasser's Egypt fluctuated. Sometimes, in the course of vitriolic mutual propaganda attacks, Nasser called H. a traitor and imperialist stooge with whom progressive A. leaders could not cooperate; at other times, when currents of inter-A. unity were emphasized, H. was the noble king of an A. sister country. In May 1967, in the frenzy of Nasser's escalating preparations for war against Israel, H. signed a defense treaty with Egypt — no doubt under heavy pressure, and on terms imposed by Nasser — and symbolically placed his army under Egyptian command. He disregarded Israel's warning and promise not to attack Jordan and entered the *Six Day War — misled, as he describes in memoirs (taken down and published by two journalists), by Nasser informing him of a victorious Egyptian advance.

Jordan's defeat in that war and the loss of the *"West Bank" were a heavy blow to H. His position was also undermined by the Palestinian-A. guerrilla organizations, their operations against Israel from Jordanian soil and their violation of Jordanian sovereignty, creating a state-within-the-state. For the Jordan-PLO crisis that culminated in 1970, see *Jordan, *PLO. When H. completed the elimination of the PLO in spring and summer 1971, he was denounced and reviled in most of the A. world and Jordan's relations with several ASt were disrupted. Syrian troops actually invaded Jordan in Sept. 1970, but were halted by Jordanian resistance — and the threat of US and Israeli intervention.

Jordan's relations with the ASt, and H.'s standing in the A. world, were rebuilt only gradually in the 1970s. H. tried to resolve the basic contradiction between his claim to the Israel-occupied "West Bank" as part of his kingdom and Palestinian-A. claims to independence by proposing a federal or confederal structure for the future Jordan, after Israel's withdrawal, with a measure of autonomy for the Palestinian part of the kingdom. He first did so publicly in Mar. 1972, but the idea was not well received at the time; Egypt even severed diplomatic relations on account of it. During the *October War, 1973, H. decided not to join Egypt and Syria in full-fledged war, a decision that was co-ordinated with and accepted by the two countries; but he sent an armored brigade to help Syrian forces — a contingent that arrived rather late, when the tide of war had already turned and Israeli forces were battling inside Syria. After the war, US-mediated talks on a "Disengagement Agreement" with Israel, similar to those Israel concluded with Egypt and Syria, failed. The gap between what Israel offered in the way of a token withdrawal and what H. regarded as a minimum requirement even for a interim agreement was too wide. In Oct. 1974, H. had to acquiesce in a decision of the all-A. summit at Rabat to reaffirm the Palestinian A.'s' right to self-determination and to recognize the PLO as their sole legitimate representative.

H. was considered a moderate in international and inter-A. affairs and concerning Israel. While he did but little openly to educate A. public opinion and guide it towards co-existence with Israel, and while his political positions changed frequently in tactical shifts, he seemed to seek a settlement based on peaceful co-existence. He had numerous secret meetings with Israeli leaders in the 1960s and 1970s, but the gap was always too wide to make an agreement possible. He insisted on complete Israeli withdrawal from the West Bank, including East Jerusalem, and even if he was ready to make some territorial concessions, those were far removed from whatever Israeli leaders demanded or proposed (e.g., the *"Allon Plan"). He continued the *de facto* co-existence of Jordan and the occupied West Bank ("Open Bridges", controlled movement of West Bank A.'s to and from Jordan, economic and trade links, aid for West Bank A. institutions, contacts with West Bank leaders, and not very intense efforts to influence West Bank public affairs); but even on interim arrangements — autonomy for the West Bank A.'s?, joint Jordanian-Israeli supervision? — he could reach no agreement with Israel.

While H. was considered pro-US, his relations with the US were strongly influenced and often irritated by US efforts to achieve progress towards Israel-Jordan peace and by H.'s hesitations and tactical shifts, his inability to take bold decisions and respond to America's pressing proposals. A particular irritant was the supply of American arms, several times decided and prepared by the US administration but reduced or even blocked by a Congress responsive to Israeli objections and the influence of a pro-Israel lobby. In his irritation, H. several times indicated that he would acquire arms from the Soviet Union. He visited Moscow in 1967, 1976, 1981 and 1982, and in 1981 concluded an arms deal.

H.'s relations with the leaders of the ASt remained complex and subject to tactical shifts (for details see *Jordan). Since 1984 he was fostered particularly close relations with Egypt's President *Mubarak. H.'s *rapprochement* with the PLO and his Feb. 1985 agreement with *'Arafat, abrogated in Apr. 1987 by the PLO, mainly because of its provisions for a joint approach to negotiations on a ME peace settlement, are described in the entries *Jordan and *PLO.

H.'s relations with the US were, in the 1980s, determined by the ups and downs of these negotiations about negotiations. H. had informally accepted the "Reagan Plan" of Sept. 1982 and committed himself to negotiate a peace settlement jointly with a Palestinian-A. delegation. He had several times assured the US that he could bring 'Arafat to agree to this course — but he was unable to live up to that assurance, and he made it clear that, contrary to US and Israeli hopes, he would not negotiate alone, or with Egypt only, and without PLO endorsement.

In home affairs, H. succeeded, since the upheavals of 1957, and after overcoming in 1970–71 the danger posed by the PLO to his kingdom, in maintaining a stable, orderly régime and impressive economic development. His régime was liberal and formally parliamentary — with Parliament suspended from late 1974 until Jan. 1984 (see *Jordan). But it was evident that King H. alone led his country. Jordanian media foster a strong personality cult of the King, but he seems to be genuinely popular. H. is also internationally highly respected — a standing which, being an excellent speaker, a master of public relations and an attractive media personality, he carefully nourishes.

H. married four times and has eleven children. His wives: a. his distant relative Princess Dina 'Abd-ul-Hamid (1955; one daughter; divorced in 1957); b. Antoinette Gardiner, daughter of a

British army officer, converted to Islam and named Muna al-Hussein (1961; two sons, two daughters; divorced 1972); c. 'Aliya Touqan, daughter of the prominent official Baha-ul-Din Touqan (1972; one daughter, one son; killed 1977 in an accident); d. Lisa Halabi, daughter of a prominent American businessman of Lebanese origin, converted to Islam and named Nur al-Hussein (1978; two sons, two daughters) (see genealogy table appended to entry *Hashemites). As Crown Prince, H. in 1965 named his younger brother Hassan (b. 1947) — and not the middle brother Muhammad (b. 1945) or one of his own elder sons (whose mother was of foreign origin) — with his third son 'Ali (b. 1975) as Crown Prince after Hassan.

Hussein-McMahon Correspondence See *Mc Mahon -Hussein Correspondence.

Hussein (al-Tikriti), Saddam (b. 1937) Iraqi politician, the strong man of Iraq since 1970–71, President since 1979. A Sunni Muslim born in the town of Tikrit, north-central Iraq, H. joined the *Ba'th party underground organization as a youth and served it as an organizer of its strong-arm squads. He was involved in plots against the royal *Hashemite régime and was imprisoned in 1956. He continued subversive activities under the *Qassem régime after 1958. In Oct. 1959, he was involved in an attempt on the life of Qassem and escaped, first to Syria and then to Egypt (where he reportedly completed his secondary education). He returned to Iraq in 1963, after Qassem was toppled in a coup, and soon joined the Ba'th leadership, named in 1963 a member of its "regional", i.e. Iraqi, command and in 1965 also of the "national", i.e. all-A. one; in 1966 he became Assistant Secretary General of the Iraqi Ba'th. In 1964, after President *'Aref turned against the Ba'th, H. was arrested, but escaped in 1966; he was pardoned later the same year.

After the Ba'th coup of 1968, H. rose to a top position of power. In Nov. 1969, retaining his post as Assistant Secretary General of the Ba'th, he became Deputy Chairman of the Revolutionary Command Council, the ruling body of the Iraqi state; and since the chairman and President, A.H. al-*Bakr, was not a strong ruler, H. in fact ruled Iraq. In the factional struggles inside the Iraqi Ba'th, H. headed the "civilian" or "party" faction against the "military" one. Having grown within the party apparatus and, in contrast to many other Ba'th leaders, with no military background, he postulated the undisputed primacy of the party. From 1970–71 he built an armed party militia and a strong secret service under party control (in fact: his own). Helped by this Ba'th apparatus, H. from 1968 to 1971 systematically "purged" the state and party establishment, and public and political life, eliminating his rivals and adversaries one after the other — first non-Ba'th elements, "rightists" and "reactionaries" (whom he accused of plots and attempted coups in May 1969 and Jan. 1970), then Ba'th "extremists" (e.g. those opposing the agreement he reached in 1970 with *Kurdish autonomist rebel leaders), and finally the Ba'th military faction and other rivals within the Ba'th (such as Hardan 'Abd-ul-Ghaffar, S.M. 'Ammash, 'Abd-ul-Karim al-Sheikhli). In June 1973 he suppressed a coup attempt by Nazem Kazzar, the head of his own security apparatus. Reportedly he had himself instigated Kazzar to plot against Bakr, but abandoned him when the plot failed.

From about 1971, H. ruled Iraq virtually as the chief and only leader, with Bakr as a near-figurehead. He completed his take-over of total power in July 1979, when Bakr resigned for reasons of ill health or, in effect, was forced to abdicate, and H. was named Secretary-General of the Ba'th, chairman of the Revolutionary Council and President of Iraq. H. accompanied the dismissal of Bakr with another bloody purge of the Ba'th command, executing, after a summary trial, 21 leading functionaries, including five members of the Revolutionary Council, and jailing 33 more. As sole leader since 1979, H. is glorified by an incessant personality cult.

H.'s methods of struggle were thus particularly ruthless, even brutal. Yet in his policies, both internal and external, he was pragmatic, with frequent tactical shifts and a capacity to adapt to changing circumstances. Despite his identification with the "party faction" he preserved, in the long run, a delicate party-army balance. He followed, sometimes, a remarkably moderate line towards the Kurdish autonomist rebels. It was H. who pushed through, in Mar. 1970, an agreement with the rebels conceding many of their demands and granting them a large measure of semi-autonomy. Yet when the Kurds rebelled again, he vigorously suppressed them in 1974–75 and used his 1975 accord with Iran to crush them. Simultaneously, he continued implementing the Kurdish semi-autonomy as he perceived it. He tried to widen the political base of his régime and in 1973 formed a "Progressive and Patriotic National Front" in which the Communists and a Kurdish faction collaborating with the government joined the Ba'th; but in 1977–78 he again suppressed the Communists. He suppressed extremist-fundamentalist pro-Iranian Shi'i organizations, but managed to prevent a general uprising or widespread resistance of the Shi'i half of the population. He held, for the first time since 1958, elections for a National Assembly, in June 1980 and Oct. 1984, with a single list of candidates endorsed by him and his apparatus.

H.'s foreign policies, too, were rather pragmatic, as evident in Iraq's alliance with the Soviet Union; her *rapprochement* with the West, since the mid-1970s; her 1975 agreement with Iran; her secession from the *Rejection Front; and her *rapprochement* with the mainstream and moderate ASt and even with Egypt — see *Iraq for details.

Since 1980, H. has been wholly immersed in the Iraq-Iran war — a war for which he is held responsible and which he leads, assuming even the supreme military command (he had himself made a General in 1976). Iran, too, holds H. personally responsible and demands his dismissal and trial as a war criminal as a pre-condition for any peace or cease-fire negotiations. Yet, despite the hardships of the war, the large-scale destruction, the stupendous casualties (and the fact that H. has no doubt numerous enemies in Iraq), his leadership seems to be firm, stable and uncontested.

al-Husseini Prominent A. family in Jerusalem, claiming descent from the Prophet Muhammad and therefore Sharifian standing (though its members do not use the title *Sharif*). A member of the H. clan was *Mufti of Jerusalem in the 17th century, and several bore the title *Naqib al-Ashraf* ("Chief of the Prophet's Descendants") of Jerusalem. Since the 18th century members of the family have held high office, particularly that of Mufti. Hassan al-H., Mufti 1789–1809, was succeeded by Taher al-H. (d. 1866). Mustafa al-H. (d. 1868), Mufti in the mid-19th century, was succeeded by his son Taher (1842–1908), Taher by his son Kamel (d. 1921), Kamel by his stepbrother Muhammad Amin al-*H. The H. clan also accumulated extensive landed property, mainly in the villages northwest of Jerusalem and Ramallah. Its members held many administrative posts in Ottoman-ruled Palestine, including several times that of Mayor of Jerusalem: Salim al-H. in the 1880s and 1890s, his son Hussein Salim al-H. (d. 1918) 1909–18, and his younger son Mussa Kazim al-*H. 1918–20. Sa'id al-H. (1878?–1945), Jerusalem Mayor 1902–06, was elected in 1908 and again in 1914 as one of the three deputies of the Jerusalem district in the Ottoman Parliament.

The most prominent members of the H. family in this century were Hajj Amin al-H., Mussa Kazim al-H. and Jamal al-H. (see entries). Among many others active in public life, the following might be mentioned: Ishaq Mussa al-H. (b. 1908), one of the few Palestinian-A. writers who attained some all-A. literary prominence; Munif al-H. (1899–1983), active in nationalist organizations, in the early 1930s edited the organ of the H.'s' political party (see below); Dr. Mussa 'Abdullah al-H. (1904–51), also active in nationalist organizations, went during World War II to Nazi Germany; when apprehended after the war, he was detained by the British in 1946 in Rhodesia; after his return, he co-organized the assassination of King *'Abdullah and was tried, found guilty and executed. Dr. Dawud al-H. (b. 1904), active in nationalist organizations and the rebellion of 1936–39, was captured by the British in Iraq in 1941 and detained in Rhodesia; after his return, he was involved in the assassination of King 'Abdullah, put on trial but acquitted, and later became a member of the Jordanian Parliament (1956, 1962); in 1965 he was reported to be a member of the *PLO executive (?); in 1967 he stayed in East Jerusalem and took part in efforts to organize the A.'s in the Israel-occupied areas and set up a Jerusalem Muslim Council; in 1968 he was expelled to Jordan; in 1970 he served briefly as Minister of Economy in the Government of Jordan. Rafiq al-H. (b. 1909), Amin Yussuf al-H. (b. 1918?), Muhyi-ul-Din al-H. (b. 1930) also were Ministers in Jordanian governments. Tawfiq Saleh al-H. (1884–1952), a brother of Jamal al-H., was acting chairman of the H.'s "Palestine Arab Party", 1944–46, in the absence, abroad, of the top leaders, and from Nov. 1945 until Jamal al-H.'s return in Mar. 1946 a member of the renewed Arab Higher Committee. Raja'i al-H. (b. 1902) served from 1945 in the Palestine-Arab information or propaganda offices established by Mussa al-*'Alami with a group of younger intellectuals; after the 1948 defeat he was a Minister in the abortive "Government of all Palestine" in Gaza, and later went to Sa'udi Arabia to become a senior official in her service. 'Abd-ul-Qader al-H. (1907/08–48), a son of Mussa Kazim al-H., in the early 1930s organized a "Congress of Educated Muslims", to fight against discrimination in government service. He was one of the few scions of notable families actually to join guerrilla/terrorist squads and became a commander of the guerrillas in the Jerusalem area both in the rebellion of 1936–39 and in the guerrilla phase of the war of 1948; he was killed in action in Apr. 1948. His son, Feisal (b. 1940), set up an "A. Studies Center" in East Jerusalem in the 1980s; he is considered close to the hard-line wing of the *Fatah and the *PLO. Fawzi Darwish al-H. (1898–1946) was an exception to the usual political orientation of the H. clan: he advocated an accommodation with the Zionists and in 1946 set up an A. "New Palestine" association to cooperate with the (Jewish) "League for Jewish-A. Friendship and Cooperation"; he was assassinated in Nov. 1946.

From the 1920s to the 1940s, the name al-H. came to denote not only an influential clan, but — mainly owing to the dominating influence of Hajj Amin al-H. and the Supreme *Muslim Council he headed — a political camp. The supporters of Hajj Amin and the Council were called *Majlisiyyin* — "Council Men", while the opposing camp was called *al-Mu'aridin* — "The Opposition"; but many simply called the *Majlisiyyin* "H.'s" (and their opponents *Nashashibis", after the prominent family heading that camp). When the *Majlisiyyin* founded, in 1935, the "Arab Palestine Party" as their political instrument, it was also often called "The H.'s". The dominating influence of the H. clan, and the political camp it represented, declined and virtually disappeared after 1948 (as did the dominating influence of other clans among the Palestine A.'s and the perception of clan loyalty as a decisive political-factional determinant). There is a prominent al-H. family also in Gaza; it is not related to the Jerusalem H.'s.

al-Husseini, Hajj (Muhammad) Amin (1893? 1895? 1897?–1974) Palestinian-A. politician and religious leader. H.'s education included a year at the Jewish French "Alliance" school in Jerusalem, one year at the al-*Azhar Islamic College in Cairo under Sheikh Rashid *Rida (without graduating), and some time at the Ottoman-Turkish school of administration in Istanbul. During World War I he served as a junior officer in the Turkish army. After the British and allied forces took Palestine, 1917–18, he was recruiting officer for Amir *Feisal's army of the *"Arab Revolt", and later an official in the provisional British military government. At the same time he became active in nationalist organization and agitation. He was president of the "Arab Club" (*al-Nadi al-'Arabi*) in Jerusalem, one of the two main associations of nationalist youth, which saw Palestine as part of an all-Syrian unity. He incited and headed anti-Jewish riots in Apr. 1920, was tried *in absentia* by a military court and sentenced to 10 years imprisonment, but escaped. In Aug. 1920 he was pardoned by the High Commissioner who had just begun establishing his administration.

In Mar. 1921, the *Mufti* of Jerusalem, Kamel al-H., H.'s stepbrother, died. H. offered his candidacy, but was not among the three candidates nominated under Ottoman law by a small body of voters, one of whom the government was to choose and appoint. However, after considerable pressure by the H. family and its supporters, as well as by some senior British officials, one of the three candidates nominated withdrew in H.'s favor, and in May 1921 the High Commissioner appointed H. as *Mufti*. The British apparently wished to keep a balance between the rival clans: the position of *Mufti* had long been held by the H. family, and that of Mayor of Jerusalem had just been taken from them and given to a notable of the rival *Nashashibi family. H. had also assured the High Commissioner that he would exercise his prestige and that of his family to keep Jerusalem quiet.

To the position of *Mufti*, a post carrying much prestige and spiritual and social influence, but no actual power, H. soon added another post with greater power potential. The British Mandatory Government deemed it inconvenient and improper to administer the communal and religious affairs of the Muslims, as the Ottoman Sultan, being Muslim, had done, and therefore in Dec. 1921 decreed the creation of a five-member

"Supreme Muslim Council", to be indirectly elected following Ottoman procedure. In Jan. 1922 the Council was elected — with H. as its president. He chairmanship of the Council, with its considerable income from and control of the *Waqf* (endowments) and its authority over all appointments of Muslim clerical functionaries and staff, gave H. much power. He used it to advance his clan's and his faction's influence and to fight his opponents among the Palestine A.'s, the Zionists, and the National Home policy of the *Mandate and the Government. He fostered the Muslim character of Jerusalem and the position of its two great mosques, and injected a religious character into the struggle against Zionism. This was the background of his agitation concerning Jewish rights at the Western (Wailing) Wall that led to the disturbances of Aug. 1929.

From the late 1920s, H. became the most important political leader of the Palestine A.'s, though he left the nominal chairmanship of the declining Arab Executive to Mussa Kazim al-*H., who died in 1934, and entrusted Jamal al-*H. with the day-by-day leadership of his faction. His politics were hard-line and extremist. In Apr. 1936, he formed an Arab Higher Committee and became its chairman. As such, he was the chief organizer of the riots of 1936 and the rebellion from 1937, as well as the mounting internal terror against A. opponents. In Oct. 1937, H. was dismissed by the government from his position as President of the Supreme Muslim Council, which was disbanded, and the Arab Higher Committee was outlawed. H. escaped to Lebanon and Syria, where he continued to direct the Palestinian-A. rebellion. In 1939 he went to Iraq, where he was close to Rashid 'Ali al-*Kilani and the pro-Nazi army officers and assisted them in their revolt in 1941. When that revolt was put down, H. escaped to Italy and Nazi Germany, where he was welcomed as a leader of anti-British A. nationalism, received by Hitler and accorded an honored position. He aided the Nazi war effort as propagandist, mobilizing Muslim public opinion throughout the world, and recruiting Muslim volunteers for the German armed forces from Bosnia and Yugoslavia.

After the war, H. was detained by the French army but escaped and in June 1946 went to Egypt. He was not allowed to return to Palestine, but was appointed by the *Arab League to be chairman of the renewed Arab Higher Committee it set up for the Palestine A.'s (Jamal al-H. actually headed the Committee, but its presidency was kept "vacant" for H.). He began organizing the final struggle of the Palestinian A.'s against partition and the emergence of a Jewish state. Actually, the ASt by now financed, equipped and directed that struggle. H. saw them only as providers of the help without which the fight could not be mounted, while claiming for himself supreme leadership, but the ASt were unwilling to grant him that position, and a great deal of half-concealed tension ensued. In the final stuggle, before the war of May 1948 and the invasion of Palestine by the regular A. armies, H. exerted some influence on the fighting in the Jerusalem area, where his relative 'Abd-ul-Qader al-H. commanded the guerillas, but he was unable to gain control of the general battle, and even less so after May 1948.

After the defeat of 1948, H. tried to form a "Government of all Palestine" in Egyptian-occupied *Gaza, but that body — welcomed at first by Egypt as an instrument to frustrate Jordan's annexation of the A. half of Palestine — failed to gain any influence on the course of events and was dissolved after a few years of shadow-existence. Attempts to create in Gaza some Palestinian-A. autonomous entity under Egyptian rule were also not welcomed by Egypt. H., still residing in Cairo, established an alternative residence in Beirut and in 1959 went to live there permanently. He endeavored to keep alive, or revive, the Arab Higher Committee and to continue sabotaging the Jordanian annexation of the A. part of Palestine, the *"West Bank", but the Committee, and H.'s own influence, continuously declined, particularly after the foundation of the *Palestine Liberation Organization (PLO) in 1964 (which H. and his Higher Committee opposed). H. spent the last decade of his life as a respected refugee, hardly involved in public or political affairs and with no influence on them.

al-Husseini, Jamal (1892? 1894?–1982) Palestinian-A. politician. Educated at the Anglican St. George school in Jerusalem and the American University of Beirut, where his medical studies were interrupted when World War I broke out in 1914. After the war, H. served in the British military administration, as an official in the Health

Department and assistant to the Governors of Nablus and Ramla. From 1921 to 1934 he was secretary to the Arab Executive headed by his uncle Mussa Kazim al-*H. and in this capacity joined, i.a., the delegation sent to London for negotiations in 1930. In 1928–30 he was concurrently Secretary of the Supreme *Muslim Council headed by Hajj Amin al-*H. After the disintegration of the A. Executive he organized the political framework of the H. faction, the "Palestine Arab Party", founded in 1935, appeared as editor of its organ al-Liwa' and represented it on the Arab Higher Committee set up in Apr. 1936 to lead the rebellion; he was the right hand of its chairman Hajj Amin. When the Higher Committee was outlawed and some of its members were arrested, in Oct. 1937, he escaped. In Feb. 1939 he was permitted to head the Palestinian-Arab delegation to the London Round Table Conference despite the arrest warrant. In 1940–41 he was active among Palestinian-A. exiles in Iraq and supported Rashid 'Ali al-*Kilani's anti-British revolt. When the revolt of 1941 was put down, he escaped to Iran, but was caught by the British and detained in Rhodesia. He was released in late 1945 — a measure that led his faction to agree to the establishment of a new Arab Higher Committee, though he himself was still barred from Palestine.

In Feb. 1946 H. was permitted to return to Palestine and assume the leadership of his party and set up a new Higher Committee (as "acting" chairman, as the chairmanship was kept vacant for exiled Hajj Amin). His factionalism, however, and the packing of the Higher Committee with his supporters, caused resentment and a split, and his opponents formed a rival committee. In June 1946, the *Arab League intervened, disbanding both committees and forming a new one. H. was again named vice-chairman, for the absent Hajj Amin. He acted as chief spokesman for the Palestine A. cause and represented it before the 1946–47 Committees of Inquiry. From 1946 he led the A.'s of Palestine towards violent armed resistance to the partition of the country and the foundation of a Jewish State. For that purpose he reorganized paramilitary youth squads, al-Futuwwa. During the war of 1948, he was in Cairo, Damascus and Beirut, endeavoring to direct the Palestinian-A. fighting forces, but he and his party and his Higher Committee failed in their efforts to maintain their leadership. After the defeat, H. was Foreign Minister in the abortive "Government of all Palestine" set up in Gaza in Sept.–Oct. 1948 (see *Palestine Arabs, *Arab-Israel Conflict). He continued his efforts to keep alive the Higher Committee, in exile, and reimpose its leadership, but had little success. He later went to Sa'udi Arabia and joined her service as a senior adviser, while in fact retiring from political activity. Al-H. wrote many articles and also two political novels, On the Hijaz Railway, and Thurayya.

al-Husseini, Mussa Kazim (1850–1934) Palestinian-A. administrator and politician. The son of Salim al-H., Mayor of Jerusalem, H. was trained at the Istanbul School of Administration and joined the Ottoman service, rising to the position of governor (Qaimaqam, Mutasarrif) of various sub-districts in Palestine, Lebanon, Anatolia and the Arabian peninsula. He retired on the eve of World War I. In Mar. 1918, the British military administration appointed him Mayor of Jerusalem, to replace his brother Hussein who had died. He pledged to stay out of politics. He did not, however, honor that condition and was dismissed.

Husseini became a political leader when he was elected, in December 1920, at the third Palestinian-A. Congress, as President of the Arab Executive then formed — a position he held until his death. From 1921 to 1930 he headed all four Palestinian-A. delegations sent to London to negotiate with the British government and persuade it to abandon the *Balfour Declaration and its commitment to the foundation of a Jewish National Home. He co-determined the Palestinian-A. leaders' decision to reject British proposals for a Legislative Council and home rule institutions — until 1929, when he agreed to the formation of a Legislative Council (but the riots of Aug. 1929 prevented the implementation of that proposal). In the late 1920s and early 1930s his leadership weakened, and his Arab Executive declined; it faded away after his death. H.'s son 'Abd-ul-Qader became prominent as a guerrilla leader in the rebellion of 1936–39 and again in 1948–49.

I

Ibadiyya, Ibadis Unorthodox Islamic sect which grew out of the *Khawārij* (Kharijite) sect of the 7th century. The Khawārij rebelled against evolving Islamic laws and practices of governance and succession, in both their Sunni and Shi'i versions, and were suppressed. Their I. heirs gradually became a separate sect — principally in the Arabian peninsula and the *Maghrib (North-West Africa). They survived mainly in *'Oman, where they form the majority of the population and their doctrine is the state religion. In the 1950s, their *Imam rebelled against the Sultan, and was suppressed — see 'Oman. Small groups of I. also exist in Libya, Tunisia and Algeria, as well as in countries reached by migrants from 'Oman, such as Tanzania.

Ibn Sa'ud (1876? 1880?–1953) The name by which 'Abd-ul-'Aziz Ibn 'Abd-ul-Rahman Aal (i.e. of the House of) Sa'ud, King and founder of Sa'udi Arabia, was best known. His ancestors, of the 'Anaiza tribe, had ruled parts of *Najd, but IS grew up in exile in Kuwait (see House of *Sa'ud). In 1902 he recaptured the town of al-Riyadh and re-established the rule of the Sa'udi dynasty in Najd. In 1913 he conquered the al-Hassa region on the Persian Gulf, and his territory thus came within the sphere where Great Britain had negotiated a series of treaties imposing her protection on the rulers of the A. coastal sheikhdoms. In a 1913 Anglo-Ottoman draft convention Britain still recognized the Sa'udi Amirate as part of the Ottoman Empire; but the outbreak of World War I changed the situation, and in Dec. 1915 Britain concluded a treaty with IS recognizing him as ruler of an independent Najd and Hassa (in fact under a veiled British protectorate; later in 1916 Britain agreed to pay him a monthly subsidy of £5,000).

During World War I, Britain encouraged IS in his fight against the pro-Turkish Rashidis, but was content with his benevolent neutrality in the war. After the war, in 1920–21, IS defeated the Rashidis and incorporated their territory into his domain, calling himself, from 1921, Sultan of Najd and its Dependencies. For his victory over the *Hashemite Sharifs of Mecca, in 1924, and the expansion and consolidation of his rule, from Jan 1926 as "King of Hijaz and Sultan of Najd, al-Hassa, Qatif and Judail and their Dependencies", and from 1927 as "King of Hijaz and Najd", and the constitution of his realm as "The Sa'udi Arabian Kingdom" in 1932, and his war with Yemen in 1934 — see *Sau'di Arabia. IS was, in the 1930s, not very active in inter-A. affairs. In 1936 he was, as arranged by the British, one of the A. rulers who induced the A.s of Palestine to end their general strike, promising them to aid their struggle, and in 1939 the British government got him officially involved in the Palestine issue, by inviting him to send delegates to the British-A. Round Table Conference. Unofficial British go-betweens (e.g. H. St.J.B. Philby) also put him, in 1939, in indirect contact with Jewish-Zionist leaders, in search for a solution to the Palestine problem, but nothing came of these contacts. In World War II, IS kept Sa'udia neutral. For his growing ties with the USA, and US oil interests, and his role in the foundation of the *Arab League, 1945, and inter-A. politics — see Sa'udi Arabia.

IS ruled his kingdom as an autocrat, consulting the princes of his dynasty and the tribal sheikhs in the traditional manner, but reserving decisions to himself. He permitted no modern representative political institutions to develop and refrained from formalizing constitutional governance, basing his rule on Islamic laws and traditions. He kept the unruly tribal chiefs — whom he had to suppress in the late 1920s by armed force — under strict control, by paying them subsidies, keeping their sons at his Courts and marrying their daughters to his sons. The tribal unrest was in part linked to a rebellion by Wahhabi "Brethren" *(Ikhwan)*, suppressed by 1929. IS continued enforcing strict Wahhabi Islam, but discontinued his initial efforts to establish a nucleus of armed Wahhabi "Brethren" in colonies. IS permitted little economic or social modernization, except for the development of the oil industry by the American "Aramco" company — which began to make the country, and the royal family, immensely rich, and which triggered a process of development and modernization that came to fruition after IS's days; he introduced, despite the rule of Wahhabi-Islamic law, increasingly luxurious ways of life which bred a measure of corruption among the dynasty and the ruling class.

IS had several wives and over 40 sons; 31 sons of legitimate full-status wives survive in the mid-1980s, in line for the succession. IS strictly controlled the large royal family and determined his succession, appointing his eldest surviving son, *Sa'ud, in 1932, as crown prince and successor, with *Feisal next in line.

Idris, King   See *Sanussi, Muhammad Idris.

Idrissi, Idrissiyya   A dynasty, and an Islamic sect or school. The I.'s, a clan or dynasty of North African origin, claiming descent from the Prophet Muhammad, the Khalifa 'Ali and the Moroccan I. dynasty (789–974), gained political power and religious influence in the region of *'Asir in Arabia (between Hijaz and Yemen) in the mid-19th century, under Ahmad al-I. He founded a Muslim school or order (*Tariqa*), similar to *Dervish orders in its structure and appearance but traditional and fundamentalist in content and influenced by the *Wahhabis. The I. state in 'Asir gained a brief semi-independence early in the 20th century, and near-complete independence in the 1920s, but was annexed by Sa'udi Arabia in 1933, and the I. dynasty lost its position. The I. school or sect has gained no significant influence in Islam.

Ifni, Sidi Ifni   Former Spanish possession in Morocco handed over in 1969. See *Morocco.

Imam   In Sunni Islam, the I. is the head of a mosque, a leader in prayer, and often also a preacher (in the larger mosques there is, separately, a preacher — *Khatib* or, in some cases, *Wa'iz*).

In Shi'i Islam, the I. is the head of the Muslim community (*Umma*) and, in theory, the ruler of its realm. He must be a descendant of the Prophet Muhammad through his daughter Fatima and his son-in-law 'Ali. Shi'i Islam gradually came to attribute to the I. mysterious, superhuman qualities. According to the main Shi'i streams, the last revealed I. disappeared, to become the hidden I. who will return at the end of time as the *Mahdi* (The Guided One) and Redeemer to institute a reign of justice. For the main body of the Shi'a — the *Ithna-'Ashariyya* ("Twelvers"), also called Ja'fariyya or Imamiyya — the last, and now hidden, I. was the twelfth, Muhammad ibn Hassan (al-Mahdi or al-Muntazar), in the 870s. The *Isma'iliyya (the "Seveners") consider Isma'il ibn Ja'far, the son of the sixth I., who died before his father, in 760, as the rightful seventh I., the hidden one to return. Some Shi'i sects, however, recognize a living I. Thus, one branch of the Isma'iliyya, regard their leader, the "Aga Khan", as the I. The *Zeidiyya, who seceded when they accepted Zeid ibn 'Ali as the rightful fifth I., in 712, and who survived in Yemen, recognize an unbroken line of revealed, living I.'s. Their I., who ruled Yemen until the civil war of 1962–67, was elected by the *Sada* (sing. *Sayyid*), the descendants of Hussein ibn 'Ali. The Zeidi-Yemeni Imamate lapsed with the termination of the civil war. The Iranian Shi'is, though *Ithna-'Ashariyya,* i.e. regarding the I. as hidden and not recognizing a living one, since the Islamic revolution of 1979 sometimes call their leader *Khomeini "Imam". Some esoteric schools of Sunni Islam which have, though orthodox, absorbed certain elements of Muslim mysticism (Sufism) and even Shi'ism — e.g., the *Mahdiyya* in Sudan — also call the head of their order I.

imperialism   The expansion of a great power through conquest of foreign countries (mainly "Third World" and under-developed ones) and/or their economic or military domination. I. is, in terms of political science and definition, not synonymous with colonialism, the more so as the latter appears on the stage of history in the 16th century, while one speaks of I. only from the 19th century. Yet, the main aspects of I. concerning the AC are described in the entry *colonialism and in those on the various imperial powers — see there.

India   On her path to independence, nationalist I. developed fairly close relations with the ME and the A. nationalists. I.'s nationalist leaders, keen to recruit I.'s large and influential Muslim minority and keep it within their movement, took care to show sympathy with Islamic problems and solidarity with the Muslims of the ME. At first, this was directed towards the Ottoman-Turkish Empire rather than specifically towards the A.'s. When the Ottoman Sultan Caliph called, during World War I, for the help of the Muslim world and a *Jihad, his call generated in I. much sympathy for the Turkish cause (though no *Jihad* volunteers) — primarily among I.'s Muslims, but also among anti-British non-Muslims.

After the war, a "*Khilafat*" movement was organized in I. to defend the Ottoman *Caliphate against Western schemes to abolish it, and the "Indian National Congress", the foremost representative of the national movement, joined the primarily Muslim *Khilafat* organization *en bloc*. The movement expired when the Caliphate was abolished, in 1924, not by Western imperialist plots but by the Turkish nationalists.

From the 1920s, the I.'n nationalists developed closer relations with the A. nationalist movements, particularly the Egyptian one, and A. nationalists were inspired by the I.'n movement and regarded it with sympathy. The leaders of I.'n nationalism had, with the exception of a few individuals, little sympathy for Zionism, the national movement of the Jewish people, and fully supported the A. view on Palestine, sometimes putting pressure on Britain in this respect. An I.'n judge served on the 1947 UN Special Committee on Palestine (*UNSCOP); he opposed the partition plan supported by the majority. I. spoke and voted against the Nov. 1947 resolution on the partition of Palestine (her opposition to partition was at least in part motivated by the trauma of the partition of I. herself, in 1947, which the nationalists had bitterly opposed, but finally had to accept).

Independent I., from 1947, continued the policy of the nationalist movement and developed close and friendly relations with the ASt, particularly Egypt. This co-operation was intensified after the Egyptian revolution of 1952, with the I.'ns regarding the new Egyptian leadership as men of their own kind — progressive, secularist, socialist and neutralist. Nehru and *Nasser were partners in the formulation of the concepts of *Neutralism and Non-Alignment, and a personal friendship developed between the two. However, planned economic, scientific and defense co-operation remained limited. I.'s relations with Israel reflected that quest for A. friendship: though I. recognized Israel *de jure* and without qualifications in Sept. 1950 and permitted her to maintain a Consulate in Bombay (much restricted in its operations), she refused to establish normal diplomatic relations and meaningful economic and cultural exchanges. I. consistently speaks against Israel at the UN and international conferences, and her attitude to Israel, cold-to-unfriendly to start with, has worsened over the years, beginning with the 1956 *Sinai War. This attitude seems to be greatly influenced, in addition to the quest for A. friendship, by the desire not to antagonize the Muslims of I.

The ASt have, despite their general sympathy for I., not responded with total support for I.'s policies. For their attitude to the I.-Pakistan dispute in general, and the conflict over Kashmir in particular, see *Pakistan. I. In I.'s border dispute with China, which erupted into open war in 1962, the ASt showed no more than benevolent neutrality, and Nasser even tried unsuccessfully to mediate, together with other neutralist leaders (a neutrality which I. resented). I. suffered a grave insult at the hands of the Islamic and ASt in 1969, when she was denied the right to participate in a Muslim "summit" meeting following a case of arson at the al-Aqsa Mosque in Jerusalem. I., however, continued her policy of close relations with the A. and Muslim states. There was no change even during the nearly three years, 1977–80, she was ruled by anti-Congress parties that had, while in opposition, frequently criticized I.'s A. policy and called for better relations with Israel.

Since the 1970s, another link with the AC has been considerably strengthened: an increasing number of I.'ns went to work in AC, mostly in Saʻudi Arabia and the Persian Gulf principalities; in the mid-1980s, their number was estimated at over 820,000 (though the recession in the Gulf countries' oil production and economic situation had begun causing a decline in their number). That I.'n presence obviously created an expanding network of relations — economic (the workers' remittances sent home amounted to over $1,500m. p.a. and their deposits in I. to some $2,500m.), trade, communications (shipping and air links) etc. It also caused political problems: the Gulf states' apprehensions that foreigners might become too numerous, and potentially too influential, and their high-handed treatment of their foreign workers against I.'s obligation, on the other hand, to protect her citizens and their rights. The increase in smuggling activities caused by the constant movement of people between the Gulf and I. also created a measure of friction.

IPC (Iraq Petroleum Company) See *Iraq, *oil.

Iran (or Persia) — herself outside the scope of

this Dictionary — is involved in many ways in ME and A. affairs. She faces A. claims to *Khuzistan, a region in her southwest inhabited in large part by A. She is in near-constant conflict, since 1980 at war, with neighboring *Iraq — over border and territorial disputes, the *Shi'is in Iraq (and particularly the Iranians among them), and general policy; and she has frequently supported, though in a sporadic and unreliable way, rebellions of Iraq's *Kurds. She has aspirations to control or dominate the *Persian Gulf — called "Arab Gulf" by the A.'s — and territorial claims to several A. islands in the Gulf (*Bahrain, *Abu Mussa, *Tanb). She aspired, at least under the Shah, until 1979, to be the strongest, the dominating regional ME power. She was a member of the *Baghdad Pact, later *CENTO, and thus in conflict with the leftist-"progressive" ASt. Her relations with Egypt, and with Sa'udi Arabia, were troubled by several issues. As the first oil-producing country of the ME, her struggles for full control of her oil had considerable influence on similar struggles by AC. As a Shi'i country, she saw herself in some measure as the protector of Shi'ites in AC, particularly Iraq, Lebanon and the Gulf Sheikhdoms. After the Islamic revolution of 1979, under *Khomeini, I. began intervening more actively and openly, especially in Lebanon. Moreover, Khomeini and his régime, as protagonists of fundamentalist Islamic rule, seemed keen to "export" their Islamic revolution and prepared to use force and subversion to instal similar régimes in the AC too. Since 1979, Khomeini's I. has been an ally of the more extremist AC of the *"Rejection Front", such as Syria and Libya, while she denounces and threatens the Gulf countries because of their aid to Iraq in her war with I.

I.'s perennial border conflict with Iraq, particularly over the *Shatt al-'Arab (the joint estuary of the *Euphrates and the *Tigris), and the attempts to settle it, e.g. the agreements of 1937 and 1975, and their failure, as well as the war of 1980 onward, are described in the entries *Iraq and *Shatt al-'Arab; for I.'s involvement in the Kurdish issue see *Iraq, *Kurds.

I.'s relations with *Kuwait were also complex. In 1961, I. was the first country to recognize Kuwait's independence and to support her against Iraqi claims and threats. Later, relations deteriorated — over the delimitation of sea borders and offshore oil rights in the Persian Gulf, the status of Iranians resident in Kuwait, I.'s condemnation of A. nationalist anti-I. propaganda centered in Kuwait, and since 1980, Kuwait's *de facto* aid to Iraq in her war with I.

I. under the Shah fostered close relations with *'Oman and aided her defense, mainly against subversion and rebellions instigated or supported by South Yemen. From about 1973 to 1979 I. maintained a contingent of officers and troops in 'Oman and a defense agreement of 1974 provided for joint Iranian-'Omani defense of the Straits of *Hormuz and the Gulf of 'Oman. Revolutionary I., since 1979, has not continued these special relations with 'Oman.

I.'s relations with Nasserist Egypt were troubled, as *Nasser regarded the Shah as a stooge of Western imperialism, while the Shah suspected Egypt in the later 1950s and early 1960s of fostering the anti-Shah agitation and subversion then spreading in I. In July 1960, following the Shah's public confirmation of trade relations with and *de facto* recognition of Israel, relations were severed altogether. They were resumed in 1970, but remained cold and mutually suspicious. The Khomeini regime, angered by both Sadat's peace with Israel and the asylum of the ex-Shah, severed relations in Apr. 1979 and I. and Egypt have since been bitterly hostile to each other.

Relations with Sa'udi Arabia were troubled by the antagonism between I.'s Shi'i Islam and Sa'udia's Sunni *Wahhabism, and also by conflicting oil interests. In the 1960s, however, a community of interests against the ambitions and policies of revolutionary-"progressive" countries brought about a *rapprochement*. Offshore oil rights were delimited (1968), and the Shah and King *Feisal exchanged state visits. After I.'s Islamic revolution the old antagonism resurged.

I.'s relations with Israel were a further irritant in her troubled relations with the ASt. She recognized Israel *de facto* in 1950, without formally announcing it, and sent a diplomatic representative with informal status. The representative was withdrawn in 1951, but relations developed — trade, Israeli technical assistance, the sale of Persian oil, Israeli airline flights to and through I., and economic co-operation in various fields; a semi-secret political alliance led to several meetings on the highest level and visits to I. by senior Israeli leaders and officials. In July 1960, the

Shah confirmed, for the first time in public, the existence of these relations and I.'s *de facto* recognition of Israel; and he reiterated similar statements and insisted on that policy despite A. protests. The presence in Teheran of Israeli representatives became permanent and grew into an establishment that was virtually (though not in name) a fully fledged Embassy. With the fall of the Shah in Feb. 1979, all these relations were severed by I.'s revolutionary Islamic régime, which has since taken an extremist stand of total hostility towards Israel and called for her liquidation by force. But continuing Israeli supplies of arms and spare parts — her own or American — were reported, frequently denied, and finally confirmed in late 1986, when the US involvement in these supplies were revealed.

Iraq Republic northeast of Arabia, the eastern part of the *Fertile Crescent, ancient Mesopotamia formed by the *Euphrates and *Tigris Rivers. Area: 170,000 sq. mi. (440,000 sq. km.). I. borders in the south on Kuwait (99 mi.) and Sa'udi Arabia (345.5 mi.); in the west on Jordan (56.7 mi.) and Syria (233 mi.); in the north on Turkey (118 mi.); and in the east on Iran (507.5 mi.).

The population in the mid-1980s was estimated at 15–16 m. About 80% of I.'s population are Arabs, i.e. speak Arabic as their mother tongue. About 25% of the population are A. Sunni Muslims, centered in the upper Euphrates region northwest of Baghdad to the Syrian border and the upper Tigris region between Samarra and Mosul. They are traditionally the politically dominant element of the country and the carriers of A. nationalism. About 50% or somewhat more of the population are A. Shi'i Muslims, inhabiting the south and the center up to the vicinity of Baghdad. *Kurds, non-A. Sunni Muslims, make up 15–20% of the population, living in the mountains of the north and north-east, with large communities in the big cities. Christians total at most 4% of the population; nearly all of them belong to Eastern churches or, the majority, to their *Uniate Catholic offshoots. An estimated break-down is: *Assyrians-*Nestorians 35–50,000; Syrian *Jacobites 40–60,000; Armenians 25–40,000; Uniate *Chaldeans 200–300,000; Syrian Catholics 70–90,000; and a few thousand Greek Orthodox, Greek Catholics, Armenian Catholics, Latin Catholics and Protestants. Smaller minorities are Turcomans (Sunni Muslims speaking a Turkish dialect), 100–200,000 of whom live in Kirkuk and along the border (but larger figures are mentioned); *Yazidis, numbering 20–40,000, mainly in Jabal Sinjar west of Mosul; Sabaeans-*Mandaeans, of whom about 20–30,000 live along the lower Tigris; and Jews, of whose ancient and large community — 100–120,000 in the 1940s — a few hundred remain, all in Baghdad. There was, prior to the I.-Iran war of 1980, an unknown number of Persians — partly along the eastern border and mainly in the cities holy to Shi'i Islam and in Baghdad. A. nomads (Bedouin) are estimated to form 5% of the population; but if semi-nomads at an advanced stage of settlement are taken into account the percentage is far higher.

I. is a predominantly agricultural country, drawing its water from the Tigris and Euphrates, and in particular from their yearly floods, with an agricultural and irrigation tradition. Swamps and salt wastes have come to cover large areas of formerly fertile land. However, over the last 70–80 years much land has been reclaimed through a number of spectacular damming and irrigation projects and modern methods of soil preservation. The main produce is subsistence crops: barley, wheat, rice and lentils. A vital cash crop is

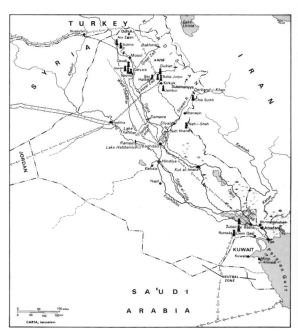

Map of Iraq

dates — I. is the largest exporter in the world. Tobacco and fruit are of importance in the north, and cotton in the center.

The main wealth of I. is her oil produced commercially since 1934 (for the terms and history of the concessions — see *Oil). In 1975 the output passed the 100 m. ton mark; it peaked in 1979 with over 170 m. tons and has declined in the 1980s to 50–70 m. tons p.a. Revenue from oil peaked in 1980 with over $26,000 m. and stands in the mid-1980s of c. $8–10,000 m. p.a. Oil production is vital for the national economy; on it depends not merely whatever development is carried out, but also the day-to-day livelihood of the country. Mining and industry are still of little importance. Of the labor force, a large majority still live on agriculture, and about 8% are in government service (including the armed forces prior to the war of 1980).

The country suffers from two main social problems — that of rapid urbanization without industrialization on a comparable scale, and the presence of an uprooted, under-employed and disgruntled intelligentsia. The Agrarian Reform Act of 1958 (see below) has been the basis for much useful work, and for the distribution of land among some 130,000 (?) peasants; but it has not solved the basic problems of rural poverty, backwardness and exploitation.

GOVERNMENT According to the Provisional Constitution of July 1970 I. is a "Sovereign People's Democratic Republic". The supreme body in the state is the Revolutionary Command Council of (maximal) 12 members who are recruited from among the Regional (i.e. Iraqi) Command of the *Ba'th party. In reality, the RCC sometimes has more than 12 members; in the mid-1980s there were nine. The chairman of the RCC is also President of the Republic and Supreme Commander of the Armed Forces. An elected National Assembly with legislative powers, provided for by the Provisional Constitution, was first established in 1980, but in reality legislative powers remained with the RCC.

POLITICAL HISTORY At the beginning of the century, what is today I. was loosely covered by the three Ottoman provinces (*Vilayet*) of Mosul, Baghdad and Basra. Though "Turkish Arabia" (Mesopotamia) was backward even by Ottoman standards, modernization had started by then in the shape of improved provincial and municipal administration (brought about by the governorship in Baghdad of Midhat Pasha, 1869–72), a rudimentary school system on the Western pattern (e.g. the Baghdad Law School, founded 1908). International rivalries, and in particular communications projects (outstanding among which was the German-inspired *Baghdad Railway scheme), and the appropriation of oil rights among British, German and Dutch interests accelerated that process. There were stirrings of A. nationalism, not easily distinguishable from a striving for greater local independence, which centered, after the Young Turks' revolution, about a group of Sunni-I. officers in the Ottoman Army, and in Basra about the Shi'i *Naqib* Sayyid Talib ibn al-Sayyid Rajab. These movements, for all their symptomatic significance, touched only a very small part even of the urban population.

Within a week of Turkey's entry into *World War I the British invaded Mesopotamia in Nov. 1914. The invasion was mounted from India, through the Persian Gulf, owing to the importance attributed to southern Mesopotamia as part of the western approaches to that subcontinent. Despite a heavy setback (the surrender of the Sixth Division under Gen. Townshend at Kut, Apr. 1916), a powerful army carried its offensive beyond Baghdad by Mar. 1917 and reached the outskirts of Mosul at the time of the armistice. At the same time a civil administration was built up under the forceful direction of Sir Percy Z. Cox and his assistant and deputy, Lt-Col. (later Sir) Arnold T. Wilson.

Declarations made by the British army and the Allies raised the expectation that I. would be granted independence. But Wilson, by then Acting Civil Commissioner of Mesopotamia, with the Government of India behind him, believed in the imperial necessity of direct British rule and was convinced that I.'s population was not capable of full self-government. Discontent grew throughout the country, uniting the Shi'i religious leaders, resentful of Christian domination, with the Sunni intelligentsia, disappointed in their hope for speedy independence; the tribal sheikhs, too, were traditionally hostile to settled authority, though Wilson and his collaborators had established better relations with them than other élite groups. In June 1920 a major insurrection broke out in the middle Euphrates and spread quickly over large parts of the country, shaking the hold of the army of occupation. Though hardly a "Great Revolution", this movement clinched the argument in London for a radical departure towards self-government. Wilson left, and with Cox's return as "High Commissioner" I. was constituted as a nominally independent country, "guided" by Britain under a *Mandate conferred by the League of Nations (*San Remo, 1920, finalized in 1922). *Feisal b. al-Hussein, recently expelled by the French from Syria, was appointed King of I. in Aug. 1921, as a result of British pressure and after a dubious plebiscite.

This arrangement — a Mandate under the League of Nations, and "a sovereign state, independent and free" (the Organic Law of 1925), linked with Britain under an Anglo-I. Treaty, 1922, on the other hand — was resented by the I. élite and marred the political atmosphere. But there were no more violent disturbances, except in the north (see below). A sound administration, guided by British "advisers", a national army (from 1920–21), a government, a constitution and a Parliament (1925) were set up. Economic progress and the development of education, starved of funds, were comparatively slow. But the newly organized I. Petroleum Company struck oil in large quantities near Kirkuk in 1927. The nationalists continued pressing for a new treaty to make I. completely independent. Negotiations, enhanced by optimism generated by public security, the good will created by Britain's success in retaining the *Mosul area for I. against Turkish aspirations (1925–26), and the philosophy of the Labor government in office in Britain since 1929, brought about the Anglo-I. Treaty of 1930 which provided for the termination of the Mandate upon I.'s admission to the League of Nations. Important strategic, economic and diplomatic privileges were reserved for Britain (and the treaty was therefore opposed by a nationalist faction). On Britain's strong recommendation, I. was admitted to the League and became independent on 3 Oct. 1932.

The political history of I. during the following nine years was not a happy one. With British prestige and responsibility removed from the domestic scene, the politicians were unable to rule the country for long. Within a year of independence the long-standing quarrel between the Baghdad authorities and the *Assyrian (Nestorian) community, displaced during World War I from their homes to the north of the later I. frontier, and British-protected under the Mandate, came to a head and resulted in the slaughter of hundreds of Assyrian men, women and children at the hands of the I. Army. Disturbances throughout the Shi'i south and center, always smoldering and often erupting into uprisings, encouraged or bloodily suppressed by the rival factions in Baghdad, assumed a far greater political importance. King Feisal was losing control and died in Sept. 1933. His son and successor *Ghazi was young, rash and unstable and, though not unpopular, had no real influence in the face of the growing political power of army officers. By the end of 1936 the situation was ripe for the first of the many military *coups* which have since shaken I. Gen. Bakr *Sidqi, at first supported by a group of leftist intellectuals (the *al-Ahali* group), was himself overthrown and assassinated in 1937; but he set a pattern of military dictatorship, thinly veiled by civilian governments, with the Organic Law nominally preserved, which lasted until 1941. King Ghazi's death in Apr. 1939 and the succession by his infant son *Feisal II under the regency of his pro-British uncle *'Abd-ul-Ilah did not change this situation. In the spring of 1941 the then ruling group of colonels, the "Golden Square", slithered into a war with Britain — caused essentially by their resentment of Britain's privileged position, and expressed in their refusal to let Britain make full use of I.'s territory and communications for the war effort. This "Rashid 'Ali movement" (named after Prime Minister Rashid 'Ali al-*Kilani — who was little more than a hesitant figurehead) threatened Britain from the rear at a most critical time of World War II. A brief campaign in May ended with the routing of the I. Army, and the flight abroad of the "Golden Square", Rashid 'Ali and the Mufti of Jerusalem who had backed and inspired the movement — some of them to Italy and Germany. After May 1941 I. was secured to the Allied side by the cooperation of the Regent and an establishment of senior politicians among whom Nuri al-*Sa'id predominated.

Post-war official I. showed an interest in various schemes for a *Fertile Crescent Federation, the real motive of which was to gain predominance in the Syrian area. These schemes were pursued intermittently, unenthusiastically and ineptly. They brought to the surface Egypt's latent mistrust of I. and caused disunity in the *Arab League and resentment in Syria.

In the post-war period, times of political liberalism alternated with strict police rule, comparative quiet with violent disturbances. A new draft treaty with Britain, signed at *Portsmouth in January 1948, was abandoned after fierce demonstrations brought the country to the verge of chaos. Steadily rising oil royalties, especially since the half-and-half profit-sharing principle was adopted in 1952, produced a surplus that was, on the whole, sensibly invested in development projects. Yet, the absence of import and distribution policies, unbridled speculation and an overall lack of social awareness on the part of the authorities more than once brought the masses close to famine. An appreciable part of the I. Army — about one division — took part in the Palestine War of 1948. It returned home in the spring of 1949 without victory and added its share to the general malaise.

Feisal II came of age in 1953 and assumed his reign, and 'Abd-ul-Ilah became Crown Prince. In Sept. 1954 Nuri Sa'id was recalled to head the government, after the freest elections I. was ever to know had returned a sizable opposition to Parliament. Nuri in practice prohibited all party activity and remained for four years the ruler of I., whether in office or out of it. He determined the country's policy, which meant externally close collaboration with the West, and domestically a police state, though in retrospect his rule may look less repressive than it did then. Economic development plans inaugurated in the early 1950s were pursued vigorously, but little thought was given to social progress or the alleviation of immediate misery. The army, well cared for and considered a bastion of the existing order, was kept strictly away from politics. The régime was unpopular with the politically articulate forces of the kingdom — whether A. nationalists, liberals, communists, traditionalists or army officers.

After 1955 discontent was focused on the *Baghdad Pact, joining I. with Turkey, Iran, Pakistan and Britain in a defense treaty backed and sponsored by the USA. Britain and I.'s common membership also provided the basis for a new Anglo-I. Treaty, Apr. 1955, which abolished most of Britain's remaining privileges and turned her air bases into joint Anglo-I. bases under the Baghdad Pact. The Pact was disliked equally as an alliance with "colonialist" Britain, as a threat to the USSR, newly regarded as a friend of the A. world, and as a separatist move harmful to A. unity and hostile, at least by implication, to its hero and protagonist, Egypt's *Nasser. Nuri's ambiguous stand during the 1956 *Suez crisis exacerbated Egyptian and nationalist antagonism. The Syro-Egyptian merger and the establishment of the UAR in Feb. 1958 was seen as a threat to I. and a federation with Jordan was hastily set up in Feb. 1958 as a counter move; but it remained unpopular and its implementation was cut short by the fall of the monarchy, in July 1958.

The Revolution of 14 July 1958 was prepared by a conspiratorial group of "Free Officers" who had come together over the previous four or five years. The leaders of the *coup* were Brig. 'Abd-ul-Karim *Qassem, a Baghdad-born Sunni of lower middle class origin, and Col. 'Abd-ul-Salam *'Aref. The takeover was effected with speed. 'Aref commanded the units which occupied the capital and killed King Feisal II and Crown Prince 'Abd-ul-Ilah at their residence; Nuri Sa'id was killed by the mob the following day while trying to escape abroad.

Qassem proclaimed a "Popular Republic" with himself as Commander-in-Chief, Prime Minister and acting Minister of Defense. 'Aref became his deputy. No officers' council was established, as the "Free Officers" had planned. The Presidency of the Republic was vested in a "Sovereignty Council" of three respected but powerless individuals. The Cabinet appointed included leading personalities representing all the shades of opposition to the defunct régime — a near-communist, liberal socialists, A. nationalists of various hues and Kurds (though not members of the autonomist-rebellious KDP — see below). However, Qassem and the officers close to him were the real rulers.

The revolution was received throughout I. with enthusiasm. The UAR and her A. allies, as well as the Communist Bloc, recognized the new régime with alacrity. The West followed within less than a month; its acceptance was made easier by soothing statements from Qassem which included promises not to touch existing oil concessions. I. even refrained for the time being from leaving the Baghdad Pact, though her membership was henceforth a mere formality (it was formally abrogated in Mar. 1959). But the atmosphere of general rejoicing and harmony did not last. Nasserists and adherents of the Ba'th group soon discovered that Qassem was determined to guard I.'s full independence vis-à-vis Nasser and Pan-Arab unity, and started undermining his position, with Qassem's deputy, 'Aref, as leader. Qassem was pushed into an alliance with the Communists who, taught by the Syrian example, bitterly opposed I. falling under Nasser's domination. An atmosphere of intrigue and violence speedily spread. 'Aref was stripped of his offices in Sept. 1958 and forced into exile as Ambassador at Bonn (a post he never took up). When he returned from Europe against Qassem's order, he was charged with an attempt to assassinate Qassem. In February 1959, he was sentenced to death in a "People's Court" presided over by Qassem's cousin Mahdawi, but reprieved.

As Communist influence and self-assurance grew, various nationalist bodies took to conspiracies — including a plot by a group around Rashid 'Ali (who had returned to I. in Sept. 1958, hoping to join or take over the leadership of the new régime) in Dec. 1958, a rising of anti-Communist officers, chiefly at Mosul, in Mar. 1959, and a Ba'thist attempt on Qassem's life in Oct. 1959. All these conspiracies were foiled and repressed — the Mosul rising with heavy bloodshed — with Communist help. By the spring of 1959 all A.-nationalist activity was virtually paralyzed, and a Communist take-over appeared possible. However, Qassem outmaneuvered the Communists, threatening them with suppression by the army after a Communist-led massacre at Kirkuk in July 1959, and at the same time promising the legalization of political parties, including theirs, from the beginning of 1960. The Communists shied away from an open contest with Qassem in the belief that restraint would bring them easy victory through their superior élan and organization. From then on their fortunes waned; the authorities increasingly harassed them and street terror started to turn against them. In January 1960 Qassem issued a decree legalizing political parties but it was hedged with safeguards enabling the régime to interfere with their activities whenever it so chose. The Communists in particular were cheated of their expectations when Qassem licensed a dissident Communist with virtually no following as chairman of a legal "I. Communist Party"; the Communists, though very bitter, acquiesced. The licensed parties quickly withered away under the unfriendliness and obstruction of the régime. In the process Qassem made enemies of the liberal-socialist National Democratic Party, hitherto generally friendly to him. By 1961 the Cabinet had lost practically all its political members, who had been replaced by technicians or protégés of Qassem. Measures of social reform passed immediately after the revolution (the most important being the Agrarian Reform Law of September 1958) came to a stop as the political atmosphere darkened. There was no internal political activity during the last two years of the Qassem period. These years are noteworthy for the Kurdish rising, Qassem's claim to Kuwait and his quarrel with the oil companies.

The Kurdish north had remained largely unassimilated to the I. state throughout its existence. Since World War I, the British occupation authorities had promised administrative decentralization and cultural self-expression, and when these promises were not fulfilled, the Kurds resisted, led in the 1920s by the eccentric personality of Sheikh Mahmud Barzenchi (Barzinji) and from the early 1930s by the heads of the *Barzani tribe, Sheikh Ahmad and his younger brother Mulla Mustafa. For this resistance, the Kurdish republic of *Mahabad, on the Iranian side of the border, Barzani's return in 1958, the Kurds' disappointment and their rebellion from Sept. 1961 — see *Kurds.

The Kuwait crisis broke out when Qassem publicly claimed the principality as a former district of Basra province, after Britain had granted it independence in June 1961. Qassem's move met with strong opposition from all other AC and an all-A. force was dispatched to defend her (see *Kuwait). But Qassem made no move to enforce his claim, and a stalemate ensued which brought him much ridicule at home and abroad. His successors recognized Kuwait's independence in 1963.

Qassem's dispute with the oil companies, the IPC and its subsidiaries, broke out in 1960 over the demand for new contracts assuring I. of greatly increased benefits. It led in Dec. 1961 to "Law No. 80" which limited the companies' concession to about one percent of their former area (areas which were actually producing were not affected).

On 8–9 Feb. 1963, Qassem was overthrown by a *coup* of the clandestine *Ba'th* group and sympathizers from among army officers. For nine months civilian leaders of the *Ba'th* tried to rule I., with 'Abd-ul-Salam 'Aref as nominal President of the Republic. They failed, through their own administrative inexperience and factional disputes, the failure of negotiations with the Kurds and defeats in the north, the antagonism aroused by the unbridled violence of the *Ba'th* militia, and the jealousy of the military, as well as the hostility of Nasser (after the breakdown of talks on a federal union of Egypt, Syria and I.). On 18 Nov. 1963 the officers around 'Aref brushed the *Ba'th* government aside, forcibly broke up the militia, and established 'Aref and themselves as rulers (for nearly five years). 'Aref died in an air crash in Apr. 1966, and was followed as President by his elder brother, Gen. 'Abd-ul-Rahman 'Aref.

The period was one of restlessness and little was achieved. For some months in 1965–66 an attempt was made to reintroduce a semblance of civilian government with Dr. 'Abd-ul-Rahman al-Bazzaz as Prime Minister. Bazzaz was forced out of office by the jealousy of the military. A settlement with the Kurds which he had negotiated was tacitly abandoned and the Kurdish rebellion flared up again. A federation with Syria and Egypt, proclaimed in Apr. 1963, came to nought; an I.-Egyptian "Union" agreement of 1964 was never implemented, except for some partial measures (it was formally abrogated in 1968, after the change of régime). Far-reaching nationalization decrees were published but not carried out. An "Arab Socialist Union" on the Egyptian pattern was founded as a single party, but never became firmly established. An end to the constitutional "transition period", a term for the resumption of some form of representative government, was fixed, and put off. In 1966 the Nasserist Brig. 'Aref 'Abd-ul-Razzaq staged an abortive *coup* attempt. An agreement with the oil companies was initialled, but remained unratified in view of nationalist and "progressive" attacks. I.'s part in the *Six Day War was limited; she sent a strong force to the north of Jordan, but it took no major part in the war and was withdrawn in 1970–71 (after much tension with Jordan because of I.'s sympathy for the Palestinian guerrillas/terrorists in their battle with Jordan).

In July 1968 the régime was toppled by a new *coup* staged by a coalition of the *Ba'th* and a group of army officers led by Col. 'Abd-ul-Razzaq Na'if. The latter was made Prime Minister, and the *Ba'th* leader Gen. Ahmad Hassan al-*Bakr became President. However, within two weeks the *Ba'th* ousted its non-*Ba'th* allies and set up an exclusively *Ba'th* régime (Col. Na'if, in exile, was assassinated later, in 1978). Another alleged *coup* attempt by Gen. 'Aref 'Abd-ul-Razzaq failed in Oct. The new *Ba'th* régime, headed by a "Revolutionary Council", systematically purged the army and all political and administrative bodies, brutally eliminating all rival groups — except for "Socialist-Unionist" factions prepared to accept the unquestioned leadership of the *Ba'th*; with such factions it established a united "Progressive and Patriotic National Front" in 1973. This Front included Kurdish factions prepared to collaborate, and the Communists (who were already *de facto* represented in the Government from 1972). But the collaboration between the *Ba'th* and the Communists, always split into rival factions, did not last; in 1978–79 the Communists withdrew from the United Front and went underground and the régime suppressed them.

However, the post-1968 *Ba'th* régime, not content with eliminating all rival groups and establishing the complete domination of its party apparatus, was embroiled for over ten years in a near-constant intra-*Ba'th* factional and personal wrangle and incessant purges. A "leftist", pro-Syrian faction headed by 'Ali Saleh al-Sa'di, had been purged and expelled in 1963. After 1968, Saddam *Hussein (al-Tikriti) gradually emerged as the strong man; dominating the party's militia and secret services and from Nov. 1969 deputy-chairman of the Revolutionary Council, he systematically eliminated all his rivals. In Jan. 1969, 'Abd-ul-Karim Nasrat of the leftist faction, a leader of the *Ba'th coup* of 1963, was murdered. In 1970 Saddam Hussein ousted Vice-President Hardan 'Abd-ul-Ghaffar (al-Tikriti) — later assassinated in 1971, and in 1971 he got rid of Vice-President Saleh Mahdi 'Ammash and Foreign Minister 'Abd-ul-Karim Sheikhli (assassinated in 1980). In 1973 he suppressed a *coup* by Nazem al-Kazzar, the head of the security services, and had him executed (though he was widely reported to have instigated the *coup* himself; during the *coup* Defense Minister Hammad Shihab was killed. With President Bakr ailing, since the early 1970s Saddam Hussein was the *de facto* ruler of I. He completed his take-over as sole ruler in July 1979, when Bakr resigned (was compelled by Saddam to resign?) and Saddam Hussein became President, Prime Minister, Chairman of the Revolutionary Council and Secretary-General of the *Ba'th*. He accompanied his take-over by another bloody purge; 21 leading officers and functionaries executed included five members of the Revolutionary Council. Saddam Hussein's rule since 1979 as the sole leader has been orchestrated by an all-embracing personality cult.

The *Ba'th* régime put I. firmly into the leftist-radical camp in inter-A. and international affairs — at least until 1980. Relations with the Soviet Union were strengthened. Agreements on economic cooperation, arms supplies, etc., included accords of 1969 providing for Soviet aid and participation in the development of I.'s oil. In Apr. 1972 I. signed a Treaty of Friendship and Cooperation with the USSR; several visits were exchanged between the heads of the two states, and though relations were not free of crises and dissent, I. became one of the Soviet Union's two major allies in the ME. In 1975 I. also joined COMECON, the Soviet Bloc's economic alliance, as an associate member. Relations with the USA, on the other hand, severed in 1967, were not resumed throughout these years (they were resumed in 1984). Relations with Britain were also precarious; severed in 1961, they were resumed in 1968, broken again in 1971 (over Britain's inability to prevent the seizure by Iran of Persian Gulf islands of the UAE), and resumed in 1974. They were also exacerbated by I.'s final disputes with the British-dominated I. Petroleum Company (IPC). In 1972 I. nationalized the IPC, and in 1973 agreement was reached on compensation and details of the take-over; the nationalization of the IPC subsidiaries, the Basra PC and the Mosul PC, was completed in 1975.

Yet Saddam Hussein's I. followed a somewhat pragmatic course. From the mid-1970s she sought a *rapprochement* with the West — mainly economic relations, investments, arms supplies — with France as a main Western partner, but also with the USA (without renewing diplomatic relations), and accordingly toned down her links with the Soviet Bloc. This trend gained further momentum after 1980, due to the I.-Iran war.

In inter-A. affairs I. followed a radical line, particularly against Israel, and supported the *"Rejection Front". In the October War of 1973 she sent two divisions to help Syria. In 1977–79 she was in the forefront of the ASt denouncing *Sadat's peace moves and ostracizing Egypt. She aided and partly hosted some of the most extremist Palestinian-A. terrorist organizations. But changes towards a more pragmatic position could be discerned on that front, too, from the mid-1970s. In 1977–78 I. walked out of the Rejection Front — in part due to such a policy change, and mainly on account of the growing rift between her and Syria and Libya.

Relations with Syria, indeed, were generally bad and a major irritant. To an old basic antagonism, deriving mainly from rivalry for the position of the dominant country of the Fertile Crescent, was added the split of the *Ba'th* into two bitterly hostile factions since the mid-1960s — with the doctrinaire "Left" in power in Syria since 1966 and the rival "Right" in I. In 1976 hostility reached a stage that I. closed the oil pipeline through Syria operating since 1952 — a closure that damaged her own oil exports (the IPC pipeline to Haifa was inoperative since 1948 and that to Tripoli since 1976) and induced her to step up the construction of an alternative pipeline through Turkey to the Gulf of Alexandretta-Hatay which was opened in 1977. In 1976–77 I.'s borders with Syria were closed altogether. There was a reconciliation in 1978-79; borders were reopened late in 1978 and the pipeline in Feb. 1979. Syrian President Asad paid two state visits — and it was agreed to unite or merge the two countries. However, negotiations on that merger plan broke down in June 1979, the union was called off and relations reverted to bitter hostility, with Syria supporting Iraqi subversives and rebels. In Aug. 1980 I. expelled the Syrian Ambassador and when Syria and Libya supported Iran in the war that I. opened in Sept. 1980, I. severed relations with both of them in Oct. In Apr. 1982 the pipeline was again closed down, this time by Syria — to deprive I. of its economic benefits. Syria has persisted in supporting Iran against I., despite several attempts to mediate and reconcile the two countries, e.g. by Sa'udi Arabia, and Syro- Iraqi mutual hostility is unabated.

Saddam Hussein's budding pragmatism was applied even to internal affairs, despite the brutality of his régime (or after all potential nuclei of opposition had been suppressed). The provision for an elected National Assembly, laid down in the Constitution of 1970, was not implemented for ten years. But in June 1980 elections were held — the first since 1958 — albeit as a referendum on a single list of *Ba'th*-approved candidates of the United Front; and in Sept. 1984 new elections were held.

A major achievement was an agreement with the Kurdish Democratic Party, i.e. the Kurdish rebels under Barzani, announced by Bakr in Mar. 1970 (and ascribed mainly to Saddam Hussein's influence) — see *Kurds for its details. (To make Kurdish semi-autonomy more acceptable to Iraqi public opinion, it was described as part of a general decentralization for all provinces, and a measure of cultural autonomy was proclaimed for the Chaldeans, the Assyrians and the Turcomans as well.) For the breakdown of the agreement, I.'s unilateral inauguration of a semi-autonomous Kurdish Region in 1974, the resumption of the Kurdish rebellion, its defeat in 1975, and its re-eruption in the late 1970s — see *Kurds.

I.'s most crucial problem in the last decade has been her relations — and since 1980 her war — with Iran. Always beset by difficulties — over border disputes, particularly in the *Shatt al-'Arab; Iranian aid to Kurdish rebels; political and international orientation; the status of Persians in I. — relations became increasingly tense in the 1960s. In 1969 the Shah denounced an agreement of 1937 setting the Shatt al-'Arab border at its eastern shore rather than along its median line or *thalweg* (except for a stretch opposite Abadan) and announced he would enforce on the waterway a régime conforming to Iranian claims. Tension and clashes ensued, relations were severed from late 1971 to Oct. 1973, and scores of thousands of Iranians were deported. But with Iran's power much enhanced, I. was not strong enough to enforce her position on the Shatt al-'Arab. In Mar. 1975 she had to accept a new agreement with Iran legitimizing Iran's position and establishing the thalweg of the Shatt al-'Arab as the border; in return, the Shah stopped his support for the Kurdish rebels, causing the rebellion to break down, as described above. But I. chafed under the agreement imposed on her by a neighbor too strong to resist.

The situation changed in 1979 with the Shah deposed, Iran in turmoil and militarily weakened, and her army in disarray. After increasing tension and border clashes, I. announced in Sept. 1980 the abrogation of the 1975 agreement and reasserted her sovereignty over the Shatt al-'Arab. On 22 Sept. she opened fully fledged military operations by a major offensive across the Shatt al-'Arab (I. reckons the beginning of the war from 4 Sept. when, she claims, Khanaqin was shelled by Iran). I.'s official war aims were the enforcement of her sovereignty over the Shatt al-'Arab; minor territorial claims, mainly in the Qasr-i-Shirin area and several small islands in the Gulf; and an end to Persian subversion and Islamic-revolutionary, anti-Iraqi instigation; but in repeated statements, mainly for home consumption, she also claimed the whole of *Khuzistan, Iran's oil-bearing southwest.

I.'s initial offensive achieved certain territorial gains, especially in Khuzistan (Khorramshahr destroyed and taken, Abadan cut off and besieged), but it did not lead to a major victory and Iranian resistance rallied. I. had a significantly superior air force (whose performance, however, was seen by experts as mediocre or low-standard), while Iran disposed of much larger man-power — and used it in massed attacks of "human waves", sacrificing many thousands. From 1981–82 Iranian counter-offensives regained most of the territory taken by I.; Khorramshahr was reconquered in May 1982, and from 1985–86 Iranian forces made inroads on Iraqi territory (in February 1986, they reached, for instance, the Fao peninsula on I.'s Gulf coast) and kept Basra and its surroundings under near-constant shelling and threat of conquest. The war was conducted with much brutality, including chemical warfare and poison gas used by I., and massive air attacks on economic targets, mainly the centers of oil production and communications, as well as civilian populations in the large cities. Casualties were numbered by hundreds of thousands. Both countries' oil exports, vital for the financing of their war effort, were gravely hit: I.'s facilities for oil loading and shipping on the Gulf were paralyzed and largely destroyed and could no longer be used, while I.

incessantly bombed Kharg Island, Iran's main loading center, and her shuttle tankers to loading points farther down the Gulf. I.'s only means of direct oil exports were the pipeline through Turkey and a new feeder linking up with the Sa'udi pipeline from the Gulf to the Red Sea at Yanbu'. Iran maintained the bulk of her oil shipping despite Iraqi attacks and great losses. From early 1984 both countries attacked oil tankers, mostly of neutral third parties, in the Gulf, and Iran extended her missile and air raids to shipping not directly linked to I., such as tankers en route to and from the A. Gulf oil ports; Iran also claimed the right to intercept and search neutral shipping en route to I. and confiscate supplies. And while the great powers tried to protect their own shipping, little action was taken to insure the freedom of shipping for all.

From about 1982–83 the war, though continuing with furious tenacity, was seen by experts as stalemated — from the mid-1980s perhaps with a slight edge in Iran's favor. I. was offering a cease-fire based on the withdrawal to the borders and negotiations for peace; but Iran refused all such offers and insisted on a list of harsh preconditions, including I.'s denunciation as the aggressor and admission of guilt, the payment of huge compensation, and the dismissal of Saddam Hussein and his régime and his trial as a war criminal. Mediation efforts — by AC and the A. League; the UN; the non-aligned group of states; the Islamic group (the ICO); and individual statesmen — have all failed so far.

The great powers were officially neutral — and caught on the horns of a dilemma; as far as arms supplies, vital to both I. and Iran, were concerned, both the Western powers and the USSR favored I., within limits (though the USSR's defense pact with I. could not be seen as fully operative), while Iran got her arms reportedly from China, North Korea and Vietnam; but, as revealed in the American "Irangate" affair, American, Israeli and other military supplies continued reaching Iran, too. The ASt, except for Syria, Libya and South Yemen, supported I. — politically and morally, and some of them also economically. Egypt supplied arms, other support and reportedly some volunteers; Jordan put her port of *'Aqaba and her communications at I.'s disposal; and, chiefly, Sa'udi Arabia and Kuwait (and to some degree the other A. Gulf states) provided economic aid without which I. could not have survived. They exported oil on I.'s account; Sa'udia allowed I. to ship oil through the Sa'udi pipeline to the Red Sea; and their aid credits and grants were estimated at over $50,000m. Iran bitterly resented that A. aid and repeatedly warned the A. Gulf states that she would regard them as I.'s allies in the war and accordingly take action against them — a threat that caused much concern, particularly in Kuwait. The Western powers were also apprehensive of the danger of an extension of the Gulf War and took certain measures to protect the Gulf — though these measures did not amount to a full guarantee.

I.'s dependence, from 1980, on the West and the mainstream AC, and particularly Sa'udi Arabia, caused her further to mitigate her radical policies and adopt a pragmatic orientation — though there was no change in her internal régime or in Saddam Hussein's rule as the sole leader. Having seceded from the Rejection Front, I. now strengthened her relations with the moderate AC — Jordan, Sa'udi Arabia, Egypt (though she has so far not resumed official relations with Egypt). She finally resumed official relations with the USA in 1984. She even somewhat toned down her anti-Israel stand and was rumored to support Egyptian-Jordanian moves for negotiations on a ME peace settlement (though she has not confirmed such rumors or taken any official steps to join these moves for a settlement). It is too soon to judge whether that shift towards pragmatic moderation is tactical and ephemeral or whether it indicates a basic change in I.'s position.

Iraq Petroleum Company See *Iraq, *oil.

al-Iryani, al-Sayyid 'Abd-ul-Rahman (b. 1905? 1910?) Yemeni politician, President of Yemen 1967–74. Member of a *Zeidi family of *Sada* (pl. of *Sayyid*, i.e. descendants of the Caliph 'Ali and his son Hussein — the institutional élite of Zeidi Yemen), I. received a traditional Islamic education and became a *Qadi* (Islamic judge). He was involved in the abortive *coup* of 1948 and was imprisoned for six years. After his release, he remained an active opponent of Imam-King *Ahmad and his régime and went into exile to Aden and Cairo, where he was among the founders and leaders of a "Free Yemen" movement. After the *coup* of Sept. 1962 he returned and joined the Republican camp in the civil war. I.

was appointed Minister of Justice, 1962–63, and of Local Administration, 1964. In the factional struggles within the Republican leadership, I. was a conservative with close links to, and influence on, the Zeidi tribes (some of whom supported the Royalists, making it urgent for the Republicans to win them over). When the power of the Republic's chief leader and President, 'Abdullah *Sallal, was restricted by the nomination of a Presidential Council (and Sallal was detained in Egypt), in Apr. 1965, I. became a member of that Council. During his tenure he was instrumental in convening a pro-Republican tribal conference at Khamir, May 1965, which tried to push the régime towards a conservative orientation and to curb Egypt's Nasserist influence. In Sept. 1966 Sallal returned, resumed power and purged his rivals; I. was sent to Egypt and kept there in semi-detention. When Sallal was toppled, in Nov. 1967, and a more conservative régime was established, I. became chairman of the new Republican (Presidential) Council, i.e. President of Yemen. Though the government was run by Prime Ministers, I. continued wielding a strong influence, maintaining his alliance with the conservative tribal leaders, especially Sheikh 'Abdullah al-*Ahmar of the Hashed federation of tribes, but keeping a balance between the various factions. I. was instrumental in ending the civil war, the Republican-Royalist settlement, 1967–70, and Republican Yemen's reconciliation with and acceptance by Sa'udi Arabia, 1970. In 1972 he also mended relations with the USA and opened Yemen to Western technology and expertise. In 1972 he helped end Yemen's war with South Yemen and re-established a measure of cooperation, re-proclaiming the common aim of an eventual merger of the two countries. During the nearly seven years of his presidency, involved in constant factional struggles, he several times threatened, or even announced, his resignation, but was persuaded to retract.

I. and his régime were overthrown in June 1974 by Col. Ibrahim *Hamdi, and he went into exile, to Lebanon and later to Syria. According to unconfirmed reports, I. was allowed to return in the 1980s.

Islam, Muslims, in the Arab countries I., which swept the ME in the seventh century, with the A. conquest, and in the centuries following, remains the ruling faith in all AC except Lebanon. A detailed description of its beliefs and practices would be outside the scope of this Dictionary (but see entries *Sunnis, *Shi'a, *Shari'a, *Imam, *Mufti, *Dervish Orders, as well as those on various sects and Islamic schools such as *Druze, *'Alawis, *Isma'iliyya, *Mahdiyya, *Sanussis, *Wahhabis). Islam shapes social patterns and deep-rooted modes of thought, behavior and customs, and the constitutions of all AC except Lebanon are based on it. M.'s are the majority of the population in all AC's, forming over 90% of the total population of the A. world. They are also, outside the A. world, the majority in Turkey, northern Cyprus, Iran, Soviet Central Asia — the Kazakh, Kirghiz, Tadzhik, Turkmen and Uzbek Soviet Republics — one Soviet Transcaucasian Republic: Azerbaijan, and several autonomous areas of the Russian SSR north of the Caucasus, Afghanistan, Pakistan, Bangladesh, Malaysia, Brunei, Indonesia and several African countries — the three non-A. members of the Arab League: Mauritania, Somalia and Djibouti, as well as Gambia, Guinea, Mali, Niger and Senegal. M. form significant minorities in India and several South- and South-East Asian countries, in the Soviet Union and Yugoslavia, and in a number of African countries. In Israel, M. form 13–14% of the population (or 15–16% if the *Druze are considered M.). Considerable non-M. minorities exist in the following AC: Lebanon (40–50%), Syria (c. 30% if the Druze and 'Alawites are considered non-M., 15% if they are counted as M.), Egypt (7–10%), Sudan (25–30% — concentrated mainly in the south, where non-M. African tribes form a large majority).

The M.'s of the world are divided into *Sunnites (who are a large majority) and *Shi'ites (see a brief explanation of that split in the two entries concerned). Sunnites form the majority of M.'s in all AC except Iraq, Yemen, Bahrain, Dubai (and 'Oman, if the *Ibadiyya are considered non-Sunni). Within Sunni I. there are four major schools (*madhhab*, pl. *madhāhib*): a. *Hanafi* — mainly in Turkey, Syria, Iraq and among urban Palestinian M., and predominant in official Islamic institutions in the countries formerly of the Ottoman Empire; b. *Shafe'i* — widespread in Lower Egypt, among rural Palestinians, the Kurds, and in Hijaz, 'Asir, Yemen and South Yemen; c. *Maleki* — in Upper Egypt, Sudan,

Libya, Bahrain and Kuwait; d. *Hanbali* — in Sa'udi Arabia. The distinction between the four *madhahib* concerns principally the interpretation and application of Islamic law, the *Shari'a, and centers on the question how far the Islamic scholars, *'ulama'*, of the first centuries of I., in the first place the founders of the four schools, in the eighth and ninth centuries (*mujtahidun*) were entitled to apply Analogy (*qiyas*), Consensus (*ijma'*) and Independent Reasoning (*ijtihad*) and how much they had to restrict themselves to the stict application of the Tradition (*hadith*). The *Hanafi* school is considered the most flexible or innovative school in that respect, and the *Hanbali* — the most conservative or restictive. However, all four *madhahib* are considered equally orthodox, and the difference between them mainly concerns fine points of the *shari'a*, and the *'ulama'* who deal with them, and little affects the beliefs and practices of the general M. population — except for the stricter fundamentalism imposed by the Hanbali school (which also gave birth to the fundamentalist-puritan movement of the *Wahhabis).

Within Sunni I., several reforming revivalist or fundamentalist movements emerged in the 18th and 19th centuries, such as the *Wahhabis* in the Arabian peninsula, whose tenets were adopted and spread by the Sa'udi clan of tribal leaders in *Najd and later became the ruling creed of Sa'udi Arabia. Other movements were influenced to a greater or lesser extent by the *Wahhabis*, such as the *Mahdiyya and *Khatmiyya (or *Mirghaniyya) in Sudan, the *Sanussis in Cyrenaica (Libya), and the *Idrissiyya in *'Asir. These movements, though orthodox and opposed to Islamic mysticism (*Sufiyya*, Sufism) and its *Dervish orders, adopted some Sufi practices and methods of oganization and set up orders of their own. Sufism itself and its orders are frowned upon by the Islamic establishment, but they remain within recognized, legitimate Sunni I.

Shi'i I. is divided into several trends or sects (see *Shi'a). The principal trend — the *Imamiyya, Ithna-'Ashariyya* (the "Twelvers"), or *Ja'fariyya* — dominates Iran and constitutes a majority in Iraq and Dubai, about half the population of Bahrain, a strong minority in Lebanon (estimates varying from c. 25% to 35% of the population), and smaller minorities in Sa'udi Arabia and several Persian Gulf principalities. In all AC, they count 7.5–8m. *Zeidi Shi'ites dominate Yemen, where they form about 55% of the population, c. 3.5 m. (a figure that is disputed by conflicting estimates). The *Isma'iliyya are a sect on the fringe of Shi'i I., and considered by many as outside I. Though they ruled Egypt, large parts of North Africa and parts of other AC from the 10th to the 12th century, few of them have survived in AC — in Syria (less than 100,000, c. 1% of the population), Yemen and the eastern al-Hasa province of Sa'udi Arabia. Two sects that grew out of the *Isma'iliyya* or were greatly influenced by it, are the *Druze (in Syria, Lebanon and Israel) and the *'Alawites or Nusseiris (in Syria, in Turkey's Hatay-*Alexandretta district, and some in Lebanon). These two sects are considered by many M. as outside the pale of I. (though the 'Alawites in Syria are in official practice treated as M.; the President, who must be a M., is an 'Alawi).

I. is the state religion in all AC except Lebanon, where there is no state religion. Sa'udi Arabia and 'Oman have no written constitution, and the provisional constitutions of Kuwait, Bahrain, Qatar, UAE, and South Yemen do not deal with basic principles — but except for some doubt regarding Marxist South Yemen's attitude, the Islamic character of these states is evident. The links between I. and the state are particularly strong in Sa'udi Arabia whose growth and conquests also spread the Wahhabi school of I., and in Morocco, where the royal dynasty is also endowed with the status of Islamic religious leadership. Similar links existed in the past in Yemen (where the Zeidi-Shi'i *Imam was king) and Libya (where the king was also head of the Sanussi order), but these special links were severed by the revolutions of 1962 in Yemen and of 1969 in Libya. However, modern Arab states, based on Western-type constitutions and administrations, also recognized I. in their constitution, while still under Western tutelage and before complete independence was achieved, either formally as the state religion (Egypt 1923; Iraq 1925; Jordan 1928), or by the stipulation that the Head-of-State must be a M. (Syria 1930). New constitutions adopted after full independence have continued that practice (Libya 1951; Jordan 1952; Tunisia 1959; Morocco 1972). Islamic law is state law in Sa'udi Arabia, the Persian Gulf principalities and Yemen. The *coups* of the 1950s and 1960s and the revolutionary, sometimes socialist or leftist character of the régimes established have effected no basic change in this context: I. figures as the state religion in the constitutions — most of them provisional — of these régimes (Egypt 1956, 1964, 1971; Iraq 1958, 1970; Algeria 1963 and 1976; Libya 1969; Yemen 1970; Sudan 1971–73 — reinforced in 1983 by the imposition of Shari'a laws and punishments). Syria does not explicitly name I. as the state religion, but her constitutions of 1950 and 1973 lay down that the President must be a M. and that Islamic law is the principal source of legislation. (For attempts to adapt the Islamic code of law to the needs of modern states — see *Shari'a.)

Radical-fundamentalist Islamic groups, however, have not been content with that official and constitutional recognition of I. They reject the law codes based in all modern AC (excepting Sa'udi Arabia and several other countries of the Arabian peninsula and the Perisan Gulf) on Western models and the fact that constitutional-political life in most AC is structured on modern rather than Islamic principles, and demand the imposition of the Shari'a and its codes of punishment as the law of the state and the social code of behavior. Many Islamic scholars have always propounded similar views or demands, and during recent decades organized militant movements sprang up to propagate and enforce them. Best known among those was the *Muslim Brotherhood, founded in Egypt in 1929, which set up tightly organized semi-clandestine cells and was prepared to use violence, even terrorist methods and assassination, to achieve its goals. Several other associations propounded similar aims without advocating the use of violence or preparing clandestine units able to use it; still others, particularly in the last decade or two, were even more extremist and violent than the Muslim Brothers. The Brotherhood in the 1940s and 1950s, and other extremist organizations in the 1970s and 1980s, were behind several terrorist plots and political assassinations in Egypt (including Prime Minister M.F. *Nuqrashi in 1948, and President *Sadat in 1981), and resistance to the government in Syria in the 1970s and early 1980s. The Islamic revolution in Iran in 1979, and the aggressively Islamic régime it established, gave a new impetus to such Islamic movements in several AC (though most of them were Sunni, while the Iranian one was Shi'i) and supported and funded extremist Shi'i organizations and "militias" in Lebanon and Iraq.

Most A. governments forcibly suppressed these Islamic-extremist organizations (e.g. Egypt 1948–49, 1954, 1965–66; Egypt and Syria in the late 1970s and early 1980s). But several governments were themselves influenced, to a greater or lesser extent, by the groundswell of Islamic fundamentalism and took steps to enhance Islamic legislation and the influence of Islamic patterns of social behavior, or at least allowed such trends to grow in their representative institutions and among the public. In doing so, they tried to accomodate the more moderate circles among the Islamic fundamentalists and enlist their support against the extremists. This goes, for instance, for Egypt since the 1970s, under Sadat and *Mubarak. Others went much farther — like *Numeiri of Sudan, who imposed in 1983 the Shari'a code of laws and punishments. Some of the Persian Gulf principalities (Kuwait, UAE) also tightened the rule of the Shari'a and its code of punishments. (The same trend is apparent in some non-A. Islamic countries, e.g. Pakistan.)

Isma'il (al-Jawfi), 'Abd-ul-Fattah (1936? 1938?–1986) South Yemeni politician, President of South Yemen 1978–80. Of (North-) Yemeni origin, I. was employed in the 1950s in 'Aden by the British Petroleum Company and was active in the *NLF, the most extremist among the various underground nationalist groups; by 1964 he was considered one of its chief leaders, in charge of its political and military/terrorist activities, and heading its leftist-Marxist wing. When South Yemen attained independence in Nov. 1967, he became Minister of National Guidance and Youth (and for some time also of Planning and Economy) in President Qahtan al-*Sha'bi's Government. But in the factional struggle within the NLF and the Government he took a radical-leftist line; in Mar.–Apr. 1968 he attempted a semi-*coup* that was suppressed and he lost his government post. In June 1969, his leftist faction overthrew al-Sha'bi and he became Secretary-General of the ruling NLF and member of the Presidential Council, under Salem Rubai' *'Ali. He continued heading a leftist, Moscow-loyal faction — together with 'Ali Nasser *Muhammad, — and built up a strong armed party militia and secret services. In the *coup* of Aug. 1971 he and 'Ali Nasser Muhammad consolidated their position, and in June 1978 they overthrew (and killed) President Rubai' 'Ali, and 'Ali Nasser Muhammad became interim chairman of the Presidential Council; in December he ceded that post to I. During the nearly two years of I.'s presidency South Yemen followed the leftist-extremist policy in international, inter-A. and home affairs. These policies, and constant factional struggle, brought I. into growing conflict with 'Ali Nasser Muhammad, who began advocating a more pragmatic, less doctrinaire orientation, and in Apr. 1980 I. was forced to resign the Presidency and go into exile. He spent the next five years in the USSR. Apparently the Soviet Union mediated between the factions and in 1985 arranged an accommodation: I. was allowed to return, and his supporters were restored to party and government positions (in the Politbureau of the ruling party, reportedly, two of his men vs. three of 'Ali Nasser Muhammad's); I. himself became Secretary-General of the party's Central Committee — a post seen by observers as mainly honorific and without real power. However, factional tensions increased during 1985, and it was reportedly only Soviet (and *PLO?) mediation that prevented an eruption. That eruption came in Jan. 1986: a *coup d'état* staged by I. and his faction led to bitter, confused fighting and the overthrow of 'Ali Nasser Muhammad. I. himself was killed (in 'Ali Nasser Muhammad's version: executed).

Isma'iliyya, Isma'ilis A sect that split off Shi'i Islam in the mid-eighth century over the identity of the seventh *Imam, recognizing Isma'il, the son of the sixth Imam Ja'far al-Sadeq, who died before his father (against Mussa al-Kazim accepted by the mainstream Shi'a). The I. later developed doctrines based on esoteric interpretations of the Qur'an and adaptations from Neoplatonic teachings. Some I. groups also propagated radical social and political ideas, such as the Qarmatians (*al-Qarāmita*) of eastern Arabia in the 9th and 10th centuries. The I. Fatimids founded a dynasty in North Africa in the 10th to 12th centuries, and ruled Egypt, Syria and both shores of the Red Sea, including Hijaz with the holy cities of Mecca and Medina, and Yemen. An 11th-century offshoot of the I. was the *Druze sect. The *'Alawi sect also grew out of the I.

Salah-ul-Din conquered Cairo in 1171 and defeated the Fatimids, and the I. were suppressed and gradually disappeared from Egypt and the Maghreb. I. groups survived mainly in Syria, Persia and Yemen. They split into two main branches — the *Musta'lis* or Western I., and the *Nizaris* or Eastern I. The former, believing in a hidden Imam were centered mainly in Yemen; but in the 17th century their center was moved to Gujarat in India and has remained there. These I. have survived in India and are today called *Bohras* or *Boharas*, or *Tayyibis*. Some *Bohra* communities exist in East Africa and Burma, mainly among Indian migrants, but none in the AC.

The *Nizaris*, who recognize a revealed, apparent Imam, ruled several regions in Persia and Syria from fortresses they built, and became known as *Hashshashiyyun* ("Assassins" in Western languages, with their legendary leader the "Old Man of the Mountain"). They developed a doctrine of holy terror, executed by "self-sacrificing" bands, *Fida'iyyun* — a term that has come in modern times to denote guerrillas or terrorists. The rule of the I. Assassins was destroyed by the Mongols in the 14th century. They survived underground and within certain *Sufi* (mystic) orders and gradually lost their violent character. In the 19th century, the Shah of Persia conferred on the 45th Imam of the *Nizaris* the title of Aga Khan; but as he developed ambitions to the throne of Persia or some territorial rule, he had to flee in 1840, to India, where the British, while firmly discouraging his territorial ambitions, accepted him as the spiritual leader and *Imam* of the *Nizari* I., called in India *Khojas*. The title "His Highness the Aga Khan" has passed to his descendants. The Aga Khan, claiming descent from the Caliph 'Ali and the Fatimid Caliphs, is considered an incarnation of the Divinity and his word is law among the *Khoja* I., who number an estimated 15–20m., mostly in India and among Indian migrants in East and South Africa. The *Khoja* I. under the Aga Khan are a tightly knit community; they have developed an elaborate network of welfare, health and educational institutions, and the Aga Khan himself is immensely rich. (The third Aga Khan, Sir Sultan Muhammad Shah, 1877–1957, was the most widely known.)

Few I. have survived in the AC — some 100,000, mainly in Syria and also in the al-Hassa province of Sa'udi Arabia and in Yemen. Their links with the *Khoja* community and the Aga Khan seem to be weak. In Syria, where they are concentrated in the Salamiyyah region, some I. were active in the *Ba'th-led *coups* and the régime they established. Most prominent was the al-Jundi clan (Sami al-Jundi — Cabinet Minister and Ambassador; Col. 'Abd-ul-Karim al-Jundi — chief of the secret service; Khaled al-Jundi — head of the trade unions) — but they were dismissed in the late 1960s ('Abd-ul-Karim committed suicide or was murdered in 1969, and Sami went into exile).

Israel Arabs (I. herself is outside the scope of the Dictionary. Her antecedents and emergence are partly described in *A.-Israel Conflict which deals mainly with her dispute with the *Palestine A. and the ASt. See also *A.-Israel Wars.)

The area earmarked for the future Jewish State by the UN partition plan of Nov. 1947 should have contained c. 400,000 A. (against c. 550,000 Jews). The larger territory emerging in fact as I. from the war of 1948 and endorsed, without prejudice to the final settlement, by the armistice agreements of 1949 would have had an A. population of more than 700,000, had all A. stayed in their places of domicile. However, as 550–650,000 A. left their homes and became *Refugees, emerging I. found herself in 1949, according to a first, incomplete census, with an A. population of c. 107,000. This figure was corrected to 150–160,000 — over 20% of the population — by accounting for more Bedouin in the Negev and for villages in the coastal plain (the Sharon) transferred by Transjordan under the armistice, as well as for c. 30,000 "present refugees" (i.e. A. who had left their domicile but not the territory of I.) and some who had drifted back, clandestinely or with permission. Of the IA, 110–115,000 were Muslims, c. 15,000 *Druze, and 30–35,000 A. Christians. About 110,000 were rural, in 85 villages, c. 30,000 urban, c. 20,000 Bedouin. The percentage of the rural population was highest, over 90%, among the Druze, high among the Muslims — c. 66% in villages and 8% Bedouin — and lower, c. 37%, among the Christians.

In the first years of the new state the percentage of this A. population declined, owing to Jewish mass immigration, to c. 11% in the 1950s and early 1960s (1961 census: 247,461 of a total population of 2,179,461). When Jewish immigration slackened, the percentage began rising. For the A. population was growing by a natural increase that was considerably higher than that of the Jews and a small number of refugees permitted to return under a reunion-of-families scheme or in individual cases (30–40,000 over the years). Since the incorporation of East *Jerusalem into Israel after the *Six Day War of 1967 (finalized in July 1980), its A. population of about 70,000 is in Israeli statistics counted among the A. of I. — though most East Jerusalem A. do not consider themselves IA and, keeping their Jordanian citizenship, make no use of the Israeli one offered to them. By the mid-1980s, the IA, including East Jerusalem, numbered some 750,000, more than 17% of the population; nearly 600,000, close to 80%, were Muslims (including nearly 80,000 Bedouin and settled former Bedouin), c. 70,000 Druze over 90,000 Christians, over 3,000 *Circassians. Of the A. Christians, c. 40% were *Greek Orthodox, c. 40% *Greek Catholics, c. 12% *Latin Catholics, c. 3% *Maronite-Catholics, and c. 5% Protestants and other denominations.

Nearly 50% of the IA live in Galilee, and another 15% — over 100,000 — in East Jerusalem; other main concentrations of A. are the northern Negev (c. 60,000 Bedouin) and the eastern part of the Sharon in the coastal plain (the "Little Triangle"). Over the years, the urban A. population — estimated in 1949 at c. 20% — has increased its share, reaching by the mid-1980s about one-third (precise statistics having little meaning, as many large villages have become semi-urban and many Negev Bedouin are being settled in towns). About 150,000 A. live in "mixed", A.-Jewish, cities such as Jerusalem (though its Eastern A. part and its Western Jewish part have remained rather separate), Haifa (c. 17,000 A.), Jaffa (10–15,000), Acre (c. 9,000). Nearly 100,000 reside in purely A. towns such as Nazareth, I.'s largest A. town, with about 50,000 A. inhabitants in the mid-1980s, Shefa'-'Amr (Shefar'am), Umm al-Faḥm, and the Bedouin resettlement town of Rahat (c. 17,000). Of the c. 85 villages, most are Muslim, but a considerable number are "mixed" Muslim-Christian, sometimes with Druze, too, and several have Christian majorities; the Druze live in 18 villages, of which 11 are purely or over 90% Druze; two villages are *Circassian.

In 1948–49 an estimated 55–60% of the IA were employed in agriculture. This percentage declined in the course of the years, conforming to general economic trends. In 1960 it was still estimated at 40% and in the early 1970s at c. 35%, but in the mid-1980s it is thought to be less than 20%. A. farming has been greatly developed and modernized — irrigation has expanded tenfold, mechanization and modern techniques were introduced, A. villages have been connected to the country's power grid, water supply and roads network. The general standard of living has steeply risen — modern housing, the exception in A. villages before 1948, has become the rule, and most IA households own electric refrigerators, washing machines, gas stoves, radio and television receivers. A. farmers hold and crop about 25% of I.'s agricultural land (formal ownership posing a complex problem, as the registration of ownership was not completed by the British Mandate authorities), and most are linked to I.'s marketing and exporting enterprises. A high percentage of the IA are employed as salaried workers — including an estimated 50% of the rural-agricultural breadwinners — most of them in Jewish enterprises (many — commuting there while residing in their villages). There are some beginnings of industry in the A. sector of the economy, but in general A. industrial enterprise has not kept pace with the general development of the country. Joint A.-Jewish enterprises, too, are only at the beginning.

A special problem is, as everywhere in the ME, the integration of the Bedouin — some 80,000 in the mid-1980s. All I.'s Bedouin are at one stage or another of the general process of settlement, sedentarization, that embraces all the nomads and semi-nomads of the ME. Those in the northern parts of the country — c. 20,000 — have become almost fully settled farmers and/or salaried workers and their encampments have turned into villages. Those in the Negev — c. 60,000 — retain a larger measure of their tribal organization and customs and their semi-nomadic economy based on animal husbandry; but with the intensification of agriculture and the shrinkage of grazing lands, their traditional semi-nomadic economy can no longer support them, let alone enable them to raise and modernize their living standards as they expect and desire. The problem is aggravated by complex issues of land ownership and grazing rights — traditional, unregistered and often disputed. The government is keen to assist and accelerate the process of Bedouin sedentarization and to provide urban or semi-urban settlements for them. Seven townships are being constructed for them, with four of them already populated, and by the mid-1980s 20–25,000 of them have settled in these towns.

There is no formal constitution in I. But under the Declaration of Independence, 1948, and the laws enacted since, the A. of I. have full citizenship and equality of status — a principle whose full implementation was not always easy, given the fact that I. was in bitter conflict with the A. of the neighboring countries (for complaints of unsatisfactory implementation, or discrimination, see below). The IA were exempted from compulsory military service, as it was held that it would not be right to demand of the IA to serve in an army engaged in operations against their A. brethren; but IA are free to volunteer for service in the armed forces — and some do, particularly a significant number of Bedouin. This exemption does not apply to the Druze and Circassians who are conscripted at their own request.

The A. of I. make full use of their voting right, and their voting percentage has since the first elections to I.'s Parliament, the *Knesset*, in 1948, been high, 75–88% (higher than that of the Jewish population). As I.'s election system is fully proportional, votes being cast for party lists, the A. voters could have carried considerable weight, had a united A. list or party been formed to represent their interests. Several A. lists were indeed presented at election time, usually linked with, or under the tutelage of, the Labour Party, which ruled I., in coalition with other parties, from 1949 to 1977. Such lists usually got 40–50% of the A. vote and after the first elections, when only two were elected, 4–5 seats in the 120-member Parliament. However, all these lists remained local, factional creations, centered around regional notables, and none developed into a permanently organized political group that could claim to represent the interests of the IA as a community — the more so as they were seen as dominated by their Jewish tutor-sponsors and serving their interests. These A. lists declined in the late 1960s. In the elections of 1973 they obtained only three seats, in 1977 — one, and in 1981 — none; in 1984 no such list was presented.

An unaffiliated, strongly nationalist A. list (*al-Ard* — "The Land") was in 1965 disqualified as anti-State and subversive, and the Supreme Court upheld that decision.

More than half the A. electorate had in the first place voted for general, not specifically A. parties; their share increased until by the late 1970s they embraced nearly all the A. electorate. These A. votes went to almost all general, mainly Jewish, parties — left, right, center, including even the (Jewish) religious parties; but their main share went either to the Labor Party (later the "Alignment") — which got, together with the Left-Socialist *Mapam* Party, c. 20% of the A. vote in the first two decades of I., somewhat less in the 1970s, and around 25% in 1981 and 1984 — or to the Communist Party (appearing since 1977 as the "Democratic Front for Peace and Equality"), which seemed to attract many A. voters not because they identified with its Communist ideology, but as a protest vote against the Israeli establishment. The Communist share in the A. vote, c. 22% in 1949, declined to 16% and then 11% in the next three elections, rose again to 23% in 1961 and 1965, 29% in 1969, and reached nearly 50% in 1977; it then fell again to c. 38% in 1981, 34% in 1984. Of the Communist Party's voters, A. were a large majority, and though the party kept a Jewish leader or two among its 3–6 *Knesset* members, two or three of them were always A. And it was the A. that were the real leaders — in recent decades mainly Tawfiq Toubi and Tawfiq Ziyad — aligning the party with Moscow's line (e.g. total Israeli withdrawal to the pre-1967 lines and support for a Palestinian-Arab state in the West Bank and Gaza).

In addition to the specifically Arab lists and the Communists, several general parties came to include A. or Druze candidates on their election lists. Left-Socialist *Mapam* had one A. MP since 1951, the Labour Alignment had 1 since 1969, 2 since 1981; the right-wing *Likud* had 1 since 1973, the "Democrats for Change" in 1977 had 2, the List for Change in 1984 had 1, the leftist *Shelli* in 1977 had 1; a new leftist "Progressive List for Peace", in 1984, stressed joint A.-Jewish political action, and 1 of its 2 MPs was A.

Regular elections were also held for two, and since 1985 three, purely A. municipalities and 45 fully-fledged local (village) councils. Since 1975 the municipality of Nazareth is controlled by the Communists, and so are, in recent years, 18 of the local councils. In the mixed towns, A.'s have been elected to the municipal councils of Haifa and Acre; the A. of East Jerusalem decline to be represented on the municipal council and only c. 15% of them take part in municipal elections.

Concerning social security, social welfare, public health and medical care, the A. of I. are covered, as other citizens, by a combination of state institutions and the widespread network of the Trade Unions (*Histadrut*) and their Sick Fund. Their health standards have significantly improved; infant and general mortality rates have steeply decreased; life expectancy and natural increase have risen; and though the birth rate is slowly declining, in line with the rise in living standards, it still is high (over 3%), and so is the resulting natural increase, particularly among Muslims. As to Trade Unions, the original conception, before 1948, had been the development of parallel, separate institutions in the Jewish and the A. sector, federated in a joint umbrella organization. This was changed in 1959–60 and direct, equal membership for A. was introduced. In the 1980s, more than 150,000 A. were members of the *Histadrut* and its Sick Fund, covering, with their families, nearly two-thirds of the A. population, and the Sick Fund maintains clinics in most of the A. villages.

Israel maintains the ME tradition of communal jurisdiction, through religious courts, over matters of personal status, as practiced in the Ottoman Empire and continued by the British Mandate. Ecclesiastical courts deal with these matters for the Christian communities, and *Shari'a courts for the Muslims. Israel has instituted a few reforms in the application of communal law — such as the possibility of appeal to the Supreme Court against judgments of the communal courts — but in substance the *Shari'a* courts are autonomous. Israel has, however, outlawed polygamy, permissible (though not mandatory) under Islamic law. There are 9 *Qadis* in 6 courts of the first instance and a three-Qadi Appeals Court; these Qadis, and their staff, are paid by the government. East Jerusalem again poses a special problem: Muslim leaders opposed the establishment of an Israeli *Shari'a* court there, and local Muslims apply in certain matters to the Jordan-directed hierarchy, and in others to the Qadi of

Jaffa. There are in I. c. 130 mosques, including some 30 built since 1948, and most of them have their own local *Imams*; all Muslim clerical staff number about 250. Since the late 1970s, Sa'udi Arabia permits IA to perform the pilgrimage to Mecca (*Hajj*), restricting the number of permits, and Jordan allows their passage; in recent years, over 3,000 IA p.a. go on that pilgrimage (not counting those from the occupied *West Bank and *Gaza).

Cultural and educational activities among IA are conducted in Arabic. I. has no official language, though most public and cultural life is in Hebrew; however, all official publications must be provided in Arabic, too, and litigants in the courts and A. MP's may demand an Arabic translation. (MP's make little use of that right, as most of them speak good Hebrew — as does a large part of the younger generation among the IA). The state provides a large network of Arabic-language primary schools, and some secondary and vocational ones and teachers' colleges; primary education is compulsory and free, secondary schooling is not compulsory. More than 200,000 A. students attend these schools, including some 30,000 on the secondary level; there are also private schools, mainly those established by Christian churches and institutions, with some 15,000 students. There is no Arabic-language university; A. students wishing to continue academic studies enrol with the Hebrew-language universities (more than 2,000 do) or go to the colleges established in the West Bank after 1967, or abroad.

There are several IA writers and poets, some of them with a certain reputation among A. outside Israel, and several periodical literary publications. However, an Arabic press had developed in pre-1967 I. to a limited degree only. A daily paper (*al-Yawm*) was published by the government and the *Histadrut* jointly from 1948 to 1968. When it was closed, the government issued another Arabic daily (*al-Anba'*), but this was also closed down in Jan. 1985. The only non-governmental Arabic daily paper is the Communist *al-Ittihad*, founded as a weekly in pre-Israel Palestine, in 1944, and resumed in 1948, a daily since 1983. After 1967, a lively Arabic press has grown in East Jerusalem. Its four daily papers (*al-Quds*, from 1968; *al-Sha'b*, 1972; *al-Fajr*, 1972; *al-Mithaq*, 1980) and several weeklies and periodicals, express various trends of Palestinian-A. opinion. They serve both the occupied areas and the IA, but consider themselves Palestinian-A., West Bank organs rather than IA. They all voice sharp opposition to I. and her occupation.

The IA are a community burdened with problems, some of which are perhaps insoluble. The very birth of the community, in 1948, was traumatic: it was a splinter of the Palestine-A. community, born out of its dissolution and in war. It had lost, in the hour of its birth, most of its élite, its leaders, its notables, most of its wealthy and middle class, who had left the country as refugees — and that included most of the teachers, the doctors, the journalists, the religious dignitaries. A large stratum of teachers, vital for the survival of the community, had to be rebuilt and trained speedily; other parts of the middle class and the intelligentsia slowly grew, but the problem of political leadership has remained painfully unsolved (one of the reasons for the influence acquired by the Communist Party was the fact that, though some Communist leaders had also left the country, and some returned later, the Communists were the only organized group to accept the partition of Palestine and to retain an infrastructure of leadership and organization). The acceleration of social change also posed problems. The extended family, the clan (*hamula*), declined as a force of cohesion, at least in the towns and in that part of the village population that became urbanized or permanently worked outside the village.

The question of full equality of rights and status, in principle and in its application, has remained an irritant. Though full equal rights were proclaimed with the foundation of the state, I. was dominated by its Jewish majority and character, and some A. saw a contradiction in principle between her definition as a Jewish State and full equality for her A. citizens. I.'s "Law of Return", for instance, conferring upon every Jew the right to migrate to Israel and immediate citizenship upon arrival, was resented by many A. as discriminatory. As I. was in conflict, sometimes at war, with the AC, there must have been a problem of loyalty. While some IA joined Palestinian-A. terrorist/guerrilla groups, the overwhelming majority of the IA was faultlessly loyal to the state — but it cannot always have been easy for them. But, mainly, many A. felt, and complained, that full equality, so solemnly proclaimed, was not actually implemented. For several years, the regions where the bulk of A. of I. lived were, for security reasons, under military government; this was relaxed in 1957, but entirely abolished only in late 1966. Even after that obstacle was removed, points of friction and complaints of discrimination persisted. Equality was lacking, it was said, in the distribution of government funds for development and services — an issue aggravated by the fact that development funds derived in large part not from taxation-earned state revenue but from Jewish-Zionist donations abroad earmarked for Jewish projects. Land ownership and land seizures also were a frequent irritant, mostly rooted in efforts to repossess land that the government considered state property but to which A. cultivators claimed title. Other irritants were the resistance of Jewish towns or quarters to A. atempts to acquire homes or take up residence, and A. resentment of many benefits granted to army veterans, a group from which most of them were excluded.

In recent years some of these irritants have been removed and complaints alleviated, but the issues involved have not been finally solved. Nor has the basic problem of identity been resolved: do the IA see themselves primarily as Israelis of A. language and ethnicity — or as Palestinian A. with Israeli citizenship? This dilemma has been thrown into sharper focus by the IA's renewed encounter, since 1967, with the Palestinian A. in the occupied areas, and it would seem that a trend of self-identification as Palestinians has been enhanced. (Most IA would probably advocate the creation of a Palestinian-A. state in the occupied areas, alongside I. and in coexistence with her — without themselves wishing to live there.) But there are no easy answers to that problem.

Israel Occupied Territories The territories occupied by I. in the *Six Day War, June 1967, included the *Sinai peninsula (Egypt), the *Gaza Strip (Egypt-occupied), the *Golan Heights (Syria), and the *West Bank with East *Jerusalem (the part of pre-1948 Palestine incorporated in Jordan). The area of these OT extended over nearly 27,000 sq. mi. (70,000 sq. km.), 3.5 times that of Israel. Their A. population was over 1m. — close to 600,000 in the West Bank, 70,000 in East Jerusalem, c. 350,000 in the Gaza Strip, 7,000 in the Golan, and c. 50,000 in Sinai. This population included, according to the figures of *UNRWA (the UN Relief and Work Agency), some 510,000 refugees of the war of 1948 — 245,000 in the West Bank (65,000 in camps) and 265,000 in Gaza (200,000 in camps); I. observers thought these figures concerning refugees to be considerably overestimated, and found their doubts confirmed by data and research prepared after the occupation.

The areas occupied were put, in accordance with international law and practice, under military government, with the laws of the previous owner or occupying country remaining in force. This rule was not applied to East Jerusalem, which was in June 1967 declared "united" with Israeli West Jerusalem, i.e. incorporated in I. — an act formally finalized in July 1980. In Dec. 1981, I. law was applied to the Golan, though no annexation was formally proclaimed. In Sinai, Egypt recovered a strip of territory in the *October War of 1973 and expanded it under the Disengagement and Interim Agreements of 1974 and 1975. Under the *Camp David Agreement of 1978 and the Egypt-Israel Peace Treaty of 1979 all of Sinai was returned to Egypt in Apr. 1982 (a small area of *Taba, near *Eilat, remained in dispute). The remaining OT had on area of c. 3,000 sq. mi. — 2,200 West Bank, 135 Gaza Strip, 720 Golan. Their population was in the mid 1980s over 1.4m. — 0.9m. West Bank (not including East Jerusalem), 0.5m. Gaza Strip, 15,000 Golan.

For the problem of I.'s withdrawal from the OT — I.'s initial offer to withdraw (except for Jerusalem) in return for a peace agreement, and the rejection of that offer by the ASt; UN resolution 242 calling for withdrawal "from OT" and peace; the ASt insistence on *total* withdrawal, unconditional and with no need for negotiations; I.'s proposal to withdraw to "secure and recognized" borders to be negotiated, i.e. partial withdrawal (with I.'s right-wing groups opposing any withdrawal and advocating the incorporation of the OT in I.) — see *Arab-Israel Conflict.

In the West Bank I. followed a policy of "Open Bridges" (and Jordan went along with that practice): mutual visits between the OT and Jordan (and through her other AC) were allowed, though under strict control, and so was the movement of goods and funds — permitting, mainly, the export of the agricultural produce of the OT to Jordan, and through her to other AC. Jordan also retained considerable influence in the West Bank and Gaza — continuing to pay salaries of former officials of her government, channelling funds to certain public and semi-public institutions, and being consulted by OT notables on steps and positions to be taken. Some institutions, such as the *Muslim Council in East Jerusalem, were directly linked to Jordan. But Jordan and King Hussein seemed to enjoy little support in public opinion, and while cultivating their half-concealed links and channels, did little to organize their supporters. From 1978, A. aid funds allotted by an all-A. Summit were to be distributed by a joint Jordanian-PLO committee in 'Amman. However, since about 1986 Jordan seems to be more active in the OT. In 1986 she launched an ambitious $1,300m. five-year plan to develop the OT economically and socially. This scheme would need foreign financial aid (and Israel's assent and cooperation), and it is too soon to judge its prospects of realization.

OT leaders maintained mostly clandestine links with Palestinian-A. organizations abroad, mainly the *PLO. However, the OT's main economic links were with I.: the bulk of their exports went to I., most of their imports came from or through I., and a large part of their labor force — an estimated 35–50% — worked in I. as hired labor. The military government, and the "Civil Administration" established in Mar. 1981 to assist it, employed many local A. officials, some in senior positions, especially in health and education, and the civil courts were manned by local A. judges and staff — though in many cases local officials refused to serve the occupation authorities. Municipalities and local councils also conducted their affairs in a semi-autonomous way. Elections for municipal councils were held in the West Bank in 1972 and 1976. Those in 1976, for which Israel amended the Jordanian election law to allow women to vote for the first time, were won in many townships by nationalists considered PLO-linked. But the military government kept a tight rein, and mayors who engaged in political, nationalist activities were dismissed — thus Fahd Qawasma of Hebron, Bassam Shak'a of Nablus, Rashad Shawa of Gaza, Muhammad Milhem of Halhul, Khalil Khalaf of Ramallah, Ibrahim Tawil of al-Bira; some of them were deported to Jordan. On the other hand, many nationalists regarded mayors serving under the occupation as collaborators, and clandestine hit squads assassinated several of them (thus Zafer al-Masri of Nablus in 1986 and Qawasma of Hebron, in 'Amman, in 1984).

Health and education services greatly developed under the occupation — three colleges, for instance, were allowed to grow into full-fledged universities (none had existed before 1967) and several more were gradually expanding; the number of children schooled increased by c. 70%, that of girls in school more than doubled. Trade unions and various associations were allowed to function, though under strict control. A lively press in East Jerusalem gave reasonably free expression to local opinion, overwhelmingly anti-occupation and anti-I., though restricted by censorship.

Political organization was banned under the military administration — though it existed, of course, underground, both by clandestine political groups and by half-hidden political activities of overt associations. The students of the new universities, particularly those of al-Najah in Nablus and of Bir Zeit, were a center of political activity, sometimes including demonstrations and acts of violence that were suppressed by the military authorities. Most political activity was dominated by sympathy for the PLO — albeit split into rival factions. There were also fundamentalist Islamic groups, sometimes in sharp rivalry with the leftist pro-PLO factions (for instance in elections for student committees). There were cells of Communists, usually cooperating with the nationalist pro-PLO groups. Many of the leading notables were supposed to be pro-Jordan, but taking their lead from Jordanian policies they usually kept a low profile.

Extreme nationalist groups were suppressed by the military authorities, and so were nuclei of a nationalist comprehensive and representative body. An informal clandestine "National Guidance Committee" was suppressed in 1967–68 and several of its leaders were deported, including East Jerusalem ex-Mayor Ruhi al-Khatib, and Dr. Dawud al-Husseini. A new Guidance Committee was formed in 1978–79 by leading mayors (Shak'a, Qawasma, Khalaf, Milhem, Tawil) and representatives of various organizations; it was outlawed and suppressed in 1982, after the dismissal and deportation of some of the leading mayors. On the other hand, I. attitudes to the formation of moderate, pro-Jordanian or potentially pro-I. groupings was fluctuating. In the late 1970s, "Village Leagues" were formed, stressing local interests and willing to cooperate with Jordan and the I. authorities. At first they got no I. support. In the early 1980s, the authorities began supporting such Leagues in various centers, but from about 1983 attitudes changed again, attempts to organize the Leagues into a country-wide federation were foiled, and the whole project was dropped. In general, I. did little to encourage the growth of moderate political groups; moderate mayors and municipal leaders, for instance, who could have grown into a nucleus of political leadership, were not allowed to do so and in several cases were dismissed when they appeared to develop a political profile. There was no progress towards a régime of autonomy, or even a significant devolution of power — though I. governmental and public opinion tended to favor such a development (while A. nationalists, and the PLO, rejected it). When in the mid-1980s the USA, Israel, Egypt and Jordan were looking for authentic Palestinian-A. representatives from the OT for planned peace talks — not PLO activists, but acceptable to the PLO as well as to Israel and Jordan — no progress was made on this either.

There was no general uprising in the OT, but a measure of violent resistance was endemic and permanent, its intensity fluctuating — sporadic acts of terrorism, seldom against I. army installations or patrols, and mostly against transportation and/or individual Israelis; and, chiefly, violent popular demonstrations and the stoning of vehicles, mainly by adolescents. The military authorities brought culprits to trial, where possible, and the courts handed down harsh prison sentences. When there was no proof, the authorities imposed administrative detention and the demolition of the houses of suspects and their families (under regulations, still valid, of the British Mandate and the Jordanian administration). Some suspects were deported to Jordan.

In addition to opposition or resistance to the occupation as a whole, which was general and total, the A. population of the OT had many specific complaints. These concerned, in the first place, Jewish settlement in the OT, and the seizure of land. Settlements were sometimes founded by non-governmental groups, whose pressure the government was unwilling or unable to resist (though in some cases the government halted or removed such groups) but in most cases by the I. government. Until 1977, the Labor-dominated government set up agricultural-military outposts mainly in areas which I. planned to retain in a future peace agreement under the *"Allon Plan", such as the Jordan Valley or the "Etzion Bloc" south of Bethlehem (where settlements had existed before 1948 and the land was Jewish-owned) — but even the Labor-led government planned and initiated some settlements in the Jerusalem area, and a Jewish suburb of Hebron (Kiryat Arba'). The right-wing Likud government, 1977–84, abandoned that restraint — in its days the emphasis was on semi-urban rather than agricultural settlements, with most of the settlers commuting to I. for their work. A special irritant for the A. was the effort to settle Jews inside Hebron — a town where Jews had indeed lived until 1929, when many of them were slain, and where Jews owned real estate. By the mid-1980s, and after the withdrawal from about 20 settlements in Sinai under the I.-Egypt peace treaty, there were about 100 settlements (versions differ as to what precisely should be counted as a settlement) — 30 in the Golan, 14 in the Gaza Strip, and c. 60 in the West Bank (of which c. 25 in the Jordan Valley) — with a Jewish population of 40–50,000 (not counting another 90–100,000 in Jerusalem suburbs built on formerly West Bank land). The militant settlers, mostly right-wing nationalist with a strong religious motivation, also sometimes used violence against A.'s they considered law-breakers (e.g. in stoning incidents), claiming the government and army were not acting firmly enough. There were even some fringe outgrowths of Jewish nationalist-religious zealot terrorism. Some such cells were discovered and brought to trial, including a group that attacked the Islamic College in Hebron in July 1983, and another one alleged to have plotted an assault against the *Haram al-Sharif*, the Temple Mount, arrested in Mar. 1984. The perpetrators of bomb attacks on several A. mayors, who were wounded, in June 1980, were not found.

Land for the settlements was in part bought from A. owners, but most of it was seized, as was land for military camps and installations and other public purposes, such as the construction of a network of roads. Most of the land seized was considered, by the I. authorities, government or state land; but the A. inhabitants, including some who cultivated parts of the land seized, claimed much of those lands as their property — claims that in most cases could not be proven in the absence of land deeds registration under the British and Jordanian régimes — or at least on the strength of old-established cultivation rights, and many cases were brought to the I. Supreme Court. A.'s questioned, at any rate, I.'s right to use state lands for settlement purposes. Of the c. 1.4m. acres of the West Bank (of which c. 0.5m. acres were cultivated), 40–50%, mostly uncultivated, were, according to various estimates, seized by the military government — most of it for military purposes, roads, etc., and c. 0.35m. acres for settlement.

A.'s also complained that large parts of the region's water resources were used for Israeli purposes, with restrictions imposed on local use. Moreover, they claimed, the economy of the OT was steered to serve I.'s interests — agriculture being encouraged, and geared to Israeli needs, while industrial growth was stymied, and the labor force was guided to serve as a reservoir for hired labor in I. Even the development of roads was, they complained, geared to I.'s needs. Foreign aid, governmental and particularly that of non-governmental organizations, also had to be vetted by the I. authorities, and not all projects offered were allowed. Incessant complaints concerned the allegedly harsh treatment of the inhabitants. I. prided herself on what she considered an eminently humane occupation régime compared with any similar occupation in modern history — no death sentences, a very sparing use of administrative detention, fair trials, a near-complete freedom of expression and the press. But the A.'s saw it differently: trial by military courts, detention without trial, demolition of houses, deportations, harsh interrogations (sometimes even violent methods and torture were charged), the denial of the freedom of association, Jewish settlement, and the economic policies described, amounting in A. view to spoliation — all these formed an ever-repeated tale of oppression. Part of I. public opinion was also increasingly unhappy with the occupation, and particularly its harsh, brutal aspects.

Large parts of world opinion, governmental and public, supported the A. position on the OT, i.e. found fault, in addition to pressing for an end to the occupation altogether, with I.'s administration and practices and frequently condemned them. This goes in particular for the Soviet Bloc, Islamic countries and most of the "Third World", and leftist circles in the West, but many Western governments were also highly critical of I. in this matter. This general trend found frequent expression in UN debates and votes. I.'s occupation practices were a near-permanent item on the agenda of the UN General Assembly and, in various contexts, of several committees and international agencies, and they were condemned in numerous votes by large majorities; I. came to regard, and disregard, these votes as a ritual performed by a hostile majority with little or no concern for facts.

Decisions of the Security Council were sometimes prevented by a veto of the USA. The UN also established special committees to investigate the occupation (see *UN). As I.'s request for a parallel investigation in the AC (e.g. concerning the human rights situation of the Jews) was rejected and, moreover, the main committee was composed of representatives of three countries maintaining no diplomatic relations with I., she refused to cooperate with the committee, and the latter could not visit the OT but was relegated to collecting "evidence" abroad.

Italy, Italian interests and policies in the Arab countries Italian interests in the ME go back to the Middle Ages, when Italian cities traded in the Eastern Mediterranean and founded large colonies, churches, monasteries, schools, hospitals, and missions in many ME cities.

In modern times, I.'s involvement in the ME began with the Italian-Turkish War of 1911–12, caused by I.'s aspirations to impose her domination on *Tripolitania and *Cyrenaica and her complaint that Turkey, suspicious of Italian designs, sabotaged her interests there. I. emerged from the war in possession of *Libya and the Dodecanese islands. Since the 1880s she also fostered interests and designs in the *Red Sea, from her colonies in *Eritrea and *Somalia. When I. joined the *Entente* in World War I, she pursued further expansionist interests in the direction of Asia Minor. In the secret Agreement of London, Apr. 1915, Britain, France, and Russia agreed that upon the defeat and dismemberment of the Ottoman Empire I. should obtain the south-western part of Anatolia. The Agreement of St. Jean de Maurienne, Apr. and Aug. 1917, designed to harmonize these promises with the *Sykes-Picot Agreement and France's aspirations to south-east Anatolia incorporated in it, assigned to I. the districts of Izmir and south-west Anatolia. In May 1917 Italy assured the Zionist leaders of her support for the *Balfour Declaration and Zionist aspirations. The secret inter-Allied agreement accompanying the Peace Treaty of *Sèvres with Turkey, Aug. 1920, confirmed that south-west Anatolia was to be an Italian sphere of influence (but Izmir was given to Greece). However, as the Treaty was abrogated, the accompanying agreement remained inoperative and I. lost her share of the spoils (she kept the Dodecanese).

Fascist I. began in the early 1930s to take a more active interest in the ME. At first she continued to support Zionism; in 1934, Mussolini suggested to Weizmann the cantonization of Palestine as a solution. But I. soon began wooing the A. of Palestine and the ME. She subsidized A. nationalists, such as Hajj Amin al-*Husseini, the Mufti of Jerusalem, and Radio Bari broadcast anti-British propaganda directed to the A.'s. I.'s conquest of Ethiopia in 1935–36 enhanced her position as a Red Sea power. She began supplying *Ibn Sa'ud with arms on favorable terms and trained his pilots, in return for his early recognition of her annexation of Ethiopia. She also renewed in 1937 a treaty of friendship with the Imam of Yemen which she had concluded in 1926, and her influence in the Yemen increased. I. also attempted to woo Iraq by offering arms on credit and free training for Iraqi air-force officers. An agreement with Britain of April 1938 provided that neither power would acquire a "privileged position of a political character" in Sa'udi Arabia and the Yemen; Italian anti-British propaganda broadcasts, which I. pledged to stop, were only temporarily halted. For I.'s colonial rule of Libya and Libyan resistance see *Libya.

When I. entered World War II, on 10 June 1940, the ME became a theater of war, with Egypt as an immediate target for Italian attack from Libya. For I.'s offensives — repelled and resumed in a see-saw sequence, with German troops playing an ever-increasing role, and finally halted in 1942 at al-'Alamein; her defeat and the loss of her North African empire — see *World War II. She had entered the war with obvious ambitions in the ME, particularly in Egypt and the Sudan, which were partly recognized by the Germans (Hitler assured Mussolini and his Foreign Minister in June 1940 that "the Mediterranean... had from ancient times belonged to the historical sphere of influence of the Apennine peninsula"). After the fall of France, 1940, an Italian military commission was stationed in Vichy-controlled Lebanon and Syria to supervise the implementation of the armistice agreement. The Commission seems to have taken no interest in A. nationalist demands, but its presence was seen as a grave threat to the Allies as preparing the ground for a German-Italian invasion; it was ended by the British-Free-French conquest of Syria and Lebanon in June 1941. In 1941, I. also lost to British forces her N.E. African empire: Somalia, Eritrea and Ethiopia.

Throughout the war I. and Germany negotiated with Hajj Amin al-Husseini and Iraq's Rashid 'Ali al-*Kilani — both in Germany since 1941, after Rashid 'Ali was defeated in his war against Britain, with Germany and I. unable to come to his rescue — on an Axis declaration in favor of A. independence and Pan-Arabism. Mussolini favored a declaration of A. independence in Iraq, Syria, Lebanon, Palestine and Transjordan, but was not eager to extend similar support to the idea of A. unity or independence for Egypt and Sudan — two countries on which he had designs. Despite propaganda broadcasts in that direction, no formal declaration was made. In May 1942 Husseini also discussed with Mussolini the formation of an A. Legion, and A. units were actually formed by both Germany and I. However, most pro-Axis A. preferred Germany to I., because of I.'s colonial record in Libya and her military weakness.

I.'s capitulation in Sept. 1943 removed her from the ME arena. After the War I. was awarded a UN Trusteeship over her former colony of Somalia, but this ended with Somalia's independence in 1960. I. also attempted to retain possession of at least part of her Libyan empire in the form of a trusteeship over Tripolitania, but failed in 1949 (see *Libya). The number of her colonists in Libya, many of whom had been withdrawn during the war, continued to decrease; in 1970 their departure was further accelerated by the confiscation of their properties by the new, revolutionary-nationalist régime, and only about 15,000 remained — no longer as colonists with landed property. I.'s interests in Libya were now mainly economic, largely oil-linked. Yet, she has retained strong economic links with Libya and a degree of influence and seems to enjoy in that country the strongest position of all European countries. I.'s activities in other AC have also been mainly economic, in particular through her vigorous national oil company, ENI, which began operating in the 1950s in several AC. In her general ME policies I. is guided by the *EEC (see there). She maintains normal relations with both Israel and most AC — though, it is felt in Israel, sometimes with a pronounced pro-A. slant. On the other hand, I. is frequently troubled, like other European countries, by acts of A. terrorism perpetrated on her soil and by the contradiction perceived between the need to take strong action against the AC considered responsible, including Libya, and the political interest to maintain good relations with those countries.

J

Jacobites Alternative name, used mainly in the West, for the Syrian-Orthodox *Monophysite Christians. The name derives from Jacob Baradaeus who reorganized the Syrian Church in the 6th century, after its beginnings in the secession of the Monophysites from the main body of the Church at the Council of Chalcedon (451). The language of the J. liturgy is Syriac-Aramaic — and a few J. still use that language as their spoken tongue. The head of the Church, the Patriarch, bears the title Mar Ignatius; his seat is in Damascus. One of the 11 dioceses of the J. Church is headed by the Archbishop of Jerusalem; the J. have certain rights in the Church of the Holy Sepulchre in Jerusalem and in the Church of the Nativity in Bethlehem. There are today an estimated 150–200,000 J. in the ME — about half of them in Syria and the rest in Iraq, Lebanon, Turkey, and a very few in Jerusalem; about 50,000 live in the Americas, and there is a strong ancient J. community numbering more than 1m. in South India (the "Malabar Christians").

Jadid, Salah (b. 1929) Syrian officer and politician. An *'Alawi born in Lataqia, J. became a professional officer. In the 1950s he joined a clandestine cell of the leftist Pan-A. *Ba'th party and soon played a leading role. He was among those who prepared and staged the *coup* of Mar. 1963 that brought the Ba'th to power. After the Ba'th group won in a bitter factional struggle with the *Nasserists, J. became, later in 1963, Chief-of-Staff. In Oct. 1964 he was also made a member of the Presidential Council, and of both the "national" (i.e. all-A.) and the "regional", Syrian, high command of the Ba'th party. In the intra-Ba'th factional struggle that erupted in 1964–65, J. headed the "military" faction that was also more extreme-leftist and doctrinaire in its political orientation (besides having a more pronounced 'Alawi profile). When the "civilian" and more moderate wing, led by *'Aflaq, *Bitar and Amin *Hafez won out, J. was dismissed in Sept. 1965 both from the Presidential Council and as Chief-of-Staff. However, in Feb. 1966 J. ousted the ruling 'Aflaq-Hafez faction in a *coup* and installed his military faction both in the Syrian state and army and in the Syrian-regional Ba'th command. As the 'Aflaq faction, now in exile, retained its leadership of the all-A. Ba'th command, J. and his associates set up a rival all-A. command in Syria.

In the new régime he established in 1966 J. took no formal post in either the government or the army but contented himself with the position of Deputy Secretary-General of the Ba'th Party, leaving the Secretary-Generalship to Nur-ul-Din al-*Atassi. In fact he was the strong man of Syria for over four years. His rule was doctrinaire and leftist both inside Syria and in foreign relations (see *Syria). The increasing isolation of Syria within the A. world caused by J.'s policies was one of the reasons for a widening further split within the Ba'th. Parts of J.'s own military faction, led by Defense Minister Hafez *Asad, coalesced in a "nationalist" faction and turned against J. In Feb. 1969 Asad, in a bloodless semi-*coup*, gained control of the government and the party command. He accepted a compromise: a coalition in which the J. group kept some important posts. In 1970 Asad, in a second semi-*coup*, seized full control. J. and his associates were dismissed and detained — as it turned out, for over 10 years. J. was released in 1983 (according to unconfirmed rumors he had rejected an earlier offer to release him, as his conditions were not met). He is kept under close surveillance and not allowed to play any rôle in public-political life.

A brother of J., Major Ghassan J., also a professional officer, was politically active in a formation very much different from, and opposed to, J.'s Ba'th: the *"Syrian Nationalist Party". He was murdered in Feb. 1957, in exile in Lebanon. Another brother, Fu'ad, was jailed in connection with the murder of Syria's leftist and pro-Egyptian Deputy Chief-of-Staff 'Adnan al-Maleki by the same "Syrian Nationalist Party" in 1955; J. released him from prison.

Jaffa An ancient town on the coast of Palestine, now in Israel. Though not endowed with a natural harbor, J. served as a port from antiquity and in the late 19th and early 20th centuries again developed into a center of economic activity and Palestine's main port (until overtaken by the modern deep-water port of Haifa, opened in 1932). J. was the town with the largest A. population in Palestine (c. 65,000 in 1944). Adjacent to it, the Jewish suburb of Tel Aviv, founded in 1909, had by that time grown into a much larger city.

The abortive partition plan of 1937 allotted J. to the part of Palestine to be kept under a British Mandate; the 1947 plan of the UN Special Committee (*UNSCOP) awarded it to the Jewish State. This was changed in the scheme adopted by the UN General Assembly in Nov. 1947, which allotted J. to the A. State, as an enclave. This idea became unworkable when fighting broke out and Palestine had to be partitioned in war rather than in peaceful cooperation. J. surrendered to Jewish forces in May 1948, on the eve of Israel's independence and before they had become the Israel Defense Forces. Most of its A. inhabitants had fled duirng the fighting, some 3,500–4,000 remained. J., which had a substantial Jewish population before 1948, now became a Jewish-majority city, with Jews settling in the abandoned houses and building new ones. In 1950, J. was joined to the municipality of Tel Aviv, now called Tel Aviv-J., and its population figures were no longer separately computed. Its A. population was estimated at 10–15,000 in the mid-1980s.

Jallud, 'Abd-ul-Salam (b. 1940/1? 1943?) Libyan officer and politician. Since 1969, Col. *Qadhdhafi's chief associate and Libya's "Number Two" leader under various official designations. A professional officer, commissioned 1965, J., then a captain, took part in Qadhdhafi's *coup* of 1 Sept. 1969. Promoted to Major, he became a member, and informally: deputy chairman, of the Revolutionary Command Council — a position he kept when that Council was renamed in 1977 "General Secretariat", until Mar. 1979. In Jan. 1970 he joined Qadhdhafi's new government as Deputy Premier and Home Minister, becoming Minister of Economy and Industry in Sept. In Aug. 1971 the post of Deputy Premier was abolished, a measure interpreted by some as the dismissal of J. from that post; he retained his portfolios. In July 1972 he became Prime Minister, replacing Qadhdhafi — a shift again interpreted by some observers as the result of a factional struggle inside the junta and a restriction of Qadhdhafi's power (?). J. became increasingly responsible for the conduct of Libya's foreign relations, particularly from 1974, when Qadhdhafi decided to devote himself mainly to basic and ideological matters and leave daily government affairs to his associates. When, in Mar. 1977, Libya became a *"Jamahiriyya"* (Polity, or Republic, of the Masses) and changed the nomenclature of her governance, J. became a member (semi-officially: deputy chairman) of the "General Secretariat" which replaced the Revolutionary Council, i.e. in effect Deputy Head-of-State.

In Mar. 1979, both Qadhdhafi and Jallud resigned their positions on that Secretariat. They have since formally held no government posts — but their real power as Head-of-State and Deputy Head-of-State is undoubted, relying on the army, the all-pervasive secret service and the "people's committees" they have built up.

Frequent rumors of factional disputes, with J. allegedly heading a faction rivalling Qadhdhafi, have never been substantiated. But J. is no-doubt very different from Qadhdhafi, both in personal character and politically. He does not have his leader's erratic firebrand charisma, and being a rather more pragmatic man of management and power manipulation he does not share Qadhdhafi's devotion to ideological doctrines with their revolutionary fervor in Islamic, social, political and international matters. He also reportedly has little part in Qadhdhafi's obsession with Pan-Arab unity and his relentless pursuit of mergers (such as Qadhdhafi's 1972–73 insistence on immediate union with Egypt), and favors an orientation towards closer *Maghrib co-operation. Yet, though rumors abound on differences and power rivalries, he has never publicly challenged Qadhdhafi's doctrines or policies, nor his support for and use of international terrorism. J. is the architect of much of Libya's foreign relations, particularly those with the USSR, where he has been, since 1972, a frequent visitor.

Japan J. was not particularly active in the ME until World War II. After the war, her growing need for ME oil and markets for her expanding industrial exports prompted her to increase her economic activities in the region, though she took care to avoid any political involvement. As J. endeavors to reduce the share of oil and gas in her energy consumption, the import of ME oil has therefore been declining over the last decade. Yet, its share in her oil imports of c. 230m. tons p.a., which was 80–90% in the 1970s, still is c. 70% in the mid-1980s, and that of the AC over 50%. J. buys nearly all of the liquified gas produced by Sa'udi Arabia and the Persian Gulf principalities. Japanese companies have also been increasingly active in oil and gas production in the AC, mostly in partnership with other companies and particularly local state enterprises. A first concession to a Japanese group was granted in 1958, for the offshore area of the Sa'udi-Kuwaiti Neutral Zone — based on a 57% share of the revenues for Kuwait (the first to break the principle of a 50:50 distribution of revenue that had become usual since the end of 1950); production began in 1961. The same and other Japanese companies in the later 1960s and 1970s took up substantial shares of existing groups and/or set up their own, new enterprises in Abu Dhabi (UAE), Qatar and Egypt. In Iraq, a Japanese group participated in a service contract. Oil and gas from J.'s own production in the AC is estimated at c. 15% of her total oil and gas imports.

J. also won a large share in the imports of the AC, particularly the newly oil-rich ones on the Persian Gulf (cars for instance), and Japanese companies participated in numerous development projects, such as the construction of power stations, harbors, dockyards, petrochemical plants etc. A Japanese concern also won a contract to rebuild the *Hijaz Railway, but this contract was later cancelled. While J.'s enterprises sometimes took minority shares in projects constructed (e.g. in Dubai's aluminum plant), they generally avoided entering into fully fledged joint ventures (an exception, outside our scope, was a large petrochemical plant at Bandar Shahpur — later renamed Bandar Khomeini — in Iran, begun in the 1970s; this project ran into serious difficulties and was halted).

J. maintains normal diplomatic relations with all the countries of the region. Her relations with Israel, though correct, have been kept at a rather low profile, and Japanese companies hesitate to become too actively involved in economic relations with Israel so as not to antagonize the ASt's where their main interests are located. J. also took a rather unfriendly attitude towards Israel in the crisis of 1973 which she perceived to threaten her oil supplies: she fully backed A. demands for a speedy and total Israeli withdrawal from all occupied territories and independence for the Palestine A.'s, and threatened to "reconsider" relations with Israel should these demands not be met.

al-Jazira (Arabic: island or peninsula.) The region between the *Euphrates and *Tigris Rivers in NW Iraq and NE Syria. The appellation al-J. is used mainly for the Syrian part. The J. is today divided into three administrative districts: Hasake, Deir al-Zor and Raqqa. It is a semi-desert area and used to be the range of the nomadic Shammar tribes. During this century there was an influx of non-A. or non-Muslim migrants, mainly from Turkey and northern Iraq, such as *Kurdish tribes, Christians (*Armenians, *Assyrians, *Monophysitic Syrian-Orthodox *Jacobites), Turcomans — and the majority of the J. population was estimated to be non-Syrian and not Muslim-Sunni.

When France obtained the Mandate for Syria (1920, formally 1922), she set up a semi-separate administration for the J. — apparently in order to weaken the Sunni-led A. nationalist movement in Syria. In 1924 the region was merged in the "State of Syria" established that year. French rule restrained the Bedouin tribes and the J. began attracting agricultural settlers and some development started. In the 1930s, the French continued to encourage separatist and autonomist tendencies in the J., but Syrian nationalism halted that trend.

Since World War II, more virgin land has been developed in the J. and Bedouin and Muslim-Sunni Syrians were encouraged to settle. The cultivated area of the J. grew from c. 50,000 acres in 1942 to almost 1.25m. acres in the 1950s, and scores of new villages sprang up. Until the 1950s the J. was developed mainly by private entrepreneurs, owners of tractors and farming machinery, through extensive cultivation of large areas and some irrigation by pumping from the Euphrates. From the 1960s, development is chiefly state-managed. Since the 1970s, it is based mainly on large-scale irrigation works linked to the new Euphrates Dam opened in 1974. The J. is also Syria's main oil-bearing region (see *oil). An oil pipeline connects the J. to a refinery built at Homs and the oil port of Tartus. Since 1974 the J. is linked to Aleppo and the port of Lataqia by a railroad.

With the influx of Syrian Sunni settlers in recent decades, the J. seems to have lost its character as a region populated mainly by minority groups.

Jerusalem (Arabic: *al-Quds al-Sharif*, or, in short, *al-Quds*). City in Palestine/Israel, sacred to Judaism, Christianity and Islam (see also *Holy Places); since 1950 capital of Israel. Population, in the mid-1980s, c. 430,000 (306,000 Jews, 120–130,000 A.'s, of whom 108,000 Muslims, and c. 15,000 Christians). Possession and control of J. has been for decades a major issue in the *Arab-Israel Conflict.

J., always the center and main city of Palestine, was in the last half-century of Turkish-Ottoman rule the capital of a Special District (*Sanjaq*, outside the jurisdiction of the ordinary Ottoman provinces, *vilayet*). It was then a small town, with a population of c. 60,000 at the beginning of the 20th century. While up to the mid-19th century Jews had been slightly less than half the population, they had by the 1890s become a majority. Until the 1860s, J. had been confined to the walled Old City; since that time, Jews had begun building new quarters outside the walls, West of the Old City, and new A. quarters (and foreign, mostly missionary ones — German, Greek, American) followed. Under the British Mandate (1920–48), J. was the capital of Palestine. It was also the headquarters of the Jewish and A. national institutions and the communal Muslim, Jewish and Christian institutions. Several disputes concerned the Holy Places — Christian communities clashing over certain rights, particularly at the Church of the Holy Sepulchre, and, mainly, a Muslim-Jewish conflict over rights at the Western Wall (the *"Wailing Wall", sacred to the Jews and seen by the Muslims as part of the *Haram al-Sharif*, the Temple Mount, sacred to them); the latter dispute was one of the main causes of the Disturbances of 1929. During the years of the Mandate, J.'s population grew to c. 165,000 (100,000 Jews, 65,000 A.). Despite the Jewish majority, the Mayor was, until 1944, an A. (Mussa Kazim al-*Husseini 1918–20, Ragheb al-*Nashashibi 1920–34, Hussein al-*Khalidi 1934–37, Mustafa al-Khalidi 1937–44).

Under the abortive 1937 plan for the partition of Palestine, J. would have remained under a British Mandate. The UN resolution of Nov. 1947 on the partition of Palestine into a Jewish and an A. State provided for J. to be internationalized, under the supervision of the UN Trusteeship Council. This recommendation was rejected by the ASt along with the whole partition resolution; the Jews, while having grave misgivings, did not formally reject it. However, when fighting broke out, the UN was unable to protect the population of J., supply it with food and water and install an administration assuring law and order, and the Jews (from May 1948: the State of Israel) and A.'s had to defend themselves, ensure their survival and establish their own administration.

The secret agreement the Jewish leadership had reached with King *'Abdullah of Jordan did not cover J. and, after months of bitter fighting between Jewish forces (the *Hagana*) and A. local guerrillas in J. and its surroundings, and particularly over the road-corridor connecting it with the coastal plain, Jordan's army, the *"A. Legion", began actively intervening in the fighting early in 1948 — even before the Mandate expired and Israel was founded. Jordan's military participation in the war from May 1948 onward also centered mainly on J. — whose Jewish part was since Apr. cut off from the rest of the country, besieged and shelled, and without supplies — and the Latrun region controlling the road to J. Israeli forces were able to hold the Jewish, Western part of the city and to take the South-Western A. quarters, but failed to hold, or retake, the Jewish Quarter of the Old City, which surrendered, with its c. 1,700 inhabitants, to the A. Legion on 28 May; it was largely destroyed — including its ancient synagogues. On 1 Dec. 1948, Jordan set up a military administration in the Old City and East J. (and the whole *"West Bank") — except for Mount Scopus, with the Hebrew University and Hadassah Hospital, which Israel held as an enclave.

The Israel-Jordan Armistice Agreement of Apr. 1949 confirmed the *de facto* partition of J. that had taken place. It provided, however, for a joint committee to ensure free access to the holy places (meaning in fact, mainly: for Jews to the Western Wall and the ancient Jewish cemetery on the Mount of Olives — which was desecrated under the Jordanian occupation, as later transpired), as well as to Mount Scopus; the Armistice also placed a limit on the arms and forces allowed into J. and dealt with J.'s water supplies and other technical questions. The joint committee never met; access to the holy places was denied to the Jews (and to Israeli A.'s), and the cultural and medical institutions on Mount Scopus were not allowed to operate, access to the enclave being granted only to changing teams of Israeli police, under the supervision of UN observers.

While the partition of the city and the incorporation of its two parts in Jordan and Israel hardened, the UN kept reaffirming its internationalization plan (also included in the abortive proposals submitted by the UN Mediator Count *Bernadotte — who had at first favored giving the whole of J. to the A. state). In Dec. 1948, the General Assembly resolved J. should be "under effective UN control", instructed the newly appointed *"Palestine Conciliation Commission" (PCC) to prepare a "detailed proposal for a permanent international régime", and asked the Security Council to ensure the demilitarization of J.; in fact nothing was done. In Dec. 1949, the Assembly "restated its intention" to establish an international régime in J. and charged the Trusteeship Council with the preparation of a "Statute of J.". At the Assembly of 1950, various proposals to effect internationalization, or at least some functional aspects of internationalization, were presented; some were adopted in committee, but none obtained the two-thirds majority needed in the plenary Assembly. While the internationalization plan has remained on the UN books, no further efforts were made since 1950 to implement it.

Israel by now firmly opposed the internationalization of her part of J. Jordan also explicitly opposed internationalization since 1950. She had transformed her military administration into a civilian-political one and in Apr. 1950 formally annexed East J. (and the West Bank). Israel began locating the institutions of her capital in J. — the Supreme Court in Sept. 1948; the *Knesset* (Parliament) in 1949; the President's official residence in 1949; ministries from 1949–50. In Jan. 1950, Parliament proclaimed J. Israel's capital since the day of her independence in May 1948. Most foreign states refused to recognize that act and kept their embassies in Tel Aviv; but several countries transferred their embassies to J. — and even those who refused did not refuse to perform in J. highly official acts, such as the presentation of their ambassadors' credentials, or official visits to the President, the Premier or Foreign Minister.

On 7 June, during the *Six Day War, Israeli forces took all of East J. The city was immediately declared united, all partition barriers were removed and movement between the two parts was made free and uncontrolled for both Jews and A. On 29 June 1967, Israel applied to East J. her "laws, jurisdiction and administration" — an act amounting to *de facto* annexation. That incorporation or annexation was formally completed by a law of 30 July 1980. Since 1967 the Jewish Quarter of the Old City has been completely rebuilt and resettled, the hospital and the university on Mount Scopus have been reconstructed and greatly expanded, and several large new suburbs have been built South, North and North-West of J. on land that was before 1967 part of the West Bank; these suburbs — with a population of 90–100,000 in the mid-1980s — have been incorporated, together with several A. suburbs North of J., in the J. municipality. Israel did not interfere in the administration of the Muslim Holy Places, the *Haram al-Sharif*, but left a Muslim Council and the *Waqf* (religious endowments) administration in charge.

East J.'s A. inhabitants — c. 70,000 in 1967, c.

130,000 in the mid-1980s — did not automatically become Israel citizens, but were entitled to apply for citizenship (very few did); they had the right to vote in municipal elections (c. 20% did in 1969, c. 10% in 1973, c. 15% in 1978, over 20% in 1983). Indeed, the A.'s of East J. did not willingly accept the incorporation of their city in Israel; most of them maintained their Jordanian citizenship and considered themselves Palestinian A.'s and their city — the capital of the West Bank (and of a future Palestinian-A. state), at present occupied. And though the city was united and open and there were economic links between its two parts, the parts remained virtually separate in their basic economy, and even more so in their social and cultural life; East J. also remained the cultural and political center of the West Bank.

There was also, since 1967, some anti-Israeli violence — terrorism or guerrilla resistance — by A.'s in J. There have been ups and downs in the number and intensity of such incidents; generally they have remained isolated and have not turned into a major resistance movement. In recent years, there have also been cases of Jewish extremist violence — both nationalist-motivated "counter-terrorism", and religious-nationalist plots to take over the Temple Mount or even destroy the Muslim sanctuaries there; some of these fanatics have been apprehended, tried and sentenced. (Many A.'s have always suspected such Jewish or even official Israeli designs and attributed to them incidents not connected to them, such as a 1969 attempt to set fire to al-Aqsa mosque committed by a demented Australian-Christian tourist — an act that was interpreted throughout the A. and Muslim world as an Israeli assault on the *Haram al-Sharif* and led to an all-Islamic summit meeting, convened to plan counter-action, and to the establishment of an all-Islamic J. Committee).

The ASt's have never accepted the annexation of East J. by Israel. They demand its restoration to A. rule (Palestinian, Jordanian, or combined), together with the West Bank, and most see it as the capital of a future Palestinian-A. state. Most Israelis consider a united J. indivisible, and the capital of Israel, and even moderates do not include it in those parts of the occupied West Bank that might be restored to A. rule in a peace settlement. Ideas of an open city serving both nations as capital, a united city divided into boroughs, joint sovereignty with A. control of *al-Haram al-Sharif*, and the like, have been mooted, but have never been seriously discussed. And the J. issue looms as a particularly intractable problem within the general A.-Israel conflict.

The international community, too, has not accepted Israel's annexation of East J. and no foreign state has recognized it. The UN General Assembly resolved in July 1967 that the steps taken by Israel to alter J.'s status were invalid and should cease. The Security Council sharply called on Israel, in May 1968 and July 1969, to cancel all measures for the annexation of J. Similar resolutions, coupled with severe condemnations of Israel, have been reiterated annually by UN institutions; Israel has disregarded them.

Jews in the Arab countries Until the mid-20th century, ancient, deeply rooted Jewish communities existed in most AC. Ancient kingdoms and tribes in the Arabian peninsula, that had been converted to Judaism, such as the Kingdom of Himyar in Yemen in the 6th century, or the Khaibar tribes in north-western Arabia, disappeared after the victory of Islam. But J. continued living in Yemen as a minority group, as *Ahl al-Dhimma* or *Dhimmis* — protected non-Muslim "People of the Book" (J. and Christians) with a second-rank status, paying a poll tax (*jizya*) and under grave restrictions and a measure of institutionalized humiliation; some Jewish tribes survived in the *Hadhramaut. In the countries of the *"Fertile Crescent" and North Africa Jewish communities preceded the A. conquest and the advent of Islam and remained throughout medieval and modern times. They, too, were *Dhimmis* until the constitutional modernization of the 19th century (though under Ottoman-Turkish rule, since the 16th century, that status had been mitigated); but some of them achieved, in the Middle Ages, a high level of cultural creativity — partly, e.g. in philosophy, science, literature and poetry, in a Hebrew-and-Arabic symbiosis.

At the beginning of our century, the number of J. in the AC (excluding Palestine) was estimated at c. 600,000 (see table), and by 1947–48, before the A.-Israel war over Palestine, at c. 725,000. After that crisis and the mass exodus of the J. of the AC (500–600,000 to Israel), only 25–35,000 J. remain in AC, with a sizable community only in Morocco (15–20,000). Most of these remnants are old people, and the communities — except for Morocco and perhaps Tunisia — are decaying and slowly dying.

JEWS IN THE ARAB COUNTRIES
Estimates (in thousands)

	Pre-World War I	1947–48	1952	1980s
Iraq	85	125	6	(a)
Egypt	60	65	40	(a)
Yemen and 'Aden	45	50	3	1.5
Syria	32	19	5	4–5
Lebanon	3	6	5	(a)
Libya	25	35	3	(a)
Tunisia	80	100	90	4–5
Algeria	100	120	100	1
Morocco	180	200	200	15–20
Arab Countries	c.610	c.725	c.450	25–35

(a) Less than one thousand.

Most of the J. in the AC were small craftsmen and traders, with some moving socially upwards into the middle class, and a few wealthy families, moving in the upper class governing élite of their respective country. Quite a few J. had acquired foreign citizenship — a measure widespread among the minority communities in the Ottoman Empire to obtain better security and consular protection. Those who were not foreign citizens, were considered citizens of the respective AC, but a measure of discrimination, of the old attitude towards the *Dhimmi*, of regarding them as second-class citizens or semi-foreigners, persisted (as it did towards other minorities); and the A.-Jewish conflict over Palestine increasingly added elements of A. antagonism and hostility (see *anti-Semitism). Sporadic acts of violence and discrimination against J. in Iraq, Syria and Egypt escalated; in June 1941 a large-scale pogrom was organized in Baghdad; and as the Palestine crisis came to a head, pogroms occurred also in Aleppo, 'Aden and Bahrain (Dec. 1947), in Libya (Nov. 1945, June 1948, June 1967), in Algiers (Aug. 1934, May 1956, Dec. 1960), and in Cairo (June 1948). Zionist, Jewish-nationalist organizations were banned, and though A. governments officially distinguished between "Zionists" and J., measures they took during the Palestine war amounted in fact to a harsh oppression of their Jewish subjects — hundreds of J. in Iraq, Syria and Egypt were detained and sent to concentration camps and many were sentenced to prison on charges of Zionism and/or Communism. Similar steps were taken again whenever the A.-Israel conflict erupted in new crises — thus in Egypt during the Suez-Sinai war of 1956 (when thousands were expelled) and the *Six Day War of 1967. Iraq in 1968–69 (when most of her J. had already left) staged show trials and executed several J. (with some A. Iraqis, too) as "Zionist and Western spies". The governments prevented or quelled anti-Jewish outbreaks in Lebanon, Tunisia and Morocco. In times of tension, such as May-June 1948, the Lebanese government posted guards to protect the Jewish quarter of Beirut (and so did the para-military *Phalanges organization). The freedom and relative safety of Beirut (until the civil war from 1975 onward) also attracted many Syrian J. to seek a haven there (though officially Syria banned their emigration).

Before 1948, there was a trickle of Jewish emigration from the AC — mainly to Europe (France, Italy) and the Americas. Though Zionist activities were permitted in Egypt and not expressly banned in Iraq (until the 1930s), Syria and Lebanon, and in the French-ruled Maghrib, few went to Palestine. The exception was Yemen; her J. had begun migrating to Palestine, for national-religious reasons and to seek a better life, in the 19th century, and between the World Wars an estimated 17,000 of them reached Palestine. After 1948–49, however, J. left the AC in a mass exodus, many of them to Europe (particularly those from the Maghrib — to France), but most — to Israel, with the help of that country and of Western Jewish organizations; the number of J. from the AC that came to Israel — most of them compelled to leave their property behind, some of them expelled — was 500–600,000. While some of these migrants were motivated by Zionist, nationalist-religious reasons, the principal motive of the exodus was the deterioration of the economic, social and political security of the J. in the ASt, and in some cases — the oppressive measures taken by A. governments or actual expulsion. About 45,000 Yemen J. were airlifted to Israel in 1949–50; these included most of the J. of Hadhramaut and most of the c. 4,000 J. of 'Aden (most of them of Yemeni origin). Some 35,000 were brought from Libya. Iraq permitted an airlift of her J. to Israel (officially camouflaged as destined for other countries) in Mar. 1950, and within a year almost the whole community had disappeared, nearly 140,000 to Israel. Some 30,000 came to Israel from Egypt — in waves as described (1948–49, 1956, 1967). Morocco virtually permitted the semi-clandestine organization of emigration to Israel, and more than 140,000 of her J. came to Israel (over 50,000 went to France, 25,000 to North America). About 40,000 came to Israel from Tunisia. Most of the J. of Algeria went to France, and only c. 15,000 to Israel.

By 1952, the Jewish communities of the *Mashriq* (the AC in the East) had already dwindled to insignificant numbers (while those in the Maghrib were not yet affected by the mass exodus): some 40,000 were still in Egypt, c. 6,000 in Iraq, 5,000 in Syria, 5,000 in Lebanon. By the 1980s, J. had nearly disappeared from the AC — a total of 25–35,000 comprising small numbers of J. mainly in Syria and Tunisia and a significant community only in Morocco (see table).

Jihad (Arabic: Holy War or, literally, great effort.) J., Holy War, is one of the fundamental tenets of Islam and an obligation on every Muslim. Its original intent, in the 7th century, was to impose on non-Muslim peoples the acceptance of Islam or the status of protected subjects (*Ahl al-Dhimma, Dhimmis*) under Islamic rule — the latter choice being open only to the "People of the Book", i.e. Jews, Christians and *Sabaeans-Mandaeans. The world is divided into *Dar ul-Islam* (the "House of Islam") — the countries under Muslim rule — and *Dar ul-Harb* (the "House of War") — countries to be conquered. Some traditions mention a third realm, *Dar al-Sulh* (the "House of Truce") — countries paying tribute to the Muslims.

Since the 8th century, when further wars of major conquest were no longer possible, some theologians have held that the obligation of J., conceived in the particular situation of the Arabian peninsula at the birth of Islam in the 7th century, had lapsed with changing circumstances. Orthodox Islam, however, holds that J. is obligatory in all generations and circumstances, and theologians have sought answers as to how that duty was to be fulfilled. Does J. mean *constant* Holy War (not actually practised in History), or should it be practised only when circumstances are favorable, as some theologians thought? And if so, who was to proclaim J. in the absence of a *Caliph, with no recognized head of all the faithful? Who proclaims it for the *Shi'i Muslims whose recognized leader, the *Imam, remains hidden until the Day of Judgment? Or is Shi'i J. altogether impossible in the absence of the *Imam*? Must J. be offensive, Muslim-initiated Holy War — or is it, as many modern theologians hold, principally the *defense* of Islam? Must all Muslims engage in J., or can selected fighters (*Mujahidun*) fulfil the injunction on behalf of the community? Must J. be actual warfare, or can it be interpreted as a "Great Effort", not necessarily military, as many theologians hold (and as the linguistic origin of the term implies)? In the absence of a recognized all-Islamic theological authority, there are no generally accepted answers to these questions.

Any war by a Muslim country against a non-Muslim one may qualify as a J., but Muslim tradition requires J. to be proclaimed officially. Many Muslim rulers did over the centuries declare J., but in most cases their pronouncement did not commit Muslims in other countries. In modern times, too, Muslim countries or movements engaged in fighting non-Muslim powers have tried to obtain the support and sympathy of Muslims everywhere by proclaiming J. The *Mahdi in Sudan, in the 1880s, used the term J., and so did the *Sanussis in Libya in their fight against the Italian conquerors, from 1911–12. The Ottoman Sultan and Caliph proclaimed a J. upon Turkey's entry into World War I, in Nov. 1914. His call aroused pro-Turkish sentiment among the Muslims of the world, e.g. in India, but it did not generate active military help for Turkey or serious rebellions in the countries of her enemies — except for some Libyan *Sanussis, who now described their fight against Italy as part of the Caliph's J., and a local Sultan in West Sudan, 'Ali Dinar. Nor did it stop the Muslim ruler of *Hijaz, the *Hashemite Sharif of Mecca, from rising against the Caliph in the *"Arab Revolt" of 1916, and a number of Muslim-Arab officers in the Ottoman Army from joining the rebels.

Muslim fighters in more recent times have continued to use the term J. and describe themselves as *Mujahidin* — mostly without formally proclaiming J. (which, strictly speaking, only a Muslim state or government can do). So did, for instance the Algerian rebels against French rule, 1954–62, and so do the Afghan rebels since

1978–79. The term J. also appeared, sporadically and marginally, in the struggle of India's Muslims against Hindu rule and for the creation of Pakistan. *Khomeini's Islamic-revolutionary Iran makes wide use of the term J. (though its main fight, since 1980, is against Iraq, a Muslim country), and "militias" and underground organizations fostered or inspired by Iran call themselves *al-J.* or *Mujahidin* — e.g., in Lebanon or in terrorist operations in Europe; but those fighting against Khomeini's régime also invoke the image of the Holy War by calling themselves *Mujahidin-i-Khalq*, fighters of the People's J. Muslim governments have also used the term J. for various purposes, e.g. their struggle for economic development or against illiteracy; thus the *'ulama'*, the Muslim sages, in Tunisia permitted the easing of the Ramadan fast because the country was waging an "economic J.".

In the *Arab-Israel conflict, too, A. leaders have tried to increase their strength and popular support by speaking of a J. While no A. government formally proclaimed a J., the sages of Al-*Azhar, the foremost Islamic center of learning, did, in 1948, and several *'ulama'* and *Muftis* repeated that proclamation in sermons, religious rulings (*fatwa*) or speeches. Even without a formal governmental declaration of J., some governments reportedly established J. funds (e.g. Libya) or collected a J. tax (Sa'udi Arabia). The Palestinian-A. guerrillas prefer to call themselves *Feda'iyyin* — "those who sacrifice themselves" (also a term from the traditional Islamic terminology) — rather than *Mujahidin*; but the latter term is also used, and according to some reports Feda'iyyin groups applied for formal recognition as *mujahidin*, so that contributions to their funds would qualify as the fulfilment of a religious duty or even as part of the charity payments (*Zakat*) obligatory for Muslims. On the whole, however, both the A. governments and the Palestinian-A. organizations have avoided defining their war against Israel unequivocally and officially as an Islamic Holy War, J.

Johnston Plan See *Jordan River.

Jordan, Hashemite Kingdom of Formerly (1921–46 or 1948) *Transjordan. A kingdom bordered in the north by Syria, in the north-east by Iraq, in the east and south by Sa'udi Arabia and in the west by Israel. Capital: 'Amman.

J. was founded in 1921 as the semi-independent principality of "Transjordan". She became independent in 1946. She was a founding member of the *Arab League in 1945 and was admitted to UN membership in 1955. The borders of Transjordan were largely defined in 1921–23, and some parts of the desert borders with the *Hijaz in 1925. The same year 'Aqaba and Ma'an, also claimed by Hijaz, were annexed (Sa'udi Arabia acquiesced in the Anglo-Sa'udi Treaty of Jidda, 1927, and formally consented in 1965 — when an exchange of territory also took place and J. acquired a coastal strip south of 'Aqaba in return for an inland area). In 1948, J. occupied — and in 1950 formally annexed — the A. parts of Palestine (except for the Gaza Strip); in June 1967, she lost them.

J.'s pre-June 1967 area was 37,000 sq. mi. — including the A. part of Palestine (the *West Bank, further on: WB) which she had occupied in 1948, and which has an area of c. 2,165 sq. mi. In the Six Day War of 1967 J. lost the WB and *de facto* reverted to her pre-1948 (Transjordanian) area of c. 35,000 sq. mi.

The population on both banks of the J. River was estimated in 1967 at c. 2 m. about equally divided between the East and West Banks. Most of J.'s inhabitants were Sunni Muslim A.'s. There were about 150,000 Christian A.'s. About 200,000 were Bedouin (nomads, semi-nomads and settled) and 15–20,000 *Circassians and Chechens (Muslims originating in the Caucasus), all of them on the East Bank (EB). The population of the EB, that had been c. 450,000 in 1948, had reached c. 1m. by 1967 mainly because of the influx of Palestinian-A. refugees in 1948 (c. 200,000) and continuing migration from the West Bank (WB), 1948–67 (various estimates ranging from 250,000–500,000, with c. 400,000 as a reasonable estimate). During and immediately after the Six Day War another wave of refugees arrived from the WB — estimates ranging from 200,000–350,000, with about 215,000 as a probable estimate (the Israelis found on the WB a population of c. 650,000). In the mid-1980s J.'s population (i.e. the EB's) was estimated at 2.6–3m. A large number, estimated at 300,000–400,000, was working and living abroad, mainly in the Persian Gulf A. oil countries. J.'s EB population included a large proportion of Palestinian A.'s — estimates as to their number vary, but they constitute a majority, perhaps up to 60–65%; about half of them still have the status of refugees, though they enjoy full citizenship. Most of the Jordanians living abroad are of Palestinian origin. The A.'s of the WB — over 1m. if East Jerusalem is included — are also Jordanian citizens.

Until the annexation of the WB in 1948–50, J.'s economy was based mainly on primitive agriculture and stock-breeding. The annexation of the WB (with a population disturbed by the Arab-Israel war of 1948 and augmented by c. 200,000 refugees) and the influx of Palestinians to the EB changed the general character of the population: that of the EB alone had more than doubled by 1967 and grown nearly six times by the mid-1980s and now included townsmen with a higher standard of living. J. was obliged to develop her resources in order to absorb the additional population. For political reasons the government gave priority to developing the EB.

Only c. 5% of the total area used to be under cultivation on the EB, with wheat, barley, vegetables, grapes and olives as the main products. The development project using the waters of the *Yarmuk River for the irrigation of the J. Valley (al-Ghor) — see *Jordan River — considerably expanded and modernized cultivation.

Two oil pipelines traversed J. — the Iraq Petroleum Company's Kirkuk-Haifa line, and *Aramco's "Tapline" from Dhahran, Sa'udi Arabia, to Sidon, Lebanon; they stopped operating in 1948 and 1975 respectively. Oil has reportedly been struck but so far production has not begun. Rock phosphates are mined since 1951–52 and constitute J.'s chief export. Deposits of potash and bromine in the *Dead Sea have been exploited since 1982–83, with several AC participating in an "A. Mining Company". Industry is limited to food processing, cement and the manufacture of soap, matches and cigarettes.

Poor communications are a major obstacle to economic development. The only railway is the single-track narrow-gauge *Hijaz line, the southern parts of which have been out of order since World War I (its joint reconstruction by Syria, J. and Sa'udi Arabia, planned for years, has not materialized). The railroad inside J. is operating, and extensions to the phosphate mines and to *'Aqaba were opened in 1975; the rail link to Syria has also been reopened. 'Aqaba is the country's only port, linked to 'Amman by a 200 mile-long road, opened in 1960, and the railroad mentioned. The port has been much improved and developed — *inter alia* so as not to be dependent on Beirut. A new, expanded port was opened in 1972. Tourism is an important contributor to J.'s economy. Many of the tourists, whose number passed the 1m. p.a. mark in the 1970s, also visit mainly Jerusalem and Bethlehem, and Israel.

Until 1956–57 J.'s public finances were heavily subsidized by Britain. Budgetary deficits were covered by Britain, who also paid the cost of J.'s Army. Since 1957, J. has received US economic aid; Britain continues to assist on a modest scale. Following decisions of the A. summits of Khartoum (Aug. 1967) and Baghdad (Nov. 1978) the A. oil countries undertook to pay J. an annual subsidy of $112m. and $1,250m. respectively; but the amounts pledged have not always been paid in full.

POLITICAL HISTORY. What is now J. was created by Britain in 1921 as the Emirate of Transjordan, and *'Abdullah b. Hussein of the Hashemite dynasty, was installed as Amir. Transjordan was under the Palestine Mandate, but excluded from the clause providing for a Jewish National Home. By installing 'Abdullah, Britain accommodated a loyal ally, prevented him from making trouble with the French (who had just expelled his brother *Feisal from Damascus) and fulfilled a British war-time pledge to his father *Hussein to recognize this area as A. and independent (under British tutelage).

Initially, Transjordan had about 300,000 inhabitants, half of whom were nomads or semi-nomads. Most of the population were A. Muslims, with about 25,000 Christians and 10,000 Circassians. The Emirate was dependent on British economic aid, as most of its area was desert and lacked economic resources. Assisted by a small number of British advisers, at the head of which was a Resident, representing the High Commissioner in Jerusalem, Amir 'Abdullah ruled his country in autocratic and patriarchal fashion. The British helped 'Abdullah create an administration and a military force, which started as a desert police unit and later was considered to be the best A. army — the *Arab Legion, commanded till 1956 by a British officer (F.G. Peake, 1921–39; J.B. *Glubb, 1939–56), with more Britons in senior command posts.

In Feb. 1928 Transjordan signed a treaty with

Britain which slightly widened her autonomy but financial and foreign affairs continued to be handled by the British Resident. A constitution of Apr. 1928 provided for a Legislative Council, in part indirectly elected. In 1934 Transjordan was authorized to establish consular ties with Egypt, Syria and Iraq. In 1939 the powers of the British Resident were reduced, a Cabinet of departmental heads, responsible to the ruler, was reconstituted and an elected Legislative Assembly of 20 members established. During World War II, 'Abdullah remained loyal to his British allies; in 1941 he dispatched a contingent of the Arab Legion to help British troops fight the Iraqi Army and the Vichy French in Syria.

In Mar. 1946 a new Anglo-Transjordanian treaty granted J. formal independence, while providing for a political and military alliance and for British aid. Britain was authorized to maintain troops and bases in Transjordan. This treaty was modified in Mar. 1948; the new treaty stressed Transjordan's independence and the equal status of the two contracting parties. 'Abdullah assumed the title of King in 1946, and re-named the country "The HK of J"; this new appellation became current from 1948–49.

'Abdullah cherished ambitions to create and rule a *"Greater Syria", i.e. a union of J., Palestine, Syria and Lebanon, to be followed by the unification of the *Fertile Crescent through the federation of Iraq with "Greater Syria". The British — or at least some British agencies and in some measure — supported 'Abdullah's aspirations (the French suspected: mainly to oust them from the Levant). 'Abdullah also received some support from the pro-Hashemite establishment in Iraq and from some elements in Syria and Palestine. He was opposed by the French, the rulers of Egypt and Sa'udi Arabia, most Syrians and the mainstream of Palestinian nationalists led by the Mufti of Jerusalem, Hajj Amin al-*Husseini.

'Abdullah felt that the first step towards the implementation of his scheme should be the merger of the A. part of Palestine with J. He maintained close contacts with the Palestinian-A. opposition led by *Nashashibi and Touqan. He also endeavored to reach an agreement with the Jews in Palestine. In 1930 he agreed to, and encouraged, Jewish settlement in Transjordan; but the plan had to be shelved because of local opposition and British obstructionism; in 1933 a law forbidding the sale of lands to foreigners was enacted. The *Peel Commission's abortive 1937 plan for the partition of Palestine envisaged the merger of her A. part with J.

Since 1946, 'Abdullah, seeking a peaceful solution of the Palestine problem, held secret talks with the Zionist leaders. He favored Jewish autonomy in part of Palestine, under his crown, but secretly accepted the partition of the country and agreed not to interfere with Jewish plans for independence — in return for Jewish support for, or non-interference with, his plan to take over the A. part. He eventually decided to pursue his plan in cooperation with the all-A. assault on nascent Israel rather than in open collaboration with the Jews; but he made it clear to the other ASt that his real war aim was the take-over of the A. part of Palestine only (and the desire to prevent that was one of the chief reasons for the May 1948 decision by Egypt and the ASt to invade Palestine with their regular armies).

In the 1948 war, 'Abdullah avoided attacking the areas earmarked for the Jewish State, and the fighting centered on Jerusalem, designated as an international enclave, and the road connecting it with the coastal plain. 'Abdullah's army took over the A. part of Palestine, except for the Gaza Strip and the Iraqi Expeditionary Force handed over to him the areas it had occupied, as Baghdad refused to sign an Armistice Agreement with Israel. In Dec. 1948, a conference of Palestinian-A. notables in Jericho — preceded and followed by similar gatherings — implored 'Abdullah to save Palestine by becoming her King. The J.-Israel Armistice Agreement, reached by secret talks with the King himself, behind the facade of the official negotiations at Rhodes, and signed in Apr. 1949, confirmed J.'s *de facto* occupation of A. Palestine. In Mar. 1949 the military government in the occupied WB was replaced by a civil administration. In May Palestinian ministers were included for the first time in the Jordanian Cabinet, and in June 1949 the country's new name of "The HK of J" was officially gazetted, thus emphasizing that J. was no longer confined to the "other" side of the River. In Apr. 1950 the Palestinians participated for the first time in parliamentary elections, and later the same month the new Parliament decreed the formal annexation of the WB. While only Britain and Pakistan formally recognized the annexation, most countries accepted it *de facto*. The A. League vehemently opposed the annexation and threatened to expel J.; in particular, Egypt, Syria and Sa'udi Arabia objected to any territorial aggrandizement of the Hashemite dynasty. A compromise formula was devised by the Prime Minister of Iraq: the West Bank would be held by J. temporarily and in trust, until its restoration to its owners would be possible. In fact a "deal" was made: the League accepted the annexation of the WB under this facesaving formula — in return for 'Abdullah's renunciation of his plan to sign a separate non-aggression treaty with Israel (of which a draft had been completed after secret negotiations in Feb. 1950).

The annexation of the WB and the influx of Palestinian refugees to the EB considerably modified J.'s ethnic and social features. The population increased nearly three times, from c. 450,000 to c. 1.2m. Of the new population, about 400,000 were Palestinians living in the WB, 200,000 were refugees who had joined them there, and 100,000 were refugees in Transjordan. Most of the new inhabitants had a higher standard of living and were used to an active and volatile political life. The population of the EB had as a whole been loyal to 'Abdullah, although pockets of opposition existed, mainly among the tribes in the north, connected by blood to their brethren in Syria, and in the towns of al-Salt and Irbid. This opposition was considerably reinforced by the Palestinians, many of whom supported 'Abdullah's foe, Hajj Amin al-Husseini. The West-Bankers, who occupied half the seats in Parliament, soon made their presence felt. While they voiced no demand for secession and a separate Palestinian-A. independence, they did demand that the monarch's powers be curtailed, the Cabinet be made responsible to Parliament and political life in J. become democratic. Opposition to the King increased as rumors of his secret negotiations with Israel spread.

On 20 July 1951, King 'Abdullah was assassinated by a Palestinian, while entering al-Aqsa Mosque in Jerusalem. (Among those tried and executed for the murder was a prominent member of the Husseini clan.) 'Abdullah's eldest son *Talal succeeded to the throne (rumors of a takeover plot by his younger son Na'if failed to materialize). In Jan. 1952 Talal gave his assent to a new constitution which made the Cabinet responsible to Parliament; a majority of two-thirds was required to dismiss the Cabinet, but this was amended in 1954 to a simple majority. The King also pursued a new foreign policy. He strove for a *rapprochement* with Egypt and Syria and joined the A. Collective Security Pact of 1950. But in Aug. 1952 Talal was found to be mentally ill. Parliament declared him unfit to rule and deposed him. His son *Hussein was crowned in May 1953 (after regents had briefly ruled for him until he reached the age of 18).

J.'s third King had to continue facing an opposition eager to shake off her financial (and political) dependence on Britain, and to improve ties with Egypt and Syria. The refugees from Palestine to whom J. gave full citizenship — the only Arab country to do so — aggravated the political unrest. Foreign policy difficulties increased as the cold war between the world powers intensified. When, in Dec. 1955, the Chief of the British Imperial General Staff visited 'Amman, it was rumored that he had persuaded the government to join the *Baghdad Pact, concluded in Feb. 1955 between Turkey and Iraq as the nucleus of a US-inspired defense treaty. Violent demonstrations against Jordanian participation forced the resignation of the Cabinet, headed by Hazza' al-*Majali, and the new government announced that J. would not join the Pact. In Mar. 1956 the King dismissed the British Chief-of-Staff of the Arab Legion, Lt.-Gen. Glubb, regarded by A. nationalists as the symbol of British imperialist domination.

In Oct. 1956 leftist-nationalist parties won the parliamentary elections for the first time, and the leader of the "National Socialist Party", Suleiman al-Nabulsi, became Prime Minister. The same month, J. joined the military alliance of Egypt, Syria and Sa'udi Arabia, and the Egyptian-Syrian Joint Military Command. During Israel's *Sinai Campaign of Oct-Nov. 1956 J. allowed Sa'udi, Iraqi and Syrian troops to take up positions on her territory (they were withdrawn when the crisis had passed). In Jan. 1957 Egypt, Syria and Sa'udi Arabia agreed to grant J. an annual subsidy of £12.5m. over the next ten years to finance her army and defense expenditures and thus enable her to abrogate her treaty with Britain. The Anglo-Jordanian Treaty of 1948 was annulled in Mar. 1957 and all British troops were evacuated by July. In Mar-Apr. 1957 the government decided to establish diplomatic relations with the USSR and to accept Soviet aid — a step still considered revolutionary.

In Apr. 1957 King Hussein decided to halt this accelerating movement towards the left. He announced the discovery of a Syrian-Egyptian plot against him and dismissed the leftist Cabinet. This led to riots and demonstrations, and all political parties were suppressed. A plot of army officers supported by Egypt was averted when the King himself appeared in the Zarqa Camp and persuaded the officers to support him. The Chief-of-Staff, Gen. 'Ali Abu Nuwar, was dismissed and fled the country. Purges in the army and the civil service followed. The USA emphasized its support of the King by sending units of the Sixth Fleet to the eastern Mediterranean, in line with the *Eisenhower Doctrine, and began supplying economic and military aid. In the years following some more unrest and attempted plots in the officers' corps were suppressed; but in general the King had re-established a stable régime. An extremist-Islamic plot by an "Islamic Liberation Party" was suppressed later, in the 1960s.

The King's reassertion of his leadership worsened relations with Egypt and Syria. The two countries did not pay the subsidy agreed upon in the agreement of Jan. 1957 (only Sa'udi Arabia paid one instalment of $5m.), launched a violent campaign of defamation against J. and encouraged subversion within J. The Feb. 1958 merger of Syria and Egypt into the *United Arab Republic was seen as a grave threat by J. and induced her to form an Iraqi-Jordanian "Arab Union" or *"Arab Federation" (14 Feb. 1958). King *Feisal II of Iraq became the Head of the Union and King Hussein his deputy. A federal parliament with equal representation for both countries was formed. A federal government was to handle foreign affairs, defense and monetary policy. Each country continued to preserve its parliament, cabinet and civil service. However, the Federation, perceived as a Hashemite dynastic arrangement, was not popular.

The "Arab Union" came to an end after the Iraqi *coup d'état* of 14 July 1958 which toppled the Hashemite régime there. Several top Jordanian leaders were killed in Baghdad with those of Iraq. King Hussein now proclaimed himself Head of the Union, called the Iraqi people to quell the revolution, and asked for US and British aid. The UAR closed her airspace and roads to Jordanian traffic; there were reports of active UAR subversion within J., and Hussein expected immediate UAR-Iraqi hostilities (possibly co-ordinated with a *coup*). Britain responded to Hussein's urgent request and a contingent of British paratroopers arrived in J. in July 1958 (covered by US jets and via Israeli air-space). J. severed diplomatic relations with the UAR and lodged a complaint against her to the UN Security Council for interference and the dispatch of armed infiltrators. US proposals to replace British troops in J. (and American troops in Lebanon) with a UN force were vetoed by the USSR and the issue was transferred to a special session of the UN General Assembly. In Aug. the Assembly unanimously adopted a compromise resolution, drafted by the ASt, noting that these states had agreed in the A. League Pact to respect each other's sovereign independence, welcoming their renewed assurances to observe that commitment, and requesting arrangements to be made that would "facilitate the early withdrawal of the foreign troops". British troops were withdrawn by October.

King Hussein abrogated the J.-Iraq Federation on 1 Aug. 1958. As it became clear that the new régime in Iraq was no satellite of the UAR, relations between 'Amman and Baghdad improved and diplomatic ties were renewed in Dec. 1960, despite the blood-feud the 1958 *coup* had caused. Relations with Sa'udi Arabia also improved. King Hussein cast aside the old enmity between the Hashemite dynasty and the House of Sa'ud which had driven his great-grandfather Hussein from Hijaz, while the Sa'udi ruler realized that his conservative monarchy was threatened by Egypt and abandoned his alliance with her. J.'s diplomatic relations with the UAR were renewed in Aug. 1959, but the latter continued to support subversion — culminating in the assassination of Prime Minister Hazza' al-Majali in Aug. 1960. Relations were again severed in Sept. 1961 when Egypt denounced J.'s recognition of Syria (which had just seceded from the UAR) and accused her of conspiring with the secessionists.

Relations with Egypt were restored in Jan. 1964, during the first A. summit conference held in Cairo. At the Conference J. agreed, reluctantly, to cooperate with other ASt to prevent Israel from diverting the waters of the J. River, and also to recognize the Republican régime in Yemen. With even greater reluctance J. acquiesced in the creation of a *Palestine Liberation Organization (PLO) with a military force, as a "Palestinian entity" authorized at a second summit conference in Alexandria in Sept. 1964. Any recognition of a Palestinian national entity was likely to cast doubts on J.'s annexation of A. Palestine. She allowed the PLO quite unwillingly to hold its founding convention in Jerusalem and to open an office. Relations were tense, and in July 1966 the Government closed down the PLO office, claiming that its Secretary-General, *Shuqeiri, was indulging in pro-Communist activities. J. also rejected proposals to station A. troops on her territory to protect her from Israel.

Israeli raids in retaliation for intensified A. guerilla activities against Israel from Jordanian territory caused retaliation and a crisis in Nov. 1966, when Israeli troops attacked the village of Samu' in the Hebron district. King Hussein was accused of neglecting the defense of his people — mainly by Syria and the PLO who called on the Jordanians to revolt against the King. Egyptian broadcasts also described the King and his government as "imperialist stooges" with whom no cooperation was possible.

As tension rose between Israel and the ASt in spring 1967, as President Nasser spoke confidently of his forthcoming victory, and war seemed inevitable, A. pressure on J. to join the camp mounted. On 30 May 1967 King Hussein flew to Cairo and signed a defense agreement with Egypt, placing his troops under Egyptian command. When the Six Day War broke out, on 5 June 1967, the Israeli government advised King Hussein via the UN to stay out of the war and assured him that Israel would not attack J. King Hussein ignored this advice and, misled by Nasser's reports of victories, joined Egypt in the war. J. lost the WB. A new influx of refugees, estimated at 200–250,000 people, crossed the J. River eastwards. They formed an additional burden on J.'s economy already hard hit by the loss of the WB. However, Israel's "open bridges" policy enabled commercial exchanges and mutual visits between J. and the WB to continue. Jordanian authorities also maintained ties with WB Arab leadership and even continued to pay salaries to many former civil servants.

In the rump-state of J., the EB, constitutional-political problems arose. As J. was not prepared to renounce the WB officially and to set up a Parliament elected in the EB only, and as elections could obviously not be held in the WB under Israeli occupation, no new elections could take place. Of the WB members of the existing Parliament — half of the House, according to the election law — some stayed on the EB, but the attendance of those living on the WB was not regular. When Parliament's term expired in 1971, it was extended for two years, but in Nov. 1973 it was dissolved; it was later considered as merely suspended, and reconvened in 1976 and again in 1984, and from 1984 it holds regular sessions. In the interim period, it was replaced by a King-appointed Consultative Council, 1978–84. No new elections have been held since 1967; for EB seats that fall vacant by-elections are held, while new members to represent vacant WB seats are elected by Parliament. The Senate, appointed by the King, was not affected by these problems and the King has regularly named new members. However, the rule that half the members should be from the WB was not kept anymore in full; nor has it been kept for the Chamber of Deputies, since members elected for vacant WB seats were frequently *former* WB men residing in the EB.

After the 1967 war, King Hussein campaigned vigorously to gain international sympathy for his country's cause. He visited several countries, including — in Oct. 1967 — the USSR (with whom diplomatic ties had been established in 1963). Closer economic relations with the Soviet bloc were initiated; however the King turned down Soviet proposals for military assistance (until the 1980s). While J. took part in the conferences of non-aligned countries, she maintained her ties with the West, especially the USA, and received economic aid and arms supplies. J.-US relations were not always smooth; but differences arising over J.'s role in US ME peace efforts, J.'s policy on guerrilla and terrorist operations, and, later, over US arms supplies, did not cause major confrontations. Whenever real crises occurred, it was to the West that J. looked for help.

Within the A. world Hussein continued to strengthen relations with Egypt. In Mar. 1969 J. joined an "Eastern Command" initiated by Egypt to co-ordinate military activities against Israel; but the Command was still-born and disbanded in 1970. With J.'s agreement, Iraqi, Sa'udi Arabian and sometimes Syrian troops were stationed on her territory with the declared aim of helping to defend her against Israel, but also with a view to looking after their own interests. There was also a large Pakistani training mission in J. Iraqi and Syrian troops were evacuated in 1970–71.

J.'s main political problem, affecting the very root of her existence, was her relationship with the *Palestinian-A. guerrilla organizations (*feda'iyyin*). The *feda'iyyin* — permitted since 1967 to grow into a large establishment, lavishly financed and heavily equipped — gradually assumed control of the refugee camps, moved their headquarters to 'Amman and took effective control of wide areas along the border. Their stepped-up operations against Israel from Jordanian territory brought about Israeli retaliations, e.g. frequent shellings and a Mar. 1968 attack on Karame, an advance base for the guerrillas. The creation of a "State within the State" not subject to Jordanian law and control created mounting tension. In Nov. 1968 serious clashes occurred between J.'s army and the guerrillas and a civil war seemed imminent. To avoid a full-scale confrontation, an agreement was reached: the guerrilla organizations were permitted to issue their own identity cards (i.e. were exempted from regular Jordanian control), but undertook not to recruit deserters from the Arab Legion or men laible for conscription; J. would permit arms destined for the guerrillas to pass; targets in Israel would not be shelled by the guerrillas from Jordanian Army positions; guerrillas would strike at targets in Israel only from positions situated at least 6 mi. inside Israel or the Israel-occupied areas; they would operate "in coordination" with the Jordanian forces; no operations against Israel would be mounted from 'Aqaba.

This Nov. 1968 agreement, vague on many crucial points, was never fully implemented. Severe clashes — in effect a struggle for the control of J. continued, with the *feda'iyyin* wielding increasing influence and the King vacillating between his hard-line army supporters and pro-guerrilla elements. There were repeated government reshuffles (invariably interpreted as either pro- or anti-guerrilla).

A new agreement reached in Feb. 1970, after an attempt to impose stricter regulations, fresh clashes, and a retreat by the King, confirmed the Nov. 1968 accord and emphasized the equality of the two parties. Yet the army Commander-in-Chief, Nasser b. Jamil, a hard-liner and the King's uncle, was taking active measures to control and restrict the guerrilla organizations; the army also resented the guerrillas' assertive behavior. Tension mounted, and in June serious clashes re-erupted, causing hundreds of casualties. The army bombarded refugee camps near 'Amman held by the guerrillas and attacked the guerrilla center in the capital; the *feda'iyyin* gained control of several districts in 'Amman, including hotels in which foreign guests were held as hostages. Several ASt, especially Egypt, Iraq and Libya, endeavored to mediate, and the King again backed down. On 10 June an agreement to cease hostilities was reached, but it was implemented only after the King yielded to the guerrillas' demand to dismiss Nasser b. Jamil (the King himself becoming C.-in-C. of the Army) and Zeid b. Shaker, the Commander of the armored division. The agreement provided, *inter alia*, for an exchange of prisoners and the creation of mixed commissions to devise measures to prevent future clashes, inquire into the causes of the riots, and supervise the implementation of this and previous agreements. An unoffficial summit conference in Tripoli (Libya) in June, set up a committee composed of representatives of Egypt, Libya, Algeria and Sudan to tackle disputes between J. and the guerrilla organizations "in a manner that both the sovereignty of J. and *feda'iyyin* action be preserved". By agreeing to the creation of this committee, King Hussein in fact accepted a sort of inter-A. guardianship, while the guerrilla organizations obtained a status equal to that of the King, Government and Army of J.

In June 1970 the King instructed his new Prime Minister, 'Abd-ul-Mun'im al-Rifa'i, to work for "national unity" and stressed the freedom of action for the guerrillas. He obviously wanted to improve relations with the *feda'iyyin* — especially with 'Arafat and his al-*Fatah. The increasing importance of the Palestinians in J.'s public life was reflected in the composition of the new Government: of the 17 ministers, nine were Palestinians, some of them sympathetic towards the guerrillas. The King also suspended conscription, thus enabling Jordanian youth to join the guerrillas. The King's retreat of June 1970 seriously undermined his position and the army's prestige and created a permanent state of crises. In a new agreement of 10 July the King had to make further concessions. The guerrillas renounced any military presence in the cities, except for some guard units for their leaders and offices, and undertook to refrain from military exercises in inhabited areas, restrict the movements of their vehicles, identify themselves at army checkpoints, and respect the civil law of J. The government undertook to abolish its emergency measures (i.e. to withdraw the army from the towns), support the propaganda activities of the guerrillas, allow them freedom of action, and (by implication) not to use the "special units" of the army against them. Mixed commissions were to supervise the implementation of the agreement.

King Hussein's agreement, in August, along with President Nasser, to American pacification plans (see *Rogers) and the renewal of the Jarring talks further strained his relations with the guerrillas, who vehemently opposed any such initiative. On the other hand, the King, pressed for anti-guerrilla action by senior army officers, now counted on President Nasser's backing. He reappointed General Zeid b. Shaker to a senior army post, and went to Cairo for talks with Nasser, 20–23 Aug. A few days later, clashes began between the guerrillas and the army. Anarchy soon prevailed in J., and the government lost control over large areas, especially in the north. On 6 Sept. the guerrillas brought to an airstrip near Zarqa two hijacked foreign airplanes, and a third plane a few days later, and prevented the army from approaching the planes or rescuing their passengers. On 16 Sept. the King proclaimed martial law. Premier Rifa'i resigned and Brig. Muhammad Dawud, a Palestinian, formed a military government resolved to crush the guerrillas. Despite more abortive cease-fire agreements, full-scale military operations erupted. An army offensive against guerrilla concentrations — many of them in towns, especially 'Amman, and refugee camps — hit civilians in large numbers (casualties were variously estimated at anything between 700 and 20,000 killed). The *feda'iyyin* now called openly for the overthrow of the King and the régime.

The AC were deeply shocked by J.'s operation (soon called "Black September"). King Hussein was denounced as a butcher and a "Nero". Kuwait and Libya suspended financial aid to Jordan, Libya severed diplomatic relations, Tunisia recalled her envoy. Iraq and Syria promised aid to the *feda'iyyin* and threatened intervention. On 19 Sept., Syrian armored units, disguised as forces of the "Palestine Liberation Army", invaded J. and occupied a strip in her north, including the town of Irbid. They were beaten back by Jordanian troops and deterred by American and Israeli threats of intervention (and perhaps also Soviet and A. advice), and retreated four days later. The Iraqi expeditionary force in J. did not intervene. The USSR, for her part, warned the USA against intervention.

At a Cairo all-A. conference (Syria and Iraq absent) President Nasser succeeded in imposing a new compromise. A four-member delegation, headed by Sudan's President *Numeiri, came to 'Amman to mediate a cease-fire; on 26 Sept. Brig. Dawud resigned, and the King appointed another Palestinian, Ahmad Touqan, as Prime Minister. An agreement to end the dispute was signed in Cairo, on 27 Sept., by J., Egypt, Libya, Sa'udi Arabia, Sudan, Yemen, Kuwait, Lebanon, and Yasser 'Arafat. A "Supreme A. Committee", under the Prime Minister of Tunisia, was to supervise and enforce the normalization of relations between the Jordanian authorities and the *feda'iyyin*. Both the army and the guerrillas were to withdraw from 'Amman; government administration was to be restored everywhere, including the guerrilla-held Irbid area in the north. Commando operations against Israel were to continue with J.'s full support, while the guerrillas were to respect J.'s sovereignty and operate "within the law, except where necessary for commando action". The A. co-signatories of the agreement undertook to intervene against whichever side broke it. Further, detailed agreements were added in Oct. and Dec. 1970 and Jan. 1971.

In fact, King Hussein continued strengthening his position. In Sept. he named a new Commander-in-Chief, Habes Majali, and in Oct. he set up a strong government under Wasfi *Tall. During 1971 he used PLO provocations and renewed clashes to continue military operations and suppress whatever remained of effective *feda'iyyin* formations — despite all-A. supervision and new Egyptian and Sa'udi mediation attempts. By July 1971 the PLO's military and organizational establishment in J. was liquidated.

Sporadic acts of terrorism continued — in Nov. 1971 Prime Minister Wasfi Tall was assassinated in Cairo (by a new, extremist terrorist group, "Black September"), and in Mar. 1973 another attempt to topple the régime had to be suppressed; but the PLO's state-within-the-state with its strong military arm no longer existed.

The King's determined action led most of the A. world to ostracize and isolate J. A July 1971 mini-summit (Egypt, Syria, Libya, Yemen, South Yemen) condemned J. and threatened intervention; Algeria and Syria severed relations, Iraq withdrew her ambassador, and new Syrian-Jordanian clashes broke out; Egypt severed relations in 1972 on another Palestinian issue described in the next paragraph. Gradually, however, relations with the ASt were normalized. Official relations with Egypt and Syria were resumed in 1973. During the October War of 1973, J., torn between the desire to show A. solidarity and the fear of another defeat, did not join the war officially and initiated no action from her territory, but dispatched an armored brigade to help Syria — a line of action that was welcomed by Egypt and Syria (J.'s troops and tanks arrived on the front on 12 Oct., when the tide had already turned, and met advancing Israeli forces in battle inside Syria).

Relations with the PLO were not as easily mended and besides the bitter memory of bloody battle — the basic conflict between the Palestinians' demand for independence and J.'s claim to A. Palestine, the WB, as part of her realm remained unsolved. In Mar. 1972 King Hussein proclaimed that after Israel's withdrawal from the WB the Kingdom would be restructured on a federal basis, i.e. the Palestinian WB would be granted a fair measure of autonomy. At the time there was little favorable response to that departure — Egypt's President *Sadat even thought it so reprehensible that he severed relations with J.; but the King stuck to it, and in later years the PLO's moderate wing accepted the idea that their demand for independence and confederal arrangements with J. might well be harmonized. In Sept. 1973, Hussein proclaimed an amnesty for those still detained in connection with the 1970–71 battle with the PLO. In the meantime, however, the ASt resolved to recognize the PLO as "the sole and legitimate representative of the Palestinian-A. people". The A. summit of Algiers, Nov. 1983, half-endorsed that recognition — which implied the rejection of Hussein's claim to be the ruler and representative of the Palestinian-A. WB. Hussein who would not openly oppose the all-A. decision, tried to forestall its final confirmation by secret diplomatic contacts; he was reported, for instance, to have reached an agreement with Sadat that the PLO should be recognized as representing only those Palestinians outside J. and the WB, and to rely on a Sa'udi veto against any resolution going beyond that (and he reportedly also held secret talks with Israeli leaders on a possible solution to the Palestinian-WB problem and an Israeli withdrawal in favor of J., but was unable to reach agreement). However, the Oct. 1974 A. summit of Rabat unanimously endorsed the full recognition of the PLO as sole representative — and Hussein acquiesced.

The mid- and later 1970s witnessed a continuous *rapprochement* between J. and the other AC, particularly Egypt and Syria (relations with Sa'udi Arabia and by now also with Iraq were in any case satisfactory). The King and President Sadat exchanged several visits, as did their chief aides. But in 1977–79 J. joined the other ASt in condemning Sadat's peace moves and the resulting Egypt-Israel agreements; reports that Hussein was trying to mitigate all-A. moves against Egypt did not materialize, and in 1979 he severed relations with Egypt, along with the other ASt. The *rapprochement* with Syria, leading to intensified consultations and mutual visits, including visits at the King/President level, from 1975, went as far as plans for a Syria-J. federation. Talks on these plans, however, broke down in 1979 and relations relapsed into a state of tension and hostility, including Jordanian complaints of Syrian subversion and plots in the early 1980s.

A gradual improvement extended even to J.'s relations with the PLO. The King met 'Arafat at the A. summits of 1977 and 1978 and later received him, mediated and arranged by Libya's *Qadhdhafi, in 1978. In 1977, 1978 and 1979, PLO delegations visited J., and from Mar. and Apr. 1979 'Arafat himself came to J. for talks with the King. In accordance with a decision of the A. summit of 1979, a joint J.-PLO committee was created to administer the all-A. aid funds allocated to the WB Palestinians. From 1979–80 J. again permitted PLO delegations and departments to establish a resident presence in 'Amman — though she banned any military/terrorist PLO activity from J. and tried to prevent and suppress any PLO operations against Israel mounted from J. against her wish. Talks with 'Arafat centered on two main issues: *a.* the possibility of a future confederation of J. and a Palestinian-A. entity to be set up in the WB and the Gaza Strip after a settlement with Israel; *b.* joint J.-PLO negotiations on an A.-Israel settlement, possibly by a joint Jordanian-Palestinian delegation.

Efforts towards resumption of negotiations on a general settlement were encouraged, even sponsored, by the USA, which regarded King Hussein as a key figure in that context and fostered close relations with him, and he was a frequent visitor to Washington. Yet, US-J. relations were strained by two complexes. One was the sale of advanced US arms to J., considered by J. to be vital. Sales were frequently held up or foiled altogether by US Congressional opposition. Thus a sale of Hawk missiles ran into difficulties; these were resolved by a compromise — *viz* that the Hawks should be in fixed positions, not mobile — but the financing and the actual supply had to overcome further obstacles. A June 1980 sale of tanks was confirmed after a wrangle. In Mar. 1984 a US sale of Stinger missiles had to be scrapped, and at the same time it was "agreed" that J. would not take part in US plans for a "Rapid Deployment Force" in the ME. In Feb. 1985 and again in Feb. 1986, it was "agreed" to postpone indefinitely a large-scale sale of US military equipment. In these circumstances, King Hussein increasingly relied on alternative sources of military supplies (Britain, France) — and these included for the first time some Soviet arms. The King visited the USSR in 1976 and 1981, and the purchase of SAM missiles was reportedly finalized in 1981.

The other complex straining J.-US relations concerned the planned negotiations for a ME peace settlement. Hussein was the only A. leader outside Egypt who did not reject President Reagan's plan for such negotiations as announced in Sept. 1982. But, hamstrung by his bogged-down negotiations with 'Arafat and the latter's constant changes of position and inability to make bold decisions, the King was unable to bring the PLO into the negotiation process — as he had repeatedly assured the US he would do. In Mar. 1984 he told the US that he would not be able to join any peace negotiations without the PLO and outside the framework of an international conference on the ME (in which the USSR and China would participate) — i.e. on conditions unacceptable to the US and Israel. Hussein remained a key-figure in the US-envisaged peace process, and the possibility of a Palestinian representation by independents approved by the PLO, rather than the PLO itself, continued to be examined; but these negotiations, and US-J. relations, were deadlocked.

King Hussein's talks with 'Arafat, in the early 1980s, had their ups and downs and were suspended several times. At the same time, the presence of PLO institutions in 'Amman increased, 'Arafat visited J. frequently, and in Nov. 1984 the 17th Palestine National Council session — boycotted by the extremist and anti-'Arafat wing of the PLO — was held in 'Amman. Finally, Hussein and 'Arafat reached agreement in Feb. 1985: when exercising, after Israel's withdrawal, their right of self-determination, the Palestinians would establish an entity in confederation with J.; the PLO and J. would jointly negotiate a ME peace settlement, based on UN resolutions, in the framework of an international conference. The idea of confederation did not arouse much further debate — though its details remained unclar-

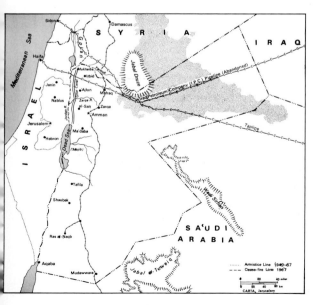

Map of Jordan

ified and controversial (mainly the question of whether the Palestinian entity would be established *ab initio* in confederation with J., as the King desired, or an independent Palestinian state would first be set up and would then join the confederation, as 'Arafat insisted. But the joint Jordanian-Palestinian negotiations did not materialize; one of the obstacles was 'Arafat's refusal to accept UN Security Council Resolution 242 (i.e. accept Israel's existence and the principle of peaceful co-existence with her) — an act seen by Hussein and by most powers as a precondition for the PLO's participation in the peace negotiations; 'Arafat also preferred the PLO to be represented by an independent PLO delegation or as part of an all-A. one rather than as part of the Jordanian delegation, as he had agreed. 'Arafat was, in any case, unable to obtain an endorsement of the Agreement by the PLO: not only did all the radical and anti-'Arafat factions oppose it altogether, but even within his own *Fatah* wing there were doubts and objections, and 'Arafat himself vacillated. Despite the Agreement, the J.- PLO situation was stalemate. In Feb. 1986 Hussein, without abrogating the Agreement, suspended all co-ordination with the PLO, and in July he closed the *Fatah* offices and institutions (though not all PLO departments) in J. and expelled several leading *Fatah* functionaries. In Apr. 1987, the Palestine National Council formally abrogated the Feb. 1985 Agreement (though reconfirming the "special relationship" with J. and half-endorsing the principal of a future confederation). King Hussein officially continued to insist that the PLO must be part of any negotiations for a settlement, but there were indications that he was again weighing the possibility of a non-PLO Palestinian representation. In the mid-1980s J. also made new low-key efforts to enhance her influence on the A.'s of the WB — *inter alia* by announcing a large-scale five-year WB development plan.

While frustrated in his relations with the PLO and concerning the ME peace process, Hussein was throughout the 1980s active in other directions. Not only was J. internally stable and progressing, but the King successfully endeavored to build up a respected international and inter-A. position. He paid many visits to foreign, especially European, capitals and received many foreign statesmen in 'Amman. In Sept. 1984 he resumed official relations with Egypt and exchanged ambassadors, and his ties with President *Mubarak personally as well as J.-Egyptian links in all fields have since become remarkably close. This breach of all-A. solidarity did not adversely affect J.'s relations with the A. world. Her relations with Sa'udi Arabia were stable, and those with Iraq grew close — particularly as she actively supported Iraq in her war with Iran. In the mid-1980s there was a new *rapprochement* even with Syria. King Hussein's inter-A. standing enabled him to try his hand — so far without much success — even at efforts of conciliation and mediation (e.g. between Syria and Egypt, Syria and Iraq). In short, King Hussein — who was given little chance of success, or even of survival, when he ascended the throne — has turned J., in the 35 years of his reign, into a country remarkably stable internally and economically, and respected in the A. world and internationally.

Jordan River The JR is formed, in Northern Galilee, Israel, by the confluence of three main sources: the Dan, the *Baniyas (with its source in Syria), and the *Hasbani (with its source in Lebanon). Its length is about 250 km. (160 mi.) in a straight line, over 320 km. (200 mi.) with its meanderings. On its way from north to south it forms the Hula Lake and marshes (drained by Israel in the 1950s), the Lake of Galilee, and finally the Dead Sea. South of the Lake of Galilee, the J. takes its most important tributary, the *Yarmuk, and farther down — Wadi al-Zarqa, (the Yabbok of the Bible) and several smaller ones. The J. Valley (Arabic: *al-Ghor* — meaning mainly the part below the Lake of Galilee) is below sea level (c. 212 meters at the Lake of Galilee, 396 meters at the Dead Sea), part of the Syrian-East-African rift. The JR carries an annual flow of c. 600m. cubic meters (mcm) on entering the Lake of Galilee. After losing much water through evaporation, 500–530 mcm left the Lake, and the Yarmuk added c. 475 mcm — before Israel and Jordan began diverting J. waters. The total quantity of water carried by the J. and its tributaries — and divertable, if so decided — was estimated at 1,100–1,400 mcm.

After the creation of political-administrative entities in Palestine and Syria, under British and French Mandates, in 1920–22, a line a few meters east of the J. was the border between Palestine and Syria from the Hula to the Lake of Galilee, a distance of about 6 mi. (10 km.). And when Britain, in 1922, created the Emirate of Transjordan, the J. from below its confluence with the Yarmuk to the Dead Sea became the border between Palestine and the new state. After the war of 1948 and the annexation of the *"West Bank" by the Kingdom of Jordan, the JR remained the Israel-Jordan border from its confluence with the Yarmuk to a point about 11 mi. (18 km.) farther south. The rest of the river was the dividing line between the kingdom's "East Bank" and "West Bank", and after the occupation of the West Bank by Israel in 1967 — the border between Israel-administered territories and the Kingdom of Jordan. The Israeli right wing, advocating the retention and annexation of the occupied West Bank, sees the JR as the natural border between Israel and the Kingdom of Jordan. But even the Left and moderates who aspire to a settlement based on Israel's withdrawal from most of the West Bank, would strive for an agreement recognizing the JR as a strategic defense line of Israel.

As the only major source of water for both Israel and Jordan ("major" — in terms of those two water-poor countries), the JR has been the object of many development schemes for the generation of power, irrigation and the supply of water to industry. A concession for a hydroelectric power plant just below the J.-Yarmuk junction was granted in 1921 (finalized in 1926) to the Jewish engineer and entrepreneur P. Rutenberg. The plant went into operation in 1932. It was partly on the Jordanian side of the border, was taken by the Jordanians in the war of 1948, became inoperative and was largely destroyed. Large-scale plans for the diversion of the J. waters — after an initial survey by Ionides in 1937–39 — were drafted by international experts from the 1940s. They envisaged lifting parts, or most, of the water to the mountainous region of Galilee and channelling them, by force of gravity, to the coastal plain and the *Negev, through open conduits or pipelines, using the Beit Netofa (Natufa) valley as main reservoir, and diverting other parts of the J. waters, and mainly those of the Yarmuk, for the irrigation of the Jordanian side (and possibly some of the Palestinian side, too) of the J. Valley below the Lake of Galilee, the *Ghor*. The basic version of those plans, the Lowdermilk Plan, 1942–44, was later amended in the Hayes Plan, the Cotton Plan, and other versions by various international consultants. The point of diversion for the Israeli scheme was originally planned to be in the Hula region, later at the Daughters-of-Jacob Bridge just South of the Hula; but political difficulties — Syrian objections, based on the area being within a Demilitarized Zone, and ensuing intervention by the UN — caused Israel to choose the Lake of Galilee as the point of diversion. Israel's "National Water Carrier" began operating in 1964. It diverts about 350–450 mcm p.a. Since the Lake is used as the main reservoir, the outflow of the JR from it has been reduced to quantities not needed for the Carrier and the maintenance of the level of the Lake. Moreover, as Israel has diverted several saline springs from flowing into the Lake and discharges their water into the J. farther South, the JR South of the Lake of Galilee has become highly saline.

Plans for the use of the J. waters by the Kingdom of Jordan were, after the preliminary survey mentioned, worked out, in various versions, by several international consultants and crystallized in the 1950s. Some of them were connected with the US aid administration and, since they could be linked to the resettlement of Palestinian-A. refugees, with *UNRWA, the UN refugee agency. They called for the diversion of the waters of the Yarmuk, and possibly some of the J., into a canal along the eastern edge of the J. Valley and the irrigation of the Valley by a network of canals branching out west- and downwards; a large dam and reservoir on the Yarmuk would further expand that scheme at a later stage, and smaller ones on the tributaries of the JR farther South would add their waters. Work on the main *Ghor* Canal began in 1958–59, its first stage was opened in 1961, and further stages, extending the canal southwards, were opened in 1963, 1964 and 1966. Plans for the Yarmuk dams and reservoirs were prepared — in alternative versions, at Maqaren and/or Mukheiba — and work was begun, but it made little progress and was suspended (*i.a.* because no final, detailed agreement was reached with Syria). On the southern tributaries, however, six smaller dams and reservoirs have been completed since the late 1960s. And in the Jordanian J. Valley impressive development has taken place under a J. Valley Authority formally established in 1977. Large areas of land have been made cultivable, and irrigated, with modern technology being used, new villages have been built and a population of c. 150,000 has been settled.

Since the USA was asked, at an early stage, to help finance both the Israeli and the Jordanian projects and feared their separate implementation might cause clashes, particularly concerning the amount of water each country was to use and divert (and Syria and Lebanon also had claims), several attempts were made, with US help, to produce a unified or co-ordinated plan. In 1953, President Eisenhower sent a special envoy, businessman Eric Johnston, to prepare a plan acceptable to all and ensuring a fair and agreed allocation of the J. waters. After lengthy negotiations with the three riparian ASt (assisted by Egypt, too) and Israel — separately, since the ASt refused to talk directly with Israel — an agreed plan was drafted in 1955. Syria and Lebanon were to use 20 and 35 mcm respectively of the J. sources (the Baniyas and the Hasbani); Syria — an additional 22 mcm farther down, between the Hula and the Lake of Galilee; the rest of the J. waters was to be used and diverted by Israel (the quantity was not specified but estimated at 375–450 mcm), leaving c. 100 mcm for Jordan flowing out of the Lake of Galilee (70 mcm with the lake's average salinity, 30 mcm highly saline). Of the Yarmuk, Syria was to receive 90 mcm, the rest going to Jordan (with the quantity not specified but estimated at 380–430 mcm), leaving 25–40 mcm for Israel's traditional use farther down the Yarmuk. Of the total combined flow of the J. and the Yarmuk, Jordan was to receive 46.7% Israel 38.5%, Syria 11.7% and Lebanon 3.1% (the tributaries below the J.-Yarmuk confluence, entirely within Jordan territory, not included). The Lake of Galilee was to serve as a reservoir for both Israel and Jordan, with parts of the Yarmuk waters diverted into it — but this was not finalized and neither Israel nor Jordan were happy with it. Experts from the four countries concerned and Egypt agreed on that schedule of distribution, as well as a régime of joint and international inspection, and technological details and procedures. In Israel, the government backed and accepted the agreement. In the ASt, however, the political authorities refused to sign any accord involving Israel as a partner and beneficiary: the "Johnston Agreement" thus remained an abortive draft.

Israel and Jordan thereupon began implementing their own separate projects; but they both did so on the tacit understanding that they would keep to the quotas of the Johnston Plan. The ASt, however, objecting altogether to Israel's use and diversion of the J., stepped up their efforts to prevent the implementation of her plan. In 1964 they decided to deny to Israel the J. sources flowing from Syria and Lebanon, the Baniyas and the Hasbani. Their plan was to divert the Baniyas southwards into the Yarmuk, to be stored in the Mukheiba reservoir planned, and the Hasbani partly westwards into the *Litani in Lebanon and partly eastwards into the Baniyas. Israel warned that she would regard any attempt to divert the J. sources as a matter of utmost gravity. When Lebanon and Syria, especially the latter, began diversion work in 1965, Israel reacted by intensive military operations, usually combined with, or presented as, retaliation for Syrian raids, and several times seriously damaged the work in progress, sabotaging its continuation. As the ASt were unwilling to give Syria and Lebanon military guarantees in case they became involved in a full-fledged battle, the diversion plan was in effect abandoned. The Israel occupation of the *Golan in the *Six Day War, 1967, put an end to its Syrian part (and Lebanon had not been enthusiastic in the first place and was in no position to continue her part alone).

Jumayyil, Amin (b. 1942) Lebanese politician. President of Lebanon since Sept. 1982. A Christian *Maronite from Beirut, J. is the elder son of Pierre *Jumayyil, the founder and leader of the *Phalanges, and the brother of Bashir *Jumayyil, elected President in Aug. 1982 and killed before assuming office. J. studied jurisprudence and worked as a lawyer and businessman with widely spread economic interests and activities. He was not very active in politics and little involved in the military activities and organization of the Phalanges; but as the son of the founder-leader and the brother of the emerging younger military commander he remained identified with them. J. entered Parliament in 1970, in a by-election. He was generally considered less determined, less hard-line, than his father (and even more than his brother) in the defense of the Christian-Maronite predominance in Lebanese politics. He was more inclined to seek an accommodation with the non-Christian communities, with the radicals striving for constitutional reforms that would abolish the communal structure of Parliament and government, with Syria, and with the Palestinian guerrilla presence and operations in Lebanon (and he did not share his brother's inclination to co-operate with Israel). He therefore played no important part in the organization and defense of the Christian-conservative camp in the civil war since 1975 and in the late 1970s maintained some contact with Syria and the *PLO leadership. Despite all this, several attempts were made in the late 1970s to kidnap and/or assassinate him.

J. was propelled into the Presidency when his brother Bashir, just elected President, was killed in the terror-bombing of the Phalanges headquarters, in Sept. 1982. Parliament elected him with a majority (and an attendance) larger than his brother's a month before, as he was seen less identified with the Maronite camp in the civil war, and as Syria did not oppose him (the only rival candidate, Camille *Chamoun, withdrew before vote). He had pledged to continue the policies of his late brother, and the first, pressing point on his agenda was the conclusion of an agreement with Israel, in occupation of large parts of Lebanon, to provide for security arrangements and a modicum of co-existence that would enable Israel to withdraw. Though J. was not enthusiastic, and the agreement was whittled down in protracted negotiations to much less than Israel desired and had hoped for, it was signed in May 1983. However, Syria and her Lebanese supporters, the rivals of J. and the Christian camps with whom J. strove to achieve an accommodation, were pressing to abrogate that agreement altogether as a pre-condition for any reconciliation. J. therefore procrastinated, delaying his final signature. He was at any rate incapable of assuring a co-ordinated withdrawal and handing-over, as Israel requested, since he and his government and army had but little effective control (his standing was also hurt on the eve of his election by the massacre perpetrated by the Phalanges in the Palestinian camps of Sabra and Shatila: if, as he insisted, he bore no responsibility at all for that operation, it showed that he had no control of the Phalanges). When Israeli forces began unilaterally withdrawing, in Sept. 1983, bitter fighting broke out between Christians and Druze in the Shuf region, spreading to Beirut, where Shi'i militias took over the Muslim western part and Druze the south-eastern suburbs and approaches, and the power and control of President J. and his government were further reduced. The army disintegrated in 1984 into virtually separate Christian, Shi'i, Sunni and Druze parts. Repeated changes in the command of the Phalanges and their "Lebanese Forces" — changes over which J. had no control — were at least in part directed against his policies and deprived him in effect of any military base of support.

Efforts for a general pacification led to a National Reconciliation Conference in Geneva in Oct. 1983 and Lausanne in Mar. 1984, in the course of which J. had to accept a large part of his rivals' and Syria's demands. He formally abrogated the agreement with Israel in Mar. 1984, before, and as the price for, the second Reconciliation Conference. He accepted far-reaching policy co-ordination with Syria. He agreed to the need for basic reforms in Lebanon's constitutional and political structure — giving more weight to Muslims, particularly Shi'i Muslims, and Druze, towards an eventual abolition of the communal system, with details and procedures to be worked out. And he set up a "Government of National Reconciliation" headed by his adversaries (Rashid *Karameh as Premier, the Shi'i leader Nabih *Berri and the Druze chief Walid *Junbalat among the Ministers). However, the hoped for cease-fire and the beginnings of reforms and reconciliation proved illusive. A bloody, nearly incessant battle continued between a coalition of Duze and Shi'i militias and Christian ones, with the army ineffective and in fact split. Berri and Junbalat boycotted the government of which they were members and in effect sabotaged it, and called for J.'s resignation or dismissal. Syria, now in effective military and political control, was pressing for a general agreement on lines acceptable to her, but was unable to enforce it (though J. was frequently summoned to Damascus. Negotiations, led mainly by the militia leaders, dragged on interminably, interrupted by bouts of bitter fighting and with the parties frequently reneging on points previously agreed. In Dec. 1985, Elie Hobeika, commander of the Lebanese Forces, signed in Damascus an agreement with the Shi'i and Druze militia leaders that provided for the dissolution of all militias, and for radical political reforms (abolition of the Christian majority in Parliament, steps towards the abolition of the communal structure of Lebanon's body politic, and a sharp reduction in the powers of the Maronite President), as well as total "co-ordination" of Lebanon's defense, foreign and inter-Arab policies, and her security services, with Syria's. Hobeika's rival, Samir Ja'ja', now rebelled, rallied to J. and those Phalange formations that had remained loyal to J., and defeated Hobeika's forces. J. himself did not reject the Dec. 1985 Agreement openly and totally. But he clearly indicated that, while accepting the cease-fire and the military provisions, he had grave reservations concerning the political reforms dictated and the reduction of the President's powers. He insisted that any reform plan should be adopted through constitutional channels, and not be imposed by the militias; and, while not daring to say so, he implied that the total subservience to Syria envisaged in the agreement was not acceptable. And J. accepted the military alliance offered by Ja'ja', who was much more radical in his rejection of the agreement, and the ensuing military clash with Hobeika and his allies. Syria did not officially join Berri and Junbalat in demanding J.'s dismissal and maintained some relations with him but her forces backed the Shi'i and Druze militias, as well as Hobeika and J.'s Maronite rival, former President Suleiman *Franjiyeh, and J.'s position in 1986-87 was precarious

Jumayyil, Bashir (1947–82) Lebanese militia leader and politician. Elected President of Lebanon in Aug. 1982, killed before assuming office. A *Maronite Christian born in Beirut, J. was the younger son of Pierre *Jumayyil, the founder and leader of the Christian *Phalanges, and the brother of Amin *Jumayyil (who succeeded him as President). He studied law and political science at the Jesuit St. Joseph University of Beirut, but did not complete his studies. From his early youth he was active in the Phalanges. In the late 1960s, he organized student agitation against the presence and activities of the Palestinian-A. guerrillas in Lebanon (1968). Considered ruthless and endowed with charismatic leadership, he rose rapidly in the organization's military command during the civil war from 1975 onward — stressing a youthful activism and a measure of disdain for the leaders of the older generation and their political deals and intrigues. In 1976, J. became the chief military commander of the Phalanges, and shortly afterwards also of the "Lebanese Forces" (at that time an umbrella formation of the Phalanges and other Christian-Maronite militias). He is credited with the bloody conquest, in Aug. 1976, of the Palestinian guerrilla camp-stronghold of Tel al-Za'tar in an East Beirut suburb.

From 1976–77, J. strove to impose on the Christian "Lebanese Forces" the complete primacy of his Phalanges, in effect the merger of all other Christian formations in the Phalanges — by force if necessary. He was held chiefly responsible for bitter intra-Maronite fighting — with *Franjiyeh's North-Lebanese militias that had seceded from the "Lebanese Forces" (in the course of which Franjiyeh's son and heir was killed, with his wife and child), and with *Chamoun's National-Liberal Party "Tigers" (which he eliminated as a fighting force, absorbing their remnants to his Phalange-Lebanese Forces). J. thus got involved in bitter blood feuds and, while adored by his supporters, was hated by many, even within his own Maronite community. He and his relatives were also targets for terrorist attacks in the civil war; in one such attempt, in Feb. 1980, his baby daughter was killed.

J.'s political line was radical. No longer content with the elder Christian leaders' struggle to maintain the inter-communal equilibrium with a measure of Christian-Maronite primacy, he aspired to a Christian, Maronite-dominated Lebanon. In the first place he wanted to defend and strengthen Maronite control of the heartland of Mount Lebanon and was apparently not averse to the thought of Lebanon as a federation of semi-independent communal cantons with the Maronite one as main and dominating part, and he seemed willing to consider even the cession of the Muslim-majority North, South and East, that had been added in 1920 to create "Greater Lebanon", and the recreation of a smaller, Christian Lebanon. He vigorously opposed Syrian intervention and the presence of Syrian troops in Lebanon, even if disguised as an "all-A." peace or deterrence force. He objected to all-A. interference, and to the integration of Lebanon in all-A. power blocs. He fought the Palestinian guerrillas' use of Lebanon as a base for their operations, did not believe in co-ordination agreements with them and wanted them out altogether.

J. strengthened, from about 1976, clandestine links with Israel that the Phalanges had maintained, on and off, for many years. He received Israeli aid in arms, training, advice, and several times met (or sent his associates to meet) Israeli leaders. The invading Israeli forces in June 1982 made it possible for J. and his Phalanges to take control of Beirut and the key levers of government. But J. understood that he could not become an accepted leader of all Lebanon being borne to power on the coat-tails of an Israeli invasion and as Israel's collaborator; he therefore began, though clearly seen as cooperating with Israel to some degree, to shun a too visible collaboration with her.

When President *Sarkis' term expired, in Sept. 1982, J. was, in the political circumstances created by the Israeli invasion and the predominance achieved by the Phalanges, the only candidate for the Presidency. It proved difficult to convene Parliament, the more so as Syria did not permit the attendance of members from the areas she occupied. But eventually, 62 of the 92 members surviving were drummed together and on 23 Aug. 1982 elected J. President, with 57 votes, on the second ballot. On 14 Sept., before he was sworn in, J. was killed in the bombing of the Phalanges headquarters (a bombing revenged by the Phalanges, three days later, in a massacre of the Palestinian camps of Sabra and Shatila). J. was succeeded by his brother Amin *Jumayyil, elected President one week after Bashir's death.

Jumayyil, Pierre (1905–84) Lebanese politician, Maronite Christian. Founder and leader of the paramilitary *Phalanges organization. Father of Presidents Bashir *Jumayyil and Amin *Jumayyil. A pharmacist, educated in Beirut and France, J. was active in sports and youth organization, reportedly much impressed by European, and particularly German, organizations. In 1936 he founded the paramilitary Phalanges Libanaises (*al-Kata'ib*). Designed to protect the Maronites (though this was never explicitly spelled out), that organization soon took a political coloring, stressing Lebanon's independence and her Christian character and opposing her integration in Pan-Arab schemes. It gradually became more of a political party, making J. one of the leaders of the pro-Western Christian camp.

In the 1930s and 1940s, J. cultivated the Phalanges as a youth and paramilitary organization and was not active in politics. He took no prominent part in the struggle of those years between pro-French and anti-French factions (*Edde and his "National Bloc" vs. *Khouri and his "Constitutional Bloc") and in the crisis of 1943. In the civil war of 1958 he was one of the leaders of the Christian-led resistance to the Nasserist, Muslim-led rebels. When that dispute was being settled, in Sept. 1958, he prevented, by threatening a *coup*, the formation of a government dominated by the Nasserist rebels and insisted on a more balanced team. In October, with the compromise that ended the crisis, he became one of the four members of the neutral government set up. He supported President *Shihab and was a Cabinet Minister during most of Shihab's Presidency (to 1964) and that of his successor Hilou (to 1970) — Minister of Finance 1960–61, the Interior 1966, and 1968–69, and most of the time Public Works and/or Health. Since 1960 he was also a member of Parliament — elected as an independent, but gradually appearing as a representative of the Phalanges (whith a handful of additional Phalangists in Parliament). J. did not take a strong stand on the basic Christian-Muslim issue, though his general attitude was well-known. He did not join other Christian factions to form a strong, united Christian bloc, and engaged in much factional-tactical maneuvering. He did, however, form, in the 1960s, a loose "Triple Alliance" with Camille *Chamoun's "National Liberal Party" and Raymond *Edde's "National Bloc". In 1970 he presented, with their support, his candidacy for the Presidency, but withdrew in favor of a more "neutral" candidate, Suleiman *Franjiyeh.

J. took, since the later 1960s, a strong position against the use of Lebanon by the Palestinian-A. guerrillas/terrorists as a base for their operations and the growth of their separate and dominant establishment in South Lebanon. He did not follow the official A. line of total hostility towards Israel, but neither did he associate himself with the willingness to co-exist in peace and cooperate evinced by some other Christian politicians (such as Emile Edde), some leaders of the Maronite Church, and his own Phalanges. He certainly was aware of Israel's low-profile aid to, and cooperation with, the Phalanges since the 1950s, but he was not directly involved in it, and he took no part in the intensification of that cooperation in the 1970s and its culmination in June 1982. Of his two sons, he seemed closer to the positions taken by cautious, balancing Amin than to those of extreme, brash, militant Bashir.

Since the early 1970s, J. was not very active in Lebanon's public and political life. He did not play a prominent role in the marshalling of the Christian-conservative camp in the civil war since 1975, though he was, of course, identified with the Phalanges and his sons. In Apr. 1984 he agreed to serve in the Government of National Unity established by Rashid *Karameh and imposed on his son Amin, the President. In July 1984, he retired from the chairmanship of the Phalanges, appointing as his successor Elie Karameh (who was duly elected in Sept. 1984, soon after J.'s death).

Junbalat (also **Jumbalat, Jumblat**) Prominent *Druze clan in Lebanon, one of the two clans struggling, since the mid-19th century, for the political leadership of the Druze community (the rival one: *Arslan). The J.'s, of Kurdish origin, claim descent from Salah-ul-Din. They were centered in Aleppo, reportedly came to Lebanon in the 17th century, invited by the Druze ruler Fakhr-ul-Din, joined his Druze community, and established themselves as semi-feudal lords of parts of the Shuf region, with Mukhtara as their center. In the clans' struggles for primacy they fought, in the 18th and early 19th centuries, against the ruling Shihab dynasty. After the decline of the latter, the J.'s emerged, from the mid-19th century, as one of the two leading clans and competed with the Arslan or Yazbaki clan for the dominant position. While their political allegiance was shifting, they were in general allies of the French during the French Mandate. Prominent figures among them in the 1920s and 1930s were Fu'ad J. (assassinated in the early 1920s) and his widow Nazira, who became leader of the clan (d. 1951), and Hikmat J., who represented the clan in Parliament and was several times Minister (d. 1943).

In independent Lebanon, since 1943, the J.'s have become increasingly assertive in their demands for the Druze community and have — under the leadership of Kamal *J. (the son of Fu'ad and Nazira), and since his death in 1977 that of his son Walid *J. — joined the Leftist-Socialist, radical camp. As the Arslans declined, the J.'s have become the chief leaders of the Lebanese Druze — and of the Leftist camp and its military formations, allied with the *Shi'is in recent years. While advocating the abolition of Lebanon's communal system of representation and government, Kamal and Walid J. have in fact enhanced the strength of the Druze community and its weight in Lebanese politics and carved out a Druze "canton" in the Shuf and upper Matn areas that is *de facto* autonomous and under their control.

Junbalat, Kamal (1917–77) Lebanese-Druze politician. The son of Fu'ad and Nazira J. (see *supra*), J. studied law and sociology in Beirut and Paris and became the head of the J. clan in the later 1940s. Considered a highly cultivated man of wide horizons and original thought, J. was a skilled politician who had, in the complex community-party-clan politics of Lebanon, no permanent allegiance but played a power game of shifting factional alliances. A supporter of Emile *Edde and his "National Bloc" in his youth, he switched his support to Bishara al-*Khouri after 1943, but soon turned against him and joined Camille *Chamoun to bring about Khouri's fall in 1952. J. first became a Minister in Dec. 1945 (Economic Affairs) and was a member of Parliament since 1947 — except for the years from 1957 to 1964.

While J. drew his political strength from being recognized as the leader of the Druze community, and later: of its armed militias — and not from the political-ideological views he propounded — he began turning Left in the late 1940s and adopted increasingly radical Socialist, and gradually also Nasserist and Pan-Arab, views. In 1949 he founded a party of his own, the "Progressive Socialist Party" and began appearing as a Socialist leader, while keeping his position as a great landlord and semi-feudal chieftain with various financial and business interests (though he distributed some of his land to his tenants). His party was mainly Druze, but claimed to be above communal interests; it advocated far-reaching social reforms and the abolition of Lebanon's system of communal representation and government.

In 1958, J. turned against President Chamoun and began organizing extra-Parliamentary, Nasserist-inspired opposition that soon became a violent insurrection and civil war. The ending of that crisis with the help of American military intervention confirmed him in his anti-Western, Leftist-Nasserist views. Under the post-1958 régime of Presidents *Shihab and Hilou, J. several times held ministerial posts — Education 1960–61, Public Works 1961 and 1966, Interior 1961–53 and 1969–70. He was prominent, and as Home Minister instrumental, in his support for the Palestinian-A. guerrilla operations and their establishment in Lebanon, and, as clashes erupted between the *PLO men and Lebanese, mainly Christian, formations, from 1970, he was involved in several crises on that issue. J. also fostered relations with the USSR and in 1972 was awarded the Lenin Peace Prize. But he also applied for membership for his party in the Socialist International, obtained observer status and was welcomed as a participant in several meetings of the International.

In the civil war since 1975, J. was one of the chief organizers of th Leftist-Muslim camp, and his Druze (or "Progressive-Socialist") militias became one of the main military formations of that camp. He also cultivated, in the context of that civil war, close relations with Syria. Yet, when Syria's involvement became a fully fledged military intervention in 1976, and Syria tried to impose a comprehensive settlement and reform plan, J. adamantly opposed the plan (which, in his view, did not go far enough and made too many concessions to the Christian conservatives). He thus was co-responsible for the strange constellation that found Syria, briefly, fighting against her allies of the Lebanese Left and cooperating with her adversaries of the Christian Right. And when J. was assassinated, in Mar. 1977, it was generally assumed, though never proven, that Syrian agents had killed him.

J., who also taught for some years History of Economic Thought at Beirut University, wrote several books on Lebanese political issues (*The Truth about the Lebanese Revolution*, 1959; *Pour le Liban* — written down by a French associate — 1978, English edition, *I Speak for Lebanon*, 1982; *In the Current of Lebanese Politics*).

Junbalat, Walid (b. 1949) Lebanese Druze politician and militia leader. The son of Kamal *J. (his mother was of the *Arslan clan, the daughter of Shakib *Arslan), J. studied at the American University of Beirut and for some time in France. He was not very active in politics in his youth, and though he belonged to his father's militia, he was considered a playboy. When, however, Kamal J. was assassinated in Mar. 1977, Walid had to succeed him — reportedly with some reluctance — as leader of the "Progressive Socialist Party" and its militias (in effect: Druze militias), and of the Druze community. At first it was thought that the community, and particularly its religious leaders, would not accept him (the more so as he broke Druze customs by marrying a non-Druze, a Jordanian of Circassian origin); but he soon asserted his leadership. At first considered moderate, he soon took his father's line of anti-Western Leftism and a close alliance with the Leftist-Muslim camp in the civil war; given to bold, somewhat erratic statements and much media exposure, he even made it more extreme. Like his father, he advocated the abolition of Lebanon's system of communal representation and government, in effect asserting the power position of the Druze community. It fell to him to enhance that power to unprecedented strength after Sept. 1983. During the first months of the Israeli occupation, from June 1982, he stayed in his home at Mukhtara and kept a low profile; notwithstanding his extremist politics, he had, as the leader of the Druze in the Israel-occupied Shuf region, some contacts with the Israelis, and the latter hoped for co-operation with him in the pacification of the area, security arrangements and the co-ordination of their withdrawal. However, he preferred to leave his occupied home, spent some time in Syria, and returned to reassert his leadership and organize resistance to Israel (and to the *Jumayyils' Christian-dominated régime set up under Israeli auspices). In Aug.-Sept. 1983 he foiled all efforts to arrange a peaceful Israeli withdrawal from the Shuf and a coordinated take-over of the area vacated, and when Israeli forces withdrew without such coordination, he organized an immediate Druze onslaught on Christian forces in the Shuf (that had been allowed by Israel to set up strongpoints) and on Christian villages (that had co-existed with the Druze for centuries — though clashes and massacres had occurred before). The Druze won that bloody battle for the Shuf, and in 1984–85 extended their control farther south and west, to the Kharrub region, reaching the coast, and to the hills dominating Beirut and its south-eastern suburbs. They also helped the Shi'i militias to take West Beirut and kept Christian East Beirut half-besieged and under constant threat, with frequent battles in the hills to its east.

In the efforts towards national reconciliation, 1984–85, J. took a hard, extremist line, insisting on speedy far-reaching reforms towards a non-communal constitution, and an immediate redistribution of power, with a larger share for the Druze (and Muslims) and a reduction of the powers of the Maronite President; he also repeatedly demanded the dismissal or resignation of President Amin *Jumayyil. He tightened his alliance with Syria, in effect becoming her client totally depending on her support, arms supplies etc.; he sometimes agreed to compromise formulas worked out under Syrian guidance, but he frequently reneged, shifted his tactical positions and burst out in new extreme pronouncements. He accepted the compromise formula of Mar. 1984 and joined *Karameh's "Government of National Unity" (as Minister of Public Works and Transportation), but boycotted and in effect sabotaged the government of which he was a member.

J. cultivated his alliance with the Shi'i *Amal militias and their leader Nabih *Berri — though that alliance, too, was unstable and punctured by crises and armed clashes. In the bitter fighting between al-Amal and Palestinian guerrillas since 1985, he took, despite his alliance with al-Amal, a rather neutral or even pro-Palestinian position, sometimes attempting to mediate. J. was instrumental in the foundation of several coalitions (a "National Salvation Front" in July 1983 — nine factions and militias of the civil war Leftist camp; a "National Democratic Front" in Oct. 1984 — six parties, including the Communists and the pro-Syrian *Ba'th). But these alliances did not turn into firm, living organisms, and J. remained a force causing instability, unreliable in his alliances and erratic in his policies, though firm in his aversions.

K

Karameh, Rashid (1921–87) Lebanese politician, many times Prime Minister. Scion of a Muslim-Sunni family of notables from Tripoli, whose sons held for a long time the office of *Mufti* of Tripoli. K.'s father, 'Abd-ul-Hamid K. (1895–1950), served as *Mufti* and was the political and religious leader of the Muslims of Tripoli and their chief representative in Parliament; he also served briefly, in 1945, as Prime Minister. K. studied law in Cairo, graduated in 1947 and opened a law practice. Upon the death of his father, he succeeded him as leader of the Muslims of Tripoli, and was elected to every Parliament since 1951. He first joined the Government in 1951, as Minister of Justice, served as Minister of Economy and Social Affairs, 1953–55, and first became Prime Minister in 1955.

In line with the traditions of the Muslim-Sunni leadership in Lebanon, K. joined shifting parliamentary factions and several times formed such groups himself, but never stabilized a permanent party organization (or, later, a "militia"). He belonged, like most of the Sunni leaders, to the mainstream faction of Lebanese politics; but he was on its "Leftist" fringe: for far-reaching reforms, and particularly for the abolition of Lebanon's system of communal representation and government, against Christian predominance, strongly nationalist and for a Pan-Arab, Nasserist orientation, radically anti-Israel and supportive of Palestinian-A. guerrilla activities. In his orientation he thus differed from most of the traditional, conservative Sunni leaders in Beirut (Yafi, Salam, *Sulh), his rivals for the top position at the head of the Sunni community. His Nasserist tendencies came to the fore in 1958, when he was one of the leaders of the resistance to President *Chamoun's régime that developed into a Nasserist rebellion and led to civil war. When that crisis ended with a compromise and the election of General *Shihab to the Presidency, K. headed a "Government of National Salvation", Sept. 1958, and remained Premier until May 1960. He was again Prime Minister in 1961–64, 1965–66, 1966–68 and 1969–70. However, owing to his extreme views and positions, his Premierships were controversial and he was involved in frequent crises, sometimes resigning and withdrawing his resignation. In Apr. 1969, for instance, no other Prime Minister was appointed after his resignation and the country was without a government for several months until he resumed the Premiership. Many of these crises derived from K.'s extreme policies concerning the Palestine conflict. During the *Six Day War, 1967, he reportedly ordered the army to enter the war — an order that was refused and countermanded by Gen. Bustani, the Maronite commander of the army. From the late 1960s, K. supported the Palestinian-A. guerrilla establishment in Lebanon and its operations. As Prime Minister he tried to reach agreements with them on a measure of co-ordination, while foiling efforts to curb them by armed action. The government crisis of 1969 was related to this issue.

In the civil war since 1975 K. at first kept his image as a mainstream man who could hold the country together and mediate. Therefore, after five years out of power, he was again made Prime Minister in June 1975. He was, however, unable to maintain an administration operating and in control, the government and the army disintegrated, and in Dec. 1976 he resigned. He now identified himself with the "Leftist"-Muslim camp, but played no prominent role in its organization and leadership. He was handicapped, like the conservative Beirut Sunni leaders, by having no Muslim-Sunni "militia" at his disposal. Moreover, as Tripoli, his own bailiwick, was torn in battle between the fundamentalist *Tawhid Islami* and pro-Syrian, *'Alawi-dominated *Ba'th militias, his leadership at his home base became ineffective.

After the Israeli invasion of June 1982, K. took an uncompromising anti-Israel line, rejected any security agreement with Israel and opposed the *Jumayyil administration that seemed prepared to sign such an agreement and collaborate with Israel. He strengthened his links with Syria and fostered an alliance with Syria's other clients in Lebanon — *Junbalat's Druze, *Berri's Shi'i *Amal, and Maronite ex-President Franjiyeh. In July 1983, for instance, he set up, with Junbalat and Franjiyeh, a "National Salvation Front", which did not become an active, effective organization. K. played a leading role in the negotiations towards a national reconciliation and reforms (the Geneva talks of Oct.-Nov. 1983 and the Lausanne conference of Mar. 1983) — representing, under Syrian guidance, the more moderate forces within the Leftist-Muslim camp, those who were prepared to accept Syrian-devised compromise plans. In Apr. 1984 he formed a "Government of National Unity", with both camps represented. But this government could not really work: it was composed of forces diametrically opposed to each other; it was mostly boycotted by some of its key Ministers (Junbalat, Berri); and it was supposed to work with a President who had been compelled to appoint it and whom some of its own members strove to dismiss. It could not even meet for many months; and it had no means to impose its will and to administer and control the country. With the army and police disintegrated into rival formations, and the country in effect divided into separate "cantons" at the mercy of rival, battling "militias". And K., who remained formally Premier, though frequently threatening to resign, was Prime Minister *pro forma* only. From early 1986 he boycotted President Jumayyil and refused to convene the government. In May 1987 he finally resigned in frustration, but his resignation was not accepted by the President. On 1 June 1987 K. was assassinated.

Khaddam, 'Abd-ul-Halim (b. 1932) Syrian, Muslim-Sunni politician, since 1984 Vice-President of Syria. After studying law, Kh. worked as a lawyer in Damascus, 1951–64. He joined the *Ba'th party and from 1963, after the Ba'th assumed power, he engaged in politics full time. In 1967 he was appointed Governor of Damascus. In May 1969 he joined the government as Minister of Economy and Foreign Trade. In the intra-*Ba'th* factional struggle he was a follower of General Hafez *Asad, and when the latter assumed power, in Nov. 1970, Kh. became Foreign Minister and Deputy Premier, and a member of the *Ba'th* high command. Considered knowledgeable, even brilliant, he has directed Syria's foreign relations ever since, interpreting President Asad's policies with suave, professional firmness. Kh. has for some years been particularly responsible for Syria's policies and operations in Lebanon, receiving Lebanese politicians and militia leaders in Damascus for countless consultations and briefings and trying to guide and instruct Syria's allies and clients, yet unable to translate Syria's undoubted domination into a full implementation of her plans. In the struggle for Asad's succession, Kh. is considered one of the potential contestants, possibly favored by Asad himself. He lacks the military background that has become traditional with *Ba'th*ist Syria's top leaders, and being a Sunni, he perhaps does not belong to the inner leadership core dominated by *'Alawis; but he might be an acceptable compromise candidate. Since Mar. 1984, Kh. has been one of three Vice-Presidents, still mainly responsible for foreign and Lebanese affairs.

al-Khalidi Prominent Palestinian-A. family in Jerusalem. Many of its sons served in senior positions in the Ottoman-Turkish administration and in public life. Among prominent members of the clan in the 20th century: Yussuf Dia al-Kh. (1842–1906) — after serving in various administrative and consular posts, represented Jerusalem in the newly established Ottoman Parliament, 1876; Mayor of Jerusalem in the 1890s; also a writer and translator. Ruhi al-Kh. (1861–1913) — an administrator, writer and essayist, Ottoman Consul in Bordeaux 1898–1908, represented Jerusalem in the Ottoman Parliament from 1911 until his death. Dr. Hussein Fakhri al-Kh. (1894–1962) — Mayor of Jerusalem 1934–37 (elected, against Ragheb *Nashashibi, with the support of the *"Husseini" faction — though he was no adherent of that faction — and most of the Jewish vote). He founded, in 1935, a "Reform Party" and joined, as its leader, the *"Arab Higher Committee", 1936, which directed the A. rebellion. Dismissed as Mayor in 1937 and exiled to detention in the Seychelles, he was released in 1938 and allowed to take part in the Feb. 1939 Anglo-Arab Round Table Conference. He returned to Palestine in 1943 and joined the renewed Arab Higher Committee in 1945, and when it split — the rival "Higher Front"; reappointed to the *Arab League-nominated Higher Committee, Kh. was the only member of the Higher Committee to stay in Palestine during the fighting, 1947–48, but had no influence on the course of events. After the war he briefly joined the "Government of All Palestine" set up in Gaza, but soon left it to join the service of Jordan. From 1953 he was several times a Cabinet Minister (1953–54 and 1956 — Foreign Minister), and in Apr. 1957, when King *Hussein reasserted his power in a royal *semi-coup*, he was Prime Minister for some ten days. Mustafa al-Kh. (1879–1944) served in the Palestine Mandate judiciary and was in 1937 appointed to replace his dismissed relative Hussein al-Kh. as Mayor of Jerusalem. Ahmad Sameh al-Kh. (1896–1951), Hussein al-Kh.'s younger brother, was a well-known educator and writer, in the Mandate government's education service, from 1941 Deputy-Director of Education; for some time, Kh. was also principal of the Arab College of Jerusalem. His son Walid al-Kh. (b. 1925) is since the 1940s an outstanding representative of a new generation of Palestinian-A. intellectuals: in 1945 — one of Mussa al-*'Alami's team of young intellectuals in his Information/Propaganda Offices; in the 1960s one of the founders and directors of the PLO's Institute of Palestine Studies, Beirut, and a professor at the American University of Beirut; since the 1970s at Harvard. Kh. is close to the PLO, though as an academic he maintains a measure of independence, and a leading exponent of Palestinian-A. political thought. He has been frequently mentioned as a potential Palestine A. representative in future peace negotiations.

al-Khalifa, Aal ("House of") The dynasty of sheikhs (since 1970: Amirs) ruling *Bahrain. The beginning of their rule is put by some in 1782–83, when the Bahrain islands were taken from Persia by raiding-invading Arab tribes from the mainland; some put it at c. 1816. From the 1820s until 1971 the sheikhs were under a British protectorate. The rulers in this century were Sheikh 'Issa ibn (bin) 'Ali al-Kh. (1869–1923) who was deposed in 1923 by his son, with British encouragement; Sheikh Hamad ibn 'Issa (1923–42); Sheikh Salman ibn Hamad (1942–61); and Sheikh 'Issa ibn Salman — since 1961. Other sons of the House of al-Kh. usually serve in key positions of government and administration, and as Ministers since the establishment of a Council of Ministers in 1970. Since 1970–71 the head of that Council, or Prime Minister, has been the ruler's brother, Sheikh Khalifa ibn Salman al-Kh.

Khanaqin Small town in eastern Iraq, in the province of Diyala, close to the Iranian frontier, on the Baghdad-Kermanshah road. Kh. lies in an oil-bearing area ceded by Persia to Turkey in 1913. Under an Anglo-Turkish agreement of that time, oil exploitation rights were to remain with the Anglo-Persian Oil Company, which in 1926 set up a subsidiary, the Kh. Oil Company — for decades the only group operating in Iraq that was not connected with the *Iraq Petroleum Company. The KOC produced oil in small quantities (200–400,000 tons p.a. in the 1950s) and built a refinery at Alwand near Kh. (capacity in the 1960s: c. 350,000 tons p.a. of finished products). The KOC was partially nationalized in 1951, along with the nationalization of the Anglo-Iranian company by Iran, and continued operating as a contractor on behalf of the government. This relationship was terminated by agreement in 1958 and the company was fully nationalized by Iraq. From about 1963, production — now by Iraq's national oil company — was stepped up, in breach of an agreement with Iran that provided for co-ordinated and agreed quantities and mutual inspection.

al-Khatmiyya A conservative-revivalist Islamic order in Sudan, opposed to Islamic mysticism (Sufism) and its *Dervish Orders, the opponent and rival of the *Mahdiyya order. The Kh., founded in the mid-19th century by Muhammad 'Uthman al-Amir Ghani, of Hijazi origin (d. 1853), is also called, after its founder, al-Amir-Ghaniyya or al-*Mirghaniyya.

Khaz'al, Sheikh (d. 1934) Semi-independent Arab tribal chief who controlled Muhammara (*Khorramshahr) in the South-West Iranian province of *Khuzistan until 1924–25.

Khomeini, Ruhullah, Ayatullah (b. 1902?) The chief spiritual and political leader of Iran's Islamic revolution, 1979, and the régime it established. His biography and activities are outside the scope of this Dictionary; but his involvement in, and influence on, the A. world should be briefly mentioned. Kh., who had to leave Iran in 1963, after the Shah suppressed unrest, went for about one year to Turkey and then spent almost 15 years of exile in Iraq, where he was kept under strict surveillance; he was unable to kindle a new insurrection in Iran, though he did exert considerable clandestine influence on the Islamic establishment in Iran and among the Shi'is of Iraq. In Oct. 1978 he was expelled from Iraq, apparently under pressure from the Shah, and went to France, where he was free to step up his political activities against the Shah's régime until he emerged victorious within a few months. It may be assumed that his resentment of the curbs imposed on him by Iraq, since 1964 *Ba'th ruled, is an element in his attitude to Iraq.

In the war unleashed by Iraq in Sept. 1980, Kh. has been the chief force rallying Iran's will and capacity to resist, despite serious military disadvantages and grave initial setbacks. It is under his guidance, or by his command, that Iran has refused for years to consider a cease-fire and negotiations to end the war and insisted on complete victory — including an international condemnation of Iraq as the aggressor, the payment of huge amounts of compensation, the dismissal of Iraq's leader Saddam *Hussein and his trial as a war criminal. He does not, however, seem to raise territorial demands beyond the restoration of the frontiers to their pre-1980 status.

Kh.'s brand of radical, revolutionary Islamic fundamentalism and the imposition of Islamic law and methods of government on the state exerts a powerful influence in the AC, too. His immediate impact and direct links are restricted, as his Islam is the *Shi'i one, to the Shi'is in the AC — who carry weight (since the *Zeidi Shi'is of Yemen seem to be largely unaffected by Kh.) only in some of the Persian Gulf sheikhdoms and especially in Lebanon; there Shi'i-Islamic extremist organizations have sprung up, inspired by Kh. and aided by his agents and Iranian "volunteers" sent to intervene in the Lebanese civil war (these agents and volunteers stress in particular the fight against Israel). However, Muslim-Sunni fundamentalist-extremist streams and movements in the AC have also derived inspiration and encouragement from Kh.'s teachings and his victory in Iran. His revolution and his régime have added impetus and strength to the upsurge of Islamic fundamentalism noticeable in the AC in recent decades. Most A. governments, taking an anti-Iranian position in any case because of their A. solidarity with Iraq (Syria and Libya being the exceptions), fear and resent that intrusion of "Khomeinism". Some of them, however, try to counteract it by giving a greater emphasis to the dominant status of Islamic law in the constitution and governance of their countries.

Khorramshahr (Arabic: Muhammara) Town and port in the South-West Iranian province of *Khuzistan, on the eastern bank of the *Shatt al-'Arab. The town, and the province, have a partly Arabic-speaking population — according to some: an Arabic- speaking majority — and until the 1920s Kh. was usually called by its Arabic name, Muhammara. The government of Iran was unable to exercise effective control, and power was in the hands of a semi-feudal A. chieftain, Sheikh Khaz'al, since 1910 protected and subsidized by Britain (in return for his pledge not to interfere with oil exploration and drilling operations begun in 1909). However, in 1924–25 Reza Shah crushed the rebellious Sheikh's autonomy and fully incorporated Khuzistan, including Kh., into Iran's administration. The town's name was Persianized into Kh.; it was developed into a major port. Its population grew to over 200,000 in the 1970s, and some estimates put it even higher. It lost some of its importance as a port when Iran began developing, in the wake of her dispute with Iraq over the Shatt al-'Arab, her ports on the Persian Gulf, particularly Bandar Shahpur (renamed Bandar Khomeini in 1979–80). In the Iraq-Iran war since Sept. 1980, Kh. was taken by Iraq in Oct. 1980; it was retaken by Iran, after the failure of several attempts, in May 1982. In the fighting, the town was almost completely destroyed.

al-Khouri, Bishara (1890? 1892?–1964) Lebanese, Christian-Maronite politician. President of Lebanon 1943–52. Educated in Beirut Jesuit schools, Kh. studied law in Paris and returned in 1911 to open a law practice in Beirut. During World War I he escaped to Egypt. He returned in 1918–19 and after a brief spell as Secretary of a government which Lebanese politicians tried to set up before the French Mandate administration was established, he reopened his law practice. He then joined the judicial administration, becoming a judge in 1923. When in 1927 the first Lebanese government was formed under the French Mandate, he became Minister of Interior, and in 1927–28, and again in 1929, was Prime Minister. In 1932 he was a candidate to succeed Charles Debbas as President, but the French suspended the Constitution. Kh. now led a group fighting for the restoration of the Constitution, formalizing it in 1934 as a party, the "Constitutional Bloc", considered anti-French and favoring the integration of Lebanon in the A. nationalist movement (against Emile *Edde with his "National Bloc", who was pro-French and, stressing Lebanon's Christian-pluralistic character, did not see her way to independence as part of the A. nationalist struggle).

In 1936 Kh. was a candidate for the Presidency, against Edde, and lost by a small margin. But in Sept. 1943, with the resumption and intensification of the struggle for independence, he was elected President of the Republic — unanimously, as Edde had not formally presented his candidacy and Edde's supporters absented themselves from Parliament. His election was due in no small measure to the alliance he had made with Riyad al-*Sulh, the leader of the A.-nationalist Sunni Muslims. The unwritten agreement he had reached with Sulh and the Muslim leaders, the "National Covenant" of 1943, laid down the details of Lebanon's communal political system, the distribution of power among the communities (see *Lebanon).

In 1948–49, Kh. sponsored a change in the Constitution to allow his re-election in 1949 for a second Presidential term. This breach of the Constitution raised a storm; it had been preceded by irregularities in the Parliamentary elections of 1947 and charges of corruption. A campaign of mounting opposition culminated in Sept. 1952 in a semi-*coup* led by his leading rival, Camille *Chamoun; Kh. was forced to resign, and his public career was ended. His brother Salim and later his son Khalil (b. 1921) succeeded to the leadership of his "Constitutional Bloc", but the party did not regain its leading position; until 1968 various Parliamentary candidates still used its name, but in effect it was no longer an organized party.

Khuzistan Province in south-western Iran, on the *Shatt al-'Arab, with a partly A. population, also called Arabistan. Iran's main oil-bearing area. Capital: Ahwaz; other main towns: *Khorramshahr, Abadan, Bandar Khomeini (formerly Bandar Shahpur). Area: c. 62,000 sq. km. (close to 24,000 sq. mi.). Kh.'s population was estimated in the 1970s at c. 2m., in the 1980s at over 3m. At the beginning of the century, before oil development began, many — perhaps most — of its inhabitants, then less than 1m., were Arabic-speaking nomadic tribesmen, largely Muslim-Sunni. As the government of Iran was weak, *de facto* control was in the hands of the A. Sheikh Khaz'al of Muhammara (in Persian: Khorramshahr). As oil development began and the area assumed a new importance, the British, protecting their oil interests, in 1910 signed an agreement with Sheikh Khaz'al: in return for his pledge to maintain security and not to interfere with oil production. Britain, while stopping short of recognizing his independence, guaranteed to protect him against external attacks and to pay him an annual subsidy. When Iran stabilized and strengthened her rule, Reza Shah in 1924–25 overcame Sheikh Khaz'al and put an end to his semi-independence.

During Reza Shah's reign, not much was heard of A. claims to the region. However, in the 1940s, when Iran was weak and tribal revolts troubled the neighboring provinces, several A. sheikhs of the area began professing A. nationalism and calling for the incorporation of "Arabistan" into Iraq. Iraqi nationalists, who had played with the idea before, increasingly voiced similar demands, with government support, though Iraq's governments stopped short of officially demanding the annexation of Kh. As revolutionary-nationalist régimes took control in Egypt (1952), Iraq (1958), Syria, they began encouraging an irredentist A. movement and demanding, if not Kh.'s cession to Iraq, at least local autonomy for her Arabs. Iran rejected such claims. In 1965 she recalled her Ambassador from Damascus when the Syrian Prime Minister described "Arabistan" as a lost A. territory to be recovered. Iran also endeavored to develop Kh. and strengthen its Iranian character. With the development of Kh.'s oil economy, the population had much increased, most of the new settlers and workers being Iranian. The proportion of the Arabic-speaking population had correspondingly decreased — estimates of their share in the 1960s and 1970s varying from one-third to two-thirds of Kh.'s population.

Kh. was the main arena of the Iraq-Iran war of 1980 on, and parts of it were conquered by Iraq in her initial offensive. Iraqi spokesmen implied that Iraq would keep and annex the region, though this was not formally stated. After the recovery of the region by Iran in 1981 and 1982, Iraq's pronouncements on Kh.-Arabistan were toned down and more or less ceased.

Kilani (also **Kailani, Gilani, Gailani**), **Rashid 'Ali** (1892–1965) Iraqi politician. Prime Minister 1933, 1940, 1941. Born in Baghdad, a scion of a leading Muslim-Sunni family, K. graduated from the Baghdad Law School. After briefly serving as a judge, he soon became active in politics. He first joined the government in 1924 as Minister of Justice and was Minister of the Interior, 1925–28. In 1931 he co-founded the nationalist *al-Ikhā' al-Watani* (National Brotherhood) party which rejected the terms of the Anglo-Iraqi Treaty of 1930. In 1933 he became Prime Minister for the first time, for half a year. He then served as Minister of Interior in 1935–36, and in Dec. 1938 became Chief of the Royal Cabinet. K. saw World War II as an opportunity to complete Iraq's independence by fully emancipating her from British influence. He was at first cautious and hesitant as to the means to oust Britain and deny her the facilities which Iraq was obliged, under the Treaty of 1930, to put at her disposal. The ex-*Mufti* of Jerusalem, Hajj Amin al-*Husseini, then in Baghdad, egged him on, and the group of rabidly anti-British and pro-German colonels then in effect ruling Iraq behind the scenes ("The Golden Square") saw him as a potential instrument of their policies and projected him into the premiership in Mar. 1940, with the help of some of the older politicians of other factions. In Jan. 1941 he had to cede the Premiership, because of factional intrigues; but in Apr. 1941 he was reinstated as Prime Minister in what amounted to a semi-*coup* by the colonels. In the grave crisis that followed — an attempt to deny facilities and services to the British that led to military operations against Britain; a call for German help; the dismissal and replacement of the pro-British Regent and a purge of his supporters and the *Hashemite-loyal and pro-British political establishment — K. was little more than a puppet. When his rebellious government and its forces were defeated by the British, at the end of May, he fled with those who had placed him in power. He went to Germany, where he served the Nazi war effort as a leading A. collaborator and propagandist.

After the war, K. lived as an exile in Sa'udi Arabia and Egypt. After the Iraqi *coup* of July 1958 he hoped that Gen. *Qassem's revolutionary régime would turn Pan-A.-nationalist and "Nasserist" and offer him an honored place among its leaders, so he returned to Iraq in Sept. 1958. His hopes were, however, soon disappointed, and he was also concerned by what he saw as the "Leftist" turn of the new régime. He became involved with "Nasserist" plotters, or gave his name to their attempts, and was arrested. In July 1959 it was announced that he had been sentenced to death in a secret trial in Dec. 1958. He was, however, reprieved. In July 1961 he was released from prison. He played no further part in public life.

King-Crane Commission A commission headed by the Americans Henry C. King and Charles R. Crane, sent in 1919 by the US administration to Palestine and Syria to investigate the wishes of the population concerning the future of the two countries. The KCC should have included experts from additional allied countries, but the British and French delegates never joined it. The KCC reported general opposition to Zionism and to the imposition of a French Mandate on Syria, and recommended the creation of a *"Greater Syria", to include Lebanon and Palestine. It reported that, if it were at all necessary to establish a Mandate, the inhabitants would prefer an American or, as a second choice, a British one. The KCC's methods of gauging public opinion were questioned by many. Its Report, in any case, was never acted upon.

Kurds A nation inhabiting north-west Iran, north-east Iraq and east Turkey — with some K. also in north-east Syria and Soviet Transcaucasia (mainly Armenia). The K. have a long history; some identify their ancestors as the Kuti mentioned in Sumerian inscriptions of the third millennium BC and the Medes in ancient Iran. They speak an Indo-European tongue closely akin to Persian (and divided into several different dialects). Most of them are Sunni Muslims. They are divided into tribes, frequently engaged in internecine rivalry and violent struggles. Since they inhabit mainly mountainous regions, they have never developed a nation-wide polity (though some K. have played leading roles in the history of the ME — Salah-ul-Din and his Ayyubid dynasty, for instance, were K.).

Kurdistan, the domicile of a population predominantly Kurdish in speech and consciousness, has never formed a political unit. Moreover, it has never been precisely defined, and its tentative, informal definitions are not accepted by all. Roughly, it is bounded in the north by the Aras river in eastern Turkey and on the Iran-USSR border; in the west by the Kara-Su and upper Euphrates rivers in Turkey and Iraq, in the south by the border between mountain country and undulating plains in Iraq, approximately along a Mosul-Kirkuk-Khanaqin line; and in the east by a line drawn from Hamadan to Lake Rezaiyeh (Urmia) and Maku, in Iran. The area of Kurdistan thus defined would be c. 135,000 sq.mi. (350,000 sq.km.). However, many non-K. live within this area, and many K. outside it. There are large and long-established urban K. communities in several cities outside Kurdistan, e.g. Baghdad, Basra, Aleppo and Damascus. (Some Iranian Shi'i tribes, e.g. the Lurs and Bakhtiaris, are thought by some to be of Kurdish origin, but are not usually considered as K.; the non-Muslim *Yazidis of Jabal Sinjar in Iraq speak Kurdish, but do not consider themselves K. and are not usually counted among them.)

There are different estimates as to the number of K.: 2–6m. in Iran, 3–10m. in Turkey, 2–3m. in Iraq, 3–700,000 in Syria, 1–200,000 in the USSR. A reasonable estimate might be: 3.5–4m. in Turkey, 3m. in Iran, 2.5–3m. in Iraq — a total of 8.5–10m. in Kurdistan, with 4–500,000 more in Syria, 150,000 in the USSR, totalling about 10–11m. K.; Kurdish sources tend to give larger figures, to a total of more than 20m. (Attempts to arrive at reliable figures are made more difficult by the fact that the official statistics of the countries concerned do not usually refer to K. as such; in Turkey particularly the term K. is unused and unacceptable and the K. of eastern Turkey are often referred to as "Mountain Turks".)

Owing to the tribal structure of the Kurdish people, organized until the mid-19th century in several local principalities under the nominal sovereignty of the Ottoman Sultan or the Shah of Iran, and the mountainous nature of Kurdistan, divided into isolated valleys, a modern Kurdish nationalist movement was late in coming. Towards the end of the 19th and the beginning of the 20th centuries a Kurdish intelligentsia in Constantinople and later in Europe began working for a national revival, at first culturally and soon politically too. Traditionally leading families, like the Badr Khan and Baban, who had recently lost their positions as local rulers, formed the nucleus and leadership of this national intelligentsia and founded the first Kurdish political societies and later parties. They had little or no effect in Kurdistan but gained a hearing in political circles in Europe. It was partly in response to their pleading that the victorious allied *Entente* powers, dismembering the Turkish-Ottoman Empire after World War I, envisaged an autonomous region of Kurdistan in eastern Anatolia and the *Mosul province of what was to become Iraq, with an option for later independence. They included a provision for such a Kurdish entity in the abortive peace treaty of *Sèvres which they imposed on Turkey in 1920. But when Turkish nationalist resistance achieved the replacement of that treaty by the new peace treaty of *Lausanne, 1923, the provision for Kurdish autonomy or independence was dropped (no Kurdish representatives had been allowed to participate in the negotiations). In the protracted wrangle over the province of Mosul, on the other hand, the problem of the K. and a possible autonomy for them played an important role, and when the *League of Nations Council finally awarded the province to Iraq in Dec. 1925, it did so on the understanding that Kurdish national "distinctness and consciousness" would be recognized, K. would play a leading role in the region's administration, and Kurdish would be a second official language there. That provision concerning Kurdish as an official language was formally reiterated by Iraq in the obligations she took upon herself in May 1932 before the League of Nations agreed to end the British Mandate and recognize Iraq's independence. Iraq did not fulfil these commitments to Kurdish satisfaction. In Turkey and Iran, no commitments were made for any kind of Kurdish semi-autonomy or the recognition of Kurdish national rights. Moreover, in Kemalist-nationalist Turkey Kurdish distinctness and stirrings of Kurdish aspirations, which erupted in 1925, 1930 and 1937 in violent rebellions, were suppressed.

The fragmentation of Kurdistan, and the very different circumstances prevailing in Iraq, Iran and Turkey, caused a parallel fragmentation in the Kurdish nationalist movement and its organizations. In any case, most of the Kurdish associations and "parties" were formed in exile and remained unrepresented in, and unrepresentative of, the homeland. The first and main organization akin to a modern political party was *Khoibun* ("Independence"), founded in 1927 in Beirut. Its chief leaders were of the old princely Badr (Bedir) Khan clan, particularly Kamuran 'Aali Bedir-Khan. *Khoibun* remained essentially an organization of exiles, mostly in Europe; it was pro-Western and non-Socialist. *Khoibun* lost influence and waned when nationalist organizations began to grow in Kurdistan itself — such as the right-wing *Heva* ("Hope") (which claimed to have been founded before World War I) and the Marxist *Rizgari* or *Ruzkari* ("Salvation") in Iraq, and the left-wing *Komala i-Zhian i-Kurdistan* ("Committee of Kurdish Resurrection"), in short *Komala*, in Iran. Late in 1945 the *Komala* reconstituted itself in *Mahabad as the "Kurdish Democratic Party" (KDP), which gradually emerged as the link between the sophisticated diaspora, the urbanized, de-tribalized K. with their educated, intellectual elements, and the incipient nationalist consciousness of the main part of the Kurdish nation, the tribes. The KDP, active in both Iran and Iraq, became the focus of Kurdish nationalism both organizationally and ideologically, with Mulla Mustafa *Barzani (or Barazani) as its main leader.

In Turkey, Kurdish nationalist organizations remained underground and were ruthlessly suppressed. They seemed to have little influence on the tribal-rural rebellions of 1925, 1930 and 1937 that were suppressed. A measure of Kurdish unrest continued, and since about 1984 it has intensified, growing into a near-constant semi-rebellion.

In Iran, relations between the Shah's government and the K. were in general much better. The régime left traditional society and its tribal patterns of governance undisturbed and did not interfere with the social-cultural activities of the younger generation as long as the K. remained politically loyal. This *modus vivendi* was broken when, in the unrest and disturbance in North Iran, during the first year or two after World War II, the K., with Soviet encouragement, attempted to set up, in Jan. 1946, a separate, independent Kurdish Republic in Mahabad. The Republic, under Qazi Muhammad and a group of urban intellectuals and merchants, with Barzani tribesmen as its main armed force under Mulla Mustafa Barzani, was defeated by Iranian troops in Dec. 1946, when the USSR abandoned the separatist government she had set up in Azerbaijan and began withdrawing her troops. Qazi Muhammad was court-martialled and executed; Mulla Mustafa and his Barzanis escaped to the Soviet Union.

Iran's relations with her K. then reverted to the previous patterns of a *modus vivendi*. Moreover, they became close as the Shah began allowing the Kurdish rebels in Iraq, from the 1960s until 1975, to establish their main supply base and staging area in the Kurdish region of Iran and aiding them with supplies, arms and ammunitions.

Relations soured when the Shah, as part of his 1975 agreement with Iraq, stopped all that and denied the rebels the facilities upon which they depended, thus causing the collapse of the rebellion. When, after the Iranian Islamic revolution of 1979, *Khomeini imposed his hard Islamic régime on the Kurdish region, too, putting an end to the *de facto* semi-autonomous *modus vivendi*, some of the K. of Iran rebelled, and the region has been in a state of semi-rebellion since 1979–80. These developments also caused a split in the Kurdish national movement. The KDP had never been fully united, and its Iraqi and Iranian branches had sometimes followed divergent policies. But in the Iran-Iraq war, since 1980, the Kurdish rebels of Iran collaborate in some measure with Iraq and her secret services, while their brethren rebelling in Iraq collaborate to some extent with Iran. The two branches of the KDP thus find themselves on opposing sides in a war — though they seem to have avoided direct clashes between Kurdish rebel forces themselves.

In Iraq, there was near-constant Kurdish unrest from the liquidation of Turkish rule in 1918, the beginnings of a British administration, and the formation of the Iraqi Kingdom in 1922. At first, this unrest was linked to Turkish efforts to keep the province of Mosul within the new Turkey; but the unrest remained endemic when the province was awarded to Iraq (1925–26) and when Turkish manipulations gradually ceased. The British in their first years also tried to manipulate various tribal sheikhs, sometimes encouraging a degree of *de facto* semi-autonomy, sometimes suppressing the sheikhs' semi-rebellion. In the 1920s and 1930s, several Kurdish uprisings occurred — but it is a question of terminology at what point the near-constant unrest should be called a "rebellion". At the same time, many Kurdish leaders collaborated with the Iraq government, and the latter always contained one or several Kurdish Ministers — mainly from the urbanized K., but sometimes also tribal leaders (and the urbanized élite in any case was of tribal origin and had tribal links). The K. also received, during those years, several half-promises and half-measures towards a degree of local autonomy (e.g., the Iraqi declaration of May 1932 referred to above); but these, hardly satisfactory in the first place, were never fully implemented.

The main leader of the tribal unrest, and/or the rebellions, in the 1920s and the early 1930s, was Sheikh Mahmud (al-Barzinji). In the 1930s the Barzanis became the chief leaders — first Sheikh Ahmad and then Mulla Mustafa. The struggle, entirely tribal at first, became increasingly "national", as the de-tribalized urban intelligentsia became more deeply involved. This synthesis of traditional-tribal and modern nationalist elements found its expression in Mulla Mustafa Barzani's assumption of the Presidency of the KDP in the 1940s. The association of the Iraqi KDP with the Kurdish Republic of Mahabad, 1946, gave further impetus to the nationalist struggle.

Barzani was permitted to return to Iraq after the *Qassem *coup* of 1958. He and his men helped Qassem against both Nasserist and Communist attempts to take over, though Barzani was kept under surveillance in Baghdad. But Kurdish hopes for a settlement that would give some satisfaction to their aspirations were disappointed by the Qassem régime, and unrest spread again. In 1960 Barzani escaped to his mountains, and in 1961 Kurdish unrest turned into a fully fledged rebellion. The military fortunes of that rebellion were changing, but Iraq's armed forces were unable to liquidate it, partly because of the help it received from Iran, as described. Barzani reportedly also received aid from Israel. The Iraqis set up irregular units from among Kurdish tribes hostile to the Barzanis and encouraged rival factions, e.g., one set up by Jalal Talabani, a former lieutenant of Mulla Mustafa; but the impact of these bodies on the struggle was slight.

During the years of the rebellion, negotiations continued, on and off, aiming to end the revolt and achieve Kurdish-Iraqi reconciliation on the basis of an agreed autonomy for the K. In June 1966, an agreement was reached with Prime Minister Bazzaz which envisaged a partial *de-facto* autonomy for the Kurdish provinces, to be based on a general decentralization of Iraq's administration; the use of the Kurdish language in local government and education; a fair, proportional share for the K. in government, army, civil service, etc.; and freedom of Kurdish political organization (with a secret clause reportedly permitting the Kurdish rebel forces, the "Pesh Merga", to remain intact as a militia). The agreement was, however, not implemented — it was not fully acceptable to the Iraqi establishment, and Bazzaz himself ran into trouble over it; the cease-fire it entailed was never complete, and in 1968 a full-fledged rebellion resumed.

The pattern repeated itself in the 1970s. In Mar. 1970, full agreement was reached with the government, now of the *Ba'ath* Party and under the dominating influence of Saddam *Hussein. The new agreement went even further than that of 1966. It formally accepted the existence of a Kurdish nation was one of the two nations forming Iraq. The local autonomy granted, and the use of the Kurdish language envisaged, were wider than in previous agreements. A Kurdish Region was to be formed by the Kurdish-majority areas, i.e. mainly the three provinces of Suleimaniyya, Arbil and Dohuk (the last one newly created in 1969–70 out of the Kurdish northern parts of Mosul province). A "High Committee" was to supervise the implementation of these measures. The leading officials in the Kurdish areas were to be K.; a K. was to be named Vice-President of Iraq, and K. were to be appointed to the Revolutionary Command Council; K. were to be represented proportionally in Parliament, government — and reportedly, informally, also in the army and the civil service. Kurdish military forces were to be dissolved (but a secret clause reportedly permitted the retention of some 10–12,000 *Pesh Merga* as border guards or militias). The agreement was to be fully implemented within four years.

The recognition of the Kurdish nation as one of Iraq's two nations was incorporated, as agreed, in Iraq's new provisional Constitution of July 1970. Five KDP-nominated Ministers joined the Government of Iraq. A Kurdish University in Suleimaniyya opened its first courses; the preparation of Kurdish-language instruction in the Kurdish-majority areas and of Kurdish textbooks was begun; Kurdish broadcasts and Kurdish publications were taken in hand. Yet, the leader proposed by the KDP as Vice-President of Iraq was rejected; no K. were nominated to the Revolutionary Council; and there was no progress in the installation of a Kurdish semi-autonomous administration in the Kurdish provinces and in the Kurdish Region envisaged to embrace them. Moreover, there was persistent disagreement on the delimitation of that Kurdish region, especially concerning its western and southern boundaries in the Mosul and Kirkuk areas. For Kirkuk, it had been informally agreed that a census would be taken to determine which parts of the province had a Kurdish majority; but this census was delayed, and the K. claimed that the government was deporting K. from the disputed area and settling A.'s in their place. The share of the Kurdish Region in Iraq's revenue, mainly the oil revenue derived in large part from the region, was also in dispute. And the cease-fire was not fully kept. Barzani and his associates were convinced that all this derived from ill will, from a deliberate sabotage of the agreement by the government, tension mounted again, and the government encouraged Kurdish anti-Barzani factions to re-emerge.

When in Mar. 1974 the deadline came for full implementation of the autonomy agreement, the government unilaterally began implementing the measures it had designed — without the approval of the KDP or its co-operation, with no agreement on any of the points in dispute, and without including any part of the provinces of Mosul and Kirkuk. The five KDP Ministers, and the Kurdish Governors of Arbil, Dohuk and Suleimaniyya resigned and went to the mountains, and the rebellion re-erupted. Iraq's new Kurdish region was set up with collaborators and anti-Barzani factions only. In Apr. 1974 a Kurdish Vice-President was appointed (Taha Muhyi-ul-Din Ma'ruf), and in Sept.-Oct. an Executive Council, headed by Hashem al-'Aqrawi, and a 60-member Regional Council (at first with 9 seats left vacant for KDP representatives) were appointed for the semi-autonomous Kurdish Region proclaimed. In the 1980 and 1984 elections for the Iraqi National Assembly, the K. of that Region — no longer called "Kurdish" in official parlance — elected 26 members of that Assembly (which would be much less than their proportional share) and, simultaneously, also elected their Regional Council. There were Kurdish Ministers in the Government, and a pro-Government section of the KDP was part of the *Ba'th*-led ruling National Front. At the same time, the rebellious parts of the tribes and the KDP were ruthlessly suppressed. These operations were, so Kurdish spokesmen claimed, not confined to actual rebels, but amounted to a suppression of the K. in general, including the forcible transfer of Kurdish populations from the

Kurdish areas and their replacement by A. settlers, large-scale arrests and executions etc.

The Kurdish rebellion that had re-erupted in 1974 again had shifting military fortunes; in any case, it tied down considerable parts of the Iraqi army, and it could not be fully suppressed. The rebellion collapsed, however, in 1975, when the Shah of Iran, following his Mar. 1975 agreement with Iraq, stopped his aid to the rebels and denied them the use of Iranian territory as a supply base and staging ground. The *Pesh Merga* disintegrated, its leaders fled, including Mulla Mustafa Barzani (who died in 1979 as a refugee in the USA), and most of its fighters sought refuge in Iran. The number of Kurdish refugees to Iran was reported as over 200,000. When they began drifting back, under an amnesty, they were reportedly not permitted to go back to the Kurdish region but transferred to A. areas in the South.

In the later 1970s, Mulla Mustafa's sons Mas'ud and Idris Barzani tried to rekindle the rebellion and rebuild the *Pesh Merga*. But the movement was split and in confusion. Parts of the KDP, including another Barzani brother, 'Ubaid-ullah, collaborated with the Government. Talabani revived his rival faction, now calling it "Patriotic Union", PUK; and Idris and Mas'ud themselves were at loggerheads. Syria, in conflict with Iraq, reportedly supported the rebels, especially the Talabani faction, but kept a low profile. However, after the Iraq-Iran war broke out, in Sept. 1980, *Khomeini's Iran resumed a degree of aid to the rebels in Iraq (which posed another problem, as described above, since Barzani-KDP collaboration with Khomeini alienated the Iranian KDP branch, in semi-rebellion against the Khomeini régime, under 'Abd-ul-Rahman Qassemlou). The rebel KDP also joined a "National Front" of several anti-government organizations underground or in exile. The Iraqis, who could ill afford to divert parts of their army for the fight against the rebels, tried to win Talabani and his PUK as collaborators and partners; but talks, from 1982, broke down in 1984–85, and from early 1985 Talabani and his group rejoined the rebellion, though not in co-operation with the Barzanis' KDP. Some of Iraq's Kurdish collaborators also defected and joined the rebel camp. Iraq again had to repress a Kurdish rebellion; reportedly she also revoked large parts of the cultural autonomy granted since 1974 and continued measures against the Kurdish population as a whole. And the rebellion continued, claiming to control a wide strip of territory along the Turkish and Iranian borders.

Kuria Muria Islands Group of five small islands off the south coast of *'Oman. The islands, only one of which is inhabited (by less than 100), were ceded to Britain in 1854 by the Sultan of Muscat and 'Oman, and a cable station was built. The islands were administered by the British Political Resident in the Persian Gulf, but legislation by the British Governor of *'Aden and the Protectorates applied to them. In Nov. 1967, when Britain granted independence to 'Aden and South Arabia, which became South Yemen, she handed the KM islands back to 'Oman. South Yemen claimed them and appointed a Governor; but when 'Oman insisted on her ownership, South Yemen did not press her claim, and 'Oman took possession without incident. An air strip was constructed and in 1980 landing facilities were granted to Britain and the USA.

Kuwait Principality, sheikhdom at the north-western corner of the Persian Gulf. Area (excluding the K.-Sa'udi *Neutral Zone): c. 6,500 sq. mi. (17,800 sq. km.), population (mid-1980s estimate) c. 1.7m., 60% foreign non-citizens. Until World War II and the beginning of oil production, K. was a small, poor settlement of Bedouin, fishermen, pearl divers and boat builders, with a population of 50–75,000. But, situated on the Bay of K., the only deep-water bay in the Gulf, it had a natural port and acquired an important strategic role as a potential gateway to Iraq and the Arabian peninsula. For this reason, Germany intended, at the end of the 19th century, to extend the planned *Baghdad Railway to the Bay of K. Britain saw these plans as a threat to her domination of the Persian Gulf and her route to India and, beyond foiling the railway extension scheme, in 1899 agreed with the Sheikh of K. to place his realm under British protection — though the Ottoman-Turkish Sultan's nominal sovereignty was not formally abolished. Under this Protectorate Britain conducted K.'s foreign affairs and supervised her administration and law and order. After Ottoman Turkey entered World War I, in Nov. 1914, Britain recognized K. as independent under British protection. The Protectorate remained in effect until 1961, when K. became fully independent, under her Sheikh of the House of *Sabah, now styling himself Amir.

The discovery of oil changed K.'s fortunes, caused rapid development and made her immensely rich. An oil concession was granted in 1934 to the "K. Oil Co.", a 50:50 partnership of the Anglo-Iranian Oil Co. and the (American) Gulf Oil Co. Oil was discovered on the eve of World War II, but production began only after the war, in 1946. Production rose rapidly, as did oil revenues — for data see *oil. The concessionaire company was taken over, in stages, and by 1975 was fully nationalized.

K.'s oil revenues have made possible a tremendous economic development — which has remained mainly oil-based despite diversification efforts. Two large oil ports have been built, Mina' al-Ahmadi, and Mina' 'Abdullah, with two oil refineries with a capacity of c. 30m. tons in the 1980s. An extensive petrochemical industry has sprung up since the late 1960s; of K.'s oil, c. 60% is now processed locally and exported as refined products. A gas liquefaction plant was opened in 1979. An oil tanker fleet was developed. K. city and its suburbs, where nearly 90% of the population live, have become a richly developed modern urban conglomeration. An extensive network of modern roads covers the country, and a large international airport has been built. K. has become an international finance and banking center (a development intensified by the decline of Beirut since the late 1970s, but not without problems — such as the growth of an "unofficial", shady stock exchange, whose billion-dollar collapse in 1982 shook K.'s economy). Extensive deposits and investments abroad were estimated in the 1980s at over $ 70,000m., and by some at c. $ 100b., and included variegated business activities in international banking and finance, participation in foreign industrial and commercial enterprises, real estate, hotels etc.; these yielded revenues of several billion dollars p.a. (though the oil recession of the mid-1980s has caused a certain decline).

With her economic development and her oil riches, and a national income p.c. that was for some years considered the world's highest (until overtaken by Abu Dhabi), K. has become a top-rate welfare state: education, including studies at the university (founded 1966), health, telephone services, are free, electric power at a low, nearly nominal price, housing is provided by the state, employment guaranteed, air-conditioning nearly universal, cars — nearly one per adult. Water supply was a grave problem, as K. has no water sources for her growing population. Water has been shipped from Iraq in container vessels; several agreements, since 1964, providing for the supply of water from the *Shatt al-'Arab, in Iraq, in pipelines and/or canals, have not been fully implemented. Most of K.'s water now comes from giant desalination plants.

As K.'s economy developed and expanded, it increasingly needed labor, and the population grew rapidly — mostly by migrant laborers from abroad: Palestinian, Jordanian, Egyptian, Iraqi, Yemeni A.'s, Iranians, Indians and Pakistanis. In 1957, these foreigners already were estimated at 35–40% of the population (then 206,000). According to a 1970 census, the population had grown to 733,000 — of whom 387,000, i.e. 52.8%, were foreigners. The census of 1975 showed a similar percentage of foreigners in a population of 1.055m.; and by 1980, 794,000 foreigners constituted a 59%-majority in a population of 1,356,000. In the mid-1980s, K.'s population was estimated at c. 1.7m., of which 60% or more were foreigners. The largest foreign group were Palestinian A.'s — nearly 350,000, c. 20% of the population. Foreigners were not only a majority of the labor force, but they occupied key positions. In the 1960s, nearly 50% of the civil service, and 80% of the teachers were foreign A.'s, mainly Palestinians and Egyptians. This is gradually changing as generations of young educated Kuwaitis grow-up.

This majority of foreigners, their key position in K.'s economy and labor, and the influence they wielded, though having no civic and voting rights, in the body politic, posed a grave problem. Moreover, foreign A.'s, and particularly Palestinians, were presumed to be the main reservoir for radical and subversive groups — whether Nasserist and leftist-revolutionary, Palestinian, or Islamic-radical (of the Sunni, *Muslim Brothers, type, or, later and even more dangerous, the Shi'i Iranian, Khomeinist one). The Shi'i share in the population, originally estimated at 15–17%, had grown with the influx of foreign, mainly Iranian, workers to an estimated 25–30%. K.'s ruling conservative élite, fully aware of this problem (and buying off Palestinian-A. terrorism by generous donations), was even more alarmed when in Dec. 1983 a series of car bombs revealed the presence of terrorist cells — apparently with Iranian-Shi'i motivation — and more terrorist attacks occurred in 1985. The deportation of illegal or undesirable foreigners that had begun in 1979–80 was stepped up, and with the recession of K.'s oil economy and the contraction of the labor market in the mid-1980s, there were plans to make larger numbers of foreigners depart.

K.'s emergence into independence met mainly one obstacle: Iraq's claim that K. rightfully belonged to her. Britain had no objections when K. from the late 1950s demanded more independence, becoming economically viable with the development of her oil resources. In 1960, the Sheikh's government began taking over departments that had been in British hands (Finance, Justice); in Apr. 1961 K. established her own currency, the K. Dinar, to replace the Indian Rupee; and in June 1961 the British Protectorate was abrogated and the full independence of K. was proclaimed. Thereupon Iraq presented a claim to sovereignty over K., basing herself *inter alia* on an Anglo-Ottoman draft agreement of 1913, never ratified, which described K. as part of the Turkish-Ottoman *vilayet* (province) of Basra, i.e. the land that later became Iraq. Similar claims had been made several times in the 1930s, but had not been pressed as long as K. was under British protection. Iraq's declaration in 1961 included an implied threat of occupation by force. K. immediately requested Britain to return her military forces and lodged a complaint with the UN Security Council. The renewed presence of British forces caused the Soviet Bloc and leftist-neutralist countries to take a position against K.; Iraq complained to the Security Council that British military intervention threatened her and made a sham of K.'s alleged independence, while she, Iraq, had no intention of using force. The Security Council was deadlocked when a resolution recognizing K.'s independence was vetoed by the USSR in July 1961 and an appeal for the withdrawal of British troops, sponsored by the UAR (Egypt-Syria), failed to secure a majority. However, the same month, the *Arab League admitted K. to membership, thus recognizing her independence (Iraq walked out in protest and boycotted the League until 1963); it also set up an all-A. force (actually mostly Jordanian and Sa'udi) to defend K. With the recognition of the A. world, and its symbolic defense of K.'s independence thus assured, the Amir in Sept. asked Britain to withdraw her troops. Britain responded immediately and the withdrawal was completed by Oct. 1961. Yet, K.'s application for UN membership was vetoed by the USSR in November.

With the immediate Iraqi threat removed, and after contacts with Iraq, K. asked the Arab League in 1962 to reduce the all-A. force to a small token contingent and then to withdraw it altogether; it was dissolved and withdrawn early in 1963. In Oct. 1963 (after the overthrow of the *Qassem régime in Feb.), Iraq recognized K.'s independence; at the same time she received a grant of $ 84m. from K. (and there were reports of additional payments). Iraqi objections to K.'s UN membership, and the Soviet veto, had been withdrawn even before, and in May 1963 K. was admitted to the UN. She had agreed in Mar. 1963 to establish full diplomatic relations with the USSR — the first Persian Gulf country to do so.

There remained an unresolved border dispute between K. and Iraq, both on the mainland and, particularly, over various branching western outlets of the *Shatt al-'Arab and the islands created by them. Iraq was especially interested in securing control of the islands of Bubiyan and Warba — either by full possession or, at least, by a lease and agreed occupation. Though this was not agreed upon, the presence of Iraqi troops on Bubiyan and elsewhere on Kuwaiti territory was reported several times. The border dispute led to several armed confrontations, and even clashes — thus in 1973 and 1976. In 1977, a provisional standstill agreement was achieved, and in Nov. 1984 a fuller border accord was reported.

K.'s foreign policy was, despite her conservative character and interests, emphatically neutralist. Getting no full satisfaction from the USA and the West for what she considered her needs for arms and military equipment, she contracted, from the late 1970s, for the supply of sophisticated arms systems from the USSR. K. also had to maneuver a complex neutral policy between Iraq and Iran — an exercise that became increasingly difficult in the context of the Iraq-Iran war, after 1980. Her sympathies were no doubt with Iraq and she afforded that country large-scale aid — direct financial grants and credits, the assurance of supplies, and help in channeling Iraqi oil imports and exports (since Iraq's facilities on the Gulf were paralyzed and largely destroyed). She feared Islamic-revolutionary Iran's aggressive and expansionist policies, reinforced by the threat of Shi'i-extremist subversion inside K. Yet, officially she maintained a neutral stance.

K. took a neutral position in inter-Arab politics, too, sometimes offering herself as a mediator. Yet, despite her concern with radical, Nasserist, Palestinian subversion inside K., she usually took a rather radical line in her verbal, declarational postures. She also used her financial resources to buy off the potential threat of radical A. countries or organizations. A "K. Fund for Arab Economic Development", set up in 1962 with a capital that was constantly increased (authorized capital, since 1980, $ 2,000m.; working capital — over $ 3,500m.), disbursed easy credits to most AC to the tune of hundreds of millions each year. K. also used her reserves for direct governmental aid in large sums: she contributed over $ 150m. p.a. to Egypt and Jordan after 1967, following an Arab League decision to aid the countries confronting Israel; $ 400m. p.a. after 1973–74, to the "confrontation countries" and Palestinian organizations; $ 550m. p.a. (other reports speak of $ 340m. p.a.) after 1978 (Egypt now excluded). Large additional sums, with no details published, go to Palestinian-A. guerrilla/terrorist formations. K. also pays a large share in other aid funds, such as that set up by *OPEC, the "A. Fund for Economic and Social Development", the Arab-African Development Bank and Fund, and international funds and organizations. Sometimes she uses her aid for political pressure — thus she suspended her aid to Jordan in 1970 out of solidarity with the Palestinian guerrillas, and her National Assembly several times resolved to withhold aid to Syria. In recent years, K. was reportedly withholding parts of the post-1978 aid to the "confrontation countries".

The régime and government of K. have remained conservative. In 1961, first elections

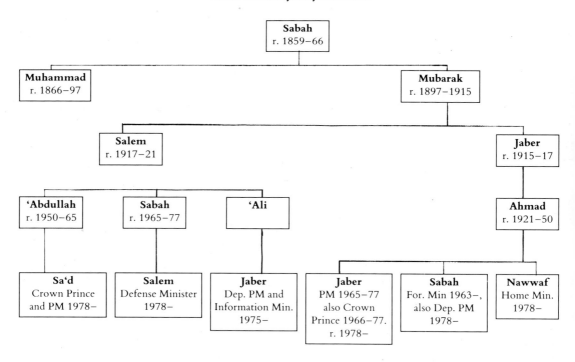

The al-Sabah Dynasty of Kuwait

Note: These scions of the dynasty, and others not listed, have filled many posts as Cabinet Ministers and in top executive and civil service positions. Listed here are only rulers and key positions, such as Prime Minister, Foreign, Defense and Home Minister.

were held (men only) for a Constituent Assembly. A Constitution was promulgated in 1962, providing for a constitutional monarchy, with a single-house 50-member parliament (with Ministers added *ex officio*), elected for a four-year term by male suffrage (a restriction that has remained in force, since the National Assembly rejected several attempts to grant voting rights to women). As only citizens could vote, the electorate has thus remained very small — 57,000 or 3.5% of the population in 1985. The first National Assembly was elected in 1963, and new elections were duly held in 1967, 1971 and 1975. Those elected were in their majority conservative supporters of the Amir and his government, with left-inclined radicals and Nasserists winning a few seats. Yet, the Assembly gradually became assertive and independent, pressing on the government more radical policies (e.g. concerning the nationalization of foreign oil interests and inter-Arab positions). By 1975–76 about one third of its members were considered "uncooperative" and oppositional, and in Aug. 1976, the Assembly was dissolved and parts of the Constitution were suspended. In 1981 the Constitution was reactivated, and National Assembly elections were held that year and in 1985. Political parties were not permitted, and the composition of the Assembly was generally unchanged: most of the 50 elected members were conservative and pro-Government, with a few nationalist "radicals", a few Islamic fundamentalists (with widely different media guesses as to their number), but the Assembly as a whole tended to assert its independence. In July 1986 this assertiveness and a dispute with the Government again led to the dissolution of the Assembly, with no date set for new elections.

Executive powers have remained firmly in the hands of the ruling al-*Sabah dynasty, whose members still hold, in the mid-1980s, 6 of the 16 ministerial posts and most of the major executive positions. The dynasty itself is divided into two branches, the Jaber al-Sabah and the Salem al-Sabah branches, who have since 1915 alternated in power, with a certain rivalry. The Jaber branch ruled 1915–16, 1921–50, and since 1978; the Salem branch — 1916–21 and 1950–77 (see Table).

Since 1965 the head of the branch not holding the Amirate has served as Crown Prince and Prime Minister.

L

Lake Asad The lake created by a dam on the river *Euphrates in northeastern Syria (the *al-Jazira* region).

Lake Nasser The lake created by the "High Dam" South of Aswan in Egypt and Sudan since the early 1970s. See *Aswan Dam.

land reform In several AC the ownership of land tended in the 19th century and the first half of the 20th to be concentrated in the hands of a small number of large landowners. By 1950–52 the distribution of ownership in some of the main AC was estimated as follows (in % of land registered):

	Landowners		
	Small	Medium	Large
Iraq	15.7	17.2	67.1
Syria	13	38	49
Egypt	35.3	30.5	34.2
Jordan (East Bank, Transjordan)	36.3	49.5	14.2

(In this tabulation, a small owner is one owning less than 25 acres in Syria and Transjordan, less than 62.5 acres in Iraq, less than 5 acres in Egypt; a large owner is one owning 250 acres, 625 acres, 50 acres, or more, respectively).

The large landowners usually lived in the city and had their land tilled by peasants *(fellahin)* who were landless or owners of plots insufficient for their subsistence. In Egypt particularly the agricultural population included a very large proportion of landless peasants. The peasant worked the land in some cases as a hired wage laborer, in most cases as a tenant share-cropper; the share he received, in kind, varied — but it was generally low, barely sufficient, and frequently insufficient, for his subsistence. There was thus a great deal of rural poverty, particularly in Egypt. In Algeria and Tunisia, the situation was aggravated by the fact that a large number of the landowners were foreign settlers, mainly French.

This system of land tenure was seen by nationalists and modernist reformers as a root evil of their countries' economy and society. It perpetuated poverty — in Egypt, e.g., for about two-thirds of the population. It caused neglect of the land and slowed its development. It held up vital industrialization, as capitalists preferred to invest their money in land rather than in industry. And it conferred excessive political power on a small number of great landowners (who came to control also large parts of the financial, commercial and industrial sectors of the economy).

LR was therefore on the socio-political program of nearly all modernist political groups and parties. Yet, in the first decades of independence or semi-independence very little was done to implement LR plans — the great landowners, who were not interested in reforms or even wished to delay and frustrate them, dominated the government (and the Western tutor power did not press for LR). It was only after the overthrow of the old régime by military *coups* — 1952 in Egypt, 1958 in Iraq — that new, reform-minded régimes instituted serious LR; in Egypt, LR was indeed a major plank of the new régime of the "Free Officers"; in Syria, LR came through the country's merger with Egypt, 1958. In Jordan and Morocco no far-reaching LR was enacted. In Tunisia and Algeria, LR was initially linked with the nationalization of the properties of the departing French settlers.

Egypt's Agrarian Reform Laws of Sept. 1952 limited the extent of landed property to 200 acres per head of family (with an additional 100 acres for children), excess land to be confiscated within five years (compensation, amounting to ten times the value of the annual rent, to be paid in government bonds) and distributed, in 2–5 acre plots (the recipient to repay the government within 30 years for the compensation it had paid); recipients of distributed lands, and owners of up to 5 acres, were to form government-supervised cooperatives. These LR laws were duly implemented, though distribution lagged behind expropriation and the LR Authority held much of the land expropriated. The 1952 laws were further tightened in 1961, the limit of land ownership was reduced to 50 acres per individual, 100 acres per family, and more land was distributed. In the two phases nearly 1m. acres were confiscated and c. 750,000 acres distributed to c. 350,000 families between 1952 and 1970. The pattern of land ownership in Egypt was changed by these reforms, as follows:

by owners of	% of land held 1952	1964
less than 5 acres	15.4	54.7
5–10 acres	8.8	10.1
10–50 acres	21.6	21.9
50–100 acres	7.2	6.4
100–200 acres	7.3	6.9
over 200 acres	18.7	–

In Aug. 1969, the limits on land ownership were further reduced and more land was ordered to be confiscated and distributed.

In Syria, a LR law was enacted in 1958, after the merger with Egypt. It limited land ownership to 200 acres of irrigated, or 750 acres of dry land per individual (plus 100 acres irrigated, or 275 acres dry land, for other family members). After Syria's secession from the UAR in 1961, the LR laws were amended several times and the limits were tightened to 37–125 acres (with a wider range of variations according to the quality of the land). Implementation was slower than in Egypt, and data as to actual confiscation and distribution are conflicting; but over 3m. acres seem to have been confiscated by the end of the 1960s and over 2m. acres distributed to some 40–50,000 families.

In Iraq, some LR laws were enacted before the revolution of 1958, but only partially implemented; some lands were distributed — but they were mostly state lands rather than land confiscated from large owners. New LR laws on the Egyptian pattern were enacted in Sept. 1958. They limited land ownership to 620 acres irrigated, or 1,240 acres dry land. There were conflicting data concerning implementation, confiscations and distribution; these were also delayed by dissension among rival ruling factions. By the 1970s Iraq reported over 7.25m. acres confiscated, and over 3.5m. acres distributed to some 130,000 families.

In both Tunisia and Algeria, LR was linked to the nationalization and take-over of lands owned by European, mostly French, settlers; it also entailed — to a much larger degree than in the AC of the East — intensive efforts, and experiments, to establish on the expropriated land cooperatives, collectives and/or state-farms. Tunisia took over some 2m. acres and distributed, according to some reports, 0.9m. acres to small peasants, while setting up state farms, cooperative "production units" or "agro-combinates" on 1.1m. acres. However, these experiments in socialist and state agro-economy bogged down, in the late 1960s, in bitter controversy and failure, and were discontinued in late 1969. The expropriation of privately owned excess land was not extensive. Algeria took over some 7.5m. acres of the French settlers' land and also expropriated a similar amount of land from large local, Muslim landowners (the key in Algeria's case being not the size of the estate but its annual revenue as compared with an acceptable maximum income of an agricultural family). Some of the expropriated land was distributed to small peasants, but most of it was handed over to a complex and frequently changing system of co-operative and semi-collectivized state farming; c. 2000 such "autogestion" units were established on land totalling, according to conflicting reports, 6–7.5m. acres. Reports of 2.5m. acres given to co-operatives seem to refer to the same "autogestion" units. Other data speak of some 1.5–2m. acres distributed to about 37,000 families of small peasants. From 1971 (actually 1973) a second phase of Algeria's "Agrarian Revolution" was proclaimed, involving the expropriation of an additional 4–5m. acres and the expansion of the co-operative state farms. In the mid-1980s it was estimated that some 700,000 private farms of small peasants still held and worked 50–60% of Algeria's agricultural land.

LR was an important part of the socio-economic and political program of the A. national movement, and particularly its reformist-progressive wing. Yet, while the time has not come to assess its long-term effects, it is evident that it has not been a panacea. It has not provided solutions to the economic and social issues involved. The problem of landless agricultural workers persists — their number has not significantly declined and at least in Egypt it continues to grow, since the increase in the rural population far exceeds the growth achieved in the number of landowners (in Syria and Iraq, this problem is much less acute). There has been little progress concerning the insufficient wage of agricultural laborers and the resulting poverty. The number of small landowners has increased, and so has their percentage of the total of landowners; the income of peasants who benefited from the distribution of land has risen. But they seem to spend the additional income mainly on consumption rather than invest it in the development and amelioration of their farms. Many plots, mainly in Egypt, remain insufficient for subsistence and many small peasants, in addition to the landless, continue working as tenants — under improved and more secure tenancy conditions. The cooperatives planned have made little progress. Generally, the socio-economic condition of the rural populations seems not to have changed very much and LR seems to have brought little social advancement to the *fellah*. The diversion of capital from the acquisition of land to investment in industry has made little progress. And the efficiency of farming, the yield per unit, seems to have somewhat declined with the fragmentarization of larger agro-economic units (though this point is disputed). Yet, despite these setbacks and reservations, there is no doubt that LR was inevitably necessary.

Latin Christians of what in European languages is called the Roman Catholic rite are in Arabic called L., while the term "Roman Catholic", *Rum Katholik* in Arabic, designates the *Greek Catholics. See *Catholics.

Lausanne The city of L. in Switzerland frequently was the venue of negotiations concerning the AC or the ME, and several agreements and treaties are called in its name. 1. A Treaty of L. of Oct. 1912 between the Ottoman Empire and Italy (after a preliminary agreement of May 1912) ended the war of 1911–12 in which Italy invaded and annexed *Tripolitania (Libya). Turkey agreed to withdraw her forces and in fact renounced her possession of and sovereignty over Libya (as well as Rhodes), though she never did so *de jure*. Italy agreed to the stationing in Tripoli of a Representative of the Ottoman Sultan in his capacity of Caliph (*Khalifa*) of all Muslims.

2. The Peace Treaty of L. signed on 24 July 1923, after 8 months of negotiations, between Turkey and her World War I enemies: Britain, France, Italy, Greece, Yugoslavia, Rumania and Japan. It replaced the Treaty of *Sèvres signed in 1920 by the Ottoman Sultan's government and denounced by the Turkish nationalists. In the Treaty of L. Turkey renounced all claims to the non-Turkish provinces of the former Ottoman Empire, i.e. mainly the A.-populated areas (for

territories that remained in dispute see *Alexandretta-Hatay — which Turkey repossessed in 1939 — and *Mosul, which was given to Iraq in 1926). The clauses of the Treaty of Sèvres depriving Turkey of Eastern Anatolia by providing for Armenian independence and Kurdish autonomy or independence (see *Armenians, *Kurds) were dropped (as were several provisions concerning Greek administration of parts of Western Anatolia with Izmir, and plans for Italian and French "zones of influence" in parts of Anatolia — these, and the Turkish nationalists' successful military struggle to prevent their implementation, are outside the scope of this Dictionary). The Treaty of L. also contained a Convention on the Straits of the Bosphorus and the Dardanelles, and clauses concerning the Aegean Sea and its islands — also outside our scope here. The Treaty also accepted the abolition of the extra-territorial rights of foreigners in Turkey (the *Capitulations).

3. L. was the meeting place, Apr. to Sept. 1949, of the *Palestine Conciliation Commission (PCC) with delegations from the ASt's and Israesl, for discussions or preliminary negotiations on the possibility of a peaceful settlement. A protocol of 12 May 1949 to establish a basis for these discussions is sometimes referred to as the Protocol of L. The discussions were abortive.

4. Negotiations between the conflicting groups and parties in the Lebanese civil war were held, as National Reconciliation Talks under Syrian guidance, in Mar. 1984 in L. (a first phase, in Oct. 1983 in Geneva, having failed). They resulted in far-reaching concessions by President Amin *Jumayyil and the conservative Christian camp and the establishment of a "Government of National Unity" dominated by the President's foes. See *Lebanon.

Lawrence, Thomas Edward (1888–1935), "L. of Arabia". British archaeologist, officer, intelligence agent, ME expert and writer. Following travels and some archaeological expeditions in Syria and Egypt, from 1909, L. was sent, after Turkey entered World War I against Britain and her allies, to join the British "Arab Bureau" in Cairo, under D.G. Hogarth. He participated in the preparation of the *"Arab Revolt" mounted by Sharif *Hussein of Mecca in June 1916, was sent with a small British expeditionary force to assist it, and took part in its sabotage and guerrilla operations. He served as chief British liaison officer, handling British subsidies and aid, from 1918 attached to Gen. Allenby's staff, and in Oct. 1918 entered Damascus with the A. forces. He described the Revolt, and his part in it, in his book *Seven Pillars of Wisdom* (privately printed 1926, published 1935; an abridgment, *Revolt in the Desert*, was published 1927). His book, considered a creation of literary value, has remained controversial; so has his true part in the events he described.

L. was a member of the British delegation to the Paris Peace Conference in 1919, chiefly as liaison to the A.'s, and acted as adviser to Amir *Feisal; he was an intermediary in the *Feisal-Weizmann Agreement. Later L. served, in 1921–22, as an adviser on A. affairs to the Colonial Office. His views on the post-World War I ME settlement seem to have been complex and torn by doubts. He sometimes felt that the A.'s had been let down by Great Britain, but several times stated that Britain had honorably fulfilled her commitments to the A.'s. He supported the *Balfour Declaration and advocated (and saw prospects for) a Jewish-A. settlement along the general lines of the Feisal-Weizmann Agreement he had helped to conclude.

League of Nations Founded in 1919–20, the LoN was involved in several issues concerning the ASt. It was entrusted with the sponsorship and supervision of the *"Mandates" system devised by the European powers, mainly Britain and France, as a compromise between promises of independence and imperial control as secretly agreed during World War I. In the ME, Mandates were imposed in 1920 (formally in effect in 1922) on Palestine with Transjordan, Syria and Lebanon, and Iraq, and the LoN, through a Permanent Mandates Commission, kept close watch on their administration. Thus, the Palestine issue was constantly kept on the Commission's agenda, with both the Jews and the A.'s of Palestine submitting frequent complaints against the British Mandate government, and the Commission often highly critical of the British administration. Britain's decision to end the Mandate for Iraq and grant that country independence in 1932 was also examined, and grave doubts were expressed, particularly concerning the fate of the minorities in the future independent Iraq. Indeed, soon after Iraq's independence, the LoN had to deal with massacres of the *Assyrians, 1933, and the future fate of that community (plans discussed did not fully materialize and action taken by the LoN was not effective). The LoN lost much of its prestige and influence in the 1930s and during World War II and was formally dissolved in 1946. It thus had no part in the termination of the Palestine, Jordan, Syria and Lebanon Mandates.

Other A. issues in which the LoN was involved were mainly the disputed question of whether the *Mosul district should be part of Turkey or Iraq — decided in 1926 in favour of Iraq; and the Franco-Turkish dispute over *Alexandretta — terminated, without the L.'s approval and in disregard of the compromise formulae it had devised, by France's acceptance of Turkey's demands and the annexation of Alexandretta by the latter in 1939.

Two AC became members of the LoN: Iraq in 1932, upon attaining independence; and Egypt in 1937, following the Anglo-Egyptian Treaty of 1936. (Three Muslim countries were also League members: Persia/Iran as a founder-member; Turkey from 1932; and Afghanistan from 1934.)

Lebanon Republic on the eastern coast of the Mediterranean ("the Levant"), with a population of 2.6–3m. (mid-1980 estimate — but there are also higher estimates). L.'s population is A., i.e. Arabic-speaking, but composed of many religious communities none of which constitutes a majority. The political-constitutional structure of the country is based on the census of 1932, according to which all Christian groups together formed 53.7% of the population: *Maronites 29%; *Greek Orthodox 10%; *Greek Catholic 6.3%; *Armenian Orthodox (Gregorians) 5.1%; Armenian Catholics 1.1%; *Protestants, *Syrian Orthodox and others 2.2%. All non-Christian communities constitued 45.3%: *Sunni Muslims 20.8%; *Shi'i Muslims 18.2%; *Druzes 6.3%. For political reasons no census has been taken since 1932. But the figures of 1932 no longer conform to recent and present-day demographic realities: the Christians have lost their overall majority, and the Maronites their status as the largest single community. Estimates of present percentages of the various communities vary widely. The following may be a realistic estimate: all-Christians — 40–45%; Maronites — 20–25%. All non-Christians — 55–60%; Sunni Muslims — 20–24%; Shi'i Muslims — 28–35%; Druzes — 7–9%. The Maronites are concentrated in the Mount L. districts; Sunni Muslims in the Tripoli district of the north, in the southern coastal area and the capital city of *Beirut; Shi'i Muslims in the south ("Jabal 'Amel") and in Coele Syria (al-*Biqā', the plain lying between the L. and Anti-L. mountain ranges); Druzes are concentrated in southern Mount L. and the south-eastern district of Hasbaya and Rashaya. 2–3m. Lebanese emigrants reside abroad, mainly in the Americas, and some 150–200,000 retain their Lebanese citizenship; most of these are Christians.

L. borders in the north and east on Syria and in the south on Israel. Her largely mountainous area totals c. 4,000 sq.mi. of which less than half is considered cultivable. The population is over 60% urban. About 25–30% engage in agriculture, 20–25% in industry, transport and construction, and over one-third in services. Of the national income, less than 15% derives from agriculture, c. 25% from industry, and more than 50% from trade, finance and services. Fruit is

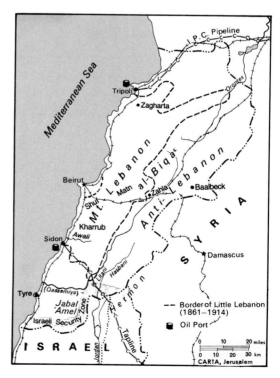

Map of Lebanon

exported, but staple foods must be imported.

L.'s economy is more modern than that of most AC and supports a higher national income. Tourism, shipping, banking and finance used to play an important role, and Beirut was a major world center for the gold trade and banking. This vital economic sector has been gravely damaged by the civil war since 1975. The nature of her economy induced L. to maintain a system of free enterprise and to eschew controls and state planning. A customs and currency union with Syria, inherited from the period of French rule, was dissolved in the 1950s soon after full independence was attained, as Syria favored a protectionist and controlled economy. Some sections of the infrastructure previously leased to concessionaires were nationalized — e.g. the railways, the port of Beirut, and the *IPC oil pipeline and Tripoli refinery; otherwise, L. has avoided any nationalization of the economy. River development for irrigation and power, reserved to the state, has not been very enthusiastically promoted. The *Orontes River, flowing north into Syria, is still untapped, and a project for the development of the *Litani River, begun in the early 1950s, has been implemented only in part.

L. is a communications and transport center. Her railways, however, are underdeveloped; a narrow gauge line runs to Damascus (opened in 1895), a standard-gauge line from Aleppo (built 1903–14) enters L. and ends at Rayak on the Damascus line, and a coastal line runs from Beirut to Tripoli, where it joins the pre-World War I Syrian Aleppo-Tripoli railway (its southern connection to Haifa and Egypt was cut in 1948). Beirut has a major port that used to serve the transport of goods by road to Syria, Jordan, Iraq and the Persian Gulf, and a large international airport, and L.'s "Middle East Airlines" (largely owned by private shareholders) is the largest in the ME; all these services have been badly damaged and frequently paralyzed by the civil war. Oil pipelines from Iraq (built by the IPC in 1934, expanded in 1949, and nationalized in 1973) and Sa'udi Arabia (the "Tapline", laid by *Aramco in 1950) terminate at the Mediterranean in Tripoli and near Sidon respectively; the Tapline stopped operating in 1975, the Iraqi line in 1976.

POLITICAL HISTORY. What is now L. was part of the *Ottoman Empire until the end of World War I. Parts of it formed the semi-autonomous district (*Sanjaq*) of Mount L. under a Christian (but non-Lebanese) Governor with a degree of Great Power supervision. This arrangement was imposed on the Empire by the Great Powers in 1860–61 after anti-Christian riots. Maronite Christians formed nearly 60% of the population in this district; the Christian communities as a whole amounted to 80%; Druzes were more than 11%, while Sunni and Shi'i Muslims represented less than 10%. The rest of what is now L. formed part of the Ottoman provinces (*Vilayet*) of Beirut and Damascus.

When Ottoman Turkey entered World War I, she abrogated the semi-autonomous status of Mount L. Beirut had been, before the war, one of the centers for A. and Syrian-Lebanese societies, some clandestine, striving for independence, autonomy or at least a decentralization of the Ottoman Empire (see *Arab Nationalism). Some of these societies also advocated a wider autonomy for L., possibly with an enlarged territory (the distinction between *Pan-Arabism and a specifically Lebanese nationalism being then quite vague). Several Lebanese A. leaders were in contact with the Western Powers, particularly France. Thirty-three A. notables, including several Lebanese, were tried and executed as rebels by the Turks in 1915–16 on the basis of suspicion and their previous contacts with foreign diplomats, though in fact there was no nationalist insurrection in L. or the other A. regions of the *Fertile Crescent. The country was occupied in 1918 by Allied Forces under Gen. Allenby and placed under a temporary Allied (*de facto* French) military administration. Attempts to establish a nationalist A. government, as was done in Damascus under British supervision, were foiled.

In accordance with the decisions of the *Paris Peace Conference, L. and Syria were placed under a French *Mandate on behalf of the *League of Nations in July 1922. On 31 Aug. 1920, before the Mandate was formally confirmed, a French decree created "Greater L." by annexing the overwhelmingly Muslim districts of *Tripoli in the north, Coele Syria (the *Biqā'), in the east, *Jabal 'Amel* and the Tyrus and Sidon coastland in the south, and the city of Beirut, to the predominantly Christian district of Mount L. This created an economically viable political entity with a major city and port, but it destroyed

L.'s homogeneity and predominantly Maronite-Christian character. Lebanese society consisted thereafter of many communities, each a minority, with about half of the population composed of non-Christian groups, Muslim and Druze.

The populations of the annexed districts had not been consulted before the annexation and most of the Muslim inhabitants opposed and resented it. Some of them advocated the absorption of all L. into Syria (as did many Syrian nationalists), while others favored that course at least for the newly annexed Muslim districts. In general, the Christian communities, particularly the Maronites, supported the new independent Greater L. and developed a separate Lebanese, as opposed to Syrian or A., nationalism. This fundamental Muslim-Christian dichotomy found little open expression in the political parties which were mainly formed by coalitions of pressure groups and networks of prominent semi-feudal families and their retainers. But it was a very real and profound ideological division which ultimately determined L.'s fate. The struggle against foreign tutelage and the Mandate, although fundamentally similar in most AC, could not be waged with the same extreme intensity in L. because of her unique conditions. France had created L.'s enlarged boundaries and French support guaranteed her existence. Protagonists of Greater L.'s independence tended therefore to be pro-French, while the radical anti-French A. nationalists had less regard for L.'s independence and integrity.

At first, France ruled with an appointed administrative commission. A Representative Council, indirectly elected by the various communities, was established in 1922. This Council participated in the drafting of L.'s constitution, enacted by French decree in 1926. This constitution, with several amendments, remains the basic law of the land. Its provisions include — as a "transitory measure" — an equitable communal representation in parliament, government and public administration. From 1926, L. was ruled by a President elected for a six-year term by Parliament, and a Government appointed by the President. The four-year-term Chamber of Deputies was two-thirds elected, one-third appointed by the President (until 1943, when it became fully elected), with the communal proportion pre-determined fo each multi-member constituency. An appointed Senate was also provided for but was abolished after one year, in 1927. Since implementation of the constitution was made "subject to the rights and obligations of the Mandatory Power", France retained *de facto* authority.

The new constitution did not work successfully and was suspended in 1932 by the French High Commissioner; the President (and the French) ruled thereafter without parliamentary sanction. A struggle to restore constitutional government ensued. The faction which most consistently fought for its restoration, and refused to cooperate with the government, was consolidated in 1934 as the "Constitutional Bloc" under Bishara al-*Khouri; it also identified with A. nationalism. Its chief rival, the "National Bloc," led by Emile *Edde, also advoated a speedy return to constitutional government but was prepared in the meantime to cooperate with France; this faction emphasized L.'s Christian-dominated special character, and opposed her association with Pan-A. nationalism. Authority to elect the President was restored to parliament in 1936. Edde narrowly defeated Khouri for the presidency, and the constitution was fully restored in 1937.

The struggle for constitutional government had temporarily overshadowed the issue of complete independence with a treaty of alliance between equals to replace French tutelage. After protracted negotiations, such a treaty was signed (parallel with a Franco-Syrian treaty) in Nov. 1936. L. was to become fully independent, and France was to defend L. in return for military bases and the right to station French troops on Lebanese soil. Signed by the Popular Front Government of Léon Blum, the treaty was not ratified by its successors and never took effect.

While French rule remained colonial, and L.'s independence was postponed, the draft-treaty had a far-reaching impact. It meant recognition for the country's independence and territorial integrity not only *vis-à-vis* France but Syria also. Indeed, the parallel Franco-Syrian draft-treaty included Syria's recognition of L.'s independence. Those elements in L. (mostly Muslim) still objecting to L.'s separation from Syria, or at least to the inclusion of the "new" Muslim districts within her borders, now resumed their agitation. Their opponents defended L.'s independence. Although the resulting tension was over a basically political problem, it had distinct communal, Muslim-Christian, undertones. Young Maronite activists founded a para-military organization for the defense of their community, the *Phalanges (al-Kata'eb) led by Pierre Gemayel (*Jumayyil). Other communities established similar groups (e.g., the Muslim Najjada). The proliferation of para-military formations was also encouraged by the growing influence of Fascist Italy and Nazi Germany. A clearly Fascist, Pan-Syrian organization, the *Syrian Nationalist Party (Parti Populaire Syrien — PPS), founded by Antoun *Sa'adeh, was outlawed in 1936.

Partial self-government in L. was further restricted with the approach of World War II. Parliament was dissolved and the constitution suspended in 1939; President Edde resigned in 1941. French administrators and officers in L. remained loyal to the Vichy government after the fall of France in 1940. Under the armistice concluded with France, a German and Italian base was gradually built in L. and Syria and full-scale German-Italian penetration into the ME seemed imminent, particularly when German assistance was requested by the pro-German revolutionary régime in Iraq in 1941. British and Free-French forces invaded and occupied Syria and L. in a brief campaign in June 1941.

Gen. Catroux now proclaimed, in the name of Free France, the termination of the Mandate and the independence of L. and Syria; British statements concurred. But France intended to retain a predominant position in L. and Syria by concluding new treaties of alliance, granting her privileges. Lebanese nationalists found this unacceptable. The elections of 1943 brought the Constitutional Bloc to power and Bishara al-Khouri became President with the Muslim Riyad al-*Sulh as Prime Minister. In Oct. 1943, the new Government and Parliament enacted the abolition of all articles of the constitution restricting L.'s independence by giving precedence to France's rights and obligations. The French arrested the President and members of his government, declared the measures taken unlawful, and appointed Emile Edde President. Some Ministers, however, escaped to organize demonstrations and resistance. Invoking the needs of security and the war effort, the British Commander of the ME supported the nationalists and, threatening armed intervention, demanded the restoration of parliamentary rule and the legitimate government. France had to yield, the national government was reinstated, and Edde was discredited. The finale of French domination came in 1945–6, when France evacuated her military forces and transferred locally recruited troops to L. to become the nucleus of her national army — after a struggle mainly conducted by Syria, and a complaint to the UN Security Council. L. was now completely independent.

On the eve of the crisis of 1943 an unwritten "National Pact" was concluded between Christians (mainly Maronite) and Muslim leaders — principally Khouri and Sulh — on the political future and character of L. The Muslims accepted the country's separate independence and territorial integrity within its post-1920 frontiers, while the Christians abandoned their dependence upon French protection and accepted independent L.'s integration into the A. family of nations. The Pact also reconfirmed the communal structure of L.'s governance and fixed a Christian-Muslim quota of 6:5 for the composition of Parliament (so that the House would always number a multiple of 11). It also ruled that the President would always be a Maronite, the Prime Minister a Sunni Muslim and the President of Parliament a Shi'i Muslim. The Commander-in-Chief of the armed forces and the Head of the Security Services were also to be Maronites. (The Minister of Defense usually was a Druze, but this was not said in the Pact.)

The National Pact also formed the basis for the country's membership, at first hesitant and reserved, in the *Arab League. Lebanese apprehensions compelled the ASt to append to the Protocol of *Alexandria (which laid the foundation for the League) an appendix solemnly recognizing L.'s independence. When the League proved to favor cooperation among separate, sovereign states, rather than a policy of Pan-Arab unification, L. became an active member and ardent supporter.

In her nation-building and internal politics, L. was less successful. The unity of 1943 proved unstable — though the National Pact's rules for the distribution of power were not seriously questioned until the 1970s. Permanent and responsible parties did not develop. Governments rose and fell in quick seccession, and accusations of nepotism and corruption were frequent. The elections of 1947, returning the Constitutional Bloc of Khouri and Sulh to power, were denounced as rigged. Louder protests were heard when an acquiescent parliament amended the constitution in 1948 to permit the re-election of President Khouri for a second term. A right-wing *coup* by the Syrian Nationalist Party (PPS) was reported to have been attempted and suppressed in 1949; Antoun Sa'adeh was summarily tried and executed (Premier Sulh was assassinated, in revenge, in 1951). A bloodless *coup* stage-managed by Camille *Chamoun (Sham'un), compelled President Khouri to resign in 1952 and Chamoun was elected President.

A grave crisis occurred in 1958. The traditional Christian-Muslim antagonism now focused upon L.'s inter-A. orientation. The left and many Muslims favored integration with an Egyptian-led Nasserist revolutionary union or bloc, strengthened by the Feb. 1958 merger of Egypt and Syria as the *UAR. Most Christians, and the Chamoun régime, opposed such an integration, insisting on L.'s separate independence, and favored a rightist, pro-Western policy and neutrality in inter-A. affairs. An opposition "National Front" was formed in 1957 under the predominantly Muslim leadership of Sa'eb Salam, 'Abdullah al-Yafi, Rashid *Karameh and the Druze Kamal *Junbalat. Officially, the aim of the Front was to prevent a constitutional amendment permitting President Chamoun's election for a second term, but the real, fundamental issue was the question of L.'s inter-A. integration. Violence flared up in 1957, turning into a general rebellion in May 1958. The government and its supporters insisted that the rebellion was a Nasserist attempt to seize power, organized and supported chiefly by Syria. The rebels consistently denied these accusations. The government submitted a complaint to the UN Security Council in May 1958, charging the UAR with interference in L.'s internal affairs. In June the Security Council dispatched an international military observers' group ("UNOGIL") to L. They failed to detect the infiltration or presence of foreign forces or arms (though such an infiltration was generally assumed). A leftist revolution in Iraq, July 1958, aggravated the crisis. Claiming that L.'s independence was being threatened, President Chamoun appealed to the USA for assistance. President Eisenhower agreed that "indirect aggression from without" threatened L. and dispatched US troops to the country. US proposals to replace her troops (and the British contingents sent to Jordan during the crisis) with UN forces were vetoed by the USSR. In view of this deadlock, the issue was transferred to a special session of the UN General Assembly. An A. draft resolution was adopted by the Assembly in August, noting that the ASt were committed to respect each other's independence, welcoming their renewed undertaking to "observe" that commitment, and requesting arrangements that would "adequately help in upholding the principles of the Charter... and facilitate the early withdrawal of the foreign troops." US troops were evacuated in Oct.

The civil war of 1958 was conducted with restraint. The Army, under the command of Gen. Fu'ad *Shihab (a Maronite Christian), did not intervene, thus avoiding a confrontation that might have destroyed the army's apolitical and non-communal character. President Chamoun let it be known that he did not intend to run for a second term. At the end of Chamoun's term, Gen. Shihab was elected President in 1958. Under Shihab's paternalistic administration, which enhanced the powers of the Presidency, the Army command and the Secret Services, the Nasserist rebels of 1958 were appeased and returned to play a leading role in the government; their leaders (Karameh, Yafi, Salam) headed virtually all governments after 1958, while Chamoun and his associates went into temporary political eclipse. An approximate balance in parliament was later achieved between the Nasserist, Pan-Arab left and a "Triple Alliance" of the right-wing moderate Christian-led factions of Chamoun, Pierre Gemayel and Raymond Edde. When Shihab declined Parliament's offer to amend the constitution and re-elect him for a second tem in 1964, this balance was preserved, and politically neutral Charles Hilou became President. Shihab retained considerable influence behind the scenes and a loose "Shihabist" faction was strong in Parliament.

However, the atmosphere of crisis and uncertainty with regard to L.'s future, created by the events of 1958, did not disappear entirely. Some violence became endemic, with occasional clashes, kidnappings, political assassinations. In 1961 a *coup* attempt by the SSNP (Syrian Nationalist Party) was suppressed. Some Christian leaders returned to the concept of a smaller, more homogeneous Christian L. that would relinquish the non-Christian districts. The country was also affected by the A.-Israel crisis mounting in the early 1960s. A. plans to prevent Israel's use of the *Jordan River included the diversion of its Lebanese tributaries westward into the Litani and eastward into Syria's *Baniyas and *Yarmuk. Such schemes called for a military protection which L. could not provide, and as she declined to invite A. forces into her territory, L. was not eager to implement the plans. While formally participating in the War of June 1967, L. escaped defeat by refraining from military action.

The political equilibrium was critically endangered again from 1968–69. Palestinian-A. guerilla groups (*Feda'iyyin*), based in L. or infiltrating across the Syrian border, stepped up their sabotage operations against Israel, and Israel retaliated. The guerillas also demanded a freedom of action tantamount to a state-within-a-state. The "Triple Alliance" of the right opposed *Feda'iyyin* presence in, or operations from, L. (although their objections were not always openly expressed), while the Nasserist left encouraged them. President Hilou and the army favored the right-wing position and objected to commando operations from Lebanese soil, but felt unable to take strong action, fearing a new left/right or Muslim/Christian confrontation. Several compromise formulas (such as commando operations controlled by the Army, use of L.'s territory for transit only, etc.) were suggested and rejected. Following a grave crisis late in 1968, aggravated by an Israeli raid on Beirut's Airport, a new crisis in Apr. 1969 left the country with only a caretaker government for seven months, with the constant threat of an army takeover or a non-parliamentary presidential government. (Gen. Fu'ad Shihab was often mentioned both as the potential author of a *coup* and as a candidate for the presidency in 1970.) In Nov. 1969 an agreement with the *Feda'iyyin* was imposed by President Nasser's "mediation". This "Cairo Agreement" laid down a *modus operandi* for the commando groups, prescribing their bases and location (in the south-eastern corner only), limiting their raids and imposing some army control.

But the *Feda'iyyin* never abided by the Cairo Agreement fully and in good faith; clashes continued with both the Phalanges and the army, and new "co-ordination" agreements brought no solution. L.'s south-eastern corner, the 'Arqoub, remained outside government control and soon came to be called "Fatahland". And the country was continuously exposed to Israel's counterblows against operations conducted from Lebanese territory.

In 1970 Shihab refused to present his candidacy since he was not guaranteed a decisive majority. The candidate he sponsored, Elias *Sarkis, lost by one vote to Suleiman *Franjiyeh, considered to be "neutral". President Franjiyeh chose Sa'eb Salam as Prime Minister, with the Leftist Nasserist Druze Leader Kamal *Junbalat in the key position of Minister of the Interior.

PLO operations in and from L. and Israeli reprisal raids, and the resulting confrontation between the PLO and the Lebanese army and the Phalanges, remained L.'s chief problem. Clashes continued, and new "agreements" in 1970, 1972 and 1973 were not implemented. In May and Sept. 1973 the army conducted serious military operations against the *Feda'iyyin*, but failed to break them (a fact that hardened the resolve of the Phalanges that L., or at least her Christian heartland, could be saved only by their military efforts). The PLO expanded its *de facto* control of southeastern L. to include also large parts of the southwest, the Shi'i-majority *Jabal 'Amel*. Its heavy hand on the local population, its operations against Israel and Israel's reprisals, caused an increasing flight of Lebanese from the south — many of them to Beirut, where large suburban quarters of Shi'i refugees sprang up in the southwest.

The intensifying L.-PLO confrontation also had grave repercussions in other fields — all-A., involving Syria, and chiefly internal. The ASt felt the duty to help an A. sister-country and the PLO solve problems arising between them, the more so as they had mediated the 1969 Cairo Accord regulating the PLO's presence and operations. In 1973 they tried again to mediate, but without success. In July 1974 an all-A. Defense Council discussed proposals to dispatch A. troops to L. to separate the forces and enforce the arrangements agreed; but, though the idea of inviting A. troops had been discussed in L., too, for some years, L. declined the offer (she might have preferred UN peace-keeping forces) and demanded, instead, a stop to A. arms supplies to the *Feda'iyyin*. The ASt were, in any case, not in a position to take effective united action. Syria, however, had her own interests in L. and regarded the country as part of her strategic defense sphere. She was backing the *Feda'iyyin* in L., and it was believed Syrian troops, disguised as *Feda'iyyin* and especially as fighters of the PLA, regular Palestinian troops forming part of the Syrian army, were operating in L. since 1970. Early in 1975 L. and Syria were reportedly discussing the entry of regular Syrian troops, but no agreement was reached.

It was, however, internal Lebanese affairs that were most gravely affected. The question of how to deal with the *Feda'iyyin* deeply divided L.'s political community: the Christian "right wing" pressed for determined action against their state-within-a-state and their terror operations, while the Muslim "Left" opposed such action and sympathized with the *Feda'iyyin*; and the army, torn by these conflicting tendencies, strained for action but did not dare take decisive steps. Home Minister Junbalat was reported to be in acute conflict with the army, denouncing its operations against the PLO; and Premier Salam, though more moderate, partly went along with him. In Apr. 1973 Salam and his government resigned, and several ineffective governments formed by second-rank leaders followed each other until 1975. Behind the split over the *Feda'iyyin* issue there loomed the danger of the wrecking of the national consensus on L.'s intercommunal structure, based on the National Pact of 1943, and the polarization of L.'s body politic into a conservative, "right-wing" camp determined to preserve the *status quo* of the communal structure (though its moderates might consent to amend the actual division of power in favor of the Muslim communities), and a radical, "left-wing" one anxious to change that structure — its moderates content with a change in favor of the Muslims within the communal structure, and its extremists bent on the abolition of that structure altogether. And such a polarization could lead to a dreaded total confrontation of Christians versus Muslims.

The dreaded split occurred with the eruption of L.'s civil war in Apr. 1975. Preceded by a violent confrontation over a local issue in Sidon, in Feb., a bloody clash between the Phalanges and PLO-*Fatah* squads in Beirut on 13 Apr. is usually seen as the beginning of that civil war. The Muslim "Left" joined the *Feda'iyyin* against the Phalanges, and soon Beirut was engulfed in incessant fighting and terror. There were innumerable attempts and agreements to reach a cease-fire, but none of them were effective; they were also marred by a constant wrangle over what should come first: a political agreement, to remove the reasons for the violence, or an end to violence, to make possible a quiet, reasoned discussion of the political issues. The government — after an attempt to form a military one that collapsed within days, headed from June 1975 by Rashid *Karameh — was paralyzed. The President and government shied away from ordering the army into action, fearing that it might split if it became involved in the civil war. And indeed, the army soon disintegrated; many officers and whole units deserted to join "their" camp and community. In Jan. 1976 a junior officer, Lt. Ahmad Khatib, broke away and formed an "*Arab* Lebanese Army" that joined the Muslim-leftist camp. In Mar. 1976 a senior officer, Brig. 'Abd-ul-'Aziz al-Ahdab, tried to stage a military *coup*, which fizzled out but further disrupted the army. Actual power was increasingly exercised by "militias", some of them communal-political and others — bands of toughs recruited by local bosses.

The right-wing Christian camp was politically represented by the Phalanges, Chamoun's National Liberals (Chamoun was also Minister of the Interior), to a lesser degree Franjiyeh's faction (as President, Franjiyeh could not identify himself fully with one of the camps — and he was not on friendly terms with the Phalanges), and even less so Raymond Edde's National Bloc. It was backed — and egged on — by communal Maronite organizations, such as the "Maronite League" and the extremist "Guardians of the Cedar". The Maronite Patriarch backed that camp, but cautiously tried to stay out of the political struggle. The Maronite commanders of the army also sympathized with the rightist camp. Late in 1975 efforts were made to create a joint roof organization; they materialized only later, in Sept. 1976, in a "Lebanese Front" chaired by Chamoun — but the Front did not become very effective. Militarily, the Phalanges were the mainstay of the rightist-Christian camp, with

Chamoun's "Tigers", to a lesser degree Franjiyeh's *Marada* militia (which controlled the Zaghorta-Batroun region in the north, but did not intervene much in Beirut and other areas of fighting), and deserting army units, mostly Maronites. The other Christian communities — the *Greek-Catholic and even more so the *Greek-Orthodox, and the *Armenians — tried to stay out of the fighting (though some of them defended their quarters with local *ad hoc* militias).

The radical-Muslim camp was far less homogeneous. The traditional Sunni-Muslim leaders — conservatives in the social sense, despite their adhesion to the "leftist"-Nasserist camp — had their factions and parliamentary blocs, but none of them had grown into a stable, permanent party. Some Sunni leaders did not fully join the radical camp but tried to maintain a "center" faction, supporting President Franjiyeh. The radical camp included Junbalat's "Progressive Socialist Party", based on Druze communal allegiance rather than ideological principles. There was the Communist Party. Various small Nasserist factions did not accept the traditional Sunni leadership. The *Ba'th party was split into mutually hostile pro-Syrian and pro-Iraqi wings, but both wings belonged to the camp. The "Syrian Nationalist Party" (SSNP), formerly pro-Fascist right-wing, now belonged to the radical camp, but had little influence. The old Muslim *Najjada* militia now appeared as a party, but it was small and had little impact. The Shi'i leadership wanted a basic change in L.'s structure, but it was antagonistic to the Sunni leaders and the Druzes — and it was only now beginning to set up a strong organization; it began defending Shi'i villages and quarters, but kept out of the civil war in its first years. All these Muslim and/or radical groups were allied with the Palestinian organizations. Attempts to set up a joint leadership, a United Front command, were made only later, from about 1976.

The military set-up of the radical camp was at first rather haphazard and disorganized. The traditional Muslim-Sunni leaders had no militia, and therefore increasingly lost influence. The *Ba'th*, the Communists, the *Najjada*, the SSNP had small squads of fighters. So had various Nasserist factions, such as a "Union of the Working People's Forces", led by Kamal Shatila and Najah Wakim; Ibrahim Quleilat's "Independent Nasserists", whose militia, *al-Murabitun*, became the main Sunni fighting group in Beirut; Mustafa Sa'd's "People's Liberation Army" in Sidon. Farouq Muqaddam headed a non-Nasserist "24th October Movement" in Tripoli. These militias were local groups, confined to their town or quarter — and were not much different from non-"ideological" bands of toughs in town quarters led by local bosses. In Tripoli, there grew also a Muslim-fundamentalist militia, "Islamic Unity" (*al Tawhid al-Islami*), led by Sheikh Sa'id Sha'ban, which later clashed with pro-Syrian *Ba'th* fighters reinforced by a growing *'Alawi population, and lost to them. Gradually, the main military effort of the Muslim "Left" was taken on by the Druze-PSP militia and the Shi'i communal organization which grew in the mid-1970s, renamed al-*Amal (Hope), turned into a militia and gradually became involved in the civil war. The Palestinian-A. *Feda'iyyin* mainstream, *al-Fatah*, tried at first to stay out of the Lebanese imbroglio (though they had triggered its eruption), but the Syria-based units of the PLA and *al-*Sa'iqa*, as well as the extremist-"rejectionist" PLO formations, took part in the fighting, and gradually all the PLO groups joined until they became the military mainstay of the Muslim "Left". The Muslim camp called itself "National Movement" or "Progressive Front" and tried to set up a joint command, but this remained rudimentary.

The civil war, accompanied by brutal terrorism, soon turned into a *territorial* fight, with each camp trying to consolidate its rule in the parts of L. it dominated — the Maronite Christians in Mount L., the coastal region north of Beirut, and East Beirut; the Sunni Muslims in Tripoli, West Beirut, Sidon; the Druzes in southern Mount L.; the Shi'is in southern L. and the Biqā'. The brunt of the fighting concerned (a) the liquidation of "enclaves" of the rival camp (such as Palestinian camps in East Beirut, mainly Tel al-Za'tar, besieged and later attacked by Christian forces, and Christian villages in the Druze-dominated Shuf and Matn parts of Mount L. and in parts of South L.); and (b) mixed and "border" areas (such as, mainly, Beirut, which eventually was divided by a "green line" into Muslim West and Christian East Beirut, its port and airport, the slopes of Mount L. southeast of Beirut, the coastal region south of Beirut, Mount L.'s eastern slopes towards the Biqā' around Zahla and its northern borders towards Tripoli). There were innumerable attempts to agree on a cease-fire, particularly in Beirut, but none of them were effective. The consolidation of regions dominated by one community gradually reinforced the idea of the establishment of "cantons" as a permanent solution and the transformation of L. into a federation of such cantons — an idea that came to dominate much Christian-Maronite thinking, but was anathema to the Left-Muslim camp (though *de facto* the Druzes and the Shi'is adamantly enforced their rule in their "cantons").

The Government was paralyzed, the army was at first kept out of the war and later disintegrated, and any central, united administration of L. as one country turned into a fiction. The civil war also destroyed the main base of L.'s economy — Beirut's rôle as an international banking and finance center (though the full effects of that process became apparent only later) — and paralyzed Beirut's port and airport as world crossroads. It also gravely affected L.'s prestigious higher education centers and her lively and diversified press (see end of entry). Parliamentary life was also crippled; no new elections could be held and the existing House could meet only rarely and with great difficulty, in no-man's-land. In early 1976, Parliament extended its term by two years (a measure repeated later several times, so that in the mid-1980s the House elected in 1972 still was the only all-Lebanese parliamentary institution).

In 1975–76 the A. League and a number of ASt made several attempts to mediate, but these attempts were half-hearted and to no avail. Syria, however, had a greater stake in L. and systematically stepped up her intervention, backing the Muslim-"leftist" camp and gradually established *de facto* control of large parts of northern, eastern and southeastern L. At the same time she tried to mediate and devise a political formula that would end the civil war. In Jan. 1976 she stepped up both her military intervention and her search for a political solution and offered a plan for a settlement. That plan was adopted by President Franjiyeh and publicly presented by him in Feb. 1976, as his proposal. It provided for a new distribution of power, *viz* a representation ratio of equality, 50:50, between Christians and non-Christians for Parliament and senior administration posts (against the 6:5 ratio established by the 1943 National Pact); by doing so, it accepted the principle of a continued communal structure and postponed its abolition to an undetermined future. It also proposed to reduce the powers of the (Maronite) President and increase those of the (Muslim) Premier. The reform plan was accompanied by Syrian security guarantees (and implied a degree of Syrian involvement and supervision).

Franjiyeh's Syrian reform plan caused a major change in the situation. The Christian-conservative camp accepted the plan, while the Muslim "Left" rejected it as going not far enough towards the abolition of the communal division of power; the Palestinian *Feda'iyyin* also rejected it — mainly because it seemed to imply a restriction of their independent action and the imposition of Syrian supervision. The situation was further complicated by a serious onslaught on Franjiyeh's position as President: he was suspected of planning to extend his term beyond its Sept. 1976 expiry, and refused to heed requests to resign earlier; the Constitution was amended to permit the election of the new President six months in advance, and in May Elias Sarkis was elected for Sept. with Syrian support — and, after reported strong Syrian pressure, with no votes against him. Franjiyeh had fled the Presidential palace in Mar., threatened by civil war and terror attacks, and gone to Christian Jouniyeh, north of Beirut.

In the spring of 1976, Syria decided to enforce her reform plan, to prevent the victory of one of the rival camps and the threatened final partition of L. Syria thus turned against her allies and clients and allied herself, *de facto*, with their foes. From Apr. 1976, Syrian regular troops entered L. in substantial strength, and in May they opened an offensive against Muslim-and-Palestinian positions. This offensive did not make much headway — the Syrians obviously wished to avoid a full-fledged battle and did not use their full strength. A new offensive in Sept. was more successful, but was not pursued to complete victory and the liquidation of the Muslim and Palestinian camp's military strength. The Syrians did, however, allow their new Christian allies to intensify *their* military offensive; the Phalanges laid siege, for instance, to the Palestinian camp of Tel al-Za'tar in East Beirut, from Jan. 1976, later attacked it and in Aug. stormed it, with bloody massacres reported (the Palestinians held Syria responsible for that débâcle).

All-A. involvement in the L. crisis was intensified in 1976. Syria's intervention caused a crisis in her relations with several ASt, particularly Egypt and Iraq. Mediatory efforts, *inter alia* by Libya's *Jallud, remained unsuccessful. But in June 1976 it was decided to send all-A. troops to L.; the plans provided for a force of 4,500–5,000, and the first contingents, mainly Sa'udi, Sudanese and Libyan, entered L. in June. This force, however, had little impact — it was instructed not to become involved in actual fighting, and despite continued cease-fires, all abortive, there were no accords or cease-fires which it could have observed and enforced. In Oct. 1976, an informal mini-summit in Riyadh (Egypt, Syria, Sa'udia, Kuwait, L. and the PLO) decided to set up a larger and more effective "A. Deterrent Force" (ADF) of c. 30,000 men, and later the same month a full summit in Cairo endorsed that decision. The bulk of the ADF was to be Syrian troops i.e., in effect, the all-A. summit accepted Syria's dominant military presence in L. and lent her troops an all-A. cloak. Token forces were sent by Sa'udi Arabia, Sudan, the Persian Gulf states and Libya (the Libyan contingent was soon withdrawn), but when the ADF reached full strength in Jan. 1977, 90% of its 30,000 troops were Syrian. During 1977 and 1978, the token contingents of other ASt were withdrawn, and by early 1979 the ADF was wholly and exclusively Syrian. Syria continued to present her troops in L. as an all-A. force, mandated by an all-A. decision. At first, the ADF was nominally commanded by a Lebanese officer, but over the years this fiction faded away.

In Oct. 1976, with the entry of the ADF and the proclamation of a general cease-fire, the civil war officially ended. Syria concentrated her troops mainly in the Biqā and the north, taking over complete *de facto* control of these regions; but smaller ADF contingents also entered Mount L., Beirut, Sidon, and parts of South L., stopping about 10 miles short of the Israel border — reportedly under a tacit "Red Line" understanding with Israel (see below). In Dec. 1976, a new government under Salim al-Huss was installed, and gradually re-established a measure of control; it also began rebuilding the army. But the army was in reality divided into formations of the different communities — with each brigade loyal to its communal leaders. And the two camps remained mutually hostile. The Christian camp, since Sept. 1976 under an umbrella "Lebanese Front", jealously guarded its *de facto* control of its "canton", the Druzes kept theirs, and the Shi'is gradually asserted a more effective control of their area. The Left-Muslim camp, now calling itself the "National Movement", still resented Syria's intervention against the Left (and when Kamal Junbalat was assassinated in Mar. 1977, it was generally assumed that the assassins were Syria's agents); but gradually, Syria's old alliance with the Muslim Left was restored. Syria and the ADF were also party to several new agreements with the *Feda'iyyin*, trying to regulate their presence in and operations from L. and culminating in the Shtura Agreement of July 1977; but this new accord, like the preceding ones of 1969 and 1973, provided no solution to the problems and dangers raised by the PLO's operations.

It was, indeed, over the PLO's presence and operations in South L. that fighting soon re-erupted, in 1977. The Shi'i population of South L. began resisting the PLO's domination of the region and its exposure to Israeli reprisals; but the main resistance came from the Christian enclaves in South L., aided by Christian militia men from their main areas farther north. The Christians of the south, and the Phalanges in general, had been secretly collaborating with Israel for some years; this cooperation became more open and publicly known from 1976. Christian South-Lebanese militias endeavored to establish, with Israeli assistance, a *cordon sanitaire* between the PLO concentrations and the Israeli border, and Israel opened that border to supply the Lebanese border region, cut off from the rest of L., and to enable its inhabitants to find work, medical treatment, etc., in Israel (the "Good Fence"). In Mar. 1978, Israeli forces invaded L. and occupied the border zone, up to the Litani River. When Israel withdrew, in June 1978, under UN and great-power pressure, she left the border zone under the control of a mainly Christian Lebanese militia, later called the "South L. Army", under Major Sa'd *Haddad, that was trained, financed and equipped by Israel (Haddad, a Greek-Catholic, was dismissed from the L. army, but appealed — and maintained links with the army and the Maronite leaders in Beirut; he died in 1984 and was replaced by a retired army officer, the Maronite Gen. Antoine Lahad). In Mar. 1978, under a UN Security Council decision, a "UN Interim Force in L." (*UNIFIL) was sent to South L., composed of c. 4,000, later nearly 6,000, soldiers from different nations. However, since UNIFIL's mandate barred it from actually fighting, it was unable effectively to prevent either intra-Lebanese clashes, soon to escalate again into a civil war, or PLO raids and intrusions into Israel and the resulting PLO-Israel confrontation. During the fighting from 1976–77 — intra-Lebanese, Lebanese-PLO, PLO-Israel, and Israeli reprisals — many thousands of South L.'s inhabitants fled the area; their number was variously estimated at over 200,000 — about one third of the region's population.

In the rest of L., too, clashes soon resumed. While Syria gradually effected a reconciliation with the Muslim "Left" and the Palestinians, her *de facto* alliance with the Christian camp revealed itself as a passing episode not in line with her basic policies and interests, and soon crumbled. The Syria-Franjiyeh reform plan of 1976 remained unimplemented, all attempts to devise a formula for a national reconciliation failed, and Syria was consolidating her *de facto* dominance — without being able to impose her formula for a settlement; Syrian attempts to formalize her presence by a Syro-Lebanese defense treaty also failed. The Christian camp resisted Syrian inroads into the "canton" it controlled, and in Dec. 1977 clashes erupted between Christian militias and Syrian troops. During 1978 they intensified and the Muslim-Palestinian camp joined the fight, and resumed attacks on, and the shelling of, East Beirut; Christian militias also resisted and prevented the dispatch of Syrian-controlled units of the Lebanese army to South L.

During those years, the Phalanges strove to unify the entity Christian camp under their leadership, to take over at least its military command — a compaign that caused grave intra-Christian clashes. From the late 1970s, an umbrella formation, the "Lebanese Forces", (LF), tried to unite all Christian militias; in fact the LF were dominated by, and almost co-terminous with, the Phalanges. In May 1978, Franjiyeh dissociated himself from the "Lebanese Front", strengthening his relations with Syria and effecting a *rapprochement* with the Muslim camp; his *Marada* militia (controlling his northern fief, but not active in Beirut and the rest of L.) thus became unreliable for the Phalanges and Lebanese Forces. In June 1978 the Phalanges attacked Franjiyeh's centers (killing his son Tony with his wife and small daughter) and eliminated his militia; in Feb. 1980, they repeated and completed that operation. In July 1980, the Phalanges also liquidated, in bloody clashes, Chamoun's militia, the National Liberal Party's "Tigers", as an independent formation and forcibly incorporated its remnants in their LF. The Phalanges now dominated the more or less united formations of the Christian camp.

On the political side, too, the Christians' resolve to keep control of their "canton" hardened, and tendencies to turn L. into a federation of cantons came to the fore. A "charter" issued by the Lebanese Front in Dec. 1980 seemed to point in that direction: it was vague about precise constitutional proposals but stressed the "autonomy" of L.'s various communities. A demand for the withdrawal of the Syrian "ADF" forces was voiced with increasing frequency, though it did not crystallize into a formal government demand; Syria did not heed such requests but claimed that only an all-A. decision could terminate the all-A. mandate conferred upon her. However, she withdrew the bulk of her force from Beirut in Mar. 1980; on the other hand, she further consolidated her control of East and North L.; Christian militias were compelled, for instance, to withdraw from the Christian-majority town of Zahla and to leave its control to local leaders — Greek-Catholic rather than Maronite — under Syrian supervision.

Clashes in South L. — Lebanese-PLO, and PLO-Israel — continued throughout the late 1970s and early 1980s. In 1981, the USA sent a senior diplomat, Philip Habib, to mediate a cease-fire (L.-PLO-Israel, with Syria as an informal partner), but his success was not complete. In June 1982, Israeli forces invaded L. in a massive operation — described in detail in the entries *A.-Israel Conflict and *A.-Israel Wars. Originally proclaimed to intend only the liquidation of the PLO's military-terrorist establishment and to halt at a line c. 25 mi. from the border, the operation continued beyond that line and soon Israeli forces occupied all of South L. and its coast up to the southwestern suburbs of Beirut, the southern

Biqā', the Shuf region and southern Mount L., reaching and cutting the Beirut-Damascus road at several points; they did not occupy Beirut, but linking up with Phalange forces in and around that city, they were free to move in East Beirut and up to the coast NE of Beirut and to besiege and shell West Beirut. The Phalanges collaborated with the invading army to some degree (though not to the extent planned and expected by the Israelis) and established their almost complete domination under the umbrella of the Israeli occupation. Indeed, Israel seemed to aim at the establishment of a Christian-dominated Lebanon under a Phalange leadership that would make peace with Israel and be her ally. And while the older conservative Christian leaders, from Pierre Jumayyil to Camille Chamoun, were cautiously reserved (and to the Muslim-Palestinian camp and its allies the Israeli plan was of course anathema), the younger, more radical commanders of the Phalanges' military formations, led by Bashir *Jumayyil, went along with Israel's design. The Israelis endeavored to foster relations also with the leaders of the Shi'is and Druzes in the area occupied (and beyond); but, while the Shi'is of South L. had at first welcomed Israel's forces as liberators from the irksome domination of the PLO, and both Shi'i and Druze local leaders had made arrangements with the occupying army, resistance grew as the occupation continued, and the main leaders of both Shi'is and Druzes, identified with the Muslim camp, encouraged that resistance.

The first aim of both Israel and the Phalanges was the eviction of the PLO's military-terrorist formations and their nerve centers not only from South L. (achieved, in the main, by the Israeli army operations) but also from West Beirut, and the goverment of L. went along. The USA again dispatched Ph. Habib to mediate, and Israel applied pressure by stepped-up shellings of West Beirut. In July and Aug. 1982, the PLO leadership agreed to the evacuation of its offices, staff and fighters from Beirut. A "Multi-national Force" of US, French and Italian troops was sent in Aug. to supervise that evacuation. It began on 21 Aug. and was completed on 1 Sept.; about 11,000 PLO men were evacuated (though other estimates cite higher figures), and so were about 3,000 Syrian troops. The "multi-national" troops were withdrawn by mid-Sept. (They returned two weeks later, after the events of mid-Sept. described in the next paragraph, but had no significant impact on the situation; they were withdrawn in Feb.-Mar. 1984, France leaving some 50 observers — who had even less impact and were withdrawn by Apr. 1986).

In Aug. 1982, with the expiry of President Sarkis' term, Bashir Jumayyil was elected President of L.; there was no rival candidate, but of the 92 surviving members of Parliament only 62 attended (including only 5 Sunni and 12 Shi'i Muslims). Three weeks later, on 14 Sept., Jumayyil was killed when his Phalange headquarters were blown up by terrorists. Israeli forces immediately entered West Beirut, to keep law and order and prevent an eruption of total violence. However, while they were in charge in West Beirut, Phalange commandos stormed the Palestinian camps of Sabra and Shatila, killing blindly; about 460 bodies were found, including 15 women and 20 children (an Israeli commission of inquiry later found — in its report published in Feb. 1983 — that Israeli commanders bore a share of the responsibility for the massacre, since they should have prevented it; a Lebanese inquiry produced no significant results). The multi-national force now returned, and Israeli troops withdrew from Beirut late in Sept.

On 24 Sept., the murdered Bashir Jumayyil's elder brother Amin *Jumayyil was elected President; there was no rival candidate, and the number of MP's attending and of votes cast in favor was higher than that achieved by Bashir. Amin Jumayyil, though a member of the Phalange leadership (who had not played an important role in its military arm), was much less militant than his late brother, inclined to seek a compromise with the Muslim-leftist camp and Syria and a formula for a political settlement (such as the Syria-Franjiyeh plan). He was also much less committed to cooperation with Israel. An agreement with Israel on the withdrawal of her forces was the first urgent point on the agenda of the new President and the new Government of Shafiq al-Wazzan he appointed in Oct. Israel was eager to withdraw from L. — on condition that a formula for co-existence could be agreed upon, optimally a peace accord (and an alliance), but at least security arrangements that would prevent clashes in the border region and the recurrence of raids on Israel from Lebanese territory. Negotiations began in Dec. 1982 and proved to be difficult, since the Lebanese side no longer shared the basic conception of L.-Israel peace and could offer only security arrangements that fell far short of what Israel expected and demanded. After a protracted wrangle, with the help of US mediation, an agreement was signed on 17 May 1983 which satisfied Israel's minimum requirements: the state of war was terminated; L. was to prevent the existence, enty or passage of irregular forces and their incursions into Israel (and previous L.-PLO agreements permitting such activities were declared null and void); a security zone in South L. would be policed by an "Army Territorial Brigade", to incorporate "existing local units" (*viz.* Haddad's Israeli-sustained South L. Army, not named); mutual liaison offices would be set up; UNIFIL would be moved from the border region to a second-line security zone farther north; Israeli forces were to withdraw from L. within three months from the ratification of the agreement (simultaneously with remaining PLO and Syrian forces — a provision not spelled out but informally understood, and confirmed in an Israel-US exchange of letters).

The May 1983 agreement was vehemently opposed by Syria and the Lebanese Muslim-"leftist" camp, and since President Jumayyil sought an accommodation with that camp, he hesitated to ratify it and finally annulled it on 5 Mar. 1984. Since the summer of 1983, Israel was unwilling to wait for the constantly delayed ratification and prepared to evacuate L., in stages, unilaterally — if possible, in co-ordination with the Lebanese army and militias. She was not prepared to bear the responsibility, as an occupying power, for the complex intra-communal problems and confrontations, particularly between Druzes and Christians in the Shuf region. Growing resistance — at first mainly Palestinians re-infiltrating from the Syrian-held regions, but increasingly Shi'i — also imposed a burden of casualties and security problems which it seemed senseless to bear. In addition to small-scale raids, suicide car-bomb attacks inflicted heavy losses — the first in Nov. 1982, another in Nov. 1983, both on Israeli headquarters in Tyre (terrorists also blew up the US Embassy in Apr. 1983, and the headquarters of US and French troops in Oct. 1983). Israel's attempts to co-ordinate her withdrawal with the government, the army or the militias failed (government and army were, in any case, not in control of the region concerned), and Israeli forces withdrew, in Sept. 1983, unilaterally from the Shuf area and the adjacent coastal Kharrub to a line beginning on the Awali River, north of Sidon. US mediation efforts to arrange talks on the co-ordination of further withdrawals met persistent obstacles and failure. When Israel-L. talks finally resumed, in Nov. 1984, and Israel re-proposed security arrangements for the southern border zone similar to those provided for in the annulled agreement of May 1983, no accord was reached: the Lebanese insisted on unconditional withdrawal with no security arrangements and no "gains derived from the invasion". From Jan. 1985, Israel therefore continued her unilateral withdrawal in stages. It was completed by June 1985, with Israel retaining *de facto* control of a "Security Zone" inside L., 3–6 mi. wide on the average and with a population of c. 150,000, mostly Shi'i, policed by the "South Lebanese Army" and by occasional Israeli patrols. L. protested and continued demanding the total evacuation of all her territory. Attacks on the South Lebanese Army, on Israeli patrols and sometimes on border villages in Israel (mainly sporadic "Katyusha" shells) continued; these were mounted by re-constituted PLO squads and Shi'i groups — *Amal* or the Islamic-extremist *Hizbullah* (see below) — from the region north of the Security Zone. Israeli preventive or punitive action sometimes extended to that region.

Within L., the resumed civil war was again escalating. In late 1982 Christian-Druze clashes erupted in the Shuf, with the Druzes resisting Phalange efforts to expand Christian domination to that area (allowed, or encouraged, by the Israeli occupying forces), and trying to reinforce Druze primacy and expel Christian strongpoints. This battle escalated after the Sept. 1983 Israeli withdrawal from the region, and the Druzes were gaining the upper hand, expelling not only Phalange military centers but large parts of the Christian village population; they were also reaching the coastal plain west of the Shuf. In July 1983, Walid *Junbalat set up an alliance with Karameh and Franjiyeh, called the "National Salvation Front", and endeavored to attract the Shi'is — among whom Nabih *Berri was emerging as the chief leader — to join. In Beirut and on the hills southeast of it, near-constant clashes were continuing. The PLO was reinfiltrating fighters into South L. and Beirut and re-establishing its domination of the Palestinian camps. In the Syrian-occupied Biqā' region, on the other hand, Syria took action against the PLO's 'Arafat wing which refused to toe her line and accept her "guidance"; in Sept. 1983 she allowed, and aided, anti-'Arafat *Fatah* rebel formations to attack 'Arafat's forces and expel them from the Biqā'. When 'Arafat concentrated his forces in Tripoli, they were attacked in that city and the Palestinian camps around it, defeated in bloody battle (despite the support of the Sunni fundamentalist *Tawhid Islami* group), and expelled from Tripoli in Dec. 1983; they were evacuated by sea with the help of foreign and international bodies.

From the summer of 1983, mediation efforts were intensified, e.g. by the USA and Sa'udi Arabia, aiming at a cease-fire and security arrangements, and at a political reconciliation conference to be held by the government, the leaders of the two rival camps (with President Jumayyil considered as part of the Christian camp rather than as a neutral head of state above the parties), and Syria. In Sept. 1983 agreement was reached on a cease-fire and a security plan (which collapsed) and on a reconciliation conference. That conference convened in Geneva on 31 Oct., but could reach no agreement on either the conflicting plans for a reform of L.'s constitution and structure or the ratification or abrogation of the agreement with Israel; several committees were set up to discuss the various proposals, but did not get down to serious work and made no progress.

The need to resume and intensify the conciliation process was urgent as the civil war continued to escalate. In Feb. 1984, Christian formations of the army entered West Beirut to impose their control. Shi'i militias, who had become a dominant element in Beirut's southwestern suburbs and approaches, resisted and, aided by the army's sixth (Shi'i) brigade, succeeded in seizing control of West Beirut. A Shi'i-Druze alliance finally formed and the militias of the two groups joined forces to seize the coastal region south of Beirut and most of the hills to its east. The Phalanges in South L., cut off by these Shi'i-Druze advances, left their positions, abandoning the Christians of the south and the coast to a process of harassment and expulsion.

In Feb. 1984, Sa'udi mediators resumed their efforts. President Jumayyil gave in on the agreement with Israel and annulled it on 5 Mar., as the pre-conditioned price for the resumption of the reconciliation process. In Mar. 1984 a new reconciliation conference convened in Lausanne. The rival camps again presented diametrically opposed plans: Junbalat and Berri demanded the abolition of the communal key in L.'s structure and constitution (while in reality they were reinforcing their communal control of their respective "cantons"), Chamoun and Pierre Jumayyil emphasized the emergence of cantons and envisaged the transformation of L. into a federation of cantons; Franjiyeh was mediating and seeking compromise formulas, and so were the Sa'udi observers and Syria. The latter sympathized with the anti-communal proposals of Junbalat and Berri, but envisaged their realization in the distant future only, while retaining for the present the traditional communal key at least for the top posts (and an intensified linkage and coordination of L.'s policies and security with Syria). Compromise plans that seemed to crystallize were akin to the 1976 Syria-and-Franjiyeh plan, i.e. a change in the communal proportion in Parliament and administration from 6:5 to 50:50, the Prime Minister to be elected by Parliament rather than appointed by the President, with the President's powers to be reduced and those of the Premier expanded; it was also proposed to institute a Senate, and to have the President elected by a majority of at least 55% of the deputies instead of the simple majority needed before.

The final declaration of the Conciliation Conference, however, did not contain an agreement on these proposals, but instituted a committee of experts to prepare the reformed future constitution of L. (a committee that did not get off the ground). The Declaration concerned mainly a new cease-fire and detailed security arrangements and their supervision (arrangements that were not fully implemented). It did not even mention the "Government of National Unity" that was the main outcome of the conference. The conference declared itself ready to continue its deliberations if reconvened by the President (it was not reconvened).

A "Government of National Unity" was formed on 30 Apr. by Rashid Karameh. It comprised the leaders of the two rival camps — Chamoun and Pierre Jumayyil on one side, and

Premier Karameh, Junbalat and Berri on the other (Berri, not content with being Minister of Justice, had extracted an additional appointment as Minister in Charge of South L.); but it was strongly weighted in favor of the Muslim camp. The "Government of Unity" never became fully operative. Junbalat and Berri boycotted its meetings, mounted an opposition campaign calling in particular for the resignation or dismissal of President Jumayyil, and continued operating their militias in disregard of government orders and security agreements; both saw Damascus as their center of operations and spent much of their time there. Syria did not go along with her clients; she demanded not Jumayyil's dismissal, but his cooperation in and acceptance of her plans for L. (and for a greatly enhanced Syrian role in L.), and frequently summoned him to Damascus for pressing consultations. Jumayyil, however, while seeking an accommodation with Syria, did not give in and withheld his approval.

The civil war situation improved for some time after the Conciliation Conference. In June 1984, a Syrian-devised security plan was agreed upon, and in July, and again in Nov., the army announced that it was taking over West Beirut (mainly with its Shi'i sixth brigade) and that Beirut was reunited and the "Green Line" dividing it was abolished. The cease-fire and the improvements did not, however, hold for long. Muslim-Christian clashes and mutual shellings soon re-erupted in Beirut, in the hills to the southeast, and in South L. In the spring of 1985, the Druze PSP militias completed their take-over of the coastal region west of the Shuf and south of it, in the Kharrub. Most of the Christian population of those areas and the northern part of South L. was expelled, but succeeded in holding the town of Jezzin and its area (protected also in some measure by Gen. Lahad's South Lebanese Army — who extended his area to include Jezzin without Israel's approval). In July 1985, the semi-alliance of the Druzes and the Shi'is was formalized in a "United Front" by Junbalat — who was speaking in the name of a "National Democratic Front" his PSP had established in 1984 with several other left-wing groups (the Communists, the Ba'th, the SSNP) — and Berri. This was preceded by a joint Druze-Shi'i operation against the Sunni-Nasserist militia of the *Murabitun* in West Beirut in Apr. 1985, intended to liquidate any group liable to compete for a position of power in West Beirut; the *Murabitun* were eliminated as a fighting force. The Druze-Shi'i alliance of July 1985 included a Syrian-sponsored agreement on security matters; some Sunni leaders also adhered.

The liquidation of the *Murabitun* was not the only instance of in-fighting within the Muslim-"leftist" camp. In Sept. 1985, the fundamentalist *Tawhid Islami* in Tripoli (Muslim, but not "leftist") was liquidated in bloody battles by its adversary, the "A. Democratic Party", largely 'Alawi and supported by Syrian forces. The Shi'i *al-Amal* refused to acquiesce in the re-establishment of PLO control in the Palestinian camps of South L., and later also in Beirut, and entered a long battle with the *Feda'iyyin*. Clashes, and a Shi'i siege of Palestinian camps, erupted in May 1985; there were several cease-fires, including one concluded in June 1985 in Damascus, with Syrian and Druze assistance, with the extremist and Syrian-dominated Palestinian "Salvation Front" — which had no effect, since the *Feda'iyyin* in South L. and Beirut were mostly of the 'Arafat wing. Fighting re-erupted in Sept. and Dec. 1985, and escalated in Sept. 1986, with an almost complete siege of the main camps in South L. ('Ain Hilweh and Miyeh-Miyeh near Sidon and Rashidiyya near Tyre) and in Beirut (Sabra, Shatila and, the largest, Burj al-Barajneh). Syria tried to mediate through "her" Palestinian organizations of the Salvation Front, but seemed to encourage and support *al-Amal* in its fight against the camps of the 'Arafat wing. *Amal*'s battle with the Palestinians put a strain on its alliance with the Druzes — an alliance that was brittle in any case and was several times disrupted by armed clashes between the allies — since the Druzes tried to stay neutral and sometimes even helped the Palestinians (e.g. by letting arms supplies pass through Druze-controlled territory).

The fight with the Palestinians involved also intra-Shi'i problems. Extremist Shi'i elements, influenced, guided and supported by *Khomeini's Iranian revolution and considering Berri and the mainstream leadership to be far too moderate, were active inside *Amal* — and outside, in radical groups that appeared under different names (*Amal Islami, Jihad Islami*) but generally became known as *Hizbullah* ("God's Party"). These Islamic radicals aimed at transforming L., or at least Shi'i South L. and the Biqā', into an

Islamic republic on the Iranian model; they also regarded a relentless guerrilla fight against Israel as a main, sacred, task; and their men were behind many of the terrorist attacks on Israeli targets in South L. and in Israel's northern border zone. They took no part in *Amal*'s battle against the Palestinians; on the contrary, they regarded the *Feda'iyyin* as allies, while they suspected Berri and the mainstream *Amal* of wishing to restrain or halt Lebanese-Shi'i attacks on Israeli targets and to reach some *de facto* accommodation with Israel in response to the interest of the South L. Shi'is to avoid renewed involvement in the Palestinian-Israeli cycle of raids and reprisals. Observers saw the influence of the Islamic radicals increasing both within *Amal* and through their separate organizations; some also thought that radical pressure was inducing Berri and his associates to take more extreme positions in order to keep their leadership.

The Christian camp, the Phalanges and their "Lebanese Forces", also experienced sharp internal crises. Piere Jumayyil, the grand old man of the Phalanges, died in Aug. 1984; he was succeeded as chairman by Elie Karameh (designated by Jumayyil), who was replaced in 1986 by Georges Sa'adeh. But the civilian-political leadership of the Phalanges was losing influence, with the center of the stage taken by the military leaders of the Phalanges and their "Lebanese Forces". In 1984, the long-time military leader Fadi Frem was eased out and replaced by Fu'ad Abu Nader. But in Mar. 1985, a more militant group under Samir Geagea (Ja'ja'), incensed by what it regarded as the overly conciliatory, pro-Syrian policy of Abu Nader (and, behind him, President Jumayyil), staged an internal rebellion and took over the command. While Abu Nader, the civilian Phalange leaders, and the President, tried to conciliate and devise a compromise, Elie Hobeika — in the past considered a hard-line militant (and the organizer of the Sabra-Shatila massacre of 1982), but by now pro-Syrian and seeking an accommodation with the Muslim-"leftist" camp — emerged as Ja'ja''s chief rival, and in a see-saw contest during 1985 Hobeika secured the top position.

In Dec. 1985 Hobeika went to Damascus and signed a Syrian-sponsored agreement with the Druze and Shi'i militia leaders Junbalat and Berri. That accord went far beyond anything any Christian leader had ever consented to. Hobeika accepted not only the old reform plan of 1976 that had been discussed again at the 1984 Conciliation Conference but had not been finalized — a reconstitution of Parliament on a 50:50 basis of equality between Christians and non-Christians, to be implemented by new elections for an expanded Parliament within three years; a reduction in the powers of the (Maronite) President; the establishment of an Upper House (probably with a Druze chairman) — and agreed to a re-escalation of the fight against Israel and her presence in the South L. security zone. But he also agreed to the complete abolition of the communal-key structure after a transition period of a maximum of ten years that could be shortened by Parliament, to the disbandment of all militias (i.e. the dissolution of the military force that kept the Christian "canton" intact and protected), and to the complete "co-ordination" of L.'s international and inter-A. policies, her army, her security and her secret services, with Syria, L. and Syria to become "complementary" (i.e., in reality, the acceptance of a Syrian protectorate).

When this agreement — which had not been authorized by the leadership institutions of the Phalanges or the Lebanese Forces — was reported, Ja'ja' and the militants violently denounced it and deposed Hobeika as a traitor whose signature did not commit the movement. And this time, Ja'ja', who took over as commander, had the support of President Jumayyil and most of the Phalange leaders. In Jan. 1986, Ja'ja' and the formations of the Phalanges and Lebanese Forces loyal to him defeated Hobeika in battle. Hobeika fled, via Europe, to Syria and Syrian-dominated East L.; there he continued to organize formations of the Lebanese Forces loyal to him. In Aug. 1986, and again in Sept., new clashes erupted, but Hobeika and his forces were defeated again. Hobeika's "Three-Militia Agreement" remained a dead letter.

The civil war was continuing and re-escalating — Muslim West Beirut *vs.* Christian East Beirut; *Amal*-Palestinian; intra-Christian. It also had mounting international repercussions. For some years a spate of kidnappings and assassinations had been extended to foreigners; the kidnappers belonged to various terrorist groups and were frequently traced to Iranian-guided Islamic extremists. Efforts by Western governments to obtain the release of their citizens, *inter alia*, through contacts with Syria and/or Iran, had little success. Lebanese terrorists also operated in foreign countries, particularly France. And L.'s Government was paralyzed, unable even to meet — the more so as since early 1986 all Muslim ministers boycotted President Jumayyil. In July 1986 a small force of Syrian commandos entered West Beirut to enforce a pacification. The move had apparently not been fully endorsed by President Jumayyil and the Christian leadership, and some of the latter protested, but acquiesced. As the small Syrian contingent failed to enforce a cease-fire, a larger Syrian force — an estimated 7,500 troops — entered West Beirut in Feb. 1987 and took over full control, again without the full endorsement of the President, the Government, and the Christian leadership. The Syrian troops met no significant resistance, except for a bloody clash with Shi'i *Hizbullah* men. They succeeded, by enforcing strict controls with a heavy hand, in calming the situation to a large extent, particularly on the *Amal*-Palestinian front, but their success was not complete and shellings across the "Green Line" and acts of terrorism continued sporadically, on a smaller scale than before. On 1 June 1987 Premier Karameh was assassinated. Syrian troops also advanced some distance southwards and took control of the coastal road, but did not enter South L. It is too soon to judge whether Syria's direct military intervention will achieve a more permanent pacification and an end to the civil war. On the political front there has been no progress and the constitutional-political problem of L. has remained unsolved and in deadlock.

EDUCATION, PRESS. Beirut used to be an important educational and intellectual center with significant influence in the A. world. Some of its most prestigious academic institutions were founded by foreign missionaries: the French-language Catholic University of St. Joseph, established in 1875, and the American University of Beirut, founded in 1866 as the "Syrian Protestant College", a university since 1920. The "University of L." was founded in 1951, and an "Arab University" in 1960. The American University attracted students from all the AC and was an important training ground for the modern nationalist A. élite. All these institutions have been gravely affected by the civil war; some, if not closed altogether, have been paralyzed.

L. also was a center of A. literature and cultural activity (outside our scope here) — though in this field Cairo always held the first place. Beirut had an active and highly diversified press, a plethora of dailies, weeklies and monthlies, most of them with a small circulation. From the nationalization of Egyptian newspapers in 1960 until the mid-1970s, Beirut was the principal source of free, uncontrolled political information in and about the AC. Some of Beirut's newspapers were propaganda organs of, and probably financed by, foreign countries, international movements, and political factions. There were several foreign-language publications — e.g., *L'Orient* and *Le Jour* (merged in 1971), *Daily Star*. Among the more important Arabic-language daily newspapers were *al-Hayat* and *al-Nahar* (pro-Western, right-wing), *al-Anwar, al-Safir* and *al-Ahrar* (left). Several weeklies were mouthpieces of leftist, Marxist, Maoist factions and guerrilla groups. Though many of the more important organs have survived even in the difficult conditions of the civil war, their influence and standing in the A. world have diminished.

Levant "Lands of the Rising Sun". Originally designated the entire East, as seen from southern Europe, but particularly the eastern coast of the Mediterranean, from Greece to Egypt. The concept and use of the term gradually changed to mean only the coastlands of Asia Minor, Syria-Lebanon and Palestine. Recent usage limits the term L. to Syria and Lebanon.

Liberal The term L. (Arabic: *al-Ahrar*) appears in the name of several political parties in the AC. The only important and influential one among them was the "Liberal-Constitutional Party" in Egypt, 1922–53 — a rather conservative group representing the great landowners, the upper middle class and the commercial, industrial and financial bourgeoisie, and much of the time close to the Royal Court. *Chamoun's "National-L. Party" in Lebanon might also be mentioned.

Attempts to found the ASt emerging into independence on L.-Parliamentary régimes in the West-European pattern have not succeeded. Such régimes have not taken root and there is in recent decades no ASt with a L. pattern of governance. The ideas of parliamentary-democratic multi-party Liberalism were expounded by a few A. thinkers in the 1920s and 1930s, mainly in Egypt; but they have not taken root.

The label L. is used also by groups that have little connection with classical Liberalism — such as the right-wing stream of the Egyptian *"Arab Socialist Union", recognized in 1976 and turned into a "Social L. party" (in opposition) in 1977–78.

Libya Republic in North Africa, on the southern shores of the Mediterranean. Official name since 1977: The Socialist Libyan Arab People's *Jamahiriyya* (a newly coined Arabic term, roughly translated as "Republic", or "State, of the Masses"). L. is located where the eastern part of the A. world (the *Mashriq*) and its western part (the *Maghrib*) meet, and some consider her — or at least her western regions — part of the *Maghrib*. The area — mostly desert — is 680,000 sq.mi. (1.76m. sq.km.). L. borders in the north on the Mediterranean, in the east on Egypt and Sudan, in the south and south-west on Chad and Niger, in the west on Algeria and in the north-west on Tunisia.

Ethnically, Libyans are a mixture of Arabs and *Berbers (and some Tuareg); their language is Arabic, and the Berber element can no longer be distinguished. About 97.5% are Muslims. Minorities include c. 15,000 Italians (after the departure of many Italian colonists following World War II and, again, in 1969–70), 2,500 Maltese, some Black Africans, 800 Greeks, and a few hundred Jews (after the departure of most of the ancient Jewish community which numbered over 30,000 in the 1940s). In recent years there were also several hundred thousand foreign workers — most of them Egyptians, followed by Tunisians; their number fluctuates according to L.'s needs, her financial resources, and the vicissitudes of her foreign relations (the expulsion of foreign workers serving as a political instrument). A similar fluctuation applies to the number of Western experts and technicians, numbering a few thousands, mainly in the oil sector. L.'s population — 1.5–1.8m. in the 1950s and 1960s, 2,257,000 in a census taken in 1973 — was estimated as 3.22m. in 1982, including the foreign workers; some 1984 estimates spoke of 3.5m.

The main economic resource of the country is oil, in production since 1959–60. But a majority of the population is still engaged in agriculture, animal husbandry (largely nomadic or semi-nomadic), and fishing. L.'s oil-bearing region is South and South-East of the Gulf of Sirte, where Cyrenaica and Tripolitania meet. Apart from oil production little industry has been developed.

L. has existed as an entity since 1934, when the country was formed out of the provinces of *Tripolitania, *Cyrenaica and Fezzan, then under Italian rule. L. has been independent since 24 Dec. 1951, a member of the *Arab League since 1953 and of the UN since Dec. 1955.

POLITICAL HISTORY. L. was conquered by the Ottomans in the middle of the 16th century. The area had a degree of autonomy between 1711 and 1835, after a Tripolitanian notable, Ahmad Qaramanli, defeated the Pasha sent from Istanbul and secured recognition for himself as Pasha by Sultan Ahmad III. His descendants, the Qaramanli dynasty, continued ruling under nominal Ottoman suzerainty and engaged in piracy in the Mediterranean. Concerted action by the European powers brought an end to their exploits and caused the ruin of Yussuf, the last of the Qaramanlis. In 1835 the Ottomans reoccupied the territory to counter expanding French influence in North Africa.

In the mid-19th century, there emerged a movement of religious reform, the *Sanussi order, which spread among the local tribes, especially those in Cyrenaica and in the desert hinterland where neither the Qaramanlis nor the Ottomans had ever exerted effective control. The Sanussi movement gave the nomads of Cyrenaica, Fezzan and southern Tripolitania the rudi-

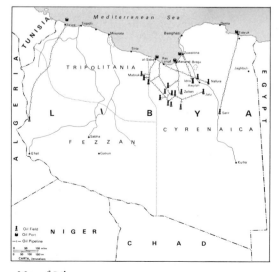

Map of Libya

ments of a social structure and a sense of national unity and grew into a political and military force.

In the late 19th century, when colonialism was at its zenith, Italy began to covet L., aspiring to acquire "her share" of North Africa, where other powers, especially France, were expanding their influence. By a series of separate agreements signed with Austria 1887, Britain 1890, France 1900 and Russia 1909, Italy secured the backing of the major European powers for the conquest of the Turkish provinces of Tripoli and Cyrenaica. In Sept. 1911 Italy declared war on Turkey and Italian troops landed at Tripoli. They encountered unexpected resistance on the part of local tribesmen and Sanussis, who fought together with the Turks under the command of a number of able Turkish officers, such as Enver Pasha and Mustafa Kemal (later known as Atatürk). However, owing to growing difficulties on other fronts, the Ottomans were compelled to make peace with Italy in Oct. 1912, relinquishing their sovereignty over L. in the Treaty of Lausanne.

Libyan tribesmen, however, continued a guerrilla war against the Italians. In Apr. 1915 after defeating an Italian force at Qasr bu Hadi, in the desert of Sirte, the Sanussis under Safi-ul-Din tried to unite the whole of Tripolitania under the Sanussi flag. But they were thwarted by the traditional feud between the Sanussi nomads of Cyrenaica and the interior and the Tripolitanian urban and coastal nationalists headed by Ramadan al-Suweihili. Safi-ul-Din was defeated by Ramadan in 1916 and thereafter resistance against the Italians, mainly in Cyrenaica, was led by the Sanussi chief, Sayyid Ahmad al-Sharif, aided by a number of Ottoman troops who had remained in the country despite the treaty of 1912.

After Italy's entry into World War I in 1915, Sanussi resistance became a part of the general war operations. The Ottomans prevailed upon Ahmad al-Sharif to attack Egypt so as to ease British pressure on them. The Sanussis first overcame the small British garrison at al-Sallum and advanced as far as Sidi al-Barrani, but a British counter-offensive forced them to retreat in 1916. Ahmad al-Sharif then left the country aboard a German submarine for Istanbul, relinquishing political and military control in Cyrenaica to his cousin and rival, Sayyid Idris al-*Sanussi, who had all along opposed any action against the British and had in fact co-operated with them.

Early in 1917, negotiations took place at Ikrima between Britain, Italy and Sayyid Idris, who was recognized as "The Grand Sanussi". Britain and the Sanussi leader agreed on mutual cooperation. Negotiations with Italy were more difficult, as the Italians could not agree to Libyan or Cyrenaican-Sanussi independence, but they eventually led to a precarious agreement on a cessation of hostilities.

After World War I the Socialist Government of Italy, pursuing a more liberal colonial policy, took steps towards granting civil and political rights to the people of Cyrenaica and Tripolitania. Separate statutes for the two provinces provided for a parliament and a government council for each province and local councils. In a new accord, signed at al-Rajma in Oct.1920, Idris al-Sanussi was recognized by Italy as "Amir" (Prince) at the head of a self-governing Sanussi régime in the interior of Cyrenaica, comprising the oases of Jaghbub, 'Ajila, Jalu and Kufra, with the right to use Ajdabiyya as the seat of his administration, which was to be subsidized by Italy. The Amir, for his part, was to ensure the disbandment and suppression of any armed Sanussi formations. The Amir was unable to fulfil this obligation, and so, a year later, the Bu Maryam accord provided that, until the establishment of full Italian control, Sanussi formations still existing would be maintained jointly by Sanussis and Italians in "mixed camps".

In view of the favorable terms obtained by Idris al-Sanussi at al-Rajma, the Tripolitanians — who had established a semi-independent régime of their own before the Italians had been able to exert full control — decided to make him their leader and invested him formally with the Amirate of Tripolitania on 28 July 1922. When the Italians took steps to prevent this extension of Sanussi self-government to Tripolitania, Idris al-Sanussi broke with them and reopened a bitter conflict. Yet he was not strong enough to fight and left the country for Egypt in Dec. 1922; his exile was to last more than 20 years.

After 1922 Fascist Italy stepped up operations to subjugate the rebellious tribes and gain complete control of the country. In 1923 she declared null and void all previous Italo-Sanussi accords, seized the "mixed camps" in a surprise action, and attacked the rebels. The renewed guerrilla war was to last nine years. It was led by a Sanussi follower, 'Omar al-Mukhtar, and based on small, mobile bands usually made up of members of the same tribe. Gradually, the Italians took the Sanussi strongholds; Jaghbub fell in 1926, Kufra — the last — in 1931. The Sanussi rebel leader, Sheikh Rida (Idris' brother) surrendered in 1928. The Italians erected a barbed wire barrier along the Egyptian frontier, to bar the rebels' arms supply routes. 'Omar al-Mukhtar, continuing a desperate fight, was wounded and captured in Sept. 1931. Tried and publicly hanged the same month, his name became a symbol of L.'s fight for freedom. With al-Mukhtar's death, resistance broke down. In 1934 Italy nominally united Cyrenaica and Tripolitania, added Fezzan and named the combined area L.

The colonization of the territory by Italian settlers started in 1920, but was hindered by the guerrilla war. In 1933 settlement was given a new impetus by the Italian administration, and agencies were created to help and finance it. By 1940 the number of Italian settlers had reached c. 90,000 in Tripolitania and 60,000 in Cyrenaica. The Italians extended the cultivated areas, enlarged cities, set up public buildings and established a network of roads. But they did little to raise the standard of living and the cultural level of the local population.

When Italy entered World War II, Sayyid Idris al-Sanussi, in his Cairo exile, endeavored, at Britain's suggestion, to recruit a Sanussi force which would help the Allied forces to liberate L. A meeting of Cyrenaican and Tripolitanian leaders, in Aug. 1940, endorsed his plans — despite the opposition of a number of Tripolitanian leaders — and asked him to negotiate L.'s future independence with Britain. The Sanussi force of five battalions took part in the campaign in the Western Desert. In return, the British Foreign Secretary, Anthony Eden, expressed in Jan. 1942 his government's appreciation of the Sanussis' co-operation and pledged that "the Sanussis in Cyrenaica will in no circumstances again fall under Italian domination".

During the war, L. became a battlefield, on which Rommel's Afrika Korps and the British Eighth Army fought for control of the Western Desert. After changing hands three times, Cyrenaica was taken by the Allied forces in Nov. 1942, and Tripoli in Jan. 1943; Fezzan fell to the Free French forces advancing from Chad. By Feb. 1943 the last of the Axis forces were evicted and Italy's rule of L. was at an end.

After the war disagreement between the Powers delayed a settlement of L.'s future and from 1943 to 1951 the country was ruled by a Provisional Military Administration, British in Cyrenaica and Tripoli, French in Fezzan. The question of L.'s future, linked with the fate of other Italian colonies in Africa, formed part of long-drawn peace negotiations with Italy. For L. a temporary UN trusteeship was agreed upon, but there were conflicting views as to its form and the identity of the trustee country or countries. Finally, in the Italian peace treaty of 1947, the disposal of the Italian colonies was deferred for a year; should no agreement be reached by the end of that time, the matter would be referred to the UN General Assembly. No agreement was reached, and the issue was discussed at the UN General Assembly in Apr. 1949.

In the meantime, Britain and Italy had agreed, in the Bevin-Sforza Plan, to place L. under three UN trusteeships for ten years: Tripolitania was to go to Italy, Cyrenaica to Britain and Fezzan to France. After ten years, L. would be granted independence upon a recommendation by the General Assembly. The plan caused sharp protests and disturbances in L. It was adopted in the UN Political Committee, in May 1949, but in the General Assembly it fell short, by one vote, of the required two-thirds majority, and was thus rejected. Instead, on 21 Nov. 1949, the Assembly ruled, by 48 votes against 1, with 9 abstentions, that "L., comprising Cyrenaica, Tripolitania and Fezzan" should become independent by 1 Jan. 1952 at the latest. A UN Commissioner was to advise and assist in the establishment of an independent government and the formulation of a constitution, in co-operation with an Advisory Council comprising one representative from each of the three provinces of L., one from her minorities and one each from Egypt, France, Italy, Pakistan, Britain and the USA.

In Dec. 1949 Adrian Pelt of the Netherlands was appointed Commissioner. With the assistance of the Advisory Council, he set up a 21-member committee to prepare the establishment of a Constituent Assembly. The Assembly convened in Nov. 1950. The main difficulty in the drafting of a constitution lay in the rivalries between the three provinces, and Cyrenaica's and

Fezzan's insistence on status and representation equal to that of Tripolitania, despite the great difference of population and area. Cyrenaica had been declared independent on 31 May 1949 by Idris al-Sanussi, with himself as Amir, with British support and for the time being under the supervision of the British military administration. Elections for a Cyrenaican Parliament were held in June 1950. Provisional representative assemblies for Tripolitania and Fezzan were also formed in 1950. Provincial Executive Councils were set up in 1950 and a provisional government of L. in Mar. 1951. The constitutional problem was solved by the establishment of L. as a federation, giving wide internal autonomy to each of her three component parts. The constitution was adopted in Oct. 1951, the throne of L. was offered to Amir Idris al-Sanussi, and on 24 Dec. 1951 L. was declared independent under King Idris.

Friction between Tripolitania and Cyrenaica bedevilled L.'s internal affairs. Tripolitania strongly favored a unitarian state, whereas Cyrenaica and Fezzan advocated federalism. Prior to the first elections of Feb. 1952, an (opposition) National Congress of Tripolitania campaigned against the federal constitution. The elections were won by moderate pro-government candidates, except in the city of Tripoli, where riots occurred. These were suppressed, the National Congress leader, Bashir Sa'dawi (holder of a Sa'udi passport), was expelled and the National Congress ceased to exist. Rivalries between Tripolitania and Cyrenaica frequently turned into conflicts between provincial and federal authorities; but the King and his government were in firm control. Subsequent elections were held without major trouble.

Nationalist elements, mainly in Tripolitania, also disagreed with the King's conservative régime and his pro-Western policy; and with the rising tide of anti-Western nationalism in the ME and North Africa their influence grew. In 1963, as a result of their pressure, the King abolished the federation and a new unitary constitution was adopted by parliament. The traditional division of L. into her three provinces was replaced by ten administrative districts. L.'s economic boom, following the exploitation of her oil resources since 1960, made the country independent of Western financial assistance and strengthened the nationalists. They were also increasingly under *Nasserist influence and favored L.'s integration in an Egyptian-led A. alliance based on socialism within and neutralism in external relations.

King Idris, 1951–69, followed a pro-Western foreign policy. Treaties signed with Britain, July 1953, and the USA, Sept. 1954, allowed these countries to maintain military bases and forces in L., in exchange for military and economic aid (then still badly needed). An agreement with France, Aug. 1955, provided for the liquidation of her military base in Fezzan by Nov. 1956, but gave her forces communication facilities in that desert region (which were curtailed late in 1963). Close ties were also maintained with Turkey and Greece. Within the Arab League, which she joined in Mar. 1953, L. supported the conservative bloc, despite insistent demands by the urban intelligentsia for a pro-Egyptian and neutralist policy. Nasserist Egypt, for her part, encouraged subversive activities in L., and Egyptian diplomats and military attachés were expelled on several occasions. However, after Egypt's defeat in the 1967 Six Day War, L. supported Egypt (and Jordan) by extensive annual subsidies. L. advocated closer cooperation among the *Maghrib* states and talks were held with Tunisia, Algeria and Morocco, but no progress was made.

Under the combined internal and external pressure for the liquidation of foreign bases, the government felt compelled publicly to favor their early evacuation, but took few practical steps. In Feb. 1964, for instance, President Nasser publicly called for the liquidation of the American and British bases in L.; a day later, the Libyan government declared that the military agreements with the USA and the UK would not be renewed upon their expiry (i.e. in 1971). The USA and Britain agreed to this, in principle, in 1964. In June 1967, the government officially requested Britain and the USA to liquidate their bases "as soon as possible". The evacuation of some bases and posts was agreed. However the matter was taken up with determination under the post-1969 revolutionary régime only.

On 1 Sept. 1969, a bloodless military *coup d'état* took place. A Revolutionary Command Council proclaimed a "Libyan Arab Republic" that would strive for a revolutionary, socialist and progressive L. and fight against imperialism. The constitution was abolished, the King deposed, and the government dismissed. All nationalist prisoners were released. There was no resistance, either by the police, thought to be loyal to the King, or the tribes of the interior, traditionally linked to the Sanussi dynasty. The King (visiting Turkey at the time) made a feeble attempt to ask for British help (rejected by Britain), but gave up without further resistance and renounced his throne.

The Revolutionary Command Council formed a government under Dr. Mahmud S. al-Maghrebi. The strong man of the new régime was Col. Mu'ammar al-*Qadhdhafi, aged 28; he was made Commander-in-Chief of the Armed Forces and emerged as chairman of the twelve-member Revolutionary Command Council, the supreme body of the new republic. In Jan. 1970, he became Prime Minister as well. His chief aide was 'Abd-ul-Salam *Jallud. Internal strife within the junta was suppressed. In Dec. 1969, a conspiracy of the ministers of Defense and the Interior to overthrow the régime was foiled. The two officers were tried and sentenced to prison for life (and in a re-trial, on popular demand, to death).

The new régime declared that it would not nationalize the oil concessions but would honor contracts with the oil companies "as long as they honor the rights of the people". Most companies soon submitted to pressure to increase tax and royalty payments to the government and follow strict government instructions as to production and development, etc. In Nov. 1969 foreign banks were nationalized by a decree that 51% of capital and full control must be in Libyan hands. The takeover by the state of heavy industry and mining was proclaimed in Apr. 1970. The use of foreign languages in public places was banned; so was the employment of foreigners, except in the case of experts and by special dispensation. The properties of Italian settlers and Jews were confiscated in July 1970, and most of the remaining Italians started leaving. At the same time, the new régime encouraged foreign invesment in fields it chose. In spring 1971, L. obtained, after tough negotiations, new, still more favorable terms from the foreign oil companies (see *oil).

L.'s new régime turned towards the "revolutionary" ASt. Of these, Nasserist Egypt's influence seemed the strongest, and an intensive tri-lateral cooperation between L., Egypt and Sudan began to develop, culminating in plans for a tripartite union. A *"Federation of Arab Republics" (FAR), to consist of L., Egypt and Sudan, was pre-announced in Nov. 1970, and proclaimed — with Syria replacing Sudan as the third member — in Apr. 1971. This FAR never really got off the ground (see *Arab Federation) and was later overtaken by more radical L.'n schemes and a deepening conflict between L. and post-Nasserist Egypt. By way of contrast, ties with Algeria and the *Maghrib* appeared to weaken; in 1970, L. ceased to participate in *Maghribi* meetings and commissions on economic co-operation. Libya, under the new régime, aided the Palestinian-A. guerrilla organizations financially and politically — to the extent that in Sept. 1970 she severed relations with Jordan in protest against King Hussein's measures against the guerrillas.

In Dec. 1969, agreements were reached with Britain and the USA on the evacuation of all their military bases. Evacuation was completed by Britain (al-Adem and Tobruk bases) in Mar. 1970, and by the USA (Wheelus Field) in June. A deal with Britain for the purchase of missile defense systems was cancelled. France, on the other hand, agreed in January 1970 to supply 110 military aircraft (mostly Mirages). The USSR also agreed to supply military equipment. L. retained pronounced Islamic features, but belonged politically and emotionally to the leftist-revolutionary camp; she professed neutralism and endeavored to keep channels open to the West too — not least for the sake of the oil sales on which her economy is entirely dependent.

Since the 1970s, L. has further radicalized her policies — both internal and foreign-international. In mid-1971, a single political party, the Arab Socialist Union (ASU), was established, similar to the Egyptian pattern. From its National Congress, at the apex of its pyramid of local and provincial congresses and committees, was to issue the state's supreme Revolutionary Command Council. Radical changes in L.'s political system were heralded in April 1973, when Qadhdhafi launched a "Popular Revolution". Existing laws were to be replaced by the *Shari'a* (Islamic law); Islamic thought was to become the basis of national life; popular committees throughout the country were to control the revolution from below and the people were to be armed to protect it. The principles of the

"Popular Revolution" of 1973 were expanded in 1976, to form the basis for a system of direct democracy, the "People's Power" (*Sultat al-Sha'b*), with a network of local and national bodies: Basic Congresses, People's Committees, and a General People's Congress. Formally charged with decision-making, in practice these institutions mainly approved decisions taken by Qadhdhafi, who continued to maintain a tough centralized rule. The new system reflected Qadhdhafi's revolutionary vision, his "Third Universal Theory", as formulated in the first part of his "Green Book", published in 1976. (Two more parts of the "Green Book" were published in 1978 and 1979.) On 3 March 1977, the People's Congress declared L. a *Jamahiriyya* (a term newly coined, instead of *Jumhuriyya*, "republic"; roughly: "State — or Republic — of the Masses"), in full: "The Socialist Libyan Arab People's *Jamahiriyya*". The *Qur'an* was declared to be the code of society; direct "people's power" was proclaimed; and since the country's defense was the duty of all citizens, general military training was decreed. The state's institutions were renamed: the Government became the "General People's Committee", the Revolutionary Command Council — the "General Secretariat". Embassies throughout the world were renamed "People's Bureaus", run by "People's Committees".

March 1979 saw the completion of the system of "People's Power" founded in 1977. Qadhdhafi and the four other surviving members of the original Revolutionary Command Council relinquished their formal posts on the "Secretariat" — officially: to devote themselves to promoting the revolution. In practice, however, there was no basic change in L.'s political system which remained a military régime completely dominated by Qadhdhafi. But Qadhdhafi increasingly relied on, and used, the "People's Committees" or "Revolutionary Committees" formed since the late 1970s under the "People's Power" system, and by the early 1980s they had become powerful organs of the revolution. They served primarily as the régime's "watchdogs". Controlled directly by Qadhdhafi, they were charged with inculcating revolutionary consciousness in the masses and eradicating any deviation from or resistance to his revolutionary ideas. They did so, *inter alia*, by physically liquidating the revolution's enemies and potential nuclei of opposition within the country and abroad.

Opposition to the régime — underground and in exile — appeared to grow since the late 1970s, culminating in May 1984 in a serious attack on Qadhdhafi's residence and headquarters in the Bab al-'Aziziyya barracks in Tripoli by men sent across the Tunisian border by the "National Front for the Salvation of Libya" (NFSL), the most significant of the opposition groups. The attack failed and a wave of executions followed. The failure of this *coup* seemed to discourage further similar ventures by other opponents in exile. Potential nuclei of opposition within the army were the only threat to the régime, since the army was the only force in the country with both the strength to carry out a *coup* and the ability to offer a feasible alternative leadership.

L.'s policies — both internal and foreign — were much influenced, and largely mitigated, by her oil economy. Since the 1960s the production and export of oil were the backbone of her economy, her only major resource, financing both her daily sustenance and her fast development, her transformation into a modern high-technology country — and despite the fervor of their revolutionary zeal L.'s leaders took care not to hurt or disturb the oil sector. Internally, for instance, the revolutionary "People's Committees", dominating all other units of economic and social activity, were not allowed to impose their control on oil installations and disturb their functioning. Externally, L.'s oil policy was tough. She drove hard bargains concerning prices, production quotas and the imposition of state control, including the nationalization of some foreign companies and the take-over of majority shares in some others (for details, and data on oil production and revenue, see *oil).

L.'s foreign policy in general, except that concerning oil, must be viewed against the backdrop of Qadhdhafi's ideological doctrine. His "Third Universal Theory" is presented as an alternative to communism and capitalism, applicable specifically to Islamic countries but also to non-Islamic Third World states, even as a world panacea. Qadhdhafi's extremely activist, unconventional and often belligerent foreign policy is both a reflection of his revolutionary idealism and a calculated attempt to advance his country's political, strategic and economic interests. Support for

Islamic causes and worldwide "liberation movements" — often indistinguishable from political terrorism — is a cornerstone of his program.

The list of foreign "liberation movements" aided by L. was headed by the Palestinian-A. guerrillas (mainly from the more extremist factions) and included the West-Saharan POLISARIO, Muslim rebels in the Philippines and Thailand, anti-government underground cells in Egypt, Sudan, Morocco, Tunisia, Chad, Niger, Mali, Senegal, extremist Muslim groups in Malaysia and Indonesia, Ceylon Tamil rebels, separatist movements in Spain (the Basque ETA, Canary Islands and Andalusian autonomists) and Italy (Sardinian and Sicilian secessionists), Latin-American leftists, particularly in Central America (Nicaragua, El Salvador), the Irish IRA, American "Black Muslims" and, according to reports never fully confirmed but persisting, extreme-left terrorists in Italy and Germany. Western observers put the number of countries affected by such Libyan activities at around 50 and many of them complained and protested, sometimes severing relations with L. The movements and countries selected for support changed in accordance with L.'s policies and perceptions. Support granted was sometimes political, often financial, and in many cases military. This included the training of foreign guerrillas/terrorists in L. From the late 1970s, L. maintained an "Islamic Legion" estimated at 5–7,000 men. In some cases, L. mediated between rebels and their government (e.g. in Dec. 1976, in the Philippines).

Qadhdhafi has always been a fervent proponent of all-A. unity, from the Atlantic to the Persian Gulf. As first steps towards such wider unity, he has consistently sponsored mergers of L. and other AC, neighboring or even remote. None of these mergers was successful. They began in 1970–71 with the federation proclaimed with Egypt and Syria, the "Federation of Arab Republics" (FAR) mentioned above. But Qadhdhafi pressed for full union with Egypt and in Aug. 1972 persuaded *Sadat to agree to a merger by Sept. 1973. As Sadat obviously had no intention to implement that agreement, Qadhdhafi in June-July 1973 made a barnstorming tour of Egypt, harangued the Egyptian public and organized a L.'n mass march into Egypt. In Aug. 1973, the merger was re-decided, but it did not take place, and L.-Egypt relations deteriorated. In Jan. 1974 Qadhdhafi persuaded President *Bourguiba of Tunisia to proclaim an immediate merger of L. and Tunisia — a proclamation that had to be scrapped by Tunisia with a great deal of embarrassment. In Sept. 1980, L. and Syria announced the merger of the two countries — but the merger has not really been implemented. In Aug. 1984, L. and Morocco (a conservative country heretofore vilified by Qadhdhafi and the target of L.'n subversion) proclaimed a "union" of the two countries. That union — which in fact was planned as a loose confederation only — was abrogated by Morocco in Aug. 1986. L.'n efforts to get Algeria interested in moves towards a union, reported for instance in 1975–76 and again in 1981, were always cautiously rejected by Algeria. Qadhdhafi went as far as proposing a union even to non-A. countries such as Chad (1981) and Malta (1971) (in both of which he strove to install a dominating L.'n influence).

While Qadhdhafi's fervent unionist zeal was no doubt sincere, his erratic and rather unrealistic merger policies and proposals were no longer taken quite seriously. In fact, L.'s relations with the countries targeted for mergers have, with the exception of Syria, deteriorated — the more so as union proposals usually alternated with, or were accompanied by, L.'n subversion. Worsening relations with Egypt led repeatedly to armed clashes, in July 1977 to warlike operations, and to near-constant complaints of L.'n plots to destabilize Egypt. L. was also, in 1977–78, in the forefront of the ASt's ostracizing Egypt and severing relations with her for her moves towards peace with Israel. Tunisia also repeatedly complained of plots and hostile action by L., including an armed intrusion and attack on Gafsa in Jan. 1980, and the expulsion of Tunisian workers in 1985; relations were severed in 1985. L.'n operations in Chad deserve a special paragraph, below.

Relations with the ASt in general were greatly affected by L.'s radical-extreme policies, her leading membership in the *"Rejection Front" and her hostility towards the conservative AC. She strongly opposed all efforts of moderate ASt to seek an A.-Israel settlement, holding that the A.-Israel conflict could be solved only by Israel's total defeat. During the Jordan-PLO crisis of 1970 she took a pronounced anti-Jordanian stand and severed relations (resumed in 1976 only).

Her relations with Saʻudi Arabia were antagonistic, as her disdain for that country's royal conservatism was reciprocated by the Saʻudis' suspicion of Qadhdhafi's revolutionary doctrines, including his revolutionary Islam. Relations with Lebanon were clouded by L.'s reported involvement in Lebanon's civil war and support for some of the rival "militias" (and by the disappearance — and assassination? — in L. of the Lebanese Shiʻi leader Mussa al-*Sadr in Aug. 1978). Relations with Iraq were troubled by L.'s friendship with Syria and since 1980 in particular by her siding with Iran in the Iraq-Iran war; official relations were severed in 1980. L.'s relations with Sudan were erratic and shifting, clouded until *Numeiri's fall in Apr. 1985 by her hosting and supporting anti-government factions (such as the "Democratic Unionists" and Sadeq al-*Mahdi's *Ansar — see Sudan), her reported aid, for some time, to the South-Sudanese rebels, and incessant reports of L.'n plotting.

L.'s relations with her African neighbors and other African countries were also frequently troubled. Mali, Niger, Senegal, Gambia (all Muslim-majority countries), Benin, Ivory Coast and others often complained of L.'n interference and subversion, and official relations were cut several times. A special case was Chad. Dominating influence in that country, or if possible its control, were seen by L. as vital to her security (and, as about half of Chad's population was Muslim, and some of it semi-A., also of Islamic and A.-national importance). L. supported certain rebelling factions in Chad from the mid-1960s, even before Qadhdhafi's *coup*, and hosted the then rebel leader, providing him with a base for his operations. Moreover, L. claimed as her territory the northernmost part of Chad, the Aouzou Strip — an area variously estimated at 70–115,000 sq.km. (27–44,000 sq.mi.) — citing a French-Italian colonial deal of 1935. The Strip was important to L. also because it was reputedly rich in uranium. She occupied the Aouzou Strip in May-June 1973 and formally annexed it in 1975. The Chad government was too weak to resist, and L. claimed it accepted her possession of the Strip. But no Chad government has recognized L.'s annexation — not even the rebel governments formed by L.'s clients.

L.'s revolutionary post-1969 régime stepped up its aid to the Chad rebel factions and turned it into direct military intervention in 1980. After mediation efforts by the *Organization of African Unity (OAU) and others, L. announced the withdrawal of her troops in 1981, but her actual withdrawal remained in doubt, and in any case she resumed her full military intervention in 1983. Renewed mediation efforts by the OAU, the UN Security Council, and particularly France (who was half-committed to the defense of Chad), led to a French-L.'n agreement in Sept. 1984, providing for the withdrawal of L.'s troops and bases. However, L. did not implement that agreement and her troops continued controlling northern Chad, far beyond the annexed Aouzou Strip. France had to acquiesce, as she did not wish to enter a fully fledged military conflict with L., but set the 16th degree as a red line whose crossing by L.'n troops would cause France to take military action. Recently the factional alignment of the Chadian rebels changed, L.'s chief client, Goukouni Wadaʻi (Ouedei), and his formations turned against L. and made peace with the Chad Government, and L. began supporting another rebel group. In Dec. 1986 L., still in actual military control of northern Chad, began a new offensive against the forces of Goukouni (himself detained in L.) and the Chad Government, meeting successful resistance (L. herself denies any direct involvement of her troops).

L.'s relations with the countries of the West were troubled — mainly because of her involvement in terrorist operations in the West (including the liquidation of L.'n exiles and dissidents who had taken refuge in the West) — and some measures were taken against L., reluctantly and half-heartedly, since the mid-1980s. Relations deteriorated even with those Western countries that endeavored to keep them stable — such as Italy (with particularly strong economic links with L.), West Germany, Spain, and France (angered and embarrassed also by L.'s operations in Chad, after she had supplied arms to L. for years). With Britain, the crisis went farther: in Apr. 1984 she severed relations with L. altogether (after someone in the L.'n Embassy fired on an anti-Qadhdhafi demonstration in London and killed a policewoman). The gravest confrontation was with the USA. In 1976, after years of tension, the US banned the export of military or potentially military equipment to L. The US had recalled her Ambassador in 1972 and reduced the staff of her embassy, and when the embassy was sacked by demonstrators in Dec. 1979, she closed it altogether. In May 1981 the US expelled all L.'n diplomats and severed relations. In Aug. 1981 a military dimension was added when L.'n war-planes attacked US aircraft on exercises over the Mediterranean Sea's Gulf of *Sirte and two L.'n planes were downed (L. had declared that Gulf, up to the degree of 32'30 latitude, c. 200mi. from its south-eastern coast, to be L.'n territorial waters, while the US rejected that claim and considered the Gulf to be international waters). Following that incident of 1981, the US imposed economic sanctions, banning the import of L.'n oil from Mar. 1982. She further tightened these sanctions in Jan. 1986, after L. was reportedly involved in a terrorist attack on Rome and Vienna airports. The 1981 confrontation over the Gulf of Sirte escalated, as the US Mediterranean Fleet and air-arm insisted on their right to sail what they considered international waters, though they actually asserted that right in infrequent test cases only. Threatening confrontations and near-clashes occurred several times in 1983, and an actual battle, followed by US retaliatory bombing raids, in Mar. 1986. In Apr. 1986 the US mounted another air raid on Tripoli and Benghazi military bases and installations — and kept up the threat of further raids and a kind of psychological war.

The only power with apparently firm and stable relations with L. was the USSR and her bloc. This was somewhat surprising, as Qadhdhafi and his L. were, despite their revolutionary zeal and anti-Western orientation, strongly anti-Communist, while the Soviet Union was aware of Qadhdhafi's erratic extremism and his questionable doctrines and could not possibly regard him as a reliable ally. Yet she and her allies supplied L. with large quantities of advanced arms and other aid (e.g. East German security expertise) and frequently proclaimed Soviet support for L. in her disputes with the West.

Litani River One of the two major rivers of Lebanon. Rising near Baalbek, it flows for most of its 105-mi. (170 km.) course from north to south through the *Biqā‘*, the valley separating the mountains of Lebanon and Anti-Lebanon (the other major river, the *Orontes, flows from the same area northwards, into Syria); near Marj 'Ayun the L. makes a sharp turn to the west, continues through a deep gorge (this stretch is also called al-Qassemiyya) and enters the Mediterranean north of Tyre (Sur). In its upper reaches, the L. is used to irrigate large areas in the Baalbek and Zahle districts.

Since the 1950s, plans provide for the erection of a dam north of Nabatiyya, in the southern *Biqā‘*, and the utilization of the L. waters — an estimated 700m. cubic meters (mcm) — for both irrigation and the generation of power; plans for an additional dam at Khardala, on the south-western stretch, the Qassemiyya, were dropped for the time being in the late 1960s. The implementation of the plans was slow and beset by difficulties; by the late 1960s a first phase was completed, the dam near Nabatiyya built and a lake, Lake Qar‘un, created with a capacity to store 90 mcm, irrigate up to 80,000 acres and generate c. 145,000 kw. The realization of further phases has been held up by the Lebanese civil war.

The L. has been linked in some measure to the Palestine problem. Before the Palestine-Lebanon borders were defined, the British proposed, in the Anglo-French negotiations of 1918–23, the inclusion of the L.'s south-western stretch within Palestine, its waters to be used for Jewish settlement and development schemes. The Zionist vigorously supported these claims. But eventually the frontiers fixed left the L. to Lebanon. Jewish-Zionist, and later Israeli, planners continued to think of gaining the waters of the L. for Israel through a mutually advantageous agreement; it was proposed, for instance, to channel them to Israel for irrigation (as no irrigation was possible in the L.-Qassemiyya gorge, west of the bend) and compensate Lebanon with electric power. However, in the light of the A.-Israel conflict there seems to be little prospect for an Israel-Lebanon agreement on such schemes. Lebanese and A. spokesmen frequently express the conviction that Israel schemes to take possession of the L. by force.

When the ASt's planned, in the 1960s, to deprive Israel of the waters of the *Jordan sources, the L. was slated to receive, through a tunnel, parts of the waters of the *Hasbani. These schemes remained abortive — see *Jordan River.

al-Maghrib (Arabic: the West). The Arabic-speaking countries of Northwest Africa — Morocco, Algeria and Tunisia, and some include also non-A. or partly-A. Mauritania as well as Libya, or at least Tripolitania, her western part. There are marked differences — ethnic, in dialect and customs — between the A.'s of the M. and those of the A. ME (the *Mashriq*). A large part of the population of the M. is of *Berber descent. Up to the mid-20th century, during the decades of the growth of A. nationalism and the struggle for independence, there were no close connections between the M. and the eastern part of the A. world — though there has always been a measure of emotional solidarity and of mutual support — and the M. was not included in the political plans of A. nationalism in its formative period on the eve of, during and after World War I. As the AC of the Mashriq attained independence before those of the M., they — particularly Egypt — provided the nationalists of the M., during the decisive years of their struggle for independence in the 1950s, with much aid and hosted the headquarters and command centers of their militant movements. After attaining independence — Libya 1951, Tunisia and Morocco 1956, Mauritania 1960, Algeria 1962 — the countries of the M. joined the *Arab League and became an integral part of the A. family of nations, though in general they were reluctant to intervene overmuch in issues of the Mashriq. The exception was Libya which has become, since her revolution of 1969, very active in inter-A. affairs, taking extremely militant positions as the mainstay of the *"Rejection Front". Algeria, too, belonged to that Front and followed militant-radical inter-A. policies, but seems to have somewhat moderated her stance over the last years. Tunisia and Morocco usually belong to the moderate-conservative camp. In recent years, King Hassan

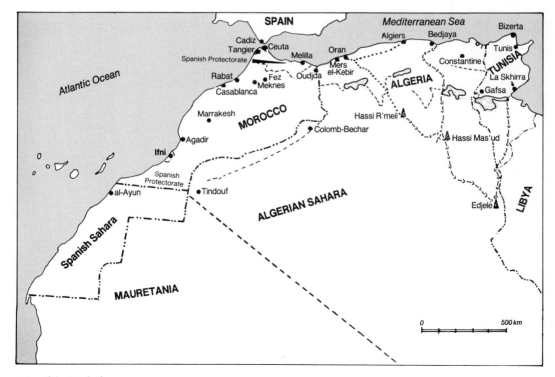

Map of the Maghrib

of Morocco has been more active in inter-A. and all-Islamic matters, as host of summit meetings and sometimes offering his mediation in inter-A. disputes.

Maghribi A. leaders have fostered, since before independence and particularly after attaining it, the idea of an all-M. union or at least close cooperation and coordination in economy, development and other spheres. Committees have been established and inter-governmental meetings and discussions held from time to time, but so far there has been no progress towards M. unity or closer co-operation. A complete union does not seem to be feasible, and conflicting interests, mutual distrust, divergent policies have foiled even modest advances in that direction. Revolutionary, socialist and radical Algeria, Islamic-socialist, extremist and erratic Libya, and conservative Morocco and Tunisia are, indeed, deeply different in basic orientation and political philosophy. Algeria and Morocco are enmeshed in a permanent dispute over borders, political orientation and the problem of Western *Sahara, and that dispute has erupted even in armed clashes and once, in 1963, in actual war. Clashes have occurred between Libya and Tunisia, too. These disputes do not augur well for M. unity.

Attempts have been made to forge partial unions between individual M. countries. Thus, the merger of Libya and Tunisia was proclaimed in Jan. 1974. This merger, which was in effect a surprise move manipulated by Libya's *Qadhdhafi, was swiftly abrogated by Tunisia and beyond contributing to the deterioration of Tunis-Libya relations had no further effect. In Aug. 1984 Morocco and Libya announced an agreement to form a "Union"; this turned out to be no more than a plan for a loose confederation, and while its provisions were implemented only slowly and partially, it caused grave misgivings in Algeria and Tunisia. The Union was abrogated in late Aug. 1986 by Morocco (after Libya denounced King Hassan for inviting Premier Peres of Israel to meet him in Morocco). In any case, these Libyan-initiated partial unions have not advanced the prospects for real all-M. unity and cooperation.

Mahabad Autonomous, break-away Kurdish republic established in 1946 in north-western Iran, with Soviet encouragement. Iraqi Kurdish rebel groups took part in the venture, and Mulla Mustafa *Barazani was its military leader. The Republic of M. was crushed by Iranian forces at the end of 1946 when Soviet forces had to withdraw from northern Iran. See *Kurds.

Mahdi, Mahdiyya The M. (Arabic: the Guided One) is in Islamic theology chosen by God at the end of time to fill the earth with justice and equity (and sanctioned to overthrow the existing régime). In 1881, in Sudan, Muhammad Ahmad ibn 'Abdullah (c. 1840–85) claimed to be the M. and *Imam* (the head of the Muslim community). His followers established a religious order, the *Mahdiyya*, with a body of activists called *al-Ansar* (Arabic: the Helpers; the original *Ansar* were the "Helpers" of the Prophet Muhammad in Medina). The M. movement was also supported by some tribal groups.

The M. called for a holy war against the infidels, including Muslims who did not acknowledge his mission. His fanatical followers, whom Europeans incorrectly called "Dervishes" (a term usually applied to members of the mystic Sufi orders, strongly opposed to and by the M.), defeated the Egyptian troops sent against them and conquered the provinces of Kordofan, Darfur and Bahr al-Ghazzal. The British advised the Egyptians to evacuate these territories and sent Gen. Gordon, former Governor-General of Sudan, to organize the evacuation. But the M. besieged Gordon in Khartoum, and took the town in Jan. 1885, killing Gordon, and established his rule over Khartoum and most of Sudan. The M. died in 1885 and was succeeded by 'Abdullah Ibn Muhammad, the *Khalifa* (successor). The order lost much of its vigor and failed to establish a well-ordered state. In 1896, the British sent an Anglo-Egyptian force commanded by Gen. Kitchener and reconquered Sudan, 1896–98. The *Khalifa* was killed in battle. Continuing resistance was quelled at the beginning of the 20th century.

The *Mahdiyya* gradually changed from a fanatic-military revolutionary force into an ordinary sect or order which, in time, gained great political influence. It later became generally pro-British, anti-Egyptian, was in favor of Sudanese independence (as opposed to union with Egypt) and supported — or sponsored — the *Umma* Party which represented that trend in the political arena. Its main rival was the fundamentalist *Khatmiyya or *Mirghaniyya order. The *Mahdiyya* is strongest in central and western Sudan. It claims 2–3m. adherents. From the 1950s it was a focus of opposition to the military-revolutionary régimes controlling Sudan. In Mar. 1970 the order was accused of mounting a rebellion which was suppressed; its last *Imam*, al- Hadi al-M., was killed, and no successor was proclaimed.

The *Mahdiyya*, and the *Umma* Party it sponsored (which was by now semi-illegal and half-underground), were partners in a "National Front" that continued opposing Numeiri and his régime (see *Sudan). The *Mahdiyya* played an important role in the overthrow of Numeiri, Apr. 1985, and in the new régime established after the elections of Apr. 1986 (see Sadeq al-*Mahdi).

The *Mahdiyya* order (*al-Ansar*) was led by Sir 'Abd-ul-Rahman al-M. (1885–1959), the posthumous son of the M. (al-M. gradually was used as the family name). During World War I he helped the British combat the Pan-Islamic propaganda of the Ottomans. He gradually took a pro-British line and was knighted in 1926. In the 1940s he became the patron of the *Umma* party. Efforts to elect him President of independent Sudan did not succeed.

Sir 'Abd-ul-Rahman's son, Siddiq al-M. (1911–61), succeeded him in 1959 as head of the order. Under him the *Mahdiyya* became the spearhead of resistance to Gen. *'Abbud's military rule.

Siddiq was succeeded as leader of the order, in 1961, by his brother al-Hadi al-M. (1915–70). He caused a schism in the *Umma* party, 1966, by patronizing its conservative right wing. He was a strong candidate for the presidency but his ambitions were thwarted by the *Numeiri *coup* of May 1969. After the *coup* he retired to the Nile island of Aba. He was considered to be a leader of the opposition to the new régime, and in Mar. 1970 was accused of fomenting a rebellion. When the rebellion was crushed, the *Imam* al-Hadi was killed, reportedly while trying to escape to Ethiopia. Since al-Hadi's death, another brother, Ahmad al-M., has been considered leader of the order, though not formally proclaimed *Imam*.

al-Mahdi, al-Sadeq (b. 1936) Sudanese politician, a member of the *Mahdiyya* sect and the son of its *Imam* Siddiq al-M., grandson of the *Imam* Sir 'Abd-ul-Rahman al-M., and great-grandson of the Mahdi himself. M., an Oxford graduate, held no position in the religious establishment of the order, but became a leader of its political arm, the *Umma* Party which advocated independence rather than union with Egypt and was considered anti-Egyptian. He became Prime Minister in July 1966, heading a coalition government, but was forced out in May 1967 by a split in his *Umma* Party, his uncle the *Imam* Hadi al-M. sponsoring the semi-secession of a more conservative faction. *Numeiri's *coup* of May 1969 put an end to his legal political activities, and he was in and out of prison or house arrest. After the alleged *Mahdiyya* rebellion of Mar. 1970 he was deported to Egypt. He returned in 1972, was again arrested, and in May 1973 went into exile in England, Sa'udi Arabia and Libya. He was one of the leaders of a "National Front", semi-clandestine in Sudan and mainly in exile, increasingly with Libya as a base of operation, and was in the forefront of the fight against Numeiri culminating in July 1976 in an attempt to overthrow him. After a reconciliation with Numeiri he returned to Sudan in Aug. 1977 and cooperated with the régime for some time, but soon fell out with Numeiri and resigned his position on the ruling single party's politbureau (*inter alia* because he objected to Numeriri's approval of Egyptian President *Sadat's peace moves towards Israel). In Sept. 1983 he publicly denounced Numeiri's decrees imposing the Islamic law (*Shari'a*) code of punishments. He was again arrested and kept in detention until Jan. 1985.

In Apr. 1985 M. was among the leaders of the *coup* that overthrew Numeiri. A year later he led his *Umma* Party to victory in the Apr. 1986 elections and formed a coalition government. It is too soon to define his policies, but he seems to aspire to *rapprochement* and a normalization of relations with Libya, while somewhat cooling down those with Egypt. While Numeiri's *Shari'a* decree is no longer followed in practice, M. has not felt able to abrogate it altogether. Nor has he found a formula to end the rebellion of the African tribes of South Sudan.

Maher, Ahmad (1886? 1889?–1945) Egyptian politician. After graduating in law (Montpellier, France), M. taught at the Law College. In 1918–19 he joined *Zaghlul's *Wafd* party and soon rose to prominence. He was elected to Parliament from 1924, but served in *Wafdist* governments only once — in 1924, as Education Minister for a few weeks. He was President of Parliament in 1936. After the accession of King *Farouq in 1936–37, he strove for a reconciliation between the *Wafd* and the King and his Court — deviating from the line adopted by the party, and in 1937 he was expelled from the *Wafd*. Together with M.F. *Nuqrashi, he then founded the *Saadist Party, which claimed to represent the true traditions and ideology of Sa'd Zaghlul, the late founder-leader, and his original *Wafd*. In fact, the Saadist party came to collaborate with the royal court against the *Wafd*. In the elections of 1938 it emerged as the second-largest faction, after the "Liberal Constitutional Party", its ally. M. became Finance Minister and in 1940 again President of Parliament. In Oct. 1944, when the King dismissed the *Wafd* government that had been imposed on him in 1942 by the British, M. became Prime Minister and Minister of Interior. Elections he held in Jan. 1945 returned his Saadist Party as by far the largest Parliamentary faction. In Feb. 1945 he obtained parliamentary endorsement for a declaration of war on Germany and Japan (he and his party had advocated an Egyptian declaration of war since 1939). He was assassinated the same day in reprisal for that declaration. The murderer, a young lawyer, according to some reports belonging to the extremist, pro-Fascist "Young Egypt" *(Misr al-Fatat)* group, was tried and executed.

Maher, 'Ali (1883–1960) Egyptian politician. A wealthy landowner and a graduate of the law school, M. in 1919 joined the *Wafd*, then emerging as the main and representative nationalist organization, but he soon seceded to join the conservative, royalist camp. A member of Parliament since its foundation in 1924, he served as chairman of the constitution committee. M. was many times a Minister (Education 1925–26; Finance 1928–29; Justice 1930–32) and Head of the Royal Cabinet in 1935 and 1937. On the death of King *Fu'ad, 1936, he was a member of the Regency Council until King *Farouq came of age in 1937. M. became Prime Minister from Jan. to May 1936, heading, as a respected independent, a government of transition slated to prepare the return to a constitutional régime and arrange elections. He again formed a government in Aug. 1939, serving (as in 1936) as his own Foreign and Home Minister. He was forced to resign, under British pressure, in June 1940, because he displayed marked pro-Axis sympathies and obstructed the services and facilities Egypt was obliged, under the Treaty of 1936, to put at Britain's disposal in time of war and was suspected of secret contacts with Axis agents; from 1942 to 1945 he was kept under house arrest. He again became Prime Minister (and Foreign and War Minister) in Jan. 1952, after the *Wafd* government had involved Egypt in a violent struggle with the British that led to bloody clashes and riots against British troops as well as foreigners and minorities ("Black Saturday"), he was in office for only five weeks. After the July 1952 revolution of the "Free Officers", M., as a respected and non-conformist, though right-wing, independent, was asked to form the new government; he again served as his own Foreign, Home and War Minister. He resigned in Sept. 1952, as he was not willing to go along with the agrarian reform and the general reformist-revolutionary tendencies of the officers, and withdrew from political activity.

al-Majāli, Hazzā' (1916–60) Prime Minister of Jordan in Dec. 1955. His (and the King's) intention was to finalize Jordan's adhesion to the *Baghdad Pact — but following protest riots he resigned and the decision to join the pro-Western Pact was scrapped. In May 1959 he again became Prime Minister and Foreign Minister. Early in 1960 he denounced Egyptian agents for plotting against Jordan's régime and the life of her leaders and predicted an attempt on his own life. He was assassinated in Aug. 1960 — it was generally assumed by Egypt's agents.

al-Maktum The clan or dynasty of sheikhs ruling the small principality of *Dubai, in *Trucial 'Oman — since 1971 the *United Arab Emirates (UAE). The present ruler is Sheikh Rashed ibn Sa'id al-M. (b. 1914), who succeeded his father, Sheikh Sa'id, in 1958, upon the latter's death. Sheikh Rashed is also the Vice-President of the UAE since its creation in 1971, and since July 1979 also its Prime Minister. His sons also occupy top positions in the UAE: the elder son, Dubai Crown Prince Maktum Rashed al-M., was Prime Minister of the UAE from its inception in 1971 until July 1979, when he stepped down for his father and became Deputy Prime Minister. Of his younger sons, Muhammad R. al-M., has been Defense Minister of the UAE since its creation, and Hamdan R. al-M. Minister of Finance and Economy. Reports speak of rivalry and friction among the sons.

The al-M. clan, as rulers of Dubai, have been in constant rivalry with the rulers of *Abu Dhabi, of the al-*Nuhayan clan — both over the primacy in the UAE, and over her shape and constitutional structure. The M.'s insist on the retention of stronger and wider powers by the individual sheikhdoms (mainly Dubai) and oppose the creation of too powerful federal institutions (with the Sheikh of Abu Dhabi as President of the UAE). The positions held by the al-M. clan in the federal government, are the result of a careful balance worked out in nearly constant struggle.

Mandaeans (also Sabaeans or Sabians, in Arabic: *Subbā'*). A small community in southern Iraq, variously estimated at 10–30,000, living mostly in towns, as artisans (mainly silversmiths). The M. faith contains Christian and Muslim elements as well as traces of other religions. The M. speak Arabic, but in their religious rites they use an ancient Chaldean-Aramaic language. Ritual immersion in a river is an important part of their religion, and they are sometimes called "Christians of John the Baptist". The M. have not played a prominent part in Iraq's national movement or in public-political life outside their own community.

mandates After World War I the victorious allies devised, as part of the peace settlement, a new system of governance for the former German colonies and the Asian areas severed from the Ottoman-Turkish Empire. The system was a compromise between the principle of self-determination for all nations, generally accepted and proclaimed in particular by US President Wilson, and secret war-time agreements to divide the non-Turkish parts of the *Ottoman Empire into imperial zones of influence (the *Sykes-Picot Agreement). Article 22 of the Covenant of the *League of Nations, instituting the system of the M., speaks of "peoples not yet able to stand by themselves", whose "well being and development... form a sacred trust of civilization"; "tutelage of such peoples should be entrusted to advanced nations... as Mandatories on behalf of the League".

Three types of M. were created. The "B" and "C" M., with wider powers for the Mandatories, comprised the former German possessions in Africa and Oceania; the "A" M. included Palestine with Transjordan, Mesopotamia (Iraq), and Syria and Lebanon. The Mandatory powers were to give administrative assistance and advice and — in the case of Iraq and Syrian-Lebanon — to "facilitate the progressive development" of these territories "as independent states"; constitutions were to be drawn up within three years. The Mandatories were to submit annual reports to the Permanent M. Commission of the League of Nations.

The distribution of the M. was decided at the *San Remo Conference of the principal allies, Apr. 1920, and finalized by the League of Nations Council on 24 July 1922 (except for Iraq). The M. for Palestine, conferred upon Great Britain, recognized the "historical connection of the Jewish people with Palestine" and obliged the Mandatory to assist in the establishment of a Jewish National Home. Under Art. 25 of the Palestine Mandate, added in Aug. 1921, the Mandatory was entitled, with the consent of the League Council, to "postpone or withhold application of such provisions... as he may consider inapplicable" (meaning those concerning the Jewish National Home) from "the territories lying between the Jordan and the eastern boundary of Palestine as ultimately determined". In Sept. 1922, Britain requested, and obtained, the consent of the Council to make the Jewish National Home provisions inapplicable to Transjordan and to create there, under the Mandate, a (separate, semi-independent) administration. The Palestine M. did not include a clause concerning independence and a constitution, but the Mandatory was made "responsible for the development of self-governing institutions, and also for safeguarding the civil and religious rights of all the inhabitants of Palestine, irrespective of race and religion". For the history of the Palestine Mandate and its termination in 1948, see *Arab-Israel Conflict.

The M. over Transjordan was terminated in Mar. 1946, when Britain recognized Transjordan's independence and signed a treaty of alliance with her. Full international recognition of that independence by the admission of Transjordan to the UN was held up by a Soviet veto and took place only in Dec. 1955.

Iraq was also an "A" M. conferred upon Britain. But, first, the territory concerned was not finally defined in 1922 with the establishment of the M.: the fate of the *Mosul province, claimed by Turkey, was left open for further negotiations and arbitration by the League of Nations — though *de facto* it was already incorporated in Iraq. The province was finally awarded to Iraq in 1925–26. Secondly, as Iraq's nationalists opposed the imposition of any form of M. and demanded full independence, Britain and Iraq reached, after two years of struggle, a compromise in the shape of the Anglo-Iraqi Treaty of Alliance of Oct. 1922. This treaty in fact incorporated most of the provisions of the M., so that Britain could present it to the League of Nations as merely an instrument to implement the M., while telling the Iraqis that relations were governed by a freely agreed treaty and not by an imposed M. An Iraqi Constitution came into effect in 1925. The League of Nations watched Iraq's progress towards independence with some misgivings. It made the award of Mosul in 1925, conditional on the extension to 25 years of the Anglo-Iraqi treaty, i.e. a measure of British tutelage (complied with in a new treaty of Jan. 1926). And when Britain agreed, in the Anglo-Iraqi Treaty of June 1930, to terminate the M. and grant Iraq full independence, the League made its approval, and the admission of Iraq to the League, conditional a solemn declaration by Iraq on the protection of minorities (made in May 1932). In Oct. 1932 the M. was terminated and Iraq was admitted to the League of Nations, the first AC to attain that status.

The M. for Syria-Lebanon was granted to France. For its history; the draft treaties of 1936 envisaging its termination, but not ratified; the declaration of its termination in 1941; the crisis of 1943–46; and the M.'s termination by the admission of Syria and Lebanon to the UN in 1945 — see *Syria, *Lebanon.

The League of Nations' Permanent M. Commission was constituted in Feb. 1921. It studied the annual reports of the governments of the mandated territories and advised the League Council as to whether the provisions of each M. were strictly observed. It summoned governors and other high officials for questioning and accepted representation from inhabitants of the territories concerned. The Commission was often critical of the Palestine Mandatory administration, particularly in response to Jewish representations concerning the implementation of the clauses concerning the Jewish National Home. In 1930 it sent a commission to investigate Jewish and A. claims concerning the Wailing Wall. In 1937 it expressed a preference for the cantonization of Palestine rather than its partition as recommended by the Peel Report. In 1939 it declared the White Paper on Palestine then issued by the British to be contrary to the spirit of the M. For its misgivings over the termination of the M. for Iraq — see above.

With the decline of the League of Nations in the later 1930s, its supervision of the administration of the M. became much less effective; it lapsed entirely when the war broke out in 1939.

Maronites An Eastern Christian church centered in Lebanon, Catholic through a *Uniate. According to M. tradition, the Church was founded in the fifth century by a monk called Maron (Maroun) in the *Orontes River valley. It seems that in the seventh century the M. adhered to Monothelism — a doctrine that emphasized the One Will of Christ and was used by Emperor Heraclius of Byzantium in an effort to reconcile, in the schism between the *Monophysite and Orthodox churches concerning the divine-and-human nature of Christ, but turned into a schismatic doctrine of its own. The Monothelites-M. sought contact with the Catholic Church during the Crusades and eventually adhered to it through the Uniate, i.e., retaining a certain autonomy in the administration of the Church and the community, headed by a Patriarch, and in its liturgy, the language of which remained Syriac-Aramaic. There are different versions as to the date of the Uniate — from a first union in 1182–84, re-confirmed in 1438–45, to a definite, formal Uniate in 1736.

Since the 17th century the M. enjoyed a degree of special relations with, and protection by, France. They were concentrated mainly in the northern and central part of Mount Lebanon. Since the late 18th century they began moving southwards, into a region mostly inhabited, and dominated, by *Druzes. The close co-habitation of M.'s and Druze in Mount Lebanon soon led to trouble between M. tenant farmers and Druze landlords. The M. church began to agitate against the Druze, an agitation that was boosted by the conversion to the M. faith of the Druze Amirs of Mount Lebanon. Relations were further aggravated when the Egyptians occupied Lebanon in the 1830s and sided with the M.'s against the Druze. Serious clashes occurred in 1840–41, when the Egyptians withdrew, and again, culminating in a Druze massacre of Christians, in 1860.

These developments led to a growing intervention by the great powers. In 1861 they induced the Ottoman Sultan to establish an autonomous District of Mount Lebanon, in which Christians were about 80%, and M.'s more than 60%, of the population. In 1920, France created, under her *Mandate, a "Greater Lebanon", by joining to the previously autonomous Mount Lebanon the Muslim-majority regions of Beirut, the South, Tripoli and the North, and the *Biqā' in the East. The M. lost their majority, but remained the largest single community, c. 29% of the total population and c. 57% of the Christians, and they wielded a decisive influence in the new state and determined its character as a pluralistic society based on a communal structure — with the Christians, and particularly the M., as the strongest partner.

The M. were the staunchest defenders of "Greater Lebanon's" independence and territorial integrity — against demands to sever the Muslim areas added in 1920 and join them to Syria and Syrian schemes, always suspected, to annex all of Lebanon — and of the communal structure of her parliament and governance. Many of them also stressed Lebanon's predominantly Christian and non-A. character. They were, however, divided as to the methods and tactics of their struggle. One camp took a strong, assertive stance, which drove it to rely on "special relations" with France, and also predestined some of its leaders to favor friendly relations with the Jews of Palestine and later Israel. The other camp favored close cooperation with the Muslims inside Lebanon, a stronger emphasis on the A. character of the country and a larger measure of integration in all-A. political structures. For the function of this issue in Lebanon's politics since the 1930s, the "National Pact" of 1943 that ensured Christian and M. predominance with a 6:5 Christian/non-Christian ratio in representation, and its breakdown in the 1970s — see *Lebanon. In 1936, the leader of the first camp, Emile *Edde, won the Presidency against Bishara al-*Khouri, leading the rival faction. Some Christian-assertive M. leaders created, in 1936, a para-military organization, the *Phalanges (al-Kata'ib), for the protection of the community (later, in the 1970s, a second, wider militia, the "Lebanese Forces", was added). Some more radical M. wanted to recreate a truly Christian Lebanon and advocated the cession of the Muslim-majority areas and the re-creation of a smaller, Christian-majority Lebanon.

The demographic basis for the predominance of the Christians, and particularly the M., had indeed become invalidated over the years. The distribution of representation and power, the 6-to-5 ratio in Parliament and the assumption that Christians were about 55%, and M. nearly 30%, of the population, were based on the census of 1932. There was no doubt that these figures no longer represented realities — but the Christian-M. leadership has, for obvious reasons, prevented a new official census. It is generally assumed that the share of the Christians has declined to 40–45% and that of the M. to 22–25%, with some setting it as low as 20% (while the Shi'is have become the largest community, perhaps 32% or even 35–40%). (These figures do not take into account Lebanese emigrants, numbering an estimated 2.5–3m. or even more, especially in the Americas, among whom the M. are a majority; it has always been in dispute whether those emigrants retaining their Lebanese citizenship should be reckoned in the calculations of Lebanon's communal structure.)

Efforts to end the civil war and devise a political solution are based on three alternative schemes: a) The retention of the communal structure, with the 6:5 ratio replaced by a 50:50 ratio (with the M. retaining the Presidency — perhaps with a reduction of powers). This formula has been advocated, since 1976, by Syria — at least for the immediate future, until a non-communal democracy can be agreed upon. It is accepted by many M.; in fact, it was proposed in 1976, with Syrian backing, by the then President, the M. Suleiman *Franjiyeh. b) The abolition of communal representation altogether and the establishment of a non-communal, one-man-one-vote democracy — now, or after a period of transition during which the powers of the M. President and his community would be much reduced. This is propounded mainly by the Shi'i and Druze leaders; few M. would accept it. This last scheme was the ultimate target of an agreement between the three main militias in Dec. 1985; but when the commander of the mainly M. "Lebanese Forces" accepted and co-sponsored it, he was ousted and disavowed. c) The division of Lebanon into cantons, each dominated by one of the communities. *De facto*, such a division has already taken place in large measure, with a Christian-M. "canton" virtually autonomous in northern and central Mount Lebanon, a Druze one in the Shuf, southern Mount Lebanon, and the Shi'is striving for one in South Lebanon (and perhaps in the Biqā'). Muslim and Druze leaders do not tend to consider such a cantonization as a solution to be formally institutionalized. Among the M., however, a growing body of opinion seems to favor it.

The M. are deeply divided concerning their political conceptions and leadership. As the old division between assertive-Christian, pro-French (Edde) vs. A.-integrationist (Khouri) gradually faded away, the problem of how to preserve the survival of the M. and their primacy has persisted — and has become more critical with the demographic decline of the community and the offensive of the Shi'is and Druze since the 1970s. Marginal, radical groups, dissatisfied with the established leadership, seek new solutions as described; thus, the "Guardians of the Cedars" organization led by Etienne Saqr (Abu Arz); the M. Monks Association under Boulos Nu'man is also activist and radical. The top leadership has been held, since the late 1970s and particularly since the Israeli occupation of 1982–83, by the Phalanges under Pierre, Bashir and Amin *Jumayyil successively, who nearly liquidated rival factions (such as Camille *Chamoun's "National Liberals") or integrated them forcibly in the Phalanges and their "Lebanese Forces". But that leadership is hotly contested, and, moreover, there is a near-constant struggle, sometimes erupting in bloody battles, between rival factions within the Phalanges and the Lebanese Forces. Rival clans — such as Chamoun in the Deir al-Qamr region of the Shuf, Southern Mount Lebanon, or the bitterly anti-Phalange, pro-Syrian *Franjiyyeh in the Zagharta region of northern Mount Lebanon — rule their traditional fiefs. And the M. Patriarch, who in the past held the community together and wielded considerable political influence — particularly Elias Howeik (Huwayyik), until 1932; Antoun 'Arida, 1932–55; Boulos Ma'ouchi, 1955–75 — seems to have lost much of his influence.

al-Masri, 'Aziz 'Ali (1878–1965) Egyptian officer and politician. Born in Cairo into an Arab-Circassian family, M. studied at the Military Academy in Istanbul and from 1901 served in the Ottoman Army. He was a member of the Young Turks' "Committee for Unity and Progress". After the Young Turks' revolution, 1908, his hopes for A. independence or autonomy within the Ottoman Empire and a joint Turkish-A. kingdom were disappointed, and he joined A. nationalist activities. M. was a co-founder of the clandestine *al-Qahtaniyya* association (1909) and of *al-'Ahd*, a secret society of A. officers in the Ottoman Army (1913). He was arrested, tried and sentenced to death, but was released and permitted to leave for Egypt. Despite the rift between him and the Turks, he at first refused to join the British in World War I. But when the *"Arab Revolt" broke out in 1916, with independence envisaged in the correspondence between the British High Commissioner, *McMahon and Sharif *Hussein of Mecca, M. joined the Revolt as Chief-of-Staff of the Sharif's army. He resigned the same year — reportedly after he attempted in vain to mediate between the Sharif and the Turks.

In the 1920s and 1930s M. was sporadically active on the fringes of Egyptian politics, taking part in several associations that advocated an A. orientation and active Egyptian involvement in efforts for all-A. unity (an orientation that became dominant in Egypt only in the late 1930s). He was close to right-wing circles and in the 1930s fostered pro-Fascist, and particularly pro-German sympathies (he had always admired Germany and had tried before World War I to enlist her influence with Turkey in favor of A. autonomy within the Ottoman Empire). In 1939 he was appointed Chief-of-Staff of the Egyptian Army by Premier 'Ali *Maher, who was also considered pro-German; but as the British considered him hostile and suspected him of sabotaging Egypt's contribution to the war effort, they compelled the government to dismiss him in Feb. 1940. He thereupon deserted and tried to reach the "Axis" forces in the Western Desert. He was caught and put on trial in May 1941, together with several other officers (his protector 'Ali Maher had been dismissed in June 1940 and was under surveillance). The trial dragged on, bogged down in legal complexities, and M. was released early in 1942 by the new *Wafd* government, without a verdict.

M. had some links with the "Free Officers" preparing the *coup* of 1952 and, being regarded as a symbol of nationalism and resistance to the foreign occupation, had some influence on their thinking; some of the officers, such as Anwar *Sadat, had been party to his anti-British activities in 1939–40. In 1953 the new régime appointed him Ambassador to the USSR; but he retired after only one year in 1954.

Mauritania Muslim country in Northwest Africa, on the western fringes of the Sahara desert, and herself largely desert, bordering in the north on formerly Spanish *Sahara (*SADR — or Morocco, if Morocco's annexation of that territory is considered valid) and Algeria; in the east on Mali; in the south on Senegal; and in the west on the Atlantic Ocean. M. is not an A. country and the details of her history and politics are outside the scope of this Dictionary. But her population, mostly tribal — an estimated 1.75m. in the 1980s — is defined largely (70–80%) as "Moors", i.e. a mixture of *Berber, black African and some A. elements and considers itself A. or semi-A. (the remaining 20–30% are black Africans). In the absence of a national language beyond the various tribal tongues the Arabic language has long served as an auxiliary language or *lingua franca*, and since 1966 it has been proclaimed the national language and the main language of instruction. Since Nov. 1973, M. is a member-state of the *Arab League.

When M., formerly a French possession, became independent — in 1958 semi-independent within the French community, and in Nov. 1960 fully independent — the ASt, except for Tunisia, did not at first accept and recognize her, nor did many other countries, especially those of the "progressive", leftist camp. They considered her an artificial creation of French colonialism. Moreover, Morocco claimed the whole of M. as part of her territory, taken from her by France; and the ASt, except for Tunisia, supported that claim — though their support was rather half-hearted and verbal only. M.'s request for admission to the UN was blocked by a Soviet veto, while A. and Third World proposals to submit her independence to a plebiscite or negotiations obtained no majority. In 1961, the Soviet veto was withdrawn and M. was admitted to the UN, with 10 ASt (of the 13 then UN members) voting against and many Third World countries abstaining. However, during the 1960s the ASt accepted M.'s independence and established relations with her, and even Morocco gradually relented — with some French mediation — and in Jan. 1970 recognized M. and established relations with her. Relations have remained cool, the more so as they were disturbed by conflicting positions on the West *Sahara dispute. M. also frequently suspects Moroccan intrigues and interference in her internal factional struggles and upheavals. Official relations were in the 1980s twice severed, and later resumed.

The fate of Spain's West Saharan territories involved M. in a protracted dispute. A gradual handing-over by Spain to the local population, with the prospect of eventual independence, had been discussed and called for by UN books. But in Nov. 1975 Spain agreed with M. and Morocco that she would hand over the territory to them; she did in Feb. 1976. In Apr. 1976 Morocco and M. agreed to divide the territory; Morocco also agreed to let M. have a share in the territory's phosphate mines, its main resource, located in Morocco's part. Morocco immediately annexed her part of Western Sahara; M. did not. Demands for independence crystallized in 1975 in a guerrilla organization, *"POLISARIO", and led in Feb. 1976 to the proclamation of a "Saharan Arab Democratic Republic" ("SADR"). While Morocco was prepared to fight POLISARIO and its Republic (and clash with Algeria which supported and aided it), M. was neither able nor willing to do the same. In Aug. 1979 M. renounced, in agreement with POLISARIO, her part in the territory. Morocco immediately annexed that part, too. M.'s abrogation of her agreement with Morocco in accord with POLISARIO was bitterly resented in Morocco and further troubled the relations between the two countries. In Feb. 1984 M. recognized SADR.

M. considered herself part of the Arab *Maghrib and whatever arrangements would eventually be agreed for Maghribi union or co-ordination, but her troubled relations with Morocco cast a heavy shadow over such aspirations. As Maghribi union was in any case not an immediate prospect, this was perhaps no acute present-day policy problem for M.; but balancing between Morocco and Algeria, to which M. was naturally drawn by the state of her relations with Morocco and over the West Sahara problem, was a cardinal issue in her foreign policy. In Dec. 1983 M. adhered to an Algerian-Tunisian Treaty of Friendship and Cooperation of Mar. 1983 — a treaty with an apparent anti-Moroccan edge.

McMahon-Hussein Correspondence Ten letters exchanged between 14 July 1915 and 30 Mar. 1916 by Sharif *Hussein ibn 'Ali of Mecca and Sir Henry McMahon (1862–1949), the British High Commissioner in Egypt, 1914–16. The letters discussed the terms under which the Sharif would ally himself with Britain in World War I and revolt against Turkish rule. H. asked Britain to recognize, and assure, the independence of the AC — meaning all of the Arabian peninsula except 'Aden, and the whole *Fertile Crescent — after the war, and to support the re-establishment of an A. *Caliphate. Britain accepted these principles, but could not agree with H.'s definition of the area claimed. In his second note, of 24 Oct. 1915, McM. excluded certain areas: "The districts of Mersin and Alexandretta and portions of Syria lying to the west of the districts of Damascus, Homs, Hama and Aleppo, cannot be said to be purely A., and must on that account be excepted from the proposed delimitation." The interpretation of that sentence later gave rise to a long argument between Britain and the A.'s as to whether Palestine was part of the area excluded (as it was west of the province of Damascus, which covered all of Transjordan, but not geographically west of the four towns mentioned). Britain always maintained that she had never intended to include Palestine in the area of A. independence — as confirmed by McM. himself in a letter to the Colonial Office of 12 Mar. 1922; but several British spokesmen admitted that the wording was not clear, and so did the Government when publishing the hitherto secret correspondence, in 1939 (". . . the language in which this exclusion was expressed was not so specific and unmistakable as it was thought to be at the time"). The A.'s claimed that Palestine was included in the area they considered promised to them and that both the *Sykes-Picot Agreement of 1916 and the *Balfour Declaration of 1917 contradicted McM.'s promises to H. and revealed Britain's bad faith. McM. also claimed a special position for Britain in the provinces of Baghdad and Basra, and H. implicitly accepted that claim. As to the coastal lands of western Syria, and Lebanon, H. did not accept their being granted to France and indicated that he would claim them after the war. The degree of great power (British and French) tutelage envisaged was also left rather vague and later generated much controversy.

No complete agreement was reached in the McM-HC and it does not constitute a formal treaty or a firm commitment. But an Anglo-A. alliance was established, and the *"Arab Revolt" started in 1916, on the assumption that Britain would generally support A. independence. The Sykes-Picot Agreement and the post-war settlement were regarded by A. leaders, beyond the Palestine question and specific territorial claims, as a betrayal, because they substituted zones of imperial influence and tutelage, or even direct imperial control, for the full independence which, the A.'s insisted, had been promised.

Melilla Spanish town in northern Morocco, on the southern coast of the Mediterranean. See under *Ceuta.

Messali Hajj, Ahmad (1898–1974) The most prominent leader of Algerian nationalism from the late 1920s to the early 1950s. Born in Tlemcen into a working class family, M. served with the French army in World War I and stayed in France after the war, marrying a Frenchwoman. He became an Algerian nationalist, rejecting the conception then prevailing of Algeria's integration in France. In 1924–25 he co-founded an organization called *L'Étoile Nord-Africaine*, which was at first linked to the Communists. M. himself was reportedly for some time a member of the Communist Party; he later severed these links and increasingly adopted Islamic tendencies, also maintaining ties with Fascist and extreme right wing groups. *L'Étoile* was banned in 1929 and M. was arrested. The organization was re-formed in 1933 but was soon outlawed again and M. was rearrested. In 1936–37 he founded the *Parti du Peuple Algérien* (PPA), which soon had to go underground. M. was rearrested in 1939 and sentenced in 1941 to 16 years in prison. He was released in 1943, after the Allied landing in North Africa, but was exiled into forced residence. In 1946 M. founded a new party, the *Mouvement pour le Triomphe des Libertés Dé-*

mocratiques (MTLD), advocating full independence for Algeria; the MTLD merged later with what remained of the PPA. In the early 1950s it sponsored a new *Mouvement National Algérien*, MNA, seen by some as a new party replacing the MTLD and by some as the military arm of the MTLD. M. himself, in and out of prison, was again imprisoned in 1952 (he reportedly spent thirty years of his life in prison). From the late 1940s he was increasingly out of touch with a younger generation of nationalist leaders (*Ben Bella, Belkacem Krim, Hussein Ait-Ahmad, Muhammad Khidr), who went underground and set up a "Special (or Secret) Organization" for armed struggle — against M.'s wishes or without his knowledge, though M. was still respected as the grand old man of Algerian nationalism. When that *Organisation Spéciale* set up a *Conseil Révolutionnaire pour l'Unité et l'Action* (CRUA) in 1953, and a *Front de Libération Nationale* (*FLN) in 1954, and launched an armed revolt on 1 Nov. 1954, the break was complete. M. denounced the revolt and the new leaders, and was denounced by them. Since the 1950s he was completely alienated from what had become the mainstream of Algerian nationalism. Though still imprisoned as a nationalist, he had no part in the final struggle, in the negotiations of 1961–62 that led to Algeria's independence, or in the establishment of the new state. Released in 1962, he stayed in France as an exile. Though he had feeble links with attempts to organize groups in opposition to the Algerian régime, mainly in France, he played no major role in them and died after a decade of isolation and alienation, a relic of earlier times.

Middle East The area east of Europe and the Mediterranean and south of Russia and Central Asia. The term came into use around the turn of the century, to designate the western approaches to India-Afghanistan, Persia and the Persian Gulf. It has acquired a wider meaning since World War I and mainly since World War II ("ME Forces"; "ME Command"; "ME Supply Center"). Previously, the term Near East was more usual. Some have tried to distinguish between the Near East — meaning Turkey, the Levant, Egypt, the Arabian peninsula and sometimes also Cyprus and Greece — and the ME, meaning Iraq, Iran and the Persian Gulf. But this distinction has not been generally accepted.

No precise definition of the term ME has ever been generally accepted. Turkey, Israel, the AC in Asia, Egypt and Iran are included by all; Cyprus, Sudan and Libya by many; Afghanistan, and sometimes Pakistan, by some; A. North-West Africa, the *Maghrib (Tunisia, Algeria, Morocco, sometimes also Libya), are usually not included in the term ME.

Racially, most of the peoples of the ME belong to mixed Mediterranean sub-groups of the white, Caucasian or Europiform race, except for southern Sudan, populated by black Africans; negroid admixtures are decreasingly noticeable northwards, in Sudan, Egypt and the Levant. Small groups in northern Sudan and southern Egypt are classified as Erythriot or Hamitic (*Nubians).

Linguistically and ethnically, roughly one-half of the nearly 200m. population of the ME (including Sudan and Libya) are A., whose tongue belongs to the Semitic group of languages. The other half are Iranian (linguistically Indo-European or Aryan) in the northeast, Turkish in the northwest, Hebrew-speaking Jews in Israel. In the AC there are some non-A. *minorities — *Kurds (whose language is Iranian) in Iraq and Syria; *Armenians in most countries of the *Fertile Crescent and Egypt, mostly in Syria and Lebanon; and speakers of Nilotic and Hamitic tongues among the tribes of Sudan.

Religiously, most of the ME population practise *Islam — most of them in its *Sunni version, those of Iran and a small majority of those in Iraq, Bahrain, Dubai and Yemen in *Shi'i versions. Most ME countries have *Christian communities (formerly a majority in Lebanon, now c. 45%). In Israel the majority is Jewish. Various small non-Islamic communities or heterodox groups on the fringes of Islam (*Druze, *'Alawis), and animist traditions in southern Sudan, add to the ME's diversity.

The whole ME was united in one political framework only once in history — in the Persian empire of the sixth to fourth centuries BC and the reign of Alexander the Great which briefly followed it; the Arabian peninsula and southern Egypt and Sudan were not included even then. The A.-Islamic empire of the seventh and eight centuries CE embraced most of the ME but left out Anatolia (later to become Turkey) and Sudan. The Ottoman Empire, from the 16th century to 1918, ruled most of the ME but did not include Iran and Sudan.

No modern political movement aimed at uniting the ME in one political entity — the *Pan-Islamic one aspired to a much larger area and had no clearly defined political aims; the *Pan-Arab movement addressed itself to the ME's A. parts only — and if it had plans for the foundation of one political unit, such plans were not effective; the aims of the *Arab League are even more restricted. The Western powers, particularly the USA and Britain, often toyed with the idea of establishing a ME Pact or Defense Treaty, but their plans affected only parts of the ME and in any case never came to fruition (see *ME Defense Organization, *Baghdad Pact). The UN and its specialized agencies, such as the World Health Organization (WHO), sometimes attempted to set up regional institutions for the ME, but these attempts were foiled by the refusal of the ASt to co-operate with Israel in a regional entity. Turkey has always preferred to be aligned with Europe rather than the ME.

Middle East Defense Organization, Treaty
With the emergence of the ASt into full independence after World War II and the withdrawal of the Western powers from military bases and positions of privilege, Western policy planners suggested a multilateral defense pact, or command, for the ME states, to be linked to and guided by the West. These plans were clearly directed against military and political penetration of the region by the USSR, and they were stepped up with the intensification of the Cold War. It was also hoped that such multilateral arrangements would solve bilateral problems that had proven insoluble — e.g., the future of British military bases and privileges in Egypt and Iraq.

Britain and the USA were the most active in the search for such a MEDO, while Turkey and for some time France associated themselves with their efforts. In Oct. 1951 Britain, the US, France and Turkey presented to Egypt a plan for a MEDO, also termed Supreme Allied Command for the ME (SACME), and invited Egypt to join as an original signatory. Other states in the region were kept informed, on the understanding that they could later adhere to the treaty. Egypt rejected the concept outright, as she had no wish to join a Western alliance and did not see Soviet policies as a threat. She did not change her position when the plan was re-submitted in Nov. 1951 in a revised version thought more palatable to her. Other ME states were not receptive either and negotiations were suspended.

Overtures were renewed in 1954–55, with the US Secretaty of State, John Foster Dulles, as the prime mover and with added emphasis on the creation of a "Northern Tier" (Turkey-Iran-Pakistan) as the first and main line of defense. This time, Iraq was persuaded to join and the Baghdad Pact was concluded. But this Pact did not turn into a true MEDO and it harmed the ASts' relations with the West — see *Baghdad Pact.

When the USA in the late 1970s again felt the need to provide for a concerted defense of the ME, and particularly the oil-producing region of the Persian Gulf and oil shipping routes, she no longer envisaged a fully fledged MEDO, but a direct American responsibility by means of a US "Rapid Deployment Force". For such a force, the US needed local facilities, especially air and sea landing rights and a possibility to stockpile equipment. But she renounced tentative plans to rally ME countries prepared to grant such facilities in a multilateral accord and to ask of then a more active participation or even a public commitment (which, for instance, the Persian Gulf principalities were reluctant to make, though they were interested to have the US defend the Gulf shipping lanes). Instead, the US contented herself with low-profile bilateral agreements on "facilities". Such agreements were concluded with 'Oman, Egypt, Somalia and Kenya in 1980.

All these MEDO plans were devised and initiated by the great powers. The ME countries themselves did not initiate similar schemes — unless we consider the *Arab League's "Collective Security Pact" ("Treaty of Joint Defense and Economic Cooperation") of 1950, as a MEDO. But that Pact was not a full-fledged MEDO since it embraced only the member-states of the League (seven at the time of its inception; the new member-states later joined the Pact). Moreover, the Pact added but little to the commitments and obligations already contained in the League Covenant; and the factors limiting the operations and the efficacy of the League applied to the Security Pact as well. In any case, though the League member-states gave each other military succour on several occasions (Kuwait, 1961; against Israel), the Security Pact did not develop into an active, effective military or defense organization. Nor can the military pacts concluded by Nasser's Egypt in 1954–55 be described as a MEDO: they included only certain ASt (Syria, Saʻudi Arabia, Jordan) and were intended to create an Egyptian-led alliance or bloc, with an edge against other ME and ASt (Iraq, Turkey).

military bases, foreign See *bases.
military coups, juntas See *army officers in politics.
military forces See *armed forces.
Millet System The Turkish term M., derived from the Arabic *Milla*, meant a (religious) community. The MS was the institutionalization in the Ottoman Empire of the Islamic principle and practice that granted the Christian and Jewish communities the right to establish their own ecclesiastic and communal organization with wide autonomy in matters of personal status, community affairs and education. The community leaders, endowed with jurisdiction in such matters over the members of their community, were held responsible for the maintenance of order within their community and the payment of the *jizya*, the poll tax, and other taxes imposed on non-Muslims. Until the 19th century there were only three recognized M.'s: the *Greek-Orthodox, the *Armenian (Gregorian), and the Jewish. Subsequently, separate M. status was given to various other denominations and sects (such as the *Greek-Catholic and other Uniate communities — but not the Protestants), until by 1914 the number of M.'s in the Ottoman Empire had risen to 14.

The MS perpetuated religious-communal divisions, and as these sometimes coincided with, or developed into, ethnic divisions (e.g., the Armenians, or Christian communities in the Balkans), it promoted the rise of nationalism among the non-Muslims of the Empire — and also encouraged foreign intervention on their behalf. Consequently, the Ottoman government sought, in the 19th century, to limit or undermine the MS, for the sake of the integrity and independence of the Empire. One method was the introduction of M. constitutions in the 1860s that sought to increase lay participation in the affairs of the community. Yet, under foreign pressure and the M.'s' own insistence on self-preservation, the MS was maintained until the end of the Ottoman Empire in 1918.

The successor governments did not formally use the term MS, but in fact the autonomy and jurisdiction of the religious communities and their ecclesiastic courts in matters of personal status and in religious affairs was maintained both by the British and French *Mandate administrations and, to a certain degree and subject to reforms and increasing state intervention, by the emerging independent ASt.

minorities The primary social and political framework of loyalty and allegiance in the AC and the whole ME was, for many centuries, the communal-religious group. This has been largely replaced, since the late 19th century, by the "nation"; but communal-religious entities and allegiances, quasi-national in many cases, still play a very important role.

In the ASt as a whole, the dominating majority is A. in language and ethnicity, Muslim-Sunni in religion. Exceptions as to the majority status of the Muslim-Sunni community are Lebanon (where no single community constitutes a majority and all Christian groups together, nearly 55% of the population in the past, still are 40–45%); Iraq (where the majority is Shiʻi-Muslim — but the Sunni-Muslim minority is in fact the ruling group); Yemen (almost evenly divided between *Zeidi Shiʻis and *Shafeʻi Sunnis, with a slight majority for the former); ʻOman (where the Muslim-*Ibadi majority is not usually counted as Sunni); and Dubai and Bahrain (whose indigenous population, not counting foreign workers, is about evenly divided between Sunnis and Shiʻis, with a slight Shiʻi majority). However, despite these partial exceptions, the dominant mainstream in the population of the ASt undoubtedly is A. in its national identity, Muslim-Sunni in its religious one. "M." are therefore all groups differing from that majority in either their linguistic-ethnic or their religious character.

Some M. groups in the ASt differ from the dominant mainstream both ethnically-linguistically and religiously: the black African tribes of southern Sudan; *Armenians; *Greeks; Persians in Iraq (if Shiʻi Islam is considered a M. religion); Kurdish-speaking *Yazidis and Shabak in Iraq; permanently resident non-Muslim foreigners; *Jews (who, though speaking Arabic, form a distinct ethnic entity). Except for South Sudan's African tribes, and the Armenian communities in

Syria and Lebanon, these are all small groups. Border-line cases consist of a few ancient communities, mostly Christian, who preserve some measure of almost-national group consciousness that goes beyond the religious-communal: Nestorian-*Assyrians and Syrian *Jacobites in Iraq and Syria, *Sabaeans-Mandaeans in Iraq, *Maronites in Lebanon (all with Syriac-Aramaic dialects as their ancient tongue — surviving in most cases only as the language of liturgy); and Egypt's *Copts (preserving remnants of ancient Egyptian). Of these, too, only the Maronites and the Copts are significantly large population groups.

M. groups differing in religion only are the Christian communities of the AC. The degree to which they regard themselves as separate, quasi-national entities or unreservedly as part of the majority nation varies — with the strongest consciousness of "national" distinction in the border-line groups mentioned, a greater solidarity with A. majority nationalism in the *Greek-Catholic, and the greatest in the *Greek-Orthodox communities. To the same category of differing in religion, but not in linguistic-ethnic nationality belong the Shi'i Muslims in most AC (for the special cases of Iraq, Yemen and Bahrain see above) and the heretic communities on the fringes of Islam — *Isma'iliyya, *'Alawis, *Druzes in Syria and Lebanon.

Differing in their ethnic-linguistic nationality only, while belonging to the Muslim-Sunni mainstream in their religion, are the *Kurds in Iraq and Syria, and some Turks and Turcoman tribes in Iraq and Syria. The *Berbers of the *Maghrib also belong to this category — to the degree that their ethnic-linguistic distinctiveness survives. So do the remnants of several ancient peoples in Sudan (Beja, *Nubians, *Nuba), who are Muslims but non-A.

Arabic-speaking or ethnically A. M.'s outside the ASt's are found — not counting A. migrants in Western countries (especially France, the Americas, West Africa, and to a lesser degree East Africa) — in the southern border regions of Turkey and the *Alexandretta-Hatay District; in south-western Iran (*Khuzistan-"Arabistan"); in some countries of Northwest Africa bordering on the A. *Maghrib (Chad, Niger, Mali) and the three semi-A. African countries that have joined the Arab League: *Mauritania, *Somalia and *Djibouti; and in Israel (where they form over 17% of the population — not counting the *Israel-occupied territories — with the percentage growing; see *Israel Arabs).

M.'s make up a considerable part of the population, and therefore pose a political problem, actual or potential, in the following AC: Lebanon — where no single community constitutes a majority, all Christian communities together form 40–45%, Muslim Sunnis c. 20%, Muslim Shi'is 30–35%, Druzes 8%; Syria (non-A. in their original language, though largely Arabicized by now — 8–10%; non-Muslim — c. 15%; non-Sunni Muslim or on the fringes of Islam — c. 15%); Iraq (A. Shi'i Muslims — c. 55%, A. Sunni Muslims — c. 20%, non-A. Sunni Muslim Kurds — c. 15%, non-A. Shi'i Muslim Iranians — c. 2%, non-A. Turcomans, Shi'i and Sunni, c. 3%, non-Muslims — c. 4%); Yemen (more than 50% Shi'i Zeidis, nearly 50% Sunni Shafe'is); Bahrain and Dubai (over 50% Shi'is, nearly 50% Sunnis); Sudan (25–30% non-A. non-Muslims, constituting almost the total population of the three southern provinces); the surviving distinctiveness of the Berbers, 30–50% in Algeria and Morocco, is in doubt.

All M.'s wish to enjoy equal rights and yet to preserve their distinctive character, whether ethnic-linguistic or religious-communal. In the past, under foreign rule, some of them were given a degree of local autonomy, such as the Syrian Druzes and 'Alawites under the French Mandate (when the French were accused of encouraging Druze and 'Alawi separatism and using it against the Syrian-A. nationalist struggle for independence); independent nationalist Syria abolished that autonomy. The Kurds of northern Iraq were supposed to receive some autonomy when the *League of Nations decided in 1925–26 to award the Mosul province to Iraq; the promise was not implemented by either the British administration or post-1932 independent Iraq. Southern Sudan with its African tribal population was deemed by the British-Sudanese administration not ready for full-fledged autonomy, but it was kept separate as a closed, protected area; independent Sudan abolished these precautions and tried to extend her administration to the South. The architects of modern Lebanon, before and after her independence, sought to protect the various M. communities by building a system of government based on a predetermined representation of the communities and an agreed distribution of power among them.

Some of the M. communities struggled for a greater measure of autonomy. The Assyrians in Iraq failed. The Kurds rebelled for decades; since 1974 Iraq has granted them a degree of local autonomy, but as they are not content with that very partial autonomy and accuse Iraq of breaking agreements and promises in that respect, a rebellion continues (see *Kurds for details). The African tribes of South Sudan rebelled from 1962–63 and eventually obtained in 1972 an agreement on a far-reaching autonomy; as the agreement was broken, they resumed their rebellion in 1983. Berber resentment and complaints create a measure of tension, and sometimes clashes, in Algeria (where Berbers were in the forefront of the nationalist struggle against France), but a clear-cut, organized movement for Berber rights and aspirations has not crystallized either in Algeria or in Morocco.

Most M.'s rely on the national state dominated by the majority and hope that their distinctive character will be preserved under its rule — a hope that is unlikely to be fulfilled in the long run, in view of the centralistic, equalizing, sometimes totalitarian tendencies prevalent in modern nationalism.

Minority groups will no doubt continue to exist, but the scope of their distinctiveness will contract and they will have to conform to the national stance and character of their respective state as shaped by the dominant majority. The exception, M.'s with realistic hopes for true autonomy and a fuller preservation of their identity, seems to be the Kurds in Iraq and the Africans in southern Sudan, as well as the main communities of Lebanon, where — despite the tragic tribulations of the last decade, or even in the wake of these tribulations — the main groups are eking out, *de facto* if not openly proclaimed, semi-autonomous regions or "cantons", each controlled by a dominant community.

MINORITIES[1]

Country	Differing ethnically and in religion (non-A. and non-Sunni-Muslim)	Differing in religion only (A., but non-Sunni-Muslim)	Differing ethnically only (Sunni-Muslim but non-A.)
Egypt	Armenians, Greeks, Jews	Copts[2] and other Christians	
Syria	Armenians, Jews	Christians[2], 'Alawis, Druzes, Isma'iliyya	Kurds, Turcomans
Lebanon[3]	Armenians, Jews	Christians[2], Shi'is Druzes, 'Alawites	
Iraq[4]	Armenians, Jews, Iranians Shi'is[4], Sabaeans[2], Yazidis, Shabak, Assyrians[2]	Shi'is[4], Christians	Kurds, Turcomans
Yemen[5]	Jews	Zeidi Shi'is[5]	
Sudan	Black Africans	Christians	Remnants of ancient non-A. peoples
Algeria	Jews	Christians	Berbers
Tunisia and Morocco	Jews	Christians	Berbers

[1] Taking Arab Sunni Muslims as the majority community, as holds true for the A. world as a whole and for most AC individually (except Lebanon, Iraq, Yemen, Bahrain, Dubai, 'Oman). As ethnic-communal identities are a complex matter, this table is a schematic one.
[2] Some Christian communities, and the Sabaeans, may be considered borderline cases, as their religious distinctiveness amounts to a near-ethnic one.
[3] No single community constitutes a majority in Lebanon.
[4] Iraq is treated in this table as ruled by the A. Sunni Muslims; but A. Shi'i Muslims are a slight majority.
[5] The Shi'i-Zeidi Muslims are a minority only in terms of the A. world; in Yemen they are a slight majority and the main rulers.

Mirghani, Mirghaniyya An Islamic politico-religious order in Sudan, named after its founder, Muhammad al-Amir Ghani (al-Mirghani) (1793–1853), generally and mainly called *al-*Khatmiyya*. The M. rivalled the **Mahdiyya* order — though both stood for a revival and purification of orthodox Islam (and both used, although not belonging to *Sufi* Islamic mysticism and its *Dervish orders, some Dervish rituals, customs and organizational methods). Unlike the *Mahdiyya*, which advocated the overthrow of existing régimes that had deviated from pure Islamic traditions, the M. recommended co-operation with the régime. Generally, the M.-*Khatmiyya* appeared, despite its basic fundamentalism, as more moderate than both the *Mahdiyya* and militant Muslim organizations like the *Muslim Brotherhood. Similar to the *Mahdiyya*, though not as publicly and vigorously as the latter, it objected to the imposition, in 1983, of the harsh *Shari'a code of punishments.

The M.-*Khatmiyya* has always been considered pro-Egyptian. In the years of the struggle between the advocates of separate independence and those of union with Egypt, it supported the pro-Egyptian *al-Ashiqqa'* party, from 1952 the "National Unionist Party"; from 1956 it backed the "People's Democratic Party", and since 1967 the "Democratic Union Party" (DUP) issuing from the merger of the two latter groups. The order also accommodated itself more readily than the *Mahdiyya* to Sudan's revolutionary régimes — that of *'Abbud, 1958–64, and that of *Numeiri, 1969–85. Its basic orientation has not changed, and it continues advocating close co-operation with Egypt, resisting Libyan blandishments more firmly than the *Mahdiyya*. It has maintained its involvement in politics, though low-profile, through the DUP.

The leadership of the M.-*Khatmiyya* order has always been held by the descendants of its founder. The leaders during this century were al-Sayyid 'Ali al-M. (1870–1968) and his son, al-Sayyid Muhammad 'Uthman al-M. (b. c.1942?), since 1968. The leaders of the order refrained in general from directly taking part in political affairs and party organizations — though their support for the "National Unionists" and later the DUP was well known. In May 1986 Ahmad al-M., the younger brother of the M. head, was elected chairman of the new Supreme Council of Sudan, i.e., Head-of-State (with little actual power).

missions, missionaries The propagation of the Christian faith through M. activities in the AC and the ME has been directed at proselytizing adherents of the Eastern Christian churches no less than Muslims and Jews. The conversion of Muslims was indeed difficult, nearly impossible, as it was illegal under Islamic law and a Muslim converting to another faith was considered an apostate and subject to harsh punishment — until the 19th century: the death penalty. Most converts made by Catholic and Protestant M.'s were therefore Eastern Christians. M.'s have also established many educational and charitable institutions open to members of all communities and not engaging in direct, immediate propagation of conversion.

Catholic religious orders have been engaged in M. activities in the ME since the Crusades, assisted since the 17th century by a Vatican Congregation for the Propagation of the Faith, and have built hundreds of educational and charitable institutions. The "Latin" (in Western terms: Roman-Catholic) communities in the AC's, as distinct from *Uniate-Catholic ones, are mainly the result of such M. activities. By a papal decree of 1894, however, all proselytizing in the ME, where Uniate churches exist (i.e. not including Sudan and the *Maghrib*) has been entrusted to the Uniate churches exclusively.

Protestant and Anglican M. were active from the 18th, and mainly the 19th century, with the first American M. arriving in Syria in 1819. Presbyterians worked mainly in Syria and Lebanon, Congregationalists in Armenia, German and Swiss Lutherans in Palestine and Lebanon, Anglicans-Episcopalians in Palestine, Egypt, Sudan and Libya; Baptists, Methodists, Pentecostals joined later. As a result of this activity, Protestant communities, practically non-existent before, grew to c. 250,000 in the AC and Palestine. In 1927 a Near Eastern Christian Council was formed as a meeting ground for the Protestant M. societies; in 1958 it became a regional component of the World Council of Churches. From the 19th century, the Russian Orthodox Church also engaged in M. activities and established institutions of its own.

Prominent M.-established Catholic educational institutions are the University of St. Joseph in Beirut, founded in 1875 by the Jesuits; the Coptic-Catholic Seminary of Ma'adi in Egypt, also founded by the Jesuits; a Syro-Chaldean Seminary in Mosul, founded by the Dominicans; the Greek-Catholic seminary of St. Anne, established by the White Fathers in Jerusalem (transferred to Lebanon in 1967); the Dominican-founded École Biblique in Jerusalem; the University of Bethlehem — a college before, granted university status in 1973. The most important educational institutions established by Protestant M. are the American Universities of Beirut (founded 1866 as a college, a university since since 1920) and Cairo (1919). The Protestant-established institutions of the YMCA also became important social-educational centers. The various religious orders and congregations have also founded numerous hospitals and clinics which have greatly contributed to the development of public health in the region.

M.-established educational institutions have since the 19th century trained generations of a modern élite, an intelligentsia that became the growing ground of nationalism and its leaders; M.-founded printing shops were the birth-place of an Arabic press, pamphlets and modern books, and thus contributed to the same process. But later, most of the emerging independent, national ASt have tended to regard M. and their activities with a measure of suspicion and resentment, as an outgrowth of imperialism and foreign rule (added to the traditional Islamic condemnation of the conversion of Muslims). Even educational and charitable institutions established by M. have been suspected as means to attract converts by the material benefits offered. M. activities by foreigners (and most M. indeed were foreigners) have been banned or restricted by several ASt. Most ASt have also restricted the independence of M.-established educational institutions, compelled them to conform to national curricula and imposed a degree of supervision by the state educational authorities.

Islamic M. activity has always been directed only to countries outside the A. world and the ME, i.e. to countries not considered Islamic — e.g. in Africa, Asia and the West. But Islamic institutions in the ASt, such as, chiefly, the al-*Azhar University in Cairo, have served as M. centers and training grounds.

Mohieddin See *Muhyi-ul-Din.

Monophysites Christian churches that split from the main body of the Eastern (*Greek-Orthodox) Church following the Council of Chalcedon, 451. The schism concerned the nature of Christ, the M. holding that there is only one *(monos)* nature *(physis)* — divine — in the person of the Incarnate Christ, while the Orthodox believed that Christ has a double nature, divine and human. However, the schism was also political-national, as it expressed the traditional hostility of the provinces of Egypt and Syria to Byzantium and their unwillingness to accept orthodox doctrine as laid down by Byzantium. And indeed, the M. organized in four separate, "national" churches: the Ethiopian ("Orthodox") church, today c. 18.5m. (outside the scope of this Dictionary); the *Armenian ("Orthodox", or Gregorian) church — today 5–6m. (of whom c. 0.5m. in AC); the *Copts in Egypt, today more than 3m.; and the Syrian ("Orthodox", or *Jacobite) church, today 150–250,000 in the ME, about half of them in Syria, and 1–2m. in India. Since the 17th century (for the Armenians — earlier), parts of the four churches seceded to join the Catholic church through *"Uniates", while retaining a measure of autonomy ("Syrian-Catholics" etc.).

Montreux Convention

  1. An agreement of July 1936 concerning the Straits of the Bosphorus and the Dardanelles — outside the scope of this Dictionary.

  2. An agreement of May 1937 between Egypt and the twelve powers enjoying privileges of *"Capitulations", i.e., extra-territorial jurisdiction over their citizens. The MC provided for the abolition of the Capitulations after a twelve-year transition period, and was duly implemented. See *Capitulations.

Morocco (Arabic: al-Maghrib — the West). Kingdom on the northwestern corner of Africa, on both the Mediterranean and Atlantic shores, bordering on Algeria in the east and southeast, Mauritania and West Sahara (SADR) in the southwest. Area: 458,730 sq. km. (172,000 sq. mi.) — or 711,000 sq. km. (270,000 sq. mi.), if formerly Spanish Western *Sahara, annexed by M. is included. Population: 22–23m. (1983 estimate). Capital: Rabat (al-Ribat) — population 435,510 (1971), c. 840,000 with suburbs (1983 estimate). Most M'ns are Sunni Muslims and

Islam is the state religion. Some 65% are Arabic speaking, concentrated in towns and the lowlands, c. 35% are *Berbers inhabiting mainly the mountain regions. There are 70–100,000 mostly Roman Catholic Christians and some 20,000 Jews.

Since the 17th century M. has been under the rule of a Sharifian dynasty, the house of al-'Alawi (also al-Hassani or al-Filali). There were Spanish enclaves of different sizes on the Moroccan shores. France started to show interest in M. in the 19th century, especially after she occupied Algeria in 1830. From the late 19th century, and particularly from about 1900, France penetrated M. and increasingly gained control of large sectors of her economic and political life, mainly those in need of modernization and reforms. This control was generally imposed on M. in the form of agreements on guidance and expert advice. France also fully occupied certain areas of M. — beginning with oases on the M.-Algerian border, 1900–03, and later adding vital and central points: Casablanca and Oudjda 1907, Fez 1911. France accompanied that penetration by a series of agreements with other Western powers granting her a free hand in M.: with Italy 1900, Britain 1904, Spain 1904 (an agreement in which France had to grant Spain similar rights of penetration and control in a Spanish zone of interest in northern M. and in the far south), Germany 1909 and 1911 (as Germany herself had ambitions of penetrating M., these agreements with her were achieved only after sharp Franco-German crises in 1905 and 1911). In 1906, an international conference at Algeciras reaffirmed M.'s independence and equal economic opportunities for all powers in M., but endorsed the predominant position of France and Spain in their respective zones, and particularly their control of police and security matters.

On 30 March 1912, in the Treaty of Fez, the Sultan of M. accepted a French protectorate over his country. A French Resident-General became responsible for foreign affairs and defense and was empowered to introduce reforms. The Sultan remained formally responsible for internal affairs, but French influence in this sphere was also significant. Later the same year a Franco-Spanish Convention defined Spain's status and her zones of influence in southern M. and on the northern shore, and a special international status for *Tangier. The status of Spain's zones thus derived from France, the protecting power, and not from the Sultan of M.

As France's actual control of M. spread gradually over the country, both France and Spain faced stubborn resistance by local tribesmen in the Rif mountains in the north. The most important resistance leader, Muhammad 'Abd-ul-Karim (al-Khattabi), a tribal leader in the Spanish Rif, in 1921 declared himself Emir over an independent state, the "Republic of the Rif". The Spanish, and later the French too, tried both to lure and fight him. He was finally defeated by the French in May 1926 and exiled from M. (in 1947, while the ship transporting him from the island of Reunion to France passed the Suez Canal, he escaped and sought asylum in Egypt; he died in Cairo in 1963). By the mid-1930s the subjugation of M'n resistance was completed.

French policy in M. was shaped mainly by the first Resident-General, General L.G.H. Lyautey (1912–25). The Sultan himself had little power even in internal affairs. Most of the urban population and the modern economy were under direct French control, including transportation, industry, mines, modern agriculture by French settlers, taxation, finance, the judiciary, security and foreign affairs. Thus the Sultan's government, the *Makhzen*, controlled only restricted sectors of public life. Moreover, in the mountainous regions the French preferred decentralized, indirect rule, based on the traditional tribal chiefs, mostly Berber, whom the French supported, not intervening much in their activities and leaving the secluded small mountain villages in their primitive state. Agriculture and industry were actively developed in the modern sector, which greatly expanded between the World Wars. European immigration was encouraged, and the European population reached some 200,000 in the 1930s. Lyautey's support of Berber tribal leaders in time developed into a general policy of cultivating the Berbers against the Sultan and his government, and against A. nationalism.

The French introduced a limited system of representation, with most of the power and advantages reserved to French settlers. In 1919 a wholly French advisory council was established, and a few years later some M'ns were included. In 1926 the council was divided into four "collèges": three of them French (for agriculture, industry and commerce) and one indigenous M'n; French representatives were elected, M'ns — appointed.

During the 1930s a national movement began to grow, struggling both against the French and the authoritarian power of the Sultan. The French tried to suppress this movement and its leaders. In 1930 the French forced the Sultan to issue the "Berber *Dhahir*" (decree) which provided for the Berbers to be under the jurisdiction of their tribal chiefs and customary courts according to their own customs and traditions, and not under that of the Islamic *Shari'a courts. Both traditional-religious Muslim leaders and educated, urban nationalists strongly opposed the "Berber *Dhahir*", and their joint resistance paved the way to a common national movement. In 1934 a "Comité d'Action Marocaine" was set up and demanded a limitation of the powers of the Protectorate, and an extension of self-rule. When its demands, presented to both the French and the Sultan, were rejected, it organized demonstrations and clashes erupted. In 1937 the Committee was dissolved by the authorities only to take the form of several other organizations, which the French also dissolved. Among the important national leaders who emerged in this period was 'Allal al-Fassi. In 1937 all nationalist activity was forbidden. The nationalist leaders were arrested or exiled, but some were given refuge in Spanish M.

The national struggle was renewed during and following World War II, after the allied invasion of Nov. 1942. In 1943 the nationalists founded the *Istiqlal* (Independence) Party, headed by Ahmad Belafreij, with most of the other leaders in exile or under arrest. The *Istiqlal* soon became the main national party, though it was backed mainly by the urban intelligentsia. It demanded complete independence, with a constitutional government under the Sultan. Other nationalist groups in French and Spanish M. seemed to have smaller support. Sultan Muhammad V, ibn Yussuf, too, began in the later 1940s making veiled declarations of support for the national movement. His aim was also to assuage the nationalists' opposition to his authoritarian rule and focus their resistance against the French. France introduced gradual reforms in M. in 1946–47, but did not intend them to lead to M'n self-rule. These reforms provided for the establishment of elected local and provincial councils, a reorganization of the Sultan's government and closer cooperation between the Sultan's government and the French directors and advisers; they also envisaged economic development, the expansion and modernization of the education network, and the foundation of trade unions. The *Istiqlal* Party rejected these reforms as insufficient; the Sultan indicated that he took the same position and in late 1950 demanded radical changes in the French Protectorate. When the French dismissed eleven Moroccan elected members of the Council who had criticized the French administration and budget, the Sultan declared a personal protest strike and refused to sign any orders or laws. In early 1951 he had to end his strike, but the relations between him and the French had deteriorated. The national struggle now became more violent, marked by demonstrations, clashes and arrests. From 1951–52 the M. issue was brought before the UN several times, but no decisive result was reached.

In 1953 the tension between France and the Sultan came to a crisis. The Pasha of Marrakesh, Tihami al-Glawi, supported by numerous other district governors and tribal chiefs — all among the traditional Berber chiefs cultivated by the French against the modernized, urban nationalists — demanded the removal of the Sultan, claiming that his cooperation with the nationalist, secular modernists was a deviation from Islam, and the French took up the demand. On 20 Aug. 1953 Sultan Muhammad V agreed to go into exile and another member of the 'Alawi family, Muhammad ibn 'Arafa, became Sultan. The nationalists considered Ben 'Arafa a French puppet, and though Muhammad V had not been a leader of the national movement, his removal made him a symbol of nationalism, and the demand for his return to the throne became dominant among the nationalists. Their general demands also became more radical; they now refused to accept a gradual transition to independence or to take into consideration French economic and security interests, and stepped up the violence of their struggle.

French policy changed in 1954 when Pierre Mendès-France came into power with a socialist government and realized that the end of French rule was inevitable. At first it was decided and agreed that Muhammad ibn 'Arafa would abdicate, and Muhammad V would move from his exile in Madagascar to France, but would not return to the throne; instead, a regency council would be established, as well as a first representative government. On 1 Oct. 1955 Ben 'Arafa stepped down without formally abdicating and moved to Tangier, and a four member regency council was sworn in. But a few days later, Tihami al-Glawi changed his mind and demanded the return of Muhammad V to the throne — apparently because he sensed the political trend and decided to join it at the last moment rather than remain in the losing camp. Muhammad V returned to France in late Oct., on 5 Nov. he was recognized once more as the legitimate Sultan, and on 16 Nov. 1955 he returned to M. Early in Dec. the first representative Moroccan government was established, including members of the *Istiqlal* party, the Parti Démocratique pour l'Indépendence (PDI) headed by Muhammad Hassan al-Wazzani, and independents. The transition to independence was completed on 2 Mar. 1956 with a M'n-French agreement abrogating the 1912 Protectorate and a French recognition of M.'s independence. However, the agreement also spoke of French-M'n "interdependence" and cooperation in defense and foreign affairs, to be defined in new agreements, and granted France the right to keep military forces and bases in M. for a transitional period. On 7 Apr. 1956 a similar agreement was signed between M. and Spain, cancelling the latter's Protectorate in Spanish M.; but *Ceuta, *Melilla and the other small "Presidios" remained fully Spanish territory, and Ifni, the Spanish *Sahara and several small islands remained under Spanish authority. In Oct. 1956, an international conference agreed to the abolition of Tangier's special international status and its integration in M. (it became a free port in Jan. 1962).

On reaching independence M. lacked experience in governing. The Sultan's authority under the French had been limited and all foreign and most internal affairs had been handled by the French. M. had to develop her system of government and legislature, and their relation to the monarchy. The division between the urban modernist population and the rural conservative one continued to affect politics. The state also had difficulties in overcoming irregular military forces and there were several clashes with them during 1956–59. Each of the three political powers — the monarchy, urban modernist nationalists, and rural conservatives — tried to gain as much authority as possible. The two latter groups were not homogeneous (though the *Istiqlal* was seen as the major national party).

In autumn 1956 the Sultan appointed a 76-member Consultative Assembly including representatives of the parties, professional, social and religious organizations. This assembly did not have much of a say and ceased to exist in 1959. In July 1957 the Sultan proclaimed his son Hassan heir to the throne (previously the succession was not decided during the monarch's life, and any member of the 'Alawi house could succeed). In Aug. 1957 Sultan Muhammad assumed the title of King.

While the monarchy remained strong, division among the parties increased. In 1957 conservative rural elements, Berber-dominated, established the "Mouvement Populaire" (MP) headed by Mahjoub Ahardan (and reportedly supported by the King). In 1958–59 a left-wing faction split from the *Istiqlal* and founded the "Union Nationale des Forces Populaires" (UNFP) headed by Mehdi Ben Barka and 'Abd-ul-Rahim Bou'abid; the Trade Unions split at the same time. Though the UNFP supported the government of 'Abdullah Ibrahim, of the left wing of the *Istiqlal*, 1959–60, it soon became the object of repressive measures by the King's security forces which were under the direct control of Crown Prince Hassan. Relations between the King and the parties worsened in 1960 and many *Istiqlal* and UNFP leaders were arrested. In May the King dismissed the government and himself headed a new one, with the Crown Prince as his deputy; as Ministers, he chose right-wing members of the *Istiqlal*, the MP, and the right-wing trade union Union Générale des Travailleurs du Maroc (UGTM) established in 1959 after the split in the Union Marocaine du Travail (UMT). The same month, country-wide municipal elections were held — the first general elections in M.; and though the candidates were forbidden to represent political parties, it was estimated that the *Istiqlal* had the upper hand in the rural areas, while the UNFP was stronger in the modern urban centers on the coast.

In Feb. 1961 King Muhammad V died and was succeeded by his son as King Hassan II, who also assumed the Premiership. He tried to consolidate his control by establishing a political party loyal to him. Following several attempts, the Front pour la Défense des Institutions Constitutionelles (FDIC) was founded in 1963. That Front was in fact based on the MP; in 1964 it split into the Parti Socialiste Démocratique (PSD) and the MP. Neither of these parties had a strong popular backing and both served the King in his endeavor to appear as supporting democracy and a representative régime and to promote economic and social modernization without introducing political liberalization and full democracy. A provisional Fundamental Law of June 1961 and a first formal constitution, approved by referendum on 7 Dec. 1962, represented such conservative conceptions; the King retained wide authority; Parliament was to consist of a House of Representatives, elected by universal, direct suffrage, and an Upper House, indirectly elected by a council of electors; Islam was declared the state religion.

The first elections under the new constitution were held in May 1963. The *Istiqlal* competed as an opposition party, as its Ministers had resigned, or been dismissed, in Dec. 1962. The newly formed FDIC was seen as King-supported. The elections failed to produce the expected clear majority for the government party: of 144 seats, the FDIC gained 69, *Istiqlal* 41, the UNFP 28, and Independents 6. In the indirect elections to the Upper House in Oct. 1963, however, the FDIC and other government supporters won most of the seats. The King did not continue as Prime Minister, but the government was composed of his appointees and Parliament had little influence. In the second half of 1963 repressive action was taken against the *Istiqlal* and UNFP, the opposition parties. Most of the UNFP leaders were arrested in July 1963 in connection with an alleged *coup* attempt, and several of them were later sentenced to death, including Ben Barka, who had fled, *in absentia*; the death sentences were commuted by the King in 1964. Tension increased, especially among the educated urban youth, and student riots broke out several times and were harshly crushed. The FDIC, with no adequate majority in Parliament, tried in vain to attract the opposition parties into forming a coalition government. In the face of a weak government, unemployment, rising prices and general discontent among the urban population, riots erupted in March 1965. The King proclaimed a state of emergency in June and, becoming once again Prime Minister, assumed full executive and legislative power. Parliament was dissolved and the opposition was treated harshly. In Oct. 1965 the UNFP leader Mehdi Ben Barka disappeared in France, never to be seen again; Moroccan prominent figures, among them Gen. Muhammad Oufkir, the Minister of the Interior and head of the secret services, were found guilty in France *(in absentia)* of complicity in his assumed abduction and murder.

In July 1967 Hassan II relinquished the Premiership. The following years witnessed repeated reshuffles of cabinets composed mainly of the King's men and technocrats. There was further student and worker unrest. As the King apparently felt the need to increase public support, there was from 1969 a gradual return to political activity — under strict royal control. In Oct. 1969 local elections were held, but boycotted by the opposition. An experiment in "directed democracy" was made by a new constitution approved by referendum in July 1970. It provided for a 240-member House of Representatives — 90 elected by direct suffrage, 90 by local councils, and 60, representing the professions and economic divisions, by an electoral college. Elections in Aug. 1970 — boycotted by the opposition — returned 158 Independents, most of them supporting the King, 60 MP, and only 22 from opposition parties.

The King-controlled government and parliament were unable to resolve the continuing tension amongst students, intellectuals and workers. The revolutionary fervor infiltrated even the army and led in July 1971 to a *coup* attempt by senior right-wing officers and numerous cadets who denounced the corruption in the royal administration and its ineptitude in dealing with the Left-instigated ferment and wanted to abolish the monarchy and establish a republic. Several senior officers were killed during the *coup*, others were later sentenced to death. Following this crisis, one of the King's closest aides, Home Minister Muhammad Oufkir, was transferred to the Defense Ministry, to purge the army of revolutionary elements; his position became so strong that he started to plan another *coup*.

While fighting the opposition and suppressing

subversion, the King tried to assuage dissent by a measure of political liberalization. A third constitution was prepared, and approved by referendum on 1 March 1972. It provided for a 240-member House of Representatives, two-thirds elected by direct general suffrage, one third by electoral councils. While the King was empowered to dissolve Parliament, the government was to be responsible to both the King and Parliament which was for the first time given the right to topple the government by a vote of non-confidence or censure. But the opposition was not reconciled. A "National Front" of *Istiqlal* and the UNFP boycotted the Mar. 1972 referendum. Parliament was suspended by the King. Meanwhile, the left-wing opposition, the UNFP, split in July into a "Rabat section", headed by 'Abdul-Rahim Bou'abid — regarded as more leftist — and a "Casablanca section" headed by 'Abdullah Ibrahim, supported by the trade unions and considered more pragmatic and ready to co-operate with the royal administration. The Left's "National Front" of the *Istiqlal* and the UNFP was now a dead letter.

A most dangerous *coup* attempt, engineered by the King's strongman Muhammad Oufkir and the Air Force, and including an air attack on the King's plane and on his palace, was suppressed in Aug. 1972. Oufkir was killed during the event, more than 200 officers were arrested and several were sentenced to death or imprisonment. Hassan II himself assumed the command of the army, and became Minister of Defense until March 1973. His position by late 1972 was precarious, because at a time of rampant political opposition and popular dissent the army had revealed itself as not reliable.

To consolidate his position, Hassan II acted on two fronts: large-scale purges of centers of dissent, coupled with nationalist policies. The attempted *coup* of 1972 and new attacks on government buildings throughout M. in 1973, seen as a new plot to overthrow the régime — presumably by the UNFP and leftist activists, with Libyan backing — served as a pretext for continuous trials and harsh sentences. On the other hand, in March 1973 Hassan II announced plans for the Moroccanization of the economy and the nationalization of foreign-owned (mainly French) lands and their distribution among the peasantry. Other expressions of a stronger nationalist stance were the extension of territorial waters from 12 to 70 miles; a more active part in the Arab-Israel conflict; and shortly after, the conflict over Spanish *Sahara (see below).

In 1974 the split within the UNFP became final and the "Rabat Section", which had been outlawed in 1973, established an independent party, the Union Socialiste des Forces Populaires (USFP). In May 1974 the veteran *Istiqlal* leader 'Allal al-Fassi died, leaving the party without a prominent leadership. The Left was further split in 1974 by the foundation of a new front for the Communists, the Parti du Progrès et du Socialisme (PPS), headed by the veteran Communist leader 'Ali Yata; in contrast to the suppression of previous similar attempts to legalize the Communist Party, the PPS was allowed to organize legally. The King, who felt he was increasingly popular because of his policy towards Spanish Sahara, continued harassing and half-suppressing the leftist opposition, while partially responding to its political pressure. In summer 1976 the King announced local and parliamentary elections for the coming months, and with the exception of the UNFP, the opposition parties agreed to participate. Municipal elections were held in Nov. 1976, provincial ones in Jan. 1977, and elections for professional and vocational chambers in Mar. 1977. More than 60% of the seats were won by "Independents", most of them conservative supporters of the King. Hoping to ensure fair general elections Muhammad Boucetta, the new leader of the *Istiqlal*, and 'Abdul-Rahim Bou'abid of the USFP joined the Government as Ministers of State on 1 March. Elections for a 264-seat Parliament were held in June 1977 (176 directly elected, 88 chosen by electoral colleges). Independents won 141 seats, *Istiqlal* 49, MP 44, USFP 16 and PPS 1 (the UNFP boycotted the elections). The new government, in Oct., included eight *Istiqlal* members, with Boucetta as Foreign Minister, MP leaders, and Ma'ati Bou'abid of the UNFP, whose party disowned him; the USFP took no ministerial posts except for the symbolic Minister of State position of its leader. Thus, the King succeeded in winning over an important part of the leftist opposition without conceding much of his authority. In 1978 the pro-government independents' group in Parliament established a "Rassemblement National des Indépendants" (RNI) headed by

Prime Minister Ahmad Osman ('Uthman). The latter resigned from the Premiership in March 1979 to devote himself to the organization of his party. In 1981 a faction based on rural areas split from the RNI, forming a "Parti des Indépendants Démocrates" (later renamed National Democratic Party) but stayed in the government.

Social and economic issues continued troubling M. Ma'ati Bou'abid, who replaced Osman as Prime Minister in 1980, himself a former trade union leader, negotiated with the unions and agreed to wage rises. This provided a temporary, partial answer to social unrest, but added to the burden on the state budget and the economy. In order to cut government spending, the education budget was cut by reducing student grants and limiting admission to the universities. As a result, student strikes broke out, and unrest continued 1981–83. The unrest increased in June 1981 following price hikes of subsidized food, and culminated in a general strike and riots in Casablanca in which some 70 people were killed (opposition sources quoted much higher figures). The USFP and its affiliated trade union, since 1978 reorganized as the Confédération Démocratique du Travail (CDT) and headed by Noubir al-Amaoui, were accused of creating this unrest, all CDT offices were closed down and its leaders arrested. Later when the USFP denounced the government's Saharan policy as too "soft", its senior leaders, including 'Abd-ul-Rahim Bou-'abid, were arrested and tried, and its newspapers suspended. Dissent increased in Oct. 1981 following constitutional changes, mainly the extension of the term of Parliament from four to six years. The opposition claimed that the 1977 elections had not been fairly conducted and that the majority parties' deputies were not fulfilling their parliamentary duties, and all 14 USFP deputies boycotted Parliament. A government reshuffle in Nov. 1981 eliminated all RNI Ministers — to create, as the King and the outgoing Premier announced, a loyal opposition.

In Mar. 1982, in an effort to improve relations with the opposition, USFP leader Bou'abid was pardoned and USFP and CDT offices were allowed to reopen in Apr. Many union leaders, however, remained in prison, and the ban on USFP newspapers continued until 1983. In 1982 Prime Minister Ma'ati Bou'abid established a new party, the Union Constitutionelle (UC). In June 1983 municipal elections took place, with the UC and other pro-government center-right candidates winning a majority. General elections, however, were delayed several times — beyond the expiry of Parliament's six-year mandate. In Nov. 1983 the government was replaced by a caretaker government of National Unity headed by Karim Lamrani (al-'Amrani), in which representatives of the six major parties took part, including the *Istiqlal* and the USFP; it was to organize general elections and draw up an economic program. But when the government announced prices hikes of basic foodstuffs and education fees in Jan. 1984, riots broke out in the urban centers; they were quelled by the army, with more than 110 killed and some 2000 arrested, but the rioting ended only after the King announced the suspension of the price increases. While Communists and the Left were blamed for these disturbances, Islamic fundamentalists were also accused of plotting to overthrow the monarchy during these riots, some of their leaders were tried in 1985 and several were sentenced to death or imprisonment.

Parliamentary elections were held in Sept. 1984. The results — including the 104 chosen by indirect election — gave the UC 83 seats, RNI 61, MP 47, *Istiqlal* 43, USFP 39, National Democratic Party 24. Lamrani formed a new government in Apr. 1985, and 'Izz-ul-din Laraki (al-'Iraqi) a new one, of similar composition, in Sept. 1986.

M.'s foreign policy after independence was achieved and M. became a member of the UN in 1956 and the Arab League in 1958, focused on relations with France and Spain and the consolidation of her authority in all regions she considered part of her territory. The French-M'n agreement of March 1956 provided for protocols on French military and economic interests in, and cooperation with, M. to be prepared. But no such accord was ever signed, as M. was not willing to establish the special relations with France that had been envisaged, and France had to realize that her formal position in M. was similar to that of other foreign states. In 1960 she had to agree to liquidate her bases and evacuate her troops; all French military left M. by 1961. Most French agricultural property was nationalized, especially in 1963 and 1973; a final agreement on compensation was reached in 1974. M. continued to benefit from French technical expertise, but the number of French citizens in M. decreased gradually. French-M'n relations worsened due to the Ben Barka affair in 1965, and were repaired only in 1969.

Agreements with Spain concerning the termination of the Spanish Protectorate were reached in 1956, but relations worsened due to a conflict over several enclaves in the southern Spanish zone which Spain was reluctant to hand over. Agreement on those was reached only in 1958, and the area was handed over, and Spanish troops withdrawn, in 1961. However, Spain still retained an enclave at Ifni; the struggle over that issue was resolved only in 1969, when Ifni was handed over. These agreements did not include several Spanish settlements ("Presidios") on M.'s Mediterranean coast, which Spain regarded as fully Spanish territory. M. claimed them — but has so far not pressed the issue.

From the mid-1960s, a dispute arose over Spanish *Sahara, claimed by M. (for details see *Sahara). From the early 1970s M. stepped up pressure and agitation; this culminated in Oct. 1975 in a peaceful mass procession, a "Green March" by a claimed 350,000 M'ns into Spanish Sahara, stage-managed by the King. In Nov. 1975, Spain gave in, and agreed with M. and Mauritania to hand the territory to them; she did so in Feb. 1976, and the two recipient countries divided it between themselves in Apr. 1976. But local organizations claiming independence, since 1973–74 set up guerrilla forces, "POLISARIO", supported, armed and maintained by Algeria and centered on Algerian soil. In Feb. 1976, POLISARIO proclaimed a "Sahara Arab Democratic Republic" (SADR). M. was now involved in a protracted, costly guerrilla war which, she claimed, only Algeria kept going. In Aug. 1979 Mauritania renounced her part of Western Sahara, M. immediately occupied and annexed the Mauritanian part, and now had to fight for the whole of Western Sahara. Against the elusive guerrilla fighters in the remote desert, M. built over years an earth wall; when its completion was announced, in 1984–85, it was about 2,500 km. long and enclosed from the Algerian and Mauritanian border to the Atlantic Ocean c. 77,000 of Western Sahara's total 100,000 sq.mi.

The Sahara issue also clouded M.'s international, and particularly her African, relations. By the mid-1980s, 65 countries had recognized SADR. The UN continued recommending a referendum under international supervision, and so did the Organization of African Unity (OAU). M. agreed in principle to such a referendum, but protracted negotiations with OAU envoys and committees brought no agreement on its actual terms and modalities (and the impression was that M.'s acceptance of a referendum was tactical only and not meant for implementation). When a SADR-POLISARIO delegation was presented at an OAU Foreign Ministers' conference, in Feb. 1977, M. walked out and suspended her active participation in OAU activities. The issue of SADR's participation of the OAU persisted and caused much bad blood between M. and many countries of Africa. In Nov. 1984, M. announced her secession from the OAU (effective Nov. 1985) in protest against the seating of a SADR delegation at the 20th OAU Summit.

M.'s relations with Algeria were troubled. Territorial disputes arose over border regions left by France with Algeria and claimed by M. — regions rich in coal and iron ores, especially the Colomb-Béchar and Tindouf areas. The conflict caused several armed clashes and erupted in fully fledged military confrontation in 1963. M. claimed that Egypt had secretly supported Algeria in this confrontation, and severed relations with Egypt (until 1964). She also refused the Arab League's mediation because of Egypt's dominant influence in the League. Following the mediation of Ethiopia and Mali on behalf of the OAU, an interim agreement was reached, based on the *status quo* — i.e., the territories were left under Algerian sovereignty. But M. did not regard this settlement as final, and her relations with Algeria remained tense and unfriendly. The confrontation over Western Sahara added bitterness.

M. claimed Mauritania's territory and bitterly opposed the full independence granted to that country in 1960. Most of the AC at first supported M. in her rejection of Mauritania's independence, with the exception of Tunisia, whose support of Mauritania angered M. and caused her to sever relations with Tunisia (until 1964). However, as most AC gradually accepted Mauritania, M. realized that she, too, had to recognize Mauritania's independence, especially when the Spanish Sahara issue became a matter of prominent common interest. She did, finally, in 1969, and official relations were established in June 1970. But relations did not become friendly; Mauritania frequently complained of Moroccan interference in her internal power and factional struggles; and cooperation over Western Sahara was short-lived and soon turned into sharp differences.

Relations with Libya were also far from friendly. M. suspected Libyan subversive intrigues behind many of her internal troubles, and also detected a measure of Libyan aid to the Sahara guerrillas. In July 1971 official relations were severed — and resumed only in Jan. 1975; in 1980 M. again withdrew her Ambassador. Yet, in Aug. 1984, M. and Libya proclaimed a "union" or merger of their two countries — a surprise move seen by most observers as a M'n effort to find allies against Algeria (and Libya's *Qadhdhafi was always eager to "merge" his country into larger A. unions). However, the few steps taken towards the very partial implementation of the "merger" agreement (e.g., a joint Secretariat) indicated that the real aim was no more than a political alliance and a degree of co-ordination. Even that alliance soured when Libya in July 1986 violently denounced King Hassan for inviting Israel's Prime Minister and meeting him in M., and called for all-A. action against M. In Aug. 1986 the King denounced and abrogated the union agreement of 1984.

All these differences with M.'s neighbors in the Maghrib dampened and retarded, of course, the chances for a union of the Maghrib — though all Maghrib countries continued proclaiming such a union as their aim. In the first years of independence, M. was driven by her differences with France and Spain (and the radical positions taken by Algeria) to seek closer cooperation with leftist-radical A. and African countries — despite her own internal conservatism. Thus M. hosted a *Casablanca conference of radical states in 1961 and took part in efforts to create a "Casablanca Bloc" of radicals (which was short-lived and abortive). When in 1961 she sent a contingent of troops to a UN Peace Force for Congo (later Zaïre), this was seen, in the political reckoning of the UN balance, as part of the radical camp's contribution. However, the improvement of relations with France and Spain, coupled with the radical states' support of Algeria and POLISARIO, caused M. to move closer to the West. The dispatch of another contingent of Moroccan troops to Zaïre in 1977–78, was in defense of a pro-Western, right-wing régime assailed by leftist radicals from Angola. M.'s relations with the USA had anyway been friendly from the beginning. She had even allowed the US to maintain several military bases in M. These were evacuated and handed over by 1963, but certain "facilities" remained at the disposal of the US, and M. received American aid. M. also fostered normal relations with the USSR.

M.'s emphasis on nationalist policies also drove her to be more active in A. and Islamic affairs, and in the A.-Israel conflict. She identified with the ASt involved in the *Six Day War of 1967, and sent troops to participate in the *October War of 1973. From the late 1960s she sided with the moderate ASt, and King Hassan II was repeatedly active in efforts to mediate between the rival camps within the A. world and renew inter-A. co-operation. M. hosted several all-A. Summit meetings (Sept. 1965, Casablanca; Dec. 1969, Rabat; Oct. 1974, Rabat; Nov. 1981 and Sept. 1982, Fez; Aug. 1985, Casablanca), as well as all-Islamic Ministers' and Summit meetings (beginning with the first Islamic Summit of Sept. 1969, Rabat). M. supported *Sadat's peace initiative of 1977, and King Hassan II played a rôle in its preparations and hosted secret Egyptian-Israeli preliminary meetings. M. went along, in 1979, with the all-A. decision to sever official relations with Egypt, but has in fact maintained links (though she has not, as had been expected, resumed official relations).

From the 1950s M. allowed most of her Jews to emigrate — many of them to France and North America, but more than 150,000 to Israel, though officially the organization of migration to Israel was illegal. In recent years she has begun cultivating relations with the former M'n Jews abroad. In this context she has sometimes invited and hosted M'n-Jewish delegations, including groups from Israel. In July 1986 King Hassan became the second A. leader (after Sadat) to establish a measure of open and public relations with Israel, by inviting Israel's Prime Minister Peres to visit M. and meet him. The talks were not, the King insisted, "negotiations", and in substance he did not deviate from positions taken by other ASt of the more moderate wing. But the invitation and the meeting were seen as a new departure of symbolic and moral significance, and was bitterly denounced by radical A. leaders.

Moslem See *Muslim.

Mosul Third-largest city of Iraq and capital of the province of Niniveh (formerly M.). Situated on the Tigris, center of an oil-bearing area and of transit trade with Turkey and northern Syria. Population: close to 1m., mostly Muslim-Sunnis, partly *Kurds. The province of M. — under Ottoman-Turkish administration, until 1918, the northernmost of the three provinces *(vilayet)* that later became Iraq — had a high percentage of non-A. populations, such as Kurds and Turcomans, and Christians, and during and after World War I attracted many refugees from Turkey, such as *Assyrians and *Armenians.

Under the secret *Sykes-Picot Agreement of 1916, M. and its region were slated to become part of a French zone of influence. However, in Dec. 1918 Premier Clémenceau acceded to Prime Minister Lloyd George's request to transfer the area to the British zone of influence, in exchange for British concessions on the Rhine and a share for France in the reorganized "Turkish Petroleum Company" (later the Iraq Petroleum Co.). In the post-World War I peace negotiations, Turkey insistently claimed M. and its region, arguing that the population was predominantly "Muslim-Ottoman" (i.e. non-A.), and that the area had not been in British hands when the armistice of Mudros was signed on 30 Oct. 1918. The dispute was not resolved in time for the signature of the peace treaty of *Lausanne between Turkey and the allied powers, 1923. The treaty therefore left the fate of the M. area open for further negotiations and eventually arbitration by the *League of Nations. As no agreement was reached in continuing negotiations, the League decided in 1925–26, after a committee had investigated the problem on the spot, in favor of Iraq (then under a British *Mandate). Turkey was awarded, in compensation, a 10% share, for 25 years, in Iraq's oil revenue. The League stipulated that the Anglo-Iraqi treaty providing for a measure of British tutelage be extended to a 25-year term, but this extension was soon cancelled by the Anglo-Iraqi treaty of 1930, endorsed by the League in 1932, which granted Iraq independence. The League also insisted on Iraqi pledges and guarantees concerning the protection of minorities and their rights, including a measure of local and cultural autonomy, in the M. province. It re-demanded, and obtained, similar, more general guarantees before endorsing, in 1932, Iraq's independence and membership in the League. Iraq never fully honored these pledges and promises, and her refusal to grant an autonomy satisfactory to the minorities led to violent clashes with, and a massacre of, the Assyrians (1933) and permanent unrest among the Kurds, erupting several times in full-fledged rebellions (see *Kurds).

In 1927 Iraq divided the province *(vilayet)* of M. into four smaller provinces *(liwa')* — M., Kirkuk, Arbil and Suleimaniyya. In 1969–70 the northern part of the remaining province of M. became a separate province, Dohuk (the term for "province" was changed into *muhafaza*). In Mar. 1970 an agreement with the Kurdish rebels, after long years of fighting, provided for large parts of the former *vilayet* of M. to become an autonomous Kurdish region. However, the agreement spoke of Kurdish-majority districts without clearly naming and defining them, and differences soon erupted concerning this vital point, as well as the extent of autonomy and the implementation of the agreement of 1970.

In Mar. 1974 the Government of Iraq unilaterally, without the consent of the rebel leaders, proclaimed a (semi)-autonomous Kurdish region — to consist of the provinces of Suleimaniyya, Arbil and Dohuk, with its capital at Arbil (see *Kurds). Kurdish nationalists continued claiming additional areas of the provinces of M. and Kirkuk. For their resumed rebellion see *Kurds.

Mubarak, (Muhammad) Husni (b. 1928) Egyptian officer and politician. Vice-President of Egypt 1975–81, President since Oct. 1981. Born in Kafr al-Musaliha village in the Menufiyya district north-east of Cairo, the son of a petty official of peasant stock, M. graduated from the Military College in 1949 and the Air Force Academy in 1950. After serving as a fighter pilot, he was an instructor at the Air Force Academy, 1954–61. He attended several training courses in the USSR, including a full year, 1961–62, at the Soviet General Staff Academy. In 1967 he became commander of the Air Academy, with the rank of Colonel, in 1969 — Chief-of-Staff of the Air Force, with the rank of General (Air Vice Marshal), and in 1971–72 — Commander-in-

Chief of the Air Force. In that capacity M. played a key role in the preparations for, and the conduct of, the *October War of 1973, and the successful manner in which the Air Force fulfilled its task in that war is usually seen as M.'s personal achievement. In 1974 he was promoted to the rank of Air Marshal.

In Apr. 1975 President *Sadat appointed M. as his only Vice-President. M. had never been active or prominent in politics and was seen as a professional rather than a political leader; he had no political base of his own. Sadat was seen to have elevated M. from political obscurity to a position of top leadership. As Vice-President, M. fully followed Sadat's lead and policies, without much independent action. He served as the President's envoy on many missions to the AC and the world, including the USSR and China. Observers thought that even as Vice-President M. did not create a political base for himself — though some saw his hand in the elimination of several potential rivals (such as War Minister and Deputy Premier Gamassy in Oct. 1978, or Mansur Hassan, Minister for Presidential Affairs and Information, in Sept. 1981). M. was fully associated with Sadat's moves towards peace with Israel, from Nov. 1977 to the *Camp David Agreements of 1978 and the peace treaty of 1979 — though he himself did not participate in the actual negotiations.

When President Sadat was assassinated in Oct. 1981, M. immediately took over as President — and within a week was nominated by the "National Democratic Party" and confirmed by a referendum (with no rival candidate). For some months he also took the Premiership, but in Jan. 1982 he reverted to the practice of having the government headed by one or the other of the President's associates. M. also became the head of the government "National Democratic Party".

M. proclaimed that he would continue Sadat's policies — and, indeed, in general did so. Yet, his Presidency was, different from Sadat's, in style and mode of operation, and gradually in some of its policies. M. was not the type of charismatic, flamboyant leader that both his predecessors, Sadat and *Nasser, had been, and put much less stress on his own personality and leadership. He appeared as a solid, hard-working, somewhat dour administrator, honest and cautious, rather than a brilliant tribune. He also emphasized, in contrast to his predecessors, an unusual modesty in his personal life style (and so did his wife, who — in contrast to Mrs. Jihan Sadat — did not appear much in public). In his policy, M. somewhat toned down the liberalization, the "Opening" and free enterprise of Sadat's régime, reimposed stricter state control, and in particular tried to eliminate the excesses and negative side-effects and the measure of corruption and nepotism that had grown under Sadat. In the face of growing Islamic fundamentalist movements he continued Sadat's policy of forcibly suppressing their extremist excesses, while emphasizing Egypt's Islamic character and strengthening orthodox Islamic elements in public manifestations of his own régime. His ability to halt the Islamic-fundamentalist threat to Egypt's modern régime was, after half a decade of his rule, still in some doubt; as was the ability of his régime to solve to Egypt's socio-economic problems.

In foreign affairs, M. made no basic changes in Sadat's policies, but certain shifts of emphasis became apparent. M. continued and developed Egypt's close alliance with the USA (while trying to keep some outward manifestations, such as cooperation in the fight against terrorism, or the military "facilities" granted to the US, under wraps, and rejecting suggestions of publicly visible joint action, e.g. against Libya) and continued relying on ever-increasing US aid. But he also made efforts to restore and improve relations with the USSR. He also endeavored to strengthen relations with the European community. M. kept the peace treaty with Israel and rejected all A. attempts to entice him into abrogating it. But he appeared to turn that peace into a "cold" one and in effect to freeze relations — he withdrew Egypt's Ambassador in Sept. 1982 (after Israel invaded Lebanon); he allowed a border dispute on the possession of a small area at *Taba near Eilat to grow into a major issue; he refrained from effectively counter-acting anti-Israel manifestations in the Egyptian media (especially those of the opposition) and public opinion; and he virtually halted most cooperation in various fields. In Sept. 1986, when the Taba issue was submitted to agreed arbitration, relations improved somewhat, a new Egyptian Ambassador was appointed and M. held a "summit" meeting with Israel's Premier — the first since 1981, and his own first.

M.'s handling of relations with Israel was probably related to M.'s desire to effect a reconciliation with the ASt and see Egypt resuming her leadership of the A. world. For, while refusing to renege on the peace treaty with Israel, and insisting that it was not for Egypt to ask the ASt for a resumption of relations but for the ASt to propose it, M. was actively interested in mending Egypt's relations with the ASt. Formally, he achieved full results mainly concerning Jordan, which resumed official relations in Sept. 1984 (whereupon very close relations began developing). But he fostered *de facto* ties to the moderate ASt (Sa'udi Arabia, Morocco, Tunisia, the Gulf principalities); he vigorously aided Iraq in her war against Iran, despite the absence of diplomatic relations; he cultivated Egypt's special relations with Sudan; and he supported and aided the *PLO (*'Arafat's wing). M. also tried — thus far unsuccessfully — to promote, in conjunction with Jordan, US-guided moves towards a comprehensive ME (i.e. A.-Israel) peace settlement — and to get 'Arafat's PLO to join it.

Mufti   A Muslim religious official who issues Islamic Law (*Shari'a*) rulings (*Fatwa*, pl. *fatāwi*), in general in response to questions. In most Islamic countries the M. is government-appointed, generally for life.

The M. has a highly respected status and spiritual and social influence, but plays no executive or political role. However, his rulings frequently concern issues of political significance and in many such cases conform to the wishes and conceptions of the government in power (see *Fatwa). A notorious exception to the generally non-political character of the office of the M. was the M. of Jerusalem, Hajj Amin al-*Husseini who exploited his position to consolidate his political leadership (see *Palestine Arabs).

Muhammad, 'Ali Nasser (b. 1939/40) South Yemeni politician, Prime Minister 1971–85, President 1980–86). Of tribal background, M. was trained as a teacher in 'Aden, graduating in 1959, and became a school principal in his Dathina tribal area. In the 1960s he was one of the founders and leaders of the *National Liberation Front (NLF), especially its fighting squads. During the decisive struggle of 1967, he commanded the NLF's guerrilla formations in the Beihan area. When South Yemen became independent under the NLF, late in 1967, he was appointed governor of several provinces successively. In 1969, when President Qahtan al-*Sha'bi was ousted by a more leftist-extremist faction, he joined M.'A. Haitham's Government, first as Minister for Local Government and later the same year as Minister of Defense. Though active in the victorious leftist faction, M. was not yet a member of the five-man Presidential Council, but some observers already saw him as one of an emerging ruling "triumvirate" (with Salem Rubai' *'Ali and 'Abd-ul-Fattah *Isma'il). In Aug. 1971 that triumvirate ousted Haitham and took over as a new Presidential Council. M. also became Prime Minister, retaining the Defense Ministry for some time.

In June 1978 Salem Rubai' 'Ali was overthrown by 'Abd-ul-Fattah Isma'il and M., and was killed. M. became President, but ceded the Presidency to Isma'il after a few months, contenting himself with the premiership and membership of the Presidential Council. Within the ruling leftist faction and the duumvirate at its head an unrelenting struggle now began escalating; it appears to have been generated by personal rivalry between M. and Isma'il, by each one's desire to wield full power, tribal-factional interests, and some political differences: Isma'il was a doctrinaire extremist, guided by a strict Moscow-loyal party line, which led South Yemen into a near-complete isolation within the A. world, while M. gradually tended to more pragmatic policies, a measure of reintegration in the A. mainstream and an improvement in South Yemen's relations with her A. neighbors, particularly Sa'udi Arabia. In Apr. 1980 M. won and Isma'il was ousted and went into exile to Moscow.

M. as President and in full power gradually implemented his more pragmatic line and achieved some improvement of South Yemen's inter-A. standing and relations. The factional struggle, however, continued even in Isma'il's absence, as other members of the ruling team turned against M. (particularly Defense Minister 'Ali 'Antar, made Vice-President in 1981, and Deputy Premier 'Ali Salem al-Beid). After several attempts at mediation and reconciliation, and apparently some Soviet pressure, Isma'il was allowed to return in 1985. His return reintensified the factional struggle. The course of the final showdown in Jan. 1986 has remained confused, reported in conflicting versions, with each side claiming that the other had attempted to stage a *coup* and assassinate its rivals. In the fighting, Isma'il, 'Antar and several others were killed. But M. was defeated and ousted. He escaped death and went into exile in Yemen and/or Ethiopia. He continued speaking of rallying his supporters and resuming the fight. In Dec. 1986 he was put on trial, *in absentia*, with about 140 others.

Muhammad V, Ibn (Ben) Yussuf (1909? 1911?–61)   Sultan of Morocco 1927–57, King 1957–61. Sultan M., addressed according to Moroccan custom also as "Sidi M." or "Moulay M.", succeeded his father, Sultan Yussuf, in 1927. Under the French Protectorate, his authority was very restricted; in fact, his administration, the *Makhzen*, was limited to the "native" sector of life and economy. Even in that restricted sphere he was repeatedly forced to take measures or sign decrees he disapproved of, such as the "Berber Decree" of 1930 (see *Morocco), and sometimes he resisted the French dictate. In general, Sultan M. was considered an instrument of the French, and the incipient national movement turned in some measure against him, too. During World War II, under France's Vichy régime, he protected his Jewish subjects to some degree (the degree is in dispute). As the nationalist movement intensified, from the late 1940s, Sultan M. began to identify himself with it in increasing measure and on account of that he entered into growing conflict with the French, while the nationalists and popular opinion began to appreciate him. In Aug. 1953 the French exiled him to Madagascar and replaced him with his relative Moulay Muhammad Ben 'Arafa (though he did not abdicate or renounce his claim). But mounting unrest, virtually a nationalist uprising, compelled them to rescind that measure and to reinstate Sultan M. In Nov. 1955 he returned to Morocco and his throne, and it was during his reign that Morocco became independent in 1956. In Aug. 1957, Sultan M. assumed the title of King. In May 1960, in one of the crises of Morocco's governance, he assumed the Premiership himself, and held it until his death. He died in Feb. 1961 and was succeeded by his eldest son, Moulay *Hassan.

Muhammara   See *Khorramshahr.

Muhyi-ul-Din, Khaled (b. 1922)   Egyptian officer and politician, leader of Egypt's Left. Born into a middle class, medium land-owning family, M. studied at the military academy and became a professional officer, reaching the rank of Major. He also took a BA in Economics at the University of Cairo. He was a member of the "Free Officers" group that staged the *coup* of July 1952, and of the Revolutionary Command Council established after the *coup*. However, as he displayed marked leftist tendencies (the "Red Major"), and also supported *Nagib against *Nasser in the Feb. 1954 showdown between those two (which Nasser won), he was expelled from the Revolutionary Council and arrested for some time. Since the 1950s, M. has been the leader of the Egyptian non-Communist but Communist-leaning Left (but some maintain that he was a member of the Communist Party for some time). He has been chairman of the Egyptian Peace Council and since 1958 a member of the World Peace Movement's Presidential Council — maintaining, in that capacity, many international contacts. He is a recipient of the Lenin Peace Prize 1970.

Despite M.'s Leftist "heresy" he remained inside Nasser's establishment and no harsh action was ever taken against him. He was a member of the Central Committee of the régime's single party, the "National Union", and from 1957 a member of the National Assembly on behalf of that party. In 1956–57 he was made editor of a new daily, *al-Massa'*, but was dismissed in 1959; in 1964 he was appointed chairman of the board of the *al-Akhbar* mass-circulation paper, but this post, too, he held only for about a year. In the new single party, the "Arab Socialist Union" (ASU), M. rose to membership of the Secretariat in 1964, but failed in 1968 in his efforts to be elected to the Supreme Executive. For some time he was chairman of the "High Dam" (*Aswan) Committee.

After Nasser's death, under *Sadat, M.'s links with the régime became more precarious. He opposed Sadat's liberalization, his policy of "Opening" for free, capitalist enterprise, and his growing alliance with the USA, and maintained a leftist "Nasserist" line. In 1979 he was formally charged with anti-state activities and security offences — but no trial was held. M. deviated from the régime's position also concerning the conflict with Israel. Conforming to the line taken by the international Left, he took part in abortive attempts to organize a conference with the Israeli Left in 1971–72, while insisting that no "Zionist" Leftists should be allowed to attend. He opposed Sadat's peace moves, from 1977. In 1976 the ASU disavowed him and called off his attempts to organize ASU volunteers to join the Leftist-Muslim camp in Lebanon's civil war.

When in 1975–77 various trends or "platforms" were allowed to crystallize within the ASU, and finally to become separate, independent parties in 1976–77, M. headed the Leftist "platform" that became the "National Progressive-Unionist Rally". In 1978 he founded the NPUR's organ, the weekly al-Ahali, and has remained its editor. The NPUR has not, however, developed into a strong organization and seems to have little influence. M.'s weekly, too, has remained a marginal sheet with little impact (its publication was suspended several times). Under the Sadat-*Mubarak régime, M. also lost his Parliamentary seat. He was still elected in 1976 — because of his family's standing in his constituency rather than his ideology and politics — but lost in the elections of 1979, 1984 and 1987 when his NPUR won no seats.

Muhyi-ul-Din, Zakariyya (b. 1918) Egyptian officer and politician, Vice-President 1961–68, Prime Minister 1965–66. Born into a midle-class, medium land-owning family in the Dakhaliyya province, M. became a professional officer, graduating from the military academy in 1938 (together with *Nasser and *Sadat). He was close to the "Free Officers" group and joined them on the eve of their *coup* of July 1952, as a Lt.-Colonel, becoming a member of the Revolutionary Command Council. From 1953 to 1962 he was Minister of the Interior, including three years of the Egypto-Syrian *United Arab Republic (UAR); he was also responsible for security and the secret service. From 1961 he was also a Vice-President — for one month of the UAR, and then of Egypt. In Sept. 1962 he gave up the Home Ministry, but continued as Vice-President (one of five, from 1964 — one of three). In Oct. 1965 he became Prime Minister, serving also as his own Minister of the Interior; there were conflicting reports as to whether he was also considered a Vice-President during his Premiership. In any case he resumed the Vice-Presidency when he had to resign the Premiership in Sept. 1966.

When Nasser resigned on 9 June 1967, after the *Six Day War, he nominated M. as President in his place — but the resignation and the appointment were withdrawn following mass demonstrations. In Nasser's reconstituted government of June 1967, with Nasser himself as Premier, M. served as Deputy Prime Minister (again with contradictory and somewhat blurred reports as to whether he was also regarded as Vice President). He was dropped from the Government in Mar. 1968 and since then has not held any government position, though he is held in high respect as a former Vice-President and long-time pillar of the régime.

M. was considered, in Nasser's days, as the chief proponent, within the ruling junta, of "right-wing" tendencies, pro-West and opposed to the tightening alliance with the USSR. He advocated a mitigation of the state socialism practised, a wider scope for free enterprise, a slower pace of development and cuts in the budget. M. formed his 1965 government with the intention of implementing these policies and recommendations, but he was unable to push them through, and his resignation (or dismissal) in 1966 was an indication that Leftist trends were gaining the upper hand in Nasser's team.

On the death of Nasser in Sept. 1970, M. was seen as a possible candidate for the Presidency, and according to some reports he did indeed struggle to win power, but failed; rumors said that Nasser himself, on his deathbed, had proposed him, but Russia had vetoed the proposal. In the crisis of May 1971 he supported Sadat against the bid for power of the Leftist-Nasserist faction. Some of Sadat's new policies of liberalization, "Opening" and alliance with the West were quite similar to what M. had proposed in the 1960s. Yet, no close alliance between M. and Sadat developed; on the contrary, Sadat seemed to regard M. as a possibly dangerous rival and kept him under surveillance. M. opposed Sadat's peace policy towards Israel, and though he did not resume political activities, he emerged from his retirement twice, publicly to denounce — together with the three other surviving former Vice-Presidents — both the *Camp David Agreements of Sept. 1978 and the Peace Treaty with Israel of Mar. 1979.

Muscat (Masqat), Muscat and 'Oman M. is a small town in the south-east of the Arabian Peninsula, on the Gulf of 'Oman, and the capital of the Sultanate of 'Oman. The country, traditionally "Sultanate of M & O", officially became the Sultanate of *Oman in 1970.

Muslim, Muslims See Islam.

Muslim Brothers, Brotherhood *(al-Ikhwan al-Muslimun)* An ultra-conservative, fundamentalist religious and political organization founded in Egypt in 1929 by Sheikh Hassan al-Banna, who became its "Supreme Guide" *(al-Murshid al-'Aam*, a title taken from the vocabulary of the Muslim mystics, *Sufis*, and the *Dervish orders, along with some organizational and missionary techniques — though the MB was strictly orthodox and its teachings had no *Sufi* or Dervish tendencies). The aim of the MB is to impose the laws of Islam (the *Shari'a*) upon the social, political and constitutional life of the Muslim nations. Though it displays certain conservative-reformist tendencies, its conception of Islam is orthodox-fundamentalist, with *Pan-Islamic aspirations and strong xenophobic, anti-Christian and anti-Jewish sentiments.

The MB has become, over the years, a strong, semi-clandestine popular organization, rooted mainly in the lower classes and strong among university students. In the 1940s — perhaps the time of the MB's greatest expansion — its strength was variously estimated between 100,000 and 1m. members. It also maintained a paramilitary youth organization and underground hit squads. The MB has generally been in extreme opposition to all Egyptian governments; its power and influence were extra-parliamentary (al-Banna stood for election to Parliament one single time, in 1945, and was defeated) and were manifested through agitation and demonstrations. Its hit squads were held responsible for the wave of political assassinations that engulfed Egypt in 1945–48 (former Finance Minister and *Wafd* leader Amin 'Othman Jan. 1946; a bomb in a cinema May 1947; a senior court official Mar. 1948; Prime Minister *Nuqrashi Dec. 1948; several attempts on the life of *Wafd* leader *Nahhas; and more). In 1948 the MB recruited volunteers to join the A. irregulars fighting the Jews in Palestine. They saw action in southern Palestine and on the outskirts of Jerusalem. After the May 1948 invasion of the regular Egyptian forces they were partly incorporated in those forces, but lost their impact.

In view of its violent, terrorist activities the MB was banned in Dec. 1948 by Premier Nuqrashi. It was in retaliation for this ban that Nuqrashi was assassinated. Measures to suppress the Brotherhood were now tightened, and the movement went underground. Al-Banna himself was murdered in Feb. 1949 — it was assumed: by agents of the régime — and replaced by Sheikh Hassan Isma'il al-Hudeibi.

In Apr. 1951 the MB was permitted to resume activity — on condition that it would limit its functions to spiritual, cultural and social matters and not engage in political activities (which, its spokesmen claimed, it did not do anyway) nor maintain any para-military formations. The MB did not seem to have regained in those years, under its new Supreme Guide, its previous strength and impact. Some of the "Free Officers" who staged the revolution of July 1952 were considered close to the MB; and when the new régime in 1953 banned all political parties, it accepted the MB's claim that the movement was not a party and did not apply the decree to the MB. However, the régime soon suspected the MB of subversion and banned it in Jan 1954. The power struggle of 1954 between Gen. *Nagib and Col. *Nasser was exacerbated by Nagib's attempt to soften the régime's attitude towards the MB, which reportedly tended to support him. When Nasser won, measures to suppress the organization were further tightened. In Oct. 1954 an attempt to assassinate Nasser was ascribed to the MB, and the régime took strong action. Thousands of MB were arrested, and their 19 top leaders were put on trial in Dec. (a show trial in which the accused did not appear with much dignity). Seven were sentenced to death — including al-Hudeibi — and nine to prison; Hudeibi's sentence was commuted to life imprisonment, but six were executed.

The MB — now reportedly under a collective leadership without a "Supreme Guide" — was not completely broken and continued operating underground. The régime, in any case, continued denouncing its plots and holding it responsible for various political difficulties. A revival of its activities was reported especially in the mid-1960s, including a plot on Nasser's life, and in 1965 and 1966 thousands were again arrested and hundreds were tried. Sentences, in Aug.–Sept. 1966, included several death verdicts and three were executed (including the MB's most prominent ideologue and writer, Sayyid Qutb); Hudeibi, who had been released in 1956 on compassionate and health grounds, was rearrested and sentenced to prison, with two sons (according to some reports he died the same year in prison, but according to others he was released in 1970 and died in 1973). Yet, student unrest in 1968 was again ascribed to the MB.

Under *Sadat, from 1970, and since 1981 under *Mubarak, the MB was treated more leniently and some observers saw a certain affinity between it and the new leadership (Sadat himself had reportedly been close to it in the 1940s and 1950s). As the MB were thought to have considerably moderated their stance — under the leadership of 'Umar Talmassani (without the title of "Supreme Guide"; he died in May 1986) — there was even talk of a sort of alliance between them and the régime: against the Left, and against more extreme Islamic groups. In any case, they were allowed to acquire an increasing influence, even a large measure of control, in lower-class quarters of the cities and especially at the universities — though it is not clear how much of that control was wielded by the MB and how much by other, more extreme groups. But the MB was not permitted to establish a political organization or openly to put candidates for public office, such as the National Assembly. Its main press organ, *al-Da'wa*, was sometimes banned. In the National Assembly elections of 1984, the MB made an informal alliance with the *Wafd* party and 8 MB entered the Assembly on the *Wafd* ticket. In the 1987 elections they were in coalition with the Socialist Labor and Socialist Liberal parties, and among that list's 60 elected some 35 were reportedly MB.

The MB had never been the only Islamic organization in Egypt, but usually it had been the most extremist one (other groups, such as *Shabab Muhammad*, or Saleh Harb's *Jam'iyyat al-Shubban al-Muslimin*, had remained part of the establishment). Since the 1970s, however, the MB were outflanked by more extremist underground Islamic organizations, using violent and terrorist means (which the MB had gradually abandoned) — such as the "Islamic Liberation" *(al-Tahrir al-Islami), al-Takfir wa'l-Hijra, al-Jihad* groups (see *Egypt; *Islam). But the MB have their own extremist wing, there are underground links, and there may be clandestine double membership.

The home and center of the MB is Egypt. Attempts to create branches in other AC have been only partially successful, and no all-A. or inter-A. association of MB groups has been founded. Apart from Islamic organizations under other names, groups calling themselves MB were established, from about 1945, in Palestine, Jordan, Syria, Lebanon, and later Sudan; some of them were short-lived, and the association of those surviving with the Egyptian movement was rather loose. The MB in Sudan, under Hassan Turabi, has mostly remained within the establishment and sometimes even participated in the government; under régimes that permitted multi-party elections, it did not field candidates under its own name, but it was reported to be behind "Islamic Front" candidates who won a few seats in the elections of 1965 and 1968 and a larger representation (51 of 264) in 1986. In Jordan, too (including until 1967 the Palestinian *"West Bank"), the MB — led by 'Abd-ul-Rahman al-Khalifa — was for most of the time a legal organization, within the establishment though often in opposition; it contested elections (though its candidates usually appeared, formally, as "Independents") and several times won seats in Parliament. Its influence seems to have declined since the 1950s and 1960s. (A more extreme Islamic group, the "Islamic Liberation Party" *(Hizb al-Tahrir)*, which split since 1952 from the MB under Taqi-ul-Din al-Nabhani and appealed to the same public, was later accused of subversion and a plot against the régime, 1969, and was outlawed).

The country outside Egypt where the MB had the strongest impact was Syria. The Syrian MB was founded in the late 1930s and became really active from 1945–46. Its founder-leader was Mustafa al-Siba'i, Professor of Islamic Law at Damascus University, who died in 1964. Until the early 1960s the Syrian MB, though often dissenting from the mainstream (and linked to, or even clandestinely founding, more extreme groups of different names, such as an "Islamic Liberation Party"), was a legal part of the establishment, and presented candidates for Parliament, usually as Independents; in the House elected in 1961, for instance, 7–12 deputies, according to different versions, were considered MB men. It even had Ministers in the Government (e.g. in Khaled al-*'Azm's Government in 1962), and its leader Siba'i was for some time Deputy President of Parliament. But after the *Ba'th Party came to power, in the *coup* of 1963, the antagonism between the MB and the ruling leftist-revolutionary nationalist trends erupted into open mutual hostility — aggravated by the ever-increasing rôle played in the ruling establishment by members of the *'Alawi sect whom the Sunni-fundamentalist MB could not but consider heretics or non-believers. The MB, now led by 'Issam al-'Attar (who soon went into exile), was outlawed in 1963 and went underground. In the 1970s it began stepping up acts of sabotage and violence, which escalated particularly from 1978–79, including, for instance, a June 1979 attack on officer-cadets, most of them 'Alawis, in Aleppo, amounting to a massacre. Counter-action by the régime and its efforts to suppress the MB were equally brutal, leading in June 1980 to a massacre of MB detainees in Palmyra prison; in Feb. 1982 a veritable insurrection in Hama and full-fledged army and special forces action against it left Hama nearly destroyed by artillery shelling and thousands killed (in the official version: c. 1,200, in other reports: 10–30,000). After these battles, MB violence and sabotage seemed to have abated; but it was by no means clear that the MB had really been decisively suppressed.

Mutawali, Mutawalis (In Arabic, the plural is *matāwila*.) The *Shi'i Muslims of Lebanon (of the mainstream *Ithna-'Ashariyya* trend of the Shi'a) are called M. This refers principally to those in southern Lebanon (the "Jabal 'Āmel"), but also to those in the northern *Biqā'* (Coele-Syria), the Baalbek region. For data about the M. see *Lebanon; *Islam; *Shi'a; *Minorities.

N

Nagib, Muhammad (1901–84) Egyptian officer and politician, President of Egypt 1953–54. Born in Khartoum, the son of an Egyptian army officer, N. graduated from the University of Cairo (law) and the military academy, 1921. He joined the regular army and slowly rose in rank, becoming a colonel in 1948, a general in 1950. He was wounded as a brigade commander in the A.-Israel war of 1948. He subsequently became commander of the frontier force and, in 1951, of the land army.

Among army officers, N. was admired for his integrity; he frequently voiced demands for army reforms and the elimination of corruption. He apparently was not a member of the "Free Officers" group, but was in touch with them through his operations officer, 'Abd-ul-Hakim *'Amer. In 1952 he was their candidate for the presidency of the Officers' Club, and his election, against the wishes of the King and the senior establishment, caused a minor crisis. N. himself claimed that he joined the Free Officers from the start, 1949–50, and was their leader in the *coup* of July 1952. However, according to the later official version, generally accepted, he did not take an active part in the *coup* but was asked by the young revolutionaries to represent them as a sort of figurehead, while *Nasser was the real leader.

After the revolution of July 1952, N. was made Commander-in-Chief of the Armed Forces and chairman of the Revolutionary Command Council. When the civilian government formed after the *coup* resigned in Sept. 1952, N. became Prime Minister and Minister of War. On the proclamation of the Republic in June 1953, the Revolutionary Council appointed N. President and Prime Minister, but relieved him of his military post. From about that time, a deep rupture evolved between him and Nasser, which led to a grave crisis in Feb. 1954. N. held that his high office should carry real authority and a decisive share in the formulation of policies, while Nasser regarded him as a mere figurehead. N. thought, contrary to Nasser, that the army should return to its barracks and political-parliamentary rule should be restored — a view supported by right-wing circles, the *Wafd*, the *Muslim Brotherhood, and the Left. N. seemed, in general, to hold more moderate views — in foreign affairs, too, such as relations with Sudan, and a settlement of the Anglo-Egyptian dispute — and wished to restrain the revolutionary fervor of the young officers. The differences came to a head when it was decided, in Feb. 1954, without N.'s knowledge, to ban the activities of the Muslim Brotherhood. N. resigned in protest, but some of the ruling Free Officers, led by the leftist Khaled *Muhyi-ul-Din, supported him, used their army units to threaten a violent showdown, and forced N.'s return as President in Feb. and as Prime Minister in Mar. Nasser now mobilized counter-demonstrations of workers and army units — and gained the upper hand. In Apr. N. was relieved of the Premiership, and while he retained the Presidency, its powers were much reduced. In Nov. 1954 N. was dismissed from the Presidency, too (which remained vacant until 1956, when Nasser assumed it), and placed under house arrest. It was even hinted that he was involved in a Muslim Brotherhood plot then discovered and suppressed. His supporters, too, were purged.

N. was released from house arrest in 1971 only, after Nasser's death. But, while *Sadat accorded him a position of respected, retired elder statesman, he was offered no post and never regained any real influence. In the few interviews and articles he published, N. strongly supported Sadat — both in his internal and general policy and concerning his moves for peace with Israel. He also voiced harsh criticism of Nasser and his régime — going in one interview as far as to regret the revolution of 1952, and his part in it, and to claim that had it not been for Sadat's efforts to "save what could be saved", Egypt "would have gone to the dogs".

N.'s memoirs (as told to a Western journalist) were published, in English, in 1955, under the title "Egypt's Destiny"; he later partly dissociated himself from this book, and a Lebanese weekly serialized new memoirs by N. in 1973.

al-Nahayan See *Nuhayan.

al-Nahhas, Mustafa (1879–1965) Egyptian politician. After law studies at the University of Cairo, N. opened a law practice, and from 1904 to 1919 was a judge. In 1918 he joined Sa'd *Zaghlul in his nationalist agitation, became a member — and soon a leader — of Zaghlul's *Wafd Party, and was exiled with Zaghlul to the Seychelles. Since Egypt's first elections under the new constitution, 1924, he was a member of Parliament. In 1924 he was Minister of Communications in Zaghlul's short-lived Government. On Zaghlul's death in 1927, N. was elected head of the Wafd Party, and remained its leader until his death. In 1928 and 1930 he was for short periods Prime Minister (keeping the Home Ministry for himself) — each time dismissed or forced to resign by the political manipulations of the King and the politicians close to him. In 1935 he led — and won — a campaign of agitation for the reinstatement of the parliamentary constitution that had been replaced since 1930. He led the Wafd to victory in the elections of May 1936 and formed a new Wafdist government. In Aug. of the same year he headed the all-party delegation which negotiated and signed the Anglo-Egyptian Treaty giving Egypt nominal full independence (see *Egypt). In Dec. 1937 King *Farouq dismissed N. and the Wafd again went into opposition.

In Feb. 1942 the British, convinced that only a nationalist Wafd government would fully co-operate with them and fulfil Egypt's obligations towards the war effort, forced the King to dismiss the Government and appoint N. Prime Minister (he again took also the Interior portfolio). In the elections of Mar. 1942, N. again led the Wafd to victory. As Prime Minister, N. chaired the talks towards the establishment of the *Arab League, 1943–44, and the League's preparatory *Alexandria Conference, Oct. 1944. The day after that conference — with the British no longer so blatantly intervening in Egypt's internal affairs — King *Farouq dismissed him. The Wafd boycotted the elections of Jan. 1945, but won the next ones, in Jan. 1950, and N. once again formed a government. He now followed a nationalist, anti-British policy. As negotiations on the termination of the presence of British troops and bases, and the amendment or abrogation of the treaty of 1936, made no progress, N. in Oct. 1951 unilaterally abrogated the treaty and proclaimed the incorporation of Sudan under the Egyptian crown. He also rejected a Western invitation to co-sponsor a Western-led ME Defense Pact (and seek a solution to the problem of British bases in the framework of such a pact). He started a popular struggle to eject the British troops that led to mounting violence and clashes, culminating in battles between Egyptian and British troops and the eruption of mob violence ("Black Saturday", Jan. 1952). In the crisis created his government fell. Corruption charges against N. and his team also contributed to that fall.

In the purges conducted by the "Free Officers" régime after the *coup* of July 1952, N. did not face trial (as many politicians of the pre-*coup* régime did), but the Wafd party was compelled to dismiss him from its leadership. His wife was tried on several charges of corruption and sentenced to heavy fines and the confiscation of most of her property. N. himself was in 1954 deprived of his civil and political rights; they were restored to him in 1960, but he did not return to political activity.

Najd The central region of Saʻudi Arabia and the Arabian peninsula, a desert plateau not precisely defined but usually taken to be about half of Saʻudia's area, c. 400,000 sq. mi. or 1m. sq. km., with a population of 3–4m. (estimate). In the past, most of the population were Bedouin, nomadic or semi- nomadic, and N. was the center of the strongest tribes and tribal federations; but in recent decades most of them have left the nomadic ways. Permanent settlements were located, in the past, in oases only (al-Riyadh — now the capital of Saʻudi Arabia, Haʼil, ʻAnaiza, Buraida et al.). Caravans used to pass through N. from the Persian Gulf coast and Iraq to Mecca, Medina and the Red Sea coast. With Saʻudia's rapid development, a network of modern communications has been built. A railway links Riyadh to the oil centers on the Persian Gulf, and a network of modern roads to the Gulf, Mecca, Medina and the Red Sea. An oil pipeline crosses N. from the Gulf to Yanbuʻ on the Red Sea, and a 460-km. pipe carries desalinated water from Jubail on the Gulf coast to Riyadh.

In the 19th century N. was in dispute between the great tribes, especially the House of *Rashid of Jabal Shammar, whose stronghold was in Haʼil, and the House of *Saʻud of the ʻAnaza tribe, centered in Riyadh — who eventually won in 1921 — see *Saʻud, House of. The name N. survived in the titles Ibn Saʻud assumed from 1926 to 1932. In the administrative structure of Saʻudi Arabia, since 1932, most of N. is within the Governorate of Riyadh and there is no administrative unit by the name of N.

al-Nashashibi Palestinian-A. family in Jerusalem which became prominent in the last century of Turkish-Ottoman rule and provided many administrators and public figures. At the beginning of the 20th century, ʻUthman N. was considered head of the clan; he was elected to the Ottoman Parliament in 1912 and 1914. After his death the same year, Ragheb N. became head of the family and its most prominent figure (see entry following).

A colorful member of the N. clan was Fakhri N., a political organizer and, from the late 1920s the family's "strong-arm man". For some time he served the Mandate government — as aide to the Governor of Jerusalem, 1920, and later ADC to High Commissioner Herbert Samuel. During Ragheb N.'s term as Mayor of Jerusalem, Fakhri was his chief aide. He later became one of the chief organizers of opposition to the Mufti of Jerusalem, his Supreme Muslim Council and his *Husseini faction, and one of the founders and organizers of the N.'s "Defense Party", 1934. He also organized trade unions. In the first stage of the A. rebellion, 1936, he was active in the recruitment of guerrilla bands, but when the Husseini-led rebellion turned against the opposition and embarked upon internal terrror (including several attempts on his life), Fakhri N. in 1938 became a chief organizer of counter-bands for the protection of the opposition leaders, the so-called "Peace Gangs" (in some cooperation with branches of the British military and the Jews). He was reportedly prepared to accept the 1937 plan for the partition of Palestine and to seek an accomodation with the Jews, and tried to revive the "Defense Party" as a moderate political force. In World War II, he promoted the recruitment of Palestinian-A. volunteers for the British Army. Detested by the Husseini-led nationalists as a traitor (accused also of corruption in his business activities) and sentenced to death by secret terrorist courts, Fakhri N. was assassinated in Baghdad in 1941.

Among other notable members of the N. family in the last generations: Muhammad Isʻaf N. (1882?–1948), the son of the family's head ʻUthman N., was a known writer, one of the few Palestinian-A. writers with all-A. renown. ʻAli N. was among the founders, in 1912, of a "Decentralization Party" for the A. parts of the Ottoman Empire; in 1915 he was suspected of subversive activities, tried and executed in 1916. Anwar N. (b. 1913) was an official in the Palestine government, inter alia as adviser to the A. section of the Palestine Broadcasting Service, and later a French-trained lawyer. He was also active as a journalist and wrote many articles. In 1945 he joined Mussa *ʻAlami's Palestine-A. propaganda offices. He then entered the service of Jordan, becoming a Cabinet Minister. ʻAzmi N. (b. 1903) — a journalist, and from the 1930s an official of the Palestine Mandate government, *inter alia* director of the A. section of the Palestine Broadcasting Service (1944–48); from 1948 in the service of Jordan — as director of the Broadcasting Service, Cabinet Minister and diplomat. Nasser-ul-Din N. (b. 1924) — a well-known journalist, living mostly in Egypt, served for some years as *Arab League emissary in Europe, mainly for information/propaganda work; N. published a book of memoirs (*Roving Ambassador*, Arabic, Beirut 1970). Muhammad Zuhdi N. has been active in the *PLO leadership, from the mid-1970s to the mid-1980s as a member of its Executive Committee.

In the 1920s and 1930s, and to a decreasing extent in the 1940s, the term "The N.'s" denoted in common usage, besides the name of the prominent family described, the Palestinian-A. political group which the family headed, *viz.* the faction of the opposition (*al-Mu'āridin*) to the Supreme Muslim Council and its Husseini leadership. The official program of the N. faction, and its "Defense Party" founded in 1934, was not very different from that of the other nationalist parties and the mainstream. In practice, however, they were ready to co-operate with the British Mandate authorities, maintained close relations with Amir *'Abdullah of Transjordan and in the 1940s advocated and prepared his take-over of the A. part of Palestine; they were also more moderate with regard to the Jews. In 1936, the N.'s joined in organizing the A. rebellion in its early stages then called "The Disturbances"; but when guerrilla formations launched a campaign of assassinations directed against the N.'s and their opposition faction, they seceded and organized counter-guerrillas, "Peace Gangs" (see above, Fakhri N.).

During the later 1930s and the 1940s, the family and its political faction declined in influence and power and many of their members took public and political positions conflicting with the family tradition. To a degree, this was part of a general decline of the role of the prominent families and their function in determining the political affiliation of their members and clients. But the decline of the N.'s was in large part the result of their leaders' disappointment and lack of assertive activity.

al-Nashashibi, Ragheb (1875? 1880/81?– 1951) Palestinian-A. politician, head of the N. family of Jerusalem (see above). A graduate in engineering of Ottoman-Turkish universities, N. was Jerusalem district engineer and from 1914 one of the representatives of Jerusalem in the Ottoman Parliament. In World War I he was an officer in the Turkish army. After the British occupation of Palestine (1918), with the first steps of Palestinian-A. political organization, he was among the founders of the "Literary Club" (*al-Muntada al-Adabi*), which competed with the "Arab Club" (*al-Nadi al-'Arabi*) dominated by the rival *Husseini family.

When Mussa Kazem al-*Husseini was dismissed as Mayor of Jerusalem in 1920, N. was appointed to that post, which he held until 1934. He co-operated with the British authorities and advised the A.'s to participate in representative, self-governing bodies which the British proposed and the nationalist A. mainstream rejected. In 1923, his adherents formed a "National Party" (*al-Hizb al-Watani*) — which in appearance and extremist slogans hardly differed from the Husseini nationalist faction, but under the surface tried to promote more moderate policies and co-operation with the Government, and to a degree with the Jews. The party did not last long. In his efforts to organize the camp opposing the Supreme *Muslim Council and the rival extremist Husseini faction dominating that Council, N. now turned to local, municipal interests and succeeded, despite the failure of his party on the national level, in recruiting many A. mayors to his camp of "The Opposition" (*al-Mu'āridin*). In the first municipal elections, held in 1927, he won in Jerusalem and his supporters triumphed in all towns except Gaza. In 1934, however, he was defeated in the Jerusalem elections.

In 1934 the N.'s founded a "Defense Party" with RN at its head. In that capacity he became a member of the "Arab Higher Committee" formed in Apr. 1936 to lead the general strike that turned into a rebellion. He supported the strike and the first stage of the "Disturbances", but when in 1937 they deteriorated into internal terror, he resigned from the Higher Committee and turned against the Husseini leadership.

In 1937, N. was inclined to accept the proposals for the partition of Palestine then announced by the British, though in public he opposed it. He supported Amir *'Abdullah of Transjordan and was one of his confidants — but this position, too, found little public expression. Nor did N. publicize his reported moderation on the A.-Jewish issue. He accepted and supported the new British policy under the White Paper of 1939 (which other A. leaders in public rejected as conceding too little). But in the late 1930s and the 1940s he was politically inactive — depressed by the Palestinian-A. internecine terror and the impasse into which the Husseini command had led the Palestine A.'s, and disappointed that the British, after the suppression of the Husseini rebellion, did not actively promote his alternative leadership. He thus allowed his faction to decline.

In 1948, N. actively promoted the Jordanian annexation of the A. part of Palestine (to become the *"West Bank" of Jordan) and organized Palestinian-A. support for that move. He was appointed as the first governor of the West Bank — but did not take active charge, seemed to regard that post as a symbolic position of honor, and kept it for a short time only. In 1950 he joined the Jordanian Cabinet as Minister of Agriculture, and later of Transport, and in 1951 he became Minister without portfolio in charge of *al-Haram al-Sharif*, the Jerusalem Temple Mount, and Guardian of the Holy Places. He died the same year.

Nasser See *'Abd-ul-Nasser, Gamal.

Nasserism The social and political doctrine of Egypt's Gamal *'Abd-ul-Nasser; the political and social attitude of A.'s in many countries, mainly in the late 1950s and the 1960s, who regarded 'Abd-ul-Nasser as the leader of all A.'s, and Egypt under his leadership as the prototype of an A. nation progressing towards national freedom and social justice. The term N. is mainly a foreign, Western creation and seldom used in Arabic; A.'s usually call it "A. Socialism" or "A. Socialist Unionism". N. is neither a well-defined doctrine nor an organized movement, but rather a general socio-political outlook. Yet, it was for some years the most popular ideological-political trend in the A. world, developing against the background of disillusionment with other ideologies and disappointment with the performance of A. leaders and governments.

Incipient N. was a strongly nationalist reformism, emphasizing vigorous economic and social development with an expanding state sector, enlarged by a process of nationalization, based on a single-party near-totalitarian populism (in fact, though not in doctrine, led by an activist core of the officers' corps). It professed a strident neutralism — with strong anti-Western undertones determined by anti-colonialist memories and the urge to eliminate positions of privilege still held by Western powers. In the early 1960s, Nasser and his régime — and therefore N. — became increasingly Socialist, adopting a populist-totalitarian version of state socialism; a *Pan-Arab element, the wish to unite all AC under similar "Socialist-Unionist" régimes, also received a stronger emphasis. Ideologically, N. had to compete with several similar "Socialist-Unionist" trends — e.g. the clandestine "A. Nationalist Movement" (*Harakat al-Qawmiyyin*, see *Arab Nationalism) and the Syria-centered *Ba'th* group — although it would be difficult to define precisely the doctrinal differences. But N., less doctrinaire and rather more pragmatic, and with Egypt's power and prestige behind it, seemed to have a stronger impact on all-A. opinion, while the *Qawmiyyun*, at first considered sort of younger, more extreme Nasserists, were drifting into an increasingly leftist-Maoist position.

However, Nasser and his associates were not content with the gradual growth of their influence, but tried to expand the power of N., as a doctrine, as a political régime, and as a tool of Egyptian predominance, by means unacceptable to the other ASt, including underground intrigues, plots, political assassination and subversion (see *Egypt, *'Abd-ul-Nasser, *Arab Nationalism). Because of these strong-arm or subversive tactics, N. lost much of its attraction. Those ASt that were the target or scene of Nasserist attempts to gain control, resisted and denounced them, and even pro-Nasserist AC or groups did not fully accept N.'s guidance, at least not in its Egyptian version. In Iraq and Syria, particularly the latter, Nasserist factions were locked in combat with the dominating *Ba'th* stream, and their claim for co-equal leadership was defeated.

As N. failed to impose itself on AC outside Egypt, doubts were cast on its success even in its Egyptian home and base. As Egypt got bogged down in her military intervention in Yemen (1962–67) Nasser and his associates in the later 1960s tuned down their efforts to "export" N. to other AC. With Nasser's death in 1970, N. lost much of what remained of its magic. Even in Egypt herself, Nasser's successor, *Sadat, changed policies in a way that amounted to a *de facto* dismantling of N. as the basic doctrine of Egypt's governance and society.

In Egypt, the officers' régime's single party — the "Liberation Organization" 1953–58; the "National Union", 1957–62; and the "Arab Socialist Union" 1962–77 (formally dissolved in 1980) — may be regarded as the organizational instrument of N. For the three years of the abortive Egyptian-Syrian union (the *UAR), 1958–61, the "National Union" operated in Syria, too, as the only legal political party. But even at its peak, N. had no organized, unified instruments outside Egypt, no all-Arab roof organization uniting the small groups or factions that could be seen as inclining to or being guided by N. Such groups, usually calling themselves "Socialist-Unionist" in different versions and split into competing factions, existed mainly in Syria and Lebanon (after N. was eliminated in Iraq, as a serious organized force in 1959). In Syria they were liquidated or driven into exile after 1963, except for splinter factions prepared to submit to *Ba'th* primacy and to join a united front led by the *Ba'th*. In Lebanon various small groups that could be described as Nasserist continue operating — such as the Muslim-Sunni "militia" of the *Murabitun* in Beirut or a similar formation maintained by the Muslim-Sunni leaders of Sidon.

Traces or elements of N., in a measure that cannot be precisely pinned down, may be seen in various leaders and organizations in AC — such as the Lebanese Druze leader *Junbalat and his "Progressive Socialist Party"; Iraqi President *'Aref, 1963–66; Sudan's *Numeiri, 1969–85; the Algerian *FLN, especially in its first stages under *Ben Bella; radical independent opposition members of the National Assembly in Kuwait. Even Libya's *Qadhdhafi, whose doctrine is quite different from N., was a fervent admirer of Nasser and would probably describe himself as his disciple. Thus, N. as a general outlook, though not as a defined doctrine or organized political force, may be said still to exert some influence, despite its decline, in several AC, and mainly in Egypt herself — where it is imbued with a certain nostalgia and absorbs feelings of discontent with the post-Nasser régime and present conditions.

National Liberation Front (Algeria) See *FLN.

National Liberation Front for Occupied South Yemen (NLF) Militant nationalist underground and guerrilla organization in *'Aden and *South Arabia (later South Yemen). Based mainly on the tribal hinterland of 'Aden, the NLF was founded in 1963, with Qahtan al-*Sha'bi as its main leader. It was considered the strongest group in the nationalist rebellion that broke out in Oct. 1963 and continued intermittently until the achievement of independence in 1967. In 1966 the NLF joined a roof-organization, *FLOSY, but it seceded the same year, re-establishing itself as a separate organization. In a violent struggle between the two factions, the NLF won out, and in 1967 it gained control of the South Arabian principalities one after the other, defeating both FLOSY and the sheikhs' and princes' armed forces and compelling the British to transfer authority to the NLF (and not to the princes, as planned, or to FLOSY).

In Nov. 1967 the NLF formed the ruling group, single party and government of the new People's Republic of South Yemen, with Qahtan al-Sha'bi as President. Although at first sometimes supported by Egypt (which in general preferred FLOSY), the NLF had been closely associated with, and influenced by, the extremist "Arab Nationalist Movement" (*Harakat al-*Qawmiyyin*, see *Arab Nationalism) and its increasingly Leninist-Maoist ideas. From 1967 it veered further to the left, gradually becoming a Moscow-guided Communist party (though for some years there was a struggle between Russia-oriented and China-oriented factions). In Oct. 1978 the NLF, still the ruling single party, renamed itself "Yemen Socialist Party". For the constant factional struggles within the NLF/YSP and the *coups* they engendered, see *South Yemen.

Negev (Hebrew: drylands, south.) The southern half of Palestine/Israel, a triangle with its apex at Eilat-*'Aqaba on the Red Sea's Gulf of 'Aqaba. Though the N. was allotted to the Jewish State under the UN partition plan of 1947, Egypt complained in 1949 to the Mixed Armistice Commission that Israel's presence at its southern tip was illegal, as her forces had reached that point in Mar. 1949 only, after the Egypt-Israel armistice; the complaint was rejected in 1950, and nothing more was heard of it. However, many A.'s saw the southern part of the N. as the land bridge between Egypt and Jordan and seemed to harbor aspirations. British plans, in 1946–48, envisaged the N. as a major British base, under arrangements to be made with Egypt and/or Jordan, rather than as part of the Jewish State; the US also thought for some time that Israel should give up the N., and Count *Bernadotte, the UN mediator, proposed in 1948 to award it to Jordan. All these proposals, rejected by Israel, were dropped. The idea of an extra-territorial Egypt-Jordan corridor through the southern N. continued to be mooted. But while Israel would probably agree to facilitate Egypt-Jordan transit in the context of peace, the idea of extra-territorial arrangements was unacceptable to her — and was, indeed, never raised officially.

Nestorians See *Assyrians.

neutralism Neutrality in time of war — an accepted and well-defined concept of international law — was practised in *World War II by the ASt independent at the time: Egypt, Iraq, Sa'udi Arabia and Yemen; but as an allied victory became certain, three of them joined the Allies. Iraq declared war in Jan. 1943, Egypt in Feb. 1945, and Sa'udi Arabia proclaimed her "adhesion" to the Allies in Mar. 1945. None of them took part in actual war operations against the "Axis" powers.

N. as a concept or a general inclination (which would not automatically prescribe actual neutrality in time of war) is quite a different matter. The desire to avoid involvement in the struggle of great powers and power blocs is natural for small states and was in fact put into practice by many countries throughout history, long before the term N. gained currency. N. as a concept — for which soon the term Non-Alignment was preferred — was born after World War II, as a growing number of Asian and African countries became independent. Several statesmen stood at its cradle. The man who gave the notion currency was India's Jawaharlal Nehru, in close alliance with Tito of Yugoslavia and Egypt's *Nasser. In 1949–50, Israel, too, inclined to N. — but she was rebuffed by the nascent non-aligned camp and in any case switched to a more pronounced pro-Western attitude from about 1950.

The new N. added several new dimensions to the natural desire to avoid involvement in power blocs. Its sponsors argued that N. was a particularly appropriate stance for the newly independent states of Asia and Africa, and gave it a sharp edge against Colonialism — i.e., against the former Western rulers, now seen by many as aspiring to "neo-colonialist" control (while most of them ignored the colonialist aspects of Russia's acquisition of and rule in her Asian parts). N. thus acquired a distinct anti-Western hue and the countries professing it were closer to the Soviet bloc than to the American-led Western one. This tendency was enhanced by the attitude of the West. Both power blocs at first disdained N.; but the Soviet bloc soon came around to favor and support it, while the USA in the 1950s still condemned N. and thought it immoral (e.g., J.F. Dulles) and changed its views much later. The fathers of N., and particularly Nehru, also endowed their N. with a moral dimension. They considered it the proper, the "right", doctrine for Third World countries and were highly critical of countries linked to the great powers, and especially to the USA.

The leftist-"progressive" ASt were among the first to adopt the new N. Egypt's Nasser was among its sponsors and its main protagonist among the ASt, naming his version "*Positive N.*", i.e., putting emphasis on active policies and doctrines of his own rather than passive-negative neutrality in relation to the powers. The other leftist ASt — in the 1950s mainly Syria and Iraq, later also Algeria, Yemen, Sudan, Libya — soon joined the camp of N. (and the rift between them and the conservative, Western-linked ASt split the *Arab League into rival camps).

The camp of N. soon expanded to include more and more Asian and African countries — even states allied to the Soviet bloc or the West which would not fit into the original definition of N. Gradually, almost *all* Asian and African countries joined the Neutralist or non-aligned group, until membership of the group had grown from an original 25 to 99 countries (plus two "Liberation Organizations"). The conservative ASt were in the forefront of that quasi-neutralist stampede. In fact, Sa'udi Arabia, Morocco and Tunisia joined the neutralist camp right at its first fully fledged congress, 1961; Jordan joined a little later, and by the mid-1960s all ASt were members.

The neutralist group had no common policy on most world issues, except for its anti-colonial stance. In fact, N. did not prescribe common policies, as it determined general attitudes only and left it to each country to interpret the principles of N. in the light of its own circumstances and interests. However, as membership expanded until it included full-fledged members of the Soviet bloc like North Vietnam and North Korea (since 1975) and allies of the USA, both South Vietnam and her Communist Vietcong rebels (since 1972–73), the group became less and less cohesive and its members took different and conflicting positions on most controversial international problems, such as Korea, Vietnam, the Congo, Cambodia, Afghanistan. In fact, within the neutralist bloc there emerged a leftist, pro-Soviet camp, a Western-inclined one, and a "neutral" one in the center. Yet, as to rhetoric and verbal declarations and resolutions, the left-inclined camp retained the upper hand. Concerning the A.-Israel conflict, the neutralist group fully supported the A. side (including countries that maintain friendly relations with Israel).

No neutralist country takes a favorable view of N. or non-alignment when its own interests are concerned. India, for example, the leading proponent of N., bitterly resents neutralist positions taken even by friendly countries with regard to her border dispute with China or the problem of Kashmir. Nor do neutralist Iran and Iraq accept a neutralist position in the war between them.

In its first years the non-aligned group of nations was content with informal meetings of its leaders or envoys, mainly at the UN during its General Assembly. Nor has the group established a formal organization in later years. But the *Bandung Conference of Asian and African states (1955) was to a certain extent a meeting of neutralist countries. Since then, the non-aligned group has institutionalized, in an increasingly formal way, regular meetings — both at the "summit" level of Heads of States and at the working level of Foreign Ministers. It has also set up a permanent co-ordination bureau of a number of Foreign Ministers. Its first summit conference was held at Belgrade in Sept. 1961, with 25 countries participating; similar meetings followed from time to time: Cairo 1964 (46 countries plus 11 observers), Lusaka 1970 (54 countries, 8 observers), Algiers 1973 (76 countries), Colombo 1976 (85 countries), Havana 1979 (96 countries), Delhi 1983 (99 countries, and 2 organizations), Harare 1986 (same attendance). Various Afro-Asian organizations, such as the Afro-Asian Peoples' Solidarity Organization and similar bodies (see *Africa) are also, in spirit and function, if not by definition, neutralist or non-aligned bodies.

neutral zones In British-led negotiations over the northern frontiers of *Najd (later *Sa'udi Arabia), in the early 1920s, large areas on the borders with Iraq and Kuwait remained in dispute. They were the domain of nomadic Bedouin tribes who ignored boundaries and resisted a centralized government control. It was therefore agreed — at a Dec. 1922 meeting in 'Uqair — between Sultan (later King) *Ibn Sa'ud and Sir Percy Cox, the British High Commissioner for Iraq, to set up two zones of "neutral and common ground", one on the Najd-Iraq frontier, the other on that of Najd and Kuwait. In the latter, oil was later discovered and exploitation rights were given separately by Sa'udi Arabia and Kuwait to different companies; since no borders between the two concessions were delineated, the companies on the two sides had to cooperate. In 1964–65; Sa'udi Arabia and Kuwait agreed to divide the NZ between them. An agreement on the border delimitation was finalized in Dec. 1969, except for two offshore islands that remained in dispute. It was, however, agreed to let the oil companies continue their operations, the two countries to share the oil revenue. However, in some statistical and other data the NZ is still separately listed. Sa'udia and Iraq also agreed, in July 1975, to divide the NZ between them by a straight line dividing it into equal parts. Some border rectifications were agreed in 1981.

Nile River in Africa — the world's longest (c. 4,160 mi., nearly 7,000 km.). Its two main sources, the White N. and the Blue N., join and form the N. north of Khartoum, in Sudan. The White N. rises in equatorial East Africa, flowing through Lake Victoria, Lake Kyoga and Lake Albert to the savannah plains of Sudan. In the flat regions of southern Sudan its waters spread and form a large swamp area, the *Sudd*, where half of it is lost through evaporation. The White N. supplies a major part of the N. waters during the eight months when the river is low. The Blue N. rises on the Ethiopian plateau and passes through Lake Tana. Plentiful rainfall in that region causes flooding from June to October. Below the confluence of the Blue and White N.'s, the N. takes in, from the southeast, one more major tributary, the Atbara, coming down from the northeast Ethiopian highlands. The N. then enters the desert and makes its way through a narrow valley. Rock barriers form five cataracts along that valley. Below the northernmost cataract, the *Aswan High Dam was built, creating a large, over 310 mi. (500 km.) long lake (Lake Nasser). North of *Cairo, the N. branches out into a large delta formed by silt deposits, and then flows into the Mediterranean.

The average annual flow of the N. on the Sudan-Egypt border is nearly 85,000 m. cubic meters (mcm) — 25,000 mcm coming from the White N., 50,000 mcm from the Blue N. and 10,000 mcm from the Atbara. The N. and its waters form the lifeline of Sudan and particularly of Egypt. The area of Egypt outside the N. valley is, except for a number of oases, mostly desert, and cultivation is confined to the long, narrow strip of land in the N. Valley and the widening area of its delta — c. 13,500 sq. mi. (35,000 sq. km.), about 3.5% of Egypt's land. Agriculture totally depends on irrigation from the N. As the quantity of water during the dry season is insufficient, the construction of dams to control and store the N. waters during the flooding season has been the cornerstone of Egypt's economic development and her ability to cope with the rapidly increasing population. It was also necessary, to a lesser degree, for northern Sudan. Such storage, as it developed from the beginning of the 20th century, has permitted a transition from basin irrigation by flooding during the high water season to perennial irrigation throughout the year and the harvesting of two or three crops.

Work on flood control barrages and later storage dams was begun in the late 19th century: the Delta Barrage was begun in 1843, made serviceable in 1887–90 and reinforced in 1898–1901; further barrages were built at Asyut (1901–02), Isna (1908), and Nag Hamadi (1930). The first major dam was completed at Aswan in 1902; its level was raised and its capacity increased in 1907–12 and again in 1932–35. Several small dams were added in Middle Egypt. In Sudan, two dams were constructed between the World Wars: at Sennar on the Blue N. (1925–26), and at Jabal Awliya on the White N. (1937). After and the achievement of complete independence, Egypt built, with Soviet aid, the "High Dam" (al-Sadd al-'Aali) near Aswan (1960–70). It is assumed that with the completion of that giant project Egypt's use of the N. waters for storage, irrigation and power, and the expansion of her irrigated land, have realized their potential to the full. Sudan constructed another major dam on the Blue N. at Russairis (completed 1966).

The division of the N. waters between Egypt and Sudan was a cause for much dispute, and as Britain was administering Sudan, it became part of the Anglo-Egyptian conflict. In 1920 Egypt objected to the allocation of water from the N. for the development and irrigation of the *Gezira region in Sudan and the plans for a Blue N. dam. The enlargement of N.-irrigated areas in Sudan was one of the measures taken by Britain against Egypt in the Anglo-Egyptian crisis of 1924. An expert commission established to resolve that crisis, recommended a mode of distribution of the N. waters, taking into account the interests of both Egypt and Sudan, but Egypt in 1925 rejected its recommendations. An agreement was reached in May 1929, allotting to Egypt 48,000 mcm and to Sudan 4,000 mcm and granting Egypt priority in the realization of her quota and the right to inspect Sudan's irrigation works.

The agreement of 1929 held good for about 25 years. Yet Egypt's resolve to control the source of her vital water supply was one of the chief reasons for her demand for the "Unity of the N. Valley", i.e., her claim to rule Sudan — dropped only in 1953. In the 1950s a revision of the 1929 agreement became necessary — both in preparation for the new Aswan High Dam scheme, and because Sudan was pressing for a more equitable share of the N. waters. After nearly five years of negotiations a new agreement was signed in 1959. On the assumption that new works would make available larger quantities of water, Egypt was now allotted 55,000 mcm and Sudan 18,000 mcm p.a.; additional waters expected with the future completion of the drainage of the al-Sudd swamps (estimated at 18,000 mcm. p.a.) were to be shared equally by the two countries.

Egyptian-Sudanese schemes and agreements were based on the assumption that the quantities of water reaching Sudan from Uganda (the White N.) and Ethiopia (the Blue N.) would not be significantly diminished by development works in those countries. There was, however, no hard and fast agreement with the two countries. Ethiopia always claimed that as the "supplier" of a major part of the N. waters (according to her: "84%") she was a partner to any N. development and should be consulted. In 1959 she laid the foundation to a large hydroelectric plant and dam at Lake Tana; and soon after that newly independent Uganda (with Kenya and Tanzania as partners) informed Egypt and Sudan that in the next decades she would, in addition to the hydro-electric plant existing at Owen Falls, Lake Victoria, use more N. waters e.g. for schemes on Lakes Kyoga and Albert. Talks with Egypt in 1961–62 yielded no agreement. The implementation of these schemes in Ethiopia and Uganda has made little progress; in fact, it was nearly halted by the internal crises of those countries. But the problem posed by them has not been resolved.

NLF   See *National Liberation Front.

non-alignment   See *neutralism.

Nuba   Negroid tribes of non-A. origin in western Sudan, mainly in Kordofan. Most of them are non-Muslim, pagan animists; but a minority is Muslim. The N. are believed to number about 600,000. Those of northern Kordofan are completely Arabicized, though maintaining their tribal customs. Some N. groups in the south of Kordofan have taken the names of the A. tribes they once served as slaves. The diversity of the N. languages has caused them to adopt Arabic as a *lingua franca*. The N. have taken little part in S.'s general national movement. They have, however, organized to protect their particularist, tribal interests, mainly against the dominating Muslim-A. northern Sudanese, and have sometimes linked themselves in some measure to the African tribes rebelling in South Sudan. A senior N. leader, Philip 'Abbas Ghabbush was active in the 1960s, underground under *Numeiri's régime, 1969–85, and several times accused of secessionist-"racial" plots. In 1985 he founded a "Sudan National Party" advocating a federal system for Sudan, with Jabal N. as one of the semi-autonomous constituent regions. In Sept. 1985 Ghabbush and his party were involved in a *coup* attempt against the post-Numeiri régime and Ghabbush was imprisoned until Jan. 1986. In the Apr. 1986 elections he won 8 seats. He was invited to join the government coalition, but preferred to stay in opposition.

Nubia, Nubians   N. is the area between Upper Egypt and Sudan, from the Red Sea to the Libyan desert — an almost rainless plateau bisected by the *Nile, mostly arid steppes and sandy desert. Politically N. is divided between Egypt and Sudan. The N., also called Barābira or Danāqila, form the majority of the population between Khartoum and Upper Egypt, estimated at 350–400,000. They are descendants of an ancient people of mixed Egyptian and Black-African origin with later A. admixture; they are Muslims, and besides their own African-Hamitic language most of them also speak Arabic. Herdsmen and peasants at home, many of them migrated to urban centers in Egypt and Sudan.

The people who were living on lands flooded by the lake created by the *Aswan High Dam in the late 1960s ("Lake Nasser") — about 100,000 — were mostly N. They were resettled by Egypt and Sudan (with Egypt paying compensation to the latter); but many of them drifted back and rebuilt villages on both shores of Lake Nasser.

al-Nuhayan (also Nahayan, Nihayan)   The clan or dynasty of sheikhs ruling *Abu Dhabi in *Trucial 'Oman, since 1971 the *United Arab Emirates (UAE). The ruler, and head of the clan, during recent decades is Sheikh Zayed ibn Sultan al-N. (b. 1918). Sheikh Zayed was for twenty years, 1946–66, Governor of the sheikhdom's al-'Ain district, with the oasis of al-*Buraimi at its center. In Aug. 1966 he overthrew — reportedly with the encouragement of the British, then still the protecting power — his brother Sheikh Shakhbut ibn Sultan (who had ruled the sheikhdom since 1928 and was considered an obstacle to development and progress) and became the ruler of Abu Dhabi. He played a major role in the negotiations towards the federation of the Trucial Coast sheikhdoms as the UAE and in efforts to overcome the rivalries and disputes between the various sheikhs (chief among which was his own clan's near-permanent rivalry with the sheikhs al-*Maktum, the rulers of *Dubai). With the foundation of the UAE, 1971, Sheikh Zayed became President of the Federation, remaining also ruler of Abu Dhabi. He was re-elected in 1976, 1981 and 1986, by the "Supreme Council of Rulers", for five-year terms. Sheikh Zayed has been pressing, with gradual, slow success, for stronger federal institutions — with the main resistance coming from the ruler of Dubai.

Numeiri, (Muhammad) Ja'far (b. 1930) Sudanese officer and politician, ruler of Sudan 1969–85. After graduation from the pre-independence Military College of Khartoum in 1952, N. served in infantry and armor units. He was suspected of participating in anti-government instigation and heading subversive cells, including a "Free Officers" group from 1963, and was suspended and arrested several times (1957, 1959, 1965), but reinstated each time. After his rehabilitation of 1966 he completed a course at an American military college and later attained the rank of Brigadier-General.

In May 1969 N. seized power in a military *coup*. He dismissed the Presidential Council and the Government, dissolved Parliament and banned all political parties, and formed a Revolutionary Council as the supreme state organ, with himself at its head. He also appointed himself Commander-in-Chief and Defense Minister, and in Oct. 1969 also Prime Minister. N. had to balance between conservative groups (such as the two great orders, the *Mahdiyya* and the *Khatmiyya* — both of which had little sympathy for his régime), the army (on which he relied), and the Communists (whose main faction he half-suppressed, while letting other factions participate in his government). In Mar. 1970 he suppressed *al-Ansar*, the militant organization of the *Mahdiyya*. In July 1971 he was overthrown in a *coup* headed by leftist officers whom he had purged in 1970; but a counter-*coup* returned him to power three days later (reportedly with Egyptian and Libyan help). He then savagely suppressed the Communists.

In Sept. 1971 N. was elected President, the only candidate in a plebiscite. He was re-elected in 1977 and 1983. As President he also retained the Premiership. In 1972 he founded a single party on the Egyptian pattern, the "Sudan Socialist Union", and headed its politbureau. From 1972 he also convened a "People's Council" or National Assembly. In Mar. 1972 he reached agreement with the South Sudan African rebels by conceding a wide local- regional autonomy — his major achievement. But his régime did not attain real stability — the single party did not take roots; he frequently changed his Vice-President and the heads of the Defense establishment; a "National Front", comprising both the *Mahdiyya* with its *Umma* Party and its adversary, the "National Unionists" supported by the *Khatmiyya*, harassed his régime, partly from bases in Libya; the settlement with the South Sudanese rebels turned sour and he began reneging on it; and the economic situation deteriorated continuously (for these developments see *Sudan). N.'s foreign policy was also somewhat erratic. In 1969–70 he planned to join a Federation with Egypt and Libya; but in 1971 he opted out. He fostered, however, close relations with Egypt, signing a Defense Agreement with her in 1976–77 and an accord on gradual integration in 1982 and instituting a joint "Nile Valley Parliament". The USA and the West came to regard him, in his later years, with sympathy.

N. gradually cultivated an alliance with fundamentalist Islamic groups, chiefly the *Muslim Brotherhood. In Sept. 1983 he decreed the full implementation of the code of punishments of Islamic law, the *Shari'a — a measure that aroused strong opposition. A new rebellion of the South Sudanese Africans also erupted. It may be reasonably assumed that these two developments hastened N.'s fall. He was overthrown in Apr. 1985 in a *coup* mounted by the Army in collaboration with his political foes. N. escaped to Egypt and received political asylum there — despite the new régime's repeated demands for his extradition. A decision to try him *in absentia* was reported, but not implemented.

Nuqrashi, Mahmud Fahmi (1888–1948) Egyptian politician, Prime Minister 1945–46, 1946–48. An engineer by profession, N. was active in the *Wafd* party. After the *Wafd's* victory in the elections of 1936, he was Minister of Transport. In 1937 he seceded from the party, mainly because he sought an accomodation with the King, as against the intransigent position taken by Nahhas. Together with Ahmad *Maher, he founded the *Sa'adist Party, which claimed to represent the true traditions of the *Wafd* and its late leader Sa'd *Zaghlul, but became an anti-*Wafd*ist ally of the King and his court. N. was a minister in anti-*Wafd*ist Cabinets — Interior 1940, Foreign Affairs 1944–45. In Mar. 1945, after the assassination of Ahmad Maher, he became Prime Minister (taking also the Interior portfolio), until Feb. 1946. When Isma'il *Sidqi's Government fell, in Sept. 1946, N. again formed a government, again serving as

Home Minister and until Nov. 1947 also as Foreign Minister. In 1947, while Premier and Foreign Minister, he took the Anglo-Egyptian dispute over Sudan to the UN Security Council, but failed to obtain the Council's support.

During his tenure, Egypt went to war with nascent Israel. After the failure of this venture, the army leaders claimed that it was N. who had decided against their advice to intervene in Palestine with the regular army. N.'s associates (he himself was dead by then) claimed that the decision had been imposed on him by King *Farouq. When the *"Muslim Brotherhood", stepped up its terrorist activities, N. outlawed the organization in Dec. 1948 and ordered measures to disband and suppress it. He was assassinated the same month by members of the Brotherhood.

Nusseiris, Nossairis See *'Alawis.

O

OAPEC (Organization of Arab Petroleum-Exporting Countries.) See *oil.

OAU, Organization for African Unity See *Africa.

October War, 1973 See *Arab-Israel Wars.

oil in the Arab countries The development of the oil industry in the ME which began in 1901 was patterned on concessions granted to foreign companies — a pattern which terminated by 1976 and was characterized by three major, at times parallel, struggles. The first was between the powers, through their companies, to obtain concessions. The participants were Great Britain, Germany, the Netherlands, France and the United States. The main struggle, between Great Britain and the USA, came to an end in 1954 when the US obtained a 40% share in the up-to-then exclusively British oil concession in Iran, giving her the lion's share in ME oil. The second struggle was among major oil companies. This rivalry ended in 1928 with the "Red Line Agreement" which admitted American companies to the British-led Iraq Petroleum Co, obliging them not to seek concessions on their own in the formerly Ottoman territory. This created an international cartel which virtually controlled the free world oil supplies and set the prices.

The third strife, the longest and most complex one, was between the oil producing countries and their foreign concessionary companies. This came to an end in 1976 when practically all the region's oil industry was nationalized. At first, the ME countries did not develop their oil resources themselves for lack of technological knowledge and financial resources and because of international political conditions. The terms of the concessions they granted were written by the foreign companies in their own favor.

As the oil producing countries began to realize the enormous value of their oil, they started a long battle with the companies to obtain basic modifications in the concession terms, which originally granted the companies, in addition to the right of exploiting the oil, extraordinary privileges. The producing countries received 16% of the profits or 4–6 shillings per ton of oil produced. The areas of exploitation were practically countrywide. The major issues of the controversy were higher royalty payments and a reduction of the concession areas. But the oil producing countries made slow progress. The first major breakthrough occurred in 1950–54 when royalties were raised to 50% of the profits — 12.5% of the price as royalty, and the balance as income tax. To guarantee stability of income the two sides agreed on a "posted price" for stated periods of time. The various companies also agreed to relinquish, at stated periods, considerable chunks of the original concession areas.

The 1950s were perhaps the golden age of relations between the producing countries and the concessionary companies. Demand for oil was high and the revenues of both the countries and the companies were steadily mounting. The oil revenue of the producing ME countries jumped from $193.3 million in 1950 to $1,274 million in 1959. However, at the end of the decade a recession set in, both in Europe and in the USA; demand for oil dropped and the companies reduced the price of oil by 10% early in 1959 and by approximately another 10% late in 1960. This 20% cut in the countries' revenue caused serious difficulties in their development programs. But the producing countries were powerless each separately to force the companies to restore the price cuts.

OPEC. On 14 Sept. 1960, the ME producers established, with Venezuela, the Organization of Petroleum Exporting Countries (OPEC), believing that by uniting they could force the companies to restore the price cuts and grant them other concessions. But OPEC was unable to restore higher prices immediately. During the 1960s the companies continued to determine both production ratios and price levels, and OPEC succeeded in gaining for its members only minor concessions (the 12.5% of the posted price royalty payment, for instance, was no longer to be counted as part of the 50% profit share and the producing country was to receive a full 50% of the profits). OPEC could not force the companies to grant its price demands because the demand for oil was low during the 1960s and because the greatest share of the ME concessions was in the hands of the major American oil companies — Standard Oil of New Jersey (Exxon), Standard Oil of New York (Mobil), Standard Oil of California, Gulf Oil and Texaco — which also produced US oil and thus had alternative oil sources and continued to dominate the international oil markets.

The period 1901–1970 was the era of the multinational oil companies — mainly eight: the five American, Anglo-Iranian (British Petroleum), Royal Dutch-Shell and Compagnie Française des Pétroles. These companies dominated the oil industry, determined production rates and set prices. But in 1970 things began to change. Prosperity returned to Europe and the US and the demand for oil rose rapidly. Yet for the first time US oil production began to drop and US reserves declined swiftly. As a result, the era of the companies began to set and that of the producing countries was dawning. On 14 Feb. 1971 a five-year agreement was signed in Teheran between the Persian Gulf oil producers and 22 oil companies, providing for an immediate price increase of 38 cents a barrel, to rise to 50 cents by 1975 (5 cents a year), a tax increase to 55% and an additional price increase of 2.5% p.a. to compensate for inflation and devaluation. The revenue for the Gulf group countries in 1971 was estimated at $1,400m. more than in 1970, and the total additional income for the five-year period at $11,700m.

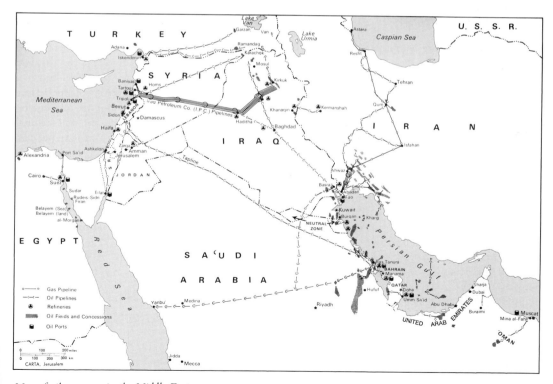

Map of oil resources in the Middle East

The producing countries formed two groups: the Persian Gulf group, and the Mediterranean group under the leadership of Libya, each group negotiating separately with the respective companies. This developed into a leapfrogging technique: the gains achieved by one group became the demand of the other. Being a latecomer to oil exploitation, Libya's concessionary pattern was the grant of small areas to many companies, among them small independent ones without any other oil sources. Thus Libya could play the small companies against the multinationals to whom Libyan oil was of little importance, and obtain better terms than the Gulf producers even before 1971.

In the negotiations of the Teheran agreement the companies negotiated as a group — and US Under-Secretary of State John Irwin was sent to support the companies. But Libya steadfastly insisted on separate negotiations, after the Gulf group would conclude its agreement. Irwin and the US Ambassador in Teheran were persuaded by the Shah of Iran to accept separate negotiations and so advised the companies. After the Teheran agreement was signed, negotiations began in Tripoli, Libya, with the Mediterranean group, including Iraq and Sa'udi Arabia which had outlets also on the Mediterranean through pipelines. An agreement was signed in Tripoli on 2 Apr. 1971. It provided for a 90 cents increase in the posted price, and an annual additional increase of 5 cents during the term of the agreement; a 2.5% annual price increase to compensate for inflation and devaluation; an increase of the tax to 55% (for Occidental in Libya to 60%); and a surcharge of 8 to 11 cents a barrel to cover past claims.

The achievements of the Teheran and Tripoli agreements were the beginning of a new era in the relations between the producing countries and the concessionary companies. The companies appeared weak, almost helpless, and conceded all the demands of the producer governments, while the governments displayed growing power, self-confidence and inflexibility, and were ready to continue the struggle. Publicly the companies expressed satisfaction with the agreements, proclaiming that five years of stablility of oil supply and price had been guaranteed, but they knew that soon they would have to concede new demands. These came rapidly. When the USA devalued the dollar late in 1971 by about 10%, OPEC asked for an equivalent increase in price — in spite of the five-year term of the agreements and the 2.5% compensation for inflation and devaluation. After long negotiations an agreement was signed on 20 Jan. 1972 for an immediate increase of 8.49% in the posted prices with a complicated formula for future contingencies. It became known as Geneva I.

The producers also demanded participation in the foreign companies. This was to be the first step towards the ultimate takeover of the industry. Some of the early concessions enabled the producing country to acquire up to 20% of the shares of the foreign companies, but until 1969 the producers did not take advantage of these provisions. However, at the June 1968 OPEC conference the Sa'udi Oil Minister raised the issue, and negotiations began. After many conferences, and after Ahmad Zaki Yamani warned the companies that the alternative to participation was nationalization, an agreement with Sa'udi Arabia, Kuwait, Qatar, Bahrain, and the United Arab Emirates (UAE) at the end of 1972 provided for an immediate acquisition by producers of 25% of the companies in Jan. 1973, with 5% more each year from 1979 to 1982, and 6% in 1983, which would give the governments a 51% control of the companies. Iran was not involved for she had nationalized her oil industry in 1951, Iraq had nationalized the Iraq Petroleum company in June 1972, and Bahrain decided not to participate. Kuwait accepted the agreement, but her National Assembly rejected the 25% rate and demanded an immediate 60% participation.

OPEC's demands continued. In Feb. 1973 the US devalued the dollar again by 11.11%. The oil companies promptly raised the posted prices in accordance with the Jan. 1972 formula, but the producers refused to accept the companies' offer. A new agreement of 1 June 1973 — the Geneva II agreement — provided for an 11.9% increase in price with a new formula for future contingencies. The Teheran and Tripoli agreements, although contracted for five years, were no longer valid, and the technique applied was "leapfrogging" between the Gulf group under the leadership of Sa'udi Arabia through its oil minister, Ahmad Zaki Yamani, and the Mediterranean group under the leadership of Libya's Colonel *Qadhdhafi.

The next objective was for the producing countries unilaterally to set the price and the production rates, and the full nationalization of the oil industry. In Aug. 1973, Libya nationalized 51% of the concessions of the American companies. In Oct. 1973 OPEC asked for a 50% increase in the posted price. The companies refused and the meeting broke up. Eight days later the Gulf OPEC for the first time unilaterally increased posted prices by 70%. This was a great triumph of the producers over the companies, and the beginning of a grave crisis — which coincided with the A.- Israel war of Oct. 1973.

OAPEC. The leaders of the ASt, realizing the political potential of A. oil resources, soon attempted to involve A. oil in the political struggle. But the major oil producers — Saʻudi Arabia, Kuwait and Iraq — resisted these attempts to turn their chief economic asset into a football in the political game. However, when the June 1967 *Six Day War emotionally swept the A. world, the A. oil producers and transporters proclaimed on 5 June a boycott to stop the flow of oil to any country that supported Israel. The negative economic consequences for the A. oil countries were soon apparent, and the major oil producing countries virtually revoked their boycott. But over its official revocation a struggle erupted between the big oil producers and the radical ASt, especially Egypt. Only after Saʻudi Arabia, Kuwait and Libya promised an annual payment of $135 million to Egypt and Jordan, the victims of the war, did the A. summit conference of September 1967 resolve to resume the pumping of oil. Thus the three major A. producers were doubly hurt by the boycott — they lost revenue, and they had to pay those who had lost the war.

To prevent a recurrence of such contingencies, Saʻudi Arabia, Kuwait and Libya established the Organization of Arab Petroleum Exporting Countries (OAPEC) in Jan. 1968. Its stated objective was the protection of the economic character of oil policies, and the protection of foreign investments in oil development. They intended to restrict membership to insure the preservation of OAPEC's aims. However, after the Qadhdhafi revolution in Libya (1969) its nature changed. Membership requirements were modified and the radical ASt became members. By Mar. 1972 OAPEC was transformed into the antithesis of its original aims and became a political instrument using A. oil resources as a political weapon.

On 17 October 1973 OAPEC proclaimed an A. oil embargo by an immediate 5% production cutback, with the same percentage to be cut each month "until withdrawal is completed from all the A. territories occupied in June 1967 and the legal rights of the Palestinian people are restored". At first the embargo was imposed on virtually all consuming countries. Later they were classified into three groups: "friendly" countries would get their regular supplies; neutrals would be subject to the monthly cuts; and to the hostile countries — the USA and the Netherlands — a total embargo would be applied. However, the embargo was not implemented as planned. The level of its percentage cuts and the classification of countries changed each time OAPEC met. Finally, after sharp divisions among the members, the embargo was lifted on 18 Mar. 1974.

Meanwhile, in Dec. 1973, the Gulf countries raised the posted price of crude oil to about $11.65 a barrel, an increase of more than 400% from the Oct. price of $2.59. The producers also pressed the companies concerning participation percentages, royalty levels, and taxation rates. By 1974 the participation percentage was raised to 60%, first by Kuwait; royalties were raised from 12.5% to 20%; and the tax rate was increased to 85%. By 1976 practically all the producing countries gained full control of their oil resources. Some producers dismissed the foreign companies and operated the industry themselves, others retained their foreign companies as operators of the industry on a fee basis. In spite of conflicting interests and orientations, the producing countries now dictated, through OPEC, oil prices which they constantly raised almost at will. As a result a goodly portion of the consumer countries' wealth passed into the coffers of the producing countries. The latter, wielding the oil weapon, also seemed to have acquired the money weapon and there seemed to be no limit to their power. Each OPEC conference was anxiously watched: by how much would the price go up?

The consuming countries attempted to adopt measures to protect themselves. The USA initiated a conference of the major consuming countries in Feb. 1974, which set up the International Energy Agency (IEA). France opposed this move and persuaded the European Economic Community (EEC, Common Market) to open a dialogue with the Arab League which began in July 1974. Finally, again led by France and initially opposed by the USA, a "North-South" dialogue was held in Mar. 1975 in a Conference of International Economic Cooperation (CIEC). But because of divisions and conflict of interests among the US, Western Europe and Japan, and differences within the European group, practically nothing came out of these three attempts.

RECYCLING To counteract the steady outflow of ever greater financial resources from the consuming to the producing countries (see Table 1), finance specialists and institutions devised recycling mechanisms for bringing them back. There were four major means: 1) getting the producing countries to invest their surpluses in the consuming countries; 2) increasing the scope of exports to the producing countries; 3) selling them sophisticated arms and ammunition; 4) obtaining contracts from the producing countries for the implementation of gigantic development projects (Sa'udi Arabia allotted for its 1975–1980 development program $ 144 b.).

These recycling devices worked well. A study for the years 1977–79 showed that the financial flow from the ME oil countries to the US had balanced the cash outflow from the US for oil imports. The high prices also seriously reduced demand for oil. A substantial drop in production first showed in 1975, after the price jumps in 1973–74, and again in 1978. In both cases prices stabilized. However, in 1979 a second oil crisis erupted. The Iranian revolution eliminated, at first, about 5 million barrels a day (b/d) from the market. A new wave of panic buying engulfed the market, resulting in enormous price jumps. By March 1979 the price of Arabian Light oil went up to $14.55 a barrel, against $12.70 in 1978, and from then until Oct. 1981 OPEC had no uniform price. Above an official bottom price every producing country set its own price, some reaching as high as $46 a barrel. Sa'udi Arabia, for reasons of her own interests, tried to stick to the official price of $14.59. However, in an effort to persuade the others to reestablish the uniform price, she increased her price to $18, then $24 and $28, finally to $32. But each time Sa'udi Arabia raised her price, the others added the differential to their prices.

The consequences of this mad rush for high prices were soon felt. The demand for oil began to drop rapidly in 1981; and by Oct. the drop reached such proportions that the other OPEC members agreed to reestablish a uniform price at $34 a barrel, provided Sa'udi Arabia raised her price to $34. Sa'udia agreed and the uniform price was reestablished. But the compromise failed; the demand continued to drop. OPEC's high prices also created a rival: the non-OPEC producers. While oil prices were low, the oil resources of several countries — North Sea and others — were not developed. However, when prices skyrocketed, a number of new producers entered the oil market and competed with the OPEC producers. For the same reason a number of alternatives to oil were activated, at first on a small scale.

With a glut forming in the world oil market the third oil crisis was setting in, in reverse. OPEC's base was still limited to price control. When it was formed, Venezuela advocated production control as the second element of a cartel. But the ME producers refused to submit, as sovereigns, to the control of production. Now, with the glut growing and demand declining, OPEC was ready to attempt production rationing for the members. In Mar. 1982 OPEC decided, for the first time, to control production and set a production ceiling of 18 m. b/d, to defend the $34 price. But the glut continued. OPEC leaders blamed it on the increased production of non-OPEC producers and the stock drawdown by the consuming countries. And despite the overall production ceiling, OPEC members produced more than their quotas.

By the end of 1982 it became clear that production ceilings alone would not increase the demand for oil. Non-OPEC producers, especially Great Britain, lowered their prices by $5 to about $30, while the OPEC price for Arabian Light was still $34. Consequently, in Mar. 1983 OPEC decided to lower the price of Arabian Light from $34 to $29 a barrel. Yet demand continued to fall and the glut kept growing. Henceforth OPEC battled on two fronts: the non-OPEC producers must curtail production and maintain OPEC prices; and OPEC members must abide by OPEC's production quotas and prices. But OPEC lost out on both fronts. Cheating on both price and production rate was widely practiced, and by many devices members tried to overcome the restrictions of price and production levels. Desperate, OPEC reluctantly abandoned the uniform price in Oct. 1985 and attempted to concentrate on production control.

Sa'udi Arabia was a victim of the situation. In 1982 she assumed the role of "swing producer", i.e. agreed to produce the quantity remaining after the fulfilment of all the others' quotas. As a result, the Sa'udi share kept dropping, until it declined in August 1985 to about 2 m. b/d from about 8 m. in 1982. Sa'udi Arabia was bitter at both OPEC and non-OPEC producers. In mid Sept. 1985, her oil minister threatened both OPEC and non-OPEC producers with a price-war which would bring down all producers. If Sa'udi Arabia were to reduce the price and increase production, her Oil Minister Yamani declared on 1 June 1985, "many oil producing countries, both OPEC and non-OPEC, would exit from the world oil market, many banks would collapse; it would shake the world economy... (and) lead to a major depression". At the same time Sa'udi Arabia gave up the role of "swing producer" and accepted a quota of about 4.35m. b/d. This created new difficulties in OPEC, for no member was ready to reduce its quota.

OPEC's turning point came in Dec. 1985. OPEC abandoned its position as the determiner of oil prices. While deciding to "secure and defend for OPEC a fair share of the world oil market consistent with the necessary income for member countries' development", and maintaining a production quota, it began, *de facto*, acting as the world "swing producer", and its share of the world market dropped from c. 45% in 1970 and nearly two thirds in 1979–80 to 32–35% in the early and mid-1980s. OPEC's abandonment of price control and the threat of a price war caused oil prices throughout the world to tumble from about $28 to $10–12 a barrel. In spite of Sa'udi Arabia's threats and dire predictions in case the price of oil dropped to $20 a barrel, the consuming world welcomed the reduced oil prices. No economic depressions set in, and the world's financial institutions did not collapse. During 1986 OPEC was bickering about quotas and ways of raising prices and by how much. Its members could not agree on any of the issues. Sa'udi Arabia's threat of a price war backfired, and King Fahd dismissed his oil minister, since 1962 a chief architect of OPEC.

TABLE 1. MIDDLE EAST[1] OIL PRODUCTION, REVENUE AND SURPLUS, 1974–1979

Year	Production (million tons)	Revenue ($ billion)	Surplus ($ billion)
1974	1,805.0	106	68
1975	975.1	99	35
1976	1,107.1	122	40
1977	1,118.4	135	33
1978	1,058.9	127	11
1979	1,076.4	175	35

[1] Including Iran, not including North Africa.
Sources: *Middle East Oil Crises since 1973*, 86.

THE OIL PRODUCING COUNTRIES:

Iran, the first ME country to produce oil since 1908 — following a concession granted to William Knox D'Arcy, an Englishman, in May 1901 and the establishment of the Anglo Persian (later Anglo-Iranian) Oil Company in 1909, with the British government as the major and controlling partner since May 1914 — is outside our scope. But events concerning her oil industry, and their political repercussions, had a deep influence on oil developments in the AC — from the first conflict between the producing country and the concessionaire company (and the imperial power behind it), in 1932, through the crisis of 1951–53 resulting from Iran's nationalization of her oil industry, to the Oct. 1954 agreement with a new International Iranian Oil Consortium, which recognized the National Iranian Oil Company (NIOC) as the owner of the former company's properties — the Consortium's production and refining operations to be based on a lease — and reduced the share of Anglo-Iranian (renamed British Petroleum, BP) to 40%, while five major American companies held 40%, Royal Dutch-Shell 14%, and the Compagnie Française des Pétroles 6%. Iran's oil industry, completely taken over by the state in Mar. 1973, was gravely affected by the Iraq-Iran war since Sept. 1980. The war wrought heavy damage on production, refining and transportation facilities, just recovering from the paralysis caused by the Islamic revolution of 1979. The giant refinery of Abadan was destroyed, and Iran's export and loading installations in the Gulf — Kharg Island, and later loading stations farther down the Gulf, like Sirri Island — and her tankers, were frequently attacked. These attacks provided the rationale for Iran's frequent attacks on A. and foreign tankers and other vessels in the Gulf: if *her* oil exports and shipping were disturbed, so would be all the others'.

Iraq. Since the beginning of the century, German, Dutch, British and American companies were seeking oil concessions in the Mosul and Baghdad *vilayets* of the Ottoman Empire. An American concession of 1909 for the construction of three railway lines (one of them through Mosul and Baghdad) included the right to exploit mineral resources 20 kilometers on either side of the lines; but it was never ratified.

In 1912 a British company, the Turkish Petroleum Company (TPC) was formed. The three European groups united in Mar. 1914 in an effort to prevent the US from entering the race: the British were to have 50% of TPC, the Dutch 25%, the Germans 25%; a 5% share was to be proportionally deducted for Colouste S. Gulbenkian, for his mediation; the partners would seek concessions in Ottoman territories, excluding Egypt and Kuwait, only through the TPC. The Ottoman government consented in principle to grant a concession, but reserved the right of Turkish participation. World War I halted further action.

During the war Britain and France agreed on the division of Turkish territories after victory. Mosul was assigned to France, but Britain wanted it to be included in the rest of Iraq assigned to her. In Apr. 1920, at the *San Remo Conference, France ceded Mosul to British Iraq, in return for the German 25% in the TPC; she also agreed to let TPC lay pipelines and build railroads across Syria to bring out the oil.

The USA accused her two Allies of depriving her of a fair share in the Mesopotamian oil and a bitter struggle ensued. After a long wrangle between the U.S. and British governments, and between American oil companies and the Anglo-Persian Oil Company, it was agreed in 1925 (finalized in July 1928) to grant an American company half of the British share, i.e. 23.75% of the TPC. The concession was revalidated by a new Iraq government concession in Mar. 1925 (the company was renamed in 1929 Iraq Petroleum Company, IPC). In July 1928 the Near East Development Co. (Standard Oil of New Jersey and Standard Oil of New York, the only two companies left of the American group) became part of the IPC, with 23.75%.

The US group had to undertake, like the other partners in the PC, not to seek separate concessions in the Asian territories of the defunct Ottoman Empire, except Kuwait — the "Red Line Agreement" of 1928 (an undertaking they broke in 1946, when they joined an American group that obtained concessions in Sa'udi Arabia.)

There were three concession areas: 32,000 sq. mi. east of the Tigris River to the IPC, for 75 years (finalized in Mar. 1931); c. 46,000 sq. mi. west of the Tigris to the Mosul Petroleum Co. (Apr. 1932); all other lands, c. 92,000 sq. mi., to the Basrah Petroleum Company (Dec. 1938). Royalties were to be 4 shillings (gold) per ton. Internal pipelines were constructed and production began in 1927. In that first year production was 45,000 tons, in the late 1930s it passed 4m. tons and in 1951 it rose to 8.35m. tons. The oil produced in the Basra region in the south moved to world markets by tankers. For that of Mosul and Kirkuk in the north a pipeline was constructed in 1934, branching out to Tripoli (Lebanon) and Haifa (Palestine) where refineries were built. After World War II, the line to Tripoli was expanded several times and a new branch to Baniyas (Syria) was added in 1950. By 1965 these pipelines conveyed 40m. tons p.a., 64% of Iraq's oil output; by 1970 a capacity of over 50m. tons was reported. In the 1970s, however, they were closed down for long periods because of the Lebanese civil war and Syro-Iraqi differences. The branch to Haifa has been inoperative since 1948, when Iraq stopped the flow of oil because of the A.-Israel war.

In Nov. 1950 Iraq obtained a 50% royalty increase, from 4 to 6 shillings per ton, and in 1951 — after the nationalization of the oil industry in Iran, and the 50:50 profit sharing arrangement in Sa'udi Arabia — a 50:50 sharing of profits. Production grew steadily — from 33.5m. tons in 1955 to 84m. tons in 1971. Oil revenue, $214m. in 1955, rose to $840m. in 1971. But the Iraqis became more and more discontented with the terms of the concessions, their pressure mounted, and relations between the government and the company deteriorated. In December

1961, 'Abd-ul-Karim *Qassem (ruling Iraq since a *coup* of July 1958) enacted a law which deprived the three companies of their concession areas except the parts under actual exploitation, 740 sq. mi., less than ½% of the original concession. Even areas already developed by the company but not yet in actual operation, such as the North Rumaila field in the south, were confiscated. An Iraqi National Oil Co. was set up in Feb. 1964, to operate the expropriated area.

Efforts to reach agreement with the *'Aref and *Ba'th régimes that succeeded Qassem after his fall in 1963, failed. On 1 June 1972 President *Bakr announced the nationalization of the Iraq concession. At first neither the Mosul PC nor the Basrah PC were nationalized. In the area nationalized France, with her 23.75% interest, was allowed to continue to lift her share for the next 10 years. The small Mosul company voluntarily surrendered its concession. With the Basrah PC the government agreed in Feb. 1973 to increase production very considerably. But during the Egypt-Israel war of October 1973, Iraq nationalized the share of the two American companies, Exxon and Mobil, in the Basrah PC, two weeks later that of Royal Dutch-Shell, and in Dec. that of the Lisbon located Partex Foundation (Gulbenkian) — to punish the US, the Netherlands and Portugal. Early in 1975, she took a 60% participation, in agreement with the remaining two partners in the Basrah PC, British and French. In December, she nationalized the remaining foreign interests in the company.

Iraq opposed OAPEC's Oct. 1973 oil embargo, explaining that the cutback unjustly harmed friendly countries and that it was preferable to nationalize and expel the foreign oil companies. The real reason for Iraq's opposition was her desperate need for markets for her nationalized oil. She now took advantage of the shortage of supply and increased her oil sales. In 1975, when other OPEC countries experienced an average drop of 19% in production, Iraq increased production by 21.5%. Algeria and Sa'udi Arabia accused her of having cut $1 a barrel off the OPEC price. Production rose to 138 m. tons in 1980, and revenue to $26b.

Iraq also met with increasing difficulties concerning her pipelines to the Mediterranean. The line running through Syria was often sabotaged or closed. Periodically the Syrians would impose higher transit fees. In Dec. 1966 Syria impounded all IPC assets until claims for back royalties and higher transit fees had been satisfied, and stopped the flow of Iraqi oil to Baniyas in Syria and Tripoli in Lebanon; in Mar. 1967 the company agreed to increase the transit fees by 50%. A similar episode occurred in 1970. When Iraq nationalized the IPC and Syria nationalized the pipeline in her territory, in 1972, Syria demanded a 100% increase, and after long negotiations a 50% increase was agreed.

In the face of these transit fee and other demands, possible sabotage and frequent interruptions, Iraq constructed a pipeline connecting the southern oil fields and their Persian Gulf ports with the oil fields in the north, completed in 1976. She also agreed with Turkey, in Aug. 1973, to build a pipeline from the Kirkuk fields to a Turkish port on the Mediterranean, in *Hatay- *Alexandretta, each country to build its part. In Jan. 1977, the 700 mi. Kirkuk-Dortyol (Ceyhan) pipeline was opened, with a capacity of 25m. tons a year; in 1980 Turkey and Iraq agreed to increase the capacity to 45–50m. tons a year (900,000 b/d).

In Apr. 1976 Iraq stopped pumping oil through the Syrian pipeline. In Feb. 1979 she resumed pumping. However, in Apr. 1982, Syria broke off relations with Iraq, in the context of the Iraq-Iran war, and closed her lines to the flow of Iraqi oil. As loading facilities on the Gulf were paralyzed by the war, Iraq's export capacity was reduced to 700,000 b/d through the Turkish line. Iraq, therefore, planned an expansion of the line through Turkey, and an outlet through Sa'udi Arabia. In April 1985, she agreed with Turkey to construct a second, parallel pipeline, to add 500–600,000 b/d. A two stage pipeline was planned through Sa'udi Arabia facilities: first, a line from Basra to the Sa'udi Ghawar-to-Yanbu' Petroline, which would then carry Iraqi oil to the Red Sea; later, Iraq would build a line of a 1m. b/d capacity parallel to the Sa'udi one and a terminal at Yanbu'. In Oct. 1981 Sa'udi Arabia consented, and in Jan. 1984 a formal agreement was concluded. In Mar. 1986, stage I was completed and Iraq demanded a 500,000 b/d increase in her OPEC quota.

Over the years, Iraq developed new oil fields, built and expanded refineries, widened the internal pipeline network, increased the utilization of natural gas and built up a petrochemical industry. She engaged in direct marketing and also organized oil tanker companies.

Sa'udi Arabia. The oil industry had its most dramatic, revolutionary impact in Sa'udi Arabia (S.A.). Nowhere in the ME, up to that time, had oil development produced such striking contrasts between the indigenous nomadic mode of life and the Western technological innovations introduced by the oil companies, and nowhere has the change been so radical.

In a Dec. 1915 treaty with Britain 'Abd-ul-'Aziz *Ibn Sa'ud, Sultan of Najd, undertook not to grant concessions without the consent of the British government. In Aug. 1923, he granted an oil concession in the al-Hasa area to Major Frank Holmes' Eastern and General Syndicate, a British group that acquired the concession not to work it, but to sell it. But its efforts to sell it in Britain and in the USA failed, and its concession lapsed. After Ibn Sa'ud's conquest of the Hijaz, Britain recognized the Sa'udi Kingdom's independence and in the Treaty of Jidda, 1927, removed the restrictive provisions of the old treaty. After preliminary studies by an American engineer, K.S. Twitchell, and negotiations with other candidates, among them IPC, S.A. awarded a concession in 1933 to Standard Oil of California (SOCAL) (H. St. John B. Philby, friend and adviser of Ibn Sa'ud, maintained that he, not Twitchell, brought SOCAL to S.A.). SOCAL set up the California Arabian Standard Oil Company and began exploration. Three years later SOCAL sold half of the company to the Texas Oil Company. In Mar. 1938 oil was discovered in Dammam. One year later a supplemental agreement extended the concession area to 440,000 sq. mi. By that year production in Dammam reached 30,000 b/d. At first the oil from Dammam was shipped on barges to Bahrain, where the company had a refinery. In 1939 Ras Tanura was selected as the terminal and connected with Dammam by a 39-mile pipeline.

During World War II, oil production was curtailed. As the king needed and demanded revenue, the company advanced him loans on future royalties; but his demands persistently increased and the company asked the US government for aid to protect their concession which they presented as vital to US national interests and security. After a number of moves the US decided in Feb. 1943 to grant S.A. "lend-lease" aid. US government plans to acquire the concession were successfully resisted by the companies. In Jan. 1944, the name of the company was changed to the Arabian American Oil Company (Aramco). In Dec. 1946, Aramco agreed to sell 30% of its shares to Standard Oil of New Jersey and 10% to Socony-Vacuum (finalized late in 1948); both these groups, partners in the IPC, broke the Red Line Agreement by joining Aramco.

Aramco planned to construct a pipeline to bring the oil to a Mediterranean port. Attempts to have the US government build it were opposed by other US oil companies, and were dropped. In July 1945 Aramco set up the Trans-Arabian Pipeline Company (Tapline). Plans to build the line through Jordan and Palestine to Haifa were dropped, and it was constructed through Jordan, Syria and Lebanon, with its terminal at Sidon. The Tapline — 1,040 mi. long (with its first 270 mi. section owned and operated by Aramco), and with a capacity of 310,000 b/d, c. 15m. tons p.a., later expanded to 400,000 b/d — was opened in Nov. 1950. Syria soon asked for increased transit royalties, and there were frequent negotiations and increases. In May 1970, Tapline was sabotaged in the *Golan, and Syria permitted its repair only in Jan. 1971, against additional payments. Since 1975 Tapline is no longer used, because of the cheaper tanker rates and the instability in Lebanon.

With the termination of the war, production increased rapidly — from 645,860 tons in 1943 to 26.2m. tons in 1950, and, after the completion of Tapline, 36.6m. tons in 1951, 46.2m. tons in 1954. In 1950, Aramco agreed to pay S.A. 50% of the company's net operating profit (the per ton royalty to be part of that profit share). Sa'udi revenues rose from $1.5m. in 1940 to $260m. in 1954 (with total profits of $520m., out of $1.75 a barrel sold by the company $1.40 was profit). S.A. also had a share in the Sa'udia-Kuwait *Neutral Zone. In February 1949 she granted a concession to the American Western Pacific Oil Corporation (later Getty) for onshore oil exploitation on terms considerably better than those of Aramco. Early in 1957, S.A. granted a concession to the Arabian Oil Company (Japanese) for the offshore area of the zone — on even more favorable terms, including a 56% government share of the profits. In 1955 Getty produced 0.6m. tons, in 1972 — 3.9m. Arabian Oil produced in 1961, its first year, 0.5m. tons and in 1972 10m. Sa'udia's revenue amounted to $2.6m. in 1955, $97m. in 1972.

S.A.'s oil reserves were constantly rising in spite of the ever increasing production rate; the Sa'udi concession obviously covered the greatest oil producing fields in the ME. Production was steadily and constantly growing and reached 375m. tons in 1973, nearing the 500m. ton mark in 1979 and 1980–81. Revenue was nearly $3b. in 1973, passed $30b. in 1976–77 and $100b. in 1980. Aramco also discovered new oil fields, onshore and offshore; expanded the internal pipeline system; enlarged tank farms, loading and port facilities; and built a sea-island for the accommodation of very large tankers. For the impact of the oil industry on S.A. and her development and modernization see *Sa'udi Arabia.

Relations between Aramco and the government were generally good and the company complied in most cases with the government's requests. After Iraq's 1961 confiscation of more than 99% of the IPC concession areas, Aramco in Mar. 1963 agreed to relinquish about 75% of its concession area, all but 125,000 sq. mi., with six additional relinquishments at five-year intervals. In Nov. 1962, S.A. established the General Petroleum and Mineral Organization, Petromin, to supervise all oil affairs, and empowered it to enter into any phase of oil and mineral operations.

S.A. also aspired to enter "downstream" operations. She set up the S.A. Refining Company (SARCO), which built and operated refineries, and a tanker company. She increased the utilization of natural gas resources aided by Aramco, and developed a large scale petrochemical industry, partly in joint ventures with foreign oil companies and other enterprises.

She began building two gigantic industrial cities: based on the oil and gas industries: on the Gulf, Jubail, and Yanbu' on the Red Sea, each estimated to cost $15–20 b. In 1976 she set up the Basic Industries Corporation (SABIC), to hold the government's share in the equities of the various joint-venture refineries, petrochemical complexes and industrial undertakings. From 1977 a 750-mile 48-inch oil pipeline from the Ghawar/Abqaiq oil fields in the eastern province to the port of Yanbu' on the Red Sea was constructed, with a capacity of 1.85m. b/d (to be expanded to 2.35m. b/d) at a cost of about $1,550m. The line went into operation in 1980.

S.A.'s takeover of Aramco, beginning in 1972 with 25% and culminating in a total takeover decided in 1976 and fully implemented in 1980, is described in the first, general part of this entry. In fact, while its judicial status and financial arrangements have changed, Aramco has continued operating on behalf of the Sa'udi government. S.A.'s role as a main leader of OPEC — her maneuvers and manipulations concerning prices and production quotas; her attempts to keep price increases to a level that would not endanger the oil economy or antagonize the USA too deeply, and her occasional sallies into Sa'udi-initiated price increases; her role as a "swing" producer, 1982–84; and her reintroduction of a higher production quota from 1985 — are described in the first part of this entry. During the oil recession of the mid-1980s, S.A.'s production declined to less than 250m. tons in 1983 and 1984, sinking to about 2,000 b/d in Aug. 1985. Her oil revenues dropped to $40b. in 1984 and $28b. in 1985, and less than $20b. were expected for 1986 (but there were also conflicting estimates). Her Oil Minister, A.Z. Yamani, was dismissed in Oct. 1986. Since 1985, S.A. has re-increased her production rate, basing herself on an OPEC quota of 4.35m b/d (about 220m. tons p.a.) and hoping that with the stabilization of the oil market the drop in prices — and in her revenue — would be halted.

Bahrain. The Sheikhdom of B., a British protectorate, obligated since 1880 not to grant any concession without British approval, granted one in 1925 to Major Frank Holmes, representing the Eastern and General Syndicate. In 1927, a subsidiary of the American Gulf Oil Corporation took an option to purchase the Syndicate rights; in 1928, Gulf transferred its rights to Standard Oil of California. After long negotiations on the provision that the company must be British registered and its managing director and a majority of the other directors must be British, the concession was granted in 1930 to the Bahrain Petroleum Company (BAPCO), a subsidiary of Standard Oil of California, registered in Canada. In 1935 that company sold one half of the concession to Texas Oil, forming a joint new company, California-Texas (Caltex). The concession was extended in 1940, to cover all of B., 1.64 m. acres, for 55 years from June 1944.

Production started in 1932. Bapco built a refinery to serve B. and mainly Sa'udi Arabia; it went into operation in July 1935.

Production reached 20,000 b/d (1m. tons p.a.) in 1939. During World War II it was reduced, but in 1946 it again attained 1.1m. tons, in 1958 2m., and in 1967 it passed the 3.5m. ton mark. Since the mid-1970s it has declined to 2–2.5m. tons. Revenue, based since 1953 on a 50% share of profits, was $1m. in 1940, passed the $8m. mark in 1954 and reached $30m. in 1970 and nearly $400m. in the mid-1970s. Thus, production and oil income, as well as reserves, were modest if compared with other A. oil countries and the ME in general. Since B. exported refined oil products, not crude oil, she did not join OPEC; she became, however, a member of OAPEC in May 1970.

Oil revenue was divided into three parts: one third to the Sheikh, one third for current expenses and development (greatly improving education and health services and the standard of living), and one third was invested abroad, mainly in England.

Relations with BAPCO were generally good. In 1965 B. granted offshore concessions to other companies. In 1971 she set up a B. National Oil Company. In Oct. 1972, B. agreed with BAPCO to take a 25% participation share, to reach 51% in 1983. She did not implement that agreement, but in Sept. 1974 she acquired a 60% participation (not including the refinery). In Dec. 1975 all the oil fields, but not the refinery, were transferred to the B. National Oil Company. In July 1980 the government acquired 60% in the refinery.

Kuwait. The Sheikh of K., under British protection since 1899, was committed to grant an oil concession only with British approval. In the early 1920s, Major Frank Holmes, representing the Eastern and General Syndicate, obtained a concession and, after the Anglo-Persian Oil Co. declined to acquire it, offered it to the American Gulf Oil Corporation. Here, as in Bahrain, the British government insisted on compliance with the British Nationality clause and from late 1931 a long British-US wrangle ensued. But the British were determined not to lose to the Americans, after Sa'udi Arabia and Bahrain, for the third time and a compromise was reached in Dec. 1933: Anglo Persian and Gulf were to form a joint Kuwait Oil Company (KOC) in equal partnership. In Dec. 1934 KOC obtained a 75-year concession covering the entire sheikhdom.

The war interrupted operations, but production began in 1946 and grew rapidly — from 800,000 tons in 1946 it reached 17.3m. tons in 1950, 37.6m. in 1952, 106m. in 1964, and rose to 152m. tons in 1972. Estimates of reserves were also constantly rising. In 1948 K. granted another concession to the American Independent Oil Co. (Aminoil) for her one-half share in the K.-Sa'udia Neutral Zone. Production in that zone reached over 1m. tons in 1955, 19m. in 1965 and nearly 28m. tons in 1972 — of which one half was K.'s. Despite the 1964 and 1970 agreements to divide the Zone, the sharing arrangements remained in force.

A 1.25m. ton p.a. refinery at Mina al-Ahmadi was completed in Nov. 1949. Its capacity was expanded to 190,000 b/d, over 9m. tons p.a., by 1959, and 250,000 b/d, 12.5m. tons, in 1970. Each of the three companies operating in the Neutral Zone (one on K.'s share, two on Sa'udia's) also built a refinery.

Royalty payments, at first 9 cents per barrel, were turned in Dec. 1951 into a 50:50 profit sharing (and in return the Sheikh extended the concession for an additional 17 years, i.e. 92 years from 1934). Oil revenue was $800,000 in 1946, $139m. in 1952, $464m. in 1960 and climbed to over $1.5b. in 1972; it reached $8–9b. in the mid-1970s and peaked in 1979–80 at over $20b. Of these revenues, one third went to the Sheikh, one third to social and economic development, and one third was deposited abroad for future contingencies and interest income. The ensuing radical changes in K.'s economic and social structure and her development into a comprehensive welfare state are described in the entry *Kuwait.

In 1961, K. established the state-owned Kuwait National Petroleum Company (KNPC). The government also set up petrochemical and transportation companies, and assigned new foreign companies to exploit the areas relinquished by KOC and offshore oil. K. was the first ME country to reduce production for conservation reasons.

As a member of OPEC and OAPEC, K. was in the forefront of the struggle with the foreign companies. She was active in the achievement of the Teheran Agreement of Feb. 1971, and subsequently demanded participation in the foreign companies. In 1972 she accepted a 25% share, but her National Assembly rejected that share as insufficient, and the government demanded full nationalization. In 1974 K. was the first to obtain a 60% participation. But late in 1975 Gulf Oil and British Petroleum surrendered their remaining 40% equity. In July 1977 K. also nationalized her share in the Neutral Zone. In the crises since 1973 K. followed, most of the time, the policies of Sa'udi Arabia. In the recession of the mid-1980s, her production declined to 45–55m. tons p.a. and her revenue reverted to about $9b.

Qatar. After Standard Oil of California obtained the oil concession in Bahrain (1930), the Iraq Petroleum Co. (IPC) authorized the Anglo-Persian Oil Co. to negotiate for a concession with the Sheikh of Q. In May 1935, Anglo-Persian was granted a 75-year concession covering all of Qatar, and in 1937 an IPC subsidiary, Petroleum Development (Qatar), took it over (it changed its name in 1953 to Qatar Petroleum Co.). Oil in commerical quantities was struck in 1939. Production was interrupted because of the war, and resumed in 1947, with first exports in December 1949. By 1950 Qatar was producing at the average rate of 33,800 barrels a day. Production was 1.6m. tons in 1950, passed the 5m. mark in 1955, reached 10m. in 1964–65, rose to 24m. tons in 1973; it dropped to 20m. in 1975, rose again, and declined since 1981 to 12–19m. tons p.a.

In June 1952, Q. granted an offshore concession to Royal Dutch-Shell, and in 1969–70 to a group of Japanese companies. From the 1960s, production was about 60% onshore, 40% offshore, from the mid 1970s it was about 50:50, sometimes with a higher offshore production. Q. also obtained half of the revenue of an offshore concession granted by Abu Dhabi in the al-Bunduq area. Q. had claimed that area as her territory, a demarcation commission ruled in 1969 that al-Bunduq was on the median line between the two countries, and they agreed to share the revenue.

From Sept. 1952, payments to the government were based on a 50:50 sharing of profits. Payments rose from $1m. in 1950 to $54m. in 1960, $198m. in 1971, reaching over $2b. from the mid 1970s and peaking at over $5b. in 1980–81. Of that revenue, 25% went to the Sheikh, 35% to public utilities, welfare services and development, and 40% to the reserve fund. The oil revenue made possible an impressive development of Q.'s economy and her transformation into a wealthy welfare state — see *Qatar.

Relations between the companies and the government were on the pattern usual in the region. The companies extended production, extended loading facilities, built refineries (for internal need), and developed natural gas resources. They relinquished portions of the concession areas, and had to comply with OPEC decisions. In 1968 the government took over the refining and distribution facilities. In Apr. 1972, Q. established the Q. National Petroleum Co, replaced in July 1974 by the Q. General Petroleum Corporation. In 1972 the government took a 25% participation, to reach 51% in 1983. In Feb. 1974 it raised its share to 60%, and in Oct. 1976 it nationalized the remaining 40%. Since Feb. 1977, the fully nationalized company is called QPC.

United Arab Emirates (UAE). The *Trucial Coast was covered by a concession of an IPC subsidiary; but this was relinquished or lapsed in most cases. In the Federation of the UAE, formed in 1971, with the abolition of the British protectorate, oil production and revenues are not a federal matter but belong to the individual sheikhdoms.

Abu Dhabi (AD) granted Petroleum Development (Trucial Coast), an IPC affiliate, a 75-year concession in 1939, and a 65-year offshore concession to AD Marine Areas (ADMA) — two-thirds Anglo-Iranian, renamed British Petroleum (BP) and one third Compagnie Française des Pétroles (CFP) — in 1953. ADMA discovered oil in 1958 and exports began in 1962 when a terminal was built at Das Island. Petroleum Development (Trucial Coast) — renamed AD Petroleum Co. (ADPC) in 1962 — discovered oil on shore in 1960 and began exporting in Dec. 1963. Production advanced rapidly both onshore and offshore — from 800,000 tons in 1962 to over 50m. in 1972 peaking at nearly 80m. tons in 1977. In the early 1980s it declined to 36–38m. tons.

The government's share was 20% of the profits for both ADMA and ADPC concessions. In 1965 ADPC raised the profit share to 50% and agreed to relinquish unexploited areas, and ADMA did the same in 1966. As the companies relinquished sections of their concessions, the

Sheikh granted them to new companies, including a Japanese consortium in the late 1960s. Revenue rose from $3m. in 1962 to $105m. in 1967, passed the $1b. mark in 1973 and peaked at over $10b. in 1979–80.

In 1971 the government established the AD National Petroleum Company, and in 1972 it acquired a 25% participation in all foreign companies to rise to 51% in 1983. In 1974 it increased state participation to 60%. However, A.D. did not follow the other producing countries in total nationalization. The government also entered into joint ventures with foreign companies on a 60:40 basis in the expansion of the oil industry. The only enterprise totally state-owned was the exploitation of natural gas, of which AD took control in Apr. 1976 after foreign companies declined to participate. AD also built new refineries and established a tanker company. A large $500m. refinery with a capacity of 120,000 b/d (6m. tons p.a.) was opened late in 1981 in the Ruweis Industrial Center. For AD's general development, based on her oil income (which gave her the highest per capita income in the world) — see *Abu Dhabi.

Dubai granted the first oil concession, offshore, in 1952 to D. Marine Areas (DUMA) — two thirds BP and one third CFP. In 1963, D. Petroleum Company (DPC), a subsidiary of the American Continental Oil Co. obtained a concession covering the mainland and territorial waters; in Aug. 1963, it also bought a 50% interest in DUMA. In 1968 DPC discovered oil and production began in Sept. 1969. It reached 4.3m. tons in 1970, 13m. in 1975, and passed the 18m. mark in 1978–79; in the 1980s it declined to 16–17m. tons p.a.

In Jan. 1971, D. raised the companies' rate of payment to 55%. Her revenues reached $1.b. p.a. in the 1970s and peaked at over $3b. in 1980. In July 1975 D. acquired 100% ownership of all the operating oil and gas companies — which were to continue managing the operations. The decline of D.'s oil exports in the 1980s was not as steep as in other countries, since she reportedly did not fully conform to OPEC policies and sold on the "spot market".

Abu Dhabi and Dubai are the UAE's main oil producers. But there are beginnings in other UAE sheikhdoms, too.

Sharja granted oil concessions to a number of companies, onshore and offshore, in the late 1960s and early 1970s. Production began, offshore, in 1972–75 and reached in the mid 1980s 2.5m. tons. In 1976 Sharja established 60% participation in all the companies. *Ras al-Khaima* granted concessions to several companies from the late 1960s. In the mid 1970s a consortium — with the national oil company taking a 50% interest — struck oil and commercial production was reportedly beginning in the 1980s. *Umm al-Qaiwain* also granted concessions to several companies from the late 1960s, mainly offshore, later also onshore. So did *al-Fujaira* in the 1970s. No major oil finds have yet been reported.

Taking the UAE as a whole, oil production was about 53m. tons in 1971, over 80m. in the mid 1970s and peaked at over 100m. tons in 1977–78 — 84.8% Abu Dhabi, 13.3% Dubai, and 1.9% Sharja. In the 1980s it dropped to less than 50m. tons, with Sharja's share rising. Total revenue was over $5b. in 1974 and $12–13b. since 1979.

'Oman. In 1937 Petroleum Development (Oman), an affiliate of the IPC group, obtained a 75-year oil concession covering the Sultanate except the province of Dhofar, and in 1953 two American companies, Cities Service and Richfield, were granted a concession in Dhofar for 25 years after commercial oil discovery. As no oil was struck all the IPC members withdrew except two: Shell retained 85%, and Partex (Gulbenkian) 15%. When oil was discovered in 1966, CFP bought back 10% from Partex. In Mar. 1966, the Sultan's share was raised to 50% of the profits. In 1968 PDO acquired exploitation rights in the Dhofar province, too, and early in 1970 it relinquished one third of its concession area, and agreed to two further relinquishments. In the areas relinquished new and offshore concessions were granted. 'O. was not a member of OPEC, but complied with most of the changes OPEC introduced. In Feb. 1974, the government acquired 25% participation in PDO and in July 1974 raised its share to 60%.

Production began in 1967 after a pipeline was laid to the coast and reached 11.75m. tons in 1968, 18m. in 1976, 14–16m. in the later 1970s and early 1980s, 20m. in 1984 and 25m. tons in 1985. Oil revenue was $6m. in 1968, $115m. in 1971, passed the $1b. mark in 1975 and $2b. in 1979 and reached $4b. in 1984. In the mid-1980s it declined somewhat. A 50,000 b/d (2.5m. ton p.a.) refinery was opened in Nov. 1982.

Syria. S. benefited from the ME oil industry as a transit land for pipelines from Iraq and Saʻudi Arabia (see above). Over the years many exploration concessions were granted (including one to an IPC subisdiary), but no oil was found. Finally the American Menhall Drilling Company reported in Oct. 1956 that it had struck oil at Karachok, in the northeast, close to the Iraqi border. In Oct. 1958 the government (now the *UAR) cancelled the Menhall concession and took it over. In Aug. 1959, a German company struck oil in the same area. But later in 1959 it was agreed that the Soviet Union would aid S.'s oil exploration. More oil fields were discovered in the northeast, and commerical production began in the 1960s.

Production reached 1m. tons in 1968, 5–6m. in the early 1970s and 10m. in 1978; it stands at 8–9m. tons p.a. in the 1980s. Oil revenue is estimated, in the mid-1980s, at over $2b.

A refinery in Homs — intended mainly to refine Iraqi oil from the pipeline — was completed in June 1959 by a Czechoslovak company; its capacity was expanded several times. A second refinery, near Baniyas, with an annual capacity of 6m. tons was opened in Aug. 1979. By 1980 S.'s annual refining capacity reached 11.5m. tons.

Egypt. Prospecting for oil in E. began in the late 19th century, and oil was first produced in 1908–09 at Gemsa, on the African side of the Red Sea at the mouth of the Gulf of Suez. In 1912–13 Anglo-Egyptian Oilfields (AEOF), a Shell subsidiary, obtained a concession from the Egyptian government. A second field, Hurghada, discovered in 1913, south of Gemsa, was for 25 years E.'s major producing field. A third field, Ras Gharib, between those two and Suez, discovered in 1937–38, was E.'s most prolific and accounted for about half of her production. Royalty payments, 5% of production until 1923, then 12.5%, were raised in 1938 to 14% of production. From 1946 oil was discovered on the Asian side of the Gulf of Suez at Ras Sudr and other locations in *Sinai, exploited by AEOF in partnership with Socony-Vacuum. E.'s production passed the 2m. ton mark in 1949 and remained 1.8–2.3m. tons p.a. until 1957.

From 1947, E. enacted several laws limiting new oil mining licences to Egyptians, restricting foreign companies as to their directors and their share in enterprises (no more than 49%) and imposed higher royalties. The foreign oil companies operating in E. refused to accept the new conditions. Standard of New Jersey withdrew in 1949; Socony-Vacuum and AEOF suspended exploration.

After the Officers' *coup* of 1952, the new régime modified these laws to permit foreigners to continue with oil exploration and exploitation. Royalty payment was set at 15% of oil produced for a number of years, then to rise to 25%. A number of foreign companies obtained new concessions and the old foreign companies returned to continue their operations (AEOF's assets were sequestrated following the Suez crisis of 1956, and though the sequestration was lifted in 1959, the government took over the major share of the company in 1964). Soon the eastern and western deserts and the Gulf of Suez coasts were dotted with oil exploration and exploitation units. (Most Egyptian oil wells have a short life-span, and to keep up production levels E. must continuously seek new sources of oil.) Offshore exploration also yielded large oil supplies, especially in the Gulf of Suez. Production rose to over 6m. tons from 1963, over 10m. from 1968, 20m. in 1970, over 15m. tons in 1971–72 (the last three figures exclude the oil produced in Israel-occupied Sinai), and, after a decline, over 20m. from 1977, over 30m. from 1980, — and over 40m. tons in 1984 and 1985 — with much fluctuation (the al-Morgan offshore field in the Gulf of Suez, for example, produced 15m. tons in 1970 but in 1973 production dropped to 7m. and continued to drop at the rate of half a million tons a year).

In 1913 AEOF erected a small refinery at Suez and enlarged it in 1919. The Egyptian government built its own refinery at Suez in 1922, to refine the oil it received as royalty, and doubled its capacity in 1938. By 1954 the two refineries had a capacity of 3.3m. tons p.a.

Later the government took over the AEOF refinery and built a new one in Alexandria, and by 1963 its three refineries had an annual capacity of 6.6m. tons. With additional refineries built, it reached 15m. tons in the 1970s. (In the 1969-70 E.-Israel war of attrition the Suez refineries were heavily damaged, but by 1972 they were repaired and enlarged.)

In 1973, E., still vitally interested in extensive and steady exploration by foreign companies, introduced a new system of small area concessions and production-sharing. Companies were to invest minimal stated amounts in exploration in a stated period of years and to pay a bonus at signature. Their concession was to run for 20–30 years after the discovery of oil in commercial quantities. They were entitled to 40% of production to recover their investment; of the balance, the government was to receive 80%–87% and the companies 13–20%. After a stated period the companies were to relinquish the non-exploited areas. The new system was very successful, and by late 1979 companies from the US, Europe, South America and Japan had signed some 60 production-sharing agreements and committed themselves to invest over $1b. in exploration, paying hundreds of millions of dollars in bonuses at signature. By 1984 the number of agreements had reached 89. The resulting rise in production is listed above. (But E. had a fast-increasing home consumption of oil, and exports that were still about two thirds of production in the late 1970s declined to one half to one third in the mid 1980s). Revenue increased accordingly until the impact of the third oil crisis which at first reduced production and forced Egypt to cut prices. The later price drop of 1985–86 caused E. a serious financial crisis. A large part of Egypt's oil is used at home; the part exported has declined in the mid-1980s to about one third. Egypt is not a member of OPEC; her OAPEC membership has been suspended since 1979.

E. was also a major oil transporter. Until 1967 the bulk of the oil coming from the Persian Gulf area passed through the Suez Canal and E. derived much revenue from the transit tolls — see *Suez Canal. After the closure of the Canal in 1967, E. proposed — to compete with Israel's pipeline from Eilat to Ashqelon and as an answer to the giant tankers which carried the oil around the Cape of Good Hope — to build a pipeline parallel to the Canal farther inland, and the Economic Council of the *Arab League endorsed that plan. The scheme presented a complex of problems: financing; commitment of the international oil companies to ship sufficient quantities of oil through the pipeline; competitiveness with the large tanker rates. Plans were changed several times; a tentative July 1969 contract with a European consortium for a $175m. pipeline to Alexandria was modified in July 1971: "Sumed" (Suez-Mediterranean) pipeline would consist of two parallel 42-inch lines from 'Ain Sukhna, 25 miles south of Suez, to Sidi Krer west of Alexandria; cost increased to $300m. In Oct. 1971 the American Bechtel corporation was awarded the contract, at a cost of $397.5m. But because of difficulties of financing a $400m. Arab stock company was set up late in 1973 to finance the scheme — E. herself to invest $200m., Sa'udi Arabia, Kuwait and Abu Dhabi each $60m. and Qatar $20m. E. cancelled the contract with Bechtel and awarded a new one to an Italian consortium (cost: $348m., Bechtel to act as adviser and superviser).

In Aug. 1976, the pipeline was completed; it was officially opened in Feb. 1977. The final cost was $480m. Shipping commitments through Sumed presented a major difficulty. Its capacity of 80m. tons was never fully utilized — in 1977 it had commitments of 20m. tons, and in 1978 its throughput reached 40m. As tanker rates came down, shipping through the pipeline was no longer economical, and in 1978 Sumed had to reduce its charge by nearly 50%. Yet throughput reached only 66m. in 1981 and in 1984 it fell to 45m. tons.

In July 1976, E.'s National Production Council recommended dropping the plan for a second parallel line, to increase Sumed's capacity to 120m. tons; instead, it opted to widen and deepen the Suez Canal — reopened in 1975 — so it could handle 250–300,000 ton tankers by 1982. The Canal had its own problem of keeping transit charges competitive with the giant tankers around Africa. Although E. envisaged Sumed as complementary to the Canal, not competing with it, many Egyptian leaders doubted whether their country could economically maintain both the Suez Canal and the Sumed Pipeline.

Libya. First oil exploration and exploitation concessions were granted in 1954–55 to several foreign companies; by 1957–58, 11 companies were prospecting, and in the 1960s about 40 companies were operating — 24 of them American (including some of the giants), with major British, French, Italian and German groups among the others. Oil was struck in the later 1950s and commercial production began in 1960–61, increasing rapidly. In the 1970s

85–90% of the oil was produced by American companies. Production reached 55m. tons in 1965, 160m. in 1970 and declined in the 1970s to about 100m. tons; in the crisis of the 1980s production further decreased to 50–55m. tons. Oil revenue passed $500m. in 1967 and $1b. in 1968; it reached $10b. in the mid-1970s and passed $20b. in 1980; in the early 1980s it declined to $10b., with a further substantial decrease expected for 1986–87 (data about L.'s oil revenue are not officially published and estimates are frequently conflicting). Of the revenues, 70% were to be spent on development, 15% to go to reserve funds.

As the oil fields were all inland, in the desert, an extensive pipeline system to the coast, with terminals and oil-ports, had to be constructed. One such system, terminating at Marsa al-Brega (Bureika) was completed late in 1961; others, with terminals at Ras Lanuf, al-Sidr and Zuweitina, followed; and a network based on the longest trunk pipeline, 320 mi., to Tobruk was completed in 1966–67. A first refinery, at Marsa al-Brega, was opened in 1974; two more, at Zawiya and Tobruk, were built in the late 1970s. An Esso-built gas liquefaction plant, also at Marsa al-Brega, was opened in 1970.

Although L.'s remarkable oil economy — and the resulting affluence and general development — were created by foreign, chiefly American, companies, L.'s relations with these companies were sometimes stormy. Since the takeover by *Qadhdhafi's revolutionary régime in 1969, L. has driven a hard bargain and constantly tightened the screws concerning production quantities, prices and royalties-and-taxes, frequently playing one company against the other. In 1971 she imposed on all companies a 51% state participation, and in 1973–74 she wholly nationalized six of the companies; additional companies withdrew subsequently and in the early 1980s, including some of the major groups. The four or five American companies still operating in L. were ordered by the US to withdraw in 1986, in the context of the deterioration of US-L. relations. For L.'s general oil policies in the context of OPEC see the first part of this entry.

Algeria. Concessions were granted in the early and mid-1950s while A. was still French-ruled, mainly during the Algerian rebellion of 1954–62. The concessionaires were four major groups of French oil companies, government and private, with the participation of international companies, mainly Shell. Production began in 1956 at Edjele, in the Sahara desert near the Tunisian border; it reached 1.25m. tons in 1959, 8m. in 1960, 20m. in 1962, 40m. in 1968, 50m. in 1971, was 45–50m. tons in the 1970s and peaked in 1978–79 with nearly 60m. tons; in the 1980s it declined to around 30m. tons p.a. (though conflicting data give higher figures, up to 50m. tons). A. also produced natural gas in large quantities. Independent A.'s oil revenue, since 1962, rapidly increased: it amounted to $50m. in 1963, $325m. in 1970, over $3.5b. in 1974, nearly $6b. in 1978, and peaked with $11b. in 1980; in the 1980s it declined to $8–10b. p.a.

As the oil and gas fields were all in the Sahara desert in A.'s far south, a large network of pipelines had to be constructed to the Mediterranean. The first, from the Hassi Mas'ud-Hawd al-Hamra fields to Bedjaya (formerly Bougie) was completed in 1959, one from Edjele to a Tunisian terminal at La Skhirra in 1960, a third one from Hassi R'meil to Arzew near Oran, with a branch to Algiers, in 1964; this was extended southeastwards to Hassi Mas'ud in 1966, and both these fields were connected with Skikda (formerly Philippeville) by new lines in 1970. A liquid gas pipeline to Italy, through Tunisia, was agreed upon in 1973, but its construction was delayed for four years by Tunisian demands concerning the ownership of the Tunisian part of the line; when the line was completed in 1981, its operation was delayed by an Algerian-Italian dispute over payments; it was opened in May 1983. Refineries were also constructed — the first, in Algiers, was opened in 1969, one in Arzew in 1973, and one in Skikda in 1977. Several gas liquefaction plants were built in Arzew, from 1964, and one in Skikda (opened in 1972).

Independent A.'s relations with the foreign companies, first and foremost the major French groups, were highly complex and beset by frequent disputes concerning production, prices and A.'s participation. In July 1965, A. imposed new arrangements of equal partnership and a 50:50 participation, and in 1971 she unilaterally took a majority share in all the French companies; some of those agreed to the new conditions, and accepted compensation terms, after a long wrangle, and some withdrew. Other foreign companies were nationalized and taken over entirely — five American ones in 1967, and five others in 1969 and 1970. Inland marketing was nationalized in 1968, and the takeover steps of 1971 included a complete nationalization of all pipelines and all gas production and processing. A.'s state oil company, SONATRACH, became a major empire and the primary power in A.'s economy (in 1982 it was decided to split it up into several smaller state companies). New agreements with foreign companies in the 1970s and 1980s were based on new principles — SONATRACH keeping full control and the foreign companies acting as operators only. Even after the nationalization process described, A.'s relations with the major buyers remained troubled; oil sales to France were regulated by long-term agreements, but large-scale long-term agreements on the sale of liquefied gas caused protracted disputes — one agreement, with the American El Paso group (1969), was cancelled in 1980 by the company, while others, with France (1970), Italy (1973) and Belgium (1975), were amended and reconfirmed in 1982.

Tunisia. Oil concessions were granted from

TABLE 2. CRUDE OIL PRODUCTION
(millions of tons p.a.)

	1950	1960	1970	1980	1985
Abu Dhabi	–	–	33.4	65	37
Algeria	–	8.6	46.4	48	50
Bahrain	1.51	2.3	3.8	2.5	2.5
Dubai	–	–	4.2	17.5	17.5
Egypt	2.2	3.1	19.0	30	45
Iraq	7.0	47.6	76.4	138	71.5
Kuwait	17.2	81.9	137.3	85	53.5
Neutral Zone	–	7.3	26.3	(a)	(a)
Libya	–	–	159.6	86	55.5
'Oman	–	–	16.4	14	25
Qatar	1.7	8.2	17.0	23	15
Sa'udi Arabia	27.3	62.1	175.7	495	170
Sharja	–	–	–	0.5	2.8
Syria	–	–	4.5	8.5	8.5
Tunisia	–	0.2	4.1	5.5	5.5
Total	57	221.3	724	1,018.5	559.3

(a) Included in Sa'udi Arabia and Kuwait.
Source: composite

TABLE 3. CRUDE OIL PRODUCTION
(daily average in thousand barrels)

	1950	1960	1970	1980	1985
Abu Dhabi	–	–	683	1,375	740
Algeria	–	183	980	960	1,000
Bahrain	30	45	76	55	50
Dubai	–	–	84	360	350
Egypt	45	62	361	600	900
Iraq	140	972	1,560	2,645	1,430
Kuwait	344	1,692	2,732	1,700	1,070
Neutral Zone	–	136	503	(a)	(a)
Libya	–	–	3,320	1,750	1,110
'Oman	–	–	323	285	500
Qatar	34	175	359	480	300
Sa'udi Arabia	547	1,314	3,548	9,900	3,400
Sharja	–	–	–	10	56
Syria	–	–	90	165	170
Tunisia	–	3	87	110	120
Total	1,140	4,582	14,706	20,395	11,196

(a) Included in Sa'udi Arabia and Kuwait.
Source: composite

1949, still under the French Protectorate, to various foreign companies — French, US, Italian and others. Independent T., since 1956, issued further concessions, including, from 1964, also for offshore prospecting, until about 15 companies were operating in T. Oil was struck in 1964 in the al-Borma region in the Sahara desert in southern T., on the Algerian border. Commercial production began in 1966, reached 3.3m. tons in 1967 and passed the 4m. mark in 1971; it stood at 5m. tons in 1979 and fluctuated between 5m. and 6m. tons in the 1980s. About half of T.'s production was used for home consumption. Oil revenue reached about $600m. in 1980 and $800m. in 1985. Relations with the foreign companies were generally smooth. T. did not join OPEC; she joined OAPEC, but seceded, 1986.

A pipeline from the far-away production area to the Mediterranean at La Skhirra was completed in 1966, using for most of its length the line which T. had allowed Algeria to lay from Edjele to La Skhirra in 1960. T. also agreed to the passage through her territory of a gas pipeline from Algeria to Italy — though she held up the final agreement from 1973 to 1977, until she was recognized as the owner of the pipeline on her territory and her demands for transit fees were met (the pipeline was opened in May 1983). T. got involved in a dispute with Libya over the offshore borderline; the matter was raised before the International Court which ruled in Feb. 1982, against T.'s petition, in favor of the *status quo*, and rejected a second Tunisian appeal in Feb. 1985.

Morocco has produced oil since the 1930s, with various companies holding concessions. However, production has so far remained very small, in the 20–40,000 ton p.a. range. M. has not joined either OPEC or OAPEC.

Oil has reportedly been struck in *Sudan*, *Yemen* and *Jordan*; but commercial production has not yet begun.

TABLE 4. OIL REVENUES (in US $ millions)

	1940	1950	1960	1970	1980	1985
Abu Dhabi	–	–	–	230	11,000[a]	8,000[a]
Algeria	–	–	50[a]	325	11,000	8,000
Bahrain	1	3.3	14	34	400[a]	350[a]
Dubai	–	–	–	40	3,500[a]	2,700
Egypt	–	–	95	200[a]	2,900	1,600
Iraq	8	14.8	267	500	26,000	10,400
Kuwait	–	12.4	450	895	20,000	9,000
Libya	–	–	–	1,600	21,000[a]	8–10,000[a]
'Oman	–	–	–	106	2,500[a]	3– 4,000[a]
Qatar	–	1	54	125	5,000	3,000
Sa'udi Arabia	1.5	112	355	1,200	104,000	28,000
Sharja	–	–	–	–	100[a]	600[a]
Syria	–	–	–	n.d.	n.d.	n.d.
Tunisia	–	–	–	–	600	800

(a) In many cases, data about oil revenues are not officially published, and as there are different methods of calculating them, estimates are frequently conflicting. The composite data given, culled from different sources, are in many cases estimates.

'Oman ('Uman) Formerly Muscat and 'Oman. Sultanate in the south-eastern corner of the Arabian peninsula, on the coast of the Gulf of 'O. and the Arabian Sea, bordering in the north and northwest on the United Arab Emirates (UAE, formerly *"Trucial 'Oman"), in the west on Sa'udi Arabia, and in the southwest on South Yemen; the borders, mostly in desert areas, are largely undemarcated. The main, central part of 'O. has a narrow littoral behind which, to the north and west, rise mountains reaching heights of over 3000 meters (*al-Jabal al-Akhdar* — the "Green Mountain"), and behind them stretches a plateau that merges into the Great Arabian Desert. The southwest of 'O. is called *Dhofar and has been fully incorporated into the Sultanate only since the 1970s. 'O. also owns — as an exclave, separated from 'O. by the UAE — the tip of the Trucial 'O. peninsula, jutting into the Straits of *Hormuz, called Ru'ūs al-Jabal or *Ra's Musandam. She also owns several islands in the Arabian Sea, chiefly Masira and the *Kuria Muria islands. She also ruled the small Gwadar peninsula on the Pakistan coast across the Gulf of 'O., but in 1958 sold it to Pakistan.

The area of 'O. was usually estimated at c. 82,000 sq. mi. (212,000 sq. km.) — and though according to some sources that figure included Dhofar, it seems to have referred to 'O. without Dhofar; with Dhofar, conflicting estimates of c. 115,000 sq. mi. (300,000 sq. km.) seem to be more correct. The population, estimated until the 1960s at 500–700,000, has by the mid-1980s passed the 1m. mark, and some estimate it at nearly 2m. It is mostly A. though in the towns there are Pakistani, Indian and Iranian minorities, estimated at 15–20%. The majority speak Arabic in the dialects current in the Arabian peninsula and the Persian Gulf area, but the ancient South-Semitic dialect spoken in Dhofar is defined by some linguists as a non-Arabic tongue. The population is Muslim — most of it of the *Ibadiyya sect usually classified as non-Sunni; Ibadiyya Islam is the state religion. A small part of the population works the land cultivating less than 1% of 'O.'s area, mostly in the mountains. Farther inland, nomadic tribes graze their animals. The inhabitants of the coast were in the past mostly fishermen, pearl-divers, boat-builders and traders. Since the late 1960s, the growing oil economy has provided an increasing share of employment.

'O., or at least strong points on her coast, were held by Portugal from 1508 to the mid-17th century, and subsequently by Persia. From the mid-18th century she has been ruled by an A. dynasty, the Aal (House of) Abu Sa'id (for rival "Imams" inland see below). The Abu Sa'id Sultans expanded their rule to parts of eastern Africa, especially the island of Zanzibar, where many 'Omanis traded and settled. But Zanzibar and 'O. were divided, in 1856, between the two sons of Sultan Sa'id ibn Sultan (ruled 1804–56), with Britain mediating the division. In 1877, Dhofar was annexed (but not yet firmly controlled).

'O. (then "Muscat and 'O.") was the first country in the *Persian Gulf area to sign a protectorate treaty with Britain — in 1798, at first: with the British East India Company; the first British governor arrived in 1800. Anglo-'Omani protectorate treaties were amended and redrawn several times. The most recent re-formulations, in 1951 and 1958, played down the protectorate and emphasized 'O.'s independence. Yet Britons, mostly under contract rather than seconded from the British government, still headed the army and directed wide sectors of the administration. As Britain withdrew her protecting presence from the Persian Gulf area — announced 1968, implemented 1971 — 'O. became fully independent in 1971. She was admitted to the *Arab League in September of that year, and to the UN in Oct. Over a thousand British officers continue serving with 'O.'s armed forces, and Britons command the navy and air force. Certain naval and air facilities also remain at Britain's disposal, mainly at Masira island and Salala (Dhofar), and since 1980 similar facilities are being granted to the USA.

'O.'s economy was extremely poor and backward until the late 1960s. Marine activities had declined, and little agriculture was practised. There were no modern roads, no airfield, no urban development, no health and education services. Sultan Sa'id ibn Taimur, ruling since 1932, deliberately obstructed all economic and social progress, let alone modernization of the régime.

The change came with the discovery of oil and the growth of a modern oil economy, which even Sultan Sa'id could not prevent. For data on oil production, from 1967, and oil revenue, see *oil. Oil revenues made possible the initiation of far-reaching modernization and development — not as rapid and luxurious as in some Gulf countries, but revolutionary in terms of 'O.'s past.

As Sultan Sa'id ibn Taimur continued resisting pressures for modernization and reforms that mounted in the late 1960s (and that were joined by British advisers and the British government), his son *Qabus, strongly encouraged by the British, mounted a *coup d'état* in July 1970 and deposed his father (who went into exile and died in London in 1972). The new Sultan, who had been kept inactive and confined to the palace for many years, now stepped up development and modernization — including the construction of ports, airfields, roads; some industrialization (mainly oil-linked: fertilizers, gas liquefaction); and a network of health and education services. By the mid-1980s there were c. 1,750 hospital beds, against a single hospital with 12 beds before 1970; 500 schools with over 165,000 students, against three schools with 900 students before 1970. Sultan Qabus endeavored to direct these economic and social changes in a conservative manner and to go slow on the introduction of representative government. However, he took first steps in that direction, too, by creating, in Oct. 1981, an appointed Advisory Council.

'O. was disturbed for many years by two separate rebellions, both with international repercussions. One concerned the emergence, among the inland tribes, of an *Imam of the Ibadiyya sect who claimed not only religious authority but political autonomy or even independence for the mountainous, inner regions. Though traditionally the Sultan had also been the Imam, the separation of the spiritual-religious Imamate from the secular-political Sultanate was an old issue and latter-day Sultans were willing to concede such a separation. But in 1913 the Imam rebelled and established himself as ruler of inner 'O. An agreement was signed in 1920 in Sib which, the Imam claimed, legitimized his rule. The Sultan, however, later contested the validity of that agreement and maintained that, even if valid, it granted only limited local autonomy. While Muhammad ibn 'Abdullah al-Khalili was Imam, 1920–53, the dispute was simmering; but in 1954 a new Imam, Ghaleb ibn 'Ali, rekindled an armed rebellion, supported by several tribes. He was defeated by the Sultan's army, with the help of British forces, in 1955 and 1957, but, usually living in exile in Egypt or Iraq, insisted on his claims and maintained that serious fighting was continuing (which was denied by the Sultan).

The ASt supported the Imam and presented his revolt as a national and anti-colonial struggle. Sa'udi Arabia also joined the campaign against the Sultan and the British and aided the Imam, for geopolitical reasons and interests of her own. From the late 1950s, the ASt with the support of the anti-colonialist Afro-Asian group, endeavored to involve the UN in the issue. In 1963, the UN sent a Swedish diplomat to investigate the problem, and in 1964–65 it set up a sub-committee for the same purpose. Neither reached clear conclusions as to the Imam's and the Sultan's claims and the guerrilla war the Sultan was denying; but the sub-committee ruled that the issue was an "international", not a domestic, problem and invited the UN De-colonization Committee to examine it. The latter, and in its wake the UN General Assembly, adopted, each year from 1965 to 1970, resolutions affirming 'O.'s right to full independence and calling on Britain to withdraw her troops. The Sultan's government, along with Britain, rejected these resolutions as unwarranted and illegal UN interference (a) in the internal affairs of 'O. (the rebellion), and (b) in the relations between independent 'O. and Britain.

After the take-over by Sultan Qabus and the withdrawal of the British protectorate, "decolonizing" UN intervention ceased, Third World pressure relented and some ASt began supporting 'O. and her Sultan (in large part in connection with the other rebellion, see below, and under the influence of Sa'udi Arabia. The rebellion was defused, in 1971–72, with Sa'udi Arabia and some Gulf sheikhdoms mediating in informal talks with the Imam. The rebellion has not been an issue since.

Another revolt erupted in Dhofar in the mid-1960s. A "Front for the Liberation of Dhofar" was set up there in 1965 — see *Dhofar. This "Front" aimed not only at the overthrow of the government of 'O., and perhaps the secession of a revolutionary Dhofar, but at the destabilization of the conservative (and in the 1960s still British-protected and -dominated) Gulf principalities in general and renamed itself "Popular Front for the Liberation of the Occupied Arab Gulf" (PFLOAG). It was closely connected with the leftist-revolutionary wing of the Palestinian-A. guerrilla groups, the *"Popular Front for the Liberation of Palestine" and the "A. Nationalist Movement" (Harakat al-Qawmiyyin, see *Arab Nationalism), and supported by the A. left, the *Nasserists and the *Ba'th, and by the leftist ASt — Iraq, perhaps Egypt and Syria, and mainly South Yemen. While it claimed to control Dhofar and to have underground cells in the Gulf area, it was obviously based in South Yemen and got its arms, finance and supplies from there (reportedly with Soviet, and perhaps Chinese, support). This rebellion engaged 'O. forces in sporadic, sometimes heavy, fighting in Dhofar during the later 1960s and early 1970s.

In the fight against that PFLOAG, however, 'O. was supported not only by the British. Both the conservative ASt and Iran, then still under the Shah, understood and dreaded the leftist-revolutionary character of that rebellion and aim to disestablish the Gulf region as a whole and gradually rallied to 'O.'s side. Of the ASt, only Jordan actually sent a military contingent (volunteers, commandos, aircraft), while Sa'udi Arabia helped financially, paying for military equipment etc., and began exerting pressure on South Yemen. Iran maintained, from late 1972, a substantial expeditionary force in 'O. (3–6,000 men, aircraft and naval equipment; an Iranian force of c. 3,000 men was actually fighting, and defeating, the rebels). In 1974, Iran's military aid was regulated in an 'O.-Iran agreement on the joint defense of the Straits of *Hormuz.

Political pressure on South Yemen grew. Several Gulf sheikhdoms tried to mediate: so did the Arab League (unsuccessfully, as the rebels refused to accept its mediation). But the decisive element was Sa'udi pressure — see *South Yemen. In 1975 South Yemen gave in and ceased supporting the rebels; this was reaffirmed in Mar. 1976 in a Sa'udi-mediated 'O.-South Yemen agreement. The Dhofar rebellion, deprived of its bases and supplies, faded out — though the Front itself maintained an organization, held congresses etc. In 1982, after further mediation, 'O. and South Yemen established full, normal relations.

In return for the conciliation with South Yemen and the end of the rebellion, 'O. undertook to liquidate British bases and end the British military presence. 'O. announced, indeed, in 1976, that the British naval base at Masira island was being closed and British air force units were withdrawn from Salala. Actually, as mentioned, "facilities" remained at Britain's disposal, and British officers continued serving in 'O.'s armed forces and heading several of their branches (the British commander-in-chief was replaced by an 'Omani officer in Nov. 1984). Iran's involvement in the defense of 'O. was also gradually toned down: by 1977, the bulk of the Iranian forces were withdrawn, and plans for the institutionalization of a joint defense of the Gulf were shelved. With the fall of the Shah and the emergence of *Khomeini's revolutionary-Islamic régime in 1979, Iran turned from a close ally into a potential threat and enemy — both to 'O. herself and, particularly since the outbreak of the Iran-Iraq war, 1980, to the security of, and free navigation in, the Gulf. While 'O. remained strictly neutral in the Iran-Iraq war (at least outwardly and formally), it was in the context of this new, sharpened concern for the defense of the Gulf that 'O. granted the USA certain air and naval "facilities" and agreed, in 1980, to serve as one of the potential staging and supply bases for a "Rapid Deployment Force" the US was planning. She also expanded, with US aid, her own defense installations, particularly in the Ras Musandam exclave in the Straits of Hormuz.

Independent 'O.'s Sultan Qabus was now free to cultivate normal foreign and international relations. He did so on a rather low profile, fostering active cooperation with Sa'udi Arabia and the other Gulf states within the *"Gulf Cooperation Council" he co-founded in 1981, but otherwise refraining from too active a foreign policy. He set a conservative, moderately pro-Western course, cultivating his alliance with Britain and the USA, but joined the group of non-aligned nations despite that alliance. In Sept. 1985 'O. established official relations with the USSR, but did not proceed actually to exchange Ambassadors. In inter-Arab politics, 'O. evidently belonged to the conservative-moderate camp, without displaying much activity. She refrained even from anti-Israel declarations. And when in 1979 the ASt ostracized Egypt and severed relations with her, because of her peace treaty with Israel, 'O. did not join the all-A. consensus (alone with Sudan and Somalia) and maintained cordial official relations with Egypt. She suffered no ill consequences and was not even denounced too harshly: apparently, the other ASt accepted her low-profile, restrained stance of moderation. Sultan Qabus has also refused the *PLO permission to open an office. 'O. has joined neither *OPEC nor *OAPEC.

OPEC See *Organization of Petroleum Exporting Countries.

Organization for African Unity, OAU See *Africa.

Organization of Arab Petroleum Exporting Countries, OAPEC Established in Jan. 1968, OAPEC soon included Algeria, Bahrain, Egypt, Iraq, Kuwait, Libya, Qatar, Sa'udi Arabia, Syria, the UAE and Tunisia — i.e. all oil-producing AC except 'Oman and Morocco; four of these countries were not members of *OPEC (Bahrain, Egypt, Syria and Tunisia). Egypt's membership was suspended in Apr. 1979; Tunisia seceded in 1986. For the circumstances and aims of OAPEC's creation and its policies — especially during the crisis of 1973 — see *Oil, first part.

Apart from its mainly political aims, OAPEC has not been very active. It has been instrumental mainly in two specific projects: the foundation of an A. tanker fleet in 1973 (established, eventually, by several AC, not by OAPEC and not as an all-A. venture); and the construction of a large dry dock in Bahrain, inaugurated in Dec. 1977 (bitterly opposed by Dubai who was building her own dry dock and wanted all-A. support to be focused on her project).

Organization of Petroleum Exporting Countries, OPEC Formed in Sept. 1960, OPEC had from the 1970s 13 members, including all the major oil-producing countries of the ME, and five non-ME ones (Venezuela, Indonesia, Nigeria, Gabon, Ecuador). The ME members were Iran and seven AC: Saʻudi Arabia, Iraq, Libya, Algeria, Kuwait, Qatar and the UAE (at first, before the establishment of the UAE in 1971, Abu Dhabi and Dubai). Six A. oil-producing countries were not members: Egypt, Syria, Bahrain, ʻOman, Tunisia and Morocco. For OPEC's aims and policies and its impact on the world's oil economy see *Oil, first part.

Orontes (In Arabic: al-ʻĀssi.) River rising in al-*Biqāʻ ("The Valley") in eastern Lebanon, flows northwards through Syria and, turning west, flows into the Mediterranean near Antakia (Antioch) in the Turkish district of *Alexandretta (*Hatay). The O., 310 mi. (496 km.) long, is Syria's largest river except for the *Euphrates that passes through her northeastern part. It carries c. 480 m. cubic meters (mcm) p.a. The utilization of its waters for irrigation is an important Syrian development project. Two dams were built north of Homs, and the extensive al-Ghab swamps, created by the river northeast of Hama, were drained — a project that reclaimed c. 55,000 acres when its main stage was completed in 1961 and that was to be further expanded. Syria had begun these works on the O. without an agreement with Lebanon about the quantities of water to be used by her. In 1972 an agreement was reported according to which Lebanon was to use c. 80 mcm of the O. waters for irrigation and let 400 mcm flow into Syria.

Ottoman Empire The OE — in itself and its history outside the scope of this Dictionary — ruled all of what are now the AC, except for Morocco and most of Sudan, from the early 16th century (Egypt was taken 1517, Northwest Africa in the decades following). In large parts of the Empire especially in North Africa, Ottoman rule was nominal, sometimes no more than a symbolic suzerainty, while local princes and chieftains in fact controlled large areas in Algeria, Tunisia, Libya. In Egypt, O. control was more effective, though the Mamluk rulers were left as local governors — under a Governor-General sent by the Sultan. In 1811 the Mamluks were removed by a new local "Pasha" and military chief, Muhammad ʻAli (of Balkanic origin), who built a new Egyptian state and established a dynasty, nominally under O. suzerainty. Direct O. control in the A. region was in the main confined to the *"Fertile Crescent" (Iraq, Syria with Palestine) and the coastal areas of Arabia (including the pilgrims' route to Mecca and Medina); but in these reigons, too, local chiefs sometimes asserted a far-reaching *de facto* autonomy.

The decline of the OE, from the end of the 17th century, began with the continuous contraction of its European-Balkanic possessions, in constant struggle against Russia and Austria-Hungary — outside our scope; but from the early 19th century it reached the heartland and central administration — also outside our scope — and the Empire's A. and African areas. In the first half of the 19th century the four major Western powers — Britain, France, Russia and Austria — increasingly intervened (in concert, or as rivals) in the OE's affairs, both internal (modernization, legislation, status of minorities) and foreign, including the Sultan's relations with his vassals ("The Eastern Question"). The settlement, in 1840–41, of a protracted Turco-Egyptian crisis that had led in the 1830s to an Egyptian conquest of Palestine and Syria and threatened Turkey's heartland, was imposed by the great powers. The latter also increasingly intervened, from the 1840s, in Lebanon and compelled the Sultan in 1860–61 to grant Mount Lebanon and its Christian-*Maronite majority a far-reaching autonomy. In the later 1870s, Britain and France imposed their joint financial and economic control on Egypt. Indeed, the dismemberment of the OE ("The Sick Man on the Bosphorus"), mainly under Russian pressure, with French and Austrian support, was prevented mainly by Britain.

Moreover, the Western powers began occupying parts of the OE's A. possessions. France conquered and annexed Algeria in 1830 and imposed a French protectorate on Tunisia in 1881. Britain occupied Egypt in 1882 — though she described her rule of Egypt as temporary and provisional, formally abolishing the OE's sovereignty only in 1914, when the OE entered World War I on the side of Britain's enemies. Italy in 1911–12 conquered and annexed Tripolitania-Libya.

A. nationalism, emerging at the end of the 19th and the beginning of the 20th century, was directed against the OE in as much as its national aspirations to complete independence necessarily meant the dissolution of the OE. Some A. nationalists, however, restricted their demands to a decentralization of the Empire and A. autonomy within it. Indeed, as the O. Sultan was also the Caliph of all Muslims, acting against the Sultan was a breach of Islamic loyalty to the Caliph. On this problem, and O. efforts to foster Islamic solidarity, see *Arab Nationalism, *Pan-Islam. When World War I broke out and the opportunity arose for an A. rebellion encouraged and aided by the Western powers, it was only Sharif *Hussein of far-away Mecca who staged such a rebellion, with British help (the *"A. Revolt" of 1916), while the bulk of the A.'s in the O. army and in the A. heartland of the Fertile Crescent remained loyal to the OE and only very few A. officers deserted to join the rebelling Sharif. Vigorous measures against leaders suspected of A. nationalist tendencies in Syria and Palestine, in 1915–16, were preventive, as no A. rebellion had broken out in those countries.

When the OE early in the 20th century allied itself to Germany and Austria-Hungary and finally in 1914 entered the war on their side against Britain, France and Russia, those three powers, later joined by Italy, resolved that after their victory in the war they would dismember the OE. This resolve, and tentative plans as to how to dispose of the regions to be severed, crystallized in a number of secret war-time agreements, chief among them the *Sykes-Picot Agreement of 1916. After its defeat in the war, the OE was indeed dissolved. With O. sovereignty removed, the princes of Arabia became independent in Yemen, Hijaz and Najd, while in the Fertile Crescent semi-independent ASt were set up under British and French tutelage. Turkey's renunciation of any claims to these regions was laid down in the Peace Treaty of *Sèvres, 1920. But this treaty, accepted by the Sultan and his government, envisaged inroads also on the integrity and sovereignty of Turkey's Anatolian heartland and a nationalist revolution under Mustafa Kemal ("Atatürk") rose against this scheme, and established a revolutionary counter-government in Ankara. The Treaty of Sèvres was replaced in 1923, after protracted negotiations, by the Peace Treaty of *Lausanne.

Kemalist Turkey abolished the O. Sultanate in Nov. 1922, and the Caliphate in Mar. 1924, and all members of the house of Osman, the former Sultan/Caliph's dynasty, were banished.

P

Pakistan The creation of P. through the partition of India in 1947 posed a delicate problem to Arab nationalists and governments. Sentiments of Islamic solidarity made them sympathize with the struggle of India's Muslims and their wish to establish their own independent state. On the other hand, A. nationalists had close links with the Indian national movement and its leaders and had no wish to jeopardize their friendship and support. Moreover, the principle that a country should be partitioned to accommodate the aspirations to independence of a religious-national minority was highly problematic to the A.'s, since it had obvious implications and parallels to the Palestine issue, concerning which the A.'s bitterly opposed partition. Owing to that dilemma, A. spokesmen and the governments of the seven ASt then independent or near-independent refrained from taking unequivocal positions on the India-P. issue.

This basic dilemma concerning the very creation of P. has continued coloring the attitudes taken to P. by the ASt, the more so as P. has been embroiled in frequent conflict with India. In general, the conservative, pro-Western ASt — such as Iraq until 1958, Jordan, Saʿudi Arabia — have tended to sympathize with P., including cautious support for her claims in the Kashmir issue, though officially even they stayed neutral. The more leftist-neutralist ASt, such as Egypt and Syria, practised a stricter neutrality, with a marked pro-Indian tinge. Their animosity towards P. intensified when the latter tightened her links with the West and in 1954–55 became a co-founder of the *Baghdad Pact (later *CENTO, inoperative since 1979). It receded when P. turned leftist-neutralist under Bhutto, in the 1970s, and though P. mitigated her neutralism under Zia-ul-Haq, from 1977, and turned right (and Islamist), the A. leftist states' animosity, and preference for India, remained muted.

P. herself has always been keen on fostering her ties to the A. world. She vigorously supported the A.'s in the decisive stages of the Palestine struggle, 1947–48, and has backed the ASt against Israel ever since, refusing, as a matter of course, to have relations with Israel. P. was also active in all-Islamic affairs; while several *Pan-Islamic organizations were founded and led by various political groups and leaders and not necessarily by the government, the latter often supported them and sometimes was itself active. Such Pan-Islamic activities of P. have lessened in recent decades. On the other hand, the Pakistani state and society have under Zia-ul-Haq, since 1977, adopted Islamic patterns — a process that enhanced and intensified P.'s links with the AC. P. was neutral concerning inter-A. blocs and rivalries and fostered relations with AC of both conservative and radical trends. Unconfirmed (and denied) reports in the 1970s claimed P.-Libya co-operation, and Libyan aid, in the development of P.'s nuclear capacity. In general, however, P.'s relations were closer with the conservative ASt, particularly those on the Persian Gulf. P. enjoyed a measure of economic aid from Sa'udi Arabia and the oil sheikhdoms on the Gulf. She provided, in return, technical services and personnel, e.g. in aviation (pilots, ground crews) and reportedly even military personnel; from 1969–70, a Pakistani army unit was reported in Jordan. There were also officers on private contract — e.g. in 'Oman. Large numbers of Pakistanis were working in the A. oil countries of the Persian Gulf; their number was reported in the early 1980s as more than 1m. (?), and their remittances as over $2,000 m. p.a.

Despite these close links, the political support P. hoped for — in her dispute with India, and especially the Kashmir problem; over the secession of Bangladesh, 1971; in the Afghanistan issue, from 1980 — was only partially forthcoming (though on the Kashmir problem the position taken by most ASt — self-determination for its inhabitants — was closer to P.'s position than to India's).

Palestine See *Arab-Israel Conflict, *Palestine Arabs.

Palestine-Arab Guerrilla ("Feda'iyyin") Organizations As the *A.-Israel Conflict turned violent, from the 1920s, guerrilla groups (terrorist squads, "gangs", 'isabāt) formed from the 1930s, particularly during the A. rebellion of 1936–39 (the "Disturbances"). While nominally under the control of the nationalist leadership, headed by the *"Husseini" faction (see *Arab-Israel Conflict, *Palestine Arabs), these squads were in fact operating separately, in most cases locally or regionally, with no central command or leadership. A large force of volunteers from the AC, semi-G. with aspirations to form a regular force, under Fawzi al-*Qawuqji, operated in P. in summer 1936, but failed to establish full control of the G.'s under a central command. None of the G. groups turned into a permanent organization. A similar pattern developed during the G. war that erupted in Dec. 1947, preceding the invasion of the A. regular armies in May 1948. After the armistice agreements of 1949, incursions into Israel and sabotage or terrorist operations in the early 1950s also were the work of small local groups of *Feda'iyyin, but Israel suspected that they were armed and encouraged, or even organized, by branches of the armies and secret services of the ASt.

Permanent GO's began forming in the late 1950s and early 1960s, at first clandestinely among young PA's in Europe and AC (Lebanon, Syria, Egypt, Kuwait). They were soon allowed to set up their centers in some of the ASt — first in Algeria and Syria, followed by Egypt and others; cells in Jordan and Lebanon, the countries closest to Israel (with Syria) and the natural bases for operations against her, were set up without the approval of their governments. The G. groups endeavored, of course, to establish underground cells in Israel (and after 1967 in the Israel-occupied areas). Most of these organizations saw themselves not only as G. groups but as political formations with a military arm. They aspired to the liquidation of Israel and the re-establishment of P. as one unit dominated by her A. inhabitants. For their policies and operations, and their conflicts with AC, particularly Jordan and Lebanon — see *PLO.

Since the 1960s PA GO's have multiplied — mostly small groups divided by political conceptions, factional loyalties, methods of operations — and several groups have repeatedly split. The more important ones are listed below; but some were ephemeral, and some — "fronts" or fictitious covers for secret operations of existing groups. Several A. host countries have formed their own PA client organizations (Syria, Iraq, Libya — see list). In 1969 the PA GO's took over the Palestine Liberation Organization, PLO, formed in 1964 as a mainly political and representative organization; Yasser *'Arafat, the leader of al-Fataḥ, was made chairman of its executive committee. Since 1969 it has assumed the overall direction and command of the various GO's — to a degree that it is sometimes left vague whether certain actions are taken by the PLO or by one of its constituent GO's. The GO's have remained independent and frequently act against the wishes and instructions of the PLO leadership; yet the PLO remains responsible for the actions of all its constituent GO's. (see *PLO).

The more important GO's are:

1. AL-FATH or AL-FATAH (*Fatḥ* in Arabic: victory, conquest; F-T.H is also the acronym in reverse of *Harakat Tahrir Filastin* — P. Liberation Movement). Founded in the late 1950s and commemorating Jan. 1965 as the beginning of actual guerrilla operations, al-F. is considered the largest and dominating constituent group of the PLO, and while formally its delegates do not have a majority in the PLO Executive, Central Committee and National Council, they usually control these bodies and command the support of their majority. Al-F.'s leadership largely overlaps, and is identical with, that of the PLO. Its top leaders are Yasser *'Arafat (Abu 'Ammar), Khalil al-Wazir (Abu Jihad), Salah Khalaf (Abu Iyad), Faruq al-Qaddumi (Abu Lutf), and the brothers Hani Hassan and Khaled Hassan. Its military arm is also called *al-'Assifa* (Thunderstorm). There is no reliable way to determine its numerical strength, i.e. the number of its full-time mobilized fighters receiving regular pay; varying estimates put it, at its peak in the mid- and late 1970s, at 6–10,000 — but considerably higher figures were also mentioned (while the other GO's were estimated to number only hundreds of full-time fighters — except, perhaps, for Syria's *al-Sa'iqa*).

Al-F.'s nationalism may be described as rightist: it rejects the Marxist or Maoist leanings of some of the other GO's, has strong Islamic links and tendencies, and holds that discussion of divisive social and political-ideological issues should be avoided until victory is won. It also opposes a pronounced orientation of the Palestinian movement towards any A. state or bloc and emphasizes political independence. Officially al-F. stands for the establishment of a democratic, secular, multi-religious state after the destruction of the "Zionist entity" (Israel); but the secular-democratic character of that future, ideal P., the dropping of its description as explicitly and exclusively A., and the acceptance of Israel's Jewish population have several times raised heated debates and have not been incorporated in the official documents of the PLO, such as its Charter (which would have to be amended to accommodate these principles).

Al-F. has always been beset by factional struggles — with Khalaf and Qaddumi considered as leading the more militant faction. In 1983, however, al-F. split altogether: a Syria-based and Syria-dominated F. formation under Sa'id Mussa (Abu Mussa) rebelled against 'Arafat's leadership and claimed the name al-F. and *al-'Assifa* for its secessionist group. For this rebellion and the expulsion of 'Arafat's forces from eastern and northern Lebanon, see *PLO.

2. AL-SA'IQA (Arabic: Lightning and Thunder) — Vanguard of the People's War of Liberation — is a GO established in 1968–69 by the *Ba'th party ruling in Syria. It is estimated to number over 1,000 full-time fighters — some reports speaking of several thousands — and is considered the second-largest GO. It is based in Syria, fully controlled by her, and in effect exists only in Syria — with some clandestine cells among PA's (and Syrians) abroad, mainly in Europe. As Syria does not usually permit guerrilla or sabotage operations by GO's directly from her territory, al-S.'s actual military or terrorist operations are less publicized, and perhaps less numerous; it usually operates from or through Lebanese territory (and has also been used by Syria in the Lebanese civil war). Its leaders have frequently changed. Chief among them was Zuheir Muhsin, and after his assassination in 1971 — 'Issam al-Qadi (Muhammad al-Mu'aita and Dafi Jumai'ani have also been mentioned as top commanders). In any case, al-S. is in effect under the direct command of the *Ba'th* party apparatus and the Syrian army and its secret service.

3. THE POPULAR FRONT FOR THE LIBERATION OF P. (PFLP), led by Dr. George *Habash (one of the few Christians among the leaders of the PA GO's), coalesced in 1969 out of several small groups ("Heroes of the Return"; "Young Avengers"). It grew out of the radical, clandestine *"A. Nationalist Movement" (*Harakat al-Qawmiyyin*) and remained closely linked with it. The PFLP, like the *Qawmiyyin*, combines a very militant nationalism and unrestrained, terrorist modes of operation with a neo-Marxist-Maoist ideology.

It advocates an all-out people's G. war and opposes any political solution to the A.-Israel conflict. It was mainly responsible for a spate of brutal hijackings of foreign civilian airliners from 1970 and continued these operations even after the mainstream umbrella PLO disavowed and banned them, from 1972. The PFLP was, indeed, in bitter opposition to the mainstream PLO and does not submit to its discipline. It boycotted the PLO Executive and Central Council from 1974 to 1981, and has done so again from 1983 to 1987. In the split in the PLO, 1983, it was anti-'Arafat, but it did not join the rebellion and its military operations and, prepared to negotiate with 'Arafat and seek a formula for reunification, kept a position between the rival camps. In 1984 it formed an anti-'Arafat "Democratic Alliance" within the PLO, which reached a tentative agreement with the 'Arafat wing — but the agreement was not implemented. In 1985 the Alliance joined forces with the pro-Syrian "National Alliance" in a "National Salvation Front". In 1987 it effected a reconciliation with the 'Arafat camp — see *PLO.

In its doctrinaire leftism, the PFLP has no permanent ties of allegiance to any of the ASt. It was reportedly cultivated for some years by Egypt's *Nasser, who hoped to turn it — and the *Qawmiyyin* — into a loyal Nasserist faction, but that alliance soon fell apart. It found support in Iraq, Libya, South Yemen, but did not stabilize these links. The PFLP's closest ties are with Syria, and since the 1970s its center and base is in Damascus; but as its doctrines are not identical with those of the Syrian Ba'th, and as it refuses fully to submit to Syrian guidance and instructions, relations even with Syria have remained reserved and critical.

The PFLP, whose strength in full-time fighters is estimated at a few hundreds, has frequently split and several of the groups listed below have grown out of it.

4. THE (POPULAR) DEMOCRATIC FRONT FOR THE LIBERATION OF PALESTINE (DFLP or PDLFP), a small group headed by Na'if *Hawatma, a Jordanian Christian, seceded from the PFLP in 1968–69 over problems of doctrine and leadership. Its Marxism-Maoism is more doctrinaire than that of the PFLP and it emphasizes its ideology and tries to keep it pure. The DFLP is politically on the extreme Left and calls for an active struggle against the conservative A. governments, such as Jordan. It conducts military/terrorist operations, but these have usually not been spectacular. It opposes the hijacking of foreign civilian aircraft and terrorist operations in foreign countries. Though strongly anti-'Arafat, the DFLP did not join the rebellion of 1983. Allied in 1984 with the PFLP in the "Democratic Front", it favored, like the PFLP, a compromise formula for an accommodation with 'Arafat. It did not join the "National Salvation Front", formed in 1985 by the PFLP and the pro-Syrian groups. Though it is based in Syria, its relations with Syria are reserved and critical.

5. THE POPULAR FRONT FOR THE LIBERATION OF PALESTINE — GENERAL COMMAND is a small splinter group that seceded from the PFLP soon after its formation. Headed by Ahmad Jibril, a former officer in the Syrian army, it seems to operate in tightly organized clandestine cells. Its military operations are usually of an extreme, terrorist character, including hijacks of foreign aircraft and the taking of hostages and their murder. The PFLP-GC's political leanings are obscure, but, based in Syria, it generally seems to follow the Syrian line. It also enjoys Libyan support. In 1983 it joined the anti-'Arafat formations. It took no part in the reconciliation of 1987.

6. THE PALESTINE LIBERATION FRONT, another extreme, terrorist GO, also split off the PFLP, and later the PFLP-GC. Since 1983 it is reportedly split — one faction, more radically anti-'Arafat, is headed by Tal'at Ya'qub and one by Muhammad 'Abbas (Abu'l-'Abbas). Politically obscure, and clandestine even vis-à-vis the ASt (and, though Abu'l-'Abbas is a member of the PLO Executive, perhaps even vis-à-vis the PLO leadership), the PLF is variously reported to be based in Syria or in Iraq.

7. THE ARAB LIBERATION FRONT is a PA GO set up in 1969 by the Iraqi *Ba'th* party. It has remained marginal and hardly any actual military/terrorist operations have been ascribed to it. Its command — Zeid Haidar; 'Abd-ul-Wahhab al-Kayyali (assassinated in Dec. 1981); 'Abd-ul-Rahim Ahmad — did not produce outstanding leaders and seemed to have little impact. The ALF was, in any case, under the direct command of Iraq's *Ba'th* party and army. Following a shift in Iraq's policies, for instance, the ALF was in the PLO split of 1983 the only group outside

the 'Arafat wing of *al-Fath* and its "independent" supporters to stay loyal to 'Arafat.

8. THE POPULAR STRUGGLE FRONT is a small, extremist group that seceded in 1969 from *al-Fath*. Led by Samir Ghosheh, Subhi Ghosheh and Bahjat Abu Gharbiyya, it joined the "National Alliance" formed in 1984 by the anti-'Arafat, Syrian-guided factions, and the "National Salvation Front" of 1985.

9. From time to time, terrorist actions are ascribed to several clandestine, shadowy extremist groups — some of them outside the framework of the PLO, some perhaps fictitious "fronts" or secret arms of other organizations. The most publicized among them is BLACK SEPTEMBER (taking its name from the Jordan-PLO war that climaxed in Sept. 1970), which made its first appearance with the murder of Jordanian Premier Wasfi *Tall in Nov. 1971. Observers think that there were in effect two different groups under the name BS. At first BS was a secret arm for clandestine operations of *al-Fath*, led by Salah Khalaf (Abu Iyad); this BS formation was apparently dissolved in or about 1973. The name BS was then taken by an extremist group of gunmen led by Sabri al-Banna, "Abu Nidal"; this group disobeyed a PLO order to cease its terrorist operations and dissolve itself and was reportedly expelled from the PLO in 1972 or 1974. However, it continued operating, and some of the most brutal terrorist crimes and assassinations are ascribed to it. It has remained clandestine and is supported only by the most extreme ASt — Libya, Syria and for some time Iraq. Its base and headquarters were in Baghdad and are now variously reported to be in Damascus or Libya. Undercover links with the "official" *Fath* are frequently rumored. Similar groups appearing from time to time under different names — "Black June", "Black March" etc. — are thought to be cover-names or splinters of the same organization.

10. Another group that has remained shadowy and in doubt, is the guerrilla arm of the Communist Party. In 1970 the party, (then still the Jordanian CP, under Ya'qub Zayyadin) reportedly set up a GO naming it *al-Ansar*. But hardly any operations on its part were reported, and its very existence remained in doubt. While the CP sometimes appears as a constituent group of the PLO (thus, e.g., as a member of the PFLP-led "Democratic Alliance" of 1984 and the "National Salvation Front" of 1985), it has according to other reports been denied full constituent membership because of its refusal to set up fully-fledged guerrilla/terrorist squads and was officially admitted only in Apr. 1987.

11. The PLO as originally conceived, in 1964, was to have a regular military arm, the Palestine Liberation Army, PLA, attached to the various A. armies. Palestinian units in battalion, and later brigade, strength were indeed set up in the framework of four A. armies — the Egyptian (the 'Ain Jalut Brigade), Syrian (Hittin and Yarmuk Brigades), Iraqi (Qadissiyya Brigade, Battalion 421), and the Jordanian (al-Badr Brigade); their combined strength was variously estimated at 8–12,000 men. The overall command of this PLA changed several times — 'Uthman Haddad; 'Abd-ul-Razzaq Yahya; Misbah Budeiri et al. — sometimes in the context of intra-PLO factional struggles or PLO-ASt differences. But anyway, the notion of an overall PLA-PLO command of the units incorporated in the various A. armies, and of PLO control of these forces, turned out to be illusory: while the ASt concerned accepted or nominated Palestinian officers for some, though not all, command posts, and Syria allowed *al-Fatah* to assume partial control of at least one of Syria's PLA brigades (al-Yarmuk), the PLA brigades within, or attached to, the A. armies became in fact part of these armies, fully integrated and under their command and control.

The PLA, as a regular force in the framework of regular A. armies was not meant to engage in guerrilla/terrorist operations, though in several cases it backed such operations. (Its Syrian brigades were also used in the Lebanese civil war — on Syria's behalf and under her orders.) Initial plans provided for PLA-linked formations, the Popular Liberation Forces. But these plans did not materialize.

Palestine Arabs As P. was not a political-administrative unit during Ottoman-Turkish rule, until 1918 (though as a general geographic term the name P. remained in use), it is doubtful whether her A.'s — c. 650,000 at the end of World War I — identified themselves specifically as PA. A population's allegiance and self-identification was, until fairly recent times, with their religious community, their village and surrounding region (sometimes even with ancient, half-legendary tribal formations, such as the division into "Qais" and "Yaman" that split the A. villages of P. until the 19th century) — rather than with wider "national" entities. As a national consciousness, and an explicit A. nationalism, spread — from the early 20th century — most PA nationalists probably saw themselves as Syrian A.'s. In any case, under Turkish rule no A. nationalist movement called explicitly for the independence of P. as a unit.

In 1918–20, while Amir *Feisal ruled in Damascus, most PA leaders called their country "Southern Syria" and opposed its separation from Syria. Two rival groups then speaking for incipient nationalism — the "Cultural/Literary Association" (al-Muntada al-Adabi) and the "Arab Club" (al-Nadi al-'Arabi) — were more or less united on that point, and several leading activists were in Damascus with the group around Feisal endeavoring to set up an A. administration for (Greater) Syria. However, when Feisal's vision of a greater Syrian A. kingdom was shattered and the partition of the area into separate entities under Western imperial tutelage became a fact, the PA began conducting their communal and political activities within the framework of P. and the new geographic-political realities led to the emergence of the PA's as a body politic. The nationalist struggle against the British *Mandate, and first and foremost against the Jewish-Zionist National Home, greatly enhanced the development of a strong national consciousness and an intense PA nationalism.

The PA rejected proposals of 1922 by the British and P. governments to set up a Legislative Council, and they did not establish binding, all-embracing national institutions of their own (like the Jews' *Knesset Yisra'el* with its elected Assembly and the National Council, *Va'ad Le'umi*, nominated by that Assembly). The Mandatory Government suggested the establishment of an "A. Agency" parallel to the "Jewish Agency for P." provided for in the Mandate, officially to represent and lead the PA; but the proposal was rejected. The PA had communal-religious representative bodies: the Christian communities had their church hierarchies with their administrative and judicial organization (local leaders struggling, in some cases, against the largely foreign hierarchy for the "Arabization" of that organization and a stronger lay representation — particularly in the *Greek-Orthodox community); and for the Muslim community, whose affairs had been managed in the Ottoman Empire by the state, the Government ordered a "Supreme Muslim Council" to be created (1922). The PA also founded many economic, professional and cultural organizations. Their political-representative organization, however, remained rather sporadic and fragmentized.

The two associations or clubs mentioned withered after 1920. From 1919–20, organizing efforts centered on "Muslim-Christian Committees", so named to stress, against the government's official classification according to communities, A. national, supra-communal unity. These committees, composed of small numbers of notables, convened several congresses; the first one, in Jaffa, Jan. 1919, still saw P. as "Southern Syria" not to be separated from Syria. The third congress, Haifa, Dec. 1920, centering now on the struggle in P. (with "South Syria" no longer mentioned), set up an "A. Executive" that turned into a permanent body, with Mussa Kazem al-*Husseini as chairman. These congresses, and the Executive, also sent several delegations to Europe, mainly to London and Geneva, for talks, contacts and to propagate the Palestinian-A. cause. The first such delegation went out in Aug. 1921; in Geneva it co-operated with the permanent "Syrian-Palestine Office" maintained there for some years by a group of Pan-A. exiled leaders, and participated in a conference convened by that group. Similar delegations were sent in 1922 and 1923. Bt as the Executive, its congresses and its delegations had no tangible success in their lobbying efforts and showed little active leadership, the Executive gradually waned. No more congresses were held after 1923, except for one in 1928 when an attempt was made to revive the Executive without much success. When Mussa Kazem al-Husseini died, in 1934, the Executive ceased to exist.

Behind the united front of the A. Executive of the 1920s, the real political leadership was increasingly wielded by Hajj Amin al-*Husseini, the *Mufti* of Jerusalem, and his faction. They used the Supreme Muslim Council, of which al-Husseini was President, as an instrument of political and factional power, and a fierce struggle of rival camps over this issue largely shaped political life among the PA. Neither the supporters of the Council — *al-Majlisiyyun*, also often called, after the clan leading them, *"Husseinis" — nor their adversaries, "the Opposition", al-Muʿāridun, also called *"Nashashibis", since that clan led them — organized themselves in the 1920s as formal political parties. Both camps derived their main strength from an informal network of urban clans supporting them, each with a network of client clans in the villages around their town, where they frequently were land-owners and held positions of economic power and patronage. While both camps had such networks, the Majlisiyyun-Husseinis were generally stronger among the urban intelligentsia and the Islamic establishment, especially in Jerusalem and Hebron, while the Muʿaridun-Nashashibis and the clans supporting them (such as the Dajani in Jerusalem, the Touqan [Tawqan] and Masri in Nablus, Irsheid in Jenin, Bitar and Abu Khadra in Jaffa, Kheiri and al-Taji-al-Farouqi in Ramla) had a stronger tissue of client clans in the rural areas and based themselves on local and municipal interests. There were also influential clans, with their rural networks, whose allegiance was fluctuating or who tried to keep their independence of the two main camps (such as the Shawa in Gaza or the ʿAbd-ul-Hadi in Nablus), and there were individuals who did not follow their clan's orientation.

In general, the Husseinis were considered more militant or extremist, the Nashashibis — more moderate and prepared to collaborate with the government and the Jews, though this found scant expression in their public statements. Publicly, both camps were strongly nationalist, rejected the Mandate and the Balfour Declaration, opposed the government and the Jews and their National Home aspirations, and neither came up with any plans for an A.-Jewish settlement or a compromise solution to the conflict. During the 1920s there were several attempts to found political parties, based in the main on local, municipal or rural-agricultural interests, some of them half-supported by the opposition Nashashibi camp, some — with clandestine government or Jewish support. None of them had much impact and most withered soon. The dominating influence among the PA remained that of the two main camps, with the "Husseini" camp setting the pace and fanning the violence that erupted again in the disturbances of 1929, and dragging the "Nashashibi" camp along.

With the demise of the A. Executive and the intensification of the political pace in the early 1930s, several political parties were founded in 1934–35. The two main ones were the "National Defense Party" headed by Ragheb *Nashashibi and rallying the Muʿaridin-Nashashibi camp, and the "P.A. Party" organizing the Majlisiyyun-Husseini camp and headed formally by Jamal al-*Husseini (really by the Mufti Hajj Amin al-Husseini, who did not wish to compromise his national, above-party leadership by formally chairing the party). A third party, the Istiqlal ("Independence"), was founded by ʿAwni *ʿAbd-ul-Hadi in 1932. This was a militantly nationalist, Pan-A. party, ideologically rooted in the pre-World War I nationalist formations and the Istiqlal group they had tried to establish after the war, and with connections to the remnants of that group (though, by now, without the links to the *Hashemites and the British that the group had in 1918–19); in P., the party grouped younger, militant intellectuals, but had little impact or influence. Three other parties seemed to have even less influence: the "Youth Congress", which grew out of a congress held in 1932 and was led by Yaʿqub Ghussein; the "Reform Party" founded in 1935 by Dr. Hussein al-*Khalidi, Mayor of Jerusalem 1934–37; and the "National Bloc" of ʿAbd-ul-Latif Salah of Nablus; these three are mentioned because their leaders became members of the Arab Higher Committee established in 1936.

When in Apr. 1936 an A. general strike was declared, beginning with acts of violence against Jews and soon turning into a rebellion (then called "Disturbances"), an "Arab Higher Committee" (AHC) was formed to assume the overall leadership of the movement. The ten-member AHC, chaired by the Mufti Hajj Amin al-Husseini, was composed of two more representatives of the "Husseini" party, Jamal al-Husseini and the Christian A. Rock; Ragheb Nashashibi and a second, Christian, representative of his party; the Istiqlal's ʿAwni ʿAbd-ul-Hadi and the "independent" Ahmad Hilmi, considered close to the Istiqlal; and the leaders of the three minor parties mentioned. This AHC provided for one brief year, or less, a united leadership. When in July 1937 the rebellion was resumed, after having been suspended since Oct. 1936 (see *Arab-Israel Conflict), that unity was broken: the two Nashashibi party members of the AHC resigned and the leadership remained with the extremist faction alone.

In Oct. 1937 the AHC was outlawed. Three of its members (Khalidi, Hilmi, Ghussein) were arrested, deported and kept in detention in the Seychelles; the *Mufti* and Jamal al-Husseini escaped to Syria/Lebanon; 'Abd-ul-Hadi had gone into exile even before, after being briefly detained. The AHC thus ceased to be an operative body, but the *Mufti*, Jamal Husseini and their associates tried to keep the rebellion going from their Syrian-Lebanese exile, through a clandestine, non-institutionalized high command. Inside P., municipal and village affairs were managed by the local notables, many of them close to the Nashashibi camp, but no alternative political leadership emerged. One chief reason for that was the brutal campaign of terror mounted by the rebel squads and the exiled leaders against the rival camp and its leadership — terror that induced the Nashashibi camp to form, from 1937–38, counter-terror squads, so-called "peace gangs", but still managed to paralyze and stifle any attempt to form a political leadership in the absence of the exiled extreme faction.

Military operations, the actual rebellion — mainly guerrilla attacks on Jewish settlements and urban quarters and road communications — were conducted by small guerrilla-type squads ("gangs", *'isabat*), most of them village-based. The AHC, and later the clandestine high command in exile, tried to set up a centralized military command, but never succeeded in imposing on the "gangs" a disciplined military command structure. In Aug. 1936 the Syro-Lebanese Fawzi al-*Qawuqji led a volunteer army into P. and assumed the supreme command of the PA rebellion. He appointed Fakhri 'Abd-ul-Hadi commander of the Palestinian contingent of his army; but he never succeeded in integrating most of the guerrilla squads into his army — which was in any case a brief episode that ended when the strike-and-rebellion was suspended in Oct. 1936 (see *A.-Israel Conflict). ('Abd-ul-Hadi later was one of the "peace gang" commanders; he was assassinated in 1943.) In the resumed rebellion, 1937, the head of the "gangs" in the Tulkarm region, 'Abd-ul-Rahim al-Hajj Muhammad from Dhannaba village, proclaimed himself commander in chief and was supported by the exiled leadership; but his command was contested by several rivals and in any case never extended to the south, where the guerrillas were controlled by Hassan Salama from the Ramla area southwards and by 'Abd-ul-Qader al-Husseini in the Jerusalem area. 'Abd-ul-Rahim was killed in 1939 by the "Peace gangs"; the absent high command appointed Ahmad Abu Bakr from Burqa village to replace him — but his command was never effective, and the rebellion was waning at that time.

The rebellion of 1936–39 had a far-reaching effect on the PA in several respects. (a) The internal terror decimated the élite and deeply affected a large stratum of PA society in both towns and villages. There are no reliable figures, but the number of victims was variously estimated at 4–8,000, and there was hardly a family of notables that was not hit. Beyond the bitter, fearful memories of those years, the climate of violence has persisted throughout the decades since the late 1930s. There is among the PA little open, reasoned debate of controversial political issues, and dissent is frequently silenced — often by the assassination of the dissenters.

b) Political life was paralyzed, and a vacuum, a near-total lack of leadership was created for almost ten decisive years, by the combination of internal terror with the absence (abroad or in detention) of many first-rank leaders of the militant, extremist camp.

c) The leadership of the PA struggle was in fact gradually taken over by the ASt — a take-over encouraged by the British from the intervention of the A. rulers in Oct. 1936 through the Anglo-A. conferences on P. in 1939 and 1946–47, and up to the involvement of the ASt in the P. War of 1948. Yet, while in fact waging the P. struggle, the ASt did not impose their views and policies, but allowed, from about 1946, an extreme faction of the PA to call the tune.

d) The domination of the PA, in 1937–39, by "gang" commanders and the internal terror accelerated a growing disintegration of the traditional structure of PA society. The dominating influence of the leading families of notables with their network of client clans in the villages, declined — and so did the decisive position of the extended family, the clan (*hamula*), in social life in general.

During the first years of World War II the PA were numbed into political inactivity. When in 1943–44 some notables wished to resume political action, towards the decisive years of the post-war settlement, the Husseini faction opposed any such resumption, and particularly the creation of a new representative body, in the absence of its leaders (many of whom had drifted in 1940–41 from Syria-Lebanon to Iraq, and from there the *Mufti* and some associates had gone to Nazi Germany, while Jamal al-Husseini and others had been arrested and deported). The Nashashibi camp, still paralyzed by the years of terror and disappointed that the Government had not encouraged it to form an alternative leadership, was inactive. Thus, activities had to be led by marginal, minor groups, non-party individuals such as Mussa al-*'Alami, and non-political associations such as the Chamber of Commerce or the Trade Unions. But even they accepted the Husseini ruling that activities should not extend to the major political issues and that no representative body should be formed, and focused their energy on the prevention of the sale of A. land to Jews, and information/propaganda efforts — see *Arab-Israel Conflict.

But the basic questions concerning the country's future, and the re-establishment of a leadership body that would deal with them, could no longer be postponed. During 1944, several of the minor parties (but not the Nashashibis) tried to re-establish their party organizations. Though they had little success, the Husseini faction felt compelled to do the same — taking care to appoint only provisional, acting officers and to leave the top posts vacant for the absent leaders. When the PA were asked, in Sept. 1944, to send a delegation of observers to the *Alexandria Conference called to prepare the foundation of the *Arab League, they could not agree on the composition of such a delegation and the Husseini faction prevented its formation; with difficulty it was agreed to send the respected non-party Mussa al-*'Alami as a single observer. But 'Alami was involved in controversy (e.g. over the rival land salvation schemes) and his position was soon contested. In Nov. 1945, the Arab League sent a mission headed by the Syrian Jamil Mardam to mediate the land salvation controversy and help establish an agreed leadership body. As Mardam brought a British promise that Jamal al-Husseini would soon be released, and helped the Husseinis to obtain a dominating position, the latter agreed to re-establish a 12-member AHC, consisting of the same six party leaders as in 1936 (with Jamal Husseini provisionally replaced by another Husseini), four more representatives of the Husseini faction, one Nashashibi (Ragheb) and two independents (pro-Husseini 'Alami, and pro-*Istiqlal* Ahmad Hilmi), with the chairmanship left vacant — meaning: for the *Mufti*. But the new AHC did not operate smoothly and soon new controversies erupted. When Jamal al-Husseini was released and returned to P. early in 1946, he vigorously assumed the leadership. In Mar. 1946 he expanded the AHC to consist of 7 Husseini faction men, 12 "neutrals" (many of them in fact pro-Husseini), and 10 for the other parties, two each.

The non-Husseini groups refused to accept this *coup* and boycotted the new AHC. Talks on a compromise (including the addition of 10 pro-opposition "neutrals") failed in May, and in June the non-Husseini groups set up a rival leadership body, the "A. Higher Front". Faced with this open split, the Arab League again intervened: it dissolved both of the rival committees and appointed a new, five-member AHC, with the *Mufti* Hajj Amin al-Husseini as chairman (still in exile — since June 1946 in Egypt), Jamal al-Husseini as deputy chairman, one more Husseini man and two pro-opposition neutrals (Hilmi and Dr. Hussein al-Khalidi). Thus the League, though it knew that the Husseinis did not accept the policies adopted by the ASt and took a more extremist line, handed the dominating influence to the Husseini faction.

The new AHC took an uncompromising line in the decisive struggle of 1946–48: it declined all British compromise proposals, such as cantonization and semi-autonomy, rejected the UN partition plan, and called for war to prevent its implementation. But the split had not been healed and the new AHC was not really in control. Even the military instrument it tried to forge towards the inevitable clash, blunt and ineffective, was split into the Husseini-founded *Futuwwa* and the opposition-leaning *Najjada*, and the decision to merge them was not realized. The PA opened violent action on the morrow of the UN decision of 29 Nov. 1947, not effectively prepared and with no strong, united leadership.

The events of 1947–48 — the guerrilla war from Dec. to May; Qawuqji's volunteer "Army of Deliverance"; the invasion of the regular armies of the ASt and the A.-Israel war; the flight of the refugees; the occupation of the A. parts of P. by Jordan and Egypt — are described in the entries *Arab-Israel Conflict and *Arab-Israel Wars. The end of the war found the PA divided and their body politic shattered. In 1947–48, the PA numbered about 1.3m. — double their number at the end of World War I and the inception of the Mandate (that remarkable growth, larger in the mixed cities and the coastal regions of Jewish settlement than in the purely A. districts, included a number of immigrants from neighboring AC — illegal and mostly unregistered; there is no way to establish their number, the usual estimate is 100–200,000, with some observers going up to 300,000 or more). Of these 1.3m. PA, c. 650,000 remained in their homes — over 400,000 in the Jordan-occupied *"West Bank" and East Jerusalem, 70–100,000 in the *Gaza Strip and 150,000 in Israel (See *Israel Arabs); 600–650,000 left their domicile as refugees — c. 400,000 remaining within P. (200,000 in the West Bank and 200,000 in the Gaza Strip), 100,000 going to Jordan, and c. 150,000 to Syria and Lebanon (and a very few to other countries). Those in Jordan and the Jordan-occupied part of P. received the Jordanian citizenship — c. 700,000 (400,000 original inhabitants of the West Bank, 200,000 refugees in the West Bank, 100,000 refugees in Jordan); the 150,000 in Israel became Israeli citizens; those in the Gaza Strip, Lebanon and Syria had no citizenship.

From 1948 to the mid-1980s the number of PA, divided and partly dispersed as they were, has greatly increased; in fact, they have tripled to c. 4m., as detailed below. In some of their divisions, this was the result of their high natural increase alone, with no major other demographic changes. Thus, for instance, in Israel: though some 40–50,000 refugees were allowed to return through a scheme of family reunion, and some may have drifted back undetected, most of the more than four-fold growth to over 700,000 was due to natural increase. The same goes for the PA in Syria and the Gaza Strip with its massive concentration of PA refugees. In Lebanon there was some additional influx of PA from Jordan after the latter expelled the Palestinian guerrillas in 1970–71 — but that influx concerned mainly PLO activists and officials and "regular" fighters, maybe a thousand or two, not a population movement of any size (the same, in reverse, goes for the evacuation of 11–12,000 PLO men from Beirut in Aug. 1982 — and the re-infiltration of a few thousands after 1984: these movements of PLO professionals meant no demographic change for the bulk of the PA in Lebanon).

Significant demographic change concerned the PA in the Jordan-occupied West Bank, Jordan herself, and the Persian Gulf. In the latter area, and particularly in Kuwait, large numbers of PA found employment and settled. In Kuwait alone, their number is estimated at c. 300,000, and in the Gulf region as a whole it may well reach 400,000. But the permanence of their settlement was in doubt: as Jordanian citizens they could return — or be made to return — to Jordan or the West Bank; and indeed, when the oil boom and its labor market began shrinking in the 1980s, a movement in that direction did set in. During the 19 years of Jordanian rule in the West Bank, 1948–67, a considerable migration of PA from the West Bank to the East Bank (Transjordan) was reported. Figures cited are unreliable and vary greatly — from 250,000 to 500,000, with c. 400,000 as possibly the best estimate. A further wave of migration occurred during and immediately after the *Six Day War of 1967 (most of the West-Bankers fleeing to the East Bank were in the West Bank since 1948, as refugees); figures vary again — from 200,000 to 350,000, c. 215,000 being a probable estimate. In any case, precise figures could not be given: the West Bank PA were Jordanian citizens and there was no way of telling whether movements from the West Bank to the East Bank or the Gulf were meant as permanent emigration. The Israelis occupying the West Bank in 1967 found a population of c. 650,000 (or 585,000 without East Jerusalem, soon separated and incorporated in Israel). Some movement — to Jordan, and to the Gulf — continued after 1967, and again, there was no telling how much was for work, how much permanent migration; it is estimated, from 1967 to the mid-1980s, at c. 185,000, but some cite figures up to 300,000. By the mid-1980s the population of the West Bank, excluding East Jerusalem, was c. 900,000.

In Jordan (Transjordan, the East Bank), the

growth of the PA population, enhanced by the migration from the West Bank, has turned the PA into a majority — even without counting the considerable part of the Transjordan population that was of Palestinian origin in the first place. Detailed figures again vary, but the fact of a Palestinian majority — put by some at over 55% — is generally accepted since the mid-1970s; Jordan herself counts her PA inhabitants, informally, at over 1.2 m., of whom she regards more than 50% as fully integrated, the rest as refugees.

The total number of PA is in the mid-1980s estimated at c. 4m. — about 1.2m. in Jordan, 0.9m. in the West Bank, 0.5m. in the Gaza Strip, 0.7m. in Israel, 0.2m. in Lebanon, 0.2m. in Syria, 0.3m. in Kuwait an other Persian Gulf countries, 0.1–0.2m. in other AC and in Europe or the Americas. Of these 4m., c. 2m. still retain the status of refugees, listed and supported by *UNRWA, the UN Relief and Works Agency (a figure regarded by many observers as inflated); of the refugees, c. 0.7m. live in refugee camps — in fact fully grown refugee towns.

The post-1948 political activities of the PA — see also *Arab-Israel Conflict — were at first final convulsions and after-throes of the war of 1948. Several rallies of notables, late in 1948, had urged King *'Abdullah of Jordan to save and take over the A. part of P., and as the PA on the West Bank welcomed, or acquiesced in, the Jordanian occupation, there was little specifically Palestinian political activity in those parts. In the Egyptian-occupied Gaza Strip, however, efforts were made — and encouraged by Egypt — to keep a PA entity alive and foil its annexation by Jordan. In July 1948, an "Administrative Council for P." was set up in Gaza under the auspices of the Arab League; in Sept., it was replaced by a "Government of all P.", claiming authority also over Israel and the Jordan-occupied parts. Set up by the remnants of the AHC, this "government" was headed by Ahmad Hilmi and included Jamal Husseini as Foreign Minister and, at first, the non-Husseinis 'Awni 'Abd-ul-Hadi and Hussein al-Khalidi; it was recognized by all the ASt except Jordan. An 86-member "Constituent Assembly" was also appointed, presided over by Hajj Amin al-Husseini. However, this experiment of a Gaza-based P. government failed utterly. It had no authority over most of what had been P., was vigorously opposed by Jordan, and even in Gaza the Egyptians did not allow it real authority. The "Constituent Assembly" met only once, in Oct. 1948, and was never reconvened. The non-Husseini members drifted away and joined the service of Jordan, and the government did not function. In Sept. 1952 the A. League announced officially that it had ceased to operate and that P. would be represented in the League by the ASt. As Egypt did not annex the Gaza Strip, some rudiments of local self-government were set up in the late 1950s and a Gaza-PA entity was maintained. In 1958, a "Palestinian National Union" was founded — parallel to, and part of, the "National Union" that was the single political organization of Egypt and the *UAR of 1958–61; but it did not take root or develop into a nucleus of a revived PA entity.

The Jordan-occupied part of P. was integrated in Jordan, with no attempt to create a Palestinian entity, though the West Bank and the East Bank *de facto* remained distinctive halves of the Kingdom. PA were appointed to local administrative positions and from 1949 also as Jordan Cabinet Ministers, civil servants, diplomats etc. In Mar. 1949 the use of the term P. in official documents was banned and the term "West Bank" substituted. A new election law of Dec. 1949 gave the inhabitants of the West Bank the right to vote (with equal, 50:50 representation to the two parts of the kingdom). In Apr. 1950 elections were held, and the formal incorporation of the occupied West Bank in the kingdom was solemnly proclaimed. This annexation caused a serious inter-A. crisis, since the ASt bitterly opposed it and threatened to expel Jordan from the Arab League. The crisis was resolved by a double formula: first, the annexation was officially termed "temporary", until the liberation of the whole of P.; second, in a secret deal, 'Abdullah consented to scrap a non-aggression pact with Israel he had negotiated; in return the ASt acquiesced in his "temporary" annexation of the West Bank.

The PA as new citizens of the Hashemite Kingdom, educationally more advanced and used to vigorous, volatile political activity and factionalism, were a fermenting element in the kingdom, and while many of them were prominent in public positions at all levels, many others were active in oppositional agitation. But during the 19 years of Jordanian rule, there was no demand for a PA state, for secession from, or even autonomy within, Jordan, no specifically Palestinian organization with specific Palestinian demands. (For the situation of the PA after 1967 see *Israel Occupied Territory.)

The question of a P. "entity" was reopened in the late 1950s and early 1960s by both PA outside the West Bank and some of the ASt, mainly in the context of, and as an instrument in, the A.-Israel conflict. This was the time when PA guerrilla organizations crystallized (see entry), and they were indeed in the forefront of the renewed PA consciousness and demands. Yet, the ASt's hesitated to adopt unequivocally the slogan of a PA state, realizing that that slogan was basically anti-Jordanian, since a separate, distinct P. state would necessarily invalidate Jordan's rule over AP. The A. Heads-of-States decided therefore, at their first summit meeting, Jan. 1964, to recognize a P. "entity" that would not be a state or a territorial unit but a national, extra-territorial, organizational entity, and to leave the future territorial shape and limits of that entity blurred on purpose. It was as such an entity that the *"P. Liberation Organization" (PLO) was established in 1964, sponsored by the A. League and the ASt. The PLO itself quite clearly demanded an independent PA State — though the term "State" does not appear in its Charter; however, it focused its emphasis on the liberation of that part of P. constituting Israel and left quite vague its attitude to the Jordanian occupation and annexation of the West Bank. Its first Charter in 1964, stated explicitly that the organization had no "sovereignty" over the West Bank or the Gaza Strip; this postscript was dropped in the reivsed Charter of 1968.

After the take-over of the PLO by the guerrilla organizations, in 1969, and its transformation into an umbrella organization for those, the demand for an independent PA state was more insistent and articulate — and gradually the ASt adopted and supported it, the more so as since 1967 all of P. was occupied by Israel and the anti-Jordanian implications of the demand for an independent AP state were blurred. Jordan herself had to accept the A. League's decision of 1974 to recognize the PLO as the sole legitimate representative of the PA people, and from 1972 King *Hussein advocated a federation or confederation between the future AP and Jordan. Several ASt's supported that idea, and at least part of the PLO, under *'Arafat, accepted it in principle in the mid-1980s; the agreement 'Arafat signed with King Hussein in Feb. 1985 was abrogated by the PLO in 1987, but the clause providing for a future confederation was not among the points denounced (the actual implementation of the confederation idea would depend in any case on Israel's withdrawal from the West Bank).

The cardinal question of whether the ASt and the PLO, when demanding an independent PA state, still mean *all* of P., i.e. the elimination of Israel (as clearly stipulated in the PLO Charter), or a PA state in *part* of P. in co-existence with Israel — remains undecided (see *Arab-Israel Conflict). Moderate A. spokesmen, and their supporters in other countries, insist that the aim is the latter; according to them this is implied in all-A. decisions of recent years (e.g. the *"Fahd Plan" adopted by the Fez Summit of Sept. 1982) and also in a resolution of the PLO's P. National Council of 1974 that a "national authority" be set up in any part of P. vacated by Israel. Certainly King Hussein's plan for a confederation with a PA entity means an entity in part of P. co-existing with Israel. But so far, only a few A. leaders have stated that aim clearly and the PLO leadership has not done so — not even its 'Arafat wing, considered moderate. The extremist factions of the PLO, and the *"Rejection Front" among the ASt, vigorously oppose the very idea of co-existence with Israel (and several PLO moderates advocating it have been assassinated).

The debate on these vital issues (confederation with Jordan, co-existence with Israel) is not conducted, among the PA, frankly and publicly, though there is a wide network of PA journals and publications. Among the PA outside P., the wider public does not seem to take part in a discussion that remains confined to the professional functionaries of the PLO — and among those it is a factional struggle, frequently violent, rather than a frank, reasoned debate of basic ideological-political problems. In the West Bank and Gaza — the core and base of any future PA entity — there are municipal institutions, in part elected ones, there are non-political professional, economic and cultural associations, and an articulate press; but political organization has been banned by Israel. As far as political public opinion can be gauged, the PA in the occupied areas are divided into a pro-Jordanian camp — not active and hardly articulate, and considered to be a minority — and a pro-PLO camp, thought to be the majority; even the former profess to accept the status of the PLO as the sole legitimate spokesman of the PA. Both camps fervently desire the termination of the Israeli occupation and the establishment of a PA entity. While the extremist factions of the PLO have underground cells and a measure of influence, it is assumed by many observers — though not confirmed by published opinion polls — that the majority would favor a PA entity alongside Israel and in peaceful co-existence with her (without committing themselves as to whether this would be a final solution or only a political settlement necessary in the circumstances) and would go along with the idea of a confederation with Jordan. Plans for ME or A.-Israel peace negotiations, discussed in the 1980s by Egypt, Jordan, Israel, and pushed by the US, envisaged PA representatives taking part — either within a joint Jordanian-Palestinian delegation or as a specifically PA delegation. Israel refused to negotiate with the PLO as long as that organization had not accepted the existence of Israel, and co-existence with her as its policy and aim, and forsworn terrorism (and the US agreed with that position). The PLO was unwilling to commit itself in that sense until the PA right to self-determination, in effect: independent statehood, was accepted — a commitment neither the US nor Israel were prepared to make. Therefore, negotiations were envisaged without the PLO; the intention was to select a group of PA not active members of the PLO but acceptable to it as well as to Jordan and Israel. By the mid-1980s this intention — one of the bones of contention in the continuing, deadlock over the plans for negotiations — had not been realized.

In Ottoman times, P. was a backwater and the PA were hardly different from the A. population of the surrounding regions in their social and educational level. However, during the 28 years of the Mandate, under the impact of the general development of P. and its Jewish sector (and the struggle with that sector), the PA greatly advanced in their health and educational standards, their social institutions, their political awareness and activity; it may be estimated that their average level was by 1948 more highly developed than that of the AC (with the exception of Lebanon). True, in the arts and literature (outside the scope of this book) very few of them attained all-A. renown. But they had a lively press (two main dailies regularly published for most of those years: *Filastin* — founded 1911, a daily from 1929, published by an A.-Christian family — and *al-Difāʿ*, founded 1934, several other dailies published for some time, and a plethora of weeklies and periodicals), a highly developed educational network (mostly governmental, some private, and some missionary) — though as yet no university, and rising average educational standards. This development continued, and was enhanced, despite the adverse general and political situation of the PA, after 1948. In fact, among the PA refugees educational standards rose most conspicuously, owing to the intensive schooling provided by *UNRWA, the UN agency caring for the refugees. A large number of young PA studied at universities in the AC and in Europe and America, and the PA are by now estimated to have a higher ratio of academically trained than any other ME population. In the Israel-occupied West Bank and Gaza, though without Israeli aid, several post-secondary colleges have turned into universities (Bir Zeit, 1975; al-Najāh, Nablus, 1977; Bethlehem — a Catholic institution — 1973; Hebron Islamic College, 1972; Gaza Islamic College, 1979). A lively press in East Jerusalem, including several dailies (*al-Quds, al-Fajr, al-Shaʿb*), serves the West Bank and Gaza, too — and, though subject to Israeli censorship, vigorously expresses its views. A wide-ranging press and periodical literature has also been created outside P. by the PLO and various groups affiliated with or financed by it. This includes the weekly, sometimes daily, *Filastin al-Thawra* ("P. Revolution"), founded in 1972 as the organ of the PLO; several *Fatah* mouthpieces; *al-Hadaf*, the organ of the *PFLP; *al-Hurriyya*, that of the *PDFLP; and a news agency (*Wikalat al-Anbāʾ, al-Filastiniyya al-ʿArabiyya*, WAFA). PA journalists also work in several general A. papers, particularly those published in recent years in European centers, and enjoy considerable influence.

An "Institute of Palestinian Studies" was established in the 1960s in Beirut, later affiliated to the University of Kuwait and connected with several institutions in Western countries; it publishes a monthly *Journal of P. Studies*, also in English and French.

Palestine Conciliation Commission (PCC)

In Dec. 1948, the UN General Assembly set up a PCC, to assist in a peaceful settlement of the A.-Israel conflict. The five permanent members of the Security Council were entrusted with the nomination of the members and chose representatives of the USA, France and Turkey. In 1949 the PCC convened a conference in *Lausanne, but since the representatives of the ASt refused to meet and directly negotiate with those of Israel, it held separate consultations with A.'s and Israelis. A "Protocol of Lausanne" emerged, setting down a number of principles for a future solution, but neither the conference nor the protocol were of consequence. In the late 1950s, the PCC tried to take a hand in the P.A. refugee problem, tentatively suggesting a three-pronged approach — an agreement on the repatriation to Israel of some, the resettlement of some in the AC, and the absorption of some in third countries. To investigate these prospects, the PCC in 1961 sent to the ME the American Dr. Joseph E. Johnson of the Carnegie Foundation; he submitted a first report in Oct.-Nov. 1961 and a final one in Sept. 1962. But Johnson's Report and proposals were inconclusive, as he had been unable to find or create a significant area of agreement; his report, unacceptable to either party, was shelved by the PCC.

Having achieved virtually nothing, the PCC has not been active since about 1962. Its American, French and Turkish members are no longer prominent political personalities but medium-level officials. Yet the PCC has not been officially dissolved and it submits annual reports of its lack of activities.

Palestine Liberation Organization (PLO)

Founded in May-June 1964 at a congress in Jerusalem — under the auspices of the *Arab League and mainly on Egypt's initiative — the PLO was conceived as a political representation of the PA's, non-territorial "entity". Such an entity, vaguely mentioned before, had been proposed and discussed in the A. League since 1963; Jordan had opposed it. To avoid that Jordanian opposition, PA demands for independent statehood, with the ensuing claim to the part of P. annexed by Jordan, were deliberately left vague and open (thus enabling Jordan, despite her misgivings, to allow the congress to be held in Jerusalem), and all emphasis was put on the struggle against Israel. The "Arab Higher Committee", surviving, in exile from the pre-1948 days, bitterly objected to the foundation of the new body, declaring itself to be the sole representative of the A.'s of P.; but its claims were disregarded. Syria voiced strong reservations concerning the non-territorial character of the PLO, preferring it to represent a clearly proclaimed PA *state* in all of P., but did not press her views. The PLO was to have a military arm, the "P. Liberation Army", attached to the regular armies of the various ASt but under the overall control of the PLO — a plan that was greatly changed in actual implementation, as the Palestinian units formed within the Egyptian, Syrian, Iraqi and Jordanian armies in fact became integrated in and were commanded by these armies and PLO control over them was ineffective.

The PLO adopted, at its first constituent congress of 1964, a detailed National Charter or Covenant (*mithaq*) that was modified and expanded at a session of the National Council in Cairo in July 1968. The Charter states that "the Palestinian A. people" (which is an "inseparable part of the A. nation") "possesses the legal right to its homeland". "The Palestinians are the A. citizens who were living permanently in P. until 1947" and their descendants; "Jews who are of Palestinian origin" (1964) — or "who were living permanently in P. until the beginning of the Zionist invasion" (1968), dated in another resolution of the Council at 1917 — "will be considered Palestinians". The Balfour Declaration, the Mandate, the partition of P. and the establishment of Israel are "null and void"; "the claim of a historical or spiritual tie between Jews and P." is denied, "Judaism... is not a nationality, ...the Jews are not one people". "The liberation of P... is a national duty to repulse the Zionist, imperialist invasion... and to purge the Zionist presence from P." "The PA people... through the armed Palestinian revolution, rejects any solution that would be a substitute for the complete liberation of P." "Armed struggle is the only way to liberate P." and "Feda'iyyun [i.e. guerrilla, commando] action forms the nucleus of the popular Palestinian war of Liberation". (A postscript to the Charter of 1964 stated that the PLO had no sovereignty over the parts of P. occupied by Jordan and Egypt; this was dropped in the Charter of 1968.)

Since that Charter was adopted, PLO thinking seems to have changed in several respects. The resolve to set up a PA independent *state* — a term not mentioned in the Charter — including the Jordan-annexed parts, has hardened. On the other hand, the idea that such a PA entity might renounce complete, separate independence and enter a confederation with Jordan, has been accepted in principle by parts of the PLO. The PLO, or parts of it, in recent years seem willing to accept all the Jews of Israel as citizens of the P. state they envisage; they also emphasize the democratic, secular character of the state they aim at (an emphasis that Israel could not take seriously, in view of the PLO's character and that of political life in the AC). A decision of 1974 to establish a "fighting national authority" in any part of P. vacated by Israel has been interpreted by some observers as meaning that the PLO would be content to set up its state in *part* of P., alongside Israel and in co-existence with her (though such an interpretation has never been endorsed by authorized PLO spokesmen). In recent years some PLO leaders have been prepared to meet Israelis of leftist-"dovish" views. None of these changes has been formalized or explicitly endorsed.

In 1964, the lawyer Ahmad *Shuqeiri, who had been Under-Secretary General of the Arab League and Ambassador to the UN of Syria and Sa'udi Arabia, was nominated as chairman of the nascent PLO's 13-member executive. His leadership of the PLO was considered a failure, limited mainly to flaming-extremist oratory, and he was dismissed in Dec. 1967 (formalized at the July 1968 Council). He was replaced by a "collective leadership" headed by Yahya Hamuda, a lawyer and not-very-prominent politician (who seems to have been even less effective than his predecessor). However, during the early and mid-1960s, various *PA Guerrilla Organizations grew and gradually assumed the *de facto* leadership of the PA struggle. They obtained increasing representation on the National Council and the PLO Executive, and in Feb. 1969, at the fifth Council session, they seized full control of the PLO, gaining the majority on the Executive (4 *Fatah, 2 *Sa'iqa, 1 pro-*PDFLP, 1 kept for the *PFLP, which refused to take its seat, 4–5 "Independents" of whom at least three were close to *Fatah*), and *Fatah* leader Yasser *'Arafat became its chairman. The PLO now became in effect a roof or umbrella organization for the various guerrilla groups. Its central leadership, dominated by *al-Fatah*, never wielded complete control over the different, rival organizations, each of which retained its operational and ideological independence, with some of them, such as the PFLP, in near-constant opposition and unwilling to submit to the discipline of the PLO Executive and its decisions (and some, such as the extremist *"Black September", even reported expelled); but by and large, the PLO, while retaining its double character as a political-representative body and an umbrella high command for guerrilla groups, was in charge of these groups. It thus assumed responsibility for their armed operations, considered terrorist by Israel, most of the West and large parts of world public opinion — including operations which its Executive had not approved. In fact, most of the PLO's activities were such guerrilla/terrorist operations. The PLO knew that these operations had little effect on the actual military situation and would not bring Israel to her knees: the rationale behind many of them was that they were needed to "put P. on the map", to awaken world governments and public opinion to a fuller awareness of the existence of the unsolved P. problem and the sufferings and demands of the PA people — an aim that was indeed achieved in large measure. Terrorist operations included the assassination of A. leaders considered too moderate, including some from the ranks of the PLO itself, and discouraged open dissent and frank debate and, even more so, A. initiatives towards peace with Israel.

The ASt increasingly accepted the PLO as the legitimate representative of the PA's, allowed it to operate freely in their territories, and supported it with ample funds — particularly the wealthy oil countries, Sa'udi Arabia and the Gulf sheikhdoms. The PLO was thus enabled to build up a growing establishment with large offices, economic and financial enterprises, social, health and educational institutions, a press, research and the publication of books and periodicals, diplomatic representation in many world capitals, and an intensive information/propaganda campaign — and a large and well-paid body of functionaries to maintain all these activities. PLO chairman 'Arafat was constantly moving around A. and world capitals for conferences, consultations, participation in international congresses (including a Nov. 1974 appearance at the UN General

Assembly, at the invitation of the Assembly) and visits, "official" or unofficial — being treated in many capitals as a foreign head of state.

PLO terrorist operations in Europe, against foreign airliners, hijacks and the capture of hostages etc. proliferated from about 1970; in the mid-1970s they were disavowed and ordered stopped by the PLO — but were continued by the PFLP and other dissident factions, and apparently also by secret PLO arms and "fronts". Such operations could be managed from command posts in various A. cities, or abroad, sometimes in collaboration with European and international terrorist organizations. Operations against Israel, on the other hand, had to be staged from the AC bordering on Israel. Until 1967, Egypt permitted such operations from the Gaza Strip — observers differing as to the degree of Egyptian control and sponsorship. Syria kept the PLO and its guerrilla squads under tight control and did not permit any independent action directly from Syrian soil — while encouraging and aiding operations from Lebanese territory. The main bases of operations were in Jordan and Lebanon. The PLO conducted these operations with no co-ordination with the governments and armed forces of the two countries, without asking for their consent, and in effect with no consideration for their interests and wishes, turning the two countries against their will into battlefields and exposing them to Israel's counter-blows. In effect, the PLO, with its ramified establishment, acted as if it ruled Jordan and South Lebanon, as a nearly independent state-within-the-state and seized *de facto* control of large sectors of the two countries (mainly those close to the Israeli border). These grave developments were further aggravated, in Jordan, by the PLO's explicit hostility towards King *Hussein and his régime, and its threat to the régime, and in Lebanon, by the apprehension that any confrontation of the PLO by the government and the armed forces might cause a polarization of Lebanon's internal-communal tensions and a civil war with the Muslims supporting the PLO. For the resulting tension, efforts to work out agreements, and clashes in both countries, Jordan's liquidation and expulsion of the PLO in 1970-71, and the PLO's role in Lebanon's civil war, from 1975 — see *Jordan, *Lebanon.

The ASts' support for and recognition of the PLO, that had been a fact for some years, were formalized in 1974, when the all-A. Summit at Rabat recognized it as "the sole and legitimate representative" of the PA people. King Hussein of Jordan had of course grave misgivings — not only on account of the deep rift between him and the PLO since 1970 but because that recognition invalidated his claim to the West Bank; but he had to accept that ruling. Indeed, from the mid-1970s a certain *rapprochement* took place between Jordan and the PLO, a limited presence of PLO offices and representatives was again permitted, and from 1982 Hussein negotiated with 'Arafat on proposals for a joint Jordanian-Palestinian delegation to take part in ME peace negotiations and the future Jordanian-Palestinian confederation. On these negotiations, the Hussein-'Arafat agreement of Feb. 1985, 'Arafat's inability to have the agreement endorsed by the PLO, and its abrogation by the PLO in 1987 — see *Jordan.

On the peace negotiations problem there was no progress. Hussein's pressure for the acceptance by the PLO of Security Council Resolution 242 has so far failed, and so has that of Egypt's President *Mubarak, with whom 'Arafat from 1983-84 resumed and strengthened relations he had cut in 1979. The real issue is a formal acceptance by the PLO of Israel's right to exist and a clear commitment to peaceful co-existence with her — evidently: in *part* of P. (which may be seen as implied in the PLO's desire to take part in peace negotiations, but which the PLO has so far been unwilling to make explicit); in the diplomatic code this is formulated as "accepting Resolution 242" (see *Arab-Israel Conflict). The PLO had an additional, specific reason for rejecting Resolution 242: the Resolution speaks of PA refugees only, not of the PA people and its rights. Formulae suggested by the USA — such as accepting the principles of the resolution while registering a reservation concerning that (legitimate) objection — proved unacceptable to the PLO. Circumlocutions, like accepting "all" UN resolutions, were unacceptable to the US and Israel, and so were PLO pre-conditions like a pre-arranged recognition of the PLO once it endorses Resolution 242, or the pre-guaranteed acceptance of its demands for PA statehood or self-determination. This vital issue therefore remained, in the mid-1980s, unresolved. In any case, beyond 'Arafat's apparent inability to take bold decisions, since the early 1980s he has been unable to commit even his own wing of the PLO, let alone the PLO as a whole.

In the course of Israel's invasion and occupation of South Lebanon and the Beirut area, from June 1982, PLO forces and establishments were expelled, a process leading to the organized and internationally aided evacuation of 11–14,000 PLO personnel from Beirut, late Aug. to 1 Sept. 1982, to various AC (Tunisia, Sudan, Yemen, South Yemen). The PLO now set up its headquarters in Tunisia, but most of its forces were dispersed and far from the borders of Israel. Efforts, in 1983, to rebuild an operative center and infrastructure in the parts of Lebanon dominated by Syria — the *Biqā', the eastern parts of Mount Lebanon, and the northern region of *Tripoli — met Syrian opposition and a Syrian-instigated rebellion within the ranks of the PLO and 'Arafat's own *Fatah*. The PLO's, and particularly 'Arafat's, relations with Syria had always been difficult, owing to their refusal to accept Syrian policy guidance and Syria's refusal to allow the PLO guerrillas freedom of action from Syrian soil. Syrian and PLO forces had actually clashed in Lebanon in 1976, when Syria intervened in that country to enforce a settlement of the civil war in accordance with a Syrian plan and the PLO resisted; Syrian forces had forcibly suppressed that resistance — in co-operation with "right-wing" Christian militias. Now, in 1983, Syria refused to allow the re-establishment of 'Arafat's forces in the parts of Lebanon she controlled. 'Arafat himself was expelled from Syria in June, and a rebellious, Syrian-controlled wing of *al-Fatah*, under Sa'id Mussa (Abu Mussa), clashed with 'Arafat-loyal forces and expelled them from the *Biqa'* in the summer of 1983, after bloody battles. When 'Arafat withdrew his men to the Tripoli area, the battle spread there, and in Dec. 1983 'Arafat and c. 4,000 of his men had to ask to be evacuated from Tripoli — by sea, and again with international help. However, in 1985–86 'Arafat succeeded in re-infiltrating some of his men into the Palestinian camps in South Lebanon and Beirut. These attempts to re-establish a dominant PLO presence were one of the chief reasons for continuous clashes between Palestinian gunmen in the camps and the Shi'i *Amal militia.

Of the various anti-'Arafat groups within the PLO, the Syrian-controlled *Sa'iqa*, and perhaps the PFLP-GC, collaborated with the *Fatah* rebels in battle. The PFLP, PDFLP, PSF, PLF (see *PA Guerrilla Organizations) did not join the actual fighting, but they stepped up their political struggle against 'Arafat and the mainstream. The anti-'Arafat factions boycotted the 17th National Council held in 'Amman in Nov. 1984. They organized themselves in anti-'Arafat fronts (split in themselves): a "Democratic Alliance", founded in May 1984 by the PFLP, the PDFLP, the Communist Party and the PLF; and a "National Alliance", founded in May 1984 by the *Sa'iqa*, the *Fatah* rebels, the PFLP-GC, the PSF and some smaller groups. The "Democratic Alliance" was prepared to negotiate with 'Arafat's mainstream — demanding more hardline policies and reforms in the structure of the PLO amounting to a paring-down of 'Arafat's powers and the formation of a "collective leadership"; but the National Alliance opposed any deal with 'Arafat, insisting that he be deposed and that the PLO as a whole accept the Front's hardline policies and a new (Syrian-guided) leadership. In Mar. 1985 the two anti-'Arafat Fronts formed a joint "P. National Salvation Front" — obviously closer to the hardline *Sa'iqa* and *Fatah* rebels than to the more flexible and independent PFLFP and PDFLP; but the PDFLP and the Communists refused to join the new Front. 'Arafat's mainstream is also not fully united behind him: a hardline faction, headed by Salah Khalaf (Abu Iyad) and Farouq Qaddumi, greatly constrains his freedom of action.

Reconciliation efforts continued from 1984 (and in the fight against the Shi'i assault on the camps in Beirut and South Lebanon the rival formations even cooperated to some degree. Finally, in Apr. 1987 a reconciliation was achieved. The 'Arafat wing agreed to the abrogation of the 1985 accord with King Hussein, to the severance of "offical" PLO relations with Egypt, and to the reconfirmed rejection of Resolution 242; and the PFLP and PDFLP rejoined the National Council and the Executive (with the Communist Party also admitted for the first time). But the extreme pro-Syrian groups, and Syria herself, took no part in this reconciliation.

Pan-Arabism The aspiration for A. unity is one of the main components of A. nationalism. As separate, divergent A. national or semi-national entities have in fact developed in the various AC, and have in modern times crystallized into separate states, the issue of all-A. unity is highly complex and elements of all- A. nationalism (*Qawmiyya*) are in constant dialectical interaction with elements of divergence and local nationalism (*Wataniyya*). P.-A., all-A. nationalism, is enhanced by a common language and civilization; a history common in large parts; Islam as a strong element of A. nationhood; a joint confrontation of, and resistance to, outside factors (the West — culturally and politically; Israel); and a strong emotional-ideological consciousness of all-A. unity. Against that unity, on the other hand, operate the emergence of local patriotisms and separate states; different geographic, economic, social conditions and interests; a history that has been in large part different and divergent; spoken dialects of Arabic very different from, and to some extent incomprehensible to, each other; political and dynastic rivalries, conflicting orientations, and the vested interests of existing separate rulers, régimes, establishments. The existence, in some AC, of non-A. minority groups — such as the *Kurds in Iraq, the African tribes in southern Sudan, the *Berbers in North-West Africa (see *Minorities) — tends to operate against all-A. unity, and so do manifestations of pre-A. memories and allegiances (*Shu'ubiyya* in Arabic), such as *Pharaonism in Egypt or *Phoenicianism in Lebanon — though these have never been a serious threat to Arabism.

P.-A. feeling and ideology are stronger in the *"Fertile Crescent" (Iraq, Syria, Palestine) than in the AC more distant from the heartland of the A. world. Egyptian nationalism, for instance, the earliest A. national movement and in many respects at the core of A. nationalism as a whole, has always been Egyptian in the first place (with some rather derisory remarks on all-A. aspirations ascribed to Sa'd *Zaghlul, its top leader) and turned to a measure of all-A. interest only in the 1930s. In general, while P.-A. sentiment, ideology and rhetoric dominated A. nationalism to a large extent, in its political-operative aspects A. nationalism was — after the failure of the first P.-A. efforts in the post-World War I settlement — mainly *Wataniyya*, "local" nationalism of the various AC. P.-A. plans were, in the period between the World Wars and up to the 1950s, nurtured mainly by the *Hashemite dynasty and small groups of activists (e.g. the *Istiqlal* group) — but even they concerned themselves mainly with the Fertile Crescent rather than the whole A. world. In recent decades, political P.-A. aspirations were cultivated mainly by the clandestine "A. Nationalist Movement" (*Harakat al-Qawmiyyin*); the Syrian *Ba'th party; from the late 1950s to the late 1960s to a certain extent by *Nasserist Egypt (though Nasser aspired to a closely knit Egyptian-dominated bloc rather than to full all-A. union); and by Libya's Col. *Qadhdhafi. But these efforts to create all-A. unions, complete or partial, had no success; see *Arab Nationalism; *Arab Federation; *Ba'th *Nasserism.

In contrast, the cultivation of closer cooperation between existing, separate A. entities — whether or not this can properly be called P.-A. — has been much more successful, both in the political and in various cultural and other fields. Such cooperation is, since 1945, mostly channelled through the *Arab League, established for that purpose, with all ASt as members (except Egypt since 1979). This, indeed, seems to be the trend of development: P.-A. is not, in recent decades, an organized movement aspiring to the creation of a political union and the replacement of the existing separate ASt by an all-A. entity; it is a general feeling of unity and an aspiration to emphasize and cultivate those aspects of the A. nation's life that are common to all its parts, and an organized effort to institute and develop as close as possible a cooperation between the various ASt.

Pan-Islam The idea and doctrine of the unity of the Islamic world-community (*Umma*) and the movement to realize and foster that unity. While a sentiment of Islamic unity has always been part of the consciousness of the world's Muslims, a modern PI movement originated at the end of the 19th century. Its principal thinker and propagator was the Persian or Afghan Jamal-ul Din al-Afghani (1837–97). Several other prominent Islamic scholars — Muhammad *'Abduh, 'Abdul-Rahman al-Kawakibi (1849–1903), Muhammad Rashid *Rida — also propounded PI ideas; most of them combined these ideas with that of a reform and revival of I.

The Turkish-Ottoman Sultan *'Abd-ul-Hamid II encouraged the PI movement and, emphasizing his position as *Khalifa* (*Caliph) of all Muslims — a position that the Ottoman Sultans had not emphasized for a long time — tried to use it for his political purposes. While he did not call for an all-Islamic empire or the extension of his rule over non-Ottoman Muslim areas, he hoped to foster a degree of allegiance to him on the part of all Muslims that would ward off European influences and interests infiltrating his empire, cultivate pro-Ottoman sentiment among the Muslim subjects of the European powers (Russia; France in North Africa; Britain in India), strengthen his empire internally and avert the disaffection of its non-Turkish Muslim subjects. 'Abd-ul-Hamid and his successors had only limited success concerning these aims. When, on the outbreak of World War I in 1914, the Sultan-Caliph declared a *Jihad (Holy War), to get the Muslim subjects of his enemies to rise against their European rulers, his call was ignored by most Muslims — at least in its political and operational implications, though it may have created a degree of sympathy for Turkey as a Muslim country. Turkish efforts to foster PI also failed to prevent the growth of an A. nationalist movement within the Empire. Yet, Islamic feelings and loyalty to the Sultan induced the *Sanussi Muslims of Cyrenaica, after the Italian conquest of Libya, 1911–12, to mount a continuous resistance to the conqueror. And while a Muslim-A. local ruler in 1916 staged a British-aided revolt against the Sultan (Sharif *Hussein ibn 'Ali of Mecca — see *Arab Revolt), and a few A. officers of the Ottoman army deserted to join the rebels, the bulk of the A. population of the Empire was loyal during World War I and did not rebel — and Islamic feelings, the allegiance to the Sultan-Caliph, had an important part in that loyalty.

Following revolutionary Turkey's abolition of the Caliphate in 1924, a new element was added to PI aspirations: the desire to restore the Caliphate. Various Muslim rulers or former rulers aspired to the position of Caliph and some even took actual steps to achieve it (thus the *Hashemite King Hussein ibn 'Ali of Hijaz), but none of them gained significant support in the Muslim world. Several conferences were held in the 1920s to discuss the renewal of the Caliphate, but no consensus was reached. PI feeling was rooted in the hearts of many Muslims, and several societies propounded it, but it created no effective political organization. Attempts to use PI sentiments for the benefit of specific political causes — such as the Palestine A. struggle against Zionism (Hajj Amin al-*Husseini in the late 1920s and early 1930s) — added an Islamic element to the activities and led to congresses and committees and their resolutions, but did not produce a strong, organized PI movement.

After World War II, several newly independent countries had Muslim majorities — such as Pakistan, Indonesia, Malaya (later Malaysia), from 1971 also Bangladesh, and several African countries (Senegal, Gambia, Mali, Niger, Guinea, the semi-A. countries of Mauritania, Somalia and Djibouti), and the AC that reached independence: Jordan, Syria, Morocco, Tunisia, Algeria, Libya, Sudan, and later South Yemen and the Persian Gulf sheikhdoms; one of these countries — Pakistan — had an official Islamic state ideology. Strongly Islamic Sa'udi Arabia, became, owing to her oil production and economic strength, significantly more influential than she had been before. These developments gave new impetus to PI trends — not towards the creation of an all-Islamic empire (which was not anymore the aim of PI, if it had ever been its aim), but towards a stronger cooperation between Muslim countries and the creation of all-Islamic institutions that would foster such cooperation.

Since 1949 several all-Islamic organizations have been founded, with Pakistani activists and functionaries in the forefront; none of these associations, loosely organized and to some extent overlapping, had significant impact or influence. They included a "Muslim World Congress" which held several sessions until the late 1960s (and presented itself as the continuation of a previous World Muslim Congress organization, electing as its President the ex-*Mufti* of Jerusalem, Hajj Amin al-Husseini, who had organized and chaired a similar Congress in Jerusalem in 1931); a "World Congress of Muslim *'Ulama*", since 1952; a Muslim Youth Congress, 1955; an "Islamic Conference of Jerusalem" (sponsored by the *Muslim Brotherhood), 1953 and 1960; a "Conference of Islamic Liberation Organizations", Cairo 1953; a "World Muslim League" (*Rabita*) — Sa'udi-sponsored — since the early 1960s; an "Afro-Asian Islamic Conference", centered in Indonesia, since 1965; and others. Most of these congresses and associations were non-governmental, but government leaders and functionaries frequently took part in them. Some of them were unofficially sponsored by governments.

The creation of an association of Islamic *states* or governments was of course more difficult, since most Islamic states were understandably cautious and hesitated to add an Islamic dimension to their international commitments — and political interests and orientations were divergent and often conflicting. Yet, attempts were made. Pakistan's first Premier Liaqat 'Ali Khan (assassinated in Oct. 1951) tried to arrange a conference of Islamic governments, and failed. So did the Malayan Premier Tungku 'Abd-ul-Rahman in 1961. Egypt's *Nasser, King *Sa'ud, and Pakistan's Governor-General Ghulam Muhammad in 1954 spoke of the creation of a Congress of Islamic states, but nothing came of it. In the mid-1960s King *Feisal of Sa'udi Arabia tried to set up an alliance of Islamic states (in effect: the conservative ones, against Egypt's revolutionary-subversive *Nasserism) — but he did not persevere. Late in 1980, President *Sadat of Egypt announced the formation of a "League of A. and Islamic Peoples" (a move against the *Arab League that had suspended Egypt's membership); but this Islamic League did not get off the ground and was formally dissolved in 1983 by Sadat's successor *Mubarak. A loose association of Islamic states was finally formed after the Islamic Summit of Rabat of Sept. 1969 (convened after a demented foreign visitor had set fire to *al-Aqsa* Mosque in Jerusalem — an act that was misinterpreted in the A. and Islamic world as an "Israeli plot" and caused great excitement and a resolve of Islamic Heads of States to consult about possible action). That summit instituted regular meetings of the Islamic states' Foreign Ministers — meetings formalized since the early 1970s as an "Islamic Conference Organization" (ICO) with a permanent secretariat (the first Secretary-General, until 1973, was the Malayan ex-Premier Tungku 'Abd-ul-Rahman, followed by the Egyptian Hassan Tihami, the Senegalese 'Abd-ul-Karim Gaye, from 1979 the Tunisian Habib Chatty, and since 1984 the Pakistani Sharif-ul-Din Pirzada). While at the first meetings 23–25 countries attended, the ICO membership is in recent years put at 42 (including the *PLO; Egypt's membership was suspended in 1980, following her peace agreement with Israel, but she was readmitted in 1984). Four further summit meetings were held (in Lahore 1974; Ta'if/Mecca 1981; Casablanca 1984; Kuwait Jan. 1987).

The Islamic countries endeavored to extend their cooperation to various fields of activity, particularly in the economic sphere. Several semi-governmental economic conferences were held from 1949 and through the 1950s. A plan to establish an all-Islamic Development Bank was worked out in 1970 and endorsed several times in 1972–75, and the Bank became operational in 1976. A separate Development Fund (to afford credit on easier, non-commercial terms) has been planned since the late 1970s. (These financial institutions, like all Islamic banks, face the problem of the Islamic ban on interest; it is usually solved by substituting other, equivalent payments — e.g. a share in profits and expenses.) An all-Islamic news agency, decided upon in 1972, has been operating since the mid-1970s, but does not seem to have much impact. An all-Islamic Court of Justice, repeatedly suggested, has not yet been established.

Generally, while the ideal of all-Islamic unity is a vision alive in the hearts of Muslims, and recent waves of radical, assertive Islamism (such as the revolutionary Iranian effort to shape a thoroughly Islamic state, and attempts in other countries to make Islamic law, the *Shari'a*, the dominant element in legislation and state and society practices) may have given it a fresh impetus, PI aspirations do not entail, in present-day realities, plans for an all-Islamic political entity. They are directed towards the cultivation of strong all-Islamic cooperation. Organizations established for that purpose have remained loose and without much clout — the ICO, for instance, has so far failed in its efforts to end the (inter-Islamic) Iraq-Iran war; but they have become part of the Islamic countries' international association and orientation.

PCC Palestine Conciliation Commission. See there.

PDFLP Popular Democratic Front for the Liberation of Palestine. See *Palestine-Arab Guerrilla Organizations.

Peel Commission, Peel Report A British Royal Commission sent to Palestine in 1936 to investigate the causes of the A. rebellion ("Disturbances") of 1936 and propose a solution to the Palestine problem. The PR, considered a penetrating study of the problem, recommended the partition of Palestine into a Jewish State, an A. State to be united with *Transjordan, and an area, including *Jerusalem, to remain under a British *Mandate. See *A. — Israel Conflict.

Perim (Arabic: *al-Mayum*) Small island off South Yemen, in the straits of *Bab al-Mandeb connecting the *Red Sea with the Arabian Sea (the Indian Ocean). P., with an area of 5 sq.mi. and a population of a few hundreds, up to 1,000–1,500, has no water or vegetation. Briefly occupied by Britain in 1799, as a strategic outpost against Napoleon's plan to advance from Egypt to India, the island was in Britain's possession from 1851 or 1857 and administered as part of *'Aden colony. P. was used as a coaling station for steamers until 1936 and later had a small military airfield. In 1967, towards 'Aden's independence as South Yemen, Britain reportedly intended handing P. to the UN or else retaining its possession, denying it to nascent South Yemen, but since the latter insisted that P. was part of her territory, Britain gave in.

South Yemeni spokesmen intimated several times that the island would be used to block shipping to Israel. An oil tanker *en route* to Israel was indeed shelled, in June 1971, in its vicinity. There were also repeated but unconfirmed reports in 1972–73 that South Yemen was allowing Palestinian guerrilla groups to use P. as a base for similar attempts, and that Egypt used it during the *October War of 1973 to enforce a blockade against Israel-bound shipping.

Persian Gulf (in Arab usage: Arab Gulf, in recent years often called "The Gulf" — to avoid that dispute of political terminology). Gulf of the Indian Ocean/Arabian Sea, separating the Arabian peninsula in the south-southwest and Iran in the north-northeast. Connected with the Gulf of 'Oman and the Arabian Sea by the shallow Straits of *Hormuz, the PG is rather shallow, its maximum depth not exceeding 328 feet (c. 100 meters). It is about 500 mi. (800 km.) long and of varying width (125–200 mi., 200–320 km.), and its area is about 90,000 sq.mi. (235,000 sq.km.). The PG contains a number of islands — near the Iranian coast the largest one of Qishn, the historically important Hormuz, and Sirri (all at its eastern end, near the Straits of Hormuz) and the small islet of Kharg (at its western end).

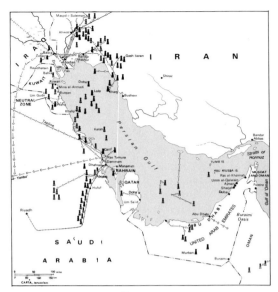

Map of the Persian Gulf

Kharg and Sirri were developed in recent years as oil loading points. Near the Arabian shore are the islands of *Bahrain and, farther east, the small islets of *Abu Mussa and the *Tanbs, both claimed and forcibly occupied by Iran in dispute with the UAE, and Huwar and smaller islets nearby disputed by Bahrain and Qatar. At the north-western end of the PG, several Kuwaiti islands, e.g. Bubiyan and Warba, have caused differences between Kuwait and Iraq. Two large peninsulas jut into the PG from Arabia: *Qatar, and *Trucial 'Oman (now the UAE, with its tip, *Ras Musandam, belonging to 'Oman); the latter peninsula, protruding into the Straits of Hormuz, separates the PG and the Gulf of 'Oman, its western coast on the former and its eastern coast on the latter.

The northern/north-eastern, Iranian shore of the PG is mountainous, nearly without streams; it has a few inlets suitable for harbors — e.g. Bandar Khomeini (formerly Bandar Shahpur), Bushehr (Bushire) and, near the Straits of Hormuz, Bandar 'Abbas. The southern/south-western, Arabian shore is sandy and mostly flat; it is unsuitable for harbors except for a few bays — e.g. at *Kuwait, which has served for centuries as the chief port of the region, and at *Dubai. At most of the modern oil ports on the PG's Arabian shore ships anchor at a distance from the shore and the oil is conveyed to them by pipes. At the northern end of the PG the only major river flows into it: the *Shatt al-'Arab, which is the joint estuary of the *Euphrates and the *Tigris (coming from Iraq), and the Karun and Karkheh (coming from Iran). The silt carried by the rivers has created a wide, marshy plain and encroaches on the sea in marshy tongues. No ports can therefore be built on the coast: the main ports (Basra, Khorramshahr) are inland, some distance up the river; but Iraq has constructed several artificial loading installations off the shore. The alignment of the Iraq-Iran border on the Shatt al-'Arab and the adjacent PG coast is in dispute, as is the Iraq-Kuwait border.

The PG has served since antiquity as an important trade and marine route. From the 16th century, PG lost some of its centrality in Europe's eastern trade, as much of that trade moved to the route around Africa and, in the 19th century, through the *Suez Canal.

From the early 16th century, the PG was dominated by the Portuguese who captured Bahrain and Hormuz and set up strong points. Their rule was ended in 1622, when Persia conquered Bahrain and Hormuz. Persia remained the dominant force in the PG, though most of the Arabian coast was ruled by local A. sheikhs and tribes; the Bahrain islands, too, were seized in 1783 by sheikhs of the al-*Khalifa clan. From the 17th century, piracy and slave-trading were rampant in the PG. The suppression of piracy was one of the main reasons for Great Britain's growing involvement in the PG from the end of the 18th and the early 19th century. Another reason was the need to protect the approaches to India — e.g. against French ambitions and plans clearly enunciated by Napoleon. From 1820, numerous agreements for the cessation of piracy were signed between Britain, acting through her governors and envoys in India, and the various sheikhs and amirs of the Arabian G. coast and islands, and gradually, in the course of the 19th century, these agreements established British protection over the various petty rulers, and the entire PG area became an area of British influence.

Concerning most of the Arabian PG sheikhs, the establishment of Britain's protectorates caused no major clash with the Turkish-Ottoman Empire, as the latter claimed no effective possession of the south-eastern reaches of the PG. It was different at the north-western end of the PG, where the Sultan claimed sovereignty over the al-Hasa coastal district (later part of Sa'udi Arabia), over Kuwait, and most decidedly over the Shatt al'Arab and the coast of the province of Basra (later Iraq). Yet Britain was increasingly interested precisely in these north-western parts of the PG, as they were potential targets of great power ambitions and intrigues. Russia's ambitions to establish a foothold in the PG, a warm-water port and an outlet to the southern seas, were thought to be evident, and her aspirations to expand in the direction of India (also perceived in Afghanistan) were a source of constant British apprehension. Moreover, a new player was appearing on the scene: imperial Germany. Turkey was towards the end of the century entering a close alliance with Germany and German enterprises were penetrating the Ottoman Empire and extending feelers towards the PG. German plans for the *Baghdad Railway, from 1899, which were opposed by Britain and her allies and transformed, after a long diplomatic struggle, from a German-Ottoman scheme into an international one, provided for that railway not only to reach Basra but to be extended to the PG at Kuwait. Britain vigorously opposed that extension and persuaded Turkey to bar it.

In a treaty with Britain the Sheikh of Kuwait in 1899 accepted British protection and committed himself to grant no concessions to other powers without British consent. While the Sultan's claim to sovereignty was not formally denied, Kuwait was now in fact a British protectorate. British interests in the region were further intensified when an oil exploration concession in south-western Iran, near the Shatt al-'Arab, was granted to British interests in 1901, oil was discovered in 1908, and the British Government in 1914 acquired control of the Anglo-Persian Oil Company formed in 1909. The local sheikh who *de facto* controlled the oil area, Sheikh *Khaz'al of Muhammara (later *Khorramshahr), in 1910 also accepted British protection, in return for his pledge to keep the oil operations secure. The sovereignty of the Shah of Iran was not formally denied, but the whole southern part of Iran, including her PG shores, were by now virtually a British zone of influence: the eastern section, with the coast of the G. of 'Oman, from Bandar 'Abbas eastwards, under a formal agreement of 1907 with Russia, and the western part, *de facto* and contrary to that agreement, through Britain's dominating influence on the tribes controlling the area (Bakhtiaris, Qashqais), though German agents were also active in the area. After the outbreak of World War I in 1914, with Turkey joining Britain's enemies, the British protectorate over Kuwait was further tightened and in 1915 *Ibn Sa'ud, the ruler of the al-Hasa coast and the *Najd hinterland, signed a treaty with Britain that was in fact a veiled semi-protectorate. A British expeditionary force that conquered southern Iraq came from India through the PG.

After World War I — with Iraq under a British *Mandate, British protectorates over all the sheikhdoms on the PG's Arabian coast, and southern Iran under dominating British influence — the PG was almost completely under British control. A British "Political Resident" for the PG was stationed in Bushir, from 1946 — in Bahrain, and Political "Agents" or "Officers" resided in most local centers (Kuwait, Bahrain, Qatar, Dubai, Abu Dhabi). The situation changed, and British control diminished, between the World Wars, as Iraq became independent (1932) and despite the Anglo-Iraqi treaty of 1930 increasingly anti-British, and Iran asserted her independence and established more effective control over her southern regions (including the liquidation of Sheikh Khaz'al's British-protected semi-autonomy in Muhammara-Khorramshahr). Yet, in World War II the PG remained a principal staging area for British and allied forces and operations — including a brief war against Iraq's rebellious Rashid *'Ali régime in May 1941 and the occupation (Aug. 1941) of southern Iran (in co-ordination with the simultaneous occupation of her northern parts by Russia), to prevent Iran from allying herself with Germany or being occupied by her.

After World War II, the erosion of Britain's dominating position in the PG accelerated. Iraq was finally moving out of the orbit of British influence; British air bases — one of them in the Basra area, at the head of the PG — were turned in 1955 into joint bases under the *Baghdad Pact and were lost to Britain when Iraq seceded from that Pact in 1959, and Iraq's alliance with Britain lapsed under Iraq's new, revolutionary régime after the *coup* of July 1958. Relations with Iran were deeply disturbed by the nationalization of Iran's oil production by the radical Mossaddeq government that also clashed with the Shah. The dispute was settled in 1954, after the fall of the radical government and the restoration of the Shah's régime, but the oil company was reshaped to include other foreign companies (35% — American) and Britain lost her exclusive control. From the 1960s, the Shah of Iran increasingly entertained great-power ambitions, presenting Iran as the principal power and main guardian of the G. Since the 1930s Sa'udi Arabia has been linked chiefly to the USA rather than to Britain. Kuwait, emboldened by the development and economic power created by her oil, demanded full independence — which Britain willingly granted in 1961.

Britain still acted, to some extent, as the policeman of the PG. She sometimes intervened in dynastic and succession disputes of the various sheikhs and rulers (mainly in Trucial 'Oman, later to become the UAE). She sometimes stepped in to settle disputes between principalities, e.g. the *Buraimi dispute between Sa'udi Arabia, Abu Dhabi and 'Oman in the 1950s, and several territorial conflicts between Trucial sheikhdoms. Even after the withdrawal of her protectorate from Kuwait in 1961, she responded to Kuwait's appeal and sent troops when Iraq refused, the same year, to accept her independence and claimed all Kuwait as Iraqi territory. Britain also guided and aided the various A. PG principalities to plan joint institutions (currency, communications, etc.) towards a future federation. But Britain felt since the 1950s and 1960s that the role of protector and policeman no longer fitted either world conditions or her own diminishing wealth and strength as a great power. In 1968 she announced that by the end of 1971 she would withdraw her protectorates and bases.

When the British Protectorates were abolished, in 1971, the seven sheikhdoms of Trucial 'Oman formed a federation (prepared before, under British guidance), the *United Arab Emirates, UAE; Qatar and Bahrain, at first slated to join, preferred to become separately independent. The states on the shores of the PG were now all independent — eight in number: Iran, Iraq, Kuwait, Sa'udi Arabia, Bahrain, Qatar, the UAE and 'Oman. In great-power and global terms, a certain power vacuum was created by Britain's withdrawal, and the USA was greatly concerned. The security of the PG, and in particular the freedom of shipping, were by now even more vital than before since a large portion of the non-Soviet world's oil supply, and far more than one-half of its oil export trade, were being loaded in the PG ports and moving through its waters. It was not only the danger of Russian penetration that perturbed the US and the West, but the threat of destabilization by terrorist groups (such as a shady South Yemen-based "Popular Front for the Liberation of the Occupied Arab Gulf", PFLOAG, that was already in rebellion in 'Oman's *Dhofar region) — groups that the West suspected of being manipulated by Russia and, for some time, China (and perhaps also Iraq). Iran under the Shah, until 1979, cooperated with 'Oman to ensure the defense of the G. of 'Oman, i.e. the eastern extension of the PG, and the Straits of Hormuz, with US and British support; in 1974 a formal Iran-'Oman agreement was concluded. Moreover, the US undertook, informally and to a limited extent, to protect the freedom of shipping in the PG and its stability. Together with Britain, to an even more limited extent, she arranged for certain naval and air "facilities" to be afforded to her — e.g. in Bahrain and 'Oman. For some years, the US thought of more permanent arrangements, such as a "Rapid Deployment Force" based on the Indian Ocean, with equipment stored, ready for use, at agreed points ashore; but the only country of the region willing to join the scheme and host US storage facilities was 'Oman (in an agreement of 1980).

In general, the newly independent PG countries were extremely reluctant to link themselves to the USA. While they were eager to obtain a low-profile *de facto* protection, they refused to enter into any formal agreements. Sa'udi Arabia's position was not much different — and Iraq was in any case no ally of the US. Even the alliance with the Shah's Iran was informal only, but the US encouraged the Shah in his stance as the chief guardian of the PG. Yet, in some respects Iran was, even during the Shah's régime, an element of disturbance for the principalities on the Arabian shore. She had renounced her old claim to Bahrain in 1970, accepting a poll conducted by the Secretary-General of the UN, according to which the majority of the population wanted independence; but with her power growing, there was no telling whether she would not reassert that claim. In 1971, Iran revived a claim to the *Abu Mussa and *Tanb islands of Sharja and Ras al-Khaima and forcibly occupied them when British protection was being withdrawn and the UAE was born. Some informal settlement was made — e.g. a reported sharing of the islands' off-shore oil revenue between Iran and Sharja — but Iran remained in occupation. Iraq, in her anti-Iranian campaign, demanded the islands' return to the UAE — but the UAE was cautiously silent. For beyond the specific case of Iranian forcible expansion, there was constant apprehension of Iran's assertion of control over the PG and potential claims to territory on the Arabian shore and islands close to it, and of Iranian subversion — using the considerable part of the population that was Shi'i, Iranian or of Iranian origin. These apprehensions grew after Iran was taken over, in 1979, by *Khomeini's assertive Islamic régime that spoke even of "exporting" its Islamic revolution. It was in large part in response to these new challenges and dangers that the six countries on the Arabian shore of the PG — Sa'udi Arabia, Kuwait, Qatar, Bahrain, the UAE and 'Oman (but not including Iraq) — formed a "Gulf Cooperation Council", GCC, in 1981. This Council, holding regular ministerial and "summit" meetings and with a permanent secretariat, has instituted, after initial hesitations and difficulties, a fairly wide range of measures designed to enhance cooperation and joint or co-ordinated action in many fields, including plans for a joint military force. The GCC has, however, taken a very cautious and low-profile line towards Iran. In the Iraq-Iran conflict the sympathies of the A. PG countries are no doubt with Iraq (despite former apprehensions of Iraqi aggressive schemes and subversion, and a lack of empathy with her revolutionary régime), and some of them have aided Iraq with huge funds, supported her war-damaged oil exports and assured her war-disrupted supplies; but the GCC has officially followed a policy of neutrality in the war.

The Iraq-Iran war, from Sept. 1980 (see *Iraq), gravely affected the PG — to a degree that it is frequently called the "Gulf War". The original, and main, arena of operations was the Shatt al-'Arab close to the shores of the G. — with *Khorramshahr and territory around it taken by Iraq (reconquered by Iran in May 1982), Abadan destroyed, and Basra under frequent Iranian shelling. An Iranian counter-offensive in Feb. 1986 reached Iraq's oil-loading installations on the PG-shore at Fao (al-Faw) and offshore (Mina' al-Bakr). Moreover, the Iraqi airforce, superior to Iran's, early in 1984 extended its bombing operations not only to Kharg island, Iran's main oil loading installation, but to shipping, and in particular oil tankers, mostly foreign, en route to or from Kharg. In 1985 Iran constructed additional or alternative facilities at Sirri island, near the Straits of Hormuz, reached by shuttle tankers and thought to be beyond the Iraqi bombers' range (but bombed from Aug. 1986). Iran retaliated by attacking oil tankers, nearly all of them foreign, en route to or from ports, on the PG's Arabian coast. Iran also intercepted and searched foreign ships in the PG, sometimes confiscating cargoes destined for Iraq. Iranian spokesmen warned several times that Iran might block the Straits of Hormuz. The vessels involved were often registered under "flags of convenience" (Liberia, Panama), but frequently European and even great-power vessels were hit. Iraq justified her attacks on ships en route to Iranian ports with a blockade she had declared. Iran claimed a belligerent's right to intercept and search neutral ships. It was more difficult to justify Iranian bombings of oil tankers serving Arabian, not Iraqi, ports (and such attacks were frequently not announced or admitted). Yet, the reaction of the powers was very restrained. The USA, Britain, France and since 1986 also the USSR sent naval patrols into the PG, indicating that they would protect their ships — and interference with their shipping diminished, though there were few actual confrontations. In 1987 the USSR provided some protection for Kuwait's oil traffic by leasing to her several Soviet tankers under the Soviet flag; the USA was preparing to allow 11 Kuwaiti tankers to fly the US flag, and was also reinforcing her own naval presence. But the situation remained explosively dangerous.

Iranian spokesmen also constantly warned the A. PG countries, especially Kuwait, that their financial and economic aid for Iraq might be seen as taking sides against Iran and lead to the extension of the war to the PG area. Thus, apprehensions of Iranian action — fully or nearly warlike — against GCC countries added to the atmosphere of tension and disturbance prevailing in the PG in the mid-1980s.

PFLOAG Popular Front for the Liberation of the Arab Gulf, see *Dhofar, *Persian Gulf.

PFLP Popular Front for the Liberation of Palestine, see there, and *Palestine-Arab Guerrilla Organizations.

Phalanges (al-Kata'ib) A paramilitary youth organization in Lebanon founded in 1936 by Pierre *Jumayyil (Gemayel), Georges Naqqash (Naccache), Charles Hilou and other young Christian-Maronite leaders to work for Lebanese independence and foster a Lebanese national spirit. Although this was not stated explicitly, the Ph. were a Christian-Maronite organization primarily intended to defend the Maronite community, and preserve the Christian character of Lebanon against suspected Muslim schemes. The Ph. adopted a pro-French attitude, seeing France as the defender of Lebanon's separate independence and Christian character; but they clashed with the French administration when France refused to ratify the Franco-Lebanese Treaty of 1936 and grant independence to Lebanon.

In time, the Ph., while keeping their paramilitary structure, became a kind of political party. In the 1940s they opposed President Bishara al-*Khouri and his Pan-A. policies. In 1949, the organization was declared illegal and operated until 1952 under another name ("Lebanese Unity Party"). In the civil war of 1958, the Ph. supported President Camille *Chamoun against the Muslim *Nasserist rebels. After the settlement of that crisis, they foiled, by threatening armed resistance and a new civil war, the formation of a government dominated by the former rebels. In the 1960s and early 1970s the Ph. operated mainly as a political faction, though they did not establish a fully organized and identified party and appeared in elections as Independents, in shifting list-alliances with other factions. They were usually represented in Parliament; their number of seats cannot be precisely determined, since their candidates were not always clearly identified as Ph. representatives; it was estimated at 3 (of 77) in 1951, 1 (of 66) in 1957, 6 (of 99) in 1960, 4 in 1964, 9 in 1968, 5–7 in 1972 (the last Parliament elected). During those years, the Ph. representatives in Parliament formed a loose alliance (the "Tripartite Bloc") with Raymond *Edde's "National Bloc" and Camille Chamoun's "National Liberals".

The ideology of the Ph., never laid down in a

major doctrinal text, rests on the premise that Lebanon constitutes a separate historic entity with an identity of her own and a continuity dating back to the Phoenicians (see *Phoenicianism). The co-existence of Lebanon's various communities can be assured only by the continuation of a community-based régime, laying down that pluralism in constitutional terms and affording the Christian communities, and especially the Maronites, a measure of predominance. The Ph. admit that Lebanon, Arabic-speaking, is culturally linked with the AC, but deny that these links should lead to a political attachment and oppose the integration of Lebanon in Pan-A. plans for A. unity (beyond the loose alliance of ASt in the A. League). While they go along with many all-A. policies, they hold that Lebanese interests have precedence over all-A. ones. Thus they conformed, in the decades since 1948, to general A. policies towards Israel, at least in public, and ostensibly supported guerrilla activities — but opposed guerrilla/terrorist operations from Lebanese soil that would involve Lebanon in clashes or a war with Israel contrary to her interests; they also opposed the growth of the increasingly powerful *PLO establishment in Lebanon creating in effect a state within the state. In fact, the Ph. — or at least some of their commanders — maintained under-cover links with Israel and received aid from her.

In the civil war since 1975, the Ph. formed the mainstay of the conservative, Christian camp, sometimes in league with Christian-commanded brigades of the army. In this process, a younger generation of military, strong-arm leaders emerged, with Bashir *Jumayyil, the younger son of the founder-leader, at their head; Pierre Jumayyil officially remained the chairman but stayed in the background (and was considered more moderate). For the Ph.'s efforts to unite under their command all Christian militias, the establishment of the "Lebanese Forces" (LF) as an umbrella formation that became nearly identical with the Ph., and their clashes with rival Maronite militias (*Franjiyeh's *Marada*, Chamoun's "Tigers", 1978-80 — see *Lebanon. From 1980, the Ph./LF now controlled most of the Christian-dominated areas — East Beirut and central Mount Lebanon.

The streak of brutality apparent in the younger Ph. leaders' treatment of their Christian rivals also colored much of their military actions against their Muslim and leftist civil war foes, and there were many reports of mutual massacres. They particularly loathed the Palestinian-A. guerrilla establishment and the camp population serving as its support and reservoir. They tried for many months to subdue the Palestinians' stronghold in Beirut, the camp of Tel al-Za'tar, but were able to eliminate it only in Aug. 1976 — during the year or so that Syria turned against her Muslim, leftist and Palestinian allies (who had rejected Syria's plan for a solution of the Lebanese crisis) and encouraged and supported the conservative-Christian camp. The LF's *de facto* semi-alliance with Syria soon broke down, and as the civil war dragged on despite its official termination in Oct.–Nov. 1976, they were able to hold most of the Christian-dominated areas but were involved, despite uncounted cease-fires, in near-constant clashes wherever that Christian region bordered on areas held or disputed by Muslim, Druze or Syrian forces.

The Ph. cooperated with Israel almost openly when Israeli forces invaded Lebanon in June 1982. Their actual military operations did not fulfil Israeli expectations (the Israeli command had expected them to take over Muslim and Palestinian-dominated West Beirut, making it unnecessary for Israeli forces to do so); but they became the dominant political-military force in most of Lebanon outside the Syrian-occupied zones. In Aug. 1982 their chief Bashir Jumayyil was elected President of Lebanon, but on 14 Sept. he was killed when the Ph. headquarters were blown up. A week later, his brother Amin Jumayyil was elected to replace Bashir as President. During the week in between, Ph. units stormed the Palestinian camps of Sabra and Shatila in West Beirut (under the nose of Israeli forces that had entered West Beirut on 14–15 Sept.) and massacred a large number of Palestinians, both fighters and civilians; they were reportedly commanded by Elie Hobeika, the head of the Ph. secret services.

The Ph./LF, leadership was much more militant than President Jumayyil and embarked on a campaign to expand the areas under their control — particularly, with Israeli connivance, in the Shuf region southeast of Beirut, where they clashed with the largely Druze population and their militias — and were defeated and expelled after the Israeli forces withdrew from the Shuf in Sept. 1983. Later they lost most of their positions in the coastal plain and South Lebanon to Druze and Shi'i militias. From 1984–85, the Ph. have also lost much of their political influence outside the Christian "canton" they still dominate, as President Jumayyil, seeking a settlement with the rival camp and with Syria, had to agree in 1984 to the formation of a coalition ("National Unity") government headed by his adversaries and to accept, in principle, a Syrian-sponsored plan for constitutional reforms.

In recent years, and particularly since the death of Bashir Jumayyil, the Ph. were deeply split. There was constant tension between their political leadership and their military establishment (coterminous and near-identical, in a vague, ill-defined way, with the LF), with the latter acting independently without the approval, and sometimes against the wishes, of the former. The (political) chairmanship was vacated in July 1984 by founder-leader Pierre Jumayyil, who died soon afterwards. The man he had nominated, Elie Karameh, was duly elected chairman in Sept. 1984, but was replaced in Aug. 1986 by Georges Sa'ādeh, long-time vice-chairman. In the military command there were frequent upheavals and changes — Fadi Fram was replaced in 1984 by Fu'ad Abu Nader, Samir Ja'ja' (Geagea) rebelling in 1985 against President Jumayyil and the Ph. leadership's policies, which he saw as a surrender to Syrian pressure, and usurping the top command. For Ja'ja''s clash with Elie Hobeika, the latter's Syrian-sponsored agreement with the Druze and Shi'i militias of Dec. 1985, and Ja'ja''s rebellion against it and victory over Hobeika — see *Lebanon. The political Ph. leadership, though not pro-Hobeika, tried to mediate and end the clashes. Thus, the situation in the Ph./LF command remained confused and weakened the organization's position, though it remains in *de facto* control of a Christian "canton".

The Ph. published a paper of their own, *al-'Amal*, from 1940 — first as a fortnightly, then a weekly, and since the 1950s as a daily. During the civil war from 1975 onward they set up a radio station, the "Voice of Lebanon", also "Voice of Free Lebanon". As they gained *de facto* control of the Christian "canton" (and as government services broke down), they began providing general services (health, communications etc.) — and collecting taxes and other fees and payments; their main source of revenue is custom duties they level on imports in several ports they control (including part of Beirut port, and Jounieh just north of Beirut).

Pharaonism Egyptian trend of thought seeing the Egyptian nation as a distinct historic entity separate from the A.-Muslim world both culturally and politically and deriving its identity from its ancient Pharoanic civilization. Ph. regards the A.'s as foreign conquerors and Islam as a passing stage and maintains that Egypt has retained, despite 1,300 years of her A. and Muslim history, her distinct, "Pharaonic" genius — re-surfacing throughout history in aspirations to re-establish her separate independence. Ph. as a general trend in literature and thought developed in the 1920s; but it was blended with other trends dissociating Egypt from her A.-Islamic heritage — such as Modernism, or an emphasis on ethnic-territorial nationalism or on E.'s European and Mediterranean cultural links — to a degree that it cannot be clearly separated from them. Ph. never crystallized as a clearly enunciated doctrine or ideology, let alone a political faction. It lost most of its influence during the 1930s, when A. and Islamic orientations became dominant and many of the prominent writers mentioned joined those trends.

Phoenicianism (also Sidonism). A trend of thought which views the people of Lebanon as the descendants of the ancient Phoenicians and emphasizes that descent as the source of Lebanon's separate, distinct character as a non-A. entity. Ph. did not crystallize into a fully developed movement or doctrine. Politically, its ideas were close to the trend wide-spread among Maronites to regard Lebanon as a distinct non-A. entity, pluralistic under Christian leadership (see *Phalanges, *Edde, *Maronites); but most of those developed their ideology without committing themselves to Ph. as a doctrine.

PLO Palestine Liberation Organization. See there, and *Palestine-Arab Guerrilla Organizations, *Palestine Arabs.

POLISARIO "People's Organization for the Liberation of Saguia al-Hamra and Rio del Oro" — a political and guerrilla formation founded in 1973–75 to fight for the independence of Spanish *Sahara, from 1975–76 in a guerrilla war against Morocco (and until 1979 also against

Mauritania). In Feb. 1976 P. proclaimed an independent "Sahara Arab Democratic Republic" (SADR). P. is armed, supplied and financed mainly by Algeria, and concentrated and headquartered there. See *Sahara.

Popular Democratic Front for the Liberation of Palestine, PDFLP Also DFLP, without the "Popular". Palestinian-A. guerrilla (*Feda'iyyin*) organization of leftist, Marxist-Maoist orientation, led by Na'if *Hawatma. See *Palestine-Arab Guerrilla Organizations

Popular Front for the Liberation of 'Oman, PFLO See *'Oman, *Dhofar.

Popular Front for the Liberation of Palestine, PFLP Palestinian-A. guerrilla (*Feda'iyyin*) organization of leftist, semi-Maoist orientation. Led by Dr. George *Habash, the PFLP is an extremist faction of the *PLO, responsible for many acts of terrorism, including attacks on foreign airports, hijacks of foreign civilian airliners etc. See *Palestine-Arab Guerilla Organizations, *PLO, *Habash.

Popular Front for the Liberation of the Occupied Arab Gulf, PFLOAG See *Dhofar, *Persian Gulf.

Portsmouth, Treaty of Draft treaty between Britain and Iraq signed in P. on 15 Jan. 1948, to replace the Anglo-Iraqi Treaty of 1930, which was considered by Iraqi nationalists as unduly restricting Iraq's independence. Emphasizing the "complete freedom, equality and independence of Iraq", the PT provided for the handing-over to Iraq of the British air bases of Habbaniyya and Shu'aiba, a Joint Defense Board, with equal British and Iraqi representation, to secure Britain's strategic interests. Despite these advances over the treaty of 1930, the PT was strongly opposed by Iraq's nationalist parties who asserted that it still granted to Britain excessive privileges. Violent demonstrations erupted, Premier Saleh Jabr, who had negotiated the treaty, was compelled to resign, and his successor, Muhammad al-Sadr, repudiated it. (The old treaty of 1930 remained in force until 1955, when it was replaced by the *Baghdad Pact.)

PPS Parti Populaire Syrien, *al-Hizb al-Suri al-Qawmi* (later changed its name to "Populaire et Social", *al-Qawmi wa'l-Ijtima'i*). Lebanese party founded and at first led by Antoun *Sa'adeh. See *Syrian Nationalist Party.

protectorates See *Colonialism.

Protestants In contrast to the old-established "Eastern churches" (*Greek-Orthodox or *Monophysites *et al*) and the *Catholic ones created since the Crusades (through *Uniates or conversion to the *Latin rite) — P. communities have grown in the AC only in fairly recent times. They therefore did not enjoy the ancient rights of communal-religious semi-autonomy under the *Millet system of the *Ottoman Empire. They have remained small communities. Missionaries of various P. denominations — mainly from English-speaking countries, Germany and Scandinavia — began operating in the late 18th, and mainly the 19th, century, creating small groups of P., principally by the conversion of Eastern Christians.

The number of Protestants in the AC is estimated at 250–300,000 — with significant communities only in Egypt (c. 100,000, mainly Presbyterians, most of them converted *Copts) and Sudan (mainly Anglican Episcopalians, nearly all among the African tribes of South Sudan).

PSP Progressive Socialist Party — a Lebanese political party founded in 1949 by Kamal *Junbalat, in fact (though not in doctrine) mainly *Druze. Since the mid-1970s it maintains a "militia" of its own which is the main fighting force of the Druze in the civil war. See *Lebanon, *Druze, *Junbalat.

Q

Qabus Ibn Sa'id (b. 1940? 1942?) Sultan of 'Oman since 1970. Educated in England (Sandhurst military academy, one year with a Scottish regiment, social studies at a British university), Q. returned to 'Oman in the mid-1960s. He was kept in total seclusion at the Salala palace by his father, Sultan Sa'id ibn Taimur (1910–72), who objected to, and prevented, the modern development of the country and maintained an autocratic régime. In July 1970, Q. overthrew his father, with active British encouragement, and became Sultan (his father went into exile in England and died there in 1972). As Sultan, Q. fostered gradual economic and social development and a measure of reform, but maintained a strictly conservative régime. He followed low-profile moderate policies in both international and inter-A. affairs and continued a close alliance with Britain and the USA. See *'Oman.

al-Qadhdhafi, Mu'ammar (b. 1942 — or, in other versions, 1938? 1935?) Libyan officer and politician, since his *coup* of 1969 Libya's top leader. Born in the Sirte desert into a poor family of the Qadhadhifa tribe originating in the *Fezzan region of southern Libya and adhering to the *Sanussi sect, Q. was imbued with a fighting tradition: his grandfather was reportedly killed in 1911 while resisting the Italian conquest, and his father and uncle fought in the resistance and were imprisoned. Q. was sent to a secondary school in Sabha, Fezzan, but was expelled for organizing a demonstration and continued his secondary studies in Tripoli and Misurata. He enrolled at the University of Benghazi to study history and geography, but transferred in 1963 to the Military Academy, from which he graduated in 1965. In 1966 the army sent him to further officers' training in Britain.

A fervent, revolutionary nationalist deeply influenced by Egypt's *Nasser, Q. agitated and organized revolutionary cells within the army and was reportedly imprisoned, but reinstated. In Sept. 1969 he took a leading part in a military *coup d'état* which overthrew the monarchy. He was promoted to the rank of Colonel and made Commander-in-Chief of the Armed Forces and chairman of the Revolutionary Council that headed the new régime. In Jan. 1970 he made himself also Prime Minister and Minister of Defense and held these posts until July 1972. In 1973, Q. proclaimed a "Popular Revolution" and began building a network of "People's Committees" topped by a general "People's Congress". In Mar. 1977, Q. declared Libya a *Jamahiriyya* — a new term he coined to mean "Republic of the Masses" — changing the structure, and mainly the terminology, of government institutions (see *Libya). He made himself chairman of the "General Secretariat" that replaced the Revolutionary Council as the supreme institution of the state. In Mar. 1979 Q. gave up this post of Head-of-State and retained only that of Commander-in-Chief. However, Q. has remained the sole and supreme leader and continues being treated as the Head-of-State.

Q. is a fervent A. nationalist, actively aspiring to *Pan-A. union. He has relentlessly proposed Libya's merger with other AC — Egypt 1969–70 and 1972–73; Sudan 1969–70; Syria 1970–71 and since 1980; Tunisia 1974; Morocco 1984 — and included in his quest for union even non-A. countries such as Malta (1971) and Chad (1981); none of these mergers has materialized — and while no-one doubts Q.'s fervent Pan-A. sincerity, his frequent merger offers are not taken quite seriously. Q. does not shun revolutionary plots and subversion to force his plans on other AC, and most AC have repeatedly denounced that subversion and sometimes severed relations with Q.'s Libya. In his overt inter-A. policy Q. takes a radical-extremist line and is the mainstay of the *"Rejection Front", including the most uncompromising hostility towards Israel and support for the most extreme Palestinian-A. terrorist groups. He is at odds with the A. consensus in supporting Iran in her war with Iraq.

Q.'s revolutionary-subversive activities were directed also against most of his non-A. African neighbors, and most of them complained bitterly and repeatedly; in Chad he has conducted actual warfare. His relations with the Organization for African Unity were troubled; in 1982 the Organization delayed for a year its summit, scheduled to take place in Tripoli, because a majority of its members refused to go to Libya and to grant Q. the status of its President until the next summit. Q.'s relations with the group of non-aligned nations were also troubled because the group did not accept either his policies or his claims to leadership.

Q. has supported and aided revolutionary or subversive movements in many foreign countries — from the Irish IRA, independence movements in the Canary Islands or Corsica, the "Red Army" terrorists in Italy and Germany, to the Philippines and the South Pacific. He is violently anti-Western and in near-constant conflict with the USA and several European countries, mainly Britain (see *Libya). (One of the reasons for his dispute with European countries is his involvement in terrorist activities there — including the systematic assassination of Libyan dissident refugees in Europe.) With the USSR and the Soviet Bloc, on the other hand, he has maintained, despite his strict anti-Communism, a close *de facto* alliance.

Q.'s doctrine is also fervently Islamic — though his revolutionary Islam is unconventional and seen by many orthodox Muslims as heretic, while he has denounced orthodox Sa'udi Arabia and fundamentalist Islamic trends (such as the Muslim Brothers). Q. himself presents his nationalist-Islamic populist-revolutionary ideology and practice as a "Third Universal Theory", neither communist nor capitalist, offering a solution to the basic problems of modern mankind. He formulated his doctrine in a *Green Book*, published in 1976, with two more parts in 1978 and 1979.

Q. has been described by his Arab foes (e.g. Egypt's *Sadat), in public, as mentally disturbed, a madman, and Western observers have also seen him as suffering from a personality disorder. But others, while conceding that his policies are often erratic and his fervor tends to lead him into wild excesses of extremism, dispute this "diagnosis". Q.'s oil policies, which are hard-line but restrained, certainly show that he is capable, when he so chooses, of cool, rational calculation.

Qamaran Islands Group of small islands in the *Red Sea, off the coast of Yemen, with an area of 22 sq.mi. and a population of c. 2,000. For some time, in the 16th century, a Portuguese strongpoint, the islands were under nominal Ottoman-Turkish sovereignty. They also served as a quarantine station for Muslim pilgrims from the East on their way to Mecca. During World War I, in 1915, Q. was occupied by the British and administered from *'Aden. In 1938, Britain agreed with Italy not to claim British sovereignty and not to erect fortifications. In 1949, Britain reaffirmed her possession of Q. — reportedly in an agreement with Yemen (which Yemen later denied).

When South Yemen became independent, in 1967, she claimed Q. as part of the formerly British territory of 'Aden, but Yemen disputed that claim. Yemen's possession of the islands was more firmly established in 1972, during the Yemen-South Yemen war, and — though not specifically mentioned in the agreement that ended that war — accepted by South Yemen. There were repeated reports, never substantiated, that Q. was used in the 1970s to enforce a blockade against Israel-bound shipping and that in the 1980s the *PLO was permitted to establish a presence on the island.

Qassem, 'Abd-ul-Karim (1914–63) Iraqi officer and politician, ruler of Iraq 1958–63. Born in Baghdad of a Sunni-Muslim lower middle class family, Q. became a professional army officer, commissioned in 1938. He served as a battalion commander with the Iraqi expeditionary forces in the Palestine War of 1948. In about 1956, by then a brigade commander, he became head of a group of "Free Officers" plotting to overthrow the monarchy and end Iraq's special relationship with Britain. On 14 July 1958, the group carried out their *coup* or revolution, led by Q. and his confederate Col. 'Abd-ul-Salam *'Aref, and proclaimed a republic. Contrary to his fellow-conspirators' plans and expectations, Q. declined to form a Revolutionary Command Council, but appointed himself Commander-in-Chief, Prime Minister and acting Minister of Defense. He did not assume the title of President but in effect became dictator and "Sole Leader" (which was for some time his semi-official title).

Though there were affinities beween Q.'s revolution and that of Egypt's *Nasser, Q. did not wish to formalize closer ties to Egypt (then the *UAR) and strove to keep Iraq independent of Nasser's dominating influence. Bitter hostility between the two men ensued. Q.'s associate 'Aref wanted a much closer co-ordination with Egypt (and also nurtured ill-disguised ambitions to become the top leader); he was deposed in Sept. 1958, and later tried and sentenced to death, but reprieved by Q. Nationalist-Nasserist disaffection soon escalated into a conspiracy and culminated in a mutiny and *coup* attempt staged in Mar. 1959 in Mosul by Col. Shawwaf. In the suppression of that mutiny Q. was aided by the Communists. This cooperation soured when the Communists began clamoring for a real share in power; when they increasingly infiltrated the administration in the summer of 1959, Q. suppressed them.

Q. was interested in social affairs and in Sept. 1958 enacted a major land reform law. Early in 1960 he tried to revive political parties; but the attempt failed, and it remains in doubt to what extent Q. had taken it seriously in the first place. He became increasingly erratic — to an extent that he was nicknamed "The Mad Dictator". Endowed with an exalted sense of his own mission, he had not created a political base to his rule, and by 1961 he had no supporters left among the political groupings and was in serious political difficulties (a rebellion of the *Kurds; his claim to Kuwait; his breach with the oil company — see *Iraq).

A combination of civilian *Ba'th* activists and nationalist anti-Communist officers toppled Q. on 8–9 Feb. 1963. Q. and his closest collaborators were shot.

Qatar Sheikhdom, Amirate on the Arabian coast of the *Persian Gulf, on a peninsula of the same name that juts northwards into the Gulf, c. 105 mi. (170 km.) long and 25–40 mi. (40–65 km.) wide. Q. borders, at the base of the peninsula, on Sa'udi Arabia; in the past she also bordered on Abu Dhabi (Trucial 'Oman, now UAE), but in 1974 Abu Dhabi ceded the strip bordering on Q. to Sa'udia. Her area, mostly desert, is usually given as c. 4,200 sq. mi. (c. 11,500 sq. km.), but some handbooks put it at nearly 8,000 sq. mi. (over 20,000 sq. km.). Q.'s population was 50–80,000 until the late 1960s, when it started rapidly growing, due mainly to the influx of foreign workers attracted by the expanding oil economy. It is estimated in the mid-1980s at c. 290,000, over 80% in the capital, Doha. The share of foreigners is variously estimated at 40–60% or even more; they include Iranians (some of whom are not recent migrants, Iranians having been for a long time an estimated 15–20% of Q.'s population), A.'s from outside Q., Pakistanis et al. With the mid-1980s crisis of the oil economy the number of foreigners has begun decreasing. Q.'s indigenous inhabitants are Sunni Muslims, mostly of the *Wahhabi school. The population subsisted, until the growth of the oil economy from the 1960s, on animal husbandry (semi-nomadic grazing), fishing, pearl-diving and some cultivation.

Q. was traditionally ruled by sheikhs of the al-Thani family. Ottoman Turkey sometimes claimed a nominal sovereignty, but never really controlled the area. When the British, from the 1820s, established a network of treaty relations in the Gulf, originally to put an end to piracy, the sheikh of Q. became part of that network. The British protectorate was formalized in treaties of 1868, 1882 and 1916, and a British Political Officer "guided" the ruler. In 1968, when Britain announced her decision to withdraw from her Gulf commitments, the sheikh envisaged, with British encouragement, joining the federation of sheikhdoms then planned for *Trucial 'Oman (the *UAE); but he abandoned that intention and preferred separate, complete independence for Q. In Apr. 1970 he provisionally declared that independence, at the same time proclaiming a provisional constitution that provided for government on a modern pattern and a semi-elected Consultative Council (the ruler selecting its 20, later 30, members from among double that number elected by limited suffrage). Q. formally declared her independence on 1 Sept. 1971, when the British Protectorate lapsed, and was admitted the same month to the *Arab League and the UN.

Oil was discovered in 1939–40 at Dukhan, on the west coast but because of World War II production began only in 1949–50. For its growth and Q.'s oil revenues — see *Oil. While productions and revenues were modest compared to other Gulf countries, they enabled Q. to finance the development both of her economy, her communications (ports, roads), and her social infrastructure (a network of health and educational institutions covering all her inhabitants, including a university opened in 1977).

Most of Q.'s economic development remained directly linked to the oil sector. A small refinery operated from 1953 at Umm Sa'id, a new industrial area being developed in the southern part of the east coast, a pipeline bringing the oil from the western fields; an expanded refinery, still small, opened in 1975, and a third one in 1983. Three petrochemical plants, mainly for the production of fertilizer, began operating in 1973, 1979 and 1980–81. A gas liquefaction plant, operating since 1975, was destroyed by fire in 1977 but rebuilt and expanded (1980); another, much larger, planned with the participation of major British and French oil companies, was scheduled to open in 1988. A cement factory was opened in 1969. A small steel plant, using imported scrap iron (and the cheap energy available), was built with Japanese companies and opened in 1978. Like other Gulf oil principalities, Q. used part of her new riches to establish a fund dispensing development aid, in modest dimensions, mainly to A. and Islamic countries.

Q.'s foreign and inter-A. policies remained low-profile, going along with the mainstream of the Arab League, the Islamic Conference Organization, the group of non-aligned nations, and the Gulf Cooperation Council (of which Q. was a founder-member, 1981). Internal politics were disturbed by conflicts and rivalries within the ruling family of the al-Thani sheikhs. Sheikh 'Abdullah ibn Qassem, ruling since 1913, was compelled to abdicate in 1949; his son and successor, 'Ali ibn 'Abdullah, suffered the same fate in 1960; and his son and successor, Ahmad ibn 'Ali (1910–77), was in 1972 ousted by his cousin, Crown Prince and Prime Minister Khalifa ibn Hamad (who reportedly had been the *de facto* ruler behind the scenes, for several years). The latter (b. 1935? 1937?) rules Q. since 1972, serving also as Prime Minister. In 1977 he named his son, Hamad ibn Khalifa, Crown Prince. Most key posts in the Cabinet are usually held by members of the ruler's clan.

al-Qawuqji, Fawzi (1890–1976) Syro-Lebanese soldier, guerrilla leader and politician. Born in Tripoli, Lebanon, Q. served in the Ottoman-Turkish army. His early life has remained rather obscure, but he took part in the Syrian-Druze revolt, 1925–27, and escaped to Iraq. There he taught at the military academy. In Aug. 1936, he recruited several hundred volunteers, mainly from Iraq and Syria, to assist the A. rebels in Palestine, and entered the country at their head, without being hindered by government troops and police. His force, centered in the A.-populated parts, mounted a number of attacks on Jewish settlements and communications, but had no major military impact or successes and his efforts to organize a revolutionary army under his own centralized command failed. The *Husseini-led command of the rebellion suspected him of being close to their adversaries. When the first stage of the rebellion ended in the fall of 1936, through the British-arranged mediation of the A. rulers, the Palestine government permitted Q. to escape across the border with his troops. In 1941, he took part in the Rashid 'Ali al-*Kilani rebellion in Iraq, and when it was quelled, he fled to Germany, where he headed an A. office for propaganda, the recruitment of volunteers and secret services. After World War II, he returned to Syria.

In Jan. 1948, he again recruited and commanded an army of volunteers — the "Army of Deliverance" (*Jaish al-Inqadh*) — that entered Palestine to assist the Palestine-A. guerrillas (see *Arab-Israel Wars for details). His force again attacked, unsuccessfully, several Jewish settlements and roads and communications, but had no major impact on the military situation; nor had officers he sent to various A. and mixed towns to organize the defense of these towns. He also failed, as in 1936, in his efforts to impose a unified command on all the A. guerrilla groups. Many units of Q.'s forces were withdrawn from May, when the regular A. armies took over and ordered volunteer formations to cease separate, independent activities. The remnants of the "Army of Deliverance" were forced by the Israel army in Oct. 1948 to withdraw to South Lebanon.

Q. retired and took no further part in public affairs. Some of his officers later became prominent in Syria's army — and in her politics, particularly her numerous military *coups*.

al-Quwwatli, Shukri (1886–1967) Syrian politician. President of Syria 1943–49 and 1955–58. Born in Damascus, Q. was active in the A. nationalist movement from his youth and one of the leaders of the secret *al-Fatat* society. During World War I, he was arrested by the Turks and according to some reports sentenced to death. Under Amir *Feisal, 1918–19, Q. was Governor of Damascus. In the years 1920–31 he was in exile in Egypt and Europe, active on behalf of the Syrian nationalists and rebels; the French reportedly condemned him to death *in absentia*. Q. returned to Syria in 1931 and became a leader of the "National Bloc", the main faction of the nationalist movement struggling for independence. He was a member of the delegation that negotiated the Franco-Syrian treaty of 1936 (never ratified by France) and became Minister of Defense and Finance in the first nationalist government, 1936–39.

From 1941 Q. was out of Syria. He returned in 1943 as leader of the "National Bloc". The same year he was elected President of Syria and led the final struggle for complete independence from France, 1943–46. He was re-elected President in 1948, but was deposed in Mar. 1949 by Gen. Husni *Za'im in Syria's first military *coup*. After spending five years in exile in Egypt, he returned to Syria in 1954, after the fall of Adib *Shishakli. In Aug. 1955, Q. was elected President of Syria for the third time. He promoted closer links with the Soviet Union and actively supported the concluson of the first co-operation and aid agreements with that country. He also followed a pronounced pro-Egyptian policy, and when a union with Egypt was considered, in 1957–58, he vigorously supported the idea — though he was no longer in the confidence of the younger officers working for that aim, and was gradually losing influence. With the consummation of the union and the establishment of the *UAR, Q. resigned and proposed Gamal *'Abd-ul-Nasser as President of the new united republic. He then retired and played no further role in Syrian politics until his death in 1967.

R

Ras al-Khaima The northernmost of the seven sheikhdoms of *Trucial 'Oman, since 1971 the *United Arab Emirates, UAE, with an area of c. 650 sq.mi. (c. 1,700 sq.km.). The population, about 25,000 by the late 1960s, is estimated in the mid-1980s as c. 75,000, most of them in the port and main town of R. al-Kh. In the past, before the advent of modern development and the oil economy, the inhabitants engaged in fishing, pearl-diving and boat-building, and some nomadic animal husbandry.

R. al-Kh. has been traditionally ruled by the sheikhs of the al-Qassemi (or also al-Jawassemi) clan which also rules nearby *Sharja. Since the 19th century the Sheikh was under British protection, along with the other sheikhs of the region. When Britian withdrew that protection in 1971, R. al-Kh. at first decided to stay out of the federation of the UAE then being formed, but eventually joined it. The Sheikh — since 1948 Saqr ibn Muhammad — is a member of the UAE Council of Rulers, and R. al-Kh. sends four Ministers to the Federal Government. In the protracted struggle between the advocates of a stronger federation and those of more power to the various sheikhdoms, R. al-Kh. vigorously backed the latter, led by *Dubai — to a degree that the Sheikh contemplated seceding from the UAE; one of the reasons was his reluctance to integrate his small motorized military force in the federal army (an integration proclaimed in 1978).

An oil concession was granted in 1964 to American companies; most of it (except for offshore areas) was relinquished after unsuccessful drillings, and later taken over by "Shell" and other companies. Oil discoveries have been announced several times since the 1970s, mainly offshore, and production was reported beginning in 1984. Though R. al-Kh. had as yet no direct oil income of her own and depended on federal UAE funds, some development was begun: an airport was constructed (1976) and the al-Saqr port modernized; a cement factory was built and an oil refinery planned (with Kuwait).

R. al-Kh. is involved in several border disputes. Some concern her borders with other sheikhdoms within the UAE and are no longer important. A dispute with *'Oman, which claimed the northern part of R. al-Kh.'s coast for her *Ras Musandam exclave, was, after smoldering since the early 1950s, raised by 'Oman in 1974; it was resolved, with Sa'udi and Kuwaiti mediation, in an agreement reported in 1979 (with no details made public). Of greater impact is a dispute with Iran over R. al-Kh.'s Tanb (Tumb) Islands. Iran's claim to these islands was pressed more strongly when offshore oil prospects became realistic, and in Nov. 1971 (while British protection was being removed and the UAE was in the process of formation) Iran forcibly occupied them, along with Sharja's *Abu Mussa island. R. al-Kh. and the UAE are demanding their return; but while R. al-Kh. would like to press that demand, the UAE pursues it with great caution.

Rashid, Aal (House of) A clan of sheikhs of the Shammar tribe in northern *Najd, centering on al-Ha'il. In the late 19th century the R.'s became rivals of the House of *Sa'ud — see there for their struggle. In World War II, the R.'s were loyal to the Ottoman Sultan-Caliph.

After the war, the Sa'udis were victorious in renewed fighting, and in the fall of 1921 the R.'s surrendered and renounced all claims to power. After winning out, Ibn Sa'ud followed a policy of reconciliation: he kept the leaders of the R. clan as guests (and hostages?) in his house and married one of their daughters (who bore him his son *'Abdullah — Crown Prince and First Deputy Prime Minister since 1982).

Rashid 'Ali See al-*Kilani, Rashid 'Ali.

Ras Musandam The tip of the *Trucial

'Oman peninsula, protruding into the Straits of *Hormuz. The area belongs to *'Oman, as an exclave separated from 'Oman by the *UAE. With a very scanty population and no major settlement, RM was a backwater to which 'Oman paid little attention. However, since the early 1980s 'Oman has begun to develop, with US assistance, defense, air and naval facilities in RM — in the context of the defense of shipping in the *Persian Gulf and the Straits of Hormuz.

Red Crescent As the symbol of the cross was not acceptable to Muslim countries, they chose that of the RC to designate their humanitarian and welfare-in-war societies parallel to the Red Cross. The first to do so was Ottoman Turkey, in 1876 (Iran chose the Red Lion and Sun), and the AC followed in the 1920s, when they became independent or semi-independent. The International Red Cross accepted and recognized these RC societies as members of its international network — informally at first, and fully and formally since 1949. In Oct. 1986 an international conference even decided to rename the League of Red Cross Societies "League of Red Cross and RC Societies". Iran decided after her Islamic revolution of 1979 to rename her "Lion and Sun" RC.

Red Line Agreement See *Oil in the AC.

Red Sea Six AC border on the shores of the RS: Egypt, Jordan (with a shoreline of a few miles only, at the head of the Gulf of *'Aqaba), Sudan, Sa'udi Arabia, Yemen and South Yemen, as well as Djibouti, the non-A. or semi-A. member of the *A. League, and non-A. Israel (with a few miles of shoreline at the head of the Gulf of 'Aqaba-Eilat) and Ethiopia's *Eritrea. At its southern end, the RS connects with the Indian Ocean (the Gulf of 'Aden, the Arabian Sea) through the Straits of *Bab al-Mandeb; in the north, it ends in two inlets, the Gulf of *Suez to the northwest, and the Gulf of 'Aqaba to the northeast. On the Gulf of Suez, Egypt's oil fields are located — on both shores and offshore.

The RS has throughout history been an important sea route for Europe's trade and communications with India and the Far East — until the opening of the *Suez Canal, in 1869, with an overland leg from the Mediterranean Sea to its northern end. The opening of the Suez Canal greatly enhanced that importance (which declined during the periods that the Canal was closed — briefly in 1956–57, and from 1967 to 1975 — and also when, in the 1970s, a large part of oil transportation was shifted to giant tankers unable to pass through the Canal; since 1975, the Canal, and the RS, have recaptured an important position in world communications).

Several powers aspired to control the RS. In the 16th century the Portuguese for some time set up strongpoints on several islands in the Bab al-Mandeb area at the southern end of the RS. From the late 19th century until World War II it was mainly Britain and Italy that competed for control, the former concerned with her imperial route to India and British colonies in Africa, the latter with her East-African Empire (Ethiopia and Eritrea, Somalia) and reported ambitions to extend her influence across the RS to Yemen and Sa'udi Arabia; Italy's presence and influence were removed with her defeat in World War II and the end of her African empire.

The West was also much concerned with Soviet ambitions in the region: first in the 1920s when the USSR was among the first powers to establish relations with Sa'udi Arabia and Yemen (discontinued, 1930s), and then from the 1960s, when Russia's alliance with Egypt supposedly put at her disposal the latter's ports and shoreline on the RS. Similar developments were feared in Sudan, Russia's position in Yemen was enhanced (even in the days of the Imam, before the revolution of 1962), and after 1967 newly independent South Yemen became a close ally and client of the Soviet Union, with Russian naval and air bases reported in *'Aden and the island of *Socotra in the Gulf of 'Aden. From 1974–75, Ethiopia, with her Eritrean RS shore, also was allied with the USSR; Somalia, on the other hand, severed her alliance with the USSR late in 1977.

Since the 1950s and 1960s, Egypt regards herself as chiefly responsible for the security of the RS; a 1980 agreement with the USA was supposed to lead to the development of the Egyptian RS port of Ras Banas as a base with some facilities for the US and a "Rapid Deployment Force" she was planning.

The RS was also involved in the A.-Israel conflict. Its northeastern prong, the Gulf of 'Aqaba, was closed to Israel-bound shipping in the 1950s, a blockade that was one of the causes of Israel's *"Sinai War" of 1956; the announcement of its re-imposition in 1967 triggered the Six Day War. The RS's northwestern prong, the Gulf of

Suez, was an arena of the *October War of 1973 and the "War of Attrition" that followed it (see *Arab-Israel Wars). Egypt, South Yemen and Palestinian-A. guerrilla groups reportedly tried to impose a blockade of Israel-bound shipping also at the southern end of the RS — see *Bab al-Mandeb, *Perim, *Qamaran.

An episode that was never clarified occurred in 1984: mines were found floating in the RS, and removed by an international operation; Libya was suspected of having floated the mines, but their origin and purpose were not clearly established.

refugees The AC and the ME have been affected by several issues of group migration and/or R. Some concern past centuries — such as the migration of Spanish Jews, as well as some from Morocco, in the 15th and mainly the 16th centuries, to the Ottoman Empire; heterodox and minority groups finding refuge in Mount Lebanon; the migration of *Druze from Mount Lebanon to south-eastern Syria ("Jabal Druze" — the Mountain of the Druze) in the 18th and 19th centuries. The Ottoman Empire allowed and encouraged Muslim R. from the Balkan (*Bushnaq*, i.e. Bosnians) and the Caucasus (*Circassians, Chechens) to settle in its realm.

The *Armenians of Eastern Anatolia were considered hostile and persecuted by the Turks, and many of them fled, particularly after the pogroms of 1895–96 and 1915–18 (when they were thought to be supporting and aiding Russia, Turkey's enemy in World War I). They settled in most countries of the region, Syria and Lebanon in particular, and ceased being "R." — though they were not fully assimilated by A. society and preserved their separate identity (see *Armenians). Many *Assyrians (Nestorian Christians) also fled from Turkey during and immediately after World War I, principally to Iraq. After much friction, and massacres in 1933, many of them fled again, and while *League of Nations efforts for a resettlement project overseas were not very successful, many of them settled in neighboring north-eastern Syria (the *Jazira*). The flight of Turkish R. from the Balkans following the Balkan Wars (1912–13) and World War I, and the exodus of Greeks and Bulgarians from Turkey, culminating in a Greek-Turkish agreement of 1923 on an organized population exchange, concerned Turkish Anatolia only, not the AC, and is thus outside our scope; so are further waves of emigration of Turks from Rumania in the 1930s, and Bulgaria in the 1930s and again in the 1950s.

Jewish R., mainly from Europe, strove to reach Palestine, but their entry was restricted by the British *Mandate authorities to a quota supposedly based on the economic absorptive capacity of the country but decisively influenced by political considerations. Yet this migration, augmented by illegal immigrant ships, reached considerable proportions decisive for the future of Palestine. The plight of survivors of the Nazi Holocaust, still in European camps after World War II, was an important moral and political factor in the deliberations on the future of Palestine, 1945–47, and in world support for the establishment of a Jewish State. Independent Israel, from 1948, instituted free and unlimited Jewish immigration; under that "Law of Return", about 1.3m. came to Israel in the 1950s. These included not only the remnants of European Jewry, but about 500,000 Jews from the AC — with the largest groups coming from Iraq (c. 140,000), Morocco (c. 140,000), Yemen (nearly 50,000), Libya and Tunisia (c. 40,000 each). (See *Jews in the AC.)

Sudan has faced a R. problem — in both directions — since the 1960s: Sudanese R. to the neighboring African countries (Uganda, Ethiopia, Zaïre), and R. from those countries in South Sudan. The Sudanese R. were almost exclusively from South Sudan's black African tribes, fleeing the vicissitudes of the civil war and the resulting destruction of their livelihood; their number — not counting those who fled their domicile but stayed in the bush, inside Sudan — has been variously estimated at up to 200–400,000. R. from the same African countries, and Chad, in Sudan have been estimated in similar figures, with some estimates going up to 500–600,000 and even 1m. and more. However, these R. movements, in both directions, are fluctuating and sporadic, with the number of R. constantly changing.

R. problems have emerged in several ASt as the result of political upheavals, rebellions, minority and community crises. Thus Kurdish populations — estimated by Kurdish sources at hundreds of thousands — have been removed by the Iraqi authorities from the Kurdish areas in northeast Iraq and forcibly resettled elsewhere. The civil war in Lebanon, since 1975, and the Israeli invasion, 1982, also created waves of R. — Shi'i Muslims from South Lebanon, mainly to West Beirut, and Christians from the Shi'i South and the Druze-dominated Shuf to Christian-controlled East Beirut and Mount Lebanon (and also abroad). Parts of these R. movements seem to be temporary, with the R. returning after the acute crisis is over, but large parts seem to have turned into a migration, an irreversible population movement.

The most persistent, and politically most important, R. problem in the region is that of the Palestinian-A. R. who fled their domiciles in the part of Palestine that became Israel in 1948, some to the A. parts of Palestine and some to the neighboring AC. This exodus was a result of the *A.-Israel Conflict in general and the war of 1948 in particular (see *Arab-Israel Conflict, *Arab-Israel Wars, *Palestine Arabs). Its origins and precise circumstances have remained in dispute. A. spokesmen have always maintained that the R. were expelled by the Jews, while Israel has insisted that, notwithstanding some cases of force or even expulsion in the course of military action, the bulk of the R. fled on their own initiative — in the confusion and fear of military operations, and following the instructions, and even more so the example, of their leaders (as later described also by several individual A. witnesses in the press and published memoirs). The right way to solve the Palestinian-A. R. issue is also disputed: Israel argues that the return of that largely hostile population is impossible and would be incompatible with the usual course of events in similar cases in recent history (India/Pakistan; Germany/Eastern Europe; Turkey/Greece), and that the R. should be resettled in the AC — with international aid. Israel has offered, since 1949, to pay compensation for landed property left behind by the R. and to allow the repatriation of a limited, agreed number of R. in the framework of a peace accord — the figure of 100,000 was usually mentioned. These offers, never formally withdrawn, have always been rejected by the ASt and Palestinian-A. leaders. For both the ASt and the Palestinian-A. leaders insisted that the R. be returned to what was now Israel or at least be given the right and the choice, to return; UN votes annually endorsed that right.

Even the figures of the R. of 1948 were in some dispute. UN agencies generally accepted an estimated total of 715–730,000; other estimated that total, more plausibly, at 600–650,000 (of the total Palestinian-A. population of c. 1.3 m., over 400,000 remained in the West Bank, 70–100,000 in the Gaza Strip, and c. 150,000 in Israel, and the R. cannot have been more than the balance). Most of these R. stayed within Palestine — c. 200,000 in the West Bank, and c. 200,000 in the Gaza Strip; c. 100,000 went to Transjordan; and c. 150,000 went abroad, mostly to Lebanon and Syria. By the mid-1980s, the estimated number of R. and their dscendants has grown to over 2m. — due to a very high birth-rate *plus* a certain tendency to inflate the lists, for the sake of rations and benefits, not to delete the deceased and not to take off the lists those who have found permanent employment and have in effect ceased to be R. Of these over 2m. R., UN agencies count over 350,000 in the West Bank, 430,000 in the Gaza Strip, nearly 800,000 in Jordan (including 200–300,000 who fled the West Bank in 1967), about 250,000 in Lebanon and slightly less in Syria (in fact, some 200–300,000 of these work and live in other countries, mainly those of the Persian Gulf, but remain registered as R. in their or their parents' place of post-1948 residence). Of the 2m. R., c. 700–750,000 live in R. camps, which have in effect become fully grown townships; most of these camps are controlled *de facto* by the *PLO. These UN figures are considered inflated by many — including UN spokesmen (see also the rehabilitation issue, *infra*); Israeli statistics, for instance, count in the occupied West Bank c. 110,000 R. and in the Gaza Strip c. 210,000 — against UNRWA's 350,000 and 430,000.

The UN began to aid the R. immediately in 1948. Late in 1949, a special agency, the UN Relief and Works Agency (UNRWA), was set up to administer that aid, mainly by providing housing in camps, food rations, health services and education. UNRWA has done so throughout the years (and thanks to its services public health and the level of school, vocational and academic education among the R. usually is superior to that of the surrounding A. population). Its budget, voluntarily contributed by member-states of the UN (with the USA always paying the largest share), $20m. p.a. at the beginning, slowly rose to $40m. after 1960, passed $100m. in the 1970s, and peaked in 1981 at $230m.; beset by constant deficits, it had to be reduced in the 1980s. After the initial outlay for the construction of camps, 40–45% of this budget paid for food rations — c. 1,500 calories per capita, 42–46% for education (UNRWA maintaining, by the 1970s, some 640 schools of its own), and 13–14% for health services (administration costs included).

UNRWA's relief operations and food supplies, and its health and education services were never in question and the UN General Assembly year after year endorsed the budgets needed. Effective action on resettlement or rehabilitation, on the other hand — though vaguely included in the mandate of UNRWA and the UN *Palestine Conciliation Commission (PCC) — never got off the ground. Several surveys and plans, usually combined with and based on general economic development schemes for the AC, were drafted — such as the Report of a PCC-appointed Economic Survey Mission (the "Clapp Report") in Dec. 1949, or that of the Carnegie Foundation's Joseph Johnson in 1962 (which was shelved by the PCC and not even submitted to the UN General Assembly); but none of them was acceptable to the parties — understandably so, as the ASt objected in principle to any resettlement. It was, indeed, basically a political issue that could not be solved by economic surveys: the head-on confrontation between the A.'s' insistence on repatriation (or at least a free choice of repatriation) and Israel's refusal to consider such a course. The UN General Assembly in its annual resolutions consistently referred to the two alternatives: rehabilitation and absorption in the host countries — or repatriation (of those "willing to live in peace with their neighbors"), and called on Israel to allow the R. a free choice.

Since the 1960s it has become increasingly evident that most of the R. have lost their rural and agricultural character and that their rehabilitation is primarily a matter of work and housing and must be mainly urban and industrial — and therefore does not require large-scale agricultural development and resettlement projects. A considerable number of R. have indeed over the years *de facto* rehabilitated themselves, i.e. have found permanent employment and housing; some have even built remarkable careers and enterprises — mainly in the oil countries. Since the early 1960s, the Commissioner of UNRWA has repeatedly estimated their number as about 20% of the R., adding that another 30–40% may still be in need of "some" assistance by UNRWA, i.e. are semi-rehabilitated. The number of those rehabilitated and semi-rehabilitated is probably much higher — there is no way of determining facts or reliable estimates, since the R. or former R. concerned do not usually delete their names from the lists of R., so as not to lose the status of R. and the benefits that go with it (and also for obvious political reasons).

Rejection Front Informal description of a group of ASt that coalesced in the 1970s to propound a hardline, radical position, particularly on the *A.-Israel Conflict, opposing any ME peace talks or great-power efforts towards a peaceful settlement of that dispute, and holding that the conflict could be ended only by the defeat of Israel — though that position was not always fully and clearly expounded. The RF called itself "Front of Steadfastness" (*Jabhat al-Sumud*). In the mid-1970s it included Syria, Iraq, Libya, Algeria, South Yemen and the *PLO; but Iraq walked out on it in Dec. 1977 (mainly because of her deepening dispute with Syria) and further drew away after 1980, when she needed A. support, and the aid of the A. oil countries, in her war with Iran, while Syria and Libya supported Iran. Algeria also toned down her support of the RF, and the PLO split in 1983, with only the extremist, anti-*'Arafat factions continuing to back the RF.

The RF never formally constituted itself. It was galvanized into stronger activity and semi-institutionalization by Egyptian President *Sadat's peace initiative of Nov. 1977, when it took the lead in the moves to denounce and ostracize Egypt. From 1977 to 1981 it held several separate summit meetings of its leaders (Tripoli Dec. 1977; Damascus Sept. 1978; Tripoli Apr. 1980; Benghazi Sept. 1981) and boycotted some of the *Arab League sessions and summits (the 11th, 'Amman Nov. 1980; the extraordinary, Casablanca Aug. 1985). It half-boycotted the first part of the 12th summit, Fez Nov. 1981, sending low-level representatives instead of the Heads-of-State, and broke it up by vetoing the *Fahd plan. In the 1980s the RF's cohesion and impact declined, and only Syria, Libya and South Yemen, with some extreme factions of the PLO, remained committed to it. On the other hand,

Iran — a non-A. country — has aligned herself with the RF and sometimes holds tripartite meetings with Syria and Libya.

The radical or extremist factions within the PLO are also sometimes called RF. They collaborated as an informal coalition from the 1970s and in 1984 formally set up a Syrian-supported "National Salvation Front" within the PLO. See *PLO.

Rida, (Muhammad) Rashid (1865–1935) Muslim-A. thinker and writer. Born in a village near Tripoli (Lebanon) and educated in traditional Qur'anic and Turkish government schools, R. became an influential Islamic scholar. From 1897 he lived mostly in Egypt, where he was a leading disciple, and to some extent a successor, of the Islamic reformer and scholar Muhammad *'Abduh, continuing and developing 'Abduh's teachings of Islamic revival and reform and of *Pan-Islamic unity. In 1898 R. founded a periodical, *al-Manar*, in which he expounded his thought. He wrote many books, some of them collections of his essays in *al-Manar*, including a *Qur'an* commentary and a biography of 'Abduh. He founded (1912) and directed for two years a seminary for Muslim scholars and missionaries based on his doctrine. R.'s teachings of a revitalized and reformed Islam were in conflict with the official Islamic establishment, but his reformism was deeply conservative. He sought to revive the pristine, simple Islam of the founding fathers (*Salafiyya*), and was thus close to the Hanbali school (*Madhhab* — see *Islam) and to *Wahhabism*. He was suspicious of Western values and thought and antagonistic to the penetration and increasing domination of the West. In the Ottoman time, until the end of World War I, he sought to keep A. nationalist tendencies within the limits of loyalty to and support of the Ottoman Islamic Caliphate, advocating a decentralization of the empire rather than A. secession; in 1913 was among the founders of the "Decentralization Party".

Yet, R. was an A. nationalist, seeing the A.'s as the nation bearing Islam and the core of the Muslim world community (*umma*), and sought to combine the struggle for their national revival with that for an Islamic renaissance and Pan-Islamic unity. He was close to a group of A. activists, mostly Syrian, who during World War I had talks with British officials in Cairo on future A. independence. He was named President of the first Syrian-A. Congress in 1920. In 1921–23 he was a member of a Syrian-Palestinian delegation in Geneva (which had talks and contacts, among others, also with Zionist leaders — though R. was deeply suspicious of and hostile to the Zionists). In 1925–26 he represented the Syrian nationalists, then rebelling against France, in Cairo and agitated for them. At the same time he continued his activities for Islamic issues — such as the abortive efforts to revive the Caliphate, and took part in the Islamic congresses of Mecca, 1926, and Jerusalem, 1931. In many of his literary and political activities he was closely associated with Shakib *Arslan — another influential but marginal figure of A.-Islamic nationalism.

R. was never fully associated with any specific political endeavor, never joined a particular political group or party, and despite the considerable intellectual and moral influence he wielded, he remained a marginal figure in the actual political struggle of A. nationalism and the emergence of A. statehood.

al-Rifa'i, Samir (1899? 1901?–1965) Jordanian politician, Prime Minister in the 1940s and 1950s (and briefly in 1963), and many times Minister, a staunch supporter of the Hashemite dynasty, a conservative and a moderate. He took a comparatively moderate attitude towards Israel, too (but King *'Abdullah did not take him fully into his confidence concerning his negotiations and agreements with the Zionist leaders). His brother 'Abd-ul-Mun'im R. (1917–85) was a senior diplomat, a Minister, and Prime Minister in 1969–70.

al-Rifa'i, Zeid (b.1936) Jordanian politician, Prime Minister 1973–76 and since 1985. The son of Samir *Rifa'i (married to the daughter of Prime Minister and Senate President Bahjat Talhuni), a confidant of King *Hussein, whose classmate he had been at college. A graduate of American Universities (Columbia, Harvard) in political science and international relations, R. joined the diplomatic service and that of the Royal Court, also attending to the family's ramified business interests and landed property (e.g. in the Jordan Valley development zone). He served at Jordan's embassies in Egypt, Lebanon and at the UN, and in 1967 was appointed Private Secretary to the King, promoted in 1969 to be Head of the Royal Cabinet, a post he held during the

Jordan-*PLO crisis of 1970. In 1970 he was named Ambassador to Britain, until 1972–73. In May 1973, still in his 'thirties, R. became Prime Minister, taking also the Foreign Affairs portfolio. While the PLO considered him to be hostile, a remarkable improvement in Jordan-Syria relations took place during his Premiership of over three years — and was ascribed largely to his efforts. Since Apr. 1985, R. is again Prime Minister — and some commentators again consider a noticeable *rapprochement* with Syria as a result of his policies. Since 1978, R. has been a member of the Senate; in 1979–80 and 1984 he was its Deputy-President.

Rogers, William (b. 1913); **Rogers Plan** As US Secretary of State under President Nixon, from Jan. 1969 to Sept. 1973, R. was much involved in ME affairs. Proposals he submitted in Oct. 1969 to Egypt and Israel (and the USSR and in Dec. to Jordan), and presented in Dec. at the UN, and in a public speech, became known as the RP. Its outline: Israel to withdraw to the international border with Egypt (i.e. that of Palestine until 1948) — with the *Gaza Strip, while not remaining occupied by Israel, to be subject to negotiations; freedom of navigation in the *Suez Canal and the Gulf of *'Aqaba to be "spelled out" and safeguarded. This first RP, concerning Egypt and Israel, was rejected by both Israel and Egypt (and the USSR). The version of Dec. 1969, addressed mainly to Jordan and Israel, envisaged an Israeli withdrawal to the armistice lines of 1949–67, with slight revisions; equal civil, religious and economic rights for Jordan and Israel in Jerusalem, the city to stay "united" while its political status "can be determined only through the agreement of the parties concerned"; a settlement of the refugee problem "must take into account the desires and aspirations of the refugees and the legitimate concerns of the Governments" — a wording believed to imply a choice of repatriation or compensation for the *refugees. This RP was accepted by Jordan, but rejected by Israel.

In June 1970, R. presented new proposals, sometimes termed RP II; these sought mainly to reactivate the mediatory mission of the Swedish UN envoy Jarring, suspended since 1969, and to end the Egypt-Israel "War of Attrition" that had dangerously escalated, with increasing Soviet involvement (see *A.-Israel Wars). The RP II proposed an immediate Egypt-Israel cease-fire; politically, it reiterated the main points of Security Council Resolution 242 — Israel's withdrawal from territories occupied in 1967, a just and lasting peace etc. It was accepted by Egypt and Jordan, but Israel considered its political clauses too vague and loosely worded and at first rejected it. She accepted it after receiving, in July 1970, detailed "clarifications" from President Nixon: Israel's withdrawal would not necessarily be to the pre-June 1967 lines, and would be demanded only within the framework of a contractual, binding peace agreement; the US would not press on Israel to accept the Egyptian and A. position regarding the borders; the Refugee problem would be solved in a way that would not impair the Jewish character of Israel (i.e. not by mass repatriation); the US would ensure the integrity, sovereignty and security of Israel, and a balance of armaments would be preserved. While accepting the RP II (causing a cabinet crisis and the withdrawal of the right wing bloc from the coalition government), Israel reiterated her rejection of RP I.

The cease-fire agreement, including a military standstill in a 30 mi. strip on both sides of the Suez Canal, came into force on 7 Aug. 1970. But Egypt immediately moved missiles towards the Canal and continued work on fortifications. Israel regarded these steps as a breach of the standstill agreement, protested vigorously, and refused to resume the Jarring talks. She agreed to their resumption late in Dec. 1970, after receiving additional US assurances and a US commitment to balance the military advantage Egypt had achieved.

When the Jarring talks proved abortive, by Feb. 1971, R. continued his endeavors to mediate an Egypt-Israel interim agreement, e.g., in one version, an accord to reopen the Suez Canal against a partial Israeli withdrawal. But President *Sadat conditioned any such agreement on an Israeli commitment to a total withdrawal, and R. was unable to achieve significant progress. (Interim agreements similar to those R. had envisaged were concluded by his successor Henry Kissinger after the *October War of 1973.)

Rumania The only Soviet Bloc country that did not sever relations with Israel in 1967. R., under Nicolae Ceausescu, took a pro-A. position similar to that of the Soviet Bloc and particularly advocated the establishment of a Palestinian-A.

independent state and fostered relations with the *PLO; but she maintained friendly relations with Israel (raising them to embassy level in 1968). Holding, contrary to the USSR, that a ME peace settlement could be achieved only through direct A.-Israel negotiations, and maintaining good relations with both sides to the conflict, Ceausescu was in a position to offer his services to bring the two sides together; and he did so, quietly and behind the scenes, several times. He was reported to have been intimately involved in the preparations for Egyptian President *Sadat's peace move of 1977, and he has continued to offer his assistance towards negotiations on an A.-Israeli settlement.

Russia, Russian (and Soviet) interests and policies in the Arab countries Tsarist R.'s contacts with the ME, from the 16th century, her main drive for expansion from the 17th century, resulting in 13 wars with the Ottoman Empire and Persia, her quest for control of the Bosphorus-Dardanelles outlet to the Mediterranean and the Capsian Sea-*Persian Gulf corridor leading to India, and the prevention of any consolidation of R. gains either by the unilateral intervention of Great Britain or by a combination of the major European powers — concerned the region of Turkey and Persia and are outside our scope. The A. region was affected only in some instances — e.g., R. supported the Ottoman Sultan in 1833 against the rebellious Egyptian Viceroy Muhammad 'Ali and the Crimean War of 1854–56 grew out of a quarrel between R. and France over the holy places in Palestine and R.'s claim to protect all Orthodox Christians in the Ottoman Empire. In World War I, R., allied with Britain and France, claimed the right to annex, after victory, Constantinople and both shores of the Bosphorus, the Sea of Marmara and the Dardanelles. These claims were accepted by Paris and London (secret agreement of Mar. 1915) in a radical transformation of Western policy; the Western powers also granted R. complete freedom of action in her zone of influence in Persia. In the secret *Sykes-Picot Agreement, 1916, R. obtained Western approval for the annexation of most of Eastern Anatolia, as well. In return R. consented to the partitioning of the A. parts of the Ottoman Empire between her two European allies. However, by the time the Ottoman Empire was defeated, the revolutionary Bolshevik government in Moscow had renounced all Tsarist territorial claims and gains.

During the interwar period the ME did not figure prominently in Soviet foreign policy. That policy was now conducted on two separate levels.

1. The USSR sought to maintain normal foreign relations, especially with her three immediate neighbors — Turkey, Persia and Afghanistan — with whom she concluded in 1921 treaties of friendship and non-aggression. The USSR was not a party to the Peace Treaty of *Lausanne, 1923; she was a signatory to the *Montreux Convention on the Straits, 1936, which permitted their re-fortification and restricted the right of warships to pass the Straits and enter the Black Sea. The USSR established commercial and diplomatic relations with Sa'udi Arabia and Yemen, in 1925 and 1928 respectively, despite the reactionary nature of these traditionalist monarchies; both missions were withdrawn in 1938.

2. On a different level, the USSR supported revolution in colonial countries, through the Communist International (Comintern). A Congress of the Peoples of the East, held in Baku in 1920 under the auspices of the Comintern, called on the inhabitants of the area to rise up against their colonial masters. Communism, however, had little appeal for the peoples of the ME. Its secularist, atheistic elements were anathema to the religious values and beliefs of Muslim society; a proletarian industrial working class did not yet exist; Communist cells were suppressed by the existing semi-independent nationalist régimes — with the full support of their Western tutors, Britain and France, who prevented any contact between these régimes and Moscow.

As the USSR resumed the position of a Great Power, penetration of the ME became a major Soviet interest. In secret negotiations with Nazi Germany in 1940, the USSR declared that she had territorial aspirations "south of the national territory of the Soviet Union in the direction of the Indian Ocean" and the Persian Gulf. She also registered her demand for "land and naval bases within range of the Bosphorus and the Dardanelles".

The occupation of Iran by R. and Britain in Aug. 1941, and her division into zones; R.'s support for separatist régimes in Azerbaijan and Kurdish *Mahabad; her reluctance to evacuate her troops after the war; and her demands on

Turkey — are outside the scope of this book.

During World War II, the USSR established full diplomatic relations with those ASt that had previously been kept out of her reach by Britain and France: Egypt, Syria, Lebanon, and Iraq. In 1945 she sought a share in trusteeships to be imposed on the former Italian colonies, particularly Libya; her proposals were, however, aborted by the West. The antagonism between R. and the West clearly manifested itself in the ME. R. encouraged ME nations in conflict with the West — such as Syria and Lebanon, 1945–46, Iran in her defiance of Western oil interest 1951–53, and Egyptian and Iraqi nationalist governments struggling with Britain. She endorsed the partition of Palestine, 1947, recognized Israel and let Czechoslovakia assist her with arms in her crucial struggle for survival, and it was assumed that her wish to get Britain out was a major reason for this change of policy (indeed, in 1949–50 the USSR reverted to the violent anti-Zionism that had been traditional with the Bolshevik party). The "Truman Doctrine" of Mar. 1947, on the other hand, committed the USA to aid Greece and Turkey against Communist aggression and subversion.

In her growing support for the A. nationalist governments, the USSR greatly diminished, or at least played down, her support for local Communist parties and for national minorities in conflict with these governments (such as the *Kurds). As such support could not be completely abandoned, however, Soviet policy continued displaying shifts and contradictions. It was obviously determined by the strategic and political interests of an expanding Great Power rather than by considerations of Communist ideology or solidarity.

In the mid-1950s the opportunity came for the USSR to make a major breakthrough. A revolutionary nationalist Egypt was locked in a bitter struggle with Britain and also increasingly isolated from the USA, resisting US pressure for a Western-guided regional military alliance, first the *ME Defense Treaty, and later the *Baghdad Pact, which Egypt regarded as a means of continuing Western domination. Intensification of the A.-Israel conflict also engendered anti-Western feelings to Moscow's profit. As of early 1954 the USSR began consistently to veto UN Security Council resolutions on the conflict that did not tally with the Arab position. A large-scale arms deal was concluded early in 1955, officially between Egypt and Czechoslovakia, but in fact including the sale of major items of weaponry directly by the USSR to Egypt. From this point on the Soviet Union had a stake in the A. world. Full political and diplomatic support for Egypt's stand in the *Suez crisis of 1956 and similarly for Syria in 1957, accompanied in both cases by threats of military intervention, enhanced the USSR's position as the A.'s' chief supporter against Western imperialism and Israel. From 1957–58 the USSR gave ever-increasing military and economic aid to Syria and Egypt. Subsequent revolutions in the A. world enlarged the camp of the USSR's clients: Iraq 1958, Algeria 1962, Yemen 1962, South Yemen 1967, Sudan 1969 and Libya 1969; but Egypt remained the USSR's single most important client and ally. Soviet aid was often geared to great show-piece schemes of national prestige, such as the *Aswan High Dam in Egypt and steel plants. The USSR also trained the officers of her A. allies' armed forces and provided most of their military equipment, thus making them more and more dependent on her. There was a growing presence of Soviet naval forces in the Mediterranean. By the end of the 1960s these forces not only enjoyed the use of strategic ports in Egypt, Syria and Algeria. Soviet naval units were welcome guests in Sudan, Yemen, South Yemen and Iraq (although the closure of the Suez Canal after June 1967 severed the sea link between the latter group of countries and the Soviet Mediterranean squadron).

The *Six Day War of June 1967 constitutes another watershed in Soviet relations with the ME. Soviet policies were among the chief factors determining the course of events before and during the crisis, and increasingly so as Moscow supported the A. cause against Israel in the UN and in Great-Power talks on the ME. The war brought to the Soviet Union Western, notably US, recognition as a ME power and for the first time US-Soviet relations came to include discussions of the ME, specifically the A.-Israel situation. The USSR speedily more than replaced all military equipment lost in the conflict by the ASt's, both quantitatively and qualitatively. In 1969–70 she went even further: she not only dispatched large numbers of Soviet officers to train and advise the Egyptian armed forces; but after the Israelis demolished the Egyptian anti-aircraft system in the War of Attrition, Soviet crews manned SAM-2 and SAM-3 missile sites, while Soviet pilots were sent to Egypt to fly operational combat missions. The USSR had severed diplomatic relations with Israel in June 1967 and supported A. demands for her total and unconditional withdrawal from the territories occupied in 1967; but since she accepted the existence of an independent Israel, she was at first hesistant about supporting the PLO, that strove for Israel's elimination. By the early 1970s, however, she was aiding and encouraging the PLO politically and militarily, without explicitly associating herself with its ultimate objective.

The USSR was also reported supporting insurgent movements in the Persian Gulf area and various leftist groupings in some of the more moderate ASt's. But while aiding mainly the radical or revolutionary régimes, she also sought to increase contacts with such generally pro-Western countries as Jordan, Kuwait, Morocco and Tunisia.

The early 1970s that saw the peak of the USSR's involvement in the A. world also witnessed the beginnings of the decline in her influence. Egypt, which under Nasser had been the main target and instrument of Soviet penetration, became under Sadat the first major trouble spot. Despite a Treaty of Friendship and Cooperation concluded in 1971, Sadat expelled the entire Soviet military presence (estimated at 15–20,000) in 1972 — reportedly because the USSR refused fully to support his plans for a further round of hostilities with Israel that would eventually enable him to negotiate a settlement from a position of strength. The Soviets, who were entering a period of *détente* summits with the US, did not wish to jeopardize their achievements on this plane as a result of A. adventurism. In a new agreement in early 1973 the USSR promised Sadat to supply military material that would change the Arab-Israeli military balance — without, however, giving the Arabs the decisive strategic weaponry that Sadat was demanding — and in the Oct. 1973 War the USSR stood by Egypt and Syria. But after that war Sadat turned to the US in his endeavors to reach a political settlement that would restore the Sinai to Egypt, and Soviet influence in Egypt continued its decline. In 1976 Egypt unilaterally abrogated the 1971 treaty. In 1977 she also withdrew her ambassador from Moscow and in 1981 expelled the Soviet Ambassador from Cairo (full ambassadorial relations were restored in 1984).

The Soviet Union sought to compensate herself by improving her ties with other ASt's and the PLO, so that she would retain clout with the US and a key rôle in any ME settlement. She scored occasional successes: she concluded further Friendship and Cooperation Treaties — with Iraq (1972), Somalia (1974 — unilaterally abrogated by that country in 1977), South Yemen (1979), Syria (1980), Yemen (1984). No such treaty was signed with Libya — though Libya reportedly proposed it. Soviet influence with the PLO grew through intense political and military assistance. There were sporadic breakthroughs with the USA, such as a Soviet-American statement of October 1977 on the ME, designed to lead to a reconvening of the *Geneva Peace Conference under joint Soviet-US aegis. The USSR also established in 1985 diplomatic relations with several Persian Gulf states that had refused them before — 'Oman and the UAE (Kuwait had already established relations in 1963).

On the whole, however, Soviet achievements in the ME were marginal. She registered apparent successes in the periphery — Afghanistan, Ethiopia — but even these turned out to be mixed blessings in themselves, as well as alienating other ME populations. Revolutionary Iran which ejected US influence did not replace the Shah's relationship with Washington by a partnership with the USSR. Moreover, the Iran-Iraq war increased Soviet predicaments. The radical states, Syria, Libya, South Yemen, with which her relations were closest and to which Moscow had far-reaching commitments, proved largely intractable and unmalleable as clients, while the PLO lost a great deal of its significance following its expulsion from Lebanon in 1982 and its internal dissensions (the USSR helped efforts to mediate and reconcile those rifts). Syria remained a strategic asset, and dependent on Soviet aid, while the USSR needed her partnership with Damascus to ensure her participation in the ME peace process; yet so intimate a cooperation with states increasingly recognized as responsible for international terror cast aspersions on the USSR's capabilities in restraining client states and her responsibility as a great power. The US also suffered a number of setbacks such as the rejection of the Reagan Plan (1982) and the withdrawal of the marines from Lebanon (1983–84); yet these have not been sufficient to reinstate the USSR as one of two world powers with more or less equal status in the region. In the mid-1980s the USSR increasingly involved herself in the Persian Gulf — acting as a guardian of free shipping.

The declining Western dependence on ME oil and the gradually diminishing importance of that commodity in the international arena; the obvious limitations of a superpower whose chief claim to influence has traditionally been the supply of arms, especially when some of its client states are intent on peace, and the superpower itself is apprehensive of an outbreak of hostilities that might jeopardize its position; the failure to win Third World states in general and ASt's in particular as adherents of Marxist-Leninist ideology and "the non-capitalist path of development"; the tendency of radicalism and nationalism to ally themselves with Muslim fundamentalism; the technological gap between East and West and the USSR's evident economic difficulties — all these combined to cast shadows on the once brilliant specter of an alliance with the USSR. While it would be rash to write off the USSR as a power in a region intrinsically conflict-ridden and in large parts suspicious of the USA, the USSR's customary policies and tactics and even her considerable investment in the area have brought her few results.

S

Saadabad Pact Treaty of non-aggression signed on 8 July 1937 by Turkey, Iran, Iraq and Afghanistan. Relations between these countries were not close, as all four focused their foreign policy mainly on relations with Europe and the great powers; and they were occasionally disturbed by tension and border disputes. However, in view of the increasing international tension and the insecurity felt by small countries after Italy's attack on Ethiopia in 1935 and the West's weakness, the four were anxious to improve their relations and strengthen their mutual security. They were encouraged in their endeavor by the West. But though the SP was hailed as an important event, it did not play a significant rôle. After the outbreak of World War II its council was never convened. Signed for five years, to be automatically renewed every five years unless annulled, it was never rescinded, but after World War II it was not considered valid.

Sa'adeh, Antoun (1902–49) Lebanese politician. Son of a Christian, Greek-Orthodox doctor who emigrated to Brazil, S. was brought up there. He returned to Lebanon in 1930 and taught German at the American University of Beirut. In the 1930s, he propounded a Syrian nationalism, based on the idea of a specifically Syrian nation — as against both *Pan-A. aspirations to all-A. unity (and Lebanon's integration in its framework) and a separate Lebanese national entity as propounded by one wing of Christian-Lebanese mainstream opinion — and propagated the creation of a *"Greater Syria". He was strongly influenced by German Fascism. He called for the immediate independence of Syria-Lebanon and the eviction of the French. In 1932, he founded a *"Syrian Nationalist Party" (al-Hizb al-Suri al-Qawmi). His party was banned and S. was harassed by the authorities, until he left in the late 1930s — reportedly first to Italy and Germany and then to South America. He returned to Lebanon, now independent, in 1947 and resumed his political activity, adding the word "Social" (al-Ijtima'i) to the name of his party; but suspected by the Lebanese authorities, he was kept under surveillance and arrested on several occasions. After Husni *Za'im's coup in Syria, 1949, S. hoped for his support, but was disappointed. In June 1949, clashes erupted between his party and the Christian *Phalanges in what was described as a coup attempt by S. He escaped to Syria, but he was extradited to Lebanon, sentenced to death by a summary military court and executed in July. His SSNP was suppressed and many of his associates were imprisoned. In revenge for his execution, his men in July 1951 assassinated Riyad al-*Sulh, who had been Prime Minister in 1949. (For the later development of the SSNP, which remained on the margins of Lebanese politics and in the civil war of the later 1970s joined the "leftist", pro-Syrian camp — see *Syrian Nationalist Party.)

Sa'adist Party Egyptian political party founded in 1937 by a faction of younger leaders seceding from the *Wafd. They presented themselves as the true heirs of the late *Wafd* leader Sa'd *Zaghlul and named their party after him. The SP was led by Mahmud Fahmi al-*Nuqrashi and Ahmad *Maher. One of the reasons for their secession from the *Wafd* was their advocacy of an accommodation with the King and his court, contrary to the *Wafd*'s position, and the SP became one of the anti-*Wafd* factions allied with, and cultivated by, the King and his court. It formed a coalition with the Liberal Constitutional Party, and the two parties won the elections of 1938 and 1945 (with the SP as the main winner and stongest faction in 1945). The SP participated in most of the non-*Wafdist* governments between 1937 and 1949, and its own leaders headed the government in 1944–46 (Maher and Nuqrashi) and 1946–49 (Nuqrashi and Ibrahim 'Abd-ul-Hadi). Two of them were assassinated (Maher in Feb. 1945, Nuqrashi in Dec. 1948). The SP was banned and dissolved in Jan. 1953, along with all political parties.

Sabaeans, Sabians See *Mandaeans.

al-Sabāh The ruling dynasty of Kuwait, the ruler using the title *Sheikh*, or in recent decades *Amir*. See entry *Kuwait, and the table at its end.

Sabri, 'Ali (b. 1920) Egyptian officer and politician, Prime Minister 1962–65, Vice-President 1965–67. S. was trained as a professional officer, graduating in 1939 from the military academy. He was not among the ten founding members of the "Free Officers" group that staged the *coup d'état* of July 1952, but was close to them and reportedly acted as their liaison to the US Embassy before and during the *coup*. He began his climb to power as Director of President *Nasser's Office. When Egypt merged with Syria in 1958 to form the *UAR, S. became Minister for Presidential Affairs in the UAR government. He kept this post in the Egyptian government, when the UAR was dissolved in 1961. As he had become one of President Nasser's closest associates, he was appointed Prime Minister in Sept. 1962, heading the government until Oct. 1965; as Prime Minister he was also a member of the Presidential Council named in 1962. From 1965, when he had to give up the Premiership, until 1967 he was one of four (from 1966: three) Vice-Presidents. In 1967–68 he served briefly as Deputy Prime Minister and Minister of Local Government.

From 1965 S. held, concurrently with his Vice-Presidency, the chairmanship of the *"Arab Socialist Union", Egypt's single party and the mass basis of her régime. He endeavored to reorganize that party into cadres, on the Soviet model, and turn it into an effective mass organization — and a base for his own climb to power. In the 1960s, S. headed the Left wing of Eygpt's ruling junta — advocating ever closer relations with the Soviet Union and, at home, a speedier and more intense advance towards state socialism, the expansion of the state sector of the economy, more vigorous nationalizations and a stricter régime. As he came to be considered "Moscow's man", his position in the leadership team was seen as an index of the régime's shifting relations with the USSR. In June 1967 he was credited with the organization of the mass demonstrations that persuaded Nasser to withdraw his resignation. After 1967, however, when Nasser felt compelled to moderate his policies in the internal, inter-A. and international arenas, S.'s influence declined. He remained, except for a few months in 1967–68, without a government position, and in 1969 he was dismissed as chairman of the ASU — apparently both because of his leftist radical tendencies and his power ambitions.

After Nasser's death, in Sept. 1970, he was seen by many as a leading candidate for the succession — the one preferred by the Soviet Union. He lost out to *Sadat, but was included in the new government as one of Sadat's two Vice-Presidents. However, a power struggle continued behind the scenes, and in May 1971 he was accused, together with a group of other leaders and administrators from Nasser's days, of plotting, treason, and abuse of power in his pre-1970 positions. He was dismissed from all governments and party posts and put on trial. In Dec. 1971 he was sentenced to death, but the sentence was commuted to prison for life. He was pardoned and released by Sadat in May 1981, but did not resume activities in political or public affairs.

al-Sadat, (Muhammad) Anwar (1918–81) Egyptian officer and statesman. President of Egypt 1970–81. Born in Mit Abu'l-Kom in the Delta province of Minufiyya into a peasant family (his father was a clerk with the army, his mother — Sudanese), S. graduated from the military academy in 1938 and became a professional officer. A keen nationalist of conservative Islamic tendency, he was close to, and for some time a member of, the *Muslim Brotherhood and the right-wing, pro-Fascist *Misr al-Fatat* (Young Egypt) party. In 1941–42 he was active in a pro-German underground group, and in Oct. 1942 he was expelled form the army. He was detained for about two years; in 1944 he escaped and went underground until the detention order was lifted in 1945. He was arrested in 1946 and charged with complicity in the murder of the former Finance Minister Amin Osman ('Uthman) and also suspected of involvement in an attempt to assassinate ex-Premier *Nahhas. In prison for over two years during the trial, he was acquitted in Dec. 1948. He then worked as a journalist, but in Jan. 1950 he was readmitted to the army.

Restored to his officer's rank and position, S. soon joined the secret group of "Free Officers" headed by Gamal *'Abd-ul-Nasser and took part — then a Lt.-Colonel — in that group's *coup* of July 1952. He became a member of the 12-man Revolutionary Council heading the new régime and remained, in various capacities, one of the leaders of the new team throughout the years of its rule — though he held no ministerial positions except for one term as Minister of State, 1954–56. In the first years of the new régime, S. served as liaison with the Muslim Brotherhood and right-wing groups. After the Brotherhood was banned and suppressed (1954) and the régime began turning to the left, he was no longer with Nasser's inner circle (and his appointment as Minister of State was a token appointment with no real power). For some time he was editor of the régime's daily, *al-Gumhuriyya*. S. was a member of the Council of the régime's single party and served as its Secretary General from 1957; this post did not carry much influence, particularly after Egypt's merger with Syria as the *UAR (1958). From 1959 to 1969 S. was chairman of the National Assembly, including one year, 1960–61, of that of the UAR. As he was, among the "Free Officers", the closest to Islamic tendencies, he was sent on several missions to Muslim countries and represented Egypt at Islamic conferences. He was also Egypt's chief liaison with Yemen.

In Dec. 1969 S. was appointed Vice-President of Egypt, as Nasser's only deputy — an appointment seen as a step to balance rightist and leftist tendencies within the ruling team and particularly to check the advance of the latter, led by the power-hungry 'Ali *Sabri. On Nasser's death in Sept. 1970, S. was chosen as President of Eygpt, and also of the single party, the "Arab Socialist Union" (ASU); he was duly elected, as the only candidate, in Oct. 1970. His selection by the ruling team was apparently intended to avoid a struggle for the succession by rightist and leftist candidates — it was assumed: Zakariyya *Muhyi-ul-Din vs. 'Ali Sabri — and S. himself was seen as a rather colorless compromise candidate, a weak *primus inter pares*. However, he soon formed his own policies and established his personal leadership with a firm grip on power. For his suppression of a May 1971 plot and the elimination of his rivals, see *Egypt.

Firmly in power, S. began changing Egypt's régime and policies. At first he did so cautiously and without admitting that he was abandoning at least some of the principles of Nasserism; he insisted that his measures were merely a "corrective revolution", restoring the true principles of the 1952 revolution. Gradually, and mainly from 1973, he introduced a liberalization of the economic régime — see *Egypt for details.

This liberalization was accompanied by a gradual change in S.'s foreign policies. He practiced moderation in inter-A. affairs, abandoning attempts to impose Egyptian domination on other ASt and moving closer to the moderate ASt, especially Sa'udi Arabia. He went along with the plan for a federation with Libya and Syria, the *"Federation of A. Republics", FAR — a scheme that did not really get off the ground — but resisted Libyan pressure for a full merger of Egypt and Libya (to which he had at first formally agreed — see *Egypt, *Libya, *Arab Federation), putting up with the resulting deterioration in Egypt's relations with Libya.

S.'s main policy change concerned relations with the great powers. He initiated a significant *rapprochement* with the USA and sought closer relations with Western Europe and the EEC. And he cut back Egypt's alliance with the USSR (which had never cultivated S. and would probably have preferred in 1970 to see 'Ali Sabri elected). In 1971 he still hosted President Podgorny and signed a Treaty of Friendship with the Soviet Union; but this was seen by observers as an effort to shore up crumbling relations rather than a sign of mutual confidence. S. visited Moscow in Oct. 1971 and Feb. 1972 to settle differences. But in July 1972 he unilaterally terminated the services of an estimated 15–20,000 Soviet experts, including all the military ones. He later explained that the main reason for that drastic step was the Russians' unwillingness to give him a free hand and unlimited support in his preparations for war against Israel and to remove their involvement in, or even control of, Egyptian decision-making. But later in 1972–73 relations were improved and the USSR resumed full military aid towards and during the war of 1973.

S.'s main concern, indeed, was with the continuing Israeli occupation of Sinai and other A. territories — a matter of vital priority and national honor. He was ready to move towards peace negotiations — as he told UN envoy Jarring in Feb. 1971 and US representatives many times; but his pre-condition was Israel's total withdrawal to the pre-1967 lines and a "just settlement" of the refugee problem. As Israel could not accept that condition, S. resolved that the occupation could be ended and Egyptian territory restored by military action only, and from 1971–72 prepared for war. The *October War of 1973 is described in the entries *Arab-Israel Wars and *Arab-Israel Conflict. In military terms, the war was not an Egyptian victory; but in a wider perspective, and in Egyptian and A. perception, it was a great achievement: Egyptian forces had won battles, displayed impressive capabilities of military planning and leadership and thus restored their pride and honor; and they had forcibly recovered part of occupied Sinai, including the vital eastern shore of the Suez Canal, and broken the deadlock. This was S.'s achievement, S.'s victory, and his prestige was at its peak, both in Egypt and in the AC.

S. now sought to resume, on the basis of the new situation created, negotiations with Israel, and he did so increasingly and almost exclusively with US mediation. However, after two major Interim Agreements reached in 1974 and 1975 following protracted, US-mediated negotiations, no further progress was achieved. The deadlock was broken in Nov. 1977 by S.'s dramatic surprise visit to Israel (which had in fact been prepared by secret diplomatic contacts). In his meetings with Israeli leaders and his public address to a solemn meeting of the *Knesset*, S. offered complete peace and normal relations against a total withdrawal from all territories occupied in 1967 and an agreed, negotiated solution to the problem of the Palestine A.'s. In substance, his proposals were thus not different from previous positions held by Egypt and other moderate ASt. His great achievement was the psychological breakthrough of meeting the "enemy" face to face and talking to him, his spelling out what before had at best been implied: a preparedness to coexist in peace with Israel once she agreed to A. demands and conditions, and his willingness to negotiate for Egypt alone, wihtout waiting for an all-A. consensus. He made it clear, though, that he would not conclude a *separate* peace with Israel but would consider an eventual agreement as a first step towards a general A.-Israel settlement.

For the negotiations that followed, the "Camp David Agreements" of Sept. 1978 and the Egypt-Israel Peace Treaty of Mar. 1979 — see *Egypt and *Arab-Israel Conflict. The official normalization of relations went into effect in Jan. 1980 and Ambassadors were exchanged in Feb.; S. did not live to see the completion of Israel's withdrawal in Apr. 1982. He had received the Nobel Prize, jointly with Premier Begin of Israel, in Dec. 1978 (after the Camp David Agreements, before the Peace Treaty), as well as several European and American medals and prizes, some of them posthumously. S.'s relations with Israel's leaders soon cooled and went through several crises. Negotiations on an autonomous régime for the Palestine-A.'s, as the first stage towards an agreed solution of their problem, soon stalled and were discontinued. Israel's formal annexation of East Jerusalem, in July 1980, was resented by S. So were her air raid on an Iraqi nuclear reactor, in June 1981, and several raids on PLO positions in Lebanon. (The cooling-off, or freezing, of Egypt-Israel relations deepened after S.'s death.

S.'s moves towards peace with Israel led the A. world to denounce and ostracize Egypt, and him personally — see *Egypt. S. bore this severance of Egypt from the A. family of nations — which was never complete, relations in many fields continuing unofficially — and the personal defamation accompanying it with angry disappointment and with a show of pride. He refused not only to abrogate his agreements with Israel, but declined actively to seek the restoration of Egypt to her natural place within the A. world, and at its head, asserting that since the ASt had severed relations it was they, not Egypt, that should seek a reconciliation.

After 1979, S. continued enhancing close relations with the USA and encouraged her to play a crucial, near-exclusive, mediating role in the peace process. During his rule Egypt also became increasingly dependent on US aid. S. received US Presidents Nixon and Carter in Egypt and himself visited the US in Oct. 1975 and several times later. In 1979–80 he became a partner to wider US strategy plans and agreed to provide low-profile facilities for a planned US "Rapid Deployment Force" (that was not fully implemented). His relations with the USSR declined. In 1976 S. abrogated the Treaty of Friendship. In 1977 he recalled Egypt's Ambassador, leaving her represented at a lower level; later he expelled several Soviet diplomats, and in Sept. 1981 requested the withdrawal of the Soviet Ambassador and the closure of the Military Attaché's office — all unfriendly gestures.

At home S. continued his policy of liberalization and de-Nasserization. He gradually dismantled the single-party system, allowing in 1975 the formation of "platforms", i.e. organized factions, within the ASU, and late in 1976 their transformation into fully fledged parties. In 1978 he formed a party of his own, the "National Democratic Party", which soon became the government party and absorbed the ASU. In the executive, no further major upheavals occurred. S. served as his own Prime Minister in 1973–74 and thereafter appointed loyal second-rank associates to that post. He dismissed Vice-President *Shafe'i in 1975 and replaced him with the commander of the air force, Husni *Mubarak. He changed his Defense Minister (considered the most important man after the President) several times. S. himself was re-elected President in 1976, with no rival candidate.

For S.'s measures against the Communists, his support for a growing emphasis on Egypt's Islamic character, and his efforts to curb, and later suppress, Islamic extremist organizations — see *Egypt. It was one of these groups that assassinated S. in Oct. 1981.

The main issue that clouded S.'s last years — and his record and memory — was the complex of Egypt's economic and social problems, the inability of his liberalization to fulfil the high-pitched expectations pinned on it and solve the country's basic problems. The growing disappointment with S.'s policies was aggravated by that policy's negative side-effects: an increasing relapse into the inequality of a free enterprise society, the emergence of a new class of profiteers flaunting their wealth in visible contrast to the poverty of large parts of the population, and a great deal of spreading corruption and nepotism. S. and his policies, both socio-economic and concerning Israel, were denounced by the Communists and the left, the Nasserists, the extreme Islamists, and many intellectuals. S. himself, aware of his inability to solve the socio-economic problems facing Egypt, turned mainly to foreign affairs. In the last years of his Presidency he tightened his régime, taking harsher measures against his adversaries on the Communist and Nasserist left and the Islamic right, including an extensive purge in Sept. 1981.

The impression was that S.'s charisma, his paternalistic leadership, his ebullient command of popular support were declining during his last years. He had also gradually abandoned the simple life style that had made him popular and adopted a more imperial style of grandeur. Ramified activities of his family were disliked. His wife, Jihan, whom he had married in 1951 after divorcing his first wife (Jihan's mother was of English origin), seemed personally popular — but her increasing involvement in active public life was not. When S. was murdered in Oct. 1981, during a parade on the anniversary of the October War of 1973, by Islamic extremists, there were few signs of genuine mourning. His memory as a leader and a statesman who had shaped Egypt's history seems to be dimmed and not very actively cultivated.

S. wrote a book on the Revolution of 1952, with autobiographical features (*Revolt on the Nile*, 1957), and an autobiography (*In Search of Identity*, 1977–78). There are several books, and numerous essays and magazine features, on his life.

S.A.D.R., "Saharan Arab Democratic Republic" See *Sahara.

al-Sadr, Mussa (1928–78?) Lebanese-Iranian Shi'i religious authority and political leader.

Born in Iran to a family reportedly of Lebanese origin, S. received both a traditional Islamic and a secular education, graduating from Tehran University in 1956. In 1959 he moved to Tyre, Lebanon, where he began mobilizing the Shi'i population with the aim of reducing the political influence of both the traditional leadership and the leftist parties. In 1967 he established, for the first time in the modern history of Syria-Lebanon, a Supreme Islamic-Shi'i Council. These activities won him wide support of the rank and file of Lebanon's Shi'is, and he was often referred to as *Imam. Politically, S. supported the integrity of the Lebanese state and its basic structure, but he demanded modifications to accommodate the growing needs of the Shi'i community and raise its status. He was pro-Syrian and anti-*PLO. In the early 1970s he founded and led a movement for the advancement and defense of the Shi'i community, originally conceived as mainly social and non-political and called "The Disinherited" (al-Mahrumin). In the mid-1970s this movement grew increasingly political and turned into the Shi'i al-*Amal organization, of which S. became the first and main leader. In Aug. 1978 S. disappeared while on a mission in Libya. The Libyans claim that he departed for Italy, but Lebanese Shi'is do not believe that and are convinced that S. was either detained (and is still imprisoned in Libya?) or killed by the Libyans. His disappearance has caused a grave crisis between Libya and Lebanon in general, and the Lebanese Shi'is in particular. The latter venerate S.'s memory as a martyr.

Sahara The northern parts of the huge S. desert are within the confines of several North-African AC — mainly Algeria, but also Libya to her east and Morocco and semi-A. Mauritania to her west. The desert of north-western Sudan and the western Desert of Egypt may also be seen as part, or extensions, of the S. Borders in the S. desert were defined only in the late 19th and in the 20th centuries, some of them not precisely (which was not very important at that time, as the territory concerned was all French-dominated). These imprecisions have resulted in some border disputes, such as that between Algeria and Morocco over the Tindouf area, important because of large iron deposits and mines; or that between *Libya and Chad with regard to the Aouzou Strip.

The western extremities of the S., on the Atlantic Ocean, were since the 19th century a Spanish possession known as Spanish S. (Sp. S.) or Western S. (WS). Formally, a Spanish province called Sp. S. was created in 1958, out of the Spanish colonies of Saguia al-Hamra and Rio del Oro, with al-Ayun as its capital and had an area of c. 260,000 sq.km. (100,000 sq.mi.). There were no precise data on the population of Sp. S. which is of mixed, Moorish-*Berber and African stock with some A. elements. The sedentary population was assumed to be c. 25,000 at most, and the number of nomads was usually estimated at 30–40,000, while some sources cited figures of 50–80,000; Saharan activists since the 1970s spoke of much higher figures. Since the late 1970s, in the course of the Moroccan-S. war (see below), most of these nomads were reported to have crossed the border into Algeria. WS's chief — or only — economic asset was large phosphate deposits developed by Spain in recent decades.

Morocco claimed the whole of Sp. S. as part of the Moroccan territories that had been a Spanish Protectorate and were handed over in the 1950s and 1960s. Spain rejected that claim and envisaged instead a gradual increase in local self-government within a Spanish commonwealth. In 1963 the territory first took part in elections to the Spanish Cortes (males only, three deputies, of whom two were tribal chiefs). In 1967 a local Assembly (*Jama'a*) was set up — 40 tribal chiefs, and 40 elected. Spain also continued investing in Sp. S. and developing the phosphate mines, including a 60-mi. conveyor belt to the coast and loading facilities, opened in 1972–73.

From the mid-1960s the UN General Assembly was discussing the problem of Sp. S. Faced with Morocco's claims vs. Spain's concepts and local demands for independence, it recommended a referendum. Spain accepted that recommendation in principle and reiterated that acceptance several times but took no action to prepare such a referendum. Morocco opposed a referendum, insisting that WS was part of her territory. Algeria, a powerful and activist neighbor, rejected Morocco's claims and favored independence; Mauritania, involved in her own conflict with Morocco, wavered. Several Moroccan-Algerian-Mauritanian summit meetings failed to reach an agreement. Local organizations, most of them advocating independence, grew in the 1970s, and around 1973–75 the "Popular Organization for the Liberation of Saguia al-Hamra and Rio del Oro" (POLISARIO) emerged as the leading one.

For Morocco's "Green March" of Oct. 1975, Spain's handing-over of Sp. S. to Morocco and Mauritania (February 1976), POLISARIO's Algerian-backed resistance and the proclamation of the "S. Arab Democratic Republic" (SADR), Mauritania's renunciation of her part (Aug. 1979), Morocco's annexation of all the former Spanish S., and the continuing war against POLISARIO-SADR — see *Morocco. Algeria-based SADR was recognized, gradually, by several countries — mainly of the leftist-revolutionary African group (not the Soviet Bloc); by 1979, some 20–23 countries had done so, 16 of which were African, by the mid-1980s some 65, among them the four radical ASt Algeria, Libya, Syria and South Yemen, and since 1984 also Mauritania. The UN refused to accept as final Morocco's annexation and continued calling for a referendum, as did the Organization for African Unity, OAU. For the resulting Morocco-OAU crisis see *Morocco. After a protracted wrangle over the admission of SADR to the OAU, half measures and postponements, SADR was officially admitted and seated at the 20th Summit, Nov. 1984.

al-Sa'id, Nuri (1888–1958) Iraqi officer and politician, the most prominent of a group of pro-*Hashemi and pro-British Iraqi leaders, many times Prime Minister. Born in Baghdad to a Muslim-Sunni family of mixed A.-Kurdish descent, NS graduated from the Istanbul Military Academy and became an officer in the Ottoman army. Active, but not prominent, in pre-World War I A. nationalist associations, NS deserted from the Ottoman army during World War I, joined Sharif *Hussein's *Arab revolt in 1916 and became Chief-of-Staff in Amir *Feisal's army (commanded by his brother-in-law, Ja'far al-'Askari). He remained attached to Feisal after the war and became the first Chief-of-Staff of the Iraqi army in 1921. He was Minister of Defense 1922–24 and 1926–28. In 1930 he became Prime Minister for the first time, founding a party — al-'Ahd, "The Covenant" — to support him in Parliament. He negotiated the treaty of 1930 with Britain which terminated the *Mandate. NS was Prime Minister 1930–32, 1939–40, 1941–44, 1946–47, 1949, 1950–52, 1954–57, 1958, heading 14 governments, and often held other or additional ministerial offices, particularly as Foreign or Defense Minister. After the defeat of the Rashid *'Ali movement in 1941, NS was Iraq's leading statesman, whether in or out of office, and the chief representative of the Hashemite establishment. In Feb. 1958 he became Prime Minister of the short-lived *Arab Federation of Iraq and Jordan. NS was murdered in Baghdad during the *coup* of July 1958.

NS believed in the need for a firm alliance with Britain and loyally supported the Hashemite dynasty — though in the late 1930s he was allied for some time with the anti-British and anti-Hashemite junta of officers ruling Iraq behind the scene, and apparently tried to reinsure with Germany in 1940. He feared and hated communism and distrusted the USSR. In A. affairs he was keenly conscious of Iraq's age-old rivalry with Egypt. He favored a Federation of the *Fertile Crescent under Iraqi leadership (with a measure of autonomy for the Jews of Palestine and the Christians of Lebanon); late in 1942 he submitted a scheme along these line to Britain and the ASt — but it met with strong A. opposition, particularly Egyptian, and he did not pursue it. In domestic affairs NS promoted administrative efficiency and economic planning. He was a conservative, even an autocrat, and did not believe that parliamentary democracy was a suitable form of government for Iraq. In his heyday Iraq was in effect a police state — though his régime seems mild and rational in the light of more recent developments. During his last years NS was not in tune with the social and political forces sweeping the A. world and seemed to have little understanding of them.

al-Sa'iqa (Arabic: Lightning, Thunderstorm). Palestinian-A. guerrilla (*Feda'iyyin*) organization established in 1968 in Syria by the ruling *Ba'th party and the Syrian army. It is under the command of the Syrian army and its intelligence service and includes Syrian soldiers. See *Palestine-A. Guerrilla Organizations.

Saleh, 'Ali 'Abdullah (b. c. 1942) Yemeni officer and politician, President of Yemen since 1978. A son of the Hashed tribes, S. was a professional army officer who came into prominence in 1977–78. A battalion commander with the rank of major, and from 1977 military commander of the Taʿizz region, he helped A.H. Ghashmi, the chairman of the Military Council after the assassination of President Ibrahim *Hamdi in Oct. 1977 and President from Apr. 1978, to consolidate his power and suppress a rebellion of rival officers in Apr. 1978. When Ghashmi was assassinated in June 1978, S. became a member of the Presidential Council as well as Chief-of-Staff and Deputy Commander-in-Chief; he was also promoted to the rank of Lt.-Colonel. A month later he was made President. He purged the officers' corps of opposing and rebellious elements, escaped several assassination attempts, and succeeded in consolidating his power and giving Yemen, torn for years by factional rivalries and internecine violence, a period of comparative stability. He was re-elected in May 1983.

At first considered dependent on and subservient to Saʿudi Arabia, and faced in Feb. 1979 by a South Yemeni invasion and warlike operations, S. succeeded in restoring a delicate balance between Saʿudi Arabia (on whose financial aid Yemen remained dependent) and South Yemen (with whom he achieved a reconciliation). He also followed a pronouncedly neutralist policy and kept Yemen balanced between the USA, who supported and aided Yemen against South Yemen, and the USSR (who had in the past supplied most of Yemen's military equipment). He visited Moscow in Oct. 1981 and concluded a Treaty of Friendship and Co-operation with the USSR in Oct. 1984. In inter-A. affairs he also followed a policy of low-profile neutrality. In domestic matters he endeavored to keep a balance beween the conservative tribal federations and leftist urban factions. In his first year or two he tried to reconcile the underground leftist "National Democratic Front" and even invited it to join the government, but no final agreement was reached, and S. soon felt secure enough to drop the offer and continue on a more median course. The stability he achieved is unprecedented since the overthrow of the monarchy in 1962.

al-Sallal, ʿAbdullah (b. 1917? c. 1920?) Yemeni officer and politician. Leader of the revolution of 1962, President of the Yemen Republic 1962–67. Son of a lower-class *Zeidi family, S. was sent in the 1930s to the Baghdad Military Academy, from which he graduated in 1938. Upon his return he was suspected of anti-régime activities and detained for some time, but was then allowed to resume his army career. He took part in the abortive al-Wazir *coup* of 1948 and was sentenced to death; the sentence was commuted to seven years imprisonment and he was released after a few years. In 1955 he was appointed Governor of Hudeida. S. was close to Prince al-*Badr, who made him commander of his guard in the mid-1950s, and of the newly established military academy in 1959. When al-Badr became Imam-King in Sept. 1962, S., then a Major, became commander of the Royal Guard and according to some reports commander-in-chief of the army. He was the main leader of the revolution of Sept. 1962 that toppled the monarchy, became President of the Republic and led the Republican camp in the civil war that erupted. He was concurrently also Prime Minister 1962–63 and 1966–67.

S. was strongly pro-Egyptian and depended on Egyptian support, not only in the conduct of the civil war, in which an Egyptian expeditionary army was the main force on the Republican side, but also in the frequent factional struggles within the Republican camp and army. He advocated a union of Yemen with Egypt and twice concluded agreements for Yemen to join Egypt-led unions or federations — in Mar. 1958 (the *UAR) and in July 1964 (a planned, abortive Egypt-Iraq union) — agreements that were not implemented. S. was immersed in factional controversies and had little influence on the officers' corps, and even less on the tribes, and he was, of course, anathema to the Royalist camp. When the Egyptians felt compelled to seek a resettlement of the Yemen conflict, they removed him in Apr. 1965 and took him to Egypt, into forced residence (while the Republic was run by a Presidential Council that formally included S. but was in fact composed of his adversaries). In Sept. 1966 S. was allowed to return to Yemen and resume power; he took the Premiership in addition to the Presidency. However, when Egypt withdrew her expeditionary force in 1967, after the *Six Day War, S. was overthrown in a bloodless *coup* in Nov. 1967. He went into exile to Baghdad and lost all influence on Yemeni affairs. In 1973 there were reports of his return, but they were false, based on plans and intentions rather than facts. Late in 1981, apparently no longer considered a dangerous rival, he was allowed to return to Yemen and retire.

San Remo Conference Convened in Apr. 1920 by the principal allied powers victorious in World War I (Britain, France, Italy, Japan, Greece and Belgium) to decide on the Turkish peace treaty and certain other matters, the SRC, *inter alia*, assigned the *Mandates which the nascent *League of Nations had decided in 1919 to impose on ME territories taken from Turkey. It gave to France the Mandate for Syria and Lebanon, to Britain those for Mesopotamia (Iraq) and Palestine, the latter to be administered in accordance with the *Balfour Declaration. The League of Nations formally confirmed these Mandates in 1922. At SR, incidentally to the SRC, Britain and France concluded an accord on French participation in the future exploitation of oil in Iraq. A. spokesmen denounced the decisions of the SRC as contrary to the independence promised to the A.'s by the allies powers during the war.

Sanussis, Sanussiyya Islamic religious order founded in Mecca in 1837 by Muhammad ibn 'Ali al-S., of Algerian origin. A Sunni order of the Maleki *madhhab* or school dominant in North Africa, it aimed at purging Islam of unorthodox accretions and returning to the original teachings of the Prophet and the Qur'an. Though orthodox-fundamentalist, the founder and the S. were influenced by certain aspects of Islamic mysticism — but they kept their rituals simple and austere and discouraged ceremonies of ecstasy, dancing and singing, as practised by the *Dervish orders.

In 1841 the founder went to Egypt and from there to Benghazi and Tripoli to teach and spread his doctrine. He was more successful among the Bedouin, especially those of *Cyrenaica, than among the peasants and in the towns, and set up a network of lodges (sing: *zawiya*) i.e. centers of residence, prayer and teaching, for the S. Brothers (*Ikhwan*). The Mother Lodge, *al-Zawiya al-Baida*, on the central Cyrenaican plateau, was founded in 1843; the center shifted to the Jaghbub oasis when the founder settled there in 1856, and later, about 1895, to Kufra. The founder died in 1859 and was succeeded by his son, al-Sayyid al-Mahdi al-S., under whose leadership the S. spread also in Sudan and the Sahara. After his death, in 1902, the order was headed by al-Sayyid Ahmad al-Sharif al-S., the nephew of the founder.

Early in the 20th century the S., dominating the Cyrenaica countryside, grew into a political force, too. When Italy invaded and occupied Libya in 1911, the S. mounted strong resistance which continued as a guerrilla war and merged from 1914 into World War I, as Turkey saw the S. as allies and aided them. However, a rival S. leader, al-Sayyid Muhammad Idris al-*S., the founder's grandson and the second leader's son, decided to support the British and their allies (who included Italy), and raised a S. force in Egypt to fight on their side. In 1916 he was recognized by Britain as the "Grand S.", the chief of the S. order. Idris overcame the rival leadership, and Ahmad al-Sharif escaped to Turkey, never to return.

For the S. between the wars and during World War II, see *Libya and Idris al-*S. Idris became King of independent Libya in 1951. Even with Idris as King, Libya was not a S. country, the S. were only one group of the population, and not the largest one; but they were the mainstay of the régime, particularly in Cyrenaica. In the years of independence, however, their strength and influence declined — perhaps inevitably, with the increasing modernization of Libya and the development of her oil economy. This decline has accelerated and intensified since the revolution of 1969 and the disappearance of the King and the S. establishment that had been prominent in government and the services. *Qadhdhafi and his régime have not taken institutional steps formally to ban the S. order, but the centralist character of the régime and its strict, all-embracing control seem to have eliminated the public-political influence of the S.

al-Sanussi, al-Sayyid Muhammad Idris (1890–1983) Head of the *S. order in Libya-Cyrenaica, King of Libya 1951–69. Born at Jaghbub, Cyrenaica, the grandson of the founder of the S. order, Idris established contacts with the British in Egypt in 1914 and stayed in Egypt during World War I, and while the S.'s' guerrilla war against the Italians became part of Ottoman Turkey's war, he recruited in Egypt a S. force on the side of Britain and her allies. In 1916 Britain recognized him as the "Grand S.", the leader of the order — in place of his uncle al-Sayyid Ahmad Sharif al-S. who fought on the other side. After the victory of the allies, Italy recognized him, in the Rajma Agreement of 1920, as Amir of *Cyrenaica heading a self-governing régime in the interior centered on the S. oases of Jaghbub and Kufra. In 1922 S. accepted the additional title of Amir of *Tripolitania offered to him by the nationalists of that region — against Italy's wish. His agreement with the Italians was anyway half-hearted and short-lived. While the S.'s resumed their rebellion and guerrilla war, he left in 1922 for exile in Cairo, and remained there for 20 years.

When Italy entered World War II, S. called upon all Libyans to co-operate with the Allies in a joint effort to drive out the Italians and initiated the recruitment of a S. force which took part in the North African campaign. In return the British recognized his claim to head an independent or autonomous Cyrenaica. After the allied victory, and while discussions on the future of Libya were still going on, he proclaimed himself in 1949 Amir of Cyrenaica — with British support, and under a provisional British military government. In 1951 the crown of a united Libya was offered to him and on 7 Oct. 1951 the National Assembly proclaimed him King of Libya. He ascended the throne on 24 Dec. 1951 when Libya became independent.

His reign was ultra-conservative and while he continued reying on his S.'s in Cyrenaica, there was frequent friction between him and the nationalists in Tripolitania. His position was weakened in 1963 by the abolition of the federal structure of Libya and the imposition of a unitarian régime dominated by Tripoli. The stability of his reign seemed to depend on his person, since he had no children. King I. al-S. was deposed by a military *coup* on 1 Sept. 1969; he was abroad at the time and did not fight for his throne. He spent the rest of his days in exile in Greece and Egypt.

Sarkis, Elias (1922? 1924?–85)   Lebanese jurist, economist and politician. Governor of the Central Bank 1967–76, President of Lebanon 1976–82. A Maronite Christian of a lower middle class non-prominent family, S. was educated at French-Catholic institutions in Beirut and graduated in law at the Jesuit St. Joseph University. From 1953 he worked as a judge at the Audit Office (cour des comptes). Involved in an investigation of irregularities in the Defense Ministry, he came to the attention of President Fu'ad *Shihab and was transferred to the President's Office. He played an important part in turning that office into a powerful institution, also in collaboration with the secret services built up by President Shihab, and in 1962 became its director-general. In 1967 he was named Governor of the Central Bank which he headed for nine years, during a time of increasing economic difficulties. In 1970 he was a candidate for the Presidency, supported by the "Shihabist" camp; he lost to Suleiman *Franjiyeh by one vote. In 1976, Syria, then in *de facto* occupation of most of Lebanon, strongly supported his renewed candidature and even applied much pressure, and S. was duly elected President. During the years of his Presidency the civil war, that had officially ended in Oct. 1976, resumed and escalated. The rival armed "militias" and/or the Syrian army dominated most of the country, the regular army disintegrated and the government was unable to function properly and virtually lost control. The last months of his term saw the Israeli invasion of June 1982. S., while personally respected, was therefore not an effective President. While doing his best to reconcile the warring factions and work out a peace settlement, he refrained from expressing forceful opinions or taking clear-cut positions in the constant struggle of the factions, coalitions and militias. Out of frustration, he was on the verge of resigning several times (e.g. in July 1978). When his term expired in Sept. 1982, he retired and in the three remaining years of his life took no further part in public affairs.

Sa'ud, House of (Arabic: *Aal*), **Dynasty**   The ruling dynasty in the largest country of the Arabian peninsula, Sa'udi Arabia, giving the country its name. The family, of the 'Anaiza tribe, first ruled the Dar'iyya area of *Najd. Muhammad Ibn Sa'ud, who ruled Dar'iyya 1726–65, adopted the *Wahhabi doctrine and set up a Wahhabi state in 1745, and as he expanded his area of control he spread the new faith over large parts of the peninsula. His son 'Abd-ul-'Aziz (ruled 1766–1803) and his grandson Sa'ud (ruled 1803–14) extended their power as far as the Syrian and Iraqi borders, raided the border areas and also Mecca and Medina. Under 'Abdullah Ibn Sa'ud (ruled 1814–18), the Sa'udis were defeated by Muhammad 'Ali of Egypt, on behalf of the Ottoman Sultan, and 'Abdullah was executed in Istanbul. During the years 1819–37 the Sa'udis reconsolidated their rule. From 1837 to about 1843 Egyptian-Ottoman units again took control, and from 1843 the HoS reasserted itself. From about

1865, however, it declined and had only limited control over the Darʻiyya-Riyadh area, the Ottomans and the rival House of *Rashid of the Shammar tribe preventing an extension of its power.

In the 1880s the Rashid clan gained the upper hand and in 1890–91 it defeated ʻAbd-ul-Rahman Aal S. and conquered the Darʻiyya-Riyadh area. Survivors of the HoS found refuge in Kuwait, among them young ʻAbd-ul-ʻAziz ibn ʻAbd-ul-Rahman, *"Ibn Saʻud" (1880–1953, ruled 1902–53). The latter resumed the fight and regained control of Riyadh in 1902. He soon began expanding his realm. In 1913 he took the al-Hassa region on the Persian Gulf and thus came into contact with the sphere of British interests and domination and in 1915 he made a pact with Britain. In the course of his expansion, he beat the Rashidis, who surrendered in 1921, and clashed with *Hussein, the *Hashemite Sharif of Mecca and King of *Hijaz; in 1924 he conquered Hijaz and deposed the Hashemites. Henceforth the HoS ruled most of the Arabian peninsula (except the southern, south-eastern and some of the eastern parts).

Ibn Saʻud, who named his kingdom "Saʻudi Arabia" in 1932, died in 1953 and was succeeded by his eldest son Saʻud ibn ʻAbd-ul-ʻAziz (1902–69). Saʻud's reign was clouded by a deep rift with his half-brother *Feisal ibn ʻAbd-ul-ʻAziz (1904–75); in 1958 he was forced to transfer wide authority to Feisal and in 1964 he was deposed and succeeded by Feisal. He went into exile and died in 1969. Feisal ruled until 1975, when he was assassinated. He was succeeded by his half-brother *Khaled ibn ʻAbd-ul-ʻAziz (1912–82). Upon Khaled's death, in 1982, his half-brother *Fahd ibn ʻAbd-ul-ʻAziz (b. 1921) became King, with another half-brother, *ʻAbdullah ibn ʻAbd-ul-ʻAziz (b. 1923), as Crown Prince. These four successions consolidated the principle laid down by Ibn Saʻud: the Kingship was to pass on among his sons, by and large according to seniority.

Other key figures among Ibn Saʻud's surviving sons (he had over 40) are Prince Sultan (b. 1924), Defense Minister since 1962 and one of the Deputy Prime Ministers since 1982, and Prince Naʼif (b. 1934), Minister of Interior since 1975 — both full brothers of King Fahd, members of a powerful group of brothers called, after their mother, the Sudairis. Other surviving sons of Ibn Saʻud serve as Ministers, provincial governors etc. and some are active in business. Many members of the third generation, Ibn Saʻud's grandsons, are also active, and some are prominent, in business and/or government and army positions. Of King Feisal's sons, for instance, one, ʻAbdullah (b. 1921), was Minister of Interior 1953–60; one, Saʻud (b. 1941), has been Foreign Minister since 1975; one, Turki (b. 1945) is Director of Foreign Intelligence.

Things are no-doubt slowly changing in Saʻudi Arabia. New strata of educated professionals, "technocrats" and businessmen are growing and political influence is being spread more widely. None of Ibn Saʻud's sons and grandsons wield the unquestioned authority the old man possessed in his later years. Yet, the HoS still effectively rules its country, reserving to itself all positions of power and decision.

Saʻud Ibn ʻAbd-ul-ʻAziz (1902–69) King of Saʻudi Arabia 1953–64. Eldest son of King ʻAbd-ul-ʻAziz ibn ʻAbd-ul-Rahman *"Ibn Saʻud" (after the death of his brother Turki in 1919). With the consolidation of the Saʻudi Kingdom, his father named him Crown Prince in 1932 (with the understanding that his half-brother *Feisal would be second in line) and Viceroy of *Najd. When Ibn Saʻud died in 1953, S. mounted the throne and also assumed the Premiership, despite reports of sharpening rivalry between him and Feisal. But differences escalated when the country underwent a severe financial crisis, despite its increasing oil revenues, as a result of extravagance and unbridled spending. At the same time, relations with Egypt deteriorated, and in Mar. 1958 President *Nasser publicly accused S. of plotting his assassination. S.'s poor health also made him go abroad frequently. In 1958 he was compelled to hand over actual executive power to Feisal. However, he continued struggling. He made a partial come-back and took the Premiership in 1960, but in 1962 he had to restore it to Feisal. In 1964 he demanded that Feisal give up his powers. In the crisis that ensued, Feisal gained the upper hand. On 2 Nov. 1964, the Council of *'Ulama'* (Muslim Sages) deposed S. and crowned Feisal in his place. S. went into exile, at first in Europe; in 1966 he settled in Egypt and allowed Nasser to use him in his conflict with Feisal. When Nasser toned down his inter-A. activities after 1967 and strove for a reconciliation with Feisal, S., was pushed into the background and ceased public and political activities. He died in exile in 1969

Sa'udi Arabia (also, informally, **Sa'udia**) (*al-Mamlaka al-'Arabiyya al-Sa'udiyya*) Kingdom in the Arabian peninsula. Area: c. 830,000 sq.mi. (2.15 million sq.km.). Capital: al-Riyadh. SA borders on Jordan, Iraq, the Persian Gulf principalities (Kuwait, Bahrain, Qatar, the UAE, 'Oman), Yemen and South Yemen. The country has two coasts: in the east the Persian Gulf, in the west the Gulf of 'Aqaba and the Red Sea. The borders with Kuwait were defined in the 'Uqair agreement of 1922, those with Iraq and Jordan in the Hadda and Bahra agreements of 1925 — all arranged with British help (as were several provisional accords preceding them). On the Kuwaiti and Iraqi borders there were two "Neutral Zones" where no agreement could be reached, but in 1969 and 1981 respectively it was agreed to abolish and divide these zones. The border with Yemen was settled in 1934, after a war, but some disagreements remain. That with South Yemen is disputed in several places. On the borders with the Persian Gulf principalities there are also some disagreements, but these are dormant and have been deliberately played down in recent years. SA is divided into the provinces of *Najd, *Hijaz, al-Hassa, the northern border, and *'Asir.

Concerning the population, there were until the 1960s widely different estimates. A census

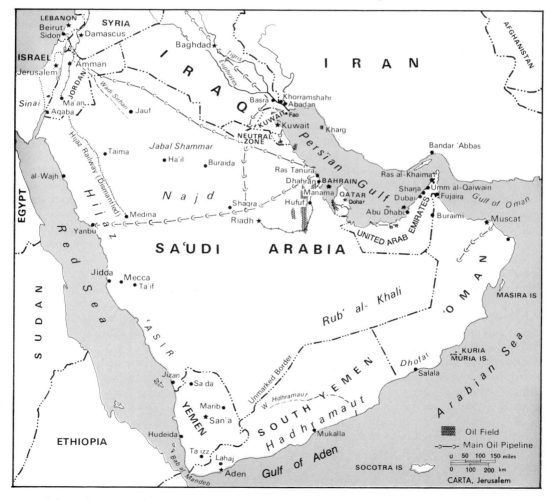

Map of the Arabian Peninsula

taken in 1964 was considered defective and was never published. A census of 1974 counted 7.013 million. In the mid-1980s, the population is estimated at c. 10 million (including 2–2.5 million foreign workers). The indigenous population is Arabic speaking. The overwhelming majority are Sunni Muslims belonging to the *Wahhabi trend of the Hanbali school. A few hundred thousand *Shi'ite Muslims live in the al-Hassa region and a small Yemenite *Zeidi minority in the 'Asir region. The majority of the population is of tribal background, and a decreasing part are still nomadic or semi-nomadic (estimated until the 1960s at 25–35 per cent, but considered in the mid-1980s to be less than 20 per cent). The urban population is estimated at c. 45 per cent.

In the past, the economy was one of desert nomads engaged in camel raising (and raiding), with a few agricultural settlements in oases, and few towns with some commerce on the coasts and in the nearby hinterland; fishing and shipping developed more on the Persian Gulf than on the Red Sea shore. For many years, a major source of income was the annual Muslim pilgrimage (*Hajj*) to the holy cities of Mecca and Medina (estimates as to the number of pilgrims from abroad in the 1920s and 1930s varied from 50,000 to over 200,000, in the 1960s it reached 200–375,000, and since the 1970s it is around 1 million. Beginning with the 1940s, oil production has become the major source of national and individual income and of development resources.

SA, under that name, came into being in 1932. In the earlier 20th century the area now named SA was divided. In *Najd, the central and northern part of the peninsula, the House of *Sa'ud, that had re-established its rule of the central region, around al-Riyadh, in 1901–02, was gradually expanding its domination (defeating the rival House of *Rashid); in 1913 it had also added to its domain the al-Hassa region on the coast of the *Persian Gulf. The Sa'udi ruler, 'Abd-ul-'Aziz ibn 'Abd-ul-Rahman *"Ibn Sa'ud", was from 1915 allied with Great Britain, but stayed neutral in World War I. Since 1921 he bore the title "Sultan of Najd and her Dependencies". The western part of what later became SA, *Hijaz, was under Turkish-Ottoman sovereignty, though Turkey exercized actual control mainly in the towns and along the pilgrims' route to Mecca and Medina. In 1916, *Hussein Ibn 'Ali, the *Hashemite Sharif of Mecca, rebelled with British aid and established himself as King of Hijaz. Clashes between Ibn Sa'ud and Hussein escalated into war in 1924 and Ibn Sa'ud conquered Hijaz and deposed the Hashemites in 1925; in Jan. 1926 he proclaimed himself King of Hijaz, too.

From 1926, Ibn Sa'ud consolidated his rule throughout most of the peninsula and integrated Hijaz, which was more developed than Najd and did not easily accept the Sa'udis' Wahhabis rules and customs. He appointed his son *Sa'ud, the Crown Prince, Governor of Najd and his son *Feisal Governor of Hijaz. He set up a consultative council (*Majlis al-Shura*) of sheikhs and notables in Hijaz. Britain recognized his independence in the Treaty of *Jidda of 1927. In 1929–30, he put down a rebellion of tribal chieftains and the *Ikhwan* ("Brethren" — the semi-settled military nuclei of the Wahhabis), who demanded the continuation of conquests beyond the northern borders.

Once stability had been achieved, Ibn Sa'ud proclaimed the union of the two parts of his kingdom, on 18 Sept. 1932, as the "Kingdom of SA". In his continuing efforts to stabilize the country, he endeavored to settle the tribes, mainly around the oases; but the establishment of *Ikhwan* settlements ceased after the suppression of their revolt. He allotted lands to sheikhs and wealthy merchants to encourage settlement, and in 1947 exempted them from paying rent on these lands. His attitude to the tribes was on the "carrot and the stick" pattern. He subsidized the sheikhs with large grants of money, took their women relatives for his and his sons' wives; but he harshly punished tribes which did not keep order, carried out traditional raids for plunder (*ghazzu*), or turned against him.

The conquest of Hijaz and the Holy Cities made SA a focus for all Islam. In 1926, Ibn Sa'ud convened an all-Islamic congress in Mecca. But he rejected a proposal by Indian Muslims to turn Hijaz into an all-Islamic protectorate and strained relations with Egypt by barring the traditional Egyptian army escort for the Egyptian *Hajj* (pilgrimage) caravan, as there was no longer any need for such protection. Ibn Sa'ud concluded a series of friendship and non-aggression treaties with AC: Transjordan 1933, Bahrain

1936, Iraq 1936, Egypt 1936 (settling also the 1926 dispute over the *Hajj* escort). But there was increasing tension between SA and Yemen. In the 1920s, SA gradually extended her protection over the *'Asir region, taking advantage of internal disputes in the ruling *Idrissi dynasty. In 1933, a revolt of Hassan al-Idrissi was put down and Ibn Sa'ud formally annexed Asir to his kingdom. Idrissi fled to Yemen where he received asylum as well as aid in organizing raids across her border; Yemen also disputed the Sa'udi annexation of 'Asir. In Mar. 1934, Ibn Sa'ud declared war on Yemen and within a few weeks conquered large portions of the country, including the principal port of Hudeida. On 23 June 1934, he signed a peace treaty agreeing to give up the occupied areas, evacuate Yemen and revert to the *status quo*. In 1937 he signed a friendship and non-aggression pact with Yemen.

In 1933, Ibn Sa'ud granted the first oil exploration rights to American interests — against stiff British competition: the Standard Oil Company of California, which was joined by the Texas Oil Company in 1934. The two companies jointly formed the "Arabian American Oil Company" (Aramco); in 1948 two more giant companies joined — Standard of New Jersey, and Sacony Vacuum. Oil was found in the Dhahran, Dammam, and Abqaiq areas. Commercial production began in 1938, but it increased significantly only after World War II, when it became the mainstay of the economy (see *oil).

In World War II Ibn Sa'ud was neutral, though leaning towards the Allies. Even when the Axis powers appeared victorious, he refused to support the anti-British revolt of Rashid 'Ali al-*Kilani in Iraq; he pointedly sent his son Mansur to Cairo on the eve of the battle of al-'Alamein, and rejected German and Japanese requests for oil concessions. On account of the sharp decline in the number of pilgrims since the late 1930s, he requested — and received — financial aid from the Allies, mostly the USA (by Sept. 1946 — $17.5m. in grants and loans). On 1 Mar. 1945, SA joined the Allies, without formally declaring war and while maintaining the neutrality of the Holy Places; this enabled her to join the UN as a charter member.

During this period, relations between SA and the USA grew closer. A US diplomatic representation in SA was established in 1940. Under a 1943 agreement the Americans in 1944–46 built a large air base in *Dhahran (with rights to use it for three years); at the same time, a US military mission began training the Sa'udi Army. The US government also decided to lay an oil pipeline from Dhahran to the Mediterranean, in Lebanon (the Trans-Arabian Pipeline, "TAPLine" — in fact later built by the oil company, completed in 1950). In Feb. 1945, Ibn Sa'ud met President Roosevelt on board an American warship. At the meeting he stressed his anti-Zionist stand and Roosevelt appeared to be impressed, though SA and the USA continued to differ on the Palestine issue. Ibn Sa'ud opposed President *Truman's proposal to permit the immigration to Palestine of 100,000 Jewish survivors of the Holocaust (1946) and resented US support for the partition of Palestine (1947), and US aid to Israel. Yet, he did not carry out threats of retaliation against American interests, such as stopping the flow of oil. In 1949, the US representation in Jidda was raised to ambassadorial level. Under a defense treaty of 1951, US rights at the Dhahran base were extended for five more years (extended again in 1956 until 1962). The supply of American arms, training and military aid continued.

In inter-A. relations growing more active in those years, SA took a moderately active part. In 1936 Ibn Sa'ud had been among the A. rulers calling the Palestine A.'s to suspend their rebellion and promising to struggle for their cause. In 1938–39, and again in 1946–47, SA was one of the ASt invited by Britain to participate in the abortive London Conferences on the fate of Palestine. In 1945, SA was among the founders of the *Arab League.

Ibn Sa'ud was absolute ruler of SA, restricted only by Islamic law and custom. Muslim law (the *Shari'a) was state law, administered by religious courts. The Consultative Council of Hijaz became progressively weaker and eventually was replaced by the King's council, which had no real powers. There was no distinction between the national treasury and the private coffers of the king. This was changed only towards the end of Ibn Sa'ud's life. In 1951–52 the first national budget was published, and the first bank in SA opened shortly after. In Oct. 1953, Ibn Sa'ud set up a modern-style council of ministers, but kept his right of veto. Despite opposition of the clergy to westernizing innovations, Ibn Sa'ud began a series of development programs — made possible by increasing oil revenues. A railroad was laid between Dammam on the Persian Gulf and Riyadh (completed 1951); a network of roads and internal air communications was developed, the number of cars increased, and radio stations were established, first by Aramco and then by the state. Ibn Sa'ud also somewhat curbed Wahhabi fanaticism. The ban on smoking, for example, was never put into effect in Hijaz and was soon abolished throughout the country, and that on music ended with the introduction of radio broadcasts.

'Abd-ul-'Aziz b. 'Abd-ul-Rahman Ibn Sa'ud died on 11 Nov. 1953. Though many expected a struggle among his sons for the succession, Crown Prince Sa'ud smoothly mounted the throne, taking also the Premiership. Sa'ud attempted to make his eldest son Fahd crown prince, but faced with his brothers' opposition he had to appoint his half-brother Feisal instead. Under Sa'ud the tempo of change increased. Income from oil passed the $300m. mark in the mid-1950s. New social strata — college graduates, army officers, civil servants and clerks, technicians and workers — demanded their share of the socio-political cake. The number of foreign technicians and experts increased. Modern schools, with mostly foreign teachers — Palestinians, Egyptians, Lebanese and Syrians — caused much ferment, and in 1955 Sa'ud expelled many of them. The royal family itself was the source of much waste and corruption. Sa'ud built for himself a marble palace in Riyadh which cost $4m. merely to plan, and $140m. to complete. A special plane brought flowers every day to the palace from Asmara in Eritrea. About 350 princes and their relatives lived at royal expense, and they, too, built themselves magnificent palaces and lived a life of extravagance. The royal household alone swallowed 17% of the state revenues. Luxury began spreading also among a new class of entrepreneurs. The power of Wahhabism declined and a way of life incompatible with its doctrine spread widely. In spite of the large oil earnings, the deficit in 1957 was $500m., state debts — $400 m., and the value of the rial plummeted.

Sa'ud was also experiencing difficulties in foreign affairs. Immediately after his ascent to the throne, a serious dispute with Britain (as the power protecting *'Oman) erupted over *Buraimi. Anglo-Sa'udi relations deteriorated until they were cut off completely in 1956 because of Britain's *Suez War. SA's rulers had always taken an anti-*Hashemite stand in the Arab League and opposed, together with Egypt and Syria, all plans to extend the influence of the rulers of Iraq and Jordan. SA was one of the principal opponents of the Western-sponsored *Baghdad Pact, worked against Iraqi influence in Syria and, together with Egypt, attempted to alienate Jordan from the West. However, an alliance with a radical-revolutionary *Nasserist Egypt, with her aspirations to hegemony in the A. world, could not last long. In 1957–58, relations worsened to an extent that Nasser accused Sa'ud in Mar. 1958, of organizing an attempt on his life.

This charge added to the unrest in SA resulting from the financial crisis and the escalating quarrel between Sa'ud and his brother Feisal, the Crown Prince and Deputy Prime Minister. On 3 Mar. 1958, Sa'ud was forced to transfer to Feisal all executive authority. Feisal placated Nasser and introduced a number of reforms. He changed the composition of the government and brought four ministries, including the Treasury, under his direct supervision. He cut royal household expenses from 17% to 5% of the state budget. The financial situation recovered, and in 1960 there was a surplus balance of $185m. The reforms aroused opposition, mainly among the princes; some of them objected to the curtailment of their purses, while others, led by Prince Talal, turned radical and demanded more drastic reforms and savings. Aided by these princes, Sa'ud compelled Feisal to resign in Dec. 1960, and resumed full authority. He promised Talal's group reforms and changes and even appointed him Minister of Finance; but he did not keep his promises and in 1961 dismissed Talal who later fled to Beirut. Because of failing health, however, Sa'ud had to go for medical treatment to America in Nov. 1961, and authority reverted to Feisal. In Mar. 1962, Sa'ud regained the upper hand, but in the summer he was compelled to go abroad again for medical treatment. This struggle between the two brothers continued until 1964. In the meantime, Feisal succeeded in removing Sa'ud's supporters from key positions, and in Mar. 1964 Feisal refused to hand over his power to Saʻud. Finally the Council of *'Ulama'* deposed Saʻud on 2 Nov. 1964 and proclaimed Feisal King. His half-brother *Khaled was made Crown Prince.

Feisal made use of the machinery of absolute power to weaken power foci that had raised their head under Saʻud — princes, the clergy, foreigners. He encouraged energetic though gradual development and progress — made possible by oil revenues, which passed $500m. in 1964, $1,000m. in 1969, $3,000m. in 1972, and $25,000m. in 1975. The network of roads was widened, ports were built and deepened and airports established. The construction of a large petrochemical oil-based industry was begun. Efforts were made to develop also other branches of the economy not directly linked to oil — agriculture, the construction of dams, and mining (e.g. gold mines in Hijaz). The school network was greatly expanded, and a second university, named after ʻAbd-ul-ʻAziz Ibn Saʻud, was opened in Riyadh in 1964 (the first had been founded in 1957). Feisal also continued efforts to settle the Bedouin. Telecommunications were developed and a third radio station was inaugurated in 1968 in Dammam. The army was strengthened, mainly the "National Guard" — tribal units, mostly of Najdi tribes particularly loyal to the king, in charge primarily of internal security, but the build-up of modernized branches of advanced military technology was also begun. Though all this modern development was quite contrary to the inclinations of the religious establishment, Feisal took care not to affect their status more than necessary. The *Shariʻa* remained the law of the land, including its code of punishments (such as the amputation of the hand of thieves, and public executions). A special "Religious Police" continued enforcing the performance of the obligatory prayer and other religious duties.

In his inter-A. policies, Feisal attempted to thwart Egyptian attempts to penetrate the Arabian peninsula. When civil war broke out in Yemen in Sept. 1962 and Egypt sent an expeditionary force to help the Republicans, Feisal gave moral and political support and increasing military and financial assistance to the Royalists, and this hostile confrontation with Egypt led not only to a war of proxy but several times to actual warlike clashes. In *ʻAden and *South Arabia, SA supported the underground "South Arabian League", which opposed the main-line Nasserist-inclined nationalist movement and Egyptian attempts to penetrate and control ʻAden. Her relations with leftist-revolutionary South Yemen, from 1967, were tense and not too friendly. As relations with Egypt deteriorated, Egypt was even accused of activating a subversive underground in SA, the "Arabian Peninsula People's Union", held responsible for several sabotage attacks in Saʻudi cities and along the pipeline (several of its members, mostly from the Yemeni minority in ʻAsir, confessed to having been trained and sent by the Egyptian army in Yemen; some of them were executed in early 1967).

The deterioration of relations with Egypt and her allies in the leftist-Nasserist Pan-A. camp induced Feisal in the early 1960s to cultivate the idea of an Islamic union — in effect an alliance of conservative Islamic states. But, while he drew closer to several conservative states, such as Jordan, Iran, Pakistan, nothing much came of the Islamic union idea at that stage (closer, institutionalized cooperation between the Islamic states was gradually implemented later, from 1969–70 — and SA was quite active in it; but by then it no longer had pronounced anti-Nasserist inter-A. implications and was in fact joined by *all* Islamic countries, not only the conservative ones).

Efforts to mend relations with Egypt and devise a solution to the Yemen conflict were stepped up from the mid-1960s, and as Egypt withdrew her expeditionary force from Yemen in 1967 and Nasser toned down his activist-interventionist A. policies, relations began to improve. Egypt's involvement in the *Six Day War of 1967 also induced SA, like most ASt, to disregard inter-A. disputes and rally to Egypt's side against Israel. On the eve of the War, SA's declarations against Israel were extremist, but her participation in the war was minimal. She sent a brigade to Jordan, but it did not arrive in time and took up positions in southern Jordan when the war was over; SA troops remained in Jordan for several years. At the Khartoum Summit of Sept. 1967, following the defeat, SA consented to grant an annual aid of £50m. to Egypt and Jordan. Open enmity between S. and Egypt ceased after the war, and broadcasts against SA from Radio Cairo stopped. Underground groups also ceased their activities, which had been anyway sporadic and very limited in scope — though some organizations claimed continued existence (in 1969 a plot was reportedly suppressed, but it was not clear whether it was connected with them or a factional or officers' intrigue).

In the later 1960s and early 1970s SA endeavored to mend her relations with the other countries of the Arabian peninsula (including the settlement of various small border disputes) and stabilize the peninsula. In 1965 the border with Jordan in the *'Aqaba area was agreed (with certain modifications, giving Jordan a somewhat longer shoreline). The same year it was agreed with Kuwait to divide the Neutral Zone (the agreement was finalized in 1969). A similar division of the Sa'udi-Iraqi Neutral Zone was agreed with Iraq in 1975 and finalized in 1981. An end to the Yemen civil war was negotiated with active Sa'udi involvement, and in July 1970 SA recognized the Yemen Republic and soon resumed aid to Yemen (and a growing influence on Yemeni affairs). Late in 1971 SA, which had for years half-heartedly supported an 'Omani-Ibadi Imam rebelling against the Sultan of 'Oman, arranged a reconciliation with the Sultan and established official relations, also renouncing her claims to the oasis of *Buraimi. In 1974 a border agreement was reached with the UAE, finalizing the renunciation of Sa'udi claims to Buraimi, and also providing for modifications of the border with the UAE's Abu Dhabi so that Sa'udi territory would extend to the coast of the Persian Gulf between Abu Dhabi and Qatar. King Feisal's campaign of reconciliation and stabilization extended also to Iran, even though certain conflicts of interest and a wide divergence of attitudes were not resolved; in 1975 the Shah paid a state visit to SA. The stabilization of Sa'udi relations in the peninsula was completed in 1976, when SA persuaded South Yemen to stop her support of the *Dhofar rebellion against 'Oman and of other subversive organizations in the Persian Gulf region, and established normal relations with South Yemen accompanied by a measure of Sa'udi aid; but this was after King Feisal's time.

King Feisal continued cultivating close relations with the USA, and was considered by the US as a moderate and an ally. This relationship was shaken by the leading hard-line rôle played by the Sa'udi Oil Minister A.Z. Yamani in the oil crisis of 1973 — the linking of supplies with political conditions, the boycott declared on the US and the West, the sudden replacement of agreed prices by the unilateral imposition of huge price increases. But even then, and more so later, the US continued seeing SA as the moderate and reasonable one among the oil-producing countries. She also endeavored to involve SA in the ME peace process after 1973, though on the A.-Israel issue SA was certainly not "moderate" — at least in her publicly declared policies. Secretary of State Kissinger paid several visits to SA from Nov. 1973 through 1974 and 1975, President Nixon did so in June 1974, and the Sa'udi princes and Ministers were frequent visitors in the US. A new agreement on economic and defense cooperation, including large-scale supplies of advanced American military equipment, was concluded in June 1974, and another one in Jan. 1975. In his efforts to build up modern armed forces with advanced military technology, Feisal also concluded contracts with France and Britain, sometimes based on Sa'udi commitments to supply oil. West Germany joined the competition for Sa'udi contracts later, but was more restrictive, refusing to supply offensive weapons, e.g. tanks that SA wanted.

King Feisal was assassinated in Mar. 1975 by his nephew Feisal ibn Musa'ed ibn 'Abd-ul-'Aziz (demented? part of a plot? revenge for a brother killed in 1965 in anti-television riots?); the assassin was executed in June. Feisal's half-brother *Khaled ascended the throne, while *Fahd became Crown Prince. Khaled ruled for seven years and in general continued Feisal's policies — perhaps with a somewhat more conservative tinge. During his rule oil production and oil revenues reached their peak; a recession in production and a fall of oil prices and of SA's revenue set in shortly before Khaled's death in 1982 and their impact was felt only after Khaled's death. In 1979, SA completed the total take-over of the foreign oil company; Aramco continued operating on behalf of the state and its national oil company, "Petromin".

King Khaled maintained close relations with the USA and the West. He received visits from President Carter in Jan. 1978 and French President Giscard in 1977, and concluded further large-scale contracts for advanced American arms in 1978 and 1981. However, these arms purchases in the US became more difficult as they aroused increasing opposition in the US Congress and public, fanned *i.a.* by pro-Israel circles who saw a danger to Israel in such sophisticated and advanced weapons going to an A. country that had not signalled much readiness for a peaceful A.-Israel settlement. These difficulties came to a head in 1981 around the sale of sophisticated American surveillance aircraft ("AWACS") which the US House of Representatives voted to ban with only a narrow majority in the Senate preventing a Congressional veto. SA had to face similar difficulties in further large sales of American weapons systems after Khaled's time. She therefore stepped up her arms purchases in Europe, particularly France. King Khaled paid state visits to France and Britain in June 1981, and received French President Mitterand three months later. Yet, relations with the US administration remained close. When the US planned in 1980 to set up a "Rapid Deployment Force" to defend the Persian Gulf and the ME in emergency, she envisaged SA as hosting some of the potential storage and deployment bases. This, however, SA was not prepared officially and openly to grant: she shied away from a formalized alliance and preferred whatever facilities she might grant to the US — and according to various reports and rumors she did indeed grant some — to remain secret and informal.

In the inter-A. crisis triggered in Nov. 1977 by Egyptian President *Sadat's visit to Jerusalem and moves towards peace with Israel, King Khaled did not, as some observers had expected and as he himself may have been inclined, display a firmly moderate or conciliatory policy but joined the hard-line confrontation states ostracizing Egypt — and by doing so, in coordination with Jordan's King Hussein, turned that hard line into the all-A. mainline. SA did not sever all links with Egypt; she did not, for instance, withdraw all her investments, trade and communications continued, as did tourism, and Egyptian technicians and workers stayed in SA and continued sending home their earnings — but official relations were broken and several joint ventures were suspended. SA endeavored to maintain a mainline, apparently moderate camp of ASt; a plan she presented, through Crown Prince Fahd, to the other ASt in 1981, was adopted in 1982, with modifications, as all-A. guidelines towards a ME settlement. In the last years of King Khaled's rule, the Iraq-Iran Gulf War caused SA much concern. She sympathized with Iraq, despite previous apprehensions of that country's revolutionary character and policies, and her relations with Iran, never cordial, were deeply troubled since *Khomeini's Islamic revolution. From 1981, several violent incidents occurred involving Iranian pilgrims who staged assertive radical-Islamic demonstrations; particularly bloody clashes occurred in 1987 leading to the death of more than 300 Iranian pilgrims.

Sa'udi Arabia came to sustain Iraq with substantial economic and financial aid, partly clandestine; she also allowed Iraq to ship oil through the Sa'udi pipeline to Yanbu' on the Red Sea, and also exported some Sa'udi oil on Iraq's account. In 1981 SA was among the founding states of the *"Gulf Cooperation Council" (GCC); in fact she was its leading and most powerful member and had a decisive influence on its policies. Officially, she followed — and made the GCC follow — a careful policy of neutrality between Iraq and Iran. But Iran was not convinced and repeatedly — and threateningly — accused SA, and the other A. Gulf states, of aiding Iraq in her war. SA took part in all-Islamic efforts (abortive so far) to mediate between Iraq and Iran and devise a formula to end their war. She also tried several times to mediate between Syria and Iraq; it was mainly Prince *'Abdullah, the King's half-brother, who was active in these efforts.

The days of King Khaled's rule also saw some internal unrest. The existence of a revolutionary underground organization had been repeatedly rumored before; so had unrest and plots among officers, and in 1969 a combined plot attempt had reportedly been suppressed. Intrigues among the princes had also led to some unrest — such as Talal's ventures, and the Sa'ud-Feisal struggle, in the 1950s. In Nov. 1979, however, there was a serious outbreak of violence when an underground group — apparently an organization of heretics, with only partly political and mainly religious-fanatic motivation — seized the Ka'ba Mosque in Mecca; they were bloodily suppressed. In Nov. 1979 and Feb. 1980 there was also some unrest among SA's Shi'is, on the Gulf coast. The ultra-conservative régime saw most of this unrest as a result not only of the rapid modernization but, mainly, of the influx of foreign workers (who constituted more than half of the work force in the 1980s and could therefore not be dispensed with.

King Khaled died in June 1982, and his half-brother Fahd ibn 'Abd-ul-'Aziz ascended the throne; another brother, 'Abdullah, was named Crown Prince and First Deputy Premier, with Defense Minister Prince Sultan assumed to be next in line. King Fahd in general continued his predecessors' policies and there were no major changes. The problems posed by the Gulf War, and the confrontation with Iran, became more acute and pressing in the mid-1980s. In inter-A. affairs, there was a measure of coordination with Jordan and some *rapprochement* with Egypt — though SA has not, as many observers had expected, resumed official diplomatic relations. Sa'udi efforts to convene an all-A. Summit and joint all-A. action on the major problems facing the A. world met with failure and SA's activity in the all-A. arena has slackened.

The main problem facing SA was the oil recession: the decline in oil production, export and prices, the resulting fall in revenues and reserves, the necessity for sharp cuts in budgets and development projects, and the vicissitudes of the oil policies devised (by SA, and by OPEC) to confront these issues — for data see *oil. Oil Minister A.Z. Yamani, in charge since 1962 and apparently held responsible for these vicissitudes, was dismissed in Oct. 1986.

SA's oil revenues, the main source of her income and the mainstay of her GDP, peaked in 1980–81 with over $100,000m. They had created huge reserves, cleverly invested world-wide and estimated at c. $150,000m., and financed gigantic development schemes, partly completed and partly still abuilding: several large refineries; a large and variegated petrochemical industry — most of it concentrated in huge complexes in a new industrial zone in Jubail on the Gulf coast; a pipeline, with a capacity of over 1.5 mb/d, from the Persian Gulf coast to Yanbu' on the Red Sea (reducing shipment through the unsafe Gulf); new ports at Jidda, Yanbu', Jubail; several new airports, including at Riyadh the biggest and most luxurious one in the world; a network of modern highways; several industries not directly connected with oil; impressive agricultural projects which, though requiring huge investments ("uneconomical" in terms of other countries), made the once barren desert country not only self-sufficient in wheat but a wheat exporter. The oil revenue also made possible the equipment of the armed forces with advanced high-technology weapons, and modern systems of communications throughout the country. It also sustained the high standard of living to which the population had become accustomed — from modern supplies of water, largely derived from sophisticated desalination plants, through advanced medical care (free) and educational institutions, including seven universities (also free), to housing provided by the state and a personal style of wealthy living for many and of extravagant luxury for some.

The decline in oil revenue was bound to affect much of that wealth. In 1983, oil income had declined to less than half of the peak, an estimated $40–43,000m., by 1985 it was thought to be around $28,000m., and in 1986 even less. Running expenses could be met only by drawing on the reserves, that were estimated to have declined to c. $70,000m. or even less by 1985–86; the budget was from 1983 in deficit to a tune of $15–20,000m. and the excess of imports over exports (mainly oil) was estimated at $25–30,000m. in 1984–85. Some development schemes had to be slowed down or halted — though by 1986 it was not yet clear which ones were affected and how far. The employment of foreign workers began to contract — some observers estimated an exodus of about 50,000 each month from 1985(?).

By late 1986, SA expected an end, or at least some alleviation, of the crisis, as she hoped that following an increase of world oil prices and of her own production her oil revenues would rise again.

Sèvres, Treaty of Peace Treaty signed in Aug. 1920 between the Turkish Ottoman Empire and her World War I enemies. Most of its provisions are outside our scope here — concerning arrrangements for the Straits of the Bosphorus and the Dardanelles, and Anatolia (an independent *Armenia, and autonomy, and possibly later independence, for the *Kurds, in its eastern parts; a Greek administration in the Izmir area in its South-West, with a future decision on its possible incorporation in Greece). The ToS also obliged Turkey to surrender all non-Turkish provinces in Africa and Asia-outside-Anatolia, *i.e.* mainly the A.-inhabited areas, renounce all claims to them and recognize arrangements for their disposal made by the Allies. The ToS was not ratified: the Turkish nationalist-revolutionary régime that replaced the Sultan and his government rejected it, mainly because it dismembered the Turkish heartland of Anatolia. It was replaced in 1923 by the Treaty of *Lausanne. The new Treaty, while scrapping the provisions concerning Anatolia and revising those on the Straits, reconfirmed Turkey's renunciation of any claims to the A. region.

al-Sha'bi, Qaḥtan Muhammad (1920–81) South Yemeni politician, President of South Yemen 1967–69. Born in Lahej Sultanate in the 'Aden Protectorates, Sh. worked for several years in the Lahej Land Department and became its director in 1955. He left government service in 1958 to work for the nationalist insurgents and joined the "South Arabian League" (see *South Yemen). He left in 1960 and fled to Yemen. Around 1963, while still in exile in Yemen, he co-founded the *"National Liberation Front for the Liberation of South Yemen" (NLF) and became one of its main leaders. He proclaimed an armed rebellion in Oct. 1963 and led a guerrilla war against the British and the *South Arabia federal authorities, as well as against rival nationalist groups, chiefly *FLOSY. In 1967 he overcame these rival factions and the NLF emerged as the only organization with which the transfer of power was to be negotiated. Sh. headed th NLF delegation to the Nov. 1967 Geneva talks on independence. With independence achieved, the same month, he became South Yemen's first President, Prime Minister and Commander-in-Chief. He was, however, soon involved in factional struggles within the FLN and the Government, and in June 1969 he was deposed. He was expelled from the ruling party, detained, and from Apr. 1970 imprisoned. He was also ailing and did not return to active public and political life until his death in 1981.

Shafe'is One of the four schools (*madhhab*, pl. *madhāhib*) of Sunni Islam (see *Islam). Though it is not of great significance in the ordinary Muslim's life to which *madhhab* he belongs, and his *madhhab* is hardly used to describe or name him, it is different concerning the Sh. in Yemen. There the Sunni Muslims, nearly all of them Sh., are usually called Sh. They are almost half of Yemen's population — estimates vary, and it is generally assumed that the Shi'i *Zeidis constitute a narrow majority. The Sh. live mainly in the coastal plain (the *Tihama*), and in contrast to the Zeidis very few of them belong to tribes. Urban elements and the intelligentsia are somewhat stronger among the Sh. than among the Zeidis. In the past, the confrontation of Sh. and Zeidis was a significant element in Yemen's history. The Sh. had no military power comparable to the great and belligerent Zeidi tribes and were subjected to Zeidi hegemony. During the Ottoman period they tended, therefore, to co-operate with the Turkish authorities. In the independent Kingdom-Imamate of Yemen, 1911 (or 1918) to 1962, they did not play a political and public-administrative rôle commensurate with their share in the population. Some of the Sh. intelligentsia played leading rôles in the revolution of 1962 — e.g. Ahmad Muhammad Nu'man and 'Abd-ul-Rahman al-Beidani. Sh. filled significant positions in the Yemen Republic from 1962 — Sh. were members of the Presidential Council (A.M. Nu'man, Muhammad 'Ali 'Uthman — 1965–73, assassinated 1973) and Prime Ministers (Nu'man, Hassan al-Makki, 'Abd-ul-'Aziz 'Abd-ul-Ghani), Ministers and senior officers. The new régime endeavored to play down the difference between Sh. and Zeidis and even "abolished" *Shafe'iyya* and *Zeidiyya* as legally and officially significant categories. The Egyptian expeditionary force also helped to promote and foster young Sh. Yet, while the distinction between Sh. and Zeidis has become less important, the Yemen A. Republic has remained Zeidi-led. No Sh. has become President or reached the top rank of the army leadership. And while the issue had not erupted in recent decades into violence or public manifestations, a measure of dissatisfaction among Sh., particularly Sh. army officers, is reported from time to time.

Shari'a (Islamic Law.) Originally and ideally intended to regulate all spheres of life without differentiating between civil, criminal, personal status law etc., the areas covered by the Sh. have in fact been shrinking in the past century, Islamic law being superseded by secular legislation. From the mid-19th century secular laws were enacted in various fields (commercial, criminal etc.), though at first not in matters of personal status. This was done either by the adoption of complete Western codes and the enactment of new

Western-inspired laws, or the codification of Islamic laws by Western methods (e.g. the Ottoman Civil Code, *Mejelle*). Such secular legislation, and the establishment of civil, criminal, commercial courts outside the framework and jursidiction of the Sh., were ostensibly designed to supplement the Sh., not to abrogate it. In fact, however, the area of Sh. jurisdiction was gradually restricted, mainly to matters of personal status and the *Waqf* (Religious Endowments). This process applied to the Ottoman Empire and Egypt as well as the French-ruled *Maghrib*, and was taken over and continued by the ASt (except for the countries of the Arabian peninsula), when they became semi-independent after World War I and fully independent later.

In the 20th century the secular legislator began interfering also with the laws of personal status, the area dominated by the Sh. Reforms were made in most AC — e.g. the enhancement of women's status in cases of divorce and the prohibition of polygamy (as in Tunisia in 1956) or its restriction by the imposition of conditions and/or the need to obtain the permission of the Sh. judge, the *Qadi* (as in a Syrian law of 1953 or in various Egyptian laws). Such reforms were effected, usually by the secular legislator, in three principal ways: 1. The adoption of suitable elements from teachings of Sh. jurists of various schools instead of such precepts of the dominant school that did not suit the purpose of the reformers. 2. Procedural devices denying legal recognition to certain acts even if valid under the Sh. (e.g. Egyptian legislation prohibiting the registration of marriages below a minimal age). 3. Penal legislation to prevent acts permitted under the Sh. (e.g. the prohibition or restriction of polygamy; Israel applies the same method). The Ottoman Family Law of 1917 is the first modern law of personal status based on this method; modern laws in the same direction have been adopted by most AC. Modern legislation has also abolished or disregarded the harsh Sh. code of punishments such as death for adultery, amputations for theft etc. Other reforms concern the administration of the *Waqf* — up to its complete abolition in Egypt.

The ASt also reorganized the Sh. courts' system along more modern, and partly Western, patterns. They introduced, for instance, a hierarchy of judicial authorities and appellate Sh. courts not previously reorganized in the Sh. system.

While the reforms mentioned considerably widened the *qadi*'s discretionary power (e.g. concerning permission for polygamy or the dissolution of marriages), the *qadi* and the Sh. court personnel were in most AC integrated to a large extent in the state-appointed and state-directed service. Egypt abolished the Sh. courts altogether in 1956 and transferred their powers to the civil court — where Sh. law still governs family matters and personal status but is applied by civil judges, with Sh. *qadis* as advisers. Tunisia has also abolished Sh. jurisdiction. A similar process has affected Islamic institutions sanctioned by the Sh. and their personnel (though its speed and extent vary from one AC to another): mosque functionaries — the *Imam*, the *Khatib*, the *Wa'iz* — are in many cases government-appointed and part of the civil service or at least placed under government control (in Egypt, this process has been opposed in recent years by Muslim radicals and has led to numerous clashes); even the *Mufti has lost some of his independence and usually implements the government's policies. Traditional Islamic institutions of education are in part being superseded by secular state schools, in part — e.g. al-*Azhar University — modernized, adding secular subjects to their curricula and revising methods of instruction (and coming under increasing state supervision).

On the other hand, secular legislation is inspired by the Sh. in most AC. As all AC except Lebanon define themselves as Islamic countries, with Islam as the state religion, their constitutions lay down, in various versions, that Islamic law, the Sh., should be "the basis" or "a principal source" (in Egypt, since 1980, "*the* main source") of all legislation. The extent to which these principles have been put into effect varies from country to country and cannot be precisely measured in any case. Radical-fundamentalist Islamic circles inside and outside government have been pressing in recent years for a stronger enhancement of Sh. influence on legislation. They demand, for instance, a systematic review of all existing laws as to their compatibility with the Sh. and the revision of those found incompatible (in Egypt, the National Assembly set up several committees to discuss possible legislation in that sphere — but the government seems to go deliberately slow). There are efforts to devise a banking and financial system replacing the payment of interest, banned by the Sh., by different formulae such as sharing costs and profits. These experiments are borne mainly by the financial institutions of states that fully apply the Sh. codes, such as Sa'udi Arabia, the Persian Gulf principalities, Pakistan. Radical Islamists oppose the increasing control by government of mosques and their staff. Inspired by Iran's radical-Islamic régime, these circles pay much attention to matters like dress, women's deportment, separation of the sexes, the ban on alcohol, etc., and sometimes employ pressure or even violence to enforce what they hold to be Sh. rules in these fields — and observers see an increase in the acceptance of these rules by growing parts of the public in Egypt and other AC. Radicals also strive to impose on the state judicial systems the harsh Sh. code of punishments (e.g. death for adultery, amputations for theft, floggings etc.) that are applied by none of the modern ASt except for those of the Arabian peninsula (but are practised by Iran and Pakistan). No AC seems to be willing to adopt that code. The exception was, for some time, Sudan. There, President *Numeiri decreed the Sh. code of punishments in Sept. 1983 and began applying it, arousing wide-spread horrified opposition. After his fall in 1985, the new régime seems not to apply it any more and wishes to do without it, but, reluctant simply to abolish it, is still searching for a more suitable (Islamic?) code to replace it.

Sharif (Arabic: noble.) A descendant of Hassan, the son of Fatima, the Prophet Muhammad's daughter, and the Caliph 'Ali, and thus a descendant of the Prophet. An especially honored position in the larger towns of the A.-Muslim world was that of *Naqib al-Ashraf*, the Head of the Sharifs in the respective area; the position usually passed from father to son. A branch of Hassan's descendants bearing the title Sh. established itself in Mecca in the 10th century and ruled it independently or semi-independently until 1924, when Mecca and the *Hijaz were conquered by the *Sa'udis. The *Hashemites of Jordan (and until 1958 also of Iraq) are descendants of the Sh.'s of Mecca. The dynasty ruling Morocco since the 17th century (the House of al-'Alawi or also al-Filali or al-Hassani), also are of Sharifian descent. So are a number of other respected families throughout the A. world.

Descendants of the Prophet Muhammad through his other grandson, al-Hussein ibn 'Ali, Hassan's younger brother, bear the title *al-Sayyid* (the master, the lord). But *al-Sayyid* is also used in Arabic as the ordinary address, "Mr.", with no connotation of noble descent.

al-Shāriqa See *Sharja.

Sharja (Correct transliteration: al-Shāriqa.) One of the seven sheikhdoms of *Trucial 'Oman that federated in 1971 to form the *United Arab Emirates (UAE). Area: c. 1,000 sq.mi. (2,600 sq.km.). The population, estimated until the 1960s at 15–20,000, engaged in fishing, boat-building, pearl-diving and some semi-nomadic animal husbandry; it increased rapidly after the discovery of oil and in the course of the general development of the UAE. A census of 1980 put it at 159,000, of which 111,000 were foreign workers, a census of 1985 counted 269,000. The sheikhs of Sh., of the House of al-Qassemi, signed several treaties with Britain in the 19th century and were under British protection, along with most of the other petty rulers of the Arabian coast of the Persian Gulf. Britain made Sh. a military base and the headquarters of the small para-military force she set up for the Trucial Coast, the "Trucial Scouts". The British protectorate lapsed in 1971 and the region became independent as the (federated) UAE. Within the UAE, Sh. tended to side with the *Dubai-led camp advocating weak federal institutions and more power to the Federation's constituent units. She was also reluctant to integrate her para-military National Guard and her units of the "Trucial Scouts" in the federal army, but eventually the integration was effected in 1968. Sh. is proportionally represented on the Federal Council (6 of 40) and the federal government. The governance of her own sheikhdom has sometimes been troubled: Sheikh Saqr ibn Sultan, ruling since 1952, was overthrown in 1965, and the new Sheikh, Khaled ibn Muhammad, was killed in Jan. 1972 in a *coup* attempt by the deposed Sheikh. Since 1972, the ruler is Sheikh Sultan ibn Muhammad.

Sh. was involved in several border disputes, some of them concerning a number of exclaves she possessed in the interior of the Trucial 'Oman peninsula and on its eastern coast. Some of these disputes were with sheikhdoms that also joined the UAE (Dubai, Umm al-Qaiwain) and were of little importance after the federal merger. Others concerned 'Oman; these were settled in a UAE-

'Oman agreement of 1979 (of which no details were made known). A dispute with Iran over the island of *Abu Mussa acquired growing importance as offshore oil was discovered in the area (the possession of the island was also in dispute between Sh. and *Umm al-Qaiwain, and the two sheikhdoms had granted conflicting concessions to different US oil companies). In Nov. 1971, when the British protectorate was withdrawn and the UAE was being formed, Iran forcibly occupied the island. While officially Sh. and the UAE protested and demanded the return of the island, some informal arrangements were made by Sh. and Iran, by which the latter endorsed the oil concession granted by Sh. and agreed to share the revenue derived from it.

Oil production began, offshore, in 1974-75 and has remained modest, and so has, accordingly, Sh.'s revenue from oil — for data see *oil. However, for her development plans Sh. did not have to depend on her oil income only but could draw on federal funds, and though the oil recession of the mid-1980s resulted in a certain slowdown, her economic and social development continued.

Shatt al-'Arab The joint estuary of the *Euphrates and *Tigris rivers in southern Iraq, on the Iranian border. From the confluence, at Qurna, to the Persian Gulf, the length of the Sh. is about 120 mi. (190 km.). About 50 mi. from its mouth, below Basra, the Sh. receives on its left (eastern) bank the Karun River, from Iran. The Sh. creates on its lower course wide areas of swamps. It used to carry, until the Iraq-Iran war from 1980 onward, much of the foreign trade of Iraq (via Basra) and Iran (via Khorramshahr) and provided the outlet for the southern Iraqi oil fields and the (Iranian) Abadan refineries.

The Sh. has long been an object of strife between Iraq (previously, the Ottoman Empire) and Iran. According to an agreement of 1937, based on previous Ottoman-Iranian accords, the Sh. was wholly Iraqi territory except for a length of three miles opposite Abadan, where the frontier was considered to run along the *thalweg* (the line of greatest depth) of the river. This arrangement proved unsatisfactory to both sides, particularly to Iran who thought the boundary should be all along the *thalweg* or the median line. Questions of piloting, dues and general procedures caused sporadic outbursts of the conflict and grave crises in 1961, 1965, and 1969. In Apr. 1969 Iran formally abrogated the agreement of 1937 and served notice that any future accord must be based on equal rights and the median line or thalweg. A period of crisis ensued, while Iran enforced shipping and piloting controls; in Dec. 1971 Iraq even severed official relations (resumed in Oct. 1973), and serious border clashes erupted in Feb. 1974. The crisis was resolved by a new agreement reached in Mar. 1975 and finally signed in June 1975. Iran, with the Shah at the height of his power, obtained full satisfaction of her demands concerning the Sh. (in return, she stopped all support for the *Kurds' rebellion — causing the collapse of that rebellion). Iraq, however, could not acquiesce in the disadvantageous accord of 1975 which, she claimed, was imposed on her. As relations with Iran deteriorated on other issues, too, Iraq abrogated the agreement of 1975 in Sept. 1980 and opened warlike operations. In the Iraq-Iran war since 1980, triggered in large measure by the problem of the Sh., the area of the Sh. and adjacent *Khuzistan were the main area of operations. Iraqi forces speedily took most of the Iranian side of the Sh., including Khorramshahr, the main town (Abadan was cut off and besieged). In 1981-82, however, Iranian forces recovered; they broke the siege of Abadan in Sept. 1981 and reconquered Khorramshahr (in ruins) in May 1982. Later they subjected Basra and the Iraqi side of the Sh. to near-constant shelling, and in Feb. 1986 they crossed the River and occupied Fao (Faw) on the Gulf coast and the area around it. As a shipping route, the Sh. was made totally unusable, and so were the oil loading facilities which Iraq had constructed over many years at its mouth and which were now for the most part destroyed.

Shi'a, Shi'i(te)s Islam is divided into two main schools or streams — the (majority) *Sunnis, and the Sh. The Sh. (Arabic: faction, party) arose in the 7th century, holding that 'Ali ibn Abu Taleb, cousin of the Prophet Muhammad and husband of his daughter Fatima, was the legitimate successor (*Khalifa*) and, later, that the leadership of the Muslim community was divinely vested in the descendants of the Prophet through 'Ali and his sons al-Hassan and (martyred) al-Hussein. The leader of the community was called *Imam*. The main streams of the Sh.

hold that a last *Imam* did not die but became invisible, hidden, to reappear at the end of time as *al-Mahdi*, the Guided One, "to fill the earth with justice".

The Sh. split several times over the identity of the *Imam*, and particularly the last, the hidden one. The *Zeidi(te)s* grew out of a schism over the identity of the fifth *Imam*; they recognize a living *Imam*. They survive mainly in Yemen and rule that country. A schism over the seventh *Imam* gave birth to the *Isma'iliyya* sect; one of their branches recognizes a living *Imam*, the Aga Khan. It is disputed whether they are part of the Sh. or on the fringes of, or outside, Islam. (Two other sects on the fringes of Islam grew out of the Isma'iliyya: the *Druze and the *'Alawis.) The main stream of the Sh. holds that the twelfth *Imam* is the hidden one; they are called the "Twelvers" (*Ithna-'ashariyya*), also *al-Ja'fariyya* or *al-Imamiyya*. It is to them that the term Sh. generally refers.

The number of the Sh. (i.e. the Twelvers) worldwide is estimated at 80–90m., 8–11% of all Muslims. They are a large majority in Iran, and Sh. Islam is the state religion of that country since the 16th century. In the AC the Sh. are 7.5–7.8m. or c. 4% of all Muslims. They constitute a slight majority in Iraq, Dubai and Bahrain, a strong minority in Lebanon (25–35% of the population, a majority among the Muslims if the Druze are not counted as Muslims), and smaller minorities in Sa'udi Arabia (2–3%) and several Persian Gulf principalities. See also *Islam, *Minorities.

The Sh. in those AC where they are strongly represented have in general not enjoyed the status and share of power apportionate to their numbers. Even Iraq, with her Sh. majority has since becoming independent been ruled mainly by Sunni Muslims. The Sh. of Lebanon have in recent years begun to assert their strength and claim a larger share of power — inspired and encouraged by *Khomeini's Iran (as are underground groups of rebellious Iraqi Sh.). In the religious-doctrinal field, both Sunni and Sh. savants tend in recent decades to play down the differences and encourage a certain *rapprochement*; the (Sunni) Islamic University of al-*Azhar, e.g., teaches Sh. law doctrine (*fiqh*) since the 1950s. But generally the Sh. Muslims have remained a distinct community cultivating its own customs and doctrines. Its main centers of learning are in Iran (Qum, Mashhad) and at the Sh. holy cities of Iraq — Najaf ('Ali's tomb), Karbala (Hussein's tomb) and al-Kazimain.

Shihab, Fu'ad (1902–73) Lebanese officer and politician, President of Lebanon 1958–64. Maronite Christian of a renowned family whose heads had in the past borne the title Amir. During the French Mandate, Sh. served in in the "Special Troops" recruited by the French, reaching the rank of Lieutenant-Colonel. In 1946, when Lebanon became independent, he was appointed Commander of the Army as a General, and did much to build it up into a modern, professional force. In Sept. 1952, when a "National Front" staged demonstrations against the corrupt administration of President Bishara al-*Khouri, Sh. refused to order the army to suppress the demonstrators, and Khouri was in consequence forced to resign. For an interim period of a few weeks, Sh. served as Prime Minister and Minister of the Interior and Defense. He adopted a similar attitude in the civil war in 1958, when fighting broke out between supporters of President Camille *Chamoun and a *Nasserist "National Front". Sh. once again refused to order out the army against the insurgents, holding that it ought to be above the rival camps and constitute a force for national unity (and fearing it might break into rival factions if used in a civil war). Sh. thus acquired a reputation for impartiality, and on 31 July 1958 he was elected President — as a compromise, the first step towards a reconciliation of the parties in the civil war. Sh. continued that reconciliation, though somewhat favoring the Nasserist Muslims. In response to their demands, and to appease them, he moved closer to Egypt and her camp. He initiated a series of reforms in the administration aimed at strengthening the Muslim population, initiated public works in the backward north and south mainly populated by Muslims, and enhanced the powers of the Presidency, striking for efficient, centralized government. His opponents claimed that he was employing bureaucratic and dictatorial methods, using the Secret Service for his own purpose and emptying the parliamentary system of its content. Even after he retired from the presidency in 1964 (declining urgent offers to arrange for an amendment of the constitution and his election for a second term), Sh. retained much influence through his supporters in Parliament, who formed a "Shihabist" bloc, through numerous army officers who remained loyal to him, and through the Secret Services. In 1970, he was urged to stand again for the presidency (as permitted by the constitution after an interval of one term), but refused.

Shishakli, Adib (1901–64)   Syrian officer and politician. President of Syria, 1953–54. Born in Hama, Sh. served in the "Special Troops" set up by the French Mandate régime. In 1948 he was a senior officer in *Qawuqji's "Army of Deliverance" which fought the Jews in Palestine. He is said to have been a member of the *"Syrian Nationalist Party" of Anton *Sa'adeh. Sh. played a major part in Husni *Za'im's *coup* in 1949, but was suspected by Za'im of disloyalty and dismissed from the army. He was reinstated by Sami *Hinnawi, after his *coup*, in Aug. 1949. On 19 Dec. 1949 he led a military *coup* which overthrew Hinnawi. At first, Sh. permitted the formal parliamentary régime established by Hinnawi to continue and himself assumed only the title of Deputy Chief-of-Staff, though in fact he ruled behind the scenes. Sh. opposed the pro-Iraqi leanings of the "People's Party" then in power, and on 29 Nov. 1951 carried out a second *coup*. His rule now became more openly dictatorial, although he appointed as a figurehead President and Prime Minister Marshal Fawzi Selo, one of his supporters. He assumed formal power in June 1953, when he became Premier and had himself elected President in a referendum. The same referendum approved a new constitution, which gave the President wide powers.

Sh. attempted to introduce several economic and social reforms, but did not persist in them. In 1952 he banned all political parties and established an "Arab Liberation Movement" as the single political organization. The ALM did not take root, and the parliament elected under its aegis in 1953 remained a non-representative shadow-body. Since Sh. created order and stability in Syria, the West supported him, and he was considered pro-Western.

In Jan. 1954 resistance to his oppressive régime and antagonism he had aroused among the *Druze erupted in violent demonstrations. On 25 Feb. 1954 a *coup* forced Sh. to resign. He left Syria and lived in Lebanon, Sa'udia and France. In 1957 he was charged with plotting a *coup* with the support of Iraq and the West, and was tried *in absentia* several times. In 1960 he emigrated to Brazil. There he was assassinated in 1964 by a Druze in revenge for the bombing of the Druze Mountain during his rule.

al-Shuqeiri, Ahmad (1908–80)   Palestinian Arab politician, chairman of the *PLO 1964–67. Born in Acre, the son of Sheikh As'ad Sh., a prominent political and Muslim religious figure in mandatory Palestine. A lawyer by profession, trained at the Jerusalem Law School and the American University of Beirut, Sh. in 1945 headed a Palestinian-A. propaganda office in the USA, and later in Jerusalem. Briefly a member of the Arab Higher Committee (Mar. to June 1946); Member of the Syrian delegation to the UN 1949–50; Under Secretary for Political Affairs of the *Arab League 1951–57 (according to his own account, he continued at the same time to represent Syria at the UN — from 1954 as Ambassador). Sh. was Sa'udi Arabian Minister of State for UN affairs and Ambassador to the UN 1957–62. During his tenure as Ambassador to the UN (Syrian or Sa'udi), he was the most active and vituperative spokesman for the A. cause against Israel. In Apr. 1963 he was appointed as the representative of the Palestinian A.'s at the Arab League and asked to prepare a plan and statutes for an organization representing a Palestinian-A. "entity". When a *"Palestine Liberation Organization" was established in 1964 under the auspices of the Arab League, Sh. became its chairman. His leadership of the PLO was considered a failure — he was later also blamed for his violent and irresponsibly extremist speeches advocating the physical extermination of the Jews of Israel — and he was relieved of his post in Dec. 1967 (formalized July 1968) and retired from the political scene. Sh. published a book of memoirs (*Forty Years of Arab and International Life*, Arabic, Beirut 1969).

Sidon (Arabic: Saida)   Town and port in southern Lebanon, 25 mi. (40 km.) south of Beirut. The ancient Phoenician city was in modern times a small town with a population estimated at 25–30,000 in the 1960s. It grew during the civil war from 1975 onward and the Israeli occupation of 1982–85, with their large movements of refugees — mainly of Shi'is from the countryside and Palestinian A.'s from the area's camps — to an estimated 100–150,000, the third-largest city in

Lebanon. Although situated on the northern fringe of Shi'i-majority South Lebanon, and a main administrative and political center of the Shi'is, the town itself has a Muslim-Sunni majority. It is also the center of several large camps of Palestinian-A. refugees ('Ain Hilwa, Miyeh-Miyeh) dominated by the *PLO and its military/terrorist establishment.

Public-political life in S. has been troubled since the late 1960s mainly by clashes with Palestinian-A. formations. The town, or at least its Sunni part, has been dominated by a Sunni *Nasserist militia set up and led by Ma'ruf Sa'd, Member of Parliament (and after he was killed in Mar. 1975 on the eve of the civil war, by his sons). This militia was in the early 1970s involved in bitter clashes with PLO squads, mainly from the al-*Sa'iqa group; but after it joined the Leftist-Muslim-PLO camp in the civil war, and after the PLO forces were expelled by the invading Israelis in 1982, it became an ally of the Palestinians.

From about 1983, S. was one of the centers of growing resistance to the Israeli forces, particularly on the part of the Shi'is. The increasing assertiveness of the Shi'is in general was also partly centered in S. As PLO fighters began returning to South Lebanon, from 1984–85, and re-asserting their domination of the camps, S. and the camps around it became a main arena of an armed struggle between them and Shi'i al-*Amal forces. S.'s Sunni-Nasserist leaders appear as mediators in that struggle.

Sidqi, Bakr (1890–1937) Iraqi officer and politician reportedly of Kurdish origin. A graduate of the Ottoman military academy, he served in command positions in the Ottoman army throughout World War I. In 1921 he joined the newly-formed Iraqi army. In 1933, as commanding officer of the army in northern Iraq, S. crushed what was described as an *Assyrian rebellion (others saw it as a massacre of the Assyrians), and was promoted to the rank of general in consequence. In 1935 he put down several tribal rebellions in southern Iraq. He headed a group of army officers who looked with distaste at the disputes of civilian politicians and wished to emulate their colleagues in Iran and Turkey who had played so prominent a part in modernizing their country. S. collaborated clandestinely with the civilian politician Hikmat Suleiman and the leftist-reformist *Ahali* Group. In Oct. 1936, when he was Acting Chief of General Staff, S. moved military units to Baghdad and forced Prime Minister Yassin al-Hashemi to resign. Hikmat Suleiman became Prime Minister and S. Chief of the General Staff and the strong man and real ruler of the country. His was the first straightforward military *coup d'état* in the newly independent AC. His reformist plans remained largely unimplemented. S. was assassinated in Aug. 1937 by a group of dissident officers.

Sidqi, Isma'il (1875–1950) Egyptian politician. Trained as a lawyer at Cairo Law School and abroad, S. was a minister in Egypt's semi-independent government from 1914 (Agriculture; *Waqf*). In 1918–19 he supported the nationalists under Sa'd *Zaghlul and accompanied him to exile in the Seychelles in 1919. He subsequently left the *Wafd* and participated in setting up the Liberal Constitutional Party in 1922. He was Minister of the Interior in 1924–25 on behalf of that party. S. became Prime Minister in June 1930 and substituted for the 1923 constitution — suspended since 1928 — a more conservative one and altered the election law. He founded a party to support him in Parliament — the "People's Party" (*Hizb al-Sha'b*) — and won the elections of May 1931 under the new election law. His rule, in collaboration with the King and under his orders, was conservative and considered by many as autocratic. His aim was also to strengthen the monarchy and weaken the *Wafd* party. S.'s harsh rule aroused much opposition and growing popular resistance. When his government became involved in a corruption scandal, he fell in Sept. 1933. As a former Prime Minister, he was a member of the delegation which negotiated and signed the Anglo-Egyptian Treaty of 1936. In Feb. 1946, he again became Prime Minister. He reached an agreement with the British Foreign Secretary, Ernest *Bevin, on the evacuation of British forces from Egypt within three years and the establishment of a joint defense council. The agreement was not ratified, as both sides published conflicting interpretations of the clause dealing with the future self-determination of Sudan, and S. was compelled to resign in Dec. 1946. He never again held government office. S. was also President of the Association of Industrialists and a protagonist of conservative capitalism. He did not believe in A. unity and in 1946, while head of the government, had contacts with Zionist envoys towards a settlement of the Palestine problem. In 1948 S. had the courage to warn in the Senate, alone, against the Egyptian invasion of Palestine. He later published a series of articles in which he advocated an understanding with Israel. His memoirs were published, in Arabic, in 1950.

Sinai Campaign, Sinai War, 1956, See *Arab-Israel Wars.

Sinai Peninsula Triangle-shaped desert area, which forms the land bridge between Asia and Africa, bordering in the west on the *Suez Canal and the Gulf of Suez, in the east on the Gulf of *'Aqaba. Area: c. 23,000 sq.mi. (59,000 sq.km.). The population was c. 38,000, mostly Bedouin, in 1948. After 1948 Egypt stepped up some development, mainly the production of oil, and also mounted a military build-up in S. and by 1967 estimated its population as 126,000(?), including c. 25,000 Palestinian-A. refugees. After the *Six Day War of 1967, under Israeli occupation, the population was estimated at c. 60,000 (of which 30–40,000 in the town of al-'Arish, on the northern shore). After S. was returned to Egypt in 1982, Egyptian estimates speak of a population of c. 200,000 — but they are doubted by observers.

Along the western shore minerals were discovered and exploited: manganese at Um Bugma and oil at Ras Sudar and Abu Rudeis.

S. was part of the Ottoman Empire since 1517. The agreements of 1840 which regulated the relations between the Sultan and his autonomous Viceroy of Egypt left the administration of S. unclear and controversial. While Ottoman sovereignty was uncontested, sporadic Egyptian administration was maintained — at least since the late 1870s — and continued under the British occupation of Egypt (1882). The Sultan claimed that Egyptian temporary rights of administration referred only to the northwestern parts of the Peninsula and to a number of posts in the southern parts, on the pilgrims' route to Mecca, while a central triangle Suez-'Arish-'Aqaba was under direct Turkish rule.

After 1882 the British claimed for Egypt — and tried to establish *de facto* — fuller rights of possession. British notes of 1892 and 1902 laid down the eastern boundary as a line drawn from al-'Arish or Rafah to 'Aqaba. (A tentative plan to develop the al-'Arish area for Jewish settlement was briefly discussed in 1902–03, but was never put into practice.) When the Turks set up a garrison in *Taba, south of 'Aqaba, in 1906, a sharp diplomatic clash with Britain ensued (the "'Aqaba Incident"), and the Sultan, while not renouncing his claim, had to acquiesce the Rafah-'Aqaba line as a border. This line became the boundary of British-Mandated Palestine (1922–48) and — except for its northern extremity, where Egypt crossed it to occupy the *Gaza Strip — the armistice line between Egypt and Israel (1949–67).

S. was a main Egypt-Israel battle ground in 1956, 1967 and 1973 (see *Arab-Israel Wars). Most of it was occupied by Israel in 1956 (up to 10 mi. east of the Suez Canal), but Israeli forces were withdrawn under international and Great Power pressure, while a UN Emergency Force (UNEF) was set up to guard the border and operated from 1957 to 1967. All S. was occupied by Israel in 1967, and Israel began exploiting the oil wells on its western coast, with considerable investment, developing tourism on its eastern coast, and also providing improved services for the Bedouin population. She also set up several settlements in the north and on the eastern coast.

In the War of Oct. 1973 Egyptian forces crossed the Suez Canal and established a bridgehead c. 6 mi. (10 km.) wide. They were left in its possession by the cease-fire and a Jan. 1974 "Disengagement Agreement" which added a 6 mi. buffer zone to be held by a UN Emergency Force (UNEF) re-established in Oct. 1973. An Egypt-Israel Interim Agreement, concluded in Sept. 1975 under US auspices, provided for a further Israeli withdrawal of a few miles to the east and an expansion of the Egyptian-held area, and moved the buffer zone farther east. It also returned the Abu Rudais oil wells to an Egyptian civil administration, demilitarized and under UNEF supervision; the Suez Canal had been reopened in June 1975. In the *Camp David Agreements of 1978 and the Egypt-Israel Peace Treaty of 1979 Israel had to agree to return all of S. to Egypt — as President *Sadat rejected all proposals for the continued existence of Israeli settlements and an Israeli presence, in one form or another, at Sharm al-Sheikh on the east coast. About half of S., up to a line from al-'Arish to the southern tip, was returned to Egypt in several stages, by Jan. 1980. Israel's withdrawal from the rest — and thus the return of all S. — was completed in Apr. 1982. What Israel had built on the east coast was handed over intact, while the settlements at the north-western end of the border were mostly demolished by the settlers. A "Multinational Force and Observers", agreed in 1978–79, with personnel from 11 countries, was in place in Mar. 1982; but there have been no crises calling for action on its part. A dispute that has so far not been solved, concerns a tiny area at *Taba near Eilat; an agreed panel of international jurists has begun a process of arbitration in 1986.

Sirte (or **Syrte**, Arabic: Sidra), **Gulf of**   Gulf in the southern Mediterranean, off the coast of Libya, bounded by the shore of Tripolitania in the south and south-west and by that of Cyrenaica in the east. The GoS became a political issue when in Oct. 1973 Libya proclaimed its eastern part to be her territorial waters, up to the 32'30 parallel, a line from north of Benghazi to northwest of Misurata, 200 km. (125 mi.) from its south-eastern tip. The USA and other maritime powers refused to recognize that claim, and the US insisted on the right of her fleet to sail, and her air force to overfly, what she considered to be international waters. Although the US asserted that right only in infrequent test cases, the confrontation escalated in the context of the US-Libyan crisis. In Aug. 1981 Libyan planes attacked US aircraft and two Libyan fighters were shot down. Further incidents, though no actual clashes, occurred in 1983, and another air battle in Mar. 1986. The dispute has remained unresolved.

Six Day War   See *Arab-Israel Wars.

slavery   Full ownership of slaves with unlimited rights to bequeath, sell, and trade them, was already forbidden in most ME countries at the start of the twentieth century (Sudan: 1898, Morocco: 1911), except for the Arabian peninsula. However, even in countries where S. was outlawed, many vestiges remained of hidden S. or of semi-S., such as "inherited" domestic servants, indebted tenant-farmers forbidden in effect to leave their master's land, and young girls sold into marriage by their fathers. Cases were also known of slaves who were formally freed, but who preferred the security of remaining attached to the household of their masters.

In the Arabian peninsula, open S. survived up to the 1960s. West African countries and Sudan supplied young men and women to slave markets openly held in Arabia. The victims were either sold by their families, abducted by force, or inveigled into slavery. The Pilgrimage to Mecca, (*Hajj*) often served as cover and pretext for slave trading, both as an inducement to the victims to join pilgrims' caravans and as a meeting and market place. Such sales were often calculated as a means of financing the pilgrimage of powerful individuals. S. in Sa'udi Arabia, 'Oman, and Persian Gulf sheikhdoms, the transfer of slaves from Africa to the Arabian peninsula and slave trading, were documented as late as the 1950s and 1960s. Estimates as to the number of slaves in the Arabian peninsula varied from 700,000 to two or even three million in the 1950s, and from 100,000 to 300,000 and more in the 1960s.

In Sa'udi Arabia a decree of 1936 imposed certain limitations on slave trade and importation, and forbade the imposition of S. on free men; but it did not forbid S. as such. The complete prohibition of S. was decreed only in Nov. 1962; to facilitate the implementation of its decree, the government allocated funds to compensate owners who freed their slaves. Since then, officially S. no longer exists in Sa'udia, but according to published evidence and reports the ban has not yet been put fully into effect. UN agencies also reported several times that Sa'udi Arabia had not replied to questionnaires on S. Only in 1973 Sa'udi Arabia deposited with the UN the instrument of her accession to the 1926 Convention banning S. and its later supplements.

Socialism, Socialist   The term S. is widely used in A. political writings and appears in the names of numerous parties and organizations in the AC. Generally, however, A. politicians and writers do not mean the Western-type S. as developed in the 20th century, in contradistinction to *Communism, and organized in the Socialist, or Second, International — i.e. a S. based on multi-party parliamentary democracy and a liberal conception of human rights, and in most cases on non-revolutionary methods, and usually calling itself Social Democracy. They mean rather a State S. based on populist-revolutionary, frequently single-party and semi-totalitarian régimes often set up by army officers (though there is of course no rigid, hard-and-fast division or definition of the two types of S.).

Before World War II, a measure of Western-type S. thinking may be discerned in the ideas and writings of several Egyptian and Lebanese writers and politicians, but no Social-Democratic party or organization was formed. Traces of Social-Democracy may perhaps be seen in the left wing of the Egyptian *Wafd* party, in the Iraqi *Ahali* group (Kamel Chadirchi), or in the Tunisian Neo-*Destour* party. After the war, the Moroccan left wing (*Ben Barka, the UNFP and USFP), and for some time Kamal *Junbalat's PSP in Lebanon, may be added. But even in these groups Western-type Social Democracy did not mature but gradually changed into other types of S. Yet the S. International was anxious to discover like-minded groups in the AC and cultivate relations with them. They were particularly attracted by the Moroccan Left and by the Lebanese PSP. The latter was even invited to join, and though its full adhesion never materialized, it was given the status of an observer, as was the Egyptian *"Arab Socialist Union"; but relations did not become close, and the two parties did not turn into Social-Democratic groups. The S. parties of Asia, coalescing in an "Asian S. Conference" in Jan. 1953 (with the S. parties of Burma, India and Israel as the chief initiators), were also keen to associate sister-parties in the AC and invited several of them to their conference. Israel's prominent role in that Asian organization induced the A. parties to decline the invitation to the 1953 Conference and additional ones held until 1972. (In a curious marginal episode, the Secretariat, judging from the names of parties, invited also the "S. Democratic Party" of Egypt; but this turned out to be a revived version of Ahmad Hussein's "Young Egypt" — a clearly and avowedly Fascist group).

Populist-revolutionary State S., on the other hand, has become since the 1950s the ruling creed in many of the left-leaning ASt. The ruling single party of the Egyptian officers' régime founded in 1952 adopted it from the mid-1950s, under *Nasser's leadership, and in 1962 changed its name into "A. S. Union". Under *Sadat, the ASU broke up into different parties and the emphasis on S. declined; the mainstream group, the "National Democratic Party", no longer has S. in its name; but two smaller opposition factions are called "S. Labor" and "S. Liberals". The *Ba'th Party in Syria and Iraq, calling itself S. since its merger with *Hourani's "A. S. Party" in Syria in 1953, has ruled Syria since 1963 and Iraq since 1968. The ruling party in South Yemen, formerly the *NLF, is called since 1978 the "Yemen S. Party". Sudan's *Numeiri called the single party he set up in 1971 the "Sudan S. Union". Algeria's *FLN, the single and ruling party, does not carry the term S. in its name, but belongs to the same trend of populist-revolutionary S. Tunisia's "S. *Destour* Party" (formerly Neo-*Destour*), ruling the country since independence, professes a S. containing elements of both the populist brand and Western Social Democracy, but its practice has not conformed to the latter; a more liberal faction that split from it in the 1970s, led by Ahmad Mestiri, calls itself "Democratic S. Movement" and seems to profess a Western-type Social Democracy. Junbalat's "Progressive S. Party" in Lebanon is not the ruling party but is highly influential; it seems to belong to the populist brand of S., and has remained a mainly Druze formation, with S. ideology as a secondary element. On the Moroccan Left, one of the main factions calls itself S. (the "S. Union of Popular Forces", USFP); it seems to belong to the populist brand of S.

In the late 1950s and the 1960s, Nasser and his disciples used to emphasize the A. national character of their S., calling their movement "A. S." and claiming that it created a special, distinctive brand of S. However, "A. S." has contributed very little to the body of general S. ideology or doctrine; it is but the A.-nationalist body representing populist-revolutionary State S. Since it was closely linked to *Pan-Arab plans for an all-A. union, most of its factions called themselves "Socialist-Unionist". They have declined since Nasser's death and the decline of the influence of *Nasserism.

Socotra Island in the Indian Ocean, c. 140 mi. east of the Horn of Africa, 250 mi. south of the coast of southern Arabia. Area: 1,382 sq. mi.; population c. 15,000 (Arabs, Africans, some people of Portuguese ancestry). S. came under British protection in the late 19th century when the Mahri Sultanate of Qishn, to which it belonged, became part of the Eastern *'Aden Protectorate (see *South Yemen). Since Nov. 1967 it has been part of South Yemen. According to persistent reports, never officially confirmed, S. has been placed at the disposal of the USSR as a naval base.

Somalia Republic in northeast Africa, on the

"Horn" of Africa, formed on 1 July 1960 by the merger of the former Italian-administered Trust Territory of S. and the British Protectorate of Somaliland. Italy had acquired "her" part of S. in the late 1880s, later made it a colony, lost it in World War II to British forces, received it back under a UN Trusteeship in 1950, and granted it independence on 30 June 1960. Britain had acquired increasing influence in the other part of S. during the 19th century, occupied it in the 1880s, made it a Protectorate in 1889, and granted it independence in late June 1960. (French S., *Djibouti, stayed out of the union and became separately independent.)

S., with an area of c. 246,000 sq. mi. (640,000 sq. km.) and a population estimated in the mid-1980s at over 6m., is Muslim (99% of the population) but not A.; the Somalis are, ethnically, of mixed "Hamitic", Berber and Negro stock, and until the 1970s Arabic was used very little, mainly by traders. The details of S.'s developments are thus outside our scope. S., however, joined the *Arab League in Feb. 1974 (one of three non-A. countries to do so). Arabic has since been cultivated and used somewhat more in education and government administration. Within the A. League, S. has not been very active. She belongs to its moderate camp, in particular since 1977, when she abrogated a treaty of friendship and alliance with the USSR which she had concluded in 1974 and adopted a pro-Western orientation (in 1980 she also granted the USA certain facilities for a US "Rapid Deployment Force"). In 1979 she was one of the three AC that maintained official relations with Egypt, while all the others severed them.

South Arabia, Federation of (*Ittihad al-Janub al-'Arabi*) Formed under British guidance, between 1959 and 1965, out of most of the sultanates amirates and tribal sheikhdoms of the *'Aden Protectorates (see *South Yemen), the FSA comprised by 1965 an area of c. 61,000 sq.mi. (159,000 sq.km.) and a population of around 700,000 consisting mainly of nomadic tribes. In Feb. 1959, six units of the Western 'Aden Protectorate — the amirates of Beihan and Dali', the sultanates of Awdhali, Fadli and Lower Yafi' and the Sheikhdom of Upper 'Awlaqi — formed the "Federation of Arab Amirates of the South". In Apr. 1962 the Federation changed its name to "F. of SA". During the 1960s nine more units of the Western Protectorate joined the F.: the sultanates of Lahaj 1959, Lower 'Awlaqi 1960, Hawshabi 1963 and Upper 'Awlaqi 1965; the sheikhdoms of 'Aqrabi 1960, Sha'ib 1963, 'Alawi and Mufalahi 1965, and the states of Dathina 1960. Fifteen units of the Western Protectorate had now joined; only the Sultanate of Upper Yafi' stayed out of the F. However, of the four principalities of the Eastern Protectorate, only the Sultanate of Wahidi joined, 1962. 'Aden town, a Crown Colony, decided to join in Sept. 1962 and did so formally in Jan. 1963 (acquiring the status of a Federal State). By 1965 the F. comprised 17 members.

'Aden's decision to join was controversial. The nationalists bitterly opposed it, considering it a British plot to submerge the politically advanced and sophisticated town of 'Aden in the backward, autocratic Federation subservient to the British. A majority in favor of the F. had been obtained in the 'Aden Legislative Council only by including a provision enabling 'Aden to secede within seven years if the Council felt her interest were harmed. The federal political structure indeed reflected Britain's intention of assimilating the potentially revolutionary 'Aden in the conservative hinterland. The Federal Legislature — named the Federal Council (*Majlis al-Ittihad*) — consisted of 103 members, only 24 of whom were from 'Aden; and the Executive — the Supreme Federal Council (*Majlis al-Ittihad al-'Ali*) — had 15 members, only four of whom were 'Adenis. On 29 Nov. 1961 a Federal Army was created out of the former 'Aden Protectorate Levies, formed in 1928; it was under the nominal control of the federal authorities, but was in fact under British command. On 1 June 1967 the five battalions of the Federal Army joined four battalions of "Federal Guards" (raised by the various petty rulers) to create a 9,000-man strong SA Army.

The federal structure remained weak: the diverging interests of the various sheikhdoms were dominant and no strong federal establishment was created. The chairmanship of the Executive (i.e. Premiership) was held in monthly rotation by the members of the Supreme Council, and no one was prepared to serve as President. The insurgent nationalists regarded the F. as a creation of British colonialism and wanted to destroy it. Their guerrilla war, 1963–67, was directed against the F. no less than the British. After 1964, when Britain announced her intention of leaving SA by 1968, it became doubtful how much British help could be expected after the envisaged transfer of power to the Federal Government. A treaty between Britain and the F., proposed and tentatively agreed upon in 1964, was never ratified. A UN mission which visited 'Aden in Apr. 1967 did not recognize the Federal Government. Between Aug. and Sept. 1967, the nationalist *NLF overran one SA sultanate after another and the Federal authorities collapsed. Britain had to admit that collapse in Sept. 1967 and to negotiate a transfer of power to the NLF. When, on 29 Nov. 1967, independence was attained, the Federal structure was abolished and SA was renamed the "People's Republic of *South Yemen".

South Yemen, People's Republic of (since Nov. 1970: People's Democratic Republic of Yemen). Country in South Arabia, on the shores of the Indian Ocean (the Gulf of 'Aden), between the Red Sea and the Sultanate of 'Oman's *Dhofar. SY is made up of the former Colony of *'Aden and the Western and Eastern 'Aden Protectorates (including those that had not joined the Federation of *South Arabia), and the offshore islands of *Perim and *Socotra. She became independent in Nov. 1967. Area: c. 130,000 sq.mi. (330,000 sq.km.). SY borders on Yemen, Sa'udi Arabia and 'Oman. The only demarcated frontier is part of the Yemen border. The population, counted as 1.59 m. by a census in 1973, was estimated in the mid-1980s at c. 2.2 m. The main town is 'Aden, with a population of 250,000. A new capital — *Madinat al-Sha'b* (Arabic: People's Town; former name: *al-Ittihad*) was built adjacent to 'Aden. The population is c. 75% Arab and consists mainly of *Shafe'i Sunni Muslims. Foreign workers — Yemenis, Indians, Pakistanis and Somalis — are all in 'Aden town (nearly all the Europeans and Jews left after independence). There is a sharp contrast between the modern 'Aden town and the underdeveloped, poor, tribal and partly nomadic hinterland. SY derives its main revenues from 'Aden harbor and the oil refineries.

POLITICAL HISTORY. Britain briefly took control of Perim Island in 1799, to prevent Napoleon from moving to India through the Straits of *Bab al-Mandeb. In 1839, the Government of Bombay Province, in British India, acquired 'Aden town from the Sultan of Lahaj, mainly for use as a coal depot. 'Aden remained under the jurisdiction of the Bombay government till 1932. As its importance grew, particularly after the opening of the Suez Canal, 1869, Britain signed almost 30 separate treaties by which the sultans, sheikhs, sharifs and amirs of the town's hinterland accepted varying degrees of British protection. Most of these were Shafe'i Muslims who resisted the intrusions of both the *Zeidi Imams of Yemen and the Ottoman Empire. Backed by Britain, these tribal leaders foiled Ottoman penetration of South Arabia in the 1870s and an attempt to conquer 'Aden in 1915 (although Ottoman troops succeeded in capturing Lahaj). The Yemeni Imam *Yahya claimed that South Arabia was an integral part of Yemen, but his demands were rejected by South Arabia's petty rulers. In 1932 the administration of 'Aden was transferred from Bombay Province to the Governor General of India. Five years later, in 1937, 'Aden became a Crown Colony, and the hinterland was termed the Western and Eastern 'Aden Protectorates.

Britain maintained stronger contacts with the chiefs of the Western 'Aden Protectorate, the immediate hinterland of 'Aden town. In the early 1950s the Colonial Office proposed to create in the Western Protectorate a federation which would later become a member of the British Commonwealth; this proposition was opposed by the tribal leaders who disliked the increasing British interference. But when Britain suggested

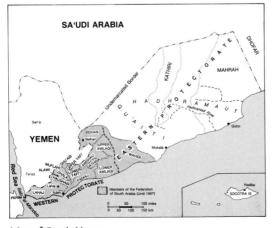

Map of South Yemen

a federation which would later become an independent Arab state linked with Britain only by treaty, the Sultans, who were under growing leftist and Nasserist pressure, agreed. From 1959, a "Federation of *South Arabia" was formed; by 1965 it had 17 members; 15 from the Western Protectorate, one from the Eastern Protectorate and 'Aden town. One sultanate of the Western Protectorate and three of the Eastern Protectorate refused to join the Federation. A political party, the "United National Party", formed mainly by middle-class pro-British and Federalist 'Adenis, supported the Federation, but it had little influence and the Federation remained weak (see *South Arabia).

The Eastern 'Aden Protectorate — mostly deserts and barren hills, with some fertile valleys (of which the most important is the *Hadhramaut) — consisted of the four sultanates of Wahidi, Qu'aiti, Kathiri and Mahra (including the island of Socotra), with Mukalla, in the Qu'aiti State, as the main town and harbor. Sa'udi Arabia claimed the Hadhramaut as part of her territory. Britain was interested in pacifying the area and strengthening it against the Sa'udi claims. Between 1936 and 1939 Harold Ingrams, the British Political Officer in Mukalla, signed about 1,400 treaties with local tribal leaders obliging them to stop fighting among themselves. The chief sultans accepted the protection and tutelage of the British Governor of 'Aden. In 1940, Britain raised a military force of c. 1,500 men, the Hadhrami Legion. Wahidi was the only one of the four Eastern Protectorate sultanates willing to join the Federation of South Arabia.

In 'Aden town, administered as a colony, the constitutional progress was that of paternalistic, British-guided gradualism: a Legislative Council, initially composed of "official" (i.e. colonial government officers) and non-official members, was established in 1946–47. Reforms of 1955 and 1957 reduced the number of official members and increased, among the non-official ones, the number of elected members, until they formed a majority; the electorate, however, remained restricted. At the same time the Governor's Council, orginally consisting of colonial officials only, was gradually enlarged to include representatives of local notables, and eventually members of the Legislative Council; it became a "Council of Ministers" in 1961, and its chairmanship passed from the Governor to a "Chief Minister" in 1963. The British wanted 'Aden to join the Federation — a highly controversial proposal, as the character and interests of the colony and the tribal sultanates were quite different: the latter were economically and socially backward, under the mediaeval autocracy of their desert chieftains, but enjoyed a larger degree of independence from Britain, while 'Aden town was economically more developed, socially sophisticated and politically active, but under a colonial form of government. Yet, in 1962–63 Britain succeeded in persuading the 'Aden government and Legislative Council to approve 'Aden's entry into the Federation — with its weight in the Federation's councils much less than that merited by its population, strength and economic contribution. In Jan. 1963, the Crown Colony became a Federal State and the British Governor's title was changed to that of High Commissioner.

Nationalists, both in the sultanates of the protectorates and, particularly, among the urban population of 'Aden, were dissatisfied and clamored for faster progress towards complete independence and the liquidation of British tutelage and privileges. Most of them believed that violence was the only way to achieve their aims.

The first insurgent organization, formed in 1951 in the Lahaj Sultanate, was the "South Arabian League" (SAL), led by Muhammad 'Ali al-Jifri and Sheikhan al-Habshi and backed by Egypt. Following the Yemen revolution of 1962, Egyptian support was transferred to a new and more militant organization — the *National Liberation Front for Occupied SY (NLF), founded in 1963 and led by Qahtan al-*Sha'bi. On 14 Oct. 1963 Sha'bi proclaimed, in the Radfan mountains north of 'Aden, an armed struggle against the Federation and any British presence. Later the main focus of the insurgency shifted to 'Aden town.

In Feb. 1965, the British High Commissioner attempted to appease the insurgents and invited 'Abd-ul-Qawi Makkawi, leader of the opposition in the Legislative Council, to form the 'Aden government. But insurgent activities increased, Makkawi gave them his open support, and in Sept. 1965 the High Commissioner dismissed Makkawi, the government and the Legislative Council, suspended the constitution and ruled by decree. Makkawi became a voluntary exile.

The Yemeni minority, constituting almost half of 'Aden's population, and deprived of electoral rights provided many insurgents. About 25,000 of them were members of the "'Aden Trades Union Congress" (ATUC), led by 'Abdullah al-Asnaj. The first of these trade unions had been organized in 1953 with British support, but gradually ATUC had adopted a leftist and pro-Nasserist line. It also founded, in 1962, a political wing, the "People's Socialist Party" (PSP). In May 1965, the PSP united with the SAL to form the "Organization for the Liberation of the Occupied South" (OLOS). A few months later the SAL, which now supported the sultans and was considered conservative, seceded. Egypt sponsored a successful effort to unite all the insurgent organizations (excluding the SAL), and in Jan. 1966, the OLOS — now made up mainly of PSP followers — and the NLF merged to form the "Front for the Liberation of Occupied SY" (*FLOSY). The deposed Prime Minister, 'Abd-ul-Qawi Makkawi, headed the Political Bureau, and 'Abdullah Asnaj became Secretary-General. FLOSY continued the armed struggle against Britain and the federation; it favored the union of South Arabia with Yemen and accepted Egyptian guidance. These two issues, and factional struggles, destroyed the recently achieved unity: late in 1966 the NLF split from FLOSY and the two organizations engaged each other in a struggle for supremacy. The NLF adopted an increasingly leftist, Marxist orientation and cultivated close links to the underground "A. Nationalist Movement" (*Harakat al-Qawmiyyin*) and its Palestinian-A. branch, the *PFLP.

Between 1964 and 1967 insurgent activities greatly increased. Since the early 1960s, the South Arabian problem had also been raised at the UN — mainly by the ASt, none of which recognized the Federation. (The *Arab League had denounced the Federation as "a creation of British imperialism and colonialism)". The UN Special Committee on Colonialism (the "Committee of 24"), and subsequently the General Assembly, endorsed in 1963 a report claiming that large parts of the South Arabian population disliked the existing régime and that the Federation was designed to prolong British rule in the area. British-Federal consultations in 1964 resulted in a British promise to grant independence, evacuate South Arabia and hand over power to the Federation by 1968. But in 1965 the UN General Assembly adopted a resolution urging elections, affirming the "inalienable right of the (South Arabian) people to self-determination and freedom from colonial rule" and demanding the "immediate and complete removal of the British bases". A similar resolution was adopted in 1966. Britain accepted the UN resolutions, again stating in Feb. 1966 that she would withdraw by 1968, and agreed to some UN supervision of the election and self-determination process. In Apr. 1967, a UN mission came to 'Aden for consultations on the organization of elections; but because of insurgent activities and a dispute with the British and Federal authorities, the mission left after a few days. Both FLOSY and the NLF refused to meet the mission, because it would not forgo all contacts with the sultans. The UN mission thus played no part in the shaping of events. In Feb. 1967 the British Foreign Secretary reiterated that Britain would leave South Arabia by 1968, transferring power to the Federal Government, to whom financial and military support was also promised. During summer 1967, Federal ministers held discussions with the UN mission (in Europe) and Britain, and made a (vain) attempt, supported by Britain, to contact the nationalists and arrange for a broad-based coalition of all groups.

Egyptian support for FLOSY was withdrawn in 1967, after the evacuation of the Egyptian expeditionary force from Yemen. Seizing this opportunity, the NLF took over most of the South Arabian sultanates. When the NLF emerged as the stronger force, the Federal Army and the ATUC gave it their support and those sultans and federal ministers who were not captured by the NLF fled the country. Egypt, who had previously ignored the NLF, now lent it her support. On 5 Sept. 1967 Britain had to acknowledge the collapse of the federal régime and to recognize the nationalists as the group with whom she would negotiate the transfer of power; in Nov. she had to state that negotiations would be conducted with the NLF alone. Negotiations were held in Geneva that same month and it was agreed that independence would be granted to South Arabia at midnight on 29 Nov. 1967. The new State was named the PR of SY, and Qahtan al-Sha'bi became its first President, Prime Minister and Commander of the Armed Forces. The

Republic was immediately admitted to membership of the UN and the Arab League.

The situation in SY deteriorated during her first year of independence. She had few, if any, economic resources of her own; British aid was meager, and was soon stopped because of incessant disputes. Her only economic asset — 'Aden's position as a transit and refuelling port — was placed in jeopardy by the closure of the Suez Canal. Government attempts to remedy the situation by tax increases and a reduction of salaries were unsuccessful. Moderate and extreme-leftist factions within the NLF were fighting for power, which caused instability and two unsuccessful rebellions during 1968. In June 1969, a *coup* replaced President Qahtan al-Sha'bi and his government with a more extremist leftist Presidential Council and government under Muhammad 'Ali Haitham, Salem Rubai' *'Ali and 'Abd-ul-Fattah *Isma'il.

During these first years efforts were made to abolish the traditional tribal system by the liquidation of the former sultanates and the re-division of the country into six new governorates — but tribal allegiances remained strong. The former sultans, federal ministers, SAL and FLOSY leaders were purged, jailed or sentenced to death and their property was confiscated. In addition to their past sins they were accused of plotting and attempting rebellion against the new State — in collusion with Sa'udi Arabia and "the imperialists". Late in 1969, SY enacted far-reaching measures of nationalization.

In foreign and international affairs, SY joined the leftist camp. She received economic and military aid from the USSR; and a close relationship developed between SY and China, who also granted aid. According to reports never officially confirmed, the USSR enjoyed naval and air base facilities in 'Aden and Socotra. Relations with the USA were severed by SY in Oct. 1969. SY also recognized East Germany — when that step still was a demonstration of a leftist orientation. Later, in the 1970s, SY joined COMECON, the economic association of the Soviet Bloc, as an observer. Her leaders visited the Soviet Union several times, Premier Kosygin was in SY in Sept. 1979, and throughout the shifts and vicissitudes of SY's politics and factional splits, close relations with the USSR and a strong Soviet influence remained constant. In Oct. 1979 she signed a Treaty of Friendship and Cooperation with the USSR. Other Soviet Bloc countries like Cuba and East Germany also cultivated relations with SY and aided her.

In inter-A. affairs, too, SY followed a radical-leftist line and became, with Syria and Libya, a mainstay of the *"Rejection Front". Though she had adopted the name "SY" to show that she regarded Yemen and SY as parts of one country and wished to unite them, no practical steps were taken towards a merger and relations wth Yemen remained cool and tense in SY's first years. In Nov. 1970 SY renamed herself "People's Democratic Republic of Yemen" (without "South-") — a step resented by Yemen. Tension and sporadic clashes, aggravated by tribal and border disputes, soon escalated and in Sept. 1972 clashes turned into warlike operations. These were halted by all-A., and particularly Libyan, mediation and renewed mutual endorsements of the decision in principle to unite the two Yemens. Such union pledges were reiterated at several meetings of the two Heads-of-State (changing ones in both countries), but relations did not improve much. In Feb. 1979 clashes again escalated into warlike operations — again followed by declarations of unity and the resolve to merge that were not implemented.

Relations with Sa'udi Arabia were hostile from the first days; Sa'udia did not even recognize SY and a border dispute soon arose. Relations with Egypt were correct but reserved; though SY applied for assistance, Egypt gave her little help. SY took a revolutionary stance regarding south-eastern Arabia and the Persian Gulf, and particularly her neighbor 'Oman. She actively supported anti-'Omani rebels fighting in adjacent *Dhofar since the mid-1960s and provided them with arms and supplies and an operational base in her territory, and she was behind the rebels when they attempted to widen their scope and to subvert and "liberate" the Persian Gulf region as a whole (see *'Oman, *Persian Gulf). SY also took an extreme anti-Israel line, and there were several reports, never fully confirmed, that she aided Egyptian efforts of the 1970s to block the Bab al-Mandeb straits to Israel-bound shipping, put the islands of Perim and/or Qamaran (which latter she claimed until 1972, when she acquiesced in Yemen's ownership) at the disposal of Palestinian-A. guerrilla groups and was involved in a

June 1971 bazooka attack on a Liberian oil tanker on its way to Israel.

In the mid-1970s, SY toned down her revolutionary zeal and adopted more pragmatic policies — a process connected also with internal factional struggles (see below). As the Dhofar rebellion was declining and being defeated, SY bowed in 1975–76 to Sa'udi pressure, accompanied by promises of improved relations and substantial aid, and stopped her aid to the rebels and to subversive schemes in the Persian Gulf, thereby causing the virtual end of the rebellion. In 1976 SY and Sa'udi Arabia established normal and official relations, and the cessation of SY aid to the Dhofari rebels was formally agreed upon with 'Oman (after Sa'udi, Kuwaiti and UAE mediation). Normal relations with 'Oman were agreed in Oct. 1982, though Ambassadors were not actually exchanged at the time. However, this gradual mitigation of SY's inter-A. policies and her growing dependence on aid from Sa'udia and the A. Gulf states did not lead to a change either in her pro-Soviet orientation or in her membership of the Rejection Front. Thus, SY refused to join the protest votes of the other A. and Islamic countries against the Soviet intervention in Afghanistan, from Dec. 1980, and sided with Iran against Iraq in the Gulf War — together with Syria and Libya, though not very actively. In Aug. 1981 she signed a Treaty of Friendship with Soviet-allied Ethiopia and Libya; but his treaty, interpreted at first as an alliance and a defense pact, had little impact on political or defense realities.

At home, SY's régime was troubled, as factional strife continued. This centered in part on doctrinal and ideological-political issues (there was, for instance, talk of pro-Chinese *versus* pro-Russian tendencies), but was determined in fact by a struggle for power and by tribal allegiances and rivalries. In Aug. 1971, Haitham was ousted and went into exile; 'Ali Nasser *Muhammad became Prime Minister and a member of the new Presidential Council, with Salem Rubai' 'Ali and 'Abd-ul-Fattah Isma'il (it was to 'Ali Nasser's growing influence that the change to more pragmatic policies was ascribed). In June 1978, President Salem Rubai' 'Ali was ousted and killed, and his supporters were purged. A new 111-member Supreme People's Assembly was elected. The new Presidential Council had five, later ten, members, but two of them, 'Ali Nasser Muhammad and 'Abd-ul-Fattah Isma'il, were the top rulers. At first, 'Ali Nasser was Council chairman, but in Dec. 1978 he ceded that position to 'Abd-ul-Fattah Isma'il, while continuing to hold the Premiership. Isma'il was also the Secretary-General of the ruling party, which had been re-formed in Oct. 1978 as the "Yemen Socialist Party". Between the two men there was an increasingly bitter rivalry — with Isma'il as revolutionary-doctrinaire hardliner (who also built up a party-dominated popular militia as the focus of his power), while 'Ali Nasser was seen as a pragmatist. Other members of the Presidential Council, the Government and the party Politbureau, such as 'Ali Nasser 'Antar and 'Ali Salem al-Baid, took shifting positions, maneuvering between the two principals.

In Apr. 1980 'Ali Nasser Muhammad gained the upper hand and took the Presidency in addition to the Premiership; he also became Secretary-General of the party. Isma'il went into exile to Russia. But while 'Ali Nasser was now the top leader, factional struggles and purges continued. In 1985, an inter-factional accommodation was reached — reportedly through Soviet mediation. It involved the return of 'Abd-ul-Fattah Isma'il and the restoration of his faction to some power positions, while 'Ali Nasser Muhammad gave up the Premiership (given to Haidar Abu-Bakr al-'Attas) and some of his dominating position in the party. But the compromise did not achieve a full reconciliation and factional strife continued. In Jan. 1986 it erupted in a major crisis, a bloody civil war whose details, related in conflicting versions, have not been fully clarified. In the fighting several top leaders were killed, including 'Abd-ul-Fattah Isma'il and 'Ali Nasser 'Antar (who had joined 'Ali Nasser Muhammad's foes). Soviet and A. attempts to mediate and restore a compromise had but little success. 'Ali Nasser Muhammad's régime collapsed, and he himself escaped to Yemen and Ethiopia. Haidar al-'Attas — heretofore a second-rank leader not fully identified with either of the rival factions — was named President, another second-rank official, Yassin Sa'id Nu'man, Prime Minister, and 'Ali Salem al-Baid Secretary-General of the YSP. The new régime purged the state and party apparatus of the deposed leader's men and then endeavored to restore normal conditions. In Oct. 1986 it held new elections to the Supreme People's Assembly. While continuing their predecessor's pragmatic policy of fostering normal relations with all ASt and paying visits to several of them, the new leaders rejected 'Ali Nasser Muhammad's proposals to work out a new compromise that would return him and his adherents to a position of shared power. In Dec. 1986, he and c. 140 of his men were put on trial, he and 48 others *in absentia*.

Soviet policies and interests See *Russia.

Spain A country with a long and rich history of ties with the A. world (with parts of her territory ruled by Muslim A. "Moors" from the 8th to the 15th century), S.'s involvement in A. affairs in this century was first and foremost in Morocco. Her Protectorate over parts of that country and its liquidation in northern Morocco in 1956, and in southern Morocco in the years following, are described in the entry *Morocco. It should be noted that S., though confronting the Moroccan national movement in circumstances similar to those of France, succeeded in general in avoiding a head-on clash with the Moroccans and maintaining reasonably good relations with them. S. continues holding a number of towns ("presidios") on Morocco's northern Mediterranean coast, chief among them Ceuta and Melilla. S. considers them Spanish territory, but Morocco regards them as part of her land. Morocco has so far not pressed her claims, and growing local unrest has not erupted in major violence; but the issue is no-doubt a focus of potential conflict. For "Spanish Sahara" and S.'s handing-over of that territory to Morocco and Mauritania in 1976 — see *Sahara, and *Morocco.

Having no direct imperial interests in the AC east of Morocco, S. has always endeavored — whatever her régime and political character: Kingdom, Republic, Franco-Fascism, or the restored democratic Kingdom since 1975 — to cultivate friendly relations with the ASt, and has been quite successful in that quest. Spanish economic interests are active in the ASt to a modest extent; Spanish oil companies have a minor share in several of them. S. was reluctant to establish official relations with Israel — no doubt because of her quest for A. friendship. In the 1950s, Israel had refused to establish relations with Franco S., but since the 1970s she was keen on establishing them with new S. Eventually, full diplomatic relations were set up in Jan. 1986.

Sudan Republic in North-East Africa (1969–85: "Democratic Republic", since Dec. 1985 again "Republic"). Area: c. 967,000 sq.mi. (2.5m. sq.km.) — the largest country in Africa. S. has existed as a political entity in her present borders since 1899 (when she was re-conquered by Anglo-Egyptian forces, after the *Mahdi*'s rule). She attained independence in Jan. 1956, and became a member of the UN on 12 Nov. 1956. S. borders in the east on Ethiopia and the Red Sea, in the south on Kenya, Uganda and Zaire, in the west on Chad, the Central African Republic and Libya, and in the north on Egypt.

The population was given by the last census, taken in 1973, as 14.17m.; in the early 1980s it was estimated variously as 19–20.5m., officially (1983) as 22m. The population is not homogeneous. Ethnically, about 50% consider themselves A. (though some surveys list only 40% or slightly less as claiming "A. origin"). More than 10% are various non-A. Muslim groups, mostly of "Hamitic" or "Nubian-Hamitic" descent — such as the *Nubians in the north, the *Beja in the north-east, the *Nuba and the Fur in the west. All these popultions, A. and non-A., have strong negroid admixtures. About one third of the population, all in the south, are black Africans of "Nilo-Hamitic" origin — with Dinka, Nuer, Shilluk as the main tribes. Some surveys estimate

Map of Sudan

the non-A. populations of the north and the south together as more than 50% of the total. Arabic is the official language and a *lingua franca* for many of the non-A. groups as well; but most of these groups have their own language — about 115 languages are counted, of which 26 are considered the main ones. In the non-A. south, English is also used as a *lingua franca* and in a 1972 agreement with the southern rebels it was recognized as an official language for the south.

In terms of religion, more than half of the population are Muslims, estimates varying from 50–60% to 73%. Christians are estimated at 7–9%, nearly all of them in the African south (where they are about 20%); and pagan animists are 18–24% of the total population, all of them in the African south (where they constitute c. 80%).

S.'s population has in recent years also included large numbers of refugees from neighboring African countries — Uganda, Ethiopia (mainly Eritrea), Chad, Zaïre. Their number has sometimes been estimated at over 1m., but, usually several hundred thousand, it fluctuates, as groups (mainly tribes from Uganda) move back and forth. There are also refugees from S. to the neighboring countries — mainly from the African south, in the context of the civil war; their number, sometimes estimated at several hundred thousands, also keeps shifting.

S.'s economy is almost entirely agricultural, and to a large extent pastoral. The most important cash crop is cotton which accounts for about half of the country's exports. In the south coffee, tea, and tobacco are grown. 80–90% of the world's supply of gum arabic come from S. There is, however, little industry. Efforts are made to explore and exploit oil and mineral deposits. Oil has already been found in the south; an American company began extracting it, but suspended operations because of the civil war. Chrome, gold and gypsum are already being mined; deposits of copper, iron, silver and zinc have been located. In recent years, S.'s economy has been in a serious crisis. Growth rates are low and S. is unable to repay or service her external debt, estimated in the mid-1980s at over $10,000m. up to $15,000m. Agricultural production and cotton exports have declined. As the government is unable to implement reform and rehabilitation measures recommended by foreign and international finance institutions, foreign aid has decreased.

POLITICAL HISTORY. *Bilad al-S.* (Arabic: "Land of the Blacks") was the name given by medieval Muslim geographers to the region lying south of the Sahara Desert and Egypt. Western S., extending to the Senegal and Niger rivers, was under French domination until the 1960s when this area became the independent states of Chad, Niger and Mali. Eastern S., or S. in the more restricted sense used from the end of the 19th century, comprises the territories south of Egypt.

Muhammad 'Ali, the Ottoman Sultan's Viceroy in Egypt who became an autonomous ruler, conquered the north-central areas of the country, i.e. Nubia, Sennar and Kordofan, in 1820–22. During the reign of the Khedive Isma'il (1863–79), the provinces of Darfur, Bahr al-Ghazal and Equatoria and the Red Sea port of Suakin were added to Egypt's possessions. Egyptian rule impoverished S., especially through the slave trade. The bitterness which the population felt towards the occupants was one of the reasons for the rebellion of the *Mahdi.

The rebellion grew out of a fanatical Islamic-revivalist movement. Its leader, Muhammad Ahmad Ibn 'Abdullah, claimed to be the *Mahdi* (Arabic: The Guided One), the divine leader chosen by God at the end of time to fill the earth with justice. The *Mahdi*'s followers (*al-*Ansar* — Arabic: Helpers, after the first supporters of the Prophet Muhammad) defeated the troops sent against them in 1881 and conquered most of Kordofan, Darfur and Bahr al-Ghazal in 1882–83. The British, who had occupied Egypt in 1882 (although nominally she remained part of the Ottoman Empire), recommended the evacuation of the rest of S. and re-appointed former Governor Gen. Gordon to organize this. Gordon negotiated with the *Mahdi* but failed to reach a compromise. In Jan. 1885, the *Mahdi*'s troops conquered Khartoum and massacred its garrison, including Gordon. The *Mahdi* died in the same year and his successor, the *Khalifa* 'Abdullahi, ruled till the liquidation of the *Mahdist* state in 1898.

In 1896 the British government decided to reconquer S., mainly to prevent other powers (Germany, Italy, Belgium and especially France) from taking over the vital area of the sources of the Nile. The conquest was carried out in Egypt's name, to reimpose Egyptian control over what was described as Egyptian territory. The expeditionary force, composed of British and Egyptian troops under the command of Sir Herbert Kitchener, took Khartoum in Sept. 1898 and by the end of that year the remaining *Mahdist* forces were defeated and the *Khalifa* 'Abdullahi was killed. The *Mahdiyya* later became a peaceful sect, although still very influential; it was opposed by the *Mirghaniyya or *Khatmiyya sect.

A "Condominium" agreement signed by Britain and Egypt in Jan. 1899 established their joint rule over S. Britain wielded *de facto* control, and the régime she set up was colonial-type, the Anglo-Egyptian partnership being virtually fictitious. The administration was along military lines, because there were frequent uprisings; pacification was completed only at the end of World War I. S. was governed by a Governor-General, appointed by the Egyptian Khedive on the recommendation of the British Government. The Governor-General, who held both executive and legislative powers, was always British, and until 1926 the post was entrusted to the British C-in-C of the Egyptian Army (the *Sirdar*). A Mar. 1899 agreement with France ended a crisis over the occupation by French forces of Fashoda in South S. which had brought Britain and France to the brink of war: France relinquished the area. In 1901 and 1902 agreements with Italy and Ethiopia defined S.'s borders with Eritrea and Ethiopia.

A nationalist movement appeared at a rather late stage, stimulated by the presence of Egyptian Army officers and civil servants (generally of lower and middle rank). In 1921, 'Ali 'Abd-ul-Latif, a former army officer, created a "Sudanese United Tribes Society", which demanded independence for S. He was imprisoned. After his release he created, in 1924, a "White Flag League" aiming to establish S. as part of a Nile Valley united under the Egyptian Crown. Supported by Egyptian circles, it organized anti-British demonstrations in which military school cadets were active. The British imprisoned 'Abdul-Latif again and suppressed these beginnings of the national movement.

On 19 Nov. 1924 Sir Lee Stack, the Governor-General of S. and *Sirdar* of the Egyptian Army, was assassinated in Cairo by Egyptian nationalists. In retaliation the British compelled all Egyptian troops and civil servants to evacuate S. As anti-British agitation was mainly conducted by educated Sudanese in the cities, the British encouraged tribalism and tribal institutions and started ruling through local chiefs and sheikhs rather than creating a central bureaucracy based on urban educated Sudanese. Courses for training Sudanese administrators were discontinued, the Khartoum military college was closed down and harsh discipline was introduced at the Gordon Memorial College of Khartoum, an institution opened in 1902 to train artisans and junior officials which had become a breeding-ground of Sudanese nationalism.

After 1924 Sudanese nationalism stagnated. From the mid-1930s its main organization was the "Graduates' Congress" based on Gordon College. Nationalist activity was revived after World War II when a decision concerning S.'s future seemed imminent. The nationalists were now faced with the alternatives of an independent state or "Unity of the Nile Valley", i.e. union with Egypt (as Egypt demanded in her persistent struggle with Britain over S. — see *Egypt). Those favoring the latter seem to have conceived it as a weapon against Britain rather than a permanent commitment to Egypt. Most of the supporters of independence joined the *Umma* (Nation) Party, under 'Abdullah al-Khalil, while the pro-Egyptian group, under Isma'il al-*Azhari, formed the *Al-Ashiqqa'* (the Brethren), which grew out of the "Graduates' Congress"; both camps, though, were continuously splitting into many rival factions. Of the religious orders, the *Mahdiyya's al-Ansar* supported independence, while the rival *al-Mirghaniyya* was pro-Egyptian.

The British started a gradual transition to partial autonomy in 1943 by establishing an Advisory Council for northern S. In 1948 a Legislative Assembly was set up for the whole of S. The transfer of power was slow, however, and caused friction with Egypt which objected to any form of self-rule under British tutelage. The pro-Egyptian factions in S. also boycotted the legislative elections of 1948 and the Assembly created. (The Sudanese members of the government — the Governor-General's Executive Council — were not, as a rule, political personalities.)

A turning point was the July 1952 *coup* in Egypt. The new rulers agreed to grant the Sudanese the right of self-determination, as they were eager to get the British out of S. as soon as possible. Late in 1952 they concluded an accord with the Sudanese parties, and on 12 Feb. 1953 Egypt and Britain signed an agreement about the future of S. A transition period of three years was set to prepare the ground for the act of self-determination that would decide the future of S. (independence or union with Egypt). During the transition period the administration would be transferred to the Sudanese, and elections held under international supervision. British and Egyptian troops would be evacuated as soon as the elected Sudanese Parliament decided that "Sudanization" was completed and the time for self-determination had come. Two international commissions were to assist that transition. Elections took place in Nov. 1953, and al-Azhari's pro-Egyptian party — by now called "National Unionist Party" (NUP) — won. In Jan. 1954 Azhari became the first Prime Minister of S.

The Sudanization of the administration was considered completed in Aug. 1955 and Parliament demanded the evacuation of British and Egyptian troops which was effected by Nov. 1955. Parliament and the government also demanded a simplification of the complicated constitutional procedure set for self-determination, and it was agreed that S.'s future would be decided by a vote in Parliament. Azhari and his supporters had by now changed their minds about a union with Egypt and preferred complete independence. A resolution to that effect was unanimously adopted by Parliament on 19 Dec. 1955 and on 1 Jan. 1956 S. became formally independent. As a Constitution, most of the British "Self-Government Statute" was taken over. This provided for an elected Parliament (elections being partially indirect, through tribal and village councils), and an Upper House three-fifths elected and two-fifths appointed. A Presidential Council, elected by Parliament, took over as Head of State.

Soon after achieving independence, Premier al-Azhari lost his parliamentary majority as his NUP split and lost the support of the pro-Egyptian *Khatmiyya* order. He had to form a coalition government that included 'Abdullah Khalil's *Umma* party. In July 1956 a new coalition was formed by the *Umma* and the "People's Democratic Party" (PDP) founded by seceding members of the NUP and supported by the *Khatmiyya*; 'Abdullah Khalil became Prime Minister. The same coalition returned to power following the elections of Feb. 1958, but its stability was threatened by disagreements between its partners over both domestic and foreign affairs. Thus the suggested appointment of the *Mahdiyya* leader 'Abd-ul-Rahman al-*Mahdi as President of the Republic (instead of the five-member Presidency Council in office since independence) was strongly opposed by the PDP and had to be shelved. The *Umma* party — pro-British and keen to strengthen ties with the West — also clashed with the PDP's pro-Egyptian and neutralist-leftist orientation. The threat of an economic crisis, caused mainly by a poor cotton crop, induced Premier Khalil to appeal for US economic aid. This was opposed by his coalition partners, and to maintain his parliamentary majority, he had to win the support of the representatives of the south — in exchange for a pledge to discuss the transformation of S.'s constitutional structure into a federal one. The coalition, and the Premier's position, were soon threatened again by feelers put out by some leaders of his own party for a new coalition with the NUP. In October 1958 talks were held in Cairo between President *Nasser, al-Azhari and PDP leaders, causing further concern to the Prime Minister and to a number of senior army officers who feared the increase of Egypt's political influence in S. On 16 Nov. the two main parties — the *Umma* and the NUP — agreed to form a coalition. But their agreement was thwarted by a military *coup* on 17 Nov. 1958. It has been suggested — but never proved — that 'Abdullah Khalil had a hand in the *coup*.

The leader of the *coup*, Gen. Ibrahim *'Abbud, abolished all political parties, "to save the country from the degeneration, chaos and instability" into which party rivalries and the politicians' self-seeking intrigues had led it, and banned all political activity. Parliament was dissolved and the constitution suspended. A "Supreme Council of the Armed Forces", composed of twelve officers, proclaimed Gen. 'Abbud President and delegated to him all legislative, judicial and executive powers, as well as the command of the armed forces. A twelve-member cabinet headed by 'Abbud as Premier, contained seven officers.

'Abbud's military dictatorship, which was rather mild and conservative, lasted for nearly six years. Several abortive military *coup*s were crushed by 'Abbud in 1959. Fifteen prominent former politicians were arrested in 1961 for causing agitation and unrest, but they were released a year later. There was no progress towards constitutional rule or the resumption of political life, little economic advance — and the problem of southern S. (see below) appeared to be deteriorating. By Sept. 1963, the southern tribes were in open rebellion.

A *coup* broke out in Oct. 1964 sparked off by the troubles in the south and general discontent with the economic situation, inefficiency and corruption. Politicians, university students and workers had started campaigning for an end to military government and the restoration of democracy. On 21 Oct. police fired on demonstrators, killing one student. A general strike was called immediately and Gen. 'Abbud was forced to negotiate with a common front comprising all the old parties and supported by the heads of the two religious orders. The Constitution of 1956 was reinstated. It was agreed that 'Abbud would stay on as President but hand over executive power to a transitional government composed of all parties and including, for the first time, the Communist Party and the *"Muslim Brotherhood". Within four weeks, however, 'Abbud had to resign as President and Commander-in-Chief. The presidency reverted to a five-member Council.

The transitional government put much emphasis on the problem of southern S. and tried — unsuccessfully — to solve it with the help of supporters among southern leaders. The freedom of the press was restored and the ban on political parties was abolished. In June 1965 elections were held, in which all parties, except the PDP, participated. As no party won an absolute majority, a coalition was formed between the *Umma* party, with 76 seats and the NUP, 53 seats. Muhammad Ahmad Mahjoub (*Umma*) became Prime Minister and al-Azhari (NUP) permanent chairman of the Presidential Council. The new régime was torn between rightist and leftist factions. In Nov. 1965 the Communist Party was declared illegal. The decision was contested in court, which declared it null and void. However, after a protracted dispute with the judiciary, the court's judgement was overruled by the Assembly, which reimposed the ban.

In the meantime, the *Umma* party was again split. A right wing under the leader of the *Mahdiyya* Order, the Imam al-Hadi al-Mahdi, supported the Premier, Mahjoub, while younger elements followed the Imam's nephew, the modernist-progressive Sadeq al-*Mahdi. The latter became Prime Minister after a vote of no confidence forced Mahjoub to resign in July 1966. The new government, also a coalition of the *Umma* and the NUP, was able to improve the economic situation owing to strict controls and loans from the World Bank. It also promised to solve the question of southern S. by a degree of regional autonomy. The drafting of a permanent constitution was speeded up. However, as the Imam withdrew his support from his nephew, one faction of the *Umma* party voted against the government and it was defeated in the Assembly in May 1967. M.A. Mahjoub again became Premier, supported by a coalition of the NUP and the Imam al-Hadi faction of the *Umma*; the PDP now also joined (it merged, late in 1967, with the NUP, to form the "Democratic Unionist Party", (DUP). This government concluded an arms deal with the USSR and lifted the ban on the Communist Party. It severed diplomatic relations with the UK and the US following the Israel-Arab *Six Day War. But the coalition was unstable; the presidency was claimed by both Azhari and al-Hadi al-Mahdi; the southern problem was unsolved; and the drafting of the constitution caused considerable controversy. The draft prepared was based on Islam, regionalist decentralization and a strong presidential executive at the center; it was strongly opposed by the Communists and the PDP. In Jan. 1968, the government decided to dissolve the Assembly. In new elections, in Apr. 1968, the newly merged DUP won 101 seats, al-Hadi al-Mahdi's faction of the *Umma* 30 seats and Sadeq al-Mahdi's *Umma* 36. The two former groups again formed a government under Mahjoub. But this government, too, failed to tackle the three major problems — the economic situation, the permanent constitution and southern S. Its position was undermined by disputes between the coalition partners and by reports that the two wings of the *Umma* had reunited and were about to re-establish their conservative rule.

On 25 May 1969 a group of army officers under Col. Ja'far al-*Numeiri staged a bloodless *coup*. The name of the state was changed to "Democratic Republic of the S.". The constitution was again suspended, and the Constituent Assembly and the Presidential Council were dissolved. Absolute powers were vested in a National Revolutionary Council. A former Chief Justice, Abu Bakr 'Awadullah, was appointed Prime Minister. His Cabinet contained several Communists. All political parties were abolished and several former ministers were brought to trial on charges of corruption. The new régime proclaimed a policy of "Sudanese Socialism", with the state participating in the economy, while maintaining freedom for foreign aid and local capital.

In Oct. 1969, friction concerning the Communist Party came to a head. During a visit to East Germany, 'Awadullah declared that the Sudanese revolution could not function without the Communist Party (which had disregarded the ban imposed on political parties and conducted public meetings and propaganda activities). Numeiri prepared to cooperate with the Communists to achieve broader support for his régime, but striving to curtail their power, disavowed 'Awadullah and himself took over as Premier, naming 'Awadullah Foreign Minister and Minster of Justice.

In Mar. 1970, Numeiri confronted the potentially most dangerous foes of his régime (and probably the strongest organized group in the country), the *Mahdiyya* and the *Ansar*. In Numeiri's official version, *Mahdiyya* demonstrations turned into a plot, a rebellion. He suppressed that "rebellion" in a military and security operation. Nuclei of *Mahdiyya* resistance forces, concentrated on Aba island in the White Nile, were liquidated — an operation in which the Imam, al-Hadi al-Mahdi, was killed. The rival, political *Mahdiyya* leader, Sadeq al-Mahdi, who was among the hundreds arrested, was deported to Egypt (and so was the Communist leader 'Abd-ul-Khaleq Mahjoub).

Relations with the Communists continued plaguing the régime and were at the root of several *coup* attempts, changes of government and purges. In Nov. 1970, leading leftists were purged from the government and army, but other leftists continued serving. The Communist Party itself was split on the question of collaboration with the régime (with the main faction, under Secretary-General 'Abd-ul-Khaleq Mahjoub, opposing such collaboration). In July 1971, a group of leftist officers — of those purged in Nov. — actually ousted Numeiri; they were, however, defeated after three days by loyal army units, and Numeiri was reinstated amidst bloody purges of leftists, summary trials and executions (including the top Communist leaders). The crisis also caused some upheaval in S.'s foreign relations — the USSR was accused of supporting the *coup*, ambassadors were recalled, and relations came close to a breach; with Iraq, similarly accused, relations were severed. Libya and Egypt appear to have helped Numeiri.

The suppression of the *Ansar* and the Communists in 1970–71 eliminated Numeri's political rivals and enabled him to consolidate his régime. In Aug. 1971 he proclaimed a transitional Constitution, and in Sept. he was elected President, as the single candidate, retaining also the Premiership. In Oct. he dissolved the Revolutionary Command Council. The same month he established a single party, on the Egyptian pattern, the Sudanese Socialist Union (SSU), which held its first convention in Jan. 1972. In Feb.–Mar. 1972, Numeiri attained the greatest achievement of his years in power: he reached agreement with the South-S. rebels to end the civil war (see below). In Sept. 1972 a People's National Assembly was elected (indirectly) and in Apr. 1973 it adopted a permanent Constitution which proclaimed S. to be a "unitary, democratic, socialist and sovereign republic", with Islam as state religion (but provided for an autonomous régime in the south). In Feb. 1974 a new National Assembly was elected.

But S.'s stability continued to be shaken by plots and unrest. One nucleus of potential opposition was the officers' corps. An officers' plot and attempted *coup* was foiled in Jan. 1973, and another in Sept. 1975. At least the second was reportedly connected with and inspired by a political anti-Numeiri "National Front" (NF) that had been formed, in exile (mainly in Libya) or half-underground, from the early 1970s by a coalition of the *Mahdiyya*'s *Umma* Party, the former NUP-DUP, and the Muslim Brotherhood. In July 1976 another *coup* attempt was staged by the NF, with active Libyan support. It was suppressed only after serious fighting.

Numeiri responded by constant purges and an

effort to tighten his government. He also tried to strengthen the SSU, but had little success. In Apr. 1977 Numeiri was re-elected, as the single candidate, for a second six-year term as President. He now felt secure enough to initiate a reconciliation with the NF. An amnesty was proclaimed in Aug. 1977. Sadeq al-Mahdi returned to S. after over seven years of exile. Another faction of the NF, the Muslim Brothers led by Hassan 'Abdullah al-Turabi, also made its peace with the régime. The third faction of the NF, al-Sharif al-Hindi's DUP, reached an agreement with Numeiri in Apr. 1978 on the dissolution of the NF (although the reconciliation process faced at the same time new obstacles because of Numeiri's half-support of Egypt's peace policy towards Israel). While promoting that reconciliation process, Numeiri continued reorganizing his Government. In Feb. 1978, elections to S.'s third People's National Assembly and the Southern People's Regional Assembly took place, with candidates sponsored by the *Umma*, the DUP and the MB successfully participating.

Meanwhile, S. was facing worsening economic problems, which caused further social and political unrest. The Numeiri régime had done very little to advance major development schemes. The only new projects were the start of work on the long-planned Jonglei Canal to drain the vast al-Sudd swamps of the White Nile (see *Nile) in 1978, with international aid and by foreign companies, and the beginning of oil production by the American Chevron company in south S. at about the same time. In general, the economy stagnated and production declined. When the government decided to devaluate the currency in mid-1978, a wave of industrial trouble swept S. During 1979, there was further economic decline, and growing public resentment led to violent riots in Aug. 1979. The reconciliation process suffered delays and was partially suspended. Renewed unrest in the south (see below) aggravated the situation. Reshuffles in the Cabinet and the SSU, as well as in the southern regional government, failed to calm the growing unrest. During 1980–81, Numeiri continued to struggle with the economic difficulties and grave and growing pressures within the régime, and a wave of violent riots swept over the Darfur region. In Oct. 1981 Numeiri dissolved the National Assembly, and the new one he convened in Feb. 1982 was appointed, not elected. In 1982 serious political-industrial unrest re-erupted in Khartoum, the Army was summoned to crush the turbulence and the régime's prestige was eroded. Numeiri put the blame on the SSU's failure to win popular support and again made substantial changes at the top of the political hierarchy, dispersed the leading SSU institutions and purged the top echelons of the army command. Gen. 'Abd-ul-Majid Hamed Khalil, since 1979 First Vice-President, Minister of Defense, Commander-in-Chief, General Secretary of the SSU and regarded as Numeiri's chosen successor, was dismissed from all his posts (Numeiri had similarly dismissed in 1978 First Vice-President Abu'l-Qassem Muhammad Ibrahim and several times changed other Vice-Presidents).

Yet, despite this continuous political and economic predicament, and with the South Sudan crisis mounting, the Numeiri régime held on. In an Apr.-May 1983 referendum Numeiri was elected, as the single candidate, for a third presidential term. In Sept. 1983 he decreed the implementation of Islamic law (*Shari'a*) and its code of punishments throughout S. — a step that was rejected by many, including both the major Islamic orders, the *Mahdiyya* and the *Khatmiyya*, and caused bitter resentment particularly in the non-Muslim south.

The steady weakening of Numeiri's position came to a climax in Mar. 1985, when massive civil disobedience erupted, paralyzing the country. On 6 Apr. 1985, it brought about the régime's overthrow. Numeiri took refuge in Egypt. Power was taken over by the army command under Gen. 'Abd-ul-Rahman Muhammad Hassan Siwar-al-Dhahab, Defense Minister and Commander-in-Chief since March 1985. The Government, the National Assembly, the Regional Assemblies, and the SSU were dissolved. In April a fifteen-member Transitional Military Council, with Siwar-al-Dhahab as chairman, and a civilian Government headed by Daf'ullah Juzuli were formed. This transitional Government led S. until Apr. 1986, when the first democratic election since 1968 were held throughout the country (excluding large areas in the south — see below). The *Umma* Party under al-Sadeq al-Mahdi emerged as the strongest faction in the new Constituent Assembly with 99 of

260 seats, followed by the DUP with 63 and the Muslim Brothers' National Islamic Front (NIF), led by al-Turabi, with 51 seats. On 15 May 1986 Sadeq al-Mahdi formed a coalition government, comprising the *Umma*, the DUP and several southern groups. The NIF and the Communists (with three seats) formed the opposition. The Presidency was replaced by a Council of Sovereignty or State Supreme Council, chaired by Ahmad 'Ali al-Mirghani, the brother of the spiritual leader of the *Khatmiyya* sect (thus balancing al-Mahdi's position as Prime Minister). From summer 1986 the new government had to cope with S.'s serious problems — with the economic crisis and the escalating civil war in the south as the most severe and urgent ones.

FOREIGN POLICY. During its first years, S.'s government followed a neutralist line, generally with pro-Western sympathies. After the 1958 *coup*, Gen. 'Abbud carried on the same policy, although he was somewhat less friendly towards the West. The civilian government which succeeded 'Abbud in 1964 reportedly for some time supported revolutionary movements in southern Arabia, Congo and Eritrea. In 1965, relations with the German Federal Republic were severed after Bonn's decision to establish diplomatic relations with Israel (re-established in 1971), and those with Britain over Rhodesia (re-established in 1966). In June 1967 relations with the West deteriorated further as a result of the *Six Day War, and S. broke off relations with the USA and UK; those with Britain were resumed in Jan. 1968, and those with the USA in July 1972. From 1967–68, the Sudanese government strengthened relations with the USSR and the Soviet Bloc and accepted military and economic aid, including Soviet military advisers. After the May 1969 *coup* the Numeiri régime also recognized the German Democratic Republic. But relations with the Soviet Bloc suffered a heavy blow in the crisis of July 1971 (see above). In the 1970s military "facilities" the USSR enjoyed in S. were cut, and in 1977 all Soviet military advisers were reportedly expelled. Generally, the Numeiri régime followed, despite its officially neutralist stance, a pro-Western, pro-US orientation. It also grew increasingly dependent on US and Western aid. The post-1985 régime seemed to take a more reserved, neutralist line.

S., admitted to the Arab League in 1956, upon attaining independence, followed a neutral policy between the rival A. blocs. In 1958 a sharp conflict with Egypt arose when the latter tried to take over disputed border areas by force. Egypt was compelled to retreat following Kharoum's firm stand, including a complaint to the UN Security Council. Another, more permanent cause of friction with Egypt, the problem of the distribution of the Nile waters, was resolved in 1959 by a new agreement — see *Nile. Yet, during the first years of independence S. remained suspicious of Egypt, resenting Egypt's "Big-Brother" attitude and reported intervention in S. politics, intrigues and the cultivation of pro-Egyptian factions. Gradually, however, relations became normal. After the A.-Israel Six Day War S. became more active in inter-A. affairs. The first A. summit conference after the war was held in Khartoum in Sept. 1967. A Sudanese contingent was left with the Egyptian Army at the Suez front. S.'s Premier also tried unsuccessfully to mediate in the Yemen war.

Following the May 1969 *coup*, Numeiri initiated a policy of close cooperation with Egypt and Libya. Leaders of the three countries met several times to discuss cooperation in the military, economic and cultural spheres. In Nov. 1970 they announced their decision to establish a federation of Egypt, Sudan and Libya. But when the federation was re-endorsed in Apr. 1971 (with Syria as an additional member), S. was no longer among its members. It was not officially clarified why S. at the last minute opted out of the Federation, but it may be assumed that the reason was the growing antagonism between her and Libya (see below). S.'s relations with Egypt were not adversely affected; on the contrary, they were considerably strengthened during the 1970s and early 1980s and became so close that a trend towards an eventual S.-Egypt confederation was indicated. In Feb. 1974 Presidents Numeiri and Sadat agreed on plans to "integrate" S. and Egypt. A Defense Pact was prepared in 1976 and signed in Jan. 1977; it was reconfirmed and renewed in Dec. 1981. It was also decided that the two National Assemblies should meet in joint session, and from 1977 they did so several times. In 1979 S. dissented from the all-A. denunciation and boycott of Egypt, supported her moves towards peace with Israel, and maintained official relations with her; all-A. pressure compelled her to recall her Ambassador in Dec. 1979, but she sent a new one in 1981. In Oct. 1982 the idea of Sudanese-Egyptian integration was institutionalized in a formal agreement. As a token of that integration, a "Nile Valley Parliament", consisting of 60 members from each National Assembly, first met in May 1983. From 1985, after the fall of Numeiri, the new régime visibly dissociated itself from Egypt. In Feb. 1987 it signed a new Egypt-S. "Charter of Brotherhood", abolishing the integration agreements. But it is too soon to say whether the trend towards integration has been decisively halted or reversed.

In S.'s relations with Libya there were ups and downs, but the trend in the 1970s was towards increasing tension and a growing antagonism. S. always suspected Libyan subversion, intervention and plots; and indeed Qadhdhafi, resenting Numeiri's pro-Western orientation and his opposition to Libyan expansionist merger schemes (e.g. in Chad), seemed to have a hand in several attempts to topple or destabilize S.'s régime. He granted asylum and operational bases to the *Mahdiyya*-plus-DUP opposition, and went as far as supporting and aiding the rebelling South S. African tribes (a strange move, in terms of Libyan principles and orientations, since that was a rebellion of non-A. and non-Muslim populations against an A.-Muslim régime). S. also complained of breaches of her sovereignty by border incursions and overflights. Official relations were severed from 1976 to 1977, and from 1981 to the fall of Numeiri. The post-1985 régime resumed relations and instituted a significant *rapprochement* with Libya (although it also complained of encroachments on S.'s territory by Libyan operations in Chad).

Relations with Ethiopia were also troubled. Ethiopia complained that S. was aiding the Eritrean rebels, or at least granting them asylum and operational bases, while S. charged Ethiopia with affording similar support to the South S. African rebels. Since both countries were interested in normal relations, there were ups and downs, from acute tension and the recall of Ambassadors to solemn state visits, and S. promised several times to end her aid to the Eritrean rebels (and did so to a certain extent). But the problem remained unresolved. An additional irritant was the transit through S. of 10–15,000 escaping Ethiopian Jews, from 1981–82 to a peak in 1984–85, their reception in transit camps, and their transportation to Israel in an airlift organized by American institutions and tacitly allowed by S. This issue also had internal repercussions in S. and led, after Numeiri's fall, to the trial and condemnation of several leading officials, including one of Numeiri's Vice-Presidents.

THE PROBLEM OF SOUTHERN SUDAN. The most acute domestic problem is the question of the three southern provinces — Equatoria, Bahr al-Ghazal and the Upper Nile, populated by 6–7m. non-A. and non-Muslim Negro tribes, mostly pagan and about 20% Christian. During the Condominium, the (British) government endeavored to preserve southern S.'s special character and to close it to northern Muslim penetration and domination. In 1955, on the eve of independence, southerners, afraid of northern domination, rebelled, starting with a mutiny of southern troops. The rebellion was suppressed, but a further revolt broke out in 1963. In Feb. 1964 the government decided to expel all foreign Christian missionaries operating in the south, accusing them of fostering the rebellion. Harsh military action against the rebels and villagers and tribes assisting them caused a great number of southern Sudanese to take refuge in neighboring countries; in July 1969 the UN estimated their number at over 150,000, while others spoke of up to 400,000. The rebellion and its suppression is said to have caused the death of hundreds of thousands of people.

The southerners were divided over their plans for the future: some wanted a separate southern state independent of S., and some a federation with the north, while others were prepared to cooperate with the existing unitary state, perhaps with increased local autonomy and decentralization, and collaborated with the government (in which some southerners, forming various shifting parties, usually held ministerial posts).

The new civilian government of Oct. 1964 declared an amnesty in the south. A Round Table Conference on the constitutional future of the south was held in Khartoum in Mar. 1965, attended by the government, representatives of southern and northern political parties and observers from seven African states. But no agreement was reached, and the problem was referred to a committee. The latter recommended a measure of decentralization and regional autonomy — a recommendation endorsed by another conference of political parties. Elections postponed in the south in 1965, could be held in 1967. But the government was still unable to agree to a basic solution to the problem and the rebellion continued.

The rebellion was centered mainly in Equatoria province. Its forces were divided by tribal differences and antagonisms. It was, for instance, reported that the Dinka, the largest tribe, centered in Bahr al-Ghazal and Upper Nile provinces, took little part. But information about the internal organization and problems of the rebels was spotty and unreliable. In 1967–68 the rebels established a Uganda-based "Provisional Government" headed by Aggrey Jaden, and early in 1969 they proclaimed an independent "Nile Republic", headed now, after factional struggles and the ouster of Jaden, by Gordon Mayen. However, some of the rebels inside S. refused to recognize the Uganda-based refugee government; in mid-1969 their military army, the *Anyanya*, proclaimed their own independent government, the *Anyidi* State, and Gen. Emidio Tafeng Lodongi formed a Revolutionary Council and Government. In 1970–71 Col. Joseph Lagu emerged as the main leader.

After the *coup* of 1969, the new Numeiri régime resolved to find a solution to the problem of the south and opened secret negotiations with the rebels, in the Ethiopian capital Addis Ababa. In March 1972 an agreement was signed, thereby ending the civil war. The three southen provinces jointly were given a large degree of autonomy (later incorporated in the new provisional Constitution of 1973). The newly created Southern Region was to be ruled by a Higher Executive Council and an elected People's Regional Assembly. The chairman of the Council was to be appointed by the Head of State and serve also as Vice-President of S. There was to be no discrimination on grounds of religion and ethnic background. The central Government remained responsible for defense, foreign policy, communications and several other matters of national concern. Education, housing, health etc. were left in the hands of the southern government. A first Regional Assembly was elected in Nov. 1973. For several years the 1972 Agreement provided the basis for peace and cooperation in the south itself and between the south and north. But in the mid-1970s, circumstances began to change. The economic crisis aggravated the south's already serious economic problems; S.'s realignment with Egypt was traditionally perceived in the south as a threat to southern autonomy and interests; the process of "national reconciliation", from 1977, seemed to strengthen the Arab-Islamic character of S.; and the Government seemed to renege on its support for southern autonomy. There was also near-constant factional and tribal friction in the southern regional institutions and they were shaken by frequent changes in the executive and by the central (northern) Government's attempts to use and manipulate these changes and frictions. Lagu, who had replaced Abel Alier, a Dinka, as chairman of the Executive Council in 1978, was out by Feb. 1980 and Alier resumed his chairmanship. But in Oct. 1981 the Council and the Assembly were dissolved, along with the dismissal of S.'s National Assembly. From the early 1980s the south was much agitated by a proposal to dissolve the three-province region and reconstitute each province as a separate entity. This idea, evidently a breach of the agreement of 1972, was supported by Lagu and other Equatoria politicians (because they resented Dinka predominance in the regional institutions), but strongly rejected by most of the south. Yet it was decreed by Numeiri in June 1983, causing bitter resentment. Even deeper anger was aroused in the south by Numeiri's Sept. 1983 decree imposing Islamic law and its code of punishments on all S. without clearly exempting the non-Muslim south. These affronts and irritations brought much support to the rebellion that had re-erupted shortly before, in 1983.

The new rebellion was led by a "S. People's Liberation Movement" that emerged in 1983 out of splits in the renewed *Anyanya* organization, with a military wing, the "S. People's Liberation Army". The dominant leader of the rebels was a former Colonel in the S. Army, John Garang, who claimed that he was fighting not only for the autonomy of the south but for a revolution in all S. The SPLA has had a considerable measure of military success and controls or half-controls large parts of the south. (Equatoria, the center of the rebellion of 1963–72, this time participates only very partially — apparently because this time the Dinka dominate the rebellion, and the SPLA.) The rebels have cut nearly all land, river and air communications and thus prevent relief from reaching a famine-stricken population, unless coordinated with them and under their auspices (which the Government will not allow). Neither Numeiri's government, until 1985, nor his post-1985 successors have so far succeeded in suppressing the rebellion by military means or alternatively working out an accommodation in secret contacts.

Suez Canal An artificial canal connecting the Mediterranean and the Red Sea. Its length is 101 mi. (163 km.). Its northern outlet is at the city of Port Sa'id and its southern outlet is at Suez. It passes through lakes the largest of which is the Great Bitter Lake. It had, until deepened and widened in a major $1,300 m. operation 1976–80, a depth of 43 ft. (13 meters) and a minimum width of 196 ft. (60 meters), able to accommodate vessels of up to 37 ft. (11 meters) draft and a load of up to 60,000 tons. Since that operation, it can accommodate vessels with a load of up to 150,000 tons (or empty vessels up to 370,000 tons).

The man who conceived the idea of the canal and was its driving force was the French engineer Ferdinand de Lesseps. France gave him support, while Britain, regarding the scheme as a French attempt to challenge her influence in the East, opposed it fiercely (and tried, as an alternative, to develop a land route from the Mediterranean to the Red Sea and, also, a railway from the Syrian coast to Mesopotamia, to link up with Euphrates and Tigris steamers). In Nov. 1854, de Lesseps obtained from Sa'id, the Pasha of Egypt, a concession for the "Universal SC Shipping Company" to dig the canal and operate it for 99 years. Due to British pressure, the Ottoman Sultan, who was nominally the Suzerain of Egypt, refused to approve the concession. A new concession, in Jan. 1856, included an Egyptian undertaking to supply free of charge the labor required for digging. In 1858, despite British opposition, de Lesseps announced the formation of the SC Company. In Nov. 1858, the company floated about 400,000 shares at the price of 500 francs each. Half of them were bought by France, and Egypt bought nearly all the other half.

Work began in 1859 under the guidance of French experts; tens of thousands of Egyptian *fallahin* labored — and many of them perished. In 1866, the company dispensed, in an agreement with Isma'il, the new Viceroy, with most of the forced labor *(corvée)*, against a substantial compensation. The agreement also stressed Egyptian sovereignty over the C. area and, in its wake, the Ottoman Sultan confirmed the concession. On 17 Nov. 1869, the SC was inaugurated with great pomp. Its cost came to 432.8m. francs.

The Egyptians held 44% of the ordinary shares, in addition to preference shares which entitled them to 15% of the profits. The Khedive Isma'il got, however, heavily into debt until he had to put up for sale all his shares. The British government bought them in 1875, at the initiative of Disraeli, for c. £4m. In 1882, the British occupied Egypt and thereby gained control over the canal zone.

In 1888, the Maritime Powers and the Ottoman Empire signed the Convention of Constantinople, in which they undertook to keep the SC "always free and open in time of war as in time of peace, to every vessel of commerce or of war, without distinction of flag". With regard to some clauses of the convention, priority was given to Egyptian security needs, but this did not apply to the freedom of passage which was established as an essential principle not limited by any conditions.

The SC became profitable several years after its opening and, by 1920, its profits had paid eight times the original investment. On the eve of World War II, over 20m. tons p.a. of shipping passed through the C. In the 1960s, the total tonnage reached 275m. and the annual income $150–200m. Until 1938, Egypt did not receive any part of the company's income or profits, because in 1880 she had mortgaged her 15% share of the profits to French banks. Under agreements in 1937 and 1949 this was corrected to some extent and Egypt began receiving 7% of the profits. Similarly, in 1937 Egypt was given representation on the board of the company; this was enlarged in 1949.

The SC is of great military and strategic importance. British reinforcements and equipment (mainly from India and Australia) passed through it during World War I. A Turkish-German attempt to capture the C. in 1915 was driven off. When Britain granted nominal independence to Egypt in 1922, she kept the right to station troops and bases in the C. Zone and to defend it. In the Anglo-Egyptian Treaty of 1936, Egypt recognized Britain's special interests with regard to the SC and agreed to the stationing of British forces of specified type and strength in the C. area; the treaty stressed that this would not be interpreted as occupation or an infringement of Egyptian sovereignty. During World War II, reinforcements for the Allied troops passed through the SC. The Germans tried to bomb it without success.

After World War II, Egypt demanded the evacuation of all British forces and bases from her soil, including the C. Zone. Negotiations met with many difficulties, and a severe crisis resulted in 1951–52 (see Egypt). Under an Oct. 1954 agreement Britain undertook to evacuate the C. Zone within 20 months; the bases would be maintained with the help of British technicians, and British forces would be permitted to return to them in the event of an attack on a member state of the Arab League or on Turkey (in other words, on any ME country with the exception of Israel). The agreement re-emphasized the freedom of passage, although for years Egypt had prevented the passage of ships to and from Israel. The last British forces evacuated the C. Zone in July 1956.

In the meantime a crisis had arisen in the relations between Egypt and the West and, on 26 July 1956, Egypt nationalized the SC, in retaliation for the discontinuation of promised Western aid. The West European countries, with Britain and France at their head, feared for the freedom of passage through the C., and especially for their vital oil supply route. They were also concerned that Egypt might not be able to maintain the C. or organize navigation through it. Egypt argued that she had only nationalized the company, as the C. itself was in any case Egyptian property, and no changes would occur in C. passage and arrangements. Negotiations on those arrangements and the safeguarding of international interests, on compensation to the company and representation on the board of management, failed in late summer 1956, and discussions at the UN Security Council were to no avail.

At the beginning of Nov. 1956, British and French troops moved into the C. Zone on the pretext of separating Egypt and Israel, then engaged in the *Sinai War. In the course of the fighting, the Egyptians blocked the C. by sinking 47 ships. Intervention by the UN, and particularly the US and USSR, forced Britain and France to withdraw their forces from Egypt (see *Suez War). In Jan. 1957, Egypt abrogated the Anglo-Egyptian Agreement of 1954 and denied Britain the right to return and operate her bases in the C. Zone. That same month the Egyptian "SC Authority" began to clear the C. and in Apr. it was re-opened to navigation. In 1957, Egypt also reiterated her undertaking to respect the freedom of navigation and announced details of arrangements for passage through the C. After lengthy negotiations with the company and shareholders, an agreement on compensation and the mutual settlement of accounts was reached in Apr. 1958. Contrary to fears expressed in 1956, the Egyptians succeeded in running the C., including navigation, without mishap. For a number of years after 1957, Egypt received loans and grants, mainly from the World Bank and Kuwait, to widen and deepen the C.

From 1948, Egypt prevented the passage of all ship on their way to or from Israel. Israel and many other countries deemed this blockade, which led to many incidents, to be contrary to the Constantinople Convention of 1888 and other international agreements (such as the Anglo-Egyptian Treaty and the Egypt-Israel Armistice), and on 1 Sept. 1951 it was condemned by the UN Security Council, which called on Egypt to "terminate the restrictions on passage", found to be "unjustified interference with the rights of nations to navigate the seas". Egypt ignored the decision, and attempts to get the Security Council to act again were frustrated by a Soviet veto. The blockade of the SC was one of the causes of the Sinai War and the Six Day War.

The SC was closed again during the June 1967 Six Day War and remained closed for eight years, as Israel occupied its East bank. Israel agreed to its reopening on condition that the freedom of navigation to and from Israel be assured. Egypt refused this; she also opposed the reopening of the C. while Israeli forces were stationed on its east bank. Attempts to arrive — through the good offices of the USA — at a separate interim agreement on a partial Israel withdrawal and the reopening of the SC failed in 1971.

In the *October War of 1973 the SC was a main battle arena. Egyptian forces succeeded in breaching the Israeli fortifications on the eastern bank (the "Bar-Lev Line") and crossed the C., while Israeli forces occupied a strip of territory on the western, Egyptian side (see *Arab-Israel Wars). The Disengagement Agreement of Jan. 1974 provided for the evacuation of the Israeli-held beachhead on the Egyptian side of the C., while it left Egypt holding a strip of territory on the eastern bank, with a *UN Emergency Force manning a buffer zone. The agreement did not specifically speak of the reopening of the SC, but in its wake Egypt began clearing and repairing the C. and rebuilding the destroyed cities on its shores. Progress was achieved in a US-mediated Egypt-Israel Interim Agreement of 1 Sept. 1975; Article 7 said: "Non-military cargoes destined for or coming from Israel shall be permitted through the SC" (in foreign-flag vessels). Towards that agreement the SC was reopened in June 1975. Finally, the Egypt-Israel *Camp David Agreements of Sept. 1978 and the Peace Treaty of Mar. 1979 provided for free passage of Israeli shipping through the C., and were duly implemented.

The vicissitudes of the SC problem had a significant impact on the world's oil economy, since most of the Persian Gulf oil used to pass through the C. Its blocking during the crisis of 1956 caused an oil shortage in Europe. After the C. was reopened in 1957, the proportion of oil tankers among ships passing through it increased, reaching 70% of the tonnage of the c. 21,000 vessels passing through it in 1966. After 1967, when most of the oil shipping had to take the route around Africa, giant oil tankers were built that could not have passed through the C. When the C. was reopened in 1975, it could accommodate only 23% of the world's tankers (against 74% before 1967). This limitation was amended in part by the widening-and-deepening operation of 1976–80. After its completion the C. could accommodate half of the world's tankers, and from the early 1980s oil tankers again constituted a large proportion of the C. traffic: 1,600–1,900 of the 22–23,000 vessels carried 100–135m. of the c. 350m. tonnage passing through. Income from the SC was a vital source of revenue for Egypt — the third-largest (after oil exports and remittances from Egyptian workers abroad). It fluctuated from $800m. to over $1,000m. p.a.

Suez War Military operation of Oct.–Nov. 1956 by Great Britain and France against Egypt. The operation was originally planned in response to Egypt's nationalization of the *Suez Canal Company, on 26 July 1956, in case negotiations should fail to secure the desired safeguards. But in the event it was presented as an operation designed to "separate the belligerents" in Israel's *Sinai Campaign against Egypt "and to guarantee freedom of transit through the Canal by the ships of all nations". As revealed later, the operation had been secretly co-ordinated and pre-arranged with Israel.

On 30 Oct., 24 hours after Israeli parachutists had been dropped at the Mitla Pass in Sinai, an Anglo-French ultimatum ordered Israel and Egypt to withdraw ten miles from the east and west banks, respectively, of the Suez Canal and to allow British and French troops to establish themselves along its length. As arranged, the ultimatum was accepted by Israel — whose forces had halted before reaching the Canal; it was rejected by Egypt. About 12 hours after the expiry of the ultimatum, British and French aircraft operating from Malta, Cyprus and aircraft carriers started bombing Egyptian airfields in the Delta and Canal areas, and an Egyptian frigate was sunk in the Gulf of Suez. President *Nasser ordered the blocking of the Canal; this was achieved by sinking 47 ships filled with concrete. However it was only at dawn on 5 Nov., when Israel had achieved her objectives and fighting in Sinai had practically stopped, that French and British parachutists were dropped outside Port Sa'id. The French and British Armada, which had been based on Malta, arrived off Port Sa'id on 6 Nov. After very little fighting, the town surrendered and light patrols started south towards Suez.

The UN General Assembly had been pressing for a cease-fire since 2 Nov. By now, the outraged reaction of the US government (which had not been consulted prior to the operation), Soviet threats of intervention, mounting internal opposition and financial difficulties, and the fact that the Sinai Campaign used as a pretext was over — compelled the British government to agree to a cease-fire. France, unable to continue alone, reluctantly followed Britain's lead. The UN continued to press for the immediate withdrawal of the invading troops. A UN Emergency Force, *UNEF, was created temporarily to take over control of the evacuated areas. Port Sa'id was evacuated in December and full possession of the Canal was restored to Egypt.

During the operation Egypt had nationalized British and French (as well as some other foreign and mostly Jewish) properties. Negotiations over claims and counter-claims for compensation — war damage, sequestrated and confiscated properties — dragged on, particularly as Egypt had severed diplomatic relations with Britain and France; agreements were reached in Aug. 1958 (with France) and Feb. 1959 (with Britain), and relations were restored in Dec. 1959 (with Britain) and Apr. 1963 (with France — delayed because of the Franco-Algerian conflict). Several other AC also severed relations with Britain and France — though none aided Egypt militarily — and only restored them after some time.

The outcome of the SW is generally seen as evidence that direct imperial military intervention overseas, of the 19th-century gunboat diplomacy type, is no longer feasible. In particular, Britain and France could no longer apply force without US support. The episode thus marked the end of Britain's position as a Great Power. (France had ceased to be a Great Power in 1940.)

al-Sulh, Riyad (1894–1951) Arab nationalist and Lebanese politician. Prime Minister, 1943–45 and 1951–56. Scion of a prominent Sunni Muslim family in Beirut (which provided also other Prime Ministers — Sami al-S. [1890–1968, several times from 1945 to 1958]; Taqi-ul-Din al-S. [b. 1909, Premier in 1973–74]; Rashid al-S. [b. 1926, Premier in 1974–75]). S. studied law in Beirut and Istanbul. He was active from his youth in the A. nationalist movement. He was sentenced to death by a Turkish military court during World War I, but was pardoned. In 1918, he joined the administration set up by Amir *Feisal in Damascus and was one of the co-founders of the *Istiqlal* party. When Feisal's rule collapsed, S. escaped from Syria. He worked in Egypt and Geneva for Syrian independence, in the framework of the Syrian-Palestinian Congress. Despite his Pan-A. views, he had contacts with the Zionist leadership in the 1920s and in 1921 tried to persuade the Palestinian-A. leaders to accept Britain's Zionist policy. He returned to Lebanon only in 1936, when relations between the nationalist movement and France improved, and rapidly became one of the most prominent Sunni leaders.

In 1943, S. helped lay the foundations for independent Lebanon by agreeing with the *Maronite Christian leader Bishara al-*Khouri on a "National Pact" which determined the régime and character of the State, based on an inter-communal equilibrium — see *Lebanon. S. became the first Prime Minister of independent Lebanon. He held this office for more than five years, 1943–45 and 1946–51. He was highly regarded also in the other AC.

In 1949, while S. was Prime Minister, the right-wing Pan-Syrian leader Anton *Sa'adeh was sentenced to death by a military court, in a summary trial, and executed. Sa'adeh's supporters held S. responsible and in revenge assassinated him in July 1951, on a visit to Jordan.

Sunni(te)s The chief and major stream in Islam, adhering to the accepted *Sunna* ("Tradition"), in contrast to the *Shi'a (the "Faction"), which reserved the leadership of the Muslim community to the descendants of 'Ali and developed traditions of its own. Several schools (*madhhab*, plural *madhāhib*) developed within the framework of Sunni Islam; for these and Sunni Islam's marginal schools or sects as well as Sunni-Muslim mysticism and fundamentalist revivalist orders, see *Islam, *Wahhabiyya*, *Dervish Orders, *Mahdiyya*, *Sanussiyya*.

Sykes-Picot Agreement A secret exchange of notes, 1916, among Britain, France and Russia, the chief Allies of World War I, relating to the partition of the Ottoman Empire after its defeat. Named after the chief British and French negotiators, Sir Mark Sykes and Charles François Georges-Picot.

According to the SPA, the non-Turkish prov-

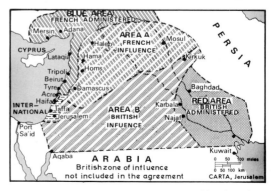

Partition of the Ottoman Empire as planned by the Sykes-Picot Agreement

inces of the Ottoman Empire were to be divided as follows: the Arabian peninsula was to become independent. Palestine, west of the Jordan River (excluding the *Negev), was to be placed under an international regime; Britain was to control Haifa and Acre and the region between them.

The French sphere was to include two zones. An "A" zone — the interior of Syria, from and including Damascus, Homs, Hama and Aleppo in the west, up to and including the *Mosul District in the east — was designated as a French zone of influence; a "Blue" zone — Cilicia in Asia Minor and all of coastal Syria and Lebanon, west of the "A" zone — was to be placed under direct French control.

The British sphere included the "B" zone — the Negev desert in Palestine, the area east of the Jordan River, and central Mesopotamia with a northern arm reaching into Persia and a southern arm descending towards the Persian Gulf — designated as a British zone in influence; a "Red" zone — the provinces of Basra and Baghdad — was to be placed under direct British control (as were Haifa and Acre).

Zones "A" and "B" were envisaged as areas in which semi-independent ASt or a confederation of ASt might be established, while France and Britain were to supply advisers and to be accorded economic privileges.

The SPA was approved by Russia in return for Britain and France's recognition of Russia's right to annex Trabzon (Trebizond), Erzerum, Lake Van and Bitlis in Anatolia. The SPA was published — and repudiated — in Nov. 1917 by the Bolsheviks who found it in the Russian Foreign Office Archives. Both Arabs and Zionists strongly criticized the SPA as being inconsistent with promises Britain had made to them (the *McMahon-Hussein Correspondence and the *Balfour Declaration, respectively).

The final distribution of the Ottoman territories partially reflected the SPA, but was greatly modified by the *Mandates System which abolished any formal, direct possession by the Powers — though it left them in *de facto* control. The SPA's territorial provisions were also changed: Palestine became a British Mandate; Cilicia remained part of Turkey: and France ceded her rights in the Mosul region to Britain (see map).

Syria Republic on the eastern shores of the Mediterranean, bordering on Turkey in the

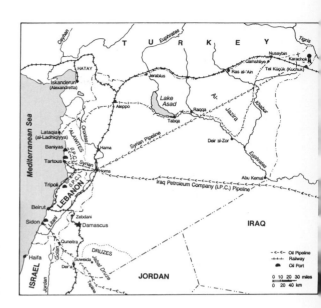

Map of Syria

north, Iraq in the east, Jordan in the south, Israel in the southwest, Lebanon and the Mediterranean in the west. Official name: Syrian Arab Republic. Area: 71,500 sq. mi. (186,000 sq. km.), including c. 720 sq. mi. in the *Golan occupied by Israel since June 1967.

The population, 10.42m. at the census of 1981, is estimated as 11–12m. in the mid-1980s. Arabic is the official language and commonly spoken; some groups speak Kurdish, Armenian or Turkish, and remnants of Aramaic survive in a few villages. About 90% of the population are A.'s (i.e. speak Arabic as their mother-tongue). But S. has a high percentage of ethnic and ethno-religious minorities, A. and non-A. Close to 70% of the inhabitants of S. are Sunni(te) Muslims. This number includes non-A. *Kurds, 6–7% of the population, mostly in the northeastern border region, the *Jazira.

The largest ethno-religious minority is the *'Alawi(te) or Nusseiri community, 10–12% of the population, concentrated in the region of the Mountain of the 'Alawites, in the northwest. The *Druzes, about 3%, dwell primarily in the region of Jabal al-Duruz (the Druze Mountain) in southern S. and some in the Golan. Christians comprise 10–12% of S.'s population; about one-third, c. 4%, are *Greek Orthodox, one-third non-A. *Armenians (most of them Orthodox

Gregorians, some — Armenian Catholics), and about one-third belong to smaller Christian communities. In addition, other religious minorities are the *Isma'ilis and Shi'is — about 1.5% together, *Yazidis, and *Jews (4–5,000 — down from over 25,000 in the 1940s). The number of nomadic Bedouin has dropped to 1.5–3% of the population.

The Syrian economy is largely dependent upon agriculture, which accounts for 30–35% of the labor force and 18–20% of the national income — though its share in both is constantly declining. The possibilities of agricultural development are still great.

In the past decades industry has grown, and its share of the national income has risen to about 20%. It produces mainly consumption goods — textiles, leather, tobacco, edible oils and cement. The important industrial areas are Damascus, Aleppo, Homs and Lataqia.

In the late 1950s, oil was discovered in northeastern S. Commercial production for export, by the government-owned "Syrian General Petroleum Corporation", began in the late 1960s, reached nearly 1m. tons in 1968, 4.5m. in 1970, and has since the mid- 1970s stood at 8–9m. tons p.a. In 1968, a 400 mi., 5m. ton p.a. pipeline was completed from the oil fields in the east to the refinery in Homs (established in 1959 with a 1m. ton capacity, expanded in 1971 to 2.7m. tons) and thence to an oil port built at Tartous. Other pipelines traversing Syrian territory are one built by the *Iraq Petroleum Company in 1952, to Baniyas, branching out at Homs from the Kirkuk — Tripoli (Lebanon) line existing since 1934; and the "Tapline" from *Aramco's fields in Sa'udi Arabia to Sidon in Lebanon (inoperative since 1975). The Syrian government received transit royalties. From the Iraqi pipeline with its 50–60m. ton p.a. throughput S. also received a substantial share for her own needs, but in the context of S.'s dispute with Iraq it was closed (by Iraq) from 1976–1979, and has again been closed (by Syria) since 1982. S.'s largest development project is the *Euphrates Dam completed in 1978 with Soviet aid and creating Lake Asad; it is to irrigate 1.75m. acres, produce 600,000 kilowatts of electricity, and make possible large-scale settlement (for details see *Euphrates).

POLITICAL HISTORY. The area known today as S. was part of the *Ottoman Empire from 1517 until the end of *World War I. Most of S. was part of the three provinces (*Vilayet*) of Aleppo, Damascus and Beirut.

With the continuing decline of the Ottoman Empire during the 19th century, Western influence grew — first through economic and cultural penetration, later through political and military intervention. France was the power with the most ramified interests in S., a result of steady commercial activity as well as ties with the Catholic, and especially the Maronite, community. Beginning in the 1830s, the Jesuits intensified their educational activity in S., opening many schools and, in 1875, a university in Beirut. American Protestants in 1834 established a modern printing press and in 1866 founded the Syrian Protestant College, later to be named the American University of Beirut. In the late 19th century the Ottoman government also opened a number of modern schools in S. A cultural revival resulted, which paved the way for the appearance of an A. nationalist movement on the eve of World War I.

During World War I, when the British discussed future A. independence with Sharif *Hussein of Mecca (with whom Syrian nationalists also had been in touch), in preparation for the Sharif's *"A. Revolt" of 1916, the future A. state demanded by Hussein included S.; however, the status and borders of the future state remained undetermined, and the British reserved the Western coast lands for a future French administration (see *McMahon-Hussein Correspondence). The Syrian nationalists did not take part in the Arab Revolt and there was no uprising in S. herself. But the Turks suspected the nationalists and condemned several of them to death.

With the Ottoman collapse in 1918, S. was conquered by Allied forces, including A. troops commanded by Amir *Feisal, son of Sharif Hussein. Feisal entered Damascus in Oct. 1918 and, with the encouragement of the British, established an A. government which gradually took over the administration in the interior of the country, where Britain supported the establishment of an Arab state. However, the secret *Sykes-Picot Agreement of 1916 between Britain, France and Russia earmarked the interior of the country as a French "area of influence", while the coastal areas were to be directly administered by France. With some flexibility and good will the two agreements might have been reconciled and a semi-independent A. State set up in the Syrian interior under French influence. But as the French became entrenched on the coast, antagonism between them and the nationalists grew more intense. In July 1919, a "General Syrian Congress" declared S.'s independence, and clashes soon erupted between A. and French forces. In Mar. 1920, the Congress proclaimed Feisal King of S. (intending, though no borders were precisely defined, a *Greater S. that would include Lebanon and Palestine). Britain and France did not recognize the declaration of independence and decided, at the *San Remo Conference in Apr. 1920, to confer upon France a *Mandate over S. French forces began moving toward Damascus and after breaking the A. resistance at Meisalun entered Damascus on 25 July 1920, putting an end to Feisal's brief rule. The *League of Nations endorsed the French Mandate over S. in July 1922.

From the start, the Syrians and particularly the Sunni-Muslim A. majority, the mainstay of the nationalist movement, hated the French rule imposed on them. The French on their part tried to weaken this majority and base their government upon the support of the ethnic and religious minorities, especially the Christians of Mount Lebanon. They set up a state of "Greater Lebanon" and added to the Christian majority area, semi-autonomous since 1861, Muslim majority districts in the north, south and Coele S. (al-*Biqa' — the Valley), and mixed Beirut (see *Lebanon) — districts that the Syrian nationalists had expected to become part of their country even if they accepted Lebanon's separation (which they did not). The French also divided the rest of S. into separate administrative units, emphasizing separatist minority interests. The Lataqia region, inhabited chiefly by 'Alawites, became a separate administrative unit, as did Jabal Druze and the district of *Alexandretta (with a sizeable Turkish minority). In the rest of S. two different states, that of Aleppo and that of Damascus, were established, linked in a federation. In 1924–25, these two states were united in the "State of S.".

The various Syrian states were given constitutions and councils, but real authority remained with the French High Commissioner in Beirut and his officials. The French Mandatory government improved public security and administration, communications, and the health and education systems. S. even became a haven for refugees, e.g. Kurds and Armenians from Turkey, and later Assyrians from Iraq. But the people of S. rejected the French administration as foreign rule. Their nationalist opposition erupted into violence several times during the 1920s. In 1925, a local uprising in Jabal Druze, led by the Druze Sultan al-*Atrash, spread to other areas of S. and was supported by the nationalists of Damascus. A national Syrian government was set up in Jabal Druze by the nationalist leader, Dr. 'Abd-ul-Rahman Shahbandar. The rebels broke through to Damascus and the city was subsequently shelled by French guns and aircraft. The revolt was finally quelled only in 1927.

The French government now agreed to grant S. independence after the manner of the Anglo-Iraqi agreement of 1922 — i.e. nominal independence based on a treaty granting the Mandatory Power special privileges and particularly the right to maintain troops and bases. Accordingly, France began to encourage increased self-government. In May 1926, Lebanon was declared a republic and granted a constitution and parliamentary institutions. In regard to S., however, similar progress was held up, mainly because nationalist demands far exceeded the concessions that France was willing to make. Only in 1928 did the French High Commissioner lift military government and allow the holding of elections for a constituent assembly. The elections of Apr. 1928 were won by the "National Bloc" (al-Kutla al-Wataniyya) — a coalition of several nationalist groups united only by their opposition to the French Mandate. Hashem al-*Atassi, Prime Minister during Feisal's reign and now leader of the Bloc, was elected President of the Assembly.

The nationalists prepared a draft constitution, which demanded, inter alia, the re-unification of all S. — implying: a *"Greater S.", mainly incorporating Lebanon. The French High Commissioner refused to endorse this draft, attempts to reach understanding failed, and the Assembly was dissolved in May 1930. The High Commissioner now unilaterally proclaimed a constitution; this established a republican régime in S. and provided for a Chamber of Deputies elected by male suffrage for a four-year term; the Chamber was to elect the President of the Republic, with limited powers; the government was to be responsible to the Chamber. "The obligations contracted by France in respect of S." were to take precedence, and in matters touching upon them the constitution was to be applied only with French approval.

The nationalists protested the imposition of this constitution, but public life began to follow its provisions. In Jan. 1932 elections were held and the National Bloc lost much of its strength. New French proposals for a Franco-Syrian treaty to replace the Mandate with nominal independence for S., while safeguarding French interests, did not satisfy the nationalist members of the Chamber and were torpedoed by them. The Chamber was suspended *sine die* in 1934. Again tension increased in French-Syrian relations, and a general strike and rioting broke out early in 1936.

New efforts to find a political solution brought a Syrian delegation to Paris. The Popular Front government of Socialist Léon Blum was more inclined to compromise than its predecessors, and, in Sept. 1936 a 25-year Franco-Syrian Treaty of Friendship and Alliance was initialled. S. was to become independent and to be admitted to the League of Nations within three years. The territories of Jabal Druze and Lataqia would be incorporated, but maintain a certain degree of autonomy. France's economic status and educational institutions were guaranteed. France alone was to equip and train the Syrian Army to be established. F. was to maintain troops and military bases in S. and aid in her defense in case of war, while S. was to provide France in that case with all facilities, communications, etc. The new Syrian Parliament endorsed the Treaty in Dec. 1936 and it was formally signed the same month.

Elections were held in Nov. 1936 and won by the National Bloc. Its leaders now took over the government: Hashem al-Atassi became President, Jamil Mardam Prime Minister, Shukri *Quwwatli, Sa'dullah Jaberi, and Fares Khouri ministers. The Lataqia and Jabal Druze districts were incorporated into S.

But France, under right-wing governments and facing the escalating menace of Nazi Germany and Fascist Italy, tarried, postponed the endorsement of the Treaty of 1936, and finally refused to ratify it.

The quest for a political settlement with France was again deadlocked. The nationalists insisted on the ratificaiton of the Treaty and full independence, but were not united as to how to achieve this aim. The National Bloc suffered from splits and instability. Dr. 'Abd-ul-Rahman Shahbandar, never a trusted member of the Bloc's dominant faction (he was pro-Hashemite and pro-British), withdrew in 1939 and established a "Popular Organization" as an opposition. He was assassinated in 1940; it was apparently a political murder, and it shocked the country and dealt a heavy blow to the beginnings of a parliamentary tradition.

Separatist movements grew with French support, in the *Jazira and Jabal Druze. French-Syrian relations deteriorated as a result of the *Alexandretta affair: the French gave in to Turkey's increasing demands and pressure, and after a brief League of Nations-sponsored autonomy the district was annexed by Turkey in July 1939. Furious protests and riots followed in S. and President al-Atassi and the government resigned. The French dissolved the Chamber of Deputies, appointed a government of officials, and announced that the Franco-Syrian draft treaty would not be submitted to Parliament for ratification. The administration of the Jabal Druze and Lataqia districts was again separated from S.

After the defeat of France, June 1940, French officials in S. remained loyal to the pro-German Vichy government. The Italians and the Germans stationed a cease-fire supervision commission in S. and Lebanon and began preparing airfields and bases and cells of agents and supporters. Their growing domination brought the British to invade S. and Lebanon together with Free French forces in June 1941. General Georges Catroux, as Free France's new "Delegate-General" (no longer "High Commissioner"), proclaimed the termination of the Mandate and the independence of S., but made actual independence conditional on the conclusion of a new treaty granting France a privileged position — which S.'s nationalists no longer accepted. The French therefore delayed transferring the government to the Syrians and re-establishing parliamentary institutions. Under British and American pressure, they agreed in 1943 to hold free elections. The National Bloc once again triumphed, and its leader, Shukri Quwwatli, was elected President.

Power was now gradually transferred to the Syrian government and administration. The article of the constitution restricting S.'s sovereignty and granting special privileges to France (Art. 116), was annulled in Jan. 1944 without a struggle (after a fierce struggle over the same issue in Lebanon in Nov. 1943). The separatist autonomy of the Druze and 'Alawite districts was ended. But Franco-Syrian differences re-erupted when the French refused to transfer the "Troupes Spéciales", Syrian units within the framework of the French ME forces, to the jurisdiction of the Syrian government and to withdraw their own troops unless a preferential treaty were signed. However, the Syrians' continued refusal to do so was winning increasing international support.

In 1944, the USSR and the USA recognized S., and Britain did in 1945, and the newly-founded *Arab League unequivocally supported S. She began to act like a sovereign state. In Jan. 1945, the establishment of a national army was announced; in Feb. S. declared war on the "Axis" powers and thus became, in Apr., one of the founding members of the United Nations. In May, anti-French riots broke out because France still refused to withdraw her troops, and the French again shelled Damascus. However, a British ultimatum forced them to cease fire, and by the end of the year the British and French had agreed on the withdrawal of their troops. This agreement did not satisfy S., as its wording implied a privileged status for France in S. and Lebanon, and (together with Lebanon) she lodged in Feb. 1946 a complaint with the UN Security Council. The USSR vetoed a resolution calling for negotiations and a speedy withdrawal; but the parties settled the matter between themselves, and by mid-Apr. 1946 France had withdrawn all her garrisons from S. 17 Apr. — "Withdrawal Day" — still remains S.'s national holiday.

It soon emerged that S. had no strong leadership. The "National Bloc", the major political force on the road to independence, disintegrated soon after that aim had been realized. Aleppo leaders, centered around the "People's Party", competed with the Damascus leadership and its "National Party". The minorities were loyal first and foremost to their communities, and the tribes to their own leaders. The 1947 elections resulted in a parliament without any strong party or leadership. Many independent deputies stood for local and clan interests. In this situation of instability, fundamental problems re-surfaced: should S. build her separate independence, or should she unite with her A. neighbors, Hashemite Jordan and Iraq? In general the Aleppo leadership supported union schemes, while the Damascus leaders and most governments opposed them together with Egypt and Sa'udi Arabia.

A serious crisis occurred as a result of the army's defeat in the Palestine War (1948). Political and military leaders accused each other of responsibility for the débâcle. On 30 Mar. 1949 the commander-in-chief of the armed forces, General Husni al-*Za'im, carried out a *coup d'état* and deposed the President, Parliament and Government. Za'im announced plans to eliminate widespread corruption and institute reforms and development schemes. In June 1949 he was elected President in a referendum.

In Aug., Za'im was deposed in another *coup* by Sami al-*Hinnawi and executed with his Prime Minister. Hinnawi tended toward union with Iraq; he restored parliament, which was dominated, under his protection, by the Aleppo leadership and adherents of union. Hashem al-Atassi was elected to the presidency. But officers opposing union with Iraq rebelled and in Dec. 1949 Hinnawi was deposed by Adib *Shishakli.

At first, Shishakli preferred to leave the President, Parliament and Government intact and to rule from behind the scenes as Deputy Chief-of-Staff. But the clash between the army's growing intervention in state affairs and the civilian leadership's desire to return the officers to their barracks, created constant tension. In Dec. 1951, Shishakli staged a second *coup* and established a dictatorial régime. He dissolved Parliament and abolished all parties, establishing a single political organization of his own, "The Arab Liberation Movement" (which, however, did not take root). In July 1953, a referendum approved a new constitution, which granted the President extensive powers, and Shishakli himself was elected to the post. The leaders of all factions were now united in their opposition to Shishakli. In Feb. 1954, a new *coup* was carried out with the help of a military junta, Shishakli's government collapsed and he fled S. The 1949 Parliament and

President Hashem al-Atassi, dismissed by Shishakli in Dec. 1951, were restored. But political stability was still lacking, and one government followed another. In 1955 Shukri al-Quwwatli was elected by Parliament to replace Atassi as President.

From the mid-1950s leftist elements began to achieve positions of strength, especially the "Arab Socialist Renaissance Party" (al-*Ba'th) and the Communists. In inter-Arab relations, S. began to adopt an increasingly pro-Egyptian line; in Oct. 1955, a Syro-Egyptian defense pact was signed and a joint command established. The USSR began fostering relations with S., concluding economic aid agreements and supplying arms (since Feb. 1956). The *Sinai and *Suez Wars of Oct.-Nov. 1956 brought S. even closer to Egypt and the Soviet Union. During the hostilities in Egypt, the Syrians blew up the oil pipelines from Iraq and Sa'udi Arabia passing through S. This resulted in tension between S. and these two countries. The pipelines were repaired in Mar. 1957, but S.'s relations with her pro-Western neighbors remained strained. Inside the country, power was increasingly concentrated in the hands of officers with Ba'th or communist leanings. These two parties sometimes collaborated, but late in 1957 relations between them deteriorated to the point that a dangerous confrontation seemed imminent. Factional disputes also led to increasing violence, assassinations (such as that of Deputy Chief-of-Staff 'Adnan Maleki in Apr. 1955), plots and trials. The Ba'th leadership found itself in a double danger: it feared a communist take-over or a general de-stabilization, and the intervention of pro-Western forces (Iraq, Jordan, Turkey, Israel) from without. So the Ba'th leadership turned to Egypt and prodded President *Nasser to "save S." by merging the two countries.

The union took place in Feb. 1958. The Egyptian President became the President of the *United Arab Republic (UAR) and S. became the "Syrian Region" of the UAR. At first S. was to a certain extent treated as a distinct entity. Although foreign affairs, security, education and industry were handled by the central government, separate governments of the "regions" dealt with financial, economic and many internal matters. But integration soon became tight and the régime centralized. The provisional constitution (on the Egyptian pattern) granted extensive powers to the President. Political parties in S. were disbanded. Early in 1960, local committees of the "National Union", the Egyptian-pattern single party were set up, and in the summer a single National Assembly — appointed from members of the defunct Syrian Parliament (one-third) and the Egyptian National Assembly (two-thirds). In Oct. the authority of the central government was considerably expanded. In effect, Egypt, the bigger, more developed country, increasingly took over control of the Union.

The union soon became unpopular in S. The dissolved Ba'th party was disappointed at the meager representation its leaders had in the régime. The upper classes were apprehensive of the socialist policies the UAR government was preparing to impose on S., while left-wing circles were disappointed at the slow pace of the socialist reforms. Above all, Syrian army officers felt that Egyptian officers were taking over key positions, and relegating them to less important posts. A further step toward full integration was made in Aug. 1961, when the separate governments of the two regions were abolished. Similarly, far-reaching steps were taken toward nationalization and reform (see *UAR).

In Sept. 1961, a Syrian officers' junta carried out a *coup* which resulted in S.'s withdrawal from the UAR and the restoration of her full independence. In Nov., a new temporary constitution was proclaimed and elections were held in Dec. The Constituent Assembly chosen elected Nazem al-Qudsi, a leader of the "People's Party", as President of the Republic. The new régime turned to the right and abolished many of the reforms of the UAR government. This policy caused renewed ferment among the army officers and in Mar. 1962 a group of officers carried out a further *coup*. President al-Qudsi and his civilian administration were dismissed; but, due to disunity among the various officer factions and unrest in the cities, they were restored to power. The government was now more leftist — and still less stable. Ministers changed frequently and the government was more than ever under pressure by the army commanders, who were themselves divided into rival factions (pro-Egyptian against anti-Egyptian; Ba'th against right-wing, etc.). Egypt refused to recognize S.'s secession, claimed the Union still existed and continued to call herself the "United Arab Republic". Mutual complaints shook the Arab League; and when the League readmitted S. as an independent member, Egypt boycotted it, in 1962–63, for half a year.

On 8 Mar. 1963, *Ba'th*-linked officers staged another *coup*. Many of these officers were 'Alawites and Druzes, but as strong man there emerged, after several months of factional struggle, the Sunni general Amin al-*Hafez. The *Ba'th* began to purge the army and government of pro-Nasserist elements. This resulted in a Nasserist attempt to overthrow the régime in July 1963; the *coup* was suppressed.

The *Ba'th* régime in S. endeavored to establish a united front with the *Ba'th* government in Iraq in power since Feb. 1963, but had little success; in any case the *Ba'th* régime in Iraq was overthrown in Nov. S. also made efforts to renew the Syrian-Egyptian union — this time as a federation, in which Iraq, too, was to participate. Discussions on the plan were held in spring 1963 and resulted in an agreement, but this broke down in the *Ba'th*-Nasserist clashes of 1963 and the elimination of the Nasserists. Relations with Egypt, which had improved slightly with these discussions, deteriorated again. An Egypt-S. military pact was renewed only in 1966 and formal diplomatic relations were resumed in 1967.

Inside S., the *Ba'th* government began implementing a socialist policy of nationalizing banks and factories and distributing land to the peasants. Merchants' and landowners' protest demonstrations and riots, Feb.-Apr. 1964, were brutally suppressed. In Apr. 1964, a new temporary constitution was proclaimed, defining S. as a "democratic socialist republic, constituting an integral part of the A. nation". The *Ba'th* leadership had by now split into two rival factions: one, based on the veteran party leadership was more moderate; the other comprising younger party leaders, many of them 'Alawites and Druzes who pressed for speedy implementation of socialist principles and were hostile to Nasser and Nasserism, won greater support among the army officers and was called the "military wing". Late in 1965, the "moderate", "civilian" faction ousted the extremists from their positions. But in Feb. 1966 the extremists staged a military *coup* and imprisoned and later exiled the old leaders, including Michel *'Aflaq, the founder and ideologist of the party, Salah-ul-Din al-*Bitar, co-founder of the party and head of the deposed government, and General Amin al-Hafez, Chairman of the Presidential Council. The exiled faction claimed to retain the "national" (all-A.) leadership of the *Ba'th* and went to Baghdad, where its supporters seized power in 1968. A bitter Syro-Iraqi rift ensued.

The power behind the *coup* was the 'Alawite General Salah *Jadid. He was supported by the 'Alawite General Hafez *Asad, the Commander of the Air Force, who became Minister of Defense and soon Jadid's rival, and the "regional" (Syrian) leadership of the *Ba'th* party — Yussuf Zu'ayyin (who was named Prime Minister) and Nur-ul-Din al-*Atassi (who became President). The elimination of the moderate faction further restricted the public base of the régime, and drove it to collaborate with the communists and to grant them, for the first time, representation in the government. It conducted purges, planted supporters in all key positions and gained control of all "popular organizations" such as trade unions, and students', farmers' and women's associations. The régime also relied on powerful and ubiquitous secret services. Nationalization was stepped up; in 1967, the party claimed that one-third of the cultivated land had already been redistributed.

In its external policy, the régime strengthened its ties with the Soviet Union. It tried to improve its relations with Egypt. It adopted an extreme line against Israel, and the Israel-S. border became an arena of violent clashes and constant tension — which was one of the causes of the *Six Day War of June 1967. The war resulted in the occupation of the *Golan Heights by Israel forces and their advance to within 38 mi. (61 km.) of Damascus. S. agreed to a cease-fire supervised by the United Nations, but continued to oppose any political settlement of the A.-Israel conflict, denounced the all-A. mainstream as too moderate, and refused to participate in the A. summit conference at Khartoum in Aug. 1967. She rejected Security Council resolution 242 of Nov. 1967, which called for Israel's withdrawal from occupied territories in the framework of a just and lasting peace, and refused to cooperate with UN envoy Jarring. S. gave unreserved support to the Palestinian guerrilla organizations (*Feda'iyyin*), and especially the *al-Sa'iqa* formation established by her own *Ba'th* party and security services; but did not allow them to set up an independent establishment in S.

Splits in the *Ba'th* leadership continued. Until Oct. 1968, the dominant group was the leftist faction led by Jadid, Zu'ayyin, Atassi and Foreign Minister Ibrahim Makhus. Its policies led to S.'s complete isolation in the A. world. In Oct. 1968, a "nationalist" group gained the upper hand; it aimed at reducing S.'s dependence upon the USSR, improving relations with the other ASt and renewing the battle against Israel. The central figure in this group was Jadid's rival Hafez al-Asad, Minister of Defense. Asad took control in Feb. 1969 in a semi-*coup*, but accepted a compromise and the continuing participation in the government of the leftist faction, with Atassi as President and Zu'ayyin as Premier. In the growing conflict between the *Feda'iyyin* organizations and the governments of Lebanon and Jordan, 1969–70, S. consistently supported the *Feda'iyyin*, and relations with these countries deteriorated. S. threatened intervention on several occasions; in Sept. 1970, Syrian forces indeed moved into Jordan to aid the *Feda'yyin* but were repulsed.

In Nov. 1970, General Asad completed his takeover. He dismissed President Atassi and provisionally replaced him with Ahmad al-Khatib (not a prominent leader), while Asad himself became Prime Minister. His opponents of the Jadid-Zu'ayyin faction were removed from their government and party posts, and most of them were arrested. In Feb. 1971, a 173-member "People's Council" was appointed, which nominated Asad, in Mar., as President of the Republic. He was endorsed, the same month, in a plebiscite (as the only candidate, 96% voting, 99.2% of the votes in favor). In April, Asad divested himself of the Premiership, appointing a loyal follower to the post. In May 1971 Asad was also elected Secretary-General of the *Ba'th* party. He was re-elected President, for seven year terms, by plebiscites in Feb. 1978 and in Feb. 1985 — nominated, as the only candidate, by the *Ba'th* and the People's Council (National Assembly).

Asad's régime at first emphasized a new "openness" in its internal policies — a slightly more liberal economic policy and an effort to associate select non-*Ba'th* but "Socialist-Unionist" factions with the régime. A new, permanent Constitution, to replace a provisional one of 1969, was passed by the People's Council in Jan. 1973 and endorsed by a plebiscite in Mar. It defined the "Syrian A. Republic" as a "popular-democratic and socialist" state, "part of the A. homeland", and its people as "part of the A. nation, struggling for the realization of its total unity". Islamic Law (the *Shari'a, al-Fiqh*) was to be the "principal base of legislation". This last definition caused protest among Sunni Muslims who considered it insufficient; to assuage that Muslim opposition, a clause was added providing that the President must be a Muslim (which raised another problem: as Asad was an 'Alawi, his endorsement as President implied the recognition of the 'Alawi community as Muslim — and many Sunni Muslims refused to accept that ruling). The President was to be proposed by the *Ba'th*, nominated by the People's Council, and elected for a seven-year term by plebiscite. The People's Council was to be chosen for a four-year term in general elections; at least half of its members were to be workers and peasants.

Elections for the People's Council were duly held in May 1973 — the first general elections since 1961 — and again in 1977, 1981 and 1986. Toward the 1973 elections, the *Ba'th* party set up a "National Progressive Front" with the Communists and several "Socialist Unionist" factions prepared to accept *Ba'th* guidance and primacy (Mar. 1972); candidates usually appeared on behalf of that Front, most of them *Ba'th* men, but independent candidates were not ruled out.

President Asad thus succeeded in giving S. long years of a stable régime — the longest-ruling President and the most stable government the country has known since independence. The régime was, despite its various outward paraphernalia of democracy, the harsh, near-totalitarian rule of an army junta and the inner core of the *Ba'th* leadership, reinforced by an ubiquitous secret service, with all media state- and party-directed. The only group resisting were Sunni Muslim conservatives and fundamentalists, mainly the *Muslim Brotherhood. Their underground resistance took an increasingly violent form in the late 1970s. In June 1979 they reportedly massacred 60 young officer cadets, most of them 'Alawis; revenge attacks and killings by security personnel culminated in a massacre of Brotherhood prisoners in the Palmyra detention camp, with several hundred killed.

New attacks and reprisal killings took place in Apr. 1981 in Hama, considered a stronghold and center of the Brotherhood. In Feb. 1982, what amounted to an undeclared war between the régime and the Brotherhood came to a head in a week-long battle in Hama, involving the use of artillery and aircraft; the government reported c. 1,200 killed, other sources spoke of 10–20,000. The events of Hama broke the back of the Brotherhood's armed resistance, though its underground cells continued existing and sporadic acts of violence/terrorism occurred.

Except for that Muslim struggle against the régime, whatever internal struggles were going on were conducted within a small group of Ba'th leaders and senior army officers, and behind a veil of secrecy. The chiefs of Jadid's defeated "military" faction were released by 1983, after 12 years of detention without trial; but they were not permitted to resume public-political activities, and their faction does not seem to have been revived. But there were new power struggles; "inside" reports of plots or even armed clashes between rival formations abounded, but usually they remained unconfirmed; by and large, Asad seemed able to resolve or suppress such crises and to keep the reins firmly in his hands. During recent years, a struggle for Asad's succession was repeatedly reported — the more so as Asad was ailing and sometimes seriously ill. This struggle often revolved around the unconventional figure of his brother Rif'at *Asad — reputedly a man without strong ideological convictions and not a loyal Ba'thist, a master of intrigue, thirsting for plots, and a wire-puller in economic enterprises (including illegal ones), residing for much of his time abroad, in France or Switzerland. Rif'at was for years the commander of the "Defense Brigades", a semi-secret formation for special operations and with special privileges, used to suppress internal unrest (e.g. that of the Muslim Brothers), and he seemed bent on using his Brigades to pave his way to power. However, a coalition of rival senior officers barred his way; early in 1984, an armed confrontation between the rival army factions was reported, but the President succeeded in defusing the crisis. During that crisis he appointed three Vice-Presidents — his loyal Deputy Premier 'Abd-ul-Halim *Khaddam, his brother Rif'at, and the Ba'th functionary Zuheir Mashariqa. However, the problem of Asad's succession, and the struggle between rival army and leadership factions, seemed to remain unsolved.

In his foreign and international policies, Asad endeavored to mitigate the doctrinaire leftism of his predecessors. While remaining an ally of the Soviet Union, he tried to tone down that alliance and to mend his fences with the West. He was reported, for instance, to have declined for ten years a Soviet offer of a formal treaty of friendship (such as Egypt and Iraq had signed). Yet, over the years S.'s dependence on Soviet aid and support reasserted itself and Asad reverted to an outspoken pro-Soviet policy. He was a frequent guest in Moscow, and in Oct. 1980 he finally signed a formal treaty of friendship and alliance with the USSR. S. also refused to denounce Russia's military intervention in Afghanistan — almost alone in the A. and Islamic world. Yet, S. did not accept Soviet guidance in all respects — e.g., concerning her support for Iran in the Gulf War, her position in the A.-Israel conflict, and her policy towards the *PLO (see below).

Asad's S. endeavored to improve her relations with the West. Relations with Britain and the USA, severed since 1967, were resumed — the first in May 1973, and the latter in June 1974 (after S. had accepted Secretary of State Kissinger's active mediation in the wake of the October War); President Nixon visited S. in June 1974. But the *rapprochement* did not go very far, and did not last. S. resisted all American efforts to associate her in further negotiations towards a ME settlement, and while she tried to foster better relations with the countries of the *EEC, she took a generally anti-US line. The West also bitterly resented her support for extremist Palestinian guerrilla/terrorist organizations and her reported involvement in terrorism in Europe, hijackings, and kidnappings in Lebanon; in Oct. 1986, Britain severed relations with her, and other Western countries, while refusing to go that far, took various diplomatic steps against her.

In his inter-A. policies, Asad at first endeavored to end S.'s isolation. He strengthened relations particularly with Egypt. In Apr. 1971 S. joined with Egypt and Libya in the "Federation of A. Republics". This FAR did not get off the ground; but S. continued fostering cooperation with Egypt, especially in the military field. This culminated in the October War of 1973 waged by S. and Egypt jointly (and described in detail in the entries *A.-Israel Wars and *A.-Israel Conflict); in that war S. also accepted the help of Iraqi and Jordanian contingents. But trust and cooperation between Egypt and S. were not complete, war aims were not the same, and policies to end the war were conflicting. S. did not share *Sadat's post-1973 US-supported endeavors to progress towards a peaceful settlement, and when they culminated in Sadat's Nov. 1977 visit to Jerusalem, and later in the *Camp David Agreements of 1978 and the Egypt-Israel Peace Treaty of 1979, she was in the forefront of those ostracizing Egypt and severing relations with her.

Asad took a very hard line in the A.-Israel conflict and in inter-A. affairs, and made S. a mainstay of the *"Rejection Front". Not content with insisting on Israel's total withdrawal from all 1967-occupied territories, including S.'s Golan, as a precondition for any further moves, S.'s acceptance of Security Council Resolution 242, i.e. of the principle of a peaceful settlement and coexistence with Israel, was at best half-hearted and in doubt and she seemed to regard a further military confrontation as the right way; Asad kept emphasizing that the achievement of a "strategic balance", a military equilibrium between S. and Israel, was a precondition for any settlement.

Since the 1970s, S. has cultivated close relations with Libya, another radical-"rejectionist" country; in 1980 Asad agreed to *Qadhdhafi's urgent demands and proclaimed a full union of the two countries — a merger that remained declaratory and was not implemented. S.'s relations with Iraq had their ups and downs; their mutual antagonism — with the rift between the two hostile wings of the Ba'th added to the deeply rooted rivalry for predominance in the *Fertile Crescent — led Iraq in 1976 to shut down the oil pipeline to and through S. and close the borders. In 1978 there was a reconciliation leading to a reopening of the borders and the pipeline and even to an agreement to establish a S.-Iraq federation. But talks on these plans broke down in 1979, and relations reverted to bitter hostility, with each country aiding subversive or rebellious foes of the other. This hostility led S. to side with Iran, Iraq's enemy, in the Gulf War; Iraq severed relations in Oct. 1980 and the borders were again closed, as was the pipeline in Apr. 1982. In 1986–87, efforts at mediation — mainly by Sa'udi Arabia and Jordan — seemed to lead to a measure of improvement; but it is too soon to judge the extent and depth of these changes.

S.'s relations with Jordan also had ups and downs. After the hostile confrontation of 1970–71, there was some improvement, advanced by Jordan's military succour in the October War. In 1975–76 there was a far-reaching reconciliation, with mutual visits and summit meetings, and an agreement in principle to set up a S.-Jordan Federation; but this plan soon broke down and relations deteriorated again in 1978–79. Another period of reconciliation and *rapprochement* set in in 1985, mutual visits proliferated, and King Hussein actively endeavored to mediate between Syria and her A. adversaries (Iraq, Egypt) and to associate her with concerted all-A. policies on a ME settlement. It is, again, too soon to judge how effective and how lasting this *rapprochement* will prove to be.

S.'s inter-A. relations were burdened by her policies towards the PLO and her ever-deepening involvement in Lebanon. S. supported the more extreme factions and formations of the PLO (see *PLO), and in the first place her own *al-*Sa'iqa*. Her animosity towards *'Arafat and the PLO mainstream *al-*Fatah* led her to support, or even initiate, a rebellion within *al-Fatah* in 1983, to expel 'Arafat from Syria and to aid military operations that evicted 'Arafat's forces from eastern Lebanon's *Biqa'* and later from Tripoli. Although some of the S.-supported PLO formations reached an agreement with the PLO mainstream in 1987, mediatory efforts to effect a reconciliation of S. herself and 'Arafat's PLO had as yet no success.

S.'s involvement in Lebanon leading to her open military intervention in 1976, the establishment of an "A. Deterrent Force" that was in reality Syrian, S.'s *de facto* occupation of eastern and northern Lebanon, her increasing intervention in Lebanon's internal affairs, and her almost complete military take-over in 1986–87 — are described in detail in the entry *Lebanon. These developments have created a situation where S. in reality dominates Lebanon — without being willing or able to impose the solutions she has devised for Lebanon's internal and political problems. It is clearly a situation that has not yet stabilized but is in many respects open and liable to change.

Generally, despite his initial efforts to end S.'s

isolation and follow a more A.-nationalist and less leftist-doctrinaire policy, Asad's inter-A. policies have, in many respects, reverted to the radical and doctrinaire line taken by his predecessors and have led S. back into inter-A. isolation. This isolation has been evident, since 1980, in particular in S.'s support for Iran in the Gulf War, a sharp deviation from the generally accepted all-A. line. However, incessant mediatory efforts have in the last few years begun to show a measure of success. It is too soon to judge whether changes in S.'s policy will be as far-reaching as to lead her back into the all-A. mainstream.

Syriac A branch of the Aramaic language, still used in the liturgy of several Eastern Christian churches. Western S. is used by the *Maronites and the *Monophysitic Syrian Orthodox (usually called *Jacobites, see there) and the Syrian *Catholics (see *Uniate); Eastern S. — by the *Assyrians-*Nestorians and the *Chaldeans. As a spoken tongue S. has died out, though remnants half-survive in a dialect partially spoken in a few villages in Syria and Eastern Turkey.

Syrian Nationalist Party (*al-Hizb al-Suri al-Qawmi*, Parti Populaire Syrien, PPS), renamed in 1947–48 "Syrian Social Nationalist Party" (*al-Hizb al-Suri al-Ijtima'i al-Qawmi*, SSNP). A group founded in Lebanon by the Greek-Orthodox Christian Antoun *Sa'adeh in 1932, propounding the existence of a specifically Syrian nation — as against both Syria's A. and Pan-A. nationalism and Lebanon's separate national entity and state. The party agitated for the creation of a "Natural, *Greater Syria" to include Syria, Lebanon, Jordan, Palestine (and ultimately also Iraq, Kuwait and Cyprus). It stood for a totalitarian régime and had pro-Fascist tendencies.

Because of its agitation for the immediate termination of the French Mandate, the SNP was banned in the 1930s. After independence it was suspected and harassed in both Lebanon and Syria. In 1949 it was accused of a plot against the Lebanese state and outlawed, and Sa'adeh was summarily tried and executed. In revenge, a hit squad of the party assassinated Riyad al-*Sulh, the Prime Minister at the time of Sa'adeh's execution, in 1951. In the 1950s, the party, never strong or influential and by now half-underground, illegal and leaderless, was further weakened by splits. It was regarded as right-wing and pro-West and even connected with the *Hashemite dynasty and Jordan (though its original Greater Syria conception had been anti-Hashemite); in Syria, several of its members were purged and tried as plotters against the leftist régime. In 1958, the party supported Lebanon's President *Chamoun against the *Nasserist rebels and provided some of the fighters in the civil war; as a reward, it was allowed to operate legally. But late in 1961 it was accused of a new plot to seize power through a military *coup* and its leaders were arrested, or fled and went underground; 79 were sentenced to death, most of them *in absentia* (those in detention had their sentences commuted). The party was again legalized in Lebanon in 1970.

What remained of the SSNP was split into rival factions in the growing crisis of the early 1970s and the civil war from 1975, with their leaders — Asad Ashqar, Georges 'Abd-ul-Massih, In'am Ra'd, 'Issam al-Maha'iri — reacting to the crisis in conflicting ways. The faction emerging as the main one, led by In'am Ra'ad, changed the SSNP's basic orientation and joined the Muslim-led "leftist" camp in the civil war, providing one of its fighting "militias". It also took increasingly extremist positions — e.g., after the Israeli invasion of 1982, against Israel; several operators of suicide car-bombs, for instance, turned out to be SSNP-recruited. Within the leftist pro-Syrian alliance, the SSNP kept its separate identity and sometimes its militia clashed with other factions of the same camp, such as the Druze fighters or *Franjiyeh's "Marada" militia, and while the alliance's main leaders accepted it as a freak group, mainly Christian, on their side, they could not fully trust it.

Syrte, Gulf of See *Sirte.

T

Taba Border post and small area on the Egypt-Israel border, in *Sinai, southwest of and adjacent to Eilat at the head of the Gulf of *'Aqaba. Possession of T. was at the center of a 1906 dispute between Ottoman Turkey and Britain (acting for Egypt), the "'Aqaba Incident", and the Sultan had to acquiesce in its incorporation into Egyptian-held Sinai, though he never recognized it. T. has been again disputed by Egypt and Israel since 1979. When Israel's total withdrawal from Sinai, as provided for in the peace treaty of 1979, was completed in Apr. 1982, the lines in the T. area remained in dispute, and it was agreed to solve the problem by conciliation talks or arbitration. As conciliation talks failed, the terms of arbitration and the identity of the arbitrators (three jurists from Sweden, France and Switzerland) were agreed upon in Sept. 1986, after protracted negotiations, and the arbitration process began in Dec. 1986.

Talal Ibn 'Abdullah (1909–72) King of Jordan 1951–52. The elder son of King *'Abdullah Ibn Hussein, born in Mecca, T. ascended the Jordanian throne in 1951, after the assassination of his father. His reign was short-lived and he had no time to leave an imprint of his personality or policy, though he was popular as being supposedly "nationalist" and "democratic". T. was found to suffer from a mental illness and was dethroned in Aug. 1952, his son *Hussein succeeding. T. spent the remaining twenty years of his life in a mental institution in Istanbul.

al-Tall, Wasfi (1920–71) Jordanian politician. Born in Irbid. A graduate of the American University of Beirut, T. began working as a teacher. From 1942 to 1945 he served in the British army, reaching the rank of captain. In 1945 he became a member of Mussa al-*'Alami's team and worked until 1947 in his information/propaganda offices in London and Jerusalem. During the Palestine War of 1948 he joined *Qawuqji's "Army of Deliverance". In 1949 he joined Jordan's diplomatic and civil service. After rising in its ranks, he was Ambassador to Iraq in 1961–62. T. became Prime Minister and Minister of Defense in 1962, for one year, and was again Prime Minister in 1965–67 and 1970–71. An able administrator, he was considered loyal to the King and a hard-line anti-Nasserist. He assumed his last Premiership during the decisive crisis between the royal régime and the *PLO and continued and completed the liquidation of the PLO establishment that had begun in Sept. 1970. He was assassinated in Nov. 1971 by Palestinian-A. terrorists, while on a visit to Cairo; his murder was the first appearance of the extremist *"Black September" organization.

Tanb Islands See *Persian Gulf, *Ras el-Khaima, *UAE.

Tangier (also Tanger; Arabic: Tanja) Town and port in Morocco, on the Strait of Gibraltar. The population, mostly Muslim Moroccan, was estimated in the 1930s at 50–60,000, in the 1950s at 140,000, and in the mid-1980s at over 300,000. Since the late 19th century, T. was the gate of entry into Morocco for European interests and became the center for foreign diplomats who conferred upon it a special status and increasingly intervened in its administration, beginning with health control and law and order. In 1904 and 1905 France and Spain agreed between themselves on a "special status" for T., and the International Conference of Algeciras, 1906, endorsed it (against Germany). That special status was upheld by the Protectorate Treaty with Morocco, 1912, and reconfirmed between France and Spain, though T. was within the Spanish Protectorate zone.

In Dec. 1923, France, Spain and Britain concluded a convention formally establishing a neutralized and demilitarized International Zone of T. and the area around the town, about 225 sq. mi. This convention was reconfirmed, and amended, in 1925 and 1928, joined by Italy in 1928, and accepted by most European countries. It provided for T. to be administered by a "Committee of Control", composed of the representatives of eight European states and the USA (the USA at first refused to associate herself, but later joined). A 26–27 member "International Legislative Assembly" was to consist of 16–17 foreigners appointed by their governments (4 French, 4 Spanish, 3 British, 2 Italian, and one each from the USA, Belgium, the Netherlands and Portugal), and 9 local representatives (6 Muslims and 3 Jews) appointed by a "Commissioner" or Envoy *(Mandoub)* of the Sultan of Morocco; the *Mandoub* was to preside, and three Vice-Presidents of the Assembly were to form a kind of executive. These arrangements were renewed in 1936 for 12 years. But during World War II, Spain seized control of T. in 1940, annexed it and dissolved its administrative bodies.

After the War, Spain was forced by the victorious allies to withdraw her occupation and was excluded from participation in the international régime that was re-established in Oct. 1945. In 1952–53 the statute was changed somewhat, enlarging US and Italian representation. T. prospered as a customs-free international entrepot and a financial center. But as Morocco approached complete independence and the French and Spanish Protectorates were abolished (Mar. 1956), T.'s international régime could not continue either. In Oct. 1956, an international conference abrogated T.'s international status and agreed with Morocco on new arrangements to maintain its position as an international commercial and financial center, while being part of Morocco. These arrangements were proclaimed by Morocco in a new charter for T. in Aug. 1957. But in Oct. 1959 the King repealed that charter from Apr. 1960. T.'s free economy was ended, taxes and customs were introduced and T. was fully integrated in Morocco. As many international enterprises withdrew, a rapid decline in T.'s economy set in. In July 1961 the King tried to repair the damage and announced the creation of a free port in T. from Jan. 1962 and the re-introduction of certain limited tax and customs privileges. But T.'s "golden" days were over. While its port and economic enterprises revived to some extent, it did not regain the lively prosperity it had enjoyed as an international city.

Tigris (Arabic: *Djila*) One of the two great rivers forming Mesopotamia, today's Iraq. Rising in eastern Anatolia, the T. forms the Syria-Turkey border for about 25 mi. (40 km.) and enters Iraq where the three countries meet. Flowing south-southeastwards, past Mosul and Baghdad, it joins the *Euphrates near Qurna, after a course of 1,150 mi. (1,850 km.), to form the *Shatt al-'Arab. In northern and central Iraq the T. receives important tributaries, all from the east; chief among them are the Greater Zab, the Lesser Zab and the Diyala. In central and southern Iraq the T. connects with the Euphrates through a number of channels and natural water courses, most of them seasonal. Its lower reaches are largely surrounded by swamps. It is navigable by shallow-draft vessels up to Baghdad.

Important development works, for flood control, irrigation and the generation of power, are based on the T. and its tributaries. The chief ones are the Kut Barrage, completed in 1939, and the Samarra Barrage (1956) which diverts flood waters into the Wadi Tharthar depression and through a canal to the Euphrates; the Dukan Dam on the Lesser Zab (1959); and the Derbendi Khan Dam on the upper Diyala (also called Sirwan), completed in 1963. A large dam at Bekhme on the Greater Zab and a major scheme on the T. itself near Mosul are in various stages of planning and construction.

al-Tikriti An epithet indicating the town of origin, used sometimes by several Iraqi personalities (as are other, similar epithets such as al-Rawi or al-Samarra'i). See *Hussein, Saddam.

Tiran, Straits of, and Island The SoT are a narrow passage connecting the Gulf of *'Aqaba/Eilat with the *Red Sea. A string of uninhabited and barren islands approaches the *Sinai coast to a distance of 4.5 m. (7 km.), with the T. Island being the westernmost of them.

The Islands, considered Sa'udi Arabian territory, were occupied by Egypt in 1949–50, with Sa'udi permission, and from the early 1950s Egypt closed the SoT to shipping to and from the Israeli port of Eilat, claiming that they were entirely within her territorial waters. While this claim could hardly be questioned, most countries, and most legal experts, would consider straits connecting the high seas with another country's territorial waters and ports to be international waterways where the right of innocent passage overrides the territorial-water rights of the riparian country. An international Convention on the Law of the Sea, adopted in 1958, confirms that principle in articles 4 and 16, but the particular problem of the SoT and the Gulf of 'Aqaba was never submitted to international judicial ruling. For Egypt's blockade, until Nov. 1956, and subsequent events concerning the SoT, see Gulf of *'Aqaba.

Transjordan (Arabic: *Sharq al-Urdunn*) Semi-independent Amirate east of the Jordan river, 1921–46, in 1946 and 1948 renamed Hashemite Kingdom of *Jordan. For its history, see *Jordan.

Tripoli (Arabic: *Tarabulus*, sometimes *T. al-Sha'm*, "Syrian T.", in distinction from *T. al-Gharb*, "Western T.", in Libya.) City and port in northern Lebanon, the country's second city and the main one in the north. Its population was estimated at c. 150,000 in the 1960s; more recent estimates are widely conflicting — from 250,000 to 500–600,000 or even more (in part depending on which suburbs are included). The population is mostly Muslim-Sunni, but in recent decades an

**Alawi population has grown, mainly migrants from the neighboring 'Alawi districts of Syria; some estimate the 'Alawis as 40–50,000. 15–20,000 are Christians, mostly Greek-Orthodox. T. was a terminus of an oil pipeline from Iraq, built by the *Iraq Petroleum Company in 1934, and a refinery was built next to it; the pipeline stopped operations in 1976.

T. and its region were incorporated into Lebanon in Sept. 1920, with the creation of "Greater Lebanon" by the French. The Muslims of T., and of Lebanon and Syria in general, opposed that incorporation and came only gradually to accept it — as finalized in the informal "National Covenant" of 1943. T. and most of the North have been controlled by Syrian troops since 1976.

There was always an element of competition or antagonism between Sunni leaders, such as, mainly, the *Karameh family, and those of Beirut. In the civil war since 1975 T. was at first little affected, having a nearly homogeneous Muslim population. But gradually the traditional leadership was pushed aside by "militias", unruly street-based formations led by toughs and strongman bosses, such as a "24 October Movement" headed by Farouq Muqaddam. There were also clashes between adherents of the Syrian *Ba'th and those of the Iraqi Ba'th and nuclei of anti-Syrian Muslim fundamentalist groups allied with the *PLO. The presence of Palestinian camps (Nahr al-Bared, Badawi) dominated by the PLO also led to tension and clashes. As Syrian domination was consolidated, anti-Syrian resistance escalated in the early 1980s. It crystallized in a Muslim-fundamentalist formation, "Islamic Unity" (al-Tawhid al-Islami) led by Sheikh Sa'id Sha'ban. Pro-Syrian elements, mainly 'Alawis, countered by forming an "Arab Democratic Party", also called "A. Knights", supported by Syria. Clashes further escalated when the Islamists supported *'Arafat and his PLO forces against Syrian troops and pro-Syrian PLO rebels in a bloody war that spread to T. late in 1983 and ended with the defeat of 'Arafat and the Islamists (see *Pal.-A. Guerrilla Org.'s and *PLO). But the Islamists continued their battle against the pro-Syrian 'Alawis and their Syrian backers. In Oct. 1985, the Islamists were reportedly beaten and ousted from the quarters they controlled, and since then T. seems to be under the firm control of Syria and her local clients.

Tripolitania The north-western, and main, region of Libya — a narrow strip of inhabited land and an extended desert hinterland. Its area is about 110,000 sq. mi., and its population is estimated in the mid-1980s at about 2.5m., constituting more than 70% of that of Libya. Its main city is Tripoli (Arabic: *Tarabulus*, sometimes *T. al-Gharb*, "T. of the West", in distinction from *Tripoli in Lebanon); the town's population, 180–200,000 in the late 1960s, has rapidly grown with the development of modern Libya and her oil economy and is estimated at about 1m. in the mid-1980s.

In the past, the name T. was sometimes used for the whole of Libya. In contrast to *Cyrenaica that was largely dominated by the *Sanussi sect, T. was non-sectarian Muslim-Sunni. While guerrilla resistance to Italian rule, from 1912 and again in the 1920s, was to a large extent Sanussi-led, T., and particularly Tripoli town, became the center of A. nationalist organizations. In 1929 and 1934, T. was united with Cyrenaica by the Italians to form Libya. When Libya became independent in Dec. 1951, she was a Federation of T., Cyrenaica and Fezzan under the Sanussi King Idris. Tripoli became one of the two capitals of Libya, alternating with Benghazi. But T.'s nationalists remained antagonistic to the federal system with its autonomy for Cyrenaica, and to the ultra-conservative Sanussi King. In Apr. 1963 the federal Constitution was abolished and Libya became a unitary state, with T.'s predominance enhanced. After the *coup* of Sept. 1969, Tripoli became the sole capital of Libya.

Trucial Coast or **Trucial 'Oman** A large peninsula on the southern (Arabian) shores of the *Persian Gulf, mostly desert. The population, estimated in the late 1960s as 150–200,000 (for later figures see *UAE), was nomadic or engaged in fishing, pearl-diving, boat-building and maritime commerce — until the development of an oil economy from the 1960s. Most of the TC consisted of seven A. sheikhdoms — *Abu Dhabi, *Dubai, *Sharja, *Ras al-Khaima, *Umm al-Qaiwain, *'Ajman, and *Fujaira. The tip of the peninsula, *Ras Musandam, belongs to *'Oman, as an exclave.

From the early 19th century, Britain took military measures against the piracy rife in the area, and in 1820 she imposed on the coastal chiefs an agreement to end it. This agreement was expanded in 1853 into a perpetual maritime truce, and the area, previously known as the "Pirate Coast", was named the "TC". These treaties, and others which followed, provided for British protection and subsidies. Subsequently, British political officers were stationed in Abu Dhabi and Dubai, under the Political Resident for the Persian Gulf at Bushire in Iran (and from 1946 at *Bahrain).

In the early 1950s Britain began to organize cooperation between the seven sheikhdoms through a quasi-federal permanent council headed by the British Resident. She also set up a small British-commanded military police force jointly for the seven, the "T. Scouts", with headquarters at Sharja. In 1959, Britain decided to create a common currency, the Gulf Rupee, to replace the Indian Rupee that had been the usual currency in the area; but this plan did not fully materialize, as several sheikhdoms preferred other currencies, such as the Sa'udi Rial, the Bahrain Dinar or a new Qatar Rial. In 1966, Britain established a naval base in Sharja, destined to replace the British base in *'Aden then due to be evacuated. But in 1968 Britain decided to liquidate her commitments in the Gulf area and remove her protection in 1971. In Dec. 1971 the rulers, with British encouragement, formed an independent federal state, the *United Arab Emirates (UAE). See there.

Truman, Harry S. (1884–1972) As the 32nd President of the USA, from Apr. 1945 to Jan. 1953, T. was immediately faced with the Palestine dispute. While he was unwilling to involve the USA actively in that dispute, he pressed for the admission of 100,000 Jewish survivors of the Holocaust. He agreed to send an Anglo-American Committee to investigate the problem, 1945–46, and a special envoy, Henry F. Grady, to work out with the British a formula for a solution. But no agreed US-British solution was reached. When the Palestine issue came before the UN in 1947, T. instructed the US delegation to support *UNSCOP's partition plan and vote for it. Later he had new doubts and in Mar. 1948 allowed his aides to propose the replacement of partition by a trusteeship to be imposed on a united Palestine. But on 14 May 1948 the US was, on T.'s decision and reportedly against the recommendation of his chief advisers, the first state to recognize Israel.

T. made his main impact on the ME by the "T. Doctrine" — a policy statement of 12 Mar. 1947 pledging US support for "free peoples who are resisting attempted subjugation by armed minorities or outside pressure". The T. Doctrine was meant to apply mainly to Greece and Turkey, for whom T. asked Congress for an emergency aid appropriation, and also Iran. But it had a major impact on the ASt, too, and the ME as a whole, since it initiated a more active US involvement in the region's affairs and heralded major economic aid efforts by the US (the "Marshall Plan").

Tumb or **Tunb Islands**   See *Tanb.

Tunisia   Republic in Northwest Africa, on the southern shore of the Mediterranean sea, bordering on Libya in the east and Algeria in the west and south. Area: 163,610 sq.km. (63,400 sq. mi.). Population: 6.73 m. (1982, official estimate) — 96% Muslims. Most of the population is Arab; of the *Berbers, in the south, few retain a distinctive Berber identity. Capital: Tunis (population, in 1975 census, 874,000; later estimates — c. 1m.).

T., under nominal Ottoman rule since 1574, was in fact ruled by a local Bey. In April 1881 she was occupied by France, ruling Algeria since 1830, to prevent her imminent financial collapse and to put an end to raids by T.'n tribes into Algeria. France, who had obtained European agreement to her takeover, concluded two treaties with the Bey which established a French Protectorate: (1) the Treaty of Bardo or Qasr Sa'id (1881), under which the Bey remained the nominal ruler while France became responsible for military, financial and foreign affairs; (2) the Treaty of Mersa (1883), which transferred the real power to the French Resident-General and his French advisers. French law and administration were applied and land was registered as a step towards colonization and agricultural development by French companies. Grants of large plots of land encouraged the influx of settlers, mainly from France and Italy, until they numbered some 150,000 on the eve of World War I (out of c. 2 m. inhabitants), and about 200,000 in the 1920s.

In the 1890s the French started to establish representative bodies. A Consultative Council was at first composed of Frenchmen only, who were appointed. From 1907 the French representatives were elected by the French inhabitants, while 14 Muslim representatives and one Jew were added, nominated by the Bey. The Council had only advisory authority in financial matters submitted to it. Since 1910 the French and the T.'n "sections" convened separately.

Early in the 20th century, Islamic and nationalist organizations began forming. An Islamic-reformist group was established in the Zeitoun mosque and college of Tunis, and a T.'n nationalist organization was set up in 1907. Inspired by the Young Turks' revolution of 1908, a Young T.'n movement formed which aimed to introduce reforms and restore the authority of the Bey. Following the establishment of semi-independent ASt and the advances of A. nationalism in the eastern Mediterranean after World War I, national consciousness in T. intensified. In 1920 the *Destour* (*Dustur* — constitution) movement was founded, headed by 'Abd-al-'Aziz al-Tha'alibi. It advocated a constitutional régime and an elected legislative assembly.

The French tried to conciliate these demands by introducing partial administrative reforms. In 1922, Regional Councils were established, as well as a "Grand Council" with limited consultative authority, mainly in financial matters. The separation between a French-European section and an indigenous T.'n one in these councils remained. In elections to the grand and regional councils, 1922, the *Destour* failed and only few of its candidates were elected. When Tha'alibi stepped up his party's activity he was exiled, returning only in 1937. In 1925 the *Destour* was banned.

In 1933–34, younger elements with western education and more radical views, led by the lawyer Habib *Bourguiba, established the Neo-Destour Party (ND). This party had strong ties with the trade unions and came to be regarded as the leader of the national movement. It was outlawed soon after its establishment and its leaders were arrested or exiled. Following the establishment of the Popular Front government in France in 1936 the activity of the ND was renewed. But after the fall of that government, and demonstrations in 1938, it was again outlawed and many of its leaders arrested.

During World War II T. came under Vichy rule. German and Italian forces were stationed in Tunisia. The Vichy government was reluctant to grant the nationalists' requests for more independence. The Germans, however, supported the nationalists' demands, released their leaders from prison and allowed some of them to go to Rome for political training. The Bey Muhammad al-Munsif (June 1942-June 1943) supported the nationalists and collaborated with the Axis forces. Following the Allies' conquest of T. in early 1943, the Bey was deposed and replaced by Muhammad al-Amin (1943–57). French rule was handed to the "Free French", and in mid-1944 the special rights of the Italian inhabitants were abolished.

When France relaxed political restrictions, local political activity increased — but it was again repressed by France. In 1945 Bourguiba moved to Cairo and joined the "Front for the Defense of the Maghreb", established in late 1944. In 1945 the French introduced political reforms. The council of ministers and the Grand Council (composed now of 53 members in each of the French and the T.'n sections) were reorganized and an elected municipality was granted to Tunis. The nationalists were not satisfied and their congress in summer 1946 demanded full independence. In early 1947, the French decided to establish a "national government"; but both the *Destour* and ND parties refused to participate until wider self-rule be granted.

In late 1949 Bourguiba returned from Egypt to head the nationalists in their negotiations with the French. In April 1950 he presented "Seven Demands" of the ND, most of which were granted during 1950–51. This made possible the formation in Aug. 1950 of a government headed by Muhammad Chenik with an equal number of T.'n and French ministers, among them Saleh Ben-Youssuf, a ND leader, as Minister of Justice, but negotiations for self-rule were opposed by the French Right and the settlers, who rejected any concessions to the T.'ns, and by more radical Muslim nationalists. Demonstrations were renewed and led to violent clashes in early 1952, mainly by T.'n "gangs", the *Fellagha*, and their French counterpart, the "Red Hand". Several ND leaders, including Bourguiba, were arrested, Chenik removed, and all power resumed by the French authorities. The latter continued unilaterally to decree reforms intended to lead to internal autonomy. The ND, meanwhile, took their case to the UN; in 1952 and 1953 the General Assembly rejected resolutions calling for speedy independence, but compromise formulae adopted recommended gradual progress towards that goal.

In July 1954 the Pierre Mendès-France government offered T. "internal sovereignty", with France retaining responsibility for defense and foreign affairs only. It also legalized the ND. In autumn 1954 a cease-fire was reached, though some of the *Fellagha* refused to accept it. On 21 Apr. 1955 a preliminary agreement was signed, accepting the "internal sovereignty" offered; it was finalized and worked out in detail on 3 June 1955. Bourguiba, who had been released from prison and exiled to France in 1953, participated in the negotiations; he returned to T. in June 1955 as a national leader of great influence though holding no official position. The more extremist ND leaders, headed by Saleh Ben-Youssuf, demanded complete independence and rejected the agreement but the majority endorsed it. Ben-Youssuf was ousted from the party in Oct. 1955 and went into exile in Cairo, where he agitated against Bourguiba and the ND leadership (he was assassinated in Aug. 1961).

In Sept. 1955 Taher Ben-'Ammar formed a new government composed only of T.'ns, six of them belonging to the ND. A party congress in Nov. 1955 re-elected Bourguiba as ND president and endorsed the agreements, but demanded complete independence and the election of a constituent assembly, a demand enhanced by the renewal of *Fellagha* activity and the fact that Morocco was reaching full independence. France went along and an agreement on 20 Mar. 1956 granted T. full independence, including authority over foreign affairs, defense and internal security. It was, however, agreed that there was an "interdependence" between T. and France and that they would cooperate in foreign affairs and defense — a cooperation to be regulated in detailed separate agreements; French forces were to remain in Bizerta and other camps.

Elections for a Constituent Assembly were held on 25 Mar. 1956 and all 98 seats were won by a National Front, of which the ND was the main component. On 11 Apr. Bourguiba became Prime Minister, with 16 of the 17 Ministers belonging to the ND. During the next year the authority of the Bey was curtailed, and on 25 July 1957 the Assembly abolished the monarchy and proclaimed T. a republic, with Bourguiba as Head-of-State. On 1 June 1958 a new Constitution was promulgated. It provided for the election of a President for a five-year term, re-eligible for three consecutive terms and endowed with wide powers, and a National Assembly elected for five years.

Relations with France dominated T.'s politics in the late 1950s and early 1960s. Judicial authority was transferred quickly. The system of financial-economic cooperation was abolished by 1957 and renewed on a different footing in 1959. The nationalization of French property (e.g. transport and power companies, and agricultural lands — French settlers holding 2 m. acres, over 20% of all agricultural lands) remained a source of much friction. Most of the nearly 200,000 French settlers had left T. by the early 1960s. A final agreement on compensation was reached in 1965.

Major differences related to military issues. T. opposed the use of her soil for operations against the Algerian rebels and from 1956 to 1961 was in near-permanent conflict with France on this issue, which erupted at times in violent clashes. Finally T. resolved to prevent France altogether from using military and naval bases in T., such as those near the Algerian border and the main one in Bizerta. The Bizerta crisis reached its climax in July 1961 when T. blockaded the base and fighting ensued with heavy casualties. Following T.'s complaint to the UN, the General Assembly supported T.'s right to demand the withdrawal of French troops. After lengthy bilateral negotiations, during which Algeria reached independence, the crisis ended with the evacuation of Bizerta by the French in Oct. 1963. No French forces remained in T.

In domestic politics Bourguiba and the ND were dominant. Conflict on the exclusion of institutionalized opposition coincided with social and economic grievances, large-scale unemployment and inflation. Soon after T.'s independence, Bourguiba consolidated his power by restructuring the ND party and getting rid of powerful rivals by court trials. Among those ousted, tried and sentenced in 1958 were Prince Chadly, the eldest son of the ex-Bey, and two former Prime Ministers, Taher Ben-'Ammar and Salah-ul-Din Baccouche (Baqush); ex-Prime Minister Saleh Mazali was tried in early 1959. Exiled Saleh Ben-Youssuf was tried *in absentia* and sentenced to death in Jan. 1957 and again in

Oct. 1959, with many of his followers (eight were executed; Ben-Youssuf was assassinated in W. Germany in Aug. 1961). The fact that Ben-Youssuf operated from Cairo was among the reasons for the deterioration of T.-Egypt relations.

In Nov. 1959 elections were held. Communist candidates challenged the ND, but the latter won all 90 seats. In 1963 the Communist Party was banned, leaving the ND completely unchallenged. Bourguiba was both President and Prime Minister until Nov. 1969, when he nominated Bahi Ladgham (al-Adgham) to the latter post, replacing him in Oct. 1970 by Hedi Nouira (Hadi Nuweira), a staunch Bourguiba follower; Nouira served until Apr. 1980, when he was followed by Muhammad Mazali. Bourguiba himself was re-elected to the presidency in 1964, 1969 and 1974; in 1975 he was proclaimed President for life. Bourguiba's old age and failing health made his succession one of T.'s main political problems.

Political purges continued in the early 1960s. Following a plot discovered late in 1962, 13 were sentenced to death in Jan. 1963, including 7 army officers. In 1964 the ND was restructured, its commitment to "T.'n Socialism" was emphasized and its name changed to Parti Socialiste Destourien (PSD). In the elections of Nov. 1964 the PSD won all 90 seats unchallenged.

Since 1958 the régime maintained a "National Work Service", under which men reaching the age of 20 were to work one year in a development project. Some 120–300,000 men served annually in this framework. In 1964–69 it was used in a drive to collectivize agriculture, carried out by the Minister of Finance and Planning, Ahmad Ben-Saleh. Massive land nationalization was undertaken and small independent farms were forcibly merged into c. 1000 agricultural cooperatives, encompassing over 25% of the rural population. But the project met massive opposition which finally forced Bourguiba to dismiss Ben-Saleh (Sept. 1969) and put him on trial for treason. He was sentenced in May 1970 to 10 years of prison. In 1973 he escaped and has since conducted anti-Bourguiba propaganda from Europe, in the name of a "Mouvement d'Unité Populaire" (MUP). After Ben-Saleh's fall most of the cooperatives were abolished and many plots were returned to their owners.

The growing emphasis on economic and social affairs and "T.'n Socialism" also led to a growing conflict between the government and the strong trade union movement. As early as 1956 the ND regarded the Union Générale Tunisienne du Travail (UGTT) as too independent and forced the replacement of its Secretary-General, Ahmad Ben-Saleh, by Ahmad Tlili, who was himself replaced in 1963 by Habib 'Ashour; the latter was ousted in 1965, but returned to his post in 1970. Labor relations were relatively stable until the mid-1970s. In 1976 large-scale strikes forced the government to conclude a "social contract" with the UGTT in 1977. However, strikes continued, and the UGTT became a vocal critic of the government and a rallying point of opposition.

Students and unemployed youth also participated in demonstrations. Opposition leaders like Muhammad Masmoudi, a former Foreign Minister in exile in Libya, declared their support of the UGTT, and the crisis caused a split also in the government. While Prime Minister Nouira took a hard line, the Minister of the Interior, Taher Belkhodja, advocated reforms. Bourguiba supported Nouira and Belkhodja was dismissed, late in 1977; six other ministers resigned in sympathy. Nouira's new government comprised mainly "technocrats".

In early 1978 'Ashour resigned from the politbureau and the central committee of the PSD in order to have a free hand and to dissociate himself from the ruling establishment. The UGTT then demanded changes in the system of government and an end to the harsh suppression of strikes and demonstrations and in Jan. 1978 called a general strike. The régime used troops to suppress the strike, mainly in the cities, with some 50 killed and several hundred wounded; hundreds were arrested, and 'Ashour and other UGTT leaders were charged with Libya-backed subversion. 'Ashour was sentenced to ten years imprisonment with hard labor, and other leaders were also imprisoned. A new UGTT Secretary-General, Tijani 'Abid, appointed in Mar. 1978, and his colleagues disavowed the unions' previous militant opposition and promised to cooperate with the government. 'Ashour was pardoned by Bourguiba in 1979, but remained under house arrest until Dec. 1981. Most of the others were pardoned as well, but only after it was evident that the UGTT had lost its power as a center of opposition. Yet at the UGTT congress of April 1981, for the first time a non-PSD man, Tayyeb Baccouche (Baqqush), was elected Secretary-General; furthermore, of the 13 members elected to the executive committee, 11 were former members imprisoned in 1978. Following his release in late 1981, 'Ashour was elected UGTT President — a post created for him; in Dec. 1984 he was re-elected Secretary-General and in Nov. 1985 again ousted (and sentenced to prison).

The increase in social and political protest achieved a liberalization in the election system, and gradually competing parties were permitted to operate. In July 1979 an amendment to the electoral law provided for two candidates to compete for each seat in the assembly. The idea of multiparty system was, however, still rejected by the PSD congress of Sept. 1979. In the Nov. 1979 elections, the first multi-candidate contest, only the PSD participated, because the opposition boycotted them.

In Jan. 1980 the town of Gafsa in western T. was attacked, apparently by militant political exiles backed by Libya, and was occupied for a week, until the T.'n army regained control. More than 40 were killed in the clashes; some 60 were brought to trial and 13 executed. Opposition groups condemned the "Tunisian Armed Resistance" for resorting to violence in collaboration with a foreign power.

Premier Nouira resigned in Feb. 1980 and was replaced by the Minister of Education, Muhammad Mazali. Some political liberalization now began to be felt. Mazali's government included ministers who had resigned or been dismissed in 1977. During 1980 most political prisoners were released and in 1981 some 1,000 UGTT members who had been involved in the 1978 riots were pardoned. The activity of parties other than the PSD was tolerated: in July 1980 the "Mouvement des Démocrates Socialistes" (MDS) — founded in 1978 by former PSD leader Ahmad Mestiri — was permitted to publish two weeklies, and in Feb. 1981 an amnesty was granted to most MUP members (a measure that led to a split, as one MUP faction made its peace with the government and tried to constitute itself as a legal party, while the main leaders in exile and a faction in T. opposed that). In Apr. 1981 the PSD was reformed and new blood was infused: 75% of the 80 central committee members were new ones. Bourguiba now declared that he would not rule out the establishment of other political parties, though he continued objecting to Communism and Muslim fundamentalism, as well as to groups linked to a foreign power. The Communist Party, banned since 1963, was officially recognized in July 1981, and thus the one-party system came to an end. Unofficial political groupings were permitted to participate in the Nov. 1981 elections, with the provision that whichever received 5% of the votes would be recognized as a party. The Communists, MDS and MUP competed in the elections; but the "National Front", composed of PSD and UGTT won 94.6% of the votes and all 136 seats. Since none of the other groups won the minimum 5% of the votes, they were not officially recognized, until Nov. 1983.

In Jan 1984 rioting and looting erupted in protest against the abolition of subsidies on basic foodstuffs and a 115% rise in the price of bread, added to long-standing dissatisfaction and unemployment, especially among educated youth. The rioting spread from the south all over T., a state of emergency was declared and the army was called in; some 150 were killed, more than 900 wounded and over 1,000 arrested. After a turbulent week, Bourguiba intervened and cancelled the price hikes, and order was re-established. An official inquiry blamed the Minister of the Interior, Driss Guiga. He was dismissed and replaced by Premier Mazali (whose position was thus strengthened); Guiga went into exile and was later tried *in absentia* and sentenced to 15 years imprisonment Further strikes in the public sector in early 1984, in demand of higher pay, subsided following an agreement between the government and the UGTT. Local elections, in May 1985, were boycotted by all groups except the PSD; even the UGTT did not form a common list with the ruling party.

As Premier Mazali consolidated his power, after over six years of heading the government, he seemed to groom himself as the eventual successor to Bourguiba. But factions opposed to him gained the upper hand, or else the President himself — ailing and very old, but still dominating T. as the sole leader — rejected Mazali as his heir (or perhaps he did not want anyone to grow too strong beside him). He dismissed Mazali in July 1986, appointing Rashid Sfar to head a new government. As Mazali was about to be arrested, he escaped from T. in Sept. 1986 (and was tried *in absentia*). Elections in Nov. 1986 re-endorsed the régime; they were boycotted by all opposition groups, except for a few Independents, and the PSD won all 125 seats.

T. was regarded as a westernized country, where traditional Islam was weak. State and religion were officially separated, law courts secularized, religious endowments *(waqf; habus)* abolished, and women enjoyed equal rights. Until the late 1960s, reaction against that secularism was generally limited to older, traditionally-minded individuals, mainly in the countryside. In the 1970s, however, urban Islamic movements began to emerge, demanding a society based on Islamic principles. Realizing the explosive potential of Islamic fundamentalism, the government at first, in June 1981, tried to channel Islamic agitation into a legalized "Mouvement de Tendance Islamique" (MTI); but the attempt to separate moderate and extremist Islamists was not effective, and the government soon turned against the MTI, too, and imprisoned some 50 of its leaders in Sept. 1981. The confrontation with Islam-extremists continued.

Apart from her conflict with France in the late 1950s and early 1960s T. took a moderate pro-Western line, but also fostered relations with the USSR, China and the other Communist countries. Relations with the West were important not only for the sake of the moderate and liberal image Bourguiba wanted to give T. but also because of economic considerations. Foreign aid came mainly from France, the US, West Germany, the World Bank and European monetary institutions, and Saʻudi Arabia, and T.'s foreign trade was mainly with Europe (France, Italy, Germany, Greece). T.'s involvement in A. affairs increased over the years. T. joined the A. League in 1958, but boycotted its sessions immediately, from 1958 until 1961 — mainly because of her conflict with Nasserist Egypt; she accused Egypt of trying to impose her domination by subversive and forcible means, and of hosting Saleh Ben-Youssuf's center of hostile propaganda and subversion. T.'s relations with Egypt were severed in 1958 and resumed only in 1961. T.-A. relations were also troubled by Bourguiba's divergent, independent position on the A.-Israel conflict. A. opinion was particularly antagonized when Bourguiba, who had voiced similar ideas earlier, called in spring 1965, during a visit to the ME, for A. acceptance of the existence of Israel and a settlement of the conflict by peaceful means through direct negotiations with Israel based on the UN partition plan of 1947 and the return of the Palestinian-A. refugees. His demands from Israel were thus hardly different from the mainline of the ASt., but his promise of peace and his call for negotiations were indeed. Bourguiba's statements caused a storm of protest in the A. world, he was denounced as a traitor, T.'s expulsion from the A. League was demanded, and several A. ambassadors were recalled. In May 1965, T. also refused to sever diplomatic relations with West Germany following the latter's establishment of relations with Israel, as the other ASt did. As a result of these conflicts and T.'s rift with Egypt, T. again boycotted the A. League meetings in 1965 and in 1966 broke off diplomatic relations with Egypt. The 1967 A.-Israel war caused T. immediately to mend her relations with the A. world; she even sent troops to the front, but they did not arrive in time. The reconciliation was short-lived and ended in May 1968, when Syria denounced T. for betraying the A. cause in Palestine. During 1969–70 T.'s relations with Algeria improved and on 6 January 1970 a treaty of friendship and cooperation was signed, leading *inter alia* to collaboration in the exploitation of oil fields along the common border.

After the death of President *Nasser of Egypt in Sept. 1970, T.'s relations with the radical ASt. improved. But relations with neighboring Libya — revolutionary since 1969 and considered erratically expansionist and aggressive under her leader *Qadhdhafi — were tensely ambivalent between apprehensive concern and a desire to foster good neighborly relations. In June 1970 Habib Bourguiba Jr., the President's son, was replaced by Muhammad Masmoudi as Foreign Minister. T. became more active in A. affairs and closer to Libya. This trend culminated in a surprise announcement on 12 Jan. 1974, after a Bourguiba-Qadhdhafi meeting, that T. and Libya would form a union (while previously Bourguiba had rejected any such merger). This step was apparently engineered by Masmoudi while Prime Minister Nouira was absent, and Bourguiba seemed not to be fully aware of its implications. Masmoudi was dismissed by

Nouira (and went into exile), and the merger plan was allowed to die. T.-Libya relations now became tense and at times even hostile. A conflict over the delimitation of the continental shelf, assumed to contain oil, was submitted to the International Court of Justice in 1977 and an agreement was reached in February 1982. But Libya was harboring T.'n political exiles, and backing subversive activities of T.'n oppositionaries. T. believed that the Gafsa attack of Jan. 1980 was backed, even initiated, by Libya, and charged her with continuous military infiltrations. A sharp conflict erupted when Libya began expelling, in Aug. 1985, T.'n workers (of an estimated nearly 100,000 T.'ns employed in Libya, 25–30,000 were reported expelled). The crisis led to bitter mutual accusations, and T. severed her relations with Libya. T. was also worried by the decision of Aug. 1984 to form a Libyan-Moroccan union.

Relations with Algeria further improved since 1977, after T. stopped siding with Morocco in the dispute over Western *Sahara and trying to mediate in a pro-Moroccan direction. In Mar. 1983 T. and Algeria signed a new border and friendship agreement. They also came closer to each other in their common concern regarding the proposed Libya-Moroccan union of 1984. After the abolition of that union in 1986, Algeria tried to mediate and heal the rift between T. and Libya.

T.'s growing involvement in A. affairs became evident in the transfer of the A. League headquarters from Cairo to Tunis in 1979 and the appointment of the T.'n Chedly Klibi (al-Shadhily al-Qulaibi) as Secretary-General of the League. T. became further involved by the transfer of the *PLO headquarters to Tunis after its expulsion from Beirut in Aug. 1982. T.'s involvement and vulnerability were further demonstrated by the Israeli bombing of PLO installations in T. in Oct. 1985 (and by her near-involvement in the aftermath of the terrorist hijack of the Italian cruise ship *Achille Lauro*, the same month). From 1985–86, T. requested the PLO to remove from T. all military personnel and installations and confine its presence to administrative and political departments; 'Arafat reportedly agreed, and a considerable number of PLO men were transferred to other AC.

Turkey Developments in T. herself are outside the scope of this Dictionary. But T.'s relations with and impact on the AC should be briefly surveyed. For the Ottoman Empire, its rule in the AC and its dismemberment after World War I see *Ottoman Empire. Kemalist T.'s relations with the AC, from the early 1920s, were at first reserved. T., despite her break with her Ottoman past, resented the war-time A. revolt and the secession of the A. parts of the Empire, seen as A. "treason". Turks also tended to look down on the A.'s as backward and unable to break through to the modernist development fostered by Kemalist T. and establish strong and well-directed states. A.'s on the other hand, while attracted to some aspects of new T., particularly her strong government and her vigorous development, could not go along with her secularism which they saw as a deviation from Islamic traditions and principles; many A. leaders also considered T.'s Europe-centered modernism as going too far.

There were also specific conflicts. T. disputed Iraq's possession of the *Mosul area. But when the *League of Nations finally awarded the disputed district to Iraq, in 1925–26, T. accepted that ruling. Moreover, of all AC, Iraq became closest to T. and was the first to conclude a non-aggression pact with her (the *Saadabad Pact of 1937, to which Iran and Afghanistan were also partners). T. and Iraq also had a common interest in fighting the separatist national ambitions and rebellions of the *Kurds. With Syria, on the other hand, T. was in serious conflict over the possession of the *Alexandretta-*Hatay district. This dispute was decided in 1939 by T.'s annexation of the district, in agreement with France; but Syria has never accepted or recognized this, and though she maintains normal relations with T., implying a recognition of her territorial integrity and her frontiers, the Alexandretta issue continues to rankle.

In the 1950s, the radical-"progressive" ASt, and particularly Egypt and Syria, resented T.'s increasingly close alliance with the USA and the Western powers and her association with attempts to recruit the ASt for Western-guided ME defense pacts — efforts that led in 1955 to the creation of the *Baghdad Pact, which was bitterly opposed by Egypt and Syria. In the mid-1950s Egypt and Syria suspected T. of plotting against Syria's régime, aiming to impose on her a pro-Western orientation and force her into the Baghdad Pact. With Iraq transformed into a revolutionary régime since 1958, the decline and demise of the Baghdad Pact, and the consolidation of a firmly leftist and revolutionary régime in Syria under the *Ba'th, this issue has disappeared. The conservative ASt, particularly Jordan and Iraq until 1958, which had no part in that A.-Turkish antagonism, cultivated friendly relations with T. even during the crises of the 1950s; Iraq continued that policy under her post-1958 leftist régimes, too. In recent years, Iraqi-Turkish cooperation against Kurd rebels has led even to an informal agreement permitting Turkish military operations in the border area inside Iraq. T. has also developed relations with Libya, including close trade and economic relations and Libyan credits and financial aid, and Turkish technicians and laborers as well as Turkish contracting companies working in Libya. T.'s relations with Egypt have also much improved under Nasser's successors since 1970.

The improvement in T.'s A. relations was greatly influenced by T.'s deliberate pro-A. policy since the 1960s and by her growing involvement in Islamic affairs (an involvement that would have been unthinkable in the heyday of Kemalism). Some leaders, including President Evren, warn T. of the danger of Islamic fundamentalism; but T.'s participation in all-Islamic activities has not been seriously challenged. She first attended an Islamic Economic Conference in 1954; she sent a delegation to the Islamic Summit of Rabat in Sept. 1969; she regularly attends the Foreign Ministers meetings of the Islamic Conference Organization (ICO) — at first without full membership, but since 1976 as a full member; and since 1981 she participates in the Islamic Summit meetings. T.'s pro-A. and Islamic policies also led her to restrict her relations with Israel. She recognized Israel in Mar. 1949 *de facto* and early in 1950, with the establishment of diplomatic relations, *de jure*. But she refused to raise mutual representation to the rank of embassy, usual by that time, and in Nov. 1956 she withdrew her Minister and since then has left her Legation, demonstratively, headed by a low rank Chargé d'Affaires and has also blocked closer economic and cultural relations.

Differences and suspicions still troubled T.'s relations with the ASt. A major problem was T.'s Cyprus policy and her occupation of the northern part of the island in 1974: no AC except Libya supported that Turkish step. Relations have remained particularly cool and suspicious with Syria. Apart from Syria's resentment over Alexandretta, there are problems concerning small minorities of Turks in Syria and Syrian A.'s in T.; T. suspects subversive Syrian activities inside T., illegal border-crossings, arms smuggling, and Syrian support for Kurdish and Armenian rebels, and resents the granting of Syrian asylum to such rebels. Syria resents T.'s close cooperation with and assistance to Iraq (including the transportation of Iraqi oil through an Iraqi-Turkish pipeline). And a possible conflict looms over the unsolved problem of the waters of the *Euphrates.

U

UAE   See *United Arab Emirates.
UAR   See *United Arab Republic.
Umm al-Qaiwain   The smallest of the seven sheikhdoms of the *Trucial Coast, now the *UAE. Area: c. 290 sq. mi. (750 sq. km.). The population — until the development of the UAE's oil economy since the 1960s mostly nomads — was given by a census of 1985 as 20,300, of whom 7,200 were indigenous and 13,100 foreigners. UaQ was, along with the other Trucial sheikhdoms, a British Protectorate until 1971, when she joined the Federation of the United Arab Emirates (UAE) then being formed and becoming independent. Within the UAE, the ruler of UaQ — of the Mu'alla clan — belongs to the Dubai-led camp that opposes too strong a federal authority and wishes more power to stay with the individual sheikhdoms. Since the late 1960s, UaQ has granted several oil concessions to Shell and American companies. No major oil strikes have yet been reported. UaQ thus has no large revenues of her own; but she has a marginal share in the general development of the UAE.
UN   See *United Nations Organization.
UNDOF   United Nations Disengagement Observers Force on the border between Syria and the

Israel-occupied *Golan Heights, set up in May 1974, with a strength of 1,200 men. See *Arab-Israel Wars (Oct. 1973 War).

UNEF United Nations Emergency Force, set up in Nov. 1956 to supervise the withdrawal of British and French forces from Egypt's *Suez Canal Zone and of Israeli forces from *Sinai and the *Gaza Strip, and to patrol Sinai and provide a buffer between Egyptian and Israeli forces. Its original strength of over 6,000 men was later reduced to 3,400–3,600. In May 1967 it was withdrawn at Egyptian President *Nasser's request — a step that was a major cause of the *Six Day War.

After the *October War of 1973 UNEF was revived ("UNEF II"), with a strength of 4,200–4,700. It supervised the cease-fire and disengagement of forces and acted as a buffer between Egyptian and Israeli forces. It operated until 1982, when the implementation of the Egypt-Israel Peace Treaty made it redundant and it was disbanded. See *Arab-Israel Wars.

Uniate The union of parts of Eastern churches, *en bloc*, with the *Catholic Church, and the Catholic communities thus created. The U. was based on the acceptance of the dogmas of the Catholic Church and the supreme authority of the Pope, while allowing the U. communities to maintain their own liturgy, including its language (instead of Latin), and a measure of autonomy, including the U. community's administrative structure and hierarchy, headed by a Patriarch. Sometimes the U. was a process in stages so that no precise dates can be given, and dates indicated are in some doubt. The U. communities in the ME (with their previous church in parentheses) are *Maronites (Monothelites, 1182, 1445, 1736); *Greek-Catholics (Greek *Orthodox, 1730, 1775); *Chaldeans (*Nestorian-*Assyrians, 1552); *Armenian-Catholics (*Monophysite Armenian-Orthodox Gregorians, 12th century, 1375, 1439); *Copt-Catholics (Monophysite Copts, 1741); Syrian Catholics (Monophysite Syrian-Orthodox, 1662). Of these U. communities, the Maronites, Greek-Catholics and Chaldeans are sizable groups (see entries); the rest are small communities.

UNIFIL United Nations Interim Force in Lebanon. Set up in Mar. 1978, to supervise the cease-fire and withdrawal of Israeli forces that had invaded South Lebanon, prevent the use of South Lebanon for hostile activities, and assist the government of Lebanon to reassert its effective control. Its original strength of c. 4,000 men was boosted in 1981–82 to nearly 6,000, but later again reduced. UNIFIL played no important role during the Israeli invasion of June 1982 and occupation of 1982–85. see *Lebanon.

United Arab Emirates, UAE A Federation set up, and becoming independent, in Dec. 1971 by the seven sheikhdoms of the *Trucial Coast or Trucial 'Oman on the southern, Arabian coast of the *Persian Gulf — *Abu Dhabi, *Dubai, *Sharja, *Ras al-Khaima, *Umm al-Qaiwain, *'Ajman and *Fujaira. The area of the UAE is 32,000 sq. mi. (83,600 sq. km.). The population, estimated as c. 200,000 when the UAE was formed, grew rapidly with the development of the country's oil economy, mainly by the influx of foreign workers from other AC, Pakistan and India. In the mid-1970s it was thought to be about 800,000, of which 75–80% were foreign workers; by 1980 it passed the 1 m. mark and in the mid-1980s it is estimated at about 1.5 m., 75–80% foreigners.

The seven sheikhdoms had been under British protection since the 1820s. Preparations for independence and the creation of a federation began in earnest in 1968, when Britain announced her decision to abolish her protectorate. Negotiations on the federation were difficult; *Bahrain and *Qatar which had planned to join it, withdrew. Even when the UAE was set up, one of the seven sheikhdoms, Ras al-Khaima, refused

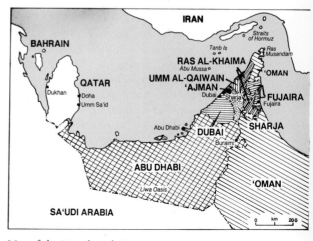

Map of the United Arab Emirates

to join; she joined early in 1972. The new independent UAE was immediately admitted to the Arab League and the UN, in Dec. 1971, and began setting up her federal constitution and administration. In July 1972 a draft constitution was proclaimed. It provided for a Supreme Council of the seven rulers and a Federal National Council composed of representatives of the seven sheikhdoms appointed by their rulers, with some account taken of the varying size of the sheikhdoms but no fully proportional calculation and much weighting for the smaller ones (Abu Dhabi and Dubai 8 each, Sharja and Ras al-Khaima 6 each, and the three remaining ones four each). Abu Dhabi and Dubai were to have a veto in both these councils. The Supreme Council was to elect one of its members as President of the UAE for a five-year term, and he was to form a Government in consultation with the other rulers and with all seven sheikhdoms represented in it. Currency and customs were to be united. Federal institutions were to be gradually established and unified. But the sheikhdoms were to retain their separate identity and to control their own economy, with the federal budget financed not by direct taxation but by contributions of the sheikhdoms (with no quotas fixed; *de facto*, Abu Dhabi and Dubai alone financed the federal budget, with Abu Dhabi paying the bulk).

The ruler of Abu Dhabi, Sheikh Zayed ibn Sultan al-*Nuhayan, was elected by the seven rulers as President od the UAE, and the ruler of Dubai, Sheikh Rashed ibn Sa'id al-*Maktum, as Vice-President; the latter's son, Maktum ibn Rashed al-Maktum, became Prime Minister, and other sons filled other key positions.

The new federation was troubled from the start by a continuous struggle over its constitutional-political structure. The rulers of Dubai wanted the powers of the federal institutions to be restricted and the main powers to remain vested in the individual sheikhdoms. This debate of principles was aggravated by the old and constant rivalry between Dubai and Abu Dhabi. Dubai, supported by Ras al-Khaima, Umm al-Qaiwain and sometimes by Sharja, obstructed or delayed the development and final endorsement of most federal institutions. When the term of the provisional constitution of 1971 ended in 1976, a permanent constitution was worked out, but Dubai and her supporters insisted on a postponement and a further five-year extension of the provisional arrangements. After five years, in 1981, the same happened again, and in 1986 the provisional constitution was extended for five more years. Sheikh Zayed of Abu Dhabi was re-elected President in 1976, 1981 and 1986.

The creation of a federal army and the dissolution of the various armed formations of the sheikhdoms met the same obstacles. Decisions taken in May 1976 caused a crisis and could not be implemented; the merger of all armed formations was re-decided in 1978 and federal forces were set up, but attempts to enforce the dissolution of the separate formations caused a new crisis in 1979. In the context of that crisis, Dubai had to be compensated by the appointment of her ruler as Prime Minister, in addition to the Vice-Presidency (his son, Prime Minister until 1979, becoming Deputy-Premier). In the mid-1980s separate armed forces still exist.

The rapid development of the UAE since the early 1970s, that has turned her into one of the world's richest countries, was the result of her growing oil economy. The bulk of the oil production is centered in Abu Dhabi, which began producing in 1962; Dubai exported her first oil in 1969; Sharja began producing, in more modest quantities, in 1974; and Ras al-Khaima in 1984. Oil production and export are not federal matters and the oil revenue is the producing sheikhdom's, not the UAE's — for details see *oil.

In her foreign and international policies the UAE takes a rather cautious and low-profile line. Within the A. League she belongs to the moderate mainline camp, refrains from spectacular initiatives, and usually follows the lead of Sa'udi Arabia. The UAE was one of the founder-members of the *"Gulf Cooperation Council", 1981. Like the other members of that group, she seems to regard the security of the Persian Gulf and its shipping lanes, and the threat posed by Iran, as her main concern; and like the other members, she handles that issue very cautiously, professing strict neutrality in the Iran-Iraq Gulf War. She applies the same caution to her territorial dispute with Iran: the forcible seizure by Iran of the *Abu Mussa and Tanb islands in 1971. The UAE is officially neutralist also in world affairs and belongs to the group of non-aligned states, and while she is no-doubt interested in cooperation with the West (and in US and Western measures for the security of the Gulf), she refuses to give any overt formal expression to such cooperation. The UAE was, in Nov. 1985, the third Gulf country to establish official relations with the USSR.

United Arab Republic (UAR) Egypt and Syria merged in Feb. 1958 to form the UAR. It broke up in Sept. 1961, when Syria seceded following a military *coup*. The initiative for the merger came from Syria — for the reasons, and Syria's fear of destabilization, see *Syria.

Egypt, though professing A. "Unionism", was seeking political coordination and a dominating influence, but not a full union. President *Nasser agreed to the merger on condition it would be based on his terms and on the pattern of Egypt's régime, including her one-party system. A provisional constitution was proclaimed by Presidents Nasser and *Quwwatli and endorsed on 21 Feb. 1958 by a plebiscite in both countries. A UAR National Assembly of 300 Egyptians and 100 Syrians was to be appointed by the President, with at least half of its members chosen from among members of the dissolved Egyptian and Syrian assemblies. A small UAR government was to deal with defense, foreign affairs, industrialization, education and "national guidance", and two "regional" governments with all other issues. A single political organization, the "National Union" on the Egyptian pattern, was to replace the parties active in Syria.

The Feb. 1958 referendum that endorsed the union and its constitution also elected Gamal 'Abd-ul-Nasser President, as the only candidate. He appointed four Vice-Presidents — two Egyptians ('Abd-ul-Hakim *'Amer and 'Abd-ul-Latif Baghdadi) and two Syrians (Akram *Hourani and Sabri 'Assali), 'Amer also to command the joint military forces, and an eight-member UAR Government (seven Egyptians and one Syrian). In Oct. 1958 the central government was expanded (14 Egyptians, 7 Syrians) and its sphere of activities and authority was greatly widened.

The government and administration of the UAR did not work well, and there were frequent reshuffles. But Syrian dissatisfaction went much deeper. The "National Union" failed to take roots in Syria, and the disbandment of the existing parties caused unrest. It was in particular the *Ba'th* leaders who were disaffected. They had pressed for the union, hoping that they would become the ideological mentors of the UAR; but Nasser, unwilling to share power or accept guidance, discarded them and ordered their organization to disband like all others. From 1959, *Ba'th* leaders resigned from government positions and went into opposition, increasingly underground. However, resentment grew in much wider Syrian circles. The posting of Egyptian officers in key positions in the Syrian armed forces; the growing trend towards centralization which put increasing power in the hands of the central government; the efforts to impose Egyptian patterns on Syria's body politic; and the application of Egyptian economic policies — beginning with land reform and some nationalization, and culminating in July 1961 in far-reaching nationalization measures and a turn to full state socialism — angered the élite who realized Syria had lost her independence and was losing her identity.

Nasser responded by tightening Egypt's grip. The economic measures of 1961 were accompanied, in Aug., by the abolition of the two regional governments. A new central government was headed by seven Vice-Presidents, only two of them Syrians (one of whom, 'Abd-ul-Hamid Sarraj, was seen as Nasser's commissar with near-dictatorial powers — and was soon involved in a struggle with 'Amer, who wished to reserve that position for himself). In Sept. 1961 a group of Syrian officers took power in Syria. They were initially prepared to discuss changes in the structure of government and a proper division of powers. But Nasser was not willing to compromise, and the officers proclaimed Syria's secession and the dissolution of the UAR.

Egypt regarded the secession as an illegal act of rebellion, refused to recognize Syria's renewed independence, and continued to call herself UAR until Sept. 1971 (after Nasser's death). When the *Arab League re-seated an independent Syria, in 1962, Egypt boycotted its meetings for six months. There was a partial reconciliation in the spring of 1963, when Syria, now under a *Ba'th* government, began discussions with Egypt on a renewed union — also to be called UAR, but on a federal pattern, with Iraq as a third partner; this scheme failed (see *Arab Federation, *Egypt, *Syria). Official Egypt-Syria relations were resumed only late in 1966, coupled with a defense pact and a significant *rapprochement*.

United Nations Organization, UN Five ASt were founding members of the UN, 1945: Egypt, Iraq, Lebanon, Syria and Sa'udi Arabia. Thirteen more ASt (and Israel) have since been admitted: Yemen 1947; Israel 1949; Libya and Jordan 1955; Sudan, Morocco and Tunisia 1956; Algeria 1962; Kuwait 1963; South Yemen 1967; Bahrain, Qatar, 'Oman and the UAE 1971. Three non-A. or semi-A. member-states of the *Arab League may be added: Somalia 1960; Mauritania 1961; Djibouti 1977. Thus, the ASt have 21 votes at the UN.

The UN has dealt continuously with many issues concerning the ASt and the ME.

PALESTINE, ARAB-ISRAEL. The ME problem most persistently on the UN agenda has been the Palestine, later the *A.-Israel, dispute. Great Britain referred it to the UN in Apr. 1947. In May 1947, the General Assembly (GA) set up a "Special Committee on Palestine" (UNSCOP) to make recommendations. UNSCOP's majority report, submitted to the GA on 31 Aug. 1947, recommended the partition of Palestine into a Jewish state and an Arab state, linked in an economic union; Jerusalem was to become an international enclave under UN trusteeship. The recommendations were adopted by the GA on 29 Nov. 1947 by a vote of 33 to 13, with 10 abstentions. A UN Palestine Commission of five nations was set up to aid the establishment of transitional régimes in the two states gaining independence; but the British Palestine administration refuse to cooperate and the Commission never came to Palestine; it was disbanded by the GA in May 1948.

Since the UN-recommended partition was opposed by force by the A.'s and hostilities broke out immediately (see *Arab-Israel Wars), a special session of the GA and the Security Council (SC) convened in Apr.-May 1948. Both considered an American proposal to shelve or postpone partition in favor of a new trusteeship, as well as other proposals for a temporary administration under UN auspices; these came, however, to naught. Late in Apr., the SC established a Jerusalem Truce Commission composed of the US, French and Belgian Consuls-General in Jerusalem, to supervise a truce to be negotiated. In mid-May, the GA decided to appoint a mediator, and the permanent members of the SC (i.e. the five Big Powers) nominated the Swedish Count Folke *Bernadotte.

As the British Mandate expired on 14 May 1948 and the State of Israel was proclaimed, the ASt invaded Palestine and a full-fledged war broke out (see *Arab-Israel Wars). At the end of May the SC ordered a four-week truce which went into effect on 11 June. The SC also established a UN truce observers' corps (*UNTSO). When the ASt refused to prolong the truce and fighting was resumed, the SC again called for a cease-fire which went into effect on 18 July. In the meantime Count Bernadotte made proposals for a settlement (see *Bernadotte); these were rejected by both sides and, later in the year, by the GA Political Committee as well. Count Bernadotte was assassinated by Jewish terrorists on 17 Sept. 1948. The UN Under-Secretary-General, Dr. Ralph Bunche, an American, succeeded him as acting mediator. When fighting broke out again in Oct to Dec., the SC again called for a cease-fire and an armistice. Negotiations were held under the chairmanship of the acting mediator in spring 1949 and resulted in separate Armistice Agreements (see *Arab-Israel Wars). The General Armistice Agreements (GAA), set up Mixed Armistice Commissions (MAC) to consider complaints of breaches of the GAAs. The four MACs were each composed of representatives of the parties and the Chief-of-Staff of the UN Truce Observers, or his representative, as chairman responsible to the SC.

Israel was admitted to the UN in May 1949. The UN has remained permanently involved in the A.-Israel conflict. Its continuous debates; the establishment of a Conciliation Commission (*PCC) in Dec. 1948 and of an agency to aid the Palestinian-A. *refugees (*UNRWA) in Dec. 1949; its attitude to the persistent breaches of the armistice, incursions, terrorism and reprisals, and to the Egyptian blockade of the *Suez Canal and the Gulf of *'Aqaba; its action in the crisis of 1956, the *Sinai War, and in that of 1967, the *Six Day War; the creation of a UN Emergency Force (*UNEF) on the Egypt-Israel front, 1956, its disbandment in 1967 and its renewal in 1973; Security Council Resolution 242 of Nov. 1967 and its significance; UN action in the crisis of 1973; the creation of an observer force (*UNDOF) on the Syrian front, 1973; the Israel-Lebanon crisis of 1978 and the creation of a UN force (*UNIFIL); and the UN continuous condemnation of the Israeli occupation of the West

Bank and Gaza since 1967, and support of Palestinian-A. rights since 1969 — are discussed in detail in the entry *Arab-Israel Conflict. For UN positions and resolutions on *Jerusalem and the *refugees see also those two entries.

The UN GA has also instituted several bodies to investigate Israeli occupation practices or otherwise express its condemnation of the occupation. A committee (Somalia, Sri Lanka, Yugoslavia) to monitor the treatment of the A. population in the occupied territories and their human rights was set up in 1968–69, and a "Committee for the Exercise of the Inalienabale Rights of the Palestinian People" in 1975 (the "Committe of 20" — in fact 23 member-states, 19 of them refusing to have official relations with Israel). The GA also ordered the UN Secretary-General to establish a special permanent unit in the Secretariat to deal with and promote the rights of the Palestinians. Other UN agencies, such as the World Health Organization, the Human Rights Commission and others, established similar committees. Israel has in general rejected these committees — in principle, and in particular because they were composed of a majority of hostile states maintaining no official relations with her — and has denied them admission to the occupied areas; their reports and activities are therefore based on information gathered outside these territories.

In all its activities and resolutions, the UN has so far been unable to provide a peaceful solution to the A.-Israel conflict. Even the Egypt-Israel Peace Agreement was not welcomed by the GA; in 1978 it denounced "separate", bilateral A.-Israel agreements, and in 1979 it declared the *Camp David Agreements invalid, "null and void", because they disregarded Palestinian-A. rights. Instead, the GA has recommended, since the later 1970s, a general ME peace conference under UN auspices.

Several other A. questions and disputes, raised at the UN by the countries involved, are discussed in the entries on the countries concerned. They are listed here briefly to summarize UN involvement.

SYRIA AND LEBANON jointly turned to the SC in Feb. 1946, complaining of the failure of Britain and France to withdraw their military forces. No binding decision was reached, because of a Soviet veto, but the debate helped resolve the dispute. In autumn 1957 the GA discussed Syria's complaint of a threat to her independence by Turkey, Iraq, Israel and the Western Powers; it took no decisions. Lebanon complained to the SC in May 1958, that the Syro-Egyptian UAR was endangering ME peace by interfering in her internal affairs, *inter alia* through the "infiltration of armed bands" and the "participation of UAR nationals in acts of terrorism and rebellion". The UN deliberations on this complaint resulted in the setting-up of an international observers' force which remained in Lebanon for several months, but achieved little.

During the civil war from 1975 onwards, proposals were sometimes voiced in Lebanon to involve the UN, request a UN peace-keeping force etc. But these suggestions did not crystallize into a formal request and apart from occasional appeals for peace or expressions of concern the UN played no role in the Lebanese imbroglio (except for its A-Israel aspects). As Lebanon did not officially complain to the UN about Syria's increasing military intervention, from 1976, that intervention did not elicit UN action.

JORDAN complained to the SC in June 1958 against interference by the Syro-Egyptian UAR. No action was taken by the SC.

EGYPT brought her dispute with Britain to the SC in summer 1947. It concerned the evacuation of British forces and mainly the future of Sudan; the Council reached no decision. The *Suez Canal crisis of 1956 was dealt with both by the SC and the GA, the *Suez War and the *Sinai Campaign mainly by the Assembly (because of the British and French veto in the SC). Egypt was deeply involved in the UN discussions and decisions on the A.-Israel problem. She appeared before the SC as the defendant in four complaints raised by ASt: in Feb. 1958 by Sudan (the issue was settled by Egypt and Sudan between themselves); in May 1958 by Lebanon; shortly thereafter by Jordan; and in summer 1963 by Sa'udi Arabia. All these problems were resolved — or left unresolved — by the ASt themselves without a UN decision on the merits of the issues.

KUWAIT complained in June 1961 to the SC about an Iraqi threat to her independence as soon as it had been granted; the dispute was resolved outside the UN.

LIBYA was discussed by the UN in 1948–49 when the GA determined the future of the former Italian possessions. In Nov. 1949 the GA decided to grant her independence as a united Libya with a federal stucture. In the same context, the GA decided in 1950 on the future of SOMALIA: a ten-year Italian trusteeship, and independence in 1960.

YEMEN. The problem of Yemen was raised at the UN in 1962, following the outbreak of revolution and civil war and Egypt's armed intervention. The UN set up an international military observers' group to supervise the withdrawal of both Sa'udi Arabian and Egyptian forces intervening in Yemen; these observers served from summer 1963 to Sept. 1964 — with no success, as the Egyptian forces were not withdrawn. In the 1960s the SC also inconclusively debated incidents and border skirmishes between Yemen and the British Protectorate of 'Aden.

SOUTH ARABIA. The Special UN Committee for Non-Self-Governing Territories and the GA dealt with the questions of 'Aden and South Arabia from 1963 onwards. The Assembly recommended the evacuation of South Arabia by British forces, refused to consider the South Arabian Federation as an independent state and recommended UN supervision of elections and the transition to independence. A UN committee tried to implement such supervision in 1967, but the events which led to the independence of South Yemen moved so rapidly that the Committee could exert no influence.

'OMAN. The anti-colonial majority in the UN decided to intervene in the problems of 'Oman (a previous attempt, in 1957, had failed). From 1961 to 1970 the GA annually recommended the evacuation of British forces from the principality. Britain and the Sultan took no account of this recommendation, which they regarded as unwarranted interference in the affairs of an independent country. The UN also tried to investigate, through sub-committees and a special envoy of the Secretary-General, the dispute between the Sultan and the Imam of 'Oman, but reached no conclusions on this problem. In the 1960s, the Secretary-General also unsuccessfully tried to mediate the dispute — see *'Oman.

BAHRAIN. An envoy sent by the UN Secretary-General in 1970 prepared a public opinion poll on the future of Bahrain, following a proposal by the Shah of Iran and with the agreement of Britain and the Sheikh of Bahrain. He concluded that the majority wanted independence (and not annexation to Iran).

SUDAN. Sudanese issues were raised at the UN since 1947 only in connection with Sudan's complaint against Egypt in 1958. The suppression and subsequent rebellion of the Negro tribes in south Sudan were not raised at the UN by any one of the nations or bodies struggling for the liberation of peoples; the rebels themselves turned to the UN in 1970 and the Committee for Non-Self-Governing Territories promised to give them a hearing, but nothing came of that.

MAGHRIB. The UN dealt with the struggle of Morocco and Tunisia for independence from 1951–52 and with the Algerian problem from 1955. UN discussions did not produce specific resolutions or tangible immediate results; but they contributed to the creation of an atmosphere in which the French had to grant full independence to the *Maghrib* countries.

MAURITANIA'S independence and admission to the UN caused a brief controversy at the UN in 1960–61, since Morocco objected. But as Morocco relented, the issue was resolved in 1961. From the mid-1960s the GA also debated the fate of Spanish *SAHARA. It recommended a referendum on its future. This recomendation is still on the books and the UN has not accepted as final Morocco's annexation of Western Sahara. But since no official request has so far been presented for the recognition and admission of the rebellious Sahara Republic (SADR), the issue is kept at a low profile.

IRAQ, PERSIAN GULF. Since the outbreak of the Iraq-Iran war in Sept. 1980, that war and its repercussions on the situation in the *Persian Gulf have been discussed occasionally at the UN. Both the GA and the SC have called for an end to the war, negotiations and a peaceful settlement, and the Secretary-General has made feeble attempts to mediate. The UN has also investigated Iranian complaints of the use of poison gas and chemical weapons by Iraq (and found them to be true). But the UN has so far taken no strong, decisive action on the Gulf War.

Besides UN discussions of ME political problems, and of complaints by or against ASt, various UN institutions and, in particular, its special agencies were engaged in the area in many fields of activity: health, education, labor relations, development, transportation, etc. The UN and its special agencies made various attempts to set up regional centers to stimulate regional cooperation (as through similar centers in the Far East, Africa, Latin America); these efforts failed due to the refusal of the ASt to cooperate in any way with Israel, and their opposition to any regional cooperation which would include Israel.

United States of America, US interests and policies in the Arab countries Except for a brief period between 1786 and 1805 when the US took diplomatic and military measures to protect her maritime rights from the Barbary rulers of the North African coast, Washington initially showed no interest in the "Eastern Question", while private US philanthropists, primarily Presbyterian missionaries, were active, establishing the Syrian Protestant College in 1866 (later the American University of Beirut), the American University of Cairo, Robert College in Istanbul and a network of smaller colleges and hospitals throughout the Levant, Turkey and Egypt. With overseas commercial interests expanding at the turn of the century, the US began to assert her "Open Door" policy for equal economic treatment with the European powers in Morocco — at the Algeciras Conference in 1906 — and elsewhere in the Middle East.

US involvement in the ME increased at the close of *World War I. While the US had not declared war against the *Ottoman Empire, President Wilson expressed American preferences concerning the future disposition of Ottoman territories occupied by the Allies. Point twelve of his Fourteen Points defining US war aims called for self-determination for these territories. American pressure led to the development of the *Mandate concept as a compromise between independence and European annexations. An appreciation of American, especially American Jewish, public opinion had also influenced Britain's support of Zionist aspirations in the *Balfour Declaration of 1917. Independent American study groups were sent by President Wilson in 1919 to Syria-Palestine (the *King-Crane Mission) and to Armenia (the Harbord Mission), but their recommendations were not followed. After the US Senate refused to ratify the Treaty of Versailles and the Covenant of the *League of Nations, American interest in the ME declined.

In the inter-war period, the US, pursuing her Open Door principle, concluded agreements to protect her cultural and economic interests in Syria-Palestine (with France, 1924) and in Palestine and Iraq (with Great Britain, 1924 and 1930 respectively). In 1928, a consortium of seven US oil companies led by Standard Oil of New Jersey succeeded in gaining a 23.75 per cent share in the Turkish Petroleum Company (from 1929: *Iraq P.C.) concessions in Iraq and other former Ottoman tetrritories. Standard Oil of California (SOCAL) acquired exploration rights in the British-protected sheikhdom of Bahrain in 1930, and a wholly American concession to Sa'udi Arabia in 1933, substantially expanded, 1939. The American Gulf Oil Company, in equal partnership with the British government-owned Anglo-Persian Oil Company, secured a concession in Kuwait in 1934.

World War II raised the level of American involvement in the ME. Great Britain held the supreme allied command for the region, and the US initially established only supply missions in North Africa and Iran (Sept. 1941). Joint Anglo-American forces occupied French North Africa (Nov. 1942 to May 1943). American pressure against restrictive British regulations and suspicions of British imperial ambitions caused tension in the British-directed ME Supply Center and American efforts to establish closer ties with the ME. By the end of 1943, the US initiated direct lend-lease aid programs with Egypt, Iran, Sa'udi Arabia, and Turkey. Rumors that Britain sought to displace American oil companies in the region led to a drive to increase US influence in Sa'udi Arabia. This culminated in Feb. 1945 in the meeting between President Roosevelt and King 'Abd-ul-'Aziz *Ibn Sa'ud and the latter's agreement several months later to grant the US an airbase at *Dhahran.

American public interest in the Palestine question grew throughout the war. In 1944, the Zionist movement brought its Biltmore program, calling for the establishment of a Jewish state, before both houses of Congress. Resolutions calling for the abolition of the 1939 White Paper were introduced; War Department and State Department intervention precluded a vote. In 1944 both presidential candidates pledged support for Jewish statehood. The Roosevelt Administration attempted to construct a neutral policy on Palestine based on prior "consultation with both Arabs and Jews", its pledges and commitments were contradictory. President Truman introduced a pro-Zionist tilt in American policy by his August 1945 endorsement of the Harrison Report determining that displaced Jewish survivors of the Holocaust had pro-Zionist preferences. He called for the immediate admission of 100,000 Jews into Palestine. Attempts to work out a coordinated Anglo-American policy on Palestine failed (for instance, the Morrison-Grady Plan).

US strategic interest in the ME increased steadily, and the region was an early focal point of Soviet-American rivalry in the emerging Cold War. This led to US resistance to the Soviet presence in Iran and Soviet demands upon Turkey (outside our scope), the *Truman Doctrine of 12 Mar. 1947, and the US take-over of Britain's responsibilities of economic and military assistance to Greece and Turkey. A transient US naval presence was transformed into the US Sixth Fleet in 1948, and a smaller US naval contingent, the US ME Force, was permanently stationed in the Persian Gulf. US ME policy was premised on the renewal of Anglo-American strategic cooperation, with primary responsibility for the defense of the region assigned to Britain. But frequent Anglo-American discord undercut the Western position. In Palestine, the Truman Administration did not follow the British lead (though both the Departments of State and Defense largely supported the British position). In Nov. 1947, the US supported the partition of Palestine into Jewish and Arab states; once the State of Israel was declared on 15 May 1948, the US granted it immediate *de facto* recognition. By May 1950, Anglo-American cohesion on Palestine was to some extent achieved by the Tripartite Declaration (US-Britain-France) which announced a semi-guarantee of the sovereignty and borders of all Middle East states and the coordination of arms supplies.

Anglo-American differences also emerged elsewhere in the ME. The US tended to come to terms with the new nationalist forces, while the British sought to preserve the political and economic *status quo*. US and British oil interests were in constant rivalry. Divergences became evident in the American acceptance of Sa'udi Arabian demands for the equal sharing of oil profits in 1950, the attitude towards the Egyptian "Free Officers" junta of 1952, and the Iranian oil crisis of 1952–53. US interests and the ARAMCO oil consortium were at least in part behind border disputes between Sa'udi Arabia and the Trucial sheikhdoms (Abu Dhabi) and 'Oman (see *Buraimi).

In the 1950s, Washington initiated efforts to create a *ME defense organization. In October 1951, the Truman Administration, joined by Britain, France and Turkey, proposed to Egypt membership in a ME command ("SACME"), which would also take over the British base in the *Suez Canal Zone as an allied enterprise. After repeated Egyptian refusals to join the command as well as a less ambitious ME Defense Organization, the new Eisenhower Administration shifted its alliance-building schemes towards the "Northern Tier" states more directly threatened by the Soviet Union. Among the ASt only Iraq showed a realization of such a Soviet threat and agreed to join the US efforts. In Apr. 1954, the US agreed to give military aid to Baghdad. In May, a US military aid agreement was signed with Pakistan. As Turkey, which had become a full NATO member in 1952, negotiated a series of agreements with Pakistan (Apr. 1954) and Iraq (Feb. 1955), a regional pro-Western bloc consisting of Turkey, Iraq, Pakistan, and Iran emerged as the *Baghdad Pact. Britain joined, while the US gave decisive political support and sat in on the Pact's committees. Hopes that other ASt would join were disappointed; on the contrary, the Pact antagonized Egypt, Syria and other ASt and created much anti-US and anti-Western sentiment. Attempts by the Eisenhower Administration to advance a settlement of the A.-Israel dispute through a solution of the refugee problem and perhaps Israeli territorial concessions in the *Negev, also made no progress. An effort to devise an agreed integrated plan for the *Jordan River development was also abortive (see *Jordan River).

US policy before and during the *Suez crisis of 1956 was contradictory. After Egypt made an arms deal with the Soviet Bloc in 1955, Secretary Dulles reneged on a promise to aid her major development project, the construction of the *Aswan High Dam, and also ensured that international aid would be denied. This led President Nasser to nationalize the Suez Canal. But when Britain and France prepared military action against Egypt, Eisenhower and Dulles refused to associate the US with the former imperial powers. In Oct.-Nov. 1956, the US pressured Britain and France to withdraw from Egypt at the outset of their military operations; simultaneous pressure on Israel compelled her to evacuate the *Sinai with uncertain political assurances and no guarantees. The US got little thanks for her support of Egypt.

From 1957, the US moved to fill the Western great power vacuum that she had brought about. On 5 Jan. 1957 President Eisenhower issued an *Eisenhower Doctrine, approved by Congress on 9 March which pledged US armed aid "to secure and protect the territorial integrity and political independence of such nations" (in the ME) "requesting aid against any armed aggression from any nation controlled by international Communism" (it said nothing about the principal danger: internal subversion). When it was actually applied, it was against threats from Nasserist Egypt rather than the USSR: in Apr. 1957 the Sixth Fleet was deployed during an attempted *coup* against the Hashemite monarchy in Jordan, and in July 1958 the US landed Marine and Army units in Lebanon to help President *Chamoun, at his request, against a Nasserist rebellion aided by UAR intervention. In Mar. 1959, after revolutionary Iraq's secession from the Baghdad Pact, now renamed *"CENTO", the US concluded bilateral executive agreements with the remaining members, Turkey, Iran and Pakistan, pledging "appropriate action including the use of armed force" in their defense in case of aggression. The agreements derived their authority explicitly from the Eisenhower Doctrine.

Several other bilateral arrangements in the ME served US nuclear strategic interests in the 1950s and early 1960s. US airbase rights in Morocco (from 1950 under French rule, 1956–63 agreed with independent Morocco) and Libya (1954–70) were of special importance to the American Strategic Air Command (SAC) before the introduction of the intercontinental range B-52. The Dhahran airbase in Sa'udi Arabia (1946–62) never became a full SAC base, but was an important US Air Force transit stop. In the late 1950s, the US deployed intermediate range ballistic missiles in Turkey. With the introduction of Polaris missile-firing submarines in the early 1960s, the Mediterranean itself became an increasing arena of superpower strategic competition. However, by the end of the 1960s, the increasing ranges of both superpowers' nuclear delivery systems caused a shift: US bomber forces and US land-based missiles no longer needed ME basing and US missile-firing submarines could hit their targets from the Indian Ocean. Intelligence monitoring from space satellites also somewhat reduced American dependence on intelligence gathering facilities based in the Northern Tier states. US military-strategic interests in the ME were thus declining in the late 1960s.

Under Kennedy, less stress was placed on establishing a ME alliance system and more emphasis was given to pre-empting Soviet-supported insurgencies by encouraging economic aid and development. The US strove to attract the A. nationalists to the West by taking new diplomatic initiatives towards Nasserist Egypt and her allies, including the new republican régime in Yemen in power since Sept. 1962 and recognized by the US in Dec. During the Egyptian-Sa'udi struggle in the Yemen civil war, the US initially served in a mediatory capacity and avoided overidentification with the conservative Sa'udis supporting the Yemeni royalists. Egyptian air attacks against Sa'udi border towns, however, soon forced increased American pro-Sa'udi alignment. In July 1963, a US Air Force fighter squadron was deployed in Sa'udi Arabia for six months in order to signal America's commitment to the integrity of the Kingdom.

Alongside of its attempted dialogue with the "progressive" régimes of the A. world, the Kennedy Administration significantly deepened US ties to Israel. President Kennedy personally described the US-Israel connection as a "special relationship" and gave private assurances of coming to Israel's defense. He approved the sale of the first major American weapons-system (defensive) to Israel: the Hawk anti-aircraft missile. A Kennedy initiative to seek a resolution of the Palestinian refugee problem through the US-sponsored Joseph Johnson mission (1962) was abortive (see *Refugees).

US efforts to draw Nasserist Egypt closer to the American orbit ended during the Johnson Administration and US ties with the A. conservative régimes as well as with Israel improved. From 1965 to 1966 the cash value of US military sales to Sa'udi Arabia increased more than tenfold; US arms transfers to Lebanon, Libya, Morocco, and Tunisia increased as well. Offensive arms were sold to Israel for the first time (tanks in 1965 and Skyhawk fighter-bombers in 1966). Johnson's sympathetic attitude towards Israel became evident in the crisis of May 1967 and the *Six Day War that followed in June. As US attempts to defuse the crisis over the Straits of *Tiran by the formation of a multilateral naval force floundered, Washington gave Israel full support. Suspicion of US-Israel military collusion led seven ASt, including Egypt, Syria and Iraq, to sever diplomatic relations with the US. On 19 June, Johnson formulated a principle on the A.-Israel situation that guided US policy for successive administrations: Israeli withdrawal from the territories taken in the war was conditional on a peace settlement. The US so interpreted Security Council Resolution 242, which she co-sponsored, and was increasingly drawn into A.-Israel diplomacy.

The Nixon Administration entered office in 1969 determined to introduce a more "even-handed" American policy in the region. During 1969, with an Egypt-Israel "War of Attrition" escalating, with increasing Soviet involvement, Nixon agreed to discuss the A.-Israel conflict in two power talks with the USSR and four power talks with the USSR, Britain and France. These talks were abortive. In December, Secretary of State *Rogers publicly announced a plan discussed since Oct. through diplomatic channels. The "Rogers Plan" called for an Israeli return to the pre-1967 borders with only minor alterations in return for A.-Israel agreements that were short of full peace. It was rejected by Israel, but later efforts for more limited disengagement arrangements ("Rogers Plan II", 1970) were accepted. Nixon's policies changed when Soviet ties with Egypt and Syria deepened and Israel emerged as an American regional ally balancing Soviet proxies. Israel's new role was demonstrated in Sept. 1970 when the US and Israel made contingency plans to use Israeli forces to block a Syrian invasion of Jordan.

New strategic dilemmas were posed for US ME policy with Britain's announcement in 1968 of her plan to withdraw from the Persian Gulf, which she executed in 1971. With excessive military commitments elsewhere, particularly in Vietnam, the US fashioned a "Twin Pillar Policy" (1970) which, consistent with the global "Nixon Doctrine", placed the burden of Gulf security on two pro-Western regional powers — Iran and Sa'udi Arabia. In May 1972, Nixon and his National Security adviser Henry Kissinger agreed to let the Shah of Iran purchase the most advanced American military equipment. US arms transfers to Iran and to a lesser extent to Sa'udi Arabia increased dramatically. As their needs for increased revenues contributed to their demands for a larger share of oil profits, the US had to accept these demands in 1972.

The 1973 *October War raised US aid to Israel to unprecedented levels — and at the same time threw into sharp profile the need for active US diplomacy in the A.-Israel conflict. Threats of unilateral Soviet intervention at the war's end, and Nixon's decision to initiate a nuclear alert, underlined the dangers which the conflict posed. The A. declaration of an oil embargo (though not fully implemented) underlined the connection between Western access to A. oil and A. demands concerning the A.-Israel conflict. The US needed ME oil only to a limited degree (though the share of ME oil in her consumption had grown from c.3% in 1970 to over 7% in 1973); but she considered the regular supply of ME oil to her allies in Europe and Japan a vital US interest.

Through the "step-by-step" negotiating strategy of Secretary of State Kissinger, his pressure, and his tireless "shuttle diplomacy", separation of forces agreements were achieved in the Sinai and the *Golan in 1974. The US and Egypt renewed full diplomatic relations, severed since 1967, in Feb.; the US and Syria in June. A second Sinai agreement leading to a further Israeli withdrawal was achieved by Kissinger under the Ford Administration in Sept. 1975. American civilian technicians were stationed in three Sinai warning stations. An accompanying Memorandum provided for the supply of advanced weaponry, including F-16 aircraft to Israel and contained new political assurances, including a US commitment not to recognize the *Palestine Liberation Organization or negotiate with it as long as it did not recognize Israel's right to exist and refused to accept UN resolutions 242 and 338.

After 1973, Egypt increasingly shifted from the Soviet to the American orbit. By early 1975, the administration agreed to sell Cairo C-130 military transport aircraft, thereby beginning a new US arms sales relationship with Egypt. In June 1974, a wide-ranging agreement for Saʿudi-US military and economic cooperation re-established and deepened their "special relationship". The US thought, however, that "the Palestinian dimension of the A.-Israel conflict is the heart of the conflict". The Carter Administration inherited its predecessor's assumption that the A.-Israel conflict was the principal problem for the US in the region. However, the Carter-Vance-Brzezinski team replaced Kissinger's step by step strategy by a comprehensive approach. This shift led to US efforts to revive the Geneva Peace Conference, suspended since December 1973, to bring the Soviet Union into the peace process and to tackle the Palestinian problem (including talks with Palestinian representatives). In Mar. 1977, Carter called for the establishment of a "Palestinian homeland", though he later explained that he did not mean an independent Palestinian state. In Oct. 1977, in a joint communiqué with the USSR, the US recognized for the first time "the legitimate rights of the Palestinians". Through Saʿudi mediation, the Administration sought to bring about a change in the PLO position on Resolution 242 and thereby open up a direct US-PLO link. US-Israel relations deteriorated in this period; tensions also arose over new Israeli settlements beyond the pre-1967 borders.

As Egypt and Israel elected to pursue their own peace strategy after President Sadat's Nov. 1977 visit to Jerusalem, US policy was forced to adapt. US and Egyptian positions converged after Carter's Jan. 1978 visit to Aswan. The Carter team sought to bolster the ongoing peace process, and to secure Saʿudi moderation on the price of oil, by proposing in early 1978 to link unprecedented advanced fighter aircraft sales to Saʿudi Arabia (60 F-15), Egypt (50 F-5E) and Israel (75 F-16 and 15 F-15) in one package. In 1978, as the Egyptian-Israeli dialogue floundered, Carter invited President Sadat and Prime Minister Begin to the US presidential retreat at Camp David and, tying up his presidency from 5 to 17 Sept., served as a "full partner" in the negotiations that produced in the end two frameworks for peace — Egypt-Israel, and general A.-Israel — known as the *Camp David Agreements. As the Egyptians and Israelis disagreed in subsequent months over translation of the frameworks into a peace treaty, Carter again directly intervened and personally engaged in his own shuttle-diplomacy (Mar. 1979) which led, by the end of the month, to the signing of the Egyptian-Israeli Peace Treaty on the White House lawn.

The second area of ME activity of the Carter Administration was focused in an area running from Afghanistan through Iran to the Horn of Africa. In 1977, the Administration showed little concern for the growing Soviet intervention in the Horn of Africa and supported the de-militarization of the Indian Ocean. But the deterioration in the political position of the Shah of Iran in late 1978, leading to his fall in Jan. 1979, demonstrated that the West could no longer rely on an Iranian surrogate to protect its interests. The crisis over Iran — the seizure of the US Embassy in Tehran on 4 Nov. 1979 by an angry Iranian mob, its staff taken as hostages, and the failure of an attempted rescue mission in late Apr. 1980 — demonstrated the limits of American military strength in the region. The US was helpless to act on the scene against the Soviet invasion of Afghanistan in late December 1979. Concerned that the Soviets might move into Iran, the US moved to fill the vacuum. The "Carter Doctrine," issued on 23 Jan. 1980, declared that "any attempt by any outside force to gain control of the Persian Gulf region will be regarded as an assault on the vital interests of the USA and such an assault will be repelled by any means necessary, including military force." In March the US established a Rapid Deployment Joint Task Force (RDJTF) — a 100,000 man intervention force to back up the new presidential doctrine. Having lost its ME bases some fifteen years earlier, the US concluded agreements with ʿOman, Somalia and Kenya on lower profile facilities and with Egypt on increased use of Egyptian airfields.

The Reagan Administration emphasized even more the military-strategic factors in US ME policy. The Reagan team helped complete the Egyptian-Israeli half of the Camp David peace process. It oversaw Israel's last withdrawal from Sinai in Apr. 1982, and established the "Multinational Force and Observers" (MFO) to patrol the Sinai. Reagan was personally warmer and more positive towards Israel than any previous president. He described Israel as a strategic asset and was the first president to call Israel an "ally", despite the lack of any formal treaty of alliance. These views were generally shared by his Secretaries of State Alexander Haig and George Schultz, but reportedly not by his Secretary of Defense Caspar Weinberger. US policy on Israel zig-zagged in response to intra-cabinet feuds. Reagan's strategic policies sometimes conflicted with Israeli interests. Thus the Administration's drive in the fall of 1981 to sell Airborne Warning and Control System aircraft (AWACS) to Sa'udi Arabia — a decision inherited from Carter and opposed by Israel who also objected to advanced arms sales to Jordan. The Israeli attack on the Iraqi nuclear reactor earlier in June 1981, air attacks in Lebanon, and the decision to annex the Golan Heights (Dec. 1981) were seen as frustrating American attempts to reach a "strategic consensus" with the A. world that might include Israel herself. Thus an essentially friendly administration suspended American arms deliveries to Israel after the Baghdad attack. In Dec. 1981, after Israel's Golan law, talks on a US-Israel strategic cooperation agreement were suspended. The Lebanon War, from June 1982, brought about further Israeli-US differences, despite the understanding shown by Secretary Haig for Israel's need to take a limited military initiative. Haig's removal in the middle of the war seemed to further tip the scales against US-Israeli cooperation, as did unfriendly American television and press coverage. Israel's war against the PLO and the plight of the Palestinian refugees raised issues that had been dormant in recent years.

On 1 Sept. 1982 a Reagan speech launched the "Reagan Plan", arguing that "self-government by the Palestinians of the West Bank and Gaza in association with Jordan offers the best chance for a durable, just and lasting peace." With the unveiling of this plan, the US expected greater Jordanian involvement in the peace process. The US also hoped for greater Syrian readiness to withdraw forces from Lebanon once an Israeli withdrawal agreement had been negotiated in May 1983. Sa'udi influence was assumed to assure both Jordanian and Syrian cooperation. But as the US was drawn into the politics of Lebanon and disappointed with the responses of Jordan and Syria to her efforts, US policy reverted to greater coordination with Israel. By Nov. 1983 a US-Israel strategic cooperation agreement was worked out and put into effect. Further peace initiatives, the Administration recognized from 1983 onward, would have to come from the parties to the conflict themselves and not from Washington. Yet the US has remained deeply involved in efforts to advance such peace initiatives.

Reagan's administration was militarily involved in the ME more than previous ones, especially in his second term. In Lebanon, Reagan approved the deployment of the US Marines in a peacekeeping capacity. From 25 Aug. to 10 Sept. 1982, 800 Marines joined a Multinational Peacekeeping Force that oversaw the evacuation of the PLO from Beirut. By 29 Sept. 1200 Marines returned to Beirut — along with French and Italian forces — to assist the Lebanese government to take control of the city. In early 1983, the Marines found themselves confronting warring Lebanese "militias" and terrorists whose truck bombs and shells, in Apr., Aug. and Oct. caused heavy US casualties. US planes also clashed with Syrian positions. In retaliation, the US struck Syrian and militia positions, but "redeployed" her Marines from Beirut to the Sixth Fleet. Relations with Syria remained troubled because of Syria's involvement with terrorism.

The US confronted Libya as well. Growing tensions led the US to close the Libyan Embassy in Washington in May 1981. In Aug. US Navy F-14's shot down two Libyan SU-22 warplanes over the Gulf of *Sirte (Sidra), claimed by Libya as territorial waters. In his second term, Reagan increasingly blamed Libya for international terrorism, including the 27 Dec. 1985 bombing of the Rome and Vienna airports. In March 1986, US naval aircraft exercising over the Gulf of Sirte came under a Libyan missile attack, and US ships and planes destroyed two Libyan ships, damaged three others and raided an SA-5 missile-radar site on shore. After linking Libya to a terrorist bomb in West Berlin that left two persons dead, including a US soldier, thirteen F-111 US fighter-bombers flying out of Britain and naval carrier-launched fighters bombed military and intelligence targets in Libya, including Col. Qadhdhafi's command and communications center, on 14–15 Apr. 1986.

While the Reagan Administration identified Iran besides Syria and Libya as a sponsor of international terrorism, US policy became more complex because of the intense interest of both superpowers in the Persian Gulf. Reagan inherited the Carter Doctrine without reservation; he deepened American commitments to the Gulf region when he declared that he would not allow Sa'udi Arabia to fall the way of Iran. The RDJTF he inherited from his predecessor, was upgraded on 1 Jan. 1983 to the US Central Command (CENTCOM) and became the first US unified command for the ME in the post-war period. In the Iraq-Iran "Gulf War" itself, the US initially observed strict neutrality, though Iraq seemed eager to improve her relations with the US and resumed official ties (severed in 1967) in Nov. 1984. Late in 1983 the US began to deepen her slight tilt to Iraq as Iran threatened to close the Straits of *Hormuz and repeatedly attacked foreign ships, especially oil tankers serving the A. Gulf ports. US token naval forces in the Gulf escorted some US merchant ships and oil tankers to protect them against Iran's threats of attack and her practice of seizure and boarding. In 1987, the US extended such protection to Kuwaiti shipping, and US-Iran tension escalated. But while the Departments of State and Defense continued to support a firm stance against Iran in the Gulf, the National Security Council initiated new contacts with Iran in 1985 and supported limited arms sales to Tehran. US interest in re-establishing relations with Iran became mixed with the wish to secure the release of American hostages held by pro-Iranian militants in Lebanon, and the arms-for-hostages arrangements became entwined with illegal attempts to conduit American funds to anti-Nicaraguan rebel ("Contra") forces in Central America. As information about these schemes became public from November 1986, it turned into a major affair in the US — "Irangate" — in which Israeli intelligence and arms dealers were also involved (and which is outside our scope). In any case, Iran troubled the Reagan Administration as much as its predecessor — with additional emphasis on Iran's involvement in the Gulf, and in terrorism in Lebanon and elsewhere.

To sum up, while US tactical policies in the ME change with changing circumstances, US basic interests and strategy have remained relatively steady, focusing on access to petroleum resources, free shipping and communications, containing Soviet expansion and influence, bringing the A.-Israel conflict to an end, and developing normal relations with both Israel and the ASt (with a preference for the moderate-conservative ones, and difficulties concerning the radical ASt).

UNRWA United Nations Relief and Works Agency for Palestine Refugees in the Near East, established by the UN General Assembly in Dec. 1949 to aid and rehabilitate the A. refugees from Palestine. The Agency provided aid — mainly in housing (in camps), health and education, by a wide spread network of its own schools and grants for studying in other institutions. Efforts towards rehabilitation and resettlement were hampered for political reasons, mainly objections in principle raised by the ASt to resettlement projects and their insistence on repatriation. UNRWA's budget — at first $8–15m., rising to over $30m. p.a. in the 1960s, passing the $100m. mark in the 1970s, and reaching $200m. p.a. in the 1980s — was raised by contributions from UN member-states (mainly the USA); it was usually beset by substantial deficits and had to be reduced in the mid-1980s. UNRWA employs a large staff (teachers, administrators etc.) — about 17,000 in the mid-1980s — most of them Palestinian A.'s, with the top echelons manned by foreigners. See *Refugees.

UNSCOP United Nations Special Committee in Palestine, set up by the UN General Assembly in May 1947 to study the Palestine problem and recommend a solution. UNSCOP's report, on 31 Aug. 1947, recommended the partition of Palestine into a Jewish state and an A. state, in economic union, with *Jerusalem as an international enclave under a UN trusteeship; this was the verdict of the majority — representatives of Canada, Czechoslovakia, Guatemala, Netherlands, Peru, Sweden and Uruguay, while the Australian member abstained, and a dissenting minority (representatives of India, Iran and Yugoslavia) recommended a united independent Palestine with a federal structure. UNSCOP's majority recommendation was adopted by the General Assembly on 29 Nov. 1947.

UNTSO United Nations Truce Supervision Organization, a group of military observers (mainly US, French, Belgian and Scandinavian officers) sent to Palestine/Israel in 1948 to supervise the truce and cease-fire. After the A.-Israel Armistice Agreements of 1949, UNTSO officers supervised the implementation of the armistice and reported on cases of violation; they chaired the Mixed Armistice Commissions (MAC), and as usually Israeli and A. complaints stood against each other, the observers had the decisive vote.

When the MAC became inoperative after the *Six Day War of 1967, UNTSO officers became observers of the new cease-fires and continued in that capacity after the *October War of 1973. In the 1970s they were attached, as observers, to the various UN forces created — *UNEF, *UNDSOF, and *UNIFIL — and lost most of their independent status; but the UNTSO Chief-of-Staff continued serving, in a limited way, as coordinator of all UN peace-keeping operations in the Middle East. See *Arab-Israel Conflict.

Wafd (Arabic: Delegation) Egypt's principal nationalist party from the 1920s to 1952–53. It evolved from a delegation sent in 1919 by nationalist leaders to the British to negotiate Egypt's independence. The delegation was led by Ahmad Sa'd *Zaghlul, as was the party until Zaghlul's death in 1927, when Mustafa al-*Nahhas became its leader. The W., with nationalism and the completion of Egypt's independence as its main plank, was modernistic and Liberal-democratic in internal matters and for many years fought the King and his Court because of their attempts to reduce Parliament's power. While the W. was a school and transition stage for most Egyptian politicians, many left it in the early 1920s to found rival, mostly more conservative parties. The W. won the elections of 1924, 1925 (a partial win), 1926, 1929, 1936, 1942 and 1950 — usually when a *Wafd*ist or neutral government held the elections. But it was in power only for short periods in 1924, 1928 and 1930 — with the King and his Court finding ways to dissolve Parliament or end the W.'s rule by other means — and later in 1936–37, 1942–44 and 1950 to Jan. 1952. It split in 1937 when it expelled a group of younger leaders headed by M.F. *Nuqrashi and Ahmad *Maher who founded the *Saadist Party, and in 1942 when it expelled the Coptic W. leader Makram 'Ubaid ('Obeid) who founded an "Independent *Wafd*ist Bloc". In the 1940s, a reformist, moderately leftist faction grew inside the W. The party also set up para-military formations (the "Blue Shirts"), but they had little impact.

Initially considered extremist and anti-British, the W. came to be regarded by the British as the group most representative of Egyptian nationalism, the one with which an agreement should, and could, be reached. Indeed, the Anglo-Egyptian Treaty of 1936 was concluded while Egypt was led by the W. In Feb. 1942 the British compelled King *Farouq to dismiss his government and appoint Nahhas Prime Minister, hoping a W. government would cooperate with the British war effort more willingly than the King's men. Farouq dismissed Nahhas in Oct. 1944, after the British toned down their interference in Egyptian politics. Eventually, it was a W. government which in 1951 precipitated a severe crisis in Anglo-Egyptian relations; it had to resign in Jan. 1952.

In 1952 the new officers' régime compelled the W. to "purge" its leadership. But in 1953 it was banned altogether, along with all other political parties. When President *Sadat reintroduced a multi-party system in 1976–77, some 24–28 members of the National Assembly joined the W. The application of the "New W." to be licensed as a party was at first rejected, because the new party law banned the reactivation of pre-1952 leaders and parties. In 1978 the license was granted; but it was hedged in by so many restrictions, including the disqualification of the party's main leader, Fu'ad Sirag-ul-Din, as a pre-1952 man, that the W. redissolved itself the same year. However, in 1983 the Administrative Court allowed its re-constitution and lifted the disqualification of Sirag-ul-Din. In the elections of May 1984, the New W. won 57–58 seats in the 448-seat National Assembly, becoming the only opposition group represented in the Assembly as a recognized faction. Its deputies included eight of the *Muslim Brotherhood, itself not licensed to present candidates; this election alliance between the New W. and the Brotherhood was terminated towards the elections of 1987. In Mar. 1987, the W. began publishing a daily paper — the first opposition daily licensed since 1952.

In the Apr. 1987 elections, the W. won 36 seats, losing its position as the principal opposition group and the only one represented in the Assembly.

Wahhabis, Wahhabiyya Puritan, ultra-conservative movement founded in the 1740s in the Arabian Peninsula by Muhammad ibn 'Abd-ul-Wahhab from 'Uweina in *Najd. His teaching was adopted and spread from about 1745 by Muhammad Ibn Sa'ud of the 'Anaiza tribe who ruled the Dar'iyya region. The W., Sunni Muslims of the Hanbali school, greatly influenced by the teachings of Ibn Taimiyya (d. 1328), claimed that Islam had been distorted by innovations, and strove to restore it to the purity of the Qur'an and the early *Sunna*. They rejected most later interpretations of Islamic theology and mysticism *(Sufiyya)*, objected in particular to the popular veneration of saints and tombs, forbade the decoration of mosques, and banned all luxuries, including coffee and tobacco. They regarded all Muslims who did not accept their teachings as heretics.

After the Sa'udis had spread the W. in Najd, they began raiding other regions in the peninsula (Hijaz, Yemen) and across its northern borders. Their zealous rejection of the cult of tombs drove them, in the course of these raids, to destroy the mosque of the tomb of Hussein ibn 'Ali in Karbala in southern Iraq in 1802–03, and the Ka'ba in Mecca and the mosque of the tomb of the Prophet Muhammad in Medina in 1803–04. They also harassed the *Hajj* pilgrims' caravans. In consequence the Ottoman Sultan took action against them, mainly through Muhammad 'Ali, the Governor of Egypt, and his troops. For the changing fortunes, and decline, of the Sa'udi W. in the 19th century and their resurgence from 1902 see House of *Sa'ud, *Ibn Sa'ud, *Sa'udi Arabia.

After Ibn Sa'ud consolidated his conquests by the incorporation of *Hijaz in 1924–25, the W. doctrine of Islam was imposed as the state religion in his realm, called Sa'udi Arabia from 1932. Ibn Sa'ud also tried to settle an order of W. "Brethren" *(Ikhwan)* in fortified villages, but these efforts were abandoned after a rebellion by the *Ikhwan* had to be suppressed in 1929–30. Moreover, W. practices and interdicts were gradually mitigated, some of them were eroded by modernization and technological developments (e.g. the strict W.'s objection to movies and television), and some of them went out of use. Also, far removed from the original W.'s destruction of holy tombs and their mosques, the Sa'udi Kings now see themselves as the guardians of the Holy Places in Mecca and Medina and the protectors and organizers of the *Hajj*.

Outside Sa'udi Arabia, there are some W. in the Persian Gulf sheikhdoms, particularly in *Qatar, where they are the majority of the indigenous population. W. teachings had some influence on other fundamentalist trends or sects such as the *Mahdiyya and the *Sanussiya, and on reformist-revivalist Islamic thinkers such as Muhammad *'Abduh and Rashid *Rida.

Wailing Wall, or **Western Wall** See *Holy Places, *Arab-Israel Conflict.

Waqf (Pl.: *Awqaf*; in North Africa also called *Habous*.) Muslim religious endowment. Property dedicated as W. is given for all time and not subject to any transaction, inheritance or sale. Its income is used for the purpose indicated in the W. deed, which may be the welfare of the dedicator's family (*W. dhurri* or *ahli*), or support for public worship, education, social relief (*W. kheiri*). Each W. is administered by a custodian *(mutawalli, nazir)* named by the dedicator, and Muslim Law *(*Shari'a)* courts have exclusive jurisdiction over W. matters.

Since the W. withdraws much property from the market, and its conditions cannot be changed even if changing circumstances would make changes desirable, many reformers and modern A. nationalists have regarded it as a backward institution in need of reform or even abolition. But the religious Islamic establishment opposed far-reaching reforms and the conservative A. régimes prior to the military *coups* confined their reforms, if any, to marginal and minor matters and applied them only to future dedications, not to existing *awqaf*; thus, e.g., Egypt in 1946 and Lebanon in 1947. The military régimes took more radical steps. Syria abolished the family W. in 1949 and prohibited the founding of new *awqaf* altogether. Egypt also abolished the family W. in 1952, nationalized the administration of *awqaf kheiriyya* (with certain exceptions) in 1953 and authorized the Ministry of W. to use the income of W. properties for purposes other than those indicated in the W. deed. In 1957 Egypt wholly nationalized W. properties, to be distributed within the framework of the agrarian reform, with proceeds of sales earmarked for development projects. Tunisia also nationalized all W. properties in 1961. In Iraq, reforms in the W. system have not been similarly far-reaching. In British-Mandatory Palestine, the government did not wish to interfere in Muslim affairs by radical reforms and handed the administration of all W. matters to the Supreme Muslim Council, which instituted no reforms.

Israel was faced by the special problem that many beneficiaries or administrators of *awqaf* had become absentees in 1948, and as the properties were administered by a custodian, changes had to be introduced. In 1965, family *awqaf* were transferred to the beneficiaries' full ownership, and W. *kheiri* properties — to Muslim boards of trustees. See *Shari'a.

West Bank The part of Palestine occupied by Jordan during the A.-Israel War of 1948 and formally annexed in Apr. 1950 was called by Jordan "the WB" (former *Transjordan, East of the *Jordan River, forming the "East Bank"), and the appellation has become widely used. The WB had an area of c. 2,200 sq. mi. (5,700 sq. km.). In 1948 the population was about 400,000 plus c. 200,000 refugees from the Israel-held areas. Jordanian statistics put it at over 800,000 in the 1960s. In the *Six Day War of 1967 the WB was occupied by Israel. The population at that time — after considerable migration to the East Bank during the 19 years of Jordanian rule, and a wave of refugees during the Six Day War (see *Palestine Arabs) — was about 600,000 (without East *Jerusalem, which was incorporated in Israel). In the mid-1980s it is estimated at c. 900,000.

Under Jordanian rule the inhabitants of the WB were about one — half of the total population of Jordan. The WB provided 35–40% of Jordan's GDP and her government revenue, nearly one-half of her industrial and 60–80% of her agricultural production. It was represented in both houses of Parliament by one-half of the members, and many of its inhabitants occupied senior positions in Jordan's administration and public life. Politically active, volatile and more sophisticated than the East Bankers, the A.'s of the WB were an element of unrest and ferment in Jordan and a growing ground for much opposition, but throughout the years of Jordanian rule there was no movement for secession and the creation of an independent Palestinian-A. state separate from Jordan.

For the WB under Israeli occupation since 1967 see *Israel Occupied Territories. Jordan continues claiming the WB as part of her territory, but since 1972 King *Hussein has proposed a federal structure for a future reunited Jordan and in 1985 he agreed with the *PLO's *'Arafat on the creation of a Palestinian-A. entity in the WB in confederation with Jordan. Jordan maintains close links with the WB, made possible by Israel's policy of "Open Bridges", pays salaries or stipends to former Jordanian officials and finances certain economic and welfare activities (in part — with aid funds provided by AC and administered by a joint Jordan-PLO committee). In 1986 Jordan announced a five-year economic and social development plan for the WB, tentatively set at $1,300m. — if foreign finance (and Israeli approval) can be obtained. The WB continues to be represented in Jordan's Parliament; but the one-half ratio is no longer maintained, and WB representatives are no longer elected by the inhabitants of the WB but are nominated by the Jordanian Parliament, some of them — East Bank residents.

women in the Arab countries W. in the ME have had since antiquity an inferior legal status and have not enjoyed equality of rights. Historically, Islam improved their status and increased and defined their rights. But over the centuries, Islam and Muslim Law (the *Shari'a) have turned, like most other established religions, into a restrictive factor, particularly if compared with the contemporary West. In recent decades, significant reforms have much improved the status of W., but wide inequalities still remain, most of them determined by the Shari'a.

Polygamy is by now restricted in many AC, but fully outlawed only in Tunisia and among the A.'s of Israel. Divorce is still easy for the husband. W.'s right to own property and inherit are limited, as is, in case of divorce, a woman's right to her own children. Bridal money is paid to the bride's father, the bride acquiring no right to it — amounting to a virtual purchase of brides. A woman owes obedience to her husband and in parts of A. society is confined to the inner chambers of the house, and her freedom of dress and comportment is restricted (e.g. by the veiling of her face in parts of society — frequently self-imposed and accepted, and again on the increase in recent years under the influence of Islamic radicals). Sexual mores are very different for men and W., with a severe punitive attitude to W. accused of pre-marital or extra-marital sexual relations (up to the accepted killing of a woman by her father or brother, to "purge the honor of the family") — as against a much more permissive attitude where men are concerned. The education of girls has made considerable progress, but is still not fully equal to that of boys in most AC. As to political rights — see below.

A movement for improving the condition of W. began emerging in the Ottoman Empire, including its A. areas, late in the 19th century. At first it was concerned principally with education — and in that field it gradually succeeded. Wherever compulsory primary education is the law — and that means, by now, nearly all AC — it applies to both sexes; and while girls do not yet constitute 50% of the primary school population, their number approaches that proportion in most AC. Since the 1920s, institutions of higher learning have opened their doors to W., including even the Islamic al-*Azhar since 1954.

Gradually, the movement began to concern itself also with the social situation of W. The first and main targets of reform were polygamy and the easiness of divorce for men. Even conservative Islamic revivalists, such as Muhammad *'Abduh, joined the struggle against polygamy. The best known among the fighters for W.'s rights was the Egyptian Qassem Amin (1865–1908), who wrote several books on the subject. In the 1920s W. themselves began to take the initiative and leadership in the fight for equal rights and to found W.'s organizations, particularly in Egypt (Huda Sha'rawi, 1880–1947; Doria Shafiq, 1910–75).

Most ASt slowly responded by cautious reforms and amendments of the laws (Muslim Turkey had preceded them). Some ultra-conservative AC like Sa'udi Arabia and the Gulf sheikhdoms have not introduced significant formal changes, though even in them the *de facto* situation of W. has begun to change. In most modernist ASt the need for change was recognized, though the Islamic establishment frequently opposed, and sometimes prevented, far-reaching reforms. Only Tunisia outlawed polygamy altogether, in 1956–58 (and Israel's ban on polygamy applied to her Muslim-A. citizens). But several AC restricted it by making each case subject to a *Qadi*'s approval that may be refused, and by giving the first wife certain rights to object or to obtain a divorce — thus, e.g., in Syrian legislation of 1953, in several amendments in Egypt's laws, in Tunisia and in Algeria. The laws of divorce were also amended, restricting the husband's right to impose it, granting the wife limited rights to demand it, and enhancing the woman's status and rights in case of divorce. W.'s rights to own property and inherit were also extended in several AC. In most AC laws were also passed fixing a minimum age for marriage. (For these reforms see also *Shari'a.)

The most progress has been made in the field of civic and political rights, especially since the 1950s. Syria granted W. the vote in 1949 — at first restricted to W. with at least primary education, but this restriction, not applied to men, was lifted in 1953. Lebanon enfranchised her W. in 1953, Egypt in 1956 (in the election law of that year, later in the provisional constitution of 1964), Iraq in 1958 and 1967 (also at first limited to W. with at least primary education). Tunisia and Morocco followed soon after attaining independence, in 1959 and 1959–62, Libya in 1963, Sudan in 1965, Yemen in 1970. Jordan needed a longer time; amendments granting the vote to W. were rejected several times, and the King's instruction to speed up progress, in 1962, was not acted upon until more vigorously repeated in 1973; the vote was granted in 1974. In Kuwait, the all-male National Assembly has persisted so far in rejecting all proposals in favor of W.'s voting rights. Sa'udi Arabia and the Gulf sheikhdoms have no W.'s vote — but most of them have in any case no elected institutions. With these exceptions, W. by now have the right to vote in all AC. The fact that in many cases the vote does not mean a free choice among competing candidates and trends, but only the endorsement of a single candidate, and even that right is not always fully implemented (the W. of Iraq, for instance, with their voting right since 1958, had the first opportunity to vote in 1980), does not detract from the achievement.

W.'s right to be elected was in several AC delayed a little longer. It was opposed by the

Islamic establishment even more strongly than the voting right; a religious ruling *(Fatwa)* by the savants of al-Azhar, for instance, held that W. should never be appointed to positions enabling them to give orders, legislate or direct men. But this right, too, was achieved with, or soon after, the voting right. The first W. took their seats as members of National Assemblies in Egypt in 1957 and Lebanon 1963, and the first W. were named as Ministers in Iraq in 1959, Egypt 1962. While the number of W. among members of parliamentary institutions and as Cabinet Ministers has remained small, such membership has by now become usual and accepted in most AC.

The increasing influence of Islamic fundamentalism in recent years will no doubt affect the status of W. In some AC W.'s manner of clothing and comportment and their status and activities in various fields of social life have begun changing and seem to revert in some measure to traditional Islamic patterns. It is too soon to judge whether and how far W.'s political rights will also be affected.

World War I As the Ottoman Empire joined the war, in alliance with Germany and Austria-Hungary, in Oct. 1914, its A.-inhabited parts soon became a battle arena. Egypt, proclaimed a British Protectorate in 1914, served as a major base and staging ground for *Entente* forces, mainly British. In Dec. 1914 Turkish forces occupied the Sinai Peninsula and early in 1915 they attacked the Suez Canal. British forces invaded Mesopotamia (Iraq) in 1914, from the Persian Gulf, and occupied its southern parts, but their advance farther north was blocked by the Turks and they suffered several defeats, including the surrender of a large British force at Kut al-Amara in Apr. 1916. (Events in non-A. areas of the ME, such as the Dardanelles, are outside our scope.)

In June 1916, an *Arab Revolt against the Turks — pre-arranged by the British with the Sharif of Mecca, *Hussein ibn 'Ali — broke out in *Hijaz, harassing Turkish communications and pinning down Turkish forces. A number of A. officers deserted the Ottoman army, or were recruited in prisoners' camps, the join the Sharif's army, but the A. population in the Fertile Crescent remained loyal to the Sultan. British-supported *Sanussi guerrillas also harassed the Turks in Cyrenaica.

British and other *Entente* forces began advancing through Sinai into Palestine late in 1916, but were halted in the Gaza area. In 1917 the Turks began retreating. The British took Baghdad in Mar. 1917 and continued advancing northwards. They also resumed their offensive in southern Palestine, under General Allenby, and took Jerusalem on 9 Dec. 1917. Troops of the A. Revolt reached *'Aqaba in July 1917 and became Allenby's right wing, advancing northwards east of the Jordan River. A final British offensive in Sept. 1918 (the battle of Megiddo) broke Turkish resistance. Damascus was taken on 1 Oct., Beirut on 7 Oct., Aleppo on 26 Oct., and on 30 Oct. 1918 the war ended with the Armistice of Mudros. Peace was concluded in the Treaty of *Sèvres, 1920, and, after its abrogation, the Treaty of *Lausanne, July 1923.

During the war, the Allies made secret agreements on the future disposition of the territories to be taken from Turkey after her defeat (see *Sykes-Picot Agreement). These were, greatly changed by political circumstances, partially incorporated in the post-war settlement.

World War II AC were a major battle zone in WW II only in North Africa west of Egypt (and if Somali is seen as an AC, in the Somali-Eritrea area). After Italy joined Germany in the war (June 1940), her forces under Marshal Graziani mounted an offensive from Libya in Sept. 1940, invading Egypt and reaching the Sidi Barrani area. A British counter-offensive under General Wavell, from Dec. 1940, took most of Cyrenaica in Jan.-Feb. 1941 (Tobruk 21 Jan., Benghazi 7 Feb.). In Feb. 1941 the Germans reinforced their Italian ally by the "Africa Corps" under Gen. Rommel, which reconquered all of Cyrenaica in Apr. 1941 (cutting off and besieging Tobruk) and halted at the Egyptian border. A new British offensive under Generals Cunningham and Ritchie again took Cyrenaica in Dec. 1941–Jan. 1942. A third German-Italian offensive reoccupied most of Cyrenaica in Jan. 1942; resumed in May 1942, it penetrated into Egypt and was halted in July at al-'Alamein. Britain's third and final counter-offensive, under Gen. Montgomery, began in Oct. 1942 and was one of the turning points of the war. By Nov. Cyrenaica was recaptured.

On 7–8 Nov. 1942 US and British forces landed at several points in Morocco and Algeria and after brief resistance by Vichy-French troops consolidated their positions in both countries, capturing Oran on 10 Nov. and Casablanca on 11 Nov. German forces occupied Tunisia, still held by Vichy-France, and stiffly resisted the allied forces. But German-Italian forces now faced giant pincers on two fronts — the British in Cyrenaica, and US and British forces in Algeria — and had to give up Libya-Tripolitania. Tripoli was taken on 23 Jan. 1943, and all of Libya up to the Tunisian border was in allied hands the same month. German resistance in Tunisia collapsed in May 1943; Tunis and Bizerta fell on 7 May, and the German forces capitulated on 13 May.

Egypt, committed by the Anglo-Egyptian Treaty of 1936 to aiding Britain in the event of war, by putting her territory and communications at Britain's disposal, broke off diplomatic relations with Germany in Sept. 1939 and those with Italy in June 1940, but did not declare war even when her own territory was invaded. The Egyptian government of 1939–40, and large segments of public opinion, were openly pro-Axis, as was the Chief-of-Staff 'Aziz al-*Masri (who tried in 1940 to defect to the Italian lines and was captured). British pressure forced the government's replacement, but Egypt's cooperation with the war effort remained unsatisfactory. In Feb. 1942 British intervention and a threat of force compelled King *Farouq to dismiss the government and appoint the leader of the *Wafd to form a new one. When an Allied victory had become certain, Egypt committed herself to the Allies, by signing the Atlantic Charter in Nov. 1943. In Feb. 1945 she declared war on Germany and Japan (the Premier responsible was assassinated the same day).

On the East African front, the Italians occupied British Somaliland in Aug. 1940. But in Jan.-Feb. 1941, British forces took both British and Italian Somalia, as well as Eritrea (and proceeded to expel the Italians from Ethiopia, liquidating Italy's East-African empire).

Syria and Lebanon were governed by Vichy-France and increasingly at the disposal of German-Italian preparations for an invasion of the ME and secret and intelligence operations. They were conquered by British and Free French forces in June 1941 in a brief operation. Iraq caused more trouble. Anti-British sentiment and German influence had been mounting in the years preceding the war. They reached their peak in Apr. 1941 when the right-wing pro-German Rashid 'Ali al-*Kilani was put in power, in a semi-*coup*, by the four colonels who were the *de facto* rulers of Iraq, and the pro-British leaders fled. Rashid 'Ali refused to grant Britain the full use of Iraq's facilities and territory, as provided for in the Treaty of 1930. The resulting dispute escalated on 2 May into military clashes around the British base of Habbaniyya. Fighting continued throughout May, and though Rashid 'Ali asked for German help, and got some (mainly aircraft), he was defeated and escaped to Italy and Germany. The pro-British régime returned and there was no further trouble in Iraq. In Jan. 1943 Iraq declared war on the Axis powers. During the hostilities of May 1941, Amir *'Abdullah of Transjordan sent a detachment of his army, the *Arab Legion, to support the British forces.

Sa'udi Arabia remained neutral and did not even formally sever relations with Italy and Germany (though she closed the Italian Legation in 1942). Only in Mar. 1945 did *Ibn Sa'ud proclaim Sa'udia's "adhesion" to the Allies, making it clear that because of the sanctity of the Islamic holy places under his guardianship this should not be regarded as a full declaration of war. Yemen, too, remained neutral.

Volunteers for the Allied forces were recruited in the ME in one country only, Palestine. About 9,000 Palestinian A.'s and 26,000 Palestine Jews joined British formations; the Jews were permitted in 1944, after a protracted political struggle, to form a Jewish Brigade within the British forces. A large segment of A. public opinion in Palestine, as in Egypt, Syria-Lebanon and Iraq, was pro-German and anti-British, and a considerable number of A. leaders and activists reached Germany on the eve or during the war and served the German war effort as propagandists, broadcasters, recruiters and organizers of volunteer formations among A.'s in Europe and Muslim populations in German-occupied territories (e.g. Bosnia in Yugoslavia). The most prominent among those were the Iraqi Rashid 'Ali al-Kilani and the Mufti of Jerusalem, Hajj Amin al-*Husseini; for additional names see *Fascism.

Y

Yahya Hamid-ul-Din (1869–1948) Imam of Yemen. Scion of a noble family of the Shi'i-*Zeidi sect, Y. was elected *Imam* — religious head of the sect, and ruler of Yemen — in 1904. He continued a rebellion against the Ottoman sovereign that had been simmering for years, and in 1911 obtained an agreement granting him wide autonomy under nominal Ottoman sovereignty. During World War I he remained loyal to the Empire, but with its dismemberment he gained complete independence for Yemen in 1918 without a struggle. In 1925 he expanded Yemen's territory by re-conquering the port of Hodeida that had been occupied in 1921 by the rulers of neighboring *'Asir with British connivance. A dispute over 'Asir itself led to war between Yemen and Sa'udi Arabia in 1934, ending in defeat for the Imam and the loss of the disputed territory. Y.'s rule was ultra-conservative and authoritarian. He prevented economic and social modernization and the creation of a modern administrative and a representative régime other than the traditional Council of Notables. He even hesitated to maintain regular economic and diplomatic ties with other nations and tried to keep Yemen isolated and closed to foreign influence. His harsh administration drove many antagonists of the régime into exile and caused sporadic plots and rebellions inside Yemen. Y. was assassinated during a revolt in 1948; but the revolt failed to topple the régime, and his son *Ahmad ibn Yahya succeeded him as Imam.

Yarmuk River A tributary of the Jordan River, joining it from the northeast, south of the Lake of Galilee, the Y. rises in southern Syria and forms for part of its c. 50 mi. (80 km.) length the boundary between Syria and the Kingdom of Jordan (with the last few miles of that border on the Syrian side, the *Golan, occupied by Israel since 1967). For the last 10–12 miles of its course, the Y. is the border between Jordan on its left, southern shore, and Israel on its right, northern one. The Y. carries an average annual water flow of c. 475m. cubic meters (mcm), with some higher estimates going up to 500–520 mcm.

The Y. forms part of the Jordan River Development Scheme. According to the *Johnston Plan, 1953–55, parts of its waters (tentatively, some 90 mcm) were to be used by Syria, with the rest, 380–430 mcm to be diverted by Jordan to irrigate the eastern side of the Jordan valley, the *Ghor*, and 25–40 mcm to be left, downstream, for Israel's traditional use. The Johnston Plan remained abortive: though it was agreed between Israel and the A.'s on the technical expert level, the ASt refused to give it their political endorsement. Jordan, however, went ahead, with Israel's agreement or acquiescence, with her scheme. Plans for the erection of a large dam on the Y. and the creation of a storage lake have not yet been implemented, but most of the waters of the Y. are diverted into the East Ghor Canal from which a network of smaller canals irrigates the Jordan Valley. See *Jordan River.

Yazidis A small community in northern Iraq, in the Jabal Sinjar and Sheikhan region north of Mosul. The Y., an estimated 20–40,000, are probably of *Kurdish extraction, but opinions on their origin differ. They speak a Kurdish dialect, but use Arabic in their religious rites. Their religion includes Muslim, Christian, Zoroastrian and pagan elements; it sees Satan, symbolized by the peacock, as a strong force contending with God and to be appeased by man. The Y. are sometimes called Devil-Worshippers.

Yemen Arab Republic, in SW Arabia. The area of Y. is variously estimated at 69–77,000 sq. mi. (180–200,000 sq. km.). She is bordered by *Sa'udi Arabia in the north and northeast, *South Yemen (the "Democratic People's Republic of Yemen") in the southeast and south, and the *Red Sea in the west. Y. consists largely of high plateaux broken in the north by deep, fertile valleys. The narrow coastal strip is called the *Tihama*. The large majority of the population earn their living from agriculture; industry and business are still in their infancy. In the 1960s and 1970s several modern roads between the major cities were constructed with foreign aid — the USA, the USSR and China each promoting and financing "their" road project. In the 1980s oil was struck in east Y. by a US company, and commercial production was expected for 1988.

The population of Y., estimated at 6–7.5m.

(including 1.5–2m. working abroad, mainly in Sa'udi Arabia), is A., except for a few descendants of Hamitic and Negroid peoples from eastern Africa in the *Tihama*. About 55% belong to the *Zeidi sect of *Shi'i Islam while the rest are *Sunni Muslims of the *Shafe'i school, and a few Shi'i *Isma'ilis (but statistics are not reliable and estimates differ). About 10% of the population live in towns. Most of the rural population belongs to about 75 tribes nominally affiliated to tribal confederations of which the most important are those of Hashed and Bakil.

Most of the tribes claim descent from Qahtan, the legendary father of the ancient tribes of South Arabia; the rest are related to the north Arabian 'Adnani tribes which migrated to Y. following the rise of Islam. The Yemeni tribe under its sheikh is an almost independent political unit with its own armed force and judicial system. As approximately 80% of the tribes, including the stongest ones, are Zeidis, the Zeidi *Imam* — who is nominally elected by the Zeidi *Sada* (plural of *Sayyid*: descendants of the *Khalifa* 'Ali and his son Hussein) — was able to establish a Zeidi hegemony over the non-militant Shafe'is.

POLITICAL HISTORY. The Ottoman Empire claimed sovereignty over Y. and officially considered her an Ottoman province. In fact the Empire controlled and garrisoned only the coast. In the interior, there was, since the 1890s, a continuous rebellion, intensified after 1904 under a new Imam, *Yahya Hamid-ul-Din. In 1911 the Turks had to conclude with the Imam an agreement granting to the interior *de facto* autonomy under nominal Ottoman sovereignty. During World War I, Y. remained loyal to the Ottoman *Khalifa* (Caliph) and the Imam refrained from hindering Turkish operations from Y. against the British in 'Aden. The dismemberment of the Ottoman Empire after the war automatically gave Y. complete independence.

The Imams Yahya Hamid-ul-Din (1904–48) and *Ahmad b. Yahya (1948–62) endeavored to keep Y. isolated from the modern world. Foreigners were forbidden to enter the country and no modernization or economic development was allowed. Relations with neighboring Sa'udi Arabia were hostile and resulted in war, 1934, over *'Asir; the Imam's tribal army was defeated. In the south, border disputes led to a permanent conflict with the British in 'Aden, which continued, despite a 1934 Anglo-Yemeni Treaty of San'a, up to the British evacuation of South Arabia in 1968. (The first British diplomatic representative was sent to San'a in 1951.) The Anglo-Y. conflict enabled Fascist Italy to become the main foreign power to have real contact with Y., with treaties signed in 1926 and 1927. Britain was disturbed both by Italian penetration — especially after Italy's conquest of Ethiopia, 1936 — and by the official relations Y. established with the USSR, 1928. However the Soviet mission was withdrawn in 1938, and Italy lost her special interest in the Red Sea following the loss of Ethiopia, 1941, in *World War II (in which Y. remained neutral). In the 1950s Y. attempted to introduce some degree of modernization by improving relations with the USSR and the People's Republic of China and accepting their aid. In 1958 Y., under Imam Ahmad, formally joined the *UAR, the Union of Egypt and Syria, in a federation that was never implemented.

The Imams established a centralist régime in San'a, paying subsidies to strong tribes and subduing rebellious ones by military expeditions in the 1920s and 1930s. They built a tribal army mobilized in rotation for short periods, encamped near San'a and used mainly to pacify Zeidi tribes and enforce taxation in Shafe'i areas. They used the detribalized Zeidi élite of nobles and religious dignitaries — the *Sada* — as the administrative backbone of their régime.

This political structure, built almost exclusively on the strictly controlled Zeidi tribes, began to fall apart in the 1940s and 1950s. Tribal unrest increased, erupting into several tribal rebellions, and finally two *coup* attempts were staged in 1948 and 1955. During the former, Imam Yahya was assassinated, but his son Ahmad subdued the rebels and assumed the Imamate. In the second *coup* Imam Ahmad was forced to leave San'a, but he was saved by his eldest son Muhammad al-*Badr, who mobilized the northern Bakil tribes. Two of the Royal princes, 'Abdullah and 'Abbas, were involved in the 1955 *coup* and executed. These attempted *coups*, launched mainly by disappointed royal princes, would-be reformers among the *Sada* and young officers, hastened the establishment of a new central, non-tribal army. Young officers were sent abroad for their military education, mainly to Baghdad (among them 'Abdullah *Sallal, Hamud al-Ja'ifi, Hassan al-*'Amri). The urban élite, encouraged by Shafe'i unrest, began to demonstrate its interest in modernization; some of its members went into exile and began a propaganda campaign against the Imam's régime; prominent among them were the Zeidi notables Mahmud al-Zubeiri and Qadi 'Abd-ul-Rahman al-*Iryani and the Shafe'i Ahmad Muhammad Nu'man. The last three years of Imam Ahmad's reign were marked by intensive unrest. Seven days after Ahmad's death, on 26 Sept. 1962, the new Imam Muhammad al-Badr was overthrown by a military coup. He escaped to the northern mountains and mobilized resistance, and Y. was embroiled in a civil war.

The young officers who overthrew al-Badr proclaimed a "People's Republic". Motivated by Nasserist aspirations, they called for a total change in Y.'s economic, social and religious structure and asked Egypt for help. A few days after the *coup*, an Egyptian expeditionary force landed in Hudeida. The revolutionaries, under 'Abdullah Sallal, named a President (Sallal), a Revolutionary Council and an Executive Council. A temporary constitution was proclaimed in Apr. 1963.

The non-militant Shafe'i population was encouraged by the anti-tribalism of the Republican government as well as by the presence of the Egyptian Army. A young member of their intelligentsia, 'Abd-ul-Rahman al-Beidani, became prominent in the government and, as Foreign Minister and economic expert, began to rival Sallal. But in Sept. 1963 the Egyptians, realizing that the Zeidis were the real power in Y., detained Beidani in Cairo; he has not returned to Y. politics. If the Shafe'is hoped to abolish Zeidi hegemony and take over the leadership of the Republic, their hopes were not fulfilled.

The Republican régime underwent frequent personal and factional changes — resulting largely from shifting Egyptian support. When on the offensive, the Egyptians supported the leftist officers, such as Sallal, Hassan al-'Amri, 'Abdullah Juzeilan, Hamud al-Ja'ifi; when on the defensive and seeking to appease the Zeidi tribes they invited Sallal for protracted "medical treatment" in Cairo and appointed non-revolutionary moderates like Nu'man, Iryani and Zubeiri to lead the Republic. Thus, Sallal held office until Aug. 1963 when he was flown to Cairo (nominally retaining the Presidency), while Iryani became a Vice-President and endeavored, with Nu'man, to win over the Zeidi tribes, organizing a pro-Republican tribal conference ('Amran, Sept. 1963). In Jan. 1964 Sallal returned and 'Amri was appointed Prime Minister. In Apr. 1965, following Egyptian defeats, Nu'man was again made Prime Minister and organized, together with Iryani (Zubeiri had been murdered in April), a pro-Republican conference of Zeidi tribes at Khamir. But in June 1965 Iryani and Nu'man were forced to resign and the leadership of the government was again taken over by Sallal. A month later he had to transfer the office to Hassan al-'Amri, and following the Jidda Agreement in August (see below) he was again flown to Cairo. 'Amri then headed the San'a régime with Iryani and Nu'man, thus appeasing the Zeidi tribes. In Sept. 1966 Sallal was returned to San'a and the above three leaders were flown to Cairo where they were detained until Oct. 1967.

When Egypt prepared her evacuation of Y., realizing that her expeditionary force was bogged down in a no-win situation, and under the shock of the *Six Day War, she released 'Amri, Nu'man and Iryani. Sallal was toppled in Oct. 1967 and left Y. for exile in Nov. The new régime, with Iryani as Head of a new Republican Council and, after a few weeks, 'Amri as Prime Minister, was supported by the military power of the tribes, particularly the Hashed. The paramount chief of this tribal confederation, Sheikh Hussein al-Ahmar, had been executed by Imam Ahmad and his son and successor, 'Abdullah al-Ahmar, had refused to join either the Royalists or Sallal's Egyptian-backed régime. Al-Ahmar's newly won support was one of the main reasons that San'a did not fall to a Royalist assault in late 1967 and early 1968. Together with Iryani, al-Ahmar became the real leader in San'a and many Zeidi tribes, under their hitherto pro-Royalist sheikhs, followed him and joined the new Republic. Hassan al-'Amri, who organized the defense of the besieged capital, thereby acquiring a considerable reputation, cooperated with Iryani and Ahmar in the policy of compromise with Zeidi tribalism. The Shafe'is on the other hand, who had for five years fought with the Republican Army and provided some of its best commanders, resented the Egyptian evacuation and the new régime. Their bitterness erupted in two intra-army clashes (also described as *coup* attempts) in March and Aug. 1968 in which Ahmar's tribal warriors joined Zeidi soldiers against leftist Shafe'i officers. The latter were subdued and some 40 under former Chief-of-Staff 'Abd-ul-Raqib 'Abd-ul-Wahhab were expelled from Y. ('Abd-ul-Raqib was killed in 1969 when he returned from his exile and resumed plotting). However, since the settlement of 1970 (see below) the Zeidi-Shafe'i antagonism has eased and the differences between the two communities have been deliberately played down by the régime.

From 1962 to 1969–70, the Royalists maintained their own régime in parts of the country. After the Sept. 1962 coup Imam al-Badr was at first believed to be dead and his uncle Prince Hassan bin Yahya, formerly a rival of Imam Ahmad and opposed to al-Badr's succession, proclaimed himself Imam. However, when Badr emerged alive, Prince Hassan recognized him as Imam and was appointed Prime Minister and Commander-in-Chief. A Royalist government formed in Oct. 1962 included some of the *Sada*, e.g. *Qadi* Ahmad al-Siyyaghi and Ahmad al-Shami. Princes Muhammad and 'Abdullah bin Hussein, and Hassan and 'Abdullah bin Hassan, were sent to the northern mountains to lead the tribes in the campaign. Zeidi tribes began to join the Royalist camp. This led to an increase in the power of the young princes in command of the tribes; the ablest among them, Prince Muhammad bin Hussein, began in 1964 to train a semi-regular tribal army of his own. Iman Badr often left Y. for medical treatment, and Prince Hassan bin Yahya was old. All this led to a certain division of power, and even pressure for some democratization within the Royalist camp. In Jan. 1965 the Imam promised to establish a legislative assembly to limit the power of the Imamate.

In Aug. 1966 Imam al-Badr was virtually deposed when a new "Imamate Council" was formed. Prince Muhammad bin Hussein was appointed Vice-President of this Council, and since Imam al-Badr was in Sa'udia Arabia from Apr. 1965 to Oct. 1968, he was now the real leader of the Royalists. Prince Muhammad commanded the Royalist offensive against San'a in late 1967 and early 1968. In June 1968 he appointed the members of a new Imamate Council and a new government under his premiership, but after failing to achieve further military successes he was ousted early in 1969 by the Imam who had returned to Y. in Oct. 1968.

The war between the Royalist and Republican camps was not really a civil war. The Egyptian expeditionary force — the war's main protagonist — was estimated at about 15,000 in late Oct. 1962, 25,000 in Jan. 1963, 50,000 in Nov. 1963 and 70,000 in Aug. 1965. Following the Jidda Agreement of Aug. 1965 this number was reduced to about 30,000. The force was evacuated in 1967, the last soldier officially leaving Hudeida on 15 Dec. 1967. This foreign military intervention attracted much support to the Royalists: the belligerent Zeidi tribes fought the Republicans and joined the Royal princes not because they wanted to revive the Imam's rule but because the Royal family was a unifying element in the war against the Egyptians. The Sa'udi government supplied the Royalists with war materials and gold. The Egyptian forces campaigned to cut off the two sources of Royalist strength: the tribes, and the Sa'udi supplies (by closing Y.'s northern and eastern borders and by bombing centers and communications in southern Sa'udia — turning the conflict into an Egyptian-Sa'udi war).

In response to a UN initiative, Sa'udi Arabia and Egypt signed, on 29 Apr. 1963, the "Bunker Agreement" to end foreign intervention. UN observers were posted along the Y.-Sa'udi border; but foreign intervention did not cease, the war continued, and as no effort was made to supervise and end Egyptian intervention, Sa'udi Arabia denounced the agreement in Nov. 1963. Fighting continued during 1964 with partial Egyptian successes. A Y. reconciliation congress in the Sudanese town of Erkwith, Oct. 1964, proved abortive because both sides insisted on their original demands — the Royalists on the revival of the Imamate and the evacuation of Egyptian troops, and the Republicans on the "continuation of the revolutionary way" and the exclusion of the Imamic Hamid-ul-Din family. In spring and summer 1965 the Royalists gained the upper hand. They captured Harib and Marib in Feb. and defeated large Egyptian forces in Jabal al-Akhdar, isolating the Egyptian garrison in the al-Jauf area.

In Aug. 1965 President *Nasser and King *Feisal signed the "Jidda Agreement" to end the war.

Sa'udi supplies were to be stopped and Egyptian forces to be evacuated within a year; the future regime of Y. was to be determined by a plebiscite in Nov. 1966; Royalist and Republican delegates were to discuss a régime for the transition period. In Nov. 1965 delegates met in the northwestern town of Harad but achieved no results. This was mainly due to a change in Egyptian policy. Egypt had stopped appeasing Sa'udi Arabia, and, following reports of British plans to withdraw from 'Aden (officially announced in Feb. 1966), decided to remain in Y. in order to achieve her long-term plans.

In Mar.-Apr. 1966 Egypt evacuated her forces — except for a number of strongholds — to the San'a-Hudeida-Ta'izz triangle, leaving the main tribal areas to their own rule, and to the new moderate Republican régime simultaneously established. When the Egyptian Army was evacuated from Sa'udia's southern border and northern Y., King Feisal stopped giving subsidies and supplies to the young Y. princes, and many Zeidi tribes switched their allegiance to the Republican government. The Royalists managed to organize only small-scale and ineffective operations, while the Egyptians concentrated on bombing the Royalist tribes. The bombing was intensified following Sallal's return to power in Sept. 1966 (there were several reports, confirmed by the International Red Cross on 2 June 1967, that poison gas had been used), and many of the tribes returned to the Royalist camp.

After the Six Day War King Feisal and President Nasser agreed at the Khartoum Summit Conference of Aug. 1967, to end the war. Soon afterwards the Egyptian Army was removed from San'a and Ta'izz and concentrated in Hudeida, from which its evacuation began in October 1967. The Royalists, under the command of Prince Muhammad bin Hussein, marched on San'a and laid siege to it in early Dec. 1967. Since the Egyptian intervention forces were gone and the régime in San'a had changed, many Yemeni tribes, mainly of the Hashed Confederation, were mobilized to save the capital. The Republican Army, which had previously left the main conduct of the war to the Egyptians, demonstrated its fighting ability, supported by civilian volunteers, and the siege was lifted.

After the Egyptian evacuation the Y. war really became a local, civil war — in many cases a diplomatic one, in which various tribes continued to change sides, and to obtain rewards and subsidies from both sides without much fighting. In fact the war began to peter out in 1969. Inter-Arab efforts to end the war were resumed, mainly by a Tripartite Committee established by the Khartoum agreement; but they were again abortive and ceased early in 1968. In 1969, however, the policy of appeasing Sa'udi Arabia followed by Iryani and 'Amri was successful and Sa'udi support for the Royalists was reduced. Drought and starvation, intense in 1970, also greatly weakened the Royalist tribes. In Mar. 1970 the Republican Prime Minister visited Jidda for the Islamic Foreign Ministers' Conference, and a general reconciliation agreement was prepared. In May, the former Royalist Foreign Minister Ahmad al-Shami — who had previously advocated reconciliation with San'a and agreed to exclude the Hamid-ul-Din family (thus following Sa'udi policy) — came to San'a with 30 Royalist leaders, none of whom were members of the Royal family. An agreement was reached that amounted to the adhesion of the Royalists to the Republic and the exclusion of the Imamic family, i.e. the abolition of the Imamate. The Royal princes and some of their tribal supporters continued to resist, and the Imam al-Badr refused to abdicate. But the war was ended. The Imam and the princes went into exile. Former Royalists were admitted to the Republican régime — Shami joined the Republican, i.e. Presidential, Council (as did the moderate Republican Ahmad Muhammad Nu'man), four Royalists joined the government, and twelve were co-opted to the National Council. (Shami and Nu'man were not included when the Republican Council was re-formed in Apr. 1971, with three members only, under Iryani; Nu'man became Prime Minister, but resigned in July.)

The Republican victory also ended a diplomatic struggle between the two camps over world recognition and international relations. After the Sept. 1962 *coup* the Republic was immediately recognized by almost all the AC — except Sa'udi Arabia and Jordan (the latter recognized the Republic in 1964) — and the Soviet Bloc, which also gave the Republic military aid, mainly through Egypt. In Dec. 1962 the USA also recognized the Republic, and, the same month, the UN accepted the credentials of the Republican delegation as the true representatives of Y. Britain and France refrained from recognizing the Republic. Despite US recognition US-Y. relations were not warm and the Republic severed relations in spring 1967. Sa'udi Arabia continued to recognize the Royalists and her aid enabled them to continue their struggle. After the Royalist defeat, the establishment of the new post-1967 Republican régime and the settlement of 1970, most of the countries still recognizing the Royalists withdrew that recognition in favor of the Republic. Sa'udi Arabia extended her recognition in July 1970, as did Britain and France. Later in 1970 Sa'udia and the reunited Republic of Y. exchanged ambassadors and Sa'udia resumed economic aid and soon acquired considerable influence in Y. A state visit by President Iryani and his Prime Minister in Mar. 1973 cemented close Sa'udi-Yemeni relations.

Post-1970 Y.'s chief problem was how to work out a reasonable, functioning balance between forces and pressures pulling in conflicting directions — both in foreign and internal affairs. The internal power struggles were aggravated by the absence of well-established constitutional and political traditions of modern state governance. The Republic had tried several times to proclaim provisional constitutional rules and set up representative-consultative councils, but none of these had taken root. In Dec. 1970, a Constitution was promulgated by President Iryani. Y. was declared an "Islamic A. Republic", part of the A. nation, with Islam as the state religion and the *Shari'a as the basis of its laws. The régime was to be a "parliamentary democracy", with equal rights for all (including women), a Consultative Council (*Majlis al-Shura*), elected for four year terms (with 20–30 members appointed by the President), to hold legislative powers. Political parties were banned. Elections for the Council were held Mar. 1971; the Council was dominated by the tribal-conservative element and elected 'Abdullah al-Ahmar, the chief of the Hashed tribes, as its chairman. It named a new Republican (i.e. Presidential) Council — Iryani as chairman, with 'Amri and the Shafe'i leader Muhammad 'Ali 'Othman. After a three month A. M. Nu'man government, 'Amri took the Premiership, too — but he was ousted after a few days, because he was involved in, or guilty of, a murder (the real reason for his ouster was reportedly his opposition to the Consultative Council and its tribal leaders); he went into exile and did not return to Yemeni politics. Thus disappeared a man who had been for years one of the top leaders of the Republic. Nu'man became a member of the Presidential Council for a few months in 1973–74, but then he, too, was ousted and removed from the political scene. M. 'A. 'Othman was assassinated in May 1973. The Presidential Council now consisted only of Iryani and Premier 'Abdullah Hajri, co-opted in 1972, and Iryani was the only one remaining of the grand old men of the Republic.

These frequent changes reflected a general lack of stability. The condominium of the Zeidi tribal leaders, the officers' corps and the modernist-leftist Shafe'i intelligentsia was uneasy. The Iryani-'Amri-Nu'man team had fallen apart. There was growing unrest among the officers. Groups of leftists were going underground — later to emerge as a "National Democratic Front" (from about 1976), rising in rebellion. It was only by a series of shifting tactical meneuvers that Iryani was able to preserve a certain equilibrium — and the maneuvering concerned Y.'s foreign orientation as well (see below). In Dec. 1972 he replaced Premier Muhsin al-'Aini with 'Abdullah al-Hajri, an ex-Royalist considered strongly right-wing, pro-Sa'udi and anti-South Yemen. But in Feb. 1974 he dismissed Hajri, who had gone too far to the right, and appointed the Shafe'i Hassan al-Makki, a moderate leftist (Hajri was assassinated in 1977).

In June 1974 Iryani and his régime were overthrown in a military *coup* led by Lt.-Col. Ibrahim *Hamdi. The new ruler dissolved the Presidential Council and governed as Commander-in-Chief with a "Military Revolutionary Command Council" which he chaired; he also suspended the Constitution of 1970, dissolved the Consultative Council and proclaimed new provisional constitutional arrangements. At first considered a right-winger and closely linked with Sa'udi Arabia, Hamdi endeavored to establish himself as a strong leader, keeping in check both the tribes and the leftists — thus reverting to his predecessor's policy of balancing maneuvers. He tried to mend relations with South Yemen, gained for a time the support of the underground "National Democratic Front", and was soon confronted by growing tribal resistance, in particular by the Hashed tribes (he was himself linked with the rival Bakil tribes); in 1977 this resistance turned into a virtual rebellion. Hamdi was assassinated in Oct. 1977. The identity of the murderers was never established, but it was assumed that they came either from the tribal right wing or from a group of officers plotting for power.

Lt.-Col. Ahmad Hussein *Ghashmi became Commander-in-Chief and chairman of the Military Council. In Feb. 1978 he revived a representative body by appointing a "People's Constituent Assembly", responding to tribal demands (Ghashmi himself was of Hashed tribal origin). In Apr. 1978 the Assembly decided to replace the Military Council by a Presidential Council and elected Ghashmi President. An officers' *coup* attempt was suppressed. But Ghashmi was assassinated in June 1978 by an envoy from South Yemen (who was killed by his own bomb in a strange episode never fully clarified).

Power was taken over by Lt.-Col. 'Ali 'Abdullah *Saleh, as Chief-of-Staff and member of the Presidential Council. A month later, in July 1978, he was made President. He purged the army of rebellious officers, suppressed another *coup* (Oct. 1978), and survived several assassination attempts. Saleh, himself of the Hashed tribes, succeeded in establishing the balance of power sought in vain by his predecessors and giving Y., after so many years of upheavals and instablity, a remarkably stable régime. The leftist underground "National Democratic Front" faded out and its rebellion collapsed in 1982, and the officers' corps ceased to form a restive political force. Saleh was re-electetd President in May 1983 for another five-year term.

The achievement of an equilibrium was Y.'s chief aim in her foreign policies, too. On the international scene she followed a neutralist policy. She resumed official relations with the USA in June 1972 and again began receiving US aid, both economic and in military supplies. At the same time she cultivated good relations with the USSR and received considerable aid from her, too. President 'A. 'A. Saleh visited Moscow in 1981, and concluded a Treaty of Friendship and Cooperation with the USSR in Oct. 1984 (without turning Y. into a close ally of the USSR).

In the inter-A. arena, Y. belonged to the mainstream and was more or less neutral in inter-A. disputes, keeping a low profile. But her main problem in foreign and inter-A. affairs was how to balance her position between Sa'udi Arabia and South Y. — an issue with important internal repercussions. Sa'udia, whose economic and political aid was a mainstay of Y.'s survival and which absorbed a large number of Yemeni workers (sometimes estimated at about 2m., with their remittances providing Y.'s main source of revenue and foreign currency), was always exerting her influence in favor of conservative policies, and particularly in support of the tribal federations, her clients, and against too close a *rapprochement* between Y. and South Y. Keeping relations with Sa'udi Arabia on an even keel was therefore always vital for Y., and since 1970 and Iryani's Mar. 1973 visit (which also yielded a border agreement in which Y. for the first time accepted the 1930 loss of *'Asir and her annexation to Sa'udia) Y. has more or less succeeded in that task.

Relations with South Y., on the other hand, were problematic from the start. Y. had always regarded South Y. — in the past 'Aden and the 'Aden Protectorates, and later the *South Arabia Federation — as part of her territory; and the South Y. nationalists had taken the same position. When South Y. became independent, in Nov. 1967, the union of Y. and South Y. became the official policy, and an unquestioned principle, of both. But the realization of that vision was a very complex matter. The two countries were socially and politically very different, and antagonistic. South Y. — since 1970 the "People's Democratic Republic of Y." (dropping the "South" — a political terminology resented in Y., who now emphasized her own name as the "*Arab Republic of Y.*") — was a virulently leftist-revolutionary, Marxist-Maoist country, and a merger with her was feared by many in Y. as a virtual take-over of conservative Y. by that revolutionary Left, or at least the introduction of a dangerous conflict into Y.'s society. Y. therefore procrastinated over any actual steps towards union — and was encouraged in that policy by Sa'udia — while South Y. was pressing for the consummation of the merger.

Meanwhile, South Y. actively aided subversive and revolutionary elements in Y., while Y. gave asylum and support to South Y. opponents of the régime — conservatives, or members of defeated factions of the leftist régime; and as the borders were largely unmarked, there were border clashes and intrusions (mainly from South Y.; Y. claimed, for instance, several times, that in clashes with leftist rebels inside Y., the rebels were men from South Y.). A state of near-constant tension resulted. Border clashes in 1972 escalated in Sept. into serious battles. A. mediation achieved a cease-fire and a reconciliation, and in Oct. an agreement was signed by the two Prime Ministers, in Cairo, confirming the decision to merge the two countries; this was solemnly re-endorsed by the two Presidents, meeting in Tripoli in Nov. 1972. Joint committees were to work out details. But despite occasional meetings no progress was made and the merger issue remained dormant, the conservative-tribal partner in Y.'s power structure blocking any advance. In Feb. 1979, border incidents again escalated into warlike operations (the "Ten Day War"). A. mediation again arranged a cease-fire and a reconciliation, and the two Presidents met in Mar., in Kuwait, and re-endorsed the decision to merge ("within one year"). Since that time there have been occasional clashes, and committee sessions and meetings at various levels, including Presidential summit meetings in 1981 (Kuwait and 'Aden) and 1986 (Tripoli). But the union of the two Y.'s — always reconfirmed, and unquestioned as a principle and goal — has not neared implementation.

Yemen, People's Democratic Republic of See *South Yemen.

Yom Kippur War, 1973 See *A.-Israel Wars.

Z

Zaghlul, (Ahmad) Sa'd (1860–1927) Egyptian politician and main leader of Egyptian nationalism. Born in a prosperous land-owning family of farmers in Ibiana in the Delta, Z. studied law, after a traditional Islamic education. At the beginning of the century he was one of the young modernists close to the *Umma* Party who opposed the conservative-Islamic trend and were seen by some as collaborating with the British administrators, although he also remained close to the Islamic revivalist circles around Muhammad *'Abduh. In 1906 he was appointed Minister of Education and in 1910 Minister of Justice. He resigned in 1913 to head the opposition in the Legislative Assembly. At the end of World War I he emerged as a leader of the nationalists and headed a delegation (Arabic: *Wafd*) to the British which demanded full independence; from this delegation the *Wafd evolved as a political party and the main proponent of the national struggle. In an effort to suppress nationalist ferment, the British exiled Z. twice — in Mar. 1919 to Malta (released in Apr.), and in 1922 to 'Aden, the Seychelles and Gibraltar. In 1923–24 Z. led the *Wafd* party to victory in nominally independent Egypt's first elections and in Jan. 1924 he became Prime Minister. However, when the British High Commissioner, Lord Allenby, reacted to the murder of the Governor-General of Sudan and Commander of the Egyptian army, Sir Lee Stack, in Nov. 1924, by presenting to the Government an ultimatum and conditions considered extreme and humiliating, Z. resigned. In new elections, Mar. 1925, the *Wafd* won a partial victory and Z. was elected Speaker of the House — whereupon the House was dissolved. In the elections of May 1926 Z. again led the *Wafd* to victory, but declined to form a government and was re-elected Speaker. His death in Sept. 1927 was a great blow to the nationalist movement. His memory as a great national leader has remained alive.

Za'im, Husni (1889? 1896?–1949) Syrian officer and politician. President of Syria in 1949. Born in Aleppo, reportedly of Kurdish origin, Z. served as a professional officer in the Ottoman Army and after World I in the "Special Troops" formed by the French authorities. During World War II Z. remained loyal to the Vichy-French authorities, and after the conquest of Syria by the British and Free French in 1941 he was detained, but returned to the army after his release. During the Palestine War of 1948, he was Chief-of-Staff with the rank of Brigadier. On 30 Mar. 1949 Z. mounted Syria's first military *coup*, deposed President *Quwwatli and dissolved Parliament. In June he held a referendum which endorsed him as President with wide powers. He dissolved all political parties and ruled without a legislative or parliamentary body. Z. had ambitious plans for reforms inspired by those of Atatürk. He was the first A. leader to give women the franchise and tried to separate state and religion. He was pro-French and anti-*Hashemite and strengthened relations with Egypt, Sa'udi Arabia and Turkey. He also tried to establish contacts with the leaders of Israel, indicating that he was interested in peace and the constructive settlement of issues in dispute, such as the refugee problem.

Z. did not have the time to implement any of his far-reaching plans. He was overthrown on 14 Aug. 1949 by a pro-Hashemite *coup* staged by Col. Sami *Hinnawi. A military court summarily sentenced him to death, together with his Prime Minister Muhsin al-Barazi, and he was immediately executed.

Zayed Ibn Sultan   See al-*Nuhayan.

Zeidis, Zeidiyya   A branch of *Shi'i Islam, dominating Yemen. The Z. split from the bulk of the Shi'a when they recognized Zeid ibn 'Ali, the grandson of Hussein ibn 'Ali, as the fifth *Imam*; Zeid was defeated in 740 by the Umayyad forces. Unlike the mainstream of the Shi'a, the Z. recognize a continuing line of living *Imams*, who must be descendants of the *Khalifa* 'Ali through his sons al-Hassan and al-Hussein. Their *Imam* is elected by the *Sada* (plural of *Sayyid*, descendants of the *Khalifa* 'Ali and his son Hussein). The election of the *Imam* caused several schisms. In recent decades the Yemeni *Imams* *Yahya Hamid-ul-Din and *Ahmad ibn Yahya broke the rule of election by appointing their elder sons to succeed them. The Z. established two states: one on the Caspian Sea up to 1126, and Yemen from the early days of Islam.

In modern times the Z. of Yemen often fought with the Ottoman Turks. While the latter controlled the coast, the Z. usually maintained a measure of autonomy in the interior or else rebelled. The founder of modern Yemen, Yahya Hamid-ul-Din, elected *Imam* in 1904, rebelled and secured his autonomy in the interior. He obtained full independence in 1918 and ruled until 1948, re-establishing Z. hegemony.

The Z. form about 55% of the population of Yemen (though there are conflicting estimates) — most of the rest being Sunni *Shafe'is — and about 80% of the powerful, belligerent tribes, of whom the strongest are the confederations of Hashed and Bakil tribes. The Z. were the military and social élite of the Kingdom. The administrative, judicial and religious backbone of the state was mostly provided by non-tribal Z. *Sada*, whose number is estimated at 300,000. Some *Sada* families claimed the Imamate, e.g. the al-Wazir clan, was behind the abortive *coup* of 1948 in which the *Imam* Yahya was killed.

The Republican régime set up by the revolution of 1962 abolished the Imamate and the *Sada* hegemony. However, as the Z. tribes were the strongest element in the civil war ensuing, the new régime had to reach some accommodation with them and gradually to revive and recognize their leading position. The Republican-Royalist reconciliation of 1970 endorsed the abolition of the Imamate, although the *Imam*, Muhammad al-*Badr, in exile, did not formally renounce it. Some *Sada* attempts to revive the Imamate were reported but not substantiated, and since 1970 there is no recognized *Imam*.

Zionism   The national movement of the Jewish people, striving for the "Ingathering of the Exiles" and the revival of an independent Jewish nation in Palestine — formally organized since 1897. In itself outside our scope, Z. was opposed by A. nationalists, indeed by most A.'s, particularly by the A.'s of Palestine, and perceived as an enemy — although there were attempts to achieve an understanding, and in the formative years at the end of World War I an agreement and an alliance were concluded but remained abortive (see *Feisal-Weizmann Agreement, *Arab-Israel Conflict). Moreover, in the perception of many A.'s, including A. political leaders, and also of many non-A. Muslims, Z. was not simply a national movement in conflict with the A.'s over Palestine, but a sinister world-wide "racist" movement. In 1975 the ASt succeeded, after a sustained campaign of propaganda and pressure, in getting a majority of the UN General Assembly (the ASt, Third World countries, the Soviet Bloc) to define and condemn Z. as "racist". Many A.'s even saw Z. as a Jewish conspiracy to dominate the world and to oppress, in particular, the A. nation. This demonization of Z. derived — though many A.'s are probably not aware of that — from European, especially German, anti-Semitic literature, such as the forged "Protocols of the Elders of Zion", which was repeatedly translated into Arabic and is still being reprinted and widely distributed. See *anti-Semitism.